THE COMMISSION OF
FINE ARTS
UNITED STATES OF AMERICA
ESTABLISHED BY THE
CONGRESS
MAY 17 1910

CIVIC ART

A Centennial History of the U.S. Commission of Fine Arts

EDITED BY THOMAS E. LUEBKE

U.S. COMMISSION OF FINE ARTS

WASHINGTON, DISTRICT OF COLUMBIA · MMXIII

PUBLISHED BY THE U.S. COMMISSION OF FINE ARTS · MMXIII

United States Commission of Fine Arts
401 F Street, NW, Suite 312
Washington, D.C. 20001-2728

TELEPHONE: 202-504-2260
www.cfa.gov

The U.S. Commission of Fine Arts offers broad public access to its resources—including photographs, drawings, and official government documents—as a contribution to education, scholarship, and public information. The submission of documents to the Commission of Fine Arts for review constitutes permission to use the documents for purposes related to the activities of the commission, including display, reproduction, publication, or distribution.

PRINTED AND BOUND IN THE UNITED STATES OF AMERICA
16 15 14 13   4 3 2 1

U.S. GOVERNMENT PRINTING OFFICE CATALOGING PUBLICATION DATA

Civic art : a centennial history of the U.S. Commission of Fine Arts / edited by Thomas E. Luebke.
Washington, D.C. : U.S. Commission of Fine Arts, 2013.
p.   cm.
Supt. of Docs. no: FA 1.2: C 87
ISBN: 978-0-160897-02-3
1. Washington (D.C.)—Buildings, structures, etc.   2. U.S Commission of Fine Arts—History.
3. Public architecture—United States.   4. Architecture—Washington (D.C.)—History.
I. Luebke, Thomas E.   II. U.S. Commission of Fine Arts.

CFA PROJECT TEAM

Editor and Project Director: Thomas E. Luebke, FAIA
Managing Editor: Mary M. Konsoulis
Historian: Kathryn Fanning, PhD
Architectural Historian: Eve Barsoum
Illustration Editor: Sarah Batcheler
Manuscript Editor: Beth Carmichael

BOOK DESIGN AND PRODUCTION

Meadows Design Office, Inc., Washington, D.C.
Art Director and Designer: Marc Alain Meadows
Assistant Editor: Caroline Taylor
Imaging Assistant: Nancy Bratton

DISTRIBUTED BY UNIVERSITY OF MASSACHUSETTS PRESS
Amherst & Boston: www.umass.edu/umpress

FRONTISPIECE: *Michael Lantz,* Man Controlling Trade, *Federal Trade Commission building, 1937–42 (CFA collection).*

*This book is dedicated
to the service of the members and staff of
the U. S. Commission of Fine Arts
in promoting excellence in the arts for the nation
and its capital city.*

⁊ℯ ⁊ℯ ⁊ℯ

Contents

1803 - 1865

in the design professions, the commission's focus demonstrated the increasing importance of the relationship of proposals to existing historic structures and landscapes; the commission staff published numerous surveys of Washington's historic resources during this period.

The crisis of the September 11, 2001, attacks emphatically marked the beginning of a new era in the national capital: unsightly security barriers—already making their appearance in the 1990s—suddenly proliferated around all public facilities, amplifying a growing trend toward limited public access to government structures. For the next decade, design issues related to security dominated the commission's agenda, from office buildings to memorials to the massive new headquarters complex for the Department of Homeland Security. Washington was forever altered from its more innocent past, when visitors could walk within a short walk of national monuments and open federal buildings were the rule. While imposing great change on the character of the public realm, the vast investment in security projects also occasioned much-needed facilities improvements for many federal buildings.

In addition, the twenty-first century has brought new issues to the discussion: most prominent has been the sustainability movement, which has dominated the professional discourse internationally. More subtle has been the impact of a technological revolution in design, one made possible by the sophistication of computer rendering, which has changed the design process itself. In the context of Washington's symbolic structures, this era has witnessed the emergence of narrative as the preponderant value in the design of memorials, resulting in the conflation of typologies such as memorials with museums and monumentality with advertisement. Commemorative works have evolved to focus more on subjective experience than on abstract ideals; allegory has been replaced by a limited palette of symbols (stars and eagles predominate) augmented by extensive narratives delivered by quotation and photographic image. The innovative use of materials, the reproducibility of images, and new technologies such as podcasts have contributed to a new frontier in the existing landscape of Washington. Under the twenty-first-century leadership of Harry Robinson, David Childs, and Earl A. Powell III, the Commission of Fine Arts has responded to this context of changing design values, using its collective professional expertise to address these trends within the framework of design excellence established more than a century ago.

Ultimately, the project of representing the American republic in physical symbols has evolved with the culture across the past one hundred years. Washington has a unique urban form and image that expresses an underlying political culture that is essentially conservative in matters of art and generally late in accepting new aesthetic trends. As our nation moves forward into the twenty-first century, the Commission of Fine Arts will continue to adapt the dreamy monumentalism of the McMillan Plan to the realities of a modern city—one that answers to both a national constituency with a need for political and cultural expression as well as a living community.

This book was conceived as a comprehensive historical summary of the Commission of Fine Arts as an institution since its establishment in 1910 and in celebration of its centennial in May 2010. In describing this century of work, the history has been necessarily organized into comprehensible pieces; the book has been structured in a generally chronological way as seven chapters corresponding to successive periods of chairmanship of the commission. As an institutional history, the book draws heavily upon resources of the commission's own collections—records, photographs, and artifacts—that may shed new light on its past and the design discussions that have shaped the national capital. The seven chapters have been researched and written by the Commission of Fine Arts staff and, in presenting a survey of the work of the commission across a century, are intended to provide a basis for further exploration by future historians.

As part of this project and concurrent with the agency's centennial celebration, a symposium was organized by commission staff in May 2010 in cooperation with the National Building Museum in Washington, D.C. The program was specifically focused on the work of the commission, composed of papers presented by scholars on salient topics in this august history—such as the role played by particular individuals in creating the capital's image and character, the conflicts that illustrate the larger thematic issues in Washington's design, and the relationship of the commission to political authority. These symposium presentations have been revised by their authors as six topical essays that punctuate the chronologically-based chapters to provide a critical perspective on the more expository material covered in the body of the book. Following the first chapter, Olmsted historian Arleyn Levee explores the legacy of Frederick Law Olmsted Jr. on the design of the city's landscapes. Washington architectural historian Pamela Scott's examination of the leadership of Charles Moore in developing its architectural framework follows the second chapter. Architectural historian Carroll William Westfall of the University of Notre Dame treats the commission's crisis of modernism in the Thomas Jefferson Memorial controversy as the classicist era ended in the 1930s, described in chapter 3. White House Historian William

Washington, an architectural assertion of imperial aspirations consonant with latent American sentiment for religious purpose: a city of heavenly beauty to represent the ideals of the democracy. The vision was powerful enough to bring about the realization of many aspects of the plan through the subsequent chairmanships of Daniel Chester French and, most demonstrably, Charles Moore, a journalist, publicist, and historian who became a powerful force in implementing the McMillan Plan. Beaux-Arts classicism remained the accepted style in Washington for decades, until the ascendance of modernism from within the professional disciplines, thus creating the first challenge to what had been a design consensus. The controversies surrounding the design of several buildings in the late 1930s—the National Gallery of Art, the competition for the Smithsonian Museum of American Art, and the Thomas Jefferson Memorial—signaled a revolution in the commission's approach to guiding the design of Washington.

The transformative events of the mid-twentieth century—the Great Depression, World War II, and the booming economic development that followed—necessitated an entirely new approach to design, one informed by the tenets of modernism and by the primacy of automobile transportation as the fundamental principle of city planning. For Washington, as well as for the country as a whole, the built environment was radically changed in this period through massive government construction projects, slum clearing and urban renewal, and the imposition of highway infrastructure through cities and across the landscape. Like the progressive idealism of the City Beautiful movement, the modernist attitude was fundamentally optimistic in its ability to solve social problems and formally inventive in abandoning historic paradigms in favor of increasing abstraction and expressionism in design. In this period, the Commission of Fine Arts exhibited a philosophical shift away from Beaux-Arts classicism and, without that unifying classical vision for the capital, was challenged with continuing the tradition of the McMillan Plan through the lens of modern design. At the same time, the commission guided great advances toward the completion of the National Mall as a public landscape and nurtured a concomitant interest in historic preservation through its oversight of the Old Georgetown historic district, established by Congress in 1950. The era was also characterized by the personal involvement of the White House in Washington design issues: Presidents Roosevelt, Truman, and Kennedy each wielded their executive influence directly to create changes, whether contrary to or in support of the Commission of Fine Arts. Thus, the chairmanships of Gilmore Clarke, David Finley, and William Walton—spanning the decades from the late 1930s to the early 1970s—reveal a more politicized relationship between the commission and the executive branch of government.

In many ways, the early 1970s present a turning point in the design of Washington, reflecting broader cultural trends that questioned government power—exemplified by opposition to the war in Vietnam and the political repercussions of the Watergate scandal—as well as an increasing reassessment of our relationship to history. With the approaching Bicentennial in 1976, Americans' interest grew in the historic architectural and urban forms of the past as an expression of our national heritage, backward-looking from the complexities of the present. Likewise in architecture, the period was marked by a rejection of the certainties of modernism and the rise of postmodernism in theory and practice. In government, broad reforms affected decision making: new laws were instituted protecting the environment and historic structures, as were procedural changes guaranteeing greater transparency in governmental processes. As a federal agency, the Commission of Fine Arts adapted to the new political climate by opening its meetings to the public and by participating in mandated historic preservation review.

For the design of Washington, a new set of issues emerged, principally concerned with urban design and the redevelopment of the city's commercial downtown. The projects attracting the most attention typically involved battles over the preservation of historic buildings and the suitable form of the city adjacent to the federal core. A new phenomenon of commemoration, the national war memorial, appeared with the controversial Vietnam Veterans Memorial and within a few decades transformed the West Potomac Park landscape of the National Mall, where the remaining temporary structures—office buildings dating from the world wars to house an expanded federal workforce—had recently been removed. The Mall itself—now completed as a coherent landscape as envisioned in the McMillan Plan—took on a new role as the home of new museums of cultural experience and a stage for political expression.

The chairmanship of J. Carter Brown defines this entire era, and his charismatic leadership dominated the commission's work for more than three decades, during which time the composition of the commission itself became less rigorously associated with the professional disciplines represented in the first sixty years of its membership. The late-twentieth-century period is characterized by a fragmentation of the consensus on styles and standards of design that had existed during the earlier Beaux-Arts and modern periods. Inevitably, there was a shift in focus from an ideological presumption of *style* to a broader consideration of design *quality*: logic, detailing, compatibility. Reflecting a broader trend

Preface

Washington, the american capital, possesses a distinctive image that is recognizable across the country and abroad for its particular character: great temples of democracy composed within a framed field of green. The image is so well established that it seems inevitable, as if it had always been so since the days of the early republic. But the design of the capital city and other national symbols did not happen by accident: They are the conscious creations first of political will, translated through the work of design visionaries who sought to communicate the political ideals of the nation into built form.

For the last century, the U.S. Commission of Fine Arts (CFA), an advisory design review agency of the federal government, has played a central role in the formation of this emblematic achievement. The CFA was established following the recommendations of the seminal Senate Park (McMillan) Commission Plan of 1901, which envisioned a new image for the nation's capital in a scale and style that was commensurate with the nation's growing economic and political power. Authorized by Congress in 1910, the CFA as an institution owes its existence to the ideals of the Progressive Era of the early twentieth century, when the problems of society were to be solved through the participation of professionals, in the case of a reimagined capital by "experts in the arts." The commission membership reflected this expertise and a spirit of collaboration across the allied arts, a hallmark of the American Renaissance period.

The underlying narrative of the commission's work has been the manifestation of political ideas into physical form. The most important issues facing the commission have been ones of national representation—memorials, monuments, museums, medals—the tangible icons of our shared national identity. Along with political and artistic trends, the commission's goals have evolved over time; its work has been enhanced or hindered by its relationship to political power. It is probably more salient in the national capital than in any other American city that issues of design are inextricable from issues of power. This book was envisioned as a comprehensive study of the CFA as an institution within the context of the physical design of Washington, D.C., and the larger political and cultural trends that have informed its work across ten decades.

There are three distinct periods in the history of the commission—eras that are defined by the coalescence of a general agreement on what is stylistically appropriate. In Washington, these eras—inextricably linked to national developments in professional design practice and aesthetics—have been punctuated by phases of transition and even political crises as the older conception gives way to the new one. From its beginnings out of the Beaux-Arts McMillan Plan, the commission's first era constitutes the triumph of classicism, the implementation of many McMillan Plan goals, and the transformation of Washington's monumental core. The second era is marked by the dissolution of that consensus about classicism and the embrace of a new design ideology, modernism, and the transformation of the built environment following World War II. The third era is associated with a reconsideration of history in design, involving the architectural trends of postmodernism and neomodernism as well as new concerns for the quality of urban life and appropriate national symbols. We are now at the beginning of a fourth era, roughly coincident with the new century, which is informed by issues that were of minor concern—or even unimaginable—for prior generations.

The visionary architect and planner Daniel Burnham, was the chief organizer and contributing designer of the immensely influential World's Columbian Exposition in Chicago of 1893–94. He was also a guiding spirit for the McMillan Plan, reimagining the national capital according to principles of the City Beautiful movement. Burnham's legacy was fundamental in establishing an image of classical style and monumental scale for

Foreword

CIVIC ART IS THE MOST PUBLIC AND DURABLE EXPRESSION OF A SOCIETY'S VALUES. We are able to understand the history of human civilization through its legacy of civic art—its monuments, public buildings, statuary, and coins—as revealing a portrait of political aspirations through the lens of artistic endeavor. Urban form itself powerfully articulates essential technological, economic, and cultural circumstances.

Washington, D.C., is a living symbol of civic culture in the American republic, and its image has been created over more than two centuries through a deliberate effort in urban design, architecture, and art. Informed by an enlightened legacy of planning from the L'Enfant and McMillan Plans, the national capital speaks eloquently of a long tradition of civic art and an evolving consensus on its many forms of expression. From its radial avenues and grand edifices of government to its parkways, memorials, and sculptures, the city provides a multilayered experience of our national culture.

Since the far-reaching proposals of the McMillan Plan more than a century ago, Washington has grown into the great scale and aesthetic ambitions of that visionary document that engendered the transformation of the city's core. The Commission of Fine Arts was established in 1910 to guide this transformation, as well as the aesthetic development of enduring national symbols such as our coins, military cemeteries, and national memorials. With this volume, we hope to tell the story of a century of design—reflecting the evolving trends in power and politics, architecture and art—and the commission's role in shaping American civic art.

—EARL A. POWELL III

CHAIRMAN, U.S. COMMISSION OF FINE ARTS

FACING PAGE: *Rear Admiral Samuel Francis Du Pont Memorial Fountain, Dupont Circle*, 1921, by Daniel Chester French and Henry Bacon.

Bushong explores the relationship of the commission to the presidency during the Roosevelt and Truman administrations following the presentation of the midcentury decades in chapter 4. Following chapter 5, historian Zachary Schrag of George Mason University examines a particular example of modern Washington architecture, the FBI Headquarters building, at the end of that aesthetic era. University of Virginia architectural historian Richard Guy Wilson presents a paradigm for understanding the multifaceted leadership of J. Carter Brown in the postmodern era through the close of the twentieth century as presented in chapter 6.

Significant aspects of the commission's additional jurisdictions have been included in the narrative—such as the Shipstead-Luce Act and the Old Georgetown Act—although most information can only be outlined for the sake of brevity. These topics constitute worthy subjects of study on their own. In addition, ancillary information in the form of supplementary texts has been provided to inform the reader of related design issues, such as the review of coins and medals produced by the United States Mint. Together, these elements are designed to suggest a detailed framework to present the work of the Commission of Fine Arts in guiding the design of national symbols, and the national capital in particular, since its creation 103 years ago.

—THOMAS LUEBKE, FAIA
SECRETARY, U.S. COMMISSION OF FINE ARTS
WASHINGTON, D.C., 2013

THE U.S. COMMISSION OF FINE ARTS *is a presidentially appointed body of "seven well-qualified judges of the fine arts," as stipulated in the 1910 legislation. Serving without compensation for renewable terms of four years, commission members meet monthly to review proposed federal and District of Columbia design projects within the nation's capital. Legislation and executive orders over the past century have amplified the commission's authority to advise the U.S. Mint on the design of coins and medals, approve the site and design of national memorials, and review the design of private construction projects that front on or abut certain federal properties within Washington, D.C. The commission, through its advisory committee of architects, the Old Georgetown Board, also makes recommendations to the District government on design matters within the historic district of Georgetown. Citations of the legislation and orders pertaining to the commission is provided in an appendix to this book.*

The commission's meetings are open to the public and are held in the agency's offices in the National Building Museum in Washington, D.C. The review process generally corresponds to the steps in a design's development. Applicants are encouraged to meet initially with the agency's professional staff informally to present an outline of the design concept and approach; staff also is available to meet with applicants throughout the process. Applicants may present the project as an information presentation to the commission for general comment. Two levels of formal review occur: the first at the concept stage and the second at the final stage of design. There may be multiple interim reviews for revisions occurring between the two formal actions. Applicants submit and then present to the commission materials for the concept review—including a variety of drawings, maps, models, and plans—before schematic design is completed, and for the final review when no substantive design changes are anticipated, prior to the issuance of a building permit. Complex or significant projects may require multiple reviews by the commission during these stages of the process. Each public review is documented by a letter to the applicant describing the commission's action; the discussions are also summarized in minutes for each public meeting; together, these documents represent the official record of the commission's actions.

Acknowledgments

A WORK OF THIS MAGNITUDE REQUIRES THE CONTRIBUTION OF MANY PEOPLE whose participation has made it possible to present the broad range and complexity of material associated with a century of history in a single volume. First, I would like to thank Earl A. Powell III, chairman of the Commission of Fine Arts, whose graceful leadership continues to set a high aesthetic standard and foster a productive working environment, as well as the other members of the commission whom I have had the pleasure to serve since 2005: Chairman David M. Childs; Vice Chairmen Pamela Nelson and Elizabeth Plater-Zyberk; Diana Balmori, John Belle, Teresita Fernández, Philip Freelon, Alex Krieger, Michael McKinnell, Elizabeth K. Meyer, Witold Rybczynski, Edwin Schlossberg, and Elyn Zimmerman.

Together with my colleagues at the Commission of Fine Arts, I am grateful for the support from many institutions in bringing this project into reality: the National Building Museum, under the leadership of director Chase Rynd with exceptional staff assistance from Scott Kratz, Chrysanthe Broikos, and Cathy Frankel for hosting the associated symposium, "Architecture, Power, and Politics," and exhibit, "A Century of Design," in 2010 as well as for providing research and event support through many years; the American Academy in Rome, which sponsored my work on this volume during an appointment as visiting scholar in 2010–2011 made possible by the advocacy of former commission members David M. Childs and Adele Chatfield-Taylor, president of the Academy; the National Capital Planning Commission, whose partnership on many projects under the leadership of executive directors Patti Gallagher and Marcel Acosta has created a fruitful collaboration between sister agencies; the many federal institutions who have contributed the effort and time of their staffs in providing information, images, and advice concerning this history, including the Library of Congress, the National Archives and Records Administration, the General Services Administration, the National Park Service, the Smithsonian Institution, and the National Gallery of Art; agencies of the District of Columbia, particularly the Historic Preservation Office and the District of Columbia Public Library; and other institutional sources including the White House Historical Association, the Historical Society of Washington, D.C., the American Institute of Architects, the Art Institute of Chicago, the Brown University Library, the Yale University Library, and the Albert and Shirley Small Special Collections Library of the University of Virginia.

Other individuals who have lent their time and attention in providing background material include many current and former employees of the National Park Service National Capital Region, especially Gregory Anderson, Glenn DeMarr, Susan Horner, Doug Jacobs, Maureen Joseph, Robert Sonderman, Susan Spain, Jennifer Talken-Spaulding, and Matthew Virta; and I thank former regional planning director John Parsons for giving his time in an extensive interview. I also recognize the contributions of former Pennsylvania Avenue Development Corporation staff members Ron Eichner, Jo-Ann Neuhaus, and John Woodbridge in providing historic background; of Julia Koster, Elizabeth Miller, Paul Jutton, and Anne Schuyler of the National Capital Planning Commission for their ongoing support in providing planning documents, images, and other advice; and Angela LoRé and Maygene Daniels of the National Gallery of Art. I also acknowledge with gratitude the body of work undertaken by former Commission of Fine Arts staff members in documenting the history of the agency and the national capital city—the late former secretary Charles Atherton, former assistant secretaries Donald B. Myer and Jeffrey R. Carson, and historian Sue A. Kohler—whose work over more than three decades created a tremendous legacy of scholarship.

I would like to thank many other individuals for their generous time and effort in assisting the Commission staff with images and other information for the book including Sarah Atherton; Davis Buckley; Patricia and Arthur Cotton Moore;

Mike Conley and Martha Sell of the American Battle Monuments Commission; Nancy Hadley of the American Institute of Architects archives; Jennifer Lynch of the Arlington Memorial Cemetery; Michelle Migliori of Brown University; Faye Haskins of the D.C. Public Library; Danielle Breaux, Jennifer Gibson, and Kathy Erickson of the General Services Administration; Barbara Natanson of the Library of Congress; Nancy Bateman, Stephanie Hess, and Martin Moeller of the National Building Museum; Julie Blake, Jean Henry, and Alan Newman of the National Gallery of Art; David Harper of Numismatic News; Ellen Alers and Fleur Paysour of the Smithsonian Institution; Tessa Brawley of the Syracuse University Library, and Caroline Cunningham of the Trust for the National Mall; as well as to the members of individual design firms including: Austin Harris of Adjaye Associates; Alan Harwood and Roger Courtenay of AECOM; Hany Hassan and Jill Cavanaugh of Beyer Blinder Belle; Anna Marich of the Freelon Group; Rick Parisi of M. Paul Friedberg & Partners; Brian Zamora of Gehry Partners; Liz Martini of Gustafson Guthrie Nichol; Mary Kay Lanzillotta of Hartman-Cox Architects; Sian Imber of Leo A Daly; Ron Kessler of McKissack & McKissack; Sahar Coston-Hardy of OLIN; Bonnie Fisher of ROMA Design Group; Kelli Quinn-Byrne of Shalom Baranes Architects; John Crump of SmithGroup/JJR; Rita Yurow of SOM; and Ignacio Bunster-Ossa of WRT. This appreciation extends to the many creators of images who have generously allowed their publication in this volume, particularly photographers Carol Highsmith, Maxwell MacKenzie, Joseph Romeo, Timothy Hursley, and Alan Karchmer; and renderer Michael McCann. I also recognize photographers Carol Clayton, Anna Frame, and Franz Jantzen for their work in documenting subjects expressly for this book.

On behalf of the Commission of Fine Arts, I am indebted to the independent scholars Arleyn Levee and Pamela Scott, Carroll William Westfall of the University of Notre Dame, William Bushong of the White House Historical Association, Zachary Schrag of George Mason University, and Richard Guy Wilson of the University of Virginia for their research and presentations on aspects of the commission's history delivered at the May 2010 symposium and for their work in revising the material as essays within this book. I further acknowledge the direct contributions of many individuals who participated closely in the production of this volume: Kathleen G. Franz of the American University and Chrysanthe Broikos for their reading of the preliminary manuscript; Beth Carmichael for her copyediting and indexing; Marc Meadows for his masterful advice, art direction, and design work; Caroline Taylor for proofreading; Tom Scibek of the U.S. Government Printing Office for managing the printing of the book; and Bruce Wilcox of the University of Massachusetts Press for his guidance and support in development and distribution of the book.

It is difficult to overstate the immensity of the task of producing this book, from thematic development through production, undertaken by the eleven members of the commission staff in addition to the normal duties associated with the design review of some 700 cases per year. I gratefully acknowledge the contributions of Frederick Lindstrom for his advice and historical knowledge; Phyllis Roderer for her invaluable management assistance; Susan Raposa for her tireless efforts in managing the commission archives and information technology; Tony Simon for his encyclopedic learning, erudite editing, and careful research; and José Martinez Canino and Raksha Patel for performing additional tasks to allow others to create this publication. The work of four individuals, without whose contributions this project would not have been possible, requires special acknowledgment: Sarah Batcheler for her tremendous dedication in identifying and finding sources for images, managing their integration into the design of the book, compiling credit information for more than 900 images, and adding her expert eye on many matters of graphic design; Eve Barsoum for her exemplary work in researching and writing Chapters 1, 2, and much of Chapter 7, as well as contributing remarkable knowledge and narrative material on the Georgetown historic district in all other chapters; Kay Fanning for her thorough and invaluable undertaking in researching and writing Chapters 3, 4, 5, and much of Chapter 6 in addition to innumerable editorial contributions, assisting in developing the structure of the book, and organizing the contributing symposium speakers; and Mary Konsoulis for her outstanding management of the centennial history project over more than three years from the organization of the museum exhibit through the many stages of editing and production of the book, for her contributions in researching and writing the urban design topics in Chapter 6, and for her herculean work in so many aspects of bringing the draft manuscript to publication, including rewriting, copyediting, identifying images, managing captions, and coordinating the work of essayists, consultants, and outside readers.

Finally, I would like to thank the many friends and family members who have given their advice and support in this four-year project, including the historians Frederick C. Luebke and David M. Luebke, and my partner Patricia Baker, whose support in all matters has made this effort possible.

—TL

Aim High in Hope and Work

POLITICS AND PLANNING IN WASHINGTON BEFORE 1910

The transformation of Washington's image from a red brick Victorian city to a unified composition of white classical monumentality was a process that took decades to accomplish and whose conceptual catalyst lay in the political and aesthetic movements of the late nineteenth century. For the United States, the geopolitical development of empire building—exemplified by the Spanish-American War, in which the country acquired remnants of the Spanish empire in the Pacific and Caribbean—was concurrent with a burgeoning interest in architecture and urban design derived from Roman imperial models. Much of Washington's physical infrastructure—its parks and major public buildings—had been built by and remained under the control of the U.S. Army Corps of Engineers. A new era coincident with the new century was marked by the influence of an increasingly professionalized cadre of other disciplines, notably architects and planners, who would bring into reality a radically different notion for the nation's capital.

The professionalization of architecture began in the mid-nineteenth century: the traditional apprenticeships gave way to an academic education with aspiring architects attending either the École des Beaux-Arts in Paris or one of the recently established American architecture programs based on the École curriculum. The systematic method taught architecture in a prescribed manner based on the analysis of a building's program and translating the requirements into design composed of hierarchical spaces established through axes and cross-axes, which informed monumental facades typically rendered in classical styles based on antiquity. The Beaux-Arts architects took pride in applying these historic principles, forms, and ornamentation to modern building types and construction techniques.[1]

The roots of new thinking about the social impact of the built environment extend back to the mid-nineteenth century, when social theorists began to characterize people as products of their environment, a contrast with earlier beliefs based on predestination and individual determinism. One manifestation of this shift in social thought was the urban park movement. Small parks had been part of New World town plans from the early years of European settlement, but following the 1853 authorization of Central Park in New York City, many American cities began to plan and develop large parks that often incorporated landscaped boulevards as approaches.[2] The parks were created in the name of health and beauty and as a panacea for a variety of urban ills. Proponents heralded the parks as fire barriers, as well as the solution

FACING PAGE: Rendering of an aerial view of the Senate Park Commission's plan for the Mall, 1901, (detail). Charles McKim designed the complex set of steps and terraces at the foot of the Washington Monument to accommodate axial differences in the plan.

9

View looking west from the U.S. Capitol, c. 1901. In the left foreground is the Botanic Garden with the Bartholdi Fountain, cast in Paris for the 1876 Centennial Exhibition in Philadelphia. It was purchased by the federal government and erected on the Mall in 1878 at the urging of Frederick Law Olmsted Sr. Lit at night by twelve gas globes, the fountain was a popular attraction at the end of the nineteenth century as one of the earliest illuminated monuments in the city.

View of the World's Columbian Exposition in Chicago (1893) looking north along the South Canal. The Machinery Building, by Boston architects Peabody & Sterns, was located to the west (left) of the canal with the Agriculture Building by New York firm McKim, Mead & White to the east (right). Open only for six months and despite the economic depression of 1893, the exposition received 27.5 million visitors, a number equal to almost half the U.S. total population of 65 million at the time.

CHAPTER I │ AIM HIGH IN HOPE AND WORK

to slums and dumping grounds, arguing that they would stimulate increases in adjacent property values to the benefit of municipal coffers.

As the public sought more comprehensive solutions to the problems associated with the ever-growing urban industrial society, the Beaux-Arts design principles and the park movement became impetuses for city planning. Confronted with labor unrest and squalor, reformers attempted to regulate industry, establish social discipline, and create visual order in overcrowded chaotic cities. The ideas behind the park movement—combined with the good-government reform measures of progressivism, international expositions, and the rampant nationalism of the late nineteenth century—crystallized in the City Beautiful movement. This national movement, led by prominent planners and lay reformers as well as politicians, was manifested in ambitious urban design schemes. Its philosophy held that city dwellers would become imbued with civic pride through elevating the design of a city's streets, parks, and buildings—particularly public buildings—inspiring residents to be more productive workers and to engage in addressing community needs, both of which would enhance urban economics. The heyday of City Beautiful occurred between 1900 and 1910. The 1901 Senate Park Commission Plan for Washington, also known as the McMillan Plan, was the most significant City Beautiful plan in the United States. The establishment of the U.S. Commission of Fine Arts in 1910 occurred, in part, to uphold the design intent of this plan. (See Arleyn Levee's essay for additional perspective on both the McMillan Commission and the Commission of Fine Arts.)

Civic Development, Parks, and Influential Men

In 1791, the location of the nation's capital was designated at the confluence of the Potomac River and Eastern Branch, straddling the boundary between Virginia and Maryland. President George Washington commissioned Major Peter Charles L'Enfant to design a plan (1791–92) for the city of Washington. L'Enfant used the Baroque design vocabulary of his native France to create a plan expressive of the new federal form of government—an orthogonal street grid overlaid with a network of diagonal avenues linking major government buildings, open spaces, and neighborhoods. The newly established Territory of Columbia—now known as the District of Columbia— comprised five independent jurisdictions: two existing small towns, Alexandria (founded 1749) and Georgetown (founded 1751); the city of Washington, encompassing

Christopher Columbus by Mary Lawrence (Tonetti) at the entrance to the Administration Building, World's Columbian Exposition, 1893. Augustus Saint-Gaudens—in charge of sculpture at the exposition—selected his assistant Lawrence for the project despite her lack of experience with large-scale sculpture. Director of Decorations Francis Millet disliked the finished piece and had it removed from the entrance; Lawrence appealed to Charles McKim, and it was returned to the original location.

the area of land demarcated by the L'Enfant Plan; and the rest of the terrain within the ten-square-mile area east and west of the Potomac River named Washington County and Alexandria County, respectively.

The Territory of Columbia's form of government was unique. The two extant municipalities retained their own governance, and Congress designated courts to administer affairs in the two counties while retaining control over the city of Washington; however, disregard and delay characterized Congress's general approach to governing. The exclusive jurisdiction of Congress established the underlying impediment to commercial development in the federal district. After complaining about the lack of responsive governance and commercial activity in their town, Alexandrians convinced Congress in 1846 to cede the land west of the Potomac River back to Virginia. In 1871, Congress revoked Georgetown's charter, combined the municipality with the other District entities, and established the first District-wide municipal government composed of a presidentially appointed governor and boards of public works and health, in addition to a thirty-three-member, locally elected legislative assembly. In 1874, Congress established a second municipal form of government, which lasted four years before a third form comprising three presidentially appointed commissioners was instituted. Consequently, a local government existed but, Congress still

controlled the appointments as well as the purse strings.

The plumber-turned-developer Alexander R. Shepherd was on the Board of Public Works and, between 1871 and 1873, became the District government's most influential leader, promoting a wide range of public works projects that laid the foundation for Washington to shed its small-town image. A critical mass of development, however, did not occur until the invention of the electric streetcar in 1888 and its introduction soon after in cities nationwide, including Washington. By 1890, several electric railway companies were operating in the District, extending outward from the central city and spurring development in the rural areas of Washington County and beyond into Maryland.[3]

Yet, even as the city's infrastructure improved over the course of the nineteenth century, the fetid Washington City Canal and the Potomac tidal flats created a noxious environment downtown. These unhealthy conditions, in such close proximity to President's Park and the White House, led the Senate Committee on Public Buildings and Grounds to direct Major Nathaniel Michler of the U.S. Army Corps of Engineers to examine land in Washington County for a site that would accommodate a new executive mansion and a public park.[4] In 1867, Michler's report recommended the creation of a park with at least 1,800 acres in the upper Rock Creek valley. Advocates of the proposal urged Congress to act quickly as land prices would continue to rise. Subsequently, Senator B. Gratz Brown of

ABOVE LEFT: *Alexander "Boss" Shepherd, shown in 1874, served briefly as governor of the District of Columbia, leaving office amid charges of mismanagement and extravagant spending. His legacy of public works modernized the city.*

BELOW: *Peter Charles L'Enfant's plan of 1791, reproduced by the U.S. Coast and Geodetic Survey in 1887 and the version used by the Senate Park Commission in developing its 1901 plan. L'Enfant's design included a greensward in the center of the city lined with civic buildings—the conceptual basis for the National Mall.*

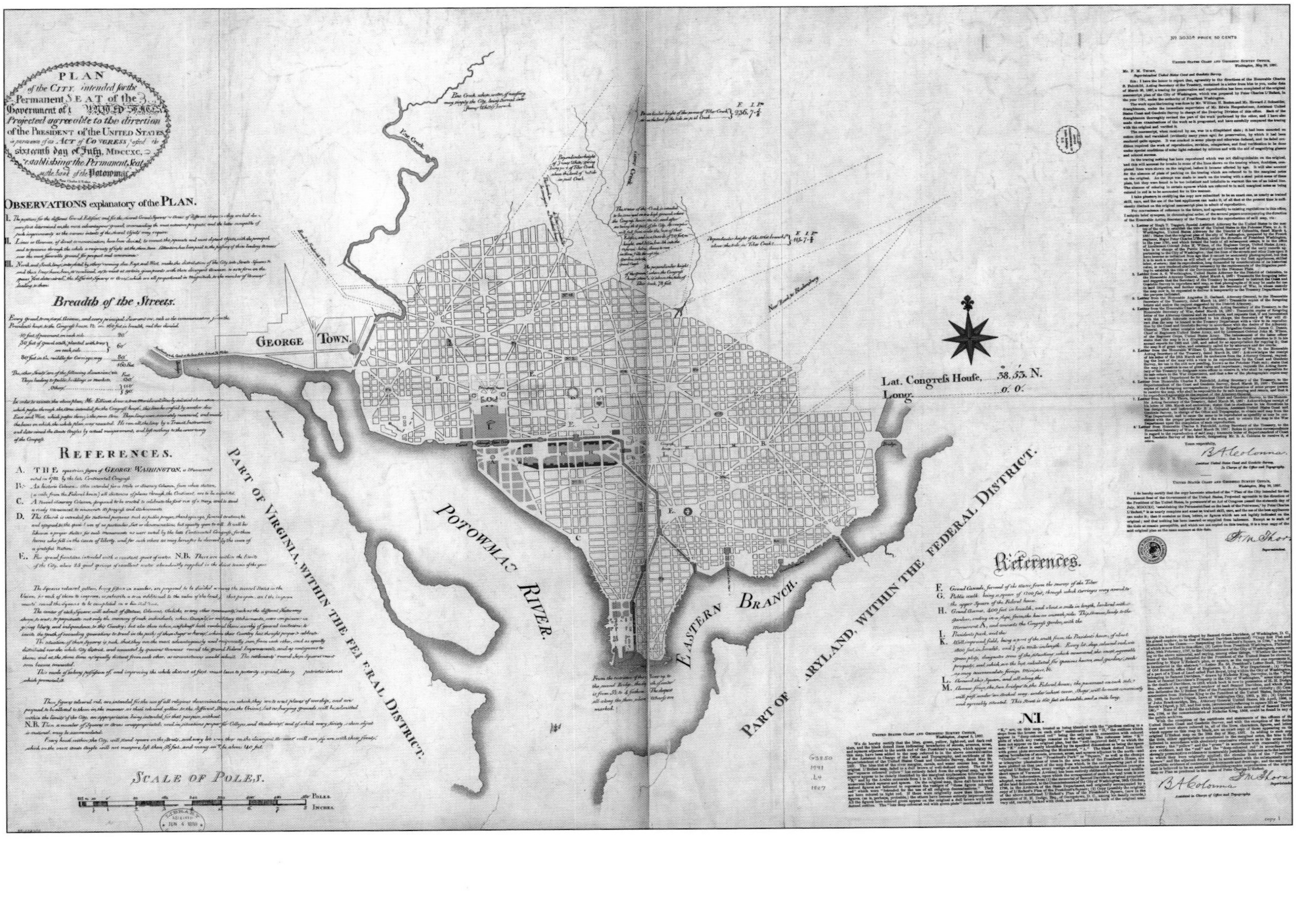

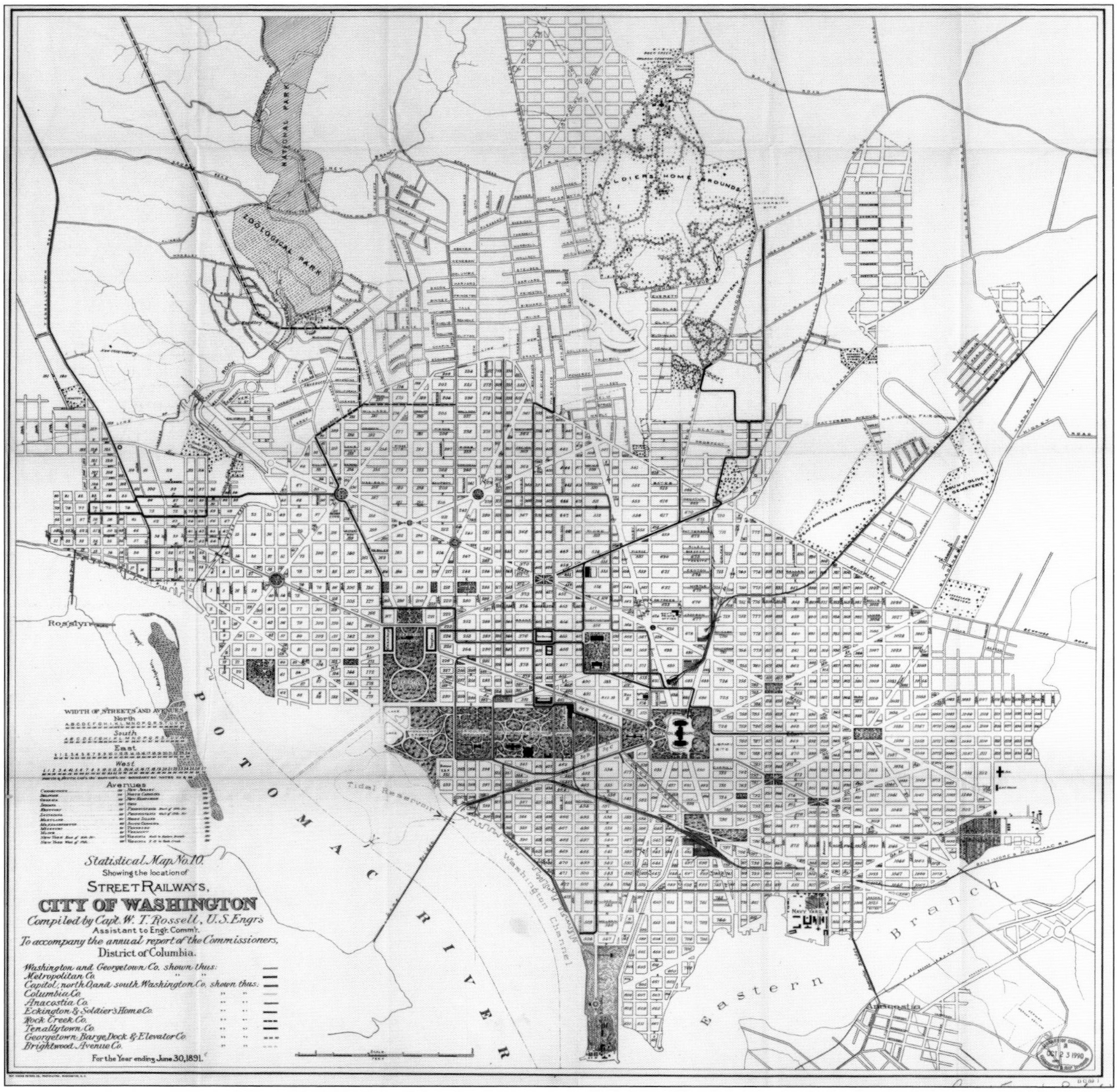

An 1891 map of the District of Columbia depicting street railway lines as well as the earliest suburban neighborhoods extending out from L'Enfant's city core.

Washington's first electric railway, the Eckington and Soldiers Home Railway, began operation in October 1888, running between 7th Street and New York Avenue, NW, and 4th and T Streets, NE. Within a year, the line was extended up 4th Street to Michigan Avenue and Catholic University.

ABOVE LEFT: *View of Rock Creek from the Pennsylvania Avenue Bridge looking south toward the Potomac River, c. 1915. Industrial development along the creek was eventually replaced by the Potomac and Rock Creek Parkway in the 1920s.*

ABOVE RIGHT: *The establishment of Rock Creek Park within the District of Columbia in 1890 preserved the largely undisturbed two thousand-acre woodland tract and made it available for recreational uses.*

Missouri, chairman of the Committee on Public Buildings and Grounds, who appreciated the beauty of the valley and restorative powers of nature, sponsored a bill for a park that year; the House tabled it, in part because the original boundaries of the city of Washington had yet to be filled with development.[5] Many conservative representatives were unsympathetic to allocating money for Washington's civic improvement projects, which they considered to be a local matter. Brown left the Senate shortly thereafter, citing poor health, and it would be nearly two decades before another member of Congress would champion park legislation. Thus, by the 1880s, Washington trailed behind many American cities in the development of large parks.

Beginning in 1884, in response to the growing public health concerns about the Potomac flats, the open sewer condition of the lower Rock Creek valley, and the dumping grounds in Georgetown, the Senate gave renewed attention to protection of the Rock Creek valley. A coalition of senators repeatedly passed bills to establish Rock Creek Park in the upper valley; the House, however, continued not to act on the bills. In 1887, the Washington Chapter of the American Institute of Architects (AIA) was founded, among other reasons, to challenge the monopoly held by the U.S. Army Corps of Engineers over civil engineering and architecture projects in the city. One of its early advocacy measures focused on opposing the corps's effort to fill in the lower Rock Creek valley. The debate—whether to fill in the valley and establish a formal boulevard on top or keep the valley open and design a naturalistic parkway with carriageways and bridal paths—would continue for more than two decades.

In 1889, civic-minded businessmen established the Washington Board of Trade, in part because they realized that coordinated advocacy regarding local issues was needed to engage Congress. The Board of Trade wanted to diminish the antagonistic relationships between the various neighborhoods and businessmen in the city that often led to failed legislation because of the lack of a united lobbying effort. With its twenty standing committees, ranging from Universities and Libraries to Streets and Avenues, the Board of Trade quickly became the city's most politically powerful civic organization.

From its inception, the Board of Trade's members sought to improve the civic stature of Washington and considered parks to be a necessary means to this end. For the Rock Creek valley, the board had a two-pronged agenda: it wanted the upper valley established as a naturalistic park and the lower valley to form the link between that park and the Washington Monument Grounds—the western end of the Mall at that time. The board prepared a report expounding the benefits of transforming the lower Rock Creek valley into a scenic parkway.

In September 1890, near the end of the congressional session, Senator John Sherman (R-OH) and Representative John Hemphill (D-SC), chairman of the House Committee on the District of Columbia, succeeded in pushing a bill for Rock Creek Park through their respective houses.[6] The establishment of the park finally allowed Washington to gain standing with the principal American cities of the day. Hemphill wrote a congratulatory note to Charles Carroll Glover—one of the founders of the Washington Board of Trade—who had lobbied the hardest for the creation of the park:

The bill to establish the Rock Creek Park, which passed Congress only after the most strenuous efforts, has been approved by the President and is now a law. As it was at your request that this bill was

CHAPTER I | AIM HIGH IN HOPE AND WORK

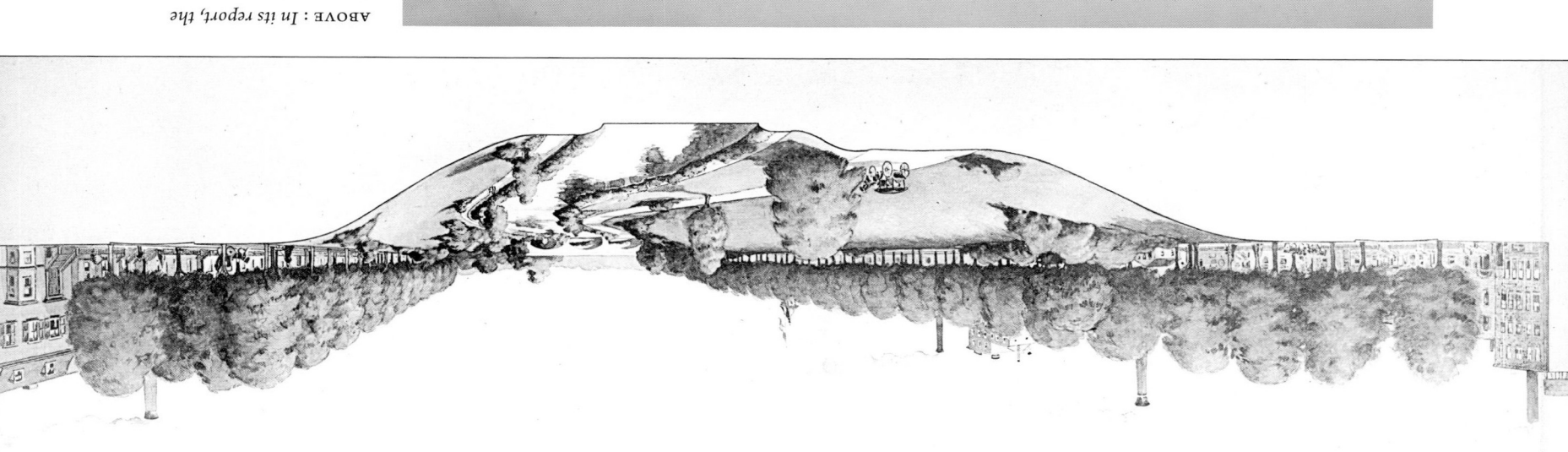

ABOVE: In its report, the Senate Park Commission recommended the open valley plan for the disposition of the lower Rock Creek valley long advocated by the Washington Board of Trade.

LEFT: View of Rock Creek with the Connecticut Avenue (now William Howard Taft Memorial) Bridge in the background, c. 1910. The new bridge, completed in 1907, facilitated the extension of development into northwest Washington.

TOP LEFT: *Charles Carroll Glover leaving his office at Riggs Bank, across Pennsylvania Avenue from the Treasury Department, in 1915. Glover began his career at Riggs & Company in 1865 and became a partner at the age of twenty-seven; when the bank adopted a national charter in 1896, Glover became its first president and held the position for twenty-five years.*

TOP CENTER: *Francis Griffith Newlands walking outside the Capitol, c. 1915. Newlands— an heir and trustee of the William Sharon estate and mining fortune—was elected to Congress in 1893 and served twenty-four years, first as a representative and then as a senator from Nevada.*

ABOVE RIGHT: *The Washington Monument and Potomac River, c. 1885. Dredging equipment is visible in the*

ABOVE LEFT: *View looking west along Connecticut Avenue Extended between Newark and Ordway Streets, NW, c. 1903. In 1887, New-lands began to sell off Sharon estate landholdings around Dupont Circle in favor of*

river; material from this operation was used by the U.S. Army Corps of Engineers to create what would become Potomac Park, abutting the western edge of the Mall.

residential property in nearby Montgomery County, Mary-land. To link his suburban development to downtown Washington, Newlands pur-chased land along Connecticut Avenue Extended in the late 1880s and established the Rock Creek Railway, which began operating in 1890.

introduced, setting aside this beautiful section of country as a park for all time, I desire to congratulate you on the final approval of the meas- ure; and to say that without your earnest, intelligent and untiring ef- forts during the entire contest it would in my judgment have failed to become a law.

Your valuable work in behalf of this great pleasure ground at the National Capital ought to be known and long remembered by the many thousands who shall hereafter enjoy it.[7]

Nevertheless, some of the advocates for Rock Creek Park supported the legislation for more than altruistic and conservation reasons. These men owned extensive tracts of land in the vicinity of the park; they included Glover, Senator William M. Stewart (R-NV), and lawyer Francis G. Newlands of San Francisco—a trustee of vast western landholdings from his wife's family, who later became a representative and then senator from Nevada. The pres- ence of Rock Creek Park—as well as the 170-acre National Zoological Park established in 1889—provided a large syl- van boundary for the adjacent residential developments they envisioned. As Stewart candidly noted, the parks took "2000 acres out of the market."[8] However, neither the zoo nor the park legislation made any provision for the future of the lower Rock Creek valley. The competing plans for the lower valley by the Board of Trade and the Corps of Engineers pitted Washington businessmen and architects against engineers and the Georgetown Citizens Associa- tion, whose members struggled to support the economic independence of the former town.

As the historian Daniel Boorstin has noted, the Ameri- can businessman emerged in the mid-nineteenth century as a unique combination of community maker and com- munity leader. His primary commodity was land, and his secondary commodity was transportation. Not to boost one's city reflected a lack of community spirit as well as poor economic sense. These businessmen sought to attract new residents with easier, cheaper, and more pleasant means of living in their city.[9] In Washington, Glover and Newlands personified the American nineteenth-century businessman and helped shape the environment that led to the establishment of the Commission of Fine Arts. In their professional careers, Glover chose banking and ulti- ately managed Riggs & Company, the city's preeminent bank, while Newlands pursued a law practice and eventu- ally political office, but their interests overlapped with busi- ness pursuits in railways and personal investments in land development.[10] They focused their energies on the pie- shaped area largely defined by Massachusetts and Con- necticut Avenues in the elevated terrain of Northwest Washington, establishing the foundation for the affluent neighborhoods that exist in this area today.

Both men also held the less common approach to real estate investment by valuing long-range planning and beauty. As a senator, in later years, Newlands endorsed leg- islation to guide harmonious development in Washington, whereas Glover was instrumental in the designation of parkland, including Potomac Park west and south of the Washington Monument. In the 1880s, dredging of the Po- tomac River in that area commenced to improve naviga- tion, and the silt was deposited on the disease-breeding tidal flats, ultimately creating 739 acres of solid terrain. With better navigation as the priority, there was no imme- diate plan for how this newly formed land should be used: buildings and structures soon arose; President Cleveland suggested the land be used by Washingtonians for veg- etable gardens. In 1897, after years of effort, Glover suc- ceeded in having the entire area designated as parkland, which would become the critical extension of the National Mall in the twentieth century.

The 1901 Senate Park Commission

Several converging factors led to 1901 becoming a critical time in Washington's planning. In 1889, the Senate Com- mittee on the District of Columbia gained a member who was highly interested in the committee's work and became its chairman within two years: Senator James McMillan (R-MI). During McMillan's tenure, important laws affect- ing the city's infrastructure were enacted, including the mandatory replacement of horse-drawn streetcars with electric cars powered from underground wires in the city of Washington (Congress prohibited overhead wires in this part of the District in 1893); the extension of the L'En- fant Plan street system into Washington County; and the establishment of a sand filtration system to purify munic- ipal water.

Before coming to Washington, James McMillan was a founder of the Michigan Car Company, a producer of rail- road cars and one of Detroit's most profitable manufactur- ing businesses; he was also a successful investor in rail- roads and utilities in the state. In 1879, he led the civic cam- paign to purchase Belle Isle, Michigan, as a public park and ensured that the plan for the island by Frederick Law Olmsted Sr. was implemented.

As the century drew to a close, efforts were initiated to commemorate the 1900 centennial of the federal govern- ment's relocation to Washington. Beyond the parades and parties, the aspirations manifested themselves in several new plans for redeveloping the area between the Capitol and the White House. McMillan endorsed a plan prepared by Chicago architect Henry Ives Cobb in 1900 that fea- tured the Mall intersected by an oblique "Centennial Av- enue" and elevated railroad tracks—a response to the re- cent law forbidding dangerous railroad grade crossings. Architect Glenn Brown, the uncontested expert on the U.S. Capitol and an authority on the early planning of the city, led the movement to kill the McMillan-Cobb plan because it obscured L'Enfant's vision for Washington; Brown instead promoted a scheme he had published in

Architectural Record in 1895." Brown—grandson of a U.S. senator, lobbyist for the Public Art League (an organiza- tion seeking to establish a national fine arts commission), and secretary of the national American Institute of Archi- tects—was well connected for the campaign. He strategi- cally arranged for the AIA's 1900 annual convention to be held in Washington with the development of the District of Columbia as the topic. Several papers were presented by leading design professionals.

Architect Cass Gilbert gave a paper about grouping public buildings in Washington and proposed a new White House on Meridian Hill. Gilbert had begun his career as a carpenter's helper and draftsman in Saint Paul, Minnesota. After studying at the Massachusetts Institute of Technol- ogy, he traveled in Europe and then worked at the Beaux- Arts–oriented New York firm of McKim, Mead & White. Gilbert opened his own practice in Saint Paul in 1882 and entered the national arena after winning the commissions for the Minnesota State Capitol in 1894 and the New York Custom House in 1899. Gilbert would later be appointed to the Commission of Fine Arts.

Landscape architect Frederick Law Olmsted Jr. from

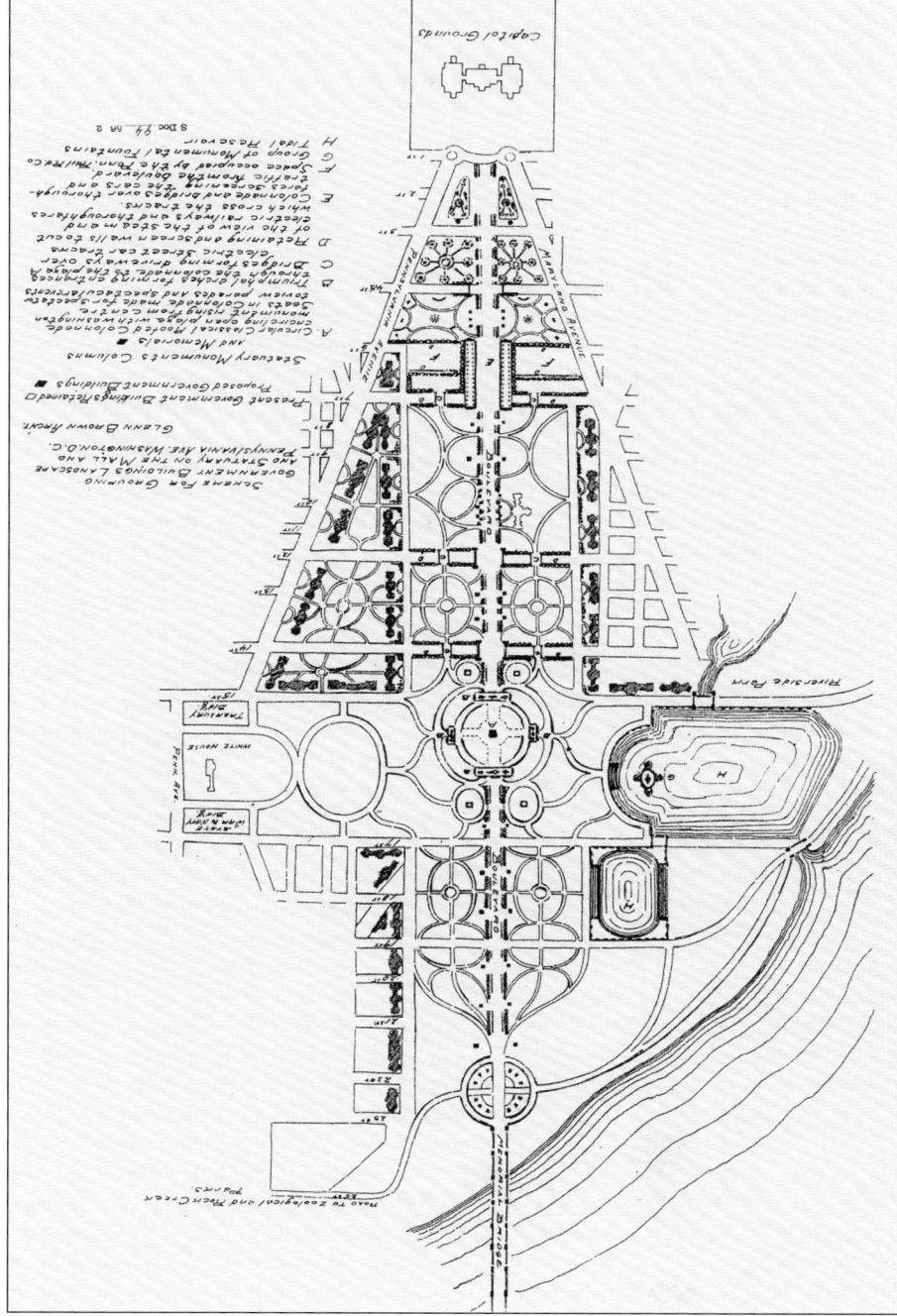

ABOVE: Glenn Brown shown in his office at the Octagon, c. 1900. Brown held an execu- tive position in the Washing- ton chapter of the American Institute of Architects during its first ten years and served as secretary-treasurer of the institute's national organiza- tion from 1900 to 1913.

RIGHT: In the mid-1890s, Glenn Brown drew this plan for grouping government buildings along an extended Mall and Pennsylvania Avenue.

FACING PAGE, TOP: As chair- man of the Senate Committee on the District of Columbia, McMillan supported Henry Ives Cobb's 1900 plan of the proposed Centennial Avenue extending from the Capitol at a slight diagonal across the Mall, nearly parallel to pres- ent-day Constitution Avenue.

BOTTOM: A 1901 study of central Washington by Fred- erick Law Olmsted Jr. shows the piecemeal development of the city outside the L'Enfant core in the late nineteenth century; the monumental precinct of the Mall is empha- sized by dark shading.

Suggestions for locating future Government Buildings in the District of Columbia.
by Henry Ives Cobb. Architect.
Washington D.C. Feby 15th 1900.
NOTE.. Shaded portions indicate Government Reservations. Proposed buildings shown in black.
LAFAYETTE SQUARE
WHITE HOUSE
Reviewing Stand
WHITE LOT
CORCORAN GALLERY
OLD OBSERVATORY GROUNDS
NEW YORK AVE.
PROPOSED MEMORIAL BRIDGE
PLAZZA
PENNSYLVANIA AVENUE
OHIO AVE.
B Street
CITY HALL
PENSION OFFICE and COURT Ho.
LA. AVE.
INDIANA AVE.
PROPOSED NEW AVENUE
UNION R.R. STATION
THE MALL
LAKE
MONUMENT
PROPOSED PARK
RIVER
AGRICULTURAL
SMITHSONIAN
BOTANICAL
CAPITOL GROUNDS
CONG'L LIBRARY
ENGRAVING BUREAU

MAP
DISTRICT OF COLUMBIA.
ROCK CREEK PARK
PETWORTH
SOLDIERS HOME
BROOKLAND
GEORGETOWN
POTOMAC
EASTERN BRANCH
RIVER
EAST WASHINGTON HEIGHTS
BARRY FARM
INSANE ASYLUM
GARFIELD

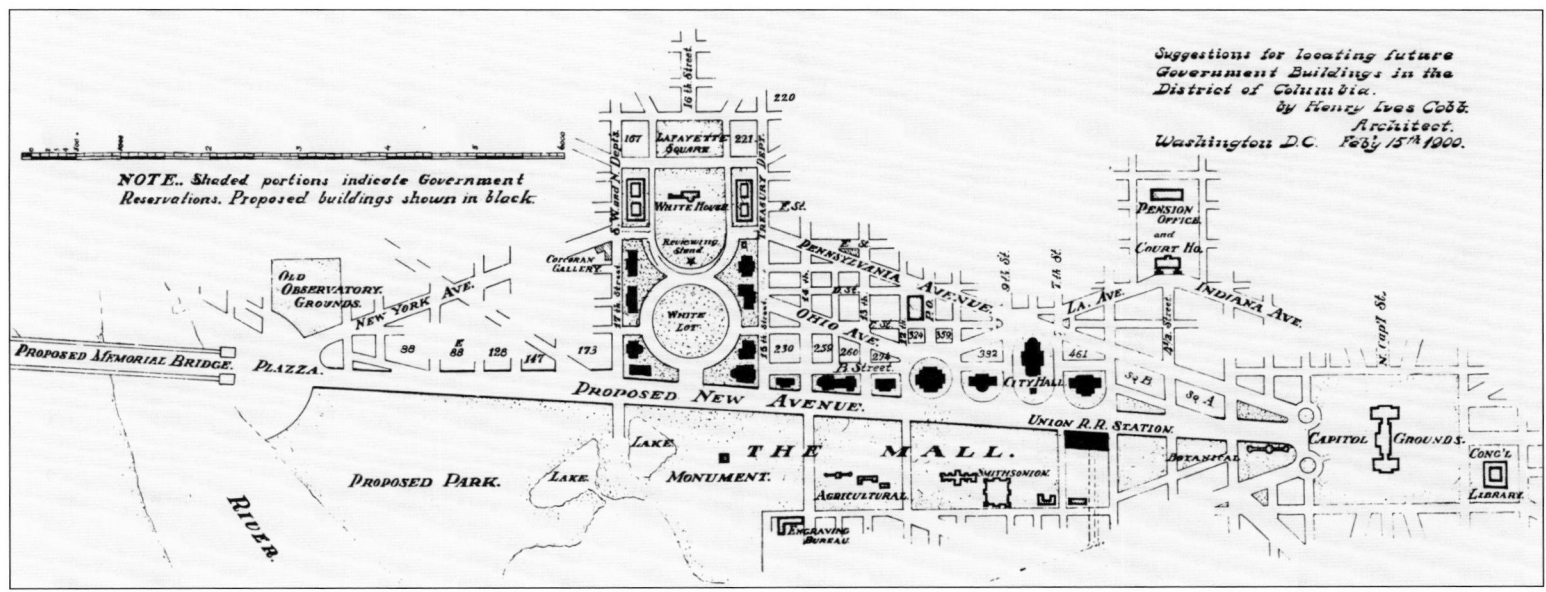

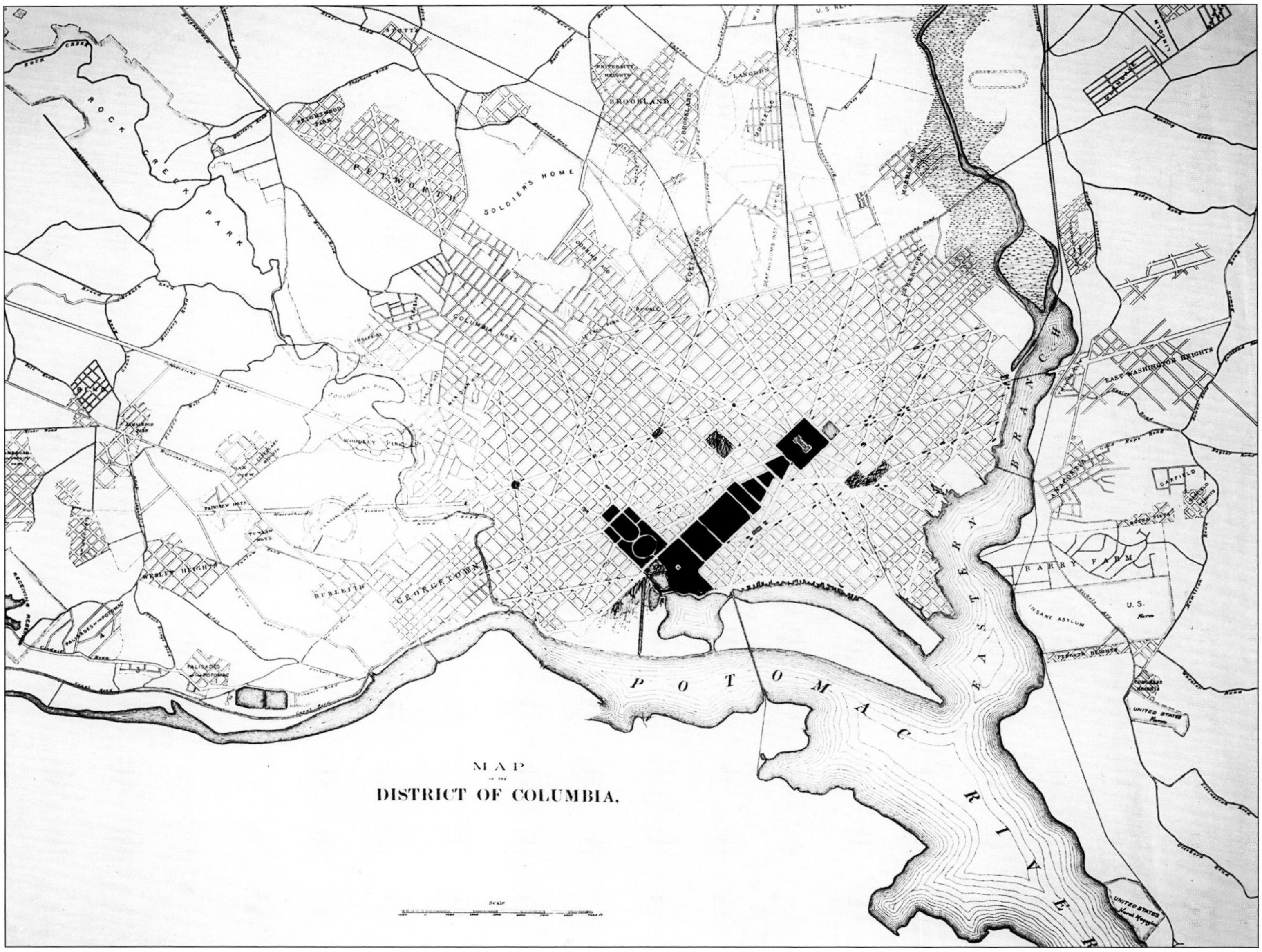

Brookline, Massachusetts, advocated for public edifices set in formal landscapes to establish a consistent whole. He also stressed the responsibility of citizens to respect history and the importance of Washington as the seat of government and symbol of a powerful nation. Olmsted was the son and professional heir to nineteenth-century America's most highly regarded landscape architect. He initially learned about Washington through his father's commission to redesign the U.S. Capitol Grounds (1874–92). While attending Harvard, the younger Olmsted worked with his father on the landscape plan for the 1893 World's Columbian Exposition. He formally entered his father's firm in 1895 and began working on the Metropolitan Park System of Boston. In 1899, Olmsted became a founding member of the American Society of Landscape Architects and the following year helped establish the first landscape architecture program in the nation at Harvard University. Olmsted would also be appointed to the Commission of Fine Arts.

At the end of the AIA convention, a resolution called for Congress to establish a professional design commission to consider improvements to the nation's capital. A few days later, a committee led by New York architect William Boring met with Senator McMillan. A mutually agreed-upon resolution was introduced in the Senate on December 17, 1900:

Resolved…that the President…is hereby authorized to appoint a commission, to consist of two architects and one landscape architect eminent in their professions, who shall consider the subject of the location and grouping of public buildings and monuments to be erected in the District of Columbia and the development and improvement of the entire park system of said District."[12]

Representative Joseph Cannon (R-IL), who chaired the House Committee on Appropriations and was opposed to spending federal money for the District, characteristically opposed the measure. After Congress had adjourned, McMillan introduced the matter at a Senate executive session on March 8, 1901, where it was approved with the expenses to be paid from Senate discretionary funds. The circumventing of the typical legislative process infuriated Cannon. Historian John Reps has argued that McMillan strategically invoked the park focus because he was well aware that other congressional committees had primary jurisdiction over Washington's public buildings, statuary, and public works.[13] It would seem that had McMillan's true interest been parkland, then a landscape architect would have been chosen to lead the commission and perhaps a second landscape professional would participate as a member.

Instead, McMillan asked Chicago architect Daniel Hudson Burnham and landscape architect Frederick Law Olmsted Jr. to serve on the panel, called the Senate Park Commission. Burnham had designed a variety of significant commercial buildings in Chicago and had coordinated the construction of the 1893 World's Columbian Exposition. After failing the entrance exams to Harvard and Yale Universities, Burnham began work as a draftsman in 1872 in the Chicago office of Carter, Drake, & Wight. Within a year, he convinced the firm's most talented draftsman, John Wellborn Root, to establish their own firm. Burnham and Root helped shape Chicago's first architectural skyline composed of tall buildings like the Rookery (1885–88) and the Monadnock (1889–92). In 1890, Congress voted in favor of Chicago hosting the World's Columbian Exposition to commemorate the four hundredth anniversary of the discovery of America. Although many people collaborated on the exposition, Burnham was the primary advocate for the notion of its unified White City. His organizational skills matched his persuasive powers: he convinced skeptical New York architects to participate in what they thought would be a regional fair as opposed to a national architectural event.[14] The exposition buildings became models and inspiration for American architecture through formal monumentality, classical designs, and a uniform cornice line. As director of works, Burnham coordinated the construction of more than two

LEFT: *The Piazza di Termini in Rome, one of the sites visited by the McMillan Commission in 1901, provided the members with a conceptual model for the design of government buildings in an urban context.*

LEFT, BOTTOM: *On their study tour in 1901, the Senate Park Commission members also visited the Place de la Concorde in Paris. Designed in 1755, it is the city's largest square and mediates between the urban architecture of the Louvre complex and the open space of the Champs-Elysées.*

TOP ROW, LEFT: *Daniel Burnham (c. 1900) insisted that the Senate Park Commission travel to Europe to study various urban and park conditions as precedents for design of Washington's monumental core.*

CENTER: *Charles McKim attended the École des Beaux-Arts in Paris from 1867 to 1870 and then worked for the eclectic French architect P. J. H. Daumet. McKim's own firm, McKim, Mead & White, founded in 1879, set the standard of Beaux-Arts architecture in America for decades.*

RIGHT: *Augustus Saint-Gaudens in Paris, 1898. The vigorous naturalism of his early work,* Admiral David Farragut *(1881) for Madison Square in New York City, inspired a new generation of American sculptors at the turn of the twentieth century.*

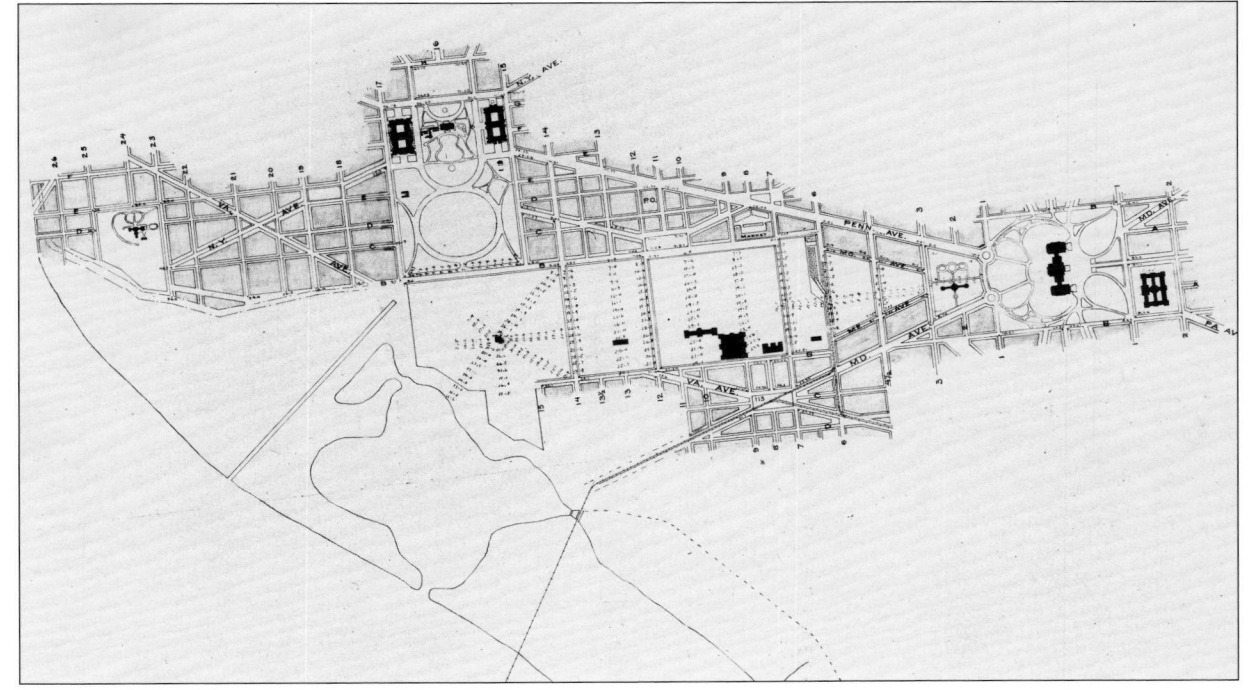

ABOVE: *The iconic aerial view of Washington's monumental core for the McMillan Plan, rendered by Francis L.V. Hoppin, 1901. Remarkably, the city's core as built is strikingly similar to this seminal image.*

RIGHT: *A preliminary anaytical drawing of the Mall prepared for the Senate Park Commission's study in April 1901 indicated streets, grade elevations, and the few existing government buildings within the Mall precinct.*

ABOVE: *View of the Mall from the Washington Monument looking eastward, 1901. Still visible are the picturesque paths designed by Andrew Jackson Downing and the Baltimore and Potomac railway crossing the Mall at 6th Street.*

LEFT: *This image of central Washington from the 1901 McMillan Report is known as the "Kite Plan." The plan integrated the vast reclaimed lands of Potomac Park as an extension of L'Enfant's Mall, culminating on the west in a rond point as a location for a memorial to President Lincoln.*

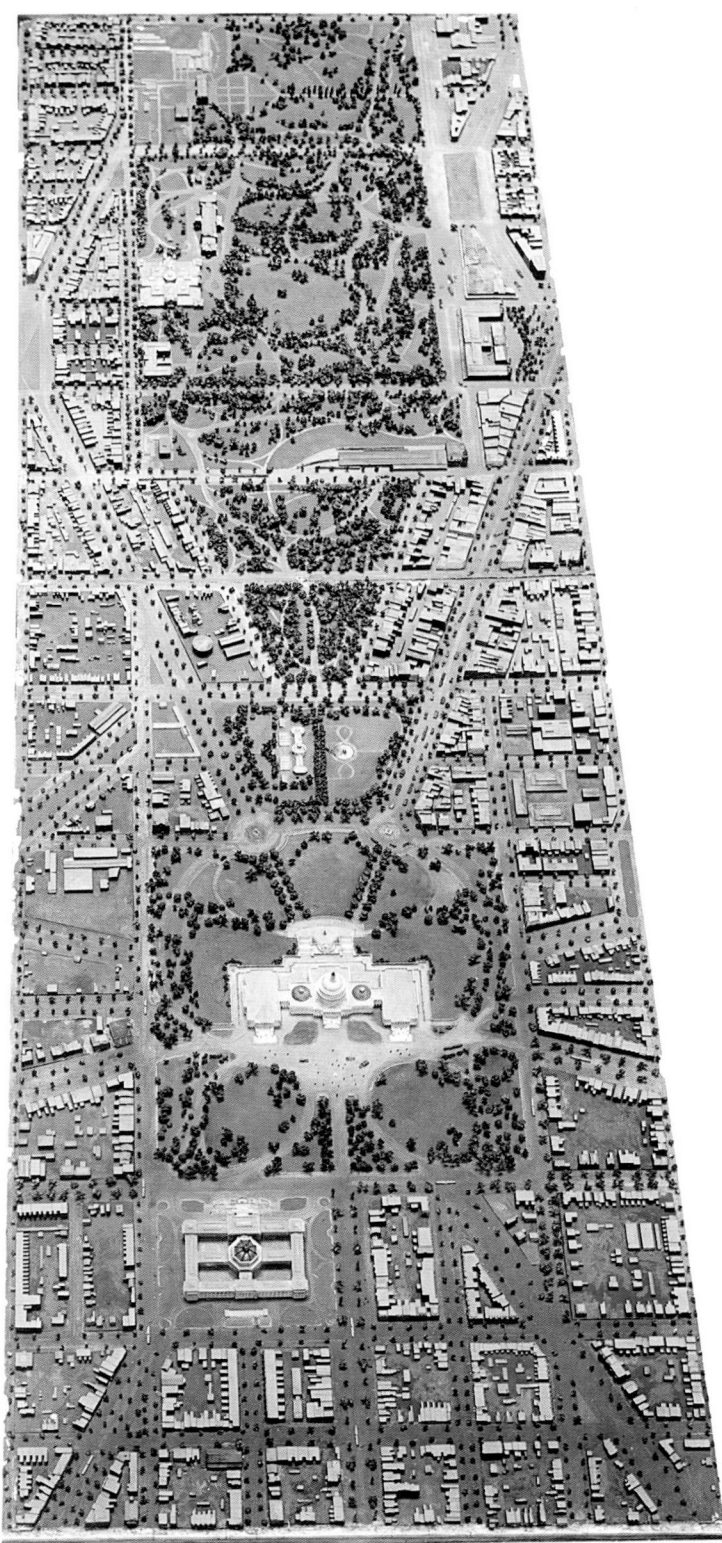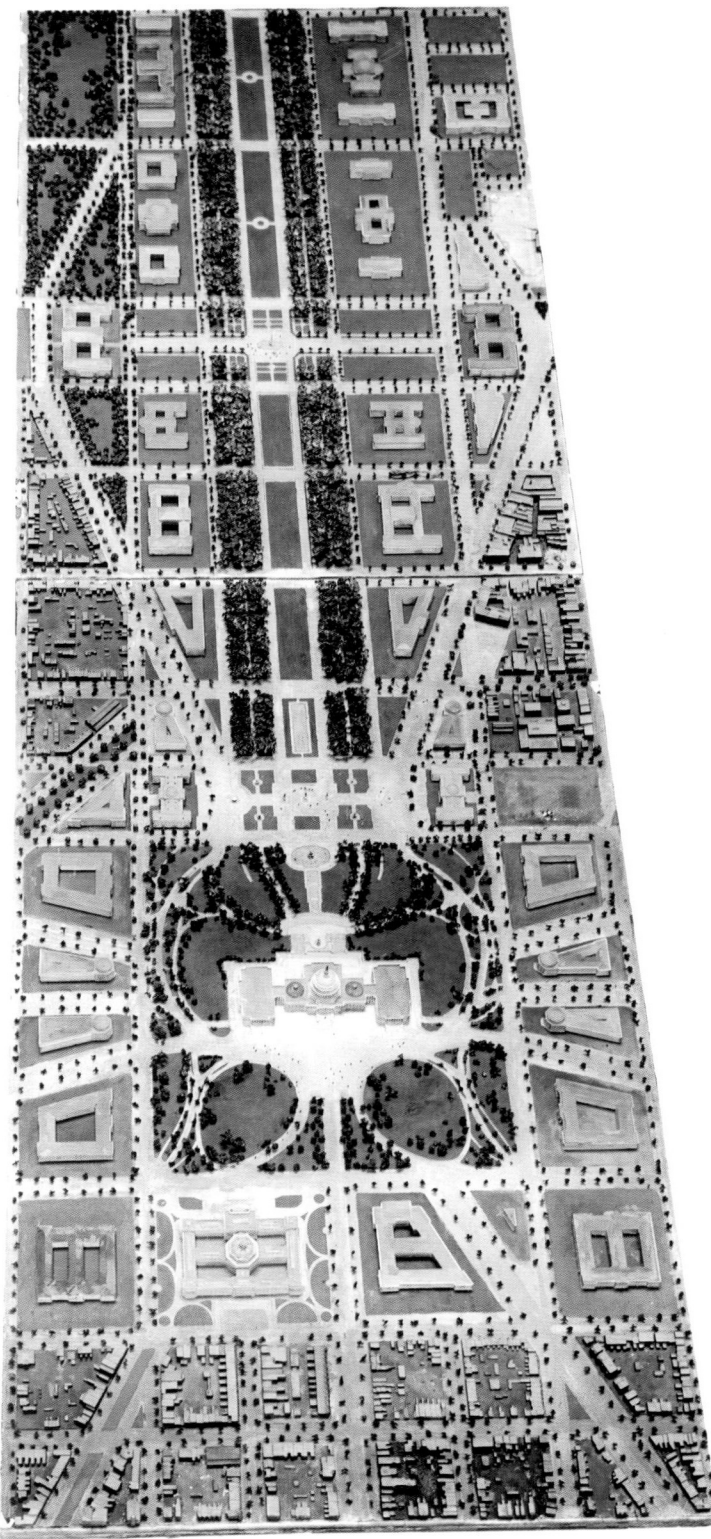

The Senate Park Commission model (1901) of existing conditions on the Mall (left) showing its picturesque and fragmented land-scape, and the proposed design for the Mall (right), imposing a wholly new order and scale to create a monumental precinct.

CHAPTER I | AIM HIGH IN HOPE AND WORK

The Senate Park Commission proposed significant additions (dark green) to the city's existing parkland (light green). The parkway along the lower Rock Creek valley, linking the Mall to Rock Creek Park, was a principal component of the proposed park system along with the Fort Circle parkway that was proposed to create a continuous ring of open space within the city.

hundred buildings in one square mile. Open for only six months, the exposition received 27.5 million visits at a time when the country's population was 65 million.

Burnham and Olmsted approached Charles F. McKim to join the Senate Park Commission. McKim had received his architectural training at the École des Beaux-Arts in Paris and was one of the country's leading proponents of classicism. A partner in the prominent New York firm of McKim, Mead & White, he had played an important role in the planning of the Columbian Exposition.

McMillan detailed his political secretary, Charles Moore, who possessed extensive knowledge of Washington, to the commission. Moore had started his career as a journalist in Michigan, which led him to meet McMillan, at the time a Detroit businessman. When McMillan was elected to the U.S. Senate in 1888, he asked Moore to join his staff; Moore served as the clerk for the Senate Committee on the District of Columbia for the period of McMillan's chairmanship, from 1891 until McMillan's death in 1902.

Burnham, Olmsted, and McKim met as the Senate Park Commission for the first time on April 6, 1901, in Washington, where Moore led them on a variety of site visits. They then traveled to Williamsburg, Virginia, and toured plantations along the James River. After the trip, McKim recommended that New York sculptor Augustus Saint-Gaudens be recruited to serve as a fourth member of

Illustration in the 1901 report of one of the six pavilions McKim proposed for the gardens around the Washington Monument to convey an idyllic and formal character to the composition.

the commission. Saint-Gaudens had also trained at the École and was recognized by many as the country's most talented sculptor. Because of the late invitation and his recent illness, Saint-Gaudens did not participate in the commission's seven-week study tour through Europe planned by Burnham that began in mid-June.

Working through the remainder of 1901, the McMillan Commission sought to blend the L'Enfant Plan with American and European precedents into a compelling vision expressing City Beautiful principles. Unveiled at the Corcoran Gallery of Art in January 1902 with large models and an extensive collection of watercolors and large-format photographs, the Senate Park Commission Plan reinforced the planning and architectural ideals introduced at the 1893 World's Columbian Exposition. The plan focused on an elaborate redesign of the Mall and called for establishing a unified collection of white, monumental classical buildings assembled around an expanded greensward.[15] Specifically, the plan allowed the national capital's monumental core to function as an expression of democracy and continuity with the Founding Fathers while reflecting an imperial scale. The proposal also made recommendations for a collection of parks, parkways, and bridges located well beyond the central core. Dedicated to recreational uses and predominantly situated along the riverfronts, through wooded valleys, and on knolls associated with Civil War forts, these naturalistic parks complemented the formal open space of the Mall. The accompanying report, titled *The Improvement of the Park System of the District of Columbia,* was principally written by Olmsted and Moore, although Burnham criticized Moore's bureaucratic tendency to edit the "color" and "life" from the text.[16]

The McMillan Plan was well received by the local and national press and in the architectural community due to a media campaign organized by Moore and Glenn Brown.[17] However, the plan was not without its detractors. In addition to congressional concern over the $2 million to $6 million cost estimate, local opposition arose regarding the relocation of the U.S. Botanic Garden with its mature trees from the foot of Capitol Hill, and from those Washingtonians living east of the Capitol who, noting the westward emphasis of the Mall planning, feared their neighborhood would be slighted economically.[18] Advocates for the plan—wary of such criticisms as well as political repercussions from McMillan's maneuver to sidestep House involvement—decided not to subject the proposal to a congressional vote. Despite the plan's lack of official standing, it became a touchstone in modern American city planning. It was not until 1910, through the efforts of the AIA, Newlands, and others, that legislation passed establishing the Commission of Fine Arts to promote the McMillan Plan.

Interim Years, 1902–1910

The members of the Senate Park Commission advocated for their plan in official and unofficial capacities for the remainder of the decade. The success of the plan hinged on removing the railroad tracks crossing the Mall in order to restore L'Enfant's vision for this area; the challenge came at a time when railroad companies were growing and increasing their power through mergers. The tracks were owned by the Baltimore and Potomac (B&P) Railroad, a subsidiary of the Pennsylvania Railroad, and served its station located at Constitution Avenue (then B Street) and 6th Street, NW. The problem was particularly urgent because of February 1901 legislation that granted the Pennsylvania Railroad the use of more land on the Mall for a larger station. Coincidentally, Alexander Cassatt, the president of the Pennsylvania Railroad, offered Burnham the project to design the new station shortly after McMillan had selected him for the Senate Park Commission. Burnham accepted the project partly in order to persuade Cassatt to relocate the station, allowing greater flexibility in designing the Mall.[19] Within a few months, the Pennsylvania Railroad had acquired a controlling interest in Washington's other railroad, the Baltimore and Ohio (B&O), which had a terminal at New Jersey Avenue and C Street, NW; the B&O also owned extensive land to the north of its station. Cassatt ultimately acceded to Burnham's wish to build the new station on B&O land at Massachusetts and Delaware Avenues. As part of the deal, Cassatt demanded that Congress compensate the company for tunneling under 1st Street east to preserve its connection with southbound tracks. Union Station, constructed between 1903 and 1908, was the first building to reflect the design principles established in the 1901 plan for Washington. Set behind a grand plaza, the station's white classical form recalled Imperial Rome's triumphal arches. Despite the transportation and architectural successes, political battles remained a concern; Moore later recalled that Cannon "made a gallant fight on the floor of the House for the elimination of the plaza."[20]

Already in the years before the establishment of the Commission of Fine Arts, City Beautiful principles guided the designs of the significant public and semipublic buildings erected in Washington: Central Public Library (1899–1902), Army War College (1903), District Building (1904–08), Senate and House Office Buildings (1905–08), International Bureau of American Republics (now known

as the Organization of American States, 1908–10), and the Daughters of the American Revolution headquarters (1910). The National Museum and the Department of Agriculture building also rose during this time; both presented challenges to advocates for the McMillan Plan.

In 1901, the Smithsonian Institution hired the prominent local firm of Hornblower & Marshall to design the new National Museum. Primarily a designer of residential architecture, the firm had been involved with the recent interior renovation of the existing museum (now known as the Arts and Industries Building). For more than three years, their designs failed to receive the necessary final approval from the Smithsonian's secretary, Samuel Langley. In early 1904, Hornblower brought a revised design to Burnham and Olmsted as well as Peirce Anderson and W. S. Eames of the AIA. Hornblower wanted general advice, such as the best alignment for the first floor, but the others sought to dissuade him from the building's contemporary French style. Nearly two years later, final drawings were approved, including a lower central pavilion and a simplified south elevation that had been reworked by McKim and Burnham; the museum opened in 1909.[21]

The battle over the Department of Agriculture building involved siting rather than style. Congress funded the design of the building in 1901; after more than two years and much negotiation, a design by Rankin, Kellogg & Crane

After years of lobbying led by Theodore Noyes, editor of the Evening Star, *Congress established the District of Columbia Public Library in 1896. With generous support from Andrew Carnegie, a national design competition for the city's new library was held; a Beaux-Arts design by the New York firm of Ackerman & Ross was selected, and the new building opened in 1903.*

TOP: *View of Union Station under construction, c. 1907. The entire plaza in front of the station was elevated approximately thirty-five feet above the bed of Tiber Creek, creating a monumental gateway to the city.*

ABOVE LEFT: *The Baltimore and Potomac Railroad Station by Philadelphia architect Joseph Wilson was erected in 1873 and represented an important example of High Victorian architecture in the city.*

ABOVE RIGHT: *Designed by the Baltimore architecture firm Niernsee & Neilson in 1852, the Italianate-style Baltimore and Ohio Railroad Station included a clock and bell tower that served as a landmark on Capitol Hill for fifty-five years.*

LEFT, TOP TO BOTTOM: *The House Office Building was completed in 1908 by the New York firm Carrère & Hastings—it was renamed in 1962 in honor of former Speaker of the House Joseph Cannon.* CENTER: *Edward Pearce Casey designed the Daughters of the American Revolution Memorial Continental Hall in 1910—the building was expanded in 1923 by Marsh & Peter.* BOTTOM: *The District Building, headquarters for the three appointed District com-*

missioners and their staffs, who administered the city's government, was constructed between 1904 and 1908 in an exuberantly sculptural Beaux-Arts style designed by the Philadelphia firm Cope & Stewardson.

ABOVE: *Philadelphia architect Paul Cret designed the Pan American Union building, the first monumental building along Constitution Avenue west of the Ellipse, completed in 1910.*

TOP: *Plaster model of one of Hornblower & Marshall's 1905 proposals for the south elevation of the National Museum (now the National Museum of Natural History), reflecting their interest in a contemporary French expression for the building.*

ABOVE: *View of the southern entrance to the National Museum, c. 1910. The Hornblower & Marshall design was revised in a Roman classical style with strong direction by Charles McKim and Daniel Burnham.*

was approved for an administrative building flanked by two laboratory wings situated on the department's land on the north side of the Mall along the 13th Street axis.[22] In early 1904, the House Committee on Agriculture—citing reasons including appropriate visibility—inserted itself in the process and opposed locating the new building on the north side of the Mall. The committee's members staunchly supported narrowing the setback of the Mall greensward by two hundred feet to allow the building's construction on the Mall's south side.

Senator Francis G. Newlands (D-NV), who had recently completed ten years of service in the House, picked up the torch for the District left by McMillan. In January 1904, Newlands wrote Brown about his concerns for Washington:

I would be pleased if the American Institute of Architects would suggest a form of legislation that would tend to uniformity and harmony in the future development of Washington! That involves the consideration and determination of the question of projections beyond the building line, the uniformity of sky line, and the treatment of buildings and the location and character of monuments, so as to produce unity in the Architectural, and Landscape treatment as a whole, also furnish me with such data as you may have as to the management of similar problems, by other municipalities in this country and in Europe.[23]

Newlands introduced a bill (S. 4845) in March concerning the location of new buildings on the Mall to counter the House committee's proposal and to preserve the wider greensward, a position Newlands passionately supported in a speech during Senate discussion of the bill. Within a few days of the bill's introduction, the Senate's District Committee also held a hearing—instigated by Newlands—on the issue of the Mall's width. A variety of design professionals attended, including Burnham, McKim, Saint-Gaudens, Olmsted, Frank Miles Day, George B. Post, George Oakley Totten Jr., and Joseph Hornblower, as well as banker Charles Glover. The Senate committee issued a report supporting the Mall's width at 890 feet, as advocated by supporters of the McMillan Commission plan, but Newlands's bill did not become law. However, the new Agriculture building eventually was built on the south side of the Mall but in accordance with the wider setback.

Within a few days of the District Committee hearing, Charles Moore, who was living in Detroit at the time, wrote a letter to Newlands:

I have been reading with the greatest possible interest your gallant defence of the Park Commission plans, especially the Mall sites and Lafayette Square plans. I think that the country owes you a debt of gratitude which you will find the people will pay you over and over again. I know of nothing in which the people are more interested than they are in the Washington plans, and they are grateful to anyone who will intelligently and steadfastly push on the good work. I am enclosing a copy of a letter I have just written to Senator Gallinger, showing how the Mall plans came to be determined as they were. Everything that is done rightly now will save a great deal of work and worry in time to come.[24]

A few days later, Burnham sent Newlands the following telegram: "I deeply appreciate the position and action you have taken regarding plans for Washington. The thanks of entire Country are due you. Please wire when you want me for any purpose and I will be on hand."[25] Frank Miles Day and architect Francis Kellogg, both of Philadelphia, thanked Newlands for his support and sought strategic advice for the future. J. R. Coolidge Jr. of the Boston Society of Architects also thanked Newlands for his speech and noted that the society advocated for the plan. McKim sent Newlands a variety of letters to indicate support from New Yorkers and at the end of the month dispatched a telegram exclaiming: "The Greatful thanks and congratulations of the Country and profession are due for the support of congress inaugu-

rated by you."[26] McKim also attempted to offer thanks by having Newlands's name listed as one of the founders of the American Academy in Rome. Newlands supported legislation for the institution dedicated to the study of classical design, but would not allow his name to be listed as one of the incorporators for reasons of propriety.[27] After this bill passed, McKim wrote: "Trustees [of the] American Academy in Rome begs [sic] to tender you their hearty and grateful thanks for your timely and valuable interference in securing passage of Bill in Senate yesterday."[28]

Following the San Francisco earthquake and fire of 1906, Newlands asked Burnham to prepare a new plan for the damaged city. Burnham declined the offer—perhaps because he thought his 1905 plan for the city would suffice—but asked if the report of the Senate Park Commission could be reissued. Newlands responded, "I think it ought to be reprinted, and will do all I can to secure a reprint.... I fear, however, there may be some difficulty in the House, as the opposition to your great work still exists there." Newlands's respect for design professionals and City Beautiful principles is reflected in his description of ongoing work in his beloved city in the west:

The rehabilitation of San Francisco... never started right. [It] should have been done under the direction of architect and administrator who had had experience in exposition building.... A certain part of San Francisco ought to have been organized into a temporary San Francisco, leaving the rest for the slow processes of permanent restoration. The work of the best architects, landscape and municipal engineers should have been employed in a harmonious development.[29]

In closing, he asked Burnham to reconsider his decision and participate in a commission that would guide the reconstruction of the city. Burnham's lengthy reply closed with a metaphysical position: "I don't believe in a com-

mittee to get up a scheme. The soul of real things does not hatch out under committees."[30]

In January 1905, President Theodore Roosevelt gave a speech, "Art and the Republic," at the American Institute of Architects' annual dinner. He argued that the nation had not yet achieved success in the field of beauty and advocated John Ruskin's approach to the spirit of doing work for the sake of the work itself rather than the fee. He asserted that he favored public buildings erected following a well-conceived plan, and he hailed the various municipal improvement commissions around the country. A few months later, Roosevelt issued an executive order establishing the Washington Consultative Board, which consisted of members of the Senate Park Commission and Bernard Green, superintendent of buildings and grounds for the Library of Congress.[31] The order dictated that the board be consulted regarding the location and design for any public building. Nevertheless, the board, sometimes referred to as the Washington Commission, did not have congressional authorization or, therefore, support.

Consequently, within two years, Burnham became frustrated with the ineffective work and quit in February 1907 in order to focus on his plan for Chicago. He wrote McKim of his decision:

I am drawing in my horns and getting out of things in which I find myself taking no active part. Therefore, I have resigned from the Washington Commissionership.[32]

In his response, McKim acknowledged the frustrations associated with their unofficial work, but not the resignation:

It is evident we cannot be expected to go indefinitely in this manner, nor count on the support of the next administration. If any blow can

ABOVE LEFT: *The old Department of Agriculture headquarters—a severe brick, Second-Empire-style building—was designed by Adolf Cluss and erected on the Mall in 1868, several years after the establishment of the department.*

ABOVE RIGHT: *The first phase of the new Department of Agriculture headquarters by Rankin, Kellogg & Crane was built between 1904 and 1908 and was ultimately located to maintain the setback recommended in the McMillan Plan; the central block was completed in a later phase after the old departmental building was razed in 1930.*

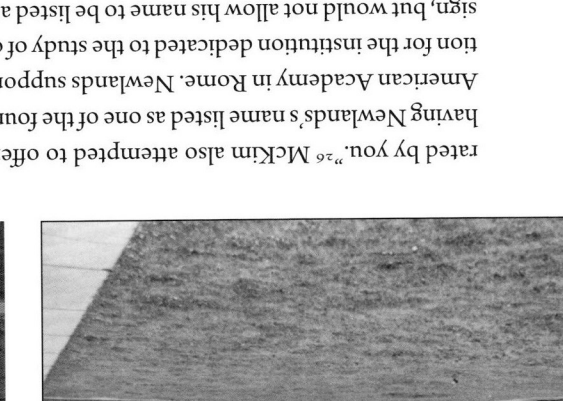

be struck by which a safe advisory board can be officially appointed during the present administration by Congress, to safeguard the development of the Washington improvement. Mr. Root or Mr. Taft are the only people I see in sight to consult. Put a wet towel around your head and think about it hard, and let us all meet in Washington before long and get together again as we did with Senator McMillan in 1901.

On the other hand, the last thing we can afford to do is to give up the good fight, and I rejoice to think that you are once more back with us; in fact, your proposition to retire has never received serious consideration by anybody.... [T]he work could not go on without you.[33]

Burnham replied:

Enough said! We stay for the present, but only long enough to effect some safe organization. It is not absolutely essential that Congress should officially create this censorship, though this would be the best thing, but it is essential that there shall be a secretary devoted to the work and that regular meetings shall be held.[34]

Thereafter, Secretary of War William H. Taft wrote a letter to Burnham expressing President Roosevelt's and his relief that Burnham intended to continue his public service in Washington.[35]

The public relations battle for a design review body continued for years, with perhaps the most vitriolic article published in January 1908 by the *Evening Star.* The lengthy piece explained that the hostility toward the "sham Commission" had intensified over time because of the persistent character of the "self-appointed" body. It claimed Congress had been tricked, especially regarding the removal of mature trees throughout the Mall, creating "desolation as bare and as hot as the Desert of Sahara." The article also complained that the often-described grand vista could be seen by only a few people.[36]

On December 15, 1908, the AIA again held its annual convention in Washington. New York architect S. B. P. Trowbridge gave an important committee report on a proposed Bureau of Fine Arts; the working group included Glenn Brown, the skilled strategist for the AIA who previously had sought lobbying advice from Newlands.[37] In an effort to educate Congress, Trowbridge began the report with a discussion of design in terms of economics rather than aesthetics. He noted that the existing public building construction situation was grave and needed immediate attention to prevent "artistic chaos" and additional money being wasted. He reported that the individual approach to particular projects led to a revolving introduction of legislation before Congress. His committee argued for a single authority "guided by the most enlightened advice which the artistic professions can furnish" and declared that "the common desire of every race in every period of their history to preserve and guard artistic treasures evidences the instinct for beauty and the aspiration for immortality."

ABOVE: *President Theodore Roosevelt depicted in a stereoscopic card, working in his office at the White House, c. 1903; he created the Commission of Fine Arts' precursor, the short-lived Council of Fine Arts.*

BELOW: *Clifford Berryman's scathing 1908 cartoon for the Evening Star critiqued the proposal to remove existing trees from the Mall and replace them with formal rows of elms. Rigid caricatures of Charles McKim, Daniel Burnham, Glenn Brown, and other proponents of a Beaux-Arts vision for the Mall carry axes and direct legions of workers to install cubic topiary.*

The group of tree-butchers and nature-butchers depicted above are represented as on their way with axes to make a "clean-sweep," as they proclaim, of all the grand old trees on the Mall. They are costumed on architectural, straight lines. Architect McKim heads the party. He is blowing a big horn—his own. He also has a big head. Architect Donn will be recognized by his corrected upturned nose. In the rear are men bearing a great number of tubbed trees intended to replace the big trees destroyed.
For further particulars inquire within.

U.S. CAPITOL

GROUP OF LE NOTRE-McKIM TREE-BUTCHERS AND NATURE-BUTCH-RS.

Architect McKim, Architect Burnham, Architect Glenn Brown, Architect Green, Architect Hornblower, Architect Donn.

Trowbridge concluded his report by emphasizing that the establishment of a bureau of fine arts was not to develop a national style for the country, "but to invest the whole subject of the fine arts with appropriate dignity, to encourage the proper schools, to stimulate the universities in this much neglected branch, and to educate the people."[38]

Senator Newlands gave the speech, "The Democracy of Art," at the convention. The importance of the democratization of art at the national level was a topic about which he had been speaking for years; however, he claimed to know little about art. Newlands remarked on the split between the support from Roosevelt's administration and the consideration within Congress. He was particularly concerned because the nation was at the beginning of a significant public building campaign. Newlands advised the AIA on how to strategize to sway public opinion and made suggestions about how to craft legislation for a Bureau of Art and Public Buildings, which would include an advisory Council of Arts. Newlands described two ways of making legislation: "You can aim high at the start, or you can rely upon the process of evolution."[39] He noted that the framework for the bureau could be developed out of the existing Office of the Supervising Architect of the Treasury.

The AIA, however, preferred to take no chances. One month later on January 19, 1909, Newlands introduced the bill S. 8606, which became known as the Bureau of Art and Public Buildings legislation. It called for the president to appoint a Council of the Arts consisting of not more than thirty "eminent" architects, painters, sculptors, landscape architects, and laymen, based on names submitted by the directors of the AIA. The duties of the council would be to advise the director of arts and public buildings, who was to be appointed by the president based on education and experience. Finally, the bill called for the preservation of historic buildings and monuments. Ultimately, the Senate never voted on the bill.

Nevertheless, on the same day Newlands introduced the bill, President Theodore Roosevelt issued Executive Order No. 1010. This presidential directive evolved out of correspondence with Glenn Brown, acting as the secretary of the AIA, and established a Bureau of Art and Public Buildings and a Council of Fine Arts. It outlined the same framework as Newlands's legislation. The large size of the council—thirty members in both Newlands's and Roosevelt's proposal—may have been a reaction to congressional criticism regarding the small size of the Senate Park Commission.

Based on a letter from Trowbridge to Newlands written shortly thereafter, it is clear that both Newlands and Roosevelt had strategized with the AIA before they issued their respective pieces of legislation. Trowbridge wrote:

We had a very successful interview with the President. He made some modifications to our letter, and . . . I cannot see that it will offend anyone, even one who is personally inimical to the President. It is so obviously, as he has outlined it, a good thing, and it is in direct line with the legislative action of which we talked. The President was very insistent upon that point, that we should do now, just as you said, only what will lead up to our ultimate action before Congress.[40]

A few days later, Trowbridge wrote Newlands a letter of thanks, which concluded: "I wish again to voice the gratitude of all the profession and of our Committee in particular for your prompt action in presenting the bill to the Senate to create the Bureau on the lines which we have laid down. . . . Your speech at the [AIA] Convention has saved us several years of hard work by pointing out to us the modus operandi."[41]

Although architects clearly respected Newlands, the following story—recounted by Roosevelt's military aide Archie Butt—suggests that politicians thought otherwise. In a letter to his sister-in-law, Butt described a dinner party predominantly consisting of senators.[42] He noted that when the topic of Newlands came up, Senator Elihu Root (R-NY) responded:

I can't make out Newlands at times. He speaks more than any man in the Senate. He makes good speeches, and no one ever listens to him, and he seems to have no desire to convert anyone to his way of thinking. He makes no effort to impress others with his theories. I think he talks for a scrapbook. Yes, that is it. Newlands talks for a scrapbook.

Butt then recounted Vice President James Sherman's candid story about the time Newlands spoke for an hour with only himself present in the chamber, quoting Sherman as saying: "I followed every word, and I was impressed with the beauty of his diction and the clearness of his thoughts and wondered why I had never heard anything else he had said."[43] Newlands's influence may have been diminished because he was a Democrat at a time when Republicans were the majority party in Congress as well as the party of the president. Newlands's 1917 obituary in the *Washington Post* suggested that his manner of work was not like the more common party-line politics associated with Capitol Hill:

Senator Newlands had no difficulty in working with his associates. He was possessed of unfailing tact and generosity, quickly recognizing and praising the good work of others and thereby arousing sentiments of friendship and a desire to cooperate. In the tempests of politics that have swept over the country since William McKinley died Senator Newlands held aloof, confining his energies to constructive legislation.[44]

The "tempests of politics" had much to do with President Theodore Roosevelt's personality and administrative style. When Roosevelt issued Executive Order No. 1010,

his predilection for action was well known; he himself ac-knowledged he operated from a bully pulpit. Others de-scribed him as a preacher of righteousness.[45] High ideals sustained his spirit, and he once said: "A practical man without ideals is a curse. The greater his ability, the greater his curse."[46] In addition, Roosevelt was an heir of the New York elite that appreciated artistic cultural awareness. Thus, Roosevelt's executive order was not surprising given his personal disposition and the well-recognized congres-sional hostility from his own party at that time.

On February 9, 1909, the Council of Fine Arts met for the first and only time. It approved the Senate Park Com-mission's site for the Lincoln Memorial to be located at the western edge of Potomac Park in alignment with the Capi-tol and the Washington Monument.

Creation of the Commission of Fine Arts

Because many members of Congress did not support the authority of executive orders, Representative Samuel Mc-Call (R-MA) introduced a bill in the House on February 25, 1909, to establish the Commission of Fine Arts. One week later Congress passed legislation that denied any ap-propriation for Roosevelt's Council of Fine Arts.[47] Three months after taking office in March 1909, President William Howard Taft rescinded Executive Order No. 1010.

Root guided McCall's bill through the Senate. The bill was much debated in Congress, whose members feared decision making by a "coterie of artists" who would be im-practical and visionary.[48] The negative beliefs were deeply held. It is important to recognize that the original bill only addressed statues and monuments, not buildings. A vari-ety of amendments were introduced to the bill in the Sen-ate: most importantly, the original language granting the commission authority to "decide" on projects was replaced with the weaker "advise." But some changes provided more clarity: the "seven artists of repute" was strengthened to read "seven well-qualified judges of the fine arts,"[49] Sena-tor Jacob Gallinger (R-NH) added fountains to the list of project types to be reviewed. On May 17, 1910, the bill be-came Public Law 181, 61st Congress, 2nd session, and read as follows:

Be it enacted by the House of Representatives of the United States of America in Congress assembled, That a permanent Commission of Fine Arts is hereby created to be composed of seven well-qualified judges of the fine arts, who shall be appointed by the President, and shall serve for a period of four years each, and until their successors are appointed and qualified. The President shall have authority to fill all vacancies. It shall be the duty of such commission to advise upon the location of statues, fountains, and monuments erected under the au-thority of the United States and upon the selection of artists for the ex-ecution of the same. It shall be the duty of the officers charged by law to determine such questions in each case to call for such advice. The foregoing provisions of this Act shall not apply to the Capitol building of the United States and the building of the Library of Congress. The commission shall also advise generally upon questions of art when re-quired to do so by the President, or by any committee of either House of Congress. Said commission shall have a secretary and such other as-sistance as the commission may authorize, and the members of the commission shall each be paid actual expenses in going to and return-ing from Washington to attend the meetings of said commission and while attending the same.

Within a month of McCall's introduction of the bill, the Senate Committee on the Library—which was chaired by George P. Wetmore (R-RI) and included Root and Newlands—began to consider who might serve on the commission.[50] Wetmore took it upon himself to assemble a short list of candidates for review by the president. He asked New York architect Thomas Hastings for recom-mendations for sculptors, painters, landscape architects, and laymen, but did not mention architects. Hastings was well qualified to provide such recommendations; he had studied architecture at the École in the early 1880s, where he met his future business partner, John Carrère. After working as draftsmen for McKim, Mead & White, they started their own firm together in New York in 1885 where Hastings served as the chief designer. Notable commis-sions included the Ponce de León Hotel (1888) in Saint Augustine, Florida; Hotel Jefferson (1893–94) in Rich-mond, Virginia; the New York Public Library (1902–11); the Manhattan Bridge (1904–11); and the Senate and House Office Building (1905–08, now the Russell Senate Office Building).

In compiling the list, Hastings sought the opinion of seven other design professionals—Whitney Warren, Francis Millet, Irving Pond, William Mead, Lorado Taft, H. A. MacNeil, and Daniel Burnham—and all of them provided lists of suggested names, including architects, despite Wetmore's exclusion of the discipline. Had the politicians followed the professionals' recommendations, the commission would have included the following men based on the number of votes: painter E. H. Blashfield, sculptor Daniel Chester French, landscape architect Fred-erick Law Olmsted Jr., philanthropist Henry Walters, and architect Walter Cook. The remaining two vacancies could have been filled by any of the following men: ar-chitects Frank Miles Day, S. B. P. Trowbridge, or Cass Gilbert, who all tied for second; painter John W. Alexan-der; sculptors Paul Bartlett or Herbert Adams; landscape architect William Manning; and laymen Charles Freer, the philanthropist; or Theodore Ely, the Pennsylvania Railroad Company's chief of motive power.[51]

In mid-May 1910, Wetmore wrote to President Taft and asked him not to make his selection until they had the opportunity to speak; the president agreed to wait. Irving Pond, in his role as president of the AIA, submitted a list of names including alternates to Wetmore. A variety of citizens and senators also wrote to Wetmore advocating one particular person or another, including the Washington sculptor Vinnie Ream (Hoxie), best known for her statues of Admiral Farragut in Farragut Square and Abraham Lincoln located in the U.S. Capitol.[52] Only Burnham provided comments on the names he submitted. He also complained about the size of the body, and, true to character, he mentioned a spirit that would be critical for success:

I am sorry that the number on the Commission is to be seven, not five. I don't believe that seven will work well. It will be a very ponderous body, whereas the work to be done needs, of all things, directness and sharpness. I further believe that the artists on the Commission should be three, not more, and that the remainder should be laymen; not millionaires, but men who will faithfully attend all meetings and do their duty fully. I am aware that many of the professional class are exceedingly anxious to 'get on this Commission,' and that they desire to do so because it will give them personal distinction. This is not a high motive; it is unworthy of the important office to be filled. No man who asks for place should be considered, the best work will come from the spirit of the Commission, and not from the brain of a genius. It must be remembered that this Commission is not to do any designing at all, but is to be a censorship pure and simple and the men who serve should be above jealousy and envy. They are to create the 'tone' which the country needs.[53]

Burnham thought Peirce Anderson—who worked for him—would be the best architect for the commission. Burnham did not recommend any sculptors because he said he did not know any "well-enough," but advised that one should be chosen "who has the severest taste, not the richest fancy." His lack of a referral for a sculptor is odd given his association with the World's Columbian Exposition and the City Beautiful movement; it may speak to his bias toward the architectural profession. He gave a lukewarm recommendation for Blashfield as a good critic of painting, "if you must have one." Ignoring Olmsted, Burnham provided only one name for the landscape position: Chicago architect Edward H. Bennett ("No one compares with him"), who also worked for Burnham. For the laymen, Burnham opposed the selection of "art patrons" but conceded, "if you must have one of this latter class, John Johnson of Philadelphia is the man." Johnson was a lawyer and art collector; his collection would become the nucleus of the Philadelphia Museum of Art. Burnham also recommended Theodore Ely of the Pennsylvania Railroad Company and Martin Ryerson of Chicago; Ely had ties to the art world as a director of the Pennsylvania Academy of

With his hand resting on a telephone, President William Howard Taft is portrayed as a modern man of the new century in this photograph from 1908. Taft's support in establishing the CFA helped to realize the formal monumentality of Washington in the twentieth century.

Fine Arts and vice president of the American Academy in Rome, and Ryerson was one of Chicago's most important art patrons.[54]

Burnham also suggested painter Francis Davis Millet as "by far the best man" for the secretary position. After graduating from Harvard University in 1869, Millet worked as a reporter with the Boston *Advertiser* before entering the Royal Academy of Fine Arts in Antwerp, Belgium. When he returned to Boston, he painted murals with John La Farge for Trinity Church and helped found the School of the Museum of Fine Arts, Boston, with La Farge and William Hunt before leaving as a war correspondent on the Russo-Turkish War; he would later serve as a war correspondent during the Spanish-American War. As director of decorations at the 1893 World's Columbian Exposition, Millet was responsible for selecting white as the typical building color. Among the many artistic works for which he was known were the 1907 Civil War Medal and the murals *The Fourth Minnesota Regiment* (c. 1904) for the Minnesota State Capitol, *Foreman of the Grand Jury* (1907) for the Essex County Court House in Newark, New Jersey, and *The History of Shipping* (1908) for the U.S.

Custom House in Baltimore. Burnham concluded his letter with the lofty and foreboding remark:

The thing needed is a noble spirit, one that will compel respect and admiration. If men are placed on this first Commission for purely political reasons, I fear that it will become a reproach to the nation.[55]

At the same time Burnham wrote Wetmore, he sent a telegram to Millet repeating his points about the composition of the commission and concluded with a clear disinterest in serving as a member:

I shrink from assuming another obligation and hope the authorities will not need me, but, if you are right and I cannot be excused I will accept the duty, hoping that the Commission will be formed as indicated above.[56]

A few days after signing the act into law, President Taft asked Senator Newlands about S. B. P. Trowbridge. Newlands replied with a letter discussing Trowbridge's education, well-known buildings, and lobbying for art legislation. He noted, "I have nothing to urge regarding his appoint-

ment, for I must say that the names which you presented were those of men singularly qualified for the position. The only opening I could see for Mr. Trowbridge would be in the place of one of the two Engineer officers whom you proposed to select."[57] In the end, Taft thought better of selecting two engineers. Within days of the act passing, he created a preliminary list of men to serve on the Commission of Fine Arts (CFA) and on June 15, Taft contacted them and requested their service: Daniel Burnham (CFA 1910–12), Daniel Chester French (CFA 1910–15), Cass Gilbert (CFA 1910–16), Thomas Hastings (CFA 1910–17), Francis Millet (CFA 1910–12), Frederick Law Olmsted Jr. (CFA 1910–18), and Charles Moore (CFA 1910–40). [58] He asked Burnham to serve as the chairman.

Only the sculptor Daniel Chester French had not been active over the years in lobbying for the arts commission. French had apprenticed with William Rimmer and John Quincy Adams Ward before winning the competition for

TOP ROW, LEFT TO RIGHT: *Daniel Burnham, Daniel Chester French, Cass Gilbert, Thomas Hastings.* BOTTOM ROW, LEFT TO RIGHT: *Frederick Law Olmsted Jr., Francis Millet, Charles Moore, Colonel Spencer Cosby (secretary).*

CHAPTER I | AIM HIGH IN HOPE AND WORK

The Minute Man (1874) in Concord, Massachusetts. He then went to Florence to study with Bostonian Thomas Ball; French was among the last of his generation to study in Florence or Rome rather than Paris. After two years, he returned to the United States and established a studio in Concord, Massachusetts. When the state of Michigan commissioned him for a portrait of Lewis Cass for National Statuary Hall in the U.S. Capitol, French decided additional training was necessary and left for Paris in 1886 to join the atelier of Marius-Jean-Antonin Mercié. Upon returning, French established his studio in New York City. His well-known works included the *Thomas Gallaudet Memorial* (1888) in Washington; the colossal *Republic* (1893) erected at the World's Columbian Exposition; and *Alma Mater* (1903) at Columbia University. His architectural sculpture included the three pairs of entrance doors at the Boston Public Library—*Knowledge and Wisdom, Truth and Romance,* and *Music and Poetry* (1902)—and four groupings for the U.S. Custom House in New York City known as *The Continents* (1907).

President Taft also selected Colonel Spencer Cosby of the U.S. Army Corps of Engineers to serve as the secretary for the Commission of Fine Arts. Cosby was the engineer officer in charge of the Office of Public Buildings and Grounds for the District of Columbia (OPBG), which had been established in 1867 when the functions of the commissioner of public buildings of the Department of the Interior were transferred to the chief engineer of the U.S. Army. This choice—the officer in charge at OPBG also serving as the secretary of the Commission of Fine Arts—would be the model followed by subsequent presidents until 1922, when the two positions were separated, severing the commission's direct tie to the chief executive. Taft appointed Cosby to these positions just after he took office and Colonel Cosby remained CFA secretary throughout Taft's term. Cosby reported directly to the president, and the new assignment allowed Taft to have close contact with the commission. Cosby had previously served under Taft in the Philippines and when the latter was secretary of war.[59] Cosby, who had graduated first in his class in 1891 from the U.S. Military Academy at West Point, had been stationed in Puerto Rico during the Spanish-American War and then in the Philippines before being assigned in 1905 to the District's water system managed by the War Department. Three years later, Roosevelt named him the engineer commissioner of the District of Columbia.

The first meeting of the Commission of Fine Arts was held in Cosby's office on July 8, 1910. Five members—all but French and Gilbert—were in attendance; they elected Millet vice chairman. In a statement from the president read by Cosby, Taft said he "desired to have their assistance in all matters relating to the location, style of architecture and general design of new public buildings in Washington, and also in regard to the laying out of grounds surrounding them." Taft was concerned about current building proposals for the Bureau of Engraving and Printing and the Departments of State, Justice, and Commerce and Labor. This request exceeded the authority granted to the commission by its founding legislation and the members requested a letter be sent to the comptroller of the Treasury regarding his opinion on the matter. By October 1910, Taft rectified the problem with Executive Order No. 1259, which added public buildings in the District of Columbia to the commission's purview for "comment and advice."

At that first meeting, the commission members inspected the recently erected statues of Generals Count Casimir Pulaski and Thaddeus Kosciuszko and the site for the proposed monument to General Friedrich Wilhelm Von Steuben, all in Lafayette Park, as well as three proposed sites for the Commodore John Barry monument. Although not certain of their authority in the matter, the members reviewed plans for the Bureau of Engraving and Printing building as requested by Taft. The meeting continued the next day for the purpose of writing two letters to the secretary of the Treasury, one regarding the plans for the Bureau of Engraving and Printing and the other establishing general design competition guidelines for the Departments of State, Justice, and Commerce and Labor to be located around Lafayette Park.

During the month after the commission's initial meeting, Burnham wrote Taft's secretary, Charles Norton, regarding stationery letterhead and asked that the president consider what to call the newly created group. Burnham noted that he preferred "The American Commission" and commented that "We are taking pains in this matter because a proper title always carries proper authority, and we want to start right."[60] After settling on a revised wording for the letterhead—"Commission of Fine Arts · Established by Congress May 17th, 1910"—Burnham wrote a letter to Norton that displayed a keen awareness of politics, a characteristic that would be shared by future commission leaders:

It seems best to let the custom grow up, of referring to U.S. matters outside the District of Columbia, before using a National heading. There are some men in Congress who will be up in arms if we take the other course in the beginning, but who will not care when custom has shown the need of a proper title. By being modest now we avoid a little fight which might annoy the President, and which is not necessary.[61]

✻

An Enduring Design Legacy: Frederick Law Olmsted Jr. in the Nation's Capital

¶ ARLEYN A. LEVEE

Frederick Law Olmsted Jr. as a young man, undated photograph, c. 1900.

Among the remarkable assemblage of experts who have guided the U.S. Commission of Fine Arts, landscape architect and planner Frederick Law Olmsted Jr. holds a unique position by virtue of the length and character of his service and the extent of his productive involvement in molding Washington, leaving an indelible artistic imprint upon the federal city. A youthful appointee in 1901 to the Senate Park Commission, the so-called McMillan Commission, he was a major contributor to this body's creative process to interpret, recast, and supplement Peter Charles L'Enfant's remarkable eighteenth-century conception for America's capital into a visionary plan for the city's renewal and future. To ensure vibrancy of the vision and artistic coherence in the city's architectural reconfiguration, the long-discussed Commission of Fine Arts became a reality in 1910 with Olmsted as one of its first members. During his eight-year tenure, with his firsthand knowledge of the McMillan Plan's design intent, he guided the implementation of its components while steadfastly guarding its aesthetic principles.

But the Commission of Fine Arts lacked authority to supplement the vision, to extend L'Enfant's ideas into the active policies required to shape and service the growing metropolitan city of a twentieth-century world power. To accomplish this expanded role of comprehensive urban planning and parkland acquisition—without compromising the balanced grandeur and artistry of the McMillan vision—required the creation in 1926 of the National Capital Park and Planning Commission (NCPPC). Again, Olmsted was instrumental in this process and among the first appointees, serving until 1932.

Beyond his duties for these three commissions, Olmsted sat on numerous Washington advisory councils with significant responsibility to study and de-velop features of the McMillan Plan. Together with his partners and associates in Olmsted Brothers, he was engaged in professional design projects throughout the metropolitan area, many of these relating back to the McMillan Commission or Commission of Fine Arts tasks; others stemmed from other associations; and still others independently commissioned but always considered according to the consummate aesthetic principles established by the McMillan Plan.[1] For much of this work, Olmsted drew little salary, barely covering the firm's overhead and contributing his services for the greater cause to ensure that Washington's landscapes of monuments and parks were unified expressions of L'Enfant's grand concept as envisioned by the McMillan Commission. America's national capital was to be an exemplary model of a comprehensively planned city, balancing architectural grandeur and landscape artistry while serving the resident and visiting public alike.

When he began his appointment on the McMillan Commission, Olmsted, at age thirty, was more than twenty years younger than his colleagues.[2] While maintaining an extensive, multifaceted design and consulting practice across the country over his wide-ranging career, Olmsted continued to remain deeply involved in Washington design for more than fifty years. His longevity, his abiding interest, and his generous commitment to public service ensured a continuity of thoughtful oversight either by him personally or by Olmsted Brothers' partners to maintain, nurture, and adapt the aesthetic vision.

Background

At the turn of the twentieth century, Frederick Law Olmsted Jr., known as "Rick" to his family and friends, was a relatively untested practitioner of the still-developing discipline of landscape architecture and of the even newer field of city planning. He brought to his challenging tasks multifaceted talents, an incisive intellect, and a well-studied comprehension of the landscape art, honed under the intense tutelage of his father, Frederick Law Olmsted Sr.; his older half-brother, John Charles Olmsted; and their partner, Charles Eliot. Each of these men had expanded the parameters of the emerging profession by their advocacy of skilled land-use planning, design aesthetics, and principles of scenic conservation and their commitment to public service.

Born on July 24, 1870, in New York, Frederick Law Olmsted Jr., originally christened Henry Perkins Olmsted, was renamed by his father sometime around 1874 to ensure that this Olmsted name would continue to be "identified with the firm and the profession."[3] As the fifth and youngest Olmsted child, he was raised in a household that was also the firm's working office.[4] He grew up surrounded by the product and passions of his father's myriad intellectual endeavors and design commissions, which ranged across the country.[5] By the time the family moved to Brookline, Massachusetts, in 1882, the home office had expanded beyond the kitchen table to include an atelier of hard-working associates implementing the senior Olmsted's aesthetic perspective in shaping land and city form and learning from his sense of social mission. As his biographer, Laura Wood Roper, noted, "In Olmsted, the artistic and the social impulse are equally strong and indissolubly joined."[6] For the senior Olmsted, landscape design was not mere decoration on the land. Rather, he conceived it as a comprehensive and integral art form, in harmony with nature, with parts subordinate to the whole, fulfilling a distinct educative, civilizing purpose often directed toward fundamental psychological needs of city dwellers. This was the credo that Olmsted's sons, protégés, and associates inherited, ex-

panded, revised, and passed on.

Educated at both private and public schools and at Harvard College, class of 1894, the junior Olmsted spent the summers of his college years either working on the grounds of the emerging Chicago World's Fair—for which his father was one of the chief planners—or in European travel with his father, exploring the design ideas expressed in major public and private landscapes. The World's Fair collaborations, learning firsthand from the artists who would later become his Washington colleagues, Daniel H. Burnham, Charles F. McKim, and Augustus Saint-Gaudens, were a highlight of his professional life. As he observed in notes for his twenty-fifth Harvard reunion report, this was

a 'rush job' full of enthusiasm and intense sustained effort, in which I first encountered the stimulus and satisfaction of working, even though as an unimportant youngster, with some of the ablest architects and other artists…. The most exhilarating and notable thing about that experience was the prevailing spirit, among these men of great individual creative ability and diverse points of view, of self-subordinating cooperation in joint pursuit of a common aim inspired by enthusiasm for an artistic ideal.[7]

During the summer following his Harvard graduation, Olmsted worked as a recorder for the thirty-ninth parallel survey, learning to read the land as his older brother John had done earlier in 1869 and 1871. He then learned the hands-on process of construction and planting as an apprentice at Biltmore, the extensive George Vanderbilt estate in Asheville, North Carolina, with increasing responsibilities as his father's health failed. He was officially added to the Olmsted, Olmsted & Eliot payroll in December 1895.[8] With the sudden death of Charles Eliot in 1897, the firm was reorganized as Olmsted Brothers in 1898 with John Charles and Rick as partners. Olmsted Jr. took over the planning role for the Metropolitan Park Commission, Eliot's innovative regional

system of parks, reservations, and parkways, which conserved for public use a network of unique landscape types linked by parkways and managed centrally without regard to municipal jurisdictions. During this early period, he also began designing the Baltimore subdivision of Roland Park, an enterprise that led to numerous related long-term commissions, including the Baltimore park system of stream-valley reservations and neighborhood playgrounds, which he worked on simultaneously with the early Washington projects.

Nineteenth-century Washington and the Transition to the New Century

Public design and planning projects in the nation's capital have a significance of their own. From the outset, L'Enfant's planning shaped a city intended for ceremonial as well as practical uses, clearly cognizant of its necessary symbolic character to represent the nation.[9] By the late nineteenth century, particularly in Europe, urban progress was measured by planning efforts designed to beautify, to improve services for citizens, and to protect municipal resources. But in America's capital, which was self-conscious about its role as exemplar for the country and the world, such efforts were invested with didactic implications. Beyond mere physical alterations, plans were considered in terms of appropriate values of a democratic society, standards of art and taste, political process, and economic justice, as well as social and racial equality.

Many of these ideas were of concern to Frederick Law Olmsted Sr. when in 1874 he began the most notable commission of his career, the design of a setting of suitable dignity and grandeur for the United States Capitol. In addition to considerable site challenges, it was the symbolic importance of this commission, this pinnacle opportunity to educate the

Frederick Law Olmsted Sr.'s plan for the grounds of the United States Capitol, 1874. Olmsted sought to balance formal elements appropriate for such a national monument with curvilinear paths and drives and artfully placed plant groupings to enhance its surroundings. His ingenious addition of a terrace for the western facade was intended to settle this very large edifice into its sloping terrain, providing a platform from which to view the dramatic sweep of L'Enfant's intended Mall and the western vistas.

taste of the nation that intrigued Olmsted. He recognized that this would be a work of generations and would be among his most important contributions to American landscape architecture.

Presaging concerns that would be articulated two decades later, the senior Olmsted expressed his dismay about the condition of the national capital in a letter of January 22, 1874, to his sponsor, Senator Justin Morrill of Vermont. Although the building of Washington represented a considerable federal investment, it was, in his eyes, "a standing reproach against the system of government." The L'Enfant Plan had envisioned the Mall as a harmoniously ordered composition, a grand axial sweep of space lined by significant institutions with a defining cross-axis at the president's house. Instead, a "broken, confused and unsatisfactory" effect had been allowed to develop, with a bewildering array of buildings intruding upon one another. In short, he continued,

The capital of the Union manifests nothing so much as disunity.... What is wanting is a federal bond. Had the buildings been ranged about a single field of landscape...consistent and harmonious one with another, a much more sustained and consequently more impressive effect would have been produced. Great breadth in this field of landscape and largeness of scale in all its features...would not be felt in the least as a disadvantage.[10]

Rather, with no controlling motive, Olmsted thought each building in the disorderly assemblage seemed to have "its own little domain."[11] Olmsted's advice was to put the control of all federal grounds and buildings under one body, which would pursue a sustained plan to elevate the capital city to "the scale of art." He further suggested at this early date that a committee of landscape architects, to include William Hammond Hall and H. W. S. Cleveland, should provide oversight over this planning.[12] Although such ideas about governance went unheeded in their day, Olmsted Sr.'s endeavors over two decades suc-

General Plan for the Improvement of the U. S. Capitol Grounds.

ceeded in surrounding the Capitol with a gracious landscape significant for its artistic merit.

It would take twenty-five years before distress at the architectural disunity of Washington's public spaces ignited a productive response to reconsider L'Enfant's design and plan for improvements with the appointment of the Senate Park Commission. It would take another nine years for the suggested advisory body of "seven well-qualified judges of the fine arts" to become a reality in 1910 with the creation by Congress of the Commission of Fine Arts and the presidential appointment of the first commissioners.[13] Yet another sixteen years would pass before the idea of a comprehensive

planning authority with a metropolitan purview was validated with the creation by Congress of the National Capital Park and Planning Commission in 1926.[14] When these three events occurred, Olmsted's son and namesake, Frederick Law Olmsted Jr., was in the vanguard of leadership.

The McMillan Commission

Rick Olmsted entered the fray over the capital's dignity with provocative observations that expanded upon his father's earlier commentary. By 1900, the Mall's clutter had worsened, leaving L'Enfant's intended grand spatial and symbolic conception unrecognizable. In his seminal speech to the American Institute of Architects in 1900, Olmsted stated with incisive eloquence, "that the purpose of the Mall, was, and ought to be, to emphasize, support and extend the effect of the Capitol as the dominant feature of the city and the most important building in the whole United States." As such, he contended, the Mall should contribute to "the effect of grandeur, power and dignified magnificence which should mark the seat of government of a great and intensely active people."[15] To recapture the greatness and unity of L'Enfant's plan, to provide suitable settings for future federal buildings, and to avoid "caprice and confusion" would require lengthy and careful study. He concluded:

Here is a plan not hastily sketched, nor by a man of narrow views and little foresight. It is a plan with the authority of a century behind it, to which we can all demand undeviating adherence in the future.[16]

He thus introduced the three tenets that would govern his aesthetic decisions during the following decades of his Washington work: First, thoroughly analyze the site, its history, its features, and its intended uses; second, develop and adhere to a controlling artistic and hierarchical plan appropriate to locale and need; and third, strive for stylistic consistency. Olmsted's tasks would vary greatly, from grand monument to urban square, from expansive greensward to wooded dell, from small park to local playground, and from parkway to neighborhood street, but each component would contribute to the overall effect of an American capital worthy of its heritage and its international stature.

Although a plaster world of monumental facades, the classical artistry of the World's Columbian Exposition of 1893 in Chicago—better known as the Chicago World's Fair—nonetheless had set transformative standards for the nation. A cosmopolitan and harmonious city seemed to offer the promise of or-

derly reform and moral uplift, a new "aesthetic language" for the nation.[17] With the mounting dissatisfaction over the capital's appearance and the impending centennial celebrations, Senator James McMillan, chair of the Committee for the District of Columbia, tapped into the planning enthusiasm that had continued after the exposition. Through astute political maneuvering abetted by powerful professional groups such as the American Institute of Architects, McMillan engineered a resolution to appoint "experts" ostensibly engaged to consult on improvement of Washington's park system. In fact, these experts had a larger objective—to develop a master plan to rehabilitate and adapt L'Enfant's design. For these tasks, McMillan reassembled the original Chicago colleagues, Daniel H. Burnham, Charles McKim, and Augustus Saint-Gaudens, with Rick Olmsted serving as the stand-in for his incapacitated father. Thus, McMillan and his able secretary, Charles Moore, set in motion that careful study Olmsted Jr. had referred to in his AIA speech, on a scale worthy of the powerful edict long-associated with Burnham, "to stir men's blood."[18]

As in the planning process for the 1893 events, Burnham set the pace with what Olmsted called his "contagious enthusiasm" to subordinate all to an artistic ideal.[19] The collaborations of this legendary 1901 commission reflected that spirit as it set forth its ambitious agenda for Washington's future, proposing improvements that would have consequent national implications. Although many pens were doubtless at work on the *Senate Park Commission Report,* better known as the *McMillan Report,* its emphasis on developing Washington's landscape opportunities to recapture the intent of the monumental core and develop the scenic promise of the city's outlying areas was typical of the planning ideals that characterized Olmsted firm work. Likewise, the admonition to

acquire land before ill-considered development destroyed its advantages was a recurring Olmsted mantra.

Evident in the greater part of the *McMillan Report* are the substantial recommendations to craft the parks, parkways, and reservations throughout the growing city. Charles Moore observed that young Olmsted's "shoe-prints marked every hill and valley" of the nearly three thousand acres already in federal control.[20] Olmsted also explored and recommended the acquisition of the ninety acres of Analostan Island, the extensive malodorous marshes of the Anacostia River, Mount Hamilton, and land for parkways and small neighborhood reservations. This ambitious list would give Washington an enviable system of varied open spaces for differing recreational uses designed to accommodate a growing population. It would take decades, however, to acquire park space in Washington approximating the McMillan intentions.[21]

Achieving parkway linkages would prove most challenging, as buildings crowded into the intended areas, elevating the cost of land takings and diminishing the political will necessary to acquire land. The park-side drives along the Mall's greensward (now known as Madison Drive, NW, and Jefferson Drive, SW); the Rock Creek and Potomac Parkway with its smaller spurs; the river-edge pleasure drive encircling

Aerial view of the Mall, c. 1900, looking east from the Washington Monument toward the Capitol. In the right foreground are the formal gardens and greenhouses of the Department of Agriculture, a building razed in 1930; beyond that, in front of the Smithsonian Castle, are the tree plantations as suggested by Andrew Jackson Downing in 1850. In the left middle ground is the roof of the station for the Baltimore and Ohio Railroad; roofs of the various U.S. Botanic Garden structures can be seen among the trees at the foot of Capitol Hill.

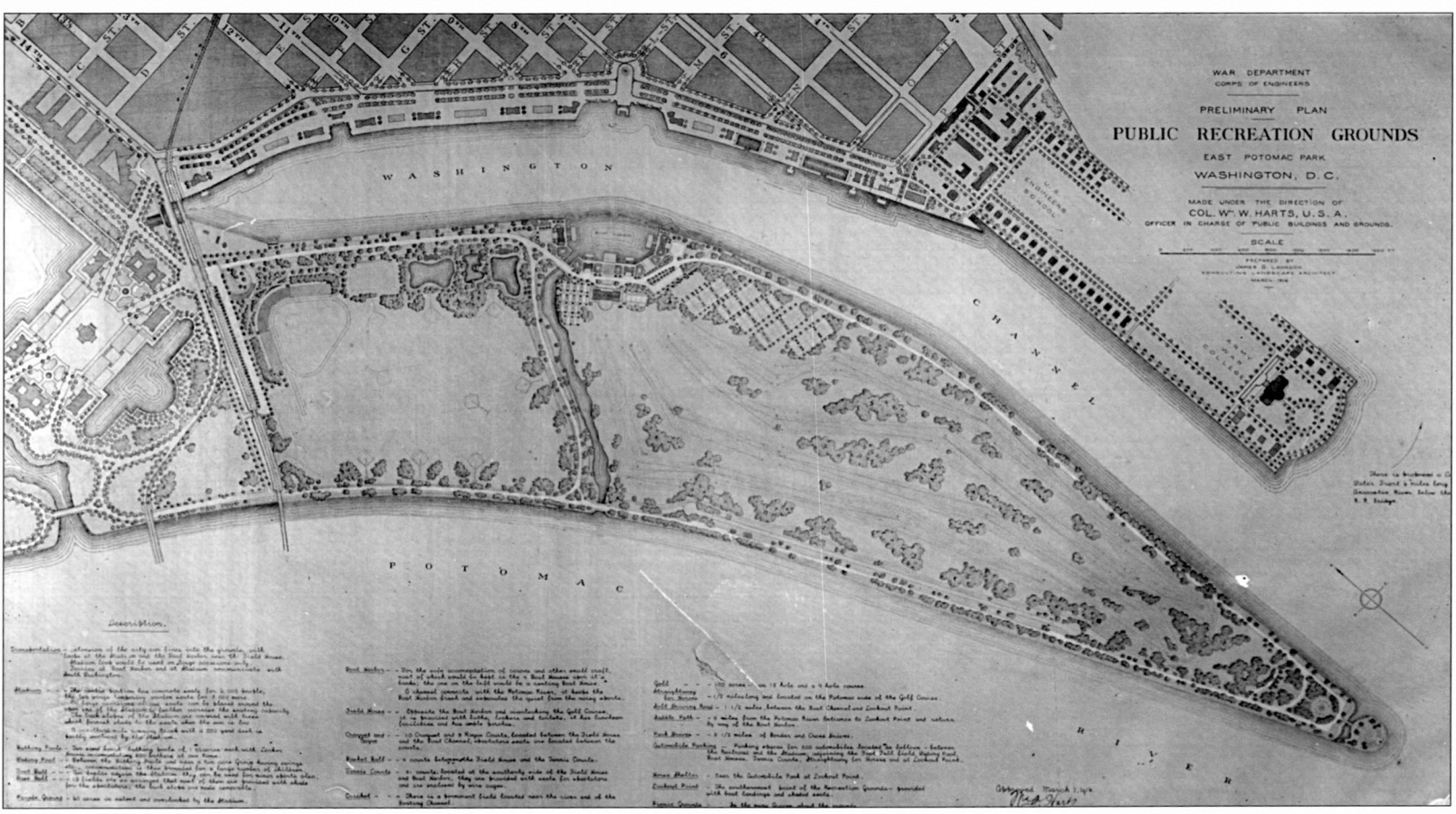

Preliminary Plan for Public Recreation Grounds, East Potomac Park, prepared for the Division of Public Buildings and Grounds of the U.S. Army Corps of Engineers, by James G. Langdon, consulting landscape architect, March 1916. The plan transformed this wedge-shaped area of land, created from dredged material from the river, into a park with various recreational facilities, surrounded by a circuit drive.

East Potomac Park; and other broad and verdant routes were achieved, many with the Olmsted firm's advice. Unfortunately, the innovative Fort Drive, a scenic circuit roadway that Olmsted proposed to link the then outlying Civil War forts and thus make their breezy hilltops publicly accessible and connected to established parks, was never completed, despite several valiant attempts to do so during the 1920s and 1930s. While the Capper-Cramton Act of 1930 gave a boost to major parkway development by providing land acquisition funding for the George Washington Memorial Parkway as well as for extensions for Rock Creek and Anacostia Parks, the Fort Drive proposal "never captured the imagination of Congress." The complexity of land acquisition in inner-city neighborhoods could not compete with the appeal of "grand approaches." In the post–World War II era, a new generation of planners trans-

ferred acquisition efforts and funding to the creation of high-speed beltway loops at the suburban edge of the city.[22]

The Washington Consultative Board

In the transitional years between the submission of the *Senate Park Commission Report* and the establishment of the Commission of Fine Arts, the former commissioners and their proponents campaigned vigorously to protect the design ideals and generate support for execution of the plan. The so-called Washington Consultative Board—Burnham, Olmsted, McKim (until his 1909 death), and Bernard Green, the congressional librarian—served as unofficial guardians of the McMillan vision. Working without pay, they monitored ongoing projects around the monumental core, negotiating with the various agencies involved, such as the Army

Corps of Engineers, to refine plans to ensure that structures and landscapes of appropriate character were located according to the plan's intentions.[23]

One such example involved placement of the Ulysses S. Grant Memorial at the eastern end of the U.S. Botanic Garden, in the area intended by the McMillan Plan to become Union Square. The monument was originally designed by architect Edward Casey and sculptor Henry Shrady for a location on the Ellipse, where its orientation was to be one-sided. It took considerable courtly diplomacy in 1907 by McKim and Olmsted to convince Casey to redesign the base for four-sided access. Additionally, careful negotiations and Olmsted's horticultural skill were required to quiet the ensuing hubbub over the necessary removal or relocation of existing Botanic Garden commemorative trees in order to accommodate the monument.[24] The future of the Botanic

Garden and its possible relocation as well as the landscape design for Union Square would continue to plague Olmsted for the next four decades. Other important decisions in process at this time concerned grading of sites such as that for the future Lincoln Memorial. Though they had some success, this board's unofficial position was somewhat anomalous, much to the irritation of Burnham. With his characteristic pragmatism, Olmsted reassured Burnham, reminding him that,

Officially and legally, our position as an Advisory Board is helpless and that of the president in having appointed us borders upon the ridiculous, but if practically we can bring about the results we want, as we are now in a good way to do, I, for one, am willing to be laughed at all day long.[25]

During this period, Olmsted was also engaged in design and initial construction for other Washington park projects.[26] He consulted with the Army Office of Buildings and Grounds on improvements for East Potomac Park, a large area of reclaimed land without "striking natural features:" Olmsted worked with his associate James Langdon to shape this space into a central meadow interspersed with recreational facilities and bounded by a tree-lined circuit drive along the water to serve as a "place of contrast to city conditions."[27] In 1906, work commenced to commemorate Senator McMillan by creating a "beautiful, dignified and enjoyable" neighborhood park located around a sand filtration reservoir at North Capitol Street in Northwest Washington that he had sponsored.[28]

The Establishment of the U.S. Commission of Fine Arts and the National Capital Park and Planning Commission

Various attempts to intrude upon the Mall made it clear that an established commission with artistic oversight would be critical to maintain and implement the McMillan vision for Washington. By 1910, this goal was achieved with the creation of a permanent Commission of Fine Arts composed of "seven well-qualified judges of the fine arts" to advise upon the location and character of monuments, fountains, and buildings and their settings. For this new commission, the surviving members of the Senate Park Commission—Burnham, Olmsted, and Moore—were reassembled with five new appointees to fulfill its mandate of oversight.[29] These pioneering members were tasked with both the evaluation of suitability and merit of various projects and the more complicated problem of developing standards and setting parameters for the Commission of Fine Art's purview. During his eight-year tenure from 1910 to 1918 on the commission, Olmsted was its hardworking landscape expert; he also served for six of those years as vice chairman. He diligently reviewed sites throughout the District and beyond, conferred on street plantings, sketched alternative layouts for monuments, and wrote definitive reports on varied projects, always maintaining his comprehensive perspective as to the appropriateness of style, scale, and the setting of the project to its intended use—all considered within the overarching design scheme.[30]

Many of the important projects before the commission in this early decade concerned the development of the monumental core and its periphery. Of particular importance were the decisions made to complete the plans for the structure and setting of the Lincoln Memorial, which finalized commitment to the Mall's westward extent. To relate the memorial's landscape to its eastern neighbor, the Washington Monument, Olmsted worked with James Langdon and Clarence Howard, a young architect who would assist Olmsted on several other Washington projects, to shape a linear reflecting pool intended to be lined by allées of English elms.[31] Unfortunately, as the United States was drawn into World War I, much of this area became the location for "tempos," block-like and hastily constructed federal office buildings that would serve a multitude of supposedly temporary purposes, some of which persisted into the 1970s.

By 1920, little had been accomplished to retrieve this seminal space from its disunity. Still populated by tempos and various athletic facilities, the central panel continued to be an irregularly graded, weedy expanse filled with remnants of bygone designs. Parsimonious appropriations and haphazard federal-local direction hindered effective planning, let alone any implementation, eroding the McMillan-L'Enfant vision before its City Beautiful goals had been achieved. However, Olmsted's "landscape emphasis" for the McMillan Plan, the "basic cloth into which the public buildings [of the monumental core] were woven," continued to generate support. Olmsted, as a member of the Committee of 100, an arm of the American Planning and Civic Association, worked with other nationwide proponents to legitimize the planning process for Washington to keep alive the verdant and comprehensive vision. By 1926, these efforts coalesced into the National Capital Park and Planning Commission (NCPPC) with vested powers to prepare, develop, and maintain "a comprehensive, consistent and coordinated plan for the National Capital and its environs," involving both federal and District agencies. As an original appointee to the NCPPC and a member until 1932, Rick Olmsted was able to continue the judicious oversight and fostering of McMillan Plan implementation that he had begun under the Commission of Fine Arts.[32]

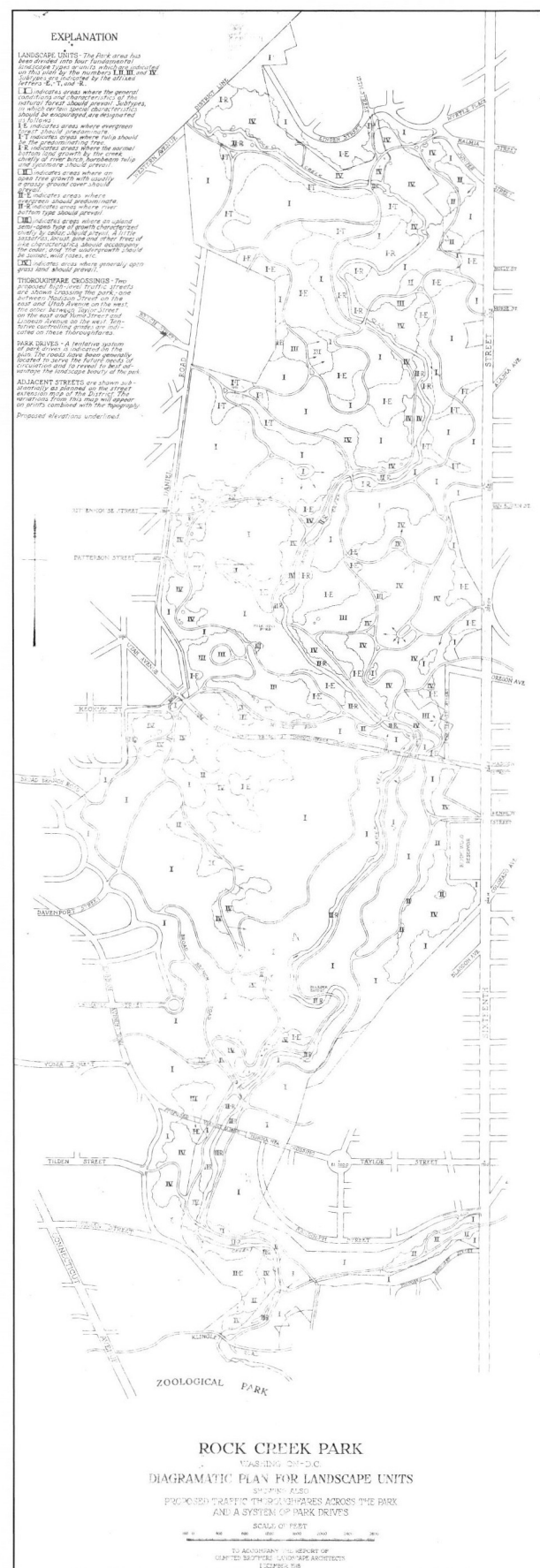

ROCK CREEK PARK
WASHINGTON D.C.
DIAGRAMATIC PLAN FOR LANDSCAPE UNITS
SHOWING ALSO
PROPOSED TRAFFIC THOROUGHFARES ACROSS THE PARK
AND A SYSTEM OF PARK DRIVES
SCALE OF FEET

TO ACCOMPANY THE REPORT OF
OLMSTED BROTHERS LANDSCAPE ARCHITECTS
DECEMBER 1918

Rock Creek Park and the National Arboretum Debate

Beginning in 1912, the problem of the Anacostia mudflats came before the Commission of Fine Arts. Olmsted, appointed as a committee of one with power to resolve design issues, reviewed the reclamation proposals from the army engineers. His plan to shape a large lake for recreation involved treating the verges of filled land as naturally as possible, reflective of healthy tidal marshes rather than the straight stiff sea walls preferred by the army engineers.[33] This issue of artistry, of appearing natural while hiding the necessary engineered constructions, would be a continual debate along most of Washington's central public waterfront, one in which the Army Corps usually triumphed. Like other projects reviewed by Olmsted during his tenure on the Commission of Fine Arts, the Anacostia issue would resurface under many guises for Olmsted's consideration over the following decades. The aspirations suggested by him in appendix E of the *McMillan Report* for "a national botanical collection," possibly even an arboretum, combined with the unresolved status of the existing Botanic Garden located in what was to become Union Square, provided continuing challenges for the Olmsted firm well into the 1950s.

The arboretum idea spawned park planning controversies well beyond Anacostia, involving both East Potomac and Rock Creek Parks.[34] The Olmsted firm's involvement in Rock Creek Park began in 1890 when the senior Olmsted and John Charles began planning for a National Zoological Park to occupy a section of the valley; however, their work left unresolved whether the zoo was to be a place for scientific investigation or public recre-

ation.[35] In the 1901 report, the junior Olmsted had recognized that this picturesque valley, a linchpin in the park system planning, was in need of careful study to protect its intrinsic landscape values while permitting public use. At this time, the lower valley from the mouth of Rock Creek at the Potomac, almost as far as the zoo, was environmentally degraded, surrounded by industry and tenements. The Georgetown Citizens Association sought a "closed valley" solution, putting the creek in a culvert and filling the valley to create more surface land for a parkway to link the monumental core to areas to the north. Alternatively, the Washington Board of Trade proposed an "open valley" solution whereby the valley would be rehabilitated to enable construction of a scenic parkway along the creek amid seemingly natural conditions. Basing their decision on "economy, convenience and beauty," the McMillan Commission put its support behind the open valley treatment rather than the dubious alternative of filling the valley. But Olmsted remained concerned over the challenges of accommodating a parkway, park use, and cross-valley access without harming the landscape's unique character.[36]

As a member of the newly created Commission of Fine Arts, Olmsted was asked to consider several legislative attempts to relocate the Botanic Garden into Rock Creek Park, responding first in 1911 to Senator Wetmore that it was "bad principle to acquire land nominally as part of a park project and subsequently divert it to other uses." However, the valley slopes were not favorable for greenhouses and other appurtenances required by a botanic garden. He maintained that a study was needed to consider a scientifically planned, well-managed national arboretum and

LEFT: *Rock Creek Park, Diagrammatic Plan for Landscape Units, showing proposed traffic thoroughfares across the park and a system of park drives, December 1918.*

ESSAY | AN ENDURING DESIGN LEGACY

botanic garden and their proper relation to the District's park system. In late 1916, when asked for advice to forestall yet another congressional plan for a botanic garden, Olmsted submitted a proposal for his firm to prepare a general report for the improvement of Rock Creek Park.[37]

Olmsted and Edward Clark Whiting (who was soon to become a firm partner) explored the park landscape in detail in 1917, mapping topographic, vegetative, historic, and other features. They assessed the impact of varying uses, evaluated needs for present and future accessibility, recommended land acquisitions, and considered methods to maintain the park. The vast acreage was divided into four major units, some with subtypes, scattered throughout the park. These were based upon the existing growth patterns: natural forest, open woodlands, wooded slopes, and open grassland, with management recommendations established for each. They looked at the differing locations of these units and their potential uses from the perspective of the park as a whole and against the city context, considering thoroughfare crossings and park roads. Their comprehensive report, a collaborative effort actually written by Whiting, recorded their recom-

mendations, enhanced by plans, sketches, and photographs.[38]

The Olmsted tenet was that the justification for any large park was the preservation of its unique qualities, in this case the "very, very precious" character and restfulness of the Rock Creek valley with its tributaries, its forested slopes and ravines, its rolling hills, and its occasional meadows. But these ideas were also pragmatic, that no matter how valuable this scenery might be, its true value remained in its enjoyment by large numbers of people, "poor and rich alike," who were, after all, the park's owners. What the Olmsted assessment provided was an analysis of various landscape types that could be made accessible, by what means, and for what type of use. It also identified areas of wildness to be protected at all costs by limiting user amenities. Enabling public enjoyment of those characteristic picturesque passages of scenery, representative of the genius loci of an individual landscape unit, was an intended goal. But preservation of the overall unity and harmony that nature had provided in the valley was foremost. Regulation and policing procedures were critical to maintain the balance of landscape protection and appropriate access, in addi-

tion to park staff knowledgeable about the essential qualities desired. Whiting concluded his report with a plea for appropriations to meet the increasing needs of the patrons while insuring protection of park values, but he counseled "the guiding policy should be distinctly one of restraint."[39]

While this report offered some protection for Rock Creek Park against future inappropriate incursions, the fate of a national arboretum was still unresolved. In 1901, Olmsted had considered East Potomac Park as a possible arboretum location, but he later decided this was too small and poorly adapted for either arboreal or botanical collections.[40] From 1918 forward, the Commission of Fine Arts championed the Mount Hamilton site, located northeast of Union Station, for an arboretum that would fulfill a component of the McMillan Plan's park mission. But Congress had to be motivated to purchase the necessary lands and provide for "the proper administrative organization of the national botanic garden."

In support of this quest, Olmsted and colleagues from the American Society of Landscape Architects (ASLA) actively campaigned throughout the 1920s to acquire this wooded and hilly site with its

Sketches of an area in the Rock Creek woods, before pruning (left), and the same area after selective pruning to open up a vista into a meadow.

potential connection to the Anacostia shore for aquatic collections. They finally achieved success by 1930 when funds were appropriated for the land acquisition under the Department of Agriculture.[41]

More than purely a place to maintain a great collection of living plants, Olmsted stressed that the arboretum should afford recreation and the enjoyment of landscape beauty. Not to compete with the scientific objective, such beauty was

as a constant guide… the peculiar beauty of certain ecological groupings of plants arising, in the absence of human interference, from the orderly operation of biological forces interacting with conditions of the environment.

As in the Rock Creek Park study, the arboretum should be planned in advance as landscape units, each distinctive for its artistic character as much as for its horticultural interest. Echoing his father's words of a half-century earlier on the need for a controlling motive in the capital's landscape, the junior Olmsted noted, "The only safety lies in a most painstaking adherence to the principle of a definite and enduring dominance of a single purpose…all other purposes being there subordinated."[42]

The Washington Monument Grounds

Lobbying efforts for the George Washington bicentennial celebration to be held in 1932 succeeded in obtaining legislative authorization to realize some of the Mall plans. But without substantial funding, this again would be a piecemeal operation. Anticipating an influx of visitors, members of the Commission of Fine Arts petitioned the congressional Bicentennial Committee for consideration of several items to ensure that the artistic intent of the founders was achieved.[43]

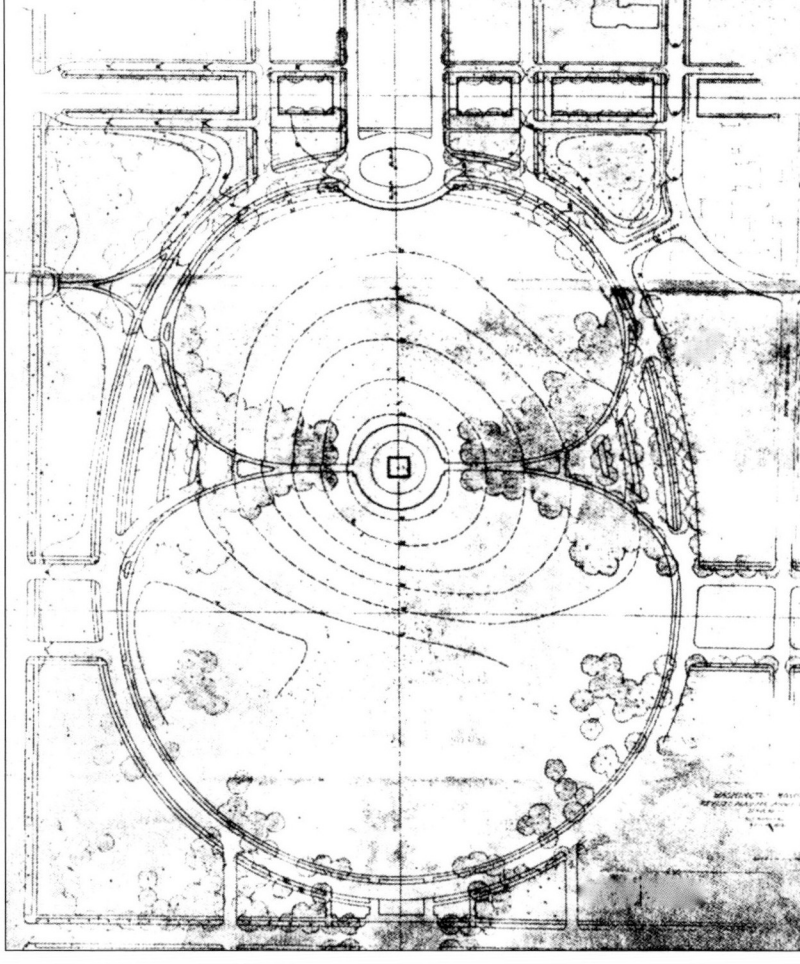

Model and plan of suggested treatment for the grounds of the Washington Monument designed by Frederick Law Olmsted Jr. and his business partner Henry V. Hubbard, c. 1932. The proposal used tree groupings to enhance vistas of the monument while keeping traffic at a distance from the monument base. Parking areas were proposed to the north and south, keeping the main east-west axis clear.

The process began with an engineering study for the Washington Monument's base. To implement McKim's elaborate garden scheme would require extensive regrading, which the engineers concluded would be most precarious since the monument did not rest on bedrock.[44] Olmsted and architect William A. Delano were commissioned to develop contrasting schemes, informal and formal respectively, for the monument's surroundings, both of which were to involve only minimal surface remodeling. Included in this challenge was the establishment of Mall traffic routes, the handling of the crossing streets, and the provision of parking areas. In the view of the Commission of Fine Arts and others, automobile traffic was usurping the streets and despoiling the dignity,

grandeur, and beauty of Washington's intended artistry.

In conjunction with his partner, Henry Hubbard, Olmsted developed a simple design based on several aesthetic principles. Instead of its existing insignificant "fringe" of trees, the monument should be flanked by masses of foliage out of which it should rise as the dominant feature at the end of the formal allée looking west and at the end of the reflecting pools looking east. Cars should be kept distant from the monument, with circuit roads and paths designed and planted to enframe various vistas. Reluctant to choose such a radical revision of the original Monument Garden plan, the commission tabled this decision, ostensibly until the Mall roads were completed and the matter could be restudied.[45]

Aerial view of the monumental core looking west, showing the cluttered conditions prior to 1932. In the foreground are the various structures and irregular paths of the Botanic Garden, with the Grant Memorial statue at its eastern edge. In the middle ground are "tempos" still in evidence in this view and on the north side of the Reflecting Pool by

the Lincoln Memorial. Some of the earlier tree plantings are visible in front of the Smithsonian Castle. The new Department of Agriculture building is set further back, respecting the lines of the Mall, but elements of the former gardens remain in front.

There was still debate in late 1932 as to the number of roads that should line the Mall and how to plant them so as to frame the central greensward. Some voices from various Washington planning agencies continued to call for a mixed planting to include tulip trees and red oaks. Olmsted labeled this idea of a varied tree palette "unfortunate" and emphasized that the distinctive essence of the 1901 scheme was the formality of its elm colonnade, with its high canopy and Gothic arch effect providing diagonal and transverse glimpses within and along the Mall.[46]

Union Square

In 1933, an infusion of money from the Public Works Administration to continue Mall construction involved Olmsted in the design for Union Square, beneath the Capitol's walls at the eastern terminus of the Mall. As in the Monument Grounds project, he tangled with some Commission of Fine Arts members committed to strict adherence to the McMillan Plan images rather than to its intent. As conceived by the McMillan Commission's watercolor illustration, this area was to consist of an open rectangular plaza spatially articulated by formal beds of lawn punctuated by fountains, pools, or statuary, which axially terminated the panels of the Mall. To create this space, the curving west wall of the Capitol Grounds would have to be straightened. The decreased area of the Capitol's western lawn was to be decorated with a central cascading water feature that terminated in a grand oval pool, with all of this supported by a series of retaining walls. All that remained of the senior Olmsted's plan were tree-lined diagonal paths that he intended to lead to the diagonals of Maryland and Pennsylvania Avenues. In the McMillan scheme, these strong diagonal lines would be interrupted by the plaza.[47]

By 1933, instead of this formal plan, Union Square existed as a rather dysfunctional trapezoidal space. The Grant Memorial, which had been located along the eastern end by McKim and Olmsted in 1907, reigned over a space now containing the Meade Memorial and an eccentric collection of noble trees and fountains along meandering paths.[48] Along the southern edge, greenhouses—remnants of the Botanic Garden—still dominated. The Garfield and Peace Monuments terminated the Maryland and Pennsylvania Avenue diagonals respectively.

Working with his associate Clarence Howard, Olmsted saw his prime task as bringing this space into proper relationship with the Capitol's west terrace and the broad reach of the Mall while reconciling serious design inconsistencies. In his April 1934 report to the commission, he noted Union Square's importance was as one unit "of a much larger whole, extending from the Capitol to the Washington Monument and on to the Lincoln Memorial." The northern and southern boundaries of the square, as defined by L'Enfant's strong diagonal avenues, had been extended into the Capitol landscape by the senior Olmsted's tree-embowered diagonal paths terminating at the western terrace.[49]

Olmsted's first step was to convince the Commission of Fine Arts that the 1901 plan, which radically shortened the Capitol's western lawn by one hundred feet in order to insert the cascade and pool, was a profound mistake. Earlier, his father had rejected Senator Morrill's desire for such a cascade, noting the importance of the simple turf panel as foreground to the Capitol's grand architecture. Observing that this area of the 1901 plan had been less studied by the commission "and was embodied in the report under pressure of time as a tentative solution in spite of expressed doubts… as to some of its features," Olmsted reminded the Commission of Fine Arts

that the plan's illustrations were never intended to be definitive in terms of their details. Reinforcing his argument that precedent did not support truncating the Capitol Grounds by a straight line, he provided seven historical plans, beginning with that of L'Enfant, illustrating that throughout all the architectural renovations of the Capitol, the western boundary had continuously been retained as a curved line.[50]

In Olmsted's view, recognizing the integrity of Union Square as a whole space, defined by strong diagonal avenues and related to the vista beyond, was critical. The square's function, he said, should be to "prepare the eye for the transition from the uniform width of the vista on the Mall to the treatment on the Capitol Grounds," where the converging lines continued as spatial definers. Alignments were complicated due to deviations from true axial projections. In 1901 adjustments had been made to align the Mall's axis from the Capitol to the off-center Washington Monument. The Olmsted team noted that the Grant Monument had been placed on a line drawn from the center of the Capitol's west facade rather than from the dome, an off-center divergence of an additional four feet. These discrepancies had to be subtly adjusted within the Union Square design, using many of the relocated mature Botanic Garden trees as screening.[51]

Again, Olmsted's tampering with the sacred lines of the 1901 plan unleashed a flurry of indignation from commission members, particularly from architect Egerton Swartwout. He insisted on the original McMillan Plan treatment of the Capitol Grounds and the intended plaza, vociferously objecting to Olmsted's informal planting scheme and to the general lack of monumentality and architectural perspective. Olmsted, in turn, reiterated that the 1901 plan never contended with the continuity of the Mall, nor with the successful termination of

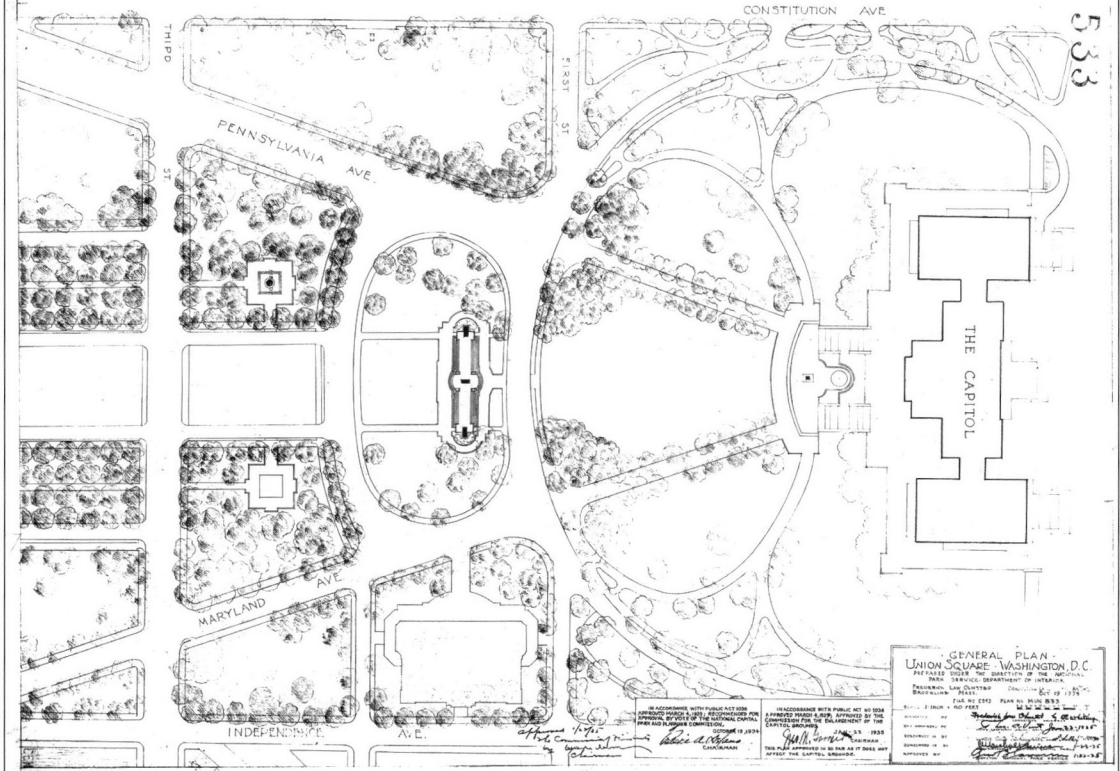

ABOVE: *Handwritten notations on a photograph of the Senate Park Commission rendering for Union Square indicate the strong diagonal lines to be retained and the various sculptural elements to be integrated.*

LEFT: *General Plan for Union Square, October 1935.*

the diagonal avenues that ended in the plaza. Moreover, he maintained, in Washington's climate such an open plaza would be "objectionable."[52]

General survey of the grounds of the Executive Mansion, showing existing conditions as of January 1935 (left), and General Plan for Improvements of October 1935 (right). The General Plan indicates a simplification of the design elements and a massing of plant materials to provide screening while retaining a clear vista to the south.

Months spent negotiating redesigns finally resulted in agreement in March 1935 among all the commissions involved. At this time, however, Rick Olmsted was recuperating from a near-fatal burst appendix, and other partners of Olmsted Brothers supervised the work.[53] Construction, completed by 1937, involved a massive tree-moving operation in which forty-one mature specimens were transplanted and 250 removed. The Olmsted design remained relatively intact until the Skidmore, Owings & Merrill redesign and installation of the re-

flecting pool about 1971, with its unequal sides to compensate for the geometric inconsistencies.[54]

The White House Grounds

Olmsted had reviewed the White House grounds in 1928, finding them "distinctly disappointing," not up to the standards of tasteful surrounds for great mansions, public and private. Concerned that this was a dwelling for a succession of families, he thought that the grounds nonetheless ought to be "in the front rank, both as expressing the honor due to the President of the United States, and as an educative example to less distinguished citizens." Specifically, the grounds lacked

"the intimate and essentially domestic kinds of beauty and usefulness that are as much to be desired for a President's family as for any other."[55]

Bringing this issue before the commission in 1934, Charles Moore noted that both Mrs. Coolidge and Mrs. Hoover had shown little interest in Olmsted's 1928 report. Since architectural renovations were planned for the building, President and Mrs. Roosevelt had consulted with Olmsted and Charles Moore, then the chair of the Commission of Fine Arts, to assess the landscape problems. Knowing that President Roosevelt had prior experience directing work on the grounds of his family estate at Hyde Park, New York, they believed

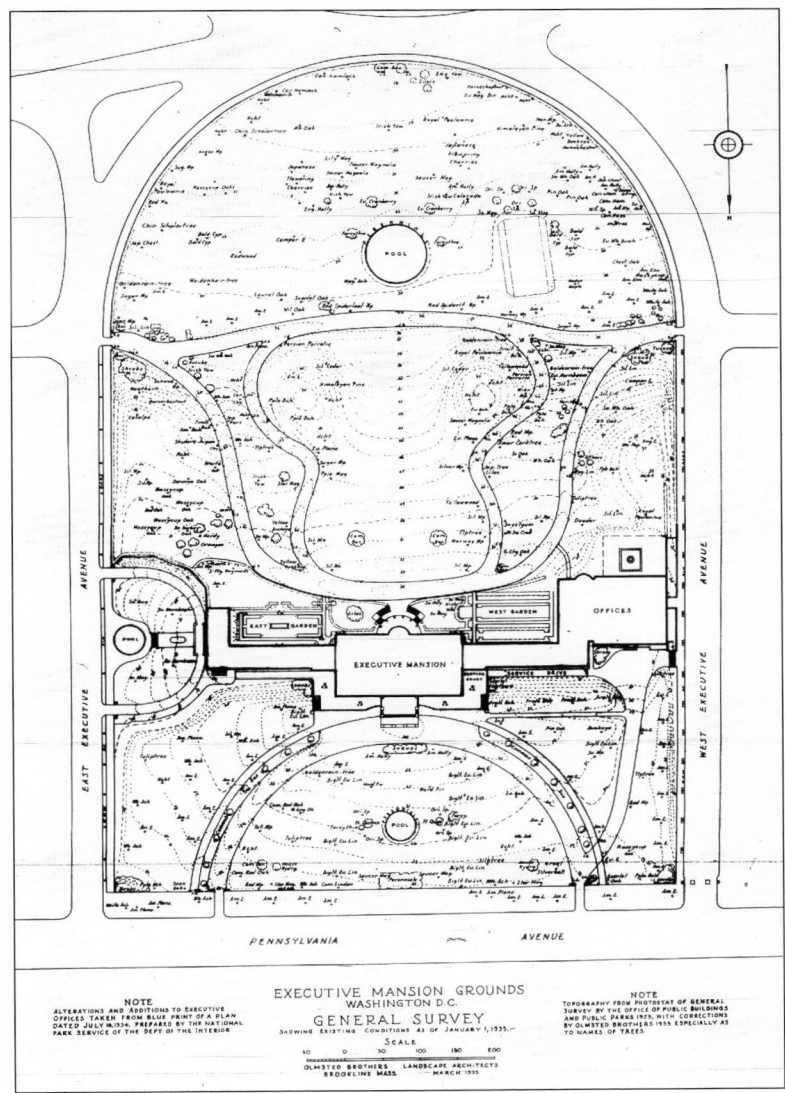

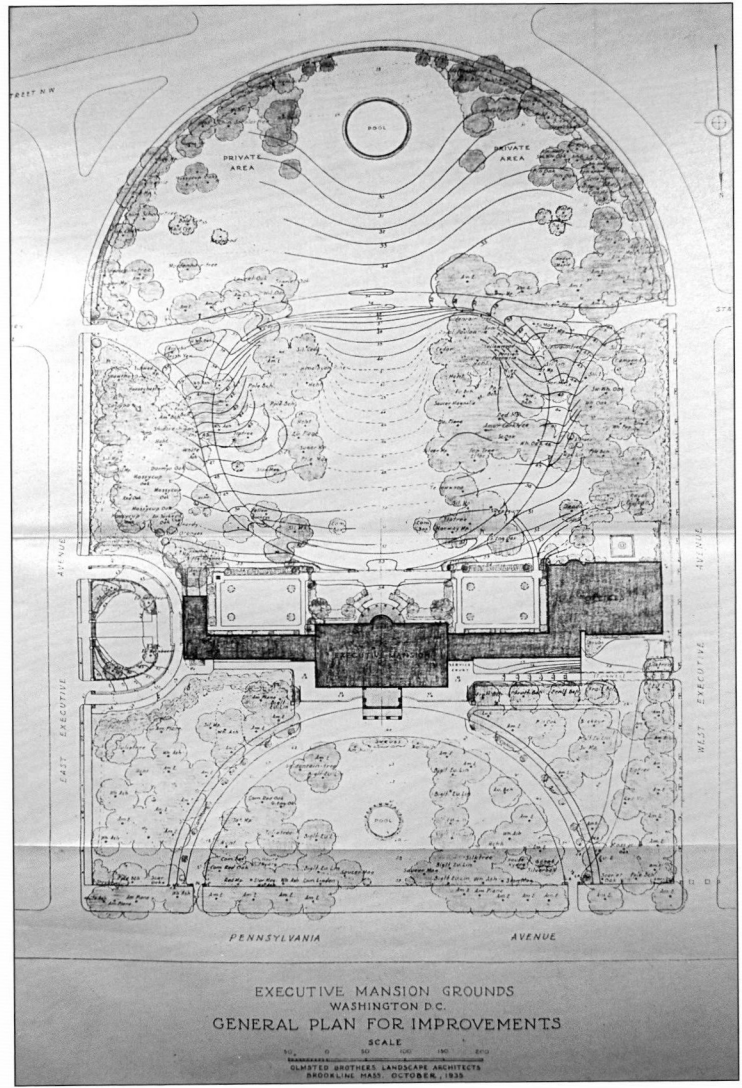

he would be a knowledgeable client with a strong interest in history.[56] Because of this, Olmsted hired Morley Williams, a professor of landscape architecture at Harvard University who was working at this time on the Mount Vernon grounds, to collaborate with him. Williams was to study "the long and somewhat obscure history of developments and changes in the White House Grounds—a thing much needed as a sound basis for guiding any changes and improvements to be made in the future."[57]

The final report, including Williams's richly illustrated historical study of the White House grounds, was presented to the commission in October 1935. Olmsted and Williams had recommended returning an appropriate historic character to the landscape in their preliminary White House report. They sought to increase the sense of privacy, to ameliorate traffic conflicts along the roads and paths, and to correct accessibility issues at the entrances. Within the grounds, Olmsted made several suggestions to improve tree and shrub compositions and to rehabilitate the formal gardens with dignified simplicity.[58]

Implementation followed a difficult course, due to cost, economic conditions resulting from the Great Depression, and jurisdictional and professional conflicts with the National Park Service. Olmsted, still recuperating from his illness, was aided on this project by Henry Hubbard, his Olmsted Brothers partner and a member of the NCPPC, which had advisory jurisdiction over the White House grounds. Hubbard noted that the firm had spent "a great deal of loving care in the investigation of this particular problem, and it certainly would be a pity and a waste if the carefully matured conception which has crystallized in Mr. Olmsted's mind were not given a fair chance of realization."[59]

Some recommendations were implemented between 1935 and 1937. These involved renovation of the east and west gardens, providing some seclusion for the residents without altering the broader visual compositions, strengthening the southern axial views, and replacing an existing pool with a simple fountain moved further south to better relate to the open areas.[60]

The Thomas Jefferson Memorial

Returning to Washington work in July 1935, Olmsted was drawn into a controversy concerning the Thomas Jefferson Memorial when he agreed to voluntarily review preliminary studies for National Park Service Director Arno Cammerer. Charles Moore had set lofty goals for this monument to be "one of the most distinguished structures in the National Capitol… to contribute to the perfection of the Washington plan."[61] Olmsted, however, had already raised concerns about the appropriateness of a grandly scaled monument in this location during his work on the Theodore Roosevelt memorial in 1922. At the time, his evaluation of the proposal led him to state that the McMillan Commission had not adequately studied the intent of the original L'Enfant Plan for this area. In looking at the view from the Tidal Basin north, Olmsted had been struck by the domestic scale of the White House as a terminus in comparison to the grandeur of the other focal points. Olmsted concluded that this southern focus should be treated less grandly than originally conceived.[62] Ultimately, the Roosevelt memorial was not built at this location, but Olmsted's concern regarding appropriate scale for treatment along the White House axis remained (see essays by Pamela Scott and Carroll William Westfall). Echoing these earlier concerns, Olmsted cautioned Cammerer that any monument placed on this axis had to visually relate to the already developed compositions along the east-west axis from the Lincoln Memorial to the Capitol and the north-south axis from the White House to the Washington Monument.[63]

John Russell Pope's plans for a grandiose monument to Thomas Jefferson on an artificial island to be constructed in the Tidal Basin aroused Olmsted's particular consternation. "From a professional standpoint and as the surviving member of the Commission of 1901, I am worried most directly about the probable esthetic outcome," he stated, adding that he did not want to see the government committed to site construction operations costing millions of dollars.[64] After Pope's death in August 1937 and the relocation of the memorial site to a peninsula on the shore of the Basin, Henry Hubbard represented the Olmsted position in ensuing discussions with the successor architects, Eggers & Higgins.[65] In the controversy surrounding the aesthetic relevance of the Pantheon form and its shoreline setting, Hubbard often found himself in debate with the architects' historical advisor, his brother-in-law Fiske Kimball.[66] From the fall of 1938, Olmsted Brothers was employed by the architects, and later by the Park Service, to provide landscape planning and implementation oversight to make the memorial's setting an effective contribution to the general plan of Washington. Complicated site conditions, conflicting transportation routes, overlapping controlling agencies, and public outcries concerning the loss of revered cherry trees frustrated attempts to produce an artistic effect. Devising an aesthetic and economical landscape scheme for such a controversial building required reconciling the opposing positions of the NCPPC, the Commission of Fine Arts, and the highway engineers from the National Capital Parks. Hubbard later commented that his role had been that of diplomat more than designer.[67]

Rick Olmsted returned to active participation in the memorial planning controversy in the spring of 1941. Because

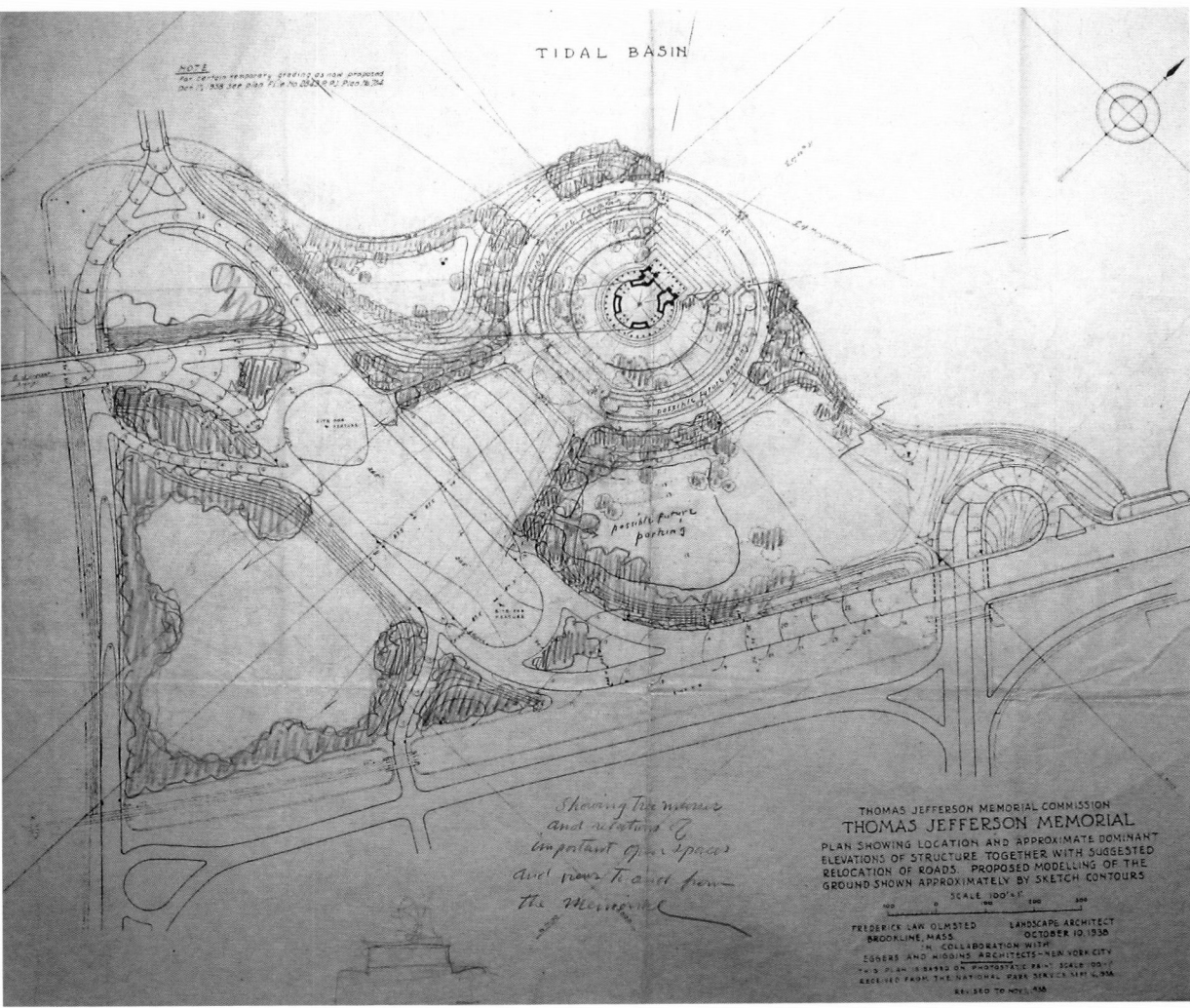

Olmsted Brothers' plan, in collaboration with architects Eggers & Higgins, showing the "location and approximate dominant elevations of the structure together with the suggested relocation of roads" for the Thomas Jefferson Memorial, October 1938. Additional notes on this plan indicate it is intended to show "tree masses and relations of important open spaces and views to and from the memorial."

Gilmore Clarke, chairman of the Commission of Fine Arts, had rejected the planting plan as "out of scale with the Memorial, and in detail, much too fussy," Olmsted agreed to reconsider the planting palette. However, agreeing with Hubbard, he still questioned the wisdom of erecting any great memorial in this location before the traffic issues were resolved and the relationship to the monumental core axes was determined.[68] Although planting supervision was under the jurisdiction of the National Park Service, implementation of the design was plagued by problems of substandard material and workmanship. While wartime exigencies and a limited budget for such a significant structure exacerbated the problems, Hubbard expressed his own dismay at the difficulties

in achieving an artistic effect. The temper of the times, the change in values, the increasing complexity of diverse pressures—particularly that of traffic congestion and altered artistic priorities—significantly thwarted the grand vision.[69]

The Theodore Roosevelt Memorial

The course of development for the Theodore Roosevelt Island National Memorial on Analostan Island is a case in point. Like the Jefferson Memorial, this is one of the last major projects involving Olmsted and his firm that emerged from the 1901 plan. From the outset, the report of the Senate Park Commission had recommended that

Analostan Island's acreage be acquired and suitably treated so that it would not come into "disagreeable occupancy."[70] Within sight of the west end of the Mall, this isle of wilderness so close by offered the promise of unique recreational opportunities in contrast to the grandeur of structures and vast sweep of formal greensward across the river. This juxtaposition was an echo of the Chicago World's Fair, where the senior Olmsted had developed the Wooded Isle as a place of verdant respite in contrast to the structured formality of the great White City.

Located at the fall line of the Potomac River, the ecologically diverse island had an interesting social history. Once owned by the family of George Mason of Virginia, by 1913 it had been purchased by the Washington Gas Light Co. and was intended for industrial uses. The Theodore Roosevelt Memorial Association rescued this prime site by purchasing it in 1931 and deeding it to the federal government for use as Roosevelt's memorial, while retaining planning rights. In accepting the deed in 1932, President Hoover commented on "the especial appropriateness" of this wooded island as this memorial, being "forever within the view of the Lincoln Memorial, the Washington Monument, the Capitol and the White House … a bit of nature within the boundaries of this city which he loved, and where he rendered such noble service."[71]

The association contracted with Olmsted Brothers in May 1932 to prepare a general plan and report, turning to Olmsted and Hubbard to advise them on whether the army engineers should be allowed to fill the island's tidal flats with dredging from the Potomac channel. Olmsted rejected the idea as too early in the planning process to be made, wisely observing that "it is a bad beginning when parts of a block of marble are carved before a clear and self-consistent artistic conception had been formed of the entirety and the spirit of the sculpture-to-be."[72]

Although Olmsted was inspired by the idea of developing the island as a "thoroughly worthy, dignified and self-sufficient" memorial park, his health delayed his early involvement, and so once again Henry Hubbard handled preliminary planning matters in consultation with Olmsted. Hubbard's list of "Considerations Affecting the Design" set forth some determining features. The island was to be "a sanctuary—a sacred grove," primarily for pedestrian use with minimal automobile access. Much of the shore would be preserved in its natural condition, subject to approval by the engineers. The architectural element, a memorial fitted to the natural conditions of the site, was to be designed by John Rus-

sell Pope. This was to be the unifying feature of the island, "expressive of the personality and work of Theodore Roosevelt," and was to be visible from various points on the mainland as a component of the central monumental composition. Thus Roosevelt would be represented among the panorama of celebrated presidential monuments with a uniquely appropriate statement.[73]

The overgrown condition of the island prevented any real examination of its topography and significant vegetative features. Therefore, in early 1934, in order to begin comprehensive planning, Olmsted requested that the Civilian Conservation Corps be brought in to clear the flammable debris, dead trees, and weedy growth. From late 1934 through 1935, crews were at work clearing stumps and brush. They also developed foot trails and bridle paths and eventually replanted thousands of trees, shrubs, and ground cover for forest improvement, while Olmsted and his firm's plantsman, Hans Koehler, marked off areas of special native vegetation to be preserved.[74]

By December 1932, Olmsted began to conceptualize the principal elements of design and preservation for the island, refining his ideas over the next three years.[75] The dominant natural feature was the woodland, which Olmsted hoped could be returned to the original of rich variety that had once covered the Potomac islands. "With skillful, yet self-subordinating and humble-minded aid from man," he said, "nature can be induced to recreate here … the very sort of climax forest, full of enduring and noble dignity and unity of character" that once had existed in this area. At the southern end of the island, the high ridge with good views to the mainland was an ideal location to have a commemorative inscription or the eventual monumental structure. While convenient access was essential, it should not interfere with the sense of seclusion proper to such a for-

est memorial. Therefore, no automobiles should be allowed; instead there should be opportunities for moving through at leisure on foot or on horseback, with access to the island by "a simple unassertive modest" footbridge and perhaps by boat. Few changes should be made to the natural ground surface, except in the flood-prone marshy areas where Olmsted recommended placing large irregular boulders to simulate a rocky shoreline.[76]

Unfortunately, throughout the late 1930s Olmsted's plan went largely unrealized except for the trail work, due to a chronic lack of funds from both the Park Service and the Roosevelt Association. The Olmsted firm, having committed itself to this task, was essentially working gratis. Nonetheless, the firm proceeded with a design for an overlook plaza at the island's southern end where a memorial could be constructed with reciprocal views toward the Mall and along the river. Olmsted's hope was for a simple unpretentious monument to emphasize to the public that the "entire beautiful island" was the primary physical memorial to Theodore Roosevelt, "embodying so many qualities which he keenly appreciated … and which he led so many others to appreciate and make a part of their enjoyment of a full, well-rounded life." But, he cautioned, until there was a permanent means of pedestrian access and a minimal amount of maintenance to stabilize the balance of nature, there was little point in building a monument. Eventually, between 1945 and 1947, the Olmsted firm finalized most of the plans, bringing the job to a point where it would be ready for construction as soon as money became available. The association had a goal of completing the work before Roosevelt's centenary in October 1958.[77]

None of this was to be. The autocracy of the automobile thwarted the careful planning for such a unique memorial. Between the early 1950s and

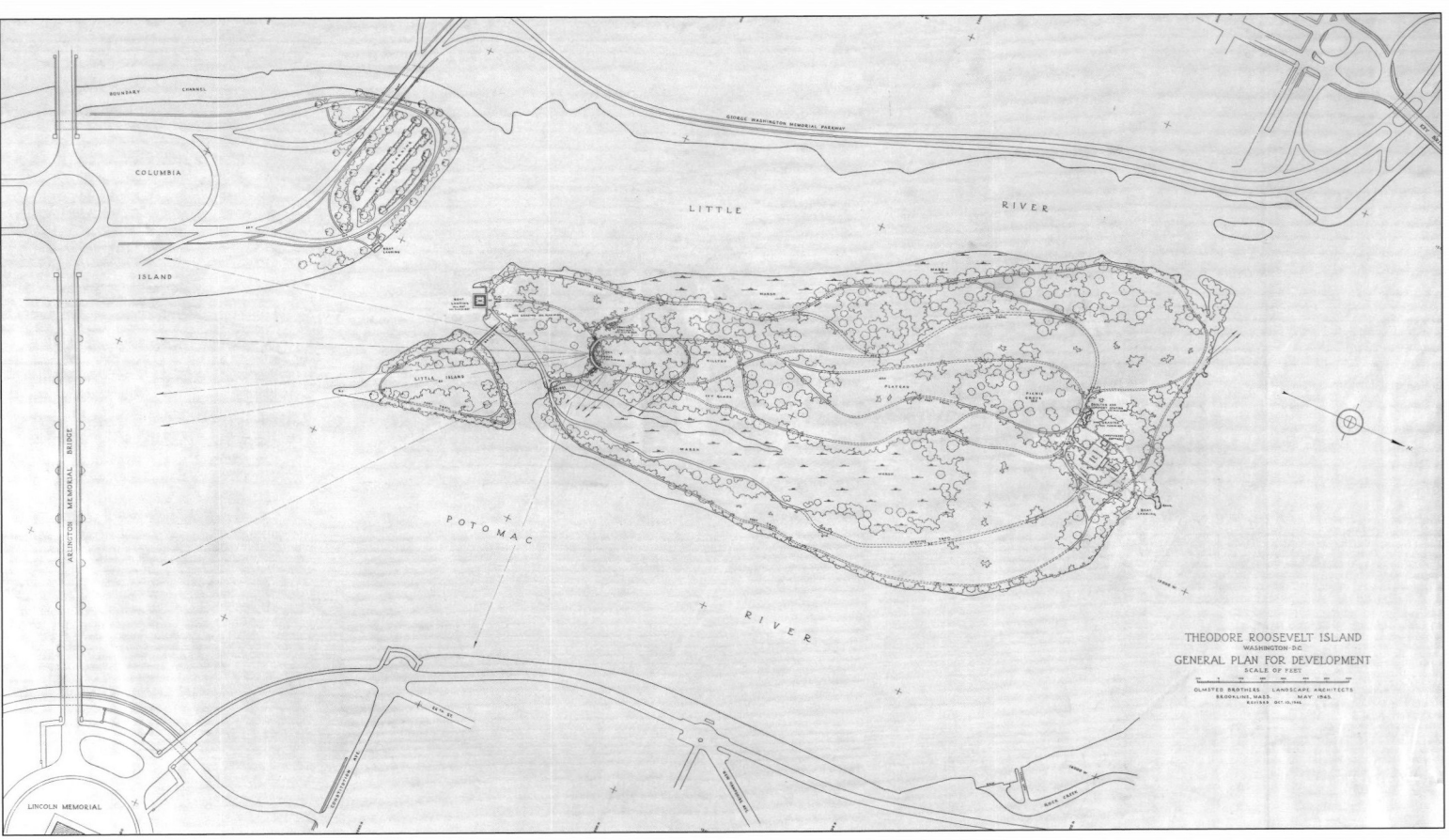

TOP: *General Plan for Development, Theodore Roosevelt Island, May 1945. Critical attention is paid to the design of the vistas east and south; a network of trails curve with the contours through woods and skirt the large marsh on the island's eastern edge. Provision is made for a comfort station and two boat landings on the north and south points.*

ABOVE: *Aerial rendering of the southern end of the island, showing the proposed primary boat landing and the curving wall below the suggested area for a commemorative element.*

ESSAY | AN ENDURING DESIGN LEGACY

1964, heated negotiations to preserve Olmsted's pioneering model of a wilderness sanctuary in the central city came to naught. The association was caught in a devil's dilemma between preserving "the integrity and sanctity of… an area of wild solitude in the very heart of the Nation" or allowing traffic congestion to disrupt the aesthetic harmony of the national capital that Theodore Roosevelt had cherished.[78] They allowed a bridge to pass over the southern end of the island, destroying all possibility of the intended visual connections. Also destroyed was the innovative concept to complement the classic architectural memorializations in the Mall with a living wilderness set aside as a monument to a president so closely associated with American conservation. In 1967 a plaza memorial to Roosevelt was inserted into the woods on the island's north side and, in 1976, a footbridge was added to provide pedestrian access to the island.[79]

The Enduring Legacy

Olmsted did not live to see the destructive intrusion into his innovative concept for the Roosevelt memorial. In the fifty-year span from the high ideals of the Senate Park Commission planning to post–World War II conditions, preservation of architectural treasures and landscape legacies was in ebb. Cities were depleted by flight to the suburbs, and the means of flight—the automobile—ruled decision making. The complexity of urban planning had moved beyond the manageable collaborative approaches that Olmsted and his colleagues had devised to new utilitarian priorities that no longer valued artistic considerations, let alone spacious greenswards and verdant passages of scenery. Well before his death in 1957, Olmsted had begun to direct his major professional efforts to planning for the acquisition, management, and preservation of scenic and natural resources as

Aerial view over Theodore Roosevelt Island with Rosslyn in the foreground and the Kennedy Center in the background, 1970s. The bridge severed all intended views toward the monumental core. A circular memorial space in the woods at the northern end of the island was designed by Eric Gugler and contains a monumental statue of President Roosevelt designed by Paul Manship.

public parks. The unique memorial idea of a public landscape consisting of a healthy, evolving climax forest abutting an intensely urban area seems to have stemmed from this thinking. From his work to establish the National Park Service in 1916 to his planning for the Florida Everglades, the California state parks, Yosemite, or the Colorado River Basin, Olmsted's endeavors ensured that America's extraordinary scenery would continue to provide opportunities for that sense of "enlarged freedom" that he treasured.[80]

Looking back over his long career from the vantage point of his fiftieth Harvard reunion, Olmsted emphasized the satisfaction he had gained from his profession, from solving problems that "would result in appropriately beautiful landscapes, whatever kind of use the land might serve." He enthused over the enjoyment of the collaborative process, the interchange of ideas, the continual learning from the reactions of people interacting with their environment. But he was equally clear that the designer's role was to steward and enhance the beauty inherent in the land, not to overwhelm it.[81]

Frederick Law Olmsted Jr. left an indelible legacy on the American land-

scape over his long and multifaceted career. Fortunately for the stewards of this landscape patrimony, he left a treasure trove of material, an extensive record of prescient reports, insightful correspondence, and imagery to guide the thoughtful evolution of his landscape creations. Nowhere are the productive results of his professional and collaborative endeavors more evident than in the diverse landscape environments of the nation's capital. Over his half century of public service to the city, he molded Washington's terrain by policy, by plan, and by shovel to ensure that the landscapes of monument and park were unified expressions of a controlling aesthetic motive, a continuing and evolving stewardship of the L'Enfant concept and the McMillan Plan. Understanding the comprehensive nature of Olmsted's thinking and his ability to integrate the grand concept with the smallest detail and to balance nature with artifice in his creations will ensure a future for his legacy of artistry for the nation's capital.

❧

Statues, Fountains, and Monuments

THE BURNHAM AND FRENCH CHAIRMANSHIPS, 1910–1915

As the second decade of the twentieth century began, the Commission of Fine Arts embarked on implementing a classical agenda for Washington grounded in the principles of the Beaux-Arts. More broadly, this agenda may be seen as exemplary of the American Renaissance—a cultural phenomenon of the era that combined national political aspirations with forms derived from imperial antiquity, with an emphasis on classical aesthetics, high technical competency, and collaboration among artistic disciplines.[1] At the same time, this steadfast embrace of the classical was occurring within a larger context of cultural change: new technologies—the automobile, radio communication, audio recordings, motion pictures, and the airplane—were already moving America toward modernity. Innovative European concepts of art and design, first introduced to the American public at the Armory Show in New York City in 1913, offered an aesthetic to represent this new age. It would be more than two decades, however, before these concepts began to make inroads into established design thinking in America; during this period, the classical vocabulary remained the accepted approach to civic architecture and the expression of national ideals.

The commission received strong support from President William H. Taft, whose interest in Washington began in the early 1890s when he first moved to the city to serve as U.S. solicitor general and was reinforced when he returned in 1904 as secretary of war. Two months after Taft became president, the local business community organized a dinner at the Willard Hotel in his honor. Taft's remarks addressed local Washington topics including governance, disenfranchisement, and planning. The speech indicates his knowledge of the Senate Park Commission's plan, contemporary trends in parkway design, and the long-time battle over the creation of the Rock Creek and Potomac Parkway:

I would like to come back here a hundred years hence and see the beauties of which this city is capable. Right here…are those beautiful Potomac flats that are going to make as fine parks and parkways as there are in the world. Those parks ought to be connected with the Rock Creek Park by means of the mouth of Rock Creek, or otherwise; and then, through them all there ought to be carried a park clear around, including the Soldiers' Home, and completing the circuit with Rock Creek at the other end…. And to think—to think that we had a genius a hundred years ago almost in his way, as matchless as Washington, to make the plan for a great Capital, like the Frenchman…whose plans were hardly changed in the new plan made by Burnham and his associates. I know there has been discussion as to the plan. There has been a feeling that perhaps it was slipped onto us at one time and slipped in at another; but we all know, even my dear friend, good old Uncle Joe [Cannon], knows, that we are

FACING PAGE: *Statue of Abraham Lincoln by Daniel Chester French within the main chamber of the Lincoln Memorial, 1922.*

RIGHT: *Daniel Burnham by Anders Zorn, 1899. Burnham commissioned the Swedish artist to paint this portrait in oil, which he hung over the fireplace in his study at the family home in Evanston, Illinois.*

BELOW: *The L'Enfant Monument, marking the tomb of Major Peter Charles L'Enfant in Arlington National Cemetery, designed by William Welles Bosworth. Among the prominent dignitaries participating in the May 22, 1911, dedication ceremony were President Taft, who gave the dedication address, and Ambassador Jules Jusserand of France. Senator Elihu Root, secretary of war under President McKinley and secretary of state under President Theodore Roosevelt, gave the concluding remarks.*

RIGHT: *Model, Manila Plan by Daniel Burnham. Shortly after Taft finished serving as governor general of the Philippines in December 1903, he selected Burnham for the commission to design the Philippine capital. Burnham traveled for six weeks in the Philippines in 1904 and produced the Manila Plan the following year. The plan featured formally arranged spaces for large civic buildings fronting the bay, recalling his proposals for Washington, Cleveland, and San Francisco.*

known as Lincoln Park on Capitol Hill in 1876. But as time passed, these memorials to Lincoln seemed to lack sufficient stature and significance as appropriate commemoration for the revered and martyred president.

The Senate Park Commission Plan of 1901 sought to resolve this issue. It extended the axis of the Mall and marked the endpoint in Potomac Park with a memorial dedicated to Lincoln. The plan evoked the Court of Honor erected at the 1893 World's Columbian Exposition, established a contrast between the federal precinct and the laissez-faire development of downtown Washington, and presented an imperial image in keeping with the country's newly recognized status as a world power that emerged following its victory in the Spanish-American War. The design of the Mall, sometimes referred to as the "Kite Plan," strove for parity with the capitals of the Old World, especially Georges-Eugène Haussmann's mid-nineteenth-century designs for Paris boulevards.

As part of the McMillan Plan, Charles McKim included a design for the proposed Lincoln Memorial, imagining a strong horizontal element to terminate the axis established by the Capitol and Washington Monument. Conceived of as a great portico set on a terrace, the design recalled Carl Langhans's late-eighteenth-century Brandenburg Gate in Berlin and was intended to serve as the backdrop to a large

sculpture of a standing Lincoln. The proposal located the memorial at the center of a *rond point* that marked the beginning of a parkway leading to the city's zoo and principal naturalistic park, and intersecting with the bridge that physically and metaphorically linked the northern and southern states by spanning the Potomac River.

Five months after the Senate Park Commission released its plan, Congress created the Lincoln Memorial Commission to determine a location and design for the memorial. It included Secretary of War William Taft; Secretary of State John Hay, who as a youth had served as Lincoln's personal secretary and later wrote a biography of him (1890); the chairmen of both congressional library committees, Senator George Wetmore (R-RI) and Representative James McCleary (R-MN); and two southern Democrats, Senator George Vest of Missouri and Representative James Richardson of Tennessee.[27] Congress established a budget for the memorial at $2 million (approximately $50 million in 2010 dollars).

Initially, the Lincoln Memorial Commission made little progress due to the personal animosities among the members. The influential Representative Joseph Cannon also remained opposed to things associated with the McMillan Plan. Moreover, Cannon disliked what the Lincoln Memorial represented, with its supporters from the

ABOVE, LEFT: *The Tripoli Monument, produced in Italy and erected at the Navy Yard in 1807, was moved to the U.S. Capitol Grounds in 1831. It was relocated to the U.S. Naval Academy in Annapolis, Maryland, in 1860.*

CENTER: *The bronze equestrian statue of General Winfield Scott—who had served every president from Thomas Jefferson to Abraham Lincoln—was designed by sculptor Henry Kirke Brown and erected at a circle on 16th Street, NW, in 1874.*

RIGHT: *The statue of General John Rawlins by sculptor Joseph Bailly was erected in 1874; Rawlins had served as Ulysses S. Grant's aide-de-camp and had also been his neighbor in Galena, Illinois.*

RIGHT: *Shortly after the assassination of Abraham Lincoln, citizens of the District of Columbia began collecting money for a sculpture to honor the slain president. Approximately life-size, the statue of Lincoln sculpted by Lot Flannery was erected in front of City Hall in 1868 atop a thirty-five-foot-tall column, where it remained until the building was renovated in 1920. Placed in storage for several years, the statue was ultimately reinstalled without the column.*

FAR RIGHT: Emancipation, *by Thomas Ball, erected in Lincoln Park in 1876. At the dedication ceremony, Frederick Douglass criticized the subservient depiction of the kneeling freed slave.*

A c. 1903 political cartoon by Clifford Berryman lampooning Representative Joseph Cannon's conservative character.

new wing of the Republican Party that emerged in the 1880s and 1890s composed of a growing urban middle class, moderate reformers, plutocrats, and, most damning in Cannon's view, easterners. He claimed to stand for the common man and the old-guard Populist Party with its base in the Midwest and West. Once Cannon became Speaker of the House in 1903, the Lincoln Memorial bill became one of many pieces of legislation that he did not allow for consideration. In response, those in favor of the Potomac Park site could only guard against infringements upon it.

As the February 1909 centennial of Lincoln's birth approached, pressure for congressional action arose along with other ideas about the best form and location for the memorial. Advocates of the McMillan Plan, including President Theodore Roosevelt, continued to champion the Potomac Park site, but several alternatives gained support. Lincoln Memorial Commission member McCleary, influenced by a trip to Italy and seeing remnants of the Appian Way of ancient Rome, changed his position from favoring the Potomac Park site to promoting a memorial road from Washington to Gettysburg, Pennsylvania. Mary

Foote Henderson, wife of a former senator from Missouri, sought to transform 16th Street, NW—including the couple's extensive landholdings in the area—into the city's *Champs-Élysées;* she supported locating a Lincoln Memorial in the form of an arch spanning the street atop Meridian Hill. Cannon was in favor of a memorial on expanded grounds of the U.S. Capitol south of Union Station. This location would have the added benefit of eradicating a lower-class neighborhood considered inappropriate at the new gateway to the city. Cannon remained vehemently opposed to the Potomac Park site, finding the former river flats inconceivable as an honorable location for the memorial; he famously quipped to Secretary of State Elihu Root:

There is a fight on about the location of the Lincoln Memorial and you keep out of it; it's none of your damned business. So long as I live I'll never let a memorial to Abraham Lincoln be erected in that God damned swamp.[28]

The short-lived Council of Fine Arts, the predecessor to the Commission of Fine Arts, approved the Potomac Park site for the memorial in February 1909, but progress remained stalled. Two years later, in February 1911, Congress

ABOVE LEFT: *Engine Company No. 24, a District of Columbia project executed in a Renaissance Revival style, was designed by architects Charles Gregg and Luther Leisenring; it began operating in November 1911 at 3702 Georgia Avenue, NW.*

ABOVE RIGHT: *The Manual Training School (also known as West Georgetown School and Public School No. 3) at Wisconsin Avenue and 33rd Street, was designed in the Georgian style by Snowden Ashford of the Office of the Municipal Architect, c. 1912.*

LEFT: *The James Ormond Wilson Normal School, c. 1912, located at Harvard and 11th Streets, NW, was designed by the Office of the Municipal Architect headed by Snowden Ashford; the CFA considered it an inappropriate style for civic architecture in the city.*

designs for a congressionally sponsored monument at Valley Forge; the Lorton Correctional Complex in Fairfax County, Virginia; and a Revolutionary War monument erected by the federal government at the Guilford, North Carolina, courthouse. When asked to consider a privately sponsored memorial to the North American Indian proposed on federal land in New York Harbor, the commission appointed New York–based members Cass Gilbert, Thomas Hastings, and Daniel Chester French to represent it and review the design. Later commissions also periodically used this practice of designating members to evaluate a project as a way to expedite the review process.

As a courtesy, the commission occasionally responded to inquiries about public works in general. This included advising against the introduction of streetcars on the Connecticut Avenue Bridge, commenting on a new lighting plan for Pennsylvania Avenue and a landscape plan for the Pan American Union building, and recommending a height limit for buildings on Squares 167 and 221, the blocks flanking Lafayette Park.

In time, Burnham became frustrated that submission materials for commission reviews were stored in various buildings, not all of which were in Washington; he also wanted a library and display space for the drawings produced by the McMillan Commission. Burnham believed that permanent quarters for the Commission of Fine Arts would serve to increase its status. Framing his desire in terms of educating the public with regard to good taste and arguing a moral imperative—while acknowledging that a permanent office would be a political issue that needed substantial support—Burnham pursued his case with Senator Elihu Root, the former secretary of war and Taft's most trusted advisor, one of the few men the president took into his confidence:[22]

If the work of the Fine Arts Commission is to be effective, it should have a building for its exclusive use, wherein the valuable books, models, documents and drawings that are rapidly accumulating can be conveniently used and taken care of. The Plan of Washington of 1902 [sic] should be permanently displayed, instead of standing, faced to the walls in various places; and such superb drawings as those of Guerin, made for Bacon's Lincoln Memorial design, should be hung permanently for merely as drawings they are inspiring—they cultivate good taste.

Above all, such a function as that of the Commission of Fine Arts needs organization, and this makes necessary plenty of well arranged rooms. That sort of moral effect which you, of all men, understand and appreciate, is now dissipated because the Commission is little known to the public and only casually to officials in Washington. If we have our own building, small though it may be, our status will be better and it will become fixed more quickly than it can be without a building.[23]

Root, however, was not successful in having a building assigned to the commission. Its offices remained at the Lemon Building until 1923, when it moved to the Department of the Interior building and then to a navy building on Constitution Avenue, before relocating to the new Department of the Interior in 1937, where the commission would remain for more than thirty years.[24] Perhaps there was no available building, or the allocation of a building was politically untenable given the commission's contemporaneous struggle to establish the site for the Lincoln Memorial at the western end of Potomac Park.

Lincoln Memorial

The Lincoln Memorial epitomized the Beaux-Arts ideals advanced by the 1901 McMillan Commission and championed by the nascent Commission of Fine Arts. The memorial was the most important project to come before the commission during its early decades.[25] Although Washington received its first outdoor sculpture in 1807, the Tripoli Monument, originally located at 8th and M Streets, SE, it would be several decades before L'Enfant's vision for public spaces occupied by "ornaments" started to take shape.[26] Memorials to the Union's Civil War heroes began to appear in the 1870s; the circles and squares closest to President's Park, such as Scott Circle, Rawlins Park, and McPherson Square, received the earliest sculptural improvements. The city's first monument to President Abraham Lincoln was erected in front of the City Hall at Judiciary Square in 1868, and a second, known as the Emancipation Monument, was installed in what became

The Connecticut Avenue Bridge, designed by architects George Morison and Edward Casey, was constructed between 1897 and 1907. When it opened, it was the largest concrete bridge in the world; it was officially renamed the William Howard Taft Bridge in 1931.

ABOVE: *An illustration in the 1901 McMillan Report of a memorial to President Lincoln designed by Charles McKim, rendered by Robert Blum.*

LEFT: *Perspective view of a memorial to Abraham Lincoln at the western end of Potomac Park, as illustrated in the McMillan Report, 1901.*

The Lincoln Memorial Commission, 1920 (from left to right): James Beauchamp Clark, William Taft, Joseph Cannon, and Samuel McCall.

reconstituted the Lincoln Memorial Commission and finally authorized action on the memorial. This time the commission members included President Taft; Senators Shelby Cullom (R-IL), Hernando Money (D-MS), and George Wetmore (R-RI); and Representatives Joseph Cannon (R-IL), James Beauchamp Clark (D-MO), and Samuel McCall (R-MA). At its initial meeting, the Lincoln Memorial Commission members decided to seek advice from the recently established Commission of Fine Arts regarding the best site for the memorial and the means by which the architect, sculptor, and artist should be selected; the Lincoln Memorial Commission also suggested several sites to consider.

The following month, Cannon—operating behind closed doors—wrote to Burnham to ensure that the architect knew which site should be taken seriously:

My recollection is that some little time ago in a conversation with you reference was made to the site between the Capitol, the Peace Monument and the Union Station. I would not if I could, and could not if I would, affect your judgment in the premises; but when you visit Washington I should be glad to have a talk with you concerning the matter.[29]

At the April 1911 meeting of the Commission of Fine Arts, it was decided that each member should send his ideas to layman member Charles Moore, who would compile the opinions into a draft report. The members of the commission considered the questions intently, including studying more than one hundred architectural designs made over the years for structures around the Capitol

building. Nevertheless, the members of the Lincoln Memorial Commission were impatient for an answer. After prodding from Taft, Burnham sent him a telegram noting that the official report had been drafted and was currently with Millet, who, like Moore, had worked as a journalist in the early part of his career. Burnham wrote:

The Lincoln Monument is the most important thing the Government has submitted to us. It seemed unwise to report until everybody who wished to, had a chance to suggest a site…. A tentative draft has been read to the Commission and sent back to the Committee for revision and at our next meeting it will be adopted as there is little left to do on it. We hope to meet in two weeks.[30]

At the same time, Burnham sent a telegram to Millet about the status of the report. Millet responded that he was "not at all satisfied." As a Washington insider (in part because he was a close friend of Archibald Butt, military aide to both Presidents Roosevelt and Taft), Millet complained that lawyers and politicians would be reading the report and that it needed to be "more concise, straightforward and orderly." He provided some specific text and then complained about the way Washington conducted business, regretted the fact that the McMillan Plan had never been adopted officially, and criticized the quality of work of the Commission of Fine Arts in general:

The trouble with the whole situation in Washington is that there is no one at the wheel. We are not beginning at the beginning. There is a plan, but not an accepted plan, and there are various commissions, but not one with capacity to carry out the whole work. The Lincoln Memorial is a very difficult and important problem, and it would be unwise to have an open competition, or any other kind of a competition, and have it be decided by a jury composed of members who know less about the problem than the competitors do. If we can get Congress to appoint a permanent jury, with authority, and instruct this jury to study the problem deliberately and seriously, it seems to me the best result can be reached and a definite step in advance will be taken.

In our own work as a Commission of Fine Arts, I think we are too casual and to[o] rapid.[31]

Millet thus put into words the general belief held by members of the commission that the direct selection of artists was preferable to competitions.

Burnham deferred to the politically savvy Millet regarding the report, but also sought to have him consider the greater context:

I am always distrustful of my own habit of hammering hard—striking from the shoulder—and, therefore, inclined to ask others to express my thoughts in a smoother fashion than is habitual with me. But perhaps you might be right in this case, and it may be better not to fire over the heads of the people we are directly dealing with.

You remember that when the Washington Monument was located on the Plan of 1791, it was then long afterward claimed by those who had opposed it, that if placed where shown by General Washington's Plan it would stand in a swamp or slough…that is now made against locating the Lincoln Memorial on the Potomac site, and this should not be lost sight of.[32]

To put more pressure on Burnham, Taft wrote him a note relaying a recent visit from the elderly Senator Cullom who wanted to know when the Lincoln Memorial Commission could expect the report from the Commission of Fine Arts. Taft responded that he "does not wish this project to take the course of so many others and die or, rather, linger along and not be realized in this generation."[33]

On July 17, 1911, the Commission of Fine Arts issued its report, which began by noting that the $2 million appropriation suggested that the memorial would be large and beautiful and, consequently, that the site design "need not be controlled or even influenced by existing surroundings." Perhaps to prevent Cannon from undermining the commission's position, the report offered one or two sentences dismissing each of the six proposed sites near the Capitol. It then established that the commission members unanimously favored the Potomac Park site:

It is impossible to overestimate the importance of giving to a monument of the size and significance of the Lincoln Memorial complete and undisputed domination over a large area, together with a certain dignified isolation from competing structures, or even from minor features unrelated to it. Upon no other possible site in the city of Washington can this end be secured so completely as upon the Potomac Park Site.

… While this site is sufficiently isolated to give it dignity, it is readily accessible, being situated in a park which even in its partially developed state has become a place of great popular resort, and which is destined to be the chief center of outdoor reunion in Washington, for people on foot as well as those in vehicles.

The commission members ended their discussion of the site with a political justification by repeating a quote from the now-deceased John Hay, who had been in favor of the Potomac Park site.

The commission members recommended direct selection of an architect; recognizing political sensitivities, they stated that if a competition was preferred, the Lincoln Memorial Commission should first create an architectural advisory committee to establish the program. The report also included an appendix addressing other sites that had been suggested over the years. In it, commission members objected to the Meridian Hill site as unsuitable because 16th Street, NW, was

so narrow and the foliage extends so far into the street that for a considerable portion of the year the memorial would be hidden from view …. Moreover, the region will soon be a busy one, and even now is occupied by residences of many and varied styles…. [T]he Lincoln Memorial would lack that isolation which is an essential element in the site of a great monument.

The commission members also rejected the Fort Stevens option because it was not located along one of the radial avenues. The appendix included a statement that the monument should be a work of art and not serve a function such as a memorial bridge. Finally, the commission members dismissed a road to Gettysburg as an option because the congressional act specified that the memorial was to be located in Washington.[34]

In August 1911, the Lincoln Memorial Commission, after meeting jointly with the Commission of Fine Arts, remained divided and could only adopt the following cautious resolution:

RESOLVED, That the advice of the Commission of Fine Arts be requested as to a designer to act as an advisor to the Lincoln Memorial Commission for the purpose of preparing designs of a memorial, within the legal limit of cost, for the site recommended by the Fine Arts Commission with a view to enable the Lincoln Memorial Commission to determine whether it will finally approve the site recommended.[35]

After the meeting, the Commission of Fine Arts returned to its offices and took an informal vote regarding the architect's name to put forward. One member advocated for William Mitchell Kendall (CFA 1916–21), the principal designer at the firm McKim, Mead & White; four members supported the New York architect Henry Bacon. After further discussion, a formal vote was taken that resulted in a unanimous decision in favor of Bacon (CFA 1921–24). Based on the recommendation from the Commission, Taft endorsed the selection of Bacon and asked him to prepare a preliminary design for the memorial.

It appears that the Commission of Fine Arts members wanted someone who could carry Charles McKim's vision to fruition. Bacon initially studied at the Illinois Industrial University (now the University of Illinois) in Urbana and then apprenticed in Boston architecture firms. He studied ancient architecture firsthand beginning in 1889, while touring Europe and Asia Minor on the Rotch Traveling Scholarship from the Massachusetts Institute of Technology. When he returned to the United States in 1891, he was hired by McKim, Mead & White; one of his early responsibilities included work on the firm's Agricultural Building at the Columbian Exposition in Chicago, at which time he met Burnham and Millet. Disliking the corporate operations of McKim, Mead & White, Bacon left after six years to open a firm in partnership with James Brite. His projects included institutional buildings, mausoleums, residences, and the professionally acclaimed competition entry for an art museum in Philadelphia, located in Fairmont Park.

The elite architectural community considered Bacon to be the personable heir (unlike the irritable William Mitchell Kendall) of McKim, who had died in 1909—and thus the best candidate for the job. Indeed, Bacon had been

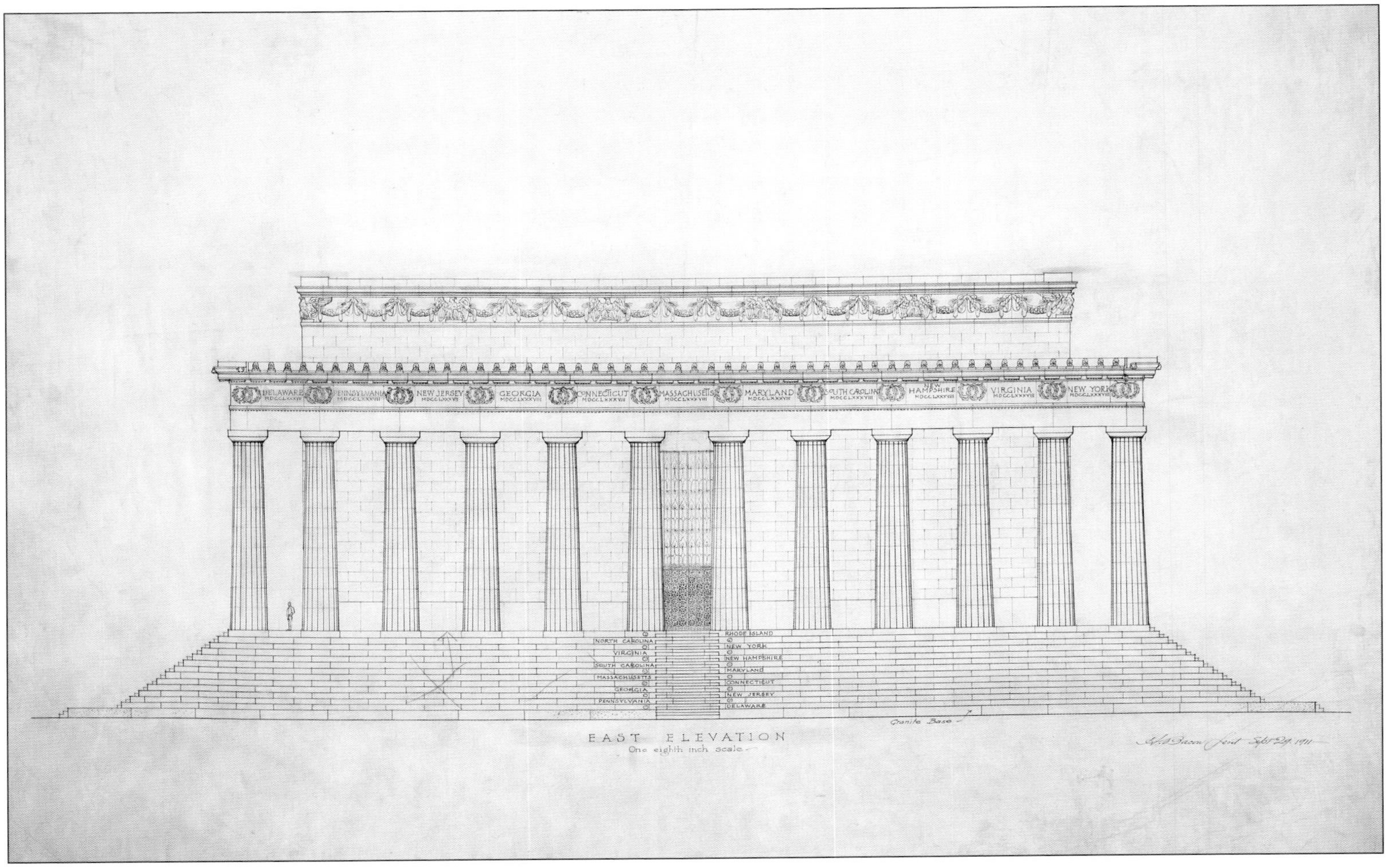

EAST ELEVATION
One eighth inch scale

ABOVE: *The preliminary east elevation of the Lincoln Memorial by Henry Bacon, 1911. The drawing illustrates a Doric temple set on a podium comprised of thirteen steps, with the names of the colonies inscribed on the risers.*

RIGHT: *A preliminary interior perspective of the Lincoln Memorial by Henry Bacon, c. 1910, rendering by Jules Guérin.*

CHAPTER II │ STATUES, FOUNTAINS, AND MONUMENTS

recognized as McKim's right-hand man.[36] It is noteworthy that Francis Millet had been Bacon's friend and mentor for twenty years. Furthermore, Daniel Chester French and Bacon had collaborated on several projects, including tombs for the Melvin brothers in Concord, Massachusetts (1897–1907), and for Marshall Field in Chicago (1906); Bacon had also designed French's summer studio on his estate in the Berkshires in 1898 and his residence there in 1900.

After Taft contacted Bacon to make preliminary designs, Bacon immediately traveled to Washington to study the Potomac Park site. His initial sketch for the memorial included a broad colonnade that clearly derived from the 1901 McMillan Plan. However, believing that the statue should be in a more secluded space, Bacon also sketched a plan of a chambered structure that became the basis for his final design.

Despite the fact that the schematic design phase had begun, politics would remain at the fore. Bacon sensed this perennial Washington issue. Following an August luncheon with the Lincoln Memorial Commission, he wrote Burnham of his initial efforts and reported that at the lunch he had sat next to Cannon, who was "very friendly when he found I was born in Illinois."[37] Notwithstanding the clear recommendations from the Commission of Fine Arts, the Lincoln Memorial Commission independently asked prominent New York architect John Russell Pope (CFA 1917–22) to prepare drawings for the memorial at Meridian Hill and at a site previously not discussed—the Soldiers' Home, a large property on elevated terrain located several miles north of the Capitol.

By early December 1911, Bacon had completed his preliminary design. Knowing that he might not receive unanimous support from the Lincoln Memorial Commission, he produced perspectives intended to express the grandeur of the site and staged an exhibition at the Smithsonian Institution's National Museum of his drawings and models. Bacon intended the exterior of the structure to express the country as a unified nation. Its pedestal incorporated a staircase with thirteen steps, one for each of the original states, with the names inscribed on the risers. A colonnade of thirty-six fluted Doric columns, modeled on those of the Parthenon in Athens, represented the number of states at the end of the Civil War. The frieze featured the names of the thirty-six states separated by wreaths comprised of northern pine and southern laurel. The attic story had garlands, ribbons, and eagles at the four corners and incorporated a secondary frieze of the names of the states that had entered the nation since 1865. Greek detailing was employed to suggest democratic ideals and the strength of the Union and Lincoln. While the plan was de-

rived from the Parthenon, Bacon opted to present his temple with a shallow vestibule and narrow portal. Within the structure, he envisioned a relatively small seated statue framed by two rows of columns and end walls featuring text from Lincoln's Gettysburg and Second Inaugural Addresses. The interior perspective suggested that Bacon wanted the memorial to inspire awe.

One week later, Pope exhibited—also at the National Museum—his concept designs for two different Lincoln Memorials at the other sites. The dramatically rendered drawings presented an immense open temple for the Meridian Hill site, whereas the Soldiers' Home site, which he preferred, featured a circular temple with a brooding Lincoln. Unlike Bacon, who represented Lincoln as the symbol of unity, Pope sought to emphasize the president's humanity. In his written commentary, Pope maintained that Lincoln should not be represented "in the form of a monument, a tomb, an arch or any form of building…but a figure of the man himself, alone, serene, above us, in a setting of simple memorial dignity…in which the man is always felt."[38]

The popular press supported Bacon's proposal. The *New York Tribune* published a lengthy article on the topic:

Mr. Bacon is a quiet spoken man of forty-five. He has designed many monuments. It is doubtful, however, if he has before in his professional life been so profoundly stirred, experienced the same poetic impulses or dreamed as many dreams as during the months since his appointment to evolve the Lincoln Memorial.

View of the December 1911 public exhibition of Bacon's preliminary design for the Lincoln Memorial presented at the National Museum.

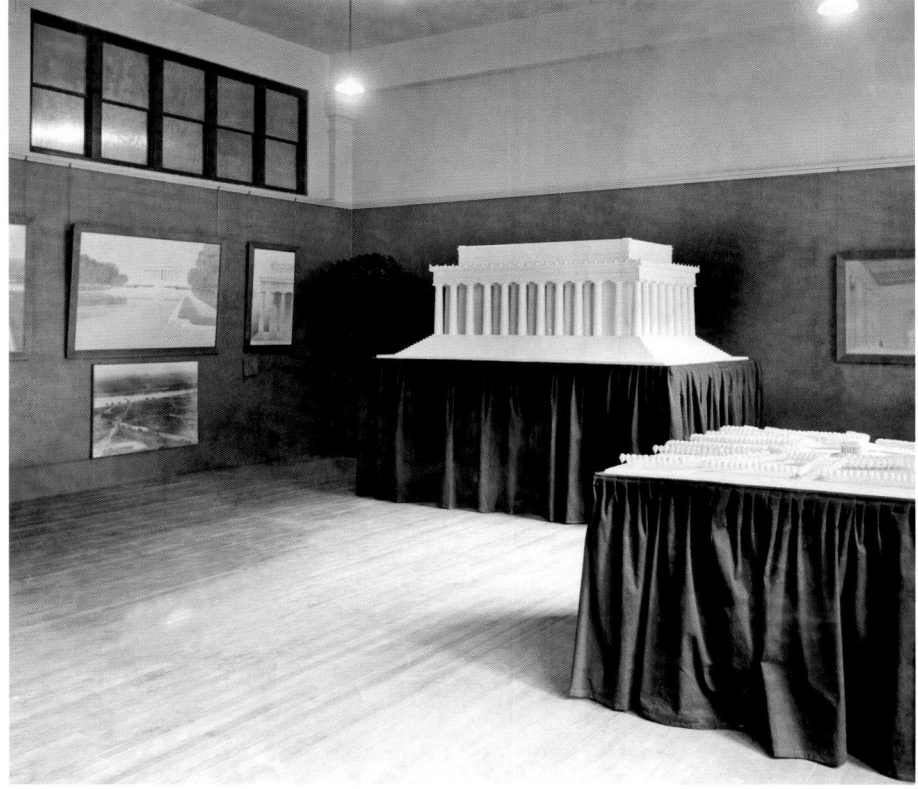

ABOVE LEFT: *John Russell Pope's Acropolis-inspired design for a Lincoln memorial on Meridian Hill, c. 1911; rendering by Otto Eggers.*

ABOVE RIGHT: *Design perspective seen from the east of the Lincoln Memorial by Henry Bacon, 1912; rendering by Jules Guérin.*

RIGHT: *An alternative design, featuring a circular colonnade by John Russell Pope, for a memorial to Lincoln at the Soldiers' Home, 1911.*

The reporter noted that Bacon considered the Potomac Park site to be the best and quoted him on the issue:

Containing the national legislative and judicial bodies, we have at one end of the axis a beautiful building which is a monument to Government, and between the two is a monument to its founder. All three of these structures stretching from Capitol Hill to the Potomac River, will lend, one to the others the associations and memories connected with each, and each will have its value increased by being on the one axis and having visual relation to the others.

The power of impression by an object of reverence and honor is greatest when it is secluded and isolated, for then, in quiet and with-out distraction of the senses or mind, the beholder is alone with the lesson the object is designed to teach and inspire, and will be subject to its meaning.[39]

Despite the positive press, many people remained opposed to the principle of constructing a Greek temple as an inappropriate form for an American hero, reflecting the conflicts arising from America's evolving cultural identity at the heart of the political and aesthetic debate.

In February 1912, Taft notified Burnham that the Lincoln Memorial Commission had requested that both Bacon and Pope make additional studies for the memorial by March 26, looking only at the Potomac Park site. Taft told Burnham that he wanted the Commission of Fine Arts to consider all of the proposals to date and provide a summary report to him a few days before the March deadline.[40] This *de facto* competition produced anxiety among the members of the Commission of Fine Arts, which Daniel Chester French expressed to Burnham:

I have just received your letter of Feb 19. I am prepared to do anything or make any sacrifice that will help to bring about the desired result in regard to the design and the placing of the Lincoln Monument.[41]

Millet sought an outside opinion on the debate. He approached the distinguished sculptor Herbert Adams (CFA 1915–20) about the form of the Lincoln Memorial. Millet asked Adams whether he thought the statue should be indoors or outdoors. Adams replied, "that depends," noted that climate destroys marble, and remarked that, "a bird perched on his thumb does not lend dignity to a statesman." Despite his flippant initial comment, Adams concluded on a serious note in favor of a sculpture located indoors:

The light and shade is the only means by which the modeling may be seen…. Out of doors we cannot control the lighting; it changes constantly…. For an important thing like the proposed Lincoln memorial, what could be more appropriate, or add more to the impressiveness of the statue than to approach it by a beautiful monumental building? When the statue itself is seen, beautifully enshrined like a precious thing, all disturbing surroundings eliminated, the lighting perfect, we have ideal conditions; and the beholder is bound to get a thrill, unless he is numb, or the sculptor has failed utterly.

In short, I can conceive of no more fitting or effective setting for a Lincoln statue than to have it placed in a simple monumental building, even if the building does cost a hundred times as much as the statue itself.[42]

In March 1912, Bacon presented three schemes: a revised version of his first design that gave greater prominence to the central chamber and eliminated the vestibule; an open memorial; and a colonnaded memorial. Pope modified his circular memorial from the Soldiers' Home site for the flat ground of the Potomac Park site. He also produced a design for a Mayan stepped pyramid and another for an Egyptian pyramid.

The Commission of Fine Arts remained unanimously in support of Bacon's reposeful temple and urged the Lincoln Memorial Commission not to be swayed by Pope's exceptional draftsmanship, adding that his romantic designs might exceed the prescribed budget. Burnham and Millet lobbied intently for Bacon's selection.[43] The Lincoln Memorial Commission members wavered on their final decision, with the minority opposition led by Cannon and Clark. Burnham expressed his ideas about the complex

matter—both the architectural basis for his position and the importance of taste—in a letter to Millet:

The argument I made before the Lincoln Commission was that the whole world is looking on and confidently expecting us to do something merely striking and picturesque and not nobly ideal; and that we must disappoint them and rise above their expectations as we did in Chicago; and that to do this we must not and cannot accept such a thing as the round, Doric design submitted, which as a piece of real fine art is not possible.

I told the Commission that … a great, round, open colonnade had never been used by any great designer, because he must have recognized as we do that the columns would jumble…. Our whole standing in architecture and our influence on the taste and architectural judgment of the community are at stake in this matter.

This is not a question of how big or how striking, but of how ideally perfect as a piece of classic art.[44]

Burnham also convinced Taft to invite Millet to the next Lincoln Memorial Commission meeting so the CFA's

Two alternative schemes by John Russell Pope for the Lincoln Memorial in the shape of a pyramid, 1912, and as a stepped pyramid, 1912; renderings attributed to Rockwell Kent.

TOP: *Laying of the cornerstone for the Lincoln Memorial, February 12, 1914.*

ABOVE: *The Lincoln Memorial under construction showing the height of the substructure needed to elevate the temple above the surrounding grade, 1916.*

position could be made clear.

On April 16, 1912, the Lincoln Memorial Commission voted four to two in favor of Bacon but insisted that he restudy his design before the commission would submit the scheme to Congress. Over the next several months, Bacon enlarged the structure and its opening and made revisions to the terraces. The Lincoln Memorial Commission gave its final approval on December 4, 1912, and forwarded its recommendation to Congress, which endorsed the design just weeks before President Taft left office.

In early 1913, Henry Bacon again restudied his design for the memorial and made minor changes, including increasing the width of the columns. The Commission of Fine Arts approved the design in May and the Lincoln Memorial Commission followed suit the next month. The groundbreaking ceremony was held on Lincoln's birthday in February 1914. By that time, Bacon had made further refinements to the design, including raising the attic story by three feet and replacing the eagles at the corners with urns. As costs increased—in part because of the inflation associated with World War I—it is ironic that Cannon advocated before the Democrat-controlled Congress in early 1916 to make an additional $600,000 appropriation (approximately $12 million in 2010 dollars) for the memorial to the Republican president; the measure passed. Cannon reflected before the House:

… I am inclined to think the Art Commission and the majority of the Memorial Commission located this memorial where it ought to be located, although I was somewhat worked up at the time. There it is, just across from Arlington, on the Potomac River: a beautiful park.… I am very glad that there has been a design for that park and for its extension. I am very glad that the park was rendered possible by producing the elevation you have there…because the tide ebbed and flowed over that park for many years after I came to Washington.[45]

The Lincoln Memorial was not completed until 1922, to some extent because of delays associated with the war; interior lighting would not be finalized until the end of the decade.

Deaths on the Commission

The first half of 1912 was marked by great change on the Commission of Fine Arts. At a critical time, Taft was forced to fill two positions on the commission that were previously held by active and highly influential members. In March, Francis Millet had traveled to Europe to attend to matters associated with the American Academy in Rome; on his return home, he sailed on the *Titanic* and died when it sank on April 15, 1912. Coincidentally, Burnham set sail with his family that same day from New York

City to take a vacation in Europe. On May 24, Burnham became sick in Heidelberg, Germany, lapsed into a diabetic coma, and died on June 1.

Senator Henry C. Lodge (R-MA) was the first to address the vacancy caused by Millet's death. He suggested his constituent, Josiah B. Millet of Boston, Francis's brother, who was an editor, critic, and publisher.[46] Taft approached CFA members for their recommendations and also consulted with Senators George Wetmore (R-RI) and Elihu Root (R-NY). In May, the commission members wrote Taft, "We feel the vacancy should be filled by a

painter of recognized ability, as well as one who would be willing to give the time required by the commission."[47] Accordingly, they forwarded the name of Edwin Blashfield, a prominent mural painter, for the position. After vetting this recommendation through Root, Taft appointed Edwin H. Blashfield (CFA 1912–16) to the commission at the end of May 1912.[48]

Burnham's death almost immediately after Blashfield's appointment created another vacancy on the commission. Senator Wetmore took up the issue, sending a letter to the president suggesting New York architect

View of the Lincoln Memorial as seen from the east, c. 1917, prior to construction of the Reflecting Pool.

Walter Cook of the firm Cook & Welch, who had been proposed for the commission when it was initially established. However, Wetmore feared that there were too many New Yorkers on the commission and thus also recommended Peirce Anderson of D. H. Burnham & Company in Chicago. Wetmore reminded the president that Anderson had been highly recommended by Burnham and reported that Senator Root concurred with his conclusion.[49] The members of the Commission of Fine Arts suggested that the seat be filled by William R. Mead of McKim, Mead & White; Mead's role in the firm involved management more than design, suggesting that his selection was based on a reflexive allegiance to the Beaux-Arts establishment.[50] Because the commission members also shared the concern of some in Congress that the commission included too many New Yorkers, they submitted the name Robert S. Peabody of the Boston architectural firm Peabody & Stearns as a second choice.[51] Three other names were also put forward for the position, including architect Austin W. Lord, submitted by the president of Columbia University, and engineer Frederick T. Barcroft, proposed by the president of the Bosserdet Yacht & Engine Company in Detroit and Senator Charles Townsend (R-MI).[52]

On July 3, President Taft himself issued a memorandum regarding the chairman's vacancy, saying that he had conferred with Root and Wetmore and that they fully agreed that the position should not be filled by an East Coast architect. Second, Taft acknowledged the decades of significant congressional prejudice with regard to art and believed that it would increase due to the absence of any representation from the West and South. Third, he argued that the vacancy should be filled by someone who lived as far west as Chicago. Taft concluded the memorandum by noting that Burnham had strongly recommended Peirce Anderson and also mentioned an awareness of the commission's favorable consideration of Anderson.[53] Two days later, Taft appointed architect Peirce Anderson (CFA 1912–16) to the vacancy and designated Daniel Chester French as the new chairman.

One year later, under a new president, the administrative leadership of the commission also changed. In 1913, recently elected President Woodrow Wilson chose Colonel William W. Harts of the U.S. Army Corps of Engineers as his military aide. That autumn, Wilson also placed Harts in charge of the OPBG and named him secretary of the commission. Harts, an engineer who would serve as secretary for four years, had attended Princeton before transferring to West Point and graduating in 1889. He was working in San Francisco as director of the California Debris Commission at the time of the 1906 earthquake; Harts helped develop plans for rebuilding the city's transportation and utility infrastructure and designed prefabricated housing for earthquake survivors.

The Second Chairmanship

The commission's first meeting with Daniel Chester French serving as chairman was held in August 1912. All members were present except for Thomas Hastings; they nominated Frederick Law Olmsted Jr. as the new vice chairman to fill the vacancy left by Millet. In a biography of French, his daughter, Margaret French Cresson, noted that the commission meetings during this period typically lasted all day and were often followed by dinner at Senator Francis Newlands's home.[54]

Items related to the *Titanic* disaster were discussed over the course of the next several months. In August the secretary relayed a request from President Taft to consider a congressional medal for Captain Roston of the steamship *Carpathia* to be presented for his efforts to rescue passengers of the *Titanic*. The commission members reviewed sixteen designs and determined that none achieved excellence. Consistent with their preference for direct selection, they recommended that new artists distinguished in medallic art be invited to present designs.[55] In the fall, Hastings and French submitted their design for the privately funded Butt-Millet Memorial Fountain; Archibald Butt had also died on the *Titanic*. The commission members recommended that Hastings simplify the architectural elements in order to meet the available budget.[56]

At the January 1913 meeting, the commission met informally with officers of the Women's *Titanic* Memorial Association to discuss a potential site for a memorial to the victims of the disaster. The commission members recommended a site along the Potomac River near the Tidal Basin and advised the women to select a prominent sculptor. Instead, the women held a design competition and returned to the commission later that year for advice on the selection of an artist from among the entries. The commission admonished the group for sponsoring a competition, but considered the memorial designed by Gertrude Vanderbilt Whitney to be the best; the final selection of the artist remained with the association.[57] In January 1914, the *New York Times* incorrectly reported that the CFA had selected Whitney's design, touching off a heated dispute among artists that included a resolution from New York City's Municipal Art Society criticizing the commission for awarding the memorial to Whitney. In a letter to the new secretary of the commission, Colonel Harts, French com-

Colonel William Harts, second secretary of the Commission of Fine Arts, accompanies President Wilson at Arlington National Cemetery, 1914.

mented on the sculpture, calling it "remarkable," but asked him to set the matter straight with the press regarding the CFA's role in the choice of Whitney as sculptor.[58]

The Panama Canal Act, passed by Congress in August 1912, stipulated that the Commission of Fine Arts could provide a report to the president regarding the artistic character of the canal structures. The Panama Canal, under construction since 1904, was an immense infrastructure project in Central America supported by the federal government that, when completed in 1914, would drastically reduce the sailing time between the Atlantic and Pacific Oceans. At the November 1912 meeting, Colonel Cosby informed the commission of the opportunity to comment on the structures and reported that the chairman of the Isthmian Canal Commission had suggested that the members of the Commission of Fine Arts visit the Canal Zone for a firsthand assessment of conditions. French eagerly looked forward to the tour with his fellow commissioners and was disappointed when only his and Olmsted's schedules allowed for the trip; the commission's clerk, Arno Cammerer, accompanied the men.[59]

They set sail for Panama in early February and submitted their draft report at the end of the month to Colonel George Goethals of the U.S. Army Corps of Engineers, the officer in charge of building the canal. Recommendations included restudying the lighthouse on the

ABOVE: *Studio portrait of Daniel Chester French, c. 1909.*

LEFT: *The Commission of Fine Arts in 1915. Clockwise from far left: Charles Moore, Peirce Anderson, Edwin Blashfield, Frederick Law Olmsted Jr., Chairman French, Colonel William Harts, Thomas Hastings, and Cass Gilbert.*

The Titanic Memorial by sculptor Gertrude Vanderbilt Whitney and Henry Bacon. The CFA officially approved the design in 1919; the memorial was erected in 1931 along the Rock Creek and Potomac Parkway near the southern end of New Hampshire Avenue and moved to its current site in southwest Washington in 1968.

Atlantic end of the canal, establishing an architectural element where the canal proper began, and marking the monument with a monumental inscription at the continental divide. The draft included the following statement:

In conclusion, since your committee during its visit to the Isthmus was constantly impressed with the feeling that the Commission was called upon too late to make its advice very effective, we raise the question whether the Commission, in its report to the President upon the structures of the Canal, ought not to take advantage of this occasion to state forcibly the necessity for taking aesthetic considerations into account at an early stage in the development of the plans for all great public works.[60]

The comment was removed from the final draft submitted to the Commission of Fine Arts in April and the official report sent to the president in July, possibly in order to maintain a good relationship with the newly elected President Woodrow Wilson.[61] Later that year, Wilson issued an executive order expanding the purview of the Commission of Fine Arts to include design review of structures in the District of Columbia as well as review of "matters of art…with which the federal government is concerned," which considerably broadened the commission's scope to federal projects outside the capital.[62]

The commission's first involvement in the design of a park began indirectly. Georgetown residents had been pressing Congress to establish the first park for the neighborhood, and in 1911 the federal and District governments jointly purchased the abandoned Montrose estate on R Street. The property contained a dilapidated Federal-era brick residence as well as a summerhouse, stables, and additional outbuildings. The OPBG, the new custodian of the property, asked the commission for advice on whether to preserve the buildings. Following a site visit at its November 1912 meeting, the commission recommended that all of the stables and outbuildings be removed, but that the residence should be preserved if Congress could be persuaded to appropriate funds to restore it in the "pure Colonial style."[63]

OPBG's landscape architect, George E. Burnap, initially designed a plan for a park that reinforced "the character of a large country place."[64] The plan established a formal entrance featuring a terrace with an ornamental fountain, along with a bandstand, pergola, and tennis and croquet courts.[65] Because Congress never authorized funds for the restoration of the house, the residence was demolished in the early part of 1914. As the officer in charge of OPBG,

Colonel Harts presented revised plans to the commission in May. The members appointed Olmsted as a committee of one to review the plans and make recommendations, and Olmsted supported the project in concept. The OPBG did not return to the commission with more detailed drawings for another year.[66]

Following the commission's May 1915 meeting, in one of his last actions as chairman, French sent a note to Olmsted and enclosed a letter about the park that he had just received from Georgetown neighborhood advocate Sarah Louisa Rittenhouse:

It is evident that Miss Rittenhouse is an old lady and I seem to see under her verboseness an affection for this whole estate that excites my sympathy. I do not know anything about these tennis courts and things that she speaks of, but I am sure you will feel disposed to respect her wish that the old place shall not be injured by any misuse of it.... I wonder what she will think of the imposing entrance that Mr. Burnhap [sic] has suggested![67]

Olmsted's reply, despite condescending remarks, indicates that he appreciated Rittenhouse's concerns and had reservations about the commission's previous action:

Like you also I feel much sympathy for the point of view of which a few lucid suggestions can be perceived through her prattle.

I don't think we have gone out of our way to do much original thinking about the park or to be sure that the designs for it were being guided by a suitable general conception of the quality to be secured in the park as an artistic whole.... At the last meeting...we recognized and pointed out a distinct lack of artistic harmony with...features of the designs then submitted and with the general atmosphere of the park as it stands today. Personally I had some doubts...about the appropriateness of the big brick-walled entrance feature. I begin to be afraid that this little park may be in the same case that has afflicted Potomac Park so badly; that there is no general conception of a controlling artistic quality as a whole, and that each little piece of work has been considered as an almost independent problem in design.[68]

The remarks indicate Olmsted's willingness to criticize the commission's work, or at least his own efforts. In its annual report for the fiscal year ending in June 1916, the commission members concluded: "Not a little difficulty has been experienced in preparing plans for turning the old Montrose estate into a park to combine the needed facilities for sports like tennis and croquet, while at the same time retaining the naturalistic features of the noble slopes and deep ravines."[69]

Despite more than four years of effort, following a site visit during its April 1917 meeting the commission members recommended that "the whole park should be

ABOVE LEFT: *The Butt-Millet Memorial Fountain (1913) was designed by Daniel Chester French and Thomas Hastings. It incorporates two low-relief sculptural panels: one representing military valor, for Major Archibald Butt, and the other representing art, for Francis Millet.*

ABOVE RIGHT: *Members of the Commission of Fine Arts traveled to Panama in 1913 to review the design of the new canal's ancillary structures; this photograph from the commission's report shows a tower to aid navigation at the canal's Pacific Ocean entrance.*

TOP: *Despite the recommendation by the CFA to preserve the Federal-era main house of the Montrose estate in Georgetown, it was demolished as part of the development of the public park.*

ABOVE: *The pergola in Montrose Park, designed by landscape architect George Burnap, located near the center of the ropewalk, c. 1915.*

redesigned." In July 1917 Harts returned with several proposals, and following another site visit a variety of issues were settled.[70] This work was carried out the following year, and in its 1919 annual report the commission members concluded that they had been

greatly interested in the development of Montrose Park…. The aim has been to adapt the landscape treatment to the topography…. It was formerly a large estate well developed, with the peculiar charm of the old colonial homesteads, and it has been the endeavor to retain this charm while adapting this place to the larger park uses by the public.[71]

A debate begun among the commission members in December 1914 suggests their residual distrust of Congress stemming from its opposition to the 1901 Senate Park Commission. Seeking advice from the politically well-connected Charles Moore, French wrote him about the request from the Joint Committee on the Library for advice on completing the frieze in the Capitol rotunda:

I wonder if there lurks in this request a hope in the minds of our enemies that we may be betrayed into giving an opinion that will embarrass us. I am sure there is no member of the Commission who would wish to have the frieze completed. In fact I am sure we should all approve of preserving it for all time by giving it a half dozen coats of white or other paint. I am writing to Colonel Harts this morning reminding him that we have no jurisdiction over the Capitol.[72]

It would seem that Moore advised otherwise. The following month, French wrote Harts that he had discussed the frieze with Blashfield and Hastings and that they had recommended it be completed, repeating the details, because the incomplete element was "unpleasant."[73] French wrote Harts a week later after a discussion of the situation with Gilbert:

I found him very averse to recommending the finishing of the frieze on any terms. He maintained that no matter what excuses or reasons we gave for advising that it be completed along the present lines, the fact that we had advised its completion would be the only thing that would be made public and we should be criticized in consequence. He was unwilling to vote for its completion under any conditions. I have to admit that I am not enthusiastic about recommending its completion.[74]

Thereafter Olmsted proposed an alternate solution that involved an altered frieze; French told Harts he would agree to it if all the members concurred.[75] In the end, the commission did not respond to Congress for a year; noting that it did not want to provide advice until after a meeting with the superintendent of the Capitol, the final recommendation was based on the existing conditions of the stone: Do not continue the frieze or alter it.[76]

A specific connection to the Senate Park Commission work was articulated by Olmsted in January 1915. His commitment to the 1901 plan and a high work ethic is evident in his letter to French, which followed ques-

CHAPTER II | STATUES, FOUNTAINS, AND MONUMENTS

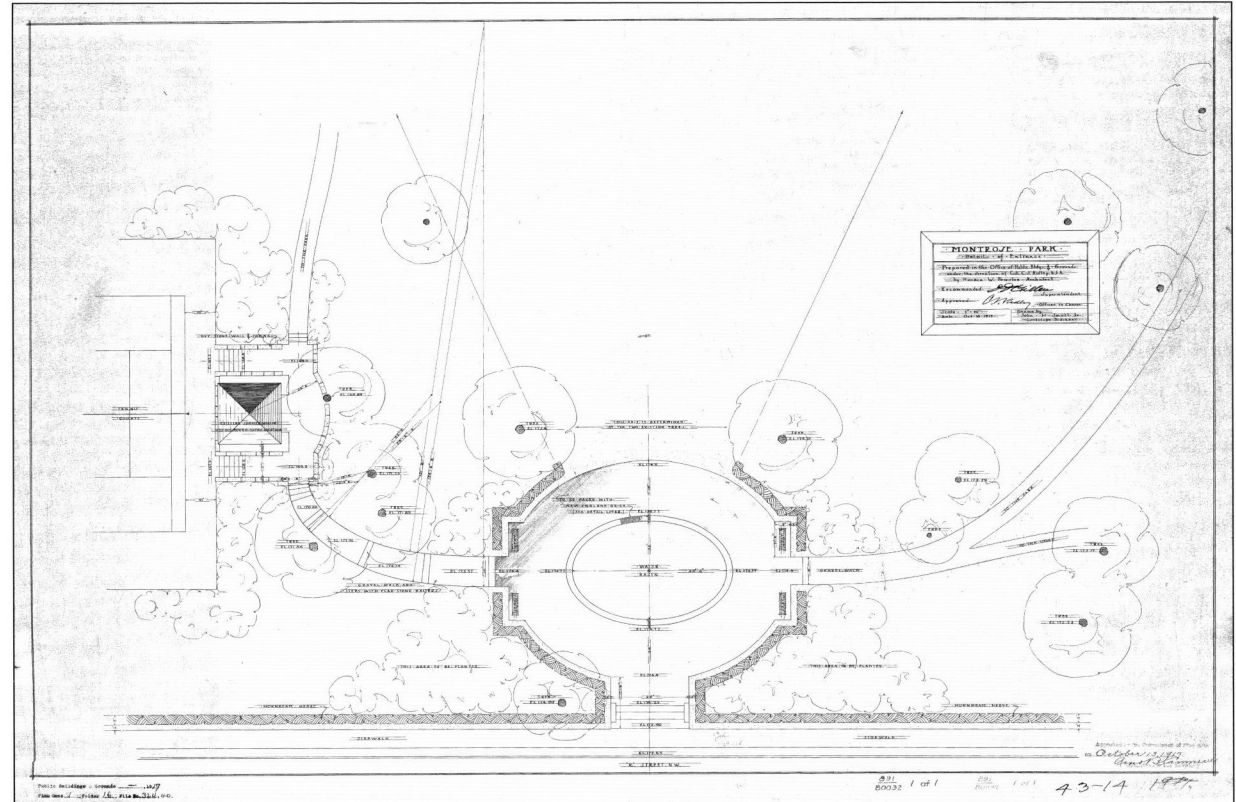

The plan by architect Horace Peaslee for the formal entrance to Montrose Park, located where the main residence once stood, was approved by the CFA in 1917.

tions by Harts about grading levels on the Mall:

I find myself so far precipitated into a study of very subtle and vitally important elements of the design that I am more than ever anxious to have it tackled seriously and comprehensively and worked on until we can feel really satisfied with result…. The old [Senate Park] Commission of course was a creative body and not primarily a critical one like the Art Commission, and as the only present survivor of the designers (indeed as the one who next to McKim was most responsible for the treatment of the Mall plan) I should hate to occupy merely the position appropriate to a member of the CFA as such, and to let some other fellow shape the plan to suit his own ideas, even though they might be just as good as mine. It is a case where I can perfectly well do my part in the designing from the background without pay or official recognition, because I had my recognition as a member of the old Park Commission…. But to sit on the side lines and let someone else overhaul the plan would be rather bitter.[77]

Olmsted's work on the Mall would continue until 1936.

Preparing for Succession

In early 1914, the commission directed Harts to meet with President Wilson because the four-year terms of five members—French, Gilbert, Hastings, Moore, and Olmsted—were about to expire, and the members were concerned about a drastic change of composition on the commission. Wilson appreciated their concern but was legally bound to nominate members to four-year terms and thus recom-

mended that they—among themselves—determine a staggered schedule with members leaving in successive years. Accordingly, French instructed Harts to establish a timetable that would have him stepping down first and Olmsted last; although French indicated that Olmsted's extensive knowledge of Washington was critical to the success of the commission's work, he did not clarify why he sought to retire first.[78] Harts determined that French would resign in June 1915, Moore and Hastings in June 1917, and Gilbert and Olmsted in June 1918; the initial terms of Blashfield and Anderson would end in May and July 1916, respectively. It seems likely that French wanted to stop serving on the commission so that he could create the sculpture for the Lincoln Memorial, a work that would fulfill a personal goal of having an outdoor statue in Washington.[79]

The Lincoln Statue

In 1913, Henry Bacon began to focus on the statue of Abraham Lincoln to be placed inside the memorial structure. Despite the concurrent artistic revolution associated with the Armory Show, Bacon knew he wanted Daniel Chester French to model a traditional sculpture in marble.[80] French had pursued idealized figures in sculpture for decades and had collaborated with Bacon on several works already. Moreover, Bacon's preference for French was consistent

with the increasingly conservative disposition of the Commission of Fine Arts and the generally slow trend of Washington to embrace change in matters of art.

Bacon's clear intent to retain French allowed him to counter the significant pressure he received from Washington architect Glenn Brown and Augusta Homer Saint-Gaudens, the widow of the late sculptor, to commission a copy of Augustus Saint-Gaudens's *Lincoln,* erected in Chicago (1884–87). Bacon responded to Mrs. Saint-Gaudens that her husband's sculpture would be too small for the space and was designed to be executed in bronze, while he wanted the new sculpture to be marble. In a letter to his friend Franklin Hooper, a professor at the Brooklyn Institute of Arts and Sciences, Bacon described the proposition of the replica as "repugnant."

French initially hesitated to accept the project because he knew it would lead to problems if he, as chairman of the Commission of Fine Arts, executed the piece. The resolute Bacon complained to Hooper:

[French] is at the height of his powers.... I have collaborated with a good many sculptors in the design of monuments, Saint-Gaudens among the number, and of them all, I have found the collaboration to be most congenial when working with Mr. French; and we each have given in to the other and stood out against each other on points that arose for discussion during our work with the result that each, at the end, has been satisfied with the combined efforts. There is much at stake in this collaboration or partnership that cannot be covered by a contract or prearranged understanding.[81]

In December 1914, the Lincoln Memorial Commission unanimously voted to give French the commission for the statue of Lincoln and its pedestal for a cost not to exceed $50,000 (approximately $1.1 million in 2010 dollars). French wrote immediately to Harts:

I consider that this is the greatest opportunity that could be offered to an American sculptor and I desire beyond anything to be permitted to execute it. As you know, however...I have answered to anyone who intimated that this statue might be awarded to me, that I felt that my position on the Commission of Fine Arts would prevent my accepting the commission.... It seems to me that this is a serious question, and one which our Commission should weigh and consider very thoroughly. I would rather relinquish my claim to this wonderful opportunity than to feel that I had been the cause of injury to a body that I feel to be a power for good in the community.[82]

Harts responded confidentially, reminding French that his term on the Commission of Fine Arts would expire on June 14, 1915, and recommended that he complete his term. In mid-January, French wrote to Taft as chairman of the Lincoln Memorial Commission:

I cannot conceive of a greater honor than that...announcing that I have been unanimously selected...to execute the statue of Lincoln for the Lincoln Memorial. Both the subject and the exalted position...

make it the greatest opportunity that could come to a sculptor. I only pray that I may prove worthy of it and of the confidence that the Commission has manifested in me.[83]

In early June 1915, Daniel Chester French submitted his resignation letter to President Wilson, indicating that he chose to leave the Commission of Fine Arts in order to ensure that continuity would be possible with staggered terms as had been established in early 1914.[84]

French attempted to leave matters as smoothly as possible. A few days after the announcement, he wrote hesitatingly to Harts regarding personal dynamics on the commission:

I do not know in the least whom you have in mind to suggest to the President as the Chairman. My own choice would be either Mr. Moore or Mr. Olmsted. I think it probable that you are not aware that the relations between Mr. Gilbert and Mr. Hastings have been somewhat strained for a number of years, each man having felt that he had a grievance against the other. Until they became so closely associated on the Commission of Fine Arts, they were for a number of years hardly on speaking terms. The fuller knowledge that they have come to have of each other while serving on the Commission has gone very far towards mitigating and even allaying this feeling of antagonism. It still exists, however, in a modified form, and I believe that if either of them was appointed Chairman it might result in friction and trouble. I may be all wrong about this, but I think it best to speak of it. You will, of course, treat my communication as confidential, and I should be glad if you would even destroy this letter after you have read it. I have so much affection and regard for both Mr. Hastings and Mr. Gilbert that I hate to write about this even to you, and I am sure you will understand my motives.[85]

Unlike Taft, Wilson was not an explicit advocate for

the city of Washington; instead of handpicking a successor, he requested the members of the commission suggest a replacement for French. At the May meeting, the commission recommended the name of sculptor Herbert Adams; before his term ended, French wrote to Adams:

It was the unanimous choice of the members of the Commission that you should fill the place left vacant by my resignation. I am sure that while you will find the duties exacting you will consider it an honor, as I did, to be a member of this body, and I am sure you will also feel that the work is worth the sacrifice. I am personally delighted that my place should be filled by one for whom I have so much affection and regard.[86]

Wilson also gave the commission the option to select its own chairman. Consequently, at the July meeting, the commission members voted Charles Moore—the assistant to the McMillan Commission and a member of the Commission of Fine Arts since it was established—as the third chairman to serve in just three years; Olmsted remained the vice chairman. The selection of chairman would remain thereafter a position elected by commission members rather than appointed by the president.

Charles Moore continued to sit on the commission for the next twenty-five years, serving all except the last three as chairman. His repeated reappointment under four presidential administrations testifies to his astute political skill and connections, attributes on which he would come to rely in his long and formative leadership of the commission.

✣

The Lincoln Memorial looking southwest on the day of its dedication, May 20, 1922. Construction of the Reflecting Pool was completed in December 1922, but it would be a decade before the Rock Creek and Potomac Parkway and the Arlington Memorial Bridge were completed.

The Improvement of Washington City: Charles Moore and Washington's Monumental Core

❡ PAMELA SCOTT

Portrait of Charles Moore, c. 1940.

"They misread history who see in the location of the seat of government at Washington only the clever bargain of scheming politicians," began Charles Moore in his lengthy and erudite introduction to the *History of the United States Capitol* (1900) by Glenn Brown. Moore went on to write about the "ideal that existed in the minds of the [founding] fathers," noting that the beginning of the Capitol building in 1793 meant that "throughout the land the idea prevailed that a permanent government had been established; that progress was assured; that law would be enforced and property be safe." Such ringing prose is not surprising, for Moore's first career twenty-two years earlier was as a journalist. He also wrote with authority about the historical context of each stage of the Capitol's history within Washington's changing political and physical evolutions, again not surprising because Moore earned a doctoral degree in history from Columbian University, now George Washington University.[1]

Moore was born in Ypsilanti, Michigan, just west of Detroit, in 1855, his parents migrating there when it was still the frontier. His mother's family was from New England Puritan stock; his father's family was Scots Irish. Moore was doubly proud of his early American ancestry and that his parents were pioneers on the western frontier. The ideas and ideals of the Founding Fathers about the federal city guided Moore's entire career in Washington. In the preface to his 1926 book, the *Family Life of George Washington,* Moore recounted that as a child, a visitor from Virginia took him on his knee and said to him: "When I was your age, I sat on George Washington's knee." Thus from his boyhood the romance of history reached out to Moore in an electrifying way.[2]

Moore's parents died when he was fourteen, and his guardian sent him to New England to be educated. During the summer of 1872, he traveled to Washington, arriving in the midst of great urban upheaval as the Board of Public Works was just beginning to modernize the city's infrastructure and beautify its streetscapes. Moore occasionally referred to his initial experience of Washington as coinciding with the city's first rebirth; he was to participate in its second. Moore graduated in 1878 from Harvard College, where he studied with Charles Eliot Norton, Harvard's first professor of the history of art. In his lengthy typescript biography of Norton, Moore quoted Norton's son, who "wittily and aptly called his father's courses 'Lectures on Modern Morals as Illustrated by the Art of the Ancients.'" Moore cited examples of Norton's influence as a teacher, his "manifestations of a sway which came to be accounted by many as the determining influence in their lives." Norton's lasting influence on Moore's intellectual life was his core thoughts about the intertwined political and cultural aspects of public life. Norton insisted, in Moore's words, that "ethos [w]as a fundamental element in beauty in art," a classical concept that very much influenced Moore's contributions to the "new" Washington and his writings about them.[3]

In his 1930 article "Standards of Taste," Moore quoted Norton at length. Next to literature, the visual arts evinced "the moral temper and intellectual culture of the various races by whom they have been practiced." Norton's thoughts about the continuum of the nation's cultural heritage, the past informing the present with its values to be transmitted to future generations, particularly influenced Moore. Norton's prose in his writings on European culture is clear, elegant, apposite, and often epigrammatic. The same is true of Moore's writings, but his were born of the impulse to prove that American democracy could also foster a rich heritage of artistic, cultural, and historical life, a view that Norton questioned in the 1870s.[4]

After graduating from Harvard, where he was the editor of the *Crimson*, Moore moved to Detroit, where he worked as a journalist. His writings soon brought him to the attention of businessman James McMillan, who, through his municipal positions, had several years of experience modernizing Detroit's urban infrastructure. When McMillan was elected to the Senate in 1889, Moore accompanied him to Washington as his secretary. Both immediately applied McMillan's urban expertise to modernizing Washington; their vehicle was the Senate Committee on the District of Columbia. Moore drafted the congressional reports on each of the projects McMillan sponsored that related to modern municipal services. These included abundant clean water, an adequate sewer system, healthy rivers and streams, and diverse recreational facilities.

Moore's friendships during the 1890s with Glenn Brown and other local architects and historians who organized celebrations of Washington's centennial in 1900 supported the precepts Norton instilled in him. By the turn of the century, Moore understood that the federal city's design and the architectural character of the Capitol, White House, and Washington Monument were inextricably linked to and expressed the political achievements of the American Revolution. By January 18, 1901, Senator McMillan was ready to implement the next step: to make "Washington a beautiful capital city," with Moore authoring the Senate report titled "Commission to Consider Certain Improvements in the District of Columbia."[5]

One of McMillan's and Moore's first steps to beautify Washington was to convince the general public that the District of Columbia belonged to the nation, with all of America benefiting from its improvement. Having first consulted with local architectural and business interests, they invoked "the remarkable success achieved at the Chicago World's Fair" of 1893 and recommended it to Congress as the model for Washington's revitalization. To gain congressional approval to hire the fair's principal designer, Daniel Burnham, as a consultant on the Senate Park Commission, Moore recalled Washington's treasured founding architecture:

The dignity and grandeur of the Capitol, the graceful and satisfactory proportions of the White House, the classic simplicity and lasting beauty of the older government buildings and the admitted excellencies of the original plan of the city of Washington… all come from the employment of trained men, selected and directed by the President of the United States. It is these precedents that the resolution seeks to follow.

Throughout their association, the two Michigan men proved to be master tacticians as well as astute politicians. Their strategy was to use the federal city's history as both the justification and basis for the beautification of Washington.[6] Moore had firsthand knowledge of Burnham's abilities as both a visionary thinker and an inspired organizer of other artists, for six years earlier he had edited, and probably written, Burnham's *The Organization, Design and Construction of the Fair*. Fifteen years later he wrote Burnham's *Plan of Chicago,* a much more significant publication.

In mid-March 1901, the three key Senate Park Commission members—Burnham, architect Charles Follen McKim, and landscape architect Frederick Law Olmsted Jr.—met in Washington. Moore introduced them to President William McKinley, whom he knew personally. Many people commented that Moore possessed the gift of friendship; fundamental to his success throughout his career was that he was the quintessential clubman with entrée to the highest political, academic, intellectual, and business circles. Remark-

ably, he was comfortable in all of them equally, and that is how he accomplished as much as he did in a very productive life.[7]

The commissioners quickly conceived their projected plan's key elements in short monthly meetings in the Capitol before they embarked in mid-June for a seven-week tour of European park precedents. Moore facilitated their meetings and accompanied them on their travels, receiving an intense education on how the integration of landscape, architecture, and public sculpture in the hands of experts results in great places. This experience was the basis for his career with the Commission of Fine Arts (CFA).[8] After the team returned from Europe, Moore remained in constant communication, especially with McKim, as the commission members made their final decisions about their five-point plan. The White House, Capitol, and Washington Monument had established three of these points, with two

Charles Moore, center foreground, in the Manuscript Division of the Library of Congress, c. 1926. In addition to his writing and service to the Commission of Fine Arts, Moore was a consultant to and later chief of the Manuscript Division of the Library of Congress from 1917 to 1927.

new monuments proposed to terminate the west and south axes of the kite-shaped outline of their plan.[9]

Burnham drafted some ideas for the commission's final report, but Moore and Olmsted wrote the final text so that the commission's visionary aims would seem grounded in a reality that would not only convince Congress but actually be realizable. Moore was also busily composing two articles promoting the commission's plan while it was still being refined. They were to be published in *Century Magazine* soon after the plan's scheduled launch at the beginning of January. Moore identified these writings as "papers" to signify their seriousness. "The Improvement of Washington City," published in February 1902, began with a more detailed account of the federal city's founding history than had appeared in popular journals to that point. Moore's goal was to provide a historically reliable context for L'Enfant's plan in preparation for arguing the legiti-

macy of the Senate Park Commission's expansion of it. By promoting public architecture steeped in the neoclassicism of the White House and Capitol, the commission avoided directly criticizing the work of contemporary architects still designing vestigial Victorian public buildings.[10]

Moore was not just reflecting the aesthetic of his time but also was acting as an activist-historian and apologist—propagandist even—when he wrote: "In a word, [L'Enfant] planned the capital city as a work of art, in which each feature should have a distinct relation to every other feature; and thus he gave to the scheme that feeling of unity which today excites the interest and admiration of the visitor to Paris." It was the opening salvo to replace the Victorian public architecture within the viewshed of Washington's monumental core. Moore praised only Thomas U. Walter's Capitol dome as he reiterated the commission's major theme: "The one thing

lacking in the development of the capital has been that unity for which L'Enfant strove." He then embarked on a communal exercise of imaging based on the grisaille halftone versions of a few of the commission's watercolors made especially to illustrate the articles. Moore concluded this first paper by noting that the visionary design was the result of careful consideration and the pragmatic need of a master plan for Washington's orderly development.[11]

"Will these plans, developed after much study by competent men, be carried out? That is for Congress to determine; but there is good reason to believe that the work will begin at once," Moore predicted. Moore's allusions to the growing "conviction that the day has come to develop Washington according to a well-considered plan" encouraged right-minded readers to support such magnificent changes to their national capital. Moore's last sentence concluded that if the new buildings and parks were

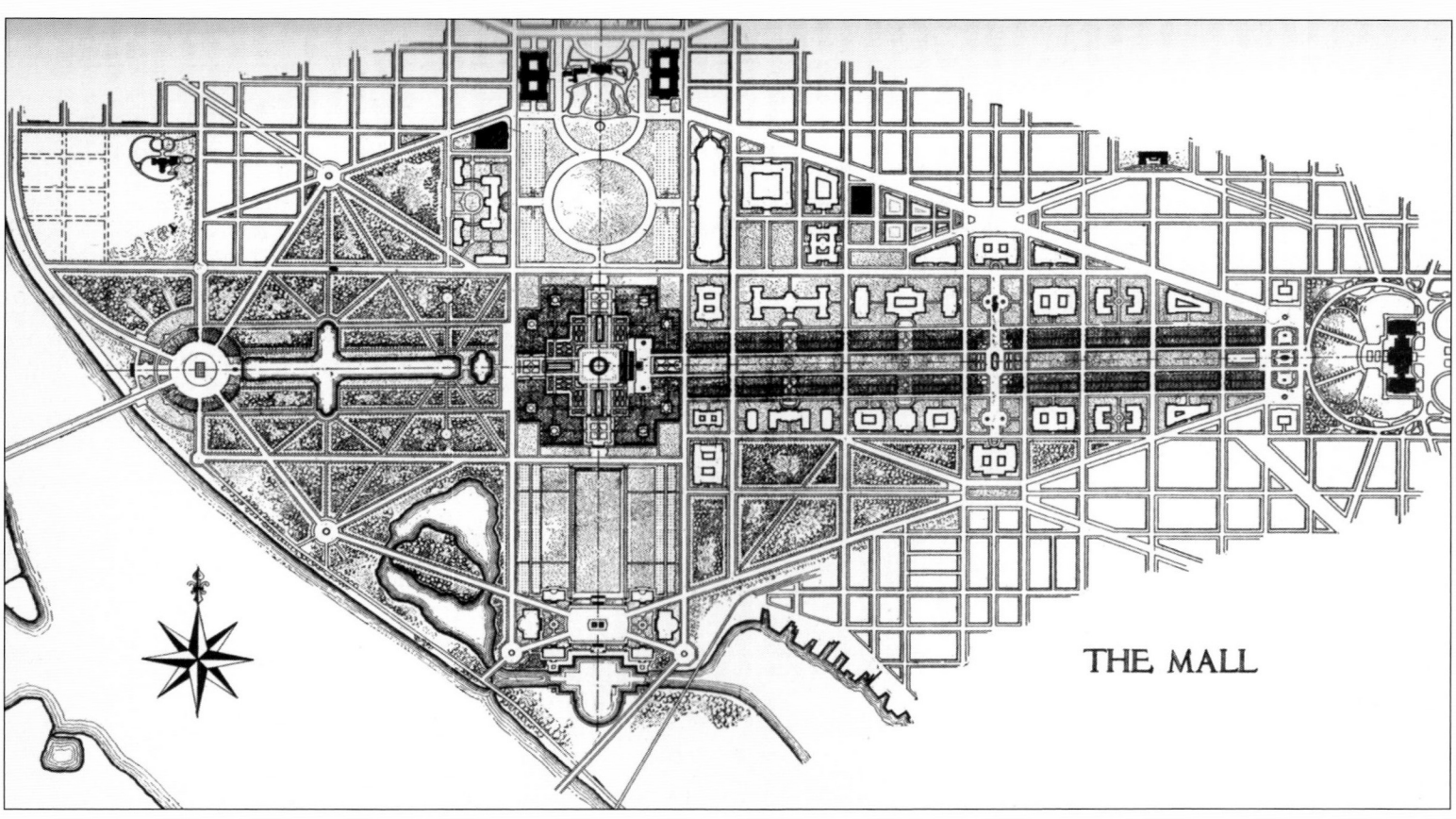

THE MALL

"developed according to a definite system…the result must follow that the capital of the United States, already beautiful in situation, will stand as one of the most beautiful cities in the world."[12]

Moore came to realize that high ideals were often and perhaps best expressed in resounding language, just as the idealized visions represented by the architecture of Union Station and the Lincoln Memorial are two examples of visual rhetoric. These modern Beaux-Arts buildings escape being utterly pretentious because their artists learned from classic exemplars how they worked on aesthetic, physical, and metaphorical levels. Their artists were serious in their intent to make America's great achievements—conquering the continent and preserving the Union—timeless within the context of the world's great accomplishments. For four decades, Moore unwaveringly insisted that the founding of the federal city as the repository of

American government was its most important historical fact. He believed Washington's aesthetic soul had been lost during the Victorian period and must be recovered by America's best artists designing modern classical buildings to house the government, honor the nineteenth century's great events, and accommodate its future.

Senator McMillan died unexpectedly on August 10, 1902, and within a few months Moore returned to Detroit where he became the secretary of the Union Trust Company, acted as the director of the Detroit Institute of Fine Arts, and was employed as a city planner. He maintained close ties with Burnham, McKim, and Olmsted and in 1905 was made an honorary member of President Theodore Roosevelt's Consultative Board of Architects, formed to promote the values and projects of the Senate Park Commission. The greatest measure of respect of his Senate Park Commission colleagues was naming Moore the

first layman member to the Commission of Fine Arts when it was founded in 1910, a position he held until he was elected its chairman in 1915. Moore returned permanently to Washington in 1918 when he was appointed acting chief of the Manuscript Division at the Library of Congress. Moore promptly began seeking out and acquiring the papers of many important early American figures; he was particularly assiduous in finding and saving Washington's history. He resigned from the library in 1927 to devote all of his time to realizing the Senate Park Commission's plan.

From the first meeting of the Commission of Fine Arts in 1910, Moore dedicated his political and literary skills to furthering the work of Burnham, McKim, and Olmsted. "The plan of 1901 was placed in the hands of its friends," as Burnham was appointed its chairman; McKim, who had died in 1909, was represented posthumously by two architects—Thomas Hastings and Cass

Members of the U.S. Commission of Fine Arts, 1912. Seated, left to right: Peirce Anderson, Frederick Law Olmsted Jr., Daniel Chester French, Thomas Hastings, and Charles Moore. Standing at rear is Arno Cammerer, clerk.

Gilbert—who had worked for him; and Olmsted was the landscape architect. The Lincoln Memorial, placed at the west end of the Mall by the Senate Park Commission, was the first great project that the Commission of Fine Arts considered; the complex debate about alternate sites endangered a critical element of the Senate Park Commission's recommendations during the century's first decade. [13]

When the Lincoln Memorial Commission was created in February 1911, its chairman was President William H. Taft, a strong supporter of the Senate Park Commission Plan. Taft required the Lincoln Commission to consult with the Commission of Fine Arts about the placement of the Lincoln Memorial and the selection of its artists. Moore's literary and organizational abilities again coincided in his draft of a report that combined the opinions expressed by his fellow members of the Commission of Fine Arts during five meetings held in the spring and early summer of 1911. Moore was at his most incisive promoting the memorial's isolated site and "a

design which combines grandeur with beauty." The report also considered various Capitol Hill and West Potomac Park sites, a delicate situation because Burnham, who signed the report as the first chairman of the Commission of Fine Arts, had been actively involved in promoting Union Station's plaza or the Capitol Grounds for the Lincoln Memorial, much to the dismay of his Senate Park Commission colleagues. While other participants in the 1901 plan were quite outspoken about Burnham's defection, Moore excused his actions as a misunderstanding.[14]

The Commission of Fine Arts unanimously approved the Potomac Park site before it considered whether the architect and sculptor should be chosen by competition or appointed. After an internal debate, the commission recommended that the Lincoln Memorial Commission appoint the artists recommended by the Commission of Fine Arts but also suggested competition guidelines, should the Lincoln Memorial Commission choose that method. Because the report by the Commission of

Fine Arts was only advisory, the Lincoln Commission held a limited competition for designs on prominent sites overlooking the monumental core. The architect that Burnham considered most sympathetic to the vision of the late Charles McKim—Henry Bacon—was selected, as was his preferred sculptor, Daniel Chester French. Moore later wrote in his memoirs: "The selection of Bacon as architect and the approval of his plans by the Lincoln Commission [in 1912] gave to the Commission of Fine Arts an established standing at this critical juncture, when its usefulness was threatened by the loss of the potent leadership of Burnham and the mastery of [artist Francis] Millet in dealing with the Washington situation." Both men had died while traveling in 1912.[15]

The Commission of Fine Arts could monitor closely the development of the Lincoln Memorial over the next ten years because the U.S. Army Corps of Engineers officer in charge of its construction also served as secretary of the commission. This dual assignment would serve the commission less well with another important Mall project, the Arlington Memorial Bridge. With the Lincoln Memorial nearing completion in 1922, long-term disagreements between the Commission of Fine Arts and the War Department concerning the location and design of the Arlington Memorial Bridge were resolved, but not entirely amicably. Earlier discussions in 1901 and 1911 about the bridge centered on whether a lofty highway bridge without a draw should connect Arlington National Cemetery with the District at the bluffs occupied by the Naval Hospital or a low memorial bridge. The War Department favored the high bridge, but in 1901 the Senate Park Commission won the first battle of the bridge with the low profile one, its landfall on the west side of the Lincoln Memorial. The bridge design, inspired by Roman aqueducts, was the solution promoted by the

Commission of Fine Arts when it advised the Lincoln Memorial Commission in 1911.[16]

The complicating factor in 1911 was exacerbated in 1922; the Commission of Fine Arts' secretary, Colonel Clarence Sherrill, was the executive officer of the Arlington Memorial Bridge Commission. He also acted as the liaison between the secretary of war, the chief of engineers, President Warren G. Harding (head of the Memorial Bridge Commission), and Moore, now chairman of the Commission of Fine Arts. The corps's pragmatic reasons in favor of a high bridge to connect the Virginia highlands directly to downtown Washington convinced the bridge commission. However, that body directed Sherrill to solicit the views of the Commission of Fine Arts and to emphasize that it was "especially desired to have this bridge of a design that will be entirely harmonious with the Lincoln Memorial."[17]

Moore's response was to ask each Commission of Fine Arts member to write his individual opinion; all strongly supported maintaining the integrity of the Senate Park Commission Plan. Moore had already informed Olmsted "that the problem is being treated entirely from an engineering standpoint, with no attention to park or memorial features." Olmsted's response was included in Moore's final Commission of Fine Arts report. In 1901 the Senate Park Commission had considered the bridge one of the plan's "most conspicuous features, intimately related for good or for ill to the Lincoln Memorial." Commission of Fine Arts member James Greenleaf, a landscape architect, wrote Moore that the bridge was "not a local city problem of utilitarian nature. It is a *Memorial*." The bridge's memorial nature had often been debated during its long and convoluted history, but in 1922 many considered it to be the Lincoln-Lee Bridge, a metaphorical as well as a physical bridge between the North and South.[18]

In mid-summer 1922, the secretaryship of the Commission of Fine Arts passed to a civilian, as conflicts of interest for corps members serving simultaneously as executive officers on more than one commission that might have rival goals became apparent. Sherrill's heart and mind were definitely allied with the War Department on the bridge issue. Moreover, Sherrill was a native of North Carolina and an officer of the Robert E. Lee Memorial Highway Commission, whose goal was to memorialize Lee in the Arlington Memorial Bridge. On September 7, 1922, Moore sent Sherrill the Commission of Fine Arts report on Memorial Bridge, acknowledging that "it is true that the plan of 1901 is not binding on any official or any commission. However, this plan has been carried out as to a majority of its elements. Therefore, no change in an essential remaining element should be made for reasons that will not clearly commend themselves."[19]

Moore's report refuted each of the Corps's arguments for a high bridge, concluding that the bridge would be "subordinate to the Lincoln Memorial only in the sense that the Union Station is subordinate to the Capitol, both being parts in one great scheme of Capitol improvement, and each taking its appropriate place in that scheme." Because Moore feared that "hidden forces were at work somewhere," he sent copies of the Commission of Fine Arts report to newspapers, contrary to the established protocol regarding confidentiality between federal commissions. Sherrill wrote Moore an icy letter on September 13, the day after large selections of the report were published on the front page of the *Evening Star*. Sherrill's response was somewhat surprising, for on September 7, the *Washington Post* had reported on the meeting of the Lee Commission during which Sherrill outlined the corps's proposed Lincoln-Lee Bridge and assured the group that it

would be completed in a year.[20]

Sherrill complained to President Harding, who wrote Moore: "I do not think the Bridge Commission has been treated in this matter in accordance with good ethics. In as much as it is a matter dealing with a commission over which the President presides I suggest before taking the question to the press hereafter any controverted [*sic*] matters be brought first to my attention." Moore apologized to the president, arguing that he was just informing the public of the issues. Elihu Root interceded on his behalf, and Harding told Moore "there will be no occasion to refer to it again." In his February 22, 1939, valedictory message to the Commission of Fine Arts, Moore recalled: "A President of the United States complained to Elihu Root that the Chairman was arbitrary. But he carried out the advice of the Commission as to the location of the Arlington Bridge."[21]

Canny publicist that he was, Moore gambled on public opinion favoring the Commission of Fine Arts's stand on the bridge, and he was right. During the next three months Moore mended most fences, for on December 18, 1922, the *Evening Star* reported on the selection of the bridge's site: "In response to one suggestion made during the general discussion, that the bridge should be run from the Lincoln Memorial through Arlington Cemetery, because of the spiritual effect it would have upon those who made the journey, as a connecting link between those two great American shrines, Mr. Harding said he did not think it was so much a matter of spiritual effect as of the artistic effect that was to be made."[22]

This response surely reveals Moore's wide influence. In his memoirs, Moore recounted that when Vice President Coolidge returned home and told his wife that Moore had won the battle of the bridge, she asked: "Did you help him?," and Coolidge replied, "No. He

Charles Moore is honored at his retirement by Uncle Sam in a 1937 cartoon by Clifford Berryman of the Washington Evening Star; *the signed inscription reads: "Mr. Charles Moore, I was delighted to have even this small part in that memorable dinner to you! Cordially and sincerely, C. A. Berryman."*

ELEVATION OF TYPICAL ARCH
PLANS FOR THE ARLINGTON MEMORIAL BRIDGE
THE ARLINGTON MEMORIAL BRIDGE COMMISSION
PRESIDENT CALVIN COOLIDGE CHAIRMAN

LIEUT. COL. C. O. SHERRILL C of E. EXECUTIVE OFFICER AND CHIEF ENGINEER
JOHN L. NAGLE DESIGNING ENGINEER

Elevation of a typical arch proposed by McKim, Mead & White for the Arlington Memorial Bridge.

didn't need it." Sherrill was not pacified; he was quoted in 1925 as saying: "We have to get rid of that Fine Arts Commission, for Chas. Moore won't let me do what I want."[23] With the Lincoln Memorial and Memorial Bridge launched, Moore still had four more key elements of the Senate Park Commission Plan to see implemented: the Federal Triangle of government office buildings; replacing the Mall's picturesque landscape plantings with formal rows of elms; the memorial at the Tidal Basin site; and the Washington Monument gardens. Realizing the Federal Triangle began in 1911 when the government purchased the land and the Commission of Fine Arts approved plans for office buildings for three executive departments: Justice, Commerce, and State. In April 1916, after a conversation with Moore and other commission members, Cass Gilbert (designer of the 1911 Justice Department building) wrote Senator Francis Newlands about forming a public buildings commission to address the govern-

ment's serious space needs.[24]

This oblique approach was necessary because the Commission of Fine Arts had no legal authority to initiate such actions, only to evaluate the suitability of sites and designs proposed by others. Yet Moore considered it crucial that they monitor such a large-scale building campaign because many other contenders also wished to have decisive voices. While a new government agency to oversee public buildings was being discussed, Gilbert told Newlands that he feared the "head of a new or special department might be a cubist, a futurist, or a Mullett," recommending instead a commission composed of experts who would be answerable to review by the Commission of Fine Arts. The long and complex history of the Federal Triangle includes many interventions by the Commission of Fine Arts. They included advising the new Public Buildings Commission to use the government's early office buildings—the Treasury building, Patent Office, and General Post Office—as

precedents to determine the architectural styles of the new offices. Moore's behind-the-scenes support for the Senate Park Commission's guiding principles again prevailed.[25]

Moore began his October 24, 1922, lecture before the Garden Club of America: "Washington, once known as the City of Magnificent Distances, may now be termed the City of Magnificent Possibilities. In spite of its century and a quarter of years, it is still a City of Beginnings. Nothing is completed. Everything is begun. It is a city of transitions." With these short, powerful declarative sentences—a natural writer on a mission—Moore was preparing the groundwork for his assault on the Botanic Garden, part of a long campaign to clear away all the remnants of the picturesque Mall. Moore proposed moving the Botanic Garden to Mount Hamilton, off Bladensburg Road NE, which had a commanding view of Washington. He may well have had in mind the location of the Royal Botanic Gardens at Kew in relationship to London, whose extent was possible because of its suburban site, as a logical model for a much larger botanic garden in Washington. While the U. S. Botanic Garden was not moved to Mount Hamilton when Congress established the National Arboretum there in 1927, its new French-inspired orangery was begun in 1931 south of Maryland Avenue, thus leaving the Mall's central axis marked only by the Washington Monument between the Capitol dome and the Lincoln Memorial in accordance with the Senate Park Commission Plan.[26]

Moore's experience as a boy of meeting a man who had met George Washington seems to have been a powerful influence in his life's work, to protect the first president's vision for the national capital. As the bicentennial of Washington's birth in 1932 neared, Moore, in his various official and honorary positions as one of America's leading popular historians, suggested completing the Washington Monument gardens as one of the bicentennial commission's official projects. He authored an article in the *Journal of the American Institute of Architects* that again combined his signature historical overview, a description of the Senate Park Commission's treatment of the monument grounds, and the Commission of Fine Arts' suggestion to implement McKim's 1901 proposed plan. National Park Service–sponsored studies in 1933 determined that the cost of underpinning the foundation would be too expensive and that steep steps on its west side leading to sunken gardens would endanger the monument's stability.[27]

By 1935 Moore faced new political, bureaucratic, and aesthetic conditions that affected Washington's buildings. New federal agencies shared oversight with the Commission of Fine Arts of the city's public buildings and landscapes. Members of commissions created for each major building took their responsi-

bilities seriously as they interacted with these agencies, for their several reports to Congress determined Washington's built environment. In 1935 the American Beaux-Arts era was rapidly passing, and Moore's mission to see the Senate Park Commission Plan completed was threatened. Until the early 1930s, Moore had successfully filled places on the Commission of Fine Arts with men trained in that tradition who fully supported carrying out the Senate Park Commission's key elements. However, younger men with impeccable public design credentials but a modernist aesthetic and ideals, were slowly added. The most significant for the outcome of the Thomas Jefferson Memorial design in the late 1930s was New York landscape architect Gilmore Clarke, who was appointed on April 21, 1932.[28]

The long and complex history of realizing the Thomas Jefferson Memorial began with the founding of the Theodore Roosevelt Association in 1919 to commemorate Roosevelt near the Tidal Basin. Moore objected to the use of this site in order to protect the 1901 plan, which had reserved it for a memorial to an individual Founding Father or all of them as a group. At the time, Moore used the public press to indicate his disapproval of the association's choice of site, an opinion he could not state in his official position. The architect John Russell Pope completed a design for the memorial based on an open peristyle design, but for a number of reasons, it was never built.[29]

Moore recalled in March 10, 1937, the main difficulty faced by the Commission of Fine Arts in protecting the 1901 plan and the commission's most successful tactic:

As to the Jefferson Memorial problems:… My only concern is that when the project is undertaken it will be well done. I got into trouble in opposing the use of the site for T. R. …What I am concerned about is loyalty to the plan under which we have worked for

36 years so successfully…. One thing is clear to my mind and that is the Commission [of Fine Arts] should be very careful not to try to exceed its power as conferred by law. We have won our battles by persuasion …. We should understand that Congress under the Constitution exercises exclusive legislation over the District." [30]

Two days later, Moore wrote Clarke—who strongly opposed John Russell Pope's Pantheon design for the Thomas Jefferson Memorial—about the history of the Tidal Basin site:

The Roosevelt Commission took umbrage at me for objecting to using that site for so recent a personage as T.R. …The objections caused the scheme to fade out…. After several meetings about which I know nothing, the [Jefferson Commission] members unanimously came to an agreement on the South Axis. I had hoped against hope that they would select another site; but they were admirers of Jefferson and they had the President with them. [31]

In this, Moore was being disingenuous as well as ambiguous. During lunch after meeting with the Thomas Jefferson Memorial Commission on May 14, 1935, Fiske Kimball noted that Moore "spoke with considerable favor of the Potomac site. [Senator Elbert D. Thomas added:] He mentioned to me that this was considered the jewel." As one of the Founding Fathers, a memorial to Jefferson would be appropriate at this site, according to the 1901 plan. When the CFA met on May 20, 1935, Moore applauded the support for the Tidal Basin site expressed by Kimball, the noted Jefferson scholar and member of the Jefferson Memorial Commission, but many of his colleagues disagreed. It seems that Moore worked quietly among those with approval powers to promote the Tidal Basin site while he publicly expressed the majority opinion of the Commission of Fine Arts against it. He was in an uncomfortable position, torn between his loyalty to the Senate Park Commission Plan and to the Commission of Fine Arts. [32]

Gilmore D. Clarke, 1934, when he was working as a consultant to the New York City Parks Department under Robert Moses. Clarke advocated for a more modern, landscape-oriented treatment for the Jefferson Memorial and eventually succeeded Moore as CFA chairman.

COMPETITION FOR A MONUMENTAL MEMORIAL TO THEODORE ROOSEVELT

TOP: *John Russell Pope's competition scheme for the Theodore Roosevelt Memorial, 1919.*
ABOVE: *View of Thomas Jefferson Memorial, c. 1960s.*

Moore's contribution to a crucial March 20, 1937, joint meeting of the Commission of Fine Arts, the Jefferson Memorial Commission, and the National Capital Park and Planning Commission (NCPPC) was to gain consensus among its attendees; the majority of members of the CFA and NCPPC voted for the Tidal Basin site. Moore had written Senator John J. Boylan, chair of the Jefferson Commission, on April 8: "All are agreed that the memorial to Thomas Jefferson should express his character and achievements. Agreement stops at this point." At the May 27 Commission of Fine Arts meeting, Clarke introduced a sketch of an informal landscape in contrast to the Pope scheme, and it was considered by the members: "The Commission agreed that some such treatment is preferable to the scheme presented by Mr. Pope." Moreover, Clarke was henceforth to represent the Commission of Fine Arts in joint meetings with the NCPPC and the Jefferson Memorial Commission. Moore realized that the views of his younger colleagues meant the end of his reign as the defender of the 1901 plan; modernism's apparent ahistoricism seemed to him antithetical to the plan's Beaux-Arts ideas and aesthetics. [33]

Pope's partners, Otto Eggers and Daniel Higgins, took over the Jefferson project after his death on August 27, 1937. They faced a changed leadership at the CFA: Charles Moore had resigned as chairman in September 1937, and Clarke was elected to fill that position. Kimball and the architects presented a revised Pantheon scheme at the September 29 meeting, which also met with disfavor by the commission. The new chairman urged revisions for political reasons: "Mr. Clarke said he felt certain that if the Thomas Jefferson Memorial Commission would present a design that has the approval of the Commission of Fine Arts and the National Capital Park and Planning Commission there

would be less difficulty about getting the approval of Congress to the site south of the Washington Monument." [34]

On February 19, 1938, Boylan wrote Clarke that the Jefferson Memorial Commission had unanimously voted for the open peristyle plan favored by Clarke but had reversed its decision five weeks later in favor of the Pantheon plan. Sadie Pope, widow of the architect, had launched a letter-writing campaign to President Roosevelt insisting that the Pantheon design be built. Kimball probably influenced her actions, his belief in the rightness of Pope's Pantheon to honor Jefferson unwavering. If Moore influenced Mrs. Pope (a personal friend) in any way, he did so quietly, his motivation "loyalty" to the Senate Park Commission Plan. Construction on the revised Pantheon scheme began in 1939. [35]

Clarke may have been defeated because he was so outspoken about disliking Pope's Pantheon—the Jefferson Memorial Commission's prerogative—and because he sought to supplant Pope's landscape with his own "sketch." Boylan defended the Jefferson Commission's actions, noting that the Commission of Fine Arts had been consulted every step of the way, and, besides, that its powers were advisory only. Moreover, if the Pantheon was a retrograde version of the 1901 design for the site, Clarke's preferred peristyle plan "was merely a rehash of the old Theodore Roosevelt Memorial design." As Moore had cautioned, Congress had the ultimate jurisdiction over Washington's development; under Clarke's leadership, the Commission of Fine Arts had attempted to impose its majority taste rather than act in its advisory role. [36]

After Moore had retired to his home, Moorelands, in Gig Harbor, Washington, his former colleagues invited him to a March 9, 1939, reunion of the Commission of Fine Arts in New

York. One main trope of his poignant reply was loyalty:

Loyalty to the nation to whose service willing allegiance was given as a patriotic duty. Loyalty to the inspired plan of Washington and L'Enfant, who by faith had the assurance of things hoped for the evidence of things now seen. Loyalty to the spirit of that architecture on which Jefferson relied.... Loyalty to the plan of 1901, modestly devised and recorded by true artists as the necessary culmination of an original design so comprehensive as to fit 'all times, however remote.' Loyalty to fellow members with respect for one another's opinions, a meeting of minds uncurbed by parliamentary forms—and invariably ending in amicable accord. [37]

Moore wrote these thoughts to his colleagues as a summing up of his own principles and legacy, as a farewell, and as a benediction on what the Commission of Fine Arts had achieved to secure Washington's aesthetic heritage.

Medal by sculptor Lee Lawrie honoring the service of CFA chairman Charles Moore, 1935. Presented to Moore at a dinner commemorating the twenty-fifth anniversary of the commission, the medal served as the model for the agency's seal.

Thine Alabaster Cities Gleam

CHARLES MOORE AND THE CLASSICAL PARADIGM, 1915–1937

I f the history of the Commission of Fine Arts can be outlined in three segments, the first period is dominated by the leadership of Charles Moore. He served on the commission for thirty years, all but seven as chairman—a record only exceeded by J. Carter Brown (CFA 1971–2002) in the last part of the twentieth century. Moore continued to promote the classical vision outlined in the McMillan Plan throughout his tenure. He found in classical architectural language an appropriate symbolic vocabulary for the public architecture and commemorative works in the capital city—and was hugely successful in guiding the remaking of Washington in the City Beautiful image as conceived by his associates and heroes, Daniel Burnham and Charles McKim.[1]

During the 1920s and 1930s, Moore played a controlling role in shaping the outcome of design through the power of his position and his extensive network of connections, both in the design and political arenas. He maintained ties to the first generation of commission members, such as Daniel Chester French, Cass Gilbert, William Mitchell Kendall, John Russell Pope, and James Earle Fraser (CFA 1920–25)—all well known for their monumental work in classical architecture or classical figurative sculpture.[2] Moore also remained on cordial terms with Frederick Law Olmsted Jr., the only surviving member of the McMillan Commission to serve on the Commission of Fine Arts during Moore's tenure as chairman.[3]

The period of Moore's leadership at the CFA may be considered the zenith of achievement in realizing the goals of the McMillan Plan. However, it was also a time of revolution in Western architecture when new architectural ideas from Europe were repudiating centuries of architectural tradition. Modernism, as the movement came to be called, rejected classical architectural language in favor of a new artistic expression and eschewed traditional ornamentation as it sought to create new forms influenced by building program and technology. By the end of the 1930s, modernist thinking had pervaded architectural education and practice; the Beaux-Arts system of education was in decline. Ironically, what had begun as visionary at the turn of the century had become conservative by the late 1930s.

In this period, the Commission of Fine Arts generally reflected the viewpoint of its leader and remained distant from these changing currents in architectural thought, maintaining adherence to the principles and classicism exemplified in the McMillan Plan. The generation of commission members in the 1920s and 1930s—notably Milton B. Medary Jr.

FACING PAGE: Heritage (1933–35), one of two massive seated figures for the Constitution Avenue facade of the National Archives by James Earle Fraser, depicts a female figure holding a child and a sheaf of wheat to symbolize the government's role in preserving the home.

CHARLES
MOORE

(CFA 1922–27), William A. Delano (CFA 1924–28), and Ferruccio Vitale (CFA 1927–32)—bore similarities to earlier members in their embrace of Beaux-Arts principles. Gradually, however, the commission began to recognize the new architectural language that ran counter to its Beaux-Arts ideals by welcoming the conservative modernism of Bertram Goodhue and Paul Philippe Cret (CFA 1940–45) expressed in simplified classical forms enclosing spaces that retained Beaux-Arts axiality and symmetry. Gilmore Clarke (CFA 1932–50), the prominent New York landscape architect first appointed to the commission in 1932, influenced the CFA in this move toward modernism, even before he became chairman in 1937 following Moore's resignation. While Clarke favored conservative work on certain projects, he tried to strike a balance between the central issues of historicism and modernism as he sought an appropriate monumental architecture—issues that would culminate in a crisis with the design of the Jefferson Memorial in the late 1930s.

During the commission's first twelve years, the position of secretary was held by a succession of four officers from the U.S. Army Corps of Engineers, Office of Public Buildings and Grounds (OPBG). Colonel Spencer Cosby, the commission's first secretary, served until 1913; he was succeeded by Colonel William Harts. In 1917, Colonel Clarence S. Ridley, a graduate of the U.S. Military Academy at West Point, became secretary, a position he held for four years. Ridley left in 1921 to serve in the Panama Canal Zone until 1940, first as an engineer and later as gov-

ABOVE: *Portrait of Charles Moore by painter and* CFA *member Eugene Savage, 1935. On Moore's lap is an eighteenth century survey of the future site of Washington; the Mall in the background is illuminated by a broad shaft of sunlight.*

RIGHT: *The Commission of Fine Arts photographed in its meeting room in the Interior Department building at 18th and F Streets in 1929 (from left to right): William Kendall, Ferruccio Vitale, Ezra Winter, H. P. Caemmerer (secretary), Abram Garfield, Charles Moore, Benjamin Morris, John Cross, and A. A. Weinman. Kendall, a former* CFA *member, was attending the meeting as a representative of the Arlington Memorial Bridge Commission. The* CFA *moved to this location from the Lemon Building in 1923.*

CHAPTER III │ THINE ALABASTER CITIES GLEAM

ernor. Lieutenant Colonel Clarence O. Sherrill was the last Corps of Engineers officer to serve as CFA secretary. A West Point graduate like his predecessors, Sherrill was secretary from 1921 to 1922; he left the military in 1926 for positions in the public and private sectors, including more than a decade as the city manager of Cincinnati, Ohio.

While the commission's chief administrator was an army officer, day-to-day operations were handled by a civilian clerk. In 1919, Hans Paul (H. P.) Caemmerer was hired for the position, beginning an association with the Commission of Fine Arts that would last for thirty-five years.[4] H. P. Caemmerer replaced his brother, Arno Cammerer [*sic*], who had joined the CFA shortly after its formation; he left to become the assistant director of the National Park Service and later, in 1933, its third director. When Congress moved the CFA from under the auspices of the OPBG and established it as an independently administered federal agency in May 1922, Caemmerer replaced Sherrill as secretary on June 30 and served in that role until his retirement in June 1954.[5] Unlike the first four secretaries of the commission, Caemmerer was not an engineer: he had a master's degree in art and archaeology from George Washington University. While at the commission, he also earned a law degree from Georgetown University and a doctorate from American University.

As secretary, Caemmerer came to "serve...as the Commission's link with the past."[6] He wrote the minutes and much or all of the regularly published five-year reports. He also wrote two volumes on the planning and architectural history of Washington and a biography of L'Enfant. In 1951, Caemmerer described his job: "The position is the most difficult and responsible of its kind in the Government service, requiring as it does high training along specialized and technical lines requiring extended artistic training and experience, and the exercise of independent judgment."[7]

By the 1930s, the commission had guided into being much of the Beaux-Arts McMillan Plan for the monumental core: a physical embodiment of American ideals at the center of the nation's capital.[8] The great commemorative landscape, although still unfinished, was now easily perceived and used as a coherent and iconic space defined by a monumental architectural frame. The successful western expansion of the Mall on reclaimed land increased the effective space of the monumental core by an order of magnitude and, with its vision of monumental white temples in a verdant formal setting, firmly established the iconic image of Washington.

The span of the CFA's history during the decades of Moore's membership is framed by the completion of two of these monumental classical temples—the Lincoln and the Jefferson Memorials—similar in their conceptual fulfillment of the McMillan Plan but radically different in the way their design was influenced by the Commission of Fine Arts. Designed in the years immediately before World War I and dedicated in 1922, the Lincoln Memorial exemplifies the collaborative artistic process of the American Renaissance realized through the Beaux-Arts tradition. Its design resembles the structure proposed by the McMillan Plan as the western terminus of the vast new Mall landscape; the strength and coherence of the design supports a unity of purpose in the commemorative task of honoring Lincoln and the preservation of the Union following

ABOVE LEFT: *Hans Paul Caemmerer, photographed in August 1922, served as secretary of the Commission of Fine Arts for thirty-two years, from 1922 to 1954. In his numerous books and articles on the federal city, Caemmerer promoted the Senate Park Commission's vision of Beaux-Arts monumentality.*

ABOVE RIGHT: *Lieutenant Colonel Clarence O. Sherrill, shown seated in a photograph from June 1922, was secretary of the Commission of Fine Arts for only one year, from 1921 to 1922. He remained the head of the Office of Public Buildings and Grounds— an agency administered by the U.S. Army Corps of Engineers and responsible for parks and public spaces in the District of Columbia— until 1925.*

BELOW: *Colonel Clarence S. Ridley, secretary of the Commission of Fine Arts from 1917 to 1921, spent the latter part of his career (1936–40) as governor of the Panama Canal Zone.*

the Civil War. The sculptural and architectural design elements are considered masterpieces of their authors, and the CFA had a central role in guiding them in their task. In contrast, the Jefferson Memorial, designed only a generation later, would be contentious to the end—a failure of consensus on the appropriate architectural expression for the American nation.

During Moore's tenure, the commission's purview was expanded by executive order and congressional legislation, a change that would have continuing importance in the remaking of Washington beyond the monumental core for decades, even into the twenty-first century. In the 1920s and 1930s, Moore and his colleagues approached these expanded responsibilities in keeping with the McMillan Plan's larger goal of treating the city of Washington as a "work of civic art" expressed in the language of Beaux-Arts classicism.[9]

Completing the National Mall

Until its great transformation following the principles of the McMillan Plan, the Mall was a picturesque landscape located between the Capitol and the Washington Monument. Based on the 1851 plan by the pioneering American horticulturist Andrew Jackson Downing, it had been built piecemeal over the second half of the nineteenth century under the U.S. Army Corps of Engineers by the Office of Public Buildings and Grounds. (In 1925 the OPBG was renamed the Office of Public Buildings and Public Parks; it eventually became part of the National Park Service after the founding of the National Capital Parks division in 1933.) The result was a series of parks, densely planted with a wide variety of trees and shrubs and joined by winding walks and carriage drives. However, two railroad lines interrupted the landscape, and the Mall's southern boundary was defined by four large, eclectic Victorian buildings built of sandstone or red brick.

The realization of the National Mall as we recognize it today—a vast space stretching from the Capitol to the Lincoln Memorial on the banks of the Potomac, with a principal cross-axis from the White House to the Jefferson Memorial—attests to a vision inspired by the McMillan Plan and shared by a cadre of planners and designers and to the influence of their leadership in agencies and organizations responsible for achieving that vision. Among these were Charles Moore as CFA chairman; Frederick Law Olmsted Jr., a founding member of both the Commission of Fine Arts and the National Capital Park and Planning Commission (NCPPC); Frederic A. Delano, uncle of President Franklin Roosevelt and chairman of the NCPPC from 1929

to 1942; and Ulysses S. Grant III, grandson of the eighteenth president and head of the Office of Public Buildings and Public Parks.[10]

Guided by the 1901 plan and by the Commission of Fine Arts after 1910, the placement, style, and setback of new buildings constructed on the Mall began to follow more formal and prescribed standards. On the north, these included the National Museum (1904) and on the south, the small Freer Gallery of Art (1928). The new Department of Agriculture building (1903–08 and 1928–30) replaced the older headquarters and, unlike its predecessor, was located out of the main greensward of the Mall's center vista. In 1920, the commission further clarified that the "preeminently important line" on the Mall was the long axis extending from the Capitol to the Washington Monument and to which all other lines must conform; this monument was the iconic presence that set the scale for the enormous composition of the Mall and made possible the reinvention of the gardenesque landscape into a national forum.[11] The commission emphasized that the need to precisely determine the central axis was demonstrated by the off-axis location of the Grant Memorial in Union Square at the foot of the Capitol. (See Arleyn Levee's essay for additional discussion of the role of Frederick Law Olmsted Jr. in these projects.) The CFA continued to advocate for the Mall's completion throughout the rest of the 1920s.

Some barriers remained on the Mall that the commission would not be able to change quickly. In the center of the east end of the Mall stood the plain plaster-and-lath temporary structures, or "tempos," that had been quickly erected to house the influx of federal employees required for World War I but were retained as government offices after the war ended and would remain to some degree until the 1970s. One of the most prominent of these tempos was a power plant occupying the center block of the Mall between 6th and 7th Streets, which provided power for the other World War I tempos; its twin smokestacks framed the views of the Capitol dome and the Washington Monument. Even the tempos, however, had been built with the McMillan Plan in mind, as described in the commission's 1923 annual report: "The temporary war buildings in the Mall were so located that upon removal the roadways will be in accordance with the Mall plan and as fast as the buildings are razed the planting of trees can be made."[12]

While the commission pursued its design review agenda to ensure that new structures and memorials on the National Mall conformed to the McMillan Plan principles, its official role remained advisory. Plans to rebuild the Mall were developed and implemented by the NCPPC and the National Capital Parks Division of the National

Park Service. Implementation of the McMillan Plan for the Mall was one of the first projects undertaken by the NCPPC; in 1929, Congress authorized rebuilding of the Mall in an act that sanctioned the creation of a continuous landscape from Union Station to the Lincoln Memorial, the first great landmarks built as a result of the McMillan Plan. Despite its advisory role, the CFA did wield influence in shaping the legislation to fulfill the McMillan Plan. Charles Moore was responsible for the language in the section relevant to the Mall and Union Square:

The Director of Public Buildings and Public Parks of the National Capital is hereby authorized and directed to proceed with the development of that part of the public grounds in the District of Columbia connecting the Capitol Grounds with the Washington Monument and known as the Mall parkway, in accordance with the plans of Major L'Enfant and the so-called McMillan Commission, with such modifications thereof as may be recommended by the National Capital Park and Planning Commission and approved by the Commission for the Enlarging of the Capitol Grounds.[13]

Frederick Law Olmsted Jr., a member of the National Capital Park and Planning Commission from its founding in 1926, worked with NCPPC chief planner Charles Eliot II to develop the plans for the project.[14] Contrary to the conceptual design of the McMillan Plan he had helped create—which would have allowed the Mall to retain its natural, uneven ground surface—Olmsted now recommended completely regrading the Mall's west end, particularly the steep elevation between 12th and 14th Streets, where the ground was raised to a level plateau; the CFA approved the grades for the four Mall roads in 1931. Olmsted then directed the removal of the Mall's picturesque groves of trees to reveal the key vista between the Capitol and the Washington Monument across a series of lawn panels flanked by phalanxes of trees. The McMillan Plan had recommended that four rows of American elms—trees known for their high, arching canopy—be planted along each side of the Mall to frame the axial vista, a recommendation that Olmsted now implemented.[15]

The Commission of Fine Arts declared its support for the Mall elm planting in January 1933; soon after, however, former CFA member William A. Delano, now with the NCPPC, warned against planting a monoculture, arguing

Aerial view of the Mall, c. 1933, looking west from the vicinity of 7th Street to the Washington Monument, showing the dense plantings and the winding roads and paths of the Victorian-era Mall just before their removal.

TOP LEFT: *The Lincoln Memorial rises above the reclaimed land of West Potomac Park as the Reflecting Pool is under construction, c. 1920.*

TOP RIGHT: *View east from the Washington Monument, 1935. The Department of Agriculture building, visible* at right, has been completed. *Four new roads have been laid out and the eight rows of American elms have been planted except on the blocks between 7th and 12th Streets, where some of the Victorian plantings remain. The power plant at 6th Street in the center of the Mall was removed in 1936.*

ABOVE LEFT: *Aerial view of West Potomac Park and the Washington Monument. The temporary Navy and Munitions Buildings abut the Reflecting Pool construction site, c. 1922.*

ABOVE RIGHT: *The Grant Memorial was erected at the east end of Union Square in 1922, which was still occupied by specimen plantings and buildings of the U.S. Botanic Garden. The Peace Monument and row houses on Pennsylvania Avenue, visible at top left, were removed in the 1930s.*

that the elms would lack uniformity and were vulnerable to disease. He urged, instead, densely planting a variety of tree and shrub species on each side of the central axis to limit side views and emphasize the main vista.[16] Concerned by his warnings, the CFA suggested substituting oaks for the elms, but Olmsted strongly defended the elms as a necessary element of the required formal character. Uniformity and limited views were not the only reason; Olmsted explained the elms' trunks would form a colonnade allowing "diagonal glimpses" from the Mall, its roads, and adjacent buildings, views that were important to animate the Mall.[17] Olmsted's argument was convincing, and hundreds of American elms were planted on the Mall in 1935. The Mall planting was almost completed by fall 1936, funded by the Public Works Administration.

The CFA's involvement extended to the lighting fixtures for the Mall. The General Electric Company designed a cylindrical lamp specifically for the Mall in a simple art deco style carried on a fluted post. The commission approved its use on all Mall roads, recommending placement of the lights in even lines a few feet before the elms to avoid emphasizing the street corners and to create the appearance of a continuous line of light after nightfall. A press release issued by National Capital Parks in the spring of 1936 commented on the CFA's role in this decision:

Another noteworthy feature of the new Mall development is the lighting installation. . . . In general appearance, by both day and night, the lights contribute generously to the beauty of the Mall development. In this respect it is interesting to note that their design was approved by the National Commission of Fine Arts, perhaps the first occasion upon which that exalted body passed upon an object formerly considered purely utilitarian.[18]

The agency's description of the CFA hints at the perception of the commission as an elite organization more comfortable passing judgment on the high arts than practical elements. But the press release also suggests the care with which each detail of the development was evaluated for its contribution to the overall beauty of the Mall. The CFA's influence and advice helped to elevate and seamlessly integrate the utilitarian into the larger, classically inspired scheme.

By the 1930s, the area designated in the McMillan Plan as Union Square at the eastern end of the Mall was the setting for two sculptures—the Ulysses S. Grant Memorial (1922) and the George Gordon Meade Memorial (1927)—set amid the remnants of the historic Botanic Garden. The little-known sculptor Henry Merwin Shrady had won an open competition to design the Grant Memorial in 1903. Shrady's depiction of Grant on a tall pedestal closely resembled the statue sketched by Charles

McKim for the McMillan Plan, but he replaced McKim's proposed statues of Generals Phillip Sheridan and William T. Sherman with bronze groups of soldiers and horses engaged in furious action at the north and south ends of a raised marble platform.[19] After a contentious site selection process, the Grant Memorial was dedicated on the centennial of Grant's birth, April 27, 1922. Five years later, the memorial to General George Gordon Meade, designed by sculptor Charles Grafly, was dedicated west of the Grant Memorial and near the intersection of Pennsylvania Avenue and 3rd Street. Grafly's scheme, which had won a 1918 design competition, depicted an elliptical grouping of marble allegorical figures in heroic scale focused on a nine-foot-tall portrait statue of Meade.[20] The statue was placed on a square marble platform oriented to the center of the Mall and aligned with its walks.

Following congressional authorization to complete the Mall, the National Park Service retained Frederick Law Olmsted Jr. as a consultant in February 1934 to prepare a general plan for Union Square. The McMillan Plan indicated the area as a memorial plaza with statues of Grant, Sheridan, and Sherman set amid extensive paving that would interrupt the continuity of the Mall landscape. By 1920, the CFA had already determined that the plan for Union Square and the Meade Memorial, as realized by the late 1920s, could serve as "a type of square for the entire Mall."[21] Olmsted's new plan for Union Square would contradict the McMillan Plan for the area and directly challenge the CFA in these long-held concepts.

As Arleyn Levee describes in her essay, Olmsted argued that the McMillan Plan had not presented a definitive concept for Union Square and that it was, consequently, necessary to adjust this area as a transitional landscape between the Capitol Grounds and the Mall. He recommended extending Union Square to 3rd Street and treating it as a more unified composition and integral part of the Mall by keeping the avenues diagonal; widening 3rd Street; and, since the Grant Memorial was wider than the center lawn of the Mall, increasing the open lawn to its west.

Olmsted presented his initial concept in April 1934 to the Commission of Fine Arts, the National Capital Park and Planning Commission, and the Commission for the Enlarging of the Capitol Grounds; all but the CFA were supportive, and his plan was approved.[22] While agreeing with the treatment of Union Square as part of the Mall, the CFA strenuously objected to Olmsted's changes: "The plan is not sufficiently monumental. The general character of the treatment of the Plaza of the 1901 Plan, designed by Mr. McKim, seems to be more appropriate."[23]

Patent drawing of the street-light designed for use on the Mall by J. W. Gosling of General Electric, 1935.

By June, Olmsted had made minor changes, and the NCPPC had again given its approval. But at its meeting that month, the CFA's opposition became more entrenched and defined. Architects Egerton Swartwout (CFA 1931–36) and John Mead Howells (CFA 1933–37) launched the attack, with Swartwout declaring Union Square "an architectural problem rather than a landscape problem" and defending features of the McMillan Plan, including a raised terrace along the square's boundary with the Capitol Grounds to make an easy transition between the two areas.[24] Swartwout insisted that the terrace be kept and adjusted to receive the diagonal lines of the two avenues.

Despite Olmsted's arguments, the commission insisted that the McMillan Plan treatment was superior and required Olmsted to restudy his proposal. Olmsted was also under pressure from Arno Cammerer—now the director of the National Park Service—to move the project toward approval because the delay with Union Square was holding up funds for the entire Mall project; both projects, noted Cammerer, were of great interest to President Roosevelt.[25]

Olmsted submitted further revisions to the CFA in September 1934 that hewed more closely to the 1901 plan, returning to the idea of a grand plaza.[26] Oddly, the CFA now preferred one of Olmsted's sketches that did not include a plaza but instead closed 2nd Street, widened 3rd Street, and created a small island around the Grant Memorial. The retaining wall was replaced with a sloping

grade between the Grant Memorial and the Capitol Grounds and included a small reflecting pool in the center lawn panel. The CFA suggested additional changes related to Mall roads, to which Olmsted agreed, and the CFA approved the concept.[27] Olmsted eventually adopted what he called a "lima bean shape" that related to the contours of the Capitol Grounds, replaced the orthogonal avenues of the McMillan Plan with diagonal roadways, and retained the curved Capitol boundary wall, features that recalled the L'Enfant Plan and offered unobstructed sight lines and intersections.[28]

Olmsted's plan more successfully united the landscapes of the Capitol Grounds, Union Square, and the Mall, defining the space and emphasizing the vista. The improvement was not lost on CFA member Gilmore Clarke, himself a landscape architect, who now supported Olmsted's plan:

The reason for a great plaza has been eliminated because of the placing of the Grant Monument at the head of the Mall…. At first [Clarke] believed with Mr. Swartwout and Mr. [John Mead] Howells that Union Square should have a rigid, architectural, rectangular treatment but … Mr. Olmsted's latest plan has good scale and carries the eye right to the Capitol.[29]

This was the last hurdle. The commission approved the plan in October, with approvals received from all three commissions by January 1935. Construction began later that year.

ABOVE LEFT: *The McMillan Plan envisioned a formal composition for Union Square with parterres and walks centered on the three equestrian statues of Grant, Sherman, and Sheridan.*

ABOVE RIGHT: *View of Union Square from the Capitol taken in February 1936, shortly after the completion of Olmsted's design. The landscape existed for little more than thirty years before it was replaced by Skidmore, Owings & Merrill's Capitol Reflecting Pool.*

LEFT: *In his proposed plan of 1935, Olmsted replaced the McMillan Commission's scheme for Union Square with a simpler treatment to create a softer transition between the Mall and the Capitol Grounds.*

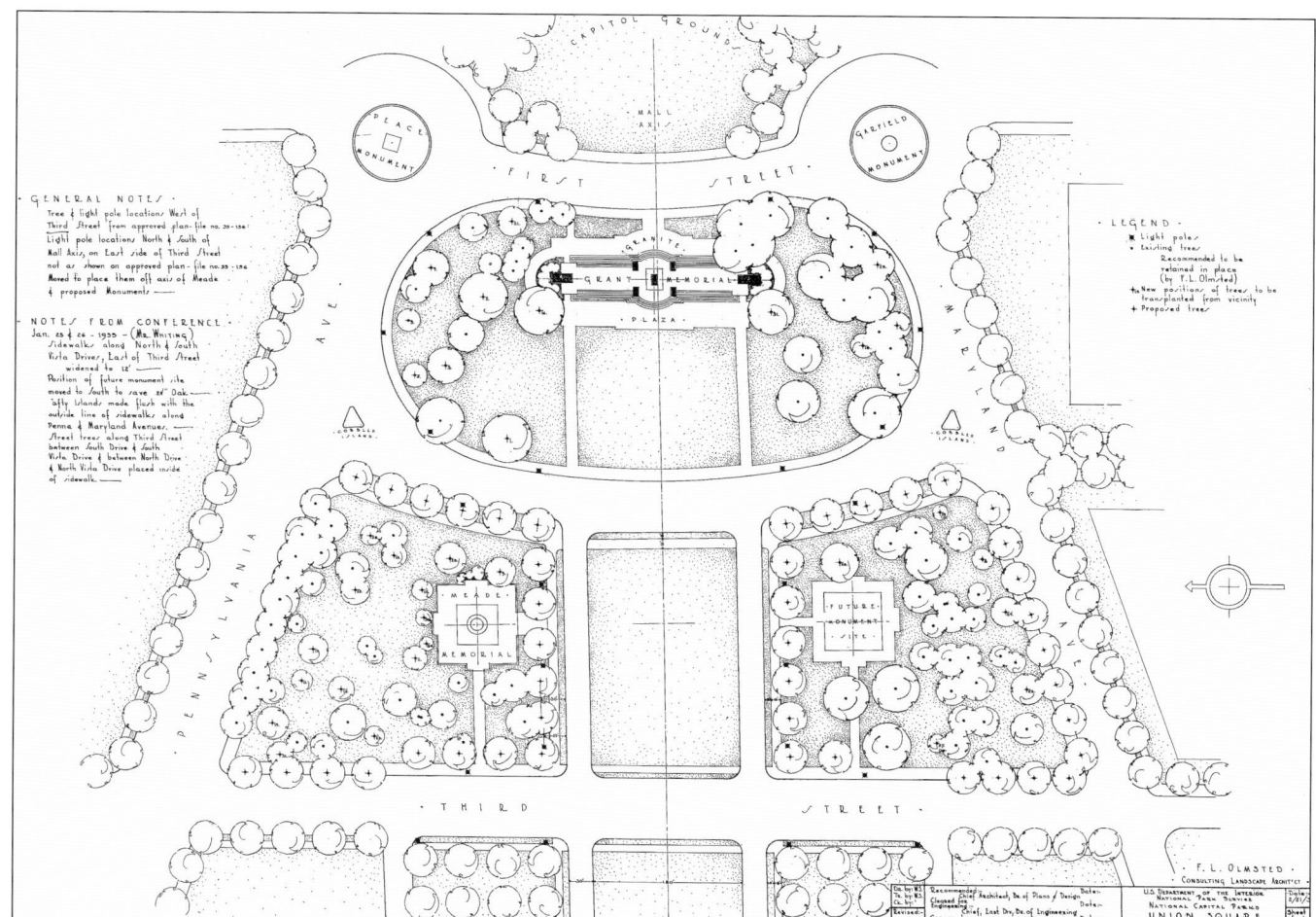

Extending the Mall Precinct and Expressing American Ideals in Works of Commemoration

Throughout the 1920s, as the commission guided into existence the McMillan Commission's Beaux-Arts vision for the Mall, it also extended the conceptual design of the monumental core beyond the Mall into other sectors of the capital city. The Great War had thrust the United States onto the world stage but at the cost of thousands of American dead; the country sought meaningful national commemoration of this sacrifice. With more than 30,000 American servicemen buried in Europe, the location of commemoration greatly expanded.[30] It became the commission's task—one which absorbed most of its attention through the first half of the decade—to express American ideals in works of remembrance at home and abroad. In this effort, the commission would continue to rely on classical vocabulary as an appropriate language to represent the American nation.

ARLINGTON NATIONAL CEMETERY AND THE TOMB OF THE UNKNOWN SOLDIER

The commemoration of the nation's military dead at Arlington National Cemetery was an important focus of the CFA's work during the 1920s. The *Senate Park Commission Report* had devoted a section to the treatment of Arlington National Cemetery and, from its founding, the Commission of Fine Arts was closely involved with its design. Although the cemetery lay in Virginia, the CFA considered it a vital part of the monumental core's future development: the cemetery would be directly linked with the Mall through the proposed Arlington Memorial Bridge and could be considered the ultimate end of the Mall as a processional route. The cemetery took on a new significance with the World War, when the nation's war dead were buried in a specially designated section of the cemetery grounds, and the Tomb of the Unknown Soldier was built in front of the Memorial Amphitheater, a structure that commemorated the dead from all the nation's wars.

A major axis through the center of Arlington National Cemetery had been established by the USS *Maine* Memorial, dedicated in 1915, which influenced the location of these later war memorials. Designed by prominent Washington architect Nathan Wyeth, the memorial commemorated the sinking of the USS *Maine* in Havana Harbor in 1898, the event that precipitated the Spanish-American War and the United States' first foray as a world power. The bodies of 229 sailors from the *Maine* were removed from Cuba and reinterred in a newly opened sec-

tion of Arlington Cemetery by 1912. Located immediately south of the burial site, the memorial consisted of a cylindrical base—recalling the turret of a battleship as well as a variety of ancient Roman tombs—that supported the ship's mast.[31] The design reflected the commission's comments that the mast be treated "frankly as an isolated relic, complete in itself, a detached fragment of the wreck...accompanied by some dignified and beautiful separate means of marking its memorial character."[32]

Thomas Hastings, a commission member from 1910 to 1917 and an architect with the distinguished New York City firm Carrère & Hastings, situated his Memorial Amphitheater (1915–20), an elliptical Doric colonnade with a Corinthian temple front, due east of the *Maine* Memorial and with a distant view of the Potomac River. The War Department then commissioned Hastings to design the Tomb of the Unknown Soldier, which would contain the body of an unidentified American soldier killed in the war.[33]

The War Department suggested placing the tomb within the amphitheater's apse; Hastings argued that the structure's foundations were not strong enough to support the added weight. With the approval of the CFA, he designed a location for the tomb at the top center of the stairway in front of the amphitheater. The first portion constructed was a low, unadorned rectangular block of marble containing the burial chamber, which was to be the plinth of a larger design that Hastings had begun to develop. This base for a future, more elaborate tomb was dedicated on November 11, 1921.

Plans for the larger tomb progressed slowly over the next decade as the commission and the War Department disagreed about an appropriate design within the context of the cemetery. In 1923, Hastings submitted a design showing an ornamental sarcophagus supported at each corner by a crouching nude figure and placed at the top of a tall shaft; the ensemble would have been twenty-eight-feet high in addition to the five feet of the original tomb, which would serve as a base. The War Department rejected the design as "too high and ornate" and likely to detract from the magnificence of the amphitheater. It submitted its own design to the commission, which was promptly rejected.[34]

As Hastings continued revising his proposal, the CFA continued to advocate for it. In 1923, Charles Moore wrote the secretary of war: "The location of the monument with relation to the Amphitheater and the city of Washington requires a monument of the general form submitted by Mr. Hastings." Explaining in a prepared statement that Hastings's design was developed within the larger ensemble of

THE TOMB OF THE UNKNOWN SOLDIER

IN MEMORIAM

TOP LEFT: *The siting of the USS* Maine *Memorial by Nathan Wyeth (1915) established a major axis within Arlington Cemetery, which governed the placement of the Memorial Amphitheater, shown here in a photograph, c. 1920.*

ABOVE: *Lorimer Rich's 1928 design for the tomb proposed a simple carved slab as the central focal point within the larger setting of the amphitheater.*

TOP RIGHT: *A model of Thomas Hastings's first proposed design for the Tomb of the Unknown Soldier on a tall pylon is presented as a montage superimposed above the original tomb, December 1923.*

RIGHT: *In a later proposal for the tomb submitted to the CFA in April 1926, Hastings eliminated the tall pylon and simplified the carving.*

TOP: *The Tomb of the Unknown Soldier, visible at lower left, was located at the top of the stairway directly in front of the Arlington Memorial Amphitheater. The USS Maine Memorial is visible on axis to the right.*

ABOVE: *The tomb designed by Lorimer Rich and Thomas Hudson Jones, featuring bas-relief panels ornamenting a massive slab of Colorado marble, was dedicated in 1932.*

amphitheater and cemetery, the commission noted that the vertical line of the monument was needed on the central axis to balance the dominant horizontal lines expressed in the terraces and balustrades of the amphitheater and in the nearby river and the horizon:

The monument should be large in scale and rich in outline and shadows, because it comes against an open and distant view…. It should rise to dominate the uninterrupted flat and distant view of the Potomac.[35]

Despite these efforts, Hastings's design continued to meet resistance from the quartermaster general, the secretary of war, and Congress, which would not appropriate money for the tomb's completion. A full-size model was placed on the tomb in December 1923; soon after, the secretary of war wrote the CFA that the War Department could not approve Hastings's design, primarily because "it has been viewed by many people, and the criticism which has come to us has been unanimously [*sic*] in disapproval."[36]

Hastings prepared a smaller, simpler version of the tomb without the dramatic plinth that had characterized his original version; but his design was set aside and, over the architect's protests, Congress authorized a design competition for the tomb in July 1926.[37] The program required a low tomb approached by steps and suggested that submissions could include an approach from the east. The winning design by architect Lorimer Rich and sculptor Thomas Hudson Jones was a simple marble block with tapered walls, its short ends facing east and west, with corner pilasters supporting a simple architrave. On the long sides, pilasters defined bays containing laurel wreaths, while the east face bore three stylized allegorical figures in relief, symbolizing peace, victory, and the valor of the American soldier. The tomb was approached by a flight of five steps, and the submission included a long entrance sequence of stairs, ramps, and lawn panels flanked by clipped trees that extended the axis begun by the *Maine* Memorial through the amphitheater to the river. The jury called the winning design austere and original and said it was the most successful viewed against the background of the amphitheater.[38]

At the request of the secretary of war, the CFA reviewed the winning competition entry in December 1928. In spite of the design's appearance, which was more restrained than Hastings's project, the commission spoke approvingly of the tomb's relation to the amphitheater and to the soon-to-be constructed Arlington Memorial Bridge but suggested moving it forward so that it could be seen from the foot of the proposed steps. The quartermaster general objected on behalf of the War Department, which did not want the existing tomb disturbed. Sculptor Lorado Taft

(CFA 1925–29) suggested instead that the stairway be lengthened, which the CFA approved.[39]

With the tomb's design now resolved, the commission urged that its landscape be designed in relation to the larger landscape of the cemetery and that the vista east from the amphitheater be developed "the same as the existing vista from the Arlington Mansion towards the Arlington Memorial Bridge," in keeping with the McMillan Plan. When a revised study shortened the approach to the tomb by fifty-four feet, Ferruccio Vitale protested that it was essential that the tomb be given an adequate landscape. Lorimer Rich pointed out the restrictions imposed on the approach by the presence of graves at the east end, to which Vitale responded that, regardless, the scheme had to be studied in relation to the vista to the river because the designers were "butchering" the landscape plan.[40] The commission agreed, asking Rich to restudy the landscape design along its original lines, to adjust the width of the stairs to the width of the amphitheater's entrance pavilion, and to extend the axis as far as possible, preparing for a comprehensive plan that would include a vista to the river. These changes were incorporated in the final design. On viewing the completed tomb in 1932, the commission noted its happiness with the result: "The massiveness of the Tomb of the Unknown Soldier and the approach provided for it makes the Tomb outstandingly distinctive among the monuments of the world."[41]

ARLINGTON MEMORIAL BRIDGE AND THE WATERGATE

The Arlington Memorial Bridge extended the composition of Washington's monumental core into Virginia and expanded the commemorative theme underlying the framework of the Mall. The Commission of Fine Arts was intimately involved in the design of the bridge and its related structures: the Watergate steps, sculpture, roads, and Memorial Avenue. More than a critical physical route across the Potomac River, the bridge was highly symbolic in its connection with Arlington National Cemetery, envisioned since the nineteenth century as a representation of national reunification after the Civil War. By the time of its design in the 1920s, the Arlington Memorial Bridge Commission (AMBC) said it would also be a "memorial to those who have died in the military service of the country," including the recent world war.[42] Among the issues the CFA would take into account when reviewing the design of the bridge and its ancillary structures were views between the encircling Virginia hills and the landmarks within the District of Columbia; views up and down the Potomac River; connections to new roads along the river;

and how to properly end the Mall axis while creating a new link across the river.[43]

The AMBC was established by Congress in 1913 to oversee the design and construction of this critical structure.[44] Federal funding for the project was delayed, however, until a massive traffic jam on the historic Long Bridge south of the Lincoln Memorial, caused by hundreds of cars traveling to the dedication of the initial Tomb of the Unknown Soldier in 1921 demonstrated the pressing need for the new bridge. The CFA first saw plans for the bridge in January 1922.

The Commission of Fine Arts was instrumental in the decision to align the bridge with the Lincoln Memorial. The AMBC had favored an alignment with New York Avenue, which would keep traffic away from the Lincoln Memorial and preserve its quality as a shrine. That alignment also offered the practicality of a direct approach to the White House and downtown Washington and an easier connection with the Lee Highway in Virginia. (See the essay by Pamela Scott.)

After consultation with his fellow CFA members, Charles Moore issued a report in September 1922 arguing against

BELOW: *Paul Pelz's 1886 design for the Arlington Memorial Bridge featured Renaissance Revival towers and articulated steel arches crossing the Potomac River.*

BOTTOM: *Competition-winning scheme (alternative #2) for the Arlington Memorial Bridge by Edward Pearce Casey, 1900. Triumphal arches on piers emphasized an imperial architectural image.*

TOP RIGHT: *Charles McKim's concept for the Arlington Memorial Bridge in the McMillan Plan was less elaborate, with masonry piers framing flat arches and gateway pylons at each end.*

RIGHT: *William Mitchell Kendall's design of 1923 adapted Charles McKim's conception of the low-arched masonry bridge, adding allegorical figures at each pier.*

the New York Avenue alignment as an unacceptable departure from the 1901 plan because it would function as a mere traffic conveyance rather than the memorial intended by the plan. To break with the 1901 plan required "cogent reasons," and Moore quoted Frederick Law Olmsted Jr. regarding the plan's primacy: "The coincident deliberate judgment in such a matter of Charles F. McKim, Daniel Burnham, Augustus Saint-Gaudens and the undersigned ought not lightly or hastily to be brushed aside by any new commission or Committee of Congress."[45] The AMBC would eventually agree to the CFA's preferred align-

ment behind the Lincoln Memorial but would require it to be a low bridge with an operable drawspan; the CFA had maintained that a fixed bridge could be built behind the memorial. The CFA also recommended to the AMBC that the bridge's architect be chosen through direct selection rather than a competition, proposing Charles Platt, Paul Cret, or the firm of McKim, Mead & White as candidates.

The AMBC chose the New York firm of McKim, Mead & White, whose partner William Mitchell Kendall would design the bridge and other features. At its meeting in December 1927, the CFA also urged that the design of the bridge harmonize with the Lincoln Memorial and be constructed of granite to be consistent with the memorial's retaining wall.[46] In his preliminary drawings for the bridge, Kendall had opted to treat the area west of the Lincoln Memorial—essentially at its back since the memorial entrance faced east—as an open plaza with roadways, all above the level of the river's shoreline and bounded by a straight retaining wall, as shown in the McMillan Plan; there were no roads along the river's edge. The scheme set in motion the most perplexing question of the review process—how to treat this area between the Lincoln Memorial and the river—and would become the predominant issue facing the two commissions and the designer in 1928. The main alternatives that evolved were an open plaza west of the memorial with free-flowing automobile traffic, as Kendall indicated in his early drawings, or a road with either a long tunnel, or shorter underpass, on the river shore below the level of the memorial. Several aesthetic and practical issues were involved: How closely should the 1901 plan be followed; should there be a watergate; how should traffic flow around the memorial to the bridge; and where should a road or tunnel be placed?

The 1901 plan had shown a watergate in the form of steps between the Lincoln Memorial and the Potomac River as a ceremonial landing place for boats carrying dignitaries up the river to the city. Such a feature also would mediate the height of the mound on which the memorial was to stand and form a visual and pedestrian connection between it and the river. However, by the 1920s, automobiles were becoming more widely used, and pedestrians walking between the river and the memorial were likely to conflict with automobile traffic. Those who supported the underpass or tunnel, including the National Capital Park and Planning Commission and some members of the CFA, claimed that routing traffic in a plaza at the base of the Lincoln Memorial would harm its character. CFA member Milton Medary said "a constant interference of traffic... would be apt to make the people lose their veneration for the Lincoln Memorial."[47] Those who argued for the open plaza—among them architect Kendall—believed that using a tunnel or underpass under the Watergate steps was too informal and would ruin the approach to the bridge.

Under protest, Kendall prepared more studies of an underpass. He developed a scheme that, instead of dividing the Watergate steps by a road through an underpass, proposed preserving the Watergate steps as he had originally presented them, including their angle of slope, with a road passing below them. Charles Moore asked whether the steps could be omitted altogether, creating a simple terrace along the shoreline, but Kendall insisted the steps

were needed to preserve the formality of that approach. The CFA approved Kendall's revised sketch as the best solution to the problem of providing a strong termination to the Mall at the Potomac River.[48]

But the argument continued. In February 1928, architect William Partridge of the NCPPC (who had been the chief draftsman of the McMillan Plan) recalled that the 1901 plan had lacked a fixed idea about the steps and had given two sketches for them. Partridge added that McKim's initial design for the Lincoln Memorial had been an open propylaeum, or gateway, facing both the river and the Mall, and all of his designs had shown steps, while Bacon's completed memorial was a closed temple with its back facing the river. Partridge also pointed out a structural problem, observing that a tunnel could weaken the mound of soil beneath the memorial, and recommended that only a retaining wall—and no steps—be used. Kendall opposed this solution because it removed the steps. [49]

A special CFA meeting to consider the problem was held on March 15, 1928, at former CFA member John Russell Pope's office in New York. Five commission members attended, along with several past members as well as representatives from the Arlington Memorial Bridge Commission and McKim, Mead & White. The men discussed several options at great length, including various combinations of a plaza, roads, watergate steps, retaining walls, and tunnels or underpasses. The McKim, Mead & White architects said they believed that the Watergate formed "the most important feature of the whole design." A road running across the middle of the steps would be inharmonious and dangerous, and they recommended building the tunnel.[50]

Opinions differed among the CFA members, past and present. Current member architect William A. Delano, speaking for the commission, said it had agreed that traffic at the Lincoln Memorial plaza would be excessive and gave four reasons why they recommended the steps be deleted from the scheme: The Mall terminated at the Lincoln Memorial rather than the river; the steps would not provide a strong abutment; they would only be seen adequately from the Virginia shore; and this was not the optimal location for a ceremonial entrance to the city. John Russell Pope observed that the steps would retain the association between the upper and lower levels, while Milton Medary found retaining walls to be a better solution than a tunnel or steps. Frederick Law Olmsted Jr., representing the NCPPC, did not believe that either a long tunnel or an underpass would be right; he preferred traffic control at the plaza on grade. Olmsted also expressed doubt that a watergate at this location would ever be used.[51] Charles Moore noted that the McMillan Commission had believed

William Mitchell Kendall envisioned an elaborate sculptural program for the Arlington Memorial Bridge, including seated figures of the first four American presidents on the D.C. side and reclining statues of ocean and river gods on Columbia Island. The bridge itself was to have forty allegorical statues; Thomas Hudson Jones prepared this quarter-scale plaster maquette of Ceres *(c. 1928) for the program of statuary, which was eventually eliminated at the recommendation of the CFA.*

ABOVE: *In addition to conventional classical ornamentation, the bridge design employed specifically American symbols. While the allegorical figures eventually were abandoned, the bas-reliefs were retained. The keystones are ornamented with bison heads designed by Alexander Phimister Proctor, completed in 1932.*

RIGHT: *The Watergate steps, shown here under construction c. 1932, were the result of an arduous review undertaken by the Commission of Fine Arts, as current and former members worked to reconcile a graceful termination to the Mall with the needs of automobiles and pedestrians.*

BELOW: *William Mitchell Kendall's 1923 proposal for four monumental pylons with figural sculptures at the bridge entrance was rejected by the Commission of Fine Arts. Kendall modified the design to include equestrian statues, which the CFA approved in 1928, but these elements would not be completed until after World War II.*

the bridge should be subordinate to the memorial and should be "a park bridge and not a traffic bridge."[52]

Once the discussion drew to a close, the CFA's current members attending the meeting unanimously decided that the Watergate steps should be built instead of a retaining wall, with a road passing under the bridge through short underpasses and crossing at the foot of the main flight of steps, with another short flight of steps extending below the road to the river's shoreline.[53] McKim, Mead & White revised their plans to reflect this approach and the commission approved them in April 1928.[54]

As part of the architectural setting of the bridge, Kendall also designed four massive pylons on Columbia Island, marking the western end of the Arlington Memorial Bridge and the eastern end of the smaller Boundary Channel Bridge, and framing the view to the central traffic circle at Arlington House in Arlington National Cemetery. He wanted to place two other pairs of tall pylons on the plaza behind the Lincoln Memorial, marking the east end of the bridge and the entrance to the Rock Creek and Potomac Parkway. When designs for these pylons were brought before the CFA in April 1928, however, the commission members found them too large in relation to the Lincoln Memorial, although in proportion to the bridge. They asked Kendall to prepare models for viewing on site the following month.

Viewing the models confirmed for the members this problem of proportion. Kendall, still insisting the pylons played an essential role in the architectural scheme of the bridge and would not interfere with the view to the Lincoln Memorial, nevertheless prepared drawings reducing their height from forty-eight to forty-three feet. The commission found even this lower height too massive in relation to the memorial's columns and suggested diminishing the pylons' apparent mass by giving them a horizontal rather than a vertical emphasis, or by replacing them with a seated or reclining sculptural figure. Kendall strongly objected to placing reclining figures so close to the Lincoln Memorial, and noted that in Europe the use of pylons in such a composition was common and "at the Place de la Concorde it is the intervening objects that make it interesting."[55]

CHAPTER III | THINE ALABASTER CITIES GLEAM

But the CFA remained firm in its views regarding the pylons' scale in relation to the memorial. Reluctantly, Kendall produced two alternatives—one for a narrower, shorter pylon and the other for an obelisk—which the commission also rejected. Finally, Kendall proposed replacing the pylons with equestrian statues on pedestals, each about eighteen feet high, and the commission accepted this concept.[56] Arlington Memorial Bridge opened to traffic in 1932, but the economic constraints of the Great Depression, and later the intervention of World War II, delayed the fabrication and installation of the statues until the 1950s.

MEMORIALS TO THE FIRST WORLD WAR IN WASHINGTON, D.C.

National interest in commemorating the Great War also extended into the fabric of Washington. In the years immediately after the war, the commission discussed the question of an appropriate national war memorial as well as its wish to avoid the creation of mediocre war memorials randomly scattered throughout the city. Contrary to the late twentieth century, when national war memorials became expected elements of the Washington landscape, a national memorial commemorating the World War was a new concept: traditionally, war memorials were erected locally to honor those in that community who had fought and died. Accordingly, the CFA reviewed designs of smaller memorials in the District of Columbia honoring the city's

own losses. The commission eventually recommended that a national world war memorial be located south of the Washington Monument, where it could be integrated into the Mall plan.[57] Although this single national world war memorial was not built, the commission did review several plans for memorials of national scope that honored the sacrifices of American military divisions within the larger framework of the monumental core, the 1901 plan, and the nascent iconography of the Mall.

In 1925, the commission reviewed the initial design for a District of Columbia World War Memorial by local architect Frederick H. Brooke. The small memorial was envisioned as a bandstand, perhaps because of the widespread desire after the war for "living" memorials that would fulfill some practical purpose or community function. The CFA recommended that Brooke consider the Temple of Love at the Villa Borghese in Rome as an example to be followed—a small pavilion referenced by the McMillan Commission in its 1901 report. Brooke revised his design according to the CFA's advice, and it was approved in May 1925.[58] Two sites in West Potomac Park were considered for the memorial, the first near an existing wooden bandstand on the polo grounds and the other in a grove of willows located between the middle of the Reflecting Pool and the Tidal Basin.[59] After inspecting the grove site in April 1928, the commission decided it "need have no axial relations with any element in the [McMillan] plan."[60] This finding did not sit well with Charles Moore, who in-

The 1925 design for the District of Columbia World War Memorial by Frederick H. Brooke was a small domed temple, or tempietto, *set within an informal landscape, completed in 1931.*

sisted that the site did indeed need to have a relation to the 1901 plan.

This difference in views prompted the CFA to ask Ulysses S. Grant III, director of the Office of Public Buildings and Public Parks, to prepare a study showing the axial relation of the willow grove site and another site on the north side of the Reflecting Pool, designated as the possible location for a structure or object in landscape plans developed for the Lincoln Memorial grounds by city planner Clarence H. Howard in 1915–16.[61] Grant's study suggested that pairing the memorial with the feature shown on the Howard plan would place the memorial too close to 17th Street, and concluded that the grove of trees would be the best location: "If in the future a memorial is contemplated for the north side of the Reflecting Basin it could be made to balance the bandstand, with little change in the Howard Plan."[62] The D.C. World War Memorial was constructed in the grove, in an area known as "Ash Woods," with no axial relation to the McMillan Plan. A

The First Division Memorial Committee sought specifically to model its monument on the columnar Battle Monument at West Point, designed by McKim, Mead & White, that supports a winged victory figure by sculptor Frederick MacMonnies.

landscape design by Horace Peaslee, first implemented in 1931 and altered again in the late 1930s, included a formal walk through an allée of trees leading north to the memorial from Independence Avenue; the temple was set on an apron of random slate paving within a loose semicircle of elms and other tall hardwoods.

Another example of Great War commemoration was a memorial honoring the First Infantry Division of the U.S. Army. A memorial committee headed by the division's commander, Major General C. P. Summerall, quickly raised $150,000, and in 1919 and again in 1920, Summerall sought the Commission of Fine Arts' advice on selecting a site and design. In January 1921, the CFA approved the committee's proposal to build a monument on a site immediately south of the State, War, and Navy Building—the imposing Second Empire office building immediately west of the White House—but the CFA advised that any memorial there should be in the form of a fountain. The CFA recommended choosing the architect and sculptor through a design competition. Disregarding the commission's advice, the First Division Memorial Committee (FDMC) instead hired architect Cass Gilbert and sculptor Daniel Chester French, both former CFA members.[63]

Gilbert submitted his preliminary design to the CFA in March 1922; at the direction of the FDMC, it was explicitly based on the 1897 Battle Monument at West Point. Commemorating army action in the Civil War, the Battle Monument was a monolithic granite column designed by McKim, Mead & White, surmounted by a winged, female allegorical figure by sculptor Frederick MacMonnies. The FDMC also required that the memorial be inscribed with the names of all battles in which the division had fought; its citation for bravery from General of the Armies John J. Pershing; and all the names of the division's 5,500 war dead—an unusual precedent for a national memorial in a civic setting.

Moore objected to the committee's prescriptive procedure for the design, which he felt constrained the creative freedom of the architect and sculptor.[64] The commission as a whole did not support placing a tall column so near the Washington Monument and disapproved the proposed design. If the committee insisted on this design, the CFA suggested it be placed at another site, possibly a location south of the National War College in Southwest Washington where the monument could perhaps form one of a group of division memorials.

This decision was not met with enthusiasm by the FDMC, and in April the First Division Memorial formed the sole subject of a special commission meeting. Six members of the newly renamed First Division Memorial Association

The First Division Memorial, designed by Cass Gilbert, was built in front of the State, War, and Navy Building (1924).

appeared with Cass Gilbert to defend the site and design proposals. The association's president, Colonel Adolphe H. Huguet, emphasized that the First Division's role in the war had been of particular significance: it had been the first to arrive in France and the last to leave, and it had fought in all the battles in France in which the U.S. Army had taken part.

Gilbert then asserted the need to build a permanent memorial that would not be subject to deterioration, as were fountains and other structures with numerous small parts. He defended the memorial's height at this location, noting that at eighty feet, including the base, it would be well proportioned in a setting defined by the State, War and Navy building and the monumental structures along 17th Street, such as the Corcoran Gallery of Art and the Red Cross Headquarters. Gilbert also argued that the column would not be high enough to compete with the 555-foot Washington Monument.

A letter from General Summerall, in which he lamented the commission's disapproval, was read into the record. Concerning the column and its relationship to the site, Summerall wrote:

The Battle Monument at West Point is the only one within my knowledge that carries a message and a conviction to uplift our people. The

First Division Monument would have [even] a greater influence upon the nation; if placed at the spot selected where it would be accessible and yet not exposed to the bustle and hurry of the working world. [65]

Summerall then threatened to move the memorial to another city if the commission failed to approve the proposal. The commission decided to recommend the site to Congress's Joint Committee on the Library, as required by the memorial's authorizing act, provided the design was somewhat altered: the shaft was lowered and the names of the war dead were inscribed on slanted, not vertical, slabs around the base, with the memorial installed on a plaza at the site.

The remaining issue, worked out between Cass Gilbert and the commission over the rest of the decade, was how to tie the memorial seamlessly into its landscape according to the precepts of the McMillan Plan. In 1916, the Office of Public Buildings and Grounds had prepared a planting plan for the area, developing the vague proposal of the McMillan Plan for "shaded walks from the hot city into the park system." Gilbert wanted to place the memorial on a broad paved terrace near the State, War, and Navy Building. The commission insisted that it be set on a gradual slope, "having the mound on which the memorial stands fade away in every direction," closely tied to the existing topography.[66] A tapis vert or green lawn panel framed by lindens would define an axis to B Street North (Constitution Avenue) and the Washington Monument Grounds. These recommendations were included in the final design, and the completed memorial was dedicated in October 1924.

OVERSEAS CEMETERIES AND WAR MEMORIALS

The commission became closely involved in the commemorative expression of American cemeteries and battle monuments in Europe following the war. Initially, acquiring the land and creating these sites fell under the purview of the Graves Registration Service of the Quartermaster General's Office in the War Department. In 1923, Congress created the American Battle Monuments Commission (ABMC) to implement their design, construction, and maintenance, and General of the Armies John J. Pershing was appointed its first chairman.[67] Advising first the

Graves Registration Service and later the ABMC, the CFA guided the design of American battlefield cemeteries, carefully reviewing all of their features including memorials, chapels, and headstones. The CFA also guided the design of battle monuments erected near the sites where American servicemen had fought in some of the war's most deadly offensives.

In September 1920, with $30 million appropriated by Congress, the Graves Registration Service appeared before the commission with tentative plans for the first five American cemeteries in France, including locations at Suresnes, Belleau Wood, and Romagne-sous-Montfaucon. The War Department asked the CFA to visit the sites at government expense and to develop guidelines for the cemeteries' designs. In March 1921, Moore and members William Mitchell Kendall and James Greenleaf (CFA 1918–27), a landscape architect, sailed for France on an army transport ship to spend two months investigating potential locations. On their return, Moore submitted a report to the CFA discussing land acquisitions and giving

The axial, symmetrical layout of the American World War I cemeteries in Europe—such as the 1921 plan by George Gibbs Jr. for Aisne-Marne near the battlefield at Belleau Wood, France—reflected Beaux-Arts planning precepts.

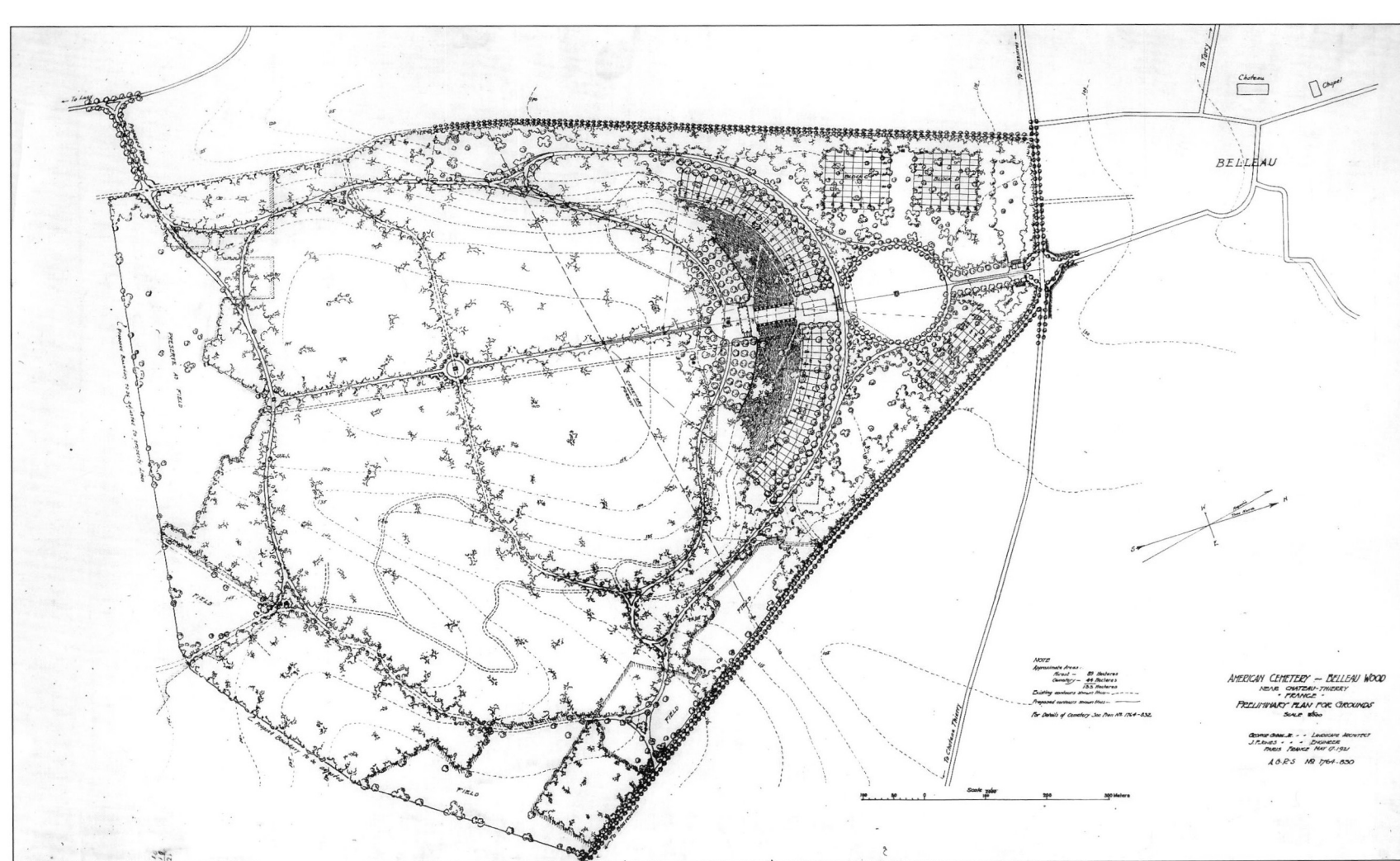

their general impressions. Moore outlined to the Graves Registration Service the two leading ideas the CFA members had agreed upon as a result of their trip: enlarging the cemeteries with appropriate landscapes that could include areas of historic interest and relating the cemeteries to nearby towns by a "suitable approach." Moore also offered recommendations for grading, structures, and walks and provided a brief description of each cemetery.[68]

Typically, the boundary of each cemetery was delineated by a wall, and the walls of each chapel were engraved with the names of the interred dead. Battle monuments included relief maps of the battlefield and bronze tablets listing the names of the dead; markers indicated where Americans had fought. Under the commission's guidance,

memorial designs adapted standard monument types in classical, often Greek, styles. Chapels were most commonly Romanesque, although not exclusively: the chapel at Suresnes, France, for example, was a classical temple that quoted the Temple of Aesculapius at the Villa Borghese— a site which was an occasional design reference for the CFA as it had been earlier for the McMillan Commission.

Returning to Europe in July 1923, Charles Moore spent the summer visiting the cemeteries. He returned favorably impressed with the progress of work and observed to the commission that the treatment of the cemeteries, following their original directive, was similar to that of military cemeteries in the United States. He noted that the approaches had a simple French character, with their

BELOW LEFT: The CFA considered the Romanesque Revival chapel (1927) for the Aisne-Marne American Cemetery, designed by Cram & Ferguson, highly suitable for its location in France. BELOW RIGHT: For the American Battle Monument at Montfaucon, France, John Russell Pope designed a colossal 185-foot-high granite column supporting a statue representing liberty; it was completed in 1933 and dedicated in 1937. BOTTOM RIGHT: For the American Aisne-Marne Monument at Chateau-Thierry, Paul Cret reconceived the classical colonnade as a modern monument (1926–32).

RIGHT: *The American cemeteries in Europe first used ranks of painted wooden crosses to mark burial sites, shown here at the American Cemetery at Meuse-Argonne, Romagne-sous-Montfaucon, France in 1919.*

BELOW: *The ad hoc solution of using a painted wooden cross to mark a grave was eventually replaced by a standard marble cross or Star of David designed by Paul Cret, as seen in this image of Suresnes Cemetery. The chapel (1927–29) was designed by Charles A. Platt, who also designed the simpler grave markers at Arlington National Cemetery.*

World War I Medals

The number of American medals issued increased substantially as a result of the World War. Compared to its European counterparts, however, the Commission of Fine Arts found the new American medals cheap and badly designed, observing, "The entire subject of medals deserves serious consideration. They represent valor, achievement, service.... They may be simple and inexpensive, but they ought to be good."[1]

While the design of medals was not officially within the Commission of Fine Arts' oversight, it became involved in the design of the Victory Medal—an honor granted to soldiers for exceptional heroism and perhaps the most important medal produced following World War I. Delegates of the Allied governments met in Paris to identify design criteria that would ensure correspondence among the medals of each country, deciding on a round bronze medal with an obverse bearing a winged figure of victory against a plain background and a reverse inscribed with "The Great War for Civilization" surrounded by the names of all the Allied nations.[2]

The army asked the commission to oversee the design for the U.S. medal. The CFA selected sculptor James E. Fraser as the artist, and he quickly developed a version of the required design for the obverse; on the reverse, he used as a vertical device the ancient Roman symbol of the fasces—a bundle of rods around an ax—overlaid on an American shield to anchor the inscriptions. The commission approved it with little hesitation one year after the armistice, in November 1919.[3]

In 1921, President Warren G. Harding made the commission's role in the review of medals official. On July 28, he signed an executive order that expanded the commission's oversight to include design review of medals, insignia, and coins produced by the U.S. Mint of the Department of the Treasury.[4] In this capacity, the CFA became involved in the review of the Distinguished Flying Cross, which was awarded to members of the armed forces for extraordinary heroism while in the air. At the CFA's May 1927 meeting, the army's quartermaster general pressured the commission to quickly select one of two designs so the medal could be produced in time for its scheduled presentation by President Calvin Coolidge to Captain Charles A. Lindbergh on June 11—an event to occur only two weeks after the CFA meeting and just three weeks after Lindbergh's historic flight of May 20–21.[5]

Both designs presented to the commission depicted a four-bladed propeller in the form of a cross. They differed in their treatment of the background: one set the cross against laurel leaves, the other against rays. The CFA reluctantly chose the latter, suggesting a few changes to strengthen the ray motif. When the cast was later produced for general issue, military officials were unhappy with the background's heavy appearance. A modified design was prepared and submitted to the CFA, which called the change negligible and advised against any alteration.[6] Senator Hiram Bingham (R-CT), who had conceived of the medal, and the assistant secretaries of war and the navy pleaded with the commission to reconsider. Charles Moore told the senator:

You are the first person in authority to express dissatisfaction with the designs for a Government award—a subject with which this Commission has been carrying on an almost hopeless struggle for many years. It is encouraging to learn that you are very much disappointed. Suppose we start there and see if the whole subject can be reopened and an entirely suitable design secured.[7]

The commission stuck to its decision but lamented that the original short deadline had led to a result "commonplace and insignificant": "Here was an opportunity to produce a medal of the highest distinction, for there are in this country medallists of high ability and approved merit."[8]

ABOVE, LEFT TO RIGHT: *In 1919, the Commission of Fine Arts oversaw the design of the American World War I Victory Medal by James Earle Fraser (depicted are the obverse and reverse sides); The Distinguished Flying Cross (1927) was designed by A. E. DuBois and Elizabeth Will of the U.S. Army Quartermaster General's Office.*

"tree-shaded avenues," and that buildings had been designed to harmonize with the local architecture. He wrote:

Everything has been done to bring out a sense of order, quiet and appropriateness to the surroundings. There is no elaboration and no striving for unusual effects, but all the possibilities of the landscape have been taken advantage of to give charm and a park-like effect, such as seen in those older parts of Arlington Cemetery devoted to the soldiers as opposed to the portions occupied by graves of officers, where elaborate monuments create disturbance. [69]

The appropriate design, religious symbolism, and size of headstones to mark American graves in the European cemeteries were persistent questions occupying the commission throughout the 1920s. Initially, American graves in Europe were marked by temporary wooden crosses; but in 1920 the War Memorial Council of the office of the secretary of war determined that a simple rectangular "American white" marble headstone, designed that year by architect and CFA member Charles A. Platt (CFA 1916–21) and based on dimensions supplied by the War Department, was suitable for the graves of all American war dead in the U.S. and abroad.[70] An enlarged version of this, inscribed with a cross or a Star of David at the top, was proposed; use of this headstone would make all American graves easily recognizable.[71]

While the original Platt-designed headstone was in use at Arlington National Cemetery, the quartermaster general thought the marker was too small compared with those in British military cemeteries. By July 1921, instead of the rectangular slabs, the quartermaster general's office had approved the use of larger marble headstones shaped in a cross or Star of David for American overseas cemeteries.[72] Moore tried to counter this decision by discussing the issue with the chief of the Graves Registration Service, who agreed that Platt's rectangular markers were suitable because 1,250 had been erected at Arlington and were thought to collectively present "a very agreeable appearance." The commission defined the distinction between the British and American type of war memorial cemetery:

The British Cemetery is usually small with stone enclosures and large headstones giving the appearance of a line of stones and emphasizing masonry, whereas the American cemetery is to be typical of Arlington, showing primarily only the small headstone, green grass, and trees.[73]

The CFA recommended enlarging the emblem for the larger headstone, but the American Battle Monuments Commission wanted the headstone itself to take the form of a cross or Star of David. In November 1923, the ABMC, now in charge of the cemeteries, presented a design for both types of markers and suggested that even a cross of painted iron might be an option. The CFA found these shapes impractical for inscriptions and less durable than a slab; the ABMC responded that the Platt grave marker resembled a milestone. By late 1924, the ABMC had developed a sample marble cross and asked for the CFA's help in obtaining a design for a Star of David. Charles Moore reminded the ABMC that the CFA had determined that small headstones—not the markers proposed by the ABMC—with trees and lawns should be the fundamental features of the American cemeteries in Europe.

Despite the CFA's warning that the design would be expensive and that, because of its shape, the stone would be likely to disintegrate, the ABMC remained adamant. The CFA finally said that if the cross had to be used, it should be redesigned as a smaller memorial with "proper proportions." Headstones remained under discussion for another four years; in 1928, the ABMC had Paul Cret design marble markers in the form of a cross or a Star of David to replace the wooden crosses over the World War graves.[74]

Framing the Mall

Perhaps the greatest achievement of the Commission of Fine Arts under Charles Moore was the development of areas adjoining the Mall into a suitable frame for both the Mall and the monumental landscape of Washington, creating by the mid-1920s a monumental core now growing recognizable as the received collective idea of Washington's urban space. In its review of both large complexes and individual buildings or elements, the commission advocated subordination or relation of small parts to the larger, unified whole of the McMillan Plan.

The work of Moore and his colleagues continued an approach to the Mall environs begun even before the establishment of the commission: Daniel Burnham had designed the city's enormous gateway, Union Station, a colossal edifice modeled on ancient Roman typologies and situated on a great plaza connected to the Mall by a new green landscape, completed in 1908. Conceived by Burnham as forming the great forecourt to Union Station and a threshold to the Capitol complex, the plaza was designed by Peirce Anderson of Burnham's office while he served on the CFA from 1912 to 1916 after Burnham's death.

The Capitol complex itself had undergone significant changes: from 1851 to 1865, two great wings—one each for the Senate and the House of Representatives—were added to the sides of the original building, creating the five-part massing that defines the building today. On either side of the Capitol Grounds, new office buildings to house the ever-increasing congressional staffs were erected, including the Russell Senate Office Building (1905–08) and the Cannon House Office Building (1905–08), both

The design for the William Howard Taft Memorial, a granite stele in Arlington National Cemetery, was approved by the CFA in 1931. Designed by James Earle Fraser, the classical Greek-style grave marker with its distinctive anthemion crest honors the former chief justice of the Supreme Court and U.S. president who supported the creation of the CFA.

by Carrère & Hastings. The Longworth House Office Building, designed by Allied Architects of Washington—whose principals included Frank Upman, Gilbert LaCoste Rodier, Nathan C. Wyeth, and Louis Justement—was subsequently added (1929–33).

THE U.S. SUPREME COURT BUILDING

The commission's involvement with the development of the area around the Mall began with the Supreme Court's desire for its own building. Although part of the judicial branch of the U.S. government, the Supreme Court remained in its historic location on the ground floor of the Capitol, which by the 1920s had become cramped. Former President William Howard Taft—a proponent of the commission's creation and an advocate for Burnham's vision for Washington—became chief justice of the Supreme Court on July 7, 1921. On that day, Taft told Charles Moore about his wish to see an appropriate building constructed for the nation's highest court. He endorsed the site—on the block north of the Library of Congress, facing the Capitol building across 1st Street, NE—indicated for the court in the 1901 McMillan Plan and the Public Buildings Plan of 1917, which contained the caveat that "[n]o building on this location should be so large as to close Maryland Avenue, one of the Capitol vistas."[75] Moore also was determined that the Supreme Court should be built here.

The Supreme Court turned to the most prominent architectural practitioner of the day, retaining Henry Bacon (CFA 1921–24), designer of the Lincoln Memorial, to prepare preliminary sketches. When Bacon died suddenly in 1924, the court hired a master of academic classicism and former CFA member, Cass Gilbert. Chief Justice Taft, however, began to have doubts about the location. The difficulty was Maryland Avenue—one of the L'Enfant Plan boulevards—which passed through the block, cutting off its northwest corner and constraining the buildable area. In 1928, Taft told Frederic A. Delano of the NCPPC that a Supreme Court building here would not be large enough to balance the Library of Congress and suggested that it be built north of the Capitol Grounds, facing Constitution Avenue.

At the February 1928 CFA meeting, Moore vigorously defended the original site: the location was designated by the 1901 plan, and Congress had passed legislation for the site and begun condemnation proceedings. The Supreme Court building would not need to balance the Library of Congress in scale, Moore said, because its design would make it compatible with the library. If it were placed north of the Capitol, as Taft suggested, the building would obstruct the vista up North Capitol Street, "one of the great cardinal thoroughfares of the city. We are trying to keep this open." Moore ended by saying: "The minute you attempt to make any changes in the location, so many things depend upon it, you are going to break into a whole series of things that have been worked out."[76]

In March 1929, Architect of the Capitol David Lynn asked the commission for its opinion about acquiring the triangle of land cut off from the main parcel by Maryland Avenue in order to enlarge the Supreme Court site and closing Maryland Avenue.[77] After polling three former CFA members—Olmsted Jr. and the architects Louis Ayres (CFA 1921–25) and Milton Medary—and discussing the matter with the present commission, Moore wrote to Lynn:

It is the opinion of the Commission of Fine Arts that under no circumstances whatever should Maryland Avenue be closed. Maryland Avenue is the great approach to the Capitol of the United States from the north and east. Nothing should block the sense of openness and directness of this approach. It is not enough to see the Dome. The steps of the Capitol should continue to be visible.[78]

The additional land was not purchased, and the design moved forward on the original parcel. The CFA quickly approved Cass Gilbert's design for the new Supreme Court building in 1929 and successfully defended it the next year when the NCPPC claimed that its size would not be in harmony with the Capitol and the library.[79]

FEDERAL TRIANGLE

In realizing the vision of the McMillan Plan, no project was more ambitious or required a more sustained effort from Moore than construction of the massive enclave of government buildings known as the Federal Triangle; its successful completion was the capstone to Moore's career.[80] The Federal Triangle was developed on seventy acres extending over a large area south of Pennsylvania Avenue and north of Constitution Avenue between 6th and 15th Streets, NW—a ramshackle neighborhood of commercial and retail establishments including saloons and boarding houses still housed largely in nineteenth-century buildings. Known historically as "Murder Bay" and "Hooker's Division," it had long been notorious for prostitution, public drunkenness, and criminal activity. The *McMillan Report* had envisioned the area functioning as a center for municipal buildings; the report's graphics depicted classical buildings that occupied entire blocks and surrounded large courtyards. Two government buildings had actually been built: the Romanesque Revival Post Office building (Willoughby J. Edbrooke, 1892–99) and the Beaux-Arts District Building (Cope & Stewardson, 1904–08). By the 1920s, many of the existing private buildings lining the

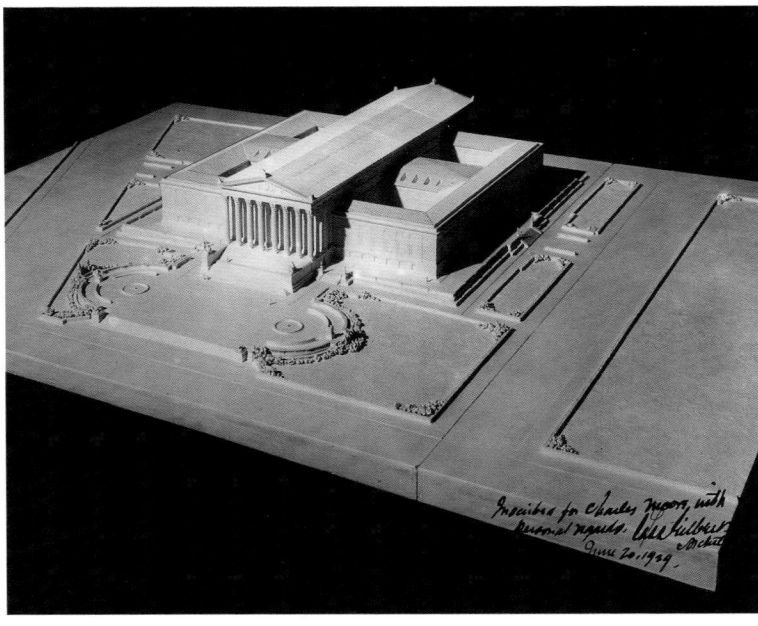

TOP: *View of the Supreme Court as built with Maryland Avenue intact, c. 1939, showing its relationship to the Library of Congress.*

ABOVE LEFT: *Model of the proposed Supreme Court building by Cass Gilbert, c. 1929, showing the diagonal of Maryland Avenue on the site.*

ABOVE RIGHT: *The massive Corinthian columns of the Supreme Court's east portico support a pediment with sculpture by Robert Aitken representing "Equal Justice under Law"; its central figure of Liberty is flanked by allegorical and historical figures, including portraits of Cass Gilbert, William Howard Taft, and Aitken himself. The flanking seated figures, both by James Earle Fraser, are* The Contemplation of Justice *on the left and* The Authority of Law *on the right.*

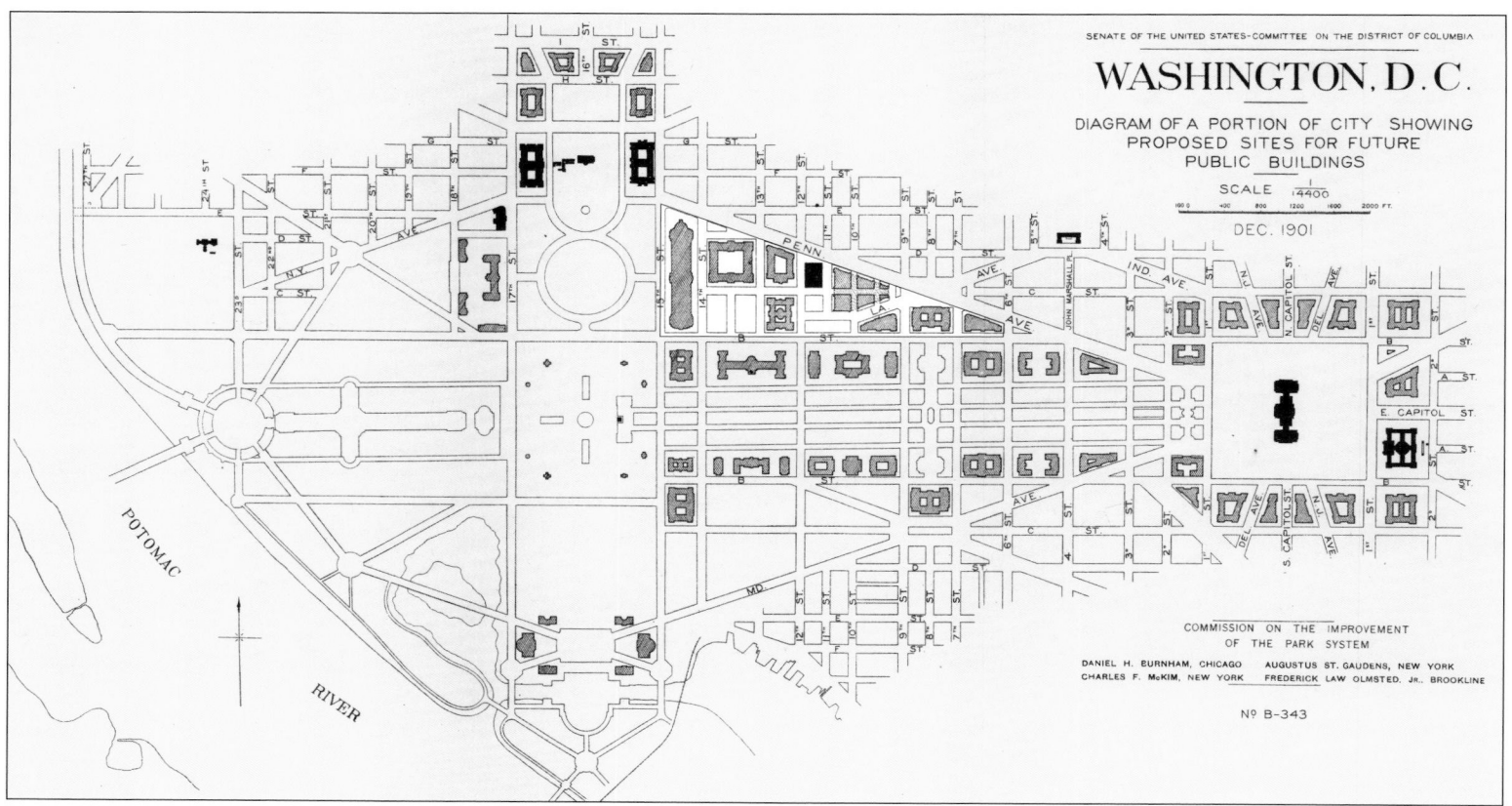

ABOVE: *The plan for the Federal Triangle presented in the McMillan Report envisioned typical Beaux-Arts blocks with central and end pavilions and enclosed courtyards situated within ample grounds.*

LEFT: *Aerial view of the Mall and the future site of the Federal Triangle in the upper right, c. 1925. Before construction of the Federal Triangle, the Old Post Office dominated its neighborhood of small-scale commercial and residential structures.*

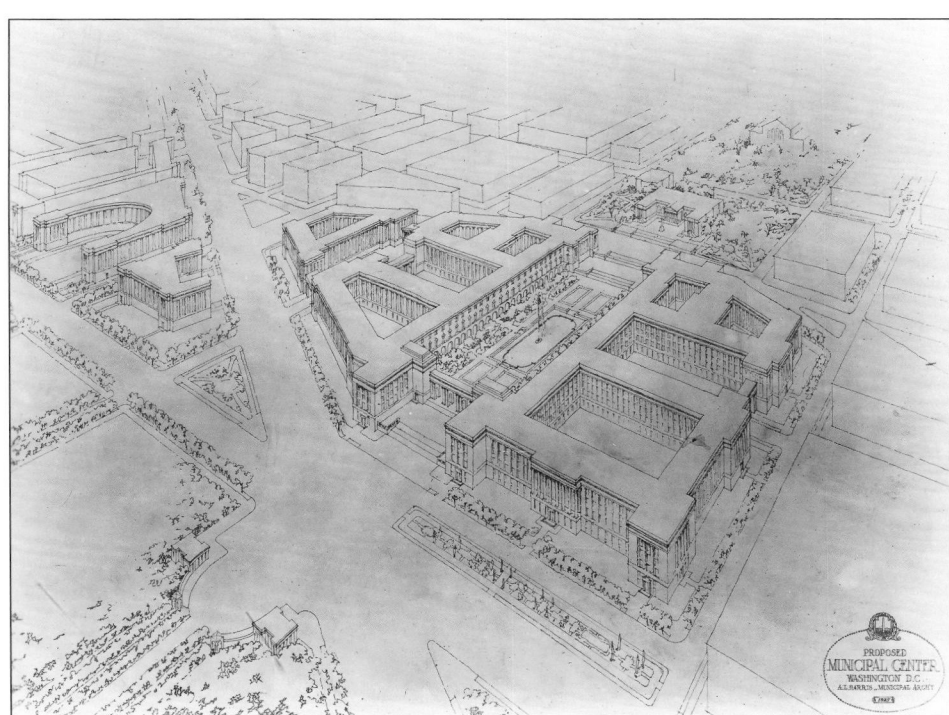

ABOVE LEFT: *The Board of Architectural Consultants, 1927. Front row, left to right: Edward Bennett, Milton B. Medary, Assistant Secretary of the Treasury Charles S. Dewey, and Louis Ayres. Back row, left to right: Louis A. Simon, Office of the Supervising Architect of the Treasury; William A. Delano; and Arthur Brown Jr.*

ABOVE RIGHT: *Concurrent with plans for the Federal Triangle, the District of Columbia developed schemes for an imposing municipal center that would extend north from the Mall along the axis of 4th Street, NW, perpendicular to the apex of the proposed Triangle complex. This early 1927 plan by municipal architect A. L. Harris was later replaced by a design by his successor, Nathan Wyeth.*

south side of Pennsylvania Avenue had deteriorated, and the impetus to create the Federal Triangle resulted partly from a desire to give the thoroughfare a dignity it had not yet known.

Even before plans for the Federal Triangle were set in motion, the Commission of Fine Arts had tried to secure a direct role in initiating a public buildings program, going so far as to propose to the Public Buildings Commission (PBC)—the agency established by Congress in 1916 to assess and recommend ways to house the burgeoning federal workforce in federally owned office buildings within the city—that the CFA might develop the plan itself. The CFA was unhappy about the lack of design qualifications among the men appointed to the Public Buildings Commission; most were chairmen or members of the Senate and House Committees on Appropriations and Public Buildings and Grounds. Moore had the CFA prepare its own report on the design of future public buildings, which the PBC published in 1918 without comment or approval as part of their official document. Moore sent copies of the CFA report to congressmen, asking them to support the CFA proposal.[81]

In its report, the CFA identified historic and contemporary models for departmental buildings—including the Department of the Treasury and the Senate and House Office Buildings—and for buildings facing the Mall, such as the National Museum and the Freer Gallery; it defined the appropriate number of stories for both and emphasized the importance of good proportions. The CFA report

explained that public buildings should "try to express adequately the simplicity, dignity, and power of this Government." It defended the use of classicism as a style best suited to convey "permanency, dignity, and grandeur," to allow variety, and to express the "various degrees of subordination" necessary to harmonize groups of buildings.[82]

The First World War put a temporary stop to federal building activity, but interest was renewed with the passage of the Public Buildings Act, signed by President Calvin Coolidge in May 1926, which authorized $50 million for construction of the new Supreme Court building and the Federal Triangle. While responsibility for the design and construction of the Federal Triangle was placed under Secretary of the Treasury Andrew W. Mellon, and the Public Buildings Commission was given authority over the selection, cost, and location of buildings, the legislation stipulated that the advice of the CFA had to be sought in these decisions.[83] Moore would call upon all his political skills and broad network of associations to make certain the planning and design of the Federal Triangle was carried out under the guidance of the CFA.[84]

Moore had advised Coolidge in August 1923 that money for the Triangle complex should be disbursed gradually, rather than all at once. In a joint meeting between the PBC and the CFA, in May 1926, commission member Milton Medary advocated comprehensive planning for the Triangle and early purchase of all the land, advice supported by the commission as a whole. The PBC and the CFA jointly allocated sites for individual buildings; the CFA was influ-

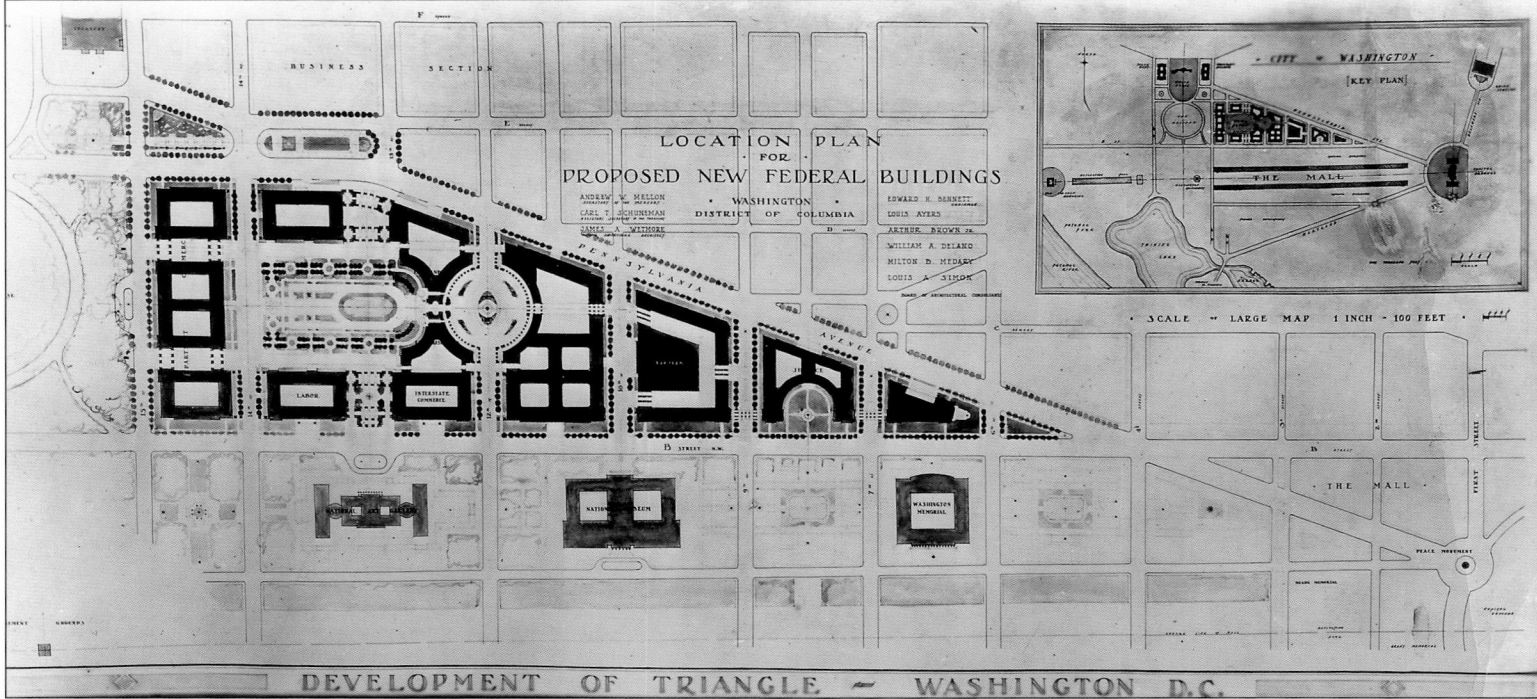

LOCATION PLAN
FOR
PROPOSED NEW FEDERAL BUILDINGS

DEVELOPMENT OF TRIANGLE — WASHINGTON D.C.

ential in protecting the Mall's open space by urging that construction should be concentrated in the Triangle and that those buildings facing the Mall should provide public amenities, such as museums, not merely office space.[85]

Architect Edward Bennett, a former assistant to Daniel Burnham on city plans for Chicago and San Francisco, was appointed architectural advisor for the Federal Triangle project. Bennett's initial plan was presented in the fall of 1926 at a PBC meeting attended by Moore. To his dismay, Moore found the Bennett plan poorly integrated, its buildings unrelated; he reported his disappointment to the commission. The CFA convened its February meeting, attended by many former members, in New York, where members agreed on "the importance of having a well-designed plan for the entire Triangle."[86] Moore sent the CFA's detailed comments on this plan to Andrew Mellon in April 1927, and they were published in the *Washington Star*.

Based in part on the Louvre and other royal complexes in Paris, the CFA plan envisioned a unified architectural treatment of related buildings in a tightly composed ensemble; the plan proposed to create larger building parcels and to close east-west streets through the Triangle while leaving some north-south routes open. Buildings would present street elevations related by colonnades and linked through arcaded passageways leading to large landscaped courtyards.[87] The Post Office building, barely thirty years old but in the now unfashionable Romanesque Revival style, was slated for demolition.

As a result of a meeting between representatives of the

CFA, the NCPPC, and the Treasury Department, and with Mellon's approval, a Board of Architectural Consultants (BAC) was appointed by Mellon to develop design guidelines for the Federal Triangle project and began meeting in May 1927. The members included two architects then serving on the CFA, Medary and William A. Delano, as well as one future member, Charles L. Borie Jr. (CFA 1936–40). Medary and Borie were partners in the Philadelphia firm of Zantzinger, Borie & Medary; Medary would later be replaced on the BAC by Clarence Zantzinger. Other members included Bennett, who was chairman and the landscape architect for the project; Arthur Brown Jr., a noted Beaux-Arts practitioner in San Francisco; Louis Simon of the Treasury's Office of the Supervising Architect; and Delano's business partner, Chester D. Aldrich. One former CFA member, John Russell Pope, was invited to join but did not respond.[88]

The BAC's guidelines for the complex included the key decision to have all the buildings present a common cornice line based on the cornice of the Smithsonian Institution's National Museum (Hornblower & Marshall, 1901–11), on the north side of the Mall between 9th and 12th Streets, NW. And each member was given responsibility for designing one Federal Triangle building: the Internal Revenue Service building (1928–35) by Louis A. Simon; the Justice Department building (1931–34) by Zantzinger, Borie & Medary; the Post Office building (1934) by Delano & Aldrich; the U.S. Customs Service, Departmental Auditorium, and Interstate Commerce Commission

The Board of Architectural Consultants' plan for the Federal Triangle, 1927. The plan proposed to eliminate several existing streets—the diagonal Louisiana and Ohio Avenues, the east-west C and D Streets, and the north-south 13th Street—to create a sequence of public spaces and monumental buildings.

Drawing showing aerial view of the proposed new federal buildings, Board of Architectural Consultants, c. 1927. The Commission of Fine Arts was dissatisfied with the Triangle plan because of what it saw as poor coordination among the buildings.

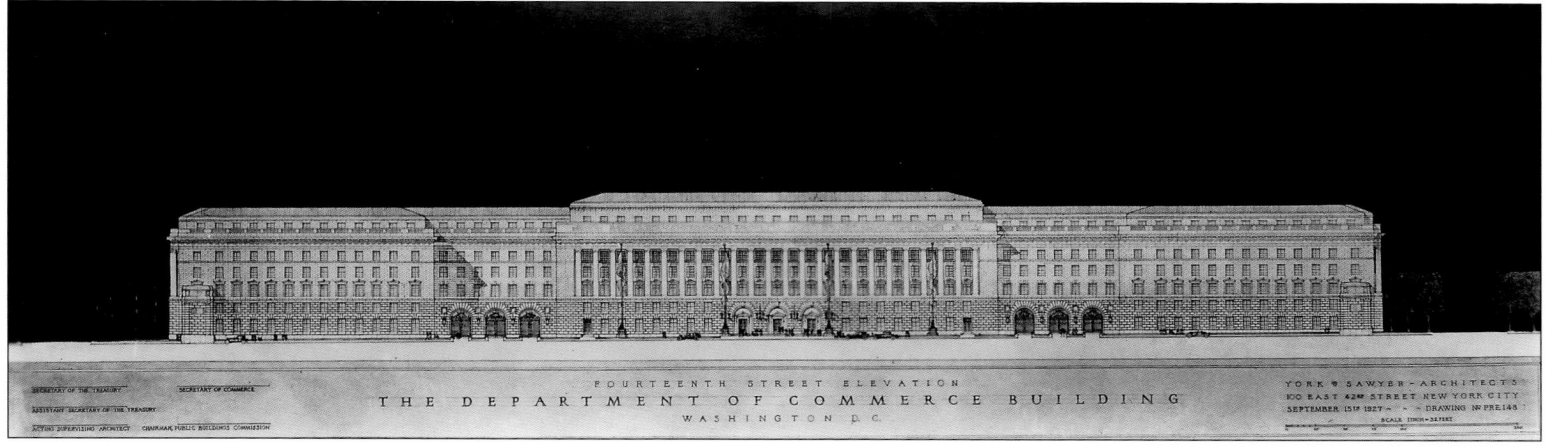

ABOVE: *The first structure designed for the Federal Triangle, the Commerce Department building by Louis Ayres of York & Sawyer, was modeled after the Louvre. Individual buildings were united as a single elevation with consistent cornice heights and bases, their separation denoted by arcaded courtyard entrances. Rendering of the 14th Street elevation, 1927.*

LEFT: *Department of Commerce, completed in 1932. Its design established several standards for the Federal Triangle complex, including a common ninety-foot-high cornice line.*

BELOW LEFT: *James Earle Fraser,* Foreign and Domestic Commerce, *shown before installation, 1934. The sculpture occupies the pediment at the north end of the Commerce Department's 15th Street facade and depicts workmen loading and unloading cotton from a ship on either side of a central figure recording the shipments. Fraser had served with Ayres on the Commission of Fine Arts.*

(1935) by Arthur Brown; and the Federal Trade Commission building (1938) by Bennett, Parsons & Frost.

As the BAC developed its guidelines and resulting plan over the remainder of 1927 and 1928, Charles Moore was kept closely informed of its progress by his commission colleagues on the board. The commission did not see the model of the BAC proposal, prepared by late 1928, until April 1929, when it was presented to senators, congressmen, architects, and other important figures at an evening reception hosted by Mellon at the Chamber of Commerce, launching a two-day conference meant to enlist support for the Federal Triangle project.[89]

The commission, however, was growing uneasy about the direction of the BAC's work, finding that, like Bennett's 1926 Public Buildings Commission plan, it lacked sufficient coherence among the individual buildings. Moore's doubts about Bennett's competence began to grow.[90] The commission suggested that Pope—because of his stature within the profession and his knowledge of Washington—be appointed to the board to bring unity and "freshness" to the plan.[91] This time, Pope accepted.

While over the next five years the Commission of Fine

ABOVE: *Delano & Aldrich's design for the hemicycle and the Great Plaza on the east and west sides of the new Post Office building (c. 1932) proposed two grand public spaces that would allow views through the buildings, linking the open spaces. Because the Old Post Office was never razed, only the west half of the east plaza was completed.*

BELOW: *Drawing of Great Plaza hemicycle, William A. Delano, 1927. Delano & Aldrich, inspired by the Place Vendôme in Paris, envisioned the dramatic curving facade of the new Post Office as framing the central public space of the Federal Triangle complex.*

Arts directed and modified the Triangle's design through its reviews and influence, it also caused delays.[92] The board continued to have difficulty producing a unified urban design under Bennett's guidance, and the commission opposed many of Bennett's ideas for common features such as landscapes, pylons, and kiosks. Moore exerted pressure on the board and on Secretary Mellon, who typically sided with the commission in disputes with the board over design decisions.

Through Moore's intercession with Mellon, the CFA succeeded in having built William Delano's understated design for the west facade of the Great Plaza—a huge open courtyard between the Commerce Department and the Post Office buildings—instead of the grander scheme prepared by Arthur Brown and preferred by Bennett. When the board proposed locating the Oscar S. Straus Memorial Fountain in the wooded area south of the Treasury Department building, across from the 15th Street facade of the Commerce Department, the CFA obtained the backing of Mellon and President Herbert Hoover to have it moved to the center of the 14th Street boundary of the Great Plaza, facing the Commerce building's opposite

TOP LEFT: *The Department of Justice by Zantzinger, Borie & Medary (1934) reworked the common vocabulary of the Federal Triangle as a thin planar articulation augmented by stylized details and ornamentation.*

TOP RIGHT: *Among the problems the CFA identified with the Board of Architectural Consultants' plan for the Triangle was the conception of the National Archives as a large, ungainly structure occupying a courtyard and facing a side street, as seen in this plaster model representing the design by Louis A. Simon, Office of the Supervising Architect of the Treasury (1929).*

ABOVE LEFT: *John Russell Pope, rendering of a proposed National Archives building, 1931. Pope insisted that the Archives should stand free of the Triangle's overall configuration.*

ABOVE RIGHT: *Bennett, Parsons & Frost's Apex Building (1938), built to house the Federal Trade Commission, terminates the Federal Triangle on the east where Pennsylvania and Constitution Avenues converge. In this view, construction is under way on Pope's National Gallery of Art; on the left is Pope's National Archives building.*

FACING PAGE: *Aerial photograph of the Federal Triangle, c. 1939. Although later criticized as ponderous and sterile, the Federal Triangle exhibits the urban cohesion and order sought by the CFA.*

side. The commission also wrested control of the Great Plaza landscape from Bennett by bringing to the attention of the NCPPC the shortcomings of its drives and street connections.[93]

Through Charles Moore's influence, John Russell Pope also received a Federal Triangle commission: the massive National Archives building. The Board of Architectural Consultants had placed it on a difficult site, an awkward interior parcel between 9th and 10th Streets. Pope preferred the block further east, between 7th and 9th Streets on the critical 8th Street alignment, halfway between the Capitol and the White House and emphasized in the L'Enfant and McMillan Plans as a major cross-axis to the Mall.

Pope submitted schemes for both sites to the CFA in July 1931. For the 8th Street site, Pope designed a rectangular block in a severe Roman classicism, similar to the style favored by his mentor, Charles McKim. Unlike the rest of the Triangle buildings, it was set back from the alignment of Pennsylvania Avenue, distinguishing the National Archives from the other buildings in the complex as befitting the importance of the site. The CFA approved both the 8th Street location and the austere classical design; the building was completed in 1935.[94]

Ultimately, Pope's plans for the National Archives were conceptually linked with those for the last remaining site within the Federal Triangle, the Federal Trade Commission building, known informally as the "Apex Building" for its location at the acutely angled eastern end of the entire complex.[95] Its spare classical design was prepared by Bennett, Parsons & Frost and was later revised by Louis Simon. Pope believed the Apex Building was necessary to frame the Archives and provide visual balance for the Justice Department building, which faced the Archives on its west side. He also thought the building was essential to connect the Federal Triangle group with the Municipal Center—a related complex of District of Columbia court and government buildings—proposed along Constitution Avenue further east at Judiciary Square along the spine of 4½ Street, NW.[96]

Moore would have to employ his powers of persuasion and considerable influence with the highest levels of power to defend the Apex Building. President Franklin D. Roosevelt—who had cultivated a strong personal interest in architecture—became interested in the design of the Federal Triangle project and expressed concern that the Apex Building would conflict with the Archives and make it appear unattractive.[97] In a December 1933 meeting with Roosevelt and Secretary of the Interior Harold Ickes, Moore responded that "Mr. Pope said if the Apex Building is not built there it will cause the Archives Building to look like a stub-end and will throw it over toward the Municipal Center group." He followed up with a letter to the president recommending "that the Apex building be built now in accordance, substantially, with the plans already made."[98] The president accepted this advice, and the Apex Building was constructed largely as intended.

The seven-building complex of federal office space was built over the period of a single decade, creating a distinctive precinct of closely related Beaux-Arts architecture. In March 1937, Charles Moore declared that "the most extensive public buildings operation ever undertaken by a government has been completed." But several factors— delays caused by the commission's numerous objections to Bennett's designs for smaller elements, a straitened economic climate, and the changing political priorities of the 1930s—prevented some major features from being built. These included completion of the great hemicycle on 12th Street facing the Great Plaza. Brick-clad building stubs where expansion was planned were left unfinished for fifty years. The factors that prevented completion of these elements unintentionally spared from demolition the 1890s Old Post Office, a relic of Washington's pre-Burnham days; several decades later, it would become the focus of the emergent historic preservation and adaptive-use movements.[99]

EXECUTIVE ENCLAVE AT LAFAYETTE SQUARE

In the McMillan Plan, the area immediately north of the White House around Lafayette Square was proposed to be an enclave of Beaux-Arts office buildings supporting the functions of the executive branch of government. Charles Moore had long championed this idea and extending it for a few blocks west along Pennsylvania Avenue up to 19th Street as a device to further unify the architectural frame of Washington's monumental core, as the complement to the Federal Triangle, and as a catalyst to redevelop Pennsylvania Avenue "as the great thoroughfare of the Nation."[100]

Moore's early efforts to achieve this classical ensemble of executive buildings adjacent to the White House included several schemes that were not realized. In 1910, at the request of Secretary of State Philander C. Knox, Congress had authorized an invited competition for a new State Department building, with the site designated as the northeast corner of the Washington Monument Grounds; the winner was Arnold Brunner of New York City.[101] The proposal was never built, but Moore believed Brunner's project—a massive classical structure with a central portico, similar to the Treasury building—would be suitable for the west side of Lafayette Square. Brunner prepared render-

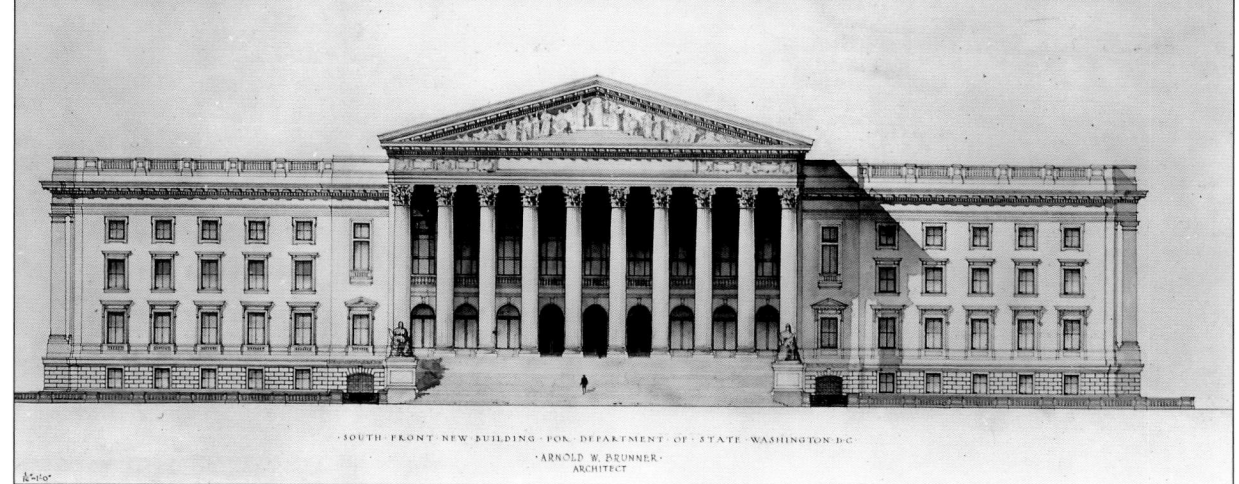

TOP: *Arnold Brunner and Charles Moore exchanged letters in April 1923 regarding Brunner's scheme for a new State Department building fronting Lafayette Square; in photographs sent to Moore, Brunner included comparison studies of the Chamber of Deputies in Paris, the Capitol, and the Treasury building. If built, the entire block west of the square would have been razed—including the historic Decatur and Blair Houses and the Renwick Gallery, used at the time as the U.S. Court of Claims.*

CENTER: *John Russell Pope's sketch (1917) illustrated a State, War and Navy Building adjacent to the White House remodeled in the Ionic order. The chimneys and mansards of the original tracing are visible at the roof line.*

BOTTOM: *Waddy Wood's reinterpretation of the State, War, and Navy Building (1930) into classical form offered a more restrained approach than John Russell Pope's earlier concept with a plain facade and punched windows.*

ings showing a similar massive structure occupying the entire block, and in 1923 Moore recommended this design to Colonel Sherrill, the commission's former secretary who was still serving as chief of the Office of Public Buildings and Grounds. Again, nothing came of this project.

Earlier, in 1917, Moore had tried to have the Second Empire–style State, War and Navy Building, located immediately west of the White House, reclad in classical dress.[102] At the time, the young Franklin Delano Roosevelt was assistant secretary of the navy, whose offices were located in that building. With his conservative architectural taste, Roosevelt loathed the building's Victorian excess, and he conferred with Moore about its possible remodeling. Moore in turn discussed this with John Russell Pope, who quickly sent him a small sketch depicting the structure with its mansard roof, pavilions, and hundreds of small columns removed, replaced with an Ionic portico and flat walls embellished with Doric pilasters to resemble

Art in Architecture

ABOVE: *As the genial and highly respected chief of the Section of Painting and Sculpture, Edward Bruce, pictured here c. 1930, secured artwork for federal buildings throughout the country.*

FACING PAGE. TOP: *George Biddle's* Society Freed Through Justice *(1936) is installed on the fifth floor stairwell of the Justice Department building.* BOTTOM LEFT: *Michael Lantz,* Man Controlling Trade, *Federal Trade Commission (Apex) building, Constitution Avenue pair, 1937–42.* BOTTOM RIGHT: *Maurice Sterne's murals for the Justice Department are more heavily allegorical than Biddle's, even employing Christian symbolism as in this painting representing* Greed *(1941).*

It was a hallmark of Beaux-Arts practice to thoroughly integrate landscape, sculpture, and ornamentation such as murals with the architecture. The CFA perpetuated this practice through its own organization—which included architects, landscape architects, painters, and sculptors—and in its review process, which considered every aspect of a building's decorative and functional program. But from the 1930s onward, the process began to change and the projects submitted to the CFA for review increasingly comprised plain boxes to which works of art were applied.

The commission remained closely involved in overseeing the ornamentation of federal buildings with sculpture and paintings during the Great Depression. In these years, two painters who later became commission members played pivotal roles in promoting and managing a federal art program that was seminal in procuring art installations for public buildings. George Biddle (CFA 1950–55), of an old Philadelphia family, followed Franklin D. Roosevelt at both Groton and Harvard, traveled widely, studied with Diego Rivera, and enjoyed a successful career as a muralist. In 1933 he wrote to Roosevelt, recommending that the president establish a national school of modern mural art: "Mural art can never be important unless it is interpreting a great social and collective idea." Biddle attached a statement requesting that selected artists be given federal wall space, specifically to create murals at the Department of Justice.[1] Roosevelt put the idea into action, charging the Department of the Treasury with administering the program.

Placed in the hands of painter and staff lawyer Edward Bruce (CFA 1940–43), the program began as the Public Works of Art Project under the Civil Works Administration, hiring unemployed artists in the winter of 1933–34 to create art for public buildings; some of the Public Works of Art projects continued under the Federal Emergency Relief Administration. Then, in the fall of 1934, the Section of Painting and Sculpture was created in the Treasury Department and headed by Bruce.[2]

The Section of Painting and Sculpture, often called "the Section," commissioned art for federal buildings with the goal of "decorat[ing] new federal buildings with work of the highest quality."[3] Most commissions were awarded through blind juried competitions and winners were often chosen from among hundreds of entries. Section projects included, most famously, the post office murals installed in towns and cities throughout the United States, and also the extensive decorative program embellishing the buildings of the Federal Triangle.

Often, the work produced under the patronage of the Section celebrated the benefits conveyed to the lives of ordinary citizens through American democracy. The use of art throughout federal buildings was not only intended to add color and interest to the daily lives of government employees; it was also a means of recalling the visual richness of historical architecture without resorting to historicist styles. Examples include the murals by commission members Henry Varnum Poor (CFA 1941–45), Maurice Sterne (CFA 1945–50), and George Biddle in the Department of Jus-

tice, and the extensive lobby mural by Kindred McLeary in the original War Department building.

The Section of Painting and Sculpture existed until 1943; the only architectural sculpture for the Federal Triangle to be executed wholly under the program was *Man Controlling Trade* by sculptor Michael Lantz, consisting of two similar groups placed near the hemicycle end of the Apex Building, one on Pennsylvania Avenue (1938–41) and the other on Constitution Avenue (1938–42). Made through a widely publicized competition, Lantz's selection reflected fulfillment of Edward Bruce's hope that the Section would support unknown and unemployed artists. The massive limestone figures of a man (representing regulation) restraining a horse (representing trade) have a Beaux-Arts pedigree but are rendered in simplified, exaggerated forms reflecting Social Realist tendencies in sculpture.[4] The action of the groups reflects the architectural thrust and then restraint of the wedge-shaped building itself.[5] *Man Controlling Trade* was the last sculpture completed for the Federal Triangle before America's entry into World War II curtailed funding for such projects. Two other important public sculptures associated with the Federal Triangle and the subjects of CFA's discussions—the Straus and Mellon Memorial Fountains—were completed after the war in 1947 and 1951, respectively.

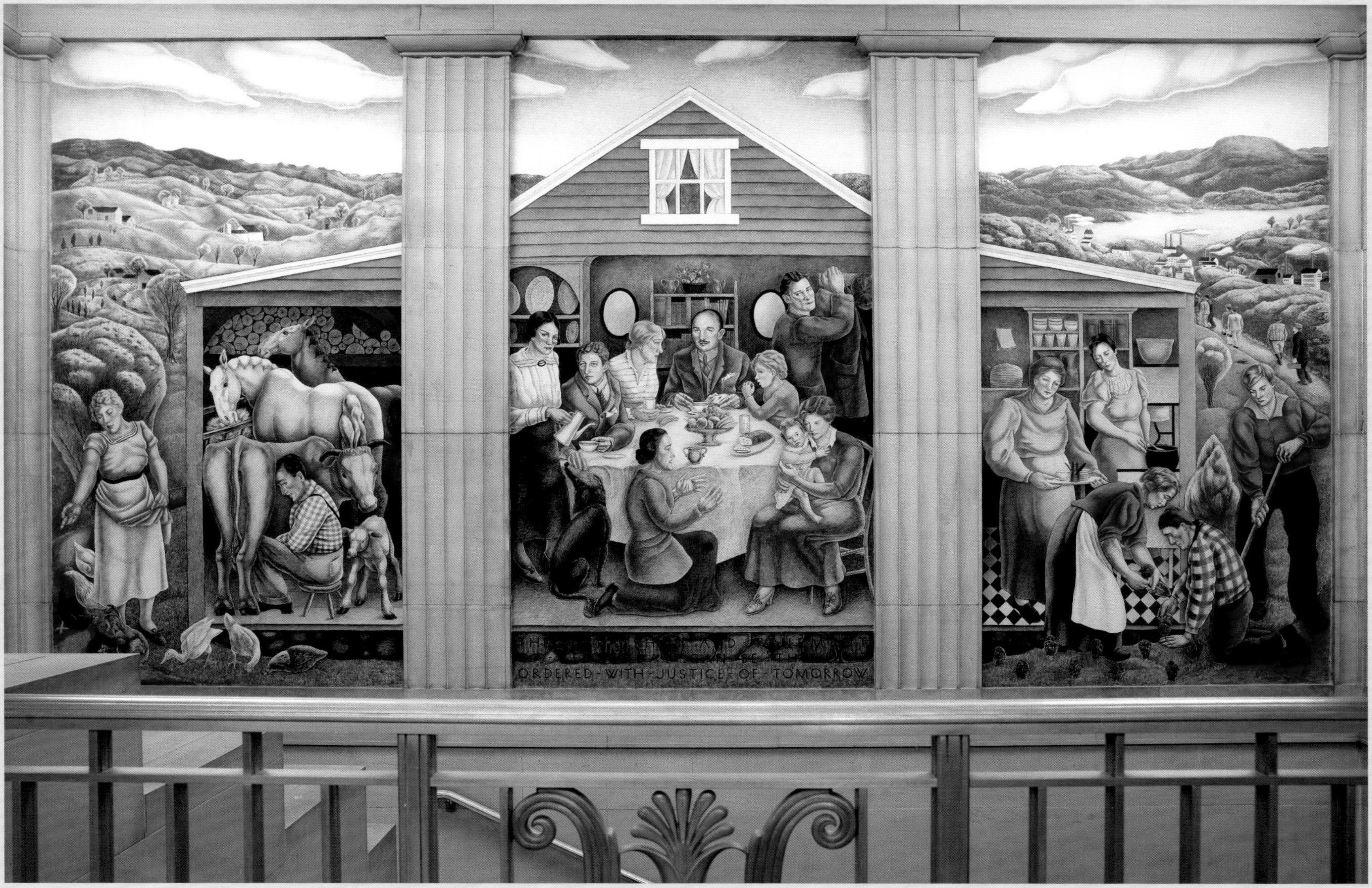
ORDERED-WITH-JUSTICE-OF-TOMORROW

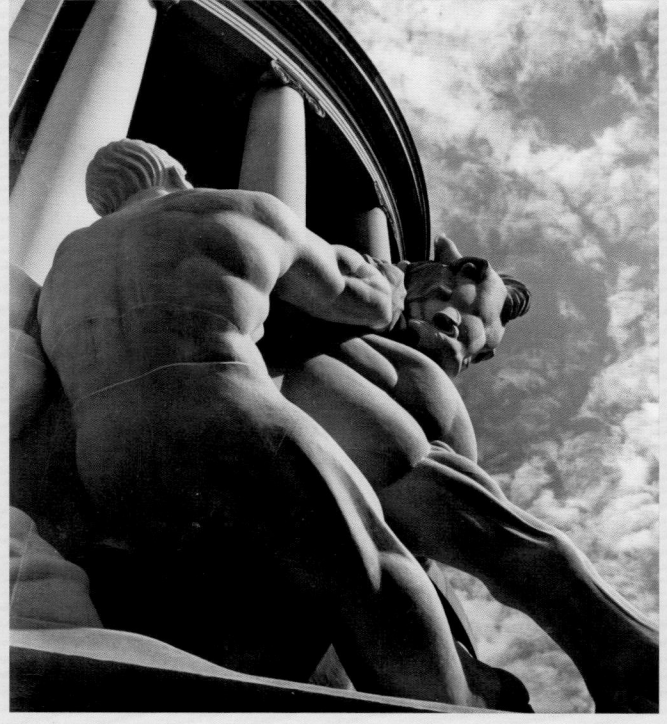

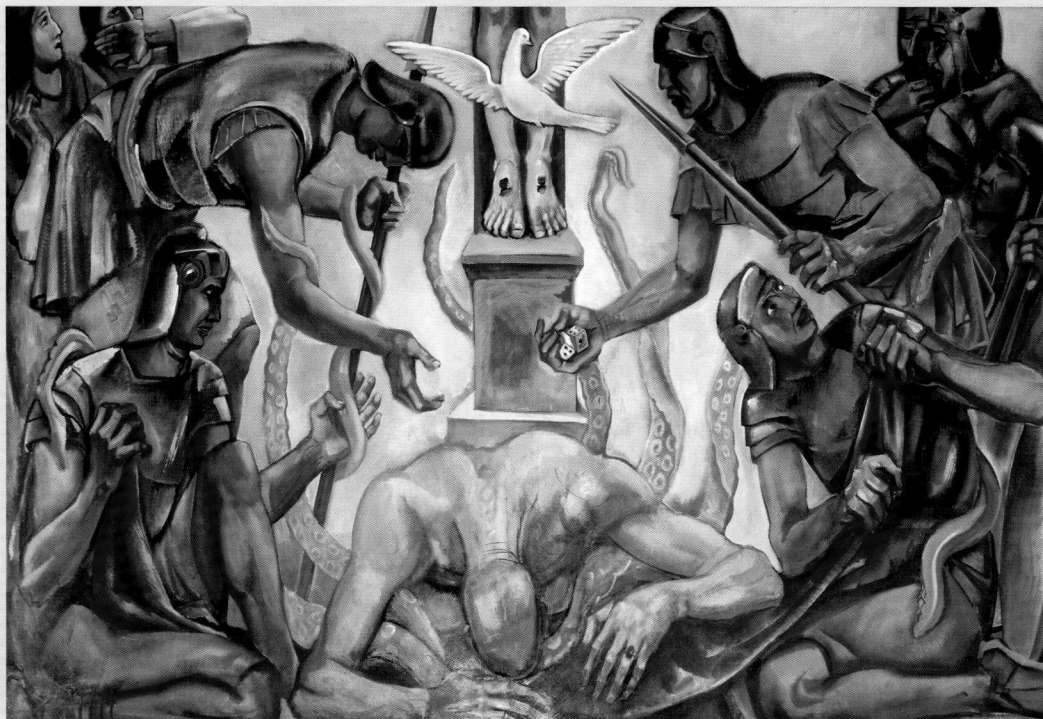

the Treasury Building. However, because of the First World War in Europe, there were no funds available for this extensive exterior remodeling. Instead, the Navy and War Departments' pressing need for additional office space was addressed through the construction of massive temporary structures on the Mall, which, ironically, would long outlast the war. The impetus to forge an image of unified classicism within the White House precinct surfaced again ten years later with another proposal for the State, War, and Navy Building by Washington architect Waddy Wood, sponsored by the Department of the Treasury and funded in 1930 by Congress. Like Pope, Wood envisioned a drastic remodeling of the old building according to classical principles; the CFA reviewed the project several times in late 1930, offering suggestions to improve the design, and approved it in January 1931. This version also remained unrealized; Congress eventually rescinded funds for the project as its projected costs grew and economic conditions worsened.[103]

The first concrete step towards implementing Moore's concept of an executive enclave at Lafayette Square was taken in 1917 with the construction of Cass Gilbert's Beaux-Arts Treasury Annex, built on the east side of the square; Gilbert also developed a plan for other buildings around the square in keeping with the McMillan Plan's vision for the area. The CFA assumed that the annex would in due time be extended north to H Street and that Gilbert's scheme for the rest of the square would be achieved.

As Moore actively pursued this vision, he tried to enlist presidential support in the crusade. In a November 1930 report to President Herbert Hoover, Moore claimed the development proposal would maintain the White House as the center of executive buildings and would promote the

As with the Federal Triangle, the McMillan Report discussed Lafayette Square in general terms and illustrated it within broad views of the monumental core. Cass Gilbert's plan (1917) shows the full conception of classical buildings framing Lafayette Square; only the Treasury Annex and the U.S. Chamber of Commerce were completed.

"uniform development of the city…to neglect this so great and so obvious an opportunity would result in throwing the city out of balance. Then the future would lament and reprobate the shortsightedness of the present."[104]

Later, in December 1933, Moore met with Franklin Roosevelt, newly elected as president, and Secretary of the Interior Harold Ickes to advocate new public buildings on Pennsylvania Avenue. Roosevelt had recently transferred the functions of the Public Buildings Commission to Ickes's department. One of Moore's chief arguments was that Pennsylvania Avenue was a more important location than the Northwest Rectangle, an area of land near West Potomac Park and the proposed site of a new Department of the Interior building; traveling to a departmental building in the Foggy Bottom neighborhood, Moore pointed out, would be like going through a "back yard."[105] Moore had been able to establish the Federal Triangle following the parameters of the McMillan Plan, but he would fail in his attempt to establish a corresponding group on the northwest side of the White House. While his argument relied on the precedence of the McMillan Plan, his notion of extending the enclave along Pennsylvania Avenue was in competition with his and the CFA's concurrent attempts to establish the Northwest Rectangle as a suitable frame for the National Mall. The Mall's potent symbolism as well as the logic of economics would trump the stylistic determinism of the McMillan Plan.

NORTHWEST RECTANGLE

Immediately north of Constitution Avenue along West Potomac Park and west of 17th Street, the Northwest Rectangle formed a defining edge for the Lincoln Memorial and the larger Mall system. As articulated by Charles Moore, the CFA's goal for this area was "to develop a frame for the Memorial itself by the use of low, marble buildings sitting behind a broad garden of trees," with a standard setback and an appropriately dignified design.[106] In this, the CFA was following the precedent of the first monumental building in the area—the Pan American Union (now Organization of American States) building designed by Paul Cret and completed in 1910.

By 1931, the CFA and the NCPPC were examining general planning issues in the Rectangle in order to achieve this goal. Frederick Law Olmsted Jr. was commissioned to develop planning recommendations for the area, and four key principles emerged that would guide its development: treat buildings as a group; emphasize the importance of circulation, including the intersection of Virginia and New York Avenues; treat structures along Constitution Avenue as "buildings in gardens"; and consider the Naval Hospital as background for the Lincoln Memorial.[107] Eventually, five new buildings were erected on Constitution Avenue from west at 23rd Street to east at 18th Street: the American Institute of Pharmacy (John Russell Pope, 1933), the National Academy of Sciences (Bertram Grovesnor Goodhue, 1924), the Federal Reserve Board (Paul Cret, 1937), the Public Health Service (now Interior Department South; Jules de Sibour, 1933), and the Organization of American States Annex (Paul Cret and Albert Kelsey, completed by Harbeson, Hough, Livingston & Larson, 1948). The commission's review of these projects was often extensive, but its main interest was less with design detail than with how each individual building would relate to the memorial as its background.

The official record of the Commission of Fine Arts implies that Bertram Goodhue's unusual and somewhat modern astylar design for the National Academy of Sciences building was readily approved by its Beaux-Arts membership, but a fuller understanding of the commission's decision is conveyed through personal letters and notes of informal meetings. Goodhue's concept for the building was presented in lifeless renderings at the CFA meeting in March 1920.[108] To his disappointment, the commission rejected the proposal; the minutes record that, "After extended discussion, the Commission took the plans under advisement."[109] In an informal meeting with William Mitchell Kendall and Charles Platt and later in correspondence with Charles Moore, it was explained to Goodhue that what the CFA sought for the building was a classic feeling appropriate to Washington, a quality Goodhue's drawings had not conveyed. Goodhue assumed that the members meant application of the classical orders and refused to revise his design beyond relatively minor alterations such as the fenestration pattern. He resubmitted the project in May 1921 but this time presented more dynamic renderings depicting the building from oblique angles within its landscaped setting, which clarified Goodhue's intent and made the proposal acceptable to the CFA, which approved it with little comment from the commission members other than the suggestion to replace a single

Plan for public building sites in the Northwest Rectangle proposed by the National Capital Park and Planning Commission, 1934, following the agency's guidance to locate federal development west of the White House instead of at Lafayette Square. The highly formal, axial plan emphasizes the geometric node in the McMillan Plan at the crossing of New York and Virginia Avenues, creating a prominent public space as the focus of the precinct.

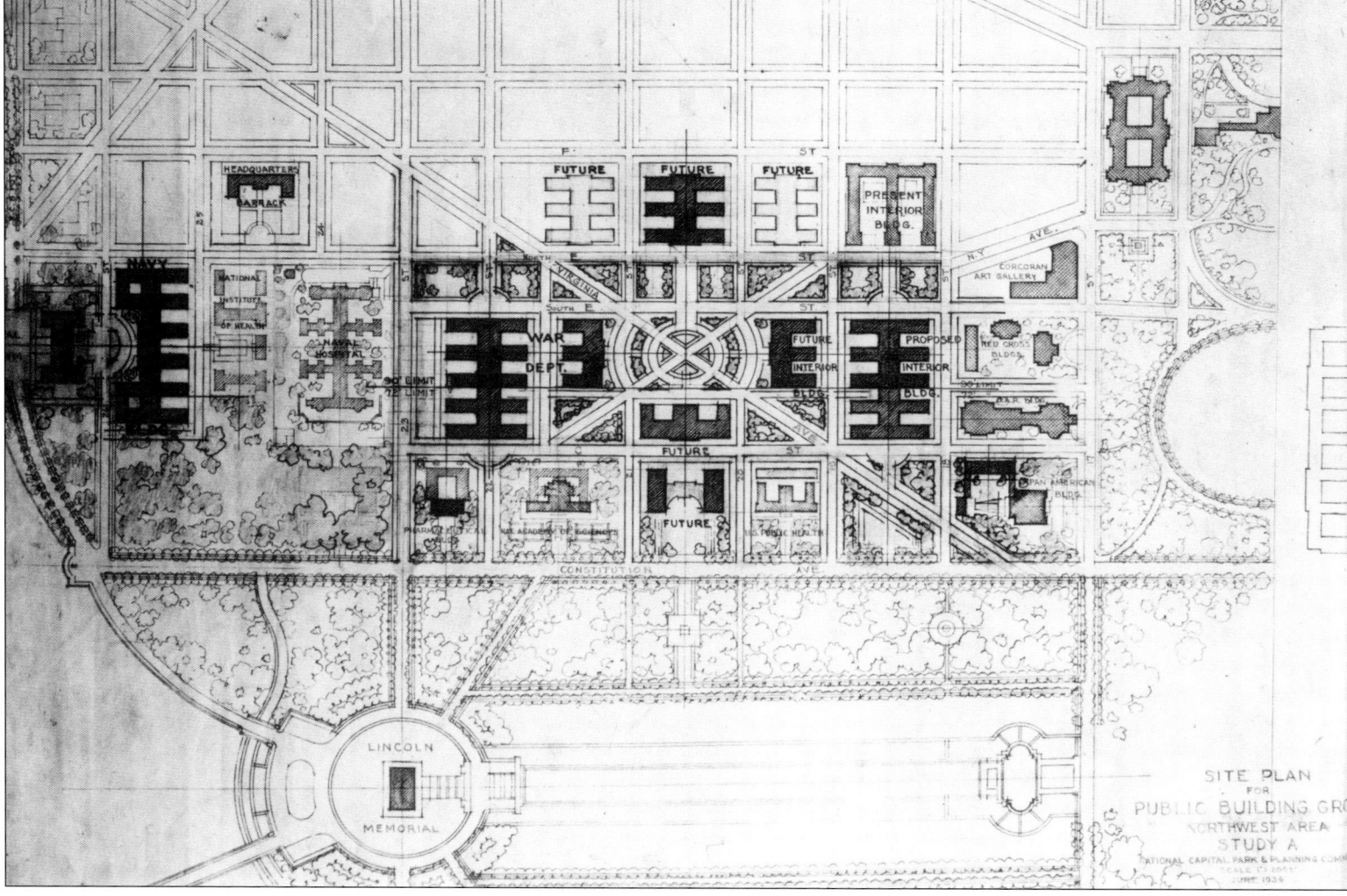

TOP LEFT: *John Russell Pope's design for the American Pharmaceutical Association headquarters (1933)— a taut box articulated by wafer-thin planes—deferred to the sculptural massiveness of the Lincoln Memorial.*

TOP RIGHT: *Bertram Goodhue's building for the National Academy of Sciences (1924) presented a distinct departure from the conservative classicism typical of American Beaux-Arts architecture.*

ABOVE LEFT: *The Public Health Service building (1933) by Jules de Sibour (now called Interior South) also passed CFA review without objection.*

ABOVE RIGHT: *The Commission of Fine Arts welcomed Paul Cret's design for the Federal Reserve Board (1937) with enthusiasm, applauding his powerful and severe adaptation of the classical idiom.*

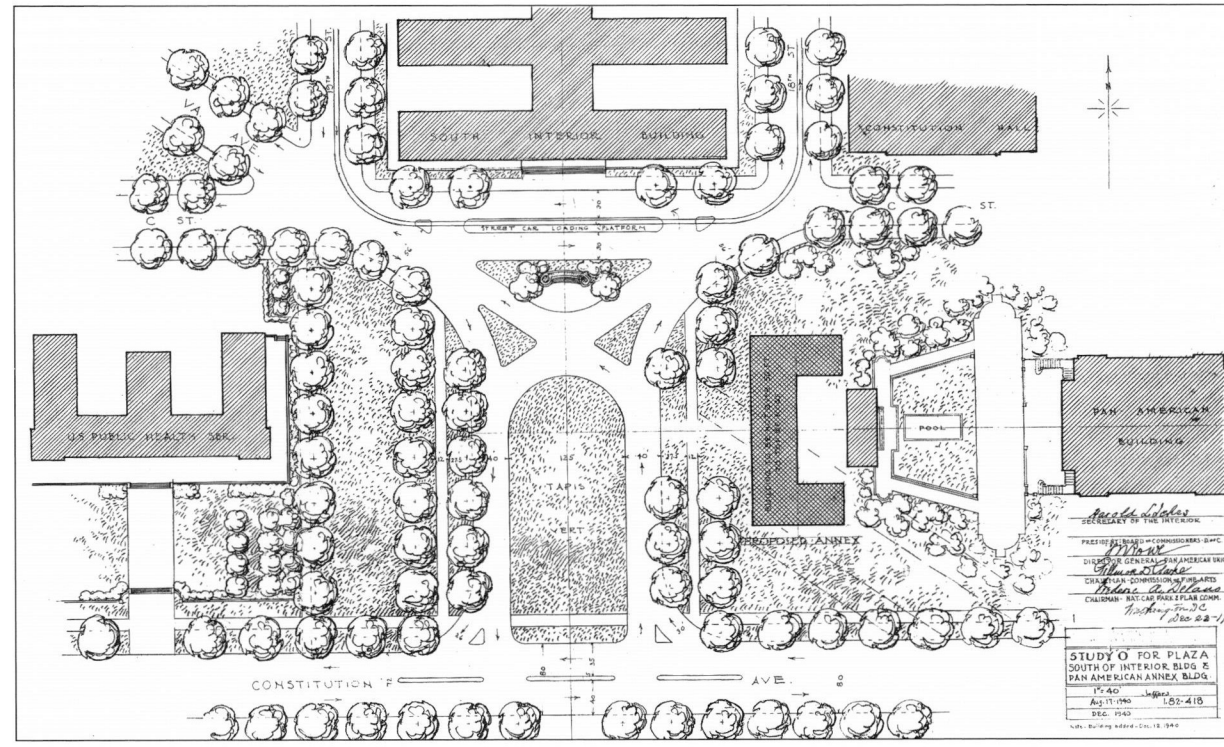

Plan for a public plaza (1940) west of the Pan American Union and south of the new Department of the Interior, illustrating Secretary Ickes's idea of connection to the Mall. The Pan American Annex by Paul Cret with Albert Kelsey to the right of the square—completed by Harbeson, Hough, Livingston & Larson in 1948—was the final structure in the imposing enfilade of buildings lining the north side of Constitution Avenue.

massive eight-story limestone building was set back at its uppermost floor; projecting from the main north-south spine were six pairs of east-west wings whose awkward proportions were treated with a high base and attic to create a nominally classical composition. Completed in 1936, the Department of the Interior building determined planning standards of height and setback for the rest of the Northwest Rectangle and remained a standard form for mid-twentieth-century office buildings until the postwar era, when the widespread use of air conditioning would transform building typology. Other federal office buildings in Washington that would follow the fishbone prototype included a suite of large buildings in the southwest quadrant: the Social Security Administration, Railroad Retirement Board, and Agriculture Department Annex buildings.

Throughout the 1930s, the CFA and NCPPC wrestled with the problem of finding a suitable location for a new structure to house the War and Navy Departments and replace the two immense World War I–era temporary complexes near the Lincoln Memorial. The NCPPC, with the Navy Department, advocated a site in Foggy Bottom at the intersection of Virginia and New York Avenues. In support of his arguments for an executive enclave on the north and south sides of Pennsylvania Avenue west of the White House, Charles Moore promoted locating the building there instead of Foggy Bottom. In 1930, a joint committee of the two commissions made several impor-

tant decisions pertinent to the dilemma: New York Avenue would not follow the McMillan Plan but would, instead, terminate at 20th Street; the American Pharmaceutical Association would be allowed to build its headquarters at Constitution Avenue and 23rd Street; and studies should be prepared for two new, separate buildings, one for the War Department and the other for the Navy, on Pennsylvania Avenue.[118]

Moore and the commission advanced various arguments for placing executive departments along Pennsylvania Avenue, beginning with the new buildings for the War and Navy Departments: the cost of purchasing land with existing improvements would be about 50 percent lower than in Foggy Bottom; there was more available space for development; and Pennsylvania Avenue—which, with proposed new connecting routes, would lead to Mount Vernon via the George Washington Memorial Parkway (1932)—needed to be redeveloped into a more dignified thoroughfare. But the NCPPC, along with the Public Buildings Commission, continued to support locating the departments in Foggy Bottom, where much of the needed land was already owned by the government, and less taxable property would be lost by the city.[119]

Beyond discussing a location at the Naval Observatory, plans for a new Department of the Navy building did not progress; no design was ever brought to the CFA, and eventually operations were moved to the Pentagon after that building was constructed. However, the secretary of war central pool with pools to the left and right sides of the lawn.[110] Despite its elements of a more modern expression, the project also presented the collaborative ideals of the waning American Renaissance, a factor that may have contributed to the commission's approval. (See Carroll William Westfall's essay.) The decorative program of the building was, in fact, undertaken with members of the commission, including sculptor Lee Lawrie (CFA 1933–37, 1945–50) and mosaicist Hildreth Meière, largely the same team that was concurrently developing the integrated program of art and architecture for Goodhue's masterpiece, the Nebraska State Capitol in Lincoln (1924–32).

The headquarters of the American Pharmaceutical Association—adapted by John Russell Pope from an early version of his 1909 design for the Abraham Lincoln Birthplace Memorial in Hodgenville, Kentucky—occupied the key site directly northeast of the Lincoln Memorial. The project was reviewed by the commission under the authority of the Shipstead-Luce Act. Throughout the commission's review, Charles Moore stressed the importance of the site relative to the memorial and to the Arlington Memorial Bridge. But the commission could be flexible; because a dirt road cut across the site, it did not object to setting the building thirty feet further north than the recommended setback.[111]

Of two designs prepared by Jules de Sibour for the Public Health Service building between 19th and 20th Streets, the CFA favored the option for a classical structure of white marble because it would complement the Lincoln Memorial. The building was given a 170-foot setback, the same as the National Academy of Sciences. When a request was made for a front driveway, landscape architect Gilmore Clarke refused: "Such a driveway would interfere with the harmonious landscape treatment of the grounds planned for all the monumental buildings created on Constitution Avenue west of 17th Street."[112]

The Federal Reserve Board building, designed by Paul Cret was a distinct departure from the standard classical federal building and Cret's most extreme statement in Washington of stripped classicism. The building retained Beaux-Arts planning and remnants of classical detailing in its square-pillared central portico and its simplified moldings. In spite of its unusual style, the Federal Reserve Board design passed CFA scrutiny with little comment. Of greatest concern was a proposed curved ceremonial driveway in front of the building; Clarke observed that the Public Health Service building had not been allowed a front driveway and stressed that "the garden treatment for buildings along Constitution Avenue should be uniform."[113] The driveway was replaced with a pair of fountains.

The administrative annex of the Pan American Union building, prepared by Cret and Albert Kelsey was the third building designed by the two architects for this organization.[114] The assigned site was a small, restricted parcel, bounded by 18th Street on the east, 19th Street on the west, Constitution Avenue on the south, and C Street and Virginia Avenue on the north. The commission's protracted discussion about the building focused on its relation to the flanking buildings—the smaller headquarters building to the east, the Public Health Service building to the west, and the new Department of the Interior headquarters to the north. Virginia Avenue also prompted much discussion: the diagonal roadway cut through the parcel on the north and affected its buildable area. Whether to close this section of Virginia Avenue, a L'Enfant Plan boulevard, and how far back to set the building from Constitution Avenue consumed years of negotiation.[115] However, the major obstacle blocking its construction was the desire of President Roosevelt's powerful Secretary of the Interior Harold Ickes to keep an unobstructed view south to the Mall from his massive new departmental headquarters. Ickes hoped to construct a monument to the American Indian in front of the Interior building, an area where the president also wanted to commemorate the liberators of Central and South America.[116]

Shortly after his appointment, Ickes made it his mission to build an enormous new headquarters for the department—which, by the 1930s, was scattered among several different locations, including within the large limestone structure between E, F, 18th, and 19th Streets designed by New York architect Charles Butler with the Office of the Supervising Architect of the Treasury, from 1915 to 1917. Now the headquarters of the General Services Administration, the building set a precedent at the time of its construction as the first modern, utilitarian federal office building. Ickes and Roosevelt wanted a new building to symbolize a heightened government role in resource management, but the structure would follow its predecessor's functional character.[117] Locating the building in the Northwest Rectangle between 18th and 19th Streets at D Street created an important visual axis from the Department of the Interior directly across Virginia Avenue to the green landscape of the National Mall. But the building's most significant contribution was its "fishbone" configuration—wings projected from a central spine forming open courts between and allowing light and air to reach almost all offices—that would become a standard type for large government office buildings in Washington for the next twenty years. Designed by the well-known Washington architect Waddy Wood, the

ABOVE: *Harold Ickes's massive new headquarters for the Department of the Interior by Washington architect Waddy Wood (1935–36) adopted and expanded the modern fishbone configuration within a classical skin.*

LEFT: *The Department of the Interior contains an extensive decorative program of large murals and bas-relief limestone wall panels. Buffalo by Boris Gilbertson (1939) is on a wall in the central corridor.*

settled the question of the new War Department building's location by approving the Northwest Rectangle block between E and F Streets and 19th and 20th Streets. The Commission of Fine Arts and the National Capital Park and Planning Commission agreed on a site for the new building immediately west of the intersection of New York and Virginia Avenues that was predicated on the closing of a portion of New York Avenue. Virginia Avenue would be left open to carry traffic between Southwest Washington and Georgetown.[120]

Funding delays pushed back CFA review of the War Department building's first phase, on the northeast por-

tion of the two-block site, to the latter part of 1938. For this portion of the building, architects Gilbert Stanley Underwood and William D. Foster of the Treasury's Office of the Supervising Architect proposed an austere and boxy design with faintly classical features, such as a severe portico and a thin cornice. The seven-story building was to be faced with rough limestone panels offset by polished pink granite spandrels, with an unornamented portico of four square piers on a two-story base to mark the entrance.[121] A series of reentrant courts would break the extreme length of the stripped classical facades.

The NCPPC recommended making the height of the

RIGHT: *Plaster model showing the proposed development in the Northwest Rectangle, c. 1938. Underwood & Foster, the architects of the War (now State) Department building (top of image), referred to the height and alignment of the Department of the Interior building (bottom of image), three blocks to its east, to govern its composition within the Northwest Rectangle. Cret's Federal Reserve building (at center left) defines the south edge of a new public space.*

BELOW: *First phase design of the War Department by Underwood & Foster, rendered by Maurice W. Kleinman (1939). The design presented a stripped classicism, derived from Beaux-Arts traditions, expressed in a starkly planar and attenuated manner.*

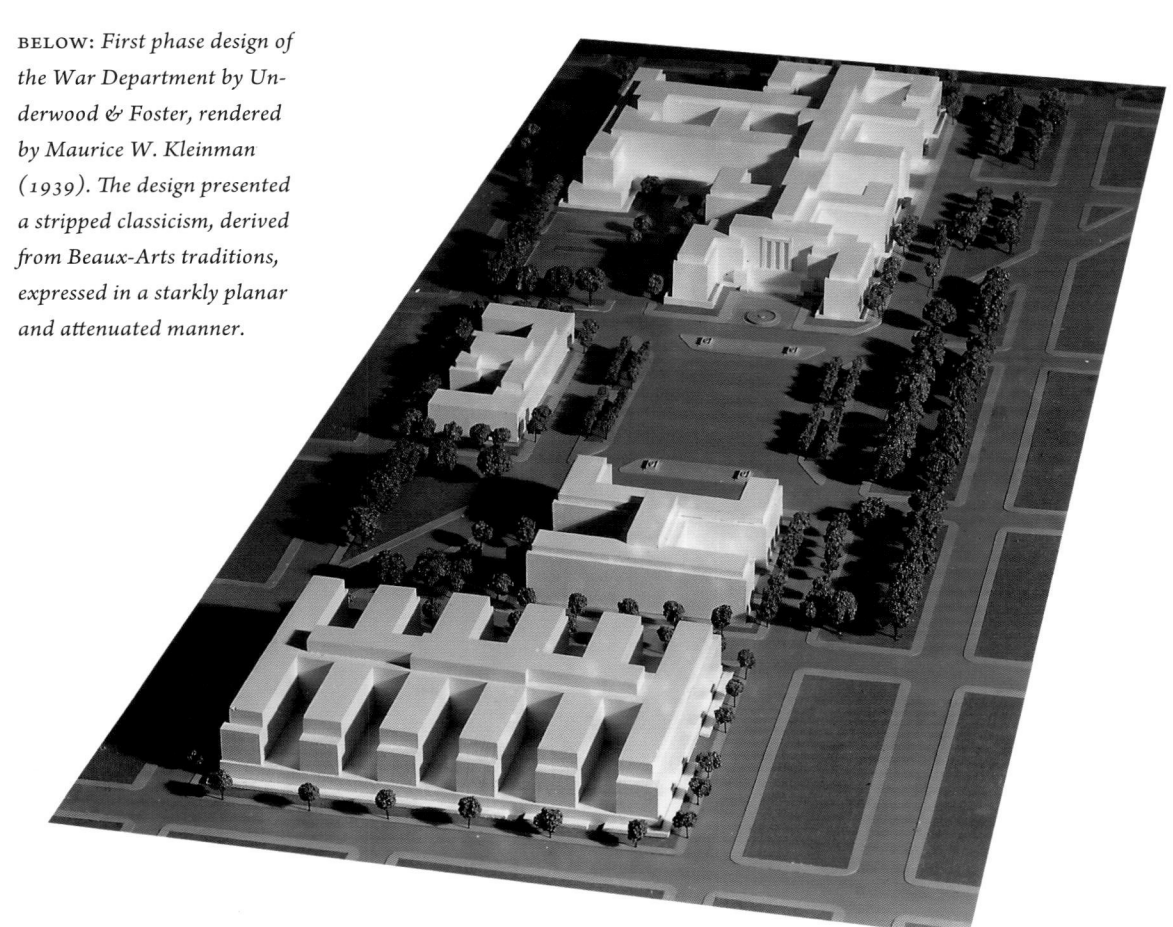

FIRST UNIT WAR DEPARTMENT BUILDING WASHINGTON D.C.
FEDERAL WORKS AGENCY · PUBLIC BUILDINGS ADMIN. · OFFICE OF THE SUPERVISING ARCHITECT · GILBERT STANLEY UNDERWOOD & WM DEWEY FOSTER CONSULTING ARCHITECTS

War Department building equivalent to that of the new Department of the Interior headquarters, three blocks due east.[122] However, the War Department site had a higher elevation, so it was built at seven stories, which, as the CFA noted, were visually equivalent to the eight stories of the Department of the Interior since the distance between the two buildings was great enough to make any difference imperceptible. The CFA agreed with the architects that the entrance block of the first unit should be aligned with a possible future south annex to the Interior building; this placement, somewhat to the north on the War Department's eastern facade, would allow sufficient room adjacent to the plaza in front of the building for a future extension to the Federal Reserve Board building. The elevations along 22nd and 23rd Streets were the same length as the corresponding facades on the Department of the Interior building.

Even before the building's completion in 1941, the War Department had begun to plan a massive new headquarters complex, the Pentagon, across the Potomac River in Virginia, the first major departmental headquarters outside the city of Washington. The Underwood & Foster building would instead become the headquarters for the U.S. Department of State.

Promoting Design Beyond the Monumental Core

During its first three decades, the Commission of Fine Arts extended the McMillan Plan's vision into areas of the city beyond the monumental core. It used its influence to guide the establishment and design of public parks and memorials outside of the Mall precinct, and it was empowered by Congress to review private projects near certain areas of federal interest. Both efforts would profoundly affect the design of the larger capital city.

Most significant of the commission's involvement in the design of new public parks was Meridian Hill Park on 16th Street, one of the first and longest-lived initiatives undertaken by the CFA. At its urging, the federal government purchased land for the park in 1912, and for more than twenty-five years the commission remained intimately involved in every step of the park's formal design, even traveling to Italy, France, and other European countries in 1914 with the park's designers to study garden precedents. Commission members regarded the park as a model of European-inspired public garden design, mostly in the Italian Baroque manner, for the nation's capital.

Meridian Hill Park originated with the redoubtable Mary Foote Henderson, wife of a former senator, who lived in an enormous Romanesque Revival mansion on 16th Street on part of the Florida Avenue escarpment called Meridian Hill.[123] Although at the beginning of the twentieth century the surrounding area was largely undeveloped, except for some small wooden buildings, it offered a dramatic view of the White House and the Washington Monument. It was Henderson's ambition to raise the stature of 16th Street and Meridian Hill, and she embarked on a series of ventures, including promoting the area as the site for a new executive mansion and as the location for Pope's scheme for the Lincoln Memorial, but without success. She was more successful in fashioning Meridian Hill as a diplomatic enclave, commissioning George Oakley Totten Jr. to design almost a dozen Beaux-Arts mansions to serve as ambassadorial residences and homes for high-ranking U.S. government officials.[124]

To support her scheme, Henderson proposed the idea for Meridian Hill Park in 1906. Taken with the site's commanding views of the monumental core, the CFA supported its acquisition as a public park. The initial design was prepared in 1914 by landscape architect George Burnap of the Office of Public Buildings and Grounds; Burnap was replaced in 1917 by the architect and landscape architect Horace Peaslee, who retained but simplified the essentials of Burnap's plan. Landscape architect Ferruccio Vitale was hired in 1919 to develop the planting plan. The park's massive retaining walls were executed by John E. Earley, a pioneer in cast-in-place concrete technology.

The park design consisted of a walled garden organized along a north-south axis with several terraced gardens set perpendicular to this center line. Every last detail of the park's architecture and landscaping, from walls and entrances to hedges and allees, came to the CFA for careful consideration. Of particular concern to the commission was the height of the southern wall along W Street, which was eventually increased to appear more substantial. The CFA also agreed with Burnap that the park should be "a general congregation point, attracting visitors from all over the city, the design for which would embrace provision for a large number of people."[125]

Lacking an explicit commemorative function, Meridian Hill Park soon became the repository for an eccentric collection of statues. Several represented European notables; most were replicas of original works located elsewhere. Although the CFA recommended specific locations within the park for all of the works, no theme appears to have guided its decisions. In 1920, for example, a bronze figure of the medieval poet Dante Alighieri by sculptor Ettore Ximenes was donated to Washington on behalf of New York City's Italian Americans; the CFA determined

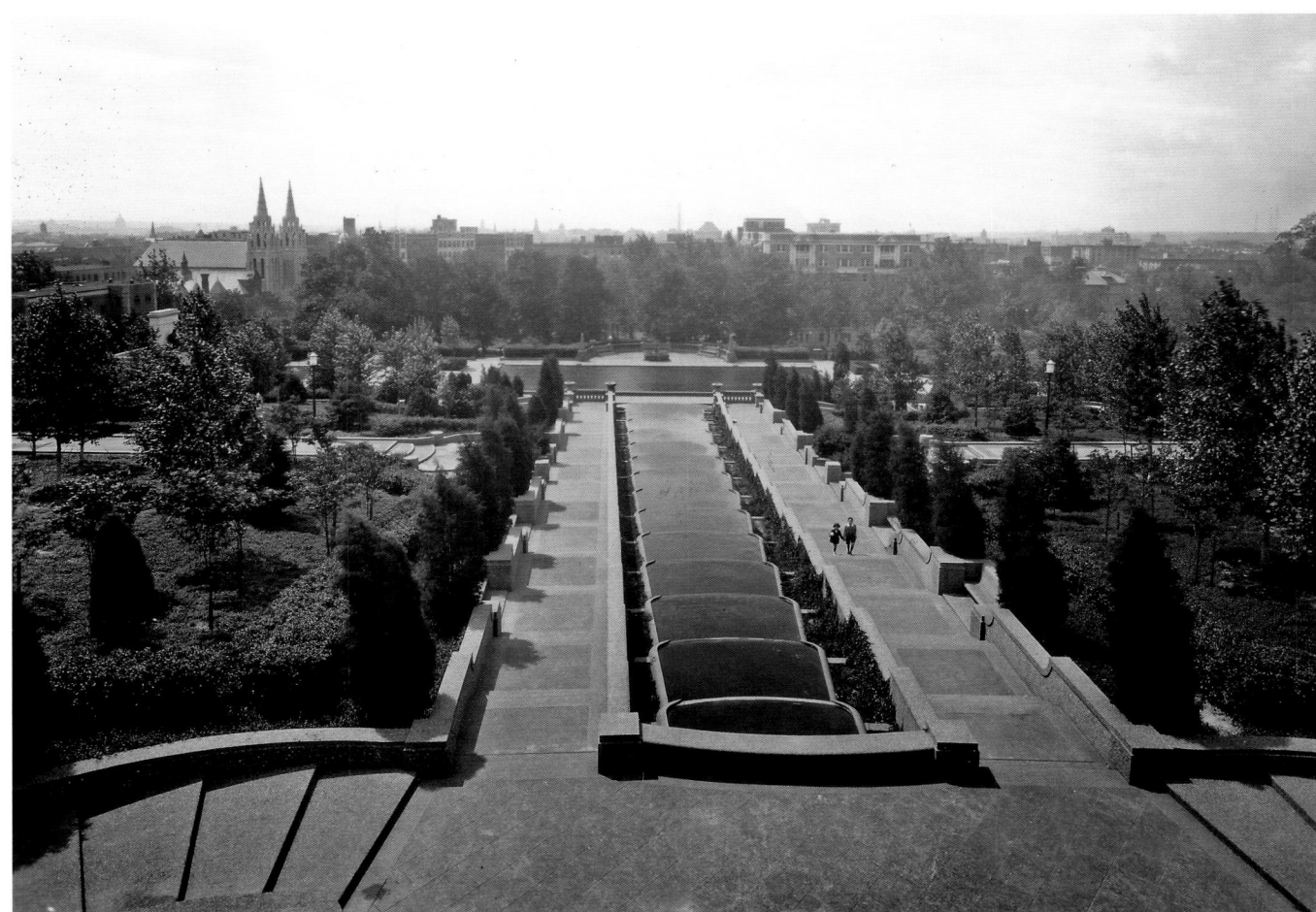

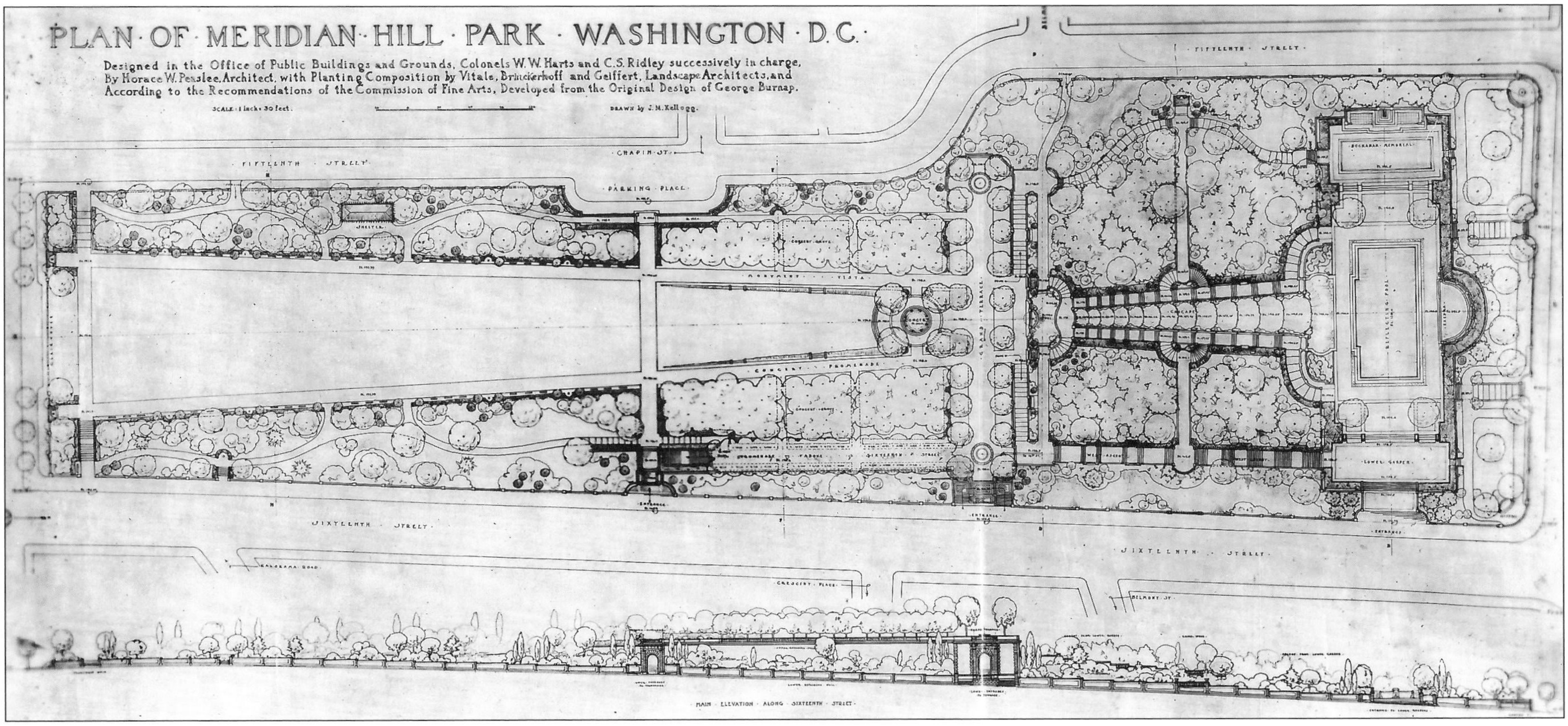
PLAN · OF · MERIDIAN · HILL · PARK · WASHINGTON · D.C.
Designed in the Office of Public Buildings and Grounds, Colonels W. W. Harts and C. S. Ridley successively in charge,
By Horace W. Peaslee, Architect, with Planting Composition by Vitale, Brinckerhoff and Geiffert, Landscape Architects, and
According to the Recommendations of the Commission of Fine Arts, Developed from the Original Design of George Burnap.
FIFTEENTH · STREET
CHAPIN · ST
PARKING · PLACE
SIXTEENTH · STREET
CRESCENT · PLACE
MAIN · ELEVATION · ALONG · SIXTEENTH · STREET

ABOVE: *Plan of Meridan Hill Park by Horace Peaslee, 1917. The CFA's close involvement with all aspects of the design for Meridian Hill Park revealed its desire to provide European-inspired models of urban landscape design for the national capital.*

RIGHT: *The Great Cascade descends the central spine of Meridian Hill Park to the Great Terrace at the south; this view, c. 1936, shows the Washington Monument in the distance.*

ABOVE LEFT: *The statue of Jeanne d'Arc by Paul Dubois (1922) was the first sculptural addition to Meridian Hill Park, in part because the French Embassy faced the park's north end across 16th Street.*

ABOVE RIGHT: *Another statue placed in Meridian Hill Park was the James Buchanan Memorial by Hans Schuler (1930), one of the lesser-known presidential memorials in Washington; it defines the east end of the lower plaza.*

LEFT: *View of the Great Cascade, early 1940s. In midcentury Washington, Meridian Hill Park was a popular gathering place for concerts and other cultural activities. The Noyes Armillary Sphere by Carl Paul Jennewein was installed in 1931.*

The art deco Navy-Merchant Marine Memorial by Ernesto Begni del Piatta (1934) did not fit with the CFA's conception for the monumental core or East Potomac Park—and was eventually placed on Columbia Island on the opposite shore of the Potomac River.

that it could be appropriately placed in Meridian Hill Park because it "is being developed along the lines of an Italian Garden."[126] A similar bequest was a bronze equestrian statue of Joan of Arc, a replica of a statue by Paul Dubois that stands before Reims Cathedral, presented to the women of America by the women of France in 1922. The CFA approved its location on the upper terrace of the park, in front of the proposed new French embassy, on the recommendation of French Ambassador Jules Jusserand and French-born architect Paul Cret.[127]

The first major sculptural addition to Meridian Hill Park was the James Buchanan Memorial. Completed in 1930 by sculptor Hans Schuler and architect William Gordon Beecher, the bronze figure of the fifteenth president is seated before a large white marble exedra, a high-backed classical bench. After first planning to have the statue terminate the park's main north-south axis in the lower garden, the commission decided it should be moved east to end the cross-axis of a large plaza.[128] The last sculpture placed in Meridian Hill Park was the *Noyes Armillary Sphere* by sculptor Carl Paul Jennewein in 1931, which anchored the south end of the central axis.[129]

The Navy–Marine Memorial project occupied an inordinate amount of the commission's attention in the 1920s and 1930s as the members tried to assess the appropriate style and monumentality for memorials on sites outside the National Mall landscape. Designed by architect Harvey Wiley Corbett and sculptor Ernesto Begni del Piatta, the proposed memorial depicted seagulls flying over a cresting curvilinear wave, its surface ornamented with decorative scrolls, bubbles, and fish. It was rendered in a fanciful art deco mode completely foreign to the solemn stone monuments typical of national commemorative art in Washington—and the CFA did not know what to make of it.

The Navy–Marine Memorial Association had envisioned its monument standing at the end of Hains Point with the Potomac River serving as background.[130] The CFA was never happy with this location: the memorial was too small, too decorative, and—to the commission—too trivial. It would not provide enough interest in the round to command this prominent position, regarded by the commission as one of the most important memorial sites, since at this time the river was still intended to

Shipstead-Luce Act

Congress codified the commission's role in shaping the city beyond the Mall through the passage of the Shipstead-Luce Act on May 16, 1930.[1] The act extended the commission's regulatory power into the private realm, giving the commission explicit authority to review the design of proposed private construction adjoining federal property within defined areas of the District. The language of the act requires

that such development should proceed along the lines of good order, good taste, and with due regard to the public interests involved, and a reasonable degree of control should be exercised over the architecture of private or semipublic buildings adjacent to public buildings and grounds of major importance.

The scope of this new jurisdiction included areas adjacent to the monumental core but also included segments of the waterfront and properties surrounding Rock Creek Park from Georgetown to the District border with the city of Silver Spring, Maryland. Several revisions over the last eighty years have further extended its reach to other areas of the city.

Through the Shipstead-Luce Act, Congress recognized that the national interest within the capital city applied not only to federal properties but also to the larger ensemble of architecture and urban design *surrounding* the built elements of the federal government and its land reserves, such as Rock Creek Park. For twenty years or more, most of the buildings reviewed were houses and apartment buildings that fronted on federal parkland. Larger semipublic buildings came under review as well, such

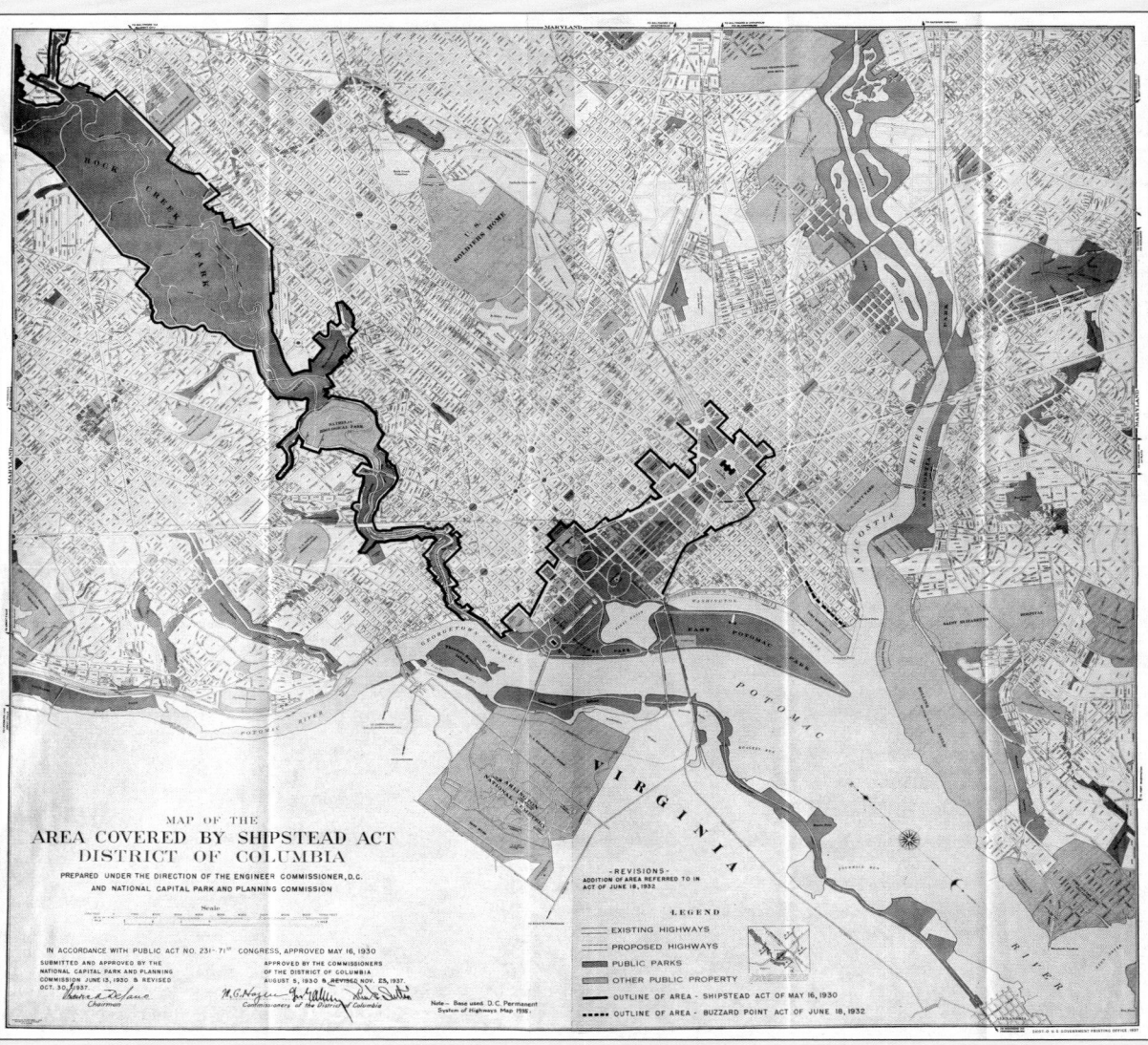

Map of the Shipstead-Luce Act jurisdiction. *The 1930 act extends the design review authority of the Commission of Fine Arts to areas adjacent to federal lands in the District.*

as the American Institute of Pharmacy building on Constitution Avenue. Increasingly, the Shipstead-Luce Act applied to more significant structures and groupings, including Lafayette Square starting in the 1950s, and the Watergate Apartments (Luigi Moretti, with Milton Fischer, 1963–67) in the late 1960s, and it would be a powerful tool employed

by the commission to guide redevelopment in the city in the last decades of the twentieth century. Whether reviewing federal or District government projects, or private projects under the Shipstead-Luce Act, the CFA's responsibility remained the promotion of good design.

be a major ceremonial route into the city.[131]

Troubled by the memorial's unconventional form, the CFA consulted with former sculptor members for guidance. Daniel Chester French and Lorado Taft, well known for their works in the Beaux-Arts tradition, both liked the piece for its unorthodox approach; Taft complimented it as "this fresh and perhaps fantastic conception." However, sitting CFA member Milton Medary insisted that Hains Point needed a monument that was "massive and strong," and the CFA disapproved the memorial, suggesting that either a smaller version of the design be placed at the entrance to a proposed canal at the north end of East Potomac Park or that something more appropriate for Hains Point be designed.[132] In the end, neither option was pursued. The canal across Hains Point was never built and the memorial was instead located on Columbia Island (now Lady Bird Johnson Park), constructed at a reduced size in cast aluminum, and dedicated in 1934.

An Evolving Design Vocabulary

By the late 1920s and into the 1930s, the Commission of Fine Arts was confronting the radical redirection that was occurring in architecture: modernism. For decades the commission, steered by Charles Moore, had been singularly successful in directing the implementation of the Senate Park Commission's vision for the capital city. The L'Enfant Plan was cited as the primary document, but this was perhaps disingenuous—the City Beautiful image of national grandeur presented by the McMillan Plan was always the touchstone.[133]

But the design vocabulary of American architects and

The CFA found Paul Cret's stripped classicism, best exemplified in the Folger Shakespeare Library (1928–32), an admirable accommodation between traditional and modern architecture.

the nature of the projects presented to the commission for review inevitably evolved; the commission had to grapple with these changes not only from the designers of the projects it reviewed, but eventually from its own membership. Charles Moore now represented a concept of public architecture in its twilight. New commission members—led by landscape architect Gilmore Clarke, who was first appointed by Herbert Hoover in 1932 and would succeed Moore as chairman—challenged that concept as they assessed the new ideas of modernism in these transitional years.

Beginning in the late 1920s, several projects reviewed by the commission epitomized the difficulty the commission had in defining an appropriate modernist style for buildings of national stature. These proposals included a range of approaches—such as the stripped classical austerity of the Folger Shakespeare Library by Paul Cret and Alexander Trowbridge; the modernist polemic of Eliel and Eero Saarinen's unbuilt project for the Smithsonian Gallery of Art; and John Russell Pope's Roman classical Jefferson Memorial—which, in their diversity, stand as symbols of this period of transition in American public architecture.

Studies for the Folger Shakespeare Library first came before the commission in May 1929. The library is notable as the first modern public building in the city—a harbinger of modernism and of the eventual end to the city's dominant Beaux-Arts ethos. The commission's response was favorable; in fact, it had little to say. In 1932, upon inspecting the Folger Library after its opening, the commission described the exterior as "somewhat modern" but, attempting to rationalize this direction in terms of classicism, added that the library had been designed as "a building which should be considered of the classical order in view of the fact that several groups of sculpture illustrating scenes in the plays of Shakespeare...are shown on the façade."[134]

More controversial was the debate over the proposed Smithsonian Gallery of Art, which played out in private meetings and correspondence; the issue surfaced in only a few documents found in the public record. Remarks by commission members, particularly Gilmore Clarke—evidence that his acceptance of modernism in Washington did have limits—helped ensure that the project never moved beyond preliminary stages; it never progressed far enough to be submitted for official commission review.

The Smithsonian Institution had been assembling a collection of American art since the nineteenth century. Plans to give the collection a permanent home emerged in the 1930s, concurrent with the development of the

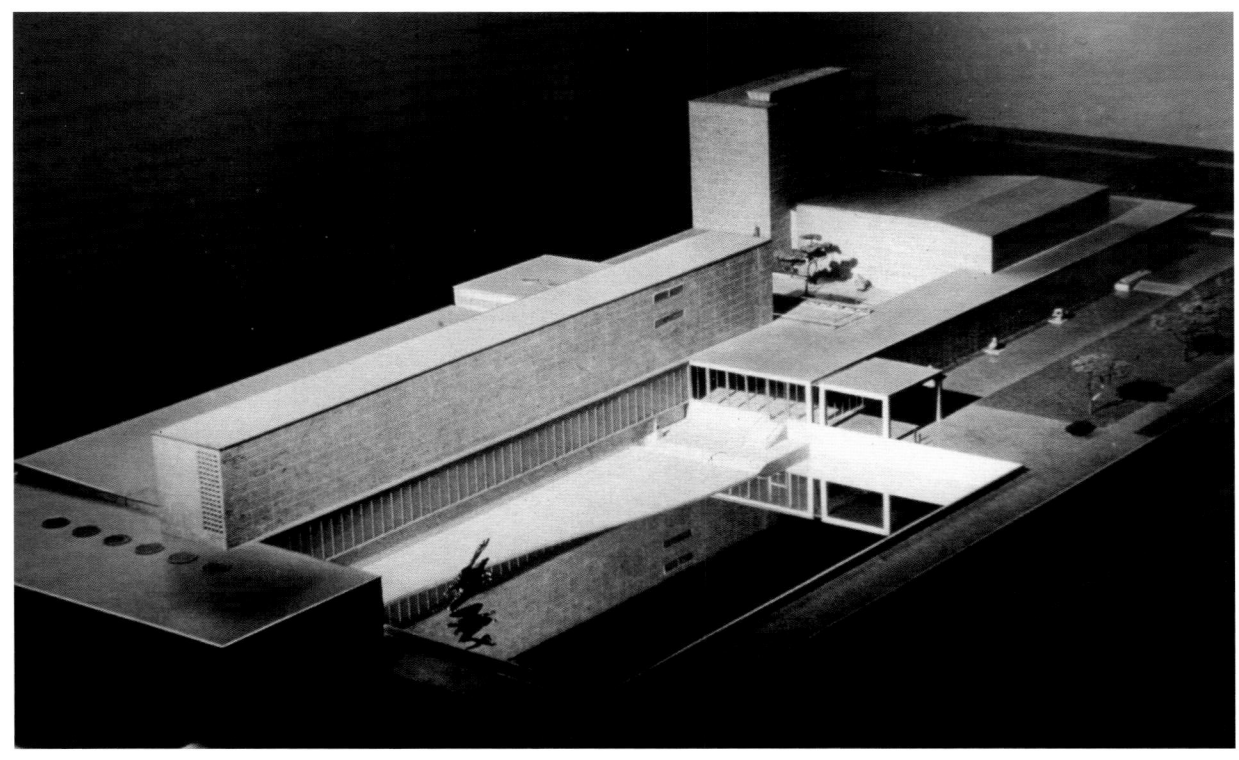

LEFT: *Model, proposal for the Smithsonian Gallery of Art by Eliel and Eero Saarinen with Robert Swanson, 1939. Although it never came before the Commission of Fine Arts for formal review, the CFA— particularly Chairman Gilmore Clarke—flatly rejected the International Style modernism of the proposal.*

BELOW: *Plan and section, Saarinen proposal for the Smithsonian Gallery of Art, 1939.*

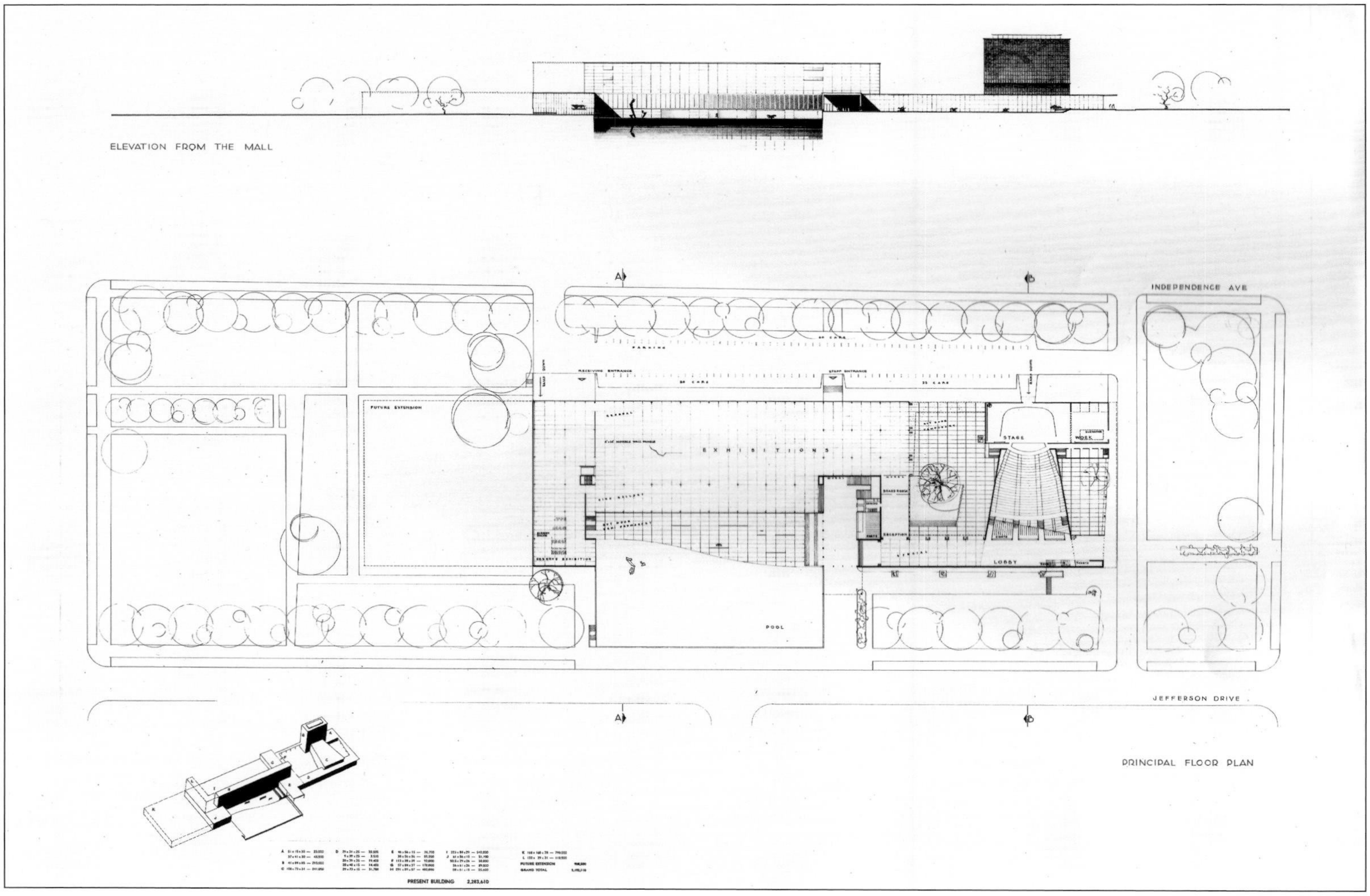

ELEVATION FROM THE MALL

INDEPENDENCE AVE

EXHIBITIONS

STAGE

LOBBY

POOL

JEFFERSON DRIVE

PRINCIPAL FLOOR PLAN

PRESENT BUILDING   2,283,610

National Gallery of Art endowed by Andrew Mellon and sited on the south side of the Mall between 4th and 7th Streets.[135] Congress established the Smithsonian Gallery of Art Commission in 1938, headed by NCPPC chairman Frederic A. Delano and composed mostly of leading modernist architects, with the exception of a current CFA member, Henry R. Shepley (CFA 1936–1940). Charles L. Borie, one of the transitional modernists on the CFA, also served on this commission.

The competition for the gallery drew hundreds of entries. The proposals were, in general, a huge departure from Beaux-Arts classicism, Washington's de facto official style. The winning entry by Eliel and Eero Saarinen with Robert Swanson was an assemblage of mostly horizontal intersecting blocks, with one vertical tower; some blocks lacked windows, some had window walls or strip windows. A sunken court with a reflecting pool separated the gallery from the Mall.[136] The proposal was the antithesis of John Russell Pope's project for the National Gallery—opposite it not only in its location across the Mall, but in its drastic departure from the Beaux-Arts ideals envisioned in the McMillan Plan.

Although the Smithsonian gallery project had not been submitted for review, the CFA borrowed the Saarinen drawings and a model of the Mall that included a depiction of the gallery to view at its meeting in July 1939. On seeing the Saarinens' design, the CFA members were aghast. The discussion was off the record, but Clarke subsequently wrote distraught letters to Frederic A. Delano and Charles Moore, who had resigned as chairman in 1937 but remained on the commission.[137] Clarke thought the proposal looked like a factory and clearly was a steel frame covered with veneer walls and bearing "offensive" ribbon windows. Moore replied with anxiety:

And now come the plans you are wrestling with for a Smithsonian Art Gallery which threaten to foist on Washington a building architecturally far inferior to the Pension Office [always reviled by Moore] and for sheer ugliness more assertive than the State, War and Navy—an epitome of the chaos of the Nazi art of today. I trust that Congress will refuse to make appropriations for a building so abhorrent to the history and architecture of the city.[138]

In his letter to Delano, Clarke said the commission could never approve the Saarinen design:

The Commission of Fine Arts must continue to act to retain a harmony of expression in the buildings to be erected in Washington, more particularly those along the Mall. The Saarinen design for an art gallery is not considered suitable and…it must not be carried out as at present planned nor with the same or similar flavor of modernism.

Anticipating Delano's objection, Clarke said:

It may seem to you to be a contradiction that the Commission of Fine Arts vigorously objected to the Jefferson Memorial, a classical 'steal' if you please, and then later object to this new architecture of the Saarinens. Well, that seems to the Commission to be a perfectly consistent policy; it shows that there is a sound middle ground which we must explore.[139]

Delano responded sharply to the CFA's circumvention of the process, pointing out that the Saarinen plan had not yet been submitted to the CFA for review and reminding Clarke that he had been invited to appear before the NCPPC to give his opinion on the design, an offer Clarke had declined. But Delano added that, while the Saarinens might have won the competition, they had not yet been given the commission.[140] Indicating the Smithsonian's own discomfort with the design, and possibly to appease the CFA, Delano noted that the gallery would not be built until its funding—to be from private sources—was in hand; if the funds were raised, the Smithsonian would have to employ the Saarinens but would tell them what type of building was wanted and would insist that the CFA review the design. However, Delano also had a vision for the gallery far different from that of the commission. He enclosed a memo he had prepared for Smithsonian officials in which he offered his opinion about the character ap-

John Russell Pope, pictured c. 1930, was considered a master of classical design by his peers. His severe monumental buildings in Washington— the American Institute of Pharmacy, the National Archives, the National Gallery of Art, and the Jefferson Memorial— spanned the Beaux-Arts era and framed the Mall.

propriate for a gallery on this site: a low building, "the reverse of a monumental structure," and relatively small. He told Clarke that if the Commission of Fine Arts required a building comparable to the National Gallery of Art, the Smithsonian should acquire another site for its museum.[141]

The Smithsonian had trouble raising money for the gallery. Delano wrote to Charles Borie:

The attitude of the Commission of Fine Arts also has added to our difficulties. I think it exceeded its authority in stating that the building designed by the Messrs. Saarinen would not be acceptable to it, overlooking the fact that the purpose of the competition was not to get a final design, but to select an architect.[142]

In the end, the Smithsonian project did not proceed because of the changing financial priorities of the nation on the eve of a new world war. In fact, no modernist building would be constructed on the Mall until 1964, with the completion of the National Museum of American History by Steinman, Cain & White, the successor firm to McKim, Mead & White. Its tepid modernism nodded toward the Beaux-Arts tradition of the Mall, but by then modernist architecture was generally accepted throughout the country as the standard and aroused no furor among commission members.

At the same time, a far less public battle erupted over the other art museum, the National Gallery of Art. The argument transpired between the Commission of Fine Arts and former CFA member and architect John Russell Pope and his patron, Secretary of the Treasury Andrew W. Mellon. The dispute arose over what the CFA did or did not say in a letter Moore sent to Mellon on January 30, 1937, after the commission first saw Pope's design. Like the controversy over the Saarinens' design for the Smithsonian, the commission's issue with Pope's design revolved around appropriateness for the Mall. However, the commission did not argue about the appropriateness of classicism itself, but, rather, the selection of an appropriate classical element—a dome or a portico—as the building's central motif. The record also gives evidence, as does the concurrent battle over the Jefferson Memorial, of Gilmore Clarke's animosity towards Pope.

Andrew Mellon donated his incomparable collection of European paintings to the nation with the stipulation that it must be housed in a gallery on the Mall. When Charles Moore learned of the gift, he arranged for Mellon to meet with John Russell Pope—widely considered the last remaining American architect up to the challenge of designing a monumental building suitable for the McMillan Plan's vision for the Mall. Mellon hired Pope in December 1935 and Moore maneuvered behind the scenes to win support for Pope's design.[143] Mellon's National Gallery plans were discussed by the CFA in joint meetings with the NCPPC in late 1935 and early 1936.

The site was on the Mall's north side, on Constitution Avenue between 4th and 7th Street, and required the closing of 6th Street.[144] Pope's design featured a central rotunda crowned with a shallow dome that reached to a height of 140 feet from the floor and two long projecting wings, each terminating in a monumental porticoed entrance.

A dispute arose over the precise meaning of a letter the commission sent to Mellon after seeing Pope's early drawings in January 1937. Mellon, Pope, and congressional committees interpreted the letter as giving full approval to Pope's design, in particular its passages stating:

These plans were unanimously approved by the Commission.... In advising that the building as planned is suited to the function to be served this Commission cannot express greater commendation. The site selected allies the National Gallery of Art to the Capitol group of buildings, while it is properly subordinate to them.[145]

In March Congress passed legislation enabling construction that President Roosevelt signed; Mellon began negotiating construction contracts.[146] When commission

With its marble cladding over a steel structure, Pope's National Gallery of Art (drawing of first study, c. 1936) combined classical form with modern technology, raising questions among modern architects about the authenticity of its expression.

members became aware in March of how their letter was being interpreted, they reacted with dismay and said the letter was only meant to assure Congress that the CFA welcomed Mellon's gift and approved the location. Gilmore Clarke and the three commission architects—William F. Lamb (CFA 1937–45), Henry R. Shepley (CFA1936–40), and Charles L. Borie)—furious that Pope considered the entire project approved, sent Moore detailed letters expressing concerns about many aspects of the proposed building—most importantly, his use of a dome as its central feature.[147]

Pope appeared at the April 1937 commission meeting to address these criticisms. He vigorously defended his decision to use a dome, explaining that its removal would ruin the design and make the building a "greenhouse" with too many skylights and insufficient height. Clarke protested that "a dome on this building will mean a dome on all other buildings on the Mall"; Pope repeated that it was necessary. Mentioning his health problems (Pope was gravely ill with cancer and would die in August), he said:

I have taken such a personal interest in the design that I am prepared to say I would be glad to build the building and die with it…. I designed the gallery to fit Mr. McKim's Plan for the Mall, who shows nine domes in his scheme…. It is more my own and simpler than anything I have done. My whole profession as an architect is standing on the defense of the design and this is all I can do.[148]

The commission acceded to Pope on most details but continued to insist that the dome be eliminated.

The conflict came to a head at the commission's May 1937 meeting, when two representatives of Mellon's National Gallery Trust attended, including Mellon's attorney, David E. Finley (CFA 1943–63), soon to be named the first director of the National Gallery of Art; he would later replace Gilmore Clarke as chairman of the Commission of Fine Arts. The commission members insisted they had not seriously considered the gallery plans in detail at the January meeting with Mellon and that the commission could not have approved these before Congress approved the concept. In the words of Gilmore Clarke:

I am sorry the architect did not present the case in full; he knows about the procedure since he served on this Commission and must realize that a group of professional men are not going to be inspired and overcome by a set of cabinet drawings. We asked him questions about the design and he did not answer them. He knew at the first meeting that the dome was not satisfactory…. Now we are not trying to embarrass Mr. Mellon but it seems that Mr. Pope is trying to embarrass the Commission, because he relies on the letter which put the Commission on record as to the size and general design."[149]

David Finley finally said that Mellon wanted to find a solution that would win the commission's support. Pope made new studies, including one showing the gallery with a smaller dome and another with a portico as the central element. However, he warned Mellon that they resulted in a monotonous interior plan and did not harmonize with surrounding buildings.[150]

On June 21, the commission met in New York at Pope's office to view the new schemes. The CFA members said emphatically that they preferred the version with the portico. A letter from Mellon, read into the record, said he would regard the use of this alternative as a "radical departure" from the plan presented to Congress.[151] Pope mounted a final defense of the domed gallery: "It has always been my effort to get a building in this location that would have an elevation or motive in the center of it of sufficient height to hold its own with the surrounding buildings, particularly the Capitol, the Archives and the National Museum."[152]

Finley requested that the CFA write to Mellon authorizing him to build the gallery with a dome. After deliberation, the commission crafted the following statement:

The Commission approve the plans as submitted, but expressed a strong preference for the scheme (E-6) showing a high central portico. This the Commission believe better adapts itself to the general composition of the Mall, of which this building is an integral part. However, the Commission are aware that circumstances appear to prevent changes in the design showing a dome, and realize regretfully that it may not be feasible to carry out their suggestions.[153]

The commission's response appears disingenuous; the January letter does not mention any reservations about design details. The original meeting minutes clearly state that the commission approved the design. Oddly, Moore himself, who had championed Pope and worked assiduously behind the scenes to secure his commission, did not defend the architect's design.

At the same time that these issues surrounding Pope's National Gallery were playing out—the first six months of 1937—the commission was also embroiled in a dispute over Pope's design for the Jefferson Memorial. The memorial's monumental classicism, almost identical to the central composition of the National Gallery, was lambasted in the architectural press by modernist critics who disapproved of what they saw as the "classical graveyard" presented by the buildings of official, monumental Washington.

The conflict over the design of the Jefferson Memorial struck at the core of the CFA's mission to define the architectural symbolism for the nation. The commission could no longer ignore the new direction in architecture, one opposed to the Beaux-Arts and City Beautiful principles espoused by its chairman, Charles Moore. Pope's Pantheon-type design—seen in the architectural profession by the late 1930s as hopelessly outdated—was at odds with the

FACING PAGE. TOP: *The 1901 McMillan Plan envisioned the Tidal Basin, on an axis due south of the White House, as the future site for a memorial to the Founding Fathers or other great Americans.*

CENTER: *Photograph of a model, c. 1937, showing Pope's first concept for the Jefferson Memorial: a temple on an extensive platform within the Tidal Basin.*

BOTTOM: *Study by Eggers & Higgins for the Jefferson Memorial composed of twin peristyles (1938), based on Pope's unbuilt 1926 project for a Theodore Roosevelt Memorial on the Tidal Basin.*

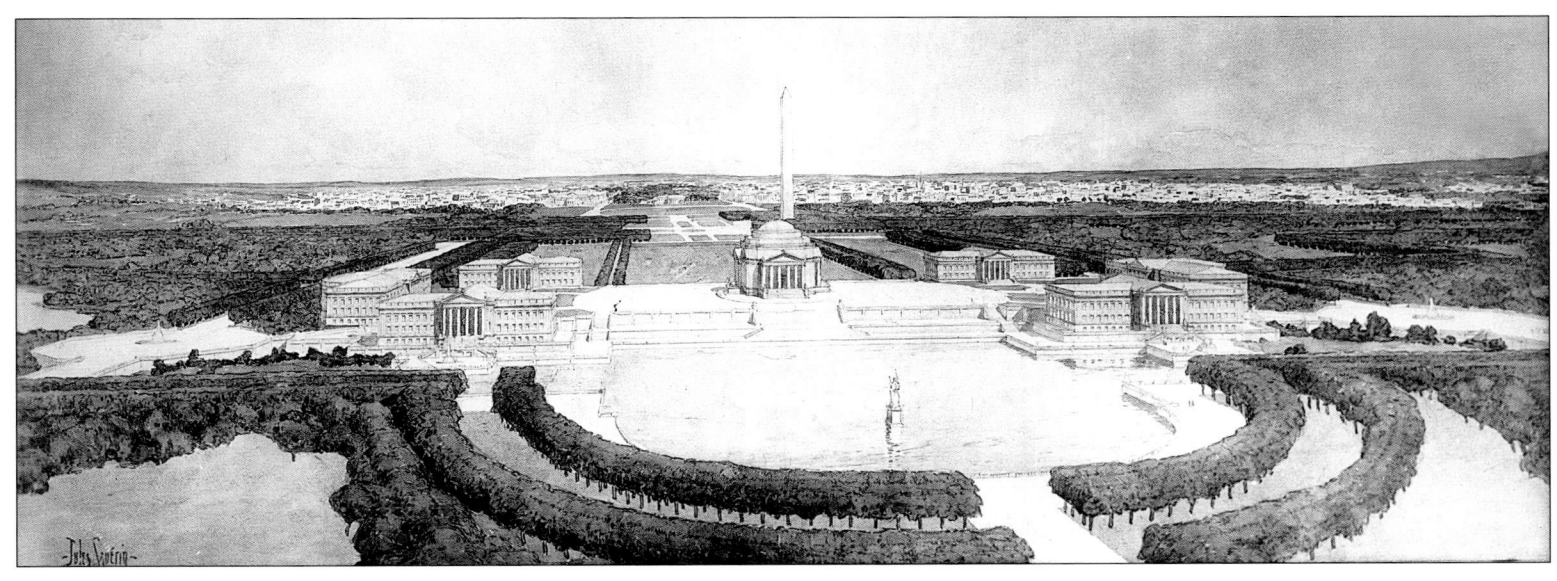

CHARLES MOORE AND THE CLASSICAL PARADIGM, 1915–1937

ABOVE: *The Jefferson Memorial under construction, c. 1942. The landscape design by Frederick Law Olmsted Jr. was never fully implemented, and the network of highways and bridges behind the memorial has compromised its setting.*

RIGHT: *The memorial, c.1945. The Pantheon-inspired temple would be the last public building in an academic classical style built in Washington.*

evolving sentiments of the commission. Even Charles Moore, chairman until his resignation from that position in 1937, did not openly support Pope's scheme, although evidence suggests he worked behind the scenes to secure its approval by the president. (See the essays in this volume by Pamela Scott and Carroll W. Westfall.)

Looking for a transitional approach—the middle ground he had earlier described to Frederic A. Delano— that would retain the best of the Beaux-Arts tradition, Gilmore Clarke led the search for, as he phrased it, a "fresh" classicism for the Jefferson Memorial, advocating for a solution that would respond more sensitively and with more originality to the Tidal Basin landscape.[154] He first encouraged an exploration of less-familiar versions of the classical vocabulary, such as peristyles within a landscape, and, as he had in the National Gallery debate, condemned the overuse of domes on the Mall. Increasingly, Clarke promoted an argument that modern architecture would be more palatable if it incorporated extensive ornamental programs into buildings integrated with their landscapes, continuing a standard Beaux-Arts practice. Ultimately, it was a futile effort to accommodate modernism with classicism: President Roosevelt would support the Pantheon design, and the Jefferson Memorial Commission would build it, disregarding the CFA's advice.

The stalemate over the design of the Thomas Jefferson Memorial signified the passing of an era for the commission: Modernism—not classicism—would come to dominate as the accepted architectural style for official Washington. More importantly, the stature of the commission's advice on an issue of national symbolism was challenged by the president. And Moore, who had begun his forty-year association with the design of Washington as the chief apostle of a new vision for the nation's capital, ended his career as the aged defender of what was now seen as a reactionary aesthetic. However, his legacy was irrefutable: the image of the city had been transformed.

ABOVE LEFT: *The bronze statue of Jefferson by Rudulph Evans, c. 1945. Due to the controversy about the memorial's design, the CFA never approved the sculpture.*

ABOVE RIGHT: *Clay study for a plaque sculpted by Laura Gardin Fraser honoring Charles Moore for his long service to the CFA and the nation's capital, 1932.*

The Jefferson Memorial: A Pyrrhic Victory for American Architecture

Will the monuments last as long as the laws? [1]

¶ CARROLL WILLIAM WESTFALL

Early in 1937, John Russell Pope's design proposal for the Thomas Jefferson Memorial was made public. It immediately provoked a controversy that pitted two very different conceptions of architecture against one another.[2] Proponents of the design argued that architecture is valued principally as a civic art. Opponents believed that architecture is principally a fine art that must be "of its time." The proponents won, but ever since, their view that architecture serves and represents the nation and its citizens' aspirations has been overwhelmed by standards set by the art world's ideological and aesthetic infatuations.

The Controversy

Pope's proposal was released by the Thomas Jefferson Memorial Commission (TJMC), which President Franklin Delano Roosevelt had brought into existence in June 1934. Earlier in that year, Roosevelt had suggested that the Commission of Fine Arts (CFA) consider either using the triangle east of the new National Archives building for a statue of Jefferson or having Jefferson replace Andrew Jackson in Lafayette Park opposite the White House. The CFA, instead, suggested the triangular site east of the Apex Building on Pennsylvania Avenue or, better, on a cross-axis at 7th Street, "which would give the statue a major location in the plan of Washington."[3] The president then enlarged his vision and had Congress establish the TJMC.[4] Its twelve members included six elected officials, three Jefferson descendants, and three appointees of the Thomas Jefferson Foundation, established in 1923, that owned and managed Monticello. Among its appointees was Fiske Kimball (1888–1955), the noted Jeffersonian scholar, historian, and architect, whose energy and expertise in matters architectural would dominate the commission. John J. Boylan (1878–1938), a long-time Jeffer-

son enthusiast, a director of Monticello's foundation, and, since 1923, a Democratic Congressman handpicked by the New York City Tammany Hall political machine, was elected chairman.[5] Outsiders, most importantly Charles Moore (1855–1942), chairman of the CFA—restrained by legislation to solely an advisory role—often attended commission meetings and the numerous site visits.[6]

The TJMC selected Pope as the memorial's architect and had him prepare proposals for four different sites. President Roosevelt reviewed them in May 1936 and selected the site south of the White House on the Tidal Basin, which the McMillan Commission of 1901 had earmarked for a memorial, and asked for further development of the two Pope schemes proposed for the site.[7] In February 1937, Roosevelt selected the design based on the Pantheon instead of the one that was "much more like Monticello."[8] On February 18, the TJMC unanimously agreed to the site and the Pantheon scheme, and the next day it made the design proposal public.[9]

The exterior and interior renderings immediately provoked controversy. The public's opposition was vociferous. It cried that the expansive, formal site plan was an unwarranted threat to the beloved cherry trees, even then a hugely popular tourist attraction.[10] And it cried that in the midst of the Great Depression a proper memorial should not be a marble mausoleum but "something useful." To this, Fiske Kimball said, "The only memorial that remains as a memorial… is not utilitarian."[11] Commissioner and Senator Elbert D. Thomas from Utah, with an eye on foreign events, responded more broadly, noting that the great question of the day was "whether you are going to have government by force or coercion or government by common consent and liberty. This is a monument to those last ideas."[12]

The CFA received the proposed memorial for review on March 20, 1937, in a

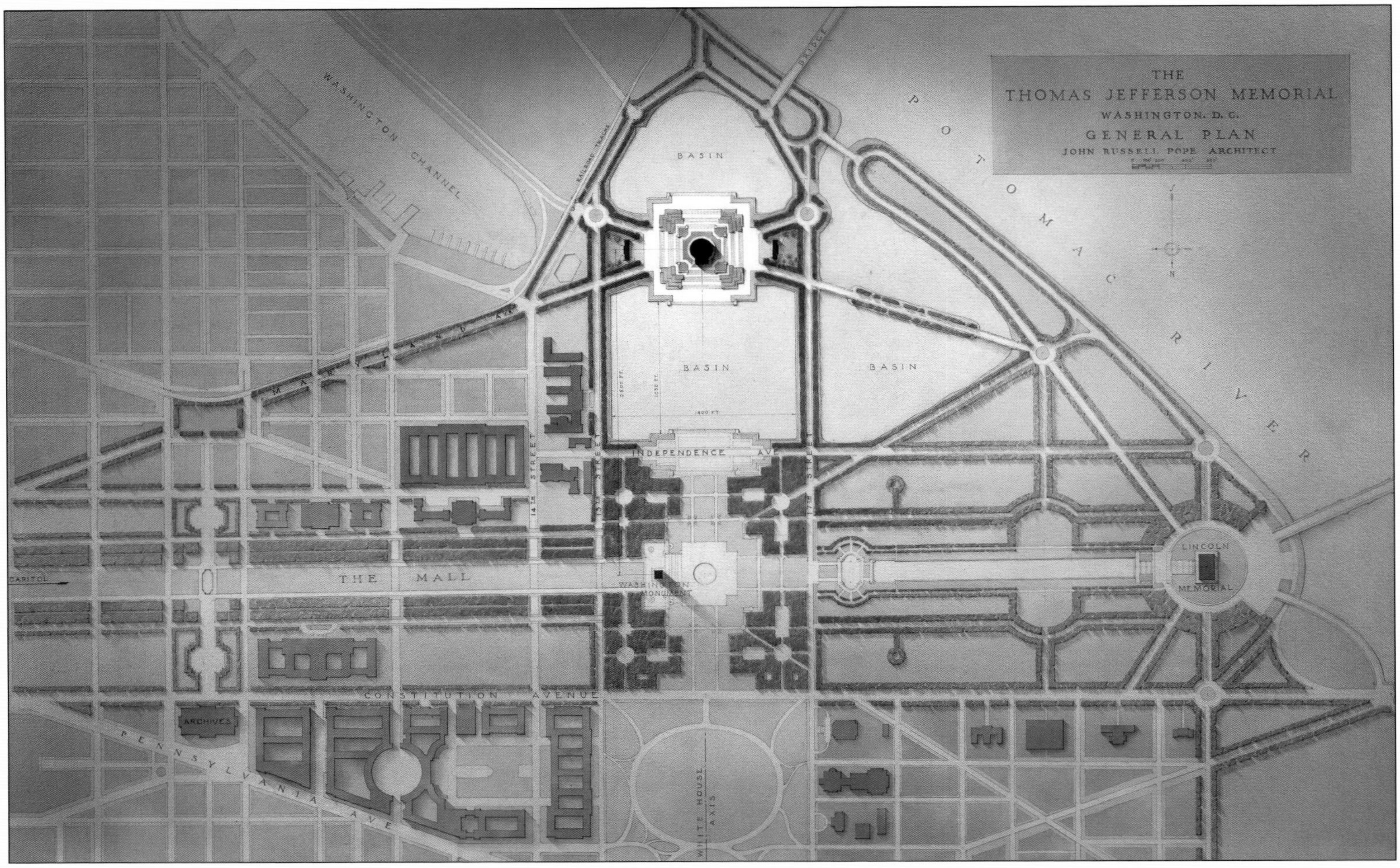

TOP: *John Russell Pope's Scheme B for the Thomas Jefferson Memorial at the Tidal Basin.*

ABOVE: *Pope's General Plan for the Thomas Jefferson Memorial showing extensive changes to the Tidal Basin.*

joint meeting with the National Capital Park and Planning Commission (NCPPC), which had an advisory role in topics concerning land use. The transcript of that meeting is extensive. The various commissioners found the site appropriate but its design flawed, which included a failure to account for the memorial's effect on roadways and the river's tidal flow in and out of the recently completed Tidal Basin. While the TJMC reported that it had followed the 1901 proposal for the area, the support of the CFA and NCPPC was clearly in the other direction, toward a smaller, less formal building in an informal setting; Henry V. Hubbard of the NCPPC cited a memorandum from Frederick Law Olmsted Jr. dated July 22, 1935, to that effect. CFA commissioner Gilmore Clarke (1892–1982), however, was the most vociferous. He objected to the lack of a competition and complained that the CFA had been presented with a "frozen" design that precluded it from offering advice.[13]

Thus, after approving the site, the CFA then disapproved the design, an action that the TJMC had expected Moore's liaison role to prevent.[14] The CFA outlined its objections in a follow-up letter to Chairman Boylan, dated April 8, 1937: "To express the character of the man to be honored," it stated, "its architectural features should not vary from the classical spirit in which he [Jefferson] practiced and which he deliberately imposed on the National Capital. Especially inasmuch as the early buildings have stood the test of time." But "quite apart from the style in which it is designed," the proposal raised other "fundamental" questions because the Pantheon scheme was so large and so similar to the nearby Lincoln Memorial, and its setting was so formal, the two "would come into competition, even into conflict." The letter suggested taking the dome and frontispiece off the Pantheon to make it a colonnade enclosing a statue or, alternatively, adapting Pope's 1925 competition-winning, but unbuilt scheme

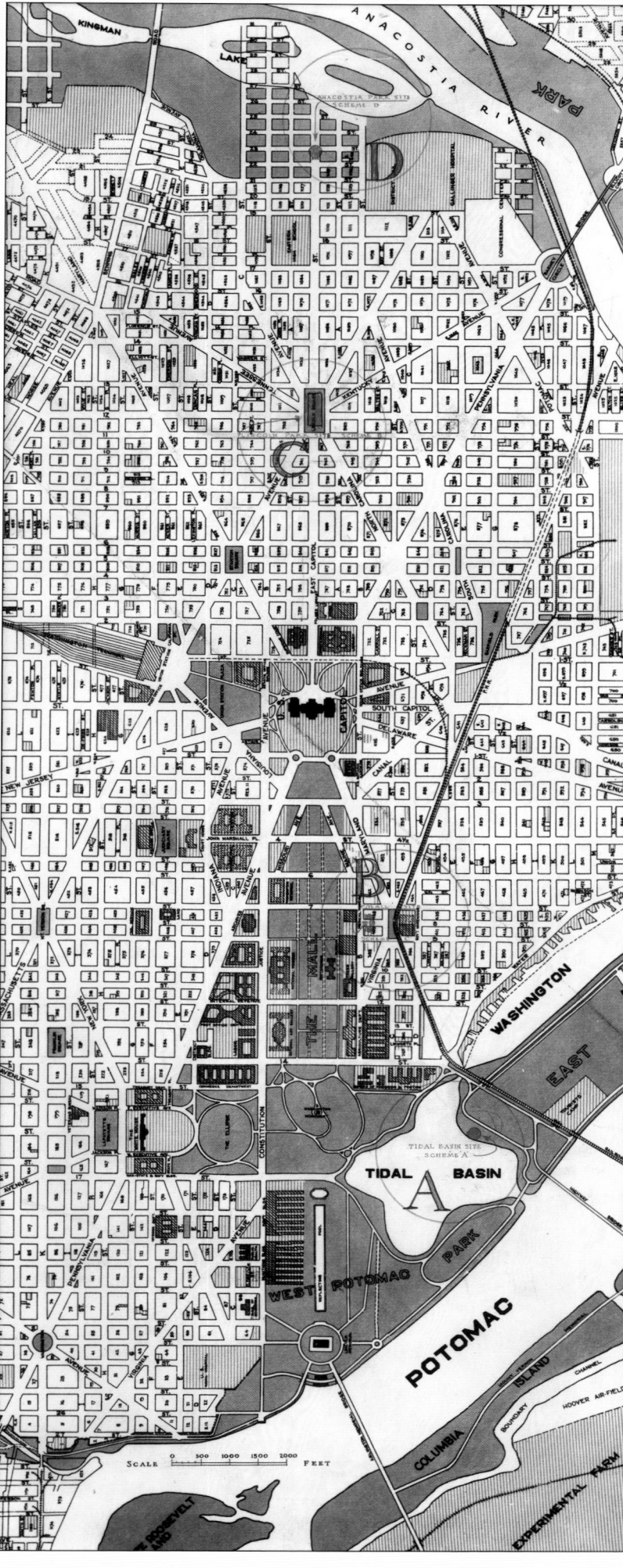

LEFT: *Map of Washington showing possible sites A, B, C, and D (noted in red) for the Thomas Jefferson Memorial, ranging west to east from the Tidal Basin to the Anacostia River, c. 1936.*

FACING PAGE: *The Thomas Jefferson Memorial Commission, February 18, 1937. Seated from left: Senator Elbert D. Thomas (D-UT), Senator Charles L. McNary (R-OR), Representative John J. Boylan (D-NY), Chairman Stuart Gibboney, and Representative Howard W. Smith (D-VA). Standing from left: Fiske Kimball, Senator Augustine Lonergan Jr. (D-CT), Joseph P. Tumulty, Representative Francis D. Culkin (R-NY), and Hollins S. Randolph.*

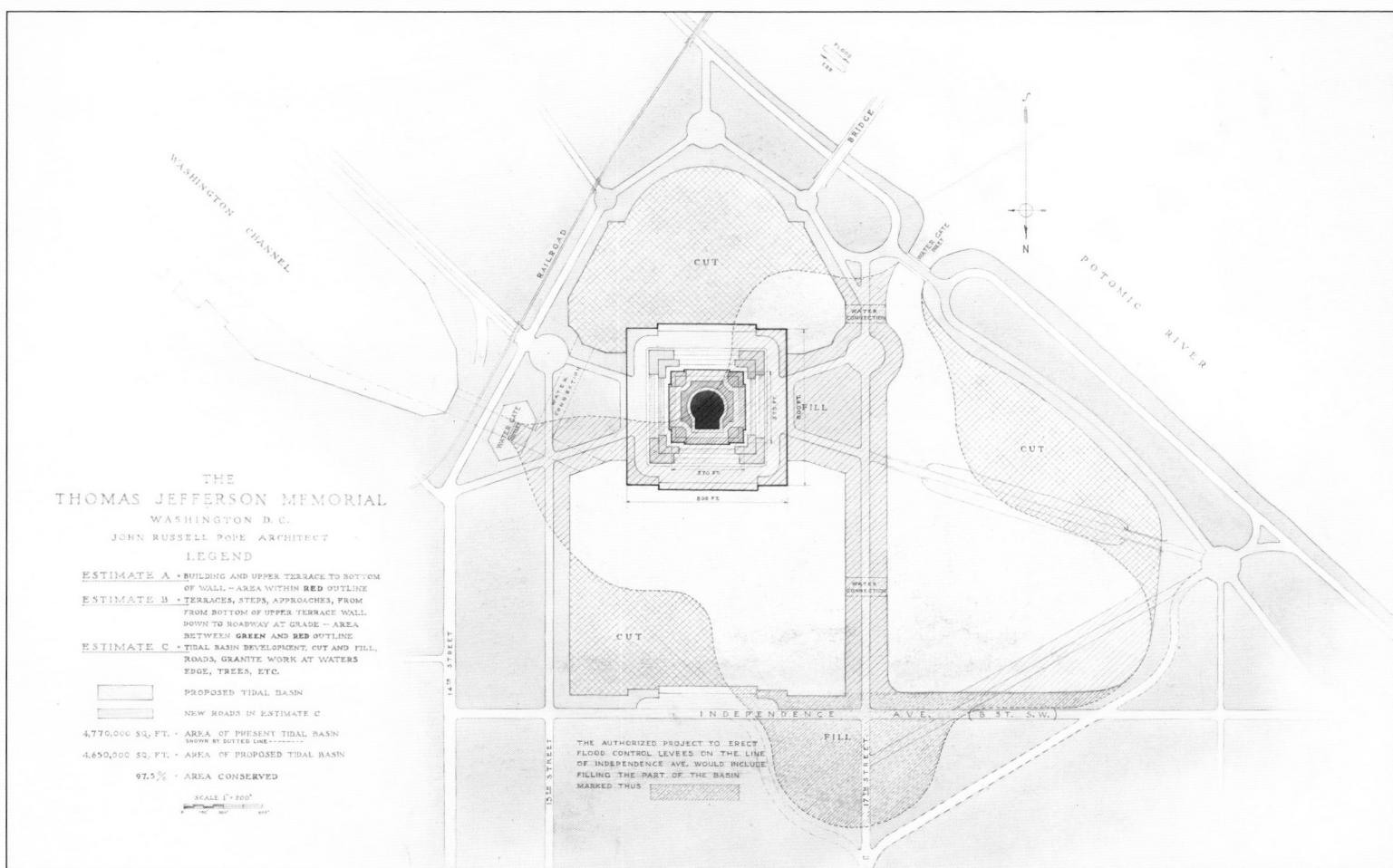

THE
THOMAS JEFFERSON MEMORIAL
WASHINGTON D.C.
JOHN RUSSELL POPE ARCHITECT
LEGEND

ESTIMATE A · BUILDING AND UPPER TERRACE TO BOTTOM
OF WALL. — AREA WITHIN RED OUTLINE
ESTIMATE B · TERRACES, STEPS, APPROACHES, FROM
FROM BOTTOM OF UPPER TERRACE WALL
DOWN TO ROADWAY AT GRADE — AREA
BETWEEN GREEN AND RED OUTLINE
ESTIMATE C · TIDAL BASIN DEVELOPMENT, CUT AND FILL,
ROADS, GRANITE WORK AT WATERS
EDGE, TREES, ETC.

PROPOSED TIDAL BASIN

NEW ROADS IN ESTIMATE C

4,770,000 SQ. FT. · AREA OF PRESENT TIDAL BASIN
SHOWN BY DOTTED LINE
4,650,000 SQ. FT. · AREA OF PROPOSED TIDAL BASIN

97.5% · AREA CONSERVED

SCALE 1" = 200'

for the Theodore Roosevelt Memorial that placed an open, split colonnade on that site.[15]

Remarks by individual CFA commissioners reveal the depth of their displeasure. Paul Manship, a sculptor, called it "cold, soulless, and too formal a representation as an expression of a memorial to so great a man who had such a warm nature.... It is just too architectural." Architect Thomas W. Lamb said it was a "reproduction of Imperial Rome.... I think it should be done in classical. It is Washington—it is the National Capital ....but I do not think it has to be done in the dry, pedantic, stilted, academic type." William A. Delano, also an architect, called it "altogether too pompous." Charles Louis Borie Jr., another architect, found that it was "too much architecture. I deplore that much architecture." Eugene Francis Savage, a painter,

was concerned about the lack of competition for the project: "I regret that this has not been exposed to the full possibility of American architecture today." And even Charles Moore said that what was wanted was something "quieter, more in keeping with Monticello."[16]

The architects Julian E. Berla and William Lescaze quickly organized the League for Progress in Architecture to fight the proposal's approval by Congress.[17] The league claimed that the site betrayed the L'Enfant Plan and thereby implicitly condemned the work of the 1901 McMillan Commission for the area with the Tidal Basin. They called the proposed Pantheon anachronistic and unsuitable for its purpose. And they especially protested the lack of a competition to select the designer.[18] The controversy persuaded Congress to declare the Tidal Basin site off limits

while it considered the matter, thereby setting the stage for round two, which unfolded out of public view within meetings of the CFA and the TJMC.[19]

Representative Boylan had already responded to the CFA's disapproval by convening a conference on April 22 involving people from Pope's office and the TJMC as well as the National Park Service, the CFA, and the NCPPC.[20] The Tidal Basin site remained in play, but the TJMC agreed to restudy the "height and design of the memorial, its terraces and immediate relations."[21] On July 13, the TJMC approved a reduced building in an informal Tidal Basin setting based on suggestions that Frederick Law Olmsted Jr., an original member of the McMillan Commission, had made in 1935 for a memorial to Jefferson on that site.[22]

External events now affected both the TJMC and the CFA. On August 23,

Cut and Fill Plan to reshape the Tidal Basin site for Pope's proposed scheme.

1937, the congressional budget deleted the request for the memorial's funding.[23] On August 27, Pope died. And at its September 29 meeting, the CFA was informed of Charles Moore's resignation as chairman, although he continued to serve as a member. CFA commissioner Gilmore Clarke, a landscape architect and strong opponent of Pope's Pantheon, was elected to succeed Moore.[24] At that meeting, Otto Eggers and Daniel Higgins, Pope's assistants who had taken over his office, made an arrangement with Boylan and presented a revised design of the Pantheon that the TJMC had not yet reviewed. The CFA rejected it with the instruction to make new designs "in accordance with the previously made suggestions."[25]

On January 25, 1938, Chairman Boylan convened a meeting of the Thomas Jefferson Memorial Commission with representatives from the CFA and the NCPPC. The participants responded to the CFA's request to review the site opposite the National Archives; and, after rejecting it, the TJMC moved into a closed executive session. It unanimously approved the revised, reduced-size Pantheon set amid cherry trees on the Tidal Basin perimeter.[26] The TJMC and the CFA then met jointly on February 3. Kimball observed that everyone wanted the memorial "to get going" and that the commissions needed to be in agreement to overcome opposition. Congress did not like the Tidal Basin site, and Boylan was ready to give up on it. But, he reported, "at the meeting [of the TJMC] last week we swung sentiment around again for the site south of the Washington Monument. Yet the members of the Memorial Commission still prefer the Pantheon design." The TJMC then presented the three requested variations for the Tidal Basin site: the Pantheon, the domeless colonnade, and the split colonnade. CFA Chairman Clarke responded, "I do not see how we [on the CFA] could conscientiously as individuals or as a group give approval to the Pantheon because in our own hearts and souls we believe it is not the thing to use." The meeting's participants agreed to have Eggers further develop the split, double semicircular colonnade scheme and have it reviewed at a special meeting two weeks hence.[27]

Two days later, an informal meeting with members of the CFA and the TJMC that included a visit to the Tidal Basin moved things along toward that February 17 meeting.[28] At the CFA on February 17, Kimball professed that, in the face of the heated opposition, he was committed to getting a memorial, and for that a united front was necessary. The TJMC now found that compromise offered the best solution. It went into what must have been a brief executive session, and when it emerged it reported that "in the interest of harmony," it had decided to accept the Theodore Roosevelt scheme's adaptation but also to "submit the question of design to President Roosevelt for final determination."[29]

But next, a bombshell: Pope's widow would not allow the use of that scheme. In an angry telephone call on February 26, beginning at 4:55 p.m. and recorded

John Russell Pope's revised site design for the Jefferson Memorial, Scheme E, July 29, 1937.

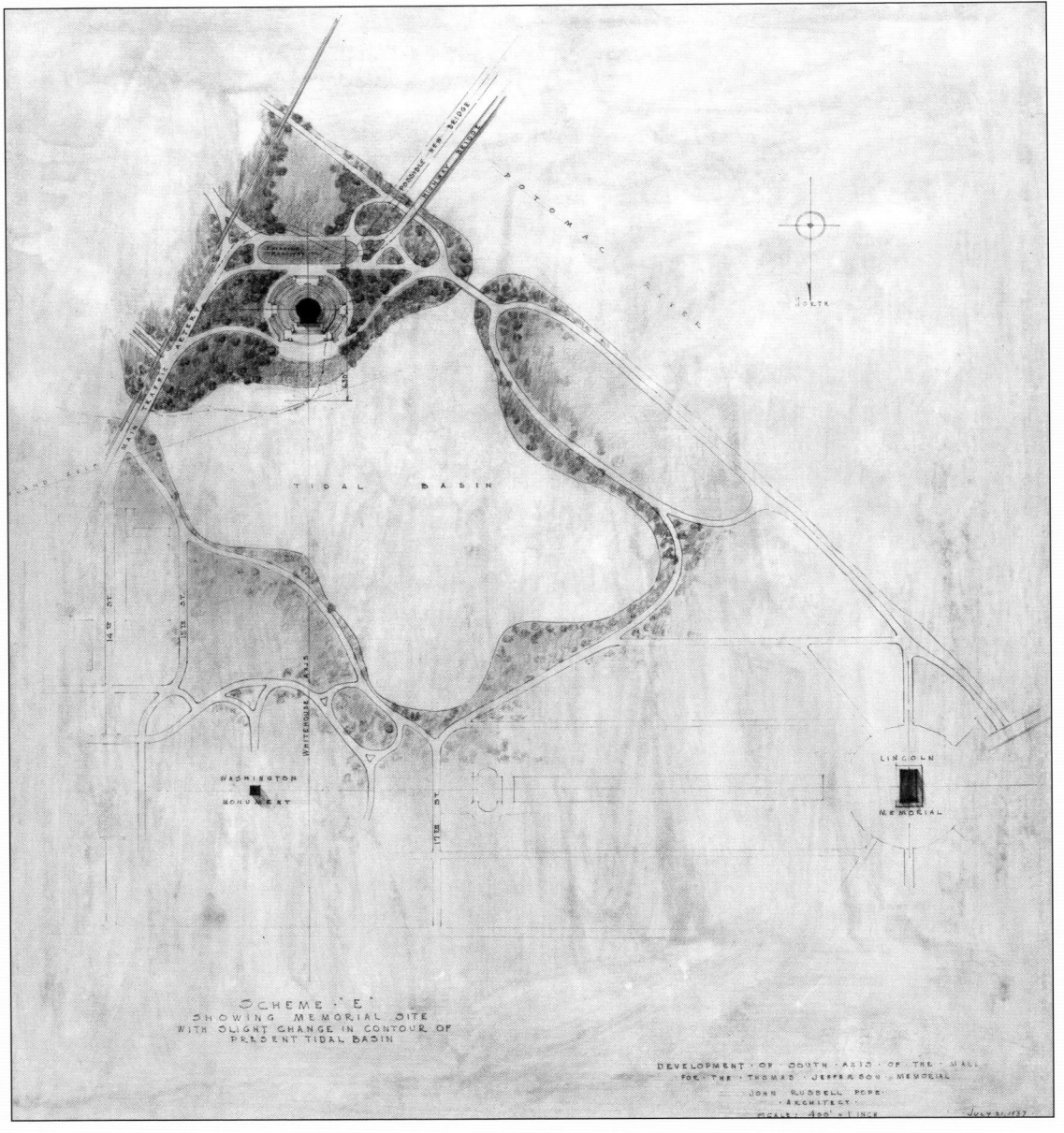

in Kimball's handwritten notes on a sheet titled "The widow," Kimball upbraided Clarke. Had he responded to Mrs. Pope? Did he know that "Eggers and Higgins *had resigned*"? Kimball pointed out that Egerton Swartwout was willing to take on the project, but "he made some trenchant criticism of the open parti and I stand with [him]." Kimball continued, "His retention would mean re-designs, re-approvals, & much delay…. When you *first* came to our board you did not object to the mass," only to the siting. But now, "You have cost us (1) our design…(we gave that up gladly for harmony) but now (2) You have cost us our architects."[30]

Eggers and Higgins were somehow mollified, but Mrs. Pope remained unmoved despite entreaties from old friends Delano and Moore.[31] This left the TJMC with only the domeless Pantheon.

However, President Roosevelt remained attached to the full Pantheon scheme, and so the TJMC now simply turned its back on the CFA.[32] On March 22, the Thomas Jefferson Memorial Commission approved that scheme and prepared Boylan's announcement. The formal presentation of the final design to the CFA produced the predicable rejection with some countersuggestions.[33] On March 29, 1938, the TJMC unanimously resolved to recommend the Pantheon design to Congress. Boylan made his announcement, and the next day President Roosevelt again requested funds to begin construction.[34]

The Issue

The funding request set off round three, which unfolded in public and revealed the underlying issue that made the controversy so intense: The opposing parties supported fundamentally different doctrines of architecture. The opponents—

led by architects, critics, educators, museum personnel, and others whose actions were channeled through the League for Progress in Architecture and who were working covertly with CFA Chairman Clarke—had broached the issue in round one, but now they were better organized in presenting it.[35]

Edwin Alden Jewell, the art reviewer of the *Sunday New York Times,* had clearly explained that doctrine in an essay in 1937. Pope's Pantheon was "first admired by citizens of an antique State." Jewell described it as at home in Claude Lorrain's Italian landscapes, presenting the "regnant ideals of the Old World." Now, with Pope's National Archives built and his National Gallery on the way, Jewell thought "[we] ought to preserve our capital forever as a mighty museum in which descendents of the pioneers might find eternally recorded the multifarious strata of our cultural life. What a rich mine it is!" But to be a "bona fide and comprehensive mausoleum for the ages," he continued, "ought not its new acquisitions to be kept in some slight degree up to date as we proceed forward upon our path of destiny? . . . We may, of course, have to wait five hundred or a thousand years for Congress to 'recognize' what today, in less exalted circles, is looked upon with a measure of diffident pride as American modernism…. The [present] curators of our great architectural museum would, doubtless with consummate argument, refute the premise that Thomas Jefferson, were he to return, might side with the rebel forces in the present crisis of blast and counter-blast."[36]

This clearly and succinctly states that the principal obligation of a building is to spurn traditional forms and be suitable for a city that is, first of all and principally, a museum that portrays the progress of architecture. This doctrine

RIGHT, TOP TO BOTTOM: *Three variations for the Tidal Basin site: Pantheon, circular temple, and open colonnade.*

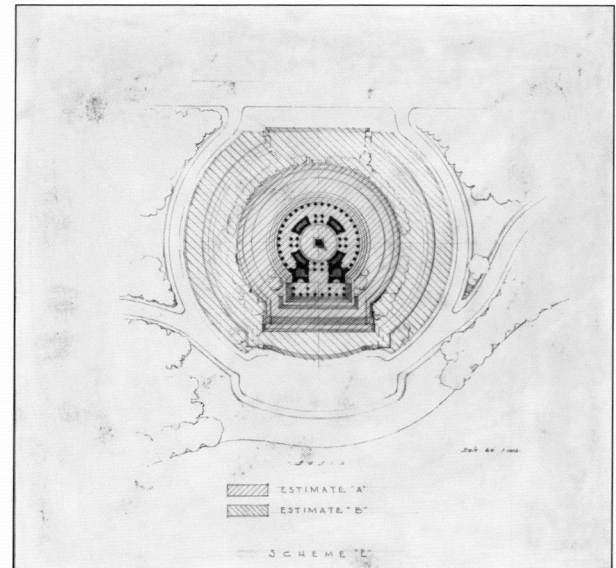

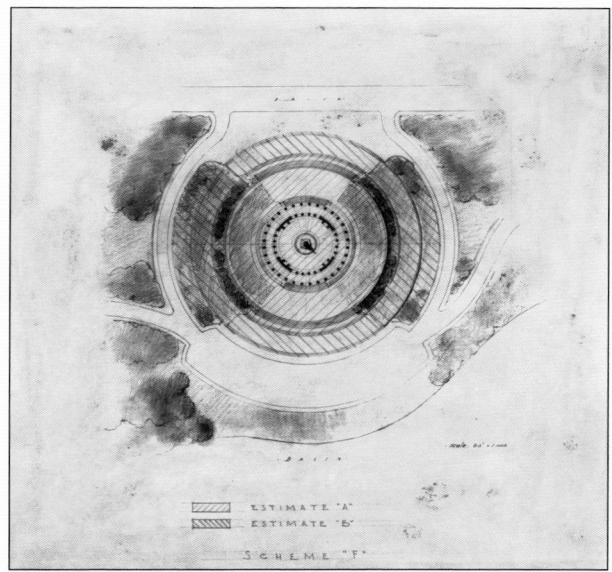

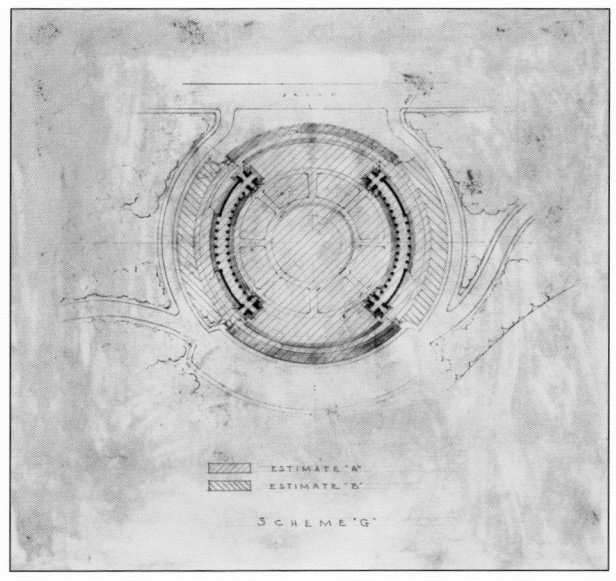

Rendering of the proposed Jefferson Memorial by the office of John Russell Pope, March 29, 1938.

was novel in the Washington of the 1930s. It was absent in 1917 when Pope, then a member of the CFA, worked up a scheme for remodeling Alfred B. Mullett's Second Empire–style State, War, and Navy Building (built from 1871 to 1888; now the Eisenhower Executive Office Building) in a classical style. Secretary of the Navy Franklin Delano Roosevelt enthusiastically endorsed it because it would "get this building to conform to the general scheme of the Treasury." A lack of funds left the building unchanged, and in 1944 the CFA found no reason to change the "interesting old office building, representing an era about seventy-five years ago when the French influence on American architecture prevailed."[37]

New styles make current styles old in changes that document progress. Mullett's was a museum exhibit, as were Pope's by the mid-1930s. They were old. The new was the newly opened Folger Shakespeare Library by Paul Cret and Alexander Trowbridge.[38] In 1929, the critic and historian Henry-Russell Hitchcock saw the future visible in the buildings planned for the 1933 Chicago fair. It "will in a sense annul finally the effect of the Chicago Exposition of 1893."[39] The 1932 Museum of Modern Art's International Style exhibition also presented the future's buildings, although purged of their socialist content.[40] Walter Gropius's installation at Harvard as chairman of the architecture department in 1936 sanctioned the

style's transplantation to America. And historians such as Sigfried Giedion and Nikolaus Pevsner spelled out modernism's inevitability.[41] In this doctrine, Pope's Pantheon was just another Pantheon—and anachronistic to boot.

Joseph Hudnut, dean of Harvard's Graduate School of Design and a Kimball protégé who had just hired Gropius for Harvard, provided a concise summary of the architecture professionals' argument.[42] Simply, Pope's design was not of its time, it was not internationalist, it was not new, and it lacked an appropriate expression. It exhibited "hyperorthodoxy," the essential creed of classicism, which contradicts a "time when architecture throughout the world is being swept triumphantly into new

· A MEMORIAL ·
TO
· THOMAS JEFFERSON ·
WASHINGTON, D. C.

OFFICE OF JOHN RUSSELL POPE
ARCHITECT
MARCH 29, 1938

and magnificent modes of expression."[43]

Hudnut put in a nutshell the anti-traditional and positivist zeitgeist argument of G. W. F. Hegel, Jacob Burckhardt, and Heinrich Wőlfflin, and soon of the modernists Giedion and Pevsner. It provides the basis for designating the period between 1876 and 1917 as the American Renaissance that Richard Guy Wilson has chronicled so well. Wilson had explained that it was acceptable to build Pantheons in America then, but not later when that style had passed into the past.[44] This was the new doctrine that gained prominence in the 1930s, especially among the vigorous critics of Pope's Pantheon. The doctrine's force persuaded the Thomas Jefferson Memorial Commission to retain

a public relations firm that soon flooded the press with photos and stories.[45] But on June 3, 1938, the memorial's funding was approved, and construction began in the fall.[46]

The Jefferson Memorial gracing the Tidal Basin today is a trophy to Kimball's Pyrrhic victory over modernism; but more importantly, it is a testimony to the energy of Roosevelt and all of the other proponents of the design. The opponents wanted a new architecture for a new age; its proponents wanted a new building that made visible the nation's ideals. As Senator Elbert Thomas, a layman in matters architectural, put it,

In the selection of the memorial and the site, we have had in mind one that would carry out the idea that this capital city of ours shall be a grand city, representing the ideals and the aspirations of the American people.[47]

This understanding is perhaps best conveyed in Kimball's *American Architecture* from 1928. "The fathers of the Republic were eager to throw off provincial dependence in other matters than that of sovereignty, to get rid of colonialism, of foreign authority," he wrote.[48] Noah Webster's dictionary did it for language, Kimball continued. The Declaration of Independence did it for the nation, and Jefferson did it for architecture. Kimball then linked architecture and the constitutional order to a common foundation in natural law. Jefferson, Kimball stated, "demanded logical system in thought" and "going to the sources in every field." "Hence the paradox that Jefferson, the apostle of individualism," went to Palladio, "who passes as the chief representative of dogmatic authority." But Palladio

had in common with nature this supposed lawfulness and reasonableness, which was doubtless what Palladio himself felt when he wrote, "Architecture, the imitator of Nature." Here was the relation to natural law, one of Jefferson's fundamental conceptions.[49]

So Jefferson turned to ancient Greek

and Roman buildings not to copy them, but to make them at once novel and correct and thereby secure the respect of foreigners.[50] "The classical ideal thus embodied was ultimately to rule in America to a degree unknown in Europe."[51] Kimball then relates how countercurrents threatened the "continuity with the past" until "the men of fundamental greatness …preserved a sense of form in…architecture. The lesser men, however, the imitators…fell into chaos." The restoration of the "supremacy of abstract form was gathering force" in the works of McKim, Mead, & White. "It was American in its origins and was to remain American in its leadership."[52] The triumph of the World's Columbian Exposition in Chicago was followed by the renewal and expansion of L'Enfant's Washington by architects who established institutions such as the CFA to "be the guardians of their established order."[53]

Kimball noted that after World War I there came "a certain loss of momentum," the result in every "artistic cycle" of the increasing distance in time between the founders and the current practitioners.[54] One result is the "disinfected classicism" in the National Academy of Sciences where Bertram Goodhue "has tried to expurgate without bringing much that is deeply creative. Beside such internal movements, a reflux for abroad is favoring the drift from the classic."[55]

Kimball doubtless knew that in 1922 the CFA had found Goodhue's initial proposal for the National Academy of Sciences unsuitably unclassical and had reluctantly approved it only after the architect made changes.[56] And he surely knew that in 1931 the CFA had approved Pope's National Archives building virtually without discussion and that in the next year it had "enthusiastically" endorsed Cret's Folger Shakespeare Library, which was even less like Pope's design and more like the building by Goodhue, whose achievement Kimball

had said "is more of a negative than a positive character."[57] It comes as no surprise then that in 1935 Kimball sought to persuade the TJMC to give Pope the job, and without a competition. In the TJMC meeting three weeks after the president on March 2, 1936, favorably reviewed "various plans and sketches" by Pope and asked for more studies along the same line, Kimball again discussed with the commission members his preference for Pope. "The old form of classical architecture is dying out, and I have not the slightest doubt that it will be very difficult henceforth to carry on that sort of thing that is wanted for Washington and to find the right man to do it. McKim is dead." So was Charles Platt, Kimball continued, and, further, Egerton Swartwout "is getting to be an old man." Who would be put up against Pope? "[I]f you look at other buildings in the [Federal] Triangle (two members of the CFA, William A. Delano and, eventually, Charles L. Borie, were involved in their design), you will see how commonplace and inferior most of them are…. He is the last great figure in the classical school which was re-founded by McKim in 1893…. [T]here is a tremendous drop after him." What would happen next? "There will be a fight to continue the classical school," Kimball said, to which Representative Howard Smith of Virginia, the TJMC secretary, added, perhaps with Goodhue's Nebraska Capitol in mind, "That is happening in the state capitols now." Then Kimball: "Very much so, and I am very strong for sticking to the last of them."[58]

Kimball was aware of the changing climate. The position that was gaining ground was clear in an early assault on Pope's Pantheon by the prominent journalist and commentator Marquis W. Childs, who noted that Pope's National Archives was "in the grandiose monumental style, its purpose more or less successfully concealed by a careful classicism." Childs then added that Boylan

said that it "makes the other new buildings in Washington look like garages. He regards Mr. Pope as the last exponent of American classical architecture…. You have Mr. Boylan's word for it."[59]

Childs's put-down of Boylan reveals a theme that was prominent among the opponents. The CFA's Chairman Clarke put it clearly in a final desperate letter to President Roosevelt after construction on Pope's Pantheon was under way: "A canvass of the architectural and artistic professions in the United States would disclose, we believe, that among those most *competent to judge* [emphasis added], a large majority is overwhelmingly opposed to the erection of a Roman Pantheon, of which there are already many in the United States."[60] Clearly, those who were "most competent to judge" were the professionals from the arts who served on the CFA, not the politicians and others who did not comprehend the anachronism of Pope's Pantheon. There had been dissension within the CFA ever since its inception, but there was also a general comity founded on the commission's commitment to the 1901 McMillan Plan's commitment to the tradition that linked its vision with that of Jefferson and L'Enfant and on back to antiquity.

Both professionals and laymen understood that the innovation that keeps any tradition alive should continue to be held within the disciplined limits defined by canonic classicism. Boylan put the matter succinctly in laymen's terms:

We wanted to have a memorial built to the honor of Thomas Jefferson, and our thought of it was that as a result of it Washington would be a better and happier and more beautiful place to live in.[61]

Arthur Upham Pope, the prominent archaeologist and historian of Persian art, had denounced the modernists' recently emerged stridency in round one as the "bombast," "abuse," ballyhoo," and "intemperance" of the small number of enthusiasts, and declared that the ba-

sis of their argument was untested by time. They did not ask:

What constitutes architectural excellence? Whence come the canons of architectural beauty? What is the aim and justification of architecture and what can it express properly?

Besides expressing its material and its milieu, architecture, if it is to be permanently effective, must express and render certain qualities that reside permanently in man's own constitutions…. Democracy, for example, is not an affair of the moment as dictators would have us believe, and it ought to be symbolized in forms that have proven their capacity to endure, in forms deeply grounded in human nature and human experience, and which carry world-wide conviction….

The new memorial accepts and honors [Jefferson's] choice, and presents it in a new guise, more ample and majestic—just as his ideal of democracy has through national growth, triumph, tragedy, and deepening experience, become a grander thing than Jefferson foresaw.[62]

Senator Thomas alluded to dictators and democracies in his testimony to the House Appropriations Committee:

I think no one in this day and age can depreciate in the least the value of monuments in reflecting the belief of the American people in democracy. I say that in the light of what is happening in the world and in the light of what is happening in our own country at the present time.[63]

Later in that hearing, Kimball defended laymen against professionals:

Gentlemen, you are laymen. Laymen are the ones who are going to see this memorial, and we think that under American traditions, perhaps it should be a body of laymen which, after hearing all the professional advice, should make such a decision [about what to build].[64]

Kimball articulated what these laymen knew but perhaps could not articulate: the union of form and content in Pope's Pantheon allied it with a tradition of architecture as a civic art that serves and represents civic institutions and builds cities. Its basis is in the imitation of the lawful order of nature and its en-

during principles.[65] The result can be beauty, which takes different forms in different times and places. Kimball's *American Architecture* recognized that such a building is a complement to a nation's constitution and, like it, gives different forms in different times and places to natural law, which is the "nature" named in the Declaration of Independence. Both the buildings and the constitutional order have the shared purpose of facilitating each individual's pursuit of happiness. The beauty of a nation's buildings and cities are visible declarations of that proposal. To achieve that purpose, both buildings and constitutions require continuity within tradition. The *Federalist Papers* are redolent with the idea, one that Kimball put this way in 1928:

Using the Roman alphabet, the established universal terms of classical form, the American designers made what had been thought a dead language the idiom of current speech, expressing with unexpected flexibility the ideas of a new age.[66]

In this face-off between laymen who would extend tradition through constant innovation and professionals who would abandon tradition to embrace novelty, Frank Lloyd Wright stood as the most conspicuous and outspoken inventor of the novel. Kimball acknowledged Wright as "a close personal friend," but in Pope's moving obituary Kimball wrote that Wright's was a voice "crying in the wilderness" and accompanied there by a "host of secondary men."[67] In his *American Architecture,* he had seen promising trends in the work of innovators, but in the obituary Kimball wrote that a lesser breed had failed to deliver. The young equate "value with style…. The 'functional' movement…[is] misunderstood by imitators and travestied by speculative builders [and] the 'international style'…[is] merely parroted and travestied by most adherents and admirers." Greatness requires a fanaticism and acceptance of the "endless flux which

brings his own work into being," knowing that it would later be renounced. Even the neoclassical architects "still involved in the passions of contemporary struggle" cannot hope to achieve "the veneration reserved only for the men who inaugurated vast movements of fundamentally original character, like Michelangelo, like the architects of Saint Denis," and like John Russell Pope: "His designs were ripened, matured, digested—transmuting the elements into a work that was his own."[68]

In a letter to the editor in the *Magazine of Art* a little later, Kimball wrote, "It may be contended that the day of the classic in American architecture is over…. I am very sympathetic with the effort to end the 'petrified forest' of columns in Washington."[69] But none of the architects who reject tradition could through argument or example persuade Kimball or the laymen to abandon their adherence to a two-millennia-long conjunction of the principles that supported architecture's quest for beauty and the civil order's quest for justice.

That conjunction was the theme of Kimball's *American Architecture,* and it was the target of the Pantheon's opponents' doctrine. The *New York Times* critic would remake the nation's capital into a museum of progress in architecture. CFA Chairman Clarke writing in 1944 said the same thing in a different way. "The strict and rigid compliance with the tenets of the classical school in architecture . . . must be abandoned in favor of a more fresh approach to the problem which will confront the designers of new buildings in the future."[70] His commission has "urged adherence to beauty of form, to excellence of proportions and to permanence of materials," but without "those details on buildings, which particularly distinguish Greek and Roman monuments," in other words, those details that connect them with their fellows across time.[71] When this new doctrine achieved hegemony, the

coin of the realm was no longer nationalism but internationalism, not beauty but novelty, and not continuity but a vigorous antitraditionalism.

Kimball explicitly rejected this new doctrine. In a book he was writing during these years on the Rococo interior in France, he dismissed forcefully and out of hand the "vicious intellectualism" of the *zeitgeist* argument.[72] His leadership allowed the laymen and politicians who understood America as he did to prevail in this battle, but it was the last such battle they would win. On the two-hundredth anniversary of the third president's birth, with Washington on a war footing to defend democracy against tyranny, President Roosevelt dedicated the last building in Washington that would make visible the lawful natural order of the nation's constitutional order and connect the nation's present and future with its roots across time and back to antiquity.

CHAPTER IV

Heroism, History, and Automobiles

THE CHAIRMANSHIPS OF GILMORE CLARKE AND DAVID FINLEY, 1937–1963

B y the late 1930s, the momentous changes occurring in American architecture finally began to have a lasting effect on the Commission of Fine Arts. Modernism was beginning to transform architectural practice, thought, and training in the United States. In its deliberations, the commission—formerly a bastion of adherence to the classical paradigm—now began to accommodate new approaches to the design of public buildings and space.

Upon the resignation of Charles Moore as chairman of the commission in the midst of the controversy over the Thomas Jefferson Memorial, the landscape architect Gilmore D. Clarke was elected chairman by his colleagues in 1937.[1] Clarke combined in his practice skill in landscape design, architecture, and civil engineering, which prepared him well to handle the complex projects facing the commission in the 1930s and 1940s. While other CFA chairmen—Moore, David Finley, William Walton (CFA 1963–71), and J. Carter Brown—had powerful political connections in Washington, Clarke did not; he seems to have compensated with a forceful personality and wide practical experience.

Early in his career, Clarke had become an authority on the design of parkways: curving roadways running through landscaped settings, which became a hallmark of American roadway design. Clarke's early parkways, including the Bronx River Parkway (1916–23) and the multiple parkways of Westchester County, New York (1922–34), significantly influenced highway design throughout the eastern United States.[2] Clarke's work in Westchester County led to his commission for the Mount Vernon Memorial Highway (completed in 1932), a George Washington bicentennial project located along the Virginia shore of the Potomac River that linked the Arlington Memorial Bridge with Mount Vernon. A commendation of Gilmore Clarke as commission chairman described his contribution:

This period was…the beginning of the "New Deal," when new ideas pertaining to architecture, sculpture and painting were being advocated, particularly in Washington. It was probably at its height when Major Clarke [Army Corps of Engineers Reserve] became Chairman and it was especially through his leadership that a compromise was reached between a hitherto severe classical style and a contemporary style in architecture, sculpture, and painting, that represented a new approach to works of art in these professions as advocated by artists of the present generation.[3]

After Charles Moore left Washington following his retirement as a commission member in 1940, he remained in contact with his former colleagues, primarily through consultation with Gilmore Clarke. Moore's death on September

FACING PAGE: *The pair of winged equestrian statues titled* The Arts of Peace (*comprising* Music and Harvest *on the left and* Aspiration and Literature *on the right) by James Earle Fraser, at the entrance to Rock Creek and Potomac Parkway, c. 1955.*

165

Portrait of Gilmore D. Clarke by Sidney E. Dickinson, 1951. Clarke served as chairman of the Commission of Fine Arts for thirteen years, overseeing the commission's review of projects during a period defined by World War II and modernism's slow ascendancy in Washington.

Most of the architects were based in New York City and were members of the Century Club. In their practices, however, they had begun to modify classical vocabulary through abstraction and simplification and to use new materials in new types of construction.

The first architect to serve on the commission who can be identified as modern was William F. Lamb. Appointed in 1937, Lamb had attended Columbia University and the École and early in his career had been a partner in the noted New York City Beaux-Arts firm of Carrère & Hastings before entering into practice with R. H. Shreve and Arthur L. Harmon, his partners in the design of the Empire State Building (1931). Charles L. Borie, appointed in 1936, designed, with his partner Milton Medary, the Justice Department building, a structure that melded suggestions of art moderne within the classical vocabulary of the Federal Triangle.

Probably the most renowned architect to be appointed in 1940 was Paul Philippe Cret, the French-born, École-trained architect based in Philadelphia who had been presenting his designs before the commission for decades. Cret was responsible for several of the most revered buildings of twentieth-century Washington—buildings that were widely regarded as successfully bridging the gap between classicism and modernism, including the Folger Shakespeare Library, the Central Heating Plant, and the Federal Reserve building.

The painter Eugene F. Savage (CFA 1933–41) was known for his murals depicting allegorical and historical scenes in Beaux-Arts public buildings executed in the Northeast and Midwest. In 1941 he was replaced on the commission by muralist Henry Varnum Poor, a regionalist painter. Paul Manship (CFA 1937–41), famous for his linear, faux-archaic sculpture, was replaced by the sculptor and painter Ralph Stackpole (CFA 1941–45). Although he had attended the École des Beaux-Arts as well as the Robert Henri School of Art in New York, Stackpole had made his career in San Francisco and was the first commission member from the West.

While the commission had fought unsuccessfully against the academic classicism of John Russell Pope, the members had also resoundingly rejected the Saarinens' modernist proposal for the Smithsonian Gallery of Art in 1939. Only in the 1940s did the commission begin to seriously negotiate an approach to accommodating modernism in Washington. In an address delivered before the Joint Committee on the National Capital in 1944—an organization comprising national civic and arts groups—Clarke expressed the tentative approach toward modern architecture taken by the conservative members of the CFA in the 1930s:

25, 1942, ended an era in the history of the Commission of Fine Arts. Testifying to his wide influence, the CFA received tributes to Moore from many state and national organizations, among them the Architectural League of New York, the National Sculpture Society, and, of course, the NCPPC and the Division of Manuscripts at the Library of Congress. Moore's successor in 1940 as the commission's lay member was Edward Bruce; after Bruce's death in 1943, David E. Finley, at the time also director of the National Gallery of Art, was appointed to fill the vacancy.

The first signs of a greater transition in the training and tastes of the commission's architect members became apparent in the members appointed in the late 1930s and early 1940s. Most appointees had received a standard training at Ivy League schools and the École des Beaux-Arts; most were fellows of the American Institute of Architects and, like their predecessors, enjoyed affiliations with leading cultural institutions such as the American Academy in Rome, the American Academy of Arts and Letters, and the National Institute of Arts and Letters.

During the last decade the Commission have witnessed material changes in the general character of artistic creation, particularly within the field of architecture…. Insofar as the National Capital is concerned, changes in architectural expression fortunately have been gradual for, as you are fully aware, the Commission have [sic] not sanctioned the abandonment of the classic background which was the basis for rebuilding the City in the years of its Renaissance, stimulated by the Senate Park Commission in 1901.

Clarke then summarized the CFA's approach: "We have urged adherence to beauty of form, to excellence of proportions and to permanence of materials, all attributes of design exemplary of the art of the architecture of the past." Noting that the Washington buildings of Cret and Bertram Goodhue had never been found incongruous, Clarke recommended that "as architectural designs are simplified, we make room for rich embellishment by sculptor and by painter and thus provide a greater distinction in our buildings, a distinction which will tend to make them wholly American in their flavor." At the end of the speech, Clarke suggested the CFA's movement toward an acceptance of stylistic change:

The strict and rigid compliance with the tenets of the classical school in architecture, which have obtained altogether too long in Washington, must be abandoned in favor of a more fresh approach to the problems which will confront the designers of new buildings in the future.[4]

Otherwise, the commission only intimated its struggles with this radical design philosophy through offhanded comments or reviews of minor projects. A few times in its deliberations, the commission referred disparagingly to William Lescaze's 1940 Longfellow Building at Connecticut and Rhode Island Avenues, NW—the first modernist

office building in the city, with ribbon windows and sheer walls expressing a functional core. Modern architecture derived meaning as well as form from the exploitation of new materials and technologies rather than from an aesthetic relying on masonry units intimately proportioned to human scale. It was left for modernist architects and for a Commission of Fine Arts increasingly composed of such architects to determine what could be meaningful and monumental for the nation's capital in this new age.

By the eve of World War II, modernism had become an acceptable style for federal and other buildings in the District, with architects trying to find appropriate modern forms for office buildings and other building types within the parameters of Washington's Beaux-Arts legacy. This change was already evident in the physical manifestation of the New Deal's response to the Great Depression: an expanded federal workforce consolidated in large box office buildings, now made possible by advances in air conditioning and artificial lighting.

At the same time, a guiding comprehensive vision for both the planning and design of the nation's capital fell victim to expediency in this time of national emergency, which would only intensify during the height of the war and through the 1950s. These years were a time of shifting paradigms in aesthetics and technology, and the importance of urban centers—as well as their design—would change radically as a result. The United States emerged from World War II with its industrial base intact and geared for production; its enormous economic capacity and vigorous embrace of the automobile would focus development toward the periphery of cities into the

Paul Philippe Cret (c. 1920) was the commission architect most successful at creating a modernist style that respected the forms, planning, and principles of Beaux-Arts design.

The Commission of Fine Arts in 1940 included architects who had begun to meld Beaux-Arts design precepts with modernism in their work. From left: Edward Bruce, John A. Holabird, Eugene Savage, Gilmore Clarke, secretary H. P. Caemmerer, Paul Cret, William F. Lamb, and Paul Manship.

ABOVE LEFT: *Cret's Central Heating Plant (c. 1934) in Southwest Washington made a simple utilitarian structure into a tautly controlled, powerfully expressive modernist monument.*

ABOVE RIGHT: *Completed in 1940, the Longfellow Building on Connecticut Avenue—designed by William Lescaze, architect of Philadelphia's iconic PSFS skyscraper—was Washington's first modernist office building, notable for its unbroken horizontal ribbon windows, expressive balconies, and streamlined form.*

expanding rings of suburbia. America's urban centers would be transformed through the federal government's well-intentioned but destructive redevelopment policies and automobile-oriented infrastructure projects; Washington would not be exempt from this transformation.

Ironically, the role of the CFA was directed in these decades less toward active engagement in city building, which emphasized wartime expediency and postwar urban renewal, and more to an intense focus on art and objects, expressed primarily in the decoration of Washington's new federal office buildings. By the end of this period, Washington was undergoing drastic physical change, and even national symbols were threatened by new tastes and priorities. The Commission of Fine Arts would find itself defending basic principles related to these sites, although not always successfully, and while the capital city was radically transformed by the implementation of a new urban order based on the movement of automobiles, the commission would also play a role in nurturing a nascent interest in the field of historic preservation.

Building for the Federal Bureaucracy

The expanded federal bureaucracy resulting from President Roosevelt's New Deal initiatives, World War II, and postwar policies was housed in new office space both within and immediately outside the District. Although two new departmental headquarters, the enormous Department of the Interior (1935–36) and the War Department (1941), had been constructed in the Northwest Rectangle, the Southwest quadrant became the focus of much of the new federal office construction. By the end of the 1940s, the War Department building was supplanted by

the Pentagon in Arlington, Virginia, as the military's headquarters—with President Roosevelt's active involvement in that decision—and the massive structure in the Northwest Rectangle area known as Foggy Bottom was transferred to the State Department. In the postwar years, the building's size was more than tripled to fill two city blocks. The potential effect of this and other federal office construction on the monumental core as well as the design implications of building typologies and improved building technology were of great concern to the Commission of Fine Arts throughout this period.

THE SOUTHWEST QUADRANT

In the late 1930s, the federal government and private developers under a federal lease program first began constructing office buildings in Southwest Washington, revitalizing what had been considered a derelict residential area. Development interest continued into the 1940s and 1950s, transforming the Southwest quadrant into the District's center for federal office construction during these years.[5] In its reviews, the CFA guided the design of these buildings to provide a frame for the Mall corresponding to the Northwest Rectangle, following one of the major planning goals of the McMillan Plan, albeit within a modern idiom.

Two main building types were explored in this development: the closed court, in which offices on both sides of central corridors could have windows facing either the building's exterior or an interior courtyard; and the open-court or "fishbone" plan with wings extending off of one main corridor, forming courts that were open at one end. The Interior Department building on C Street, NW, in the Northwest Rectangle served as the general model for the

In the Social Security building (c. 1941, now the Wilbur J. Cohen Federal Building), architect Charles Z. Klauder solved the awkward facade interruptions resulting from the fishbone plan's open courtyards by inserting a pier in the center of each opening and using a continuous base and entablature.

latter type of courtyard office structure. Advantages of the open-court typology were more extensive views and greater amounts of natural light in interior offices, making them comparable in this respect to offices along outside walls. However, the fishbone form resulted in a choppy and disjointed appearance since at least one side of the building was composed of wings with short end elevations alternating with the open courts. The closed court, used in many of the Federal Triangle buildings, had the advantages of better internal circulation and unbroken elevations, lending greater dignity and monumentality to a facade. The disadvantages were restricted views and limited natural light entering facing offices.[6]

The Social Security building (1939–41, now the Wilbur J. Cohen Federal Building; built concurrently with the Mary E. Switzer Memorial Building to its south)—among the first federal projects built specifically to house New Deal programs—also was among the first federal buildings in the Southwest quadrant, prominently located on the large block facing Independence Avenue between 3rd, 4th, and C Streets, SW.[7] In presenting preliminary sketches to the Commission of Fine Arts, Charles Z. Klauder, consulting architect for the Treasury Department's Office of the Supervising Architect (OSA), described a building that "in some respects...will have the severity of an Egyptian facade," with cavetto cornices reminiscent of Egyptian temples, deep window reveals, and a general lack of articulation, which heightened the impression of mass.[8]

Klauder's sketches also showed a fishbone plan that featured wings projecting from a long central corridor running east-west midway through the block, which resulted in courts opening to both north and south. The commis-

sion's remarks focused less on the building's decorative elements and more on this basic choice of building typology, which the members did not find appropriate for a building facing the Mall "or in any part of the Central Composition." Agreeing that fishbone buildings were unsightly, Klauder restudied the building's Mall facade and developed a sketch in which he massed the projecting wings and used a common low base to give the appearance of pylons, added a uniform cornice line, and placed piers at the ends of the courts to serve as screens. The commission found these changes to be an improvement.[9] Klauder also sheathed the facade facing Independence Avenue and the elevations along 3rd and 4th Streets with limestone. The commission noted that the changes made the projecting wings unobtrusive, and members praised the results. Clarke described it as "a building monumental in character, which at the same time is unique in that Mr. Klauder makes use of projecting wings without giving them the appearance of the undesirable fishbone type."[10] Cret commented that "Mr. Klauder did a fine job with this building; it is classic in feeling."[11]

Projects for sculpture and murals in the building, commissioned under the Section of Fine Arts of the Public Buildings Service, came before the commission between 1940 and 1942. Large bas-relief panels for placement over the entrance doors of the building included *The Growth of Social Security* by Henry Kreis, which illustrated two men clasping hands after planting a young tree. Panels were executed in dark red granite, contrasting matte surfaces for the figures with polished surfaces for the backgrounds, and employed stylized, abstracted heroic figures. The CFA also reviewed murals for the interiors, including works by Ben Shahn and Philip Guston.

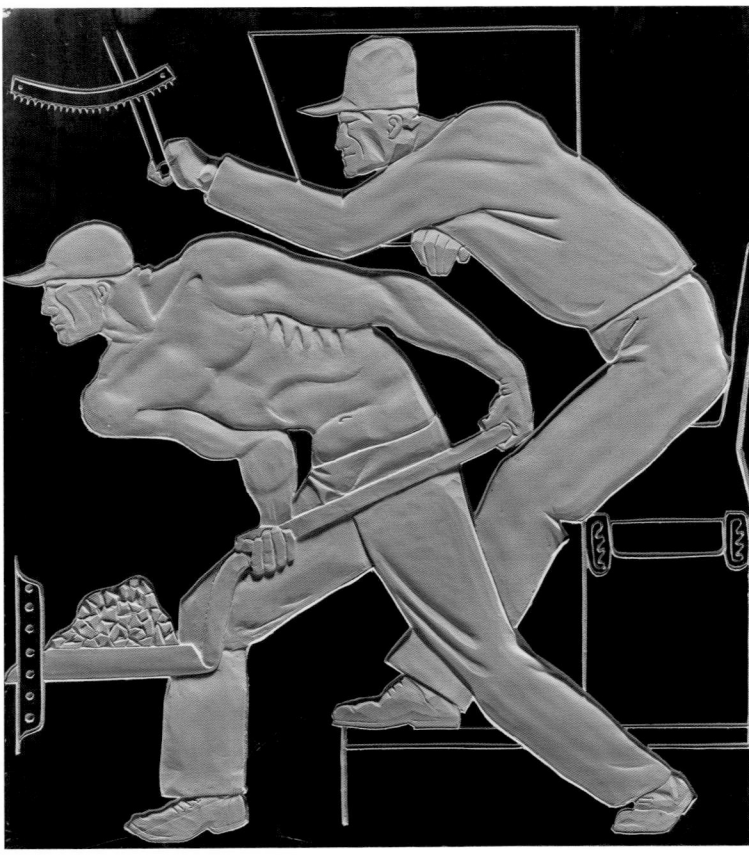

TOP, LEFT AND RIGHT: *Bas-relief panels celebrating the dignity of labor rendered in an abstracted social realist style include* The Growth of Social Security *by Henry Kreis at the Social Security building, 1941; and* Railroad Employment *by Robert Kittridge at the Railroad Retirement Board building, 1941.*

ABOVE AND RIGHT: *Frescoes at the Social Security building depicting the social benefit of the economic productivity and security of workers include* The Wealth of the Nation *by Seymour Fogel, 1942, and* Reconstruction and Well-Being of the Family, *by Philip Guston, 1943.*

Commission commentary on these panels and ornamental pieces for other buildings frequently showed members struggling with the new movements in art. Paul Manship, in particular, seemed ill-disposed to the changes in artistic representation. He described the preliminary designs for the sculptured overdoor panels for the Social Security building by Emma Lu Davis as displaying an "emotionalism suggestive of sur-realism[sic]"; his stance led the commission to disapprove Davis's first studies for the work. Commenting on bronze sculpture panels by Robert Cronbach for the Social Security building's auditorium, Manship wrote:

I realize that progress does not always follow tradition, but I am convinced that any new form must show seriousness of intention and integrity of technique and handicraft…. It is not within the province of the Commission of Fine Arts to approve perpetuation in bronze of psychopathic experiments which may be appropriate to the laboratory or studio.[12]

THE PENTAGON

By far the largest of Washington's great office complexes was built under the shadow of impending war: a new headquarters for the War Department to house the growing number of defense personnel as America anticipated entry into World War II. With conflict imminent, the War Department was determined to construct its new office building—the largest such structure in the world at the time—in only one year. The project, first presented to the commission in August 1941, faced strong opposition from numerous quarters, including the *Washington Post* and the *Washington Star,* Secretary of the Interior Harold Ickes, and Gilmore Clarke. Frederic A. Delano, chairman of the NCPPC and uncle of the president, favored the idea at first

but soon changed his mind, and the two commissions united to defeat it.

The War Department, and the project's pugnacious leader, Brigadier General Brehon Somervell, expected to locate the complex on sixty-seven acres of the former Arlington Experimental Farm, lying north of the proposed route of Memorial Avenue and within full view of the Lincoln Memorial and the historic Arlington House in Arlington National Cemetery. The question of an appropriately respectful treatment of Arlington National Cemetery had long concerned the CFA and the Senate Park Commission before it, whose 1901 report called for the cemetery's protection:

Nothing could be more impressive than the rank after rank of white stones, inconspicuous in themselves, covering the gentle, wooded slopes, and producing the desired effect of a vast army in its last resting place…. This is one of the most beautiful spots in the vicinity of Washington; it should not be defaced or touched in any way, and a law or rule should at once be passed forbidding the placing of any monument on this hill.[13]

As early as 1919, after construction had begun on the Lincoln Memorial and with planning for the Arlington Memorial Bridge soon to begin, the CFA had provided the army with recommendations for the cemetery's proper treatment and expansion: "Arlington prospectively is a portion of the great central composition of Washington… [which] imposes…certain restrictions in the location of grave areas…. It is time now to see about recovering those portions of the Arlington estate which have been given up to the Agricultural Experimental Station."[14]

Now, in 1941, the commission maintained its long-held opinion: the former Agricultural Experimental lands should be included within Arlington National Cemetery,

Ben Shahn, Unemployment panel on the east wall of *The Meaning of Social Security mural, Social Security building, 1942.*

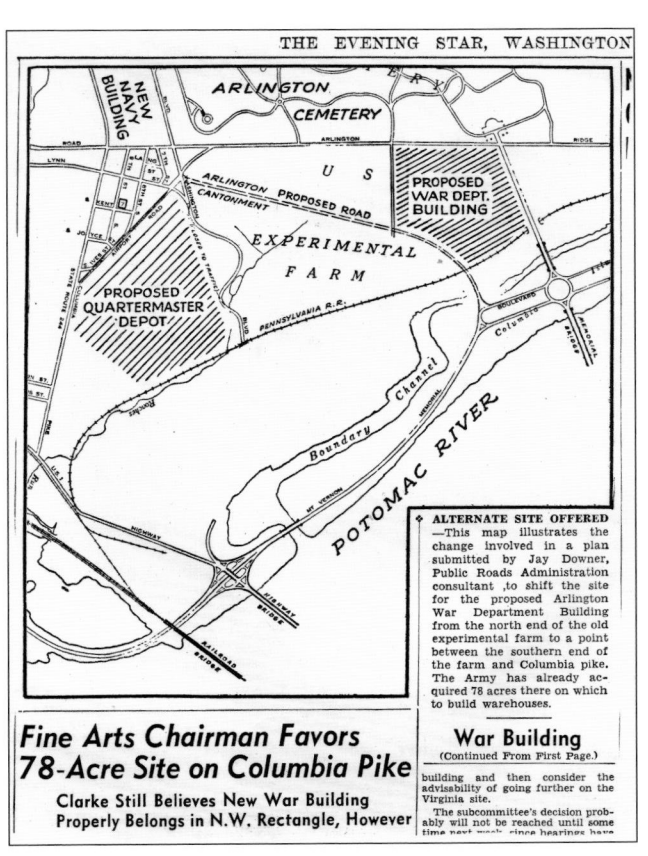

ABOVE LEFT: *Article in the Washington* Evening Star *of August 6, 1941, showing the original proposal for the Pentagon placed almost directly across the Potomac River from the Lincoln Memorial. The quartermaster depot site further south, supported by the CFA, removed the building from this critical viewshed.*

ABOVE RIGHT: *Clifford Berryman's* Evening Star *cartoon of August 20, 1942, caricatured President Roosevelt advocating to move the Pentagon site away from Memorial Bridge.*

and the cemetery itself, including its vistas, should remain inviolable. Gilmore Clarke took the lead in fighting against the site.[15] He railed against the location and the design, calling the pentagon shape "atrocious…a bull's-eye."[16] Clarke and the CFA issued a press release on August 1, 1941, which pointed out that both the CFA and the NCPPC had for twenty years urged that this property be included in the cemetery and warned that, if constructed on the proposed site, the thirty-five-acre roof of the War Department structure would be visible from Arlington House and the Lincoln Memorial. Further, immense traffic problems would result from the huge number of workers entering and leaving the complex. The statement concluded: "The Commission of Fine Arts…do [*sic*] not look with favor upon the proposition to erect buildings of any description upon lands which for years past have been designated as open area to be unencumbered save with the graves of the honored dead of the Army and the Navy of the United States." Its most appropriate use, the commission argued,

was as parkland: "a foreground or a background for the Central Composition of the great Capital City of Washington."[17] In a joint meeting with the NCPPC on August 1, 1941, other sites were discussed adjacent to the new War Department building in the Northwest Rectangle or at the eastern end of East Capitol Street.[18] Clarke denounced the building and site at a Senate Appropriations Committee hearing on August 8, but his sarcasm irritated many senators. Countering Clarke's remarks in his statement before the committee, Somervell argued that the building's stature as headquarters for the War Department in fact deserved this important location within view of Arlington House. A few days later, the Senate authorized construction on the Arlington Experimental Farm site.[19]

The CFA intervened by suggesting to the president another location farther south, on the site of a planned quartermaster depot on Columbia Pike, next to Hoover Airport and situated in a dilapidated industrial neighborhood south of Arlington Cemetery. According to information

CHAPTER IV | HEROISM, HISTORY, AND AUTOMOBILES

TOP: *A complex network of highways—including bridges and abutments designed by the firm of Paul Cret—would be required to handle the huge influx of employees commuting to the Pentagon as illustrated in this 1942 proposal by the Federal Roads Agency.*

BOTTOM: *Aerial photo (c. 1945) of the recently completed Pentagon surrounded by automobile infrastructure; it is still the largest federal office building in the United States.*

Clarke had obtained through a colleague, the site was readily available.[20] By this time, Roosevelt was having second thoughts about the Arlington Farm site. As assistant secretary of the navy in 1917, he had played an instrumental role in having the huge Navy and Munitions temporary buildings constructed on Constitution Avenue, believing that the structures were so unattractive that their demolition was assured after the end of the World War.[21] In 1941 the buildings remained, and Roosevelt's regret made him wary of imposing further intrusions on the plan for Washington. In late July, Roosevelt also was persuaded by close associates, including his uncle Frederic Delano, to reduce the number of employees in the new building by half, from forty thousand to twenty thousand workers. This action acknowledged the traffic problems likely to result from the limited capacity of the Virginia roads and the Potomac River bridges to handle the surge in commuter traffic, a decision announced to the press shortly afterward.

Roosevelt asked Clarke and Somervell, along with the War Department's consulting architect, Edwin Bergstrom, and a representative of the NCPPC to accompany him on a visit to the depot site following a meeting at the White House on August 29. Significantly, and to Clarke's great satisfaction, Roosevelt had the CFA chairman sit by his side in the backseat of the presidential limousine, with Somervell on Clarke's other side. Roosevelt made it clear that he

had already accepted the depot site as proposed by the commission, refusing even to stop by Arlington Farm on the return trip to the White House.[22]

Edwin Bergstrom presented a preliminary design for the Pentagon at the depot site to the commission at its September 1941 meeting, which was attended only by Clarke, William F. Lamb, and Paul Cret. Architect John A. Holabird (CFA 1940–45) could not attend but said he would agree with whatever Lamb and Cret decided. Lamb and Cret stressed the vital role that circulation would play in such a large building, with Cret noting it was almost a city plan. Lamb expressed a preference for a rectangular building, and both architects suggested that Bergstrom carefully study the proportions of the facades because his first versions lacked personality; Bergstrom revised the elevation drawings based on these recommendations. Acknowledging the rushed schedule of the emergency measure, the CFA expressed its satisfaction with the site but requested further study of the elevations and the interior circulation.[23]

That afternoon, following the commission meeting, Clarke, Cret, and Lamb met with the president to discuss the design. Roosevelt emphasized that he wanted the building to be shaped like a pentagon—a shape derived from the original site—and not a rectangle, so that it would be unique. Yet, Roosevelt thought that after the war this uniquely designed building would be used solely for file stor-

The Pentagon's relatively low profile and its location across the Potomac River beyond an island and a lagoon belie the building's massive scale, which is further modulated by abstracted classical porticoes and pavilions (1945).

CHAPTER IV | HEROISM, HISTORY, AND AUTOMOBILES

age and that the War Department would return to its former headquarters in the Northwest Rectangle. Roosevelt assured the three men that all plans would be reviewed by the commission despite Somervell's continued insistence that a structure in Virginia would lie outside the CFA's jurisdiction. The president then requested a report on the design and the new site from the commission, which was prepared and submitted within hours. The report noted the CFA was "greatly pleased," emphasizing that "the important termination of the Central Composition is no longer endangered by the too close proximity of the overwhelming mass of building at one side of the Arlington Memorial Bridge."[24]

GENERAL ACCOUNTING OFFICE

As both the federal bureaucracy and the need to house it continued to grow, a third typology for federal office buildings was developed: one without courtyards at all. The first of these buildings was for the General Accounting Office (GAO, now the Government Accountability Office), an agency authorized by Congress in 1921 and located in the Pension Building in Judiciary Square in 1926. In the 1930s, remodeling and enlarging the Pension Building was considered as a way to house the agency's expanding workforce, as was relocating the agency to a new building in the Southwest quadrant. However, the agency favored remaining downtown, and funds were appropriated by Con-

gress in 1940 to secure the site and construct the building on Square 518, immediately north of the Pension Building.

In 1951, the agency finally moved into its boxy, seven-story headquarters, a block building designed to gain the greatest efficiency through housing the largest number of workers within a given area. Occupying almost the entire square between G, 3rd, H, and 5th Streets, NW, the building had no internal courts or fishbone-type wings. The massive new structure, which housed 10,000 employees, was designed by Gilbert Stanley Underwood of the Office of the Supervising Architect, who, with William Dewey Foster, had also designed the War Department building in Foggy Bottom. Its enormous size was mitigated by a setback of the top two stories over the central bays. The decorative use of stone and sculpture at the G Street entrance relieved the long, plain facade.

Initial sketches for the building by Foster and R. Stanley Brown presented to the commission in January 1941 showed a fishbone plan with pavilions resting on a colonnade. The commission urged that the building be relocated to East Capitol Street "instead of crowding so many Government buildings in this section of the city," but the GAO kept the intended site. The commission then focused on the building's bulk, recommending revision of the colonnade to reduce its prominence and further careful study of the entrances.

The General Accounting Office (now the Government Accountability Office) was completed in 1951, the first federal office building to dispense with internal courtyards. Architect Gilbert Stanley Underwood employed setbacks, a red granite base, bas-relief panels at the entrance, and shot-sawn limestone panels to enliven its bulk (c. 1958).

mer student of both the Beaux-Arts Institute of Design in New York and of cfa member Lee Lawrie, who was himself chosen to execute panels for the H Street entrance. Lawrie's work was never completed, however, due to a lack of funds. The commission approved Kiselewski's panels in 1950, which depicted professionals, such as medical doctors and teachers, on the left side of the entrance and laborers, including farmers and miners, on the right; both groups were arranged in three tiers on the curving wall surfaces and were rendered in a stylized art deco mode.[26]

THE NORTHWEST RECTANGLE AND THE ADDITION TO THE DEPARTMENT OF STATE

More than in the Federal Triangle or the Southwest quadrant, development in the Northwest Rectangle involved the careful fitting in and manipulation of structures to protect views of the Lincoln Memorial area and to accommodate the raking angles and awkward relationship of the two L'Enfant Plan boulevards crossing the site—New York and Virginia Avenues. The sequence of white marble buildings along Constitution Avenue was finally completed in 1948 with the construction of the Pan American Union administration building after fifteen years of wrangling, largely due to Harold Ickes's obstructions. Disagreement over size, setback, possible street closings, and placement of the building on its small polygonal lot contributed to the delay.

The second phase of the former War Department headquarters building—by this time occupied by the State Department—advanced in the 1940s and 1950s. Working drawings for an addition that dwarfed the original were developed in 1947 by the architects Graham, Anderson, Probst & White with Harley, Ellington & Day. The new block, completed in 1958, was three-and-a-half times the size of the first, extending from 21st Street and Virginia Avenue south to C Street and west to 23rd, with entrances on C, E, and 23rd Streets; 22nd Street was closed to accommodate the new building. The building's height was lowered along C Street to six stories, in deference to the height of the Lincoln Memorial and the buildings along Constitution Avenue. Two interior courts provided natural light within the new structure, and the south half of the building was lowered one story to conform to the C Street facade of the Department of the Interior building. The design of the addition was derived from the original, although with a smooth rather than rough limestone facing and red-brown granite spandrels.

By 1956, the design had been revised, giving evidence of the gradual transformation of stripped classicism to a

Sculptor Joseph Kiselewski's clay study (c. 1949) of solid and simple bas-relief figures flanking the G Street entrance of the GAO building suited its sober and powerful facade.

The project was not resubmitted to the commission until after the war. The design was now for a block building, and the architects suggested using polished red granite as a base material to contrast with the more textured shot-sawn limestone panels used as facing on the elevations. The CFA recommended providing a visual base for the facades through the addition of a level line of granite around the building at the first-floor window sills, except at the entrances, where for emphasis the granite should be broadened to extend around the openings. The members also advised eliminating the sculpture proposed for the southwest and southeast corners and, instead, pulling the landscape treatment around the sides of the building. After these changes were made, the commission approved the design in 1949.

The commission also reviewed the program for bas-reliefs at the building's entrances and supplied names of possible artists to the OSA in 1949.[25] As sculptor for the G Street entrance, the OSA selected Joseph Kiselewski, a for-

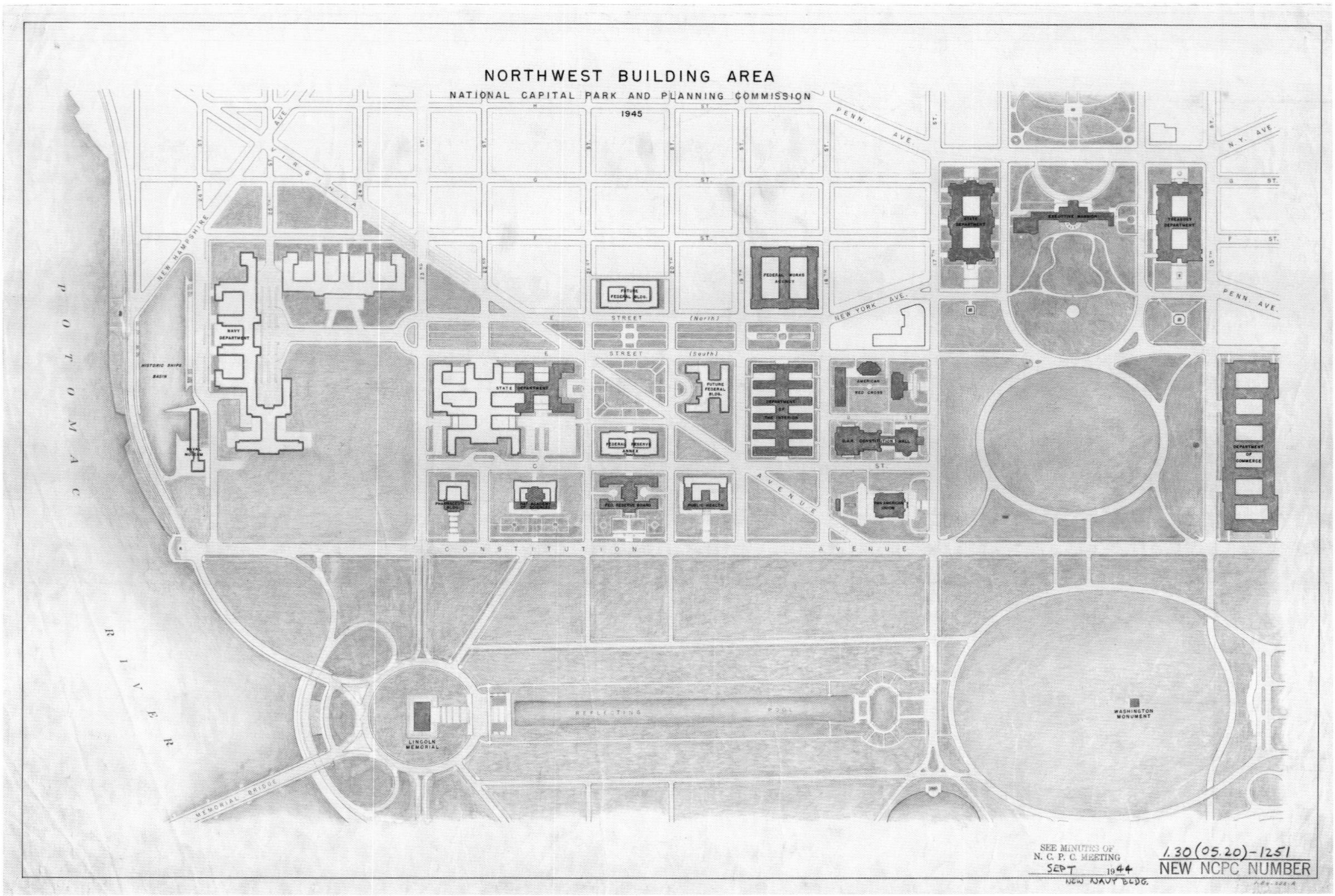

NORTHWEST BUILDING AREA
NATIONAL CAPITAL PARK AND PLANNING COMMISSION
1945

LEFT: *The War Department building, a deco-classical composition by Underwood & Foster, was completed in 1941; it became the headquarters for the Department of State in 1949 and would be expanded substantially over the following decade (c. 1950).*

ABOVE: *NCPPC Plan of the Northwest Rectangle, 1945, showing the massing and setback of buildings along Constitution Avenue in relation to the Lincoln Memorial. The radials of New York Avenue and Bacon Drive have been removed in favor of a symmetrical park between 20th and 21st Streets at Virginia Avenue and E Street. The existing War Department building is shown with a significant addition planned to the west. The massive Navy Department complex proposed to the west—on the site of the future Kennedy Center—was never executed.*

DEPARTMENT OF STATE BUILDING EXTENSION
WASHINGTON, D. C.

GRAHAM, ANDERSON, PROBST & WHITE, INC.
CHICAGO
HARLEY, ELLINGTON & DAY, INC.
DETROIT
ARCHITECTS & ENGINEERS
A. R. CLAS ASSOCIATE ARCHITECT
WASHINGTON, D. C.

GENERAL SERVICES ADMINISTRATION · PUBLIC BUILDINGS SERVICE · WASHINGTON, D. C.

ABOVE: Rendering by Graham, Anderson, Probst & White of the extensive new additions to the State Department proposed in 1947 to extend many classical features of the original structure—such as corner pavilions and the suggestion of a colonnade in the arrangement of vertical windows separated by wall sections.

RIGHT: In 1956, a new design by Graham, Anderson, Probst & White for the State Department's second phase abandoned many of the classical references used in the first. Instead, the building was treated with the language of International Style modernism: pilotis at ground level, expressive floating canopies, and an unadorned exterior skin.

spare modernism that showed the influence of the International Style. It also rejected any distant classical notion of columns, pilasters, or massing into pavilions; instead, the main block was raised off the ground on pilotis, with the first two floors encased in glass so that the block appeared to float. Walls were treated as thin planes covered with a smooth limestone facing and punched with windows; the focus was now on articulating surfaces of the volume.[27] The CFA agreed with the architects' decision to abandon "the attempt to make an architectural juncture between the existing building and the new parts of the expanded build-

ing," a problem that did not "seem to have any acceptable solution."[28] The addition was completed in 1958.

Impact of the War: Commemoration On and Off the Mall

The physical impact of World War II on Washington, particularly the Mall, was drastic. With the huge influx of workers, the population of the District of Columbia swelled to almost one million by 1945, and housing and office space was at a premium.[29] With the nation's ener-

gies focused on the war, no large-scale commemorative structures were proposed on the Mall for the duration of the conflict. The elaborate and costly plans for the huge architectural ensemble marking the western terminus of the Arlington Memorial Bridge on Columbia Island were largely abandoned. In fact, the war's most prominent legacy on the Mall was not a monument, but acres of hastily-constructed temporary office buildings. Beginning with Franklin D. Roosevelt's declaration of the war emergency in September 1939, the commission approved numerous new wood and stucco temporary buildings—popularly known as "tempos"—both on and off the Mall on the presumption that they would be torn down at the end of the crisis.[30] The power plant built to serve the World War I tempos was torn down in 1936, but several of the tempos themselves still remained, which the commission saw as a troubling precedent. This concern was well founded as the tempos from both wars proved too useful to easily discard, and most remained standing for decades, marring views and hindering plans for the appropriate development of parkland.

Among the tempos approved by the commission was the congressionally authorized addition to the Navy Department building, which was, along with the Munitions Building, one of two huge temporary buildings lining the south side of Constitution Avenue between 17th and 23rd Streets, north of the Lincoln Memorial Grounds. The CFA and the NCPPC imposed the condition that the addition should be placed "to allow a fringe of trees along 17th Street to hide the building."[31] However, this only increased the density of development in a circumscribed area. Except for the installation of these tempos, few other war-related changes were made to the Mall.

In the years following the war, no serious plans arose for a national World War II memorial in Washington. Instead, the immediate commemoration of World War II was enacted through smaller projects, such as the addition of plaques to existing World War I memorials and the construction of a Tomb of the Unknown Soldier of World War II at Arlington National Cemetery. This reticence regarding a national war memorial was not unusual: the national commemoration of war as such had never played a major role in the capital city's memorial landscape. The Grant and Lincoln Memorials transcended celebration of the Union victory in the Civil War, transmuting these monuments to individual leaders into vehicles bearing larger notions of reunification, healing, and lasting American ideals. As was typical across the nation, World War I memorials in the capital were relatively small structures honoring particular groups or the fallen of the local community, such as the First Division Monument and the District of Columbia World War Memorial.

Lorimer Rich's first plans for the Tomb of the Unknown Soldier of World War II were considered grandiose, involving removal of the Memorial Amphitheater portico and expanding a new memorial tomb into the resulting space. Under the commission's guidance from 1948 to 1950, the proposal was scaled down to a simple slab set flush in the paving behind the existing Tomb of the Unknown Soldier of World War I. The architect of the D.C. World War Memorial, Frederick H. Brooke, came to the commission with a proposal to expand that structure into a national memorial to World War II through the addition of flanking exedra or semicircular colonnades; the CFA discouraged the idea, and the memorial was never built. At the commission's request, member David Finley prepared the *Report on War Memorials* in 1947, an illustrated booklet that presented design guidelines to help communities outside Washington develop appropriate and tasteful commemorative structures.[32]

THE U.S. MARINE CORPS WAR MEMORIAL

The Commission of Fine Arts' first major effort after its establishment had been implementing the McMillan Plan's extension of the Mall vista west from the Washington Monument, securing an appropriate iconic monument—the Lincoln Memorial—on the new land forming the west end of the Mall. Preserving this Mall vista became a primary concern of later commission members and, in the 1940s and 1950s, grew to include the visual coherence of Arlington National Cemetery across the Potomac River and the surrounding backdrop for Washington's monumental core.

Under the chairmanship of Gilmore Clarke, the CFA made it a priority to ensure that the visual terminus of the Mall remained open across the river to the Arlington hills, toward the large area lying immediately north of the cemetery and including land within the cemetery encompassing the former Arlington Experimental Farm, and, to its north, another parcel of land known as the Nevius Tract. The heavily overgrown, twenty-five-acre parcel included the precise termination of the Mall axis. Because of its prominence, the site appealed to many federal and private interests, and numerous projects were proposed for construction there over the years.[33]

Several World War II–related memorials were eventually erected on land near Arlington National Cemetery, the best known and most controversial of which was the U.S. Marine Corps War Memorial.[34] The event depicted in the Marine Corps Memorial occurred during the marines'

The Nevius Tract (lower right, c. 1954) occupied a highly sensitive location at the west end of the Mall's visual axis in Virginia immediately north of Arlington National Cemetery.

invasion of the Japanese Island of Iwo Jima in February 1945, the first step in a crucial victory for American forces in the Pacific Theater. Six marines raised an American flag on Mount Suribachi; this heroic action was then repeated with a larger flag and recorded by Associated Press photographer Joe Rosenthal. Rosenthal's image showed the men in a pyramidal composition evocative of sustained and victorious effort; it quickly became an American icon.

A young navy artist, Vienna-born Felix de Weldon (CFA 1950–55), used the photograph as the basis for a sculptural study, a small model in wood and wax. Impressed by his work, the marines commissioned de Weldon to create a larger maquette, which he presented to President Truman on June 4, 1945. The next year, de Weldon created a thirty-six-foot-tall plaster study of the statue, which was placed on the north side of Constitution Avenue facing the World War I–era Navy building on the anniversary of the founding of the Marine Corps in November 1775.[35] This mock-up helped to build public sentiment for a national memorial.

A House bill in February 1946 proposed that the Navy Department erect a World War II memorial "portraying the flag raising on Iwo Jima" based on the Rosenthal photograph. Although no site or design was mentioned, it was understood that the memorial would replicate the de Weldon plaster maquette. While the CFA maintained doubts about the proposed size and the suitability of building a sculpture derived from a two-dimensional image, they became more concerned about its potential visual impact on the Lincoln Memorial were it to be built on the Nevius Tract. Presented with the statue at its meeting of February 22, 1946, the CFA disapproved its use as a model for the memorial; no site was discussed. A report prepared by sculptor member Lee Lawrie on behalf of the commission was sent to the House Committee on Public Buildings and Grounds; the report recommended that an invited competition be held for the "best known and ablest" sculptors and architects, but the recommendation was not acted upon.[36]

The July 1947 authorizing legislation for a Marine

ABOVE LEFT: *The iconic 1945 photograph by Joe Rosenthal of marines raising the American flag on Iwo Jima. This image would be the direct inspiration for a sculpture by the Austrian-emigre artist Felix de Weldon.*

ABOVE RIGHT: *Felix de Weldon (center), with Joe Rosenthal (right), presents his clay maquette of the flag raising to President Truman in the Oval Office in 1945; Truman became an ardent champion of de Weldon's concept and career.*

LEFT: *The U.S. Marine Corps War Memorial, 1954, interpreted Rosenthal's photograph in bronze on a grand scale. From the site, the memorials of the National Mall are clearly visible across the Potomac River to the east.*

World War II Overseas Cemeteries and Memorials

In 1946, Congress expanded the mandate of the American Battle Monuments Commission to include developing overseas cemeteries for American troops killed in World War II and erecting memorials at these sites to honor their sacrifice. As in previous authorizations, the new legislation required that the designs of these new cemeteries and memorials continue to be submitted to the Commission of Fine Arts for review. In its considerations of the projects, the CFA generally expressed strong support for the proposed designs.

Each cemetery comprised a landscaped burial ground; a chapel; a museum with battle maps executed in permanent materials, such as stone or mosaic; and sculpture. Cemetery sites were established in the various theaters of military action in Europe, Africa, and the Pacific and were often selected for their dramatic views of areas where significant action had occurred. For example, the American cemetery in Normandy, France, overlooks the D-Day beaches; in Italy, the Sicily-Rome American Cemetery is near the battleground at Anzio. In the tradition of achieving a high quality of design, all the projects were collaborations among architects, landscape architects, and sculptors. The ABMC chose the architects from a list supplied by the CFA; the architects then selected their team, subject again to CFA approval. Although generally based on classical prototypes, the architectural and sculptural forms were strikingly modern in comparison to the forms of the World War I overseas cemeteries and memorials developed a quarter century earlier.

ABOVE: *Sicily-Rome (originally Anzio) American Cemetery and Memorial, Nettuno, Italy, dedicated 1956.* Brothers in Arms *by sculptor Paul Manship is set within an austere classic frame by Eric Gugler of Gugler, Kimball & Husted.*

LEFT: *The Honolulu Memorial of the National Memorial Cemetery of the Pacific, Honolulu, Hawaii, dedicated 1966. Located within a volcanic crater called the Punchbowl, this memorial by Weihe, Frick & Kruse within a*

Veterans Administration cemetery honors military service in World War II, the Korean War, and the Vietnam War.

ABOVE: Cambridge American Cemetery and Memorial, Cambridge, England, dedicated 1956. The only World War II-era American cemetery in England, it was designed by Perry, Shaw, Hepburn & Dean with landscape design by Edmund Whiting of the Olmsted Brothers.

RIGHT: Ardennes American Cemetery and Memorial, near Neupré, Belgium, dedicated 1960. The massive stone marker by sculptor C. Paul Jennewein is the focus of the overall design by Reinhard, Hofmeister & Walquist.

Corps memorial honoring all marines killed in service to their country specified that it be built with private funds on public land in Washington and mandated CFA approval; authority to build the memorial was soon granted by the secretary of the interior to the Marine Memorial Commission. Gilmore Clarke reported to the CFA that the bill was not specific about site and design. At this point, however, the site considered by the memorial commission was the southern end of Hains Point, and the American Battle Monuments Commission submitted plans by de Weldon and architect Paul Jaquet to the CFA in August.[37] The design included a Court of the Four Freedoms with a memorial sarcophagus, twin reflecting pools, and a place to lay wreaths. To alleviate Clarke's concern that the high flagpole might obstruct flights from National Airport and other airfields, Jaquet told the commission that certain people, whom he did not name, had assured him it would not be a problem. When the CFA members viewed a full-size model in de Weldon's cavernous Washington studio, they unanimously decided it would be too large in scale for the site and in relation to other D.C. monuments. Commenting on the model's poor workmanship, the commission once more encouraged securing a design through competition.[38]

The commission soon received letters of protest from several government agencies, including the Civil Aeronautics Administration at National Airport, the National Park Service, and the NCPPC, all opposing the Hains Point location because of the project's size and excessive height, and because the site itself—created from reclaimed land—was slowly sinking and prone to flooding.[39] The CFA also received letters of support from military leaders, among them the commandant of the Marine Corps and Admiral Chester W. Nimitz, commander in chief of the U.S. Pacific Fleet during World War II and leader of the assault on Iwo Jima. Both men referred to the positive interest expressed by visitors who had seen the version of de Weldon's statue temporarily installed on Constitution Avenue. Their letters also noted that the sculpture appropriately illustrated the sacrifice and duty of the marines at Iwo Jima.

The commission remained concerned about the quality of the statue's artistic expression. Clarke emphasized to the commandant that the piece "should be superbly done by an artist of the first rank" selected through "a limited competition among artists of established reputation." He added that the commission was not convinced that the Iwo Jima flag raising was the best subject for a sculpture in the round and that it might be better rendered as a bas-relief.[40]

By the early 1950s, the composition of the commission had been drastically changed by President Truman, who had not reappointed Gilmore Clarke and five other members, leaving the CFA without a staunch defender of the Nevius Tract. In 1952, CFA chairman David Finley suggested that the Marine Corps Memorial be placed there instead of Hains Point, although Joseph Hudnut (CFA 1950–55) did offer a resolution stating that retention of the Nevius Tract for public use was essential for the preservation of the overall Mall plan.[41] The next year, the land was transferred to the General Services Administration by President Truman.

An amendment to the authorizing legislation allowed the monument to be built within the larger metropolitan area, and the accompanying House report indicated that Congress wanted the memorial placed on the Nevius Tract, although not on the exact Mall axis. The Department of the Interior consented to a request by the Marine Memorial Foundation (formerly the Marine Memorial Commission) to build the memorial on the Nevius Tract as part of a larger memorial composition; the National Park Service submitted a plan to the CFA showing the Marine Corps Memorial located at the north end of the tract with two other future memorials to its south. The CFA gave its approval; but to make its position clear, Finley later wrote to the secretary of the interior explicitly stating that the commission had approved only the site for the Marine Corps Memorial; the other two memorials required further study.[42]

Construction of the U.S. Marine Corps War Memorial began in February 1954, and it was dedicated in November of the same year. It included a seventy-eight-foot-tall rendition of the de Weldon statue set in front of a berm at the west, intended to shield the memorial from surrounding roads and apartment buildings. Sour gum trees were planted on the berm to form a brilliant red backdrop for the statue in the fall as seen from the Lincoln Memorial.[43]

OTHER MEMORIALS IN ARLINGTON AND THE MALL PRECINCT

Several other memorial projects in Arlington associated with the composition of the monumental core crossing the Potomac would be completed in the 1950s. The paired equestrian statues behind the Lincoln Memorial flanking the entrances to the Arlington Memorial Bridge and the Rock Creek and Potomac Parkway—the *Arts of War* by Leo Friedlander and the *Arts of Peace* by James Earle Fraser—were finally completed after twenty years of design, review, and construction delays. The sculptors had initially proposed that the pieces be carved in granite or marble in the 1930s, but the high cost of these materials became an issue for the National Park Service. In response,

The Netherlands Carillon, dedicated in 1960, commemorates American support of the Netherlands during World War II and in the immediate postwar years. The modernist style of the carillon by Dutch architect Joost W. C. Boks could not differ more profoundly from the heroic realism of de Weldon's nearby sculpture.

the Commission of Fine Arts recommended that the sculptures be cast in bronze; that decision coincided with World War II, which caused construction to be delayed since bronze was reserved for defense use. After the war, in gratitude for American aid under the Marshall Plan, Italy offered to cast and gild the statues. Casting took two years; the finished works were shipped in crates up the Potomac River and installed in 1951.[44]

The Netherlands Carillon, a gift to the United States from the Dutch people in thanks for American assistance during and after the war, was the second memorial placed on the Nevius Tract. The Dutch government insisted on a site within the Nevius Tract for the forty-nine-bell carillon because of the location's strategic relation to the Mall. At the May 1954 CFA meeting, the director of the National Park Service, Conrad Wirth, discussed the general scheme of development for the site. Opposition by the Commission of Fine Arts, the National Capital Planning Commission (NCPC; "Park" was dropped from the organization's name in 1952), and the National Park Service had stopped earlier efforts to cede the land to Arlington County for apartment development. Wirth observed that this effort, along with the construction of the Marine Corps Memorial, had kept the land under federal jurisdiction. He noted, however, that the Marine Corps Memorial was a relatively small structure occupying only a few acres and that other memorial projects were needed to further preserve the site, among them the Netherlands Carillon.[45]

Earlier in the year, CFA member Elbert Peets (CFA 1950–58), a landscape architect and planner, had written two memoranda on behalf of the commission, one ana-

lyzing the proposed location of the Netherlands Carillon on the Nevius Tract and the other setting out CFA policy regarding design criteria for the parcel as a whole. Peets did not believe a physical marker on axis with the Mall was needed because the tract's primary purpose was to strengthen the forest background for the Mall. Specifically regarding the carillon, he said, "The proposal indicates a misunderstanding of the purposes and technique of axiated [sic] planning. The crude centering of structures on a straight line has no aesthetic virtue. It is the design of the space in which the monuments stand, or of the subsidiary spaces connecting the structures that gives the composition unity and rhythm."[46] Nevertheless, President Dwight D. Eisenhower approved the carillon's location on the tract in August 1954. Dutch architect Joost W. C. Boks designed the Netherlands Carillon as an open steel tower. When that design was presented to the commission by the National Park Service in January 1957, the CFA considered the structure too "mechanical" in appearance and, at 250 feet, too high for the site, explaining that it had long been CFA policy not to approve any structure that would dominate the Lincoln Memorial. At the CFA's request, Boks reduced the height to 127 feet and added steel plates to partially enclose the skeletal steel framework.[47] The CFA approved the revised design, and it was dedicated in 1960.

For several years, the Marine Corps War Memorial and the Netherlands Carillon were considered as potential components of a larger composition focused on an extraordinarily large and ambitious monument to the five political freedoms guaranteed by the Bill of Rights: the

ABOVE LEFT: *Plaster maquette (1931) by James Earle Fraser for the* Music and Harvest *grouping of* The Arts of Peace; *the design displays an accommodation of academic classicism with the heroic realism of the mid-twentieth century.*

ABOVE RIGHT: *Two pairs of heroic equestrian statues—* The Arts of War *by Leo Friedlander at the entrance to the Arlington Memorial Bridge (left) and* The Arts of Peace *by James Earle Fraser at the entrance to Rock Creek and Potomac Parkway (right)—were planned from the 1930s atop massive granite plinths to complete the setting of the Lincoln Memorial. The CFA had worked closely with architect William Mitchell Kendall to adjust the height and mass of the two statue groups, which were installed in 1951. View looking north, 1955.*

Medals and Coins as Commemorative Objects

Between 1941 and 1943, the War Department presented some twenty new or revised war medals to the commission for review. By June 1942, with several bills pending in Congress for new or modified war medals, Gilmore Clarke circulated a letter to federal offices reminding them of the 1921 executive order requiring CFA review of coin and medal designs. Clarke also asked that the services of the country's many able sculptors and medalists be used "to give assurance that each medal may be a work of art and worthy of the service which it commemorates."[1] Despite this request for early involvement, the commission often found itself presented with a design so far along in

Paul Manship, maquette of Maritime Commission Distinguished Service Medal, 1942.

the development process that it was too late for its judgment to have any effect. In 1944, for example, the War Department ordered the production of 1.5 million bronze stars before the design was even submitted to the CFA.

After 1946, the number of medal submissions abruptly declined. With the exception of the Korean Service Medal (1954), the subjects also changed from awards for military service and bravery to medals honoring ancillary military actions or civilian achievements, such as the Armed Forces Reserve Medal (1951), two Civilian Service Medals (1956), and a medal honoring Dr. Jonas A. Salk (1956).

The commission continued to stress simplicity of composition and lettering, which it found submissions seldom possessed. Designs were often too complicated to read at a small scale. Members repeatedly recommended the hiring of competent sculptors skilled in the medallic arts, and the commission often supplied lists of artists' names or advised that a specific artist be hired, such as Paul Manship for the Maritime Commission's Distinguished Service Medal and the War Department's Legion of Merit Medal, both in 1942.[2] The CFA sometimes recommended a more symbolic rendition of a subject, reflecting a lingering preference for allegory. A proposal for the obverse of the War Department's Typhus Commission Medal in 1944— control of the disease contributed greatly to American victories in World War II— depicted a doctor carrying a victim. Called too literal by the CFA, an image of Hippocrates was initially substituted. However, after objections were raised by the U.S. Typhus Commission, the alle-

gorical figure was eventually replaced by portraits of two pioneers in the control of the disease, Howard Taylor Ricketts and Charles Nicolle.

Between 1940 and 1959, the Mint submitted designs for only two circulating coins, the Roosevelt dime and a new reverse for the Lincoln penny. After Roosevelt died in office on April 12, 1945, a new dime bearing his likeness was developed to recognize his role in founding the March of Dimes (originally the National Foundation for Infantile Paralysis) and to inaugurate a national fundraising campaign. The design, by the Mint's chief engraver, John R. Sinnock, was submitted in November 1945 with production slated to begin on Roosevelt's next birthday, January 30, 1946. Dissatisfied with the quality of the portrait, the CFA did not approve the coin and urged the Mint to consider using another artist, but the Mint went ahead with production.[3]

A new reverse for the Lincoln penny, designed in 1958 to honor the 150th anniversary of Lincoln's birth in 1959, replaced the twin wheat heads of the 1909 design by artist Victor Brenner with an image of the Lincoln Memorial. To meet the Mint's production goals, the CFA gave advance approval before the regular commission meeting of November 1958, cautioning that the changes were not desirable and the image should be limited to an accurate "replica of the Lincoln Memorial itself." Privately, the commission described the design, which included a ring of stars and the words "Lincoln Memorial" as overloaded, with the structure shown disproportionately large.[4]

ABOVE LEFT: *The terra cotta study for the Commission of Fine Arts seal was designed by Lee Lawrie for the fortieth anniversary of the agency in 1950. The seal is still used as the commission's logo.*

FAR LEFT AND LEFT: *Colonel Robert Townsend Heard, Legion of Merit Medal, obverse, 1942; Colonel Robert Townsend Heard, Legion of Merit Medal, reverse, 1942.*

ABOVE RIGHT, TOP TO BOTTOM: *Edmond Amateis, maquette of Typhus Commission Medal, 1941; John R. Sinnock, Roosevelt dime, obverse, 1946; Frank Gasparro, Lincoln penny, reverse, 1959, featuring Henry Bacon's design for the Lincoln Memorial.*

ABOVE LEFT: *Aerial rendering of the Mall axis extending from the U.S. Capitol to the proposed Freedom Shrine designed by Eric Gugler, c. 1954.*

ABOVE RIGHT: *Gugler's plan for the Freedom Shrine would have placed the massive open-air structure on the exact termination of the Mall axis, immediately between the Marine Corps War Memorial and the Netherlands Carillon.*

RIGHT: *Night rendering of the Freedom Shrine, c. 1954. The massiveness of the proposal—colossal square columns enclosing a court of honor—was criticized by the CFA for being too great a scale within the existing landscape.*

freedoms of speech, religion, press, assembly, and petition. The National Freedom Shrine, a proposal of Roosevelt's favorite architect, Eric Gugler, was intended to be a living memorial with a component, such as an auditorium, that could benefit the community.[48] Disregarding Peets's advice, the shrine was planned for the precise termination of the Mall axis. (Gugler had redesigned the West Wing of the White House in the 1930s and, in the 1960s, designed the Theodore Roosevelt Memorial on Roosevelt Island. See essays by Arleyn Levee and William Bushong.)

Gugler worked on the memorial throughout the 1950s, reluctantly reducing its size and scale at the commission's request. At a status meeting held at the White House in July 1959, David Finley noted the commission's sense that, along with the Marine Corps Memorial and the Netherlands Carillon, the Nevius Tract "would be unduly crowded with a monument of the scale of the Freedom Shrine." Finally, in August 1959, the CFA approved a memorial much reduced in size from the original proposal. The commission noted particularly the grove of trees surrounding the memorial: "We feel that this treatment will preserve the integrity of the wooded hillside as viewed from Washington and will make a handsome setting for the monument."[49] Cost, however, proved the memorial's undoing; with construction estimates running into the millions of dollars, plans for the Freedom Shrine were abandoned once Eisenhower left office in 1961.

Historic Preservation

Even as the commission gradually shifted from the context of Beaux-Arts design into the modernist age, it maintained its allegiance to the basic principles of the McMillan Plan. This allegiance fit within the beginnings of the historic preservation movement, which was a reaction in part to the postwar period's optimism about technological and social improvement that facilitated the wholesale destruction of older neighborhoods, buildings, and landscapes. The commission was intimately involved in the issues that set the stage for the preservation of some of Washington's—and the nation's—most significant historic resources. One critical milestone was the creation in 1950 of the Old Georgetown Historic District by Congress, designed to protect the oldest neighborhood within the District of Columbia and authorized to be administered by the Commission of Fine Arts. Another was the highly contentious plan to modify the White House south portico; its involvement in the ensuing debate would have great consequences for the commission as it tried to protect, unsuccessfully, the transformation of one of the most iconic American structures.

CHANGES TO THE WHITE HOUSE AND THE COMMISSION

In July 1947, President Truman returned to the White House from a trip to the University of Virginia in Charlottesville, taken with the idea of adding a second-floor balcony to the south portico of the White House. As White House historian William Bushong details in his essay, Truman's balcony idea set off a chain of events that drastically altered the relationship between the White House and the Commission of Fine Arts.

Initially, Chairman Clarke and commission members David Finley and Frederick V. Murphy (CFA 1945–50) met informally with the president's representatives at the White House to review the idea. Rather than openly oppose the balcony, they suggested hiring an architect familiar with the White House—ultimately William Adams Delano, a former member of both the CFA and the NCPPC—to review the idea, assuming these studies would dissuade the president from the inappropriate modification of the historic building. Delano's involvement had the opposite effect, however, creating support for the president's idea.

The situation presented the commission, an advisory agency to the president, with a politically difficult dilemma: how to preserve the historic integrity of the White House if it meant opposing the president's wishes. At its meeting in August 1947, the CFA concluded that the balcony posed a significant alteration, and in a letter to Howell G. Crim, chief usher of the White House, Clarke advised that the CFA "cannot approve any plan which will destroy the original design of an historic monument of the importance of the White House."[50] On September 23, 1947—in a memo recording the event, Clarke even noted the exact time— Crim called him to say that, in spite of the Commission of Fine Arts' objection, the president would proceed with the construction of the balcony. Crim asked what further action the CFA would take in the matter, to which Clarke replied that, while the commission felt it unwise to proceed with the balcony, if the president wished to build it, the CFA was powerless to do more "since they are not clothed with a power of veto." Crim then asked a slightly different question, wanting to know what action the CFA would take if the president requested them to formally pass judgment on the balcony. Clarke replied that the commission did not wish to embarrass the president, and it "would not issue any statement to the Press with respect to the matter unless called upon to do so." But, Clarke added, if asked by the press for a statement, he would need

to tell the truth. Clarke's final admonition was that if the balcony had to be built, the president should have Delano design it.[51]

In November 1947, Clarke prepared a formal letter for the commission to send to the president, reviewing the course of actions that had led to this point and, in a political misstep, admitting that the commission had expected Delano to find that the balcony damaged the building's integrity. Clarke wrote that he was astonished when he found out that Delano had endorsed the idea, which included enlarging a window to create a door, and that Delano had indicated he thought the porch "would not in any way detract from the dignity of the south portico." Clarke ended by saying the commission members hoped the president would not make a formal request to change the exterior because they still believed it would mar the facade.[52]

Truman's response in a letter dated December 2, 1947, was characteristically acerbic:

> My understanding was when the matter was discussed with you with regard to the arrangement on the south portico that when Mr. Delano made up his mind, the situation would be satisfactory to you. Now you confess that you hoped he would make up his mind in a manner that you approved of and that you didn't enter into the matter at all with an open mind—that is a great statement for the Chairman of The Commission of Fine Arts to send to the President.
>
> I can't understand your viewpoint when those dirty awnings are a perfect eyesore with regard to that south portico....
>
> Of course, I wouldn't expect you to take into consideration the com-
> fort and convenience of the Presidential family in this arrangement. The President is not to be considered but the outside appearance of The White House it seems to me to be your principal reason for existence and I can't see how anybody could come to a conclusion that those dirty awnings are better looking than an arrangement which is approved by The White House architect and by Mr. Delano.
>
> I certainly would like to have your reasons for preferring the dirty awnings to the good looking convenient portico and then maybe I'll come to a conclusion on the subject, I don't make up my mind in advance. However, I'll have to be convinced.[53]

Clarke wrote back a carefully worded reply assuring the president that the commission did indeed want him and his family to be comfortable, but noting that the awnings could be easily removed and did not alter the architecture. He repeated that the CFA can "act only in an advisory capacity" to the president, and Truman was free to carry out the changes he wished. But Clarke did not back down regarding the central issue: that the balcony would do irrevocable damage and "that nothing should be done to impair the integrity of the original design in the case of one of the most important and best loved national monuments in the country." Truman quickly responded that he appreciated Clarke's letter, adding, "I hope everything works out to the best advantage for all concerned. I am sure it will."[54]

The controversy quickly became public. The Washington Star condemned the CFA for not taking a stronger stand against the balcony and for recommending Delano:

Awnings above the first-floor windows on the south portico of the White House were a discordant but removeable feature within the neo-Palladian architectural design (c. 1940).

"The real powers of the commission may be limited. But the moral force of its decisions, when supported by a strong commission, is great." In its defense, the commission issued a press release explaining its decision, emphasizing its purely advisory role, and expressing its satisfaction that Delano would carry out the work. The next day the *Star* noted the commission's statement and expressed its opposition to the portico.[55]

Public opinion ran against the president. The *Washington Post* blasted Truman for his "specious" pretext for "meddling with a structure that does not belong to him and which is precious in its present aspect to millions of Americans." The *New York Times* also opposed the portico and the *New York Herald Tribune* said that "to override . . . the Commission appointed to advise on these matters seems to us to argue a certain want of taste and decency."[56]

Despite the uproar, Truman had the balcony built in March 1948 to Delano's design. The Truman Balcony, as it came to be called, was not to be the last radical change made to the White House during Truman's tenure. The Public Buildings Administration, based on earlier recommendations from the Secret Service, developed plans in late 1948 to make the building more structurally sound. The project was eventually overseen by the Commission on the Renovation of the Executive Mansion, created by Congress in 1949 and composed largely of its members. This project, approved by the president—who had unexpectedly won a second term—ultimately led to the complete demolition and rebuilding of the historic White House interior. So great was the demolition that the historic White House was essentially lost, replaced by a 1950s steel-framed structure within the original sandstone exterior.[57]

The Commission of Fine Arts played only a limited role in the White House renovation. As White House historian William Bushong discusses in his essay, the 1949 legislation for the renovation did not specify the commission's design approval for the project. After his experience with the commission during the balcony incident, Truman also was not inclined to ask its advice; moreover, Truman chose not to reappoint Clarke and five other members of the commission when their terms expired in 1950 in apparent retaliation for their refusal to approve the balcony. Only David E. Finley was retained. Bushong suggests that Finley likely remained because of his service on the Committee on White House Furnishings and the trust and relationships he had cultivated at the White House through that work.

Finley was a diminutive, soft-spoken man who founded and led many of Washington's most important cultural institutions. Born in 1890, the son of a South Carolina congressman, Finley completed law school at George Washington University and began federal employment in 1921, moving to the Treasury Department in 1922. Treasury Secretary Andrew W. Mellon appointed him his special

The balcony added to the south portico of the White House at the insistence of President Truman interrupts the plain vertical lines of Ionic columns and crowds the pediments above the windows (c. 1948).

Under President Truman, the Federal-era White House was almost completely demolished and rebuilt. Interior view of construction within the remaining historic exterior sandstone walls, May 17, 1950.

assistant in 1927. In this position Finley helped Mellon create the National Gallery of Art, traveling with him on buying trips to Europe and New York, meeting with architect John Russell Pope, and planning the design of the galleries. The year after Mellon's death in 1937, Finley was appointed the gallery's first director, a position he held for eighteen years. During his tenure, he obtained major American collections of European art for the gallery, securing its preeminent place among American museums.

Finley played an instrumental role in numerous other national and D.C. arts organizations. He was vice chairman of the American Commission for the Protection and Salvage of Artistic and Historic Monuments in War Areas, a founder and chairman of the National Trust for Historic Preservation, a founder of the National Portrait Gallery, president of the American Association of Museums, chairman of the White House Historical Association, and a board member of the National Cathedral. In the early 1960s, Finley became friendly with First Lady Jacqueline Kennedy through his work on the CFA's Committee on White House Furnishings and their mutual dedication to the preservation of Lafayette Square. An article in the May 1962 *Washington Star* described him as "a small deceptively frail-appearing man who has a record of successive retirements into ever-more-important jobs on the Washington scene."[58]

David Finley's quiet but adroit diplomacy also made him an effective leader of the Commission of Fine Arts. As chairman, he spent five days a week in the CFA office. At the time of his retirement from the commission after twenty years, including thirteen as chairman, he spoke to a reporter concerning his beliefs about how the CFA had maintained its effectiveness:

Mr. Finley has resisted efforts to give [the Commission] more power. Its weakness, he believes, is its strength. "We make recommendations," he says, "but they're not mandatory. They should never be mandatory or the commission would be destroyed."[59]

Truman's almost-clean sweep of appointees in 1950 significantly changed the composition of the commission. Included in the new commission were recognized proponents of modernism: Joseph Hudnut and Pietro Belluschi (CFA 1950–55). As dean of the faculty of design, Hudnut had brought Walter Gropius and Marcel Breuer to Harvard University in the late 1930s.[60] The innovative Belluschi, a regional and international modernist architect, was famous for the pioneering curtain wall design of the Equitable Building in Portland, Oregon (1948), which predated Skidmore, Owings & Merrill's Lever House by four years.

Other new members included the respected landscape architect and planner Elbert Peets, who replaced Clarke,

and the painter George Biddle. As a young man in 1922, Peets had collaborated with Werner Hegemann on *The American Vitruvius: An Architects' Handbook of Civic Art*, a compendium of City Beautiful planning. In the 1930s, Peets was a member of the team that planned Greendale, Wisconsin, one of the New Deal's three greenbelt new towns; he went on to serve as the chief of the site-planning section of the U.S. Housing Authority. Biddle had completed murals for the Justice Department like his predecessor on the commission, Maurice Sterne, and had been instrumental thirty years earlier in fostering the Federal Art Project, under the New Deal's Works Progress Administration, which employed artists to create public art.

But among the members appointed by Truman were two men—sculptor Felix de Weldon and architect Edward F. Neild Sr. (CFA 1950–55)—who had collaborated on the

Portrait of David E. Finley by Gardner Cox, 1956. An experienced arts administrator with well-developed diplomatic skills, Finley served as the CFA's chairman for thirteen years.

By late 1951, only Finley remained from the previous commission. This photograph shows President Harry S. Truman with his newly installed CFA (left to right): Pietro Belluschi, David Finley, George Biddle, Joseph Hudnut, Truman, Edward F. Neild, Elbert Peets, Felix de Weldon, and secretary H. P. Caemmerer.

design of the U.S. Marine Corps War Memorial in Arlington, Virginia, a design roundly criticized by an earlier commission. Both men had a personal connection to Truman. Neild, a Louisiana architect who had built few structures outside of his home state, had been a friend of Truman's since about 1930, when the future president commissioned him to design a courthouse in Missouri. De Weldon had come to Truman's attention for his model of the famous flag raising on Iwo Jima; he subsequently created a bronze bust of the president as an inaugural gift from the Democratic National Committee.

As its membership continued to change during the 1950s and 1960s, the commission began to slowly move away from Clarke's accommodation of modernism. New members no longer fought a rearguard action to preserve classicism, but began to reinterpret the McMillan Plan to suit modern times instead. They were proponents of modern architecture—often noted practitioners of the movement—and recognized that the CFA had a role to play in Washington planning. And, in the context of a city whose image was now well established, they also began to address the need to protect valuable historic resources—such as the National Mall, the Potomac River waterfront, the Arlington hills, and historic Georgetown—in the face of new economic and social forces.

The first major staff change to affect the commission in thirty-five years also occurred in the 1950s. After a period of illness, Hans Paul Caemmerer retired from the commission on June 24, 1954. His replacement as secretary and administrative officer was Linton R. Wilson, who was fifty-two years old and had trained in art history and

architectural design at Princeton University, along with two years of study in Sweden.[61] In the 1930s, Wilson had worked for the firm of Voorhees, Walker, Foley & Smith in New York; a firm partner, Ralph Walker (CFA 1959–63), would join the commission during Wilson's tenure as secretary. Wilson also worked on architectural projects in Scandinavia before spending eighteen years in the navy, becoming an expert on radio communication before retiring as a lieutenant commander. Wilson came to the CFA from the Office of Naval Research in Washington. His fluency in many languages—French, Italian, German, Spanish, Danish, and Norwegian—was noted in his introduction to the commission. Wilson remained at the commission for ten years until his retirement in 1964.

OLD GEORGETOWN

Georgetown was founded as a tobacco port located on the Potomac River at the southern end of the rolling road for barrels of tobacco from Frederick, Maryland; the first tobacco warehouse was erected in 1745. Responding to petitions from merchants and planters in 1751, the Maryland General Assembly authorized the acquisition of sixty acres for the platting of streets, lanes, and eighty lots for "George-Town."[62] Named in honor of King George II, the port town became Maryland's largest tobacco market in the 1780s, during which time adjacent land was annexed, the cornerstone of Georgetown Academy (now University) was laid, the town was incorporated, and a bridge spanned Rock Creek—all fundamental features of the Maryland town circumscribed by the District of Columbia in 1791. By the end of the century, the town occupied the area between Rock Creek and the academy, with the northern edge along Road (now R) Street. Most buildings represented the vernacular building tradition of the mid-Atlantic region; several buildings of architectural significance were erected on Prospect and Gay (now N) Streets in the heights of Georgetown.[63] The Chesapeake and Ohio (C&O) Canal, which opened in 1831, expanded the port's reach into Appalachia and drove the town's commerce and industry in the nineteenth century. During this period, Georgetown lost its independent administrative status: Congress revoked its charter in 1871 and in 1895 renamed its streets to conform to the L'Enfant city's grid system.

At the beginning of the twentieth century, Washingtonians—especially the socially prominent—considered the building stock in Georgetown to be aged and inferior in comparison to other neighborhoods, particularly the fashionable areas developing west of Dupont Circle. This impression began to change in the 1920s for a variety of reasons, including the arrival of prominent residents from out of town, the promotion of local history by the Progressive Citizens Association of Georgetown (PCAG), articles by the *Evening Star* columnist John Clagett Proctor, and *House Beautiful*'s series, "Gardens of Old Georgetown."[64] During the New Deal, leaders in the administration moved to the neighborhood, and the documentation of Federal-era buildings by the Historic American Buildings Survey and the Federal Writers' Project began. Years of local residents lecturing or writing articles and books about Georgetown's early history, combined with the threats of a strong real estate market in the 1940s, led the PCAG to seek legal protection for Georgetown's buildings in the late 1940s.[65]

During and immediately after World War II, several Federal-era buildings were demolished, the most historically significant of which was the Francis Scott Key house.[66] These losses raised concern among residents about the future of the remaining Federal-era buildings in the face of economic pressure.[67] In 1949, members of the PCAG—who had familiarized themselves with the preservation ordinances of Charleston, South Carolina, (1931) and Alexandria, Virginia, (1946)—approached CFA member David Finley with draft legislation for creating a historic district in Georgetown.[68] They likely targeted Finley because he had lived in Georgetown since 1931 and served as chairman of the National Council for Historic Sites and Buildings, organized in 1947 to raise public awareness about historic preservation.[69]

Finley raised the topic of protection for Georgetown at the Commission of Fine Arts meeting in June 1949. Commission members offered support for the PCAG's goal

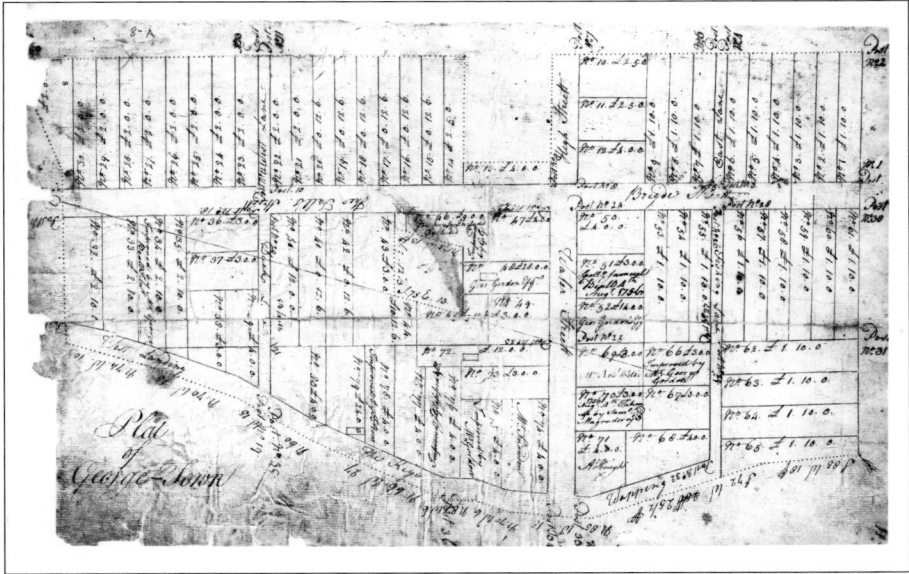

ABOVE: *The original plat of Georgetown, 1751. The tobacco port settlement centered on the intersection of M Street (named The Falls Street and Bridge Street) and Wisconsin Avenue (Water Street and High Street), with the northern limit around what is today N Street.*

LEFT: *The Old Stone House, photographed in 1935, is the only remaining Colonial-era building in Georgetown. It was built in stages between 1765 and 1775 by the cabinetmaker Christopher Layman for his shop and residence; the masonry walls included locally quarried stone and ballast.*

and suggested that the Shipstead-Luce Act of 1930 could be revised to include Georgetown. An amendment to the act was drafted at the meeting that would establish approximate boundaries for the area extending between Rock Creek, Whitehaven Parkway, 37th Street, and the southern bank of the C&O Canal, and would require the commission's review of all projects proposing the demolition or alteration of structures erected prior to 1830. It would also authorize the commission to appoint an advisory review board of three architects to evaluate applications.[70]

The commission's draft legislation quickly found political support. In July 1949, Georgetown resident Representative James Wadsworth (R-NY) introduced H.R. 5769, which was identical to the commission's amendment, apart

ABOVE LEFT: *The Whitehurst Freeway, viewed from the foot of Wisconsin Avenue, was constructed along the Georgetown waterfront in 1949; it removed commuter traffic from local streets but created an uncomfortable relationship with adjacent historic structures and blocked views to the river.*

ABOVE RIGHT: *The Francis Scott Key residence, 3518 M Street, NW, was built in 1802 and was the Key family home from 1805 to 1833. The historic building was demolished in 1948 for the construction of a ramp between the Whitehurst Freeway and the Key Bridge.*

from establishing 1850 as the critical date and Glover-Archbold Park as the western boundary. A month later, NCPPC chairman William Wurster wrote to Gilmore Clarke, suggesting that Georgetown be handled separately from the Shipstead-Luce Act authority.[71] In September, Secretary Caemmerer and NCPPC staff drafted a new bill to protect Georgetown that removed the reference to a specific building date and added language limiting the CFA's review authority to locations visible from public space such as streets and alleys.[72] The bill also clarified the district's northern boundary and extended the southern boundary from the canal to the river. Inclusion of the entire waterfront—primarily zoned industrial with no new residential uses permitted—extended protection to the whole Colonial town. The expanded area would encompass important buildings such as the Dodge warehouses, Grace Church, and the Brickyard Hill House. Nevertheless, most of the area was occupied by industrial buildings and other structures not considered "historic" as the term was understood at the time: an incinerator, power stations, concrete factories, coal and lumber yards, sand and gravel operations, gas works, steel, fertilizer, and fat rendering plants, automotive repair shops, junk yards, and the B&O Railroad spur along K Street.

Wadsworth used H.R. 5769 as the basis for H.R. 6403, which he introduced in October; the construction date of 1850 had been returned to the bill. The CFA voted to officially support the legislation at its meeting that month and issued a letter stating that the protection of Georgetown

was "an eminently worthy project."[73] The D.C. commissioners opposed the bill; writing to Representative John McMillan (D-SC), chairman of the House Committee on the District of Columbia, they questioned the bill's constitutionality and predicted that it would create hardships for property owners in the areas zoned for commercial and industrial uses. They also argued that the law would be hard to enforce because building permits had been issued only since 1877, making the dating of earlier buildings a difficult task. The D.C. commissioners advised that if the bill went forward, it should be amended to ensure that local laws associated with the repair or demolition of insanitary or unsafe buildings would not be superseded. Likely suggested as a practical measure, this amendment ultimately created a demolition loophole that would be exploited as late as 1997. At its January 1950 meeting, the CFA voted to support this revision.

A House subcommittee held a hearing on a third version of the bill, H.R. 7670, on June 22, 1950. The specific building date had been struck from the bill, and CFA review for new construction was added as well as two new sections: one regarding unsafe buildings, as recommended by the District commissioners, and another stipulating that the commissioners were to survey the designated area. In his opening remarks, Wadsworth noted that the purpose of the legislation was to perpetuate historical interest and "prevent, if possible, the erection of buildings that mar the general character of the area."[74] Representatives from government agencies and several planning, cultural, and civic

TOP: *The C&O Canal looking east from the Wisconsin Avenue bridge, 1951. Once proposed as the route for a multilane traffic by-pass, the National Park Service recreated the towpath in the early 1970s.*

ABOVE: *Aerial view of the Georgetown waterfront looking east (c. 1965) showing the Whitehurst Freeway and the continuing presence of industrial uses between the Potomac waterfront and the C&O Canal.*

BELOW: *The house at 3245 O Street, NW—unusual for its gable-fronted facade and large setback from the street—was built c. 1812 and razed in 1997 despite objections from both the CFA and the D.C. Historic Preservation Review Board (c. 1993).*

RIGHT: *Mount Zion United Methodist Church was*

founded in 1814 by 125 African Americans who left the segregated Montgomery Street Methodist Church. The original Mount Zion church, located near 27th and P Streets, NW, was destroyed by fire; the lot at 1334 29th Street, NW, was purchased in 1875, and the new Gothic Revival church was dedicated in 1884.

organizations—D.C. Corporation Counsel, National Trust for Historic Preservation, NCPPC, CFA, Committee of 100 on the Federal City, National Capital Committee of the American Institute of Architects, and Progressive Citizens Association of Georgetown—testified in support of the bill. Architect Chloethiel Woodard Smith (CFA 1967–76) and architect W. Dewey Foster, who would become a member of the first Old Georgetown Board, also offered testimony in support.

Voices of dissent, however, raised the underlying issues of racially and economically based inequality in the city. The Reverend J. D. Foy of the Mount Zion Methodist Church, a leader of the long-standing African American community in Georgetown, spoke in opposition to the bill:

I am concerned to what extent this might become a process by which a squeeze may be put on people to push them from the community.... It could actually become, in some form, a restricted covenant to restrict certain movements.[75]

The House approved the bill on July 13, the Senate passed it after the August recess, and it became law on September 22, 1950 (the Old Georgetown Act, 64 STAT. 903). The law directed the District government, in coordination with the National Park Service and NCPPC, to survey the buildings in the designated area and authorized $8,000 for the work.

In anticipation of the bill's passage, the commission—following President Truman's sweeping replacement of six members—discussed the bill at length during its July 20 meeting. Finley, the only member remaining following Truman's new appointments and elected chairman earlier in the day, suggested the group consider who should serve on the architectural board of consultants. By the October meeting, the commission had made its decision and appointed three architects as the panel of consultants: Walter M. Macomber, Mount Vernon's restoration architect, who previously had been the associate of Perry, Shaw &

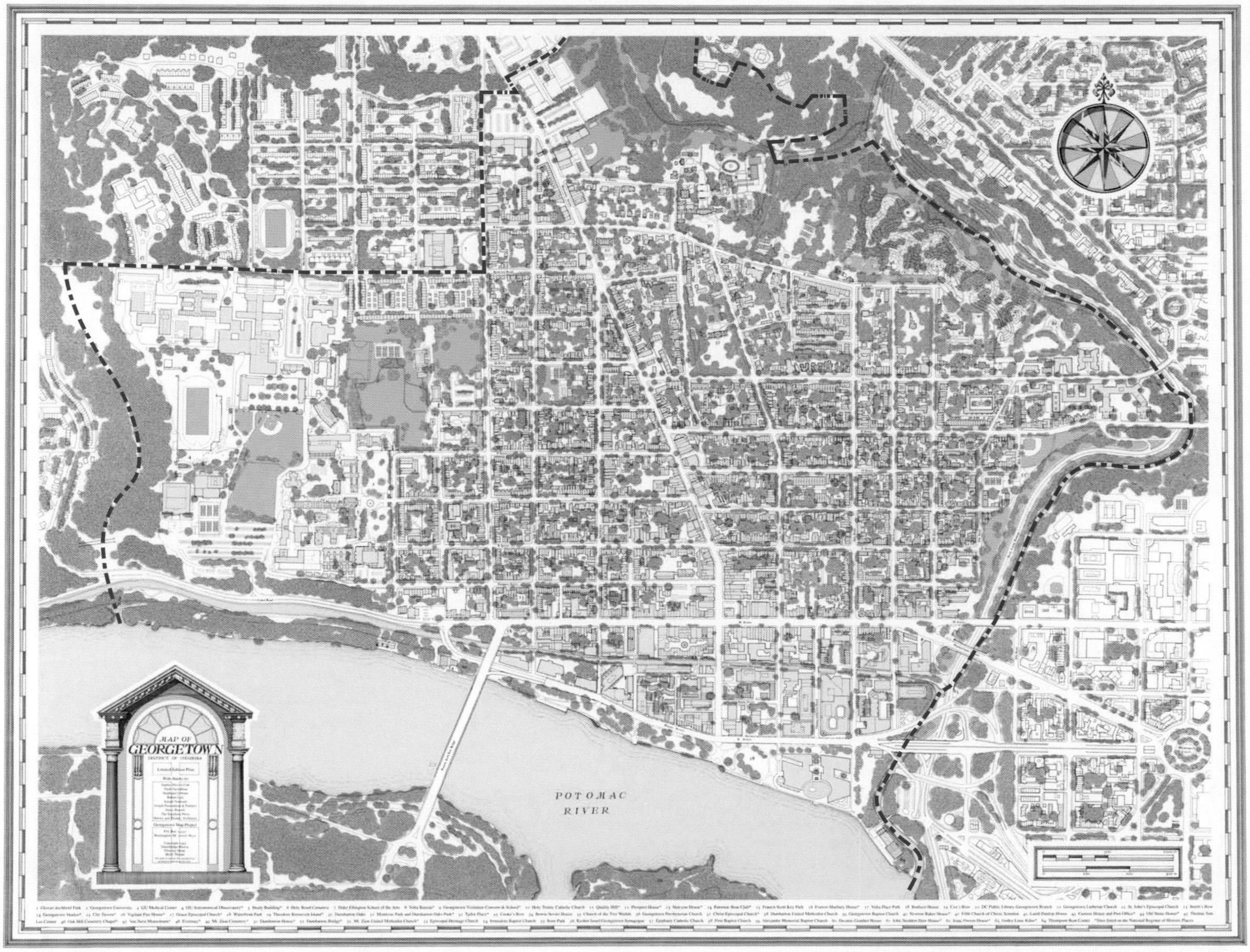

ABOVE: *Map of Georgetown (1993) indicating the boundaries of the Old Georgetown historic district as established by Congress in 1950.*

FAR LEFT: *Architect Walter Macomber, the first chairman of the Old Georgetown architectural board of consultants, at Mount Vernon where he worked as the restoration architect. (1962)*

LEFT: *Lorenzo Winslow (second from right, c. 1952), was the staff architect for the White House reconstruction and served on the first Old Georgetown architectural board of consultants. His colleagues on the renovation include (left to right) Colonel Douglas H. Gillette, Major General Glenn E. Edgerton, and Harbin S. Chandler Jr.*

2817 Dumbarton Street, NW, designed by Katherine Gibbs in 1951, led to extensive discussion about the appropriate design of windows for new structures within the Georgetown historic district (1993).

Hepburn assigned to supervise restoration at Williamsburg; Lorenzo S. Winslow, the White House architect; and W. Dewey Foster, a Washington architect who specialized in Colonial Revival residences.[76] The commission also designated Macomber to serve as the board's chairman.

While it was some time before the commission settled on the name Old Georgetown Board (OGB), the panel quickly began work, meeting weekly to review 163 cases during the first year, of which sixteen proposals were denied. The most problematic case was the new residence at 2817 Dumbarton Street by owner-architect Katherine Gibbs.[77] The issue concerned the design of the windows: Gibbs wanted sliding windows with horizontal mullions whereas the board recommended vertically proportioned, six-over-six, double-hung windows. Macomber offered an economic argument in favor of double-hung windows, citing the lower cost of replacement.[78] After initially agreeing to do what the board advised, Gibbs appealed the decision to the District commissioners, who granted her approval to install the sliding windows.

Discouraged, the board members wrote to Finley requesting that he discuss the matter with the District commissioners and concluded: "horizontal [window] panes… are truly accepted as a sign of contemporary architecture, the architecture which Public Law 808 proposes to elim-

inate from the area of Old Georgetown."[79] This interpretation of the law was overstated as the law did not prohibit contemporary architecture. In fact, when Foster had testified before Congress on the pending legislation, he noted:

This bill does not condemn modern or contemporary architecture. It only provides guidance for protecting and preserving the general character of a limited area of the City…. There is no reason why restrained and well-designed contemporary facades cannot fit in with this older work.[80]

Nearly a year after the law went into effect, the commission invited the Old Georgetown Board members to its August 1951 meeting in order to discuss problems and establish procedures. Reading from a prepared statement, "Preliminary Indoctrination for Officials Enforcing the Old Georgetown Law," commission member Elbert Peets said that Congress had passed the law because it appreciated the "evident danger that commercial exploitation—perhaps also the erratic tastes of individuals—might seriously damage the area." He added that the act's purpose was

first to save old buildings from demolition, second to save them from desecration, and, third, to create and maintain a suitable setting for them. The first two parts of the assignment, though likely to be less in number of cases, are pretty sure to be the most difficult. Abstractly considered, preservation is the most important part of the whole movement. For the demolition of the past we curse the past: let us try to save the present from the curses of the future. Each case will be a battle—it is hard to lay down rules as to which buildings justify the longest fight. This much can be said, that both the wording of the law and the best practice of architectural restoration justify dependence largely on aesthetic criteria.

While he described Georgetown as "a good local museum of late-eighteenth- and early-nineteenth-century architecture and town planning," Peets stressed that an overemphasis on the Colonial led to little appreciation of buildings constructed thereafter, and he maintained that these later buildings should also be preserved and not "remodeled under the influence of the Colonial slogan." However, he defended a limited use of the Colonial for new construction in Georgetown:

Undated contemporary Colonial…should give us the essence and not the externals of the style. It should give us simple, familiar and well-loved materials and designs that are in harmony with the scale and form and color of the neighborhood.[81]

After Peets finished, Macomber asked for guidance on handling typical issues associated with Georgetown cases. He acknowledged the full spectrum of styles existing in the neighborhood but argued that, "The great common interest in Georgetown is created by late-18th and early-19th-century houses rather than the ones built after 1850." He conceded that differences of opinion may exist, but said

CHAPTER IV | HEROISM, HISTORY, AND AUTOMOBILES

the board believed interpreting the law "requires architectural detail and mass sympathy with that period described in the law."[82] Sidestepping the Colonial Revival debate, Finley said his greatest concern was that the law did not address a particular style for new construction in Georgetown. Macomber wanted to know what kind of support the commission would give the board on this matter and reminded them that the window problem associated with the Gibbs residence highlighted concerns regarding contemporary design.

Commission member Joseph Hudnut entered the discussion:

We certainly don't want any modern gadgets in the way of chromium steel and huge plate glass walls, flat roofs and all those clichés of modernism in Georgetown. On the other hand, if you are going to encourage the use of detail copied from early American…you will presently have your old building surrounded by a considerable number of imitation buildings, like the woman [who] displays paste diamonds. I think that would be a great pity.

Nevertheless, Hudnut considered the central issue to be plainness:

I would like to make a suggestion that the only thing you insist on in the new buildings is good design. Now, if they are perfectly plain buildings, buildings that do not pretend to architectural virtuosity, but just plain, I think your setting will be better and your atmosphere more preserved because it will be obvious that here are fine old buildings, but you have refrained from parroting them or competing with them by insisting on the plainest kind of structures…plain walls of good materials, good proportions, but without detail, no detail, and no modern clichés.[83]

Apparently unaware that Macomber had been involved with the restoration work at Williamsburg, Hudnut went on to describe the often-referenced town as "imitation Colonial":

They have tried to introduce colonial detail and the consequences are perfectly dreadful. You have these stunning old buildings like the Governor's Palace and the Capitol, but these new buildings designed by modern architects just scream at you as fakes.

Macomber defended his work and did not bother to point out that the Governor's Palace and Capitol had been reconstructed in the 1930s. Hudnut conceded that the new buildings were good but emphasized that he did not want imitation Colonial buildings competing with authentic ones.

Returning the discussion to Georgetown, Macomber asked if the commission considered replacing single-light window sashes with multi-light sashes to be an inappropriate alteration. In response, Finley attempted to address public perception while acknowledging the untested terrain of historic preservation:

Wouldn't we have a greater chance of success if we let the people do what they wanted to do, whether to make it look like 1900 or a little

earlier, or to leave it as it is provided it is not offensive to the area…. If the people either remodel the building or put up a new building that is plain and not offensive, we have more or less kept the atmosphere of Georgetown but we are not trying to impose rigid standards of how they shall build a building or remodel.

Commission member George Biddle remarked that the discretion of the board members would ensure flexibility, and Edward Neild added that their "good taste" would serve as a guiding force provided that simplicity was upheld and good materials used to harmonize with the nineteenth- and early-twentieth-century buildings. Hudnut supported Neild's comment, saying the board should encourage buildings that "show good manners and are gentlemanly and can acknowledge [their] secondary role in Georgetown." Finley also espoused flexibility, but raised the problem of the tendency to aggrandize buildings and mentioned his desire to avoid lawsuits:

Give them as much leeway as possible to follow their own ideas so long as they are not offensive and conflict with the whole area around. Then encourage them not to put a grandiose…[element] on a building…. That is what they try to do…. That kind of thing is bad and I think hurts Georgetown as much as anything else. But I think the root is good taste and common sense and not to be too rigid in enforcement of ideas so we will be thrown out of court.[84]

As the discussion drew to a close, Foster asked Finley if the board could continue working with Elbert Peets; Finley agreed, further suggesting another joint session. Peets readily accepted the responsibility despite expressing discouragement about the meeting's lack of clear direction

Landscape architect and planner Elbert Peets, co-author of the 1922 publication American Vitruvius: An Architect's Handbook of Civic Art, *photographed in 1936 while serving as a federal housing planner. In the 1950s, Peets was a member of the Commission of Fine Arts, where he helped to articulate principles to guide the review of projects in the Georgetown historic district.*

RIGHT: *The Gothic Revival West Street Presbyterian Church (1873) and Chapel (1865), designed by James McGill, were notably expressive pieces of Georgetown's extensive late-nineteenth-century Victorian architecture.*

BELOW: *The 1955–56 renovation of the church was designed by Lorenzo Winslow, who refashioned the Georgetown Presbyterian Church as a Colonial Revival building suitable to contemporary tastes for new architecture in the historic district.*

for the board and suggested that the two bodies meet monthly, adding:

I must say that I feel that we are not making great progress. I think what these gentlemen say about some kind of rules, that go beyond merely saying "use your good taste," is sound. It is necessary to convince people that we are not making arbitrary individual special decisions for every one of them. That is what starts a fight. Instead of saying "make the wall openings harmonious," we should say in addition that the openings must be vertical in their proportions. That sounds very arbitrary but isn't it that kind of thing that would help you? [85]

Peet's effort to stress the importance of buildings erected after the Federal era was seemingly ignored by the board. In February 1955, Secretary Wilson presented plans to the commission for the renovation of the Georgetown Presbyterian Church, located at 3115 P Street, NW. He mentioned that the board had not taken an action on the project because the chairman had not been present and that it was awkward because the architect, Lorenzo Winslow, was a board member. Following the direction of the Reverend Russell Stroup, the congregation sought to replace the facade of its Victorian church, demolish the adjacent Victorian chapel, and build new Colonial Revival

buildings that would recall the congregation's original church built in 1821, which had been located on M Street. Winslow used the preliminary sketches for the Federal church for his inspiration.[86] The commission members did not like the proposal, and Belluschi objected strongly, explaining that "it is a statement of contemporary thought in church design and it is bad for Georgetown.... I am not against Georgian, but this is not it. It is not good proportion." No comment was made on the demolition of the chapel. The commission chose not to take action on the proposal because the congregation had supported the project.

No other joint session between the board and the commission took place during the decade; however, during that time, the commission initiated a meeting with the District commissioners, its Corporation Counsel, and the board in October 1958 to consider a long-simmering dispute regarding federal versus local jurisdiction in demolition decisions. Since 1950, the number of applications forwarded to the CFA from the District for review had decreased. In addition, several raze applications for early-nineteenth-century buildings denied by the commission had been overruled by the District. The October meeting was precipitated by the District commissioners' recent reversal of two raze applications denied by the CFA.[87] The parties discussed an opinion issued by the Corporation Counsel on the constitutionality of the Old Georgetown Act.[88] The District commissioners asserted that the law was vague and only applied to existing buildings in which significant historic events occurred; the CFA and the OGB held that the law applied to all buildings—including new construction—as well as structures and signs.

After no agreement could be reached, the three Old Georgetown Board members maintained that they could not carry out their responsibilities and resigned in protest; Finley pleaded with them to remain without success.[89] Consequently, the commission's secretary, Linton Wilson, acted in lieu of the board—reviewing and making recommendations to the commission on building permit and demolition applications—from January 1959 until the matter was settled a year later when, following a written request by Finley to President Eisenhower, the U.S. attorney general issued a position statement to the president that supported the CFA's broad interpretation of the law.[90]

Despite Wilson's shouldering of the workload, the commission sought to relieve itself from the obligation of administering the Old Georgetown Act during this time. The commission members were opposed to the responsibility for several reasons: the District did not forward all

building permit applications to the commission; the applications produced a burdensome caseload; the projects were small in scale; and there was limited federal interest due to private ownership of most structures. Concurrently, the Progressive Citizens Association of Georgetown spearheaded a movement to amend the Old Georgetown Act in order to strengthen the law with revised language.[91] The community group also approached the National Capital Planning Commission to discuss that agency's willingness to accept the responsibility to administer the law.

In the midst of these efforts, the District government—for the first time—requested funding from Congress to undertake the survey of Georgetown prescribed in the legislation. At the hearing, Representative Louis Rabaut (D-MI), who chaired the House Committee on the District of Columbia, mentioned he had read about disputes in Georgetown and preferred not to take a position, adding that "perhaps we should stop all improvements in the area."[92] The appropriation was denied.

Immediately after the attorney general's opinion was issued, Finley appealed to the former board members to resume service to fill two positions on the board. In an effort to create better working relations with the District government, he suggested that the D.C. commissioners appoint someone from the Office of the Municipal Architect for the third vacancy.[93] In March 1960, the commission issued a press release announcing the appointment of

The pre-Columbian art gallery at Dumbarton Oaks by Philip Johnson represents a notable departure from the historicist approach to new architecture in Georgetown. Commissioned by the estate's owners in 1959, the pavilion is a cluster of domed spaces enclosed with curving glass set within the renowned landscape of the estate, whose main residence was renovated in the Colonial Revival style in the 1920s.

three board members as well as the rationale for continuing to review projects in Georgetown:

The rehabilitation of this section of Washington, which has been so largely accomplished since the First World War, is a notable example of urban renewal by private initiative without the use of government funds. As a result there exists not only a large number of small and moderate size houses with gardens, many of architectural excellence, but the value of taxable property in this area has greatly increased, so that Georgetown has become a more valuable asset to the City of Washington.[94]

Despite problematic relations with the District government, the commission or its Old Georgetown Board had reviewed 2,317 permit applications by the end of the decade. The overwhelming number of projects was for alterations in keeping with Colonial Revival remodeling; 5 percent of the cases were demolition applications. The D.C. commissioners ultimately approved several demolition applications for Federal-era buildings that the Commission of Fine Arts had denied, but the CFA nonetheless supported 113 demolitions. The change occurring throughout the historic district would become more pronounced in the following decades.

Postwar Change: Highways and Urban Renewal

The midcentury decades were a time of explosive suburban growth in the Washington, D.C., metropolitan region. The decentralization of federal office centers outside the District's boundaries—a move fueled, in part, by civil defense concerns and supported by both the CFA and the NCPPC—encouraged this trend. Among the new suburban agencies were the federal office complex in Suitland, Maryland; the National Institutes of Health in Bethesda, Maryland; the National Security Agency in Fort Meade, Maryland; and the Central Intelligence Agency in Langley, Virginia.[95]

The ideal of suburban living also drew people to new homes outside the city, creating commuters who relied more on cars than public transit. Without planning authority, the Commission of Fine Arts could only attempt to make the design of utilitarian features more palatable. But through its persistence in raising concerns about the impact of highways and bridges, the CFA became an early leader in preservation of the larger urban environment. Only gradually were its members able to assert the commission's role in new urban planning efforts.

Within Washington, the new federal policy of urban renewal was drastically changing the face of the city. As with the new highways and bridges, the commission pressed for greater coordination and consideration of design in these massive redevelopment projects. Redevelopment also included the proliferation of box-like office buildings south of the Mall in response to a continuing need for federal work space despite decentralization to the suburbs; of great concern to the commission was the design compatibility of these projects with the Mall.

Many of the other projects submitted to the commission in the midcentury decades were relatively minor and often unrelated to architecture, such as the acquisition of paintings and the design of military medals, insignia, and, for a brief period, postage stamps. The Commission of Fine Arts also found itself involved with federal art programs and exhibitions.[96] In 1942, at the invitation of the Architectural League of New York, the CFA and the NCPPC collaborated on an exhibition in New York City of plans and images of Washington, D.C., to commemorate the 150th anniversary of the L'Enfant Plan.[97] Later in the decade, the commission advised on various events planned for the sesquicentennial of the District of Columbia, including another exhibition on Washington's history, which was displayed at the Corcoran Gallery of Art in 1950 and two years later at the Ford's Theater museum.[98]

The commission did not lose sight of its central concern: the physical effect of change to the setting of the monumental core—not only on the Lincoln Memorial and the Mall but on the larger area of the Potomac River Gorge as well. When the U.S. Engineer's Office revived a scheme to flood the valley for hydroelectric power, the CFA referred to its role in persuading Congress to pass an act preventing the earlier proposal.[99] Gilmore Clarke addressed the issue in a speech before the Joint Committee on the National Capital in February 1944:

Even a compromise scheme is undesirable here; we cannot build dams, no matter how well done, and at the same time continue to enjoy the beauty of this indispensible asset of the Nation's Capital. The Commission of Fine Arts took an important part in defeating the last attempt to despoil this single remaining untouched remnant of Nature's achievement in this region, and we shall continue to advocate the full protection of this magnificent valley for enjoyment by future generations of Americans.[100]

AUTOMOBILE INFRASTRUCTURE

An even greater threat to the fabric of the national capital came after the war: the impact of the automobile, brought about by large-scale road projects inserted through the city's existing neighborhoods and monumental landscape. Almost since its founding, the Commission of Fine Arts had contended with the various problems posed to the District by vehicles. In the 1920s, the number of private automobiles driven by Washington commuters increased sub-

stantially; buses and cars began to replace the ubiquitous Washington streetcar. By the 1930s, parked cars had become a visual blight on the geometric purity of the Mall roads. In the Federal Triangle, the expansive and unfinished Great Plaza—envisioned as the centerpiece of that complex—was a commercial parking lot: the vast sweep of William Delano's hemicycle on the west facade of the Post Office building was barely visible above a sea of parked cars.

In the 1950s, highway plans promised to increase the speed and efficiency of travel for the federal workforce while threatening to destroy historic neighborhoods and parks throughout the city. As much as it could within the limitations of its status as a review agency, the commission attempted to preserve the scenic and landscape qualities of Washington. The commission was particularly concerned about the visual and physical imposition of automobile traffic and its attendant highways and bridges on the Lincoln Memorial and its setting.

Plans to bridge the Potomac River from the west end of Constitution Avenue to the Virginia shoreline to reduce downtown traffic congestion were first made public in the early 1950s. District transportation planners insisted that traffic demands required a location over or near Theodore Roosevelt Island, and the House authorized a study.[101] However, a bridge at this location was problematic because of the proximity to the Lincoln Memorial and the island's function as a presidential memorial, albeit one that had not yet been completed. As Arleyn Levee discusses in her essay, the Theodore Roosevelt Memorial Association (TRMA) purchased the island in 1931 and donated it the next year to the federal government, arranging for its redesign by Frederick Law Olmsted Jr. as a landscape memorial to Roosevelt and his role as a national conservation leader.[102] A booklet published by the TRMA in the 1950s, intended to promote the memorial and defeat the bridge, explained its goal: "The Association has given the nation the makings of a monument not only to Theodore Roosevelt but also to the primeval America that the explorers and first settlers saw when they came to these shores," if people will only "keep the hand of the despoiler off it."[103] The association intended to place a single structure on the island, a paved terrace at the south end where visitors could look out to the Lincoln Memorial, establishing the kind of reciprocal view between monuments that formed a vital element of both the L'Enfant and McMillan Plans.

Legally, the TRMA possessed veto power over any construction on the island, and for a number of years it succeeded in stalling bridge plans. The bridge also faced significant opposition from Ulysses S. Grant III, the vice chairman of the Committee of 100 on the Federal City and

TOP: *Despite grand intentions, the Great Plaza of the Federal Triangle remained a parking lot for half a century. Automobile traffic engendered by rapid suburbanization and the decline of the streetcar system by the end of the 1950s made parking a necessary priority.*

ABOVE: *The CFA and the NCPPC created an exhibit at the Corcoran Gallery of Art in 1950 that explored the history of the city's design since the L'Enfant Plan and the role that transportation and dispersed development would play in the growth of the Washington region.*

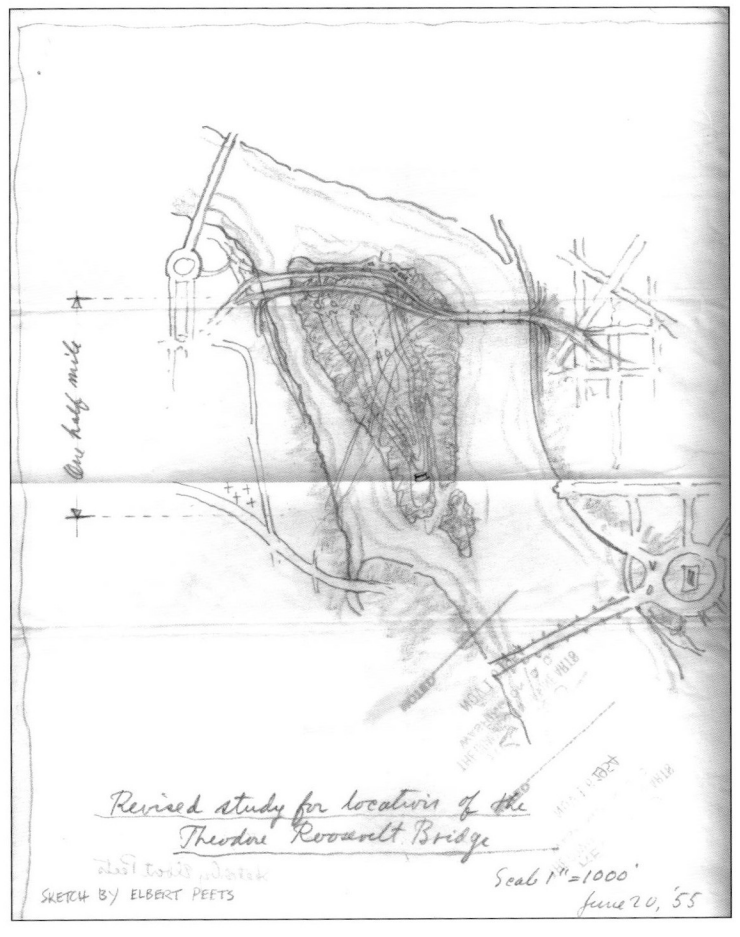

ABOVE LEFT: *In 1955, CFA member Elbert Peets developed his own study for the location of the proposed Theodore Roosevelt Memorial Bridge, keeping it on the north end of Roosevelt Island well away from the axis of the Mall.*

ABOVE RIGHT: *The utilitarian design of the Theodore Roosevelt Bridge (aerial view c. 1970) compromised the vision of creating a memorial to the president at the south end of Roosevelt Island. Initially opposed to its construction, the CFA tried to improve the bridge's appearance through refinement of its structure and abutments as well as details such as lighting.*

formerly the director of the NCPPC and the National Park Service. The Commission of Fine Arts favored a tunnel instead of a bridge in this location to protect the Potomac landscape. Legislation for this more expensive alternative was introduced in the House, but a tunnel was never built.

To meet the TRMA's objections, in 1954 Congress authorized construction of the bridge on Little Island, a smaller land mass immediately south of Roosevelt Island. However, a bridge in this location would impede views from Roosevelt Island to the Lincoln Memorial, undermining the island's memorial character. Faced with the loss of this important aspect, the TRMA conceded to a bridge over Roosevelt Island. Explaining its change of heart, the association said that "the trustees recall the part that Mr. Roosevelt as President played in conserving and developing the grand plan of the National Capital," referring to the establishment of the McMillan Commission's plan during his presidency, and recognized that "their paramount obligation is to the National Capital."[104] However, they imposed conditions: the bridge had to be low and screened by trees; it had to allow access to the island; it had to be named after Theodore Roosevelt; and it had to be approved by the Commission of Fine Arts.[105]

After the location was determined, the D.C. Department of Highways and Traffic brought its bridge designs to the CFA on many occasions between 1957 and 1959 as it changed from a reinforced concrete to a steel girder bridge. The commission's primary concern remained the mitigation of the bridge's effect on views from the Lincoln Memorial and from parklands along the river's shore. Over the course of the review process, the commission urged the Department of Highways and Traffic to consult with them and, in particular, to show renderings or models of the project in context with other structures and approach roads. The department was less than cooperative. David Finley repeatedly asked the district engineer, Commissioner Brigadier General A. C. Welling, to provide these tools of visual analysis since Finley was convinced they would make the "destructive nature of the bridge plan clear." After Welling said he did not believe a model would be useful, Finley warned him that the commission's endorsement of the design did not constitute endorsement of its location.[106] So strongly did the commission regard the project that it took the unusual step of issuing a press release in late 1957 outlining its position.[107]

Even former chairman Gilmore Clarke commented

ABOVE: *The 1959 rendering of the West Leg of the Inner Loop Freeway at Rock Creek and Potomac Parkway, shown adjacent to the heroic moderne West Power Station of 1948 across Rock Creek in Georgetown.*

LEFT: *Plan of the West Leg of the Inner Loop Freeway, G Street to Pennsylvania Avenue, NW, 1959. The Inner Loop threatened to sever historic neighborhoods such as Georgetown and would have replaced existing blocks with massive highway infrastructure.*

Power, *one of four high-relief sculpture panels proposed for the eastern abutments of Theodore Roosevelt Memorial Bridge, by Laura Gardin Fraser, 1959. The CFA approved Fraser's maquette designs of heroic allegorical figures representing key aspects of Roosevelt's character: power, courage, leadership, and foresight. Fraser died in 1966, and the sculptures were not completed; a subsequent proposal in 1985 depicting wildlife in bas-relief panels was also approved in concept but never installed.*

formally on the Roosevelt Bridge design, pushing the commission to consider it as part of the Theodore Roosevelt Memorial and to require the construction of a monumental stone bridge—the type of bridge that had been his specialty. But architect member Douglas Orr (CFA 1955–63) argued that the design should use a different material in order to differentiate the new bridge from the Arlington Memorial Bridge. The commission agreed and in January 1959 gave final approval for a steel bridge of equal 252 feet spans with large stone abutments at each end, having noted that by this choice "there was a good possibility of getting a handsome bridge."[108]

The commission's relationship with Welling remained contentious, however, as he continued to refuse to show the commission drawings of the entire setting, including the approach roads. In 1959 the commission obtained two-year-old plans from the NCPC, which the members called "disturbing in their disregard for proper use of park areas and for the way in which they crowded the Lincoln Memorial." The commission emphasized that it would withhold its approval of the bridge until the city supplied sufficient contextual information.[109] After a period of months, the District began to provide plans for approach structures, which lacked topographical information. The commission members decided to approve solely the design for the bridge and its approaches while making it clear that it refused to approve the location in the park.[110]

The Roosevelt Bridge was only a small part of a larger effort to create a comprehensive freeway system in Washington. Plans for three circumferential highways and connecting routes were developed and promulgated by the new chairman of the National Capital Planning Commission, the prominent planner Harland Bartholomew, appointed by President Eisenhower in 1953. Only the outer highway—the Capital Beltway—was fully built; stopping the others was an intense struggle that united citizens from all neighborhoods in the city in the 1960s. The proposed Inner Loop highway and its related Three Sisters Bridge crossing the Potomac just above Georgetown were of great concern to the CFA because both would have affected the monumental core, most importantly the Lincoln Memorial. Beginning in 1956 and into the 1960s, the commission reviewed projects related to the Inner Loop and the Three Sisters Bridge nearly four dozen times.[111]

The Three Sisters Bridge formed a critical link in the Inner Loop proposal. Named for three prominent rocks rising from the Potomac River a short distance above the Key Bridge, the bridge would have connected Virginia's I-66 with a Potomac Freeway that would have followed the river in the bed of the C&O Canal through Georgetown

to a tunneled K Street.[112] When the CFA saw preliminary plans for the bridge in 1959, it stressed the need to preserve parklands and the gorge's natural beauty while creating a "handsome addition to an important landscape of the National Capital."[113]

Eight years passed before further studies for the Three Sisters Bridge were presented to the Commission of Fine Arts, including a design for a single-span bridge, which the commission preferred for its simplicity. However, the members observed that the approaches were not related to the bridge structure, a problem "all too painfully evident on several recent bridges in Washington, notably the Theodore Roosevelt Bridge."[114] CFA architect member Gordon Bunshaft (CFA 1963–72) urged the engineers to continue the same arch construction at both ends to ensure that the structure flowed in a continuous line with the highway.

The revised design, presented at the April 1967 commission meeting, proposed a steel beam span on concrete posts, causing Chairman William Walton to exclaim: "We think it is a disaster…it is a bad version of the Roosevelt Bridge, which is exactly what we hoped to prevent ever happening on this site." Bunshaft brusquely told the engineers that they needed to hire a nationally known structural engineer to design a concrete bridge. The engineers protested that the constraints of site and program precluded what the commission demanded; Bunshaft again asserted that all they needed was a designer with the ingenuity to come up with "the greatest damn bridge ever built."[115] Consultants were hired and the proposal revised as a single concrete span of hollow, reinforced box girders, with the same arch construction continuing into the embankments on both ends. The commission supported this design for its imagination and daring.[116]

The early plans for the proposed Inner Loop scheme also called for a six-lane road and tunnel that would circle around the Lincoln Memorial on the river side, emerging from the south onto Independence Avenue and from the north near Constitution Avenue, where it would connect with the approaches to the proposed Theodore Roosevelt Bridge. The tunnel beneath the Lincoln Memorial area would have included ventilation exhaust structures and other intrusions into the landscape. Related changes called for two one-way drives directly on the Mall flanking the Reflecting Pool, with a new plaza between the pool and the memorial. Grudgingly, the commission approved most of these features. In a letter to Conrad Wirth, the director of the National Park Service, David Finley wrote: "The intrusion of this and other highways into the park land near the Lincoln Memorial now seems to be inevitable. It is accordingly believed that the proposed tunnel is the only fea-

sible way to preserve at least some of the serenity and dignity of the Lincoln Memorial, providing these plans are properly developed."[117]

The commission members attempted to keep portals to the tunnel at some distance from the Lincoln Memorial and recommended that they be screened with heavy vegetation. They eventually agreed with a National Park Service recommendation for a highway route that would tunnel under the Tidal Basin before emerging in West Potomac Park that purported to retain more trees and save more parkland than other alternatives, leaving the setting of the Lincoln Memorial undisturbed.[118] The commission came to reject the plan, however, when it became clear that it would require the removal of thirty-three elms along the Reflecting Pool. In defending this landscape, the commission noted:

Much more is involved than tree conservation. These trees are an integral part of an architectural design which is one of the most revered places in America. The proposed tree removal would require at least a generation to restore the quiet scene and it is by this standard that the cost of realignment of the highway must be judged.[119]

Elsewhere in the city, some components of the Inner Loop were built, most significantly the elevated highway across the Southwest and Southeast quadrants of the city and the "center leg" freeway, which connected the southwest highway across the Mall to the north. Most of the Inner Loop projects reviewed by the CFA were bridges, interchanges, and overpasses in the western Mall and

ABOVE: *The* CFA *rejected the aesthetically uninspired preliminary studies for the Three Sisters Bridge in 1967 and urged the District to hire a nationally recognized engineer to improve the design.*

BELOW: *Demonstrators clashed with police on the Three Sisters Islands in October 1969, protesting the proposed eight-lane highway connecting Route 66 with Georgetown's Whitehurst Freeway.*

Postwar infrastructure construction near the monumental core of the city transformed the character of the waterfront. The building of the Southwest Freeway (left foreground) included the massive eight-lane Francis Case Bridge across the Washington Channel as well as a series of access ramps at the rear of the Jefferson Memorial, 1961.

Potomac Parkway area and Southwest and Southeast Washington; many of the elements were designed by Harbeson, Hough, Livingston & Larson—the successor firm to Paul Cret. Most were constructed of stone and concrete with single aluminum railings along the sidewalks. The CFA usually approved these features while advising restudy of particular elements, such as the type of facing stone or railings.

Even when giving approval, the CFA repeatedly indicated its unhappiness with the overall project, although this highlighted the limits of its advisory authority. Approving one overpass, the CFA noted: "Approval of the inner belt system itself should not be implied by approval of this structure." Concerning several overpasses in the Southwest quadrant, the CFA said: "The members of the Commission had misgivings about the ability to retain the vista of the memorial area. While the members were not happy with the whole project, there seemed to be little they could do except make suggestions as to structural and architectural details on the overpasses." In late 1959, Finley wrote to the engineer commissioner: "The Commission of Fine Arts has never approved the location of the Inner Loop, but the members strongly recommend that the structures which compose it shall conform, so far as may be possible, to the principles which underlie the design of other similar structures in the nation's capital."[120]

As with the Theodore Roosevelt Bridge, the CFA was unhappy with the reluctance of the District to provide it with plans for the Inner Loop. In November 1959, after yet another piecemeal submission of studies, this time for in-

terchanges between K Street and the Whitehurst Freeway, the CFA again turned to the press and prepared a statement saying it had never seen a general plan for the Inner Loop nor given approval to a plan "which threatens to mar and in many places change the appearance of the city. The Commission of Fine Arts is particularly concerned where the Inner Loop and connecting roadways invade the parks as in the case which has been brought to the Commission today."[121]

Issuing the press release had the desired effect. The following day, the D.C. director of highways and traffic gave the commission the general plan for the Inner Loop, asking the CFA's advice about an underpass at Virginia Avenue and the viaducts and overpasses from the Inner Loop to the Whitehurst Freeway at K Street. About the latter, the CFA said it was "impossible to approve these plans...which impinge on the park land, giving it a chaotic appearance."[122] Continued opposition by the CFA and growing protests by citizens were factors in eventually halting work on the Inner Loop project, including the Three Sisters Bridge. In 1970, the U.S. District Court finally ruled that the planning process for the entire urban highway project had been flawed. Plans were dropped and funds were eventually shifted to subway construction.[123]

URBAN RENEWAL IN THE SOUTHWEST QUADRANT

A central goal of the McMillan Plan was the creation of a dignified district of government buildings that would de-

fine the city's monumental core and frame the Mall and its institutions. By the mid-twentieth century, when the desire for monumental classical edifices had passed, the Commission of Fine Arts continued to try to guide the character of development near the Mall—this time, in a redevelopment district in the Southwest quadrant, the most radically altered section of the city during the capital's midcentury urban restructuring. This historic residential neighborhood, which lay immediately south of the Mall, experienced near-total demolition and reconstruction as the District's most extensive urban renewal effort. While the Commission of Fine Arts attempted to exert control over these changes, its efforts were again hampered by the agency's lack of authority over large-scale planning.

Bounded on the west by the Washington Channel and the Potomac River, Southwest was by far the smallest of the city's four quadrants; the precinct was also known as The Island because of its isolation from the rest of the city by the elevated railroad viaduct on Maryland and Virginia Avenues and the remnants of the Tiber Creek Canal to the east. Associated with the working waterfront on the channel, Southwest was a racially mixed area, home to various immigrant and African American communities. Larger-scale industry and government offices began encroaching into the neighborhood of small-scale Victorian row houses and small businesses by the 1920s, causing neglect and deterioration as uses began to change.

Starting in the early 1940s, planning and other studies focused on the deterioration, which—given the area's proximity to the Mall, the downtown business district, and the U.S. Capitol—had aroused concern among city and federal officials, social scientists, planners, and others focused on improving conditions in the city. In the 1950s,

Southwest became an early testing ground for urban renewal, the newly developing national policy to solve the physical and social consequences of inner-city blight. The proponents for change overcame lawsuits and in 1954 won a landmark U.S. Supreme Court decision in *Berman v. Parker* that cleared the way for the demolition of Southwest to begin. By 1960, most of the quadrant between the railroad and the waterfront had been razed with the attendant displacement of thousands of residents.[124]

Early in discussions regarding the redevelopment of Southwest, the commission reviewed a report prepared by Arthur Goodwillie, director of the Conservation Service of the Home Owners' Loan Corporation. Prepared in 1942 in the early days of World War II, Goodwillie's plan put forth the idea that, rather than invest in widespread new construction in Southwest, it would be far more economical to take advantage of "existing community assets" such as infrastructure and to improve substandard housing as a way to quickly house war workers, clean up blight, and provide quality low-income homes for postwar residents. The commission concurred with CFA member William Lamb, who argued that economic and social issues needed to be addressed separately—and solved first—before "questions of design." While its response to Goodwillie was not explicit, it suggests that the commission of the early 1940s did not view wholesale demolition and redevelopment as a means to solve the problems of slums.[125]

The mechanisms to redevelop Southwest were initiated when Congress passed the District of Columbia Redevelopment Act in 1945 and the Redevelopment Land Agency (RLA) was established the following year as a branch of the District of Columbia government. The RLA was specifically empowered to rehabilitate Southwest

Before urban renewal, Southwest (pictured in 1939) was a densely built working-class neighborhood of row houses and small retail establishments that had developed near the commercial Washington Channel waterfront.

TOP: *Located within sight of the U.S. Capitol, the Southwest neighborhood had been the subject of numerous plans for improvement since the 1930s.*

BOTTOM: *By 1960, urban renewal efforts had razed the Southwest's historic fabric, as shown in this aerial view looking west toward the Jefferson Memorial.*

CHAPTER IV | HEROISM, HISTORY, AND AUTOMOBILES

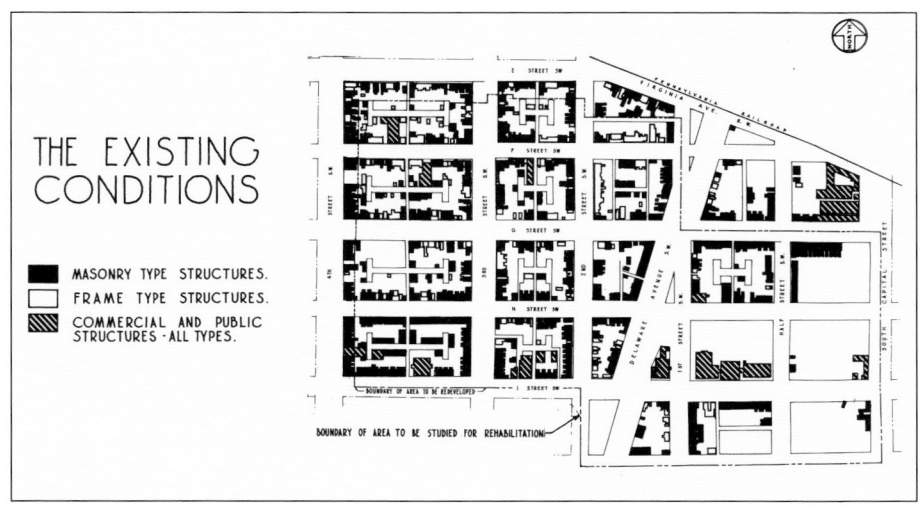

THE EXISTING CONDITIONS

■ MASONRY TYPE STRUCTURES.
□ FRAME TYPE STRUCTURES.
▨ COMMERCIAL AND PUBLIC STRUCTURES - ALL TYPES.

ABOVE: *In his 1942 plan for Southwest, Arthur Goodwillie analyzed the neighborhood's existing building types.*

BELOW: *Based on his analysis, Goodwillie proposed a nine-block test area in the neighborhood where new construction would be mixed with improvements to existing housing.*

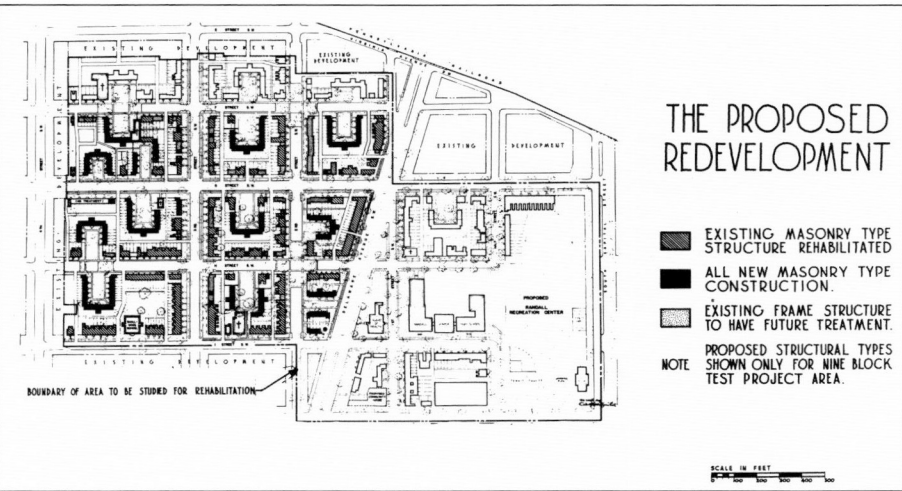

THE PROPOSED REDEVELOPMENT

▨ EXISTING MASONRY TYPE STRUCTURE REHABILITATED
■ ALL NEW MASONRY TYPE CONSTRUCTION.
░ EXISTING FRAME STRUCTURE TO HAVE FUTURE TREATMENT.
NOTE PROPOSED STRUCTURAL TYPES SHOWN ONLY FOR NINE BLOCK TEST PROJECT AREA.

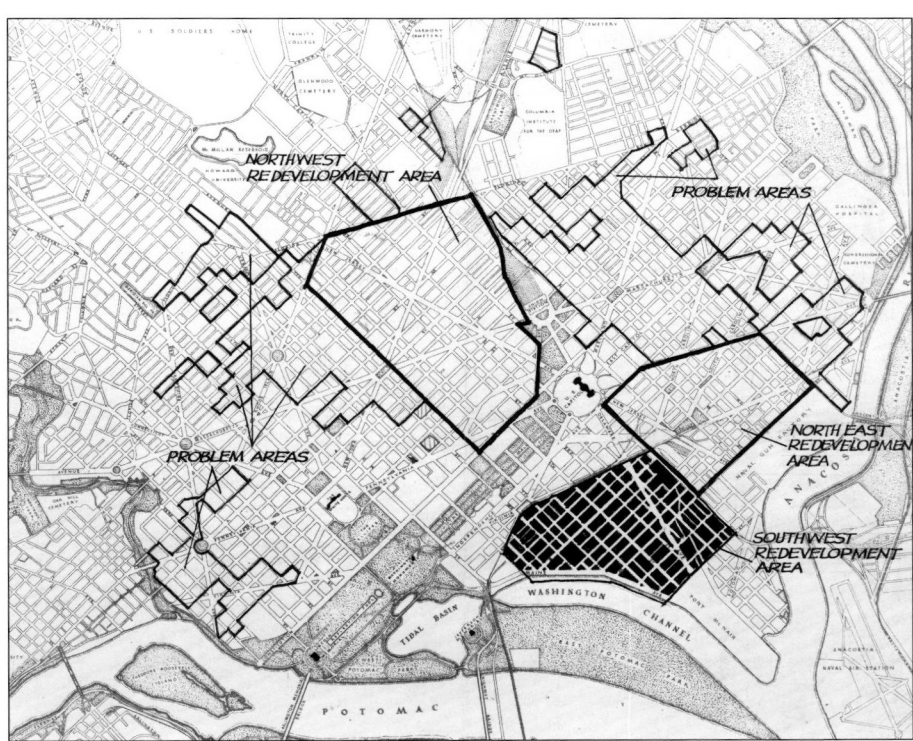

LEFT: *Redevelopment in Southwest (shaded area) was part of a larger urban renewal effort in Washington, D.C. In 1950, the* NCPPC *prepared a multivolume report,* Comprehensive Plan for the National Capital and Its Environs, *which analyzed physical and social conditions in the city and proposed responses. This plan by Keyes, Smith, Satterlee & Leth-bridge from the early 1950s was based on the* NCPPC *report and indicates the extent of the proposed redevelopment: Tracts generally correspond to areas of obsolete dwellings (more than 50 percent lacking indoor plumbing or requiring major repairs) and areas noted as blighted (with a lower percentage of substandard housing).*

The 1952 plan for Southwest developed by Louis Justement and Chloethiel Woodard Smith recommended a new urban neighborhood of six- to eight-story apartment buildings, hotels, office buildings, and a shopping mall organized around the proposed Inner Loop Freeway.

through condemnation and acquisition of property for redevelopment; the agency became active following passage of the National Housing Act of 1949, which provided its funding. While the Commission of Fine Arts' mandate required its involvement in the review of public projects within the redevelopment area, its review of the city's plans through the RLA was not assured. During the early years of redevelopment planning in the 1950s, the commission struggled with the District government over the RLA's reluctance to involve it in the review of Southwest development plans as a whole. Chairman Finley even suggested to the RLA that the Southwest waterfront be included within the Shipstead-Luce Act jurisdiction so that projects there would remain subject to design review after the agency released parcels for development.[126] However, the CFA's fight for greater oversight over the Southwest plans met with only partial success.

The large-scale development plans for Southwest evolved during the early 1950s. In 1951, the NCPPC retained Elbert Peets to create an overall blueprint for the area's redevelopment. Like Goodwillie's earlier plan, Peets's plan proposed saving the existing community by rehabilitating deteriorated housing, which would allow lower-income residents to remain in their homes. One year later, Washington architect Louis Justement—an advocate of solving urban problems through new construction and author of *New Cities for Old* (1946)—collaborated with local architect Chloethiel Woodard Smith on a far different plan for the RLA, one that proposed the demolition of existing structures and a thorough reconstruction of the neighborhood with modern buildings.

While Peets's approach was the least disruptive to the community, it was not clear that such a plan would qualify as redevelopment for purposes of federal funding. At-

tempting to steer a middle course, the agency—newly renamed the National Capital Planning Commission (NCPC) that July under the National Capital Planning Act of 1952—prepared a compromise document late that year that proposed clearing a significant portion of the neighborhood but incorporating a townhouse typology in the new construction that was similar in configuration to the original neighborhood.[127] While housing would be reintroduced in a mix of townhouses and apartment towers, a significant focus of the redevelopment was new office blocks and commercial construction.

The RLA approached the redevelopment process by delineating the Southwest into separate subareas with separate plans and developers. Early plans were presented to the Commission of Fine Arts as diagrammatic site plans and models, which the commission found to be weak both as designs and in their responsiveness to the larger city. At one

such review of "Area B" in September 1955, the commission called the plans "monotonous and poorly designed" and openly voiced opposition to wholesale demolition, commenting that it would be "far wiser" to retain buildings that were in good condition. Pressed by the RLA to choose among the schemes presented, the commission declined, calling the diagrammatic materials insufficient and instead requesting detailed site and architectural plans along with information on the overall planning program. The commission also stressed the need for coherence, preferably by using a single designer, especially along Delaware Avenue. Noting its own commitment to the principles of development inherent in the L'Enfant and McMillan Plans, the commission bluntly told the RLA it should consider an "architect's ability to realize these standards."[128]

In "Area C," the CFA raised questions about appropriateness and scale and the relationship of new development

Plans for a 10th Street Mall by developer William Zeckendorf's firm, Webb & Knapp, 1959, reflected the modernist approach to redevelopment set forth earlier in the Justement and Smith plan.

FACING PAGE. TOP:
Rendering of the functionalist-modernist FOB 6 *for the recently created Department of Health, Education, and Welfare by Faulkner, Kingsbury & Stenhouse, 1958.*

CENTER: FOB 10A *by Holabird, Root & Burgee, completed in 1963, was designed at ten stories for a prominent site terminating the 8th Street axis at Independence Avenue. Its design exhibits many of the hallmarks of the International Style: a repetitive gridded curtain wall, pilotis, and a flexible interior.*

BOTTOM: *A companion building to* FOB 10A *also completed in 1963 and designed by Holabird, Root & Burgee,* FOB 10B *is smaller in size but is expressed in a similar International Style vocabulary.*

to the Pennsylvania Railroad tracks, which had been a physical barrier in Southwest since the mid-nineteenth century. To clear the tracks, an elevated roadway was proposed by the area's developer, William Zeckendorf, as part of his redevelopment of 10th Street into a new office, commercial, and residential complex—the 10th Street Mall. In January 1956, the project was presented on an informal basis to the commission, which urged that the tracks be placed underground. After learning in May 1956 that the NCPC was moving forward with public hearings on the proposal, the CFA directed David Finley to write a letter to Robert E. McLaughlin, president of the District's Board of Commissioners. Finley noted in the letter that "no formal request has been made for the opinion of the Commission of Fine Arts," but gave it nevertheless, outlining four critical shortcomings that the commission found with the Zeckendorf proposal. Chief among them was that it competed with the L'Enfant Plan and would change the development pattern that L'Enfant had envisioned for the federal city. In addition, Finley wrote that the Zeckendorf proposal could not be successful with the railroad tracks in place and that the scale of the proposed office buildings would not be in harmony with the city's architectural development. Finley closed with the warning that the proposed scheme could do more harm than good.[129]

Development of the 10th Street Mall eventually moved forward, however, with Zeckendorf's young in-house architect, I. M. Pei, who was given design responsibility for the L'Enfant Plaza office and commercial complex, the centerpiece of the project. Pei's initial designs for the three office buildings framing the plaza would later be revised by other architects.[130]

FEDERAL OFFICE CONSTRUCTION IN SOUTHWEST

The redevelopment of Southwest coincided with a new program of federal office construction immediately south of the Mall along Independence Avenue, continuing the federal development in the area that was started in the prewar years. The Public Buildings Service of the Government Services Administration (GSA), created in 1949 out of the Treasury's Office of the Supervising Architect and other related agencies, administered these midcentury federal building projects.

Like the Social Security building of twenty years earlier, these new federal office buildings were designed to house large numbers of workers, many of whom were finally being moved out of the outmoded and deteriorating tempos. However, the new buildings were designed according to a new federal office development paradigm: no longer permanent homes for specific departments, they would provide generic office space that could be occupied by any department or by bureaus from different departments. Reflecting this expedient approach, they were typically called Federal Office Buildings—or FOBs—and designated by number rather than name.[131]

FOBs were designed to provide maximum flexibility by offering large spans of open space to be subdivided by partitions, an office plan made possible by new building technologies and advances in heating, air conditioning, ventilation, and artificial lighting. As a result, the buildings took the form of enormous masses and, despite their size, tended to lack monumentality or distinction. Their design reflected a new attitude toward housing government departments: federal office buildings were no longer grand and distinctive edifices reflecting the importance of government to society, but anonymous and interchangeable boxes built for efficiency and economy.

Federal Office Buildings planned in Southwest in the late 1950s included FOB 6, facing Maryland Avenue between 4th and 6th Streets (the Department of Education); FOB 8, on C Street between 2nd, 3rd, and D Streets, originally occupied by the Food and Drug Administration; FOB 9, built for the Civil Service Commission; and FOBs 10A and 10B, on Independence Avenue between 7th and 9th Streets and 6th and 7th Streets, respectively (the Department of Transportation, the National Air and Space Administration, and the Federal Aviation Administration).

The design for Federal Office Building 6 included a large plaza on the north side—a response to Maryland Avenue crossing in front of the site—that would separate the building from Independence Avenue and from a large tempo, which at the time occupied the site where the National Air and Space Museum now stands. The design of the box-like structure met with little opposition from commission members. Their principal advice was to scale the building to the site, setting the top story back, and omitting a proposed grille to expose the glass; the architects, Faulkner, Kingsbury & Stenhouse, made these adjustments. The commission was also concerned about the building's length, but believed treatment of the plaza, which they found carefully executed with pools and sculpture by landscape architect Lester Collins, could mitigate the problem.[132]

In the commission's view, the greatest challenge to cohesion among the federal buildings of Southwest was presented by FOB 10A, designed by Holabird, Root & Burgee as a featureless, ten-story block at a prominent location on Independence Avenue, facing a Mall site partially occupied by the nineteenth-century American Medical Museum.

A smaller companion building to the east by the same architect and designed concurrently was known as FOB 10B.

The chief difficulty of this project lay in its location at the southern terminus of the 8th Street axis across the Mall, a major feature of the L'Enfant and McMillan Plans. Any building here would face the National Archives on the north side of the Mall. The commission stated that the design of such a building was "of paramount importance, as it will be seen across the Mall and will dominate the group of buildings on the south side of the Mall.... We believe that, in view of its position, this building should be monumental in character and not convey the impression of merely another office building."[133]

The commission found the initial designs for FOB 10A too large, "bulky and out of scale," and "too overpowering for the area"; if built as proposed, it "would destroy the opportunity for later cultural development of the general area." Consequently, the building was lowered by a story and set further back from Independence Avenue, but its mass still presented problems. The commission emphasized that its final design should depend on the agency that will occupy it; when the occupant had been chosen, the commission expected the GSA to confer with them early in the design process and regularly thereafter.[134]

As plans for these new office buildings progressed, the commission grew increasingly alarmed by a seeming lack of coordination, and by 1957 it was trying to obtain further information and further review authority over FOB development in Southwest. What the commission knew of these plans came from material provided in a brochure distributed by the Public Buildings Service two years earlier, which described twenty-two buildings to be constructed under the Lease-Purchase Act, through which the government assumed ownership of privately developed buildings through gradual amortization. In May 1957, Chairman David Finley wrote to the commissioner of public buildings regarding FOBs 6 and 10A, inviting the GSA to share plans with the CFA; in August, the commission convened a special meeting to discuss the problem.[135] Participating members included the early modernist architects Wallace Harrison (CFA 1955–59), Douglas Orr, and William Perry (CFA 1955–63), along with Finley and Elbert Peets.

The members' main complaint was that, although the plan for Southwest had been in existence for two years, it had yet to be shown as a whole to the commission. They then agreed on some general observations about the plan: cultural buildings, not office buildings, were more appropriate for this location adjacent to the Mall; the GSA's drive to quickly move workers out of the tempos valued expediency over coherence in the plan; all the proposed buildings—particularly FOB 10A—were too massive for their sites; a lack of design quality and cohesion—qualities so evident in the Federal Triangle—were producing blandness and disunity; and sufficient open space was sorely lacking.[136]

The meeting precipitated a second, held two weeks later in New York City; it was attended by Harrison, Orr, and Perry and representatives of the Public Buildings Service and their FOB architects. The purpose was to discuss these planning issues in reference to specific building projects, primarily FOB 6 and FOB 10A. At the New York meeting, the assembled group viewed models of 10A and 10B set next to a model of FOB 6 and immediately questioned the scale of the ensemble. Although the heights of FOB 10B and FOB 6 were considered reasonable, the commission architects unanimously decided that FOB 10A, on the site opposite the Archives, was "impossible in scale, character and size. This particular location is the only one really on the Mall."[137] The commission approved the NCPC recommendation that FOB 10A be moved fourteen feet east to allow more space between the individual buildings and to align it more closely with the Mall cross-axis.[138] While approving the general design of 10A and 10B, the commission recommended embellishment: "The members emphasized their belief that buildings of such a severe and plain design especially require ample provision of sculpture, painting and plantings, and that consideration of these features is important before the architectural design has progressed to completion."[139]

The Commission of Fine Arts at the End of the 1950s

At the end of the 1950s, the commission—reluctantly and under pressure from Washington newspapers—began opening some meeting items to the press, although the meetings themselves were not public. The first occasion was the afternoon session of the October 1958 meeting, when the Corporation Counsel's opinion on the constitutionality of the Old Georgetown Act was discussed with the D.C. commissioners. The CFA decided that, in the future, its policy would be to invite reporters only when matters of public interest came up "since the Commission is an advisory body only and its recommendations are transmitted to the submitting agency, which usually prefers to make its own announcement." J. R. Wiggins, executive editor of the *Washington Post and Times-Herald,* responded that reporters had open access to the meetings of the NCPC and the District Board of Commissioners, and there was "no logical distinction between their situation and yours.... It really is the public's business that is

ABOVE: *The commission and its staff photographed in late spring of 1963, several months before Finley's retirement. Front row, from left: Peter Hurd, Felix de Weldon, David Finley, and William G. Perry. Second row, from left: Ralph Walker, Hideo Sasaki; staff members Marilyn Shaw, Larry Lusky, and Myra Younker; Douglas Orr; staff members Susan Bennett, C. L. Martin,* Linton Wilson (secretary), and Charles Atherton (assistant secretary).

LEFT: *David Finley presents* The White House: An Historic Guide *to President and Mrs. Kennedy, 1962. Finley's friendship with the First Lady afforded the commission an unusual degree of influence at a time of burgeoning development in Washington.*

being transacted in your sessions and it seems illogical to withhold from them information about their own affairs." The commission remained adamant that open meetings would preclude frank discussion.[140] Commission of Fine Arts meetings would not become public until the mid-1970s, under legislation designed to make the federal government more transparent.

In 1960, the commission celebrated its fiftieth anniversary. In five decades, the focus of design culture in official Washington had evolved from advancing the visionary monumentalism of Charles McKim and Daniel Burnham to mitigating the more pragmatic developments of modernism and highway engineering. At the commission meeting on May 17, Felix de Weldon presented Chairman David Finley with a commemorative green marble panel with Burnham's apocryphal "Make No Small Plans" exhortation inscribed in gold letters, a gesture reflecting on

the commission's beginnings. An assessment of the commission's continuing importance at its half-century mark was offered by the *Washington Star* in an editorial tribute to David Finley on his retirement from the CFA in 1963:

Probably no comparable period in its history has offered such a challenge to the commission. Certainly none has been as stormy. Contrary to popular opinion, the large majority of the commission's recommendations have been followed, and no one knows how many aesthetic monstrosities have been avoided as a result. Those which have come most prominently to public attention, of course, have involved controversy. In some instances…the commission's advice prevailed. Even when this was not so, however, as in the case of the Theodore Roosevelt Bridge, the fine arts group usually succeeded in gaining concessions in the location or design of major projects which have served to minimize the disruptive impact on historic values of the Nation's Capital.[141]

Presidential Influence: F.D.R., Truman, and the Design of Washington's Icons of Executive Power, 1933–1953

¶ WILLIAM B. BUSHONG

The design of Washington has been shaped by the personal taste and influence of those in power. In the middle decades of the twentieth century, two presidents, Franklin D. Roosevelt and Harry S. Truman—both with firmly held opinions on matters of design and boldly outspoken about them—exerted their authority to influence the design of many Washington landmarks, chief among them the foremost symbol of executive authority, the White House. Their personal design interests and the degree to which they involved themselves in the White House and other architectural projects also reflected their broader interest in federal design policy in the capital, which brought them into close contact and sometimes conflict with the U.S. Commission of Fine Arts.

President Roosevelt, in particular, was comfortable in the company of architects and artists. He was famous for dashing off sketches on the backs of discarded memos or envelopes to convey design ideas. The president's keen interest in Washington's architecture had a profound influence on the final appearance of such major landmarks as the Jefferson Memorial, the Pentagon, and National Airport.[1] But a central architectural concern of his presidency was the White House itself and the continuing issue of housing the burgeoning executive branch. The West Wing expansion, construction of the East Wing, and a landscaping program for the White House grounds—all conceived, built, or put into effect under Roosevelt—were ambitious and high-profile federal projects, and would be among his lasting legacies.

President Truman also sought a solution for the continuing issue of executive office expansion and had his own decided ideas about changes to the historic White House. His architectural legacy

Vice Presidential candidate Harry S. Truman lunches with President Franklin D. Roosevelt on the White House lawn in 1944.

will forever be associated with the massive structural and interior reconstruction of the White House and the addition of the famous Truman Balcony.[2] That addition and the modernization of the White House—involving the entire reconstruction of the interiors on a steel frame—were no less significant or symbolic.

The interaction among Roosevelt, Truman, and the members of the Commission of Fine Arts reflected the most overt examples of presidential influence on federal design in the era that followed the City Beautiful movement. The 1902 White House renovation by McKim, Mead & White that was commissioned by Theodore Roosevelt set the precedent for presidential recognition of qualified experts in the fine arts that was prelude to the movement that shaped the modern transformation of Washington, D.C.[3] After the formation of the U.S. Commission of Fine Arts in 1910, presidents had a formal agency from which to seek design advice. The degree to which Roosevelt and Truman would accept this advice would greatly affect the history of Washington, the White House, and the commission.

A Plan for an Executive Enclave

In December 1933, President Roosevelt asked Secretary of the Interior Harold Ickes to arrange a meeting with Charles Moore, chairman of the Commission of Fine Arts, to discuss plans for new public buildings in Washington, D.C. At the meeting, Moore promoted the idea of locating new public buildings into an executive group adjacent to the White House as contemplated by the McMillan Commission in 1901 and elaborated in a plan by architect Cass Gilbert in 1920; only Gilbert's Treasury Annex (1917–22) and Chamber of Commerce (1929), a private building, were built from that overall concept.[4] Moore also pressed for support of the commission's recommen-

dation to site the new War and Navy Department buildings west of the White House on Pennsylvania Avenue.[5]

Moore reported back to the commission on December 15 that the president was in accord with the commission's suggestion to create an executive enclave with the White House at its center—just as the Capitol was at the center of a legislative group.[6] Moore told his colleagues that the time had now come to complete the executive group at Lafayette Square, with the Department of the Treasury Annex extended northward to H Street and a new building for

ABOVE: *Aerial view of Lafayette Square in 1919 showing small scale development on the westside of the square with the White House at lower left. Cass Gilbert's Treasury Annex (lower right) indicates the scale of government office development envisioned.*

BELOW: *Lafayette Square looking northeast with the Treasury Annex at right, 1920s.*

the State Department on the square's west side. He also wished to revive earlier proposals by John Russell Pope (1917) and Waddy Wood (1930) to remodel the existing State, War, and Navy Building into a classical structure to match the Department of the Treasury, thus providing the president with ample executive office space.[7]

The federal office enclave on Lafayette Square advocated by Moore and the commission was not realized; Congress stalled all plans for new office buildings in 1933 as an emergency public works law prevented expenditures for

new federal construction due to the growing economic stress of the Great Depression. Instead of creating a concentrated enclave, the buildings over time were dispersed around the city and into Virginia. A pivotal battleground became the river lowland area of Arlington between the 14th Street Bridge and Arlington National Cemetery, the proposed site of a massive War Department complex across from the Lincoln Memorial. The commission considered the prospect of a virtual self-contained city—with railroad and bus stations, shops, churches, and recreational facilities surrounded by parking lots and an extensive network of highway interchanges—across the river from monumental Washington to be "a destruction of the central composition of the Washington Mall." President Roosevelt and the commission did agree that the initial site would block the view of Arlington National Cemetery and spoil the plan of the national capital. However, the president did not agree that the War Department should be sited in Washington. He settled the issue in August 1941 by selecting the Pentagon's present location south of Arlington National Cemetery.[8]

The Department of the Treasury Annex was not extended on Lafayette Square. In fact, President Roosevelt inadvertently contributed to the later preservation of the square by rejecting art moderne designs for a new State Department building on its west side; his taste ran to a more classical design for federal offices. Roosevelt also insisted on the preservation of Blair and Decatur Houses in 1942 and their incorporation into any office expansion plans in that area.[9]

Expansion of the West Wing

Franklin Roosevelt enjoyed the study of architecture and engaged in many of the decisions that influenced the history of the public building program of the New Deal era. However, what occupied Roosevelt's personal interest and brought him into close contact with the Commission of the Fine Arts most often were changes to the White House and its environs.

With the great increase of his New Deal staff in the 1930s, overcrowding in the West Wing of the White House had become dire. The president looked for a solution to cramped executive office space that Congress would fund and the American public would accept. Roosevelt explored his options for expansion of the West Wing by conferring with government architect Lorenzo S. Winslow. As an architect with the Office of Public Buildings and Public Parks, Winslow had been assigned in 1933 to assist in the design of an indoor swimming pool and soon became the White House "fixer." During the 1930s, Winslow was assigned White House duty to modernize the kitchen, workrooms, and service rooms.[10] President Roosevelt created the job title "Architect of the White House," but the position was not made permanent by Congress. However, Winslow would culminate his career as a public architect a few years later by directing the design services for the renovations to the White House during the Truman administration in 1952.[11]

Winslow had proven himself an able architect on the pool project and he catered to President Roosevelt's architectural predilections and taste from the outset. When the president called Winslow to the White House in February 1934 to discuss plans for executive office space, he shared his sketches of a scheme for a completely new office building on the site of the existing West Wing. Winslow took the sketches and began to develop plans for the West Wing "with the active advice and interest of the president in all the various details." The proposed plan evolved into a massive extension thirty-six feet south-

ward with a full second floor built over the existing single story and basement offices. The new structure added numerous new spaces, including an auditorium for press conferences and adjacent lounges.[12]

The Commission of Fine Arts first heard of the president's shift in office plans from the president's uncle, Frederic A. Delano—the president and chairman of the National Capital Park and Planning Commission—who brought the proposed plans to enlarge the executive offices in the West Wing to Charles Moore on March 21, stating the president needed an additional 31,000 square feet to accommodate the rapid expansion of the correspondence office, now handling 16,000 letters and telegrams a day. The original 1902 annex designed by McKim, Mead & White had been doubled in size in 1909 by Washington architect Nathan Wyeth to about 15,000 square feet. A newspaper article on April 22, 1934, broke the news of Roosevelt's plans to the public a day before the Commission of Fine Arts met to consider the enlargement scheme. The commissioners noted that this project would be treated as a temporary proposition just as the original annex had been "in the days of Theodore Roosevelt."[13] That statement reflected the commission's awareness of the president's determination to have his office space, and it was ironic, as the commission knew from past experience that temporary construction, like the World War I tempos and 1902 West Wing expansion, often proved permanent.

Charles Moore, using his influence as Commission of Fine Arts chairman, publicly supported the president's wishes to expand the executive offices, announcing to the press that the offices should be enlarged as a temporary measure until such time that a renovation of the State, War, and Navy Building could be completed for use as an executive office building. Moore privately opposed

the expansion plans and searched for a way to stop the president without damaging the commission. He decided to ask Eric Gugler to manage the task.[14]

Gugler, handsome and charismatic, had studied at the American Academy in Rome after finishing his courses in architecture at Columbia University; he was a devoted admirer of Charles McKim and a committed practitioner of the Beaux-Arts ideal of architectural design. The young architect struck up a friendship with Moore on trips to Washington to discuss McKim's career and work.[15] Moore thought the gifted young architect, formerly a partner of Henry Toombs, might have influence with the Roosevelts. The New York architects had collaborated with Mrs. Roosevelt on the design of her cottage at Val-Kill on the Roosevelt estate and had prepared designs for Franklin D. Roosevelt in 1927 to design and remodel buildings at Warm Springs, Georgia, along Colonial Revival lines. After the Gugler-Toombs partnership dissolved in 1931, Gugler practiced alone on small residential commissions. In 1933, Mrs. Roosevelt called on Gugler to consult with her on the design of the experimental town of Arthurdale, West Virginia, a public housing project she supported for low-income farmers and miners.[16]

Moore was not pleased with the scale or appearance of Winslow's expansion drawings and, according to Gugler, was "at the end of his tether" fearing the president would want to adopt them. Considering Gugler's personal connections to the Roosevelts, Moore asked him to sell the president on the permanent move of the executive offices into the State, War, and Navy Building with a tunnel connection to the West Wing. In his memoir, Gugler could not recall the date or circumstances of the meeting with the president except that it was a luncheon and that he was forceful in presenting the case that friends and supporters of the

president would be unhappy with any plans that upset the proportions of the White House. Roosevelt rebuked him for his impertinence, but, after a long discourse, the storm subsided and Gugler convinced the president to let him make a study that offered a solution to enlarge the executive offices to three times their size "without increasing the apparent size of the building to anyone who might look at it from any side, no change to the eye."[17]

The president dismissed Moore's suggestion of dropping his office expansion plans and converting the State, War, and Navy Building to office space with a tunnel connection. The need for more office space was critical, and the project could not be delayed by pursuing an option likely to be vetoed by the Secret Service, who feared that the wheelchair-bound president could be trapped in a tunnel. Roosevelt also stressed his need for the convenience of office space in close proximity to the White House, and called the seventy-nine-year-old Moore an "old fuddy-duddy."[18] Gugler continued to press the case against marring the architecture of the White House and proposed a solution to the president's problem of office space. In his memoir on his work on the West Wing project, Gugler recalled:

Henry Toombs and I both knew that F.D.R. thought of himself as an architect in a way that we both excused. He was likely to credit himself with those parts of the work he especially liked. Henry and I, what with Georgia Hall and the Little White House in Warm Springs and the work in Hyde Park, were used to this and almost always liked it and always forgave him.[19]

Within five days, Gugler, with the help of volunteer draftsmen, developed and presented to the president and, within weeks, to the Commission of Fine Arts, a skillful solution for the expansion that concealed the large volume of space he would need to add. President Roosevelt, reluctant to abandon his

own plans developed with Winslow, agreed to hire Gugler as a consultant and, by June 26, entrusted the planning to him. He also continued to assure the commission that he would remodel the State, War, and Navy Building, but money was not available and the need to enlarge the executive offices met a "present emergency."[20]

The young architect proposed a penthouse story and the excavation of a large subterranean office area. This included the basement beneath the exposed building and also expanded an equal area to the south with a light well (now filled in by offices). Gugler planned a fountain and fishpond in a lush garden within the courtyard, which would bring greenery, light, and air to these underground offices. His design included the major change of moving the Oval Office to its present southeast location adjacent to the Rose Garden. Gugler's work was rendered deftly into presentation drawings by accomplished delineator Schell Lewis, which were widely published in the press along with a photograph of the model of the expansion, all now lost.[21]

Eric Gugler at work on the West Wing plans, 1934.

Construction to enlarge the West Wing of the White House, 1934, by Eric Gugler, architect. The steel structure outlines the new spaces of a penthouse and underground offices and light well.

By July 24, 1934, bids for the expansion according to Gugler's design were opened, and the construction contract was awarded to the N. P. Severin Company of Chicago in the amount of $303,087.00. Demolition of the old West Wing structure, with the exception of the north and west walls, began in early August, and construction started on August 24, 1934. The contractors were given one hundred days to finish the job, which required construction to be carried out on a twenty-four-hour basis. President Roosevelt and his staff temporarily worked in cramped quarters at the White House or the State, War, and Navy Building across Executive Avenue.[22]

In October, the commission in-spected the progress of the work. Escorted by Gugler, they toured the new Oval Office, the Cabinet Room, the spacious new Waiting Room, and the offices of the secretaries before descending to the mail and file rooms built around the open courtyard. The work was completed on November 22, 1934.[23]

Changes to the White House Grounds

The demolition of the rambling complex of White House conservatories in 1902, directed by McKim, Mead & White to make way for a West Wing annex, radically altered the appearance of the west side of the South Grounds. In the early twentieth century, Edith Roosevelt had designed an old-fashioned boxwood colonial garden (1902) planted by White House gardener Henry Pfister. Later, Ellen Wilson replaced that garden with the first rose garden (1913), a rigid, green, and formal design with the long vistas found in seventeenth-century Italian gardens that remained intact until the Kennedy administration.[24]

With the West Wing expansion nearing completion in 1934, the issue of improving the South Grounds had again become timely. Eleanor Roosevelt found in the First Lady's office an unpublished study by Frederick Law Olmsted Jr.— prepared during the Coolidge administration for the Office of Public Buildings

and Grounds—that detailed their unsatisfactory condition and roundly criticized haphazard changes in the past. Mrs. Roosevelt, knowing of the president's interest in improving the grounds, brought the report to his attention.[25]

On October 9, 1934, Moore, Gugler, and Frederick Law Olmsted Jr., an original member of the McMillan Commission and the Commission of Fine Arts, were requested by the president to join him in his car for a ride around the White House grounds. They discussed design ideas, and the president explained what he would like to see achieved.[26] This meeting with the president spurred the creation of a master plan for the White House grounds by the National Park Service that was based on studies produced by Olmsted's office with minor changes suggested by Commission of Fine Arts member Gilmore D. Clarke, himself a landscape architect. However, without sufficient funds to execute the plan due to Depression-era budget cuts, only small improvements could be made at that time. But the Olmsted plan embraced by President and Mrs. Roosevelt would influence the Park Service's later plans for the care of the White House landscape into the twenty-first century.[27]

The Thomas Jefferson Memorial and Its Impact on the Commission of Fine Arts

A reflection of Roosevelt's regard for Charles Moore's leadership of the commission is suggested in December 1934 when he reappointed Moore, whom the commission members unanimously re-elected as chairman. Moore reported to his colleagues that "President Roosevelt had told Mr. Rudolph Forster, his executive clerk, that it was not necessary to bring a memorandum recommending the re-appointment of Mr. Moore to him but to go ahead and order it." The commission chairman was in a heady

mood and also noted "he has been having several talks with [the] president recently and he is much interested in the work of improving and developing the city of Washington."[28]

The president's reappointment of Moore preceded what would become a contentious situation involving the Commission of Fine Arts and one of Roosevelt's pet projects—the design of the Thomas Jefferson Memorial. During the winter of 1933–34, President Roosevelt asked the commission's opinion about a proposal to erect a memorial to Thomas Jefferson on Pennsylvania Avenue at 7th Street, NW, the site of the Federal Trade Commission building (Bennett, Parsons & Frost, 1938) at the apex of the Federal Triangle. Moore eventually dissuaded Roosevelt from the site, convincing him that the Trade Commission building was vital to the composition of the Federal Triangle complex.[29]

In 1934, Congress enacted legislation establishing the Thomas Jefferson Memorial Commission (TJMC), and Moore was the Commission of Fine Arts' representative to that organization; the relationship proved collegial at first as he informally attended its meetings. However, relations between the commissions frayed badly in 1938 over the design and location of the memorial. Adding to the tension was Moore's sudden resignation as chairman of the Commission of Fine Arts in 1937 and the election of Gilmore D. Clarke to succeed him.[30] Clarke would take a determined—and losing—stand against the domed Pantheon-like design created by John Russell Pope and approved by the TJMC.[31] Ultimately, the design issue was decided by President Roosevelt, who supported the Pantheon at the Tidal Basin; Congress approved the plans, which the Commission of Fine Arts had publicly and bitterly criticized.[32]

The status of the commission at the White House was well captured by

Eleanor Roosevelt's jocular tone in her "My Day" column on October 1, 1939:

Since Mr. Moore has retired, I have not had the pleasure of coming into contact with the present chairman, and the other members of the commission have always been vague, but very important figures in the background, as far as I am concerned.

To find our friend, Mr. Paul Manship, is one of the vague figures gives me great confidence for I have always looked upon this commission with such awe! The reason for this it that they can at any time step in and object to whatever changes I want to make to the formal rooms at the White House![33]

Roosevelt's Appointee and a New Direction for the Commission

On April 17, 1939, President Roosevelt wrote his uncle, Frederic A. Delano, for advice regarding the appointment of a new member of the Commission of Fine Arts to fill the vacancy created by Charles Moore's resignation.[34] Delano's advice was to bring in someone local to sit on the commission, which had skewed toward a membership of almost all New Yorkers. Delano noted:

I find the Commission of Fine Arts feel that they have been a good deal ignored and perhaps slighted. In other words, like all prima donnas, they are sensitive. I am, of course, anxious to meet the situation. There is not a single member of the Commission who comes from Washington, and it is exceedingly important that at least one man on this Commission should be sufficiently familiar with Washington to his opinion be of value.[35]

President Roosevelt's choice was artist Edward Bruce, whom he appointed in January 1940.[36] Bruce was born in New York, had studied art in Italy, had an illustrious career—as a lawyer, businessman, art dealer, and newspaper owner—and had lived in Washington, D.C., since 1933. With American artist George Biddle, he promoted and initiated the New Deal's Public Works of Art Program (PWAP), later known as the Section of Painting

and Sculpture in the Department of the Treasury. The PWAP and the Section embraced realist and representational murals in America's public buildings and ran counter to the commission's conservative, antimodernist views.

While head of the Section, Bruce promoted a design competition for a new Smithsonian Gallery of Art building that would produce "something genuinely simple and beautiful—without columns of any kind."[37] However, the 1939 competition winner by Eero and Eliel Saarinen and Robert Swanson was rejected by the commission for its modernism and went unrealized.[38] In light of this defeat, Bruce's ascendancy to the commission was a personal triumph and a clear signal that a bona fide New Deal Democrat would bring substantial changes to the commission's attitudes toward modernism and a move away from the Beaux-Arts.[39]

A New East Wing

The East Wing was another White House project that highlighted the diminished influence of the commission with Roosevelt. At the president's request, Winslow prepared designs and supervised construction in 1942 of a new East Wing to house executive offices and, in the future, a museum—an addition the president had long hoped to install at the White House for tourists. In fact, Gugler had prepared plans for the museum and additional offices in the East Wing in 1938. However, his design was considered too expensive to build during the Depression. Although the commission had been consulted about Gugler's design, the need to build became urgent after the bombing of Pearl Harbor. The pressing need for a bombproof shelter and office space for military staff led to expedited construction, and the commission had no official input on the final design prepared by Winslow.

The new East Wing contained a formal entrance for guests, offices on the first and second floors, and an air raid shelter underground. Winslow and his draftsmen worked frantically sixteen to eighteen hours a day to complete the plans and supervise construction. As the building neared completion, Roosevelt wrote the commission on September 9, 1942: "Owing to the emergency and the need for additional space and for a bomb-proof shelter, the old East Wing of the White House was torn down and the new building is now practically completed. The plans had, I think, the approval of the Commission of Fine Arts." The president then went on to ask the commission to send their views on the proposed use of rooms after the war for a museum and, in the meantime, to consider and advise on the objects and artifacts being offered to the White House.[40]

The Commission of Fine Arts and a New President

The sudden death of Franklin D. Roosevelt on April 12, 1945, marked the end of one of the most powerful presidencies in American history. As for the new president and his relationship to the commission, the end of both the Roosevelt era and World War II represented an adjustment to the times where anything seemed possible, technologically and socially. Into this era of accelerating change and the beginnings of Cold War anxiety, Harry S. Truman brought a striking change in leadership style.

Almost immediately upon entering office, President Truman began to consider plans to expand the executive office space. The West Wing extension made in 1934 already proved an inadequate solution for the everyday needs of the White House. In November 1945, President Truman invited the members of the Commission of Fine Arts to the White House and greeted them all in the

Blue Room. The commission was eager to move forward with new ideas and projects for a postwar program of development that had been held in abeyance because of the war. The president's mind was on the presentation of his own modernization plans for the White House.

He led the group into the Red Room, where a set of drawings rendered by Winslow depicted a major southward extension of the executive offices that, in the president's words, met "urgent needs." First among them was an auditorium that could seat more than three hundred people with a rostrum equipped with broadcasting facilities. Likewise, the building expansion would address the need for a pressroom to provide space for 419 correspondents. Finally, there was the pressing need to accommodate offices for six administrative assistants to the president who were inconveniently located in offices in the State Department building across the street.[41]

The president's launch of the office extension plans went smoothly with the commission, and on November 30, 1945, Clarke wrote Winslow: "The Commission were pleased with your studies and congratulate you upon being able to provide the interior space required without serious encroachment upon the grounds of the White House."[42] But the public's reaction to the announced plans created a storm of protest against the project. The president held a press conference to rebut what he called "a tempest in a teapot."[43] Truman defended his plans as not being visible from Pennsylvania Avenue and read Gilmore Clarke's letter publicly supporting the extension with design modifications. The inclusion of a cafeteria and conversion of part of the East Wing into a museum garnered the most derision from the public, and the commission recommended in a January 28, 1945, memorandum to President Truman that both elements be abandoned.[44]

Opposition to the project from professional architects and civic leaders was fierce, and the argument that the White House would lose its character as a home resonated with the public. The Commission of Fine Arts received its share of criticism for its support of the president's extension plan, but it maintained that the expansion would be a temporary expedient until suitable offices could be provided elsewhere. The House of Representatives settled the matter by blocking the West Wing project at the White House in an amendment passed 110 to 41 to recall and reallocate the construction funds on the day of Truman's press conference.[45]

The President Wants a Back Porch

The next White House improvement suggested by President Truman appeared a simple matter to him, but its ramifications rocked the Commission of Fine Arts and endangered its survival as an agency. That request was for the construction of a second-floor balcony on

the south portico of the White House where the president and his family could retreat on warm summer evenings. Gilmore Clarke recalled that the president had returned from Charlottesville, Virginia, where he made a speech on the Fourth of July in 1947, impressed by the upper balcony on one of the Lawn buildings at the University of Virginia.[46] The insertion of a balcony cutting the axis of the columns would be the first significant change in the design of the White House's core structure since the south portico's completion early in the administration of Andrew Jackson. The Truman Balcony controversy became one of the most infamous incidents in the development of the White House's architecture.

Truman presented the idea of a porch to Chief Usher Howell Crim and architect Lorenzo Winslow, firmly believing that Thomas Jefferson would have approved.[47] The chief usher then telephoned David Finley, director of the National Gallery of Art and a member of the Commission of Fine Arts since 1943. Finley was an active member of

the White House Furnishings Committee—a subcommittee of the Commission of Fine Arts since the Hoover administration that advised in the decorating of the executive mansion— and Crim considered him a friend and the perfect intermediary.[48] Finley suggested a conference at the White House on July 29, 1947, with Crim, Winslow, commission chairman Gilmore D. Clarke, and commission member and architect Frederick V. Murphy. The result of the meeting was a course of action the commission had taken before when confronted by a thorny issue related to the White House's alteration: recommending that an architect of note who had previously worked at the White House be consulted. Eric Gugler and William Adams Delano were the obvious candidates, and Delano—who with partner Chester Aldrich had designed the classical Post Office building in the Federal Triangle—was hired.[49]

The trouble arose from the president's assumption that the commission had approved his scheme with the stipulation that he hire Delano as a consultant.

He later stated that he did not feel the commission "misled him, but that the Fine Arts Commission gets scared when you start throwing bricks."[50] For its own part, the commission expected Delano to oppose the balcony and help them appease the president. However, the strategy backfired as Delano sided with the president and proceeded to work with Winslow on a solution to adding the porch. The issue came to a head in November, when Clarke sent a detailed letter to the president explaining why the commission could not support any alteration to the south portico as it would seriously mar not only the south portico but the entire south facade.

Truman's reply dripped with angry sarcasm, accusing the commission of trying to manipulate him, hoping he "would make up his mind in a manner that you approved of," and adding, "you didn't enter into the matter at all with an open mind—that is a great statement for the Chairman of the Commission of Fine Arts to send to the President."[51] Nor did Truman accept Clarke's argument that the alteration would be the first substantial change to the exterior of the White House in 118 years. The president noted that the "dirty awnings are a perfect eyesore" and he bitterly complained that Clarke did not take into consideration the needs of the presidential family in this situation.[52] Undeterred by the commission's objections, the president went on to build the Truman Balcony, as it has come to be known.

As news of the balcony and the commission's opposition became public knowledge in 1948, Truman faced a storm of criticism from the architectural profession and the media. Despite the furor, Truman persisted, and the controversy quickly entered the political mainstream. Editorials about the president's porch compared the project to his blustery presidential style and bandied terms like "Back Porch Harry" and "balcony statesmanship."[53] The

president's hardheaded reputation and unbending certainty that he was right were fair game in an election year.

Impact of the Truman Balcony on the Commission

The real casualty of the Truman Balcony controversy was the Commission of Fine Arts, which, in the president's mind, had betrayed him. Truman's subsequent communications with the commission were polite, but his brevity spoke volumes about his contempt for the agency.

In November 1948, Clarke wrote a confidential letter to David E. Finley to discuss the commission's problematic relations with the president and the part it should play in the upcoming reconstruction of the White House contemplated by Truman. Clarke noted that Congress since 1910 had inserted the phrase "shall have the approval of the Commission of Fine Arts" in legislation for any important project. After discussing the furnishings committee work and his frustrations with lay members who insisted on a period restoration of the public rooms to the style of the Early Republic, Clarke described just how sensitive relations had become:

In the present circumstances it seems to me, and I know you agree, wise not to kindle the fire of the President by suggesting in legislation any statement which might be traced back to our initiation, if we do have to tolerate for longer than the Ladies like the red plush on the chairs and sofa of the Red Room. [54]

Following the president's surprising election victory, the commission came clearly into the line of fire. In December 1948, Howell Crim; Lorenzo Winslow; Charles Barber, engineer with the Public Buildings Administration; and W. W. Reynolds, commissioner of public buildings, presented drawings to the Commission of Fine Arts proposing "fire-proofing and alterations in the White

House." The proposal was an outcome of a Secret Service investigation into the structural integrity of the White House conducted immediately after the attack on Pearl Harbor. The White House, an iconic and historic wood-framed building, was found to be structurally vulnerable, especially to fire. The report made caretakers of the executive residence acutely aware of the sagging floors, faulty wiring, crumbling plaster, and general decay of the old house. What had been antique and quaint was now thought dangerous. Truman, with a hearty appetite for building, finally acted on the report and ushered in a demolition almost as radical as the fire set by the British forces in 1814.[55]

The commission reviewed the plans and noted the radical changes proposed for the north entrance hall and stairway and recorded that, "in view of the great public interest in the White House, an outstanding firm of architects should be appointed as consultants to prepare the architectural plans for the reconstruction of the White House, inasmuch as they do not have confidence in Mr. Winslow's ability to prepare them." This latter point was reiterated in a memorandum titled "Restoration of the White House."[56]

By the following June, Congress had enacted legislation for the renovation and modernization of the White House. The bill established a Commission on the Renovation of the Executive Mansion composed of senators, house members, and two advisors: engineer Richard E. Dougherty and architect Douglas W. Orr, both members of the committee that had initially investigated the structural condition of the White House in 1941 and recommended its reconstruction. Eighty-year-old Senator Kenneth McKellar of Tennessee was chairman of the new commission. Noticeably absent from the bill was any mention of design approval by the Commission of Fine Arts.[57]

In June 1950, the *New York Times*

noted in its article "Truman Shakes Up Arts Commission" that an "artistic bombshell with a delayed action fuse was exploded by President Truman today."[58] The president let the outgoing members dangle as their terms expired one by one and then in one fell swoop appointed four new members to replace the opponents of his celebrated balcony.[59] The sole survivor of the Truman Balcony fight was David E. Finley, who emerged as the new chairman elected by his fellow members in July 1950. He had remained in the confidence of the White House through his active role on the White House furnishings committee, advising on the selection and acquisition of artwork and furnishings for the executive mansion.[60]

The reaction of the press in 1950 to Truman's modernizing of the Commission of Fine Arts ranged from articles on political payback to a concern that the commission might now follow a policy of "toadyism." The president publicly stated that changes were made because he wanted the commission in its capacity as an advisory body on public buildings and monuments to work with the National Capital Park and Planning Commission in a "dynamic combination." Although this proposed synergy was not explained, Truman's statement about planning to modernize the commission had been followed by the remark that "they had never been constructive."[61]

Chairman Finley and the Survival of the Commission of Fine Arts

The commission's survival was due in no small measure to the tact and leadership of David E. Finley. As the Truman renovation progressed and the need for decisions related to the interiors became pressing in the spring of 1950, Howell Crim, as chief usher, asserted himself and demanded control of the interiors

and their designs. Finley, the new chairman, saw the opening provided by having a friend in charge of these interior design decisions and was able to gain recognition of the commission. He obtained invitations to meetings and slowly gained influence, eventually overcoming the embarrassing omission of the Commission of Fine Arts in the legislation authorizing the White House renovation. Finley—a South Carolinian who could spin a funny yarn—was determined to reestablish the commission's authority regarding decisions about the decoration and interior design of the White House. In the end, the Commission on the Renovation of the Executive Mansion genuinely appreciated the hard work and valuable advice that Finley offered, even though he had no official role in the project. However, the chairman got what he desired—official recognition of the Commission of Fine Arts.[62] On June 19, 1951, at the suggestion of Crim, Winslow, and Reynolds, the Commission on the Renovation of the Executive Mansion decided to seek approval of all of its designs and plans from the Commission of Fine Arts, which had not been consulted officially since 1949. The grand tour of inspection was a formality, and the Commission of Fine Arts members approved the work without comment. Chairman Finley wrote a gracious letter to President Truman blessing the renovation and reviving the agency's historic tradition of design review at the White House. Finley thus smoothed over a scenario where the commission might have been absorbed into the National Capital Park and Planning Commission and made the best of a bad situation.

The remarkable talents of David Finley played no small role in saving the Commission of Fine Arts and maintaining its importance to the cultural life of the nation's capital. Several years later, Finley also played a central role in the restoration of the White House during

the Kennedy administration, rectifying the widely disparaged Truman and Eisenhower redecorating. While still serving as chairman of the Commission of Fine Arts, Finley also served as the first chairman of Mrs. Kennedy's Fine Arts Committee for the White House, which was established by executive order in 1964 as the Committee for the Preservation of the White House, which replaced the Commission of Fine Arts' subcommittee on furnishings.[63]

Presidential Influence and the Role of the Commission of Fine Arts

In his relations with the Commission of Fine Arts, Roosevelt was a conciliator rising above the fray of conflicts in Washington, D.C., concerning building and monument design or the development of the city. He kept relations cordial with the commission but had no qualms making decisions that ran counter to their recommendations, most notably in the Pentagon and Jefferson Memorial projects. Truman's relations with the commission were amicable as long as their counsel coincided with his ideas. When the commission opposed his plans, Truman took the heat of negative public opinion and forged ahead. He got his back porch and accomplished a complete interior modernization of the White House despite or without Commission of Fine Arts review.

As illustrated by its contentious relationships with Presidents Roosevelt and Truman, the Commission of Fine Arts suffered a decline in stature between 1933 and 1953. The experience was a keen reminder that the commission's advisory power emanated from its access to the president and his advisors, its persuasive influence with Congress, and its ability to form public opinion to preserve and enhance the civic heart of the nation.

Modernism and Monumentality

THE CHAIRMANSHIP OF WILLIAM WALTON, 1963–1971

W ith the election of John F. Kennedy as president, Washington culture entered a new era—bringing with it the goal of raising aesthetic standards for government buildings. At a time of enormous change in American society, new federal programs and policies resulted in an expanded government workforce and a boom in federal office construction not seen since the 1930s. This expansion of federal development within Washington brought about a sharp increase in the volume of government building projects reviewed by the Commission of Fine Arts from the late 1950s to the early 1970s, typified by the massive new federal enclave rising south of the Mall and significant changes planned and completed on and around the symbolic core. By 1962, the General Services Administration announced a plan to add almost 9 million square feet of new office space in Washington, and a young assistant secretary of labor, Daniel Patrick Moynihan, advocated for improving the national image with the far-reaching policy document, "Guiding Principles for Federal Architecture."

Just as the enormous Federal Triangle project of the 1920s and 1930s represented the culmination of Beaux-Arts classicism, the new federal buildings of the 1960s reflected a strong consensus for modern design, albeit one that would be short lived. Concomitant with an optimism about modernism's capacity to address a wide range of social issues, the design of federal buildings evolved with a new confidence: from the somewhat tentative, boxy style of the 1950s into more expressive forms of modern architecture, often designed by leading practitioners and promoted by powerful advocates with strong political ties.

In Washington, forward-looking planning and infrastructure projects continued to transform the urban fabric during the high tide of the modernist period. However, a new focus toward architectural expression, a sense of history, and urban experience increasingly entered the discussion. Although many projects related to the Inner Loop highway systems still raised concern among the commission's members, a regional transit system was planned and designed, and its construction was begun during these decades, signaling a shift in federal support away from automobile-focused infrastructure. The Mall itself was largely completed during this period, emerging as a coherent landscape freed from the temporary buildings that had encumbered it for decades.

FACING PAGE: *The Department of Housing and Urban Development headquarters building by Marcel Breuer (c. 1968) expressed a muscular and dramatic modernism for a federal office building.*

Portrait of William Walton by Alice Neel, 1967. A journalist by profession, a painter, and a close friend of President Kennedy, Walton embraced modern trends in art and architecture.

It is noteworthy that, in this era of change, there were few commemorative projects reviewed by the commission in comparison to earlier—and particularly later—periods: virtually no coin designs of the U.S. Mint were reviewed, and a few commemorative medals were issued for achievement in the arts and new technologies such as space exploration. Only a handful of national memorials—for Presidents Theodore and Franklin D. Roosevelt—were in development, but it would take decades to complete them as the political will to move forward with these projects proved inconclusive, especially in resolving traditional forms of commemoration with new modernist principles.

Under the leadership of William Walton, who served as commission chairman from 1963 to 1971, the CFA's review of projects reflected a wide cultural consensus on modernism as the appropriate expression for Washington's built environment from the monumental core to Georgetown. By the 1960s, commission members were dealing with the issues that this acceptance of modernism raised in the capital city regarding monumentality, historicity, and the manifestations of modern architecture's evolving language, such as brutalism and formalism. Their embrace of modernism was tempered by an appreciation of the underlying design principles that had shaped the monumental core, and members attempted to formulate a modern architectural and urban design expression appropriate for the nation's capital.

During this period, as advocacy of Beaux-Arts classicism finally vanished from the commission's discourse, fundamental changes in training and taste became evident among the members. Ralph Walker (CFA 1959–63)—named Architect of the Century by the American Institute of Architects (AIA) in 1957 when awarded its Centennial Gold Medal—was the last to serve on the CFA as a proponent of an early transitional modernism informed by both the Beaux-Arts and art deco. From the early 1960s, the majority of commission members had practiced as modernists throughout their careers, including such nationally known designers as Gordon Bunshaft of Skidmore, Owings & Merrill; Eero Saarinen's protégé, Kevin Roche (CFA 1969–80); landscape architect Hideo Sasaki (CFA 1962–71); and later the locally prominent Washington architect Chloethiel Woodard Smith.

Other new members included architect John Carl Warnecke (CFA 1963–67), a close personal friend of John F. Kennedy and his advisor on architecture; lawyer-turned-planner Burnham Kelly (CFA 1963–67); and sculptor Theodore Roszak (CFA 1963–69), a specialist in welded steel whose most prominent work was the monumental eagle over the facade of Eero Saarinen's U.S. Embassy in London. Continuing the close relationship between the leadership of the National Gallery of Art and the commission, the gallery's second director, John Walker, would serve on the commission from 1967 to 1971. Of the first four directors of the National Gallery, he was the only one not to serve as CFA chairman.

The *New York Times* art critic Aline Saarinen (CFA 1963–71) helped to shape the commission's views on modernism, becoming a close ally of Gordon Bunshaft on the commission, and together they strongly influenced the decisions of their fellow members. When Saarinen, widow of the architect Eero Saarinen, was appointed to the commission in 1963 (only the second woman to hold that position after Emily Muir, who served on the CFA from 1955 to 1959), a journalist recorded her impressions of Washington: "One just hopes it isn't too late to save it. Most of the modern buildings are deplorable; planless and ugly. It is very sad, I think. It should be the most beautiful city in America. When you are in it, you should know that you are in the center of a great nation."[1]

Journalist and painter William Walton was appointed to the commission by President Kennedy in 1963 and soon replaced Finley as chairman, a position he would hold until 1971.[2] A resident of Georgetown, Walton was a neighbor and close friend of then Senator John F. Kennedy and wielded considerable political influence. He had organized the Wisconsin and West Virginia Democratic primaries for Kennedy and, after the 1960 convention, helped manage Kennedy's New York campaign. In addition to his role on the Commission of Fine Arts, he became an informal advisor on architecture to President Kennedy and later to President Lyndon B. Johnson.

Like his predecessor David Finley, Walton became a leading figure in the historic preservation movement in Washington. Even before he was appointed to the commission, Walton worked closely with Jacqueline Kennedy on the preservation and rehabilitation of Lafayette Square, the preservation of the Renwick Gallery and the Eisenhower Executive Office Building (EEOB; the former State, War, and Navy Building, also known as the Old Executive Office Building or OEOB), and the expansion of the National Gallery of Art. In 1964, he organized opposition to plans to demolish the west front of the Capitol. Architecture critic Wolf von Eckardt wrote that Walton "managed to endow the advisory Fine Arts Commission with a de facto power that it had never enjoyed before…. Walton saw to it that only outstanding experts were appointed to the commission. This made the commission, without doubt, the country's most effective spokesman for good

architecture and urban design in the country."[3]

Kennedy's final appointee, architect Gordon Bunshaft (CFA 1963–72), became the dominant voice on the commission for the rest of the decade. Bunshaft trained at the Massachusetts Institute of Technology and began his association with the nascent architecture firm Skidmore, Owings & Merrill (SOM) in 1937, where he was hired to assist on work for the 1939 New York World's Fair; he became a full partner in 1949. With the exception of several years of military service during World War II, Bunshaft would spend his entire professional career at the firm.[4]

Bunshaft was influenced by Le Corbusier early in his career and by Mies van der Rohe in his mature work. As design partner, Bunshaft helped move SOM into the forefront of American architectural firms, developing the European modernism of the International Style into a robust mode for postwar corporate America. Bunshaft's design for the Lever House in New York (1952) became the epitome of the sleek glass tower block, breaking the streetline with its perpendicular orientation and allowing for civic space by opening a plaza beneath the building.[5] In his institutional projects, including Yale's Beinecke Library (New Haven, 1963) and the Lyndon Baines Johnson Library and Museum (Austin, Texas, 1971), Bunshaft thoroughly analyzed programmatic requirements to create buildings that united efficient structure and robust form; his great ability was "to take Modern architecture and make it part of the vernacular."[6]

Bunshaft was notoriously blunt and irascible, and even while serving on the commission he often dominated the members' discussions. He loathed postmodernism and famously locked horns with Robert Venturi over Venturi's

BELOW: *Gordon Bunshaft of Skidmore, Owings & Merrill (1963) was an outspoken advocate for modern design on the commission.*

BOTTOM: *The Commission of Fine Arts in 1967. Pictured (left to right): Hideo Sasaki, Theodore Roszak, Burnham Kelly, William Walton, Gordon Bunshaft, Aline Saarinen, and John Carl Warnecke.*

proposed design for a building in Southwest that was rejected by the commission in 1968.

In September 1960, a young government architect, Charles Atherton, was hired as assistant secretary to the commission; he replaced Linton Wilson as secretary in January 1965. Atherton served the commission until his retirement in 2004 after almost forty-four years, longer than any other secretary or staff member. During Atherton's tenure, the commission staff grew in number and professional stature at a time when the commission itself was evolving away from its once clubby atmosphere, a legacy of its earlier decades. This change in the commission's culture was reflected, in part, by Atherton's approach to the keeping of the minutes of commission meetings. Under Wilson, the minutes had become brief recitations of facts that were written for a time by CFA staff counsel C. L. Martin. Minutes written by H. P. Caemmerer, although succinct, had reflected the flow and conveyed the tenor of the discussions. Now written by Atherton, the minutes, although still brief, again reflected the character of the reviews. Atherton often included transcripts of the discussions of the more controversial reviews as exhibits.

Commission staff assumed a more active role in the commission's proceedings during the Atherton years; CFA responsibilities came to include historic and other research, analyses of projects and their presentation at commission meetings, and coordination with agencies and applicants. In his four decades as secretary, Atherton also instituted a publications series to document Washington's architectural heritage, including the embassies and residences of Massachusetts Avenue and 16th Street, the bridges of the District, and comprehensive surveys of historic Georgetown.

A New Consciousness of History

The relationship between Washington as a modern city and its history emerged as a contentious issue in the early 1960s as many parts of its prewar urban fabric were being dismantled: the wholesale demolition of the Southwest neighborhood, the insertion of highways throughout the city center, and the replacement of neglected mansions on K Street with boxy curtain wall office buildings were among the most notorious examples. Most emblematic of the tension this created among CFA members was their discussion about the future of Lafayette Square, immediately across from the White House, which had been developed in the nineteenth century with three-story brick residences and in the twentieth century with the fragments of an un-

Charles Atherton became secretary of the commission in 1965 and would continue in that position for almost forty-four years.

completed monumental scheme intended as an enclave for executive departments of the federal government. The discussion divided the commission deeply.

LAFAYETTE SQUARE

Early in his administration, John F. Kennedy became involved in the rehabilitation of Lafayette Square, an urban space he considered to be the forecourt of the White House; he engaged the advice of his friend William Walton in this endeavor. First Lady Jacqueline Kennedy supported the preservation of the square's nineteenth-century residential architecture and was advised initially by David Finley. Finley exerted influence not only as CFA chairman but also through his positions as a founding member and first president of the National Trust for Historic Preservation; as a member of the Committee of 100 on the Federal City (an important force for local preservation) and the First Lady's Fine Arts Committee for the White House; and as chairman of the White House Historical Association.[7]

An important residential area in the nineteenth century, Lafayette Square still had many historic structures remaining in 1960: Jackson Place on the west retained several nineteenth-century residences, among them the Decatur House at the north and two midcentury row houses at the south that were adjacent to the Blair-Lee House on Pennsylvania Avenue. Across from the Blair-Lee House and west of the White House stood the old State, War, and Navy Building, a huge and ornate Second Empire edifice that was widely reviled at the time for its exuberant interpretation of seventeenth-century French architecture. Another Second Empire building occupied the corner of 17th Street and Pennsylvania Avenue, the small former Corcoran Gallery, which housed the U.S. Court of Claims.

Its strategic location across from the White House had made Lafayette Square a focus of plans for federal office development since the 1901 McMillan Plan. Built projects included Gilbert Cass's Beaux-Arts Treasury Annex—originally meant to stretch the entire length of the square on the east along Madison Place—and the U.S. Chamber of Commerce, a private building and another element of Gilbert's scheme located on the northwest corner of the square. There also had been various proposals in the Herbert Hoover and Franklin D. Roosevelt administrations for a State Department annex on Jackson Place. Franklin Roosevelt did raise concerns about preservation, however, saying that at least two of the historic structures, the Decatur House and the Blair-Lee House, had to be preserved.

By the late 1950s, three small high-rise office buildings had been constructed on the western side of the square, along with the 110-foot-tall National Grange headquarters on H Street. To continue development, the General Services Administration hired two Boston firms, Perry, Shaw, Hepburn & Dean, the architects of Colonial Williamsburg, and Shepley, Bulfinch, Richardson & Abbott to develop studies for a new building that would house presidential commissions and three federal courts on Jackson Place; the architects were required to retain the historic residences. When the first plans were submitted to the CFA in February 1959, commission members struggled with the question of how to combine new construction with the older structures but were unable to reach a consensus.[8]

By the fall of 1960, the GSA had split the program into two buildings, with presidential offices on Jackson Place and federal courts on Madison Place. Once in office, President Kennedy entered the process and enlisted Walton to meet with the GSA, who persuaded the agency to retain the former Corcoran Gallery, the two row houses on Jackson Place, and the Treasury Annex while building two new structures around them. In its review in March 1961 the CFA agreed, although expressing a preference for replacing the Treasury Annex with a modern structure to achieve a unified appearance on the east side of the square.[9] Both Boston firms developed their designs further, using a pre-cast modular cladding system similar to one used in Eero Saarinen's U.S. Chancery in London, and presented these concepts to the commission.

The early modernist architects on the commission— Ralph Walker, Douglas Orr, who had served in the early 1950s on the commission overseeing the reconstruction of the White House, and the landscape architect Michael Rapuano (CFA 1958–62, and a business partner of Gilmore Clarke)—resisted any notion of accommodating the square's historic structures. Instead, they supported demolition of the Treasury Annex and construction of an entirely modernist building.[10] Opposed to the commission

architects was a group led by Finley, which included sculptor Felix de Weldon and painter Peter Hurd (CFA 1959–63), who wanted the square's historic character to be respected. Finley secured Kennedy's support, and Walton developed his own sketch for a large building on Jackson Place that displayed historicist touches in its use of brick, pilasters, and small-scale windows. Walton showed this sketch to the Boston architects, and eventually President Kennedy indicated his preference for a new building featuring a flat roof, brick exterior, and windows at the scale of those of Decatur House. But the division among commission members only intensified.[11]

Between 1960 and early 1962 and concurrent with the development of proposals by the Boston firms, various members of the Committee of 100 began promoting their own concept for Lafayette Square to the public and to Kennedy, Walton, and Finley. Their proposal involved tearing down the three high-rise buildings while using historic and new historicist row houses on Jackson Place as a screen in front of a new federal office building. At Finley's gentle prodding, Jacqueline Kennedy became a strong

TOP: *Even when taller stone office buildings were inserted between the nineteenth-century houses, they largely maintained the existing overall scale of Lafayette Square as shown in this 1950s view of Jackson Place.*

ABOVE: *Jackson Place looking southwest from H Street, c. 1910. In the early twentieth century, Lafayette Square had a distinctive character derived from brick residential buildings of similar height, treatment, and material.*

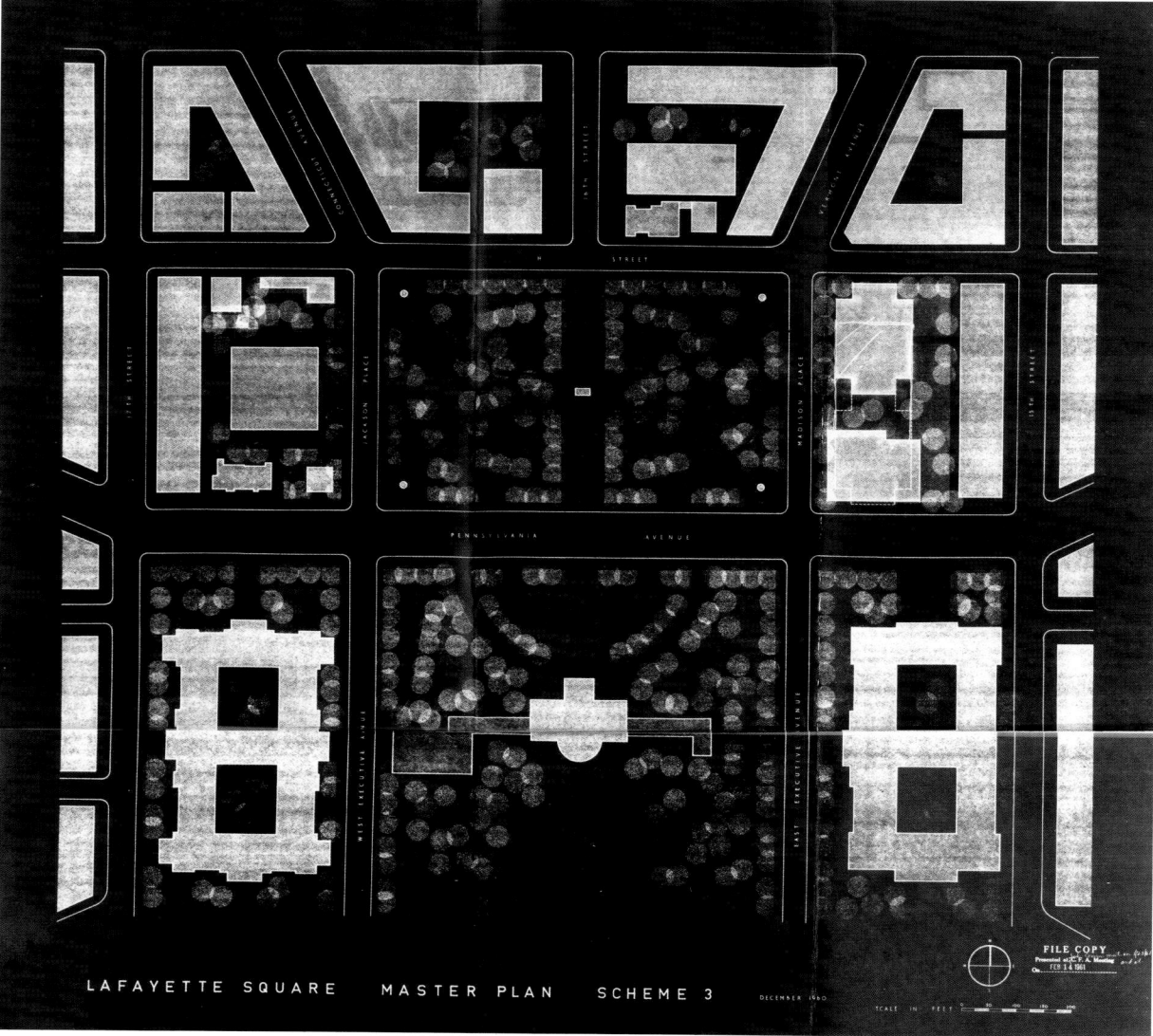

Beginning in the late 1950s, numerous schemes were proposed to remodel Lafayette Square— including this 1961 master plan by Shepley, Bulfinch, Richardson & Abbott— that were generally predicated on the demolition of most of the existing buildings.

LAFAYETTE SQUARE   MASTER PLAN   SCHEME 3

advocate of the scheme; she made certain both the president and the administrator of the GSA were aware of it, and she persuaded the GSA to direct its Boston architects to adapt their plan accordingly. At the same time, President Kennedy discussed the problem with California architect John Carl Warnecke, who developed his own adaptation of the Committee of 100's design idea.[12]

The GSA soon hired Warnecke to replace the Boston firms and, by the early fall of 1962, he had designed two new high-rise structures that would be set back behind a screen of historic and new row houses on Jackson and Madison Places. The high-rises would be large, red brick buildings with small-scale windows, a hybrid type of modern architecture that took cues from historical context, observed the residential scale, and allowed the White House to remain the dominant building facing the square.

Warnecke presented his proposal at the commission's October 1962 meeting. It met with condemnation and ridicule by the architects on the CFA, who viewed such accommodation as unnecessary preservation of old buildings lacking in architectural merit and, further, as anathema to the principles of modern architecture. Ralph Walker, in particular, spoke against it with considerable force:

We live in an age of bigness. We don't live in an age of tiny little things put together—this is an opportunity we had of making that one of the most important squares in the whole world and it should be that. What we have done is frivolously piddled it away in the restoration of unimportant buildings.

Walker also expressed the opinion that Finley had wielded undue influence with Jacqueline Kennedy, who he thought was not dealing with the realities of the times: "I hope Jacqueline wakes up to the fact that she lives in the twentieth century." Walker's tirade against the project was countered by several other commission members, including the landscape architect Hideo Sasaki, who noted that heritage and history, not just architectural merit, needed

FROM TOP TO BOTTOM: *A preliminary scheme for Jackson Place development, 1957, by the General Services Administration featured a modern four-story office building for the executive branch and the courts inserted on Jackson Place between the Blair House and the Decatur House; William Walton's sketch of a historicist design for a new Jackson Place office building was favored by President Kennedy, June 1961; The response by Perry, Shaw, Hepburn & Dean, 1961, treated the new office building in a style recalling the remaining Federal-era houses on the block; A 1961 scheme by Shepley, Bulfinch, Richardson & Abbott—a narrow, modern office pavilion in front of a nine-story office block in keeping with the firm's master plan for the square—was approved by the CFA but was not built.*

ABOVE: *Lafayette Square Plan Model, c. 1962. John Carl Warnecke's scheme to retain most of the historic buildings facing the square won the support of the preservation-minded members of the CFA but not its modernist architects.*

RIGHT: *Warnecke's design as built in the 1980s, showing the integration of historicist infill buildings along Jackson Place with the New Executive Office Building behind it.*

First Lady Jacqueline Kennedy and John Carl Warnecke inspecting his model of Lafayette Square, September 1962. The First Lady took a keen interest in the White House's historic surroundings as well as in its interior.

to be considered. Sasaki added that once destroyed, there was no way to reclaim the past:

I think both Mr. Walker and Mr. Orr, being architects, realize there are many good architectural gems that were destroyed in the name of progress.... If we made a mistake in preservation, I would rather have an error this way than the other.[13]

The commission approved Warnecke's plan at the meeting although Walker and Orr dissented emphatically. The project would be a harbinger of a new era: the compromise of received ideas of modern design to accommodate the preservation of historic structures.

New Urban Vision

While the controversy of Lafayette Square set an example for preserving historic fabric within Washington, in other parts of the city the promise of the new created an urban vision defined by modern principles—a distinct departure in scale and character from the Beaux-Arts vision of the McMillan Plan. These new urban designs, involving the massive redevelopment of megablocks, featured grand ceremonial spaces and addressed the impact of the automobile by separating it from view—usually on a level below the street. In all cases, the modernist CFA advocated for

simplicity and uniformity in the design, often emphasizing the scale of the proposals that were, in essence, a modern rethinking of both L'Enfant's grid and the Beaux-Arts vision of the McMillan Plan. In the Southwest sector of Washington, on Pennsylvania Avenue, downtown, and on the western edge of the monumental core, several urban projects of the 1960s attempted a new synthesis of modern architecture and Washington's monumental context.

As in the preceding decade, the increasing need for roadway and bridge infrastructure to serve Washington's burgeoning automobile traffic in the 1960s challenged the CFA's mission to protect the scenic qualities of the capital city. Under the chairmanship of William Walton, the commission reviewed—and typically approved—a series of bridges and overpasses for Southeast and Southwest Washington that were associated with the proposed Inner Loop highway inserted around the perimeter of the city's monumental core. As it had in opposing a tunnel beneath the Lincoln Memorial, the CFA continued to consider visual disruptions to the monumental landscape, such as the tunnel passing under Union Square at the foot of Capitol Hill. By the end of the decade, popular and political opposition to automobile-dominated infrastructure gained strength, and a rail transit system for the Washington region—

Metrorail—began to take shape. The commission played an important role in that project by guiding its designers toward a modern interpretation of monumental architecture for urban transit in the nation's capital.

PENNSYLVANIA AVENUE PLANS

Historically, Pennsylvania Avenue reflected Washington's dual nature as both a national symbol and a living city. As defined in the L'Enfant Plan, the avenue served as the ceremonial axis linking the Capitol and the White House and had been lined with commercial activity from the earliest decades of the nineteenth century. In the 1930s, the federal government redeveloped a hodgepodge of land uses along the avenue's southern edge into the massive Federal Triangle project, fulfilling L'Enfant's vision of the monumental core extended to the capital's main ceremonial route. The north side of the avenue remained the city's commercial and entertainment hub, housed in buildings largely dating to the nineteenth century.

After World War II, Washington, D.C.—and Pennsylvania Avenue—did not escape the economic decline and physical decay rampant in America's cities. John F. Kennedy's inaugural parade on January 21, 1961, traveled along Pennsylvania Avenue, and the newly sworn-in president was dismayed by the deterioration of the historic street. Kennedy shared his concern with Assistant Secretary of Labor Arthur J. Goldberg, who, with his executive assistant Daniel Patrick Moynihan, quickly acted on

Kennedy's comment. Thirty years after the Federal Triangle project, the Kennedy administration thus initiated what would become a decades-long process under several administrations to reverse these conditions. As a first step, Kennedy appointed an Ad Hoc Committee on Federal Office Space, which, in its 1962 report, committed to revitalizing Pennsylvania Avenue as the capital's ceremonial and commercial center.[14]

The following year, a team of architects, planners, and other experts was appointed as the President's Council on Pennsylvania Avenue. Chaired by architect Nathaniel Owings, a founding partner of SOM, the council was charged with preparing recommendations for improving Pennsylvania Avenue and imparting greater dignity to its appearance. CFA chairman William Walton served on the council, and two other members had or would have connections to the CFA, Ralph Walker and Chloethiel Woodard Smith.

The group issued its report in 1964, which served as an idea book for the avenue's redevelopment.[15] The report outlined a design vision and urban design principles for public and private development that incorporated sweeping changes for the avenue. Focused primarily on the blocks of rundown nineteenth-century buildings along the avenue's north side facing Federal Triangle, the plan proposed various visual devices to create a more uniform monumentality: a shared cornice line, broad setbacks, special paving and street furniture, and raised terraces for parade viewing. New buildings along the north would incorporate

BELOW LEFT: *Pennsylvania Avenue looking west from 9th Street, January 1963. The south side of Pennsylvania Avenue was defined by the monumental classicism of the Federal Triangle while the north side was a mix of small-scale retail uses in mostly deteriorated nineteenth-century buildings.*

BELOW RIGHT: *Pennsylvania Avenue from 15th Street looking east in the late 1950s. The foreground includes World War II–era temporary buildings where Pershing Park and Pennsylvania Avenue are now located.*

ABOVE: *The 1964* Report of the President's Council on Pennsylvania Avenue *sought to impose order on Pennsylvania Avenue through the wholesale demolition of buildings on its north side, replacing them with massive modern structures meant to define and dignify this ceremonial route.*

LEFT: *The model shown in the 1964 report featured a new formal termination to Pennsylvania Avenue at the Department of the Treasury at an enormous ceremonial public space called National Square.*

TOP: *Rendering of National Square by Nicholas Solovieff (1964) illustrates the proposal for a huge fountain on the avenue's axis; a vast new retail and office complex modeled on Moscow's* GUM *Department Store would have been located to the north.*

ABOVE LEFT: *Rendering of the proposed Market Square from the 1964 report, featuring an elevated public plaza, set within bosques of trees along the 8th Street axis, with public exhibition space for material from the National Archives below.*

ABOVE RIGHT: *Illustration of the E Street Distributor in the 1969 Report of the President's Temporary Commission on Pennsylvania Avenue, showing the separation of automobile and pedestrian traffic on multiple levels for E Street, which was vastly different from the urban experience then existing in Washington.*

CHAPTER V | MODERNISM AND MONUMENTALITY

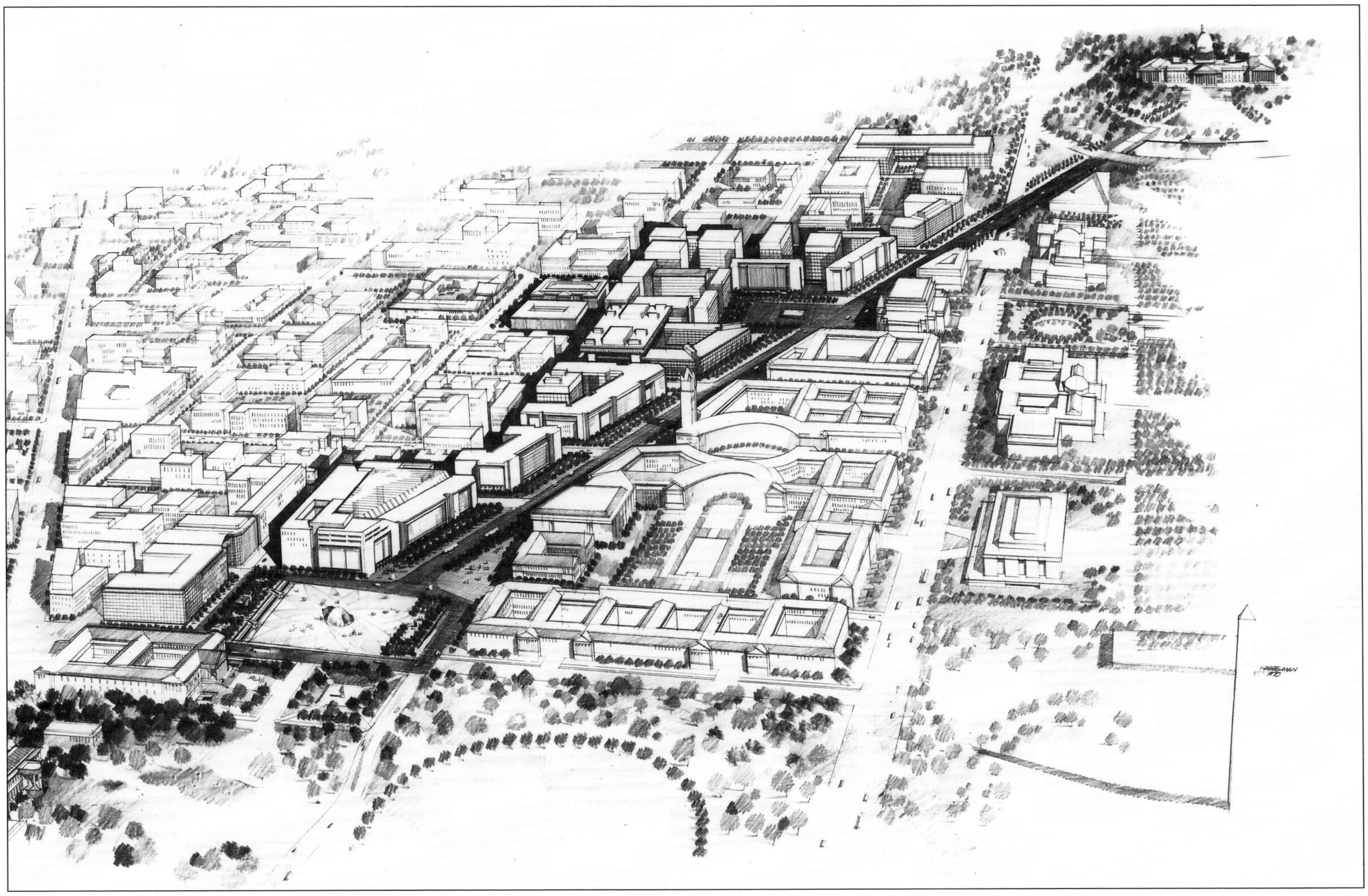

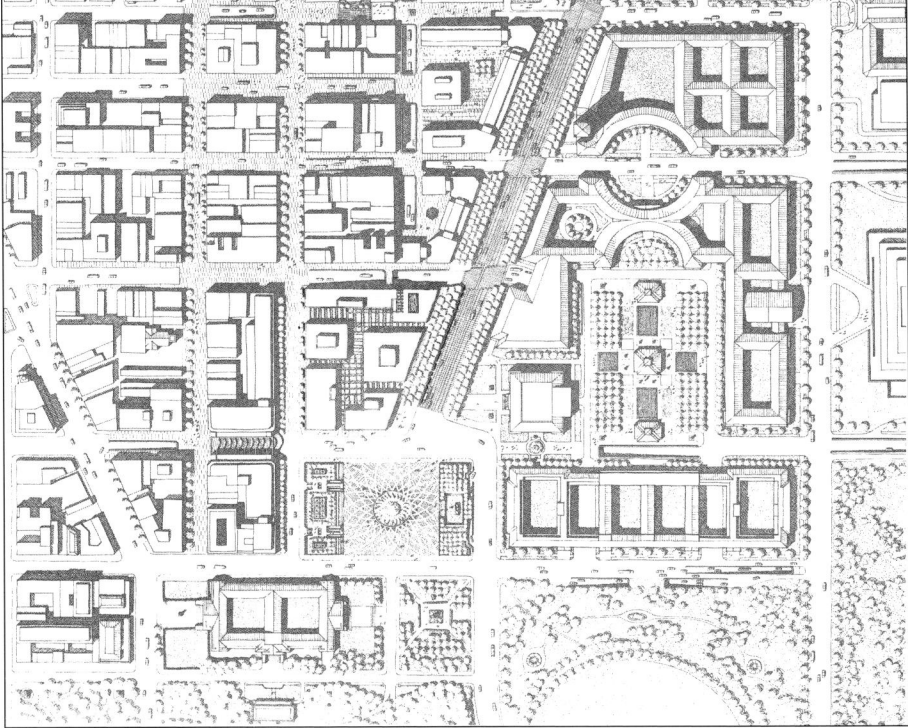

LEFT: *The plan for the western segment of Pennsylvania Avenue in the 1969 report proposed superblock development to define the north side of the avenue but reduced the size of National Square, saving some of the historic buildings, and introduced small-scale gardens flanking the central fountain.*

ABOVE: *Aerial rendering of the Pennsylvania Avenue landscape plan by Dan Kiley, 1969. CFA members were particularly concerned about the three rows of linden trees that Kiley proposed for the street's north side, which they believed would obscure rather than emphasize the unified architecture proposed for the avenue.*

arcades to provide shade for foot traffic, and three rows of clipped linden trees would give more shade and architectural definition.

The plan suggested substantial modifications to specific nodes along the avenue: Union Square at the foot of Capitol Hill would be redesigned, and a new urban square facing the Archives would enliven the avenue midway at the 8th Street axis. The plan's most prominent element, and the focal point for the avenue's western end, was a massive National Square modeled after the Place de la Concorde in Paris, which closed Pennsylvania Avenue between 14th and 15th Streets, NW; razed all the buildings on that block north to F Street, including the Hotel Washington and the Willard Hotel; and located a 150-foot-wide fountain at the square's center. The design vision addressed the area's traffic problems by separating vehicular from pedestrian traffic at E Street and along portions of 7th to 14th Streets, closing F and G Streets to vehicles, and lowering Constitution Avenue under Pennsylvania Avenue at the National Gallery of Art.

In January 1966, four alternative schemes for National Square were brought before the commission, which approved a reduced version that moved the central fountain to the west, nearer to the Department of the Treasury, while noting the ambitious plan "still contains numerous unsolved problems," such as a failure to clearly define the avenue's terminus. Although the plan proposed closing the historic avenue to traffic and destroying historic buildings, the commission voiced particularly strong views about the landscape component of the plan, designed by the modernist landscape architect Dan Kiley. The members objected to Kiley's plan for three rows of lindens planted close together on the north side of the street, which they suggested would "obscure the buildings designed specifically for the avenue." They asked Kiley to restudy this feature and eventually approved a revised plan for two rows of lindens on the north.[16]

A subsequent 1969 report, issued by the President's Temporary Commission on Pennsylvania Avenue, chaired by Moynihan, expanded on the earlier plan: it provided design and financing details for specific areas along the avenue including Union Square; Market Square at 8th Street; and a somewhat reduced National Square at 14th Street, although Pennsylvania Avenue was still to be closed at this location. For typical blocks lining the avenue, the plan put forward the concept of the superblock, the coordinated development of entire city squares to ensure efficient use of space and services. The plan also provided recommendations for a new Labor Department building, a new Smithsonian Institution art museum named after Joseph H. Hirsh-

horn, a new headquarters for the Federal Bureau of Investigation, and an addition to the National Gallery. By the end of the 1960s, some progress had been made regarding Pennsylvania Avenue: it had been designated a National Historic Site, which would encourage preservation of historic structures along the route; initial steps had been taken to modernize the city's zoning code; and new investment was in evidence with the FBI building under construction and the privately developed Presidential Building at Pennsylvania Avenue and 12th Street recently completed. However, to achieve the scale of redevelopment envisioned in the reports and plans, an entity capable of implementing change was needed. Congress would create such an entity, the Pennsylvania Avenue Development Corporation (PADC) in 1972, with which the Commission of Fine Arts and other reviewing agencies would work for more than two decades to restore the ceremonial significance and economic vitality of Pennsylvania Avenue.

METRORAIL

Perhaps no other project better exemplifies the role of the Commission of Fine Arts and its influence on the design of Washington in this period than the regional rail transit system, or Metrorail, a project of the National Capital Transportation Agency. The initial program included a four-line rail system with underground stops within the center of Washington. The commission's goal was a modern rail transit system station design that conveyed an appropriate image for the capital city, and commission members—particularly Aline Saarinen and Gordon Bunshaft—focused on guiding the system's architect, Harry Weese & Associates of Chicago, toward that end.[17]

The commission generally approved the two concepts Weese had initially submitted in September 1966 for a "simple depression and [a] massive concrete tunnel."[18] However, as Weese developed these preliminary concepts in the fall of 1966 and through much of the next year, his approach broadened to include different designs for each station, resulting in part from cost and engineering concerns—a move commission members found profoundly troubling. By the fall of 1967, the CFA feared that Weese was going in too many directions.[19]

In April 1967, Weese presented a detailed treatment of one station featuring an arched ceiling above natural rock walls and noted that variations of this design could be used for other stations. The commission responded that all stations should be designed in a simple and unified manner, perhaps using graphics to give them individuality. The remarks of Aline Saarinen and Gordon Bunshaft were most pointed: Saarinen termed the approach "Hansel and Gre-

LEFT: *Weese's initial model for the Woodley Park station (September 1966) featured exposed, rough rock walls, following his concept to create designs in response to different types of soil conditions.*

BELOW: *Harry Weese, concept sketches for an oval-section Metro station prototype, 1966.*

tel," while Bunshaft said, "I think the idea of folk art underground is for the birds."[20] Two months later, commission members were dismayed to see Weese return with yet another station design, and the minutes reflect their concern:

His studies still seemed to be probings in a variety of directions with no particular conviction evidenced in any one. A unified design could be achieved, in his opinion, through coordinating the many details, e.g. signs, graphics, ticket booths, lighting, etc. The Commission, on the other hand, had repeatedly urged the entire system be developed as a unified whole.[21]

Further, the commission rejected Weese's notion of using three different structural systems based on soil conditions: columns and slab for cut-and-cover construction; shell vaults for solid stone boring; and high vaults for deep but unstable soils. The members again questioned his proposal to use natural stone on the station interiors, to which he was adding unfinished concrete; it was an approach that they considered conveyed an "overall impression of a rustic quaintness," and Bunshaft again referred to that proposal as folk art.[22] Bunshaft urged Weese to grasp the "serious [and] marvelous opportunity to do something significant" that the Metro project offered to the national capital and encouraged him to think more comprehensively about what a subway should be—something "between a palace and a concrete shelter."[23]

The commission's September 1967 meeting proved pivotal for the project, although Chairman Walton first had to rein in Gordon Bunshaft, whose comments tended to dominate the proceedings. In executive session, Walton suggested that Aline Saarinen open the meeting by summarizing the commission's position, adding: "If she stated the position in the beginning, Gordon, without

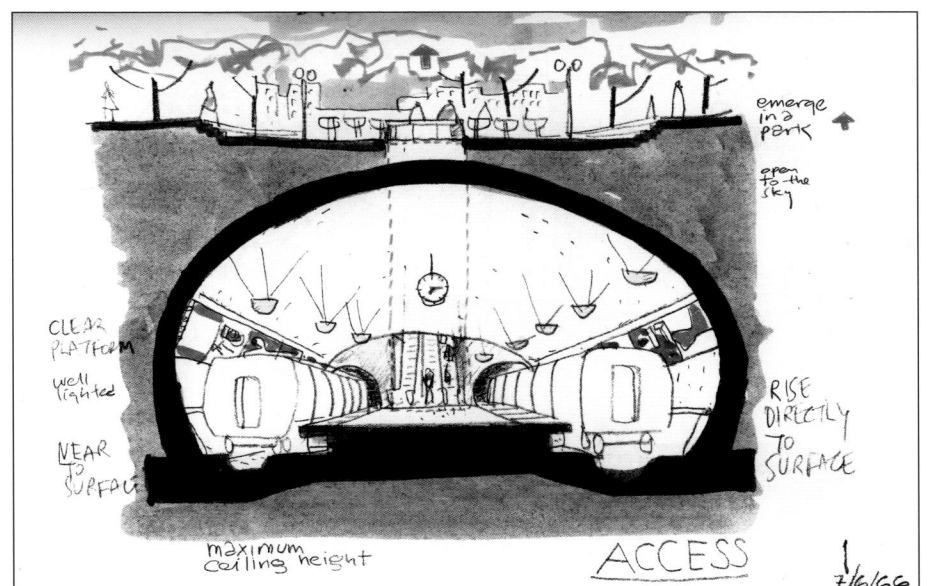

*Studies by Harry Weese &
Associates (1967) for alternative Metro station designs
using X-shaped beams to
provide internal bracing
(top) and using side-mounted
diagonal struts to create a
more vertical interior space
(bottom).*

interruption, and later you can talk all you want … and you know, not aggressively."[24]

Saarinen summarized the commission's position, reiterating that Weese's variety of designs lacked the necessary dignity appropriate to the nation's capital, which should be expressed in "not classic style but the spirit of the classic style." She said:

We feel the system should not be a series of separate experiences … but a system with continuity.… What we were looking for is a lucid expression of a continuous transportation system."[25]

As the meeting progressed, Weese continued to explain his position, which the commission members continued to question. Bunshaft became so involved in the exchange that he took a pen and, turning over one of Weese's presentation boards, began to rapidly sketch an oval-shaped space with a freestanding mezzanine inside a massive concrete vault, with tracks and platforms on either side separated from the walls and escalators.[26] The sketch, which recalled an earlier concept Weese had presented but had then abandoned as he developed the multiple station design approach, catalyzed the participants. Weese left the meeting with a clearer idea of how to proceed, and within weeks he and his team had developed the unified concept that the commission had sought.

Rather than appearing monotonous, as the Transit Authority feared, the commission declared that a single station design had much to offer: "The unique unity instilled by this kind of design would in itself be exciting because of the contrast with the relatively uncontrolled appearance of the rest of the city." The commission unanimously approved the new Weese scheme at the October 1967 meeting.[27] Aline Saarinen said of the new design: "It's beautiful, a hell of a long way from Hansel and Gretel in the beginning—we had rocky crags and Old Heidelberg."[28]

Weese's associate, Stan Allen, later recalled the exchanges with the commission and the September 1967 meeting in particular as critical to the station design process:

We had acquired another client—one who would not be rebuffed—whose ideas in effect would eclipse the approach dictated largely by engineering and budgetary considerations. This meeting proved to be the turning point in the balance of power over the nature of the situation. The Commission members really interceded to become a design participant with Harry Weese through the sheer power of persuasion.[29]

Pleased with finally having a clear direction, the CFA continued to respond positively to Weese's work as it progressed toward a unified station design for the system. Although a modern vision of monumentality, the commission's insistence on a consistent and cohesive approach to the Metrorail stations aligned this major addition to

CHAPTER V | MODERNISM AND MONUMENTALITY

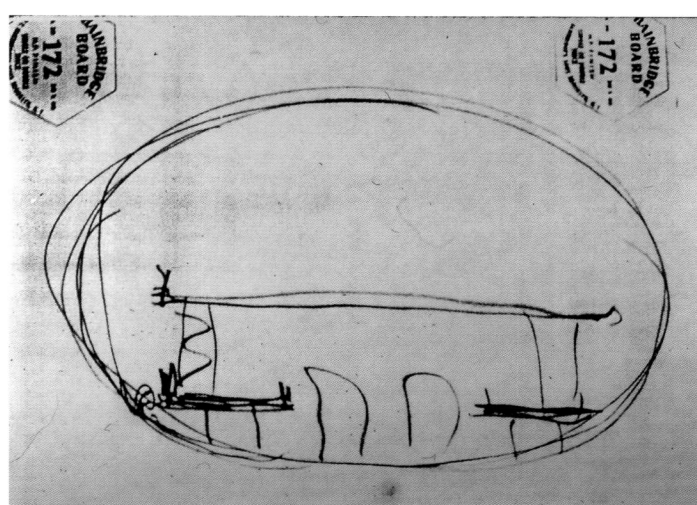

TOP LEFT: *At the September 1967 CFA meeting, Gordon Bunshaft clarified Weese's own intentions with a single sketch for the prototypical oval-section station.*

TOP RIGHT: *Model by Harry Weese & Associates (1967) of the sketch realized as a continuous concrete barrel vault to create a single monumental space.*

ABOVE: *Rendering by Harry Weese & Associates for the Metro Center station, 1968. The concept of a deeply coffered elliptical vault—with platforms, train tracks, and*

other elements set within as independent elements—gave the Washington Metro system a distinctive identity.

The Redevelopment Land Authority's (RLA) plan of 1964 (revised, 1969) indicated massive construction on the 10th Street Mall extending southward from the Smithsonian Castle and at the new L'Enfant Plaza complex, as well as new housing units in a mix of low- and high-rise types clustered around a megablock Town Center at 4th and M Streets, SW.

Washington's infrastructure with the classical-inspired monumentality promoted by the McMillan Plan.

REDEVELOPMENT IN SOUTHWEST WASHINGTON

Strikingly modern in its architectural vocabulary, a new Southwest arose in the 1960s from the bare earth left after the wholesale demolition of urban renewal. Several planned communities designed by local modernist architects, such as Charles Goodman (River Park, 1962) and Chloethiel Woodard Smith (Harbour Square, 1966), were built during the decade. These complexes employed inno-

vative combinations of low- and high-rise apartments and row houses; two—Tiber Island (Keyes, Lethbridge & Condon, 1965), and Harbour Square—even included existing eighteenth-century houses. The commission's comments on these projects were generally favorable and limited to minor recommendations, such as adding more trees for shade in open spaces between the residential buildings. The CFA also praised the preservation of the historic structures and applauded such features as parking concealed beneath plazas.[30] Commercial development occurred along the waterfront, and north of the Southwest Freeway, which cut across the neighborhood, a new enclave of federal office buildings took shape. These new office buildings, concentrated south of Independence Avenue, formed a unified frame for the southern edge of the Mall as the Beaux-Arts Federal Triangle had on its northern edge thirty years before.

Development for federal office use also occurred along a redesigned 10th Street corridor, focused at L'Enfant Plaza, William Zeckendorf's new office and commercial center. Using the NCPC's 1952 plan as a basis, the Redevelopment Land Agency had granted Zeckendorf, owner of the New York real estate firm Webb & Knapp, an option on Southwest's largest redevelopment parcel, which extended along 10th Street. As the primary formal axis from the Mall into the new Southwest, the redesigned corridor, to be known as the 10th Street Mall, would run for six blocks from Independence Avenue toward the waterfront and assert a wholly new character: widened to two hundred feet, it would feature a broad central median with special paving and lighting and would terminate in a landscaped park pro-

viding a dramatic view of the waterfront, the Washington Channel, and Hains Point. Below the park, a pedestrian bridge with stores and restaurants—called the Ponte Vecchio and to be designed by Chloethiel Woodard Smith—was planned to cross over the channel to link Southwest with a new National Aquarium on Hains Point in East Potomac Park.

As these plans began to take shape in the mid-1950s, the commission had strongly expressed its concerns about the rise in 10th Street required to clear the railroad tracks along the Maryland Avenue right-of-way. The tracks remained a point of concern and comment throughout the commission's involvement with the project, as did open space, landscaping, and a general lack of coordination regarding these features across the multiple projects in development within the sector. In 1961, the CFA reviewed study drawings of the roadway and complimented the design concept and treatment but reiterated that the "success of the design hinged on lowering the elevation of the

ABOVE: *Charles Goodman's River Park Apartments, 1962, integrated the traditional row house typology with modern design elements, such as the distinctive barrel-vaulted roofs, within the new redevelopment district.*

LEFT: *At Tiber Island, designed by Keyes, Lethbridge & Condon in 1965, a central plaza figured prominently as a focal element for the apartment buildings; courtyards, greenways, and walks played a similar organizational role for the townhouses.*

Architect Cloethiel Woodard Smith discusses a model for the Harbour Square development in Southwest Washington, c. 1960.

February 1965 included the federal Housing and Urban Development (HUD) building by Marcel Breuer, the federal Forrestal Building (FOB 5) by Curtis & Davis, and two office buildings by I. M. Pei. A meeting of the concerned parties was arranged for the following month, including officials of the RLA and the General Services Administration, representatives from Pei's office, Marcel Breuer, and one of the architects of FOB 5. The CFA plainly stated its objective for the conference: to "coordinate landscape plans for the various projects along the Tenth Street Mall into one unified plan."[34] The first thing the commission advised was the relocation of a proposed hotel in L'Enfant Plaza far enough west of the property line to allow sufficient space between it and Breuer's housing administration building. The commission then suggested and the participants agreed to unify the different properties by using the same lighting standards throughout, treating all paving and landscape walls consistently, and expanding the water feature and the number of pedestrian bridges crossing it.[35]

As on Pennsylvania Avenue, Dan Kiley had been engaged to design the landscape, this time for the overlook marking the end of 10th Street, which he proposed as an elliptical landscaped plaza embellished with trees and a central fountain. Adjoining parking in a fan-shaped configuration would be screened overhead by concrete trellises. The RLA claimed a parking structure was necessary to support commercial activity on the proposed Ponte Vecchio and to meet the parking needs of workers in nearby government buildings. The commission was particularly interested in the issue of parking, emphasizing the need for underground rather than surface lots, a solution that the RLA considered to be too expensive. Hideo Sasaki did not find the RLA's economic argument against underground parking convincing, pointing out that after the agency had spent so much on plans, it would be a "false economy" to stint on the first phase of development. At the September 1966 meeting, the commission disapproved outright any surface parking.[36]

At the January 1967 commission meeting, Kiley presented a design for an oval concrete garage with a pierced facade, supporting the overlook park on its roof and connecting the 10th Street Mall with the waterfront and the proposed pedestrian bridge. The commission praised the parking garage as a solution that effectively separated foot and vehicular traffic as well as providing a "clearly defined terminus…well integrated with the site."[37] Four months later, however, the commission was dismayed to find that the RLA had abruptly dropped plans for the garage, pleading the need to complete the 10th Street Mall quickly. The

tracks."[31] By 1965, plans for the 10th Street Mall developed by Philadelphia architects Wright, Andrade, Amenta & Gane were moving forward with the elevated roadway intact, lined with bollards and paved with red brick and gray granite.[32] Cascades of water would embellish the area where the grade rose to bridge the railroad tracks. In its review, the commission emphasized the "paramount importance" of giving spatial definition of the 10th Street axis, noting this "scheme failed to provide the three-dimensional definition required [for a] formal linear space" or to "fully recognize the disruptive visual effects" of the railroad tracks and the Southwest highway. They advised the architects to increase the sense of enclosure through such features as light standards, high parapet walls, and—most importantly—trees "to define and give shade," an amenity without which the commission members believed many pedestrians would be kept from walking along the median. Finally, the commission recommended strengthening the cascade feature.[33]

The architects added lighting standards to give some definition and extended the length of the cascade but failed to add more trees. Because of this, the commission refused to consider the plan further until it was more closely aligned with the designs of proposed adjacent buildings, which by

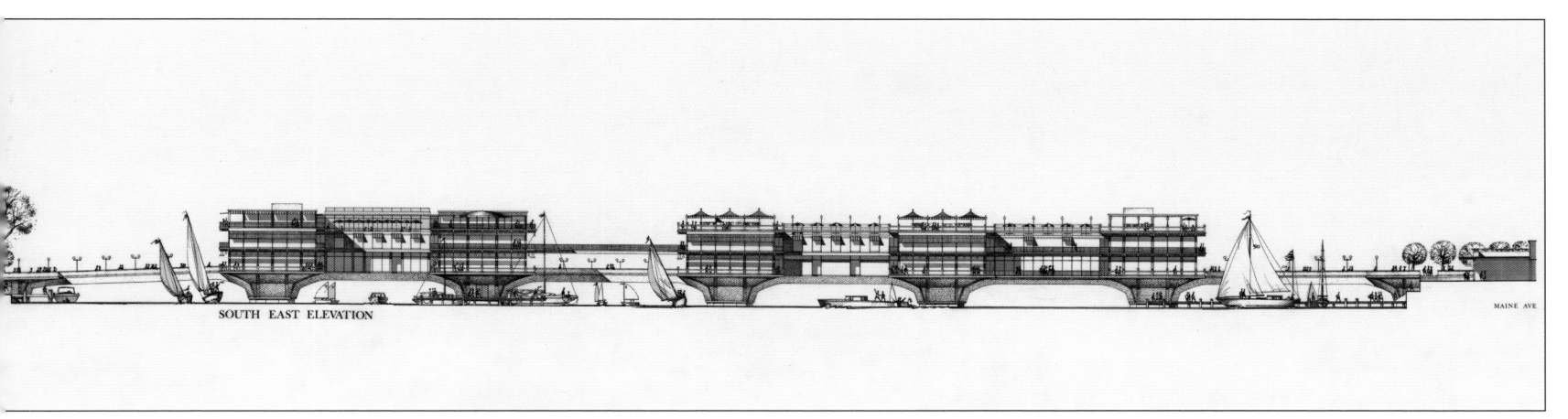

SOUTH EAST ELEVATION

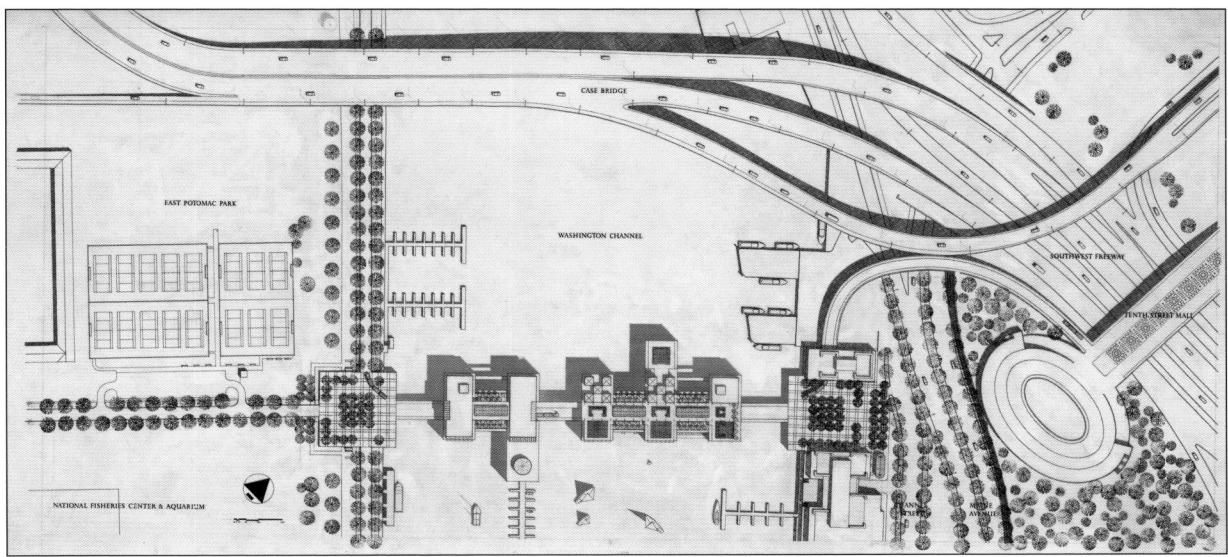

ABOVE AND LEFT: *Southeast elevation and plan of the Ponte Vecchio, a proposed pedestrian bridge spanning the Washington Channel from the foot of the park terminating the 10th Street Mall to East Potomac Park, 1966. Designed by Cloethiel Woodard Smith, the bridge was envisioned to contain multiple levels of retail uses.*

BELOW LEFT: *Model illustrating the heavy concrete forms of the proposed brutalist-style buildings at L'Enfant Plaza—including the Forrestal Building by Curtis & Davis and the L'Enfant Plaza Hotel by I. M. Pei—which were formally dramatic but proved to be uninviting to pedestrians.*

RIGHT: *Model of the first
landscape design proposal for
Overlook Park (now Banneker
Overlook) by Dan Kiley,
1966. Parking lots sheltered
by trellises would have extended down the steep hillside
to the southeast.*

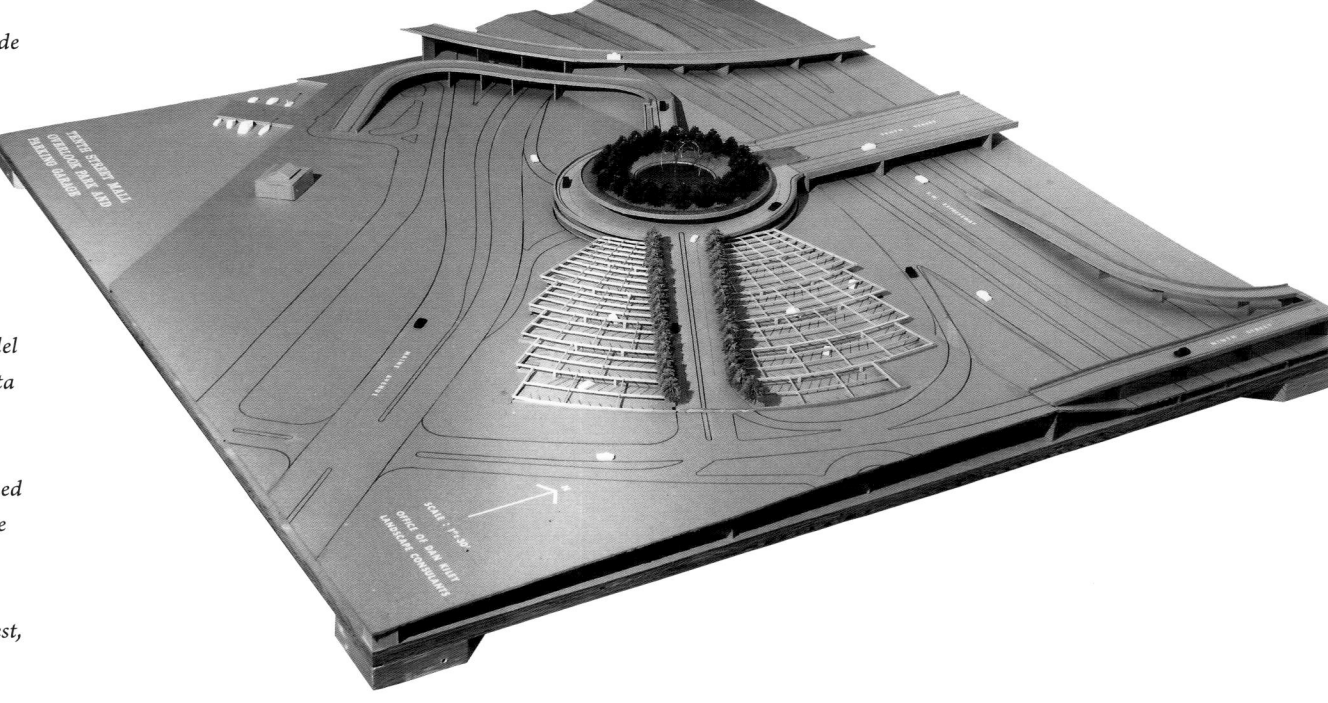

BELOW: *Plan view of a model
by Wright, Andrade, Amenta
& Gane for the 10th Street
Mall and L'Enfant Plaza,
c. 1965. The street was widened
to two hundred feet to create
a ceremonial link between
the National Mall, the new
federal buildings in Southwest,
L'Enfant Plaza, and the
Southwest waterfront.*

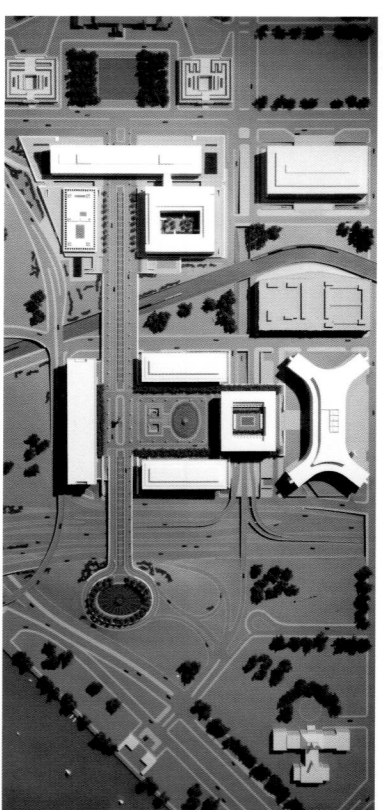

commission insisted that parking was essential to the design of the larger area and refused to grant approval. In
spite of the CFA's position, the overlook was built as an elevated park without a garage.[38]

NEW PUBLIC BUILDINGS IN SOUTHWEST WASHINGTON

By the early 1960s, many of the cleared redevelopment
parcels south of Independence Avenue had been filled with
new federal office buildings. Their bland style generally followed the postwar commercial standard of a box on pilotis
in a modified International Style; Washington's version
would be limited in height and often clad in a masonry skin,
a nod to the monumental tradition. During the 1960s, however, a new vocabulary began to emerge, a more expressive
brutalism featuring cast-in-place concrete structures.

The GSA's FOB 5 typified this evolution; its final design,
worked out over a period of four years, presented a generic
brutalism using heavy concrete members to convey an image of strength, monumentality, and seriousness of purpose. Constructed for the Department of Defense for its
energy programs and known at the time as the "Little Pentagon," the complex was later designated the Forrestal

Building after James Forrestal, the former secretary of defense under President Truman, and afterward became the
home of the Department of Energy.

The CFA expected FOB 5 to fulfill several planning
needs: to create an entrance to the 10th Street Mall and
L'Enfant Plaza; to mitigate the problem posed by the rise
in the 10th Street Mall caused by the Pennsylvania Railroad
tracks; and to complete the southern framing of the National Mall directly across Independence Avenue from the
Smithsonian Castle. Originally conceived as two L-shaped
buildings flanking the 10th Street Mall, the project first presented to the CFA by the architects Curtis & Davis in December 1961 was for an eight hundred-foot-long, north-
facing building bridging 10th Street with lower wings at the
rear parallel to the 10th Street axis.

The commission approved this basic concept, agreeing
with the architects that "because of the unusual profile of
10th Street resulting from the presence of the Pennsylvania Railroad tracks…preserving the continuity of the vista
along Independence Avenue would be more desirable
than to introduce a new and somewhat incomplete view
along 10th Street." The CFA said the presence of Independence Avenue as a major axis had merit and recommended

Aerial view of the 10th Street Mall and L'Enfant Plaza from the Southwest waterfront, c. 1980. With its austere design character and bridged by the Forrestal complex, the 10th Street Mall never became the effective connection between the National Mall and the Southwest waterfront envisioned by its planners.

reducing the length of the building to "achieve a setting more sympathetic in scale with the buildings of the Smithsonian Institution."[39]

When the project was resubmitted in more developed form over two years later, the main building was still eight hundred feet long. Its proposed six-story block had been raised about thirty feet above 10th Street on precast concrete columns and moved back from Independence Avenue. One-story projections at each end would create a forecourt along this road, while at the rear two lower wings would extend along and frame 10th Street. The architects explained that the height of the main block had been determined in reference to adjacent buildings—it would be slightly lower than FOB 10A to the east and about the same height as the 1930s extension to the Department of Agriculture to the west. The facades would be composed of a curtain wall system of glass pyramid units projecting eighteen inches from the building.

At this April 1963 meeting, one of the last under the chairmanship of David Finley, the commission approved the idea of elevating the main building on pilotis but noted that it would be a "complete departure from the basic character" of the existing Mall buildings, which were all masonry structures, as were the buildings intended for L'Enfant Plaza. Further, the commission feared the unbroken length of the glass facade would be monotonous and disruptive to the building line along Independence Avenue. Commission member Ralph Walker—who was serving on the President's Council on Pennsylvania Avenue at the time—cautioned that FOB 5 could set a design precedent for Pennsylvania Avenue, the city's most important ceremonial street.[40]

The commission recommended breaking up the expanse of glass by introducing vertical masonry elements. They stressed to the GSA "that the monumental composition of the Mall should be completed, and that the concept of the proposed design was fundamentally opposed to this principle." Finley noted: "The basic question to be determined... was not one of uniqueness of individual design but of appropriateness in terms of context of the building's setting and of its relation to other important buildings in the area and to the plan of the Mall, itself." The commission disapproved the proposal and requested new studies that would emphasize solid elements.[41]

Between this review in April and the next submission in September 1963, the composition of the commission changed almost completely. Gone were the transitional modern architects Walker, Orr, and Perry, along with David Finley, Felix de Weldon, and Peter Hurd. Appointed in their stead was a new generation of modernists: Gordon

Bunshaft, John Carl Warnecke, Aline Saarinen, Burnham Kelly, Theodore Roszak, and William Walton, who was elected chairman. Hideo Sasaki, an earlier Kennedy appointee, was the only member retained.

In the new submission, the architects had added masonry piers along the facade but had not changed the massing. Reversing its earlier stance, the new commission members rejected the proposal outright, strongly objecting to the building's unbroken mass: "The sheer size and height of the building would create an effective barrier between the Mall and the Tenth Street Mall and L'Enfant Plaza and would completely destroy the effectiveness of the Tenth Street Mall as an entrance to the Southwest Urban Renewal Project."[42] They requested new studies that would further explore solid elements, reduce the area of glass, and provide a strong accent, such as a glass bridge, at the span: "Without any interruption to the building at this point, the members believe that the whole purpose of creating this entrance will be lost."[43]

But the next revision presented in October also failed to meet the commission's objections. Discouraged, the CFA asked the architects to prepare entirely new studies for a single large building without wings, raised on pilotis, and set as far back from Independence Avenue as possible while still spanning 10th Street. They suggested various means of reducing the massive appearance, such as enclosing street-level entrance lobbies in glass and treating the ground plane beneath the building as a plaza. Gordon Bunshaft said its architecture should be a "strong, structural expression, not just a skin with decoration."[44]

The architects returned in January 1964 with four alternatives, all showing the building as a single mass of varying heights and configurations. The commission approved a scheme for a five-story building, 750 feet long and 200 feet wide, agreeing with the architects that a wider building would appear tunnel-like, losing the effect of an entrance to 10th Street. While the building would be in line with the Health, Education, and Welfare building, FOB 10A, and the Department of Agriculture building along Independence Avenue, it would not be symmetrical over 10th Street.[45] The glass pyramids were replaced with a deep, precast concrete frame.

Discussions with the NCPC in early 1964, however, led the commission to agree to further modifications, including a reduction in width from 200 feet to 120 feet to avoid an "excessive amount of deep interior space." The height was also lowered, a change made possible in part by construction of a separate, attached building to the southeast. The commission also agreed with the NCPC's argument for a further setback along Independence Avenue so that the

FACING PAGE. TOP: *Final design of FOB 5 by Curtis & Davis (rendering, c. 1965). The CFA supported the idea of treating the Forrestal Building as a framing element for the National Mall along Independence Avenue.*

CENTER: *Rendering of scheme for FOB 5 (the Forrestal Building, headquarters of the future Department of Energy) by Curtis & Davis, c. 1965. The elevated office building along Independence Avenue is split to create a gateway to the 10th Street Mall.*

BOTTOM: *The Forrestal Building, as built in 1969, was elevated above 10th Street and was intended to act as a gateway into Southwest as well as serving as a visual boundary for the Mall.*

new building would not overpower the Smithsonian Castle and to assure that "the values gained by spanning Tenth Street as the entranceway to L'Enfant Plaza" were not lost by aligning buildings along the roadway.[46]

Under the approved plan, FOB 5 was four stories of precast concrete panels, 660 feet long, and raised 40 feet on pilotis.[47] Two rear buildings were also included, one to the southwest as a one-story cafeteria, continuing the original idea of flanking the 10th Street corridor with structures—built on the recommendation of the CFA to preclude development as a parking lot. The building on the southeast was designed as an eight-story masonry block with an interior courtyard, treated as a solid mass to act as a quiet foil to the forceful, busy designs of the FOBs along Independence Avenue. The commission advised creating windowless, strongly textured walls to contrast with the main building. Later, at the insistence of the Defense Department and the NCPC, which were concerned about a windowless box as a working environment, fenestration was added at the ends of interior corridors. However, the commission objected to what it considered the arbitrary placement of the window openings, which it said made the walls appear like "wallpaper"; instead it requested a clear expression of a structural module and floor levels and the clear termination of the walls. The commission finally approved the design for the Forrestal complex in January 1965.[48]

Several other federal office projects developed in the 1960s would challenge Washington's stodgy architectural image as modernism evolved toward more expressionistic idioms and away from the International Style. Marcel Breuer, the prominent modernist architect, designed two major brutalist buildings in the Southwest redevelopment area: the Housing and Home Financing Agency (HHFA, later the Department of Housing and Urban Development or HUD) in 1964; and the Department of Health, Education, and Welfare (HEW, later known as the Hubert H. Humphrey Building, Department of Health and Human Services) in 1969.

Breuer's project for the HHFA building only came before the commission once, in June 1964. The building was to occupy a difficult site—long and narrow, oriented north to south—and adjoined a lot to the west that was to be occupied by the hotel that would form the centerpiece of the L'Enfant Plaza development. The hotel was to span 9th Street, SW, and preliminary plans indicated that it would be built right up to the property line, crowding Breuer's proposed building.[49]

Breuer had developed a precast concrete structure elevated on massive cast-in-place piers in a curving shape

FEDERAL OFFICE BUILDING Nº 5, WASHINGTON D. C.
CURTIS AND DAVIS FORDYCE AND HAMBY ASSOCIATES FRANK GRAD AND SONS ASSOCIATED ARCHITECTS
GENERAL SERVICES ADMINISTRATION WASHINGTON, D. C.

Rendering of Marcel Breuer's sculptural design for the HHFA building (the future Department of Housing and Urban Development), 1964.

that branched into double-wyes at each end. The form had grown out of the very difficulties posed by the site: to fit in the requisite office space while allowing as much open space as possible, he developed "a system which is concentrated and it branches up in the corners."[50] The building was clad in precast units sloping inward to small windows; granite was proposed for the short end walls, with their sculptural treatment of fire stairs.

The commission was generally favorable to Breuer's proposal, expressing support for the building's shape and mass. There was no objection—barely even a comment—on architectural style, except from Aline Saarinen. In closed session before Breuer appeared, Saarinen asked, "Has anyone explained why Mr. Breuer has made such a brute of a building? I think the scale is absolutely brutish…. It's a jarring scale with nothing to relate it down finally to human scale by detailing or anything." However, she did not raise this issue during his presentation, and no other members objected to the scale. The commission members focused on the large amount of surface parking, the proposed four-foot interior height of the window sills, and the relation of the building to its site—expressing concern that the building would occupy only two-thirds of the site, with the re-

maining third held for the air rights hotel project at L'Enfant Plaza. This configuration would leave Breuer's building too crowded on the site; the commission suggested it should instead fill the entire square. Bunshaft repeatedly brought up the issue, annoyed that the corners were so tight when the building "ought to float."[51] The commission encouraged the GSA to acquire the remainder of the square, but the hotel was built as planned over 9th Street on a massive parking and retail base along the lot line immediately adjacent to the HUD building.[52]

Five years after that first commission, the GSA hired Breuer to design a building for the Department of Health, Education, and Welfare. The commission recognized that the site, near both the Capitol and the Mall, offered the potential to mask the entrance to I-395, thus improving the visual quality of the monumental core. The CFA therefore recommended that the structure span the highway entrance, although it would require the incorporation of massive ventilating shafts into the building.[53] A feasibility study that included a model by Breuer for a concrete and glass structure was presented to the CFA in September 1966. The commission's review was largely confined to details of height in relation to surrounding buildings and the material to be used for the roof trusses that were needed to suspend the building over the highway tunnel. Breuer wanted them made of steel, if fireproofing code allowed. CFA members, in particular Gordon Bunshaft, questioned this decision; he noted that rendering the trusses in steel made the wall appear as if it were not hung and recommended concrete for a harmonious appearance. Despite this comment, the CFA readily approved the study; even Bunshaft, contradicting his earlier statements, called the design "beautiful."[54]

When the project appeared before the commission a second time, it was approved promptly.[55] Breuer had reduced the building's size and set it back from its previous northern alignment in response to the Office of the Architect of the Capitol, which had jurisdiction over a portion of the site. The only substantive matter discussed by the commission was the replacement of the proposed steel roof cables with concrete-covered steel piers. Walton said to Breuer, "We want to congratulate you on a very handsome building which we think will be an enormous addition to the official landscape of Washington.... We only feel guilty that you came just to get words of praise. Usually architects appear when they're not getting words of praise." Bunshaft added: "It will be a nice, strong building—and, being square, will be very powerful."[56]

NEW PUBLIC BUILDINGS IN DOWNTOWN WASHINGTON

Following a similar trajectory of monumental brutalist architecture, the first major building designed for the redevelopment on the north side of Pennsylvania Avenue was the massive Federal Bureau of Investigation (FBI) headquarters located on a site across from the Department of Justice. Designed by Chicago architect C. F. Murphy, the project was reviewed by the commission between 1964 and 1967. The contradictions inherent between program and proposal are explored in Zachary Schrag's essay in this volume.

The project closely followed the concept for the building devised by the President's Temporary Commission on Pennsylvania Avenue, providing such features as a ground-floor arcade open to the public, an effort that the CFA found to be a weakness. Bunshaft observed that the proposals for Pennsylvania Avenue incorporated so many interruptions, such as plazas, that no real continuity along the street would be possible.[57]

The commission's major interest was in achieving an appropriate balance between the two opposed concrete masses constituting the building: the lower 110-foot-high block creating a formidable public facade on Pennsylvania

Avenue and the four-story cantilevered block above it, conceived of as a "floating tray." The base, with its diagonal corner portals, was meant to express openness and invite public access to an interior courtyard—clearly a problematic goal for this particular building. Nathaniel Owings wanted the interior space to be a courtyard with "sculptural protrusions" extending out to Pennsylvania Avenue; the CFA disapproved this gesture as clumsy and lacking in scale.

Faced with an increasingly irresolvable design, the commission advised the architects to balance the two halves and achieve an appropriate expression of proportions through simplifying and organizing the elements. The CFA encouraged them to unify the elevations through more careful expression of structure and floor levels, and advised them to lengthen the top cantilevered portion and reduce the number of floors from three to two in order to lessen its "excessive heaviness."[58]

As Schrag observes, before too long commission members began to have doubts about placing such a large building on Pennsylvania Avenue. Following the CFA approval of the building in 1967, Walton said in a closed session that the design "was so unbearable before. It's still the scariest thing going up in the city."[59]

TOP: *Wood model of Breuer's 1969 concept design for the Health, Education and Welfare (HEW) headquarters building on a site partially over the Center Leg freeway (I-395) tunnel at 3rd and C Streets, SW.*

ABOVE: *In its review of Breuer's HEW building, the Commission of Fine Arts was highly supportive of the brutalist concrete design, questioning only its relative height and the material to be used for its expressed roof trusses.*

Renderings of the proposed FBI Building (above) and its internal courtyard (left), by C. F. Murphy Architects, c. 1964. Occupying a prime site along Pennsylvania Avenue, the building projects a fortress-like presence in the heart of the city with its large setbacks, deep areaways, and heavy concrete exterior. The goal of public accessibility to new buildings along Pennsylvania Avenue was in conflict with the agency's desire for a secure facility.

In contrast, the design by Ludwig Mies van der Rohe for the District of Columbia Central Library was praised by commission members when it was presented in February 1966 by Mies himself.[60] The design was in Mies's well-established style, with a clear structural system articulated on the exterior by applied steel beams and expansive public rooms within. The commission had no criticism of the design by one of the twentieth century's architectural luminaries who had been a potent influence on Bunshaft and most other American modernists. Rather, the commission fawned: Bunshaft, Walton, and Saarinen said repeatedly that the library was "beautiful." Bunshaft observed it was warehouse space but hastened to add that "it certainly would be an enhancement to the chaos of this city."[61] The director of the library gushed that it was "the most functional, the most beautiful and most dramatic public library building in the United States."[62] Saarinen declared it was "a fabulous pleasure" to have Mies attending the meeting and Walton said, "We are prepared to listen to anything that you have to say about your project, your process, and your product."[63] Mies spoke briefly, explaining that it was simply a matter of translating a clear program into an architectural language. He mentioned that he wanted to pave the plaza and sidewalk on the entrance side in granite and the commission members assured him they would support the use of granite wherever he would like.[64]

Nearly eighty years old at the time of the meeting, Mies would die three years later, before the library was complete. Some changes were made in the building as constructed. The front and rear overhangs were to have been the same depth, but the main floor was expanded to the rear, reducing the depth of the rear overhang by two-thirds. Mies had proposed facing the four service cores of the building with green marble, but changed the specification to tan brick to reduce costs.[65] Opened in 1972, the library—the District's only building by Mies—would function for decades in the midst of an economically depressed city center.

In the case of the late-modern scheme of the United States Tax Court by the Sarasota-based architect Victor Lundy, the CFA sought to relate the design to the broader architectural pattern of Washington. First presented to the commission in November 1965, the Tax Court was originally proposed for a small, awkward site confined by large buildings at 2nd Street and Indiana Avenue, NW, which the commission had called inadequate for any monumental building.[66] In addition, the commission believed that Lundy's design was "totally out of context to the classical character of buildings in the Nation's Capital." Lundy had developed the structure as a sculptural cube with its center carved out for a courtyard and its sides composed of deeply-cantilevered floors; the cubical mass was turned away from the orthogonal geometry of its site, oriented instead to the diagonal of Pennsylvania Avenue two blocks away. Lundy claimed the form was a response to Washington's sweltering summers and that the internal court would provide a sense of shelter from the sun. The commission members said they found it difficult to understand how a project of this importance "could go so far awry at such an early stage." They continued:

Model photograph of the proposed D.C. Public Library (the Martin Luther King Jr. Memorial Library) by Ludwig Mies van der Rohe, 1966. The classic modernist steel-and-glass box scheme was highly acclaimed by the CFA.

ABOVE: *Models of the initial concepts for the U.S. Tax Court by Victor Lundy, November 1965. The CFA criticized the first scheme's diagonal orientation and strongly expressionistic form (left) as inappropriate to the established urban character of Washington. An alternative design (right) featured two U-shaped building forms lined with curving glass.*

RIGHT: *Lundy presents a new proposal to Chief Judge William Drennen (left) and associated architect Homer Blackwell (right), 1972. The model illustrates the abstract forms of the building fronted by a landscaped plaza constructed over the Center Leg freeway.*

Apart from the site, however, there was little excuse for the architect's apparent disregard of the character of the Capital. It was clear in his presentation, in fact, that he had made a deliberate attempt to strike out into an area of his own personal expression with little reference to the traditions of Washington.... Obviously we are not saying that tradition has to be interpreted literally in design, but there are certain elements classic in nature that have been common to the roots of the plan and the development of the city over a long period of time. Under no circumstances could we ever accept the architect's arguments for a departure from these general principles.[67]

The commission recommended starting completely afresh. The Tax Court judges and the GSA accepted the commission's suggestion to shift the project north to a new site, a half- block between D, 2nd, and E Streets, and after this, the reviews went smoothly. Presented only one month later, Lundy's new project featured a massive central can-

tilevered block suspended between end blocks and projecting over a grand stairway facing west toward 2nd Street.[68] The facades of the blocks were sheathed in dark gray granite; other elevations, as well as areas between them and beneath the cantilevered mass, were covered in bronze reflective glass. The courtrooms had been raised from below ground to the first floor, with a central Hall of Justice connecting all components.

The commission commended the symmetrical massing and recognition of the street grid, calling the design greatly improved and commenting that "the architect has apparently grasped the import of the remarks we made on the earlier design and we are confident that he will be able to develop a solution that will not only fit in with the city of Washington, but will also possess excellent contempo-

rary qualities."[69] The commission gave a final warm approval in November 1966, with Bunshaft expressing the commission's admiration and Walton offering congratulations "on achieving the commission's aim, an excellently designed building." However, not all the functions of the site's existing user, Federal City College, could be relocated, forcing the Tax Court project to move once again. In 1971, the CFA approved the decision to shift the building to a site immediately to the west, reorienting its facade from west to east, facing a landscaped deck over the sunken Inner Loop Freeway (I-395). Funding problems further delayed construction, and the building was not completed until well into the 1970s.[70]

Modern Design for Washington's Cultural Institutions

In addition to the numerous office structures built for the growing federal bureaucracy, Washington in the 1960s saw a resurgence in the construction of arts and cultural institutions, each a significant new building with monumental aspirations commensurate with the scale, if not the style, of the Beaux-Arts vision. The John F. Kennedy Center for the Performing Arts, once planned for the south side of the Mall, rose instead on the Potomac River near the Lincoln Memorial and adjacent to the eccentric curved structures of the Watergate apartment complex. The Smithsonian Institution constructed three major museums: the National Museum of History and Technology, the National Air and Space Museum, and the Hirshhorn Museum and Sculpture Garden—the first new buildings on the Mall in decades. Plans for the East Building of the National Gallery of Art by I. M. Pei presaged more dramatic formal changes to the ensemble of buildings lining the Mall. In its review of these projects, the Commission of Fine Arts evinced its continuing concern—a principle inherited from the McMillan Plan—with the architectural setting of the monumental core.

THE KENNEDY CENTER FOR THE PERFORMING ARTS

The John F. Kennedy Center for the Performing Arts was a pioneering project exemplifying modern design in the 1960s. A national center for the performing arts had been under consideration since the Truman administration and had gained momentum in the late 1950s. For years, the strongest contender for its site had been the square designated in the 1930s for the Smithsonian Gallery of Contemporary Art, directly south of the National Gallery of Art between 4th and 7th Streets along Independence Avenue, SW. Eventually this site was abandoned in favor of a location in Foggy Bottom adjacent to the Potomac River—a choice supported by the CFA as a way to focus cultural activities into this section of the city and as a natural extension of institutional development west of the White House. Soon after President Kennedy was assassinated in November 1963, the project was named in his honor to serve as a memorial to the slain president.

The Tax Court, located adjacent to the Center Leg freeway, presents an austere composition of volumes. The building was completed in 1976.

ABOVE: *Rendering of an unbuilt design for the National Performing Arts Center by Edward Durrell Stone, c. 1959—an expressive curvilinear design with a massive circular terrace and stairs extending into the Potomac River.*

BELOW: *Rendering for the revised design of the performing arts center by Edward Durrell Stone, c. 1962, featuring a more classically derived modernist scheme of a white box surrounded by pilotis with a massive but seemingly weightless terrace projecting toward the river.*

ABOVE: *Aerial view of the Kennedy Center surrounded by highway infrastructure, c. 1971. The CFA expressed concern—without effect since the site had been determined by Congress—about how well a cultural institution could function in the tangle of highways and ramps along the Potomac River north of the Mall.*

LEFT: *Kennedy Center, view of the terrace, 1980.*

Throughout its review of the project, which took place largely under the leadership of David Finley, the commission linked the project to questions raised by the proposed Inner Loop highway intended to run beneath the Lincoln Memorial and used its comments to urge a solution to the traffic problems at the west end of the Mall.[71] The commission also raised questions about the Kennedy Center's size as it would affect views from the Arlington Memorial Bridge north toward Georgetown. Another concern was the location of the proposed Watergate complex; commission member Douglas Orr pushed the CFA to issue a statement advising that the arts center site extend to the banks of the Potomac River, which Orr intended to prevent the Watergate from being constructed between the river and the Kennedy Center. CFA members raised few objections, however, to the initial design of the Kennedy Center by the New York architect Edward Durrell Stone. In October 1959, Stone presented his proposal for an enormous building overlooking the river and containing an opera house, a symphony hall, and a theater opening on to a circular central hall intended to provide a new ceremonial space for official Washington functions. Stone also had explored extending the building to the bank of the river, which would have required diverting the Rock Creek and Potomac Parkway around it. Chairman Finley—who among his many official roles was a member of the Executive Committee of the National Cultural Center Board—

informed the CFA members of that board's enthusiasm for the project, and they quickly gave their commendation. In a press release, the commission said it heartily endorsed the magnificent concept but, alarmed about the impact on traffic, advocated acquiring more land for the project.[72]

The estimated cost for the original design, $70 million, proved to be too expensive, and the project was scaled back. By the time revised designs were brought to the commission in September 1962, the program had been substantially reduced and the design altered to a rectangular box with three auditoriums placed side by side—in form similar to Stone's U.S. Embassy in New Delhi, India (1957)—for an estimated cost of $30 million.[73] Unlike the previous project, this design would be located entirely on the allotted land and would preserve the river shore; the affected section of the parkway would pass beneath a cantilevered terrace overlooking the Potomac.

But the commission members raised the same reservations as before: that the project was too large for the site and that the future complex of roads would sever the cultural center from the city. They questioned whether one or two of the three huge auditoriums could be moved to another location entirely. Finley pointed out, however, that this was the only site that Congress had made available and that any public statement by the CFA questioning its suitability might adversely affect the national fundraising campaign that was about to begin. The commission

Rendering by Hugh Ferriss of the 1958 design for the National Museum of History and Technology by Steinman, Cain & White—the first modern museum on the National Mall.

CHAPTER V | MODERNISM AND MONUMENTALITY

agreed to hold its remarks, at least for the time being, but the design was never submitted for final review.[74]

MUSEUMS ON THE NATIONAL MALL

The Smithsonian Institution's expansion in the 1960s added three significant buildings lining the great east-west space in the heart of Washington's monumental core. All were in some way consistent with the McMillan Plan idea of using important cultural pavilions as a mediating element between the Mall's greensward and the surrounding architectural frame. However, the language had undergone a fundamental change: instead of the columned white temples of the Beaux-Arts, these institutions would present the same monumental scale but in an abstracted architectural language.

The first modern museum on the Mall occupied a key site on the north side between 12th and 14th Streets—one that had been discussed by the CFA and the NCPC for many years. Yet, when the project for the Smithsonian's National Museum of History and Technology was presented to the CFA in 1956 (completed in 1964), this watershed for modernism on the Mall went largely unremarked by the commission. The design for a marble-clad box by Steinman, Cain & White—the successor firm to McKim, Mead & White—was an abstraction of a classical temple, even more reductive than the Kennedy Center. The commission merely said that it "conformed nicely to the accepted planning of the area."[75]

The commission led by Walton in the 1960s was far more engaged by the Hirshhorn Museum and Sculpture Garden, designed by commission member Gordon Bunshaft of SOM, which transformed the architectural language of museums on the Mall. The museum and garden were built to contain the important modern art collection of the industrialist Joseph Hirshhorn. Both are located on the south side of the Mall on the axis of 8th Street, lying midway between the Capitol and the White House; L'Enfant had designated the 8th Street axis where it crossed Pennsylvania Avenue and his proposed Tiber Creek Canal as the place for a special feature.[76] By the late nineteenth century, the Army Medical Museum (1887), a red-brick Romanesque structure by Washington architect Adolph Cluss, had been built on the site; this building was razed in 1969 to make way for the new museum and garden.[77]

The Hirshhorn Museum project was submitted to the Commission of Fine Arts in June 1967, after Bunshaft had served as a member for four years. He recused himself from the initial discussions, and the project was presented by another architect from the New York office of SOM, associate partner Frederick Gans. Radically different from anything on the Mall, the brutalist concrete structure—often described as a concrete doughnut—was designed as a ring defined by inner and outer walls slightly off-center from each other, resulting in gallery spaces of different sizes.[78] Four massive piers raised the sixty-foot-high structure fifteen feet above a plaza. The reductive geometry of the concrete cylinder can be interpreted as having precedents in the severity of late-eighteenth-century European neoclassicism; it serves as a spatial complement to the square massing of Pope's National Archives building. The proposed design also included a large sunken sculpture garden spanning the width of the Mall along the cross-axis, connecting with the National Gallery of Art sculpture garden proposed for the north. The garden was to be depressed seven feet below grade to preserve an unbroken east-west vista and was to contain a long pool as its central feature.[79]

Although the proposed design differed so drastically from other Mall buildings, the commission raised no questions or concerns about the museum's style. Gans explained that the circular shape had been chosen by considering the building in relation to the proposed Air and Space Museum to the east; the completed FOB 10A to the south; and the historic Arts and Industries Building of the Smithsonian to the west—like the Army Medical Museum, a red-brick Romanesque Revival structure by Cluss. Gans said they had considered designing a rectangular building, but it would not effectively terminate the 8th Street cross-axis, while a circular building would create a "strong sculptural shape floating on this podium" that would also function well as a museum. He said using a circular form would give the museum "a sort of gaiety" that would not destroy the character of the Arts and Industries Building.[80]

Gans also commented on how effectively the museum's strong mass would appear in contrast to the banal boxiness of FOB 10A. Although approved by an earlier commission, these commission members evinced a strong distaste for FOB 10A, a raised eight-story box with repeated window modules that were flush within a marble veneer grid. Chairman Walton said the new museum "makes the horror behind it almost look good, the contrast, no fenestration almost in this new unit."[81]

The commission's discussion centered on the museum's exterior cladding and the sunken garden and its pool. Travertine had been selected for the exterior because of its warm color, which the architects felt would work well in relation to the pale pink aggregate intended for the Air and Space Museum and the pink marble of the National Gallery of Art. Funding, however, only allowed for the use of a sand-blasted, cast-in-place concrete, contributing to the starkness of the museum's ultimate appearance.

For the sunken sculpture garden extending into the Mall, Bunshaft first designed a pool with dimensions similar to those of the Lincoln Memorial Reflecting Pool, about one hundred feet wide by fifteen hundred feet long; this was soon reduced to eighty by five hundred feet. The garden was depressed so it would not destroy the "grand sweep" of the Mall; Gans claimed it would be invisible except when seen up close or from high on the Capitol steps, although it would be surrounded by a three-foot-high railing.[82]

The CFA members readily approved the design of the museum and said they considered it suitable for the Mall: "The circular form and the general massing fit in quite well in this particular location which, of course, is on the [8th] Street cross-axis of the Mall."[83] The commission expressed reservations only about details of the sculpture garden,

such as the nearly sixteen-foot height of the walls, which would "constitute a definite cut across the Mall," and requested that they be further studied. They recommended that SOM consider using low uniform walls around the pool terrace and compensate for differences in grade by installing sloping grass berms on the east and west sides, which "would probably eliminate the trench-like effect of the present scheme and also reinforce the continuity of the center grass panel as seen along the axis of the Mall." Otherwise, the commission only questioned the large expanse of stone paving intended to surround the base of the museum, always a concern in Washington because of the intense summer heat.

The revised design for the sculpture garden plaza was presented to the commission in November 1967. The height of the wall had been lowered from sixteen to twelve feet, and the garden had been simplified. The CFA requested

ABOVE: *Model of the design by Gordon Bunshaft of SOM (1969). The strong circular form was intended to punctuate the city's 8th Street axis crossing the Mall.*

RIGHT: *Model of Bunshaft's first scheme for the Hirshhorn Museum and Sculpture Garden (1967). The design would have extended a long pool across the Mall's greensward.*

CHAPTER V | MODERNISM AND MONUMENTALITY

more information about lighting, landscaping, paving, and parking, and how the architects proposed to prevent staining on the museum's sheer walls. Walton said: "It's certainly the biggest project by a member in our time. So we should proceed with double caution and should not be accused of having let him do anything he wanted in the monumental heart of Washington and we have to regard ourselves as an intimate at the same time."[84]

But an obstacle arose in July 1970 when the Subcommittee on Libraries and Memorials of the Committee on House Administration called for two weeks of hearings on the Smithsonian's plans for an ambitious expansion of its facilities and activities. Although it was only one topic among many, the subcommittee's primary interest was the 1966 agreement entered into by Joseph Hirshhorn and Secretary of the Smithsonian S. Dillon Ripley for Hirshhorn's eponymous museum on the Mall. The hearings explored a number of issues related to the bequest, including the terms of the gift, the museum's location, and the selection of an architect concurrently serving on the CFA. The subcommittee was most concerned, however, about "whether it was esthetically wise to intrude upon the central portion of the Mall with the sculpture garden portion of the museum, when it seemed clear that the traditional development of the Mall was directed at preserving the integrity of an unbroken sweep of grass linking the Capitol to the Washington Monument." The subcommittee recommended that no further action be taken to carry out the sculpture garden plans without a complete review by appropriate congressional committees.[85] Following the hearings, the Smithsonian eliminated the immense cross-axial projection of the sunken garden, reworked it as a smaller rectangular garden parallel to the Mall, and confined it to a site directly north of the museum contained within an elm tree panel. The CFA called this a "far more satisfactory solution."[86]

Like the Hirshhorn Museum, the uncompromisingly modern design of the enormous new National Air and Space Museum built directly east of the Hirshhorn site aroused no concern among commission members over the architectural style itself. However, after expressing enthusiasm for architect Gyo Obata's initial concept for the project, the CFA began to have reservations about its lack of scale and overpowering massiveness. The record of project reviews from the early 1960s to the early 1970s shows the commission fully accepting modern architecture but wrestling with an inherent weakness of modern design: the lack of standard devices to give scale to or to modulate between large and small elements, and consequently the need to invent an architectural vocabulary with each new building. Aline Saarinen commented on

TOP: *Rendering of the museum (c. 1967) showing the heavy concrete vaulting below the elevated gallery floors, which were intended to be faced in travertine;*

CENTER: *Bunshaft's second version of the Hirshhorn sculpture garden (1972) was scaled back as a sunken court without crossing the central panel of the Mall.*

ABOVE: *Completed in 1974, the Hirshhorn Museum remains the most starkly abstract of Smithsonian Institution museums lining the National Mall.*

this difficulty: "This is one of the problems, obviously, of modern architecture, where we have nothing that measures as a Greek order used to do."[87] With this project, the commission also began to confront the question of how to relate a building that had been designed to express new materials and construction techniques to the classical stone buildings of the Mall.

The idea for an Air and Space Museum first came to the Commission of Fine Arts in 1949. At that time, the CFA objected to the proposed location on the south side of the Mall, between 3rd and 7th Streets and directly across from John Russell Pope's National Gallery of Art, the site intended for the Saarinens' Smithsonian Gallery of Art. Their main concerns were about size, access, and the suitability of such artifacts for a site on the Mall.[88]

In June 1964, Gyo Obata of the St. Louis firm Hellmuth, Obata & Kassabaum (HOK) presented studies to the commission for a massive building with huge boxed windows protruding from a rectangular mass capped with a modernist cornice.[89] Obata suggested using precast concrete panels on a steel structure; the CFA recommended that, because of its size, the building should be made of poured-in-place concrete wherever possible to make it appear more vigorous.[90] In his revised design, Obata incorporated the commission's suggestion and proposed poured-in-place concrete for the building's piers and other solid portions of the facade. In response, the commission advised Obata to further emphasize the strength of the piers in order to enhance the scheme's monumentality. Nonetheless, Bunshaft told Obata the design was "wonderful," and Saarinen and Walton agreed that, "it is unquestionably still the best building we have seen."[91]

As work on the design progressed, however, Bunshaft began to express reservations. He believed a certain delicacy of scale was lost as Obata made the top floor thicker, "detract[ing] from the monumental appearance." Obata said he would add scale by detailing the soffit; Bunshaft recommended that Obata also reconsider proportions between the different bands of the cornice. Soon Bunshaft was saying to the commission: "It seems to me the building is gradually getting kind of clumsy and heavy…. It really looks like it is sinking into the ground."[92] Addressing Obata, Bunshaft said: "We love the building…. What we're wondering about is some place to get something that has a little subtlety or contrast that will take away from this overall…heaviness." Bunshaft was convinced that the problem lay with the cornice, which lacked variation and subtlety among its parts. Having previously approved Obata's design, the CFA was now unable to determine a solution to the problem of scale and suggested further studies.[93]

However, the commission did not see the project again for almost seven years; funding for the museum was preempted by the cost of the escalating war in Vietnam.[94] It was not until November 1971 that Obata returned to the CFA with an entirely different design. While Bunshaft remained on the commission, all the other members had changed, and J. Carter Brown, director of the National Gallery, had just replaced Walton as chairman. Nationally known architect Kevin Roche had been appointed, as was Jane Dart, former movie actor, a California arts patron, and a personal friend of California govenor Ronald and Nancy Reagan.[95]

Obata's new design reflected a program that had been reduced in volume by about 30 percent; he had replaced the boxed window masses and heavy cornice with a precast structure arranged in a series of horizontal setbacks and vertical towers. The building's Mall facade would be mostly glass while the Independence Avenue side would be almost solid masonry.[96] In executive session Bunshaft questioned the "inadequate articulation of [the] vertical elements," and Roche asked if more openness or glass could be provided on the Independence Avenue side. In open session, Obata agreed to restudy both issues. Although the commission noted the improvements Obata had made in design and scale, the members concluded that the "modifications…had not been able to salvage the design, and that therefore their previous encouragement of the present direction could no longer be sustained."[97]

In January 1972, Obata presented models of several new proposals. The commission preferred one that displayed a regular rhythm of solid and glass elements, saying it had a "more appropriate sense of scale." Bunshaft commented that the scheme contained the embryo of a great building but needed much refinement, and he advised Obata to improve the joining of vertical elements with the ground plane.[98]

When the architect returned with massing studies for a building composed of four solid blocks joined by three glass links, the commission said the idea had little to offer over the volume study seen the previous month. In closed session before Obata joined the meeting, Roche said: "I don't see how you could possibly approve it. There is nothing to approve." After Obata entered, Bunshaft noted: "We feel maybe [this has] been forced on you and you don't have enthusiasm for it," adding, "it looks a little dull." When Obata objected that the commission had told him to keep it simple, Brown said the massive scale was "like having a transformer that punches up all the voltage…. If you do a peaceful building, all of a sudden it becomes almost soporific." Members suggested the architect treat the joints between exterior panels as design elements and express the interior space frame. Reaffirming their approval, the CFA told him to continue with this scheme.[99]

The design Obata next presented to the commission in April 1972 was for a steel structure covered with marble panels. A facade composed of marble-sheathed blocks separated by large expanses of glass faced the Mall, while the Independence Avenue elevation was dominated by projecting cantilevered cubes. The commission members said they were disappointed that they could not be more enthusiastic but found the design still needed refinement; in particular, they objected to a series of vertical notches on the north and south facades as too "decoratorish." They requested further study of the scale and of the solid-void relationship between the glazed areas and projecting cubes of the Independence Avenue facade. The commission wrote: "The points had been made repeatedly that the design had not matured to the degree of excellence which the Commission was demanding for this very important site on the Mall."[100]

After yet more changes, the CFA still found fundamental problems with the design. In private discussion among the members, Roche said: "I just plain don't like it, and I don't think it should be built on the Mall." Bunshaft responded: "Well, it's a cold, tough building, but here we are." Brown said he disliked how the cornice pierced through the building on the Independence Avenue side; others objected to the vertical slots that Obata had retained in the marble masses. The commission considered not approving the project and advising the Smithsonian to hire another architect. Roche finally said: "This kind of sugar-cube architecture is not appropriate." He continued: "I think we still have the responsibility not to place this thing on the Mall if we don't really believe in it…. We are supposed to be establishing minimum acceptable standards at least." Bunshaft countered that the commission had told Obata to go ahead with this scheme, and the CFA was morally committed to both the design and the architect.[101]

By August 1975, Obata finally came up with changes that satisfied the commission. He had placed the museum

ABOVE: *The first study by Gyo Obata of HOK for the National Air and Space Museum (1964) was strongly criticized by the CFA for its large scale and proposed use of precast concrete.*

LEFT: *Obata's second proposal for the museum, presented in 1971, was one-third smaller but still used precast concrete panels with vertical towers and a stepped horizontal massing.*

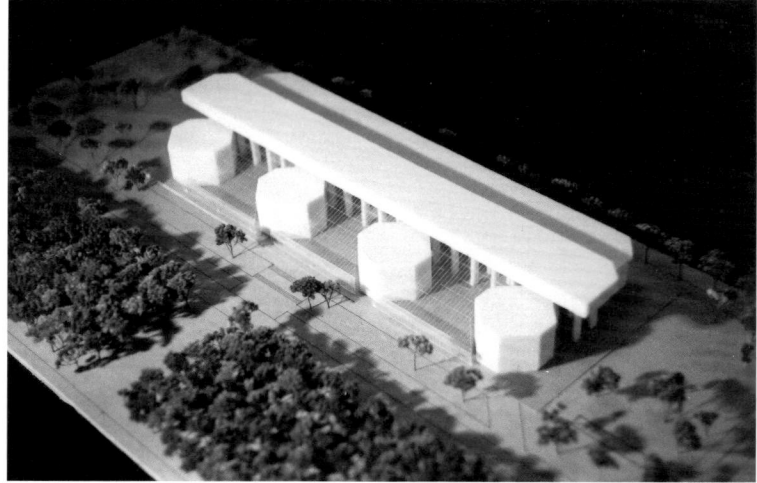

ABOVE, LEFT AND RIGHT: In 1972, Obata presented a series of models showing revised concept schemes. One scheme showed trapezoidal building forms connected by space frame–enclosed galleries; Another was asymmetrical, with long central spine connecting octagonal pavilions.

RIGHT: A third alternative design depicted an array of six solid volumes intersected with an even pattern of glass courts. The CFA expressed its preference for this scheme.

BELOW: The National Air and Space Museum as built, 1976, a sequence of pavilions clad in marble facing the National Mall.

CHAPTER V | MODERNISM AND MONUMENTALITY

on a monumental terraced base and added a broad entry stair mirroring that of the National Gallery of Art. He extended the glass areas of the north and south ends into the roof, surrounded the three cantilevered masses on Independence Avenue with glass, and eliminated the troublesome vertical slots from the Mall elevation. The commission noted the project's "substantial improvement," advising Obata to emphasize the central axis to provide a sense of entrance, and approved the design.[102] Twelve years after Obata presented his first concepts for the new museum to the commission, the National Air and Space Museum opened in 1976.

The East Building of the National Gallery of Art was commissioned from I. M. Pei almost thirty years after completion of the original Beaux-Arts structure by John Russell Pope, which, by the time it opened in 1941, was already viewed as a stylistic anachronism. In contrast, the strikingly modern East Building was conceived as a structure to house public activities, such as a center for advanced scholarly study, more than as a repository for artistic treasures.[103]

J. Carter Brown oversaw the design of the East Building for the National Gallery. Brown had joined the gallery in 1961 and became its director in 1969. In 1967, the gallery's trustees had given him responsibility for planning the new building, for which Pei had already been selected as architect. It was Brown who presented the building's design to the Commission of Fine Arts for review, beginning in 1967; the commission gave its final approval of the design in April 1971. Five months later, Brown was appointed a member of the commission, filling the seat vacated by John Walker, his predecessor at the National Gallery; Brown was elected chairman at his first CFA meeting in November 1971.

While a thoroughly modern structure, the East Building made references to its prime site on the Mall at the foot of Capitol Hill through its materials, massing, and geometric gestures. Pei combined marble sheathing on the walls with an innovative, finely crafted architectural concrete for structural members, such as beams and the space frame of the atrium ceiling, which incorporated marble dust; all marble was taken from the same Tennessee quarry as the marble of the original Pope building.[104]

The enormous atrium, counterpart of the West Building's central rotunda, played a more dominant role than the small gallery spaces contained within the three trapezoidal towers. Pei and his associated architects generated the form—a combination of two isosceles triangles with a right triangle—from their analysis of the awkward trapezoidal site located at the acute angle formed by the convergence of Pennsylvania Avenue and Madison Drive; the

building is the only Mall building to face Pennsylvania Avenue directly. With a central east-west axis bisecting two of the triangles, the plan has been said to recapitulate the larger form of the McMillan Plan's Mall. The building responded to the city's geometry: the orientation of the three towers and the incisions cut into the building's volume were all oriented to the axes of the McMillan Plan. As J. Carter Brown wished, the atrium continued the open space of the Mall within the gallery, becoming an urban plaza defined by the towers.[105] The new museum opened in 1978 to glowing reviews from architectural critics. Its strong geometries also attracted the public, whose many handprints left on the knife-edge wall of the building's southwest corner attest to its popularity as a spot for memento photographs of Washington.

Model of I. M. Pei's design for the East Building, 1970. The new gallery was aligned with the original National Gallery (West Building), but its form boldly addressed each of its four elevations through a composition of two triangles on the irregular trapezoidal site.

TOP: *Rendering by Steve Oles (1971) of the East Building's entrance facing 4th Street and the West Building, forming an urban plaza between the two galleries.*

ABOVE AND RIGHT: *The East Building's triangular geometry is expressed in dramatic volumes clad in pink Tennessee marble; the knife-edged southwest corner has become an iconic element on the Mall for many visitors.*

The National Mall

In the mid-twentieth century, the Commission of Fine Arts worked to accommodate modern design principles within the compelling framework established by the McMillan Plan earlier in the century. Despite the radical change in architectural language, the commission continued to support fundamental principles of the plan, particularly in achieving the spatial organization of the Mall and monumentality appropriate to the national capital. The National Mall as a coherent landscape of commemorative space from the Capitol to the Potomac River had emerged, recognizable but incomplete, as early as the 1930s; at midcentury, its further development was interrupted first by the war effort's physical impact on Washington and then by the distractions of reordering the city to accommodate new scales of transportation and workplaces for an enlarged bureaucracy. By the 1960s, however, planning and construction work began to bring the National Mall to fruition as a completed urban park. By the time of the Bicentennial in 1976, no wartime tempos remained, and West Potomac Park offered hundreds of acres of unencumbered parkland—an opportune location that would be devoted to the development of new memorials in less than a decade.

PLANS BY SKIDMORE, OWINGS & MERRILL

By the early 1960s, the threats posed to the Mall by highway development, automobile parking, and insufficient maintenance, along with the construction of several new museums, inspired the National Park Service (NPS) to develop a master plan that would impose controls on vehicles, emphasize new mass transit systems for visitors, and create easier access and increased amenities for pedestrians.[106] The first plan, produced by landscape architect Richard K. Webel in 1963, replaced roads with walks, placed crossroads in tunnels, increased the amount of recreational activities, and established a national visitor center, but it was not implemented. In 1965, the secretary of the interior directed the NPS to retain Skidmore, Owings & Merrill to develop another version of a Mall plan, based in part on Webel's ideas. Through firm partner Nathaniel Owings, SOM had earlier been involved in the President's Advisory Council on Pennsylvania Avenue (1962–64) and was participating in the President's Temporary Commission on Pennsylvania Avenue (1965–69).

Owings and SOM developed two master plans for the Mall over the course of eight years. Key objectives of both plans were the removal of automobiles from the Mall, an emphasis on the vista between the Capitol and the Washington Monument, and the provision of more visitor at-

tractions. For the first report, submitted in 1966, Owings brought in members of SOM's San Francisco office as well as landscape architect Dan Kiley and traffic engineers Wilbur Smith & Associates. Later, the NPS asked Owings and SOM to revisit the earlier plan in anticipation of the nation's Bicentennial; the new plan was submitted in 1973 by a Washington-based SOM team that included the young architect David Childs (CFA 2002–05). Owings had earlier appointed Childs chief designer of the President's Temporary Commission on Pennsylvania Avenue (1968–69); Childs joined the newly opened Washington, D.C., office of SOM after serving on that commission.[107] Architect Richard Giegengack and landscape architect George Dickie worked with Childs, concentrating on an element of the plan that would become Constitution Gardens in West Potomac Park. Kiley and Wilbur Smith & Associates again served as consultants to SOM, joined by engineer Kurt Pronske and landscape architect Henry Arnold, who later developed technical specifications for plantings and worked with Giegengack and Dickie on Constitution Gardens.

The 1966 Washington Mall Master Plan examined circulation problems and the need for visitor services on the Mall. It proposed the wholesale removal of roads and parking, replacing the four Mall roads with pedestrian walks supplemented with shuttle and tour buses.[108] While some cross-axial streets would be tunneled, most others would

HAPPY SENDOFF

Tempos Get A Big Bang From Sledge

The demolition of the World War II tempos on the Mall gets under way as William Walton, chairman of the Fine Arts Commission, pounds the corner of Tempo 4 with a sledge hammer yesterday. Mrs. James T. Rowe, chairman of the National Capital Planning Commission, and Bernard L. Boutin, General Services administrator, look on.—Star Staff Photo.

William Walton wields a sledgehammer at Tempo 4, located on the Washington Monument Grounds, in January 1964, beginning the removal of the remaining tempos on the Mall. In the background are NCPC chairman Elizabeth Rowe and GSA administrator Bernard L. Boutin.

RIGHT: *Nathaniel Owings (far right) presents the Skidmore, Owings & Merrill (SOM) model of the Mall to Lady Bird Johnson and others at the White House, including Secretary of the Interior Stewart Udall (second from right), 1966.*

BELOW: *The first SOM Mall Plan, submitted to the National Park Service in 1966, proposed the removal of automobiles from the Mall and the creation of a continuous landscape from the Capitol to the Lincoln Memorial.*

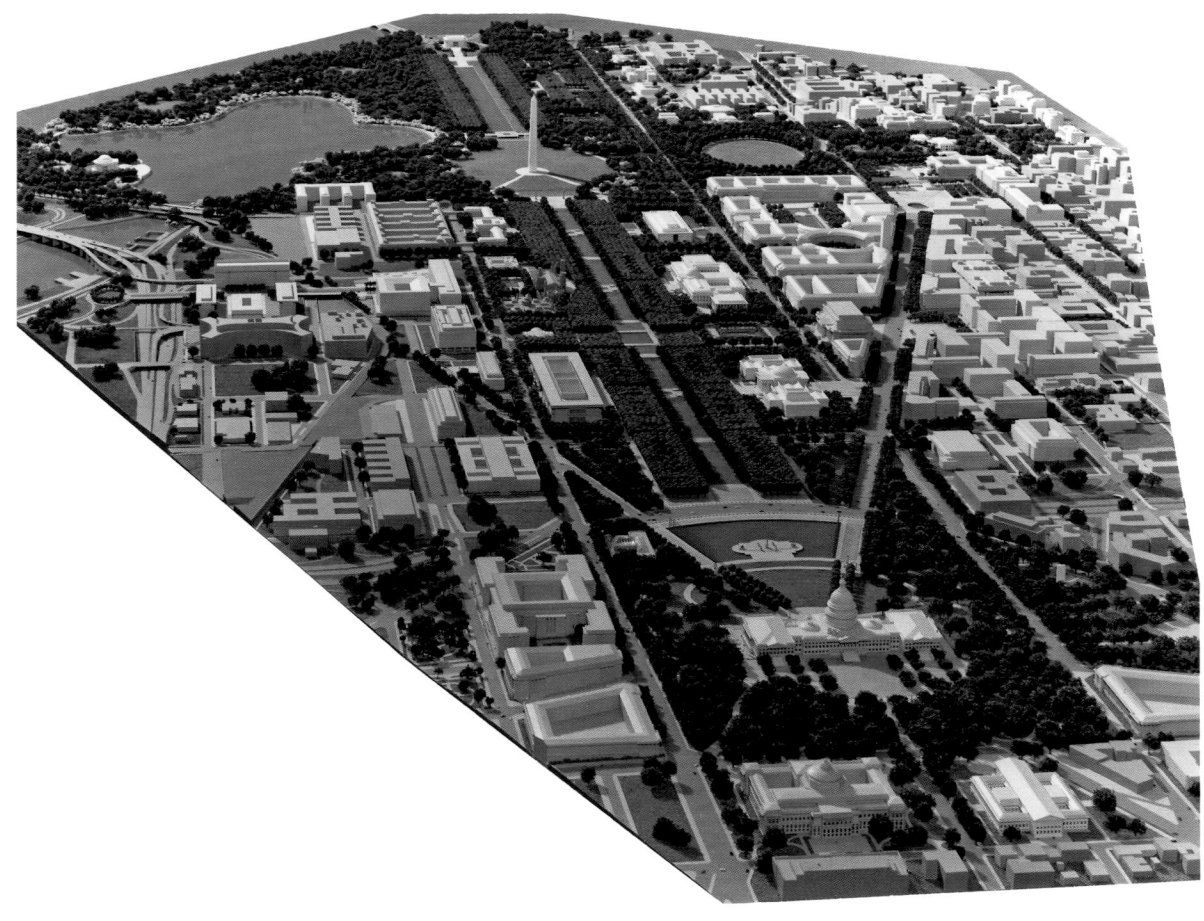

LEFT: *Model of the* SOM *Mall Plan, c. 1966. The design was intended to strengthen the spatial sequences of the McMillan Plan, reinforcing major axes and public spaces with densely planted trees.*

BELOW: *The* SOM *plan defined the Mall's main axis more narrowly with the planting of additional lines of trees inside of the existing panels of elms.*

TOP: *Rendering of the Capitol Reflecting Pool in the 1966 SOM plan. The Grant Memorial on the far side of the pool is barely visible across the expanse of water.*

BOTTOM: *The 1966 plan proposed replacing the Olmsted-designed landscape of Union Square with the Capitol Reflecting Pool and expanding 3rd Street into a broad ceremonial drive as a setting for inaugural parades.*

FACING PAGE: *Aerial photograph of the Capitol Grounds and Union Square with the reflecting pool as built at left, 1992. The landscape was built beginning in 1969 in conjunction with the construction of the Center Leg (I-395) tunnel beneath Union Square.*

be eliminated. The central Mall axis would be punctuated at a few points with fountains, with a larger fountain on the 8th Street axis to signify its historic importance.

Visitor services included the addition of an underground parking garage beneath the Mall between 12th and 14th Streets and an overlook on 15th Street offering views of the Washington Monument Grounds as well as the Mall. The plan proposed building an enormous reflecting pool in Union Square that could serve as a skating rink in winter as well as a national sculpture garden on the Mall's north side between 7th and 9th Streets. It recommended doubling the rows of Mall trees, from four to eight on each side, and introducing other tree species in addition to the American elms.[109]

When the commission reviewed the first SOM Mall plan in November 1966, the members were not convinced that cars could be totally banned from the Mall "without turning the area into a park preserve which is not the true purpose of the Mall." The CFA rejected outright the notion of the 15th Street overlook and said the Washington Monument mound should be retained as a distinct element. And in deference to the McMillan Commission's plan for the Mall's landscape, the CFA struck down the notion of adding trees to the existing elms, maintaining that the east part of the Mall should have the same number of tree rows as the west and should retain the same width of open space throughout.[110]

The 1966 plan was never approved. In 1972, as part of planning for the bicentennial, the NPS hired SOM to revise its earlier report. This document, issued in October 1973 and titled "The Washington Mall Circulation Systems," explored in more detail the problem of automobile traffic and parking on Mall roads. The plan advocated eliminating car and bus traffic entirely, replacing the inner Mall drives with walks and the outer drives with narrow roads for tour buses licensed by the NPS. Visitors who drove would park at remote locations and take shuttle buses to the Mall.[111] The plan discussed the threats posed to the Mall elms by disease and construction.

Inspired by the Tuileries Gardens in Paris, the designers proposed walks repaved in crushed compacted stone, which would provide a more comfortable walking surface than concrete or asphalt.[112] The plan also placed 12th Street in a tunnel and eliminated fountains at the cross-axes. Double rows of trees would be planted on 7th Street and along the axis of 9th Street to highlight the 8th Street axis between, and an inner row of trees—specified as American lindens—would be planted along the inner edge of the Mall elms to provide a clean edge.[113] Visitor amenities such as concession kiosks, bike racks, and benches would be added beneath the elms. Formal tree panels would extend across the block between 14th and 15th Streets; other landscaping would be added to further define this area as a transitional zone between the formal landscape to the east and the picturesque informality of the Washington Monument and other grounds to the west.[114] Both the Commission of Fine Arts and the National Capital Planning Commission found the proposed row of lindens to be problematic. They eventually disapproved the addition of this fifth line of trees as well as the idea of introducing another species to the American elm planting, which had come to characterize the Mall.[115]

As a result of the SOM plan and the construction of the Inner Loop Freeway underneath it, Union Square was redesigned, beginning in 1969. While the project radically changed the Union Square landscape, it came before the commission only a few times for review of the Capitol Reflecting Pool's design. Significantly, the project resulted in the loss of the existing Union Square landscape designed by a founding member of the commission, Frederick Law Olmsted Jr., which had served for thirty years as a transitional element between the Mall and the Capitol Grounds; this loss went unremarked by the CFA.

As first planned, the freeway had a curved alignment to save some of the historic trees, but Nathaniel Owings pointed out that if it were straightened, money would become available to build the new Capitol Reflecting Pool.[116] Construction began in 1969 and resulted in the relocation of the General George Gordon Meade Memorial, the loss of a corresponding site for a future navy memorial, and the removal of dozens of trees, many of them historic. Few subsequent changes have been made to Union Square since the SOM plan was completed in the early 1970s.

A recurring suggestion for the Mall was the introduction of an outdoor skating rink as an amenity. In September 1966, the Temporary Commission on Pennsylvania Avenue submitted a design for a three-part pool at Union Square, the center section of which would serve as an ice skating rink in winter. Soon after, the NPS proposed a skating rink as the central element of the new Capitol Reflecting Pool. However, the CFA disapproved building a skating rink anywhere on the Mall's central axis at either the east or west end and said any such feature should be placed in a peripheral area: "The central area of the Mall must remain uncluttered."[117]

More than five years would pass before an appropriate location for a skating rink was found: as the main feature of SOM's proposed National Gallery of Art sculpture garden.[118] SOM first submitted a design for a garden with a central circular pool containing a square island, framed by additional pools and cascades on the east-west axis and a restaurant to its north. Hedges and trees separated the garden into sections.[119] The CFA said it might be preferable to have a traditional garden for sculpture and recommended that the scheme be more open and clearly define the axial pattern, suggesting the garden could be sunk below ground level so that pedestrians and bus passengers could see across it to the Mall. They concluded that the SOM plans were "out of scale and overdone, shapes of sections unresolved, and the sculpture incidental to the design." SOM revised the scheme, which included a redesigned glass garden pavilion with steel pointed-arch tracery. In November 1971 the CFA accepted the changes, approving the pavilion and calling it "pleasantly in character" with the garden and skating rink.[120]

CONSTITUTION GARDENS

Another significant advance in the completion of the monumental landscape was Constitution Gardens, occupying the northwest corner of West Potomac Park, which had been built to extend the western end of the Mall on land reclaimed from the Potomac River in the late nineteenth century. The prolonged occupation of this area by the huge temporary office buildings for the Department of War and its visual separation from the immediately adjacent Lincoln Memorial grounds by a flood control levee precluded its incorporation into the larger design of the Mall for more than fifty years. Its development in the 1970s resulted in part from the commission and SOM reinterpreting the McMillan Plan in a modern vein.

Concerning the development of West Potomac Park, the 1901 *McMillan Report* is more allusive than detailed; the area of the future Constitution Gardens is discussed in only one or two places. In the section on the Lincoln Memorial, the report says: "For the most part this area from New York Avenue to the river should be treated as a wood, planted informally, but marked by formal roads and paths, much as the Bois de Boulogne at Paris is treated."[121] Renderings suggest that the McMillan Commission considered

TOP: *The 1901* McMillan Report *did not describe the landscape character of West Potomac Park north and south of the Reflecting Pool in any detail.*

CENTER: *West Potomac Park (1943) was gradually filled with tempos built during World War I, including the extensive Navy and Munitions buildings (right) and tempos from World War II (left).*

BOTTOM: *Model (1972) following the initial 1966 SOM design for Constitution Gardens inspired by the Tivoli Gardens in Copenhagen. The plan proposed an intricate and densely planted landscape with recreational and decorative elements focused on a sequence of water features.*

a system of identical walks or roads north and south of the Reflecting Pool traversing thick woods on orthogonal and diagonal lines leading to the Lincoln Memorial and other key sites.

However, the area had long been used to accommodate a more utilitarian purpose: to support U.S. participation in World War I, two enormous temporary buildings for the Navy and War Departments were built in 1918 south of B Street North.[122] Known as the Navy and Munitions buildings, they housed the offices of the secretary of the navy and the chief of naval operations. The two buildings extended for almost one-third of a mile between 17th and 21st Streets.[123] Following a severe flood of the river in March 1936, a temporary levee was constructed in West Potomac Park to protect downtown Washington from future flooding. The levee ran north of and parallel to the Reflecting Pool and was soon rebuilt as a permanent structure; in the 1970s it was incorporated into the landscape as a grass-covered slope.[124] Additional temporary buildings were added on both sides of the Reflecting Pool, with linking footbridges crossing the pool, to accommodate defense personnel during World War II. In its 15th annual report, issued in 1948, the Commission of Fine Arts recommended

that the area along the south side of Constitution Avenue, then occupied by temporary buildings, be planned as a naturalistic park area, within the rigid borders of the straight avenues, roads, and walks, with broad expanses of lawn with trees in mass, in groups, and singly, composed in a manner appropriate for passive recreation and in keeping with the immediate environment of two of the greatest memorials ever erected, the Washington Monument and the Lincoln Memorial.[125]

However, no work was carried out, and the tempos remained for decades.

The Navy and Munitions buildings were finally demolished in late 1970 through the efforts of President Richard M. Nixon; they were among the last tempos to be removed from the Mall.

Nixon's bicentennial message of February 4, 1972, announced that, by 1976, a park would be created on the site of the old tempos. That park, Constitution Gardens, would be among the most ambitious of several bicentennial projects completed by the NPS in the National Capital Parks.[126]

SOM's 1966 plan had contained extensive recommendations for the future site of Constitution Gardens, envisioning a looser, more picturesque treatment of the Mall west of 14th Street to contrast with the formal landscape of the 1st through 14th Street area: "Much of the aesthetic pleasure of the Mall landscaping is derived from this very juxtaposition of the romantic pastoral landscape with the more formal garden, and the contrast should be preserved."[127] Under David Childs and with the involvement of Nathaniel Owings, SOM developed a new, less formal series of plans for Constitution Gardens.[128] The central concept was an amusement park contained in a picturesque setting centered on a small lake, based on Copenhagen's nineteenth-century Tivoli Gardens.[129] In preparing this plan, the designers closely studied the McMillan Commission's models and drawings.

The CFA reviewed the Constitution Gardens designs several times between 1971 and 1975, a period spanning the transition between the chairmanships of William Walton and J. Carter Brown. Although the Commission of Fine Arts had hoped the redesign of the western end of the Mall would more closely follow the McMillan Plan, generally the CFA, along with the National Capital Planning Commission, supported SOM's aims. In December 1971, the commission considered the relation of the design to the McMillan Plan, commenting that the designs "appeared complicated and divergent from the original Olmsted and McMillan Commission plans to keep the area wooded and simple in character." Two months later, it noted: "The historical intent was to have this section of the Mall a green, wooded retreat from the formality of the Reflecting Pool and the scale of the remainder of the Mall."[130]

In a letter to Secretary of the Interior Rogers C. B. Morton, Brown summarized the arguments opposing the complications of the design. Saying that Constitution Gardens "should not provide this much presence on the Mall," he continued:

In general, the Commission felt that the design was too inward-looking, that it in effect turns its back on the rest of the city. As a self-contained entity, it could be located just about anywhere. The Commission is sympathetic to the need for breaking down the scale of the Mall and humanizing it into sub-spaces. It felt this proposal, however, was overdesigned.

Brown attempted to define the desired character:

The panel between the Reflecting Pool and Constitution Avenue should breathe easily and with dignity as part of an overall scheme, and enhance the experience of the monuments and of the city plan, with its increasingly precious provision of open green space.[131]

Adding to the difficulties posed by the complicated design was its high cost, estimated at $49 million. In response, the SOM design team altered the Tivoli plan to a simple, picturesque park.[132]

When SOM presented its revised design to the commission the following year, it met with immediate approval because it resembled the McMillan Commission's intent to create a wooded park in this area—although the CFA questioned the proposal for a visitor pavilion and a curved

entrance road. The CFA approved the project on condition the road be eliminated, allowing only pedestrian access. Brown wrote: "The essential simplicity of the design complements the great formal composition of the Reflecting Pool and surrounding areas."[133]

A variety of mostly European historic gardens and landscapes provided sources for particular features of Constitution Gardens.[134] A bowl-shaped landscape contained a small curvilinear lake on a broad, low plane at its center. An undulating border of trees on the surrounding slopes created a transition between the formal lines of street trees and the picturesque park. On the east, a paved terrace overlooking the lake was to have been occupied by a large food service pavilion, but it proved to be too expensive.[135] On the west rose a broad knoll with many mature trees.

Constitution Gardens was dedicated on May 27, 1976, in time for the nation's bicentennial celebration. Almost twenty years later, J. Carter Brown extended the commission's thinking, suggesting the McMillan Plan was a document that allowed interpretation:

Skidmore, Owings, and Merrill's initial scheme created a new precinct in response to the president's wishes, but the Commission rejected the scheme as being far too busy and functionally inappropriate. Our idea was quite different. Tastes were changing: people were rediscovering Victorian architecture and the naturalistic landscape plans of Andrew Jackson Downing and Frederick Law Olmsted. Moreover, we believed that the structure of the Mall was now so established that something of a much more relaxed nature was warranted for this space.[136]

The Memorial to the 56 Signers of the Declaration of Independence (completed 1982) occupies a small island in the Constitution Gardens lake. Designed by Joe Brown of EDAW, the blocks of granite, one for each signer, form a low wall defining a semicircular granite plaza and framing a dramatic view of the Washington Monument.

Presidential Commemoration in Midcentury

During the middle of the twentieth century, no new memorials were erected on the National Mall, although commemorative works for three U.S. presidents were constructed within the city's wider monumental composition on sites along the Potomac River. Similar to other contemporary memorials, all three are focused memorial precincts inserted within larger landscapes and include routes of pilgrimage through the landscape to reach the memorial sites. As with other contemporary memorials, they comprise sculptural features set within landscaped grounds.

Although the ambitious plans to create a memorial to President Franklin D. Roosevelt in West Potomac Park stalled in the early 1960s, the Theodore Roosevelt Memorial was successfully completed during the same decade. The memorial is located on Theodore Roosevelt Island, a 1930s landscape developed by Frederick Law Olmsted Jr., and relies on a typical memorial typology of the modern era: a heroically scaled figure positioned in front of a masonry slab. The memorial sits within an oval plaza lined with fountains and additional stone slabs incised with quotations. The design was heavily revised according to the CFA's recommendations to reduce the formality of the ensemble and avoid a jarring contrast with its forest setting.

The gravesite of John F. Kennedy in Arlington National Cemetery and the Lyndon B. Johnson (LBJ) Memorial are noteworthy for their relative modesty and abstraction in comparison to other presidential memorials and burial sites. Located on the west side of the Potomac River, both the Kennedy grave and the LBJ Memorial are oriented toward major vistas of the Mall within existing federal land. John Carl Warnecke was a member of the CFA when Jacqueline Kennedy asked him to design the gravesite; he presented the project to his commission colleagues, and it was quickly approved without substantial discussion.[1] In reviewing the design of the LBJ Memorial, the CFA recommended adjustments to the site plan to ensure a more consistently curving treatment of the memorial's circulation.

TOP RIGHT: *Lyndon B. Johnson Memorial Grove, Lady Bird Johnson Park, 1977, by Meade Palmer, landscape architect, and Harold Vogel, sculptor.*

RIGHT: *Theodore Roosevelt Memorial, Roosevelt Island, 1967, by Eric Gugler, architect, and Paul Manship, sculptor.*

FAR RIGHT: *Concept design by John Carl Warnecke, for the John F. Kennedy gravesite, Arlington National Cemetery, 1964.*

Historic Preservation in a Modern Era

While the 1960s were marked by the apogee of modern architecture, the decade also witnessed the beginnings of the modern historic preservation movement. In 1960, the secretary of the interior initiated the National Historic Landmark program as a means of encouraging the preservation of nationally significant properties, including those held by private parties. More galvanizing was the destruction of McKim, Mead & White's Pennsylvania Railroad Station in 1963, which generated support for the establishment of the New York City Landmarks Preservation Commission in 1965. In the same period, the federal government passed the National Historic Preservation Act of 1966, and the Venice Charter of 1964 established international conservation and restoration guidelines for historic monuments.

In Washington, the local federal response was the establishment of the Joint Committee on Landmarks in 1964, an initiative sponsored by the National Capital Planning Commission and the Commission of Fine Arts. Chaired by architect Francis Lethbridge, the Joint Committee included four architects, a landscape architect, a historian, and two laymen; the members evaluated buildings and structures based on their three-tier classification system and issued a list of 289 properties designated as Landmarks of the National Capital. As a review panel, the Joint Committee functioned as the District's de facto historic preservation review body until these functions were formally assumed by the city under the D.C. Historic Landmarks and Historic District Protection Act of 1978.

The success of the milestone Lafayette Square adaptive reuse project in the early part of the decade redefined what was possible in maintaining historic structures within the modernizing city. Many government buildings—such as the Old Executive Office Building, the Patent Office building, and the Old Post Office, once thought to be white elephants—were being reconsidered for their potential reuse as museums or their value as civic monuments. Of particular concern was the preservation of Federal-era properties—the uncommon remnants of Washington's architecture from the early decades of the nineteenth century— which were often threatened by demolition for redevelopment. In most cases, the commission's focus was on the appropriate integration of modern architecture within a historic setting, whether for individual properties such as the Octagon (Tayloe) House, or for the larger historic fabric of the Old Georgetown historic district.

View of the Old Post Office at 1100 Pennsylvania Avenue in 1967, prior to its renovation. Saving the building was an early focus of the nascent preservation movement in Washington.

TOP LEFT: *Model, American Institute of Architects (*AIA*) headquarters building, Mitchell/Giurgola Architects, 1968. The* CFA *found the proposed design too complicated and feared a massive beam above the garden would overwhelm the adjacent and smaller-scale eighteenth-century Octagon House.*

TOP CENTER: *The Mitchell/ Giurgola scheme was revised in response to the* CFA's *comments, expressing the new building as two wings separated by a vertical notch.*

TOP RIGHT: *Model for the* AIA *headquarters by The Architects Collaborative (*TAC*), 1970. The* CFA *considered this proposal more successful as a background building to the Octagon House and an appropriate preservation strategy.*

ABOVE: *As built in 1974, the* AIA *headquarters by The Architects Collaborative frames the Octagon property with a gently inflected massing.*

A new headquarters building for the American Institute of Architects was one of the first projects submitted for an individual building where a concern for historic property played a decisive role in the commission's deliberations. The competition program required preservation of the Federal-era Octagon House and its garden, a decision with which the CFA agreed. In addition to the Octagon House site, the AIA owned the adjacent historic Lemon Building to its east, on New York Avenue, which had once housed the offices of the CFA.

Romaldo Giurgola of the Philadelphia firm of Mitchell/ Giurgola had won the competition in 1964 with a design that placed the building behind the garden, enclosing the rear of the site on two sides. Despite the massive beam overhanging the corner of the garden, Giurgola claimed the project was sympathetic to the scale and character of the Octagon House. The commission called his design an overscaled and theatrical collection of "current cliches" that threatened to overwhelm the historic building's simplicity.[137] The members advised the AIA to leave the site alone and adapt the Lemon Building for its needs.

Giurgola returned with an entirely different design, comprising two rectangular wings articulated with different fenestration patterns and connected at the inside corner facing the historic house by a glass well or notch, to mediate between the two blocks. The commission members approved the proposed building's location, massing, and height, while expressing reservations among themselves that it was confused and unresolved.[138] Their concerns only grew as Giurgola developed the project further, with Bunshaft eventually declaring: "I think it's a tour de force of a goulash of all kinds of things."[139] The crux of their objection was the notch; calling it illogical, the CFA insisted the feature be removed. Giurgola claimed the architects could not do this "without abdicating our integrity" and withdrew from the project.[140]

In 1969, the AIA hired The Architects Collaborative (TAC), the Cambridge-based firm founded by Walter Gropius, which developed a project for a concrete structure that occupied a footprint similar to the previous proposal but that deferred more to the Octagon with a more sinuous horizontal massing of a seven-story structure along the site's north and east sides. The CFA publicly commended the project as straightforward, but in executive session Bunshaft said he disliked it and John Walker said it was "terrible."[141] Many members objected to the way the board room was handled as a large concrete box project-

TOP: *Row houses on 30th Street, built in 1879, exemplify the practice typical in Georgetown in which many of the original architectural elements of Victorian buildings were removed or covered in favor of Colonial Revival detailing.*

BOTTOM: *The Lauinger Library at Georgetown University was designed by John Carl Warnecke and completed in 1966; the bold tower created a dramatic addition to the existing neo-Gothic campus skyline.*

ing above the entrance, saying it was too aggressive in relation to the Octagon House. Bunshaft even expressed regret for the Giurgola design, which he said at least had more character: "I don't know that this Commission achieved anything except to make it a little quieter and make a pretty good-sized garden."[142] In response to the commission's objections, TAC made several changes in the final building, subduing the board room element and adding diagonal walls on the first floor that were set parallel to the axis of the historic house.[143] The new AIA headquarters was completed in 1974.

OLD GEORGETOWN

Initially, the modern preservation movement arose partly in response to the destruction of historic urban fabric and was focused on architectural form; it also encompassed other motivations to protect place and values—ranging from patriotism to urbanism—and, sometimes, a sentimental understanding of architectural history. Understandably, many early historic districts were created in reaction to palpable changes in the physical environment brought by modernity—widespread demolition, the

imposition of automobile infrastructure, and planar and abstract architecture—that would threaten the district's sense of place.

In Georgetown, the notion of place was associated primarily with the Colonial and Federal-era history of the neighborhood, and consequently the popular understanding was to perpetuate this image—whether it was authentic or the recreation of an imagined past. The overwhelming majority of projects submitted by applicants and approved by the Old Georgetown Board at this time represented Colonial Revival designs characterized by brick veneer, gable roofs, front entrances without stoops or transom windows, doors flanked by pilasters supporting triangular pediments, windows with squat proportions, and brick sills—elements that generally did not exist in Georgetown's Colonial or Federal-era architecture.

Submissions for residential proposals in a contemporary modern idiom receiving positive recommendations by the board represent exceptions to the rule of historicist designs. The challenges associated with modernism were mostly avoided, but explicit opinions about the hundreds of proposals reviewed by the board cannot be known as OGB meetings were not recorded at the time. Change was most apparent on the Potomac waterfront—which emerged at the end of the decade as a prime location for development and included the first adaptive reuse of an industrial building—but typically, the waterfront projects constituted new construction of an unprecedented scale

and mass. Throughout Georgetown, the demolition of historic buildings remained the basis for change, occurring at a regular pace throughout the decade. Inconsistency in design review would emerge as a problem over the years, an unavoidable matter given the great variety of buildings in the historic district and the human dynamics of public meetings.

The first sizeable project representing modern architecture was the library at Georgetown University designed by sitting CFA member John Carl Warnecke in 1966.[144] Because it was an entirely new building, the project was presented to the commission for review after the board made its recommendations. The commission members offered few comments apart from expressing concerns about the siting of the building and the color of the aggregate, and did not discuss the brutalist style or the impact of the stair tower on the picturesque skyline at the western edge of the historic district.

For residential projects, modern design was generally avoided with a few exceptions. One such case began with a demolition application submitted in October 1966 for the three-story, gable-roof, frame residence at 1348 27th Street built circa 1840. In an unusual action, the board forwarded the application to the commission without taking a position on it. Secretary Charles Atherton reported that neither the architect—specifically not named—nor the commission staff had inspected the property, although the architect had submitted an estimate to renovate the building that was "fairly high."[145] After briefly looking at the photographs, the commission members supported demolition without discussion. Despite the cursory review by the architect, staff, and commission, the application was returned to the District government with the following explanation:

There is good evidence that [the residence] dates back to 1840. Normally we would recommend that a building of this sort be restored if at all feasible. However, the condition that this structure is in would impose, we believe, an unnecessary burden on the owners. We therefore, with some reluctance, interpose no objection to razing this building.[146]

The demolition permit was approved by the CFA in November, and in March 1967, architect Hugh Newell Jacobsen submitted plans for a new house on the property; Jacobsen had recently completed the highly acclaimed modern addition to the Lee House at 2813 Q Street, NW, featuring a contemporary mirroring of a Victorian row house. The new proposal, the Trentman Residence, would be the first modern house to be proposed since the Old Georgetown Act had passed. The three-story brick design incorporated a variety of types and sizes of openings; the board directed Jacobsen to simplify the design. The project precipitated the second joint session between the board and the commission; the previous meeting had occurred sixteen years earlier in 1951.

The board members attended the commission's April meeting for direction regarding the role of contemporary design; their comments suggest a range of support.[147] Frank Cole, who had served on the board since early 1964, began the discussion:

Well, we are being confronted more and more by designs which we don't think are bad, scale-wise and detail-wise, but they are not Federal, and. . . the time has come for some guidance from the Commission whether we're going to deviate or not deviate…. Are we to look at these with an open mind or with a closed mind?

Commission chairman Walton, who lived in the neighborhood, responded first:

One of the charms to me of Georgetown is a mixture, through all stages of the nineteenth century. We are not trying to create Williamsburg. But harmony is terribly important, and some delicate balance of allowing deviation from Federal but keeping it harmonious with the neighbors, whatever the neighbors are in a particular block.

He went on to describe recent new construction:

The new buildings in Georgetown, the ones that have rather unimaginatively stuck to semi-Georgian motifs, have given us some of our least attractive buildings…with windows too small…the quality has been awful.

Board member William Haussmann, who had served since late 1963, described these new buildings as "dull mediocrity." Commission member Gordon Bunshaft maintained that the old buildings should be distinguish-

able from the new ones and argued that only scale and materials should be similar:

If you wanted to preserve a great Rembrandt painting, you wouldn't put imitation Rembrandts next to it…. Reproducing is not preserving at all…. This is not new, retaining an old area. This is done all over Europe and in Europe they don't build archaeological projects next to old buildings but they do fuss about materials, scale, and let them be what they are: good design first.

Specifically addressing Jacobsen's drawings for the Trentman Residence, Bunshaft observed that the scale was not correct:

Those three windows are confused. Actually that building should be asymmetrical on the second floor, and there should not be such an abrupt change in it with all those little windows at the top.

Walton similarly emphasized composition and harmony rather than style:

This facade looks slightly chaotic to me. There are three different things on one facade: two arches, three rectangles, and that row of windows up there…. I would do less things. Flatten the arches. It seems to me it would be a quieter facade.

The commission, though less conservative than the board, sought good design rather than modern design for its own sake. Walton asked board member Mario Campioli whether he would prefer that only Federal-style designs be approved. Campioli, who had been on the board for two years, responded "not necessarily Federal, but forms that would…preserve the historic value of Georgetown." Referring to the three stories in Jacobsen's elevation, he said:

I personally find this rather revolting architecture. This is neo-Federal, this is contemporary, that is Richardson[ian], and they're all in one building.

During the discussion, the commission members repeatedly commented that the first floor should have rectangular openings, and the board concurred. Yet the official written recommendation noted that arched openings could be studied; it also recommended a metal roof rather than slate. One month later, approval was given for a revised design that incorporated the rectangular openings. The written record and files do not explain why the Trentman Residence was built with arched openings at the first floor but reveal an ambivalent attitude on the part of the commission and its staff toward modern design in the historic district.

The topics of demolition and the waterfront were also raised during the joint session, which indicated differences of opinions between the board and commission. Board members referred to a Federal-era building on Wisconsin Avenue the demolition of which they had not recommended but had been overruled by the commission. When

Canal Square, designed by
Arthur Cotton Moore in the
late 1960s, included the rehabilitation of a historic warehouse with new construction
arranged around a central
court.

Warnecke mentioned that new construction in the waterfront should reflect contemporary architecture, Campioli
said:

*I think if the intent was to have buildings of contemporary style, obvi-
ously I have nothing against contemporary architecture, I don't want
to convey that picture, but I assume people whose names are attached
more to forms of contemporary architecture would probably be sitting
in this group.*

Like design review for new construction, historic
preservation met with its own set of challenges during this
decade: perhaps the most complicated was an appreciation of historic fabric in the predominantly industrial waterfront. The Old Georgetown Act had stipulated that the
D.C. commissioners, with assistance from the NCPPC and
NPS, conduct a survey of all buildings in Georgetown for
the CFA's use, although Congress had never appropriated
the necessary funding. Responding to community requests, the National Capital Planning Commission undertook a study of the waterfront in 1960 and concluded
that 66 percent of the buildings served industrial uses, 8
percent were occupied residences, and many vacancies existed. The summary report maintained that "the waterfront
has a truly enormous potential for predominantly residential use" but asserted that this prospective was constantly threatened by changes such as a recently proposed
ice skating rink and office buildings.[148]

In 1966, the staff of the Commission of Fine Arts, in co-

ordination with the Historic American Buildings Survey,
established a plan to document Georgetown. The undertaking began with select buildings on M Street and Wisconsin Avenue because of a combination of blight, intense
economic pressures, and the growing number of parking
lots on these commercial streets; the data were published
in 1967. Two books on waterfront buildings were produced
the following year. During this time, the commission staff
also worked with volunteers to survey residential buildings
north of M Street; this information was published in 1969
and 1970.[149] The goal of the documentation was to inform
the decision makers in anticipation of redevelopment proposals. The entire historic district was surveyed for the first
time in 1993 in a project sponsored by the State Historic
Preservation Office of the District of Columbia.[150]

In April 1968, two developers sought a general reaction from the commission regarding an unprecedented
proposal.[151] Their architect, Arthur Cotton Moore, submitted schematic drawings showing a nineteenth-century
warehouse, located at 31st Street and the C&O Canal,
incorporated into a new office and retail complex surrounding a courtyard.[152] The project, named Canal
Square, was the largest development in Georgetown in
seventy years and the first sizeable preservation project
south of M Street. Chairman Walton asked Chloethiel
Smith to speak first due to her familiarity with the waterfront—her office was located a block from the site—and

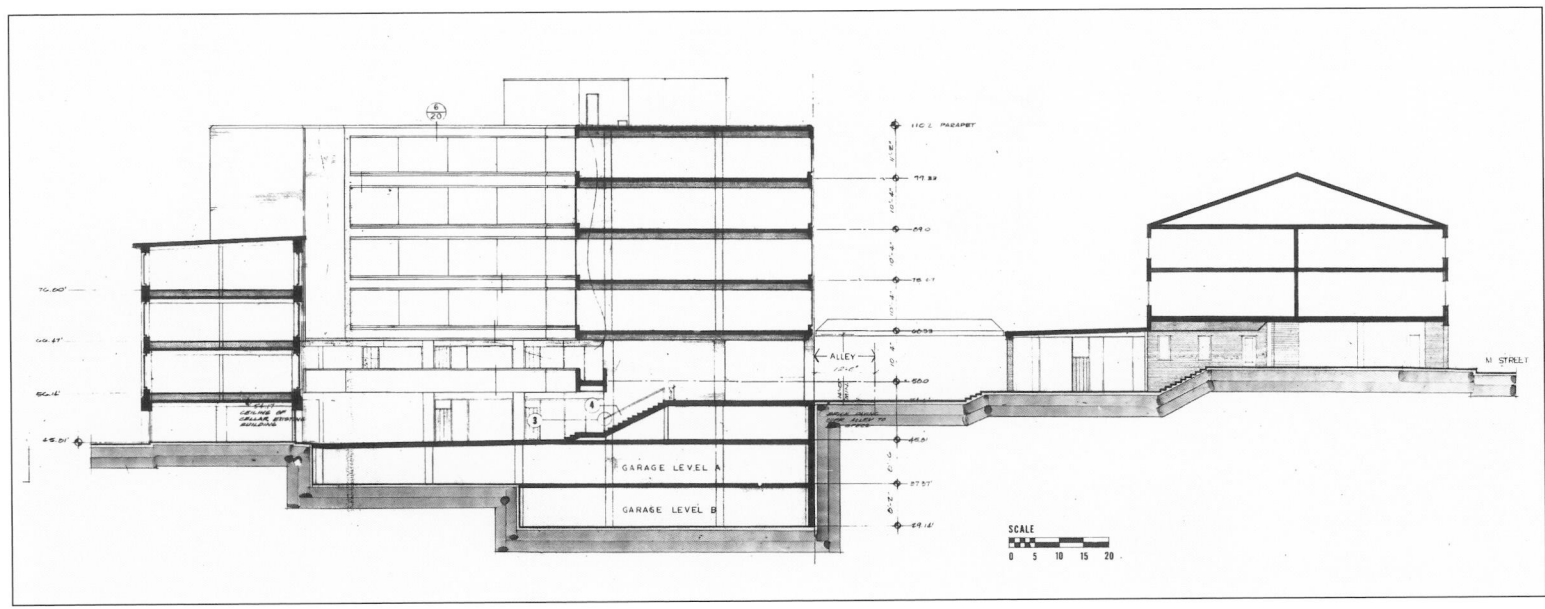

TOP: *Longitudinal section through Canal Square (looking west) illustrates the renovated warehouse (left) and the central courtyard and office building (middle)* *connected across the alley by a canopy to the gabled structure (right) facing M Street.*

ABOVE LEFT AND RIGHT: *The principal achievement of Canal Square was the incorporation of a nineteenth-century warehouse situated along the C&O Canal, restored for new office space,* *within a modern mixed-use development; Canal Square's central court featured horizontal walkways and sculptural elevator towers behind the historic warehouse building.*

ABOVE: *The Georgetown waterfront, 1975, showing the transition from its historic industrial character to commercial redevelopment. In the foreground are structures of the Smoot Sand & Gravel Company; the Dodge Center is visible in the middle distance.*

BELOW: *The Dodge Center, designed by Hartman-Cox Architects as an office complex in 1971, incorporated the Federal-era Dodge warehouses within a ninety-foot-tall modern building sloping away from the Potomac waterfront.*

to specifically address the sixty-foot-tall new construction. Smith noted that the zoning law allowed for this height, characterized the relation between the new and old as successful, and expressed admiration for the historic warehouse. During the proceedings, no comments were made about the proposed demolition of a two-and-a-half-story brick Victorian row house in good condition located on 31st Street, a one-story vernacular brick building on M Street, and various brick structures located at the rear of the lots. The commission members supported the proposal unanimously, and subsequent reviews were carried out by the board. During construction, *Washington Post* architectural critic Wolf von Eckardt wrote an article praising the project but included scathing remarks about the commission:

The Fine Arts Commission rightly insists that highly visible new buildings conform in their architectural style with Georgetown's architectural character, which is about as hard to define as the collective zoological character of all the animals that run, fly, crawl or burrow in Rock Creek Park. Its own past rigidity, combined with illiterate architectural insensitivity to what that character is all about, has resulted in some revolting, phony-Colonial horrors.[153]

Von Eckardt, like many, did not make a distinction between the board and the commission; his criticism aimed to educate the public by raising the issue of Colonial Revival hegemony and reflects an important part of the cultural context.

Canal Square's financial and critical success demonstrated the viability of preserving waterfront buildings and was soon followed by the first large-scale development project south of the C&O Canal.[154] The Maloney Concrete Company had retained Hartman-Cox Architects to design an office building to be located around the three Federal-era warehouses situated at the northwest corner of Wisconsin Avenue and K Street. In September 1971, Secretary Atherton presented to the commission the proposal for the Dodge Center, a ninety-foot-tall, stepped red-brick-clad office building. He did not summarize the board's position but assured the commission members that the proposed design did not exceed the zoning (industrial) limits and that the existing dead end alley could be closed and developed. After a brief discussion about the penthouse, the commission members approved the project. In turn, the Dodge Center would touch off a heated community debate about the existing zoning law and efforts to reduce the ninety-foot height limit. The alley closure—the first of several in the waterfront—began a trend that would have more impact on the waterfront than the height limit in creating megaparcels for large buildings of unprecedented mass to be developed through the combination of adjacent lots.

As industrial uses along the waterfront declined and market pressure increased to develop unoccupied parcels, Chairman Walton advocated the creation of a waterfront park to link West Potomac Park with the Palisades and envisioned the removal of the Whitehurst Freeway. Walton recognized, however, that these political matters involved stakeholders well beyond Georgetown, in particular commuters from Maryland and Virginia.[155] However, it would be three decades before the design of a public park at the waterfront was accepted and implemented.

In contrast to much of Washington, D.C., into the 1970s, Georgetown was a magnet for building development, emerging as one of the only areas of retail growth in the city at that time and the site of numerous redevelopment projects that would transform the historic district between M Street and the river. The riots of 1968 had dampened development generally in many parts of Washington, particularly in the old downtown area lying east of the White House; the growing attraction of the Georgetown historic district to the wealthy and well-connected ensured its position as a focus of investment.

A resident of Georgetown, the young new chairman of the Commission of Fine Arts, J. Carter Brown, would bring an intense personal interest to his work on the CFA, the caseload of which began to focus increasingly on Georgetown in the 1970s. Along with Brown, most of the membership of the commission was new; by 1972, the outspoken modernist advocates from the Walton era were gone. In the coming decades, Brown would preside forcefully over the commission's review of projects in which history—its preservation, its architectural language, and its cultural expression—would be at the forefront.

"Rather Strong Advisory": William Walton's Commission and the Challenge of the FBI Building

¶ ZACHARY M. SCHRAG

Prior to his appointment as chairman of the Commission of Fine Arts, William Walton was close enough to the Kennedys to share their architectural hobby horse. Cartoon by Edward Sorel, 1963.

The Federal Bureau of Investigation (FBI) headquarters, known since 1972 as the J. Edgar Hoover Building, should have been a proud achievement of Washington architecture in the 1960s. It was a federal office building commissioned not long after President John F. Kennedy had called for better federal office buildings. It occupied a prominent spot on Pennsylvania Avenue at the time when the president was also calling for a better Pennsylvania Avenue. It had a big budget: $60 million at the start, $126 million by the end.[1] Its intended occupant was one of the most powerful men in government, FBI director J. Edgar Hoover. And understanding the project's importance, the Commission of Fine Arts (CFA) took almost three years deliberating over the design. As chairman William Walton noted in 1967, "We have been on it longer than almost anything."[2]

Yet the end result of all of this is a building that the *AIA Guide to the Architecture of Washington* calls a "swaggering bully...ungainly, ill-mannered, and seemingly looking for trouble."[3] Critic Benjamin Forgey bemoaned "a national symbol of the cold, the imperious, and the off-putting in federal architecture."[4] J. Edgar Hoover himself is said to have termed it "the greatest monstrosity ever constructed in the history of Washington."[5] Critic Wolf von Eckardt had praised a preliminary design in 1964, but when the building opened in 1975, he derided it as "alien to the spirit of the capital and the architecture of the Avenue...a matter of a needless and heedless quest for novelty for its own sake gone slightly berserk." And, he continued, "I don't even blame the architects.... I blame the Fine Arts Commission which, under the influence of Gordon Bunshaft...tried so hard to make its imprint on Washington and Pennsylvania Avenue that it delivered a painful kick instead."[6]

Even the CFA has had its doubts. In 1986, Charles Atherton, the longtime secretary of the commission, called the building "eerie, uneasy and disturbing, like a surrealistic Italian movie of 1960." He applauded a proposal by commission member Frederick Hart to transform the building's exterior with sculptural panels.[7] (A letter writer to the *Washington Post* upped the ante with a call for "kinetic electronic billboards with computer-generated sound effects [rat-a-tat-tat].")[8]

The question, then, is how did the talented Commission of Fine Arts of the 1960s approve a design so bad that, for the last four decades, it has been universally condemned?

Emphasizing this question may be unfair. As Sister Helen Prejean has said of death row inmates, "We are worth more than the worst act we commit."[9] And von Eckardt was probably not alone when he singled out the FBI building as the greatest mistake of Walton's commission.[10] Yet we learn more from our mistakes than from our successes, and tracing the history of the FBI building can tell us much about where the commission stood half a century after its founding and half a century ago. The story of the FBI building and other federal buildings of the period tells us what the commission had and what it lacked.

A Commission with Clout

The commission's chief asset was that valuable, even indispensible resource for which so many in Washington compete: clout. The commission of the early 1960s could draw from a particularly deep well, the White House. According to his friend and neighbor William Walton, John F. Kennedy "had lived [in Washington] most of his adult life. He knew the streets, the parks, the surrounding countryside."[11] As a senator, Kennedy helped sponsor legislation to preserve historic buildings in Lafayette

Square.[12] That interest continued after his ascent to the presidency. Once, when he was supposed to be taking a nap, Mrs. Kennedy found him in his underwear playing on the floor with a model of Lafayette Square.[13] One of the last requests he made before his departure for Dallas in November 1963 was that a model showing Pennsylvania Avenue be set up in the West Wing for him to study on his return.[14] His personal involvement led *Architectural Forum,* in its January 1963 special issue on Washington, to conclude that Kennedy had "taken more interest in the face of the capital than any President since Jefferson."[15]

Of course, Kennedy could not devote too much of his own time to questions of architecture, but he did lend the prestige of his office to those who would do the actual work of rebuilding Washington. One was assistant secretary of labor Daniel Patrick Moynihan. Witold Rybczynski—who became a CFA member in 2004—rightly credits Moynihan as an important force for architecture within the administration, but there were others as well.[16] In 1961, New York City arts commissioner August Heckscher was appointed as the first special consultant on the arts.[17] He took pride in pointing out that architecture and city planning were as much a part of national culture as the performing arts, and he discussed both topics with President Kennedy.[18] Karel Yasko, assistant commissioner for design and construction of the Public Buildings Service of the General Services Administration, proved himself a proponent of modernism in federal architecture.[19] Another key player was First Lady Jacqueline Kennedy. Famous for redecorating the White House—an act she considered one of historic preservation—she played less public but still important roles in Lafayette Square and, later, Pennsylvania Avenue and the Kennedy Center.[20]

For the history of the Commission

of Fine Arts, two of Kennedy's personal friends stand out. One was William Walton, a journalist, painter, Georgetowner, and, in 1960, Kennedy campaign aide. After the inauguration, he became Kennedy's unofficial advisor on architecture. A second was California architect John Carl Warnecke. He had met Kennedy briefly in the early 1940s, and they reconnected after their mutual friend, Paul Fay, helped Warnecke crash a White House cocktail party.[21] That led to a plum commission for Warnecke: to take over the redevelopment of Lafayette Square, whose remaining Federal-style townhouses were threatened by demolition for new government office buildings. Like Walton, Warnecke was impressed by Kennedy's concern for architecture. "He really loved architecture," Warnecke recalled decades later. "He loved to talk about it. He couldn't conceive that I could know so much about a building that I was in charge of designing."[22]

For a president interested in architecture, a natural area of concern was the CFA, which, by the mid-twentieth century, had gained a certain reputation for stodginess. Kennedy started by appointing Hideo Sasaki of Harvard University to fill a landscape architecture seat. Then in the spring of 1963, the terms of the remaining six members expired almost at once. Kennedy named Walton, whose connections to the first couple and residence in Washington made him the natural choice when the commission members elected him chairman in July.[23] Since Walton's personal connection to the president was well known, this added greatly to the commission's stature.[24] Kennedy also appointed Warnecke as a member. Another appointee was architect Gordon Bunshaft, a partner at Skidmore, Owings & Merrill (SOM), a design firm known for sleekly modern corporate architecture. Bunshaft was slightly less prominent than another candidate, Philip

Since its construction, the FBI building has been condemned as "ill-mannered," "imperious," and "eerie."

Johnson. But Johnson was still tarnished by the Nazi and fascist sympathies he had displayed in 1939 and 1940, making Bunshaft a better political choice.[25] Architectural critic Aline Saarinen was appointed in part to meet Jacqueline Kennedy's wish for a woman to join the commission. Kennedy also appointed sculptor Theodore Roszak and planner Burnham Kelly. Like Sasaki, they tended to defer to the others when discussing federal office buildings. It was very much, then, a Kennedy commission.

Even after Kennedy's death that November, the commission retained the prestige and self-confidence of Camelot. Walton was close to Lady Bird Johnson.[26] And Lyndon Johnson retained Charles Horsky, the White House staffer who had advised Kennedy on D.C. affairs, including architectural matters. Commenting in 1965 on the multiplicity of agencies involved in approving buildings, Walton exclaimed, "I want to make it clear this is the only one with any current legal authority on these designs." When informed that, in fact, his commission had only an advisory role, he was unfazed: "Well, as long as we have the District Commissioners backing us, ours is rather strong advisory."[27]

The CFA members could not have sustained that strength unless they had talent along with connections. As Atherton later explained, "When you have advisory authority only, you've got to be sure it is darn good advice, for one thing, that will carry and will stick. If nobody listens to it, you lose your respect, and you're sunk as an agency." And Kennedy's commission worked hard to give good advice. But there is a fine line between a confident commission and an overconfident commission, and Walton's group often crossed that line. The commission members were assertive—willing to state their positions bluntly and forcefully, rather than deferring to the architects before them.

One striking case concerned the de-signs for underground stations of the Washington Metro. The CFA members ignored architect Harry Weese's wishes for maximum volume and structural expression in favor of their own more abstract concepts of what subway stations should look like in the nation's capital. They insisted that Weese revert to one of his preliminary designs for use in all the stations—a vaulted arch—dramatically reshaping what has become one of Washington's most recognizable works of architecture.[28]

That intervention was extreme, but it does represent the belief of the commission members—particularly Bunshaft and Saarinen—that they best served the nation by speaking freely and flexing whatever powers an advisory commission could muster. Speaking of the U.S. Tax Court in 1965, Bunshaft boasted, "We really laced into [architect Victor] Lundy, and I've talked to several friends of mine about Lundy and they say he needs it." Aline Saarinen concurred. "I was very brutal but I meant every word of it and I'm glad because this is infinitely better."[29]

Strong and Simple

It might have surprised the founders of the CFA to learn that their successors of the 1960s would spend so much of their time talking about office buildings. Public buildings in the District of Columbia were added to the commission's mandate as something of an afterthought. In May 1910, Congress established the commission to advise on statues, fountains, and monuments. It took another five months, until October 1910, for President William Howard Taft to sign an executive order adding public buildings to the charge.[30] In 1916, Congress extended this responsibility by requiring a new Public Buildings Commission to "avail itself of the advice of the Commission of Fine Arts."[31] This led to substantial input by the latter commission on the design of the Federal Triangle.[32]

In the 1960s, office buildings became a particularly prominent concern for two reasons. The first was practical: The federal government needed more space. In 1962, the Ad Hoc Committee on Federal Office Space found that more than 50,000 federal employees in the Washington area worked in crowded, poorly lit, poorly ventilated, obsolete or temporary buildings.[33] (One of the office buildings termed obsolete was the Pension Building, now a museum and office space for nonprofit organizations and federal agencies, including the Commission of Fine Arts. In 1962, there already was talk of turning it into a museum.)[34] Moreover, departments and agencies were scattered among multiple sites, making administration difficult. In an effort to upgrade federal work space in response to this report, the General Services Administration launched an ambitious ten-year plan to build 8.7 million square feet of new office space.

The second reason office buildings became important was cultural. In the 1950s, Washington had become known for second-rate architecture. As Walton lamented,

The less said the better about the buildings of the first postwar decades, the vast ill-planned State Department addition, the cold marble Federal Aviation Building, the tasteless office building next door. No administration will ever point with pride at these exercises in construction without principle.... A retired general in the White House spread a mantle of mediocrity and middle age over the city.[35]

Because the office space committee was co-chaired by his boss, Secretary of Labor Arthur Goldberg, Moynihan saw a chance to raise the standards.[36] He inserted in the office space report the famous "Guiding Principles for Federal Architecture":

The design of Federal office buildings, particularly those to be located in the Nation's Capital, must meet a twofold requirement.

First, it must provide efficient and economical facilities for the use of Government agencies. Second, it must provide visual testimony to the dignity, enterprise, vigor, and stability of the American Government.

The report also urged that "the development of an official style must be avoided."[37]

These requirements were difficult to reconcile, for "visual testimony" is not necessarily efficient or economical. The Washington Monument and the Lincoln Memorial offer visual testimony, but they house no office workers. The temporary buildings still cluttering the Mall were economical, but if they testified to the stability of government, inertia was not the kind of stability the Ad Hoc Committee had in mind. Throughout the 1960s, the Commission of Fine Arts, along with the rest of Washington, struggled to balance function and design.

In some ways, the most important member of the commission in this effort was the ghost of Eero Saarinen, Aline Saarinen's late husband. Several of the CFA members had personal connections to the late architect. Aline Saarinen, Walton, and Bunshaft had served together on an advisory board to help complete the furnishing of Dulles Airport; and Theodore Roszak, another new appointment, had worked with Eero on a chapel at MIT and the U.S. Chancery in London. Warnecke had also considered Eero a role model and a friend.[38]

More importantly, two of Eero's commissions—the Dulles Airport terminal and the U.S. Chancery in London—were widely regarded as exemplars of federal architecture, combining some classical symmetry and formality with modern simplicity. Bunshaft, the most assertive commissioner on matters of architecture, championed such designs by repeating two favorite words: strong and simple. When an applicant told him that a tight budget had forced a simple structural system, Bunshaft remarked, "I think that the structural system is so simple and strong, it's kind of nice there were some economic problems."[39] Solid was another favorite. Conversely, he and Aline Saarinen disparaged more complex designs with the pejoratives *decorative, wallpaper,* and, worst of all, *fussy.*[40]

Warnecke's vision of modernism was more nuanced. Coming from the West Coast, he was influenced by William Wurster and other regional modernists who believed that modern forms could be integrated into geographical and regional contexts. At Stanford, Warnecke designed buildings with precast concrete and modern arches, but also with red tile roofs to match the rest of the Spanish Revival campus. Not only did they respect the past, but they would, he believed, last far longer than orthodox modern flat roofs. By contrast, he disapproved of Bunshaft's Beinecke Library's intrusion in Yale's Gothic courtyard.[41] But both could agree on their admiration for Eero-like designs.

In short, the commission wanted buildings that combined classicism and modernism without being too predictable. When a senator complained that Warnecke's new executive office building in Lafayette Square looked like a "big red barn" and suggested that all federal buildings should have "a Federal style," Walton politely disagreed. He reminded the senator that "the construction costs of something like the Federal

Federal Office Building 5 embodied the strong, simple forms favored by the Commission of Fine Arts, but the commission's wish that the rear block be built without exterior windows raised controversy.

Triangle are monumental, if you do it today." And, he suggested, the buildings of L'Enfant Plaza—south of the Mall in the urban renewal area of Southwest Washington—formed the 1960s equivalent of the Federal Triangle. "I would think that those buildings were rather harmonious, even though they are not of identical styles," he testified. "The materials that have been chosen go together pretty well. They are obviously not all by the same hand, which in a way, I think, you are recommending, almost, that the same hand design all the buildings." The argument was persuasive. "Yes," said the senator. "I think so too."[42]

In quest of this harmony, the commission insisted that architects take account of Washington's existing architecture. In 1965, for example, Victor Lundy submitted a design for the U.S. Tax Court incorporating elements from buildings in hot climates in an effort to shield the judges from Washington's summer sun. After a contentious meeting, the commission rejected the design, accusing Lundy of "a deliberate attempt to strike out into an area of his own personal expression with little reference to the traditions of Washington."[43] The commission was much happier with the next design, which was more formal and more classical. And the result is a widely admired building.

Unfortunately, vision—like clout—can do harm as well as good. For in its quest for firmness and delight, the commission could lose sight of commodity. A striking example concerned Federal Office Building (FOB) 5, known today as the Forrestal Building, the headquarters of the U.S. Department of Energy. As is well known, the Forrestal Building blocks the visual connection between the 10th Street Mall and the Smithsonian Castle. That was not the fault of Walton's Commission of Fine Arts; the previous commission approved the basic scheme in 1962, and Congress authorized the bridge not long after.[44] It may be worth

noting, however, that Bunshaft thought a bridge building with thirty feet of space underneath would be less tunnel-like than two much taller buildings flanking the 10th Street Mall.[45]

A more interesting dispute concerned the rear block of the building. The architect, Nathaniel Curtis of the New Orleans architectural firm Curtis & Davis, wanted to have the exterior walls as opaque as possible, in part to contrast with the front block of the building along Independence Avenue.[46] He was supported in this by Bunshaft and Saarinen. Bunshaft argued on the grounds of aesthetics: "I think that plan makes sense without windows and I think it ought to be without windows and ought to look like a structural wall." (He would later argue along the same lines for his Hirshhorn Museum.) Saarinen extolled "artificial lighting and ventilation," which, she claimed, met the needs of many corporate employees.[47] Making the case for windows was the tenant, the Department of Defense. "We feel our people are entitled to or would be much more happy and work in a better environment if they had natural light coming in," its representative told the commission. Within the commission, Warnecke was inclined to subordinate the "pure design esthetic view" to the concerns of "the people who are going to work there for the next 70 or 80 years."[48] In the end, the two factions compromised, permitting windows on two of the block's four sides.

Along with its clout and its vision, the Commission of Fine Arts was defined by what it didn't have: an overt emphasis on city planning. This was not a formal exclusion, but those appointed to the commission tended to replicate the interests of the McMillan Commission of 1901: architecture, landscape architecture, and sculpture. And the split between architecture and planning was reinforced in 1926, when the National Capital Park Commission became the National Capital Park and Planning

Commission. In 1952, it was renamed the National Capital Planning Commission (NCPC) and given additional powers. From then on, the two commissions would each have some responsibility over federal buildings in Washington, with the CFA responsible for the buildings and the NCPC responsible for the site. As Walton told Congress in 1969, "Our voice should be in the design of the building, theirs in the use of the land."[49]

In practice, that was not an easy division, and by the 1960s the fine arts and planning commissions had formed something of a rivalry. Walton complained that the planning commissioners "often try to perform our functions."[50] Bunshaft agreed, noting of the NCPC, "The Commission is on planning, not on architecture."[51] When architects added windows to the proposed design of FOB 5, partly in response to NCPC concerns, Bunshaft angrily exclaimed, "I don't see what the Planning Commission has to do with the exterior skin."[52] On the other hand, the Commission of Fine Arts had no hesitation in discussing, at some length, issues of planning, as when they debated whether the area north of the Capitol should consist exclusively of federal buildings or include private, commercial buildings.[53]

Nor should there have been this firm division between building and land. Warnecke in particular understood that a well-designed building could fail in the wrong site. "As much as you admire the scale and detail of [the Federal Triangle,]" he later explained, "boy, are those cold potatoes."[54] And if we were to seek the CFA's greatest achievement of this era, it might be the relocation of the Tax Court and the Labor Department—planning decisions. Ideally, then, the CFA members should have collaborated with the planning commissioners. But they lacked respect for what was a very different body. Unlike the "seven well-qualified judges of the fine arts," whose only loyalty was to their own aesthetics, the planning commission included representatives from various federal agencies, making it a much more pragmatic and political body. "They are a bunch of lay people and some of them are political," said Bunshaft. Walton agreed: "The membership is terrible."[55]

The planning commissioners returned the sentiment. When FOB 5 came before it for review, the NCPC tried to make the front portion of the building thinner, to admit more light. When told that the CFA wanted no exterior windows on the rear block, members of the planning commission asked if the Commission of Fine Arts wanted people to work in the dark, and warned that a windowless block would resemble Moscow's Lubyanka Prison.[56] (This was unfair; the Lubyanka has exterior windows.) The planning commissioners got their windows, but months later they were still making jokes about windowless buildings, mocking the building's client, the General Services Administration (GSA), and complaining about the CFA.[57]

Thus, the Commission of Fine Arts combined political clout; a taste for solidity, simplicity, and hints of classicism; and a certain disregard for the National Capital Planning Commission, one that was returned. And the result of this combination was, alas, the FBI building.

The FBI Building

When it came to the FBI building, matters were complicated further by the creation in 1962 of the President's Council on Pennsylvania Avenue, which was given the task of redesigning what was considered the shoddy northern side of the famous street. Officially, the President's Council reported to the National Capital Planning Commission; unofficially, there was some tension between the two groups.[58] So along with its tenant (the FBI), its client (the GSA), and its funder (Congress), the FBI building would have to please three separate com-

missions: planning, fine arts, and Pennsylvania Avenue. Despite various overlapping memberships (including Walton) and staff liaisons, each of them remained somewhat jealous of its turf and suspicious of the others. As architect Carter Manny of C. F. Murphy & Associates complained in 1965, "There are so many bases that have to be touched on this thing, this has been frustrating."[59]

The President's Council on Pennsylvania Avenue tried hard to humanize what it knew would be an imposing building. As early as July 1963, its staff architects were fretting that a 2.2 million-square-foot building would ruin the avenue. But J. Edgar Hoover himself had insisted on remaining across the street from the Justice Department, and he had even more clout than the Commission of Fine Arts.[60] To compensate, the President's Council on Pennsylvania Avenue suggested a "symbolic FBI Building" along Pennsylvania Avenue backed up by a taller, more prosaic part to the north that would house the clerical operations.[61] The commission's chairman, Nathaniel Owings, a founding partner of SOM, also quickly rejected a proposal from architect Stan Gladych to

build a rectangular, Miesian building; he wanted a diagonal along the avenue.[62]

Equally important, the President's Council on Pennsylvania Avenue stressed the importance of circulation. It wanted the FBI building to welcome public circulation from north to south and to serve as a balcony for viewing parades. It also wanted the first floor of the building set back ten feet from the front column line in order to provide a portion of the arcade that was supposed to run the length of the avenue.[63] As Owings put it, "I would like to have it as open through there as we can possibly get."[64]

One problem with this vision is that the building was supposed to house J. Edgar Hoover's FBI, an agency born in part from the terrorist bombings in American cities of the 1910s and 1920s, an agency full of secrets.[65] While the FBI was happy to provide tours, it also wanted some physical barriers against attack. A plinth two or three feet high wasn't enough; the bureau wanted a moat. Openings in railings for public access were only acceptable when lockable gates could be thrown across them.[66]

A bigger problem was the Commission of Fine Arts. As a group, it proved

For the FBI site, the President's Council on Pennsylvania Avenue proposed a taller mass on the north and a lower building aligned with Pennsylvania Avenue

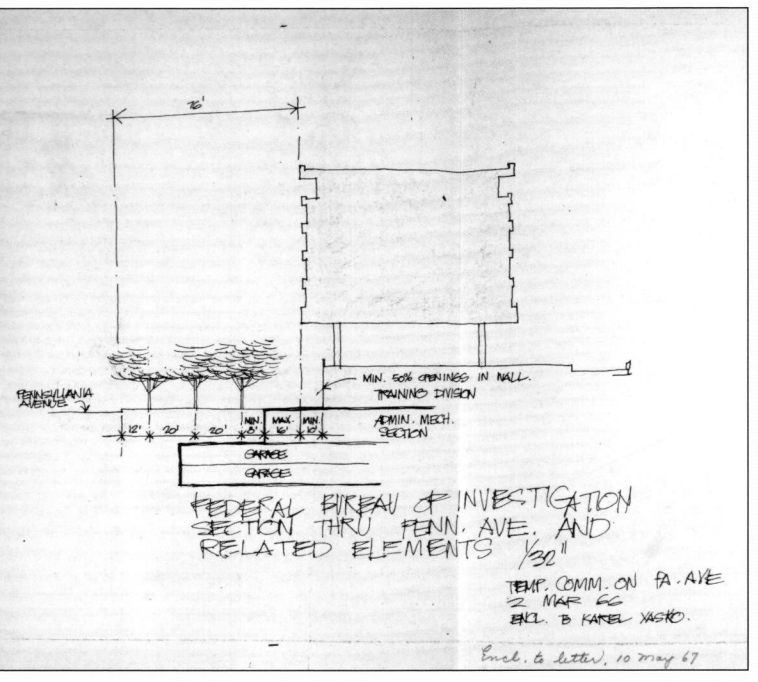

uninterested in Owings's wishes for circulation. It cared about proportions and contrast, not a continuous arcade along the avenue.[67] Bunshaft termed the Pennsylvania Avenue Commission concept "for the birds, when you get right down to it. When you have all this walk," he asked, "what [sic] the hell do you need loggia in here?"[68]

Yes, the commission members cared about Pennsylvania Avenue, at one point objecting to what they called a "particularly oppressive" treatment of the base.[69] But in the end, they came down firmly on the side of solidity rather than openness for the Pennsylvania Avenue face of the building.[70] "The base of the main terrace adjoining Pennsylvania Avenue should be treated as a solid mass with only one major penetration for the entranceway," they resolved. "To incorporate glassed-in store areas or exhibition spaces along the sidewalk would completely deny the structural purpose of the base and as a result give a superficial character to the design."[71] Their only dispute was about who would have to break the news to Owings.

The commission's dismissal of the planners' hopes for a continuous arcade

raises the question of whether the commission of the 1960s embodied planning concerns as much as Daniel Burnham might have wished. It lacked architects who were as interested in planning as Nathanial Owings, or Harry Weese, or Chloethiel Woodard Smith, who was appointed to the commission in July 1967, after the most important decisions about the FBI building had been made. While Bunshaft and Saarinen talked about avenues and looked at models showing broad sections of the city, it is not clear they had a good feeling for Washington and for the people who moved through it. Yet thanks to the Kennedy clout, they won the day.

What were later considered the building's flaws could be read—were read—as virtues. One of the chief criticisms of the FBI building is its solidity. In 2009, for example, architectural columnist Roger Lewis complained of "the massive building's hard-edged, fortress-like image" and "its opacity at street level." He claimed that "aesthetic concerns were voiced but ignored."[72] But the thing to remember is that for the Commission of Fine Arts of the 1960s—and for Bunshaft in particular—opacity

was an aesthetic concern and a positive good. Reviewing the FBI proposals, Bunshaft repeated his basic vocabulary. "Why does it wiggle around each lump?" he demanded of one detail. "Why does this wall have to go in like that?" And, in a line he could have used for just about any project he reviewed: "Why can't it just be a strong, simple thing?"[73]

From the beginning, the commission members liked the vast forms. The first presentation in October 1964 ended with Chairman Walton telling the designers that "we are pleased by the approach and very excited by it, and all those words we tell you when we're happy."[74] By late 1965, Bunshaft remarked of the FBI building that "it's marvelous and it shows how wonderful it is if we can participate in the various rough studies."[75] Rather than reconsideration, he offered only minor changes. "I think the proportions of all this sort of thing [indicating on model] are wonderful," he remarked. "I don't like that [indicating], but I think this is kind of clumsy for this [indicating]. This ought to be bigger, and this ought to be smaller [indicating]."[76] Indeed, his vision was so close to that of the building's architects,

Carter Manny and Stan Gladych, that they considered Bunshaft their champion against Owings.[77]

The fact that it was a building for the FBI only encouraged Bunshaft to expound on the virtues of solidity. "The general principle around here could be solid as a sense of security," he argued.[78] "I think personally it would be wonderful if FBI looked kind of closed in."[79] And, "You'll be aware it's FBI, not the Department of Agriculture."[80] When the architects proposed the moat, Bunshaft helpfully suggested adding snakes.[81]

When the design came before the National Capital Planning Commission in September 1967, an FBI spokesman muddied the waters by claiming that the bureau objected to the arcades on the grounds that "there would be muggings. The undesirables would congregate there."[82] Atherton had to assure a senator that whatever the FBI thought, the decision had been made "purely on aesthetic grounds."[83] Indeed, if a critic like Lewis had told Bunshaft that the building looked "hard-edged," he would likely have regarded it as a compliment. For all its monstrosity, the FBI building does express some of the aesthetic values of the Walton commission.

Conclusion

Soon after its approval of the building, the Commission of Fine Arts began expressing doubts. By 1969, Walton was telling Congress, "We are happy with it as far as the design goes, but we are all scared of the size of it. It is a blockbuster. And the symbolism of putting this size building for the FBI right in the heart of the city is terrible."[84] Indeed, it is not a beautiful building. Nor, however, is it a mediocre building. As Ada Louis Huxtable wrote in 1972, "It will look like a modern dinosaur. Washington is the great architectural boneyard. But it could be a lot worse. It could have looked like the Rayburn Building."[85] Instead, we

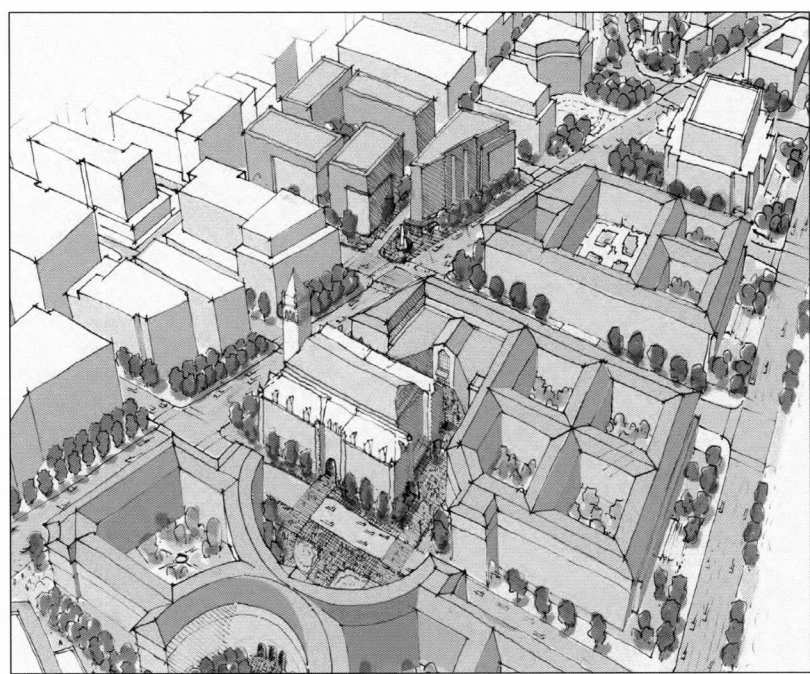

In 2009, the Commission of Fine Arts joined with the National Capital Planning Commission in recommending the demolition of the FBI building and redevelopment of the site with institutional and commercial usage.

have something that is strong, solid, intimidating, offensive, and eerie, but not boring or mediocre. Thus, while the FBI building lacks the grace of Marcel Breuer's buildings for the Departments of Housing and Urban Development and Health, Education, and Welfare, or Victor Lundy's Tax Court, it shares some of their spirit of simplicity, solidity, and distinctiveness. Faced with a difficult, perhaps impossible, program, its designers did create something impressive. That was thanks, in part, to the assertive Commission of Fine Arts of the 1960s.

And that commission left us not only the building, but also a guide to appreciating that building for what it is— its flaws and its virtues. In the project files and transcripts of the commission, we can find a vision for federal architecture. We may disagree with that vision, but we can still learn from it. Half a century later, there's even something charming about being harangued by Gordon Bunshaft.

Ultimately, the commission of the 1960s consisted of an extremely talented set of people who did not always fit easily into the constraints of the commission's structure and who struggled to

reconcile the grandeur of their vision with the limits of their power. While sometimes helpful, they were too often perceived by designers and by other government bodies as an obstacle rather than a partner in the design process.

The Commission of Fine Arts of the early twenty-first century has a different approach. In 2009, rather than maintaining the rivalry with the National Capital Planning Commission, it joined that commission to produce the *Monumental Core Framework Plan*. In their boldest proposal, the two commissions took a fresh look at the FBI building and decided that the best thing to do would be to demolish it and replace it with several smaller buildings north of a reestablished D Street, with a museum between D Street and Pennsylvania Avenue.[86] Thus in 2010, as in the 1960s, the FBI building tells something about the Commission of Fine Arts. Its collaboration with the NCPC suggests that it has a better sense of its place in Washington as both a city and a power structure. If so, its lasting monument may someday be the absence of the FBI building.

CHAPTER VI

The Past Is Present

J. CARTER BROWN AND THE POSTMODERN ERA, 1971–2002

By the early 1970s, more than two decades of postwar planning policies, development practices, and modernist design had transformed the physical form of American cities, often engendering disaffection with the impact of highway construction and urban renewal efforts. Washington and other cities were further damaged by the devastating riots of the late 1960s, and this era of social upheaval was soon followed by other political events—the denouement of the war in Vietnam, the Watergate scandal, and the oil embargo fuel crisis—that left the nation searching for values and reassessing its past on the eve of its bicentennial. As the fundamental belief in modernism's capacity to address social problems was being challenged, the destruction of urban fabric, historic buildings, and traditional neighborhoods instead contributed to a renewed interest among planners, design professionals, and the public in the urban context and architectural forms of the past. Concepts of historicity were increasingly applied to architecture and urban design, and the period of the late twentieth century was marked by the ascendance of historic preservation and the influence of postmodernism in the design of the built environment.

Washington, D.C., was substantially influenced by these trends. With the bicentennial of U.S. independence in 1976 approaching, a renewed and widespread interest in American history and its architectural record emerged; the National Mall was essentially cleared of its decades-old clutter of temporary buildings as part of a conscious plan to beautify the capital city. This set the stage for entirely new subjects of national commemoration and display: narrowly focused cultural institutions and war memorials. In contrast to the preceding two decades, the years from the early 1970s through the rest of the twentieth century saw relatively few new federal office buildings constructed in Washington. Instead, development in the city's core was focused on the rising tide of private redevelopment along Pennsylvania Avenue, in areas of Shipstead-Luce review, and in the historic district of Georgetown—and these projects dominated the Commission of Fine Arts' agenda for decades, requiring the balancing of historic preservation with the demands for change.

From the 1980s through the end of the century, the CFA also found itself deeply involved in the redefinition of commemorative language on the Mall, as the demand for new commemorative and cultural institutions—primarily war memorials and museums—grew significantly. As a new typology of commemoration for national war memorials emerged, one often focused on the subjective experience of individuals rather than a distillation of collective ideals.

FACING PAGE: *Dedicated in 1982, the starkly modern Vietnam Veterans Memorial, with its wall of inscribed names of the fallen, introduced a new typology into the design of memorials and a new theme of explicit commemoration of wars on the National Mall.*

*Portrait of J. Carter Brown by
Nelson Shanks, 1998. During
his long tenure as chairman
of the Commission of Fine
Arts, J. Carter Brown exerted
unparalleled influence on the
design of the nation's capital.*

The language of remembrance evolved, reflecting the general changes in stylistic expression taking place during these decades: abstract forms gave way to more traditional and representational elements, but both emphasized expansive use of landscape. However, as the symbolism employed referenced more and more traditional elements, the meaning of heroic language seemed to become less clear.

As part of the larger trend of rethinking the relationship to the past, the role of historic preservation in assessing development projects, both public and private, became an increasingly central aspect of the design review process. Concurrent with this was a change in stylistic expression: the certainties of modernism—its rejection of history and emphasis on simple forms often expressed in large and highly resolved buildings—gave way to postmodernism, which derived inspiration from past architectural styles and urban forms and combined them in new ways. While the CFA would, at times, find the more overt historicist appliqué of the style difficult to accept, the commission's emphasis on context and architecture as part of an urban composition would be compatible with the movement's underlying principles and its evolving emphasis on architectural complexity.

The CFA, during the last three decades of the twentieth century, was defined by the leadership of J. Carter Brown. Throughout his long tenure, Brown's influence as chairman rivaled that of Charles Moore and the other early CFA members in shaping its decisions and the visual and physical composition of the capital city. As Richard Guy Wilson discusses at length in his essay, Brown's personality and talents were multifaceted. The child of wealth and privilege, educated in both business and the fine arts, politically astute, and well connected, he had a seemingly innate understanding for marketing and promotion. He was also keenly interested in architecture and urban design, in historic preservation, and in the integrity of Washington as an urban place and a symbol of the nation. Yet as CFA chairman, he would on occasion guide decisions that, to some people, seemed to contradict these values.

J. Carter Brown was serving as director of the National Gallery of Art—a position he held from 1969 to 1992—when he was appointed to the Commission of Fine Arts by President Richard Nixon on September 22, 1971; he was elected chairman by his fellow members at the commission's meeting on November 17, 1971. Brown chaired the commission under seven presidents, and his tenure spanned the service of thirty-five commission members.

He remained commission chairman until his resignation in May 2002 due to ill health, dying less than a month later at the age of sixty-seven.

Of the six commission members who elected Brown chairman at that November meeting, three were noted modernist architects and fellows of the American Institute of Architects—Gordon Bunshaft, Chloethiel Woodard Smith, and Kevin Roche—and had served on the commission for several years or more. Bunshaft was known among his peers for speaking his mind and, of the group, had served on the commission the longest. Chloethiel Woodard Smith, only the third woman to serve on the commission after Emily Muir and Aline Saarinen, was a prominent Washington architect and planner well known for her work in the redevelopment area of Southwest. Of these projects, Smith's Capitol Park (1959–63), a row house and apartment tower development, and Harbour Square (1963–66), an apartment tower, gained renown for sensitive design and integration within modernist landscape settings designed by Dan Kiley. Kevin Roche, along with his future architectural partner, John Dinkeloo, had worked in Eero Saarinen's office for more than fifteen years, completing such projects as the St. Louis Arch and Dulles International Airport after Saarinen died in 1961. The two founded their own firm in 1966 and earned acclaim in their own right for the design of buildings such as the Ford Foundation (1968) and the Robert Lehman Wing of the Metropolitan Museum (1975), both in New York City. Roche, like Bunshaft, was later awarded the Pritzker Architecture Prize in the 1980s.

Along with Brown, three other commission members—Nicolas Arroyo (CFA 1971–76), Edward Durell Stone Jr. (CFA 1971–85), and Jane Dart—were appointed in 1971. Only Nicolas Arroyo was an architect. Arroyo had practiced in his native Cuba and served as its ambassador to the United States from 1957 until the Communist revolution in 1959. He relocated his practice to the Washington area and also pursued business interests in South America. Edward Durell Stone Jr., son of architect Edward Durell Stone, designer of the Kennedy Center, was a Harvard-educated landscape architect who succeeded Hideo Sasaki on the commission. Stone's work included several projects for The Walt Disney Company, golf courses, corporate campuses, and, locally, Lady Bird Johnson Park.

The appointment of Jane Dart—a museum trustee and former movie actor—indicated a new trend in the members' professional credentials that would dominate the commission by the mid-1980s; in fact, from 1985 to 1989, there were no architects on the commission. Brown's leadership and reputation in matters of taste would come to predominate in those years. In balancing his responsibilities at the National Gallery and the commission, Brown worked closely with Secretary Charles Atherton and an increasingly more professionalized staff of registered architects, architectural historians, and historians.

Thanks to the close ties established by William Walton with the White House, the commission's offices had moved from the massive Department of the Interior building at 18th and C Streets, NW, to a renovated row house at 708 Jackson Place, facing Lafayette Square, in August 1971, which the commission under David Finley had helped to save. New protocols for transparency and public involvement—the result of a series of new laws enacted in the early 1970s—also led the commission to a more open meeting process, transforming it from an insular closed-door culture toward a more modern standard of openness in government.

In 1971, the Commission of Fine Arts faced a changed and changing city. Just three years after extensive riots had erupted and burned much of the city's commercial center following the assassination of the Reverend Dr. Martin Luther King Jr., Washington seemed awash in plans for revival. The Redevelopment Land Agency, the city authority responsible for the demolition and rebuilding of Southwest Washington, was moving ahead with plans to take urban renewal into the city's old downtown, close to the monumental core. A new congressionally mandated

CFA members in the commission's office at 708 Jackson Place, NW, 1975. Left to right: (standing) Edward Durell Stone Jr., Kevin Roche, Nicolas Arroyo, George A. Weymouth; (seated) Chloethiel Woodard Smith, J. Carter Brown, and Jane Dart.

organization, the Pennsylvania Avenue Development Corporation, would soon be created to encourage private development along the city's main ceremonial street. The region's new rail transit system was under construction and fueling development pressure around the planned downtown stations. And city leaders expected the nation's upcoming bicentennial to prompt long-term reinvestment across the city, from the Georgetown waterfront to new entertainment and tourist-oriented venues downtown, intended to draw visitors away from the Mall and into the rest of the city.[1]

In fact, the economic revival of Washington was neither immediate nor tied to a specific event, but evolved over decades. Private reinvestment in the city during these years was influenced by federal and local development incentives ranging from land-use policies and zoning regulations to tax incentives and historic preservation laws.[2] Attitudes about the value of cities also changed in general, from the tear-it-down-to-make-it-better modernist mindset to an appreciation of the existing physical and social structures as popularized by writers such as Jane Jacobs.[3] Adaptive reuse—a new concept for urban rebuilding when used at Lafayette Square in the 1960s—was, by the end of the century, an accepted approach to both preservation and redevelopment in Washington and elsewhere in the country.

While not a planning agency and by law limited for the most part to an advisory role, the CFA exerted its influence to guide the outcome of policy, as well as design, in order to protect the visual and historic integrity of the national capital. Toward that end, CFA Chairman Brown frequently turned to and interpreted certain themes—the significance of context, the evaluation of historic merit, the importance of urban design, and the benefits of active public uses—in addition to aesthetics. These themes surfaced repeatedly in the commission's recommendations during his tenure, reflecting the dominance of his point of view in its deliberations.

Protecting the Scale and Context of the Capital City

While Washington was poised for change, Brown and his CFA colleagues remained as committed as earlier members to preserving the capital city's unique scale, a critical component of its urban design and image. On the agenda at the commission's November 17 meeting in 1971 was a proposal by the District of Columbia's Zoning Commission to increase allowable building height in downtown. The CFA's discussion that day underscored its commitment to preserving the capital's height limit.

The Building Height Limitation Act, first passed by Congress in 1899 and amended in 1910, limited the height of buildings in the city based on a formula related to street width plus twenty feet.[4] The resulting Washington skyline was distinctively low in scale without the skyscrapers common in other large cities. Increasing allowable height in the city was occasionally revisited, however, and Congress amended the act seven times between 1910 and 1945, primarily to allow exemptions for specific buildings such as St. Matthew's Cathedral at Rhode Island and Connecticut Avenues.[5] The issue arose anew in the late 1960s as efforts moved forward to redevelop the downtown, concurrent with Metro subway construction in central Washington and the RLA's plans in Metro Center, the area of F and G Streets between 7th and 12th Streets, NW.[6]

The city undertook a thirty-month study to review the full impact of the proposed changes.[7] The outcome was a proposal by the zoning commission to increase the allowable height from roughly thirteen stories to twenty-five stories in the Metro Center area. CFA members responded to this news at the November 17 meeting with concern. Gordon Bunshaft, among the most vocal against the option, argued strongly for the commission to go on record against the idea, noting: "If this isn't a horizontal city, I will eat my shirt. And it ought to stay that way. That is the best thing about Washington."[8]

Brown shared with his fellow members his talking points for an upcoming city-sponsored forum on the topic that reflected his personal view of the city:

Washington…is unique. It is the only Federal city. It is the capital. It was planned in the Eighteenth Century. It has green open space, wide streets, trees, and buildings symbolic of our national life and purpose. One of its greatest glories, however, is that a building height limitation has prevented it from becoming an American cliché. I am deeply committed to the economic health of the Federal City. Part of that is based on the unique appeal it has for people to visit here and to move here. I believe that appeal, as well as the whole leadership function of this city visually, would be severely compromised if the height limitation on its buildings were ever abandoned.[9]

While Brown's view considered economic realities, it was largely consistent with those held by earlier commission members regarding Washington's unique urban design.[10]

The CFA was joined by the National Capital Planning Commission in opposing the zoning commission proposal; but by February 1972, despite the efforts of the CFA and other agencies, the city prepared legislation for Congress to increase the building height in certain areas of the city up to 250 feet.[11] The issue remained under study in Congress, however; J. Carter Brown and Charles Atherton were among the noted architects, urbanists, planners,

scholars, and federal and local officials interviewed by the staff of the House Committee on the District of Columbia.[12] The staff's final report, produced in 1976, emphasized that those interviewed supported keeping the building height limitation intact to preserve the city's "unique human scale quality."[13] The Building Height Limitation Act was not amended.

Protecting the visual context of the National Mall from the impact of large-scale development across the Potomac River in Arlington County, Virginia, proved more problematic. In the late 1970s, road improvements and a new Metro station encouraged the rapid redevelopment of the Rosslyn section of Arlington County from an area of used car lots and low-scale industrial uses into a residential and office center. Developers saw the profit potential of high-rise development—with valuable views of the Mall and monuments—and pushed the Arlington County Planning Commission and Board of Supervisors to permit development more than double the allowable height of 125 feet under the existing county zoning code.

CFA members were acutely aware that this development had the potential to significantly affect the views from and the setting of the Mall. They also knew that they did not have jurisdiction in this area of Arlington County but nevertheless pursued actions to protect the monumental core. The commission participated in the rezoning process by delegating Charles Atherton to represent it at a series of public meetings held by the Arlington County

Planning Commission in the summer of 1978. Atherton explained the impending damage to the viewshed of the Mall by the proposed development:

The current limit to the building height was arrived at a number of years ago to specifically protect the natural skyline west of Washington's monumental central axis. The tree-lined ridge of Arlington has provided for many years a beautiful setting for the views of our great national memorials. Even today… the vista is still virtually intact…. The added height of the building you are considering today will further mar the skyline—and for the first time a building will be in view immediately next to the Washington Monument.[14]

Despite Atherton's remarks, the building was approved.

Atherton soon learned that more large buildings were being planned and, at the CFA meeting on August 22, noted: "All these years we have been holding the height line here in the District—and there has always been a tacit agreement amongst the surrounding counties to respect the general skyline around Washington. This [increased height] is just blossoming over there."[15] The commission members directed Atherton to check into the options they might have to draw attention to the situation.

At the October 24, 1978, CFA meeting, Atherton reported on the staff's analysis of development projects proposed or under way in Rosslyn and the preparation for an upcoming presentation before the Arlington County Board of Supervisors. The CFA was now joined by the National Park Service and the National Capital Planning Commission in objecting to the development, and all three

View of Rosslyn, Virginia, across the Potomac River in 2008 showing high-rise development visible from the National Mall, a significant change from the historically green western backdrop to the monumental core.

agencies would be at the presentation to outline their concerns. The CFA members also strategized about enlisting other organizations such as the AIA and the National Trust for Historic Preservation in the fray. Brown speculated that the GSA, as a prime tenant for any new office space, might be useful on their side: "Wouldn't it help to get GSA interested in the problem? Perhaps I could call [GSA administrator] Jay Solomon and find out and see what they might do. Just at present, a meeting might have some effect. Then I think publicity is important. And I think we ought to alert the papers and the TV to be there [at the upcoming presentation]."[16] Brown also wondered if, as elected officials, the county supervisors might be more responsive with greater media attention, and he directed Atherton to find out if any were coming up for re-election the following month.[17]

The efforts of the CFA and other agencies proved insufficient to persuade the county to limit development height, however, and in December 1978, Secretary of the Interior Cecil Andrus turned to legal action, suing Arlington County over the height of five projects, one of which was nearing completion.[18] The federal government claimed the buildings created a nuisance and would harm the "visual integrity of our nation's capital."[19] J. Carter Brown testified at the January 1979 trial, calling the buildings "a visual intrusion akin to an act of urban vandalism."[20] Although U.S. District Court Judge Oren R. Lewis (Eastern District of Virginia) found the federal government had standing to sue in the case, he ruled against its attempt to cap building height in Rosslyn at twenty stories, stating in his February 20, 1979, decision: "Height alone is not enough…and offense to the esthetic senses is not sufficient to constitute a public nuisance."[21] High-rise towers in Rosslyn now serve as a backdrop to the National Mall.

Guiding the Revival of the Nation's "Main Street"

By the early 1970s, the redevelopment of Pennsylvania Avenue was moving toward implementation—the result of ten years of planning and support from both the federal and local governments. In October 1972, Congress created the Pennsylvania Avenue Development Corporation, a temporary federal agency empowered to comprehensively plan, enable, and regulate public and private redevelopment on Pennsylvania Avenue from the Capitol to the White House; it would remain in operation for twenty-four years. Under the leadership of J. Carter Brown, the CFA worked with the PADC and other agencies to guide

change along the avenue while protecting and enhancing its ceremonial importance to the nation.

In addition to a staff of design and real estate professionals in charge of day-to-day operations, the PADC was governed by a fifteen-member board of directors that included several cabinet secretaries, private citizens, the GSA administrator, and the District's mayor.[22] Eight nonvoting members served as a design advisory panel to the board, a group that included the leadership of several agencies responsible for reviewing the PADC's plans.[23] J. Carter Brown held two of the advisory seats as chairman of the CFA and as director of the National Gallery of Art.

Brown's advice carried considerable weight in the PADC's design deliberations; his input was actively sought for design insight and to avoid delay in the CFA's review process.[24] His influence also derived from the fact that the PADC board viewed him as an ally, especially in obtaining funding from Congress.[25] Brown's influence was tempered, however, by Nathaniel Owings, the PADC board's vice chairman and chairman of the design advisory panel. Owings, a founding partner of Skidmore, Owings & Merrill, was an influential man in his own right, having chaired both the Council on Pennsylvania Avenue and the Pennsylvania Avenue Commission in the 1960s.

A PLAN FOR PENNSYLVANIA AVENUE

The PADC released its comprehensive plan for review in October 1974, following a year of development that included outreach to the various reviewing agencies. The plan incorporated land use, financial analysis, circulation, public improvements, building preservation, and urban design guidelines for the multiple parcels identified. While the new plan avoided the massive destruction of the 1960s concepts, it still showed Pennsylvania Avenue closed between 14th and 15th Streets, with a scaled-down version of the grandiose plaza and central fountain from the 1964 plan's National Square. The long-delayed memorial to World War I's General John Pershing, designed by Wallace K. Harrison and on hold since the late 1950s in deference to the developing 1960s plans, was accommodated in that public space. Additional public space was carved from roadways between 13th and 14th Streets to create a Western Plaza, an open square evident in both the L'Enfant and Ellicott Plans, but in the PADC plan still crossed by roadways and functioning largely as a series of traffic islands despite designations as parks for statues of General Casimir Pulaski and Alexander Shepherd.

While not empowered to make direct recommendations regarding the plan, the CFA was asked to provide an assessment by the city's mayor and the secretary of the interior.[26] Couching its response in terms of the aesthetic impact, the CFA commended the plan elements that strengthened the avenue's visual continuity, such as the fifty-foot setback and a new facade line, as well as the retention of old buildings along the avenue, including the Willard and Washington Hotels, the Old Post Office, and the Evening Star building. It also favored the introduction of housing at Market Square, but not the closing of Pennsylvania Avenue between 14th and 15th Streets, which the commission said "would provide no visual or movement amenities."[27] By 1975, having survived the review process with these major elements intact, the PADC's plan was approved by Congress.

The treatment of the western end of the avenue and the proposed design of the Pershing Memorial there triggered the CFA's eventual challenge to the PADC plan. Certain elements of the memorial's concept—a water feature, statue of the World War I general, and walls—had been approved by the CFA in 1959.[28] Revised designs for the project—now coordinated with and approved by the PADC—were presented at the March and June 1974 CFA meetings at which the commission grew increasingly concerned with the memorial's design direction, in particular the scale of the walls in relation to the avenue. At the March 1974 meeting, members Chloethiel Woodard Smith, Jane Dart, and Edward Stone Jr. also urged that the memorial components become elements of a larger park, with Brown concurring: "I think the park is the modern way to solve a memorial."[29] By July 1975, however, the concept had grown less park-like, and the commission recommended that the entire site become less formal.[30] In effect, the memorial's design was again on hold until the PADC's vision for that end of the avenue was revised.

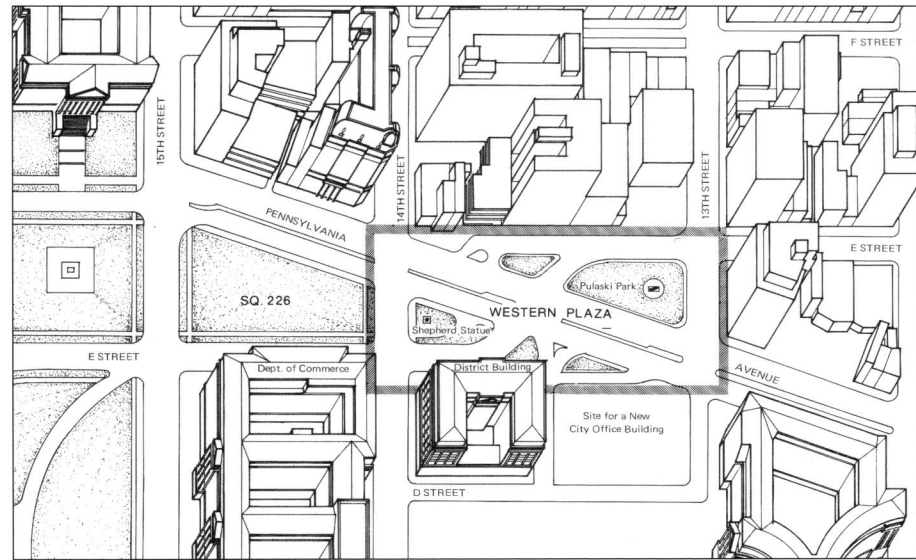

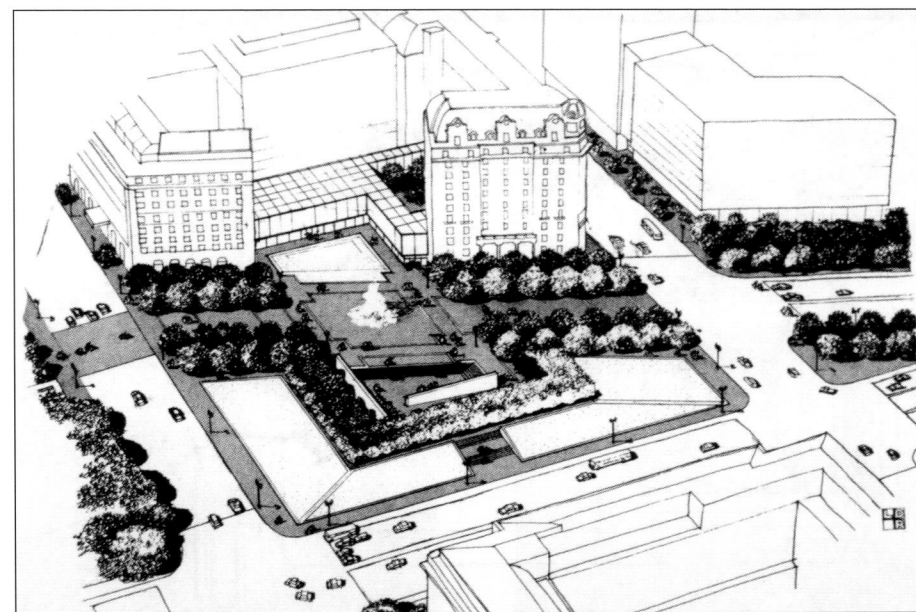

TOP: The 1974 Pennsylvania Avenue plan by the PADC proposed a "Western Plaza" between 13th and 14th Streets composed of separate parcels crossed by roadways in front of the District Building.

CENTER: Like the 1960s redevelopment plans, the 1974 PADC plan closed Pennsylvania Avenue between 14th and 15th Streets to create a plaza, but preserved the historic buildings along the north side of the avenue. A memorial to General John Pershing was located in the southern part of the plaza.

BOTTOM: In the spring of 1974, CFA members reviewed the revised Pershing Memorial concept by Wallace K. Harrison, which they found out of scale with Pennsylvania Avenue.

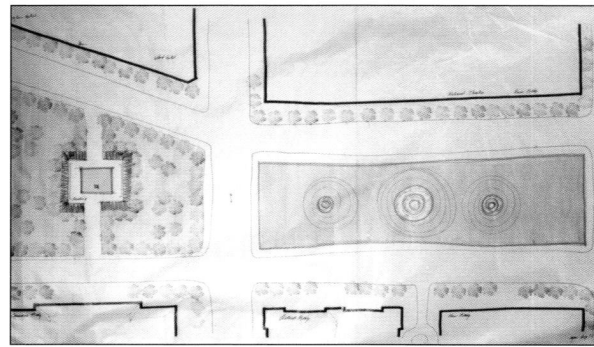

The issues arising out of the Pershing Memorial design prompted the CFA staff to undertake a detailed historical and design analysis of the area during the spring and summer of 1975. At a briefing for the commission prior to its September meeting, Charles Atherton presented the staff's findings and recommendations, noting that "it was the feeling here that maybe the problem of Pennsylvania Avenue is that a lot of attention was being focused on the wrong block, that somehow this area [13th to 14th Streets] was being considered as an afterthought."[31]

The staff proposed creating a true urban square—called Washington Plaza in their study—in the axis of Pennsylvania Avenue between 13th and 14th Streets, instead of land fragments crossed by roadways.[32] Rather than closing Pennsylvania Avenue, traffic on it and E Street would flow around the new plaza. Square 226, the parcel of land between 14th and 15th Streets, would remain intact and could be developed or used for the Pershing Memorial. The scheme retained the block's existing building setbacks, preserving the historic National Theater and Munsey Trust building. The commission cited the L'Enfant, Ellicott, and McMillan Plans as historic precedents—noting Rawlins Park at 18th and E Streets, NW, as an analogous prototype—all of which showed "an architecturally framed space" in this area of Pennsylvania Avenue.[33]

The commission was on record opposing the closure of Pennsylvania Avenue in the PADC plan, although J. Carter Brown had made more recent statements suggesting that he, personally, was not opposed to making it a pedestrian street.[34] Despite Brown's sentiments, the commission unanimously approved the staff's further exploration of its concept but noted that the CFA "would furnish no design and that the Pennsylvania Avenue Development Corporation would be given the opportunity for introducing a definitive design."[35]

The CFA staff followed this directive. By the October CFA meeting, Atherton and the CFA's assistant secretary, Donald Myer, reported that they, along with J. Carter Brown, had met informally with PADC executive director John Woodbridge, whose response was tepid at best.[36] Atherton and Myer had also met informally with staff from the NCPC, the District's Office of Planning, and the Department of the Interior, who were generally positive about the idea and were soon to meet with the District's Department of Transportation. Given the serious traffic issues at the western end of Pennsylvania Avenue, Brown emphasized that vetting the scheme with the transportation department was critical if the PADC was to take the CFA's suggestion seriously. The CFA members talked at length about how to officially reopen study of the PADC's plan and decided to pursue the discussion at a PADC board meeting where all the agencies would be present.[37]

Following through on that decision was tabled, however, until after the CFA meeting of November 1975, when the PADC tried to address the CFA's issues with new concept studies but with the avenue still closed. For his part, Woodbridge wanted to avoid reopening the congressionally approved plan.[38] At the CFA meeting, he tried to focus the discussion away from the closed avenue and back to the traffic solution of E Street crossing between 13th and

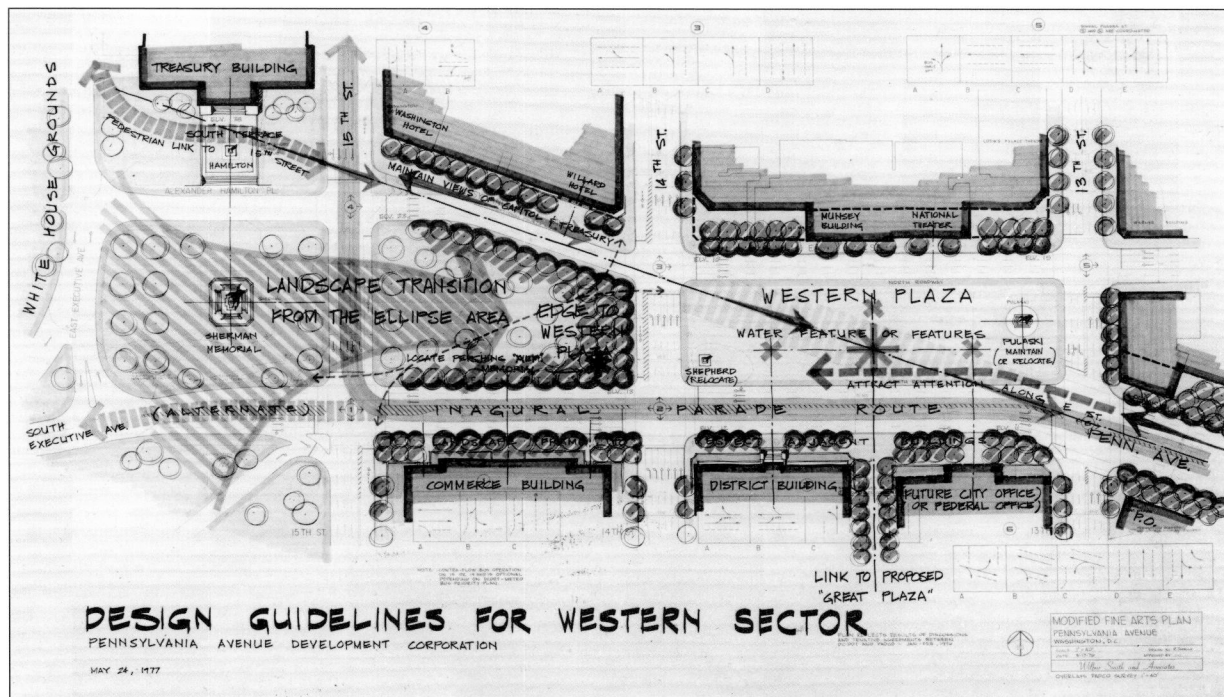

The PADC's plan was eventually changed to include an open Pennsylvania Avenue, as shown in these 1977 design guidelines.

14th Streets, to the additional pedestrian space created by closing the avenue, and to creating a park-like context for the Pershing Memorial. CFA members were skeptical, with Kevin Roche the most vocal, finding the solution unconvincing as pedestrian space: "I don't feel that the design has resolved as being either one thing or another. It is neither a street nor is it a park. Putting a fountain in the middle as a terminus is not going to solve that problem."[39]

After the meeting, Brown sent a tactfully worded letter to E. R. Quesada, the PADC board chairman, expressing the CFA's continued concern with the PADC plan. He requested that the PADC again meet with the CFA so that the commission could "get a better feeling about the whole matter, especially the issue of closing the Avenue between 14th and 15th Streets," before it brought the matter to the PADC board with its recommendations. In his manner of expression, Brown also suggested his personal willingness to now consider keeping the avenue open—the CFA's official stance—since the PADC designs showing it closed hadn't been convincing:

Although we have never been in favor of closing the Avenue, we have been open to designs based on this assumption, with the hope that a distinguished and exciting solution could be found. So far, none has materialized, and I think it may be the appropriate time to reexamine the premise of closing the street.[40]

As requested, the PADC returned to the CFA in January 1976, this time with a scheme showing Pennsylvania Avenue open and a square between 13th and 14th Streets; analysis by the PADC's traffic consultants and the city's De-

partment of Transportation found this a workable approach. Development potential north of the avenue also was improved.[41] In executive session, Brown still expressed a lingering preference for closing the avenue for pedestrian use; he wondered whether anyone would cross traffic to use either the park or square. In Kevin Roche's absence, landscape architect Edward Stone Jr. took up the counterargument:

I think the utilization of park space in the District really relates to two things: one is the density of population around it for using it during off hours, and, two, the amenity of space itself. Not so much, Carter, that the fact you might have to cross an avenue to get to it. Obviously the continuance of pedestrian space would be the most desirable. I think, all things considered, if they [the PADC] develop something that really becomes a people's space, and not something just to make a perspective, I think you will get that utilization, even if people do have to cross a traffic way.[42]

In the public portion of the meeting, Brown diplomatically addressed the issue by suggesting that the open avenue be treated as I. M. Pei had handled the 4th Street plaza between the National Gallery and the new East Building with special pavers that form a "sort of carpet of stone... with the analogy that Pei makes to squares in Rome... where the architecture and the urban design give us the basic integrity of the space, and the fact that latter-day automobiles were allowed to go across...doesn't really break up the essential integrity."[43]

The PADC moved forward with the revised concept. Design studies, expressing a park setting for the Pershing Memorial and the new plaza as very simple and open to maintain the vista with some low plantings and a fountain, were presented and approved at the CFA's April 1976 meeting. Members cautioned, however, that a treeless plaza could be too severe and uninviting for Washington's climate, with Kevin Roche summarizing the CFA's main critique: "We would like to see…more grass, more flowers—a little bit less of a horizontal direction, maybe some vertical elements."[44] By the summer of 1977, the revised PADC plan had passed the necessary review hurdles. It now included new design guidelines for the western sector of Pennsylvania Avenue consistent with the CFA's concept. The revised plan also dropped the numerous tunneled road sections that had been part of the earlier plan.[45]

NEW PUBLIC SPACE: WESTERN PLAZA AND PERSHING PARK

With the planning and design guidelines and the concept now set for the western sector, the PADC could initiate an $80 million public improvements program to develop five public open spaces along the avenue. Western Plaza and Pershing Park were to be the first, but their design process proved difficult from the start.[46] The PADC turned to the CFA for guidance as the evolving issues grew increasingly complex.

Significantly, the design teams were selected through a federal procurement process, not a competition; and this method led to unanticipated complications as the designs proceeded. Qualifications were requested in August 1977, and, by December, an independent panel appointed by the PADC board chairman chose the architecture firm of Venturi & Rauch with the landscape architecture firm George Patton, Inc., to design the area that would become Pershing Park. The landscape architect M. Paul Friedberg, in joint venture with Jerome Lindsey, Inc., was selected to design the plaza between 13th and 14th Streets.[47] In a separate process, a panel appointed by the National Endowment for the Arts selected the sculptor Richard Serra in January 1978 to design a sculptural piece for Western Plaza.

The PADC staff, which was managing the project, considered the designers mismatched to the sites; early in 1978 this concern precipitated an internal design charrette that evolved into an internal design competition between Venturi and Friedberg over Western Plaza.[48] At this stage of conceptualization, Venturi—a leader of the postmodern design movement—quickly developed what would become the signature elements of his proposed Western Plaza design: a large rectangular plaza incised with L'En-

Drawing of Robert Venturi's 1978 scheme for Western Plaza looking west along Pennsylvania Avenue with the Treasury building framed by monumental pylons.

fant's map of Washington lined by low landscaping, with two one-hundred-foot-tall marble pylons framing the Treasury building.

By March 1978, the PADC had not yet decided how to assign the sites and sought the CFA's advice. Venturi, Friedberg, and Serra each presented their early study drawings for the plaza at the CFA's meeting that month. The day before this meeting, the presentations were previewed to the PADC's design advisory panel, of which Brown was a member and a vocal supporter of the Venturi scheme.[49] That meeting concluded with the advisory group supporting Venturi's concept along with the idea of locating a smaller piece by Serra in what would become Pershing Park.[50] Venturi was thus at a distinct advantage as he went before the CFA.

At the CFA meeting, Venturi discussed four assumptions to which he tried to respond: the federal scale (L'Enfant Plan and Federal Triangle) and the local scale (commercial Washington) apparent at the site; the provision of an appropriate western termination of Pennsylvania Avenue that captured the intent of L'Enfant's plan; the PADC's guideline to create "a plaza as an open space, hard-edged…[and] lot 226 as more or less a background for that space…green, soft"; and the need to relate the plaza to adjacent architecture.[51] Venturi then described his inclusion of the two tall pylons as a way to both terminate the avenue and frame the axis, recalling the baroque technique used in the garden at Versailles. In contrast, the Friedberg-Lindsey scheme seemed less a compositional statement than a way to energize the space through grade change and active uses such as shops, cafes, an amphitheater, and a skating rink.[52] Although directed to work within Venturi's scheme, Serra, in his studies, struck out on his own, conceptualizing a two-hundred-foot-tall piece that people could enter, set on a plaza of inclined planes.

The CFA members liked Venturi's use of the pylons as a framing device, with Kevin Roche calling it "brilliant." Brown, already a supporter of the scheme, suggested adding flagpoles for symbolic value.[53] By the end of March, the PADC made its decision: Venturi had Western Plaza and Friedberg had Pershing Park, and, after an acrimonious meeting of the design teams with the PADC, Serra's contract was terminated.

The CFA reviewed Venturi's progress at its May 1978 meeting; his plan continued to have Brown's strong support. The plaza was now a raised terrace edged with trimmed shrubs; added to the scheme were flagpoles and miniature marble depictions of the White House and Capitol atop the incised L'Enfant Plan. Venturi's accompanying printed statement couched his design solution as a descendant of

Model of Venturi's Western Plaza with pylons, the L'Enfant Plan delineated in the pavement, and miniature replicas of the White House and Capitol, 1978.

the Baroque, but also as intrinsically American:

Our framed image doesn't make a bad picture—and it is picturesque in several ways. It is an asymmetrical composition, a Romantic scene of a Classical portico in a rural landscape whose prettiness [Robert] Mills in mid-century would have appreciated. It is reminiscent too of the oblique view of the portico of San Giorgio across the lagoon framed by the two columns on the Piazzetta of San Marco. And it is a symbol of American pragmatism, perhaps—framed in a Baroque plan and developed not with the authority of a prince but through the vagaries of checks and balances.[54]

The concept was presented to and approved by the CFA in July 1978. It included the open plaza with hedges on the north and south, the incised L'Enfant Plan centered in the plaza, and the one-hundred-foot-tall pylons framing the Treasury, as well as the relocated Pulaski statue at one end of the plaza surrounded by trees and grass, and a pool of water at the plaza's west end.[55] The White House and Capitol miniatures were still under study as were the flagpoles, but the PADC found them problematic. The CFA suggested adding trees at the plaza's edge and possibly a fountain in the pool to create a more welcoming environment for users.

Despite the CFA's approval, resistance to the Venturi concept was building. By September 1978, the District of Columbia government, which had long thought the new plaza should function as a public space focused on the District Building, officially made its objections known to the PADC. In a letter to PADC chairman Quesada, the District's

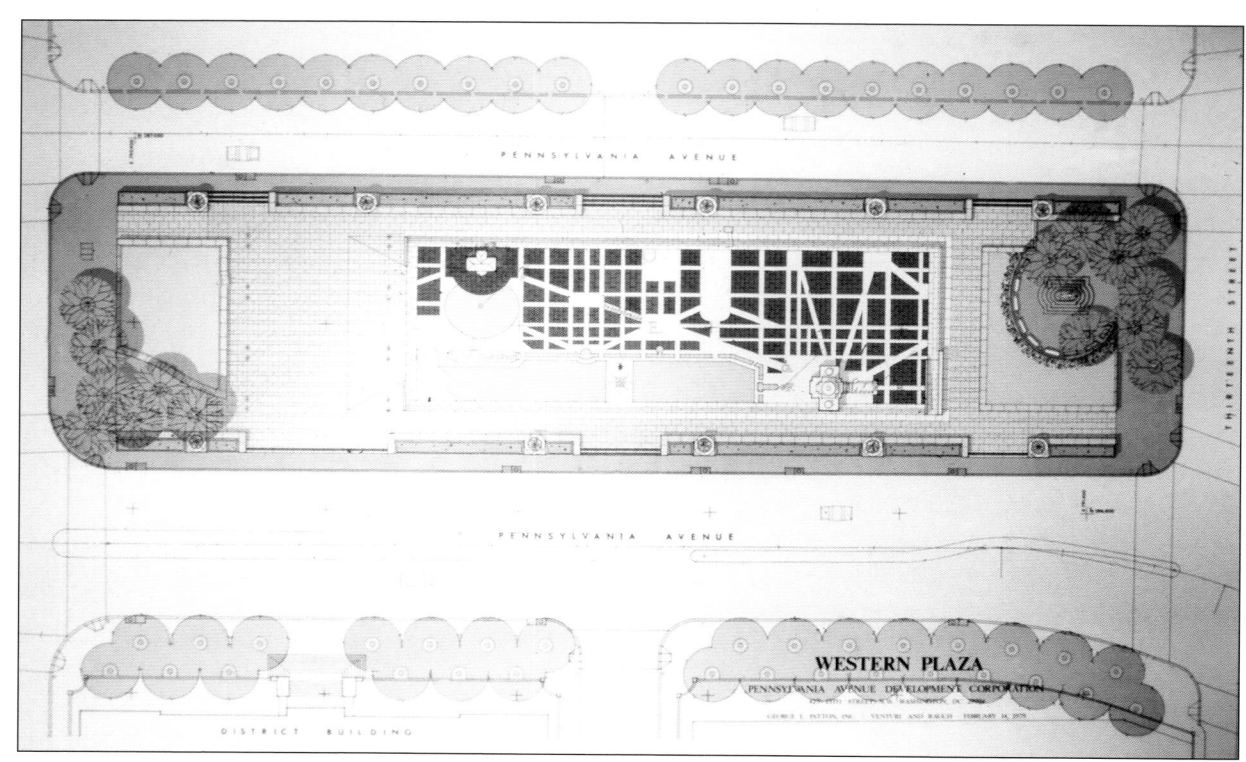

RIGHT: *Venturi's revised 1979 design for Western Plaza retained most of the earlier elements except the pylons.*

BELOW: *Western Plaza, later renamed Freedom Plaza, shown as built in the mid-1980s.*

director of planning, Ben Gilbert, urged that the plaza design be kept simple—the pylons being an unnecessary "complicating factor" and the "miniature buildings and other sculpture pieces…not appropriate for this location." The District did not want the plaza elevated, nor did it find the scheme sufficiently dignified or "people-oriented," adding:

The true function of the plaza, we believe, is to be a crossroads in the City, a meeting place, and a space for a variety of functions, relating to the surrounding buildings. In seeing the problem as primarily one of making a design statement, we believe the designer is sacrificing some of the main values of this important place in the city.[56]

Gilbert's letter noted that the PADC board's design advisory committee had itself expressed second thoughts about the pylons and the miniatures and had asked that they be reexamined. Nathaniel Owings—a modernist whose design philosophy differed greatly from Venturi's—now openly opposed the pylons; Marion Barry, the District's new mayor, also came out against the scheme.[57]

Pressure was also being exerted from other quarters and on J. Carter Brown directly. Because Brown was a member of the PADC design advisory committee, Cyril (Cy) Paumier—whose firm Land Design/Research, Inc., had been a consultant to the PADC on the Pennsylvania Avenue plan revisions in 1976—lobbied Brown to revisit those more landscape-oriented schemes, a stance supported by the American Society of Landscape Architects.[58]

By March 1979, the project presented to the CFA members for final design approval reflected these objections. Essentially, it was a *fait accompli:* the PADC board had already approved it, and the project was in working drawings, the stage just prior to construction. The board-approved design focused on the plaza's ground plane with the incised L'Enfant Plan pulled closer to the plaza's center, kept a pool at the western end, and, in deference to the city, enlarged the paved area in front of the District Building. Large urns for seasonal flower displays were added around the plaza's periphery. The White House and Capitol miniatures were retained, but the pylons were replaced by flagpoles. When asked about the missing pylons, the PADC said they were still under study but were not part of the board-approved scheme. Brown tried to quickly move the CFA toward accepting the design, but CFA members objected to the changes.[59] No formal vote was taken.

At its review of design details in June 1979, the CFA found all the vertical elements deleted and the White House and Capitol represented by bronze inlays on the L'Enfant Plan. CFA staff and J. Carter Brown met with PADC staff over the summer to work on lingering design issues related to materials and inscriptions, which were

approved at the September CFA meeting as was a nine-foot kiosk with an eleven-foot conical roof situated across from the District Building; that element was never built.[60] The project proceeded to construction, and the plaza was opened in 1980. It was renamed Freedom Plaza in 1988 in honor of Dr. Martin Luther King Jr.

Responding to criticism that the plaza was too large and barren, the PADC continued to modify the design into the 1990s, suggesting the addition of a pergola, fountain, and viewing platform.[61] Of these, the CFA approved the fountain in January 1994, observing that the plaza would finally have its long-missing vertical element. The fountain

BELOW: *Adjustments to Western Plaza's design continued after its opening. In 1982, full-size mock-ups of Venturi's proposed miniatures of the Capitol and White House were studied on site.*

BOTTOM: *J. Carter Brown and Robert Venturi examine the Capitol mock-up on Western Plaza, 1982.*

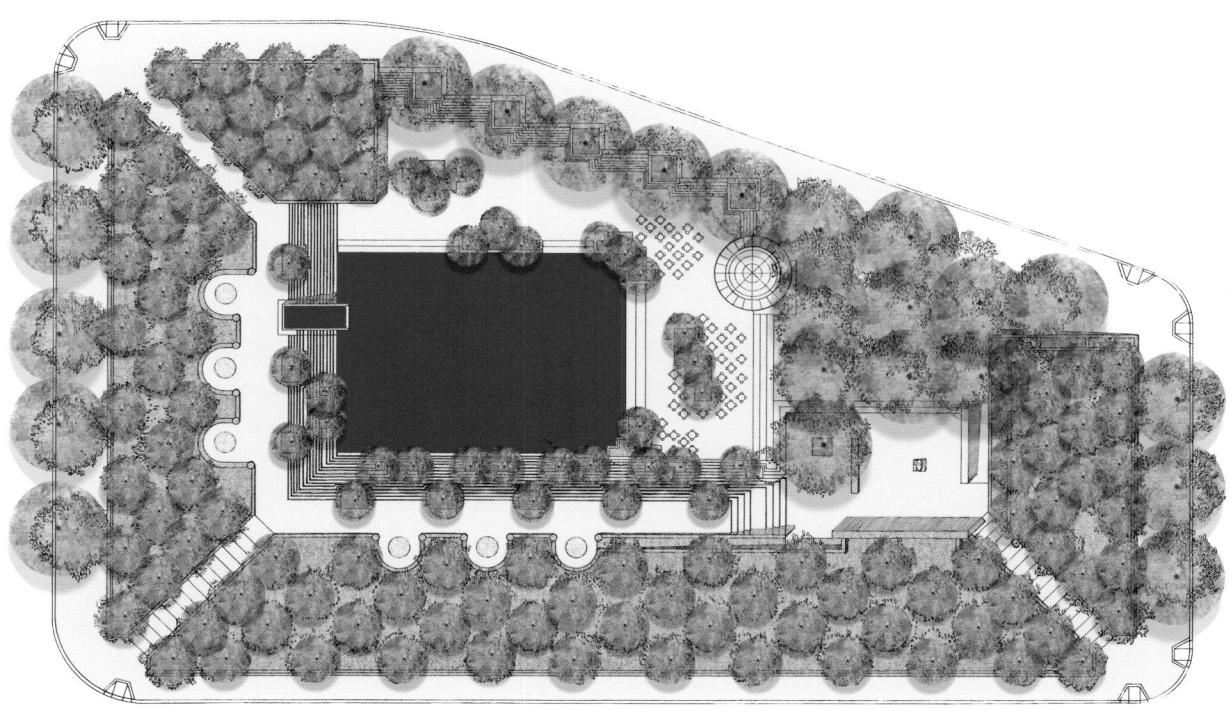

RIGHT: *M. Paul Friedberg's design for Pershing Park incorporated elevation changes and a central water feature to create an active public space; with minor changes, it was approved by the CFA in December 1979.*

FACING PAGE: *The stepped landscape surrounding the central water feature in Pershing Park, completed 1981.*

ABOVE LEFT: *Visitors enjoying the visually rich landscape of Pershing Park, 1980s.*

ABOVE RIGHT: *The Pershing Memorial includes a statue of the general by Robert Winthrop White, installed in 1983, framed by walls describing his leadership in World War I.*

was incorporated into the plaza's pool, with a domed shape bearing a striking resemblance to the fountain imagined thirty years earlier for National Square. Brown also suggested that Freedom Plaza would be a good site for the proposed World War II memorial.[62]

Pershing Park's design went far more smoothly than did Venturi's design of Western Plaza. In a series of presentations to the CFA in the spring and fall of 1979, Friedberg proposed a scheme similar to his original concept for Western Plaza, using elevation change, water, and activities to enliven the park space. His Pershing Park was a garden ringed on three sides by trees, depressed in the center with a café, fountain, waterfall, and pool that would double as a skating rink in the winter; the memorial to General Pershing was closer to 14th Street, framed by a low wall.

The CFA approved the Pershing Park design in December 1979, and it opened to the public in May 1981.[63]

From the CFA's earliest review of Friedberg's Pershing Park scheme in March 1979, J. Carter Brown was effusive about the project:

I like the concept around the Pershing cupping the space and giving a sense of enclosure…. You have something which will wall away the sense of all the traffic. That is a completely different concept from the square to the east where the tourist is invited to stand on this raised platform and orient himself with the L'Enfant Plan as to what the bigger picture is.[64]

Brown's comment highlights the very different conceptual underpinnings of these two urban spaces and suggests why Freedom plaza has not been considered a success. Pershing Park was to be a sheltered but active gathering place

for people, reflecting the "local scale" of which Venturi had spoken. In contrast, Western Plaza was a spatial device to convey a larger meaning—a symbolic space—making it part of the monumental city and not necessarily a place to be experienced for its own sake.

NEW PUBLIC SPACES: MARKET SQUARE

As the CFA and PADC were considering the design of Pennsylvania Avenue's western end, the two entities were also engaged in discussions about the urban design of Market Square, a public space several blocks east between 7th and 9th Streets and north to D Street. The area had housed the city's main food market well into the twentieth century; by the 1970s, it was a declining commercial node of small retail businesses in nineteenth-century buildings.

The PADC envisioned Market Square as a vibrant mix of residential and commercial uses organized around an open space to encourage gathering and outdoor activity. At the CFA meeting in April 1976, the PADC presented an urban design framework plan for the area that preserved some of the nineteenth-century buildings, or at least their facades, to form a historic precinct at Indiana and C Streets to attract tourists. The majority of the area, however, was converted into a superblock of housing, offices, shops, and cafes—all set well back from Pennsylvania Avenue. Open space faced the Archives across the avenue to function as "part neighborhood park, part town square...a canopy-treed room, flexible space under which various activities take place." Eighth Street, running through the center of the development, was to be closed to vehicular traffic and maintained as a paved pedestrian way to preserve the vista between the Archives and the National Portrait Gallery.[65]

The PADC specified building heights—the cornice line set at 90 feet with a maximum height of 110 feet—in proportion to the Federal Triangle. J. Carter Brown was particularly taken with the scale of the proposed housing, which tapered downward to relate to the 8th Street pedestrian way, although he disparaged the Italian hill town–inspired design by architect Hugh Newell Jacobsen as a "Mediterranean bowl."[66] The CFA members supported the overall compositional vision, asking only a few questions about pavement material, tree species, and height. It would take another two years for the plan to wend its way through all the agency reviews, including a federal environmental impact assessment.

Once the framework plan was in place in 1978, design of Market Square's open space could begin, with the addition of a commemorative element. During the CFA's July 1979 review of legislation for a navy memorial, members discussed what the nature of the memorial should be. Charles Atherton mentioned that the PADC and the U.S. Navy Memorial Foundation had informally suggested it be "useful," taking the form of a band shell for concerts in Market Square. Both Brown and member Frederick Nichols (CFA 1976–81), a professor of architecture at the University of Virginia, supported the idea as a way to activate the space rather than simply erecting another statue.[67]

The band shell idea gained traction as the design of Market Square moved forward. By 1982, the PADC and the Navy Memorial Foundation were working together to develop "a living memorial" to U.S. navy personnel at what would now be called Market Square Park.[68] The memorial was to be a concert stage for the U.S. Navy Band and other

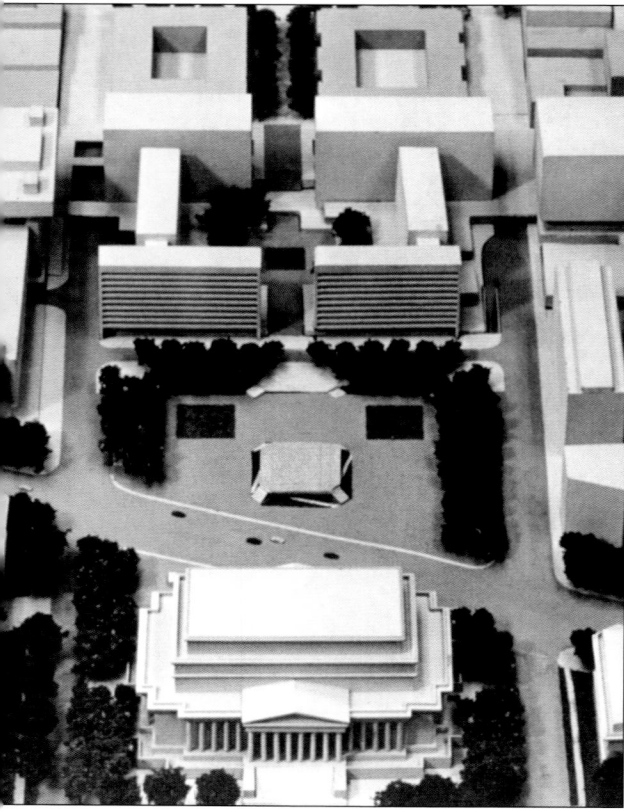

performers that would draw people to the space. The New York architecture firm of Conklin & Rossant with landscape architect William Wilson had won the competition for its design, and they presented their preliminary scheme to the CFA in February 1982.

Drawing inspiration from the classical language of Washington architecture, the architects described a wedge-shaped plaza rising away from Pennsylvania Avenue to form an amphitheater lined with a shopping arcade. A fountain and navy-themed sculpture edged the plaza on the north. The centerpiece of the scheme was a classically inspired triumphal arch at the plaza's base near Pennsylvania Avenue that rose to the cornice line of the proposed new superblock and spanned 8th Street to frame the vista. Sculpture would embellish the arch's south face, with moveable acoustic panels on its north face framing a performance space.[69]

Several members of the public spoke out against the arch at the meeting, citing issues ranging from the "overprogramming" of Market Square to the arch's odd placement at right angles to Washington's principal avenue rather than spanning it, which would be more historically accurate. CFA members were divided regarding the arch's appropriateness as a "contemporary statement."[70]

As he so often did as chairman, when it was Brown's turn to speak, he reflected on the aesthetics and meaning

of the design as part of a larger urban composition. He wholeheartedly supported the arch element as a complex work of public art and as a device that solved a difficult urban design problem. It was a postmodern approach because the arch, though referencing classical antecedents, was not historically canonical in its execution. Brown observed:

It is a visual pun. It does two things at once…. It pushes the borderline between architecture and sculpture because it functions …largely as a form, as a piece of sculpture…yet it has this function…. When we have more perspective and time and we see it is being built within a generation of the Federal Triangle whose vocabulary comes out of the same classical tradition—it won't be quite such a difficult adjustment to make after this great spree of Bauhaus architecture we have all been on. I think it has a particular plus because it brings the vocabulary over to the north side of the avenue.[71]

Brown's remarks suggest his bias toward the neoclassical over the modern but also clearly state his view that the primary role of the design was to make a compatible compositional statement in this urban space. Despite concerns expressed by some of the members during the meeting, Brown closed the navy memorial segment by drawing a conclusion from the discussion that the commission members had a "positive attitude" about the arch, "a direction we would like to see pursued."[72] None of the members dissented at this summation.

Despite Brown's encouragement, by the time the CFA

*Rendering from the 1974
Pennsylvania Avenue plan
featuring a monumental
fountain framed by Jacobsen's
proposed housing.*

next saw the design in July 1983, the arch had been eliminated in response to the PADC's further consideration of
the site's overall urban design and the Navy Memorial
Foundation's search for appropriate iconography. The
open space changed from a wedge to a semicircle, geometry derived from the curved exterior spaces of the neoclassical Post Office building, and in size it matched the
width of the Archives' portico—both changes the PADC
said better established a visual link to the monumental
buildings across Pennsylvania Avenue.[73]

The memorial design had also changed significantly:
water was now the main iconographic element, a symbol
the Navy Memorial Foundation found more fitting to its
mission and one in keeping with the water features envisioned for the area in the L'Enfant Plan. Flat pools framed
a raised circular stone platform that could be used as a
stage; a huge granite wave, expressing the power of the sea,
was this central plaza's most prominent element. A map of
the world was incised on the surface of the plaza, and the
statue of a solitary sailor stood to the side.[74]

The CFA members supported the overall concept but
cautioned that the memorial was trying to say too much.
In particular, they found that the granite wave overpow-
ered the design. Drawing a contrast to the Vietnam Veterans Memorial, attorney and developer Alan Novak (CFA
1981–85) described the underlying problem:

*One of the things we were all struck with in the Vietnam Memorial is
that it isn't doing something fifty times to capture the essence of the
message; it is just doing it magically right, and there is some right
memorialization for the Navy here, and I think you have the framework for it, but you have to figure out what that summarization
should be.[75]*

As he had with the triumphal arch, Brown encouraged
the designers to consider a classical element for that "magically right" solution—in this case, a rostral column as the
memorial's focal element. Such a column, decorated with
the prow of a ship and suggested for the site in the L'Enfant Plan, had been used by navies since the Roman Empire as a symbol to commemorate achievement. He pointed
out that as an urban design device, it could be used "to
bring out the neoclassical character of the Archives Building and bring it across the avenue.... It is the kind of thing
that seems right, because it has been in the folklore for at
least 2,000 years."[76]

The designers continued to explore the metaphors of
water and solitude, revising and editing the design over
the next few months and eventually deleting the wave and
focusing on the fountains and the granite map inlaid on
the plaza ground plane. The "lone sailor" statue was retained as an emblem of the loneliness of life on the sea.
Two dozen bronze bas-relief plaques depicting naval
themes were added on the periphery of the memorial; a

TOP: *Model of the 1982 scheme for Market Square by Conklin & Rossant showing a monumental arch as the central element of the Navy Memorial.*

CENTER: *Rendering by Steve Oles of the proposed arch parallel to Pennsylvania Avenue, looking east to the Capitol, 1982.*

BOTTOM: *By 1983, Conklin & Rossant had revised the Navy Memorial design, the arch was replaced by the figure of a sailor (foreground) and a large granite wave.*

rostral column was not included in the design. With minor changes, the CFA approved the final design in January 1984. The plaza was dedicated in 1987, but design review of the individual sculptural elements by the CFA continued into the early 1990s.

PRIVATE DEVELOPMENT AT MARKET SQUARE: POSTMODERNISM ON THE AVENUE

Neoclassicism was more overtly visible as a design influence in the privately developed Market Square complex than in either Market Square Park or the Navy Memorial. The new mixed-use buildings framing the north side of the site were among the most prominent postmodern designs built in Washington during the height of the movement in the 1980s.

The Washington architecture firm Hartman-Cox Architects, teamed with Western Development Corporation, won the PADC's development competition with the design of a two-building scheme for retail, office, parking, and residential uses. The project had to address the site constraints caused by the intersection of the 8th Street axis with Pennsylvania Avenue and respond to the complex context created by the monumental architecture in Federal Triangle and the commercial architecture of the nearby historic buildings.

The designers met these challenges by setting the pair of symmetrical buildings slightly forward of the FBI building's southeastern corner and retaining open space at Indiana Avenue. The buildings defined the northern edge of the open space of Market Square Park as a split semicircle, and their facades incorporated monumental classical elements—including pediments and a multistory colonnade of Roman Doric columns above a rusticated base—derived in part from the hemicycle of the Post Office building in Federal Triangle. Windows were inserted into the metopes of the frieze. Facades facing away from Pennsylvania Avenue were less ornate, in keeping with the nineteenth-century commercial buildings. As the concept was further refined, the pediments were deleted and loggias added to the residential floors.[77]

The CFA's review process for the Market Square project was swift. The concept was first presented to the commission in December 1985. Some members suggested that the project follow the example of the Federal Triangle buildings by adding more sculpture and other public art, but there were no comments on the design.[78] Taking that as a consensus, J. Carter Brown announced that the conceptual design had been approved. The CFA saw the full project only once more, in November 1986 at the final approval

TOP LEFT: *Rendering of the Navy Memorial as approved in 1984, incorporating the figure of a sailor standing on a projection of the globe framed by bas-relief panels and curved pools.*

LEFT: *The Lone Sailor by Stanley Bleifeld, completed 1987.*

ABOVE, LEFT AND RIGHT: *Unbuilt curvilinear design for Market Square development by Arthur Cotton Moore, 1983. Hartman-Cox Architects, with Western Development Corporation, won the PADC's Market Square development competition in 1985*

with a pair of symmetrical buildings expressed in a classical vocabulary.

RIGHT: *Market Square was completed in 1989; the Navy Memorial is in the foreground, looking north along the 8th Street axis.*

stage of design immediately prior to construction. The discussion focused on design details—color and finish of materials, color of the awnings, design of the metal grillwork and hardware—and the project was approved, with an additional review of an on-site mock-up of materials that the CFA also approved. The Market Square buildings were completed in 1989.

In his letter to the PADC after the December 1985 meeting, Brown summarized his view of the importance and appropriateness of the postmodern approach for this project at this location:

The use of a neo-classical style in the architectural solution as proposed ... will not only form a fitting backdrop to the Navy Memorial and a frame to the Portrait Gallery, but more importantly will unify the north and south sides of the avenue, a critical element in the treatment of Market Square that up to now has been absent in other proposals.[79]

COMPLETING THE FEDERAL TRIANGLE

As redevelopment progressed in other areas of Pennsylvania Avenue, gaps remained in the neoclassical fabric of the Federal Triangle. The economic constraints of the

Great Depression had left the Post Office and IRS buildings with unfinished facades and open spaces and a parking lot in place of the landscaped Great Plaza. Ultimately, the Ronald Reagan Building and International Trade Center would replace the sea of parking, and the ragged ends of the Post Office and IRS buildings would be finished, all due in no small measure to the stubborn conviction of the CFA and J. Carter Brown that the Federal Triangle had to be completed.

While the commission had supported completion for decades, the renovation of the Old Post Office building in the late 1970s created an opportunity for the CFA to press forward toward that goal. The stately Romanesque building had been slated for demolition since plans for Federal Triangle were first developed in the 1920s, a fate supported in the 1964 Pennsylvania Avenue plan and only slightly modified by that plan's 1969 revision—supported by the CFA—which saved the clock tower but would have razed the rest of the building. By 1971, public sentiment favored saving the entire building, and developers saw it as a prime candidate for adaptive reuse as a mixed commer-

cial and retail center oriented toward tourists.[80] These plans moved forward, and in January 1978 the commission reviewed the GSA's renovation scheme for the Old Post Office developed by architect Arthur Cotton Moore, which would eventually be completed in 1983.[81] Although the CFA commended Moore's design, the members considered certain exterior changes contingent on resolving the larger contextual issue of the unfinished Federal Triangle buildings. Frustrated with the GSA's unwillingness to do this, the CFA voted to withhold its approval of the project until it had an assurance that the problem would receive attention.[82]

This act ultimately pushed the GSA to hold a competition for a new Federal Triangle master plan, which was won by Harry Weese & Associates in 1979. The Weese competition entry included planning studies for the unfinished ends of the two buildings. Brown urged the GSA to take advantage of the public's support for the Old Post Office renovation to move this aspect of the Weese proposal forward.[83] However, the focus of the project came to rest on the space where the Great Plaza was to have been built.

The Weese conceptual plan was presented to the CFA in April 1982. As explained by the GSA, the concept responded to three goals: complete the Federal Triangle; increase the amount of federal office space; and create an opportunity to attract people to the Federal Triangle—an ongoing effort of the Pennsylvania Avenue redevelopment in general and the GSA's mixed-use renovation of the Old Post Office in particular.

The most significant finding of Weese's two-year study was that the large expanse of park provided by the Great Plaza was no longer needed; new public space at Western Plaza and Pershing Park, plus the nearby Ellipse and Mall, met the area's open-space needs. This opened the door to

ABOVE: *Model of a design by Vincent G. Kling & Associates to complete the Federal Triangle (1969) that would have demolished the Old Post Office except for its tower which is shown incorporated into a new neoclassical structure.*

LEFT: *Sketch of the Old Post Office tower within the new Federal Triangle development proposed by Vincent G. Kling & Associates, 1969.*

development for most of the Great Plaza site. Weese's conceptual plan took advantage of this opportunity, providing 1 million square feet of office space plus more than 300,000 square feet of retail uses and underground parking.[84] The plan introduced two other guidelines that were important to future development: the new building would not be physically connected to the existing buildings, and it would create a setting for the existing Oscar S. Straus Memorial, which included a large fountain. The overall scheme also suggested landscaping improvements in the Federal Triangle courtyards. A second, connected building located adjacent to the District Building—the designers proposed a

RIGHT: *The Harry Weese & Associates Federal Triangle competition model (1978–79) emphasized the completion of portions of the IRS building facades, shown in white.*

BELOW LEFT: *In its competition-winning 1979 Federal Triangle master plan proposal, Weese & Associates retained the Old Post Office building within redesigned public space framed by existing Federal Triangle buildings.*

BELOW RIGHT: *The Federal Triangle master plan model by Harry Weese & Associates showing development filling the Great Plaza to the rear of the District Building, 1982.*

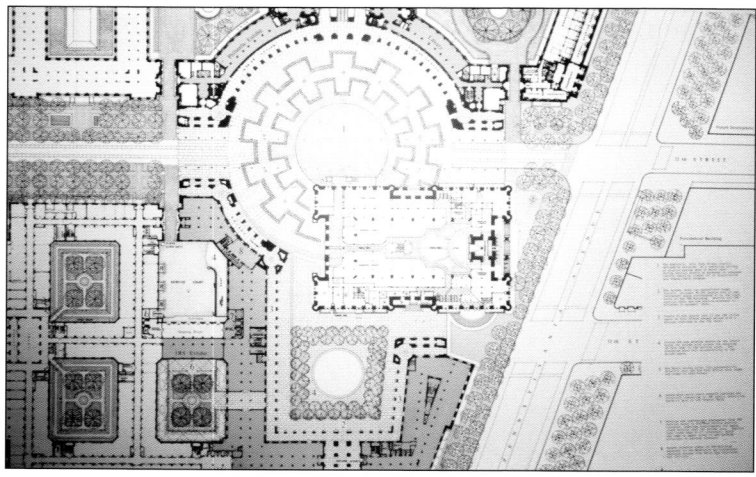

curved facade to draw people into the building complex— would complete the face of Federal Triangle along Pennsylvania Avenue.[85]

The CFA members approved the plan's underlying principles but were concerned that the curved facade on Pennsylvania Avenue weakened rather than strengthened the avenue's visual continuity.[86] Further work on the project was delayed for five years, however, until an intended user could be identified: the International Cultural and Trade Center (ICTC), a joint creation of the Department of State and Federal City Council. It was to be a centralized location for public access to foreign chanceries and trade offices as well as a tourist-oriented exhibition space and retail and restaurants showcasing international products and cuisine.

At the CFA's April 1987 meeting, representatives of the participating agencies and organizations involved in the ICTC project informally presented a preliminary concept prepared for a prospectus to be sent to potential devel-opment teams. The building's massing concept heeded the CFA's earlier advice to maintain an "urban edge" along Pennsylvania Avenue and incorporated columns and arcades to link the building to its context without quoting it directly. The CFA also learned that the ICTC program had doubled the building's intended square footage to more than 2.2 million square feet with 2,600 underground parking spaces, and a height of 120 feet. [87]

Brown supported the scheme's overall approach, but other CFA members were less pleased, in particular the sculptor Frederick Hart (CFA 1985–89), who found the building too large and the concept confusing and not in keeping with is architectural context: "I heard quite a lot about being devoted to the scale and idioms and original vocabulary of the Federal Triangle…and I couldn't tell… whether this was sort of post-modern…[or] whether it is cut down and abstract."[88] He also argued strongly for a greater integration of art into the design and for a reduction

TOP LEFT: *A competition prospectus for a vast new building—the International Commerce and Trade Center (ICTC)—was developed by a design team led by George Notter and Ted Mariani, 1987.*

TOP RIGHT: *Harry Weese & Associates' entry in the 1989 ICTC design competition presented a deeply inflected elevation along 14th Street.*

CLOCKWISE FROM CENTER LEFT: *The relationship of new development to the neoclassical architecture of Federal Triangle and its monumental context were the major issues* addressed by the four principal architectural firms chosen as finalists from among the seven entries in the ICTC competition. (Skidmore, Owings & Merrill, center left; Michael Graves, center right; Pei Cobb Freed & Partners, above right; Kohn Pederson Fox Associates, above left)

of density, which would allow more open space.

A year later, the newly enacted Federal Triangle Development Act authorized the multiagency International Culture and Trade Commission to oversee the development with the PADC managing the project. At the CFA's April 1988 meeting, the PADC presented the proposed design guidelines for the project's soon-to-be-announced design and development competition. In response to the issues of architectural compatibility and open space, the guidelines did not prescribe a style, but they did propose consideration of roof slope and material (red clay tile), building material (limestone), building setbacks similar to the existing buildings, a tripartite composition, a glass-to-solid wall ratio of 20 to 30 percent, access to air and light, a new open space of roughly two and a half acres, and a setback from 13th Street to encourage north-south pedestrian access into the site.[89]

According to the guidelines, height was defined by the ridgeline of the Federal Triangle buildings, with an exception on 14th Street where the Commerce building's portico was slightly taller; this allowed a building height of 137 feet.[90] The ICTC legislation, however, hadn't backed down on square footage and, in fact, increased it in order to support the economics of the multiuse program: 3.1 million square feet.[91] Both the NCPC and the District's Office of

Historic Preservation had reviewed the guidelines and questioned the allowable height and density. At their April 1988 meeting, the CFA members also found the larger numbers difficult to accept, which precipitated a lengthy discussion about costs and ways to cut the program.[92]

By the early fall of 1989, the project had progressed to an open competition run by the PADC, and four finalists were selected from seven submissions: Pei Cobb Freed & Partners Architects; Michael Graves; Kohn Pederson Fox Associates; and Skidmore, Owings & Merrill. J. Carter Brown remained an advisor to the PADC board; in that capacity, he, or Charles Atherton as his representative, could express opinions about the design approach for the massive project. At the PADC selection meeting on October 18, Atherton spoke out for a design that took risks and didn't veer into the mundane in an effort to be broadly appealing.[93]

The following day at the CFA monthly meeting, Atherton reported on the selection of Pei Cobb Freed, teamed with the developer William Zeckendorf of the Delta Group. Unlike the other finalists, Atherton said James Ingo Freed's design captured the quality he had spoken of before the PADC: it gave some relief from the massive quality of the Federal Triangle by "going out on a limb a little bit...which interjected in a sense a new feeling of design...even though there was a certain element of risk

A model of the winning ICTC entry by Pei Cobb Freed & Partners (1989) illustrates how the new building would engage Pennsylvania Avenue (left) as well as the hemicycle of the Ariel Rios (Post Office) building (top) and the Straus Memorial and 14th Street (bottom).

there, but they felt that just recreating…very detail at that mass…was not the best thing to do."[94]

A month later, the CFA members got to see the architectural concept for themselves. Freed described the complex project, which had to draw people in, accommodate multiple uses, and respond to differing urban contexts. Many of the public uses were concentrated on Pennsylvania Avenue between 13th and 13½ Streets. Here the building framed the District Building and quoted its massing without imitating its classical elements. A curved tower and an opening perpendicular to the angle of Pennsylvania Avenue led into a plaza defined on one side by a seven-hundred-foot-long building wall, the mass of which was broken by a low and transparent octagonal pavilion, ending in a curve that responded to the existing hemicycle of the Post Office building. The building's west facade facing 14th Street was a long concave curve, creating a space along the street to accommodate the Straus Memorial, and a curved glass-roofed arcade extended through the building. The cornice height and window-to-wall proportions were the same as in the other Federal Triangle buildings. In response to the CFA's advice, Freed had included areas for the display of artwork.[95]

Even the usual CFA skeptics were enthralled by the concept. Landscape architect Neil Porterfield (CFA 1985–92) called the design's relationship to Pennsylvania Avenue "a small stroke of genius," adding, "I think the exterior facade along the two avenues has done its job and you have…introduced the 21st century." Frederick Hart, who had long advocated for saving the Great Plaza and adhering to neoclassicism, admitted to being "spectacularly impressed…as a person who insisted we keep traditional classic orders, I withdraw that…this has so much originality…a wonderful conception." Arts patron Diane Wolf (CFA 1985–90), known for her often outspoken manner during CFA meetings, also commended the work, although she questioned whether the designers wouldn't later be forced by economics to replace the limestone and granite with less luxurious precast concrete. The concept was approved without anyone mentioning the fact that the program was still 3.1 million square feet.[96] In his letter to the PADC chairman, Brown summarized the significance of Freed's approach:

While respecting the existing architectural character, this new design offers a freshness in the special way it relates to Pennsylvania Avenue, through the introduction of a new geometry that sounds a keynote to the character for the rest of the design. It is the strength of the idea that will allow the subsequent architectural features to develop in their own way rather than be slave to the literal reproduction of the details found on the surrounding buildings.[97]

The project returned to the CFA for review twice more in 1991.[98] At the CFA's February 1991 meeting, Freed presented a further elaboration of the facade design. He looked to the facade organization of the Archives—the window placement, relationship to the pilasters, horizontal moldings at floor lines, and rusticated base—to inform the facade organization of his own building. He also described his use of certain geometries and elements, such as a pavilion, to define the plaza between the ICTC and the Post Office building and to punctuate the new building's long facade.

The members complimented him for a deft interpretation of Washington's classical architecture and approved the basic schematic design. They cautioned, however, that his suggested diagonal axis into the project from Pennsylvania Avenue created both a powerful and complex plaza space and that the geometry and placement of elements within it had to be carefully considered.[99] Further detail refinements were reviewed in June 1991, and the members were generally pleased. The program was still something of a moving target, however, and the design was modified to include usable space in the entrance "drum" at Pennsylvania Avenue. The CFA suggested some adjustments to the domed profile to make it appear less awkward.[100]

With construction under way, the Bush administration's January 1992 decision not to proceed with the ICTC concept forced the PADC and the designers to delete aspects of the public program and to rework interior spaces for more federal office use. At the CFA's April 1992 meeting, the PADC assured the members that a significant amount of public program remained, a use that had been such a driving force in the design and one the CFA had supported as a way to draw people into Federal Triangle. The members then reviewed the material samples, paving patterns, and tree planting and approved Freed's design refinements. The building was officially designated the Ronald Reagan Building and International Trade Center by Congress in 1995, and, three years later, it was dedicated and opened, twenty years after the CFA had pressed the GSA to complete the Federal Triangle.

Even as the Old Post Office project and the Great Plaza redevelopment moved forward in the 1980s, the IRS and Post Office buildings remained unfinished. Congress finally approved completion of the IRS building at the end of the decade, but completion of the Post Office building, renamed the Ariel Rios building, stretched into the mid-1990s. The Washington architectural firm Karn, Charuhas, Chapman & Twohey (KCCT) designed both projects.[101] The CFA reviewed and approved the IRS project in October 1990, commending the design restraint of the new

TOP, LEFT AND RIGHT: In 1991, James Ingo Freed presented studies of the facade's organization based on the window placement, pilasters, base rustication, and horizon-tal moldings of the National Archives building. Freed presented additional facade refinements on a model at the June 1991 CFA meeting.

ABOVE: Refinements included design development of the public space between the Ariel Rios building and the new complex.

CHAPTER VI | THE PAST IS PRESENT

LEFT: *Ronald Reagan Build-ing and International Trade Center, facing 14th Street, completed 1998.*

BELOW, LEFT AND RIGHT: *The unfinished facade of the IRS building at Pennsylvania Avenue and 11th Street, 1991. Rendering of the proposed completion of the IRS build-ing's facade designed by Karn, Charuhas, Chapman & Twohey, approved by the CFA in October 1990.*

New Approaches in Public Art

In a city traditionally known for statues of generals on horseback, new public art was installed in many locations in Washington during the last third of the twentieth century, much of it designed to contribute more to the experience of urban life than to commemorate political leaders. Examples range from the figural to the abstract, from park settings to architectural contexts; these sculptures display a lighter sensibility than the soberness of typical commemorative works.

The *Mary McLeod Bethune Memorial,* a sculpture by Robert Berks (1974), is composed of three bronze figures, including a more than life-size image of Bethune, the pioneering African American educator, and was the first portrait statue of a woman of any race erected in the District of Columbia. The site at the east end of Lincoln Park, situated midway on East Capitol Street between the Capitol and the Anacostia River, corresponds to the location of the Freedman's Memorial featuring *Emancipation* (Thomas Ball, 1876) at the west end. In its reviews, the CFA recommended simplification of the statue's surroundings, such as the elimination of radial walks.

Also by Robert Berks is *Albert Einstein* (1979), a sprawling, three-times life-size figure of Einstein seated on a bench located at the southwest corner of the grounds of the National Academy of Sciences facing Constitution Avenue, NW. The CFA was not supportive of the artist's conception of Einstein in its massive scale or rough texture, giving only its qualified approval to the landscape plan.

The redevelopment of Pennsylvania Avenue under the guidance of the Pennsylvania Avenue Development Corporation brought further opportunity for more lyrical public art in a park setting. A pair of small fountains created for the north end of John Marshall Park comprises bronze water lilies, lily pads, frogs, and turtles to evoke features of a nearby historic spring that first supplied water to central Washington. The elements rise to a common height of eight inches, recalling water level even when the granite basins are empty in winter. The CFA praised the varied decorative elements of this urban park, which also features a seated statue of Marshall but was not intended to serve as a memorial.

The Kahlil Gibran Memorial, authorized under the Commemorative Works Act and located on a site in northwest Washington near the British Embassy, was completed in 1991. The HOK landscape design features a bust of the Lebanese American poet within a composition of curved granite fountains, walls, and benches inscribed with his verses. The CFA expressed admiration for the memorial's subtlety and restraint; J. Carter Brown advised against the use of brilliantly colored azaleas that could conflict with the delicate tones of the stone paving.

In the heart of monumental Washington, the forty-foot-tall bronze *Bearing Witness* by sculptor Martin Puryear was erected in a courtyard within the Ronald Reagan Building and International Trade Center commissioned by the Art in Architecture program of the U.S. General Services Administration. Assembled of beaten copper alloy plates attached to a metal armature, the artist sought to give its surface a handwrought quality, and composed the monumental elongated form—inspired in part by African tribal figures and masks—of articulated horizontal layers to lend it human scale. The sculpture is first seen when entering Woodrow Wilson Plaza from Pennsylvania Avenue; although Puryear purposely did not relate his work to its architectural background, the CFA approved his minimalist addition to the Federal Triangle with enthusiasm.

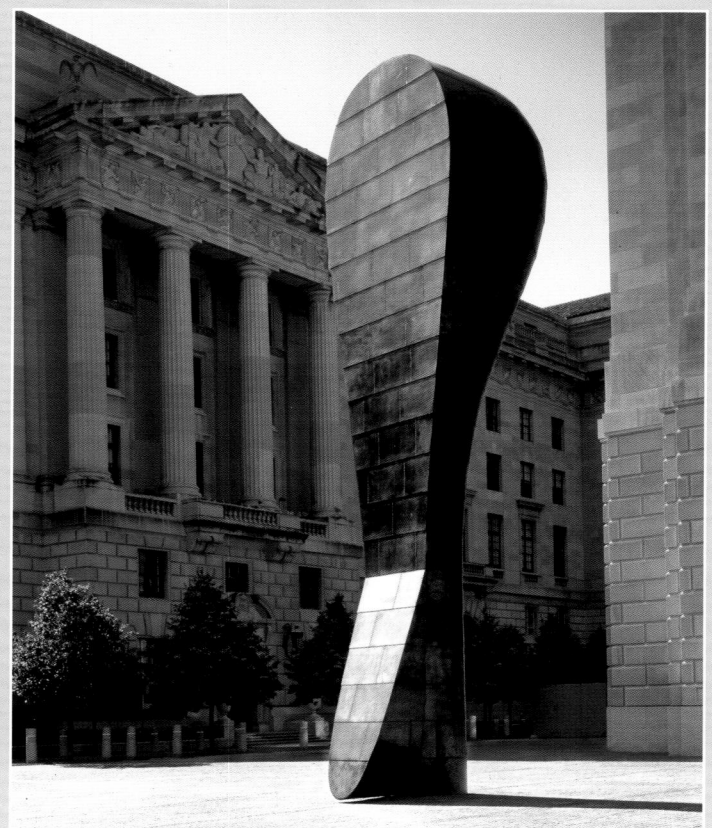

LEFT: Bearing Witness *by Martin Puryear, Ronald Reagan Building and International Trade Center, 1997.*

ABOVE: *Maquette for* Kahlil Gibran *by Gordon Kray, 1991.*

LEFT: Mary McLeod Bethune Memorial *by Robert Berks, 1974.*

BELOW, LEFT AND RIGHT: Albert Einstein *by Robert Berks, 1979;* Lily Pond *by David Phillips, 1982.*

facade and lobby entrance facing the Old Post Office and the simply finished 12th Street facade.[102] With the Ronald Reagan Building as its new neighbor, the end wall of the Ariel Rios building at 12th Street had to relate to the new spatial conditions created by the plaza. At its March 1994 meeting, the CFA reviewed and approved a concept design, which recessed the upper levels of the facade and sparingly introduced elements from the main facade. The GSA pressed the architects to include additional detailing, but the CFA disagreed, supporting the more simplified approach that was carried forward into construction.

FEDERAL DEVELOPMENT IN DOWNTOWN WASHINGTON

Proposals for private development in downtown Washington would dominate CFA discussions in the 1980s and 1990s, and, aside from the massive Ronald Reagan complex, from the mid-1970s onward relatively little federal development occurred in this period—most of it undistinguished. An early exception was the Federal Home Loan Bank Board building at 17th and G Streets, NW, located across from the Old Executive Office Building (Alfred B. Mullett, 1871–88) and adjacent to the historic Winder Building (1848). The Commission of Fine Arts reviewed the proposal, designed for the GSA by Max O.

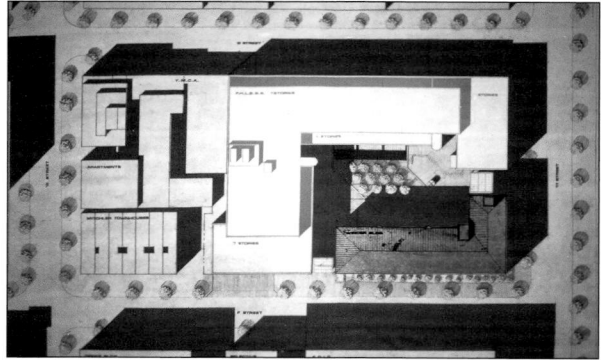

ABOVE: *An early concept study by Max O. Urbahn Associates for the Home Loan Bank building at 17th and G Streets, presented informally to the CFA in November 1973, suggested a relationship to the historic Winder Building and introduced commercial uses and a central public courtyard. The CFA endorsed these urban elements but found the corner entry problematic.*

ABOVE RIGHT: *Plan for the Home Loan Bank building by Max O. Urbahn Associates presented to the CFA in April 1974 refined the spatial relationship with adjacent buildings and the creation of internal public space.*

RIGHT: *The Home Loan Bank building employed a modern vocabulary of limestone panels and toned concrete, completed 1977.*

Urbahn Associates, in 1974 and 1975, when it supported Urbahn's expression of OEOB facade characteristics in his design, translated into modern vocabulary through the "use of fin walls, exposed slabs, and large glass area… breaking from other buildings in the neighborhood." The CFA cautioned, however, for restraint, simplification and a greater relationship with the Winder Building, which had been used for federal offices since the 1850s. The Home Loan Bank Board building was completed in 1977.[103]

Another noteworthy example of federal architecture was the new regional FBI headquarters, located at 4th Street, NW, between F and G Streets in Judiciary Square, first reviewed by the CFA in 1992. Unlike the overbearing FBI headquarters on Pennsylvania Avenue, the regional FBI headquarters reflected sensitivity to its context, drawing inspiration from its relationship to older historic structures.

At the July 1992 CFA meeting, the designer of the regional headquarters, SOM's David Childs, a future CFA member and chairman, presented preliminary concepts that responded to the strongly symmetrical facade and dominating presence of the historic Pension Building across 4th Street. The massive brick building by Montgomery Meigs, inspired by palaces of the Renaissance and

completed in 1887, had recently been spared from demolition and adapted as the National Building Museum.[104] Rather than centering the FBI entrance in the 4th Street facade, SOM aligned it with the Pension Building's east entry, creating an asymmetrically placed and projecting entry pavilion to the new building. Childs also presented a vaulted roof among the schemes and proposed limestone for the building and clear glass in the windows, rather than the precast or poured-in-place concrete and tinted glazing called for in the 1970s plan for the area.

J. Carter Brown and architect George Hartman (CFA 1989–94) both expressed concern with Childs's suggestion to stray from the modernist vocabulary outlined in the earlier plan. Hartman found the modernist WMATA building to the west of the Pension Building a worthy example while Brown did not like the new building's proposed vaulted roof. But the CFA members considered that SOM's urban design approach relating to the Pension Building merited further study.[105]

SOM's refinement of the design over the next few months changed minds on the commission at reviews in September 1992 and January 1993. The design retained the asymmetrical entry pavilion with some added rustication, lowered

ABOVE LEFT: *SOM's design for the FBI Washington Metropolitan Field Office in Judiciary Square, completed in 1997, presents a moderately historicist version of the Washington office box; the ground level terraces addressed nascent concerns for building perimeter security.*

ABOVE RIGHT: *The neutral brick facade of a new federal building on H Street between 9th and 10th Streets, NW, by Hellmuth, Obata & Kassabaum (1999), is interrupted by the striking verticality of a protruding glass element.*

CHAPTER VI | THE PAST IS PRESENT

the curve of the vaulted roof, and improved the facade articulation to emphasize verticality, reflecting the spirit of the "modernized classicism of Paul Cret."[106] Limestone and granite were the principal materials with a gray metal cornice and clear glazing. The design was unanimously approved by the commission. Ironically, cost cutting by the client, GSA, during design development required the designer to replace almost all the stone with precast concrete finished to look like limestone. The CFA approved this change with reluctance and recommended that it continue to review on-site material mock-ups.[107]

A NEW DOWNTOWN SPORTS ARENA AND CONVENTION CENTER

By the 1990s, downtown revitalization was dominated by significant public-private projects that would emphatically reverse a thirty-year trend of decline. In the spring and summer of 1995, the CFA reviewed the design for a new sports arena at Gallery Place, located on F Street between 6th and 7th Streets and encompassing G Street, filling almost the entire block. The CFA had initially opposed this site for the new facility, preferring Mount Vernon Square as more appropriate for redevelopment. However, the District's mayor, Marion Barry, with the support of the new arena's owner, Abe Pollin, pursued the fast-tracked public-private partnership at Gallery Place.[108] A significant challenge was fitting the facility on a single block; concept studies eventually led to the closing of G Street to accommodate the arena.

In May 1995, the architecture firm Florance Eichbaum Esocoff King presented preliminary ideas for the massive structure and, with the CFA's input at meetings in June and July, gradually refined the concept to be lower, more light and transparent, and responsive to the distinctly different urban contexts created by the Portrait Gallery, F Street, and nearby Chinatown. By September, the CFA approved the arena's contemporary design but with reservations about the bowl-shaped top of the signage pylons.[109] The project moved forward, and the architects returned in May 1996 with revisions to the signage elements, which were approved. In a cover letter to the city conveying this approval, J. Carter Brown addressed the need for continued revitalization in the area and expressed the hope that "the current Arena momentum can be directed to opportunities on adjacent sites with great advantage for all downtown Washington."[110]

The District hoped to do just that with the construction of a new convention center at Mount Vernon Square. The existing convention center on H Street—completed in 1983 and itself the result of protracted planning, debate, and review—was now deemed to be too small and out-moded to attract larger and more lucrative convention business. While the CFA had questioned the need to replace the convention center in its April 1995 report to the mayor regarding the arena, the city moved forward with these plans as well.

In March 1997, the city's Washington Convention Center Authority and its architectural team—a joint venture of Devrouax & Purnell; Thompson, Ventulett, Stainback & Associates of Atlanta; and Mariani & Associates—began a series of informational presentations to the CFA to refine the design concept for the large, contemporary building. Scale, street closings, and contextual compatibility with the historic Carnegie Library on the south, the residential neighborhood to the north, and the historic 8th Street axis were among the issues discussed by the commission at presentations over the next four months. In June the CFA approved the concept, noting that the "dynamic articulation" of the south facade at Mount Vernon Square should be extended to the other elevations.[111] The final design was approval in October.

The CFA and Historic Preservation in an Era of Redevelopment

By the mid-1960s, the philosophy of the Commission of Fine Arts had begun to reflect the era's growing interest in the history of architecture and the city. Chairman William Walton led the CFA to adopt preservation as an explicit interest, and in 1964 the Joint Committee on Landmarks was formed with the NCPC and the District of Columbia to consider cases involving historic properties in the city. Under the direction of Charles Atherton, the CFA staff began an ambitious program of publications beginning in the late 1960s that would extend throughout the next decades, focusing on the architectural heritage of areas under the commission's jurisdiction. In cooperation with the Historic American Buildings Survey (HABS) of the U.S. Department of the Interior, Atherton undertook the publication of a seven-volume documentary survey of Georgetown architecture, organized geographically by commercial, waterfront, and residential neighborhoods between 1968 and 1970, with research conducted by a growing number of staff members as well as summer interns. In 1977, a foldout photographic pamphlet, "A Georgetown Panorama," was edited by Old Georgetown Board chairman Wynant D. Vanderpool and published by the CFA to document the significant change taking place in the 1970s along Georgetown's principal commercial streets.

From the 1970s onward, the CFA's publication program widened its scope to include a greater range of historic

Downtown's Revival on and off Pennsylvania Avenue

By the end of the twentieth century, the mix of retail, entertainment, dining, office, and residential uses provided through redevelopment drew both residents and tourists alike to Washington's revitalized city center, expanding the Washington experience beyond the perimeter of the monumental core.

An early project of the Pennsylvania Avenue revival was the Willard Hotel renovation and addition by Hardy Holzman Pfeiffer Associates for the Oliver Carr Company. Once threatened with demolition, the landmark building designed in the Beaux-Arts style by Henry Janeway Hardenbergh in 1901 had survived under the PADC's plan. The design proposed restoring the limestone and buff brick facade and mansard roof of the original with the addition of an adjacent "small Willard" with quadruplicate forms of a cascading mansard roof and profile inspired by the original building. Commission members were enthusiastic about the design when it was presented to them in December 1979; Kevin Roche called it "marvelous." J. Carter Brown added that he had seen the submissions for the Willard competition at a PADC meeting and had thought this design was "the one they ought to build. I am delighted that it has come to the Commission now, and I think it has been a blessing."[1] Final design was approved in May 1981. As the project continued through to working drawings in 1983 and 1984, the CFA offered advice related to details such as joint color and paving surfaces.

The Cabot, Cabot & Forbes development at 1201 Pennsylvania Avenue, designed by SOM's David Childs, met with equally swift approval. Unlike the Willard, the 1201 project was all new construction and did not incorporate historicist elements. The front elevation of the sleekly modern, pink-tinged granite building followed the diagonal line of Pennsylvania Avenue; it was set back 50 feet and rose to a height of 135 feet. It contained a central atrium that formed the main lobby and was topped with a skylight. The CFA members complimented the design at an informational presentation in January 1979 and remained equally pleased in March 1979 when both the design and material samples were formally presented and approved.

The design of another new project, National Place, at 1301–1331 Pennsylvania Avenue was quickly approved in concept when presented to the commission in July 1980, but at a subsequent review in January 1981 the choice of material color raised concern among CFA members. The site presented several distinct urban characters and included a change in grade: commercial F Street on the north, the monumentality of Pennsylvania Avenue, the adjacent historic National Theater, and the Willard Hotel across 14th Street. The Philadelphia architecture firm Mitchell/Giurgola, associated with Washington architect Frank Schlesinger, responded to these distinctions by using a range of materials and colors in the 1.5 million-square-foot office, retail, and hotel project for Quadrangle Development. Limestone was proposed for the facade of the office building adjacent to the theater and a light-toned brick elsewhere.

In an attempt to make the Pennsylvania Avenue facade of the hotel "a foil to the lighter color of the Willard" and to recede in relationship to the lighter colored National Theater, the designers chose a dark, almost-black glazed brick accented with dark mortar and dark windows in black frames. CFA members, particularly architect Walter Netsch (CFA 1980–85), a retired partner with SOM and an often vocal member of the commission, disagreed with this choice: "You are not trying to make it recessive, but a wham-o, black, shiny event." The designer argued that using a lighter gray brick, especially in strong sunlight, ran the risk of being bland and noted that a similar dark/light technique had been used in other cities, such as Philadelphia on the Bulletin and PSFS buildings. To this Netsch replied, "That may fit fine in Philadelphia, but not in Washington," reiterating the special quality and requirements of designing in the nation's capital and especially along Pennsylvania Avenue.[2] The question of brick color stretched on for more than a year and included reviews of on-site mock-ups of materials.

The CFA's review of the Evening Star project at 1101 Pennsylvania Avenue, de-

veloped by the Jonathan Woodner Company, led to extensive modification of the proposed design. In late 1981 and early 1982, the architectural firm of Harry Weese & Associates presented concepts to the CFA for renovation of the existing building—originally designed by Marsh & Peter in the Beaux-Arts style in 1898—and its annex, as well as construction of an addition adjacent to the original building. In its review, the CFA suggested improvements to the proportions and rhythm of the addition as well as the way the old and new buildings were joined; the CFA members also found that the curved corner facade did not relate well to Pennsylvania Avenue. Modifications to the design were eventually approved, but the developer did not proceed with the project at the time. Four years later, the Woodner Company returned with a new designer and a new design for the project. At the February 1986 CFA meeting, David Childs presented an SOM design that incorporated an addition extending from Pennsylvania Avenue around the old building, replacing the annex on 11th Street. Although the original building held the historic right-of-way of Pennsylvania Avenue, it was now projecting into the fifty-foot setback established for the avenue under the PADC. As the concept of the building was to follow closely in form and character—if not the detail—of the original, the addition was allowed to follow that same setback. The SOM design deleted an arcade proposed in the earlier scheme, and the concept design was approved, as were the final design and materials when presented nearly a year later, in January 1987.

A new Canadian Chancery had been planned by the PADC since the late 1970s for a prominent site on Pennsylvania Avenue that was somewhat larger than the embassy's programmatic needs. In May 1984 the CFA reviewed the concept design by the Canadian architect, Arthur Erikson. The commission addressed the diverse building styles represented by the nearby U.S. District Court, the classically inspired Federal Triangle, and the modern East Building of the National Gallery of Art as well as the views of the Capitol and the Mall. Given the context and the lack of program to fill the site, the designer proposed a courtyard scheme defined with columns, a rotunda colonnade, and fountain. Following some questions about materials and a suggestion to reconsider adding a glass-covered canopy to support the columns, the concept was approved.[3]

The design was further developed during the course of the year, and the CFA members reviewed and approved a more refined design at their meeting in December 1984. Windows were shown in horizontal bands with vertical mullions, building height was reduced, and the penthouse was simplified. An entrance was added on Pennsylvania Avenue but the rotunda at the corner with John Marshall Park—a park honoring the nation's longest-serving chief justice and one of the PADC's new public spaces—remained largely the same. Security gates were retractable to maintain the effect of openness, and the building was clad in a Canadian marble with cast aluminum on the colonnade and concrete forming the rotunda columns.[4] Working drawings were reviewed and approved in February 1986.

TOP TO BOTTOM: *SOM's design for the restored Evening Star building and addition reinterpreted the florid detail of the original Beaux-Arts building in an abstracted contextual treatment, completed 1989. The* CFA *approved the concept design for National Place by Mitchell/Giurgola and associated Washington architect Frank Schlesinger in 1980 but later found the designers' choice of a very dark brick inappropriate for Pennsylvania Avenue. The Canadian Chancery on Pennsylvania Avenue by Arthur Erikson, completed 1989.*

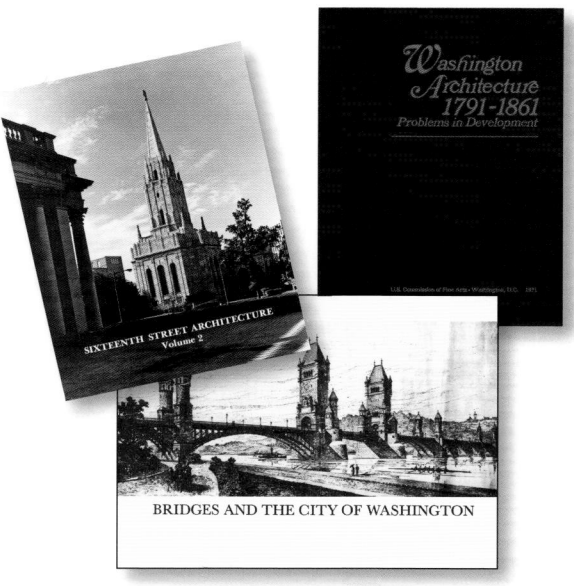

CLOCKWISE FROM UPPER RIGHT: *CFA publications include Daniel D. Reiff,* Washington Architecture 1791–1861: Problems in Development, *1971; Donald Beekman Myer,* Bridges and the City of Washington, *1974; Sue A. Kohler and Jeffrey R. Carson,* Sixteenth Street Architecture, *Vol. 2, 1988.*

Members of the CFA in 1984 (left to right): Alan R. Novak, Sondra G. Myers, Edward D. Stone Jr., J. Carter Brown, John S. Chase, and Walter Netsch.

neighborhoods and topics. In 1971, Daniel D. Reiff, an architectural historian and acting assistant secretary, produced *Washington Architecture, 1791–1861: Problems in Development,* a study of the notably conservative architectural context of the national capital before the Civil War in comparison to the grand ambitions of the L'Enfant Plan. Atherton had hired architect Donald Beekman Myer in 1966 as assistant secretary and staff architect Jeffrey Carson in 1971; together they would produce the next publications, *Massachusetts Avenue Architecture,* volume 1 (1973) and volume 2 (1975), with staff members Lynda Smith, Sibley Jennings, and Sue A. Kohler. Myer produced *Bridges*

and the City of Washington in 1974, and Kohler and Carson collaborated on *Sixteenth Street Architecture,* volume 1 (1978) and volume 2 (1988). Kohler, who served as the commission's historian for thirty-three years, expanded a pamphlet history of the commission from the 1950s by H. P. Caemmerer into a larger book format entitled *The Commission of Fine Arts: A Brief History, 1910–1976;* Kohler revised the book four more times through 1995. Kohler's last publication for the commission, *Designing the Nation's Capital: The 1901 Plan for Washington, D.C.,* was begun under Atherton's direction, coedited with architectural historian Pamela Scott, and published in 2006. J. Carter Brown himself sponsored and contributed to a symposium held at the National Gallery of Art in 1987, resulting in the volume *The Mall in Washington, 1771–1991,* edited by architectural historian Richard Longstreth and published in 1991 with a new edition in 2002.

As redevelopment drastically changed the city's urban landscape in the 1970s and 1980s, it reflected evolving national attitudes and policies toward historic preservation as well as the thorny issues of context and significance, urban design, economics, and appropriateness pertinent to the nation's capital. Under the influence of J. Carter Brown, the CFA's stance often inflamed the debate.

An exchange between Charles Atherton and J. Carter Brown at the May 1976 CFA meeting sheds light on Brown's attitude toward historic preservation in the nation's capital and, consequently, many of the CFA's responses to preservation questions that arose during his tenure. At the meeting, Atherton reported on an ongoing staff project to collect information about nineteenth-century properties in the 2000 block of I Street, NW, facing Pennsylvania Avenue, whose facades were proposed for historic designation. Although the properties were not within the CFA's purview, staff recommended that the CFA use its influence to support the facade designation of the largely intact residential block.[112] At the time, saving only building facades was considered in development circles—although debated in preservation ones—to be an acceptable way to encourage investment while preserving an old building's aspect on the street.

Taking on his self-described role of devil's advocate, Brown saw the block as one of "many, many blocks in the city which have the same or greater historical or aesthetic interest" and was not "particularly distinguished." What seemed important to Brown was building pedigree: "One of the great buildings in town is right across the street . . . miraculously preserved [2015–2017 I Street, NW, Abbe House/Arts Club of Washington and former home of James Monroe]." He added that "it would be hard for the

Fine Arts Commission to come out in a vacuum saying that … [preservation] is a better solution for that block than any other conceivable solution." Atherton countered that the block was important because it represented the capital's early history, and the goal was not to prevent development but to call attention to that history so future planning for the area would place some value on it.[113]

Brown agreed to a carefully worded recommendation for designation. His final remarks, however, reflected his fundamental political nature and a bias against vernacular architecture when it couldn't be connected to some larger significance:

You know, the trick in this game is to keep your priorities, so that you don't spread yourself so thin that just everything, by virtue of it being there already is therefore historic, which is arguable, and therefore had to be preserved, and then you get shunted aside by the builders, developers, saying those people are just crying 'wolf' all the time.

I think we have to save our fire for things. General political machinery is not set up to make distinctions in priorities and they get the idea we just immediately say everything that exists ought to be kept by definition, then we lose our clout when it comes to saying something we really feel strong about.

So I think the classification of landmarks is a useful thing. The one good building from a historic point of view has already gotten classification; it is a class 3 [2030 I Street, the Joseph Cooper House.] I wouldn't want this commission to suddenly say the whole block is class 1…just by virtue of it being there…that is why we are trying to make some differentiation. We are all allies in the same cause. It is a question of strategy and tactics of how do you get the maximum clout.[114]

The chairman's remarks also reflected the new reality of the CFA's position in the late twentieth century. Fifty or sixty years earlier, the CFA was the authority on aesthetics in the capital, and its focus was on government-related projects in the monumental core. By the 1970s, private development occupied much of the CFA's attention and the proliferation of stakeholders and reviewers in development matters meant that the CFA made recommendations in a far more complex and potentially contentious political landscape.

In addition to building significance, Brown's support of preservation was influenced by the larger compositional question of urban design, as exemplified by the 1919 F Street project by the George Washington University and the World Bank, first reviewed by the CFA in July 1976. The project included the preservation or relocation of several historic buildings and the demolition of a row of mixed nineteenth-century vernacular and historic row houses on G Street at 19th Street, NW, in order to construct a large office building. Here Brown found the small vernacular row houses compelling:

Well, our first reaction is there is a very beautiful urban scale expressed by the row of old houses . . . and would help reinforce the visual scale of the two earlier [Lenthall Houses] and obviously more important houses you are preserving."[115]

The preservation of urban character was often more important to Brown than the authenticity of building fabric. Under pressure from the preservation community and the media, George Washington University eventually returned to the CFA with several design alternatives in September and December 1976, which included appending

ABOVE LEFT: *Rendering of 1919 F Street, Vlastimil Koubek, 1976.*

ABOVE RIGHT: *SOM's design for Michler Row at 1777 F Street inserted a new office building behind the partially retained facade of a nineteenth-century house and the reconstruction of several other facades, essentially creating new structures in a historicist vocabulary. Although little authentic fabric remained of the old houses, the CFA supported the approach to preservation and approved the concept in October 1979.*

facades of the vernacular row houses to the side of the new building facing a park.[116] While several members of the commission found this solution artificial, Brown found it far less troubling:

I think conceptually it is a new idea. Erase the blackboard . . . take all that off, say here is this park. . . . And that park has various features, it has trees, has steps, has some houses which recall the kind of urban scale that used to be in that park. If you think of it that way, you really are providing a setting . . . from scratch, rather than the fact that you are somehow trying to work out a compromise. . . . Maintain that scale as a recall, as an amenity.[117]

The CFA eventually acquiesced to the relocation of the historic row houses off-site and the preservation of the other historic buildings. By 1979, the new building was redesigned, and the row houses were demolished.

RHODES TAVERN AND METROPOLITAN SQUARE

Among the city's most hard-fought preservation battles was the Metropolitan Square project on 15th Street across from the Department of the Treasury. Rhodes Tavern, an early nineteenth-century building that had been the site of numerous formative events in the capital's history, occupied a portion of the redevelopment parcel. Like 1919 F Street, urban design and historic merit shaped the recommendations of J. Carter Brown and the CFA regarding the fate of the tavern, decisions that produced an outcry from the preservation community that continued to resonate for decades.

In 1977, the Oliver Carr Company acquired much of the block known as Square 224, which contained four designated landmarks: the Keith-Albee Theater, the Metropolitan Bank building, Rhodes Tavern, and a building housing the interiors of a historic restaurant, the Old Ebbitt Grill. Although the developer considered the area a risky investment, the site had a number of assets, including a location across from the landmark Treasury building and on the national parade route, proximity to the still-thriving Garfinckel's department store, and support from the city for redevelopment.[118] The developer knew that the historic buildings added complexity to the site's redevelopment potential and hired SOM to analyze different development alternatives.[119]

As with 1919 F Street, the CFA was authorized to review the project under the Shipstead-Luce Act. At its March 1978 meeting, the members heard SOM partner David Childs present a range of development options prepared by his firm, from full preservation to a brand-new building. The firm's recommended option—based on economic, functional, historic, and urban design consid-

erations—was a brand-new building incorporating the facades of the Beaux-Arts Metropolitan Bank building and the Keith-Albee Theater as well as the interior of the Old Ebbitt Grill. Although the Rhodes Tavern was among the oldest buildings in Washington and used by the British during the burning of Washington in 1814, Childs argued that it had been drastically altered over the years and lacked historic integrity. Unlike the bank and theater, the tavern also lacked the architectural presence—even if restored in place—to establish a strong visual relationship with the neoclassical Treasury building across 15th Street; it could be demolished or moved under the SOM preferred scheme.

Brown acknowledged the difficult preservation decision posed by the project but supported SOM's preferred scheme based on urban design context. In contradiction to his earlier comments regarding the authenticity of the G Street row houses, he explained:

This is a complicated one, and a classic case of overlapping priorities in preservation. . . . From the Commission's point of view . . . we agree the Albee and the bank buildings have a marvelous dialogue going with the Treasury. And to tear those down and put a modern office building there, right next to the White House precinct and the Capitol of the United States would be a crime, no matter how sensitively designed that might be. It would be throwing away a real part of our past and part of the urban design consistency. . . . There is a whole atmosphere which is terribly important.

The real toughy is the little Rhodes Building because if one tried to rebuild it, one would no longer have a historic building but a fake. At what point do you release the idea that this is a nice throwback to our past? Our feeling around the table is that, in architectural terms, it is not significant enough to upset the whole urban design of that part of town . . . a cornice height established, and that this [Rhodes Tavern] comes out as a kind of gaping into the smile of 15th Street. This has been seen in other parts of the city and country where . . . a critical mass has tilted the scales and that one cannot hang on to a little building whose aesthetic impact is demolished by the buildings surrounding it.[120]

Brown concluded by suggesting the tavern be acknowledged in the new building by a plaque or small exhibit. There was no discussion among the CFA members or a vote about the project. Brown, speaking for the commission, saw no reason a demolition permit for the tavern should not to be granted, although the Advisory Neighborhood Commission (ANC) representative for the area spoke on the record for reconsideration of that decision.

In September 1978, the CFA was drawn further into the growing Rhodes Tavern controversy. At that month's meeting, David Childs returned to the CFA for clarification about building setbacks and height and preservation of the historic buildings. Rising costs to save elements of the theater and bank—to be borne by the developer—and the growing public sentiment to preserve the tavern meant

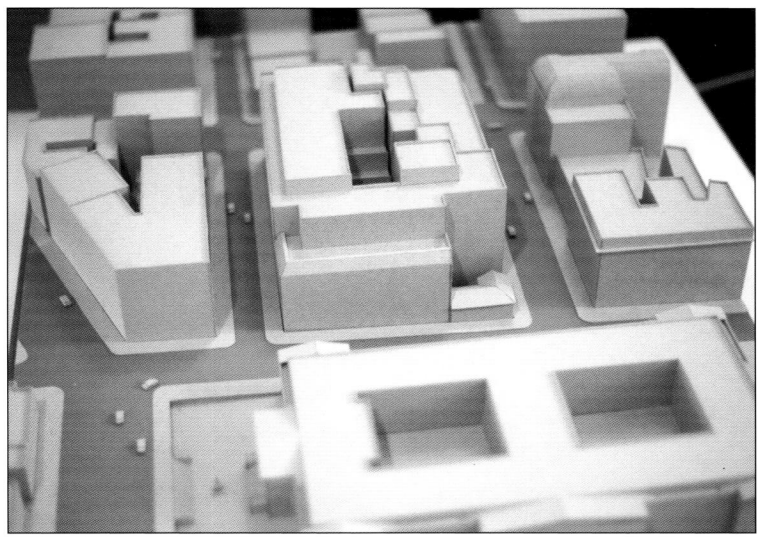

that the developer could not proceed with the original scheme. Childs pointedly asked the commission for its advice: "We would like to have your consensus [on] the question of priorities…as to the Rhodes or the Metropolitan Bank Building. In no case do the numbers work so that it would be the Rhodes or the Theater Building."[121]

In his remarks, Brown contrasted the merits of the bank building and tavern:

There are competing kinds of values here, the value of the bank building is very much an aesthetic one which has to do with historic values of that set of facades which were designed specifically with the Treasury Department in mind…. The Rhodes Tavern is a very different kind of situation…the visual values must be seen in terms of the broader sociological values, the association that we have of the building which just happens to have survived a long time and happens to have had some historic events connected in and around it…. The historical integrity of the building is not there. You don't feel the quality detailing and structure and all the things that you…looked for in the original building.[122]

TOP LEFT: *The historic Rhodes Tavern at the corner of 15th and F Streets in use as a drugstore, c. 1913.*

ABOVE LEFT: *An early* SOM *massing model of the Metropolitan Square project shows the disparity in scale between the proposed development and the existing Rhodes Tavern, 1978.*

TOP RIGHT: *Corner of 15th and F Streets in 1979, showing changes to the Rhodes Tavern facade from the early twentieth century; National Metropolitan Bank and the Keith-Albee Theater are in the background.*

ABOVE RIGHT: *Rendering of* SOM's *Metropolitan Square project; new construction on the right covered the former site of Rhodes Tavern, completed 1986.*

Brown added that the CFA was "sensitive of the nostalgia" associated with the tavern and would not prevent its preservation if that was economically feasible. Childs pressed Brown on this point, adding that the design team recommended that a preserved Rhodes Tavern still be moved from its existing site and wanted the CFA on record about the idea. Instead, Kevin Roche responded that the CFA would not take the position that "taking the Rhodes Tavern away is an improvement from an urban point of view," and the question was dropped.[123]

By April 1979, preservation efforts had stalled the full demolition of the Keith-Albee Theater, and the CFA pressed the District to save the facade.[124] Within a few months, the District government offered the developer $1.25 million from local and federal funds to subsidize that preservation. The developer was already committed to keeping the Metropolitan Bank building facade and offered $100,000 toward the removal of Rhodes Tavern from the site. However, the Committee to Save Rhodes Tavern, a preservation advocacy group, was adamant that the tavern's historical significance was derived from its location and had to remain on the site.[125]

The developer moved forward with the project, despite the controversy.[126] At the CFA's October 1979 meeting, Childs presented a concept scheme that included the theater and bank facades. While demolition of Rhodes Tavern and the small row house containing the Old Ebbitt Grill interiors was not yet determined pending a hearing under the city's new historic preservation law, the SOM scheme assumed they were no longer on the site. The proposed new limestone building, a "contemporary design" using design language compatible with the adjacent historic facades, ranged up to 130 feet, with setbacks up to 35 feet at 15th Street.[127]

Members of the public at the meeting spoke out against the new building's height, and several presented alternative schemes that incorporated Rhodes Tavern. SOM revised the scheme's setbacks in response to CFA concern that the new building could overshadow the Treasury; and, subject to the city's preservation hearing, the concept was approved at the December 1979 CFA meeting. By February 1980, the District found the Metropolitan Square project of "special merit" based on the economic benefits it would bring to the city, legally clearing the way for the tavern's demolition.[128]

With the controversy focused on Rhodes Tavern, the developer proceeded with development on the northern portion of the site at 15th and G Streets in 1980, incorporating five bays of the Keith-Albee facade into the new Metropolitan Square building; this phase was complete by 1983. The developer then moved ahead with Phase II, which would finally resolve the issue of Rhodes Tavern's preservation.

In May 1983, Childs presented Phase II working drawings to the CFA, the final step before a building permit could be issued. Brown opened the meeting with a review of the commission's actions in the project, noting that the "importance of the site" led the CFA to support preservation of the theater and bank facades, which had occurred and which was "a major victory for the cause of preservation in the city." He noted that the CFA was told by the development team it was "not economically feasible to retain…the small building which is now in rundown condition but had once been the Rhodes Tavern." From among the design options presented, Brown said that the CFA "concurred with the architect that retention of the building on that site was a lower priority than the other scheme," which preserved the bank and theater. He then emphasized that the CFA's mandate under the Shipstead-Luce Act extended only to "height and appearance, color and texture of the materials of external construction," and not matters of preservation.[129]

Several members of the public criticized the new building's height, including an individual who questioned its relationship to the White House, recalling the CFA-supported suit against Arlington County over the impact that building height in that jurisdiction would have on the monumental core. But the bulk of remarks by the public centered on Rhodes Tavern. Among the speakers was Nelson Rimensnyder, a staff member of the House Subcommittee on Government Operations and Metropolitan Affairs, who countered Brown's statement about the CFA's authority under Shipstead-Luce, noting that legislative history indicated the commission should consider historic character in its deliberations, adding "I think the action of this Commission is going to go down in the history of the city as a very, very tragic mistake."[130]

A testy exchange then ensued between Rimensnyder and Brown. Rimensnyder quoted testimony by developer Oliver T. Carr before the subcommittee in its November 1982 hearing on the tavern's preservation wherein Carr placed the decision about Rhodes Tavern squarely with the CFA: "The Commission of Fine Arts wanted a design conception for Metropolitan Square excluding a restored Rhodes Tavern and preferred extending the Beaux Arts design to the corner of 15th and F Streets." Brown repeated that it was the developer who said the only economically viable scheme was the one without the tavern, adding, "We are here to review design proposals that represent reality—and to the extent that design considerations are constrained by reality, naturally that is what we have to deal with."[131] Rimensnyder pointed out that, whatever its basis, the CFA's decision affected support of tavern preservation by Washington's cultural leadership: "Specifically, when those interviewed [by subcommittee staff] were asked to pursue some leadership role to advance the preservation of Rhodes Tavern, they declined, often citing perceived Commission of Fine Arts objection or design consideration to their preservation of Rhodes Tavern on its present site."[132]

Among the last speakers was Joseph Grano, head of the preservation group Committee to Save Rhodes Tavern, who noted that 25,000 signatures had been gathered to place the question of the tavern's preservation on the upcoming November ballot. Once the CFA approved the working drawings, however, the developer could apply for a demolition permit within thirty days. Grano asked the CFA to "show your moral support for this issue" and advise the mayor to delay the demolition permit until after the election.[133]

Grano's request prompted CFA members Sondra Myers (CFA 1980–85), an arts and humanities advisor, and Edward D. Stone Jr. to ask if the commission's recommendation letter to the mayor could reflect its sense that the city should delay issuing a demolition permit until after the election. Brown said this would be done, and the session concluded with the members' vote on the working drawings. Myers and Stone voted to approve the submission, but architect John Chase (CFA 1980–85) voted against it, preferring the commission take no action in deference to the upcoming ballot question. Walter Netsch had earlier recused himself from the proceedings because of his past relationship with SOM. Claiming his vote was only needed to break a tie, J. Carter Brown abstained from voting.

The way was now clear for the developer to apply for a demolition permit, but a series of lawsuits forced a delay until after the November election when the voters overwhelming endorsed the initiative for the District to develop a policy to preserve the tavern building. The controversy continued into 1984 with more suits and countersuits over the demolition permit, and media coverage kept the question of Rhodes Tavern preservation before the public. By the end of the summer of 1984, the preservationists were losing ground: the November ballot initiative was declared unconstitutional, and, by the end of August, the preservation group found itself unable to raise a $100,000 bond for the Court of Appeals to hear further arguments. The group then appealed to the U.S. Supreme Court, which declined to block demolition. Rhodes Tav-

ern was razed on September 10, 1984. Phase II of Metropolitan Square was completed in 1986.

The CFA's role in the Rhodes Tavern story was not easily forgotten by those involved in the efforts to preserve it. At the June 7, 1999, dedication of a plaque commemorating the building, Charles Atherton wryly noted:

I am happy to be asked to join you on behalf of the Commission of Fine Arts and its chairman, Carter Brown. He long ago urged a plaque of this sort, and is glad it is to be finally in place, just in time to mark the 200th anniversary of this historic site. The real credit, however, goes to those of you who stuck it out all these years in support of the cause. You never gave up, and just to be sure no one forgot, we all received cards once a year on the anniversary of the demolition."

And, finally acknowledging what was lost, Atherton added: "It is sad that its walls are not here to which we could affix a plaque, a plaque not marking a mere site, but a plaque worn like a medal proudly proclaiming its old campaigns."[134]

While the fight to save Rhodes Tavern was lost, the controversy helped focus attention on the question of preservation and redevelopment in downtown Washington in the last decades of the twentieth century. Other struggles, such as the successful preservation of the Old Post Office in the 1970s and its adaptive reuse in the 1980s, showed that old buildings could still have economic value and made preservation advocacy more mainstream. The National Historic Preservation Act of 1966 shaped a legal framework for preservation, with several federal tax reforms in the 1970s and 1980s providing economic incentives for the preservation and rehabilitation of historic buildings.[135] Although the reuse of old and historic buildings remained more complex than new construction, by the 1990s preservation had become an accepted approach to redevelopment in downtown Washington.

Preservation and Redevelopment in Old Georgetown

By the 1970s, Georgetown had become the city's primary center for development as other parts of the District, particularly the shabby downtown sector east of the White House and the riot-ravaged 7th and 14th Street retail corridors, struggled to attract commercial investment. When the Old Georgetown Act passed in 1950, active heavy-industrial uses dominated the Georgetown waterfront; but by the early 1970s, many of these operations had closed, and their buildings were considered obsolete. Real estate speculation had driven costs associated with waterfront development from thirteen dollars per square foot in 1965 to fifty-five dollars per square foot in 1972.[136]

ABOVE: *Aerial view of the Georgetown waterfront shows the dominance of automobile infrastructure and industrial uses along the river, c. 1967.*

RIGHT: *Members of the Old Georgetown Board, 1974 (left to right); Wynant D. Vanderpool Jr., Thomas J. Stohlman, and Warren Cox.*

The Commission of Fine Arts had taken a hands-off approach to project review in Georgetown during the 1950s and 1960s, typically accepting the recommendations of its appointed Old Georgetown Board, but this would no longer be the case after J. Carter Brown became chairman in late 1971. Brown's leadership style was engaged and compelling; moreover, as a resident of Georgetown, he was acutely familiar with the historic district. During Brown's thirty-year chairmanship, architectural trends evolved, and the historic preservation movement matured, although many of the issues from earlier decades affecting historic character—megablock development and the imposition of historic details—remained prevalent.

As pressures from competing interests in the waterfront mounted, the District government initiated a review of the zoning regulations. Brown hoped to guide the imminent change: while testifying before the D.C. Zoning Commission on the Georgetown waterfront in August 1973, Brown described a historic town that predated Washington, comparing it with the beauty of Charleston and Savannah but arguing that Georgetown was more important because of its "historical value." He noted the different characteristics of the urban fabric north of M Street versus the waterfront. To Brown, the most architecturally significant—and therefore historically valuable—area was the northern part, where he considered the scale to be consistent, and the many "beautiful features" imbued the public with a "sense of well-being."[137] Brown characterized the area south of M Street as "a very mixed bag," remarked upon the "beautiful opportunity to ascertain its market use," and declared that control of building "heights are the key" regarding new construction.[138] Brown's comments indicate some inconsistencies. For example, when comparing Charleston to Georgetown, historic value mattered most. But when evaluating the two areas of Georgetown, he did not emphasize the historic value south of M Street—apart from the buildings along the canal—as compared to the area north of M Street, even though the waterfront was the oldest part of the historic district. Similarly, whereas Brown recognized the importance of *scale* in the urban fabric north of M Street, he said *height* was the critical issue in the waterfront. Brown also stressed to the D.C. Zoning Commission that the CFA was a longtime advocate for a public park along the riverfront and recommended a fifty-foot setback from the water's edge.

LARGE PROJECTS SOUTH OF M STREET

Shortly after Canal Square opened in the summer of 1970, its developers approached the Inland Steel Development Corporation about developing twelve acres located south

of the C&O Canal between 30th and Thomas Jefferson Streets, then occupied by a sand and gravel plant.[139] The Foundry, as the project came to be known, included the rehabilitation of the mid-nineteenth-century Duvall Foundry and a new retail and office block with approximately four hundred feet of street frontage in angular masses rising eighty feet high, ten feet less than the zoning regulation permitted. Before architect Arthur Cotton Moore began his presentation to the commission at the April 1972 meeting, Brown—who had been elected chairman a few months earlier—took a preemptive stance against the height of the project:

I believe the majority opinion is that it is not in our purview to rule on land uses, but we are specifically designated by legislation to advise on height and bulk and esthetics in Georgetown. And after studying this very carefully, we feel the proposed building is too high in view of the historic nature of the site, and the unique esthetic values around it.[140]

When Moore described the proposal, highlighting the planned restoration of the old foundry and the substantial setback from the canal, he twice stated that "something has to give" to make the project work. Brown's response combined practical issues and hyperbole:

[I]f something has to give, we feel that it should be the amount of cubic volume required by the owner, rather than the amenities that have to do with public happiness and this is where we come in…. We are talking about sheer esthetics and we are talking about the scale, the sense of place that is there, and has been handed down to us in a rather unique area of this country. Those few blocks around that canal are as impressive, I think, as anything in the United States. It is a very moving part of the world and that is what we're trying to preserve.[141]

Brown wanted the proposed office building to be no more than sixty feet tall.

Moore returned the next month with a revised design that had removed the top two stories of the office building but raised the ground floor, creating a net loss of fifteen feet. The revised scheme rose sixty-four feet above the sidewalk; it also achieved five-sixths of the permissible density. Brown declared, "I think it's a hell of a lot better-looking building," and proceeded to compliment how the new building related to the old foundry, pulled back from the canal, and established a pedestrian place next to the canal. However, his characterization of the project's architectural compatibility with the surrounding neighborhood was far-reaching, saying that the fenestration pattern along the Thomas Jefferson Street elevation "partakes of the modular rhythm and scale of the Georgetown Federal."[142] Moore's design was approved in concept, and subsequent reviews were carried out by the commission's OGB. Upon completion, the Foundry became the first preservation success south of the canal.

TOP: *The Foundry project south of the C&O Canal by Arthur Cotton Moore adapted the nineteenth-century Duvall Foundry (left) into office space and added additional office and retail uses in an adjacent new building (right), completed 1976.*

BOTTOM: *View looking west along the C&O Canal, 1979. The redeveloped Duvall Foundry is visible to the right of the canal at the street; the new office and retail building is adjacent. Also visible are pedestrian amenities along the restored historic canal and existing commercial and industrial uses west of the site.*

ABOVE, LEFT AND RIGHT: *The revised design for Georgetown Park by Alan Lockman with Chloethiel Woodard Smith, completed in 1981, inserted an enclosed shopping mall and residential units within a historic commercial block between the C&O Canal and M Street; and*

view of the condominium apartments above the Georgetown Park retail base overlooking the C&O Canal, 1993.

LEFT: *The Four Seasons Hotel by SOM, completed 1979.*

In November 1976, developer Herbert Miller submitted partial-raze applications for a variety of large brick warehouses between 3222 and 3248 M Street and at 1070 Wisconsin Avenue that had been associated with maintenance of the streetcars owned by the Capital Transit Company. Miller hired architect Chloethiel Woodard Smith, who had recently completed nine years as a CFA member, to develop schematic designs for the large mixed-use project known as Georgetown Park, which proposed the retention of the warehouses' M Street facades and the massive stone retaining wall along the C&O Canal. The project included commercial space that would be accessed from M Street, sixty row houses surrounding landscaped courtyards that opened up along the canal, underground parking, and condominiums along Grace Street south of the canal.

Because a modest-scale residential project was proposed, the OGB recommended approval for the demolitions. Even though these warehouses incorporated large-

span spaces—relatively simple buildings to renovate—the proposed facade retention was typical of the 1970s and 1980s approach to preservation.[143] The commission also did not question the amount of demolition of historic fabric, although Chairman Brown took issue with the repetitive character of the residential component and said to Smith, "The charm of Georgetown depends largely on its irregularity.... I would just hate to see it have sort of a housing-project look."[144] In May 1977, Smith presented a revised design in which the residential courtyards had been filled with eighty-foot-tall new construction rising behind the forty-foot-tall M Street warehouse facades; the new development featured an A:B:A fenestration pattern typical of all four elevations. The commission gave the project preliminary approval apart from the height and fenestration treatment of the Wisconsin Avenue elevation.

By the time the project returned to the commission in November 1978, Miller had retained Alan Lockman as the architect with Smith as consulting architect. Lockman maintained the general massing of Smith's revised design but introduced punched openings to the elevations; the project was again granted preliminary approval, although commission member Frederick Nichols directed Lockman to simplify the staggered footprints of the row houses and restudy some of the roof configurations. In December 1980, the project team returned to the commission with a revised scheme that replaced the previously approved row houses with condominium apartments. The commission members agreed that the revised plan was an improvement but asked for further simplification of some elements. When next presented to the CFA in March 1981, the design instead included ornamental ironwork at various points on the facade. The developer described its purpose as "architectural embellishment," to which commission member Walter Netsch retorted, "In other words, you don't really like basic Georgetown buildings? Is that the problem?"[145]

The design was refined twice more before the OGB supported the final design for the residential portion of the project in July 1981. The nineteenth-century brick facades and the other twentieth-century exterior walls enclosed a three-level, neo-Victorian interior shopping mall that opened in September 1981. Architectural critic Paul Goldberger wrote, "The entire complex from its Victorian lamps to its mock-Georgian doors is something of an event in the evolution of popular taste. It is hard to be quite sure, however, whether this is low art gone fancy or high art gone popular."[146] Similarly, Benjamin Forgey said the mall "satisfies the contemporary architectural sweet tooth," but noted that the large-scale project was not compatible with the historic residential neighborhood.[147] The $100 million project was a catalyst for more large-scale waterfront development.

The large parking lot in the 2800 block of Pennsylvania Avenue provided an opportunity for redevelopment with significant visual impact on the neighborhood. In April 1976, following two reviews by the OGB, David Childs of the SOM Washington office submitted a massing study for a speculative hotel and office building on the parcel that wrapped around the diminutive commercial row houses comprising Diamond Row. The commission was especially engaged in this review, expressing concerns about the height of the building, its relationship to the adjacent Rock Creek and Potomac Parkway, and its role as the eastern gateway to Georgetown. Eliciting unusual dissension among the members led by painter George Weymouth (CFA 1972–77), who considered the sixty-foot height to be too tall, the project was seen as a tipping point between big-block and smaller-scale waterfront develop-

ment. Brown characterized the proposal as the "great wall of China" and directed Childs to return with massing studies that focused on addressing conditions particular to the parkway and avenue.[148]

When the project returned in June, Childs presented a single model and developed elevations without changes to the overall height. Childs's presentation addressed mechanical equipment and fenestration detailing and stressed the importance of having the clock tower become the third "exclamation point" along M Street, after the Car Barn tower and Riggs Bank dome. The commission members' comments focused on the corner of the building where Pennsylvania Avenue met M Street and how deference to the smaller scale of residential Georgetown should be handled; apart from this corner, the design was approved.

Childs submitted a revised design for the July meeting with the main block pulled back from Pennsylvania Avenue, the clock tower more perceptible, and the Diamond Row mass extended to 29th Street because the Four Seasons Hotel had become interested in the project and wanted larger rooms. Despite Weymouth's previous objection to the height of the project, the commission approved the revised design—now conceived of as a gateway instead of as a barrier. A few months after the project was approved, Brown described it as "part of the wall of a medieval town." After the Four Seasons opened in August 1979, Wolf von Eckardt noted that the six stories "beautifully fitted into the slopes," but disliked the design of the tower, labeling it "a clockwork lemon…a bland, insipid slab, standing there like an actor who forgot his lines."[149]

DEVELOPMENT ON THE WATERFRONT

Washington Harbour, located on a six-acre site formerly occupied by a concrete factory on K Street between 30th and 31st Streets, was a mixed-use development and the first project to be proposed for the Potomac River shore. Originally known as Georgetown Harbour and reviewed by the commission in October 1972, the project became enmeshed in years of litigation that touched on issues ranging from the definition of urbanism to a politically charged effort to create a waterfront park. Ultimately, the project became Washington's most significant waterfront development of the 1980s.

The proposal, submitted for the developer Robert Larsen of the Inland Steel Company by Arthur Cotton Moore and landscape architect Hideo Sasaki—who had recently served eight years on the CFA—was a ninety-foot-high, 650,000-square-foot multiuse building complex. Brown opened the proceedings with the ominous statement: "The most important thing we have to do today and

maybe this year is to focus on this whole Georgetown [waterfront] question."[150] Following the presentation, commission member Kevin Roche described the project as "fortress-like." The chairman agreed, adding:

What the building says—I think Kevin is right—is the hell with the rest of the city. We are going to do our thing. We have our little piece of property and we are just not going to play ball with anybody else. We are just going to do our thing and make the fast buck and the hell with the rest of the city.[151]

However, Chloethiel Woodard Smith challenged Brown's view of the developers and pressed for consideration of increased height limits, as she had in other discussions:

I personally feel, as I told you before, that the way things are heading now we are putting the city in the suburbs and the suburbs in the city, and the Georgetown citizens are trying to get zoning for 40-foot… houses throughout and I think it's anti-city. I think it is a terrible thing. I think also that the assumption that all private developers have a black heart, I don't think is right. For years people have been trying to do something with the Georgetown waterfront. Nothing has ever happened. I for one feel that it is time something happened.[152]

Smith's remarks were based on personal knowledge of the neighborhood; her architectural offices at 1056 Thomas Jefferson Street were located a block away from the project site. Inconsistent with the normal procedures, the commission advised the developer that a recommendation would not be issued until January 1973 to allow the commission to consider the pending waterfront study by the NCPC. In January, the applicant presented minor variations to the east and west elevations without changing the mass. The chairman advised the commission members to recommend a sixty-foot general height limit, with the potential for taller punctuating elements up to ninety feet, and a landscaped fifty-foot setback from the water's edge. A revised design with a smaller mass, with some sections remaining at ninety feet, was approved in April, albeit with the preference for park development instead of the mixed-use project.

The project then became enmeshed in a complex review process—among the NCPC waterfront study, its 1968 comprehensive plan, the D.C. Zoning Commission, and

The Georgetown waterfront in 1979 near 30th and K Streets, where the mixed-use Washington Harbour project—the first such redevelopment along the river—would be built in the late 1980s following a protracted process of review and litigation.

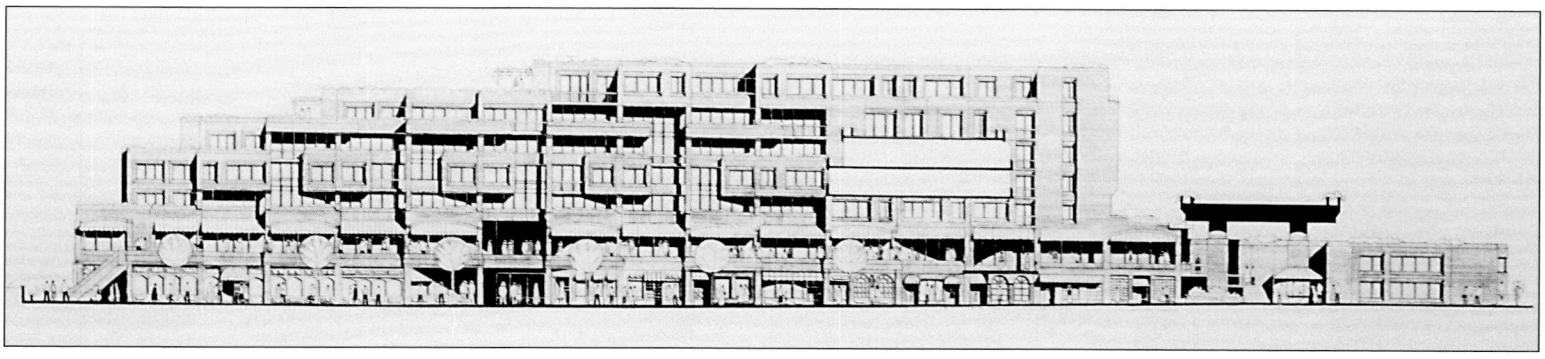

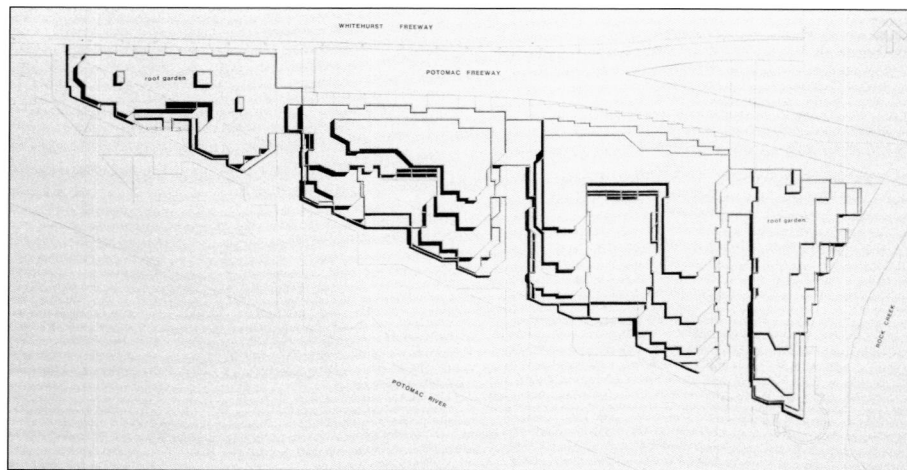

the Home Rule Act of 1973—and lawsuits brought by the Citizens Association of Georgetown and two other community groups to the D.C. Superior Court and the D.C. Court of Appeals. The litigation slowed construction across the waterfront for several years as developers and lawyers waited for clarity on legal issues. During this time, the CFA advocated for a riverfront of continuous parkland.[153]

In 1978, Senator Charles Mathias (R-MD) established a task force on the waterfront with representatives from the Department of the Interior, the District government, the NCPC, the CFA, and the Citizens Association of Georgetown to establish an agreement allowing for both park and development with minimum government expense.[154] The following year a group of senators led by Mark Hatfield (R-OR) sponsored legislation to acquire the last remaining private parcels along the Georgetown waterfront in order to integrate them into continuous national parkland along the Potomac River shoreline in the capital.[155]

By 1979, CSX Resources, in partnership with Western Development, had acquired the property and presented a new design by architect Elliot Gitlin—whose massing conformed to the allowable building envelope—to the CFA. The mass of the 1,180-foot-long brick building with narrow passageways allowing for glimpses of the river was described derisively by CFA members as "a Georgian Mediterranean fishing village," "a beached whale," and "bogus Georgetown" and was unanimously disapproved at the December meeting.[156]

Herbert Miller of Western Development, now the sole owner of the property, returned to the commission in March 1980 with an entirely new scheme by Arthur Cotton Moore. The design, well within the existing zoning requirements, featured a plan focused on a central elliptical space containing a boat basin; the axis of Thomas Jefferson Street extended through the site as well as a diagonal axis labeled as "Virginia Avenue" (but in fact aligned with the distant U.S. Capitol dome.) The buildings incorporated commercial uses surmounted by residences and fea-

TOP AND CENTER: *Proposed elevation and plan of Georgetown waterfront project for Western Development Corporation at 3020 K Street by Elliott Gitlin, 1979.*

ABOVE: *Conceptual rendering of the waterfront park by Pete Hasselman, from the 1976 plan by Keyes, Condon & Florance with Wallace, Roberts & Todd. The CFA supported plans for a continuous park along the Potomac River in Georgetown.*

tured twenty-two different facades with an agglomeration of arches, columns, ribbon windows, canopies, bay windows, domes, and corbelled chimneys—an exceptional example of postmodern design.

Although CFA members reiterated their desire for a continuous park along the Georgetown riverfront, they expressed support for the new design, particularly its reduction of mass, increased public access to the waterfront, and opening up of views along the north-south streets. However, they still considered the complex to be too tall and massive. Following further reduction of the height to seventy feet and a reconfiguration of the mass, the project was given preliminary approval in October 1980, with the commission repeating its position that it preferred an all-park solution.

Over the next four months, President Carter appointed five new commission members. Two of the members—Washington attorney and developer Alan Novak and public relations executive Harold Burson (CFA 1981–85)—attended their first meeting in March 1981, the same month that the Georgetown Harbour proposal was returned to the commission for review of the final design drawings. Following a site visit, the lengthy proceedings included a staff presentation on the project's history for the new members and testimony by community members opposed to the project. In their discussion, commission members considered the role of institutional history as well as the idea of public access to the river. The newly appointed architect Walter Netsch said:

I was not here on earlier discussions of this building, and I am at a loss to understand how this building does fulfill our charge relative to Georgetown in terms of the character of the building and the place…. I find it peculiar that this Committee allowed this sort of sybaritic symbol to appear out on this plaza…. I find this very elitist interpretation of land use in the guise of commercial and social development really contrary to the edge of the river. You see, I come from Chicago, where we have a phrase 'forever open, free and clear,' where we fight to the death for our waterfront…and so I find myself not in agreement with the plan on an architectural basis. I do think the site plan and the port concept is brilliant…but for…people to participate in this kind of a Roman holiday, I think is inappropriate to the waterfront. I just had to say my piece.[157]

Netsch's statement elicited an uncommon round of applause. Moore complained, and Novak tried to mollify him, but architect John Chase added:

I think in order for us to really justify our position as members of this Commission, we need to keep the interest of not only the citizens of Washington, but those of the entire country, in mind and if we do that, I can't see us doing anything other than denying approval of this project. I so move.

The chairman called for a second, which was given by Burson. The meeting minutes indicate that five members—

An early version of Arthur Cotton Moore's postmodern scheme for the 3020 K Street project, later known as Washington Harbour, featured a central boat basin with pedestrian access and amenities along the riverfront, 1980.

Washington Harbour, completed in 1987, features a plaza and elaborate fountain in place of the boat basin.

Brown, Burson, Chase, Netsch, and Stone—voted to disapprove Georgetown Harbour and two—Novak and Sondra Myers—voted to approve it. Following the vote, Arthur Cotton Moore quipped, "Well, I guess now we will end up where we expected we would—in court."[158] A few days after the meeting, Myers wrote a letter to Brown expressing her concern about the proceedings. Mentioning the complexity of the case, she did not believe enough time had been allowed for careful deliberation and complained of the rush that led to a potential miscount of the vote.[159]

Nevertheless, due to a zoning review technicality and because the developer wanted to present the project in greater detail, the case was heard again the following month, during which time the seven members reaffirmed their previously recorded positions. Following the meeting, Senator Hatfield, who had sponsored legislation for parkland along the shore, wrote Brown:

Congratulations for the firm stand you took yesterday in support of preserving the Georgetown Waterfront as a park for the people! The Fine Arts Commission has led the way on this issue, exhibiting a vision for the city that few others have been able to match.[160]

Miller pursued an appeal under the D.C. Historic Landmark and Historic District Protection Act of 1978. Following six days of testimony, the District's administrative law judge ultimately determined that the design of the building was not incompatible with the character of the historic district, and the city issued the building permit.[161] The $175 million complex was completed in 1987 as one of the most exuberant postmodern designs in the city; the remainder of the riverfront would be developed as parkland in the first decade of the twenty-first century.

Development of the project known as the incinerator began in the late 1990s and epitomized dominant themes of the late twentieth century: megablock development, the

accommodation of modern design in the historic district, and the value of preserving intact historic fabric. In March 1998, the commission visited the waterfront site bounded by 31st, K, and South Streets and Wisconsin Avenue, which included the 1932 Georgetown incinerator; seven late nineteenth- and early twentieth-century industrial, commercial, and residential structures; a 1956 commercial building; the alley known as Copperthwaite Lane; and the circa 1800 Brickyard Hill House—the oldest residential building in the waterfront neighborhood.

In the public meeting later that day, the architect Shalom Baranes, on behalf of Millennium Development, gave an information presentation on the proposal. The project called for the demolition of all buildings apart from the incinerator and Brickyard Hill House (which would be moved off-site during construction) and the closure of the alley to be replaced by residences, a hotel, movie theaters,

ABOVE LEFT: *Model of the 1984 conceptual design for Phase II of Washington Harbour by Arthur Cotton Moore in a style complementary to the earlier project. The CFA was concerned about the project's height and voted not to approve it, asking for additional study; the site was eventually developed in the early twenty-first century with a different scheme.*

TOP RIGHT: *The Georgetown incinerator project called for the demolition of a number of nineteenth- and early twentieth-century buildings and the relocation of the Brickyard Hill House, shown here c. 1998.*

ABOVE RIGHT: *An early twentieth-century industrial building on the site of the incinerator project housed The Bayou, a well-known music venue, 1982.*

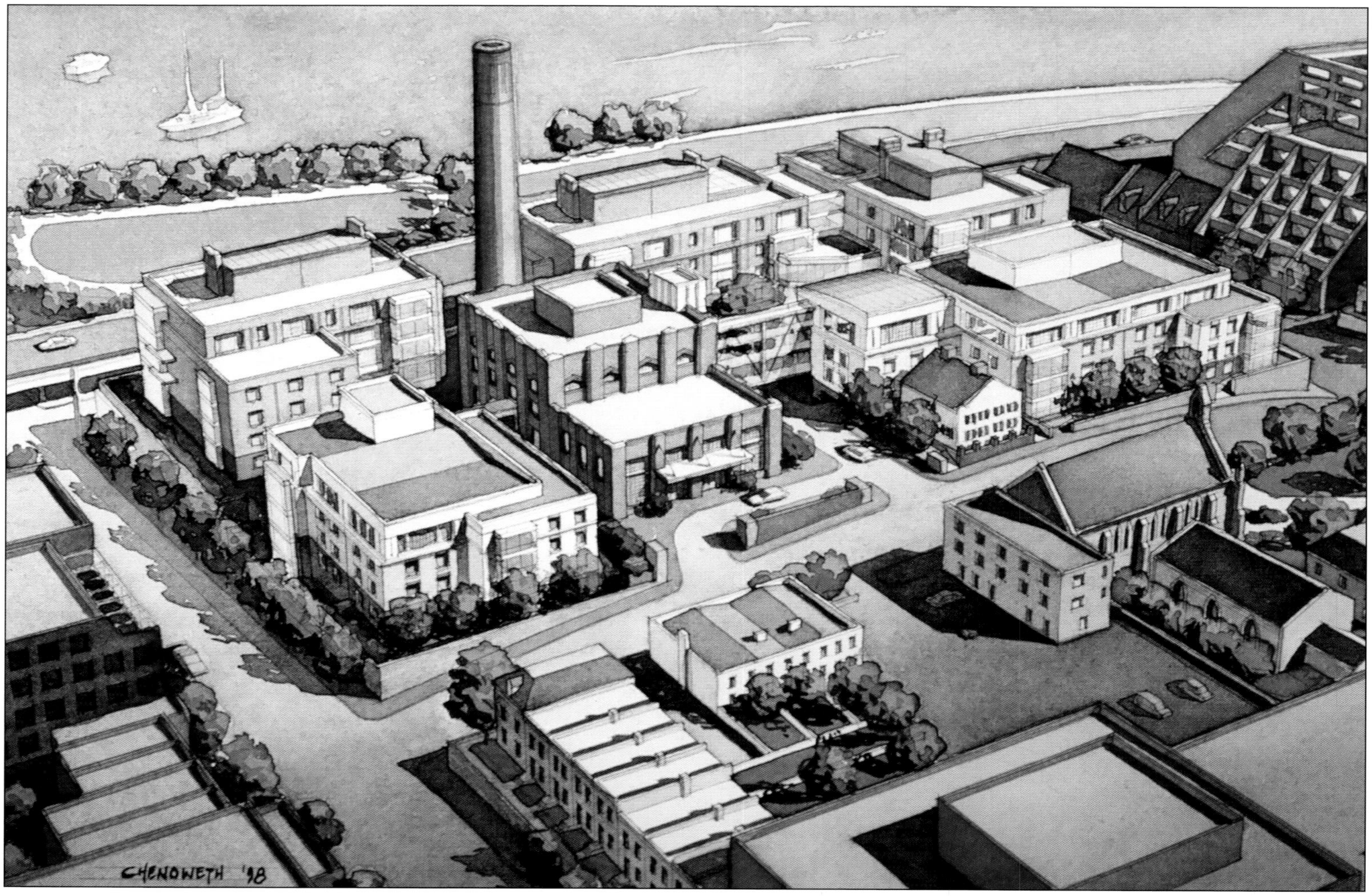

ABOVE: *Rendering of the proposed Georgetown incinerator project by Shalom Baranes Associates and Handel Architects, 1998.*

RIGHT: *Elevation of the Georgetown incinerator project viewed from Wisconsin Avenue, showing the extensive change in grade from South Street to the Whitehurst Freeway above K Street, 1998.*

The Georgetown incinerator project, completed in 2003, includes a new Ritz-Carlton Hotel, condominiums, and retail.

retail, and underground parking. At the end of the presentation, the chairman noted that a determination on "the little industrial buildings" was in order. Although they had been described by the commission staff and the architect as late nineteenth- and early twentieth-century structures, Brown concluded:

They're in the 1950s style and I don't think anybody's crying over it.... We inspected them today and I must say our impression was that we're not too sure what they're contributing to.... And we don't really have a street that is anything but post-Whitehurst Freeway and I worry that those little buildings are not contributing in real life to anybody's love of Georgetown, and nobody loves Georgetown more than I do.... [W]e felt to the extent the Old Georgetown Act charges us with keeping an eye on demolitions, those can go.... So although I would really lie down in front of the bulldozers if anybody tried this north of M Street anywhere, I do think down here with the grade change and the Whitehurst and the existing structures that are there and the history it's something that we can approve in principle.[162]

The determination characterized Brown's opinion of historic vernacular architecture: his favor for the residential neighborhoods north of M Street did not extend to the varied scale and uses within the historic waterfront. There

was no dissent from the other commission members, and the project was eventually approved. The project demonstrated the balance often necessary to create development in the historic district: in this case, between the creation of a megablock project on a site that had been partially vacant for decades and preserving historic fabric. Designed to reuse the abandoned industrial incinerator property, the success of the project came with the cost of losing a historic alley and the setting of the Brickyard Hill House—the reconstruction of which revealed the paradox of replacing actual history with its simulacrum.

RESIDENTIAL GEORGETOWN

Development pressure extended to residential properties in the 1970s, when the owner of one of the remaining mid-size estates north of P Street sought to subdivide the property. The Commission of Fine Arts, the U.S. Department of Justice, the D.C. Corporation Counsel, Mayor Walter Washington, and the D.C. Superior Court all played a role in the case that represented the first time that the setting for a historic building was considered.

was not the best example of Downing's work; the highly-altered Italianate residence had lost some integrity, the size of the garden had changed over time and was in poor condition when purchased by the owners in 1967, and a rear garden of 80 feet (rather than the historic 120 feet) established a sufficient setting. Malarkey's neighbors argued that the entire garden was critical to the suburban villa as described in Vaux's book. The mayor authorized the construction permits in March 1977, and although the neighbors filed a suit in Superior Court to enjoin the mayor from issuing the permits, the mayor's decision was upheld. The CFA has no record of review for the two row houses on Q Street; nevertheless they were designed in a modified Georgian style with mansard roofs.

The character and preservation of open space remained a prominent issue in the late twentieth century when increasing wealth generated a trend of innumerable applications for rear additions to expand the historically small-scale living quarters of most Georgetown houses. Consequently, the Old Georgetown Board—composed of architects Hugh Miller, Peter Vercelli, and J. Richard Andrews—issued its first policy statement in 1986. It emphasized that new additions should be subordinate to existing buildings and not "impinge" on open space, noting that the zoning concept of "matter of right" was not applicable to the act. The policy stated that additions should have minimal visibility from the street and should have materials consistent with those predominant to the block, concluding with the caveat that all applications would be considered on a case-by-case basis.[164]

In the 1990s, following decades of residential new construction in the Colonial and Federal styles, the question of Victorian styles was posed to the commission. In November 1997, the CFA reviewed a master plan for Cranberry Hill Associates by architect Suman Sorg that included the renovation of the Phillips School at 2706 N Street into condominiums with fourteen new row houses on the playground. Following the brief presentation, Chairman Brown complimented the architect for her stylistic range, saying, "I'm particularly interested that you have understood that Georgetown architecture is not all Federal and that there's a lot of wonderful Victorian architecture in Georgetown which gives it its texture and its charm, and you need a mix." However, when the commission staff relayed the Old Georgetown Board's desire for the commission to comment on the design of particular row houses, the chairman deflected the request: "Well, that's what they're there for. I think that they're right there on the firing line and generally we like to back them up, unless we think they've had a bad day."[165] Brown, who

ABOVE: *The Robert Dodge House, pictured in 1968, was designed in 1850 by Andrew Jackson Downing and was featured in* Villas and Cottages *(1857), Calvert Vaux's influential work on the suburban house.*

RIGHT: *Residences built on a portion of the original Dodge House garden, c. 1993.*

In early 1976, Martin Malarkey pursued a subdivision to build two semi-detached houses at the rear of his property at 1534 28th Street, which extended along Q Street for most of the block. The residence, known as the Robert Dodge House, had been designed by Andrew Jackson Downing in 1850 and was published in Calvert Vaux's seminal book *Villas and Cottages* (1857). The director of the D.C. planning office requested an opinion from the CFA, which opposed the subdivision as it would impair historic value and change the character of the open space and streetscape. In May the Department of Justice issued an opinion that clarified the CFA's authority to make recommendations on subdivisions because of the concomitant building construction.[163]

The owner's attorney argued that the Dodge House

Postmodernism and Infill Projects in Georgetown

In the 1980s, development increasingly expanded beyond the waterfront to the commercial corridors of M Street and Wisconsin Avenue as establishments changed from neighborhood-oriented shops to national retail stores and destination entertainment. In addition, postmodernism became popular in design as a superficial return to historic styles in its use of architectural fragments. While buildings inspired by the architectural vocabulary of the past might find easy acceptance with the CFA, in Georgetown this was not always the case; context remained a critical factor, and commission members often disagreed on how well individual designs fit within it.

One of the earliest postmodern designs was approved in 1980 for the Madison Bank building at 2833 M Street, a conflation of Georgian and Federal motifs designed by Martin & Jones Archi-

tects for Deanwood Development. The mixed-use development included the bank, offices, and apartments. The facades suggest residential architecture with a pastiche of gables, dormers, Palladian arches, and multilight windows. Other postmodern designs approved by the commission included two by Arthur Cotton Moore: the Corcoran School at 2715 M Street, derived from Victorian motifs, and the rooftop pavilions added to the Car Barn at 3600 M Street.

In June 1984, a proposal for speculative retail construction on a parking lot at 1229 Wisconsin Avenue was presented to the commission by Washington architect Shalom Baranes. The commission members compared the neo-Palladian design to the nearby historic Riggs Bank as overscaled and found the new design lacking in comparison. Walter Netsch concluded the review with advice for Baranes: "The conflict is the grace that existed in the

past and the kind of exuberance architects want to do today. I suggest you study a little bit more a sense of grace as you refine it."[1] Proportions were adjusted and the OGB soon approved a revised design. Interestingly, when the building was demolished in 2008 for redevelopment, some considered it historic.

Postmodernism in Georgetown continued into the 1990s with projects such as the neo-Federal bank building by Leo A Daly at Wisconsin and Q Streets, which was reviewed by the OGB in February 1996. Although it accepted the historicist building design derived from William Thornton's Octagon House, the OGB criticized the geometric relationship of the small dome to the mass of the building and found the site plan awkward as it located a parking lot along the Q Street frontage.

ABOVE: *In his design for a speculative retail building at 1229 Wisconsin Avenue, architect Shalom Baranes used a Palladian motif as the building's central element, shown as built in 1986.*

LEFT TO RIGHT: *Martin & Jones Architects combined residential architectural elements such as dormers, gables, and a classical column in a postmodern treatment of mixed-use development in their 1980 design for 2833 M Street. Arthur Cotton Moore quoted Georgetown's Victorian architecture in his postmodern design for 2715 M Street, including a prominent corner turret and glass mansard roofs, 1985. Chevy Chase Bank at 1545 Wisconsin Avenue by Leo A Daly is derived from Federal-style precedents reinterpreted at a reduced scale, completed 1997.*

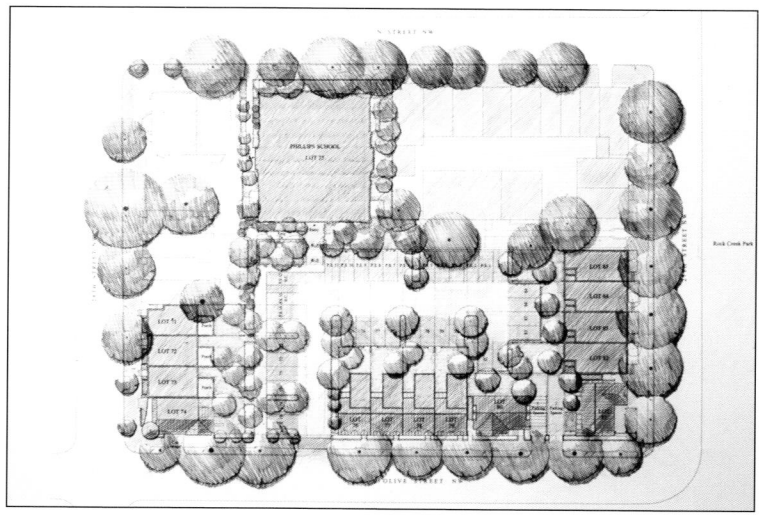

TOP LEFT: *The Phillips School, view of south facade from Olive Street, 1950.*

TOP RIGHT: *Plan of the Phillips School project proposed new row houses occupying the former school playground, 1997.*

RIGHT AND BOTTOM: *The design of the infill row house development by Suman Sorg & Associates incorporated precedents from Georgetown's Victorian-era architecture, 1998. Depicted here are street and building elevations.*

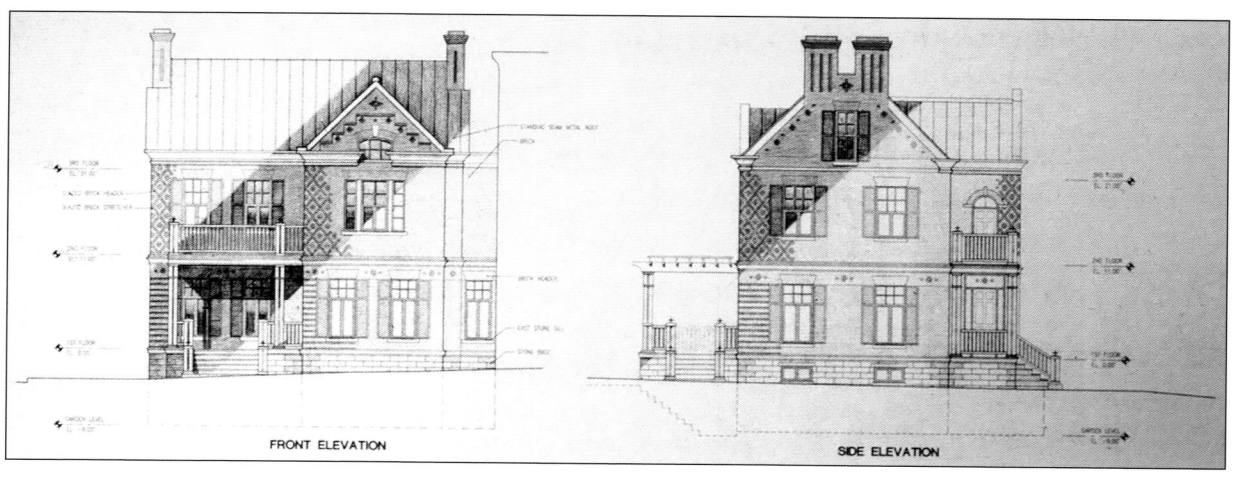

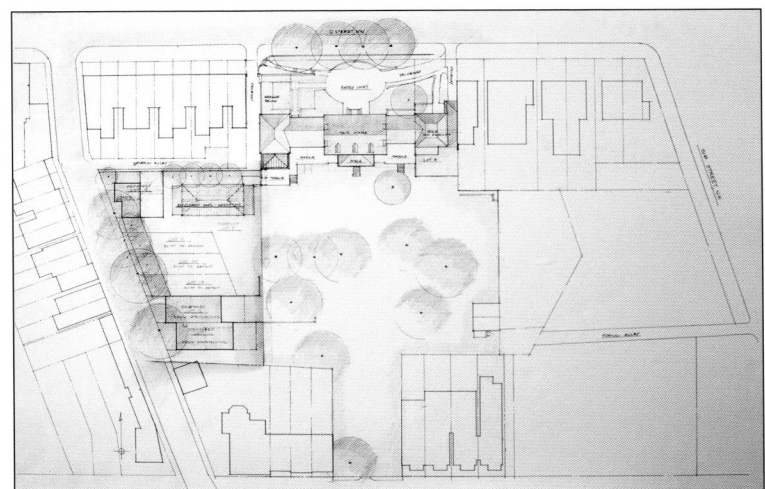

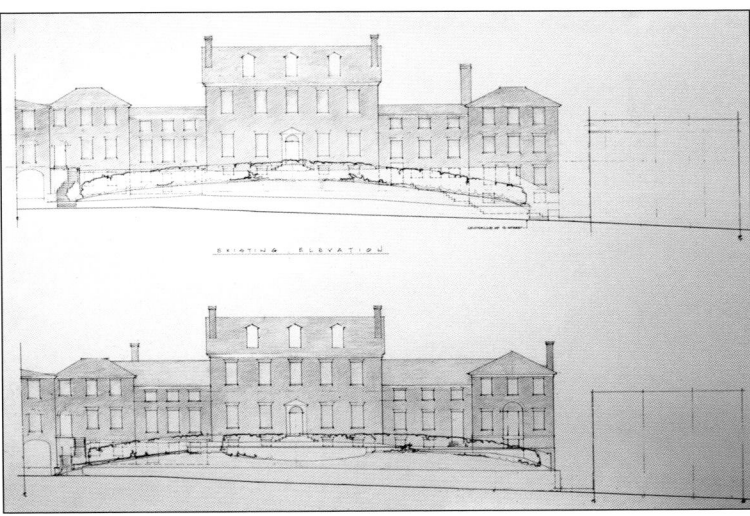

typically spoke profusely, did not want to address the board's questions or hold discussion on the first instance of neo-Victorian residential design in nearly fifty years.

A complex case involving subdivision, demolition, alteration, and new construction arose in early 1998, offering the commission a rare opportunity to review alterations to a historic building; the outcome gave preference to the extension of historic architectural principle while implying a historical past that had not actually existed—a central conflict in guiding new architecture in historic districts.[166] Herbert Miller, the developer of Georgetown Park and Washington Harbour, purchased the Bowie-Sevier House at 3124 Q Street, one of Georgetown's large estates located in the higher elevations north of P Street. A retirement home had occupied the property since 1956, and Miller wanted to remodel the main house for use as his family residence with several parcels subdivided to build new row houses. In addition to the design and preservation issues, the case involved a prominent owner and significant neighbor opposition.

TOP LEFT: *A view of the south facade of the Bowie-Sevier House shows the west wing of the main house prior to the mid-century institutional addition, c. 1910.*

ABOVE LEFT: *A series of architects were associated with the expansion of the Bowie-Sevier House; view of the south facade shows the redesign of the west wing as a hyphen end pavilion, completed 2004.*

TOP RIGHT: *Plan of the 1998 Bowie-Sevier project by Horsey & Thorpe showing the expanded main house, pool house, and new row house development on a portion of the property facing 32nd Street.*

ABOVE RIGHT: *Options by Horsey & Thorpe for the proposed alterations, refashioning the property as a symmetrical five-part composition, 1998.*

The concept application was before the commission at its March 1998 meeting to review the three row houses proposed for the portion of the estate along 32nd Street. Following a morning site visit, the commission members chose not to discuss the new construction but to address only the alterations to the site and the historic residence. The design proposed by Horsey & Thorpe to expand the residence would create a five-part house—a main block flanked by two hyphens and then two end pavilions—where only one end pavilion had existed historically. The commission members supported the changes; and, when the chairman discussed the importance of having the correct relationships between the five parts, the architect proposed increasing the roof height of the existing pavilion to "correct" its relationship to the other roofs. Despite the impact on the historic integrity of the house, Brown thought it a good idea. The comments of the D.C. Historic Preservation Division's architectural historian, who explained that for most of its existence the house had only consisted of the main block and eastern hyphen, were met with silence.[167] The project was approved in concept with a request for more information regarding the substantial reconfiguration of the front driveway.

Evolution of the Commission of Fine Arts as an Agency

While the constitution of the commission itself changed substantially over the years of Brown's chairmanship, the commission staff had grown to a half-dozen professionals, many of whom remained in their jobs for decades. In addition to the long service of Sue Kohler, Donald Myer remained as assistant secretary until 1997, when Jeffrey Carson was promoted to that position, in which he stayed until his retirement in 2001. Frederick Lindstrom, an architect from HABS, was hired to replace Carson in 1998 and subsequently was promoted to assistant secretary in 2001. The professional capacities of the staff increased dramatically under Atherton's leadership, evidenced in one notable case by the analysis and presentation on the design of Western Plaza (now Freedom Plaza) on Pennsylvania Avenue, resulting in a change to the PADC plan as previously discussed. In contrast to the practices of the commission's earlier history where the members met in closed session, new federal requirements for transparency in government resulted in open deliberations at the meeting table with cases introduced and presented by staff members—a substantial change in the institutional culture concomitant with an evolution in commission appointments from experienced practitioners to a preponderance of lay members.

The change in the credentials of appointees to the CFA may be exemplary of a larger political shift, reflecting the decline of the progressive idea of the expert panel toward a model emphasizing citizen engagement. Likewise, the very issues of architecture and design—of great importance to Franklin D. Roosevelt and the Kennedys—were less obviously an interest for successive presidential administrations. Once the working base of some presidents' close advisors, such as William Walton, the commission had been ensconced in Jackson Place within sight of the White House since 1971; in 1989 the commission was asked to vacate those offices for other entities of the Executive Office of the President. The CFA relocated in February 1990 to offices in the Pension Building in Judiciary Square, a property administered by the GSA and, by that time, the home of the National Building Museum.

With the long-standing association of the director of the National Gallery of Art with the commission, the CFA increasingly took on other functions related to the arts in Washington. Given the early prominence of the commission, the CFA chairman had been named in a codicil to the will of donor Charles Lang Freer in 1919 to approve acquisitions to the permanent collection of the Freer Gallery of Art of the Smithsonian Institution. Due to the work of David Finley, the CFA chairman was named an *ex officio* member of the National Trust for Historic Preservation in 1949 legislation and of the White House Historical Society in its 1961 charter; a 1964 executive order stipulated that the CFA chairman would serve on the Committee for the Preservation of the White House. Under William Walton, the CFA chairman was designated as an *ex officio* member of the board of the Kennedy Center for the Performing Arts in its authorizing legislation of 1964; in 1965 Congress established what became the National Endowments for the Arts and for the Humanities, designating the CFA chairman as an *ex officio* member of the ancillary board, the National Council of the Arts and Humanities. During Brown's chairmanship, Congress established the National Capital Arts and Cultural Affairs (NCACA) program in 1986 to administer grants to support the operations of major institutions located in the District of Columbia dedicated to exhibiting, presenting, and performing arts at a professional level; the administration of the program was transferred to the CFA in 1988. Through its first three decades of existence, the NCACA program was a source of public funding in lieu of a larger state arts agency to support its institutions, a period concurrent with the flourishing artistic milieu of Washington in the 1990s and 2000s. The program reached its highest historic level of funding in 2010 at $9.5 million, although over the

years it was proposed to be eliminated numerous times by several presidential administrations.[168]

The most significant change in this period to the work of the Commission of Fine Arts by congressional legislation came in 1986 with the passage of the Commemorative Works Act (CWA). Enacted in the wake of the high-profile controversies over the design of national memorials in West Potomac Park, the CWA established an advisory body, the National Capital Memorial Advisory Commission (NCMAC), to advise Congress on proposed legislation to establish national memorials on public lands in Washington, D.C. Administered by the National Park Service's National Capital Region, the NCMAC included *ex officio* representation from the Department of the Interior, the CFA, the NCPC, the GSA, the Department of Defense, the American Battle Monuments Commission, the Architect of the Capitol, and the Mayor of the District of Columbia as an advisory body to consider how proposals "(A) are appropriately designed, constructed, and located and (B) reflect a consensus of the lasting national significance of the subjects involved."[169] The CWA may be understood as a mechanism to depoliticize controversial issues of what to commemorate and where to locate memorials; it placed unusual authority for approval for the design of all com-

ABOVE LEFT: CFA *staff on the steps of 708 Jackson Place, NW, 1987 (from left): Donald Myer, Charles Atherton, Jeffrey R. Carson, Elizabeth Hannold, José Martínez Canino, Sue Kohler, and Patricia Cosimano.*

TOP RIGHT: CFA *members seated at the conference table at the commission's Pension Building office, October 1994 (from left): Adele Chatfield-Taylor, George Hartman, Joan Abrahamson, J. Carter Brown, Susan Porter Rose, Jeannine Smith Clark, and Robert Peck. Staff members are in the background.*

ABOVE RIGHT: *Charles Atherton with maquette of the George Mason statue by Wendy Ross in the sculptor's studio, 2001.*

memorative works on the CFA, the NCPC, and the Department of the Interior.

The authorization, location, and design of national memorials had historically been the most controversial of issues facing the commission—from its work on the Lincoln Memorial in its first decade to the furor over the Jefferson Memorial before World War II. While there were no national memorials erected on the Mall from 1943 to 1982, the restoration of West Potomac Park as a completed landscape created a new opportunity for commemorative sites, one coincident with a seemingly urgent need for symbolizing the national collective memory.

A New Vocabulary for Architecture on the Mall

The Commission of Fine Arts's greatest achievement during the first half of the twentieth century was the implementation of the McMillan Plan's vision for the National Mall. The chaotic mix of nineteenth-century romantic garden and industrial uses was replaced by a formal green space with self-contained neoclassical memorials as objects on axis with the White House and Capitol, framed on its northern edge by Beaux-Arts architecture.

Implementation continued at midcentury, although the architectural vocabulary of buildings on the Mall evolved from the unity of the Beaux-Arts to the unity of modernism, as expressed by the National Air and Space Museum, Federal Office Buildings in Southwest, and, later in the period, by the Hirshhorn Museum and the East Building of the National Gallery. In the last quarter of the century, however, unity of architectural expression ebbed, replaced by a rapid succession of styles with more eclectic and an often contextually or historically based vocabulary; this change was visible in the new museums proposed for the Mall. The subject matter of new Mall museums also changed in this period, becoming more focused on specific events or cultures, which added complexity to the architectural approach.

SMITHSONIAN QUADRANGLE

The earliest of the new generation of museums—a companion museum to the Freer Gallery to house the Asian art collection donated by Dr. Arthur M. Sackler and a national museum for a newly acquired collection of African art—were sited in the Smithsonian Quadrangle, south of the Smithsonian Castle on Independence Avenue at 10th Street.[170] Both were to be largely underground structures with only small pavilions at grade to protect the existing landscape south of the Castle. In a letter to Senator Claiborne Pell (D-RI) in April 1979, Carter Brown expressed the commission's support for the museums' authorizing legislation and highlighted two factors, context and setting, that would come to influence the commission in its later review of the designs: "There is already a rich diversity of both architectural character and scale...and two relatively small structures flanking the 10th Street vista of the Castle Building, screened from the street by low walls with landscaping in front, should fit in quite well."[171]

Early pavilion designs by Japanese architect Junzo Yoshimura were inspired by African and Asian cultures, "simple...garden houses...contemporary structures, not copies of traditional buildings," with two deeply sunken courts. In its April 1980 review, the CFA gave preliminary approval to the concept, massing, and site plan but found the depth of the sunken courts, at nearly two stories, problematic.[172]

When the commission next saw the schemes in September 1981, the designs had drastically changed. Ill health had forced Yoshimura to resign from the project, to be replaced by Jean-Paul Carlhian of the Boston architectural firm Shepley, Bulfinch, Richardson & Abbott, which had developed the site plan and massing. Gone were the sunken courts and the culture-specific influences on the architecture; Carlhian described his designs as contextually, rather than culturally, influenced: pyramidal roofs for the Asian art pavilion drawn from the adjacent nineteenth-century Arts and Industries Building and domes and arches for the African art pavilion inspired by the nearby Freer Gallery, with ornamentation and surface articulation on both pavilions. CFA member Walter Netsch objected to the change, terming it "elitist" and lacking in the qualities of "modesty" and "vigor" associated with Asian and African art, respectively. In response Carlhian said he wanted to move away from the literalness of a "World's Fair pavilion."[173]

J. Carter Brown supported Carlhian's change in direction as a way to make the pavilions cohesive and the entire complex more unified. He urged the designer to continue to explore in simplified form the precedents of Victorian eclecticism visible in the nearby Castle and Arts and Industries Building.[174] The revised preliminary design studies presented at the CFA's December 1981 meeting reflected these suggestions with simpler surface ornamentation and aligned horizontal elements to visually link both pavilions. Sasaki Associates also presented a preliminary landscape plan featuring the pavilions and Castle set in distinct "garden rooms"; both the landscape and revised pavilion designs were approved at the meeting.[175]

During 1982, the commission continued to review the project's progress, eventually focusing primarily on the

LEFT: *The model of Junzo Yoshimura's 1980 scheme for the Smithsonian Quadrangle shows the relationship of the new museums to the Castle and garden and indicates the depth of the proposed sunken courts.*

BELOW: *The 1981 revised design by Jean-Paul Carlhian of Shepley, Bulfinch, Richardson & Abbott eliminated the sunken courts and introduced a landscape design by Sasaki & Associates organized as outdoor rooms with trees and a water feature.*

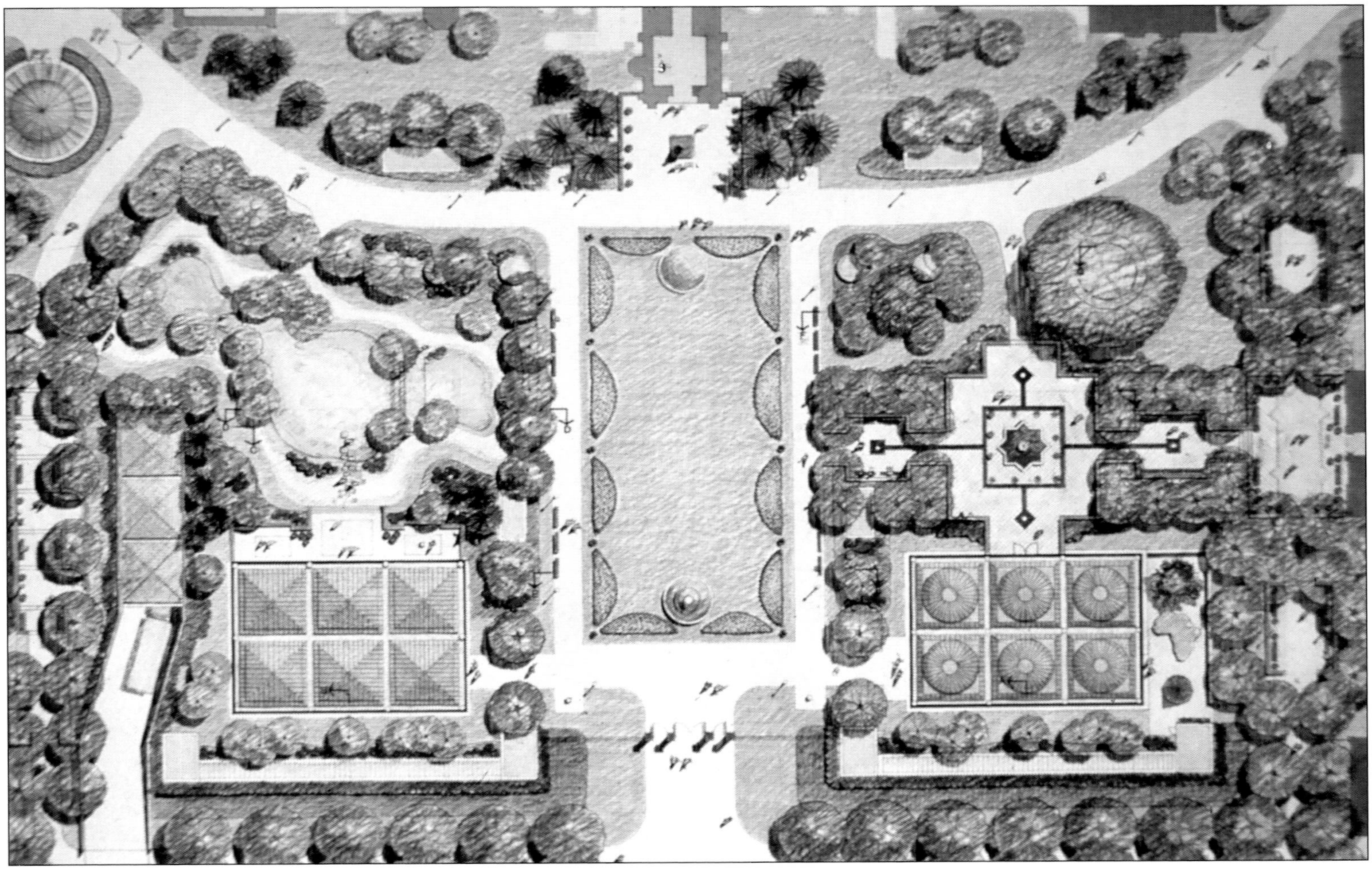

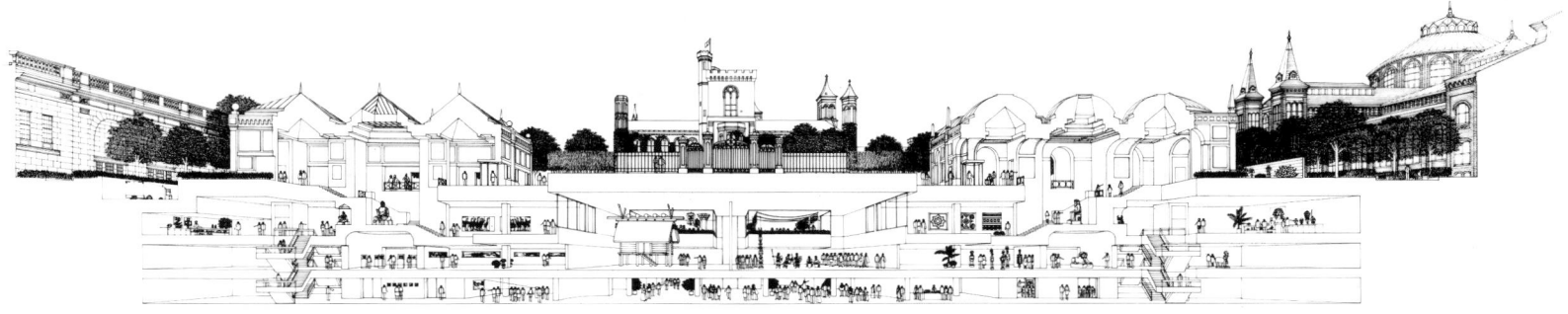

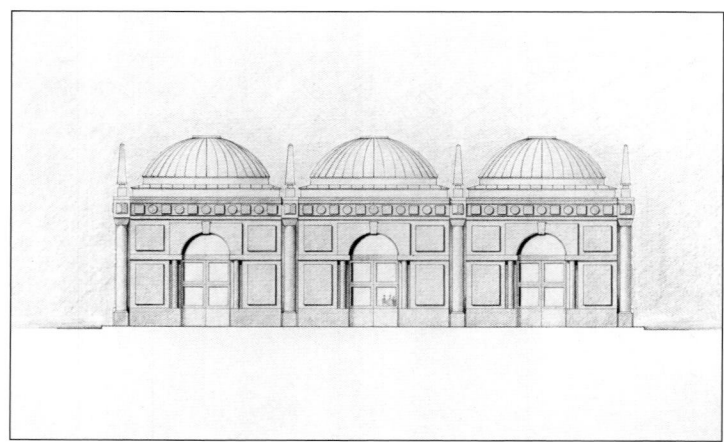

TOP: *Section through the two new museums (1981) shows the extent of the largely underground facilities and the buildings' relationship to the Castle (center), the Freer Gallery (left), and the Arts and Industries Building (right).*

ABOVE LEFT: *The south elevation of the National Museum of African Art, presented by Carlhian to the CFA in September 1981, incorporated domes and arches inspired by the Freer Gallery.*

ABOVE RIGHT: *View south from the Smithsonian Quadrangle, showing the relationship of the museums and garden to the Forrestal Building spanning 10th Street, 1993.*

RIGHT: *Aerial view of the Smithsonian Quadrangle as built, 2006.*

landscape setting for the pavilions and the Castle. Water features shown in the preliminary designs were eliminated early on for practical reasons, and the planting schemes became lower and less distinctive for each pavilion and the Castle. The CFA found this approach less compelling than the "fresh, compatible, room-like quality" of the earlier designs.[176] After reviews in July, September, and November failed to produce satisfactory revisions, the CFA asked member Edward D. Stone Jr., a landscape architect, to examine the schemes with the design team. Reporting on that meeting to the commission in December 1982, Stone noted it had become clear that S. Dillon Ripley, secretary of the Smithsonian Institution, preferred the "oriental carpet" approach of low plantings over the entire space to provide an unimpeded view of the Castle rather than the distinctive "three-room" approach preferred by the CFA. Reluctantly, the members chose to approve Ripley's preferred garden design "with regret," but asked that structural specifications and soil depth allow the inclusion of taller trees in the future.[177] The new museums opened in 1987 with their presence announced by the pavilions but their primary functions located underground.

NATIONAL MUSEUM OF THE AMERICAN INDIAN

Cultural expression within the context of the Mall was a more manifest issue ten years later with the design of the National Museum of the American Indian (NMAI). Conceived as a hybrid of cultural center and museum, the NMAI was sited directly opposite the East Building at the base of the Capitol. The commission's first involvement with the NMAI was in February 1992, when the project's preliminary program was presented for comment by the Smithsonian Institution. W. Richard West Jr., the NMAI's director, outlined the guiding programmatic principles for a museum that was to be far different from others on the Mall: a museum not solely about material culture but about Native American people and their ideas; and a cultural institution expressive of a living people informed by collaborative input from a broad spectrum of members of that community.[178] Denise Scott Brown, a partner in the architectural firm Venturi, Rauch & Scott Brown that was developing the program, explained the extensive process of interviews with Native American communities that her firm had undertaken to elicit that input, noting that these constituents wanted neither a "Neo-Classical temple" nor a "tepee" to represent them on the Mall.[179]

J. Carter Brown summarized the commission's advice in his letter to the Smithsonian. While the NMAI's planners wanted to avoid "the conventional interpretations of the museum" and include a complex array of functions, Brown advised:

There are a wide range of architectural forms presently on the Mall, especially on the south side…. All of these are held together by the strength of the surrounding spaces that comprise the essence of the Mall, and the adherence to certain parameters such as building heights and setbacks. While this suggests considerable freedom in developing a unique design, the proximity to the Capitol as well as a location on the Mall itself will call for some measure of restraint.[180]

In the hands of Douglas Cardinal, a Canadian architect of Native American ancestry, the NMAI design had evolved to be far from conventional, yet the CFA came to consider it both exciting and appropriate to the Mall. Cardinal's design—a sweeping, organic architectural expression in rough and smooth stone—and the integrated landscape plan developed by EDAW incorporated key elements the Native American communities had asked for in the building and its grounds as expressed in the program planning document *Way of the People:* natural materials, an east-facing entrance, an amorphous structure without right angles, a natural habitat of trees and water, performance and dining spaces, and a tactile and visual experience.[181]

At the CFA's September 1995 meeting, Cardinal and Roger Courtenay of EDAW introduced the design concepts. Courtenay described a landscape setting with water features and wetlands and lowlands habitats, hardscapes for ceremonial purposes, and visual and spatial linkages to the Capitol. Cardinal emphasized his design's respect for the formal composition of the Mall defined by height and setback and its strong east-west axis, but equally important in his vision was the building's organic relationship to the earth and celestial elements, expressed through curvilinear components and a cantilevered overhang on the northeast facade connoting sheltering rocks and cliffs. A domed interior space near the entry would provide a gathering

Douglas Cardinal's sweeping, curvilinear composition for the National Museum of the American Indian (NMAI) presented to the CFA in September 1995.

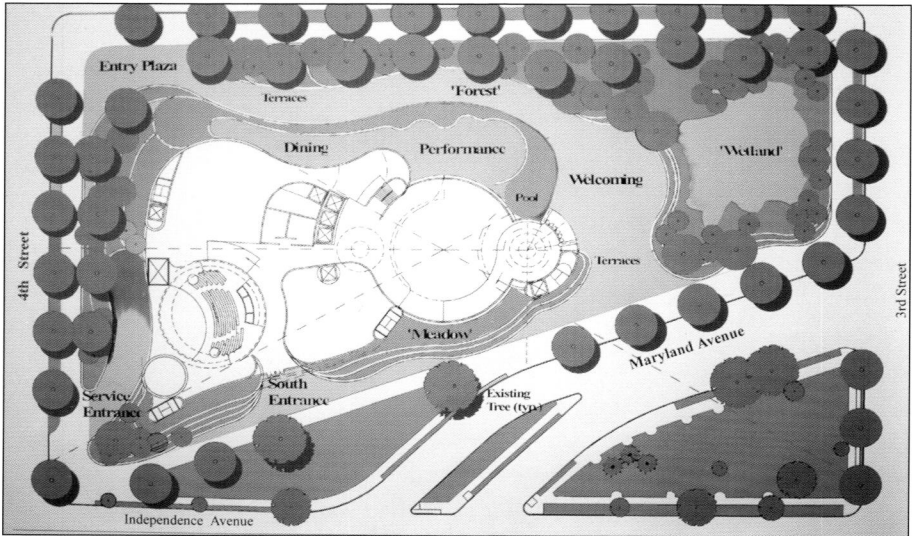

TOP: *The revised design concept developed by the Polshek Partnership in 1999 included a large column to support the projecting roof.*

ABOVE: *Like the building design's, the 1996 landscape plan for the NMAI by EDAW evolved in response to principles established during program development with the Native American community.*

place for rituals, dances, and celebrations as well as food and shops, and would lead to three floors of gallery space. The commission members recognized the building's unique program and purpose and were enthusiastic about the project, approving the design's direction despite its unprecedented appearance for a Mall museum.[182]

The following year, the commission reviewed the design twice more, in May and October, approving the concept and design development and tentatively approving the proposed materials. Few comments were made, most related to the penthouse and window "slits" on the Maryland Avenue facade. The commission expressed support for the project: "Clearly, the proposed building, together with its integral landscaping, appears well on the way to providing Washington with a first rate facility within the context of the foreground of the Capitol."[183]

The commission was far less pleased when it next saw the project in April 1999 for revised design development. Contractual problems had led the Smithsonian in 1998 to terminate its relationship with Cardinal and the Philadelphia architectural firm GBQC that was associated with him on the project.[184] The Smithsonian hired the New York architecture firm Polshek Partnership, which had designed the NMAI's associated Cultural Resources Center facility in Suitland, Maryland, to finish the project based on Cardinal's design.[185] The Polshek team addressed the slit-like windows on the south facade, shortening them and also adding horizontal windows. Most significantly, a large column was inserted to support the projecting roof, which had been unimpeded in Cardinal's original design.

Douglas Cardinal attended the meeting and asked to speak after the Polshek presentation. Cardinal described his design, with its curvilinear expression, as a counterpart to the angular geometries of the East Building. He showed changes he had made to his design based on the commission's comments, a process that involved simplifying the forms but keeping the building's spirit and sculptural essence intact.

The commission members acknowledged that the new design team had produced a good building, but Cardinal's presentation had reminded them of the "poetic" vision that had been lost. In particular, J. Carter Brown noted the added column was "the saddest thing…it looked like a crutch…ugly." The commission voted unanimously to disapprove the submission, finding the "revisions to Mr. Cardinal's unique, eloquent, and very personal statement fell short of capturing the heart and essential nature of the concept that in 1996 so captivated the Commission."[186]

The project returned to the commission for review in June 1999 with Smithsonian secretary I. Michael Heyman

ABOVE: *With further design refinement, the column was reengineered as a series of cantilevers; the National Museum of the American Indian was completed in 2004.*

LEFT: *Flowing water for the museum's extensive naturalistic landscape emerges from the rough stone base of the building, creating a sequence of pools leading to the museum's main entrance.*

New Trends in Commemoration for Coins and Medals

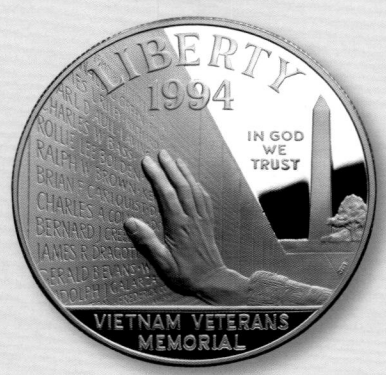

With the exception of the Kennedy half-dollar (1964) and the Eisenhower dollar (1971), no new circulating coins were issued by the U.S. Mint during the mid-twentieth century. The Mint had also produced dozens of special commemorative coins in the early twentieth century, but this program was discontinued by Congress in 1939 with the exception of three coins issued through 1954. By the 1980s, however, a new national interest in commemoration—most visible on the National Mall with the development of war memorials—was manifested in the authorization and design of American coins and medals. Congress began authorizing commemorative coins again in 1982; not only did the number of commemorative coins and Congressional medals increase substantially in this period, but the range of their subjects expanded well beyond the historic depiction of allegorical and political figures.

ABOVE: *William C. Cousins, Bicentennial of the U.S. Capitol silver dollar, obverse, 1994; John Mercanti, Vietnam Veterans Memorial silver dollar, obverse, 1994.*

RIGHT: *Diane Wolf testifying before the Senate Banking Committee on a bill to redesign U.S. coins, 1988.*

The first eloquent example of this trend was the issue of the Susan B. Anthony dollar in 1978—the first American circulating coin to bear the image of a woman and a private citizen—to honor the nineteenth-century suffragist leader. In its review, the CFA recommended that the coin's design should convey the strength of character evident in historic photographs of Anthony. The design was also notable for its distinctive eleven-sided border. The next circulating coin to be issued, in 1998, honored another historic woman: the Native American guide Sacagawea. When obverse designs by Glenna Goodacre—sculptor of the Vietnam Veterans Women's Memorial—were submitted for the gold-toned Sacagawea quarter, the CFA supported a design depicting Sacagawea with her infant son, who served as a symbol of peace as the Lewis and Clark expedition encountered native tribes.

The issue of numismatic design took on greater importance for the CFA with the appointment in 1985 of Diane Wolf, an ardent supporter of the redesign of the nation's coinage, both for its symbolic value and for its capacity to increase federal revenue through seigniorage and the direct sales of special-interest commemorative coins. Wolf drew up a resolution, adopted by the CFA in 1987, recommending that Congress and the secretary of the treasury consider changing the obverse and reverse designs of the penny, nickel, dime, quarter, and half-dollar by invited compensated competition. Her efforts eventually led to the enactment of legislation in 1992 authorizing the redesign of the reverses for the penny, nickel, and quarter. Her influence increased the public profile and number of

the Mint's commemorative noncirculating coins and helped initiate a prolific new era of circulating coin production that would continue into the early twenty-first century.

Accompanying the era's increase in the production of commemorative coins, new artistic approaches in the design of coins also emerged in the late twentieth century, particularly in the use of novel pictorial devices that adapted conventions taken from photography to expand the traditional compositions of coin design. In contrast to historic numismatic conventions, these new designs were often characterized by asymmetrical compositions, the juxtaposition of figures of dissimilar scales, and close-in, partial views of subjects. Reviewing the commemorative one-dollar coin issued for the bicentennial of the U.S. Capitol (1994), the CFA commended the massive strength of the off-center dome depicted on its obverse. A similar composition was employed in the commemorative one-dollar coin issued for the tenth anniversary of the Vietnam Veterans Memorial (1994), where the obverse illustrates the memorial wall at a raking angle with a hand reaching out to touch a name inscribed on its surface. The CFA approved the design but raised concerns that the stylized aerial view of the memorial on the reverse could be mistaken as a graphic chevron shape rather than as a representation of the memorial.

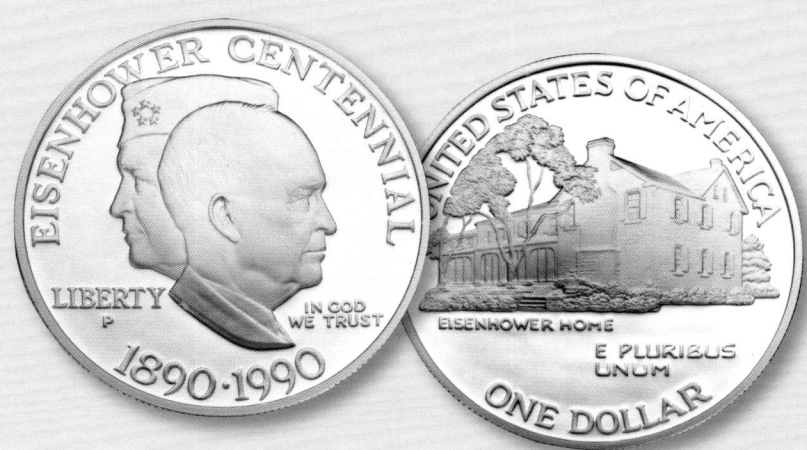

ABOVE LEFT: *Frank Gasparro, Susan B. Anthony dollar coin, 1978 obverse and reverse (1999 reissue).*

ABOVE RIGHT: *Glenna Goodacre, Sacagawea gold dollar coin, 1998 obverse (2003 reissue).*

LEFT: *Eisenhower Commemorative Silver Dollar, 1990, John Mercanti, obverse; Marcel Jovine, reverse. While traditional in its subject, the*

Eisenhower commemorative coin was unusual in featuring a double portrait of Eisenhower as general and president; the obverse presented a picturesque and almost photographic image of the leader's home in Gettysburg, Pennsylvania.

BELOW: *The CFA reviewed the Rosa Parks Congressional Gold Medal, designed by Artis Lane, in July 1999. The members found her portrait on the obverse (left) to be admirable but objected to the reverse (right)—the scales of justice balanced on a globe— as symbolically obscure.*

and the Institution's entire executive committee attending the public meeting, suggesting the high level of concern that the commission's decision had prompted within the Smithsonian's hierarchy. More importantly, the design had been revised, with instances of awkward handling refined and the column removed, restoring the cantilever and cascading quality of the facade. The commission approved this phase of design development with recommendations for further detail study, including the south facade's windows.[187]

The NMAI's final design was approved by the commission in May 2000, although the members reviewed material samples on site in October 2002, where they continued to try to preserve the language of the original design. At that review, the members found that the stone surface had been modified—from a roughly textured base gradually changing to a smooth finish on the upper stories—to a random pattern of rough bands, coarse stones, and smooth ashlar across the facade. They urged the Smithsonian, unsuccessfully, to return to the original concept's "metaphorical qualities of a mountain."[188] The revisions to the surface treatment remained intact; the museum opened in 2004.

HOLOCAUST MEMORIAL MUSEUM

Like the NMAI, which it preceded, the United States Holocaust Memorial Museum was envisioned as a hybrid institution, but rather than an expression of a distinct culture, its purpose was commemorative and educational: a living memorial to the millions of victims of Nazism and a museum to display and study the artifacts and experience of tyranny. The memorial museum was authorized by Congress in 1980 and assigned a site within the Mall precinct between 14th and 15th Streets south of Independence Av-

enue, flanked by the historic Auditors Building and Bureau of Engraving and Printing. Finding the appropriate language and expression for its complex mission and program proved a daunting task for its sponsors, designers, and the commission.

The commission first reviewed the building's concept design in May 1985. George Notter of the architecture firm Notter, Feingold & Alexander presented a scheme that included three key elements defined by the Holocaust Memorial Council, the fifty-five-member presidentially appointed group leading the project: a Hall of Remembrance, the memorial component for the victims; a Hall of Witness for permanent exhibitions; and a Hall of Learning containing the archives, library, classrooms, and temporary exhibition space. These components were organized into a large, unadorned building on columns whose most distinctive feature was a central, suspended box-like element that contained the Halls of Remembrance and Witness.

The commission members found the scheme badly lacking in commemorative expression and as an element of urban design on the Mall. Noting it spoke more of "muscle than of soul," Alan Novak suggested that the designers look to the Vietnam Memorial, which had recently been dedicated on the Mall, for guidance: "[S]implicity and delicacy are provocative, and it is something that the average person can relate well with."[189] Sondra Myers and Edward Stone Jr. concurred, finding the design emotionless and severe. Both Frederick Hart and J. Carter Brown mentioned the building's problem with scale and suggested that it be set back in line with its neighbors. Brown further suggested changes in the treatment of the windows and the columns that could improve the sense of scale, although he thought even with these changes the building remained too large.

The CFA reviewing the revised design for the Holocaust Memorial Museum by I. M. Pei & Partners in June 1987 at its Jackson Place office. Seated (left to right) are: J. Carter Brown, Frederick Hart, and Diane Wolf. Standing are staff members Charles Atherton (left) and Donald Myer (right).

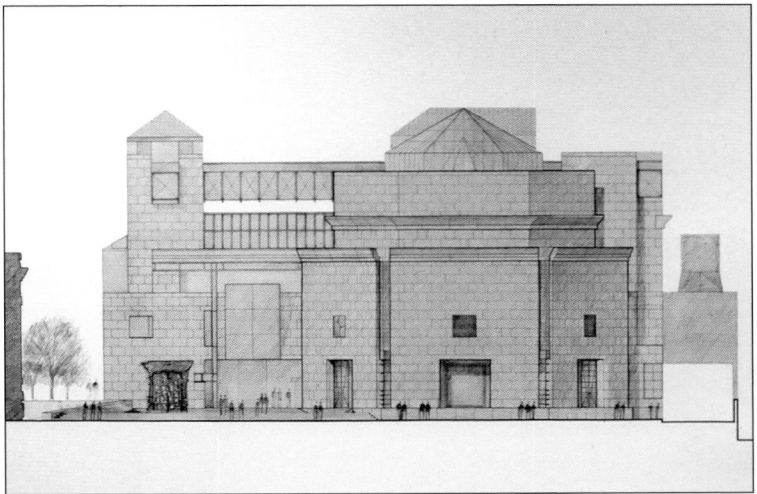

Albert Abramson, secretary of the Holocaust Memorial Council, countered the criticism, saying that the intent of the design was to be large and imposing, to bluntly "hit the conscience of the visitor." The commission advised that the scheme be restudied.[190]

The designers returned to the commission the next month, with the scheme reduced in scale with better delineation of the museum and memorial elements and set back closer to the adjacent historic buildings. The columns had been modified, reducing the original scheme's "exaggerated forcefulness." The commission approved the revised conceptual design, although "with misgivings," and suggested that the 14th Street entrance, the main entrance for the museum, needed revision to reduce its "overbearing character."[191]

Two years later, in May 1987, the Memorial Council returned to the commission with a new designer and scheme.[192] James Ingo Freed of I. M. Pei & Partners (the firm became Pei Cobb Freed & Partners in 1989) presented a scheme influenced by the building's context as

well as its program. Smaller in size, with 40 percent of its 250,000 square feet underground, the new concept incorporated a vocabulary of materials from the adjacent structures—limestone from the Bureau of Engraving and Printing and brick from the Auditors Building—and was set back to fit within this context. A notable feature on the 15th Street facade was a hexagonal commemorative pavilion containing the Hall of Remembrance, which extended beyond the established setbacks to create a visual relationship to the Mall.[193]

Except for Frederick Hart and J. Carter Brown, the commission's membership had changed entirely in October 1985, four months after the last review of the project: it now included landscape architect Neil Porterfield; Carolyn Deaver (CFA 1985–90), a business consultant and wife of Michael Deaver, an advisor to President Reagan; businessman and New York state senator Roy Goodman (CFA 1985–89); sculptor Pascal Regan (CFA 1985–89); and Diane Wolf. The members withheld approval of the conceptual design until the June 1987 meeting when

CLOCKWISE FROM TOP LEFT: *The west elevation of a proposed design by Notter, Feingold & Alexander for the Holocaust Memorial Museum, 1985.* TOP RIGHT: *The I. M. Pei & Partners design for the museum treated the Hall of Remembrance as a pavilion located forward of the building's 15th Street facade, May 1987.* ABOVE RIGHT: *West elevation of the Holocaust Memorial Museum as built, 1995.* ABOVE LEFT: *Revisions to the west elevation of the museum by I. M. Pei & Partners added greater articulation to the facade and vertical elements, 1988.*

East elevation of the Holocaust Memorial Museum with its curved portico framing the entrance as built, 1995.

issues of height, scale, and the setback of the Hall of Remembrance were addressed.

Throughout the review process in 1987 and at the meeting in February 1988, public testimony questioned the meaning and expression of the museum as a national memorial; at the February 1988 meeting, commission members themselves began to question the commemorative message expressed by the architects. Porterfield and Wolf, in particular, thought the building needed to better express a "sense of hope."[194] The commission also suggested design refinements simplifying the entrance on 15th Street and on the 14th Street facade.

This second-guessing continued at the March 1988 meeting, where members focused on the use of bricked-in blind windows on the Hall of Remembrance facade and the narrow corner slits that allowed filtered light to the interior. Freed explained that this subdued natural lighting created a contemplative space within the Hall but still let in sunlight as a symbol of life. Diane Wolf found the blind windows troubling, as did Carolyn Deaver, arguing that the windows should be glazed to allow full light into the Hall and better "express hope and triumph over the grimmest actions of man." Goodman thought Wolf's comments overstepped the commission's mandate; Hart supported Wolf, finding her comments spoke to the "artistic spirit" of the building, but he found the controlled use of interior light a powerful statement. Porterfield objected to the windows because they were decorative rather than functional. Brown tried to move the meeting forward by

noting that the technique of controlled lighting employed by the architect was also used in the chapel at Ronchamp by Le Corbusier and the MIT chapel by Eero Saarinen. He added that the blind windows were "poetic elements" employed to relieve the hall's blank exterior walls.[195]

Instead, the meeting devolved into further contention. Porterfield raised the issue of whether or not a building on the site, Annex 3, would be torn down; he found that the building contributed to the scheme's context and should remain. Brown agreed and suggested that the sense of the commission was to approve the design with additional study of the window details, all contingent on Annex 3 remaining. Wolf interjected with a motion that the Hall of Remembrance be reworked to "produce something more uplifting to the spirit" and appropriate to the Mall, with Goodman objecting. The members struggled to formulate a motion that conveyed their discomfort with the commemorative message without suggesting a complete redesign. The language of the resulting motion, offered by Frederick Hart and reflected in the minutes, seems to try to appease everyone without requiring that any changes actually occur:

The Commission had subjective reservations about the spirit of the Hall of Remembrance…and while not requesting that elements be redesigned, would ask that these reservations [be] considered and responded to at the next meeting, understanding that the architect might again present the same design if he so desired.

Senator Goodman was the sole member present to vote against the motion. A second motion, which stated

Aerial view of West Potomac Park looking west, 1895. The former tidal marshes, reclaimed in the late nineteenth century, would become the locus of national commemorative works in the late twentieth century.

that the commission's previous design approvals of the project had assumed the Annex 3 building would remain and would be void if it were demolished, also carried.[196]

The April 1988 meeting was brief and anticlimactic. Freed's presentation included a revised sectional model of the Hall of Remembrance and a slide show on the use of blind windows on significant buildings elsewhere in the city. He emphasized the contemplative quality of the interior provided by controlling natural light, and proposed changing out the brick in the blind windows with stone. He offered to add blind panels for inscriptions at the Hall's ground-floor level. With some reservations regarding the addition of inscriptions—and Wolf and Porterfield receiving assurances from the council that Annex 3 would be retained—the design development of the Holocaust Memorial Museum was unanimously approved.[197]

Commemoration on the Mall: Layered Meaning in a Symbolic Landscape

As with the Mall museums, the language and subject of commemoration on the Mall also changed in the last decades of the twentieth century. Earlier memorials were largely self-contained objects set at the end of processional routes through architecturally defined landscapes. Their meaning came from art or architectural forms recognized as symbolic—obelisk, temple, column, statue—to commemorate commonly held cultural ideals usually represented by a noteworthy individual. By the late twentieth century, Mall memorials had evolved into complex experiences in an expansive landscape. They expressed layers of meaning through extended narratives using words or images and included a multiplicity of parts, most frequently to recall the personal involvement of those who had served in military action.

This evolution in commemorative language and subject matter can be traced in the memorials the development of which spanned the century's late decades. The Franklin Delano Roosevelt and Vietnam Veterans Memorials represent pivotal works, modern in vocabulary but expansive in the use of and relationship to the landscape. In its several iterations, the Roosevelt Memorial also incorporated narrative elements within an extended spatial experience. The Vietnam Veterans Memorial and its additions reflect the movement toward memorials dedicated to subjective experience. The Korean War Veterans Memorial and the National World War II Memorial—both overtly dedicated to the wars themselves—are characterized by complex symbolic programs.

THE FRANKLIN DELANO ROOSEVELT MEMORIAL

Franklin Roosevelt's own preference for a memorial was a plain and simply inscribed desk-sized block of stone located near the National Archives; this modest monument was eventually installed in his honor on the north lawn of the Archives in 1965.[198] For some, however, such a simple remembrance seemed insufficient for so popular a

Franklin D. Roosevelt said that any memorial dedicated to him should be simple and small. Such a memorial—an inscribed block of stone shown here in 1983—was placed on the north lawn of the National Archives building in 1965.

president, and, in a separate process, the Franklin Delano Roosevelt Memorial Commission was established by Congress in 1955 to develop a suitable memorial for the thirty-second president. Unforeseen at the time, this pursuit would span nearly forty years.

In 1959, the memorial commission secured a 26½-acre site immediately west of the Tidal Basin on recreational fields in West Potomac Park.[199] The legislation authorizing a design competition called for the memorial to "be harmonious as to location, design, and land use with the Washington Monument, the Jefferson Memorial, and the Lincoln Memorial."[200]

The winner of the 1960 competition, the Boston firm of William F. Pedersen and Bradford S. Tilney, with associated architects Joseph Wasserman and David Baer and sculptor Norman Hoberman, proposed a composition of eight precast concrete slabs—the highest rising 167 feet—arranged asymmetrically on a terraced plaza. Each stele was inset with excerpts from Roosevelt's speeches in bronze letters.[201]

The press derided the design as "instant Stonehenge... left-over parentheses from an architect's apologia or tired

gravestones from a country of broken dreams."[202] The Commission of Fine Arts's own review of the memorial in February 1962 found certain qualities of the composition praiseworthy: "those of great dramatic force and impact, of imaginative and stirring effects of light and shade, and the expression of much that is characteristic of our times."[203] Yet, it was the scheme's embrace of other examples of contemporary expression that the commission found inappropriate: it was out of scale with the nearby major memorials—conflicting with the authorizing legislation—and lacking "repose, an essential element in memorial art, and the qualities of monumental permanence." They also questioned the durability of precast concrete.[204] In June 1962, CFA chairman David E. Finley testified before a House subcommittee against funding the design, and in October 1962 the design was rejected by Congress.[205] The memorial commission and the design team returned to the CFA with a revised design in May 1964. They faced an entirely new membership under the leadership of Chairman William Walton, and they made it clear they felt at a disadvantage. Walton had recently written an article, published in the *New York Times,* critical of the original de-

CHAPTER VI | THE PAST IS PRESENT

sign. Based on that publication, the memorial commission asked him to recuse himself from deliberations. Asserting that his remarks only applied to the competition design and backed by the other CFA members, Walton remained in the meeting.[206]

The revised concept was essentially the same in content as the original, although the height of the tallest stele was reduced from 167 feet to just under 139 feet, about one foot less than the Lincoln Memorial. The shapes and positions of all the slabs—still of precast concrete—were slightly altered and occupied a smaller footprint, and, at the request of the memorial commission, an eighteen-foot-high statue of Roosevelt had been added. The commission delayed its decision until June, when it approved the design on a split vote: Gordon Bunshaft, Aline Saarien, planner Burnham Kelly, and John Carl Warnecke voted for the concept; sculptor Theodore Roszak and William Walton voted against it with Hideo Sasaki abstaining due to his earlier involvement in the competition. Somewhat dramatically, Walton received a telephone call during the meeting from James Roosevelt, Franklin Roosevelt's son, conveying the Roosevelt family's opposition to the scheme

and their preference for a garden or arboretum as a more fitting memorial. James Roosevelt also suggested that the memorial commission be disbanded and the CFA placed in charge of the design selection. The intervention did not affect the CFA's decision, but ultimately the Roosevelt family's public opposition successfully killed the scheme.[207]

The memorial commission began again two years later, interviewing dozens of designers before hiring Marcel Breuer, who presented his concept to the CFA in January 1967. The commission found Breuer's design derivative of the Pedersen-Tilney scheme with its use of large slabs, although only seven in number, triangular, and of granite rather than precast concrete. The slabs adjoined narrow pools and were set in a pinwheel configuration on a plaza, at the center of which stood a granite cube with an image of Roosevelt engraved on one face. The commission unanimously rejected this proposal, calling it crude and unfocused and likening the slabs to "stage settings rather than serious architecture." The CFA also condemned as unsuitable "pop art" the photo-etching technique Breuer suggested for the portrait and found his plan to include recordings of Roosevelt's speeches unsuitable

Aerial montage of the Mall looking west showing the future site of the Franklin D. Roosevelt Memorial on the western edge of the Tidal Basin in West Potomac Park between Arlington Memorial Bridge (upper right) and the Thomas Jefferson Memorial (left), c. 1942. Construction of the Kutz Memorial Bridge, designed by Paul Cret to cross the northern bay of the Tidal Basin, can be seen in the right foreground.

The 1960 design competition for the Franklin D. Roosevelt Memorial in West Potomac Park elicited submissions that broadly explored abstract form in the modernist language of the time.

ABOVE LEFT: *Douglas Honnold and John Rex.*

RIGHT, TOP TO BOTTOM: *Abraham W. Geller; Philip Johnson; and Hideo Sasaki.*

to timelessness and reflection.[208] The Roosevelt Memorial was placed on hold once again.

Nearly a decade later, after reviewing proposals by several architects, the memorial commission hired landscape architect Lawrence Halprin to prepare yet another memorial design for the West Potomac Park site. Halprin discussed his preliminary studies with the Commission of Fine Arts in April 1975, and the CFA formally reviewed them in June.[209] Once again, there was an entirely new commission, now chaired by J. Carter Brown; members included architects Kevin Roche and Chloethiel Woodard Smith as well as landscape architect Edward Durell Stone Jr.

Halprin's memorial proposal was a massive stone wall, rising as high as twenty feet and loosely defining a series of spaces, one for each of Roosevelt's four terms as president, and stretching 1,400 feet along the west bank of the Tidal Basin. A four-hundred-foot-long entrance corridor led from the west through a national rose garden past a visitor center and theater.[210] At the south, a large berm screened the site from the noise of nearby National Airport; another large, crescent-shaped berm curved along the memorial on the east next to the Tidal Basin, extending north to Independence Avenue.[211]

The commission approved the concept, although critiquing its scale as excessive and finding the vista of the Jefferson Memorial from Independence Avenue blocked by the berm on the east. The members also objected to Halprin's proposal to use different sculptors to create works within the rooms.[212] Brown commended the conception as "essentially a landscape solution," an approach to memorials that he had earlier favored in the commission's review of the Pershing Memorial on Pennsylvania Avenue in 1974. Brown also praised Halprin's plan to retain both the playing fields and the existing landscaping along the Tidal Basin.[213]

By the next month, July 1975, Halprin presented to the commission a design considerably reduced in scale and shortened in length by a third, with the crescent-shaped berm eliminated. The memorial, a series of "linear events" comprising landscape, water, and sculpture, still had a long approach from the west. Although the commission again approved the scheme, it suggested further refinements, suggesting that the proposal was too architectural in character and that Halprin's decision to replace the long wall with a series of rooms weakened the design. The CFA also recommended emphasizing landscape over hard-edged urban geometries. Halprin explained that the architectural elements would be smaller in scale than the trees and that the rooms would essentially be gardens.[214]

When Halprin returned to the commission the following year, the CFA still had concerns about the size and complexity of the water features and the memorial's architectural character; the members wanted a "dignified landscape solution" rather than "complexity and frivolity."[215] But they once again gave concept approval, commending the improved spatial flow, the softened treatment of the rooms, and the emphasis on the final space, opening to the view of the Jefferson Memorial. They advised Halprin to focus on integrating the details of stones, inscriptions, sculpture, and water. In the summary letter from the commission, Brown advised: "The end result must have the dignity and elegance of a memorial in the Capital, and not end up more like an urban playground than an inspiring, contemplative water garden."[216]

In February 1977, Halprin presented his final version, which included quotations from Roosevelt's speeches, bronze bas-reliefs, and both still and flowing water. The commission commended it as more simple and clear.[217] Kevin Roche called the design "excellent," and Brown commented that the "overly complicated 'urban playground' aspect…had been eliminated."[218] The CFA approved the final design.

Over the next year and a half, the commission reviewed the further development of the landscape, the walls, and the numerous pieces of sculpture.[219] Throughout the process, the members encouraged Halprin to maintain what they, like their predecessor commission of the 1960s, identified as the key quality of a memorial: repose.[220] In July 1978, Brown wrote to Senator Claiborne Pell:

Rendering by Hugh Ferriss of the winning competition entry by William F. Pedersen and Bradford S. Tilney, 1960; although narrowly approved by the CFA, the controversial design was eventually dropped by the Franklin Delano Roosevelt Memorial Commission.

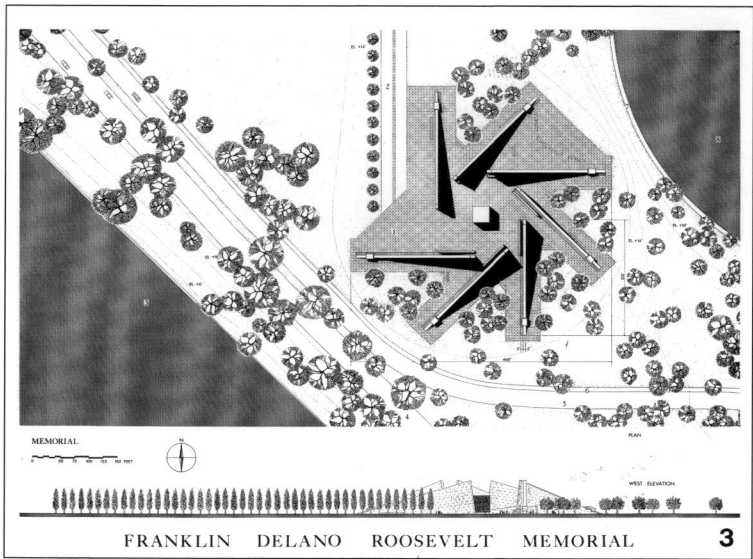

ABOVE LEFT: *Site plan of design by Marcel Breuer and Herbert Beckhard for the Roosevelt Memorial showing a pinwheel arrangement of seven stone slabs, presented to the CFA in January 1967.*

ABOVE RIGHT: *Breuer's proposal for the memorial included photo etching on the central cube and the use of sound, which the CFA found inappropriate, January 1967.*

RIGHT CENTER: *A new scheme for the memorial by landscape architect Lawrence Halprin created a series of landscape "rooms" along 1,400 feet of the Tidal Basin's western shore, June 1975.*

RIGHT BOTTOM: *By 1978, Halprin's scheme had been reduced in size but retained the primary design idea of a series of landscape rooms through which visitors progressed.*

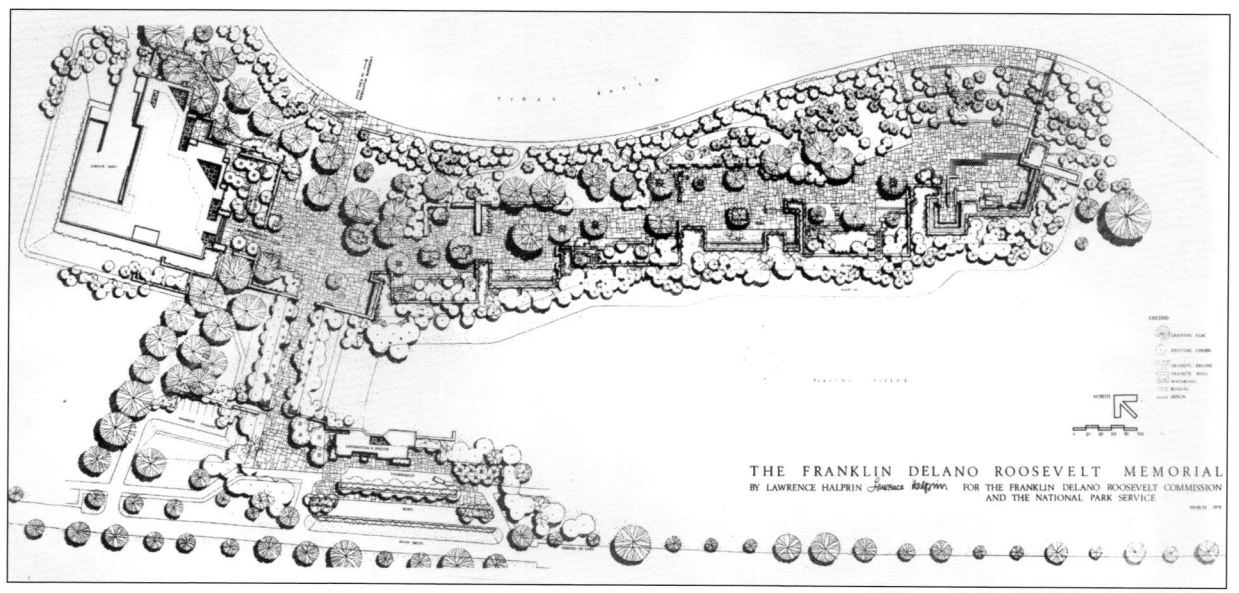

The Commission believes that the present solution finally meets all of the objectives we felt were necessary to achieve. It has a sense of dignity and repose that is entirely fitting for its setting near the other memorials. It respects in every sense the landscape of the park, its trees, and the walkways and views of the Tidal Basin. In fact its pools and fountains should do a great deal to enhance the quality of the site, and at the same time lend a feeling of uniqueness that will set it apart from the other memorials, one of the most difficult features that has eluded all other design efforts up till now.[221]

Halprin continued to simplify and reduce the monument's size, shortening the length by almost half and eliminating many features, all of which met with the commission's approval.[222] However, in 1979 the project stalled again. The Department of the Interior balked at the estimated construction cost of $50 million and yearly maintenance of $1.5 million and revoked its endorsement. A department spokesman was quoted as saying it was "not just backing away from the memorial. We're turning our backs on it completely."[223]

It would be another eleven years before the project was revived and resubmitted to the CFA for review. In April 1990, Halprin's design once more faced an entirely new membership; only J. Carter Brown remained as chairman, and the project now encountered a less enthusiastic response. The commission asked Halprin to defend the proposed memorial's size and grandiosity and criticized the change it posed to the character of the meadow in West Potomac Park. Landscape architect Neil Porterfield found the design's extensive hardscape "foreign to the context of the site." Attorney and government administrator Robert Peck (CFA 1990–94) wondered why the memorial would not offer any view from the Tidal Basin to the Potomac River.[224] Others commented on the enormous amount of

CLOCKWISE FROM TOP LEFT: *Water was a significant feature in Halprin's revised design of 1979, including a water garden that opened to the Tidal Basin; water garden, completed 1997; sculptural vignette,* The Rural Couple *and* The Breadline, *by George Segal, completed 1997; sculpture of President Roosevelt with his dog, Fala, by Neil Estern, completed 1997.*

granite Halprin proposed; he agreed to consider making his design more gardenesque.[225]

By his next submission in June 1990, Halprin had responded to these concerns. He had shifted the memorial closer to the Tidal Basin, partly beneath the existing canopy of flowering Japanese cherry trees.[226] He had reduced the extent of the granite paving by more than a third and greatly reduced the length of the entrance by moving it from west to north. Finally, he had created an opening in the berm to provide a vista to the river. The commission was pleased with the changes and approved the design. Brown commented that Halprin had created a "physical sequence of time" and a "historical drama depicted in a garden setting" enacted in four dimensions. Five more years of review and adjustments to the sculptural program followed, as well as legislation requiring the addition of a sculpture depicting Roosevelt in a wheelchair, before the memorial was finally dedicated in May 1997.[227]

With the introduction of architectural garden rooms, Halprin solved a problem that had stymied architects and review agencies since the 1950s. The sequential arrangement of partially enclosed spaces imposed an overall structure that accommodated the ahistorical forms. The simplicity of this central notion overrode the visual complexity of the innumerable sculptures, plantings, and water features and made them into a coherent whole. Brown's emphasis on integrating the memorial into its landscape through additional plantings and views enabled a memorial to Franklin Roosevelt to be realized after almost four decades.

THE VIETNAM VETERANS MEMORIAL

In contrast to the protracted and convoluted process leading to the Franklin Roosevelt Memorial, the solution for the Vietnam Veterans Memorial arrived as a single concept of exceptional clarity. J. Carter Brown recognized the strength of designer Maya Lin's idea and from the beginning of the commission's involvement in the memorial's review process was its staunch champion: he led and dominated commission discussions of the design, with architect Walter Netsch a secondary supporting voice addressing practical concerns.[228] Yet the memorial had its detractors among the public, who questioned its symbolic vocabulary, ultimately forcing additions that the CFA had to knit carefully into the memorial's precinct.

The Vietnam Veterans Memorial fundamentally changed the symbolism of the west end of the Mall and created a new memorial paradigm for the United States. Its modernist horizontality introduced a dominant typology into the vocabulary of American monuments that en-

tirely altered the way memorials have been designed since that time. It also introduced the overt national commemoration of war and its participants into the Mall's iconography: the Washington Monument commemorates the nation's founding through the American Revolution—an association not often recognized—and the Lincoln Memorial honors the sixteenth president for his unification of the country through the Civil War, but the memorialization of war had not been an explicit part of the symbolic content of the Mall.

The impetus for the Vietnam Veterans Memorial came from Jan C. Scruggs, a young Vietnam War veteran who established a memorial fund, won congressional authorization, secured a site in Constitution Gardens, and sponsored a competition in 1981 for a memorial to honor those killed in the Vietnam War and all its veterans. This was an unprecedented program, a memorial to victims and veterans—not the ideals—of war. The professional jury was charged with selecting a design that would not challenge the dominance of the Washington Monument and the Lincoln Memorial. The competition, open to all adult Americans, drew an enormous number of entries: 1,451. From these, the jury chose a small, evocative sketch of an angled black wall set in a green field. The artist was a twenty-year-old Chinese American woman, Maya Ying Lin, a second-year undergraduate architecture student at Yale University.

The commission saw Lin's design for a preliminary review at its July 1981 meeting at which she read the statement that had accompanied her competition entry: "Walking through this park, the memorial appears as a rift in the earth—a long polished black stone wall, emerging from and receding into the earth." Lin said it was "a moving composition, to be understood as we move into and out of it."[229]

The memorial was to be sited within the open meadow at the west end of Constitution Gardens, hidden from the gardens' ornamental lake by a low knoll. At the time, the sole structure at the western end of the Mall was the Lincoln Memorial, a Doric temple of white marble rising above its surroundings on a terraced mound. Before it lay the long, rectangular Reflecting Pool, which at the east terminated in the smaller, separate Rainbow Pool, set perpendicular to it and defining a north-south axis to the Mall. To either side of the Reflecting Pool rose a grassed terrace; on top of each ran a walk shaded by a double row of English elms. Beyond the walks on the south lay recreational fields and groves of trees; on the north were the flood levee and Constitution Gardens. East of 17th Street was the grass-covered mound of the Washington Monument.

The Vietnam Veterans Memorial, placed within this context, was to be composed of two black granite walls

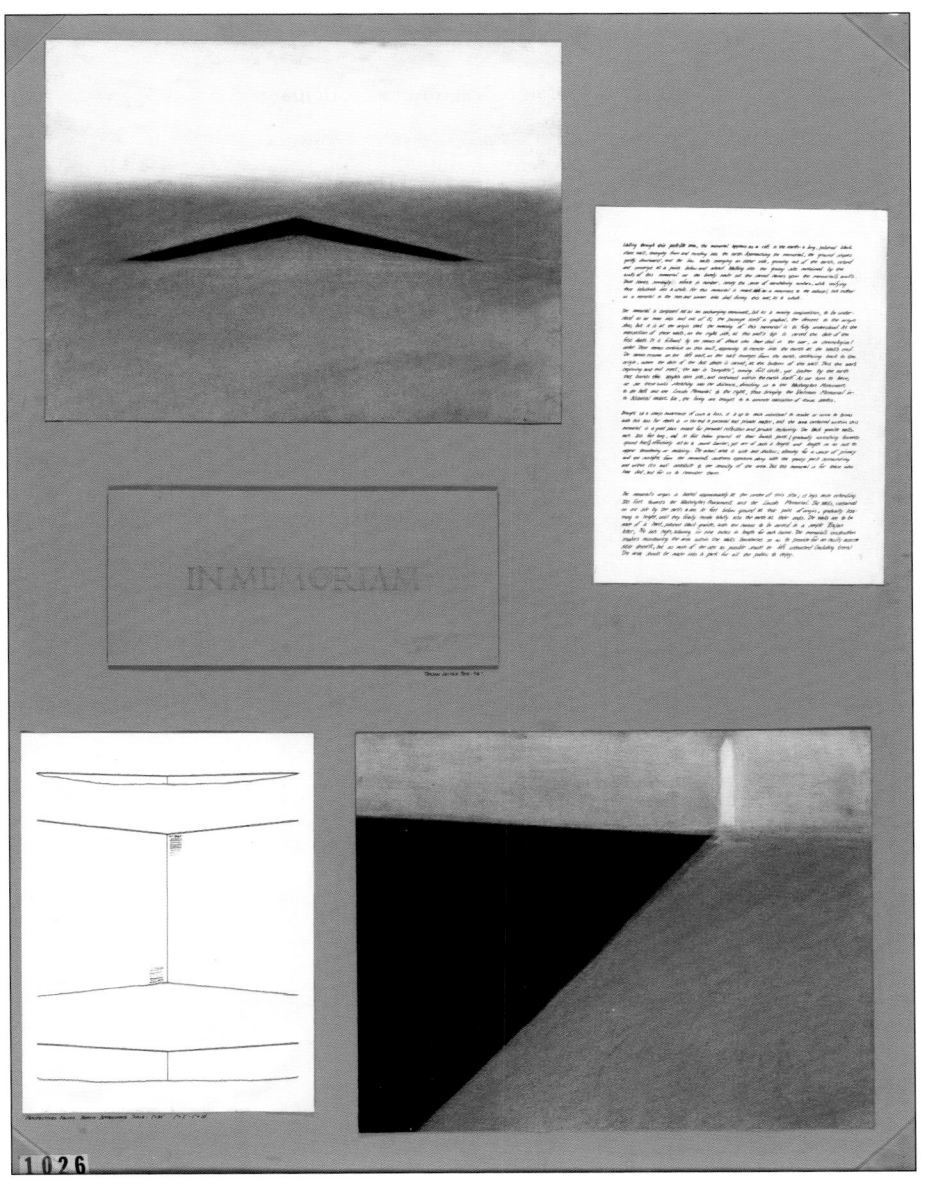

TOP LEFT: *Winning competition entry for the Vietnam Veterans Memorial by Maya Lin, 1981.*

BOTTOM LEFT: *Model of the Vietnam Veterans Memorial presented to the CFA, July 1981.*

BELOW RIGHT: *The CFA's October 1982 hearing was held in the Treasury building Cash Room to accommodate the crowds wishing to speak about the addition of a flag and other elements to Maya Lin's design. Members of the CFA seated at the far side of the table are (left to right): Alan Novak, Sondra Myers, Edward D. Stone Jr., and J. Carter Brown. On the near side of the table are (left to right): Harold Burson, John Chase, and Walter Netsch.*

BOTTOM RIGHT: *One of the studies presented to the CFA in October 1982 suggested a flagpole at the apex of the walls and sculpture on the slope leading to the memorial.*

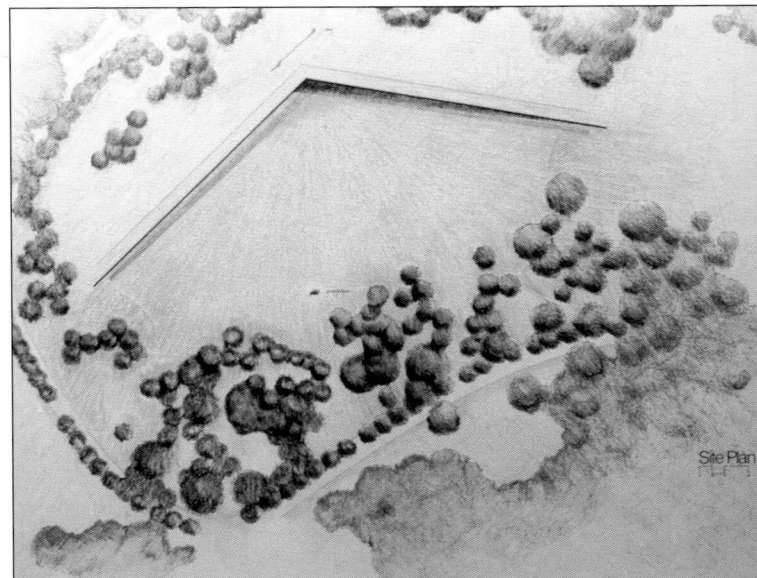

bearing the names of the 57,692 American men and women killed or missing in the Vietnam War, arranged in the order in which they had died or disappeared. Forming a v-shape oriented to views of the Lincoln Memorial and Washington Monument, the walls would be set within the ground and backed by earth to the north with a bowl-shaped slope descending in front. Lin had wanted the lawn to run unbroken to the walls and to have visitors approach the memorial directly down the slope.

A member of the public attending the meeting raised concerns about the site's potential drainage and accessibility problems and objected to the design's minimalism, which he said lacked nobility. Walter Netsch and J. Carter Brown quickly defended the proposal: Netsch called it modest yet impressive while Brown said the design's nobility came from its quiet strength and from the context of its siting between two of the nation's greatest memorials. The commission approved the concept unanimously: "The design has a simplicity and sense of dignity that befits an important memorial for this site and complements the character of the park."

A groundswell of opposition to the design soon arose. One of most prominent voices against it was a civilian lawyer with the Pentagon, Thomas Carhart, a West Point graduate and Vietnam veteran who had formerly been associated with the Vietnam Veterans Memorial Fund.[230] When the commission reviewed granite samples for the memorial in October 1981, opponents of the design spoke out at the meeting. Carhart called Lin's proposed design "insulting and demeaning: black instead of white, hidden in the ground instead of raised above it…a black gash of shame and sorrow."[231] He described his dismay that no Vietnam veteran had served on the jury and asked the CFA to reopen the competition.

Brown repeated that the commission believed in the concept's great dignity and simplicity, which it did not owe to "corny" and "superficial" references. He said the solution "had to do with nature…the modulation of the ground plane, the openness of the sky and the view of the other great historical monuments around on our National Mall…with the extraordinary litany of names, [it]…would call up in the visitor's heart a tremendous admiration and gratitude for the extraordinary sacrifice made on behalf of all of us."[232] Brown noted a trend away from the traditional type of monument "whose symbols now seem inadequate" and a resultant move toward a landscape solution. The commission unanimously approved the proposed unveined black granite for the memorial.

As the design was further developed, the commission readily approved all proposed solutions to questions of safety and drainage, the size and font of lettering, and the width and slope of the walk in front of the memorial.[233] But resistance to Lin's design continued to grow, winning the support of powerful individuals, including congressmen and Secretary of the Interior James C. Watt. This opposition led the Vietnam Veterans Memorial Fund to propose adding two traditional elements to their memorial: a fifty-foot flagpole and a figural sculpture of soldiers. The statue by sculptor Frederick Hart depicted three weary American soldiers of diverse ethnicities looking toward the wall as if they had just come across their comrades. The commission members considered the proposal in March 1982, agreeing it might be possible to add these new features but deciding they would need to see specifics before approving them.[234]

In October 1982 the commission heard four hours of testimony concerning inclusion of the new elements and their location.[235] The Memorial Fund proposed that the flagpole be placed above the memorial behind the apex of the two walls, with the statue located within the field between the two walls on axis with the flagpole. Testifying in favor of this addition were Assistant Secretary of the Interior Donald Hodel, a congressman, veterans groups, and private citizens. Those testifying against the additions included Maya Lin; Paul Spreiregen, the architectural advisor to the competition jury; and Robert Lawrence, president of the American Institute of Architects.

The commission members called the proposed location of the statue in the middle of the site "episodic" and lacking in any relation to the flagpole. While finding the flagpole an appropriate addition, the members said it might set a dangerous precedent and warned against the proliferation of flagpoles on the Mall. They approved the addition but not the location of the new elements.[236] The commission recommended, instead, that the features be grouped at the southwest entrance of the site, where they would possess greater meaning and, importantly, would not disturb the original design. Dedicated on Veterans Day in November 1982, Lin's Vietnam Veterans Memorial immediately became an enormously popular destination on the Mall.

Site proposals for the added sculptural group and flagpole continued to be refined after the memorial's dedication and were presented to the commission in February 1983.[237] The Memorial Fund favored grouping them near the entrance where the statue's three figures would look toward the memorial without turning their backs on the American flag. The opponents of the original design still preferred setting them adjacent to the memorial.

J. Carter Brown spoke at length, providing aesthetically based observations against placing the additions at

FACING PAGE, TOP AND BOTTOM: *View from the Vietnam Veterans Memorial looking west toward the Washington Monument, c. 1987. Visitor viewing names engraved on the polished black granite walls of the Vietnam Veterans Memorial, 2005.*

TOP: Three Servicemen *by Frederick Hart was completed 1984 and provided a figural representation of the thousands of soldiers who lost their lives; its location away from the memorial wall of names was championed by the CFA.*

ABOVE: Vietnam Women's Memorial *sculpture by Glenna Goodacre, completed 1995. Goodacre's composition, reminiscent of religious* pietà *works, commemorates the service of military and civilian women during the conflict.*

the memorial. While the symmetry of that scheme was appealing, he said the elements would never line up unless they were approached strictly on axis. Looking up at the flag, the pole would be cut off by the memorial wall in front of it; furthermore, the flagpole would be difficult to approach and so the inscription on its elaborately detailed base would not be seen by most visitors. Regarding the sculpture, Brown commented that, as director of the National Gallery, he had extensive experience in locating sculpture outdoors and had realized that, while it was an appealing notion to place a piece in the open, this seldom worked because of the lack of any nearby features to give scale. He said the size and monumentality of the memorial's walls would diminish Hart's sculptural group, which was slightly larger than life size. On the other hand, Brown noted, the site near the entrance had many advantages. The existing trees would provide scale; the statue group would actually be closer to the wall than in other options; and the flag would be situated at the intersection of the walks, where its inscription could be easily read. The commission voted unanimously in favor of the entrance location.

As Hart developed his statue, the CFA's main concern was his use of differences in patina to emphasize the faces. Brown advised Hart to do this subtly or risk having the figures look like waxworks.[238] Otherwise, the commission had little to say about its design. When Netsch questioned its quality—"the sense of pain and character of the whole situation…I still find missing on these figures. It is a long way from the *Burghers of Calais*…. Why can't we get the sculpture improved?"—Brown quickly ended the discussion.[239]

The commission continued to act as a watchdog for the Vietnam Veterans Memorial, endeavoring to preserve the essential simplicity of Lin's design through changes to paving and the addition of lighting.[240] In 1984 Netsch commented: "I think the proudest thing that this Commission has done this last four years is to preserve the integrity of the original design and find an appropriate location for the sculpture."[241]

In the late 1980s, another sculpture was added to the Vietnam Veterans Memorial precinct: the Vietnam Women's Memorial, honoring women's service in the war. In 1987, the commission disapproved the initial proposal for a statue of a standing female figure holding a helmet, with members objecting that the addition could destroy the emotional impact of the existing memorial.[242] J. Carter Brown observed that Lin's memorial bore the names of all the dead and missing and that Hart's sculptural piece symbolized all participants, so the monument was complete as it was; adding a new figure would imply that every group associated with the war should be literally represented.[243]

Another proposal was chosen through an open competition. The CFA assisted in selecting a site southeast of the Vietnam Memorial that was partially screened from view by an existing grove of trees.[244] The winning design by Glenna Goodacre depicted four bronze female figures in varied postures; one cradled the head of a fifth figure, a wounded male soldier. Composed in the round, the sculpture occupied a low pedestal in the center of a small plaza.[245] The landscape architect for the Vietnam Women's Memorial, George Dickie—a principal designer of Constitution Gardens for SOM—attempted to integrate the new feature into the existing landscape design, particularly what he called its "necklace" of trees, the informal groupings of trees that bordered the park's sloping lawns.[246]

Reviewing the proposal in 1991 and 1992, the CFA was generally pleased. Brown commended the statue's "centripetal strength" and said it conveyed "an immensely powerful idea." Most members agreed that the statue was well designed but regretted its addition; architect George Hartman said the Vietnam Memorial "does not need this piece and this piece does not enhance it." The commission's main recommendation was that Dickie add plantings to soften the plaza's geometric lines, with Brown observing: "The whole design concept of Constitution Gardens was to break out of the stiff geometry of the overall Mall and introduce this sort of English garden in a vast rural soft scape [sic]."[247] The statue eventually was approved in April 1992.[248]

THE KOREAN WAR VETERANS MEMORIAL

The theme and form of the Korean War Veterans Memorial—honoring on the Mall the American soldiers who fought in the conflict and those who were killed or missing—clearly echoes that of the Vietnam Memorial. The process of arriving at a final design, however, could not have been more different. The Korean War Veterans Memorial project was plagued from the beginning by the lack of a clear concept, and the architects and the commission faced an arduous process of trying to extract an organizing principle from among the numerous and disparate elements in the memorial's sprawling landscape.

Congressional authorization was secured for the memorial in 1986 by the Korean Veterans Memorial Advisory Board, and construction was placed under the auspices of the American Battle Monuments Commission. The memorial was to honor the "spirit, sacrifice, and dedication to freedom" of the 5.7 million Americans who had served in the Korean War and the 54,246 who had died, as well as the wounded and missing."[249] A national competition, open to all U.S. citizens eighteen or older, was held in 1989

for a site in Ash Woods, on the Mall south of the Reflecting Pool, corresponding to the site of the Vietnam Veterans Memorial to the north.

The winning design—out of 543 entries—was announced in June 1989, a collaborative effort of a team composed of architecture and landscape professors at The Pennsylvania State University known as Burns Lucas Leon Lucas.[250] When the ABMC brought the project to the CFA for preliminary review in July 1989, its representative told the commission that the design had been chosen because it was unique, uplifting, and captured the essence of the war, which, unlike Vietnam, had been a victory.[251]

The design consisted of a grouping of thirty-eight larger than-life-size statues of soldiers characterized by the designers as "elusive figures" moving through running water in a distant landscape. A walk extending through their midst would ascend a long slope; a red granite line would extend down the center of the walk toward a horizon line, at which point the ramp would descend to a segmental plaza separated into ceremonial and contemplative areas and centered on an American flag. Three white marble squares within the walk would designate significant points in a sequential movement through time, meant to evoke a passage through war toward peace.

Vegetation would be used in a theatrical manner: fields of thorny barberry would flank the statues, symbolizing pain and conflict; on the south, a screen of plane trees pollarded to create a tortured appearance would separate the memorial from the Mall; dogwoods would surround the area designated for contemplation at the end of the journey; and a hedge of arborvitae would extend along an arc-shaped walk curving south of the site and leading back to the entrance plaza.

At the July 1989 meeting, the commission approved the concept and congratulated the design team on its sensitive handling of the scheme. However, J. Carter Brown advised that translating a poetic vision into reality was difficult. He noted the circular quality of the proposed route, and warned against letting visitors feel they were caught in an endless cycle of leaving one war only to begin another. In his letter to the National Park Service, Brown expanded on the circulation problem:

The point of exit should avoid being too literally the point of beginning with the possible risk of misinterpretation. The Vietnam Memorial also has a sense of returning in time where endings meet beginnings…. The difference is, and it is a most important one, that nearly everyone who visits the Vietnam Memorial leaves from the opposite end from where they entered, and with a very strong focus on two other memorials (Lincoln and Washington), which suggests there is a way out of this circle of repeated conflict.[252]

TOP: *The winning entry in the 1989 design competition for the Korean War Veterans Memorial by Burns Lucas Leon Lucas introduced multiple elements into a sloping landscape.*

CENTER: *Presentation model of a substantially modified scheme of 1990 by project architect Cooper–Lecky, which revised many of the design's metaphorical elements and focused on the thirty-eight figures.*

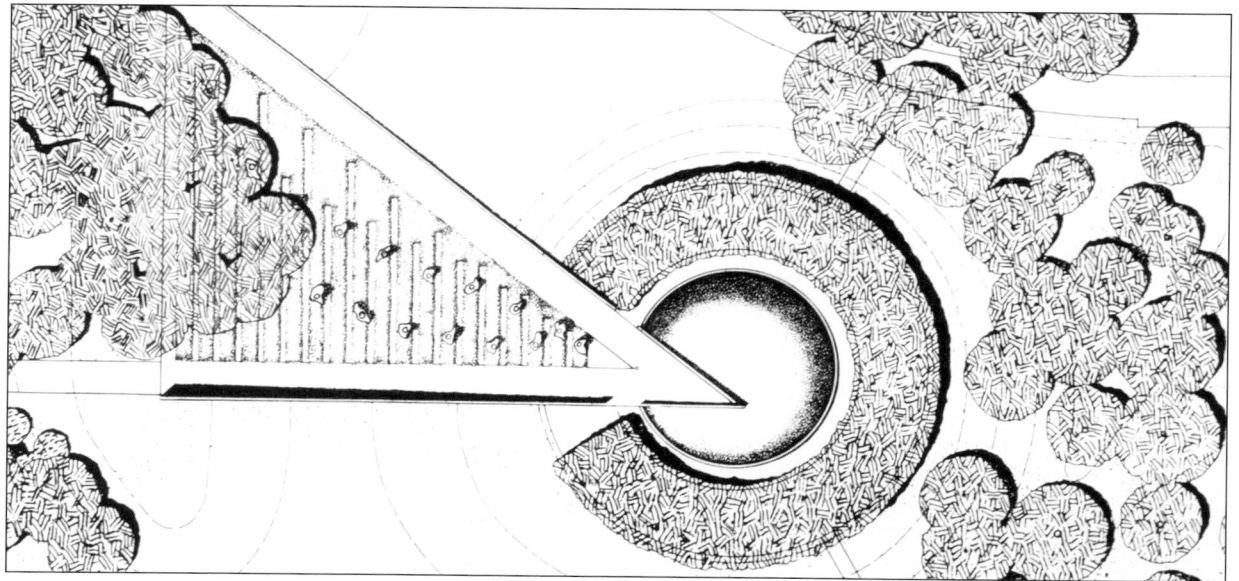

BOTTOM: *Plan showing further design modifications by Cooper–Lecky, including a polished granite wall upon which photographic images from the war would be etched, located at the southern edge of the triangular composition of figures and plantings, 1992.*

ABOVE: *Clay study of a figure for the Korean War Veterans Memorial by Frank Gaylord, 1991.*

LEFT, TOP AND BOTTOM: *The Korean War Veterans Memorial showing several figures within a planted landscape and the etched granite mural wall, designed by Louis Nelson, completed 1995. Aerial view of the Korean War Veterans Memorial as built, c. 1995.*

The memorial's own sponsors began to have serious doubts about the design. They hired Washington architect W. Kent Cooper, architect of record for the Vietnam Memorial, and his firm of Cooper–Lecky, in the fall of 1989 as project engineers and architects. Cooper–Lecky began working with Burns Lucas Leon Lucas in May 1990, but relations between the two groups soon broke down, with the original architects protesting the changes that were being made to their design; Cooper–Lecky had altered the circulation and eliminated the west-to-east axis, the white marble squares, and the entire concept of a journey through time.[253] By October 1990, the Burns Lucas Leon Lucas team was claiming to the press that the memorial had lost "the experience of moving into and through war, of release from war into the embrace of peace, and of reflection upon war." Cooper, in turn, defended his work, saying the Korean Veterans Memorial Advisory Board had determined that the column of soldiers was the main element and that other features were peripheral.[254]

Cooper—joined by project team members Henry Arnold, the landscape architect, and sculptor Frank Gaylord—then entered a difficult two-year period of attempting to make the redesign work through adding, eliminating, and altering features, with the result that the memorial as built barely resembled the original concept.[255] The CFA first reviewed the revised scheme in December 1990, with member Joan Abrahamson (CFA 1990–94) noting that the Cooper–Lecky concept, which had broken the original design down into three separate elements of entry plaza, line of soldiers, and terminal plaza, was in danger of losing the purity and strength of the original concept.[256] This issue—the change in the purity of a design idea from competition through implementation carried out by someone other than the competition winner—was not unlike that faced by other commission members with the NMAI and its design ten years later.

Cooper and his team labored to find a balance between opening the memorial to the Mall and providing enclosure to give it definition. They tried to integrate the landscape with the Mall by eliminating most of the innovative vegetative features and changed the topography to a lawn surrounded by low berms surmounted by high plantings, trying to create a resemblance to Constitution Gardens. At the January 1991 presentation to the CFA, Brown told the Cooper–Lecky team this solution would be too visible. The Vietnam Veterans Memorial, he said, was successful because it was nearly invisible on the Mall and left the existing meadow landscape undisturbed. On the other hand, if the Korean War Memorial included representational elements, they would need to be screened to

avoid a "Disney World" effect. What had been appealing about the original design, Brown said, was that it didn't mimic the Vietnam Memorial but had figures, formal landscaping, and a strong sense of containment and focus. The designers abandoned the berms and added a grove of trees at the beginning and end of the memorial to partially screen the memorial site.[257]

To define the circulation route, the architects eventually added a curved brown granite wall etched with images of support personnel and developed the circular memorial area—earlier referred to as a "chapel" or contemplative space by both the original designers and Cooper—as an exit to avoid any suggestion of a cyclical nature of war. The commission members approved the introduction of the wall, even though it might recall the Vietnam Veterans Memorial; Brown said the brown color would be enough to differentiate it. The architects later straightened the wall feature and placed it south of and parallel to the line of soldiers.[258]

Finding an appropriate expression for the setting of the statues, the one element retained from the initial proposal, also caused the Cooper–Lecky team difficulty. After discarding the thorny barberry, Cooper and Arnold had to define the field through which the soldiers were walking. They added parallel lines of granite to define a triangular field so visitors could walk among the soldiers and immerse themselves in the experience. The commission discouraged this notion, feeling it would add to the visual clutter. The designers then raised the field, narrowed the granite lines to discourage walking, and added strips of juniper shrubs between the granite. They replaced the central walk with two, one on each side, which ascended a gentle slope to a flag plaza circled by trees.

Cooper–Lecky also struggled with the treatment of the statues themselves. They altered their placement from a west-to-east axis parallel to the Reflecting Pool to an alignment following the diagonal between the Lincoln and Jefferson Memorials. Sculptor Frank Gaylord tried to balance an evocative abstraction with the realism that he believed was necessary to hold viewers' interest. He distinguished the ethnicities of individual faces and added various insignia. The commission repeatedly warned against excessive realism; Brown told the design team that realistic statues would fail to engage the imagination.

The commission began to question the necessity of including thirty-eight figures, which the original designers noted in an earlier presentation represented the number of months of the war's duration, not the 38th parallel separating North and South Korea.[259] At the October 1991 meeting, the Cooper–Lecky team showed a scheme that reduced the number of figures to nineteen, arranged in two compact s-curved lines emerging from a grove of trees at the memorial's entrance. The height of the stainless steel figures was reduced from eight feet to seven feet, and they were clad in large ponchos in an attempt to avoid the problems of excessive detail, which the CFA members had continued to critique. The wall and triangular field of soldiers now extended into a circular pool within the terminal plaza.

By January 1992, Cooper–Lecky had made all these changes, and the commission finally approved the design. Brown declared himself "delighted," complimenting the way Cooper had overlapped elements, raised the wall to contain the space, and reduced the size of the images on the wall to appear as a wavelike pattern when seen from a distance. Joan Abrahamson was the lone dissenting voice, saying it was still a "clumsy and ill-conceived scheme" set within the sacred precinct of the Mall that bore no message about the Korean War.[260] The memorial was built and dedicated in 1995.

THE AIR FORCE MEMORIAL

Another example of the trend to create memorials on military themes was a proposal for a memorial to the U.S. Air Force submitted to the commission for review in 1994. The discussion of the site selection process was revelatory in demonstrating a lack of confidence in how powerful the landscape-oriented model of commemoration had become. Several sites were under consideration—including two urban sites near the Mall—but the review focused on a site on the Arlington Ridge between the U.S. Marine Corps War Memorial and the Netherlands Carillon. The Arlington site was preferred by the Air Force Memorial Foundation; the commission warned that the location—so near to the Marine Corps Memorial and terminating the axis of the Mall—would constrain the design.

At the second review of the project in September 1994, Brown continued to express favor for an urban site but acknowledged the difficulty in getting a suitable sculpture for such a setting. He questioned the role of photography, the impact of which on the conception of commemorative works was increasingly evident:

I mean, if we had Saint-Gaudens still with us, or even Schrady, and we say: Great, take the Maryland Avenue site and put up a statue of an airman that would bring us all to tears. I don't see that happening. I think we are going to get kitsch *if we do that. And face it—I mean, on the record, I would say that the Iwo Jima Memorial is* kitsch. *It was taken from a photograph…and yet it is very effective, largely because of its site.*[261]

Opposition to the project, begun by neighborhood activists in Arlington Ridge who did not want more local

TOP: *Model of the Air Force Memorial by Pei Cobb Freed & Partners at the site initially considered between the Netherlands Carillon and the U.S. Marine Corps War Memorial, 1995.*

ABOVE: *Controversy over the original site led the Air Force Memorial Foundation to locate its memorial near the Pentagon. Pei Cobb Freed & Partners won the design competition for the new site with an abstract interpretation of flight, 2003.*

RIGHT: *The stainless steel spires of the Air Force Memorial, completed 2006.*

BELOW: *An additional element, representational figures of the Air Force Honor Guard by sculptor Zenos Frudakis, was located on the memorial's plaza near the wall of inscriptions, completed 2006.*

CHAPTER VI | THE PAST IS PRESENT

traffic, touched off a passionate dispute between the two different branches of the military. Brown's "kitsch" comment, however, would create controversy four years later, when several congressmen and supporters of the U.S. Marines, who wanted the Air Force Memorial located away from the Iwo Jima statue, called for his resignation based on this remark.

In 1996, the CFA approved a design for a fifty-foot-tall, three-dimensional star for the memorial, set within two acres situated west, and at a lower elevation, than the nearby eight-acre site of the U.S. Marine Corps War Memorial. The marines believed the broader setting of their memorial was sacred space and would be compromised by a nearby large structure. In addition to its proximity to the Fort Myer parade grounds, the location of the first military aircraft flight in 1908, the memorial foundation considered the location of its memorial to be complementary and not competitive.[262] The disagreement between the air force and marines resulted in a halt to the new memorial's design process.

At the end of the decade, the air force resumed efforts to establish a memorial and selected one of the twenty prime locations identified by the *Memorials and Museums Master Plan,* the Navy Annex site in Arlington. The Air Force Memorial Foundation held a second competition and selected a bold design, informed by the promontory point, by architect James Ingo Freed of Pei Cobb Freed & Partners.[263]

In March 2003, the commission granted conceptual approval for Freed's proposal, an abstract representation of flight: three curved stainless steel spires ranging from 200 to 270 feet. The memorial program also incorporated a meditation chamber, inscription wall, and four oversize bronze figures representing an Air Force honor guard— reprising a trend to include figural elements in an otherwise abstract design. In its discussion, the commission recommended that the figures by sculptor Zenos Frudakis be located off the memorial's primary axis. When the project returned for final approval in April 2004, landscape architect Diana Balmori (CFA 2003–12), who had not been on the commission for the concept review, commented that the expressive memorial did not need an additional figural component. David Childs, now chairman of the commission, noted the sensitive topic and compared the grouping to those added to the Vietnam Veterans Memorial; he recommended an abstract element because the sculptural figures would appear "insignificant" in comparison to the soaring spires.[264] In its action at the meeting, the CFA approved the final design with the exception of the figures; nevertheless, the memorial, including the

bronze sculptures, was constructed on the Navy Annex site and was dedicated in 2006.

THE WORLD WAR II MEMORIAL

By the late 1980s, with the Vietnam Veterans Memorial completed and the Korean War Veterans Memorial in progress, support began to grow for a third national war memorial in Washington, this one to honor all Americans who served in World War II, arguably the single most transformative event of the twentieth century on the nation. J. Carter Brown, in his role as CFA chairman, proved a successful advocate for the memorial's siting at the Rainbow Pool—directly on the National Mall's central axis between the Washington Monument and the Lincoln Memorial. With the help of Charles Atherton, he exerted an equally strong influence on the memorial's design, which continued the movement toward the use of multiple and disparate symbolic elements in an expansive landscape as seen in the Korean Memorial, albeit in a classical vocabulary.[265]

In April 1988, Congress requested testimony from the CFA on a House bill authorizing construction of a World War II memorial with a museum on federal land in the District of Columbia or immediate area. While the CFA supported the creation of the memorial, it opposed the inclusion of a museum, as did the NCPC and the National Capital Memorial Advisory Commission. Brown cited the Vietnam Veterans Memorial in a letter to the Subcommittee on Housing and Memorial Affairs that detailed the commission's opposition to a museum: "One can only point to the Vietnam Memorial and question what effect any kind of museum would have on the enormous emotional impact conveyed by this remarkable memorial."[266] The museum requirement was removed from the final authorizing legislation, which passed in 1993.[267]

One year later, in October 1994, the memorial project moved forward with the passage of a joint resolution authorizing its location within the monumental core. By early 1995, the ABMC and the World War II Memorial Advisory Board—the project's sponsoring organization—began the site selection process with input from the CFA, NCPC, NCMAC, National Park Service, and U.S. Army Corps of Engineers.[268] Of the sites considered, the strongest contenders were the Capitol Reflecting Pool in Union Square and the unoccupied terrace at the east end of Constitution Gardens, the preferred site of the ABMC and the advisory board. The NCMAC endorsed both sites at its September 1995 meeting "on the condition that the Rainbow Pool and site guidelines be accommodated" in the Constitution Gardens site, but it expressed a strong preference for Union Square.[269] Charles Atherton, representing the CFA

Memorials under the Commemorative Works Act

By the 1990s, a new generation of memorials was being developed in the monumental core, in neighborhoods of Washington, and at Arlington National Cemetery through new legislation—the Commemorative Works Act—that defined a process for authorizing, locating, and designing commemorative works in the national capital's monumental core. Two—the Women in Military Service for America Memorial and the African American Civil War Memorial—share the theme of military service. Others recognize such disparate themes as heroism, freedom, and the support of human rights.

Typically, these memorials featured realistic figural sculptures, larger than life size, on granite plazas within landscaped settings. Architectural elements were often limited to smaller features such as statue bases, garden walls, and benches. The Commission of Fine Arts was usually receptive to these projects. For those incorporated within an existing landscape, the CFA advocated respect for and careful accommodation of the original design. In their reviews, commission members emphasized simplicity of design to clarify a memorial's message.

An early example from this group is the National Law Enforcement Officers Memorial (completed 1991), which occupies Judiciary Square, a major public space within the L'Enfant Plan. The original proposal, presented to the commission in 1988, contained multiple elements including sculpture, inscribed walls, laser lights, and an elliptical colonnade as the memorial's main feature. The commission objected to the numerous elements and to the colonnade, which the members said would obscure the open spatial char-

acter of the historic square. The concept was simplified to be more parklike and included a pergola, a design enhancement suggested by J. Carter Brown.[1]

Arlington National Cemetery is the site of the Women in Military Service for America Memorial (completed 1997), which was inserted within the existing classical architecture of the hemicycle at the cemetery's entrance. The memorial omits sculpture to focus on words, water, light, and interpretation. The commission was most concerned about the proposed use of formal tree plantings, which members felt would provide too strong a contrast with the cemetery's picturesque landscape. Another commemoration of military service is the African American Civil War Memorial (completed 1998), located at 10th and Upshur Streets, NW. It is dedicated to the nearly 200,000 African American soldiers and sailors who fought for the Union during the Civil War. In its review, the commission addressed the central sculptural piece, *The Spirit of Freedom* by Ed Hamilton, considering whether the cylindrical backdrop was too abstract in contrast with the realism of the figures.

ABOVE: *The Spirit of Freedom by sculptor Ed Hamilton depicts African American soldiers, a sailor, and their families; it was conceived as a focal element within the central plaza of the African American Civil War Memorial, designed by Devrouax & Purnell at the U Street Metro Station, completed 1998.*

RIGHT: *The Law Enforcement Officers Memorial was designed by Davis Buckley and completed in 1991; the oval-shaped plaza defined by inscription walls accommodates the entry (foreground) to the Judiciary Square Metro station.*

Situated in a small triangular park between the Capitol and Union Station, the National Japanese American Memorial to Patriotism During World War II (completed 2000) tells the story of the internment of thousands of Japanese American civilians by the U.S. government during the second World War. The commission was impressed with Nina Akamu's primary sculptural element of twin cranes, a Japanese symbol of longevity and luck, intertwined with barbed wire to represent bondage and freedom. To balance this sculpture effectively with a second large element—a bell—the commission supported the designer's decision to change the orientation of the bell from vertical to horizontal.

The memorial to Mahatma Gandhi (completed 2000), a gift to the United States from India, is situated in front of the Indian Embassy, off Massachusetts Avenue. Since the bronze statue by Gautam Pal had already been cast, the commission limited its review to consideration of the site. The members advised that the figure of Gandhi should be oriented slightly to the south, off the street grid, to present a strong profile portrait when seen from the primary pedestrian and traffic routes to the east and west.

The George Mason Memorial (completed 2002) includes a statue by Wendy Ross that depicts the author of the *Virginia Declaration of Rights* seated as though at ease in the garden of his Virginia estate, surrounded by the emblems of his life and career. The site is a historic fountain in West Potomac Park at the eastern end of the George Mason Bridge; the commission advised the landscape architect, Rhodeside & Harwell, to retain as much of the garden's original design and plant material as possible. New elements in the park include the curved pergola and benches and the sculpture of Mason, which looks toward the Jefferson Memorial and other national landmarks.

LEFT: *The National Japanese American Memorial to Patriotism During World War II, designed by Davis Buckley, and completed in 2000, features a central sculptural element within a setting of water and a gently curved wall.*

ABOVE LEFT: *Model of the winning competition design for the Women in Military Service for America Memorial at Arlington Cemetery by Weiss/Manfredi, 1992.*

ABOVE RIGHT: *The Mahatma Gandhi Memorial features a bronze statue by Gautam Pal, completed 2000.*

LEFT: *A bronze statue of George Mason by sculptor Wendy Ross is the focal element in this memorial dedicated to the author of the Virginia Declaration of Rights, completed 2002.*

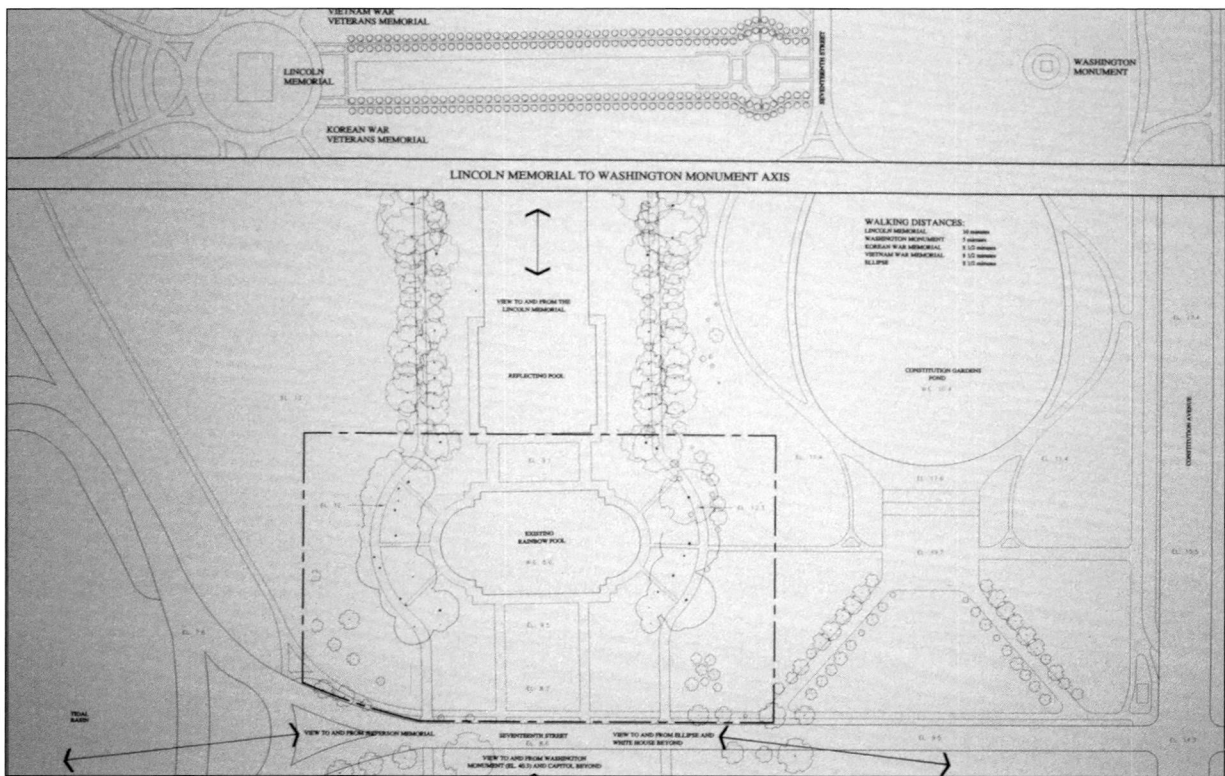

Study plan of the Rainbow Pool site in the central axis of the National Mall, September 1995.

on the NCMAC, asked for clarification about the Rainbow Pool site, broaching the idea that it, rather than the other sites, was the best location for the memorial: "Is there an implication that the Rainbow Pool might or might not be included in site four [Constitution Gardens]?...I would stick the memorial out in the Rainbow Pool and forget site four...because there you have a tremendously powerful axial relationship."[270]

The CFA discussed site selection at its July 1995 meeting.[271] A representative of the ABMC reported its continuing support of Constitution Gardens because that site met the standards of the Commemorative Works Act and also criteria devised by the ABMC: the site was on or near the Mall; it allowed a memorial to be freestanding, accessible, and relevant to its surroundings, i.e., nearby memorials and structures; and it could evoke the "profound importance" of World War II in the twentieth century.

J. Carter Brown read letters opposed to the Constitution Gardens site into the minutes of the meeting: one was from architect David Childs of SOM, the park's architect, who said it had been meant to be a pastoral area; and another was from Frederick Hart, former CFA member and sculptor of the statue group of three servicemen at the Vietnam Memorial, who proposed the erection of a memorial gateway in the traffic circle at the end of Arlington Memorial Bridge.

Brown supported Hart's proposal as offering a new opportunity in the treatment of memorials in the Mall

precinct. Here was a location, he said, for an entrance gate to the "memorial experience" on the Mall. Brown also observed that the Vietnam and Korean War Memorials had advanced the concept of the horizontal memorial; in contrast, the Memorial Circle site would allow room for a vertical expression. Brown added that Constitution Gardens would be a "cop-out." The rest of the commission agreed.

When the ABMC defended Constitution Gardens because it would allow a memorial to be placed in perspective with monuments to Vietnam and Korea, Brown countered that the problem with the site was its location off the Mall's main axis, adding that the commission might support the Rainbow Pool because of its axiality. Brown said that although "people liked what they know"—a landscape memorial like Vietnam and Korea—he still didn't think Constitution Gardens was a worthy site for this memorial. He later wrote to the ABMC:

What distinguished World War II from all other wars in which the U.S. has been involved before or since, however, was the total involvement of the citizenry, and the victorious response to totalitarian aggression on a global and unequivocally evil scale. This site [the Rainbow Pool], and that at Freedom Plaza, would allow for height, which the Commission felt will be the only viable design element capable of achieving the relative significance proportionate to the existing, spread-out memorials to the far smaller and less all-encompassing conflicts of Korea and Vietnam. It was unanimously agreed that this was a suggestion that warranted further study.[272]

Brown left open the possibility that Union Square or Arlington Memorial Circle could work as well.

Two months later, in September 1995, the ABMC returned with an examination of Memorial Circle and the Rainbow Pool.[273] They had now abandoned Constitution Gardens as a site except perhaps as an auxiliary to a memorial at the Rainbow Pool, offering space for a contemplative area. The Rainbow Pool was also favored by the World War II Memorial Advisory Board. The ABMC outlined the difficulties with the Memorial Circle location and the advantages of the Rainbow Pool. Brown, supported by the commission, offered general guidelines that would affect the Rainbow Pool site: the east-west axis had to remain open, and no vertical element would be appropriate except using two high jets of water to frame the vista, as had been proposed for the pool when it was first built.[274]

Brown also mentioned difficulties posed by the site, such as incorporating an underground visitor center, a reference in the program to the earlier museum idea; the traffic noise from 17th Street; potential damage to the historic elms; and the loss of this area for staging the July 4 fireworks and as a landing pad for official government helicopters. However, Brown concluded that these issues could be worked out.[275] In the site's defense, Brown pointed out that the Vietnam and Korean Memorials were not visible from the site and would not serve as a distraction.[276] Brown wrote to the ABMC: "The members recognize that any change to the Capitol–Washington Monument–Lincoln Memorial axis will require a deft and sympathetic hand. Therefore, the commission should be involved from the beginning in the development of design guidelines for the memorial."[277]

The Rainbow Pool site was selected and dedicated in 1995. The design guidelines for the competition—developed by the Site and Design Committee for the World War II Memorial—gave the height of the surrounding elms as a reasonable height limit; Brown commented that no structure should rise as high as the elms. Concerning fears that a memorial here would obstruct the vista, he wrote to the ABMC: "Often a vista can be enhanced by the introduction of properly-scaled elements along the line of sight. They need not detract from the view despite the fact that they could be construed by some as a possible intrusion into the vista."[278]

The design was selected through an unusual two-stage competition. The first stage, open to all Americans over the age of eighteen, drew more than 400 entries. From among these, the jury chose six finalists to be interviewed by a second jury, who selected the winning design by the architect Friedrich St. Florian. In January 1997, his design was presented to an executive session of the CFA by the ABMC with the name of the designer withheld. Bill Lacy, an architect who had served as a professional advisor to the competition, told the commission that the design had been chosen because it was "uncomplicated, easy to remember…could be altered without changing the basic diagram," and it would not interfere with the Mall vista.[279]

In July 1997 St. Florian presented his design to the commission, describing a plaza of more than seven acres around a reconstructed Rainbow Pool, which would be lowered fifteen feet below the level of the Mall.[280] Defining the plaza to the north and south would be two massive forty-foot-high walls lined with fifty freestanding columns. In his presentation, St. Florian described the individual columns as representing the strength and independence of the American character and symbolizing the unity of the nation during the war. Further, the truncated columns would suggest young lives cut short. Behind the semicircular walls would be a pair of huge berms planted with white roses. Inside the berms, large chambers would present different aspects of the war, a remnant of the earlier, discarded museum idea. The west end, facing the Lincoln Memorial, would have waterfalls and a "memorial platform."

J. Carter Brown immediately expressed his pleasure with the selection, as it did not impinge on the McMillan Plan vista, and noted that the sensitivity of the site kept the design from becoming too exuberant. Brown then asked the commission members for their opinions, telling them that it was now the time to "voice any serious dissent." All said they were impressed; Brown noted that the ability of this site to define space was of the "utmost importance."

The Commission of Fine Arts retained the same membership throughout the numerous reviews of the memorial's design: J. Carter Brown, Harry Robinson (CFA 1994–

CFA members visit the memorial site with members of the design team, May 1998 (left to right): J. Carter Brown, consulting architect George Hartman, Barbaralee Diamonstein-Spielvogel, Eden Rafshoon, architect Friedrich St. Florian, and sculptor Ray Kaskey.

TOP AND ABOVE: *Bird's-eye view of Friedrich St. Florian's winning competition design for the World War II Memorial presented to the CFA in 1997. Rendering of St. Florian's design showing the arc of freestanding columns and forty-foot-high berm viewed from the central plaza, 1997.*

2003), Barbaralee Diamonstein-Spielvogel (CFA 1996–2005), Carolyn Brody (CFA 1994–2003), Ann Todd Free (CFA 1997–2001), Emily Malino (CFA 1997–2001), and Eden Rafshoon (CFA 1994–2003). Robinson was dean of the architecture school at Howard University, Barbaralee Diamonstein-Spielvogel was a well-known preservation advocate in New York City, and Carolyn Brody had been trained as a planner. Both Emily Malino and Eden Rafshoon had worked as interior designers. Ann Todd Free was active in educational and preservation efforts. The records of the meetings indicate that J. Carter Brown typically spoke first, at length, and favorably about the memorial, subtly directing all discussion of the design. Through speeches at commission meetings and in numerous letters representing the commission, he defended the design vigorously against all arguments. Whether or not Brown intended to direct the other members in how to proceed, he certainly set the agenda and maneuvered to ad-

vance the siting and design, and members seldom voiced any opposing opinions.

During the course of the commission's reviews of the design, Brown voiced what he found to be the memorial's positive implications for the Mall. He believed that such a major structure should be built on the Rainbow Pool to dramatize the north-south axis, balance the Washington Monument and its mound, and frame the crucial east-west vista between the monument and the Lincoln Memorial. He repeatedly said World War II was the only event important enough to memorialize here, and that it was of such overwhelming importance that it deserved no other site. For the ABMC, the design offered somewhat more practical benefits: it was simple and memorable and created a distinctive precinct; it was classical, in keeping with the tradition of memorials on the National Mall as well as the McMillan Plan; it would offer ample space for ceremonies; and it could be altered without losing integrity. But the group did recognize implications to the Mall as well: the memorial "creatively conjoined" the Rainbow Pool with the Reflecting Pool and would not interfere with the Mall vista.[281]

As with the Vietnam Veterans Memorial, a cohort of prominent and vocal opponents soon formed a campaign against the site and the design. In a series of reviews at commission meetings over the next three years, beginning with the July 1997 meeting, the CFA provided a public forum for the memorial's supporters and opponents, which on both sides included senators, congressmen, World War II veterans, architects, preservation advocates, planners, critics, and other citizens. Under Brown's leadership, the commission displayed no evidence of being swayed by any of the arguments put forward by the many opponents of the memorial and its site.

The fundamental arguments presented by both supporters and opponents remained consistent, even as the design was radically altered. They revolved around notions of whether the Mall was complete as it was and should be preserved or whether the Mall's design could support change and evolve. The main premise of the memorial's opponents was that a design this large on this key site would compromise the Mall's open character and block the central vista; some went so far as to say it would destroy the design of the Mall. Many insisted that the way St. Florian had designed his classical elements recalled the official architecture of the very German and Italian fascist states that had been defeated in the war. It was also claimed that by sinking rather than raising the plaza, the design presented a confused message of both triumphant and funereal architecture.

The memorial's supporters spoke of the overwhelming importance of World War II to the United States and the need to honor its veterans before their generation passed away. Further, they argued that the Mall already had memorials to the wars in Vietnam and Korea and that World War II held far greater significance than either of those conflicts. Against the charge that its architecture was fascist, they claimed it was no more fascist than any other midcentury stripped classical building in Washington.

Brown remained consistent in his response to opponents. At the first presentation of the design at the July 1997 meeting, he said the magnitude of the war and the sacrifice of its soldiers could not be exaggerated, and that "the Commission was even more dedicated than ever to this site for the memorial, so that the site itself would serve to remind future generations of the sacrifices and the coming together of the nation at that time."[282]

At that meeting, the CFA "vigorously and unanimously reaffirmed" its site approval and approved parts of the design, including the concept of a symmetrical north-south composition on the Mall's east-west axis, the lowering of the pool and the plaza, and the ample use of fountains and water. However, the members called the architectural elements "too bulky and massive" for the park and said the columns were a "confusing and not readily accessible set of symbolic features.... Both triumph and tragedy are appropriate references in such a memorial, but it is a lot to ask of the visitor to feel the two simultaneously on the basis of a single design element."[283]

A revised design was presented in May 1998 as the team addressed criticism. The immense walls had been eliminated, and the columns were reconsidered as fifty-six metal, "shield-like" tablets for each of the U.S. states and territories, arranged in two semicircular arms reprising the shape of the deleted berms. On the west, a curved granite wall flanked by waterfalls was introduced to define the most hallowed area within the precinct. Fifty-two-foot-high pavilions would stand at the north and south ends. The plaza, now lowered only seven feet, would be a mix of paved and grass surfaces—although the paving material was not specified—and planted with grass and shrubs.

Two prominent designers added their support: David Childs—the designer of Constitution Gardens, a future chairman of the CFA, and a member of the World War II Memorial Design Selection Committee—testified that the memorial's revised design would resolve the Rainbow Pool area and define space "without adding architecture"; and Laurie Olin, landscape architect of the new barrier walls on the Washington Monument Grounds, called it a vast improvement over the previous design and said it would enhance an area that was now "a bit vapid."[284] Opponents still claimed the memorial would destroy the axis

TOP: *Model of St. Florian's revised scheme for the World War II Memorial, with the berms and columns replaced by pavilions, stone pylons, and other architectural details, 1998.*

CENTER: *Night rendering depicting further evolution of the design featuring pavilions enclosing sculptures of eagles and wreaths, and the pylons encircling the plaza adorned with bronze wreaths and twisted ropes, 1998.*

ABOVE: *Rendering of the Wall of Stars (Freedom Wall) for CFA review of star design, 2002.*

Detail of the eagles and wreath sculpture within a pavilion, by Ray Kaskey, 2005.

ground plane as the "Light of Freedom" and set before an inscribed "Wall of Freedom."[287] A cenotaph symbolizing war dead buried elsewhere had been added as a central feature. St. Florian said the changes clarified the intersection of the basic geometries of an oval and a rectangle and emphasized the sacred precinct as the memorial's emotional focus.

The remarks of the CFA members about this design were generally positive, although several criticized the cenotaph feature, fearing it would block the view of the flame to its west and would evoke death; others added minor criticisms of particular features. Brown was more laudatory, commending the design's retention of all the neighboring Mall elms, "preserving history and giving the memorial a sense of place." The concept presented in July 1997 had removed some of these historic trees; at that meeting, Brown had commented that the elms were needed as a framing device for the vista, although neither he nor any of the other members explicitly commented then or at later meetings about their potential loss.

When citizens spoke once more against the site, Brown said plainly that it was already approved. He delivered a ringing endorsement of the changes: the design was extraordinarily improved and would enhance the neglected area of the Rainbow Pool without interfering with the openness of the Mall. He defended the interrupted pedestrian access to the Lincoln Memorial on the west, saying that the sacred precinct needed a "sense of enclosure and inviolability."[288] In his letter to the NPS conveying the commission's approval, Brown concluded that the revised design was "an eloquent and effective statement worthy of the subject and the site."[289]

The CFA reviewed the final design of the architecture and landscape in July 2000. Because of the number of people who wished to speak, that meeting was held in the auditorium of the Department of the Interior. Brown opened the meeting with a lengthy discussion of the Mall's history. He noted that the McMillan Commission had not anticipated automobile traffic, but now the heavy traffic on 17th Street and Independence Avenue detracted from the quiet atmosphere of this area, which Brown said needed screening and the creation of a special place around the Rainbow Pool. Reviewing the commission's involvement with the project, he explained why it had rejected the site in Constitution Gardens as inappropriate and the decision that "if the memorial were going to be on the Mall, then it had to be on the main axis."[290]

St. Florian modestly described his design as "fitting, beautiful, and a welcome addition to the National Mall." He described two major changes: the addition of yet another symbolic element—a 120-foot-long wall of stars at the west,

and lacked a clear concept, adding that the wall at the west end blocked passage to the Lincoln Memorial.

However, Brown read a unanimous resolution of the commission: "RESOLVED, That the Commission of Fine Arts unanimously and enthusiastically approved the site plan, location, and concept of the World War II Memorial as presented at its meeting today, May 21, 1998." The CFA looked forward to a "continuing dialogue" with the designers as details were refined.[285]

Beginning in 1998 and continuing over the next three years, the design team, which now included the architecture firms of Hartman-Cox and Leo A Daly in addition to St. Florian, met informally with the ABMC and CFA staff, Chairman Brown, and other CFA members in a series of regular working sessions, usually held at the Leo A Daly offices in downtown Washington. Brown took a great interest in the process and was actively engaged in the design development. This collaborative effort among the CFA, the design team, and others was reminiscent of activities in the early days of the commission when members were detailed to talk directly with artists in their studios about design.[286]

The ABMC presented another revision in May 1999 that layered onto the memorial more detail and an expanding program of symbolic components. At the "sacred precinct" on the west, the designer proposed placing a yet-to-be-designed sculpture embodying a flame rising from a tilted

with each star representing one hundred American soldiers killed—and the relocation of the still-undesigned Light of Freedom sculpture from the west wall to the center of the pool.

Opponents and supporters delivered the same arguments as in previous years: the design and its elements lacked meaning and would destroy the vista and the Mall; and the project deserved the profound meaning offered by this site and would expand the meaning of the Mall. The CFA and Brown once more defended the appropriateness of the site, which he reiterated would give the memorial meaning and gravitas. Brown also observed that a great strength of the Vietnam Veterans Memorial was Maya Lin's warping of the ground plane down, so that visitors standing at the apex concentrated only on the memorial, and had no view of other memorials until they turned to leave. It would be the same at the World War II Memorial, Brown said, where the lowered ground plane would keep the vista open to the east and to the west, blocking it only immediately in front of the wall of stars; the World War II Memorial would frame and enhance the view along the central axis of the Mall. The CFA approved the concept at the meeting.

The memorial's groundbreaking occurred in November 2000, but construction was stalled by lawsuits brought by the opposition. The National Coalition to Save Our Mall, founded in 2000 and led by historian Judy Scott Feldman, became the leading voice of those committed to

stopping the memorial and would evolve into an advocacy group for the Mall's preservation.

J. Carter Brown would not live to see the World War II Memorial dedicated in 2004. Brown, who had served as the commission's chairman for thirty-one years, resigned his position shortly before his death in June 2002. With his unique combination of political acumen, intellectual facility, and a dominant personality, he was the foremost spokesman of the era on matters of art and design in Washington, and he presided over a period marked by the ascendancy of history, both in the maturation of the historic preservation movement as well as in the rise and fall of postmodernism in design. Under his powerful leadership, the Commission of Fine Arts had helped to establish and achieve a vision for the national capital that, while informed by Brown's own aesthetic sensibilities, recognized and preserved the city's unique qualities. In the twenty-first century, however, the commission would be faced with a new set of concerns when the demands of security, opportunities for sustainability, changes in technology, and the continuing evolution of design expression would pose new questions about how that vision would be redefined or maintained.

LEFT: *Detail of wreath and rope elements on a column, by Ray Kaskey, completed 2004.*

RIGHT: *Visitors to the World War II Memorial, 2004.*

Washington Aesthetics: J. Carter Brown and the Commission of Fine Arts

¶ RICHARD GUY WILSON

J Carter Brown held the chairmanship of the Commission of Fine Arts from 1971 to 2002—the longest of any individual in the century since its establishment. The projects and the issues with which Brown and the commission dealt were some of the most controversial in the agency's history, ranging from a mania for memorials and museums to the rise of historic preservation in Washington. All of this was accompanied by a general aesthetic unrest, or the lack of any clear dominant style or national image for public buildings and memorials. How to define Brown's tenure can be controversial, and different descriptions can be employed, such as the reigning monarch or the patron of Washington's architecture. Alternatively, he was accused of being a political accommodator and of holding an anti–historic preservation stance. He saw his role with the commission as extremely important, and, coinciding with his other positions, it became part of his mission as America's arts czar,

or as one of his long-time secretaries observed: "Carter sought the role of America's arts ambassador to the world."[1]

Brown's time on the commission coincides to some degree with the so-called postmodern period in American art and architecture wherein no one aesthetic ruled the day. Postmodernism in architecture is complex and lacks a clear definition, except that it embraced a variety of approaches to design and at times looked to the past for guidance in contrast to more orthodox modernism, which disowned history.[2] Brown's taste in architecture might be considered multivalent, or postmodern in that he advocated the diametrically opposed aesthetics of the radically abstract Vietnam Veterans Memorial by Maya Lin as well as the traditionalist or neoclassical World War II Memorial by Friedrich St. Florian. Similarly, he could support the figurative sculptures in the Franklin Delano Roosevelt and Korean War Veterans Memorials while also supporting the wildly curving and modernist forms of the National Museum of the American Indian—again, indicating the diversity of taste of the period.

Likewise, Brown could argue for the U.S. Navy Memorial and the surrounding buildings of Market Square by Hartman-Cox Architects, and the Holocaust Memorial Museum and the Ronald Reagan Building and International Trade Center, both by Pei Cobb Freed & Partners. All of these buildings were very different stylistically, but could be considered postmodern in their attempts to fit in contextually to their site. On the other hand, Brown was a fierce advocate for Frank Gehry's proposed addition to the Corcoran Gallery of Art, which was composed of wild forms and angles totally at odds with the existing building, the site, and the city. The Gehry addition came to naught as did Robert Venturi's proposed Freedom Plaza pylons at the juncture of Pennsylvania Avenue and 15th Street, NW, which Brown supported. Gehry and Venturi occupy two different extremes of American architecture of the last quarter of the twentieth century; Gehry was wildly sculptural and ahistorical while Venturi referenced the past with a cartoony wit. And preservation was no small issue: it was amplified by the contentious destruction of Rhodes Tavern (which stood at 15th Street and Pennsylvania Avenue, NW); the retention of remnant historic building facades as on G Street, NW; the preservation of the Old Post Office; and the reconstruction of the West Front of the U.S. Capitol.

One thread that runs through this tremendous variety of projects was J. Carter Brown's attempt to recognize and promote a special aesthetic for Washington, D.C. With a spirit of promotion, he claimed: "Washington is, quite simply, the most beautiful city in America."[3] He knew the history of the city, its plan, and development, and he argued that the most "important thing for our future agenda . . . is to keep the essential quality of the City, which is that of a horizontal city, with open space, green trees, and beautiful buildings."[4]

Brown's thirty-one-year chairmanship included more than 300 public meetings, the review of perhaps 3,000 projects, and the signing of at least 10,000 letters—not to mention the many testimonies and public speaking engagements connected with the commission. He also wrote a number of articles regarding the commission and Washington, D.C. While evidence suggests that staff wrote most of the letters signed by Brown that summarized the commission's recommendations and that staff provided him with images and information, it also indicates that Brown wrote all of his testimony and articles, sometimes in several drafts.[5] Other issues included the unsuccessful attempt by the Reagan administration to disband the commission in 1981, which failed partially because of Brown's influence.

However, the commission did suffer severe budget cuts. In another political move, the commission was relocated from Lafayette Square—in close proximity to the White House and near the center of power—to the old Pension Building (now the National Building Museum) at 4th and F Streets, NW, in Judiciary Square. Another aspect of Brown's tenure involved membership on the commission. Traditionally, the commission's members were leading architects, landscape architects, artists, sculptors, and knowledgeable lay people; however, beginning in the Nixon and Ford administrations, wives of politicians and individuals whose main qualifications were their substantial campaign contributions were appointed to the commission while the design membership decreased.[6] Certainly not every person appointed in these years lacked professional knowledge, but some commission members had little expertise in the substance of the commission's work; and Brown dominated the deliberations.

The commission staff that assisted

Brown included many individuals, most notably Charles H. Atherton, FAIA (1932–2005), who served as commission secretary from 1965 to 2004, a period of thirty-nine years.[7] Atherton—whose father was an architect and the designer of the American Battle Monument at Varennes, France—attended Princeton University and graduated with architecture degrees (AB 1954, MFA 1957). He had an early interest in the commission and joined its staff in 1960 after service in the navy and the Central Intelligence Agency. Atherton helped make the commission an advocate for historic preservation in the city and worked very closely with J. Carter Brown, whose tenure closely followed his.[8] Their relationship could be contentious, but a mutual respect was also evident.[9]

To understand Brown's approach to Washington's aesthetics and also his effectiveness as the chair of the commission, some personal background is necessary as architecture played a role throughout his life. Brown in many ways was one of the last of a tribe of socially elite individuals whose power and

Members meet in 1998 at the CFA offices located in the Pension Building; staff and applicant representatives are shown in the background. Seated (from left): Emily Malino, Harry G. Robinson III, J. Carter Brown, Eden Rafshoon, Carolyn Brody, and Ann Todd Free.

FACING PAGE: *J. Carter Brown at the National Gallery with Henri Matisse's* Acanthes *in the background, 1996.*

The Brown family playing music at the Windshield House, 1938 (left to right): Nicholas Brown, J. Carter Brown, Angela Brown (Fischer), John Nicholas Brown, and Anne Kinsolving Brown.

influence was rapidly waning in the late twentieth century. John Carter Brown III (1934–2002) was the second of three children of Anne Kinsolving (1906–85) and John Nicholas Brown II (1900–79). His mother had been a violinist with the Baltimore Symphony Orchestra and a reporter; his father was the scion of a distinguished Rhode Island family whose origins go back to 1638 and the initial settlement of Providence. An ancestor, Joseph Brown (1733–85), designed numerous buildings in Providence such as University Hall (1771–73) and the First Baptist Meeting House (1774–75). In 1804, the College of Rhode Island received a new name—Brown University—recognizing the contributions of the Brown family. Part of J. Carter Brown's youth was spent in the Nightingale-Brown House (1791), which he and his brother and sister gave to Brown University in the late 1980s. His father was known as the "richest baby in America" when he was born; Brown's grandmother, Natalie Bayard Dresser Brown (1869–1950), commissioned the Boston firm of Cram, Goodhue & Ferguson to design Emmanuel Episcopal Church in Newport (1901–02) in memory of the death of her husband and Harbour Court (1905) in Newport, which served as a family summer house until 1988 when it was

sold to the New York Yacht Club. In addition, the Brown family had been involved with the commissioning of a new public library in Providence and the John Carter Brown Library at Brown University.

Brown's father attended Harvard University, where he fell under the influence of Paul Sachs and A. Kingsley Porter, two of the most eminent and early academic art historians in America. He took a master's degree and developed a lifelong passion for collecting ancient and modern art. The elder Brown commissioned Ralph Adams Cram in 1926 to design a monumental Gothic Revival chapel for his prep school alma mater, St. George's, in Middletown, Rhode Island. In 1936, he gave Richard Neutra, the California modernist, his first East Coast commission, the design of Windshield House on Fishers Island, New York. A leading example of the International Style, the house received extensive publicity, especially after a hurricane severely damaged it only a month after completion in 1938. Rebuilt, it stood until a fire destroyed it in 1973; J. Carter Brown devoted a significant portion of his last years to documenting the house.[10]

As a youth, J. Carter Brown grew up in Providence and Newport and also traveled extensively. He attended boarding school at Stowe (the noted eighteenth-century house and garden in England). His father served as assistant secretary of the navy during the Truman administration, and Carter lived sporadically in Washington, D.C. He followed in his father's footsteps and attended Harvard, but majored in history and literature with his eyes set on a career in art museums. Following the advice of some of his father's friends in the museum world that a business background could be important, he attended Harvard Business School, graduating in 1958. He spent the next year in residence at Bernard Berenson's Villa I Tatti

in Florence and then entered New York University's Institute of Fine Arts, following the advice of Fiske Kimball, the noted art historian and architect and long-time director of the Philadelphia Museum of Art, who Brown quoted as saying: "It was easier to get a Ph.D. than to explain why you hadn't."[11] J. Carter Brown wrote a master's thesis on the seventeenth-century Dutch master Jan van Goyen, and in February 1961 at the age of twenty-six, began work as the assistant to John Walker, the director of the National Gallery of Art in Washington, D.C. Brown never received his PhD and in 1967 he took charge of a proposed expansion to the National Gallery of Art that would become the East Building. Upon the retirement of John Walker in February 1969, Paul Mellon, the son of the museum's founder, Andrew W. Mellon, and director of the National Gallery's board of trustees, asked Brown, then only thirty-four, to become the National Gallery's new (and only its third) director. Quite clearly Brown benefited from his family ties and social status, but as also became evident, he was a very able museum director, personnel manager, and public persona.

Between 1969 and 1992, Brown transformed the National Gallery of Art. Until Brown was promoted to director, the National Gallery contained very little modern and contemporary art; under him, it became a major repository for paintings, sculpture, and photography of the twentieth century. Brown, along with Thomas Hoving, who was director of the Metropolitan Museum of Art in New York City between 1967 and 1977, introduced the concept of the blockbuster exhibition, along with the use of extensive publicity for these huge, popular exhibitions. Though frequently rivals, Brown and Hoving together changed the nature of the American museum in the late twentieth century. Some of the exhibitions under Brown's direction displayed a showman's flair with lavish installations. For the *Eye of Thomas Jefferson* in 1976, Brown had recreated on the Mall the fireworks seen in Paris by Thomas Jefferson in 1786. Under Brown's direction, many exhibitions from small to large were held at the National Gallery, the most famous of which included: *Circa 1492; Japan: The Shaping of Daimyo Culture;* and, perhaps his crowning achievement, *The Treasure Houses of Britain.* In 1992, Brown left the National Gallery to set up a cable television arts network and curate other exhibitions, including *Rings* for the Olympic Games in Atlanta. He continued to live in Washington, D.C., and served as chairman of the Commission of Fine Arts until a month prior to his death in June 2002. The National Cathedral served as the setting for his memorial service.

As this short biography indicates, J. Carter Brown occupied a unique position not just in Washington, D.C., but in the larger world of art and culture. He had connections and knowledge along with the personality to exploit them. But also, and of vital importance, Brown's

deepest interest lay with architecture, both contemporary and historical. Several individuals recall him saying that, "If I had to do it all over again I would be an architect."[12]

Although architecture played a role during his youth, it was the construction of the East Building of the National Gallery of Art (1968–78)—about which he has written—that became a turning point for him as he climbed on scaffolds, watched the pouring of concrete, and made decisions on the minutest details.[13] He was intimately involved in the design and became a very close friend of I. M. Pei, the building's architect. Brown's role in the design process was critical to the outcome of the building, and, while he never claimed it, the atrium of the East Building was at least partially Brown's conception.[14] The personal connection to Pei became extremely important. They toured European art museums together and, as Pei recalled, "Here was a man who was an art historian, and he knew as much about architecture as I can claim to," and "He was very much interested in ur-

ban design."[15] Brown freely gave Pei his opinions on projects such as Pei's early design in 1973 for the John F. Kennedy Presidential Library and Museum—at the time still planned to be constructed at Harvard University in Cambridge, Massachusetts, which Brown felt was not appropriate. Brown expressed concern about the urban nature of the design and its modernist elements and noted: "If Sert is too much of a Latin to capture the New England twang of that community, he has at least produced, in Holyoke Center, a structure that responds well to the pedestrian world of its site. Corbu's [Le Corbusier's] little blockbuster [Carpenter Center] gives its pseudo-Georgian neighbors the treatment they deserved, without itself breaching the over-all good manners of the cityscape." About Pei's design for the library, he wrote, "I can only say that if it were to have come before the Commission of Fine Arts, it would not have received my vote."[16]

Implicit in the above and essential in understanding Brown's approach is his sense of urban aesthetics. In articles, letters, and statements, Brown acknowledged the importance of his upbringing: "Having lived most of my life in areas that embody this scale, first College Hill in Providence, then six years at Harvard, and then in Georgetown in Washington, I am perhaps overly sensitive to that particular rhythm and text, but it works in Europe, and there is no reason it should not work in those cities of America that have a rightful claim to it."[17] He recognized the different character of cities such as New York's extraordinary skyline—"maybe a bit more beautiful to look at than actually to be within"—but, in the end, he claimed that Washington, D.C., was unique and had a character that needed to be respected.[18] His writings and talks reveal a deep sense of the history of the location and plan of Washington (and, interestingly, he gives great prominence to Thomas Jefferson) and

LEFT: *J. Carter Brown with President Ronald Reagan and First Lady Nancy Reagan in the exhibition* The Treasure Houses of Britain: Five Hundred Years of Private Patronage and Art Collecting, *National Gallery of Art, October 30, 1985.*

its development. Brown was acutely aware of the role of Boss Shepherd and the political aspects of Washington's growth as a city. Brown's heroes were the original McMillan Commission members, whom he called an "all-star team."[19] He also paid much attention to Washington's waterfront, which is a subtheme that runs through many of his writings on cities.

Brown had an urban vision and understood the importance of sight lines and how they should be treated, which came into play with the World War II Memorial and the decision to locate it slightly below grade in order to keep the views open. Or, as stated in the notes of a commission meeting, "the great east-west axis had to remain open," and "the chairman added that another thing to consider was the view towards the Jefferson Memorial; he noted the heavy traffic on 17th Street and thought perhaps a berm might ameliorate this disturbing aspect of the site."[20] Brown focused lots of attention on Washington's

streets and avenues as connecting links in the city along with the variety of squares and circles, and he believed that specific areas were appropriate for certain building types. His notes for one talk specify "16th Street and Massachusetts Avenue as a setting for foreign embassies, 16th Street as an avenue of churches, Constitution Avenue and Independence Avenue as a setting for the museums and monumental government buildings—New Hampshire and Connecticut Avenues and Logan Circle as great residential streets—K Street as a commercial way."[21] Another of Brown's passions was to promote the use of street trees, which he believed were essential, "one of the great assets of Washington." He frequently wrote for himself notes and memos on the condition of trees on certain streets.[22] Some of these were undoubtedly passed on in telephone and personal conversations. But what becomes apparent was a passion for the city.

The height of buildings played a crit-

ical role in defining Washington's cityscape, which the federal Building Height Limitation Act generally limits to a height the width of the street plus twenty feet; defense of this law led Brown and the commission to deplore the destruction of some buildings or in some cases advocate the "facadomy" of others. He believed that the nineteenth-century street scale should be kept, and that even if the buildings must go, the older facades—as for instance on the 1900 block of G Street, NW—must be preserved.[23]

A major issue that arose during Brown's tenure was the growth of the skyline across the Potomac; and he, along with commission secretary Charles Atherton, provided testimony to the Arlington County Council on four high-rise towers proposed in Rosslyn, Virginia, in view of the National Mall. The press covered the event where Brown railed against the towers' impact on the Mall landscape and proclaimed, "[Only] if a building were wrapped in neon and allowed to blink" would it be worse.[24] Unfortunately Atherton and Brown lost the argument, and Rosslyn along the river became the site for tall glassy skyscrapers that marred the view from the Lincoln Memorial.

Brown demanded that the commission's members visit the sites under consideration, which was important since many of the members, appointed by the president and usually from out of town, really didn't know Washington that well. Frequently, a caravan of vehicles would descend on a location as the group could easily be ten or more. In some cases, one of the cars would carry only Brown and his driver because he would conduct business on his cell phone en route.[25]

To Brown, consideration of site included more than just a visit; one needed knowledge about its background, how it had been used in the past, and what the alternatives were. One example was his attitude toward the Federal Tri-

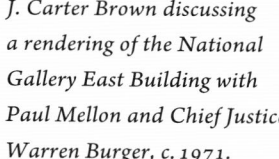

J. Carter Brown discussing a rendering of the National Gallery East Building with Paul Mellon and Chief Justice Warren Burger, c. 1971.

angle. Planned and largely built in the 1920s and 1930s, portions had never been finished, such as the removal of the Victorian-era Old Post Office. By the 1970s, times and appreciation of the past had changed. Brown supported preserving and renovating the Old Post Office, but he complained that "the plan did not solve…the most important problem: the truncated stumps, the bleeding amputated limbs" of the "eyesore…the present parking lot in the [Great] Plaza."²⁶ Ultimately the parking lot was replaced by the Ronald Reagan Building designed by Pei Cobb Freed in what might be called postmodern classicalism, and supported by Brown.

He became deeply involved in projects and frequently offered advice, as with the World War II Memorial. A strong advocate for the memorial, Brown pushed the commission hard to agree to the final site location on axis with the Lincoln Memorial, and, after a long series of meetings, finally persuaded the commission members to accept the Rainbow Pool site. He also wanted the World War II Memorial low-

ered and slightly below grade so the sight lines would stay open. But on an even more intimate level, Friedrich St. Florian gives Brown credit for one of the design features, the linking together of the state pavilions by the cast rope under the surrounding balustrades. St. Florian says the idea "was very imaginative, a real breakthrough," and that on the question of the memorial's style, Brown "stood by me—he would not waver, I was very fortunate to have a person of his knowledge and intelligence as head of the Commission of Fine Arts."²⁷ Just as the Vietnam Veterans Memorial was deeply mired in controversy for being too modern, the World War II Memorial was attacked from the opposite direction as being too traditionalist or classical in style. As noted, Brown supported both.

During Brown's tenure, historic preservation became a major concern in Washington, D.C. The history of preservation in the United States can be traced back to the saving of Mount Vernon in the 1850s, and during the first half of the twentieth century, some further strides

were made with local governments creating historic districts in Charleston, South Carolina, in 1931, and in Alexandria, Virginia, in 1946. Still, it was not until the passage of the Historic Preservation Act in 1966 as part of Lyndon B. Johnson's Great Society that the federal government became involved in historic preservation by mandating that each state and the District of Columbia set up historic preservation offices, survey their resources, and nominate buildings to the National Register. Although the Commission of Fine Arts was not a preservation agency, under Brown's leadership it increasingly took on preservation issues, some of which caused great uproar in the preservation community.

The most contentious—and one that gave Brown a negative reputation with some members of the preservation community—involved the Rhodes Tavern, located on 15th Street, NW, between F and G Streets and across from the Treasury building. Built in 1799, the structure had been the site of many meetings by important individuals; it was one of the few remaining structures

CFA chairman J. Carter Brown gestures to commission members, consultants, and staff during a site visit to West Potomac Park for the World War II Memorial, July 1997. From left: Jeffrey Carson, José Martínez Canino, George Hartman, Emily Malino, Carolyn Brody, Brown, Charles Atherton, Harry Robinson III, Eden Rafshoon, and Barbaralee Diamonstein-Spielvogel.

dating from Thomas Jefferson's presidential inauguration in 1801, the first in the new capital city. It was listed in the National Register in 1969. The developer, Oliver Carr Company, purchased Rhodes Tavern and several adjacent buildings during the 1970s, including the classical Metropolitan Bank, and filed for demolition permits with the intention of erecting a new office complex designed by David Childs of Skidmore, Owings & Merrill (SOM). SOM submitted several designs that preserved the classical facades of the adjacent structures and portions of the interior of the Old Ebbitt Grill, which also stood on the site, but the Rhodes Tavern itself would be razed. A huge preservation battle broke out with numerous public hearings, and experts on both sides were called in to testify. Some of these experts concluded—and this became the crux of the argument against saving the Rhodes Tavern building—that very little of the original tavern remained.[28] Although Brown at various times stated that he hoped what was left of the tavern might be preserved, he also stated that, "on aesthetic grounds, the Commission would prefer to see the Metropolitan Bank building saved rather than Rhodes Tavern."[29] As Brown's later comments indicated, he saw the issue as one of scale; this was one of the great monumental centers in Washington, D.C., where Pennsylvania Avenue turned the corner, and the monumental Treasury building and the other surrounding structures overwhelmed the small tavern. The battle went on and on, and Brown was quoted as saying: "The poor little beat-up derelict is sadness [sic] from the urban design point of view."[30] In the end, Rhodes Tavern—or what was left of it—was demolished.

Brown's personality and his method of working, especially with the Commission of Fine Arts, could at times seem idiosyncratic. He could become very intent on the subject at hand, and while

listening, especially in a discussion, he would close his eyes and sometimes hum; but at the end, he knew all that had been said. He knew what he liked, but Brown also listened to what experts had to say and would learn from them. In commission meetings, he deferred to architects Kevin Roche, Gordon Bunshaft, and David Childs and other knowledgeable commission members. But tensions could ensue; in particular, he and Walter Netsch, known for his testy personality, did not get along. Another figure with whom Brown had some angry exchanges was Diane Wolf, a young New York philanthropist who wanted to redesign all of the nation's coinage and had an opinion on everything but whose professional training was not in design. How much Brown influenced appointments to the commission is unknown; no records have come to light of his conversations with the White House. The issue of the lack of professional expertise among some commission members in the 1970s, 1980s, and 1990s prompted Brown's take-charge leadership style. As one staff member observed: "Carter at times was the only one on the commission who had any sense of what was going on."[31] Similar comments were expressed by other observers, that he had a point of view and was up to date on the issues.[32]

However, sometimes Brown's overly frank language could get him into trouble, as with this very impolitic observation at a commission meeting: "The Iwo Jima memorial is kitsch."[33] Made during the discussion of a proposed Air Force Memorial in 1994, the quote remained dormant until 1998, when it was found by a reporter and it became an immediate press sensation. Brown was blasted as the "fine arts poohbah" and accused by Marine Corps veterans, politicians, and some of the press as purposely denigrating and belittling the marines' sacrifice. Calls went out for his resignation.[34] Charles Atherton, in an interview, re-

marked: "When I heard the word uttered, I said, 'Here come[s] trouble.' I don't think he meant to be greatly disrespectful of the monument. . . . The irony of it [is] he's usually very, very discreet."[35] His full comment, which was never reproduced in the press, came in the midst of a discussion concerning the low quality of figural sculpture for the air force site, which was adjacent to the Marine Corps Memorial: "And face it—I mean on the record, I would say that Iwo Jima memorial is kitsch. It was taken from a photograph, it is by a sculptor [Felix de Weldon], even though he was a member of this commission at one point, who is not going to go down as a Michelangelo in history, and yet it is very effective, largely because of its siting."[36] Although his statement was politically a problem, Brown's point lay with the fact that the Air Force Memorial would not work on the proposed site and needed to be placed elsewhere. A new site for the Air Force Memorial was eventually found near the Pentagon, and the memorial was dedicated in 2006.

From his letters and interviews, it is apparent that Brown was conscious of what history would say about him, or how later generations would evaluate the decisions of the commission and his role in making them. He respected history, but also recognized that change happens; as he commented concerning the placement of the World War II Memorial on the Mall, history was a condition "of evolutionary change." The commission always adhered to a policy of reason and balance where historic preservation was concerned, but for Brown, it "could not subscribe to any ideology that viewed the status quo as always incapable of improvement."[37]

Brown possessed a political astuteness and recognized the need to reach a consensus. He realized that the aesthetic sense of the political decision makers in Washington was essentially conservative, and, consequently, when necessary he would adopt that position. For instance, Brown advocated very strenuously that Allyn Cox, an artist already known for his traditional murals in the Capitol's Great Rotunda, be engaged to paint additional murals in the Capitol.[38] Brown explained to the member of Congress in charge of the project that Cox would follow the "tradition of Brumidi... as an integrated architectural scheme;" and, of course, Brown knew full well that the aesthetic tastes of Congress would never accept an artist of a more modernist bent. Equally, regarding the Vietnam Veterans Memorial, which Brown also promoted strenuously, he knew that the modernism and minimalism of Maya Lin's design was so controversial that some compromise was needed if the design was to be saved. He explained in an essay that some commission members, such as Walter Netsch, felt "nothing should be added" and that while "I too thought the memorial so superb," still, "if we refused to compromise, there was the risk that the whole design would be discarded." He was referring to the anti-modernist attack on the memorial as too abstract and that figurative elements needed to be added. Brown explained: "I persuaded my colleagues to agree unanimously...that in principle, the sculpture and flagpole be added."[39] However, he saved the integrity of Maya Lin's design by having Frederick Hart's sculpture and the flagpole placed off-axis in a shaded grove and not right at the apex of the memorial as some wanted.

J. Carter Brown ranks with Charles Moore as one of the most important figures in the one-hundred-year history of the commission. Over the many years of his leadership, Brown certainly helped to save the commission from being shut down, and he increased its prestige. His elite background and his lifelong interest in architecture helped, as did his personality, but also he was an intelligent individual who understood that design in Washington, D.C.—whether a museum, a monument, or a commercial structure—was not just an issue of style, but part of a wider understanding of the aesthetics of the city. He knew the city, but he also continually learned new things about the city, as he also tried to understand both the most recent trends in architecture along with reexamining the architecture of the past. He could support designs of many different styles and approaches, provided they met a larger aesthetic goal, that of Washington, D.C., as the national capital. Brown promoted young talent such as Maya Lin and also figures not that well known on the national stage such as Friedrich St. Florian; he advocated for the memorial arch on 8th Street, NW, by Conklin & Rossant, which was not built. Equally, he wanted Washington to have the work of the best—of individuals such as I. M. Pei and Frank Gehry. Sometimes he won; other times he lost. For him, the city's streets embodied the capital's characteristic plan—how the sight lines were used; the placement, size, and bulk of buildings; and the treescape all were essential. Certainly, there were pitfalls during his tenure—unappealing buildings were constructed, while aesthetically appealing older buildings disappeared. Brown attempted to suggest that an aesthetic ruled Washington and that, if the different elements could be recognized and respected, the usual battle over appearance could be, in part, avoided. In spite of certain problems, Brown's tenure as chairman of the Commission of Fine Arts was one of the organization's most illustrious and, ultimately, one of its most influential; he helped to both make and save Washington, D.C.

ABOVE: CFA *members and staff place a wreath at the tomb of Pierre Charles L'Enfant at Arlington National Cemetery in honor of the seventieth anniversary of the Commission of Fine Arts, May 13, 1980 (left to right): Charles Atherton, Victorine du Pont Homsey, J. Carter Brown, Donald Myer, Frederick Doveton Nichols, and Kevin Roche.*

BELOW: *Atlantic Pavilion of the World War II Memorial in winter, 2004.*

CHAPTER VII

To Every Age Its Art

THE ROBINSON, CHILDS, AND POWELL CHAIRMANSHIPS, 2002–2012

Since its establishment in 1910, the Commission of Fine Arts had experienced three major phases informed by a larger aesthetic philosophy, each lasting roughly thirty years: Beaux-Arts classicism and its derivative expressions into the 1930s, modernism in the middle decades of the century, and a general approach informed by historicism and contextualism through the 1990s. Coincident with the beginning of the new century, several new cultural, economic, and political trends began to pose entirely new issues for the work of the commission in guiding the design of the physical symbols of the nation. These trends included the impact of information technology on the process of design in art and architecture, an economic and development boom in the national capital region, a changing philosophy about the built environment based on concepts of sustainability, and a preoccupation with building security in reaction to a rapidly evolving geopolitical context. Within the commission itself, considerable changes in its membership, its caseload, and its culture reflected the priorities of a new era.

Following J. Carter Brown's death in 2002, the commission was entrusted to new leadership of two short-term chairmanships: Washington architect and planner Harry Robinson III (CFA 1994–2003) was elected chairman immediately after Brown's resignation in May 2002; following the expiration of Robinson's appointment less than one year later, New York architect David Childs (CFA 2002–2005) became chairman in May 2003. Upon Childs's resignation in May 2005, Earl Powell III (CFA 2003–) was elected CFA chairman, the third director of the National Gallery of Art to serve in that position.

Security, sustainability, and technology became the most prominent design issues faced by the commission in the new century. After the terrorist attacks at the World Trade Center and the Pentagon on September 11, 2001, there was a significant shift in the types of projects submitted to the commission: security matters dominated the monthly agendas, driving the planning and design of new federal buildings, prompting the renovation and augmentation of existing ones, and retrofitting the major memorials. Safety concerns also affected urban design in Washington, from the placement and design of bollards and perimeter security to street closures and increased building setbacks as a countermeasure to potential damage from vehicle-borne explosives. Concurrently, the first years of the new century saw the practice of sustainability—energy-conserving and environmentally considerate design and construction—gain acceptance nationally;

FACING PAGE: Completed in 2009, the north pavilion addition to the D.C. Court of Appeals by Beyer Blinder Belle created a new entrance and accommodated security screening for the judicial complex.

commensurate policies, approaches, and technologies were developed and continued to evolve, all influencing building design.

In the first decade of the twenty-first century, contemporary aesthetic expression also displayed a renewed boldness in the architectural design of cultural institutions in the monumental core. Technological advances allowed far greater fluidity in the conceptualization and presentation of design ideas with advances in structural and materials sciences supporting the realization of these ideas in built form. This trend is evident in the design of new memorials, in which the language of commemoration was increasingly connected to the innovative use of materials such as glass as well as the reproduction of photographic imagery. New technologies also created an explosion of factual and visual information as well as the emergence of social media—undoubtedly with far-reaching effects on the future of politics, architecture, and aesthetics.

The trends of improving federal facilities and developing new commemorative works, coupled with renewed investment by the District of Columbia and a boom in private development, resulted in major increases in the num-ber of projects submitted for review by the commission. In addition, the physical age of the federal government's real estate portfolio in Washington meant that change dictated by security needs or encouraged by sustainable design led to projects brought before the commission with preservation requirements under national historic and environmental protection laws. In general, the regulatory context in which the commission functioned had become more multilayered, necessitating increased interagency cooperation and increasing the role of the commission staff in consultation on projects before review by the commission.

Perhaps the most notable case illustrating the congruence of the period's many issues was one outside the commission's jurisdiction: the U. S. Capitol Visitor Center. Designed and built over a ten-year period, the massive underground facility was envisioned to create a new experience of education, comfort, and security screening for visitors while enhancing operations of the U.S. Congress. At almost 600,000 square feet, the center is approximately three-quarters as large as the existing Capitol complex; its five-acre footprint required the complete reworking of the Capitol Grounds landscape designed by Frederick Law

Olmsted Sr. in the late nineteenth century. The project is typical of the era, when the once-grand entrance sequences of Washington's major public buildings were replaced by entry through a rear, lower-level, or convoluted access; the actual observation of the government in session is substituted in large part with exhibits. With some 2.5 million visitors per year by 2011, the project also exemplified another trend in monumental Washington: the redefinition of visitors' experience of the symbolic through the addition of increasing quantities of didactic information.

These issues illustrate the tremendous changes in the design of the built environment that emerged in the new century, in many ways constituting a distinctly different period from the preceding decade. For the Commission of Fine Arts, these issues would present a new array of challenges as it worked to ensure design quality and continuity within the context of great change.

Security in the Monumental Core

Before September 11, 2001, the commission had reviewed isolated security issues following a series of national and international incidents: attacks on American embassies in the 1980s, a truck bomb in the World Trade Center garage in 1993, and a truck bomb at a federal building in Oklahoma City in 1995. Often, the initial stopgap response was to encircle buildings or close streets with concrete planters or Jersey barriers, and "temporary" perimeter security barriers proliferated. The image of Washington was transformed profoundly; its monuments and grand edifices of government were suddenly barricaded, imparting a new image of retrenchment and unsightliness. After the September 11 attacks, security-related projects commanded much of the commission's attention throughout the first decade of the new century. As the decade progressed, the temporary barriers were slowly replaced with permanent treatments as the perimeter security requirements coalesced with master planning, sustainability, historic preservation, and design quality to establish adequate safety and greater aesthetic integrity within the urban environment.

Attitudes about federal perimeter security were influenced significantly by the commission's sister agency, the National Capital Planning Commission (NCPC). In December 2000, President Bill Clinton selected his friend and real estate developer Richard Friedman of Massachusetts as a member and chairman of the NCPC, one of the last political appointments of his second term in office. Friedman immediately focused on the appearance of security in Washington with a goal to remove the streetside fortifications that had sprung up around the city. He held that perimeter security did not have to look oppressive and argued, "Why must barricades be ugly? We can have both good urban design and good security, but now we have neither."[1]

Aerial view of the U.S. Capitol, east front, 2008. In the foreground is the new five-acre plaza and entry to the subterranean visitor center designed by RTKL and Sasaki Associates.

Although President George W. Bush soon appointed his own chairman, the Virginia land-use attorney John Cogbill to head the federal agency, Friedman remained one of its twelve commission members and was directed to establish an interagency task force to assess the long-term necessity of the highly controversial 1995 closure of Pennsylvania Avenue to vehicular traffic in front of the White House.[2] Voting members of the task force included Cogbill and Friedman as well as representatives of the Department of the Interior, the General Services Administration, the District's mayor, and the chairman of the city's council. The Commission of Fine Arts, the National Park Service, the Architect of the Capitol, federal departments, agencies of the District of Columbia, and the various police and security forces in the capital were among the participating members of the task force. Although serving in a nonvoting capacity, these agencies provided extensive insights that helped to shape the final recommendations.

The task force first met in March 2001 and quickly re-alized that the security of the entire monumental core needed to be addressed. Accordingly, the task force solicited information from the participating members, established various parameters, and then approached nationally prominent landscape architecture firms to assist with particular design solutions—resulting in the publication of *Designing for Security in the Nation's Capital* in October 2001. The report offered an aesthetically based kit of parts for security elements in urban conditions generally, while also focusing on the two blocks of Pennsylvania Avenue in front of the White House, which would remain closed. The report also recommended that the federal government immediately fund the design and construction of a landscaped civic space, by one or more nationally recognized urban designers, along this portion of the avenue. In the following months, the interagency task force engaged in the same collaborative process and, in October 2002, issued a document with more specific guidelines, *The National Capital Urban Design and Security Plan* that addressed

ABOVE: *Pennsylvania Avenue in front of the White House was closed to vehicular traffic in 1995. Temporary measures to limit access included lift-up plate barriers, guard booths, and concrete planters within the right-of-way of the city's principal ceremonial street.*

RIGHT: *The streetscape design for permanent security on Pennsylvania Avenue at the White House was won in a national competition by Michael Van Valkenburgh Associates. The design accommodated security while addressing the urban quality of the space with bollards, trees, and differentiated paving, and was completed in 2005.*

the overall monumental core and became the touchstone for perimeter security in Washington.[3]

WASHINGTON MONUMENT

While the task force was making a concerted effort to produce coherent perimeter security direction for the monumental core—both before and after the September 2001 attacks—the National Park Service (NPS) was proceeding with its own response for particular monuments on the Mall. Congress had directed the NPS to improve security at seven national sites nationwide, including three in Washington. Between June 2001 and June 2002, the National Park Service submitted proposals to the CFA to surround the Washington Monument and the Lincoln and Jefferson Memorials with hundreds of steel, cast stone, or granite bollards. In their discussions, commission members likened these early bollard concepts to "oil cans," "missile silos," and a "comb" and demanded more aesthetically appealing solutions.[4]

At the June 2001 CFA meeting, John Parsons, associate director of lands, resources, and planning for the National Capital Region of the NPS, presented a concept for security improvements to replace the two rings of concrete Jersey barriers located around the Washington Monument since 1998, part of a larger restoration project that began in 1996. The proposal called for a circle of 370 steel bollards situated 200 feet from the monument, halfway up the grassy mound that is its base; the commission members had previewed a mock-up of the proposal on-site earlier in the day. At the meeting, Parsons explained that a security analysis had determined that less secured locations such as the monument became more vulnerable as security was increased at other federal locations, which had led to the earlier placement of Jersey barriers and now the proposed bollards. J. Carter Brown, still presiding as chairman in the last year of his life, summarized the unanimous response of the commission members to the mock-up as "totally unacceptable."[5] Brown suggested that either nothing be placed at the monument or that the secure perimeter be pulled back away from it, similar to the treatment at the Ellipse, where the perimeter would be experienced as an element on the street and not of the monument.[6]

The events of September 11, 2001, led the NPS to expand the scope of work for security improvements at the Washington Monument to include a visitor center, which had been under consideration for the site since 1973 but now would have the added elements of a permanent screening facility and a tunnel connecting to the base of the monument through which the public would enter the structure. In November 2001, the NPS invited four landscape

TOP: *Aerial view of the Washington Monument Grounds, 2003, showing the haphazard arrangement of paths prior to the redesign of security elements.*

ABOVE: *Following the terrorist attacks of September 11, 2001, temporary perimeter security elements were installed around major monuments in Washington. The visitor experience of the Washington* Monument was compromised by concrete barriers, construction fencing, and a "temporary" screening pavilion, 2004.

The 2001 competition-winning scheme for perimeter security at the Washington Monument by Olin used two intersecting oval paths to integrate barriers within the landscape and to resolve the site's geometric irregularities. A skylight for a proposed subterranean visitor center and tunnel connecting the Monument Lodge to the obelisk is shown in the lawn to the east of the monument.

architects to participate in a closed competition for perimeter security and the new visitor center. The invited participants were landscape architects Henry Arnold, Laurie Olin, and Michael Van Valkenburgh and landscape designer Diana Balmori, most of whom collaborated with architects for the visitor center component of the project. The Olin Partnership, with the Washington-based Hartman-Cox Architects, was selected by the competition jury the day prior to the CFA's December meeting; the team gave an informational presentation of their design as a preliminary concept to the commission at its meeting.

The Olin design derived from the eighteenth-century English garden tradition, but also recalled A. J. Downing's 1851 picturesque design for the Public Grounds at Washington and Samuel Parsons's 1900 plan for the Mall.[7] Olin proposed a series of interlocking elliptical paths, parts of which were sunken to accommodate retaining walls unobtrusively.[8] As specified by the NPS, the historic Monument Lodge would function as the entrance to the subterranean visitor center and security screening; Hartman-Cox's design featured a large skylight for this space on the Mall axis.[9] Although highly complimentary to Laurie Olin and his site

design, the CFA members had concerns about the visitor center—specifically the skylight and the implications of air conditioning equipment on the landscape. Following the meeting, J. Carter Brown sent the customary summary letter to the NPS, which included a request to see the other competition entries in order to better understand all design possibilities.

The Olin/Hartman-Cox competition design was submitted by the NPS for formal concept design review in February 2002. After it was presented, the meeting was opened to members of the public, who spoke out against the design, questioning the tunnel in particular as inappropriate both symbolically and structurally for the Washington Monument. Despite these remarks, in a summary statement at the meeting, Brown described the experience of entering through the tunnel as a "very exciting kind of adventure" and commented that the design was "creative and sensitive and has minimal impact."[10] The commission members approved the concept design; Brown's summary letter to the NPS indicated the commission's satisfaction with Olin's approach, noting that it no longer wished to see the other competition schemes:

When first presented by Mr. Olin at the December meeting, the members were enthusiastic about the scheme, but requested additional information. Since then, the Commission has had time to consider the merits of the proposal for this most important of projects and have concluded, with their unanimous approval, that Mr. Olin's preliminary scheme, as presented, is an appropriate design solution to improve the Monument's physical perimeter security.[11]

However, when the NPS presented a revised concept for the visitor center to the CFA the following month, the changes soon led to problems for that portion of the project. The original competition scheme incorporated a stair descending from the lobby of the Monument Lodge to the underground visitor center, which the National Park Service later determined to be too narrow to accommodate the anticipated number of visitors. In the revised scheme, Hartman-Cox redesigned the entry sequence and included a glazed polygonal addition to the west end of the lodge. Brown's reaction was that the addition was too large, saying that it "chokes the old building."[12] Architect Don Hawkins of the Committee of 100 on the Federal City testified in opposition to the proposal; he offered another stair configuration and strongly objected to the visitor center skylight "floating" in the landscape.[13] Brown expressed interest in Hawkins's comments and urged further study of alternative designs; he also raised concerns about emergency egress stairs. Other commission members also expressed reservations about the revised design and feared piecemeal alterations in the future. Brown closed the discussion by noting that the commission could not approve the revision as presented and suggesting further exploration of the design based on the comments made.

In addition to this cautionary response from the commission and the explicit opposition to the visitor center scheme by both the Committee of 100 and the National Coalition to Save Our Mall, the press began to take notice of the Washington Monument debate. In early May, Jonathan Yardley, a *Washington Post* columnist and Pulitzer Prize winner for criticism, wrote a scathing commentary about the National Park Service as "a wily, secretive player in the Washington power game…that…railroaded through the aesthetically calamitous and environmentally questionable World War II Memorial…and that now proposes to do comparable aesthetic and environmental damage… at the Washington Monument.[14]

By the commission's May 2002 meeting, the NPS had entered into a formal programmatic agreement with the Advisory Council on Historic Preservation, the D.C. Historic Preservation Office, and the National Capital Planning Commission regarding historic preservation aspects of the proposal; significantly, these organizations had urged the

NPS to move more slowly in its design process.[15] Although the CFA was not a part of this agreement, the NPS wanted its input on the newly revised landscape and visitor center designs and presented these schemes at the May meeting on an informal basis. The commission members found that the revised designs still contained significant weaknesses.

With J. Carter Brown absent because of illness, Harry Robinson, CFA vice chairman, presided at this meeting. Notably, he was the only architect-planner on the commission at this time. When President Clinton appointed Robinson to the commission, he had been the principal of his own urban design firm as well as the dean and professor of urban design at the Howard University School of Architecture and Planning for nearly two decades. The commission members had elected Robinson vice chairman in February 1995—his second month on the commission.

Following extensive testimony by a geotechnical and structural engineer assuring that drilling at the monument's foundation and constructing an underground tunnel were feasible, Olin discussed the dimensions and details of the paths and retaining walls, the tree removal and planting plans, and the regrading of the knoll to diminish its "lumpy" character.[16] He also presented a plan for a plaza at the base of the monument featuring an eight-point star paving pattern composed of three types of stone, suggesting a traditional compass. Barbaralee Diamonstein-Spielvogel repeatedly questioned Olin regarding the appropriateness of this design; Olin said the star would be less perceptible in reality than as rendered in the drawing, but she challenged his prediction.

Robinson and Eden Rafshoon also questioned Olin's star and evoked Brown, suggesting that the chairman would regard it as contradictory to his perception of the "prairie-like" Washington Monument Grounds.[17] Warren Cox then presented a revised design by his firm for the glazed addition to the lodge and the tunnel to the monument. The commission members had numerous questions and concerns regarding glazing details, stair and tunnel configurations, and emergency exit hatches that would be located flush with the lawn. Don Hawkins of the Committee of 100 and George Idelson of the National Coalition to Save Our Mall also testified at the meeting, urging the commission to consider more alternatives. Diamonstein-Spielvogel's final remarks encouraged the NPS to consider the viewpoints of the commission members and the witnesses and further study the problem.

After the meeting, commission secretary Charles Atherton, who had favored the Balmori competition entry, which did not incorporate a tunnel, told a *Washington Post* reporter: "Nobody is happy to see people approach the

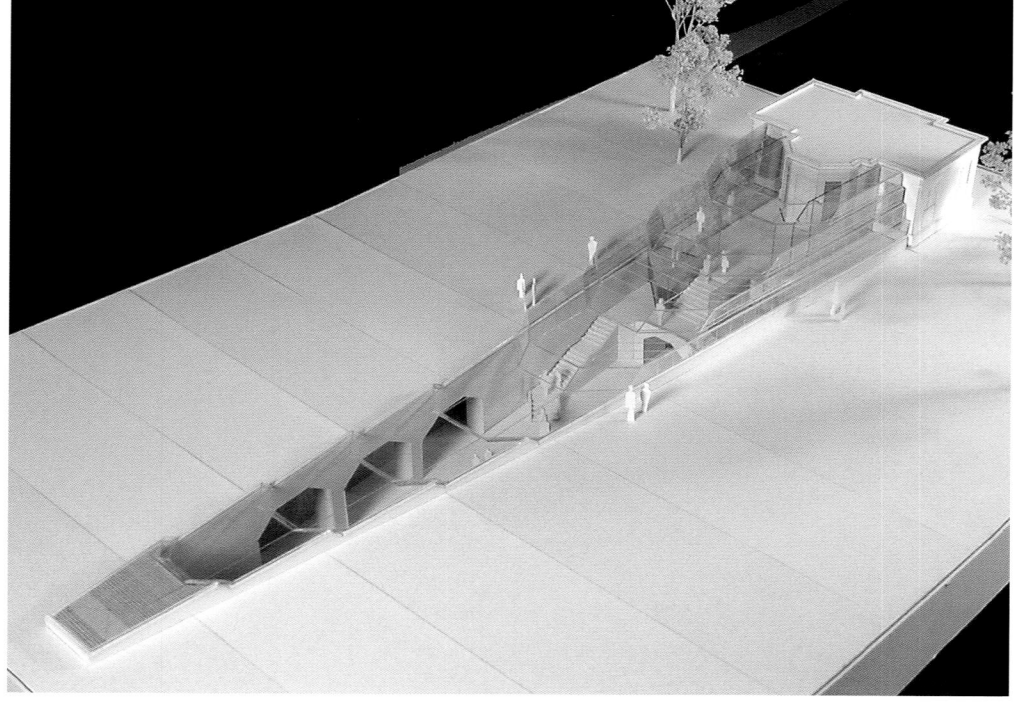

ABOVE LEFT: *Study model of the revised design by Hartman-Cox Architects for a glazed addition to the Monument Lodge to accommodate entry to the underground visitor center and access tunnel, September 2002.*

ABOVE RIGHT: *Interior rendering of the underground visitor center with the Washington Monument visible through the glazed ceiling, September 2002.*

Washington Monument in a tunnel, although it may be a reality we cannot escape."[18] Benjamin Forgey, the *Post's* architectural critic, hoped this would not be the case. He began his piece on the Washington Monument by mentioning various current underground construction proposals in the city. After discussing the symbolism of the monument, he described the tunnel as "something terribly wrong" and concluded that "this burrowing mania has got to stop."[19]

Due to failing health, J. Carter Brown resigned from the commission in late May and died less than a month later. In July, the commission members unanimously elected Harry Robinson chairman and Barbaralee Diamonstein-Spielvogel vice chairman. Robinson became the first African American to serve as chairman of the commission and Diamonstein-Spielvogel was the first woman to hold a leadership position on the CFA. In September 2002, architect David Childs (CFA 2002–05) was appointed to fill the vacancy left by Brown. Childs had served as the chief designer of the President's Temporary Commission on Pennsylvania Avenue beginning in the late 1960s and had then joined the Washington, D.C., office of SOM in 1971, where he worked for more than a decade before moving to SOM's New York office to assume a national leadership position with the firm. Between 1975 and 1981, Childs served as the presidentially appointed chairman of the NCPC. SOM, under Childs's direction, also had teamed with Diana Balmori in the National Park Service's invited competition for the Washington Monument security and visitor center project.[20]

In September 2002, the NPS returned to the commission with yet another revised concept. The landscape presentation included further developed details of the paths and retaining walls that doubled as seating as well as a new paving pattern: rather than the eight-point star, the circular plaza featured six rings composed of four types of stone. The alteration to the lodge was significantly different than the previous scheme; it now incorporated a telescopic glazed addition that extended approximately 150 feet westward, nearly half of the distance between the lodge and monument.

The commission members generally supported the configuration and detailing of Olin's paths but repeated concerns about the need to simplify the "fussy" design for the circular plaza; they also said that the proposed addition to the lodge would overwhelm the diminutive historic structure.[21] The discussion concerning the addition raised questions about the appropriateness and viability of using the lodge as the entrance point to the underground tunnel; for example, some thought the Sylvan Theater in the southeast quadrant of the monument grounds would be a more successful entrance location.

For Childs and Robinson, the fundamental issue of the design was how one should experience the monument, a point about which they did not agree. Childs argued that the Washington Monument's essential design function was as an enormous sculpture—not a platform from which to view the city—and that to emphasize an underground approach to the monument was incorrect: "This monument

RIGHT: *Model of a new design developed by Hartman-Cox Architects in spring 2003. The revised scheme included a more historicist addition to the Monument Lodge as the entry to the visitor center and tunnel.*

LEFT: *Aerial view of the Washington Monument Grounds showing the perimeter security elements as built, 2005; the proposed visitor center was not built.*

BOTTOM LEFT: *Detail of the retaining walls and bollards of the Olin perimeter security design on the approach pathways to the Washington Monument. The temporary visitor screening facility, appended at the base of the monument, serves in lieu of a permanent solution.*

BOTTOM RIGHT: *Model of one alternative design for a permanent Washington Monument visitor screening facility by Beyer Blinder Belle, 2012. This scheme would locate the facility beneath the circular plaza with access created by a pair of curving switchback ramps to a portal in a new wall along the east side of the plaza.*

can be seen in the landscape as the centerpiece of the city, as a piece of Classicism on this green verdant lawn, and to celebrate the security and that sort of deviant [underground] procession into the building I think is a mistake."[22]

Robinson disagreed, saying that the underground approach offered opportunities to enhance the experience of the monument: "[T]his experience has to be more than the travel distance from security to the top of the Washington Monument....I think it's very important to open this up and to create...the approach to the monument experience as best we can...that it should be a procession through light, through ideas, to the top of the Washington Monument."[23] Robinson added that the surface and underground "pilgrimage" to the monument need not be viewed as separate: "I see that this lets you, in fact, have a part of that pilgrimage underground and still experience this vertical obelisk that sits at the symbolic center of the city."[24] Childs countered: " If you want to go up and use this as an observation deck, then I think you should not alter the primary experience—this inviolate place—as a way of celebrating an unnatural way of getting to this monument, which is ducking down in a hole and coming up to it."[25]

Ultimately, Robinson ended the discussion by making a motion directing the National Park Service to further study the visitor center and underground access; the motion carried unanimously. In closing the discussion, however, Robinson failed to allow for public remarks; consequently, the National Coalition to Save Our Mall, the Committee of 100, and the National Trust for Historic Preservation gave their testimony in opposition after the vote. In time, parties opposed to the tunnel succeeded in enlisting congressional support to defeat the underground entrance, and only the landscape plan was implemented.

Instead, a temporary screening facility was erected at the monument in 2001 without commission review; the metal-clad box appended to the obelisk's entrance would remain for more than a decade. The idea for a permanent facility was revived in 2010, when five design options were developed by Beyer Blinder Belle and presented for informal comment by the commission in October. None of the options included a long tunnel or extensive visitor programming as had the scheme eight years earlier. Echoing the sentiments of David Childs regarding that earlier concept, artist Pamela Nelson (CFA 2001–11), the CFA's vice chairman, noted that the monument's greatest significance was as a visual icon and national symbol, rather than as a visitor attraction of an elevated viewing platform. The presentation was not a formal application, and no action was taken by the commission; the project was pending further review in 2012 as the National Park Service

considered a range of options to accommodate the screening.[26] A significant earthquake in August 2011 closed the interior of the monument to public visitation and required an extended period of repair to the unreinforced masonry structure.

LINCOLN MEMORIAL

Like the Washington Monument project, security enhancement for the Lincoln Memorial encountered a protracted review process due to specific design conditions. The National Park Service had initially approached the project in 2002 with the same proposed solution: a ring of bollards around the memorial. Rather than rejecting the bollards altogether, the commission accepted the notion that some might exist near the Lincoln Memorial. Despite this acknowledgment, the solution of how best to cross the Mall's principal axis with security elements led to years of deliberation on the location and style of the barrier and was not resolved until 2010.

At the June 2002 meeting under the leadership of vice chairman Robinson, the commission approved the installation of a proposed curving retaining wall around the north, west, and south sides of the memorial, but rejected the bollards running across the central axis of the Mall— beginning along the circular roadway at the intersections of Henry Bacon and Daniel French Drives, extending down the lower flight of steps, and meeting at the center of the lower plaza.

When the NPS presented revised plans in November 2003, the commission's membership had changed greatly: David Childs had been elected chairman the previous May with New York City developer Donald Capoccia (CFA 2001–04) serving as vice chairman; and the following month, Diana Balmori replaced Eden Rafshoon, and sculptor Elyn Zimmerman (CFA 2003–08) replaced planner and arts patron Carolyn Brody (CFA 1994–2003). Balmori, a noted scholar, educator, and advocate of sustainable design, was the first landscape designer to serve on the commission in a decade; Zimmerman, a New York-based artist best known for her large-scale outdoor sculpture, represented the first sculptor on the commission since 1989.

Earl A. Powell III also joined the commission in June, 2002, replacing Robinson. Powell was the director of the National Gallery of Art and an expert in nineteenth- and twentieth-century American art. Formerly executive curator of the National Gallery in the late 1970s under J. Carter Brown, Powell had left Washington in 1980 to serve as the director of the Los Angeles County Museum of Art. He replaced Brown in 1992 as director of the National Gallery, and his appointment to the commission continued the

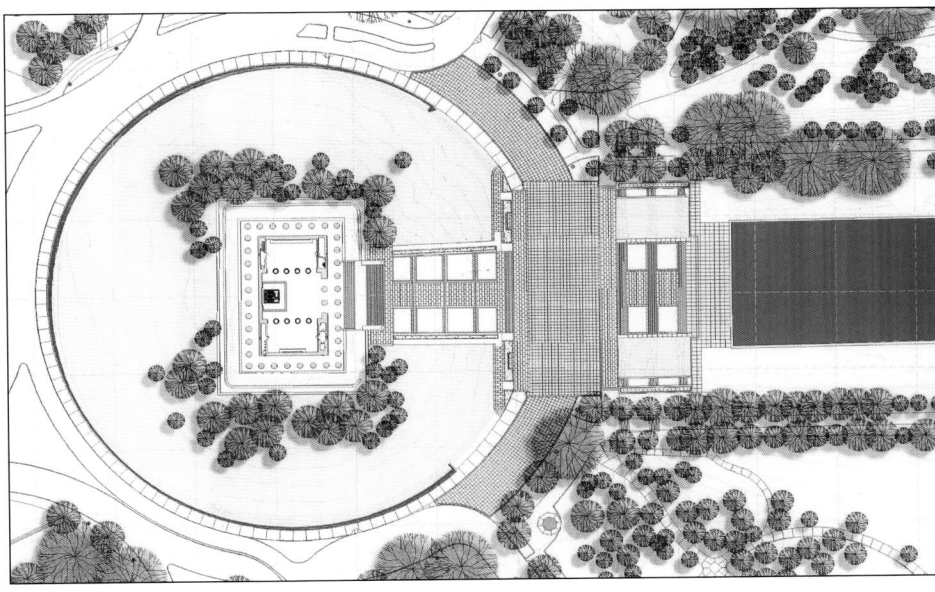

TOP: *View of the Lincoln Memorial, c. 1930, showing vehicles in the memorial's circular road and the simple treatment of the grounds; pavement at the bottom of the stairways was added in the mid-1970s*

ABOVE LEFT: *The Commission of Fine Arts, November 2003. Standing (from left): Charles Atherton (secretary); Elyn Zimmerman, Pamela Nelson, Earl A. Powell III, and Diana Balmori; seated are Vice Chairman Donald A. Capoccia (left) and Chairman David M. Childs.*

ABOVE RIGHT: *A 2005 scheme by McKissack & McKissack for permanent perimeter security at the Lincoln Memorial employed a retaining barrier wall on three sides of the memorial and the development of the plaza on the east side to limit vehicular access. Lines of bollards were proposed parallel to and across the bottom landing of the landscape stairways adjacent to the Reflecting Pool.*

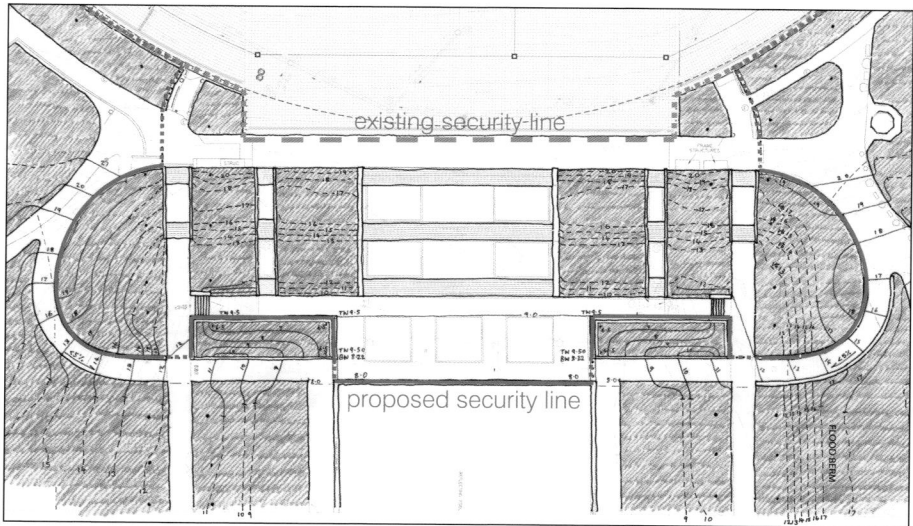

existing security line

proposed security line

TOP: *Plan of the perimeter security design by Sasaki Associates approved in February 2010. The design created the security line using a combination of low retaining walls, fewer bollards, and the Reflecting Pool itself without interrupting the axial view of the Lincoln Memorial.*

ABOVE: *Perimeter security at the Lincoln Memorial was installed at the top of the stairways adjacent to the plaza in 2009 to accommodate events associated with the bicentennial of Lincoln's birth. Although the circular granite retaining wall was constructed on the north, west, and south sides of the memorial, these large concrete blocks with battered sides created an interim solution while the design for the problematic east side was developed.*

practice of associating CFA membership and the position of National Gallery director.

At the November 2003 meeting, the commission approved a plan incorporating a fixed bollard configuration that extended from the radial streets, around the roadway, and squared off at the eastern edge of the pedestrian plaza with retractable bollards at the top of the Reflecting Pool steps. The NCPC, however, did not approve this scheme in its review. In an effort to resolve these differences, the National Park Service met with a working group of staff from the NCPC, the CFA, and the District's Historic Preservation Office, as well as interested citizens, over the course of the next year.

Three revised alternative schemes were developed, which the NPS considered to represent a consensus of the working group; these were presented by the architecture firm of McKissack & McKissack at the February 2005 commission meeting. Despite the working group's input, the commission—which now included architect, author, and educator Witold Rybczynski (CFA 2004–12), who had replaced Donald Capoccia—found all three schemes either too large or too detailed and requested a site visit and a mock-up of the bollards located to the west of the pedestrian plaza.[27]

That site inspection occurred on the morning of the commission's next meeting in March 2005; it served to reinforce rather than reduce the commission's concerns. At the meeting, Childs summarized the commission's lack of enthusiasm for any of the proposed bollard schemes: "There are lots of solutions but each one is compromised."[28] Diamonstein-Spielvogel, serving at her last meeting as a commission member, was particularly pointed, adding, "I don't want to be guilty ... of defacing our national symbols.... [W]hat I saw out there today was very distressing to me.... It just looked like fear incarnate is what we were creating. I don't want to be a part of that."[29] When it came time to vote on a recommendation, Childs acknowledged the National Park Service's long-standing efforts to resolve the issues but emphasized that a successful solution had not been found. He added that new technology could provide improved solutions, noted a preference for retractable bollards, and then supported the alternative with the line of bollards at the base of the memorial's main steps. The commission voted to approve the motion but the vote was split: Zimmerman and Rybczynski agreed with Childs, but Diamonstein-Spielvogel challenged the reference to future technology and opposed the motion, as did Balmori. Pamela Nelson abstained from voting, and Powell was absent from the meeting. Subsequent misgivings about this recommendation

prompted Childs to write to the NPS after the commission's April meeting and retract the official position it had taken the previous month:

I have continued to think about our recent consideration of your proposal for security measures at the Lincoln Memorial, and I brought the matter up again briefly with the other Commissioners at our meeting last week. The consensus is that we just are not comfortable with the position stated in our last action letter of 18 March.... I therefore ask that you return to discuss the issue of the bollards.... Thank you for your understanding.[30]

The letter led the National Park Service to pursue additional alternatives and reviews, which would take five more years to conclude. In 2008, the commission reluctantly approved an interim solution of precast concrete barrier elements in order to improve the appearance of the memorial grounds for the upcoming bicentenary year of Lincoln's birth in 2009—on condition that the entire west end of the Reflecting Pool landscape be designed as part of the memorial's perimeter security design.

The issue was finally solved at the end of the decade: in July 2009, the Park Service submitted designs from the landscape design firm Sasaki Associates, which had developed schemes incorporating landscape improvements and accessible circulation into the original scope of perimeter security. The proposed options included using the Reflecting Pool as part of the security system, thereby removing any barrier elements across the critical Mall axis. Instead, a configuration of sunken barriers, a small number of bollards at path openings, and low retaining walls along the North and South Elm Walks provided the opportunity to make the security line all but disappear from view. The commission enthusiastically approved the general concept and, following a variety of suggestions during design development, approved the final design in March 2010; construction began in 2011.

JEFFERSON MEMORIAL

The addition of perimeter security to protect the Jefferson Memorial proved to be a more difficult task than adding barriers at the Lincoln Memorial, where they could be inserted almost seamlessly into an existing structure of walks, stairs, and terraces. The Jefferson Memorial, a domed temple on a terraced podium, is a formal composition surrounded on three sides by an informal landscape. The original design by Frederick Law Olmsted Jr.—a spreading lawn planted with bosques of shade trees and evergreens defining views—was not fully implemented and had been compromised by the addition of other plantings over the

A rendering of the 2010 approved perimeter security design illustrates the use of retaining walls and other landscape elements to limit visual intrusions on the memorial.

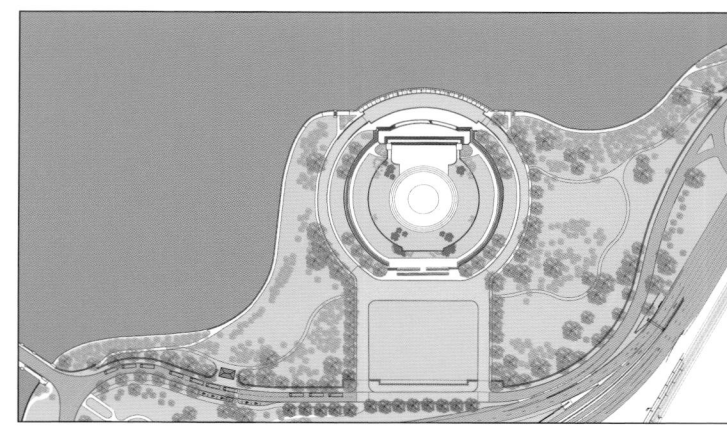

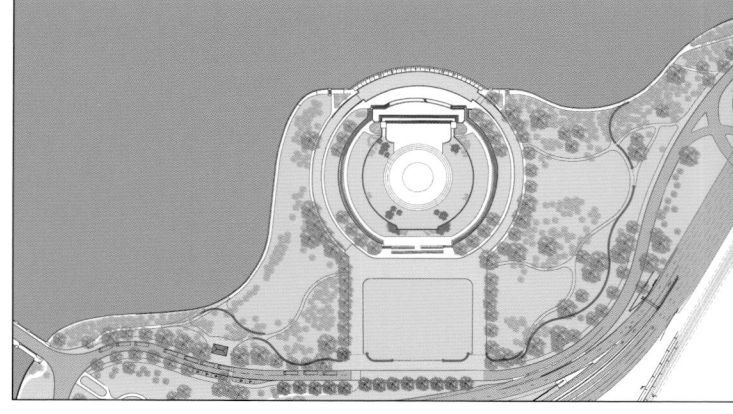

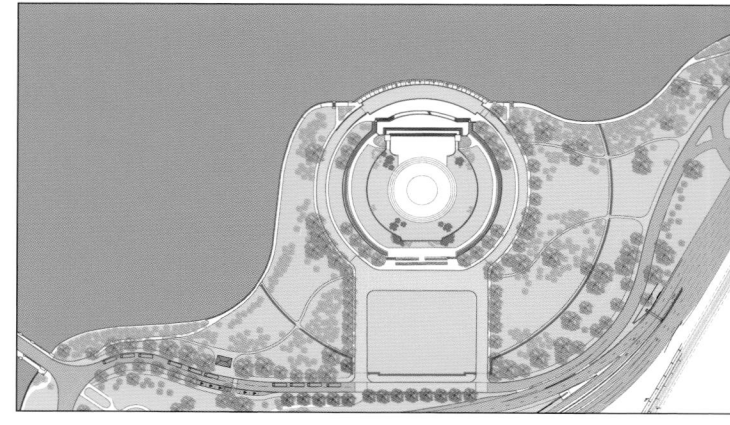

TOP LEFT: *Jersey barriers and lift-up plate barriers installed in response to the attacks of September 11 serve as temporary perimeter security and compromise the setting of the Jefferson Memorial.*

ABOVE LEFT: *In 2002, landscape architect Laurie Olin proposed a concentric perimeter security wall at the Jefferson Memorial designed to blend unobtrusively with the existing retaining walls.*

ABOVE RIGHT, TOP TO BOTTOM: *In 2010, Wallace, Roberts & Todd developed three alternative schemes for the placement of security perimeter elements (shown in red) around the Jefferson Memorial.*

TOP: *Alternative 1 located the security elements along the road at the perimeter of the site. While this scheme pre-*

sented the longest barrier system, the CFA eventually supported a version of this alternative as having the least impact on the memorial.

CENTER: *Alternative 2 proposed a meandering wall located slightly away from the road, following along historic pathways through existing trees.*

BOTTOM: *Alternative 3 constituted a more architectural solution: to integrate perimeter security in a semicircular landscape wall concentric with the geometry of the memorial.*

All three alternatives proposed a barrier across the lawn south of the memorial.

The security perimeter in Alternative 1 included stone wall segments composed of piers, benches, and cable.

years. The complex of bridges, abutments, and roadways bordering the grounds on the south detracted from the dignity of the memorial's setting—as did the recent installation of temporary Jersey barriers around the memorial.

In response to the congressional directive to protect major national memorials, the National Park Service initially planned to simply place a line of metal bollards around the memorial. However, in 2002, Laurie Olin, who had designed the barrier walls for the Washington Monument Grounds, developed a scheme for a security barrier on his own initiative. Olin proposed replicating the existing granite terrace wall situated 140 feet from the memo-

rial with another wall 30 feet beyond, filling the area in between with earth planted with turf. In May 2002 he presented this general proposal to the commission, which supported the concept. However, the National Park Service determined that this distance would not provide sufficient security and, instead, increased the required distance to 500 feet. The NPS hired architects McKissack & McKissack, with landscape architects Lee & Liu Associates, to prepare options for a barrier with a wider perimeter; these were presented to the commission in July. This team recommended replacing all vehicular circulation on the Jefferson Memorial grounds with pedestrian walks either with a barrier of bollards at the outer edge of the ring road or with a barrier wall farther out on East Basin Drive. The options would protect the surviving Olmsted landscape and would include security elements such as berms and low walls integrated within the existing landscape. The commission also approved this concept, but requested further study of the design elements.

Both versions of the proposal were abandoned as the NPS focused on perimeter security for the Lincoln Memorial and the development of the National Mall Plan. Eight years later, in April 2010, the National Park Service returned to the CFA with a new proposal by a different designer, landscape architect Ignacio Bunster-Ossa of Wallace, Roberts & Todd. The requirement of a 500-foot setback located the barrier within the existing landscape, and the design team had conducted a more thorough analysis of the historic landscape than had previously been done, identifying the "lobes" of vegetation Olmsted had used to accentuate orthogonal and diagonal views to and from the memorial. Bunster-Ossa presented three alternative security barrier configurations: a perimeter wall along the site's irregular boundaries generally following the existing infrastructure of roadways; a picturesque masonry wall running through the landscape; and a formal wall reflecting the circular shape of the memorial, similar to Olin's proposal replicating the existing granite terrace wall. All three options proposed to incorporate solid sections of wall with bollards only where the barriers crossed paved areas and to minimize the disturbance of historic and mature trees.

The design had to resolve several major issues: it had to reduce conflicts with pedestrian routes; improve the appearance of the landscape; and reduce the visibility of any barrier wall by altering the grade of the south lawn panel, the sole formal element within the landscape. After a lengthy discussion, the CFA members chose not to endorse any of the three alignments without seeing the barrier designs developed, but supported the development of simple barriers that would be transparent and permeable, responsive to the existing topography, and have a limited impact on the vegetation.

The design team returned in September 2010 with treatments developed for each of the three alternative alignments, all of which separated bicycle and pedestrian traffic. Alternative 1 was presented as the most transparent option; it combined piers and cables at the perimeter of the site, incorporating benches and allowing for a more varied spacing than a line of bollards. Alternative 2 featured a rough-faced, stone barrier wall with a flowing alignment as a feature within the Olmsted landscape. Alternative 3 was a simple, formal circular stone wall creating a

slightly elevated landscape within the barrier; the wall system would be discontinuous in key special locations to allow for passage or to frame axial views. Alternative 1 would impose the least change in the existing landscape but would result in the greatest loss of trees, particularly at the perimeter of the site. Alternative 3, shortest in length but within the existing landscape, would result in the fewest trees lost.

The National Park Service expressed its preference for Alternative 1 as the option with the least impact on the historic landscape; it also could be treated as part of the streetscape, following NPS guidelines of locating barriers where edges of landscapes are already evident. The CFA members supported this position as well, noting that it would allow the greatest amount of design control over the long barrier system in order to avoid monotony and would offer an opportunity to realize the intended Olmsted landscape. The members approved Alternative 1 in concept but recommended that features from other options also be explored, such as the treatment of the south lawn panel. In 2012, the project remained in development by the NPS.

SMITHSONIAN INSTITUTION

The Smithsonian Institution approached the problem of security design for its Mall facilities as a master plan, responding to it in terms of landscape design rather than physical barriers alone. Initiating its formal response to security issues later than the National Park Service, the Smithsonian submitted a perimeter security master plan for its museums on the Mall to the commission in January 2004.[31] Harry Rombach, the Smithsonian's associate director for facilities and master planning, introduced the project and acknowledged that the Smithsonian had been installing Jersey barriers and concrete planters around the museums for some time: "We tried to doll up the planters" with flowering plants, he said, but admitted "it really was an exercise of putting a bonnet on a pig."[32] Unlike the recommendation in the NCPC's *Urban Design and Security Plan*—which called for agencies to erect security elements that produced aesthetic continuity along streets rather than individual designs for each building—the concepts presented by architect Hany Hassan of Beyer Blinder Belle and landscape architect Roger Courtenay of EDAW showed unique design solutions that responded to specific conditions in the immediate area of each facility.

The possible vocabulary of proposed perimeter security elements included boulders, granite piers with metal infill panels, bollards, retaining walls, and posts linked by cables; plantings were specified to obscure hardened elements while maintaining the open quality characteristic of

TOP LEFT: *The 2004 perimeter security design by Beyer Blinder Belle at the National Air and Space Museum incorporates a composition of bollards and stone plinths to control vehicular access while maintaining the appearance of accessibility.*

TOP RIGHT: *Detail of a granite plinth with cast aluminum decorative relief, depicting the theme of the jet engine, part of the perimeter security at the National Air and Space Museum.*

ABOVE LEFT: *A proposal in 2004 by SOM and EDAW for building security and public space renewal involved substantial changes to the modernist National Museum of American History, including a new security screening and entrance addition on the north side of the building as depicted in this study model.*

ABOVE RIGHT: *Completed in 2008, Beyer Blinder Belle designed a perimeter security fence of granite piers and metal railings for the National*

Museum of Natural History to compliment the building's Beaux-Arts architecture.

RIGHT: *A less intensive security solution at the National Museum of American History was completed in 2008, following a design by Beyer Blinder Belle for a perimeter security barrier that echoes the abstract forms of the building's mid-twentieth-century design.*

TOP: *Photograph of the old City Hall, c. 1908, showing the building's mid-nineteenth-century north portico.*

ABOVE: *In the early twentieth century, the portico was removed, and the facade was recomposed with limestone cladding as shown in this photograph, c. 2000.*

the Mall. Commission members praised the plan, encouraged the architect to develop a single contemporary design for the eight guard booths, and approved the project in concept. The Smithsonian developed a proposal for the National Air and Space Museum first; the design team followed the direction suggested by the commission for the overall plan, which gave its final approval a few months later. Security schemes followed in the next several years for the National Museum of Natural History in 2005 and 2006—with modifications, including changing a barrier wall to a cable system in shrubs along Madison Drive and 12th Street, approved in 2008—and the National Museum of American History in 2007, both by Beyer Blinder Belle.

DISTRICT OF COLUMBIA COURT OF APPEALS NORTH ENTRANCE ADDITION

The entry pavilion addition to the District of Columbia Court of Appeals building in Judiciary Square by Beyer Blinder Belle is a prominent example of integrating new screening requirements into an existing federal facility. The historic 1820 Greek Revival structure, designed by George Hadfield, had served as the District's city hall until 1873, when it became a federal court building; east and west wings were added to the original building in 1826 and 1849, respectively.[33] Additional court buildings by Nathan Wyeth were added in the early twentieth century on the north side of Hadfield's building facing Judiciary Square; these new buildings were complementary to the original structure and created a unified complex surrounding a courtyard. At that time, the portico at the historic building's north entrance was removed and the facade redesigned; the exterior of the entire building was rebuilt in limestone as part of the Judiciary Square complex. By the early twenty-first century, the D.C. Court of Appeals was housed in the old city hall building.

To accommodate new security requirements, Beyer Blinder Belle reoriented the entry sequence of the building, recalling the location of the original north portico and proposing a transparent steel and glass pavilion as the new entry whose rhythms related to the historic building's facade. The program also included a complete renovation of the building's interior and the construction of a large courtroom beneath the building's south portico. The CFA first reviewed concepts for the pavilion in October 2003; the commission members acknowledged the addition as light, transparent, and deferential to the historic building but suggested restudy of the proposed height, roof, and columns to avoid drawing attention away from the historic structure. During the next several months, the design was refined and the height and mass reduced. At the commission's meeting

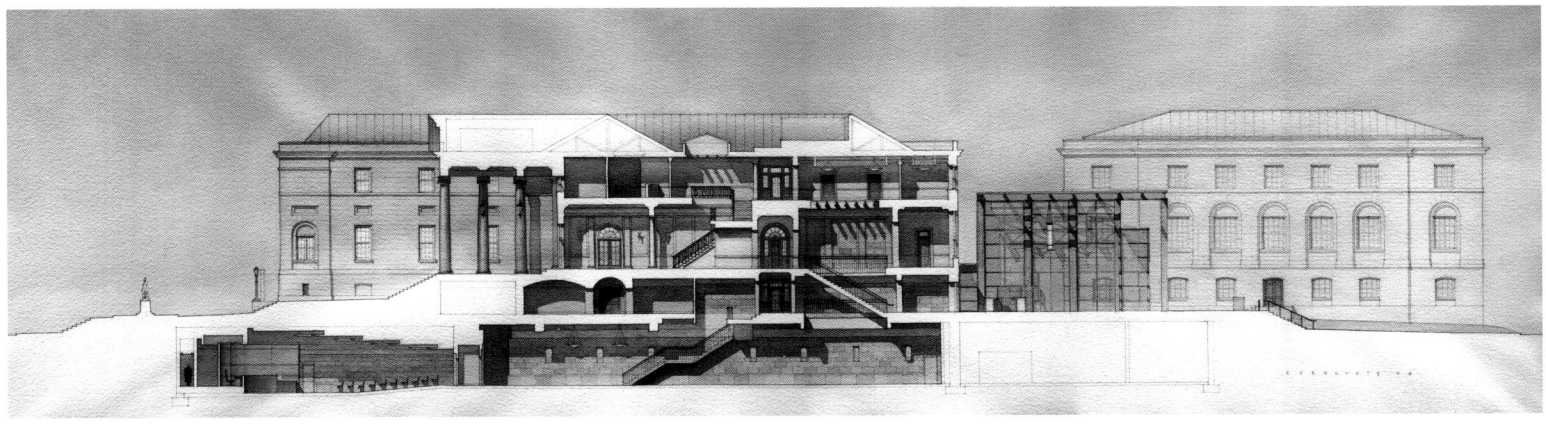

ABOVE: *Rendered section looking west by Richard Chenoweth illustrates Beyer Blinder Belle's reworking of the building's interior for use by the D.C. Court of Appeals with the addition of a new courtroom beneath the D Street portico (lower left) and a glazed security screening pavilion on the north side (right), 2004.*

CENTER LEFT: *The new entrance and security screening pavilion, completed 2009, reoriented the main building access to the north side of the complex.*

BOTTOM LEFT: *Rendering by Davis Buckley Architects of the 2003 proposal to build a new National Law Enforcement Museum beneath E Street with glass access pavilions adjacent to the D.C. Court of Appeals. Despite its impact on the setting of the D.C. courts, a final design of the museum was approved by the CFA in 2008 but remained unbuilt in 2012.*

Portrait of Earl A. Powell III by Dennis Brack, 2002. Powell is the third director of the National Gallery of Art to serve as chairman of the Commission of Fine Arts.

above-grade elements and proposed paving, noting that these could have an impact on the court's desire for a plaza design that addressed its security, access, and use requirements. The CFA recommended that the two groups jointly develop a plan for the plaza that addressed these needs.[35] In separate reviews of the museum project from 2003 through 2007, the CFA called for simplification of the pavilions' design and raised concerns regarding the design of skylights on the plaza, access for emergency vehicles, the height of bollards, and the location of sidewalks and curbs. The final design of the museum was approved in May 2008, but it remained unconstructed in 2012.

New Leadership for the Commission

During these protracted review processes, the commission's leadership changed once again. Citing a pressing work schedule associated with the rebuilding of the World Trade Center site in New York, David Childs stepped down as chairman at the May 2005 meeting but intended to continue serving as a member. He nominated Earl Powell as the next chairman, who was elected unanimously; Pamela Nelson became the vice chairman. David Childs attended one more commission meeting in September before resigning in November 2005. His vacancy was filled the next month by Boston architect and educator N. Michael McKinnell (CFA 2005–12), founding partner of Kallmann McKinnell & Wood Architects and designer of the Boston City Hall and the American Academy of Arts and Sciences in Cambridge, Massachusetts. Earlier in the year, architect John Belle (CFA 2005–11) had replaced Barbaralee Diamonstein-Spielvogel on the commission. A founding partner of the New York–based architecture firm Beyer Blinder Belle, he was known for his work on the Ellis Island Museum and the restoration of significant historical buildings such as Grand Central Terminal and Rockefeller Center.

The year 2005 also marked a time of transition for the commission staff. The position of secretary had been vacant since June 2004, when Charles Atherton had retired following forty-four years of service to the commission, with thirty-nine of those years as secretary.[36] In March 2005, architect Thomas Luebke, who had been serving as the city architect for Alexandria, Virginia, became secretary for the commission. Unlike the secretaries who had preceded him, Luebke had substantial professional experience as a designer in private-sector architectural firms on a range of institutional, commercial, and redevelopment projects. Frederick Lindstrom, an architect who had been hired in 1998 from the Historic American Buildings Sur-

in March 2004, CFA chairman David Childs noted, "I think its transparency is exactly right, the sense of arrival and the dignity."[34] Following additional refinement of the pavilion's depth, access ramps, and terrace, the revised concept was accepted in April 2004; and the final design was approved three months later.

A concurrent project, the National Law Enforcement Museum, was authorized by legislation to be located underground below the north courtyard plaza facing Judiciary Square; the design by Davis Buckley included two pavilions at grade serving as entries to the three-level, subterranean museum structure. Throughout the development of both the court and museum projects, the CFA urged coordination and repeatedly expressed its concern regarding the relationship of all the new elements proposed. At the CFA meeting of November 2005, the judges from the D.C. court specifically addressed the museum's vey, continued to serve as assistant secretary since the retirement of Jeffrey Carson in 2001. As the number of projects began to increase rapidly in the late 1990s—more than doubling from 327 submissions in 1994 to 680 in 2001—the commission staff was also increased in 2005 to create two full-time staff positions for the burgeoning Old Georgetown historic district cases and adding professional capacity to fulfill the CFA staff's growing role in regulatory and interagency consultations in a period of extensive government building activity.[37]

Under the direction of Chairmen Childs and Powell, Secretary Luebke instigated several changes in the commission's operations that reflected an increased profile for the professional staff. By 2005, the volume of cases to be reviewed by the commission at its one-day public meeting was often more than twenty—far too many for the volunteer members to reasonably adjudicate in a single session. In response, the commission adopted a consent calendar procedure, allowing staff to take action on many cases in its jurisdiction according to specific guidelines and reducing the annual average number of cases reviewed openly by the commission by roughly half.[38] Another example of the increased role of the CFA staff was the decision by Childs to assign the authorship of the case summary letters to the secretary instead of the chairman. Also very significant was the reconfiguration of the meeting room, completed in 2007, which changed the traditional arrangement of commission members around a single table to a broad arc facing the public. The new configuration allowed for improved visual and auditory access to the CFA proceedings and, for the first time, brought the secretary to the table to provide guidance on the review process.

With the new century also came an increased program of public information. In recognition of the centennial of the *Senate Park Commission Report,* historian Sue A. Kohler and architectural historian Pamela Scott edited a volume of contributed essays, *Designing the Nation's Capital: The 1901 Plan for Washington, D.C.* The volume was published in 2007, shortly before Kohler's retirement after thirty-three years as the CFA staff historian. In 2006, the commission staff helped establish the Charles H. Atherton Memorial Lecture program at the National Building Museum in honor of the former CFA secretary who had recently died. Former CFA chairman David Childs gave the inaugural lecture; other speakers included commission member and author Witold Rybczynski. Secretary Luebke also initiated two symposia held at the National Building Museum: "Framing a Capital City" in 2007 in collaboration with the National Capital Planning Commission; and "Power, Architecture, and Politics: The U.S. Commission

ABOVE: *The Commission of Fine Arts, February 2009 (standing from left): Elizabeth Plater-Zyberk, Witold Rybczynski, N. Michael McKinnell, and John Belle; (seated from left) Vice Chairman Pamela Nelson; Chairman Earl A. Powell III, and Diana Balmori.*

LEFT: *Thomas Luebke, an architect with private and public-sector professional experience, was named secretary of the Commission of Fine Arts in March 2005.*

of Fine Arts and the Design of Washington" in 2010 in conjunction with the centennial of the commission's founding. (Papers delivered at the 2010 symposium have been developed as essays by their authors and are presented in this book.)

Planning the Monumental Core for the Twenty-first Century

The profusion of perimeter security projects was only one aspect of the broader story of long-range planning for the Mall. As the twentieth century drew to a close, citizens, designers, planners, and members of Congress raised concerns about the condition of the Mall as well as its increased development with an ever-growing list of memorial and museum proposals. Mounting pressures and demands for new memorials in the late twentieth century had led to the

ABOVE: *Concept rendering by Michael McCann for the expansion of Washington's monumental core from* NCPC's Extending the Legacy: Planning America's Capital for the 21st Century, 1997. *The vision plan's key goals included emphasizing the U.S. Capitol as the symbolic center of the city, using federal development to extend development throughout the city, and integrating its two riverfronts into the city's public life.*

RIGHT: *Rendering from the* NCPC's 2003 South Capitol Street Urban Design Study *envisioned a new mixed-use neighborhood extending from the U.S. Capitol to the Anacostia waterfront.*

enactment of the Commemorative Works Act of 1986.[39] The act and its amendments changed the process of securing a site for a memorial on or near the Mall, encouraged private funding of memorials, and created a new entity, the National Capital Memorial Commission— in 2003, renamed the National Capital Memorial Advisory Commission (NCMAC)—to advise on site selection and design. Membership of the new commission included the chairmen of the Commission of Fine Arts, the NCPC, and the American Battle Monuments Commission, as well as the Architect of the Capitol, the director of the National Park Service, the District's mayor, the commissioner of the GSA's Public Buildings Service, and the secretary of defense. The Commission of Fine Arts and the NCPC also had separate review responsibilities for memorial site selection and design. While the act clearly gave the commission a significant role in the process and approval authority, it also involved the CFA directly with the other empowered agencies.

Subsequent to the new law, under the leadership of executive director Reginald Griffith, the staff of the National Capital Planning Commission undertook a special study of the monumental core. Incorporating input from nationally prominent designers, the federal planning agency issued a vision plan, *Extending the Legacy: Planning America's Capital for the 21st Century,* in 1997. This conceptual guide for long-term growth located future monuments, museums, and other development on the ceremonial routes extending outward into all four of the city's quadrants from the central node of the U.S. Capitol, rather than further concentration at the National Mall, thus expanding the monumental core into the city.

The development of the Mall also came under greater scrutiny from the public in this period. The contentious multiyear fight over the location of the World War II Memorial on the central axis of the Mall and subsequent disputes during design review had intensified the debate regarding a twenty-first-century vision for the monumental core. In 2000, Judy Scott Feldman, a historian and a prominent opponent of the World War II Memorial's design, established with other concerned citizens the National Coalition to Save Our Mall, a nonprofit group dedicated to the Mall's preservation.

The NCPC, in cooperation with the CFA, began work on a plan to guide future Mall development and issued the *Memorials and Museums Master Plan* in 2001, which built upon the L'Enfant, McMillan, and *Legacy* plans. Although the title referenced both memorials and museums, the plan generally emphasized the siting of memorials since government-sponsored museums are typically authorized by a federal law that specifies location. In an effort to balance

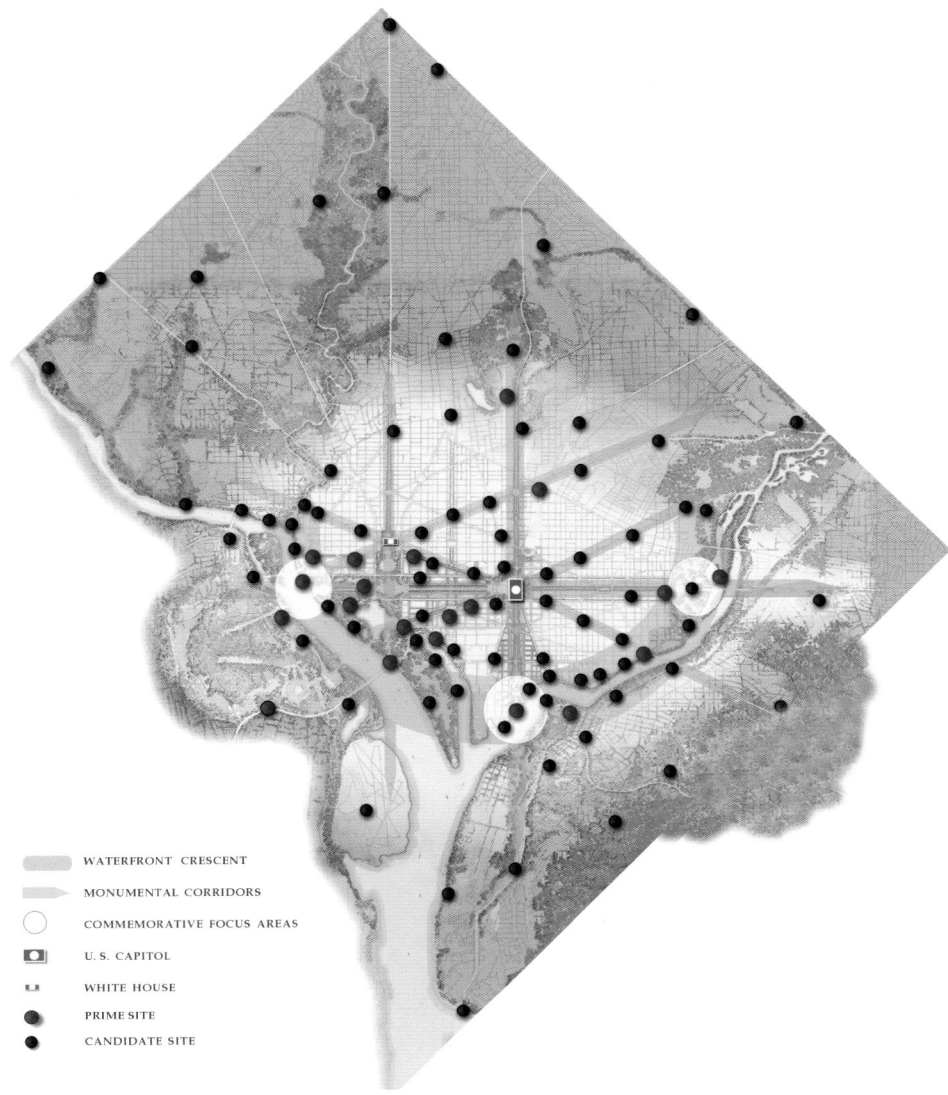

WATERFRONT CRESCENT

MONUMENTAL CORRIDORS

COMMEMORATIVE FOCUS AREAS

U. S. CAPITOL

WHITE HOUSE

PRIME SITE

CANDIDATE SITE

sociopolitical demands with the qualities of openness and historic design integrity, *Memorials and Museums* recommended the "Reserve," or no-build zone, on the National Mall and identified and evaluated one hundred potential sites throughout the city and the environs for future development. As a result, Congress amended the Commemorative Works Act in 2003, characterizing the Mall as a "substantially completed work of civic art" and establishing the Reserve. While limiting new development on the Mall, the legislation did not rescind existing authorization for the planned National Museum of African American History and Culture or the Martin Luther King Jr. Memorial, and it simultaneously created a new element, the Vietnam Veterans Memorial Visitor Center, "at or near" the Vietnam Veterans Memorial.[40]

In April 2005, following urging by the National Coalition to Save Our Mall, Senator Craig Thomas (R-WY),

The Memorials and Museums Master Plan of 2001 by the NCPC drew upon the principles of the Legacy plan to distribute commemorative sites throughout the District of Columbia.

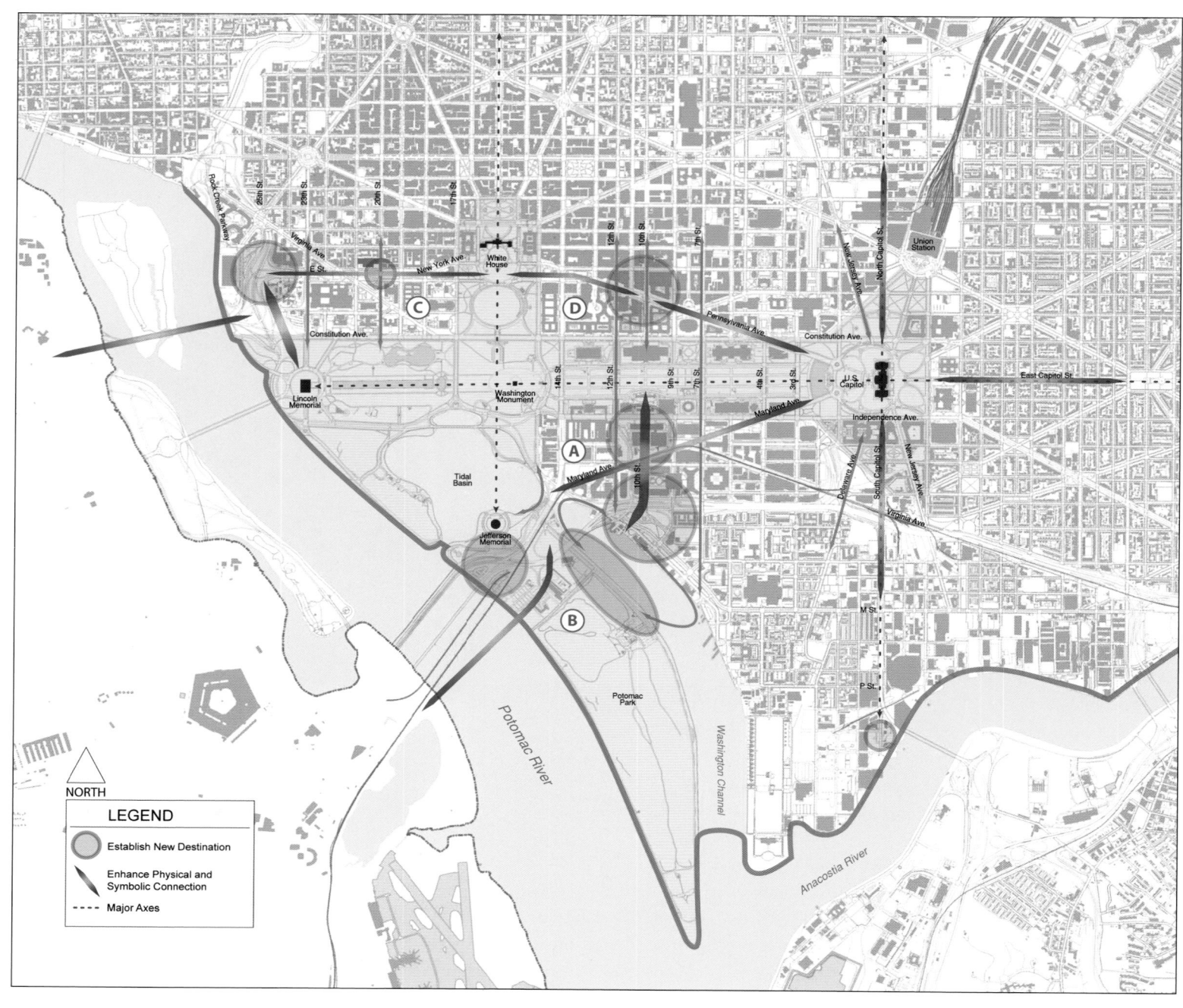

NORTH

LEGEND

⬤ Establish New Destination

◣ Enhance Physical and Symbolic Connection

- - - Major Axes

ABOVE: *The Monumental Core Framework Plan, a cooperative effort led by the CFA and NCPC completed in 2009, proposed to transform areas adjacent to the National Mall by creating sustainable and vibrant settings for new commemorative works, cultural institutions, and government facilities. The concept diagram illustrates the areas where symbolic and physical links to new destinations adjacent to the National Mall are proposed.*

FACING PAGE. TOP: *Detail of aerial rendering by Michael McCann illustrating a new mixed-use corridor along 10th Street, SW, linking the Mall with the Washington Channel and waterfront development in East Potomac Park.*

CENTER: *Street view along 10th Street, redesigned with commercial and residential activity and restoring the axial relationship to the Smithsonian Castle with the redevelopment of the Forrestal complex.*

BOTTOM: *The proposed transformation of utilitarian areas adjacent to the Jefferson Memorial to festival grounds could provide an alternative to intensive programming on the Mall while still within sight of major monuments.*

chairman of the Subcommittee on National Parks within the Senate Committee on Energy and Natural Resources, held a hearing on the future of the National Mall. Judy Scott Feldman testified on behalf of the coalition, which recommended the creation of a new super-agency oversight body for the Mall. NCPC chairman John Cogbill, John Parsons of the National Park Service, and CFA chairman David Childs also testified. In his remarks, Childs opposed the idea of a new oversight body, advocating instead for an updated comprehensive master plan for the Mall and the establishment of a nonprofit conservancy to support the maintenance responsibilities.

Consistent with Childs's testimony before the Senate committee, CFA secretary Thomas Luebke initiated with NCPC executive director Patti Gallagher a joint project between the staffs of the NCPC and the CFA—a process that led to the 2009 publication of the *Monumental Core Framework Plan: Connecting New Destinations with the National Mall.* As with preceding plans, the underlying goal was to protect the Mall from overuse. The *Framework Plan*'s first purpose was to create new settings for cultural facilities and commemorative works in areas adjacent to the Mall. Inevitably, the scope expanded to address broader needs, including the demand for federal office space and the planning and economic interests of the city, with the intention to transform federal precincts adjacent to the Mall into vibrant, sustainable destinations served by improved connections between the city, the Mall, and the waterfront.

Developed over several years with input from public and agency stakeholders, the *Framework Plan* was an elaboration of the McMillan Plan that acknowledged the need to expand the Mall. Instead of a monumental frame for the Mall, the new plan sought to dissolve the hard edge between commemorative landscape and living city with new commemorative and cultural development permeating the line between the symbolic core and the rest of the capital. The plan also addressed land use, urban design, and transportation improvements in four precincts: the Southwest Rectangle, East Potomac Park, the Northwest Rectangle, and the Federal Triangle. The goals for each precinct were articulated as extensions of Washington's planning tradition while addressing contemporary ideas of urbanism and sustainability and incorporating principles of mixed use, transit, and walkability to connect the National Mall to the waterfront and adjacent commercial areas. Conceived as a decision-making tool for planners, developers, and institutional interests seeking a presence in the monumental core, the *Framework Plan* received honor awards in planning from the American Institute of Architects and the American Society of Landscape Architects. Under the

The Evolving Landscape of the National Mall

RIGHT, TOP: *Temporary scaffolding around the Washington Monument was designed by Michael Graves and created a new image for the national icon during extensive repairs to the exterior stone from 1998 to 2000.*

BELOW: *A comprehensive program of wayfinding was developed in 2009 by Hunt Design for the NPS using a system of pylons with stone bases. The CFA advised against the use of bright colors to differentiate between destinations, finding it distracting within the experience of the landscape.*

In addition to the development of West Potomac Park as a memorial precinct, the National Mall as a whole underwent a series of changes in its physical design to improve the visitor experience and protect the landscape beginning in the last decades of the twentieth century. Increased use of the Mall—created by such programs as the Smithsonian Folklife Festival, the Library of Congress Book Fair, the U.S. Department of Energy's Solar Decathlon, as well as other demonstrations and events— began to pose new problems for the maintenance, access, and programming of this iconic national landscape.

Several major projects were undertaken in the 1990s to maintain or improve the National Mall resources. The most visually prominent of these projects was the temporary scaffolding erected around the Washington Monument to facilitate repointing of the exterior marble blocks constituting the self-supporting masonry structure, undertaken by the National Park Service and completed in 2000. Four visitor services buildings in a historicist design by architect Mary Oehrlein were added along the Mall and completed in 1999, as well as a larger visitor pavilion on the Ellipse in 1993. Another NPS project was the reconfiguration of roadways at the east side of the Washington Monument Grounds in 1997 to improve traffic flow, which changed the straight alignment of 15th Street to a gently curving arc; Jefferson and Madison Drives were also realigned as radial lines oriented toward the monument between 14th and 15th Streets. Farther east along the Mall, the National Gallery of Art Sculpture Garden—first envisioned in the SOM Mall Plan—was completed in 1999 as a circular park and monumental fountain at the 8th Street axis, designed by landscape architect Laurie Olin.

In response to increasing concerns about the condition of the Mall, the NPS initiated the National Mall Plan in 2006 to create a comprehensive and sustainable approach to problems of resource protection and management, visitor experience, and public access to the landscape of this national park. Concomitant programs included the reconstruction of the Mall lawn panels from 3rd to 14th Street as engineered and irrigated turf, begun in 2011; the installation of a comprehensive wayfinding and sign program, completed in 2012; stabilization of the Jefferson Memorial plaza at the Tidal Basin; and the reconstruction of the Lincoln Memorial Reflecting Pool to improve water quality and reduce energy use in West Potomac Park. Another significant project within the National Mall landscape was the construction of a levee barrier at 17th Street to protect downtown Washington from Potomac River flooding. In 2007, the Trust for the National Mall was established as a nonprofit organization to raise money to support improvements to the park; by 2012, the Trust had raised tens of millions of dollars—including a major gift to repair damage to the Washington Monument resulting from the 2011 earthquake— and instituted competitions to redesign several significant components of the National Mall landscape.

ABOVE: *A complete reconstruction of the Reflecting Pool in 2011–12 created a more sustainable system of hydrology while repairing the deteriorating structure of the ninety-year-old basin.*

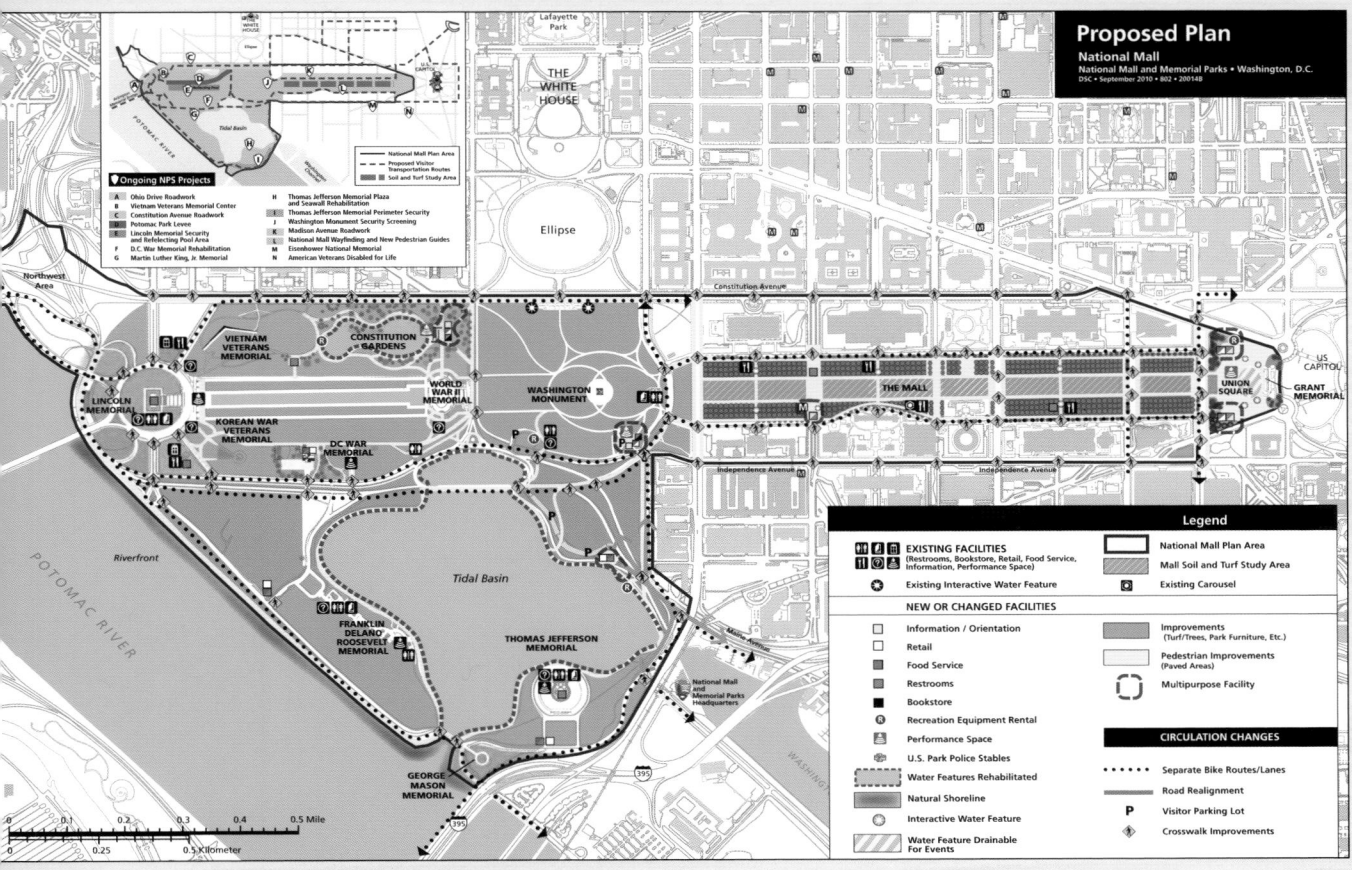

Proposed Plan
National Mall
National Mall and Memorial Parks • Washington, D.C.
DSC • September 2010 • 802 • 200148

LEFT: *In 2009 the NPS released the National Mall Plan, a comprehensive management plan intended to restore physical resources and improve the visitor experience in this national park landscape.*

BELOW: *The National Gallery of Art Sculpture Garden, designed by Laurie Olin, was installed in 1999, completing a key public space proposed by SOM in 1971.*

ABOVE. LEFT: *Heavy use of the Mall for events and programming in past decades has resulted in degraded conditions of the monumental landscape.* RIGHT: *As part of the NPS initiative to restore the Mall greensward, HOK proposed several schemes in 2012 to reconstruct the central lawn panels while providing dedicated paved areas to accommodate events. This alternative proposed several wider paved crossings with an emphasis at the 8th Street axis; the CFA rejected this scheme in favor of a more consistent pattern of panels with narrower crossings.*

leadership of Gallagher's successor, Marcel Acosta, the NCPC advanced a key objective of the plan—connecting the Mall to the waterfront—as the basis for a multiagency effort to create the Southwest Ecodistrict strategic plan beginning in 2009.

Boldness of Expression for Cultural Institutions in Washington

In contrast to the foregoing postmodern period, the design of new or the substantial renovation of existing cultural institutions in Washington evolved toward more bold and evocative expressions of contemporary architecture—following a larger worldwide trend in the late twentieth century of a prolific flourishing of cultural institutions. The role of the museum had been transformed, from the display of ennobling art to the presentation of exhibits designed around the experience of the visitor. And the museum building typology itself had undergone a revolution: from the Beaux-Arts conception of an ornamental edifice built for displaying artifacts to an expressive architectural experiment designed to attract visitors, often serving as the primary artifact itself. The phenomenon brought a new social prestige to the institutions, whose leadership, in turn, hired high-profile architects to design iconic structures to feature the institutions' cultural offerings. Notable examples included I. M. Pei's pyramid addition to the Louvre in Paris and, most notably, the Guggenheim Museum in Bilbao by Frank Gehry—a magnetic object generating its own audience that suddenly magnified that provincial city's prominence.

Washington participated in the trend, albeit within a comparatively strict regulatory framework of design review; the commission worked to guide projects toward design excellence and within the complex context of the city's legacy of urban design. By the turn of the century, the projects were increasingly informed by computer-aided drawing, rendering, and modeling, allowing the designs to be developed aesthetically by the possibilities of new materials, shapes, and easily generated perspective views—a great departure from the city's Beaux-Arts legacy, or even from modernist rationalism.

Diller Scofidio & Renfro's 2010 proposal for an inflatable blue structure in the interior court of the Hirshhorn Museum would create a new type of temporary activity space along the Mall.

CORCORAN GALLERY OF ART AND
COLLEGE OF ART AND DESIGN

Washington's oldest art museum, the Corcoran Gallery of Art, has been located in a Doric classical building by Ernest Flagg since 1897 on a site overlooking the Ellipse. Various additions to the west and north portions of the site had been built in the twentieth century, including the 1928 west wing addition by Charles Platt and the art school annex.[41] An area of about 14,000 square feet, used as a parking lot, remained undeveloped on the property; it became the location of a series of notable development proposals, the first of which was a design for an office building by Hartman-Cox Architects in 1986 that extended the granite solemnity of the museum's institutional architecture westward. The CFA members approved this concept design, commending the design as "beautiful." They were more critical of a revised scheme in 1987 that more literally replicated Beaux-Arts architectural elements of the addition. J. Carter Brown commented that "it was better before…. You have the great historic building and you want whatever gets added on to it not to compete, and as you begin to ape it closer and closer, you begin to try to sing its song and you steal its thunder." The following year, Warren Cox presented a revised version of the first concept, which the CFA approved with little discussion, but the project was never built.

Ten years later in 1999, the Corcoran's new leadership—perhaps hoping for the architectural success of the Guggenheim Museum Bilbao—selected a design by Frank Gehry featuring undulating stainless steel forms for an addition that would more than double the size of the historic building, creating new space for the school and relocating the main entrance to New York Avenue. In October 2001, David Levy, the Corcoran's director, introduced the project to the commission, saying: "Through its creative power and its commitment to new and imaginative ideas, the building we are presenting today will stand as a beacon of those values which are at the very core of civilized society…. We see our new building as an act of civic responsibility, a gift to future generations of Americans and to visitors from every land."[42] The commission agreed; it was enthusiastic about Gehry's highly individual design with some suggestions for further study of details, such as the feasibility of the skylights at grade, the loading dock, and consideration of a knee wall as opposed to security bollards. Barbaralee Diamonstein-Spielvogel said, "I saw the entrance almost as an embrace to the visitor as the building billows and flows…it [has] a peaceful and lofty quality."[43] J. Carter Brown summarized:

Dealing first of all with the entrance, I think the element of surprise is going to be very exciting. I think of Petra when you come in…. I find that the emotional content of [the building] is really one of joy. It has a certain whimsy but it also has the staying power and that solidity which you expect in a great art museum…. I would say go in peace.[44]

Before calling for a motion on the submission, however, Brown took the opportunity to scold Benjamin Forgey, the architecture critic for the *Washington Post,* who had written a piece on the Corcoran addition the day before, mentioning that a negative review by the commission would compromise the institution's ability to raise the requisite funds and "send a chilly message to all architects working in Washington that only the tried and true need apply for major civic jobs."[45] Brown said, "We are somewhat insulted that the press should assume we don't know what we're doing and have to be instructed." He also criticized the Corcoran leadership for "totally out of line" lobbying: "The management…can cool its jets and allow this Commission to do its business its way." Despite the heavy-handedness of these supporters, Brown reiterated his enthusiasm for the project; the commission approved the concept submission.[46]

In April 2003, when the project returned as a permit application, the commission members again only had a few comments and, despite the not insignificant questioning of the need for four entrances, the design was approved with enthusiasm. Harry Robinson, the commission's new chairman, said: "I think that the city needs this piece of

The Corcoran Gallery of Art is a National Historic Landmark and the home of Washington's oldest art museum, 2011. The Doric-style 1897 building by Ernest Flagg and 1928 addition by Charles Platt exemplify a Beaux-Arts typology for the presentation of art to the public. A vacant part of the property to the rear (at right) of the complex has been the subject of numerous proposals for development since the 1980s.

ABOVE LEFT: *Winning competition model of a proposed museum addition to the Corcoran Gallery and the College of Art and Design by Frank Gehry, 1999. Gehry's signature use of sculpturally curving planes would clearly set the new building apart from the original and create a radically new image for the museum.*

ABOVE RIGHT: *The model of Gehry's revised design for the Corcoran addition of October 2001 illustrates billowing metal-clad forms at the addition's entrance and highlights*

its relationship to the Corcoran's existing west wing by Charles A. Platt.

RIGHT: *Frank Gehry presenting the Corcoran addition to the Commission of Fine Arts, October 2001. From left: J. Carter Brown, Eden Rafshoon, Carolyn Brody, Donald A. Capoccia, Barbaralee Diamonstein-Spielvogel, Frank Gehry, and Harry Robinson III. Although CFA meetings had been open to the public since the 1970s, the commission continued to hear presentations seated around a central table.*

sculpture. It is as much a gift to the city in sculpture as it is a building."[47] Ultimately, however, the project was not built; the Corcoran, a private institution, could not commit to raising the needed funds to build Gehry's iconic proposal. Within ten years and with increasing financial strains, the Corcoran instead entered into an agreement to develop an eight-story office building on the vacant site, effectively ending any possibility of the museum's expansion—or its redefinition by architectural means. In 2008, the commission reviewed and approved a revival of the his-

toricist concept design by Hartman-Cox for a commercial office building on the site, but this proposal did not proceed. Beginning in 2009, a new design by Smith Group was proposed by Carr Development for a speculative eight-story office building, this time in a highly contemporary style executed in angled glass planes and a program of vertical and horizontal glass fins. The CFA raised numerous concerns about the relationship of the proposed building to its neighbors and to the context of New York Avenue, NW; the project was approved in November 2011 with di-

rection to refine the design of the building's yard and exterior where it would abut its neighbors.

THE NEWSEUM

The issues associated with the private Newseum revolved less around its design expression—which confirmed steel and glass as an acceptable part of the vocabulary of the monumental core—and more around process, the District's desire for redevelopment, and the consequences of development to Pennsylvania Avenue's symbolic importance in the nation's capital. Zoning at the project site, the northeast corner of Pennsylvania Avenue and 6th Street, NW, and across the street from John Russell Pope's National Gallery of Art, required a mix of uses, including 145,000 square feet of housing and 30,000 square feet of retail. As part of the development process, the sponsoring organization, the Freedom Forum, and its architect, Polshek Partnership (now Ennead Architects), met with and received input on the design from community organizations, civic groups, and city and federal agencies, including the Commission of Fine Arts and its staff through the agency's purview under the Shipstead-Luce Act. The designers specifically referenced these many reviews as the commission came to focus on the project's impact on the monumental core.[48]

In November 2002, the Polshek Partnership submitted its design to the commission for concept review. A glass building was proposed to symbolize the nonpartisan foundation's commitment to free press and free speech with the various elements of glazing representing transparency. The front elevation—the main facade—featured a seventy-four-foot-tall limestone panel inscribed with the First Amendment and an immense glass recess into the atrium

containing a forty-foot by twenty-foot media screen; the amount of glass on the building would be unprecedented for Pennsylvania Avenue. As the building turned the corner at C Street, the housing component was positioned to address the city's traditional orthogonal grid and the neighboring twentieth-century architecture.[49]

The commission was generally enthusiastic about the design, which represented a pronounced philosophical shift from the promotion of masonry facades erected along the avenue as recently as the Ronald Reagan Building in the 1990s, a project still comfortably within the tradition of the avenue's Beaux-Arts legacy. Rather, the commission's concerns focused on what would be seen inside the building, the amount of illumination that emanated from it at night, and the immense media screen proposed. Diamonstein-Spielvogel, in a statement that reflected the commission's continuing concern with the dignity and uniqueness of the avenue, specifically posed this issue to the project presenter, James Polshek:

So you know as well as I that the vocabulary du jour is to involve the public in the building by huge plasma screens…. If this is an [information technology] building—and it is—it's also a testimony to intellectual property. That most vivid representation may be too honky-tonk. It may be [that] what we like in Times Square, we do not like vis-à-vis…John Russell Pope or in the view of the Capitol.[50]

The commission directed the architect to further study the level of transparency and illumination, height of the building, and the details associated with incising the First Amendment on the building's front elevation.

The project team returned to the commission the next month with what they considered responses to these questions, again pursuing a formal review rather than submitting

ABOVE LEFT: *The proposed 1987 office building addition to the Corcoran Gallery of Art and College of Art and Design by Hartman-Cox would have extended the historic Beaux-Arts aesthetic of the original building and its later additions.*

ABOVE RIGHT: *Rendering of the Smith Group design for the proposed eight-story office building as seen from New York Avenue, 2011. The Corcoran's decision to develop the site as a separate commercial property would definitively limit future use of the parcel by the institution.*

TOP: *Concept model of the 2002 proposed design for the Newseum by Polshek Partnership shows the building's relationship to Pennsylvania Avenue, the Canadian Chancery, the National* Gallery of Art, and the Federal Triangle's Apex Building.

ABOVE: *Rendering of the final design for the Newseum complex in 2004, with the apartment tower as a backdrop to the exhibit areas* facing Pennsylvania Avenue. *A stone panel inscribed with the First Amendment of the U.S. Constitution and large media screens are dominant elements of the front facade.*

the plans for comment. In his opening remarks, Polshek reminded the commission that his office had been working on the project for nearly two years and noted that the team had analyzed Washington's plan from the beginning of their efforts, which led them to an unusual conclusion: "We came to understand that Pennsylvania Avenue…may be called the Nation's Main Street, but it's not necessarily the most important street in Washington, at least historically. But nevertheless, it's very powerful."[51] Then Polshek gave lengthy commentary on the illumination associated with the building and sought justification for the overall height of the building through a discussion of program, design elements, and the removal of mechanical systems on the roof—all warranting a taller height for the complex building.

The members continued to raise questions about the building's transparency and the balance of interior and exterior illumination as well as illumination from the media screen. However, Polshek's position regarding Pennsylvania Avenue and an acceptable height for development led to the most heated exchange. David Childs strongly disagreed with Polshek's views, pointing out that building on Pennsylvania Avenue came with certain limitations for an owner:

I remember once Carter Brown talking about a project on Pennsylvania Avenue and talking about caveat emptor, *the buyer beware. Your client bought this piece of property and with it came not only this wonderful view but also some obligations. So I don't think it's this Commission's responsibility to live up to the economics or the program if it doesn't fit with the piece of property. And the fact is that what we're charged with…is the aesthetics of this. And the argument that we bought this piece of property and we've got to make so much money from the housing or we've got this much program is really not a basis here.*[52]

Polshek's response returned to the point that housing was part of the program because it was required by the District, not because of the Freedom Forum's development bottom line. [53]

Harry Robinson entered the discussion by suggesting that the most important view of the building was from the pedestrian's vantage point in the immediate surroundings, and thus the proposed height was not an issue as it would not be discernible. Childs acknowledged that most people would not notice the additional height, but argued that the views down the avenue were more important and, in a specific reference to Polshek's introductory remarks, underscored that Pennsylvania Avenue, in fact, was the most important street in the city. After much back and forth, Childs made an uncommonly strong motion that "remanded" the issue of the height back to the architect for a solution; the motion passed.[54]

The Newseum project team intended to present in January 2003 for a third consecutive month, but bad weather prevented the New York City–based Polshek from traveling. The next month, the team returned for concept approval with a design reflecting minor revisions, including a slight reduction in square footage, and with advocates to speak in support of the project. During his presentation, Polshek pointed out the numerous community and agency reviews of the design, which had garnered wide favor among these groups. After Polshek's presentation, a roster of community leaders and high-ranking District officials spoke in favor of the project, including Andrew Altman, director of the Office of Planning.

Diamonstein-Spielvogel, presiding as vice chairman, called for a short recess when it came time to deliberate. Before leaving the room, Childs asked for a clarification on the building height; the actual number—134 or 137 feet—was in question due to conflicting and ambiguous drawings and models showing a variation of three feet. Upon returning, Diamonstein-Spielvogel offered a motion recommending concept approval that included the wording, "We accept the offer of the architect to further reduce the building to 134 feet." Although noted as inaudible in the meeting record, Polshek seems to have objected to that wording, prompting Diamonstein-Spielvogel to modify the motion to include the less specific, "[The] architects will continue to develop and adjust the design." This led to some confusion among the members and a short discussion. Polshek commented that the project had in fact given up square footage and reduced the height from 140 to 137 feet, adding, "I think that's a tremendous amount to give and I think that holding this building up or withholding conceptual approval based on three feet for a building of this importance is astounding…. We can't go lower." The motion failed. There was reluctance, however, to end deliberation in this way for a project that even David Childs acknowledged was conceptually strong and offered "life-giving spirit to this end of the avenue." Childs offered a motion to approve the concept design with the height reduced to 134 feet, which Polshek repeated could not be done; the motion passed four to two.[55]

When the project was resubmitted a year later, only information on the lettering of the First Amendment panel and the large interior media screen were provided; height was not discussed. That submission was approved and final review delegated to staff. During the permitting

Completed in 2008, the Newseum presents a departure from Washington's traditional masonry architecture along Pennsylvania Avenue with the highly modeled and transparent quality of its facade.

process, however, the Freedom Forum had appealed the commission's height requirement to the District government, who sustained the appeal. The Newseum was built at the taller height and opened in 2008.

U.S. INSTITUTE OF PEACE

The United States Institute of Peace (USIP), established by Congress in 1984 as a forum for the peaceful resolution of international conflicts, occupies an unusually sensitive site immediately north of the Lincoln Memorial at Constitution Avenue and 23rd Street, NW, part of the historic Old Naval Observatory. The building terminates the long row of classical marble structures housing public institutions on the north side of Constitution Avenue intended to be a backdrop for the Lincoln Memorial and its grounds; it also serves as a gateway element between the Mall and the Kennedy Center area.

Designed by Moshe Safdie, the large, cubic building with masonry walls bears a regular pattern of punched window openings; two large atria inside the block are covered by translucent curving roofs formed of spherical segments—a variation on the Washington dome. When Safdie first presented his concept to the commission in November 2002, he stressed his desire to create a building that would achieve transparency through large expanses of glass. Safdie set the cornice height both in relation to the buildings behind it and, particularly, to John Russell Pope's American Institute of Pharmacy building (now the headquarters of the American Pharmaceutical Association) to the east; this height was intended to keep the new building shorter than the Lincoln Memorial.

While the commission approved the concept, it voiced concerns addressing the protection of the monumental context. The CFA members advised Safdie to consider the appropriate scale for this location since the building had to be large enough to anchor the corner but not so large that it would overshadow the Lincoln Memorial; and they recommended subordinating the illumination of the translucent dome to that of the Lincoln Memorial. The members also suggested developing a landscape design that would respond to the urban condition of 23rd Street. Safdie assured them that the building would be lit from within, with no exterior lighting; the roof would appear opaque during the day but would glow softly at night. Donald Capoccia said Safdie should work out the security aspects of the design at the outset so that it would not be necessary to resort to the ubiquitous line of bollards.

Safdie did not return with a revised concept until three years later, in November 2005. By then, the program had expanded by 20,000 square feet. Safdie reduced the massing by placing most of the new volume below grade and slightly lowering the height; the cornice and the apex of the roof were still lower than the corresponding points on the American Pharmaceutical Association headquarters. Material details had been developed; the building would be constructed of acid-etched concrete, an artificial stone, to resemble limestone.[56] To address security, Safdie planned to use shatterproof glass and such landscape features as water and topographic changes instead of bollards. The CFA members approved Safdie's approach. Witold Rybczynski observed that there was always a tension resulting from modern buildings confronting the classical space of the Mall, commenting that he was impressed with how Safdie had handled this by designing two buildings in one: a classical block surmounted by a modern roof.

Two years later, in February 2007, the landscape design concept developed by Balmori Associates was presented for the project; CFA member Balmori did not attend

ABOVE: *Aerial rendering of the U.S. Institute of Peace and the undulating terraced landscape design by Diana Balmori on the steeply sloped site, 2007.*

LEFT: *The building, completed in 2011, comprises curving glass roofs over courts located between three masonry volumes.*

the meeting. The scheme featured long, sinuous walls undulating up the steeply sloping site—relating to the curving lines of the roof rather than the classical geometry of the building itself. The terrace walls, reinforced by lines of planting, also defined a circular public entrance plaza to the south; a similar treatment was used along the narrow border with 23rd Street. The planting scheme of trees, shrubs, and flowers emphasized white and light green colors juxtaposed with dark green and purple, a palette intended to symbolize peace. Two adjacent rills of water, one fast flowing and the other slow, were meant to enhance the sense of peace and serve the practical purpose of partially masking traffic noise emanating from the adjacent bridge and highway ramps.

Rybczynski again emphasized the unique character of the building, with its classical box and the modern roof, but he warned that the landscape design was undermining this contrast: the design was playing off one element of the building, rather than the conditions of the site, the structure, and the urban condition. He advised designing the landscape along the 23rd Street edge in response to the urban condition of regular rectilinear blocks to the east; John Belle also recommended that the landscape design of the narrow edges along the roadways be reconsidered. Consequently, when the building and landscape designs were submitted for final review in May 2007, the curving, insular garden spaces along the road had been abandoned and redesigned as a more integrated space, with a line of trees ascending the slope. The commission approved the project with praise; Michael McKinnell called the landscape "delightful," although he did recognize the high degree of maintenance it would require. The building was completed in 2011, but some design issues remained unresolved: an interagency agreement was signed that year to reduce illumination of the dome, and the USIP began plans to add perimeter security bollards in 2012.

ARENA STAGE

Vibrant architectural expression transformed an existing complex of experimental performance spaces for a District-based repertory company, the Arena Stage, at 1101 6th Street, SW. The country's first permanent structure devoted to theater-in-the-round, the original Arena building by Harry Weese was completed in 1961. Ten years later, Weese designed an addition, the Kreeger Theater, which was also intended for experimental theater productions.[57] Together, the concrete and brick structures with metal roofs in the Southwest waterfront neighborhood had become icons in the city's cultural and visual landscapes of the late twentieth century. However, by the early twenty-

first century, the existing complex was perceived as programmatically obsolete. Concurrent with the city's plans to revitalize the Southwest waterfront, the management of the Arena Stage complex decided to renovate and expand the existing facility. The result—a sensuously sculptural glass, wood, and concrete expression of contemporary architecture—was designed by Bing Thom Architects and reconceived as the Arena Stage at the Mead Center for American Theater, a keystone in the revitalized urbanism of the waterfront.

Under the Shipstead-Luce Act, the project was first reviewed at the CFA's July 2002 meeting, following a site inspection earlier in the day to examine the context and conditions. Thom's concept proposed the two existing theater spaces, the Fichandler and the Kreeger, be joined by a new theater, all under a single curvilinear roof pointing toward the Washington Monument. The three building components, plus related service, administrative, and public spaces beneath the roof, would be wrapped in a glass curtain wall; recycled heavy timbers would support the roof. The CFA members noted the light-filled and transparent treatment of the structure, raising questions about the materials and technology of the singular design. Chairman Harry Robinson's remarks summarized the commission's response:

"[It's] a wonderful jewel box.... I think we're all in love with the project." The concept was approved.[58]

The concept, described by the architect as "three temples on the mount of the Acropolis," was further developed over the next three years, and even as the membership of the commission changed, the response of CFA members remained enthusiastic.[59] In April 2003, the CFA reviewed design refinements that included a tension structure to support the large cantilevered roof and increased roof height. Again, the members' comments focused on more specific elements such as materials and signage. Chairman David Childs described the added height and glass walls as appropriate, adding that he liked the "confusion of inside and outside." Pamela Nelson found the design theatrical, but appropriately so: "It's perfect for what it is... it's going to add so much to the area of town."[60] The members unanimously approved the refinements. The waterfall at Maine Avenue was later deleted due to maintenance concerns and replaced by a ramp with the lettering "Arena Stage" as a supergraphic visible to drivers along Maine Avenue. The final design was approved in September 2005; review of adjustments to the roof profile was delegated to staff and approved in November 2008, and the building was completed in 2010.

The new theater complex, completed in 2010, presents a dramatic swooping roofline along Maine Avenue, SW.

CONNECTING TO THE RIVER: THE KENNEDY CENTER STAIRS

In an early design for the Kennedy Center for the Performing Arts, Edward Durell Stone presented an exuberantly curved building, massive in size, with a terrace extended over Rock Creek Parkway to the Potomac River. Later scaled back due to cost, the building was realized as a modernist marble-clad box that retained a western terrace cantilevered over a portion of the parkway but without a connection to the park and pathway along the river's shore. This condition—coupled with the center's isolation from the street grid by highway structures on the east and south—would cause a reexamination of the center's connections to the city and waterfront during the late twentieth and early twenty-first centuries.

A concept presented by Arthur Cotton Moore to the CFA for an informal review in July 1992 extended the center portion of the existing terrace outward as a monumental 250-foot-wide staircase descending to the narrow strip of embankment below. The stairway was bracketed by masonry elevator towers providing vertical access for those pedestrians who could not negotiate the stairs. The CFA members supported a connection between the Kennedy Center and the river, calling it "a good urban amenity," but found the steps themselves too steep and the elevation change inadequately accommodated.[61] Three years later, in October 1995, the Kennedy Center formally submitted a concept design, part of a larger scope to expand parking facilities and renovate the concert hall, by the architecture firms of Hartman-Cox and Quinn Evans. Instead of the grand monumental staircase, however, the new proposal created two narrower flights of stairs parallel to the river, leaving a maximum amount of space along the river's edge. Small elevator towers were integrated with the stairways and connected to the existing terrace with minimal walkways, allowing the terrace's floating character to remain legible. The CFA again expressed support for connecting the center to the river and found that the design respected the building's horizontality without overwhelming it but suggested shifting the base of the stairways slightly toward the river.

In 1997 and 1998, Benjamin Thompson Associates and Sasaki Associates presented concept studies to the CFA for parking expansion and improved approaches to the center that included renderings with a split stairway connection to the river. However, budget constraints prevented the Kennedy Center from including the stairway connection as part of the project.[62]

By 2003, the Kennedy Center hired Rafael Viñoly to develop a plan for the facility's expansion. Viñoly's design pushed development eastward toward the city, adding new buildings on decking over the coils of highway ramps; the Kennedy Center itself would be encircled by an ellipse-shaped terrace connected to a new trumpet-shaped plaza and water feature at the east. The new elliptical terrace on the west would cantilever over the parkway to the river with ramped connections to the embankment. The CFA approved the concept design in February 2003. Although in support of the project, the Federal Highway Administration noted that decking over the federal roadways would be a budget-driven, long-term project; in fact, Congress did not appropriate funding for the project.[63]

In the same period, the District of Columbia govern-

In 2011, the CFA approved a design by KGP Design Studio for a pair of cantilevered stairways, lightly articulated in glass and steel, to connect the floating terrace to the river's edge.

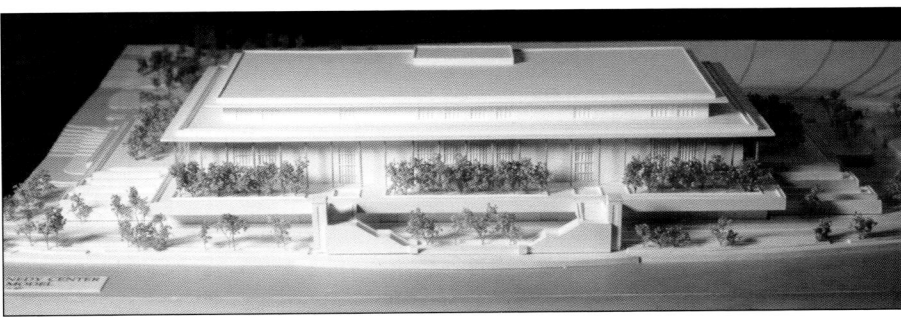

ment actively supported the reestablishment of Washington as a waterfront city. One manifestation of this vision was an access study undertaken with the Federal Highway Administration with the support of the Kennedy Center. Released in 2005, the study supported many of the goals of the Viñoly scheme, including air-rights development, a public plaza, and improved connections to the street grid. The study also continued to emphasize the need for a pedestrian link between the Kennedy Center terrace and the river. By 2007, the District's Department of Transportation, in cooperation with the National Park Service and the Kennedy Center, had engaged KGP Design Studio to revisit the idea of a pedestrian connection between the center's west terrace and the riverfront path leading to Georgetown.

KGP's concept, presented to the CFA in October 2007, reinterpreted the earlier Hartman-Cox diagram of delicate walkways leading to a pair of stairways—but in a modern expression of metal and glass. As in earlier concepts, elevator towers, now articulated in translucent glass, were integrated with the stairs; the stairs were proposed as gradually arcing trusses with glass treads and side panels. The commission was enthusiastic about the design, finding it a graceful complement to the floating quality of the terrace; with some suggestions regarding careful selection of

TOP LEFT: *Arthur Cotton Moore's concept proposed a grand masonry stairway from the Kennedy Center terrace to the Potomac shoreline that was flanked by monumental piers.*

ABOVE LEFT: *The Hartman-Cox concept of 1995 incorporated two narrower flights of stairs turned parallel to*

the river, rather than a single, steeply pitched central stairway.

TOP RIGHT: *The 2003 concept design by Rafael Viñoly for Kennedy Center expansion included decking over highway ramps and creating an enormous elliptical terrace cantilevered above the existing roadway along the river.*

ABOVE: *As part of a larger project of parking and access improvements for the Kennedy Center in 1997, Benjamin Thompson Associates and Sasaki Associates presented another scheme with two curving stairways connecting at a lower plaza.*

materials and an emphasis on simplicity, the CFA voted in favor of the concept. In October 2011, the CFA approved a revised design with recommendations to refine the landscape design at the level of the parkway.[64]

NATIONAL PORTRAIT GALLERY AND SMITHSONIAN AMERICAN ART MUSEUM RENOVATION

As part of its extensive renovation and restoration of the National Portrait Gallery and the Smithsonian American Art Museum, begun in 2000, the Smithsonian Institution proposed covering the historic open courtyard with a contemporary roof designed by the London architecture firm of Foster & Partners. The gallery and museum were housed in the landmark Old Patent Office, a mid-nineteenth-century Greek Revival government office building by Robert Mills. Located on the slightly elevated block at 7th and F Streets, NW, the building was assigned to the Smithsonian Institution in the early 1960s for use as a museum, which opened to the public in 1968. Plans for the expressive, undulating roof structure were met with enthusiasm by the Commission of Fine Arts. However, questions raised through the historic preservation review process led to mitigation measures that the commission found far less acceptable.

In 2003, the Smithsonian Institution invited seven design firms to submit plans to enclose the courtyard. Foster & Partners won the competition with a warped lattice steel canopy of glass—dubbed a "magic carpet"—that seemed to float over the courtyard without touching the walls of the structure. The goal was to create a flexible, enclosed public space in the courtyard that could serve a variety of uses from catered functions to recitals or educational programs. Associated with the courtyard enclosure project, a new 346-seat auditorium was to be constructed beneath the courtyard, which required its demolition.

When the concept proposal was presented to the commission in June 2004, it generated a warm response from the members, who thought the design was a positive addition to the historic building. David Childs's remarks were representative: "The attitude of this roof, floating over the space…is entirely appropriate…you've been able to separate out this modern piece from something that is a wonderful old building." The members' questions revolved around technical aspects of the project, such as roof drainage; detailing of elements, such as further study of the supporting columns to enhance their sense of lightness; and the control of possible light pollution emanating through the canopy at night. The commission voted for concept approval and looked forward to seeing the project again as the detailing was further developed.[65]

Significantly, the Smithsonian had not completed the mandatory Section 106 review under the National Historic Preservation Act and had demolished the historic courtyard without the necessary approvals. As a result, the NCPC and the District's Historic Preservation Office, under the mandate specified in their preservation review processes, determined that mitigation measures for the enclosure of the courtyard should include reduction of the canopy height and the addition of a new element in the Smithsonian's overall renovation project—the reintroduction of a monumental stone stairway on the F Street facade that had been demolished in the 1930s.

The revised canopy design was presented to the commission for final approval in January 2005. The members found the grace and ethereal quality of the original design somewhat reduced by the lowered height, but their enthusiasm for the project remained, and again they praised it as a welcome addition to Washington. Rather, their comments focused on how the canopy would be accomplished—structural solutions and ventilation—and details such as the color of the stone flooring, treatment of the "service wall" for catering functions and storage, and the level of transparency and color of the roof's glass. The commission requested additional study of these detail items.[66]

The meeting's next agenda item was concept review of the proposed reconstruction of the building's south exterior stair, now required as mitigation for the loss of the historic courtyard. Designed by Hartman-Cox Architects, the scheme replicated a staircase added in the early 1870s when the streets around the building were lowered; the entrance to which the stairs once led, however, would remain closed. The stairway design tried to present a historically accurate duplication of the original stair, with modifications based on grade change and modern code requirements of the Americans with Disabilities Act.[67] The main access to the museum would be through three new entry doors at street level cut into one of the museum's original stone walls.

David Childs noted the dilemma that this posed for the commission: "We want to be constructive in our responsibilities, but we also want to make clear our feelings … leave it alone, is our opinion."[68] The commission found the scheme "unwarranted and inappropriate" for a number of reasons: the CFA considered the building's period of significance earlier than the 1870s; the scheme modified original building material and altered the street grid; and it did not reopen the portico entrance at the top of the reintroduced stairway, creating a confusing message about access to the building. The commission's vote was unanimous against approval of the submission.[69]

ABOVE: *Section model of the 2005 concept design by Foster & Partners of the warped steel and glass lattice canopy to cover the historic courtyard. Supported by eight columns without bearing on the historic Patent Office structure, the enclosure was intended to create a common atrium for the Smithsonian's National Portrait Gallery and American Art Museum; a new auditorium was proposed beneath it.*

TOP LEFT: *A photograph of the south facade of the Old Patent Office on F Street, the principal commercial street of Washington, c. 1869. The original monumental stairway of Robert Mills's design is evident, though it would be demolished in the 1870s when F Street was lowered.*

TOP RIGHT: *The Old Patent Office courtyard in 1968, with its simple landscape of two fountains, lawn panels, and trees, had remained intact for more than a century.*

ABOVE LEFT: *The billowing forms of the courtyard skylight hovering above the historic building as completed in 2007. Although the initial scheme was endorsed by the CFA, the mounded profiles of the skylight structure design were lowered slightly in response to historic preservation concerns.*

ABOVE RIGHT: *Courtyard landscape plan by Gustafson Guthrie Nichol, 2004.*

Interior view of the completed canopy and courtyard landscape featuring large marble planters and seating platforms as well as a shallow scrim of water, 2008.

By June, the canopy project had become more enmeshed in repercussions from the preservation review. That month, Earl Powell, the newly elected commission chairman, summarized the CFA's actions regarding both the enclosure and the stair in testimony before the NCPC, which was reviewing the final plans for the canopy. However, the NCPC did not give its final approval because of misgivings about the canopy's impact on the historic building expressed by the Advisory Council for Historic Preservation, a federal historic preservation advisory agency. The Smithsonian and its designers met twice more with the NCPC to show additional design revisions. Of special concern was light from the courtyard overpowering the building at night; the revisions assured that the classical build-

ing itself would be well lit.[70] By September, the NCPC had approved revisions for a final design but still required the stairway to mitigate for the enclosure; it also approved a landscape scheme for the courtyard.[71]

The CFA reviewed this revised canopy at its September meeting, giving final approval to the design although expressing concern regarding the visual impact of shadows cast on the walls of the historic courtyard by the thick ribs of the gridded roof structure. The members also reviewed the courtyard landscape design by Gustafson Guthrie Nichol, which—with its shallow scrims of water, water jets, planters and climbing vines, and blue glass balcony—they found too complex in its segmentation of the space, and asked for revisions. The Smithsonian also requested

TOP LEFT: *Stereograph image from the 1890s illustrates how the stairway of the Patent Office's F Street entrance was modified when the street was lowered. This configuration remained in place until the 1930s, when the stair was demolished, and a new entrance was created at the street level.*

TOP RIGHT: *Late twentieth-century view of the Old Patent Office F Street portico and entrance. In addition to the courtyard enclosure, the building underwent a comprehensive renovation from 2000 to 2006.*

LEFT: *Photomontage of the proposed design by Hartman-Cox for a replacement stairway at the F Street entry to the building. The contested replication of the 1870s stairway remained unbuilt at the time the courtyard reopened.*

approval of the stairway, which was a requirement of the NCPC's approval, but the commission declined, referring to its previous decision, which the applicant noted put them "between a rock and a hard place."[72]

The commission finally gave its approval to the stairway at the March 2006 meeting with an expressed preference for allowing public access to the stairs and landing at least during daylight hours. Following further refinement of the courtyard scheme, the commission gave its final approval of that design a few months later. When the renovated building reopened to the public in July 2006 as the Donald W. Reynolds Center for American Art and Portraiture, plans to construct the F Street stairway had not been undertaken, and it remained unbuilt in 2012.

The new interior space—the Robert and Arlene Kogod Courtyard—features planters, white marble benches, and a water scrim under the gridded glass canopy and acts as a common orientation space for the museum.

NATIONAL MUSEUM OF AFRICAN AMERICAN HISTORY AND CULTURE

A major new project for the Smithsonian Institution, the National Museum of African American History and Culture presented the complex architectural problem of building a new museum within a highly sensitive historic landscape: the northeastern corner of the Washington Monument Grounds. The selected site involved the balancing of many delicate issues of historic preservation:

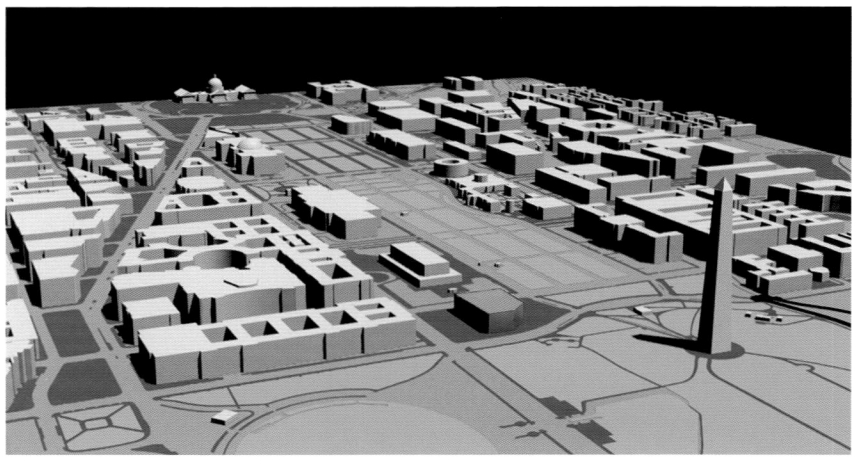

TOP LEFT: *Analysis drawing of the 15th Street and Constitution Avenue site of the Smithsonian National Museum of African American History and Culture (NMAAHC), 2005, occupying a corner of the Washington Monument Grounds.*

CLOCKWISE FROM TOP RIGHT: *Competition entries of five of the six finalists for the NMAAHC, 2009. Diller Scofidio & Renfro; Moody Nolan in association with Antoine Predock Architect (center right); Devrouax & Purnell Architects/Planners* *and Pei Cobb Freed & Partners (bottom right); Moshe Safdie & Associates (bottom left); Foster & Partners (center left).*

how to build on a site that had been vacant since the L'Enfant era, one within the perceived landscape of the National Mall, and in the shadow of Washington's most iconic memorial—but a site that, in the McMillan Plan, was illustrated as a location for a building.

Congress enacted legislation to establish the National Museum of African American History and Culture and set up a commission to determine a site "on or adjacent to" the Mall in December 2001.[73] The museum commission gave an informational presentation to the CFA in February 2003 to present the eleven sites studied, of which five were designated as preferred.[74] The members of the Commission of Fine Arts enthusiastically supported the concept of the museum but cautioned about protecting the open space on the Mall. Harry Robinson pointed out the conundrum of locating the museum on the monument site:

It is the perfect site in terms of presence in terms of the importance of the issue that's going to be housed in this museum . . . . But in terms of the front yard of the Washington Monument, I think it'll create a problem . . . to essentially truncate the front yard of the Washington Monument as the building is currently laid out may be a mistake.[75]

A year later, Congress authorized the Smithsonian Institution Board of Regents to select the site, and in April 2005 the Smithsonian gave an informational presentation to the Commission of Fine Arts on the site selection process. The CFA members commented that the Washington Monument site was problematic in that it had four fronts, creating difficulties of access and service. They shared thoughts on several of the other sites considered, noting that the Liberty Loan building and Banneker Overlook sites offered high visibility and recommending that the Arts and Industries Building, which occupied an exceptional location, be further analyzed for the new museum. However, the regents confirmed the highly prominent five-acre monument site as their choice in January 2006.

In an information presentation to the CFA three years later—February 2009—the Smithsonian project team discussed the established design principles that were distributed to six design teams competing for the project. The new building would serve as a "hinge point" between the line of Mall buildings and the Federal Triangle, and the design would need to address the building's relationship to the Mall's axis, the Washington Monument, and the larger context of the city as well as urban design issues of scale, views, current use patterns, and landscape. The Smithsonian noted that the commission's staff had been involved in the information development regarding the site and these design principles and had provided input for the Section 106 Historic Preservation Review.[76] The Smithsonian's project leaders commented that, in addition to a design

proposal, they wanted to understand how the architect worked, because they intended to select a designer rather than a design.[77]

The design collaborative of three architectural design firms, Freelon Adjaye Bond, won the competition in April 2009. Their proposal, submitted to the commission for informational purposes later that year, drew inspiration from the role of the porch in African American life and the Yoruban column of West African architecture, represented by a large podium with open ends supporting a "corona" of two inverted pyramidal segments. As part of the federal environmental review process, the project team had to design three alternative schemes, which were presented to the commission in April 2010. Each option incorporated a corona with different relationships to the site and with or without a podium. The commission members preferred the boldness of the simplest alternative with the corona atop a transparent base as well as a location for the building mass that centered on the adjacent buildings across 14th Street and Constitution Avenue. The CFA also commented that the building program was too large for the site, requested more information on the landscape design, and cautioned against a scheme with large water elements as being contrary to the character of the reflecting pools on the National Mall.

In September 2010, the design team presented a revised concept proposal that addressed many of the commission's issues: it incorporated the bronze-colored corona on a transparent base with a canopy, and the site design was further developed with curvilinear pathways related to the overall context of the monument grounds. The commission members encouraged the design team to further explore the relationship between the museum and the buildings on the north side of the Mall, the remnants of the monument grounds, and the urban grid. They expressed support for the picturesque approach to the landscape scheme and paths but raised concerns about the size of the water elements. The CFA members advised the architect to give careful study to the material, color, and transparency of the corona; they also suggested coordination with the National Museum of American History for service access to the site to avoid the unsightly necessity of a ramp along the building on 14th Street.

The commission members reviewed a revised concept in March 2011, following a visit to view a mock-up of elements on site. Overall, the designs for both the landscape setting and the building itself had been further refined and simplified, which the members found responded well to their earlier suggestions. However, they recommended reconsideration of the site design at Constitution Avenue,

David Adjaye's concept design was inspired in part by a carved wooden veranda post by the West African (Yoruba) artist Ọlọ́wẹ̀ of Isẹ̀, depicting a mounted hunter with a tiered headdress whose stepped form was expressed in the winning competition design as its most iconic element, the "corona."

ABOVE: *Rendering of the winning competition entry for the* NMAAHC *by Freelon Adjaye Bond. The multistory corona and extended podium are prominent in this view from Constitution Avenue.*

RIGHT: *David Adjaye and Kathryn Gustafson presented their concept designs for the* NMAAHC *building and landscape to the Commission of Fine Arts in April 2010. Shown discussing the model are (from left): David Adjaye, John Belle, Thomas Luebke, Kathryn Gustafson, Witold Rybczynski, Michael McKinnell, and Pamela Nelson.*

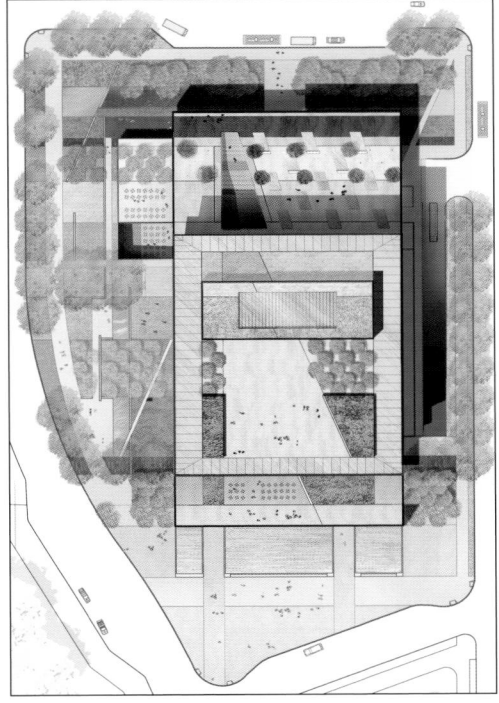

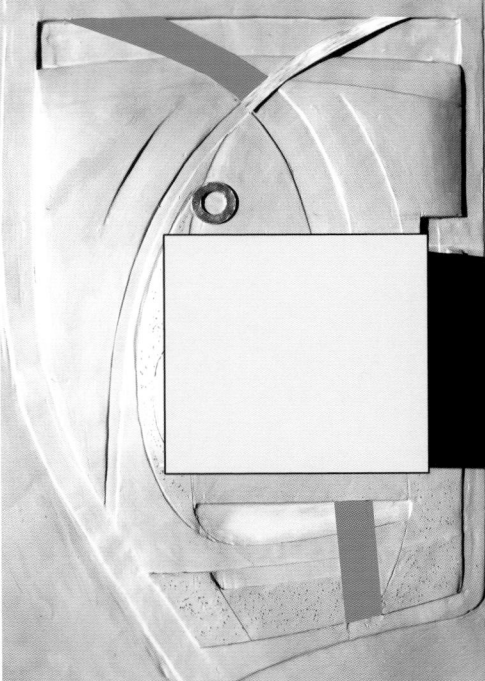

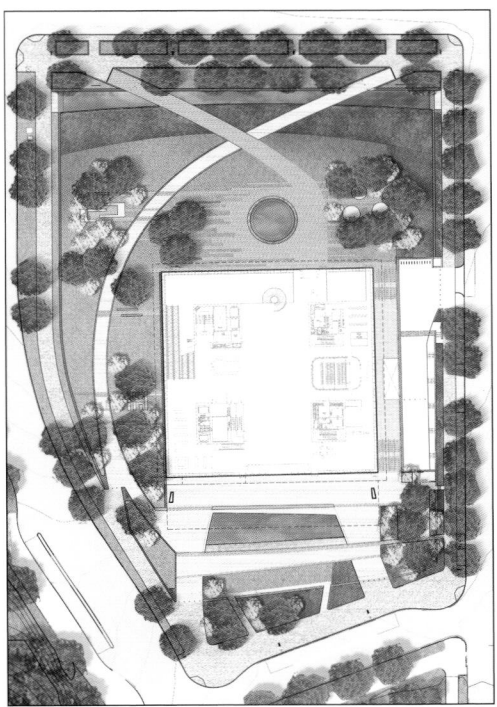

Rendering of the revised concept design for the museum as viewed from Constitution Avenue, March 2011. Freelon Adjaye Bond/Smith Group *simplified the design after restudying the transparency and material of the building's base and corona.*

ABOVE LEFT: *Site plan by Gustafson Guthrie Nichol from the 2009 winning design showing a geometrically patterned landscape surrounding the building.*

ABOVE CENTER: *Concept model in plaster for the site and landscape design, 2011, by Gustafson Guthrie Nichol. The square plan of the corona is mediated within the irregular site with gently curving walks inspired by the Washington Monument Grounds; an oculus in the north building yard would provide illumination to the extensive below-grade galleries.*

ABOVE RIGHT: *Final rendered landscape site plan, October 2011, featuring a linear water garden along the Constitution Avenue frontage and a wide reflecting pool on the south side of the main entrance facing the Mall.*

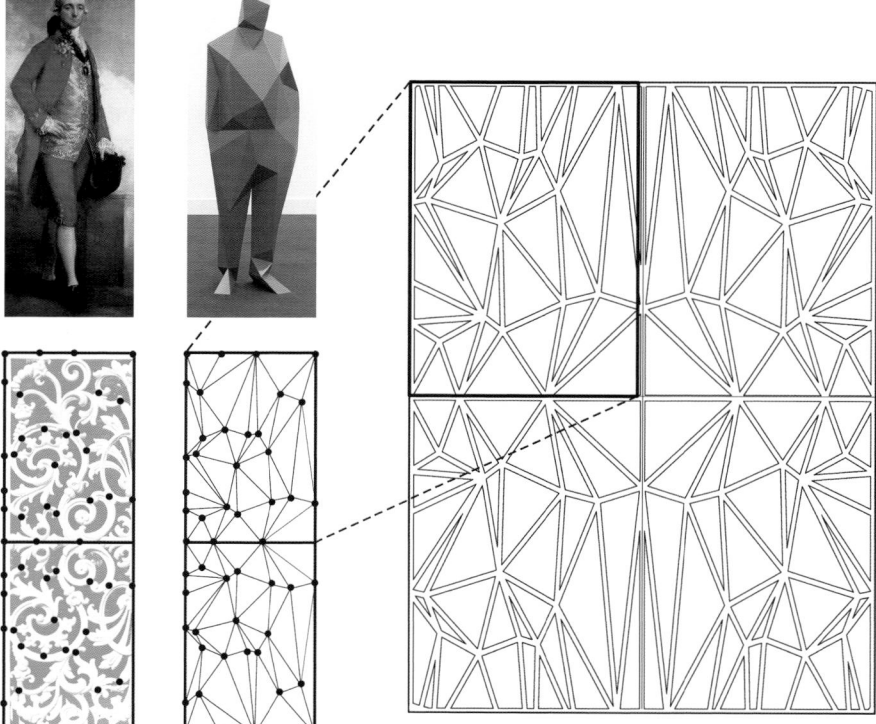

ABOVE: *Rendering of the revised concept design, October 2011, showing the south entrance porch viewed from the southwest, creating a cantilevered overhang above the reflecting pool.*

RIGHT: *Study from the October 2011 presentation by Freelon Adjaye Bond showing the development of the corona screen design derived from the geometric abstraction of traditional figures of cast-iron railings.*

LEFT: *Maquette presented at the CFA meeting of September 2012 as a study for a bronze-finished cast-aluminum corona screen unit developed from the abstract geometric design.*

noting that the naturalistic pond and rain garden there appeared incongruous with the urban quality of the street. The members also praised the direction that the designers were taking with the canopy and corona design and made suggestions for additional detailing. The revised concept was approved with the commendation that "the development of the design now illustrates how this museum will become part of the community of other buildings along the National Mall."[78]

In October 2011, the design team returned with a revised concept design that addressed many of the issues raised regarding the impact of the building: its height had been adjusted to align with various roof and balustrade lines of the Federal Triangle, and the projection of the front porch was reduced. Adjaye's design of the corona, now proposed as a shell of patterned cast metal panels pierced by geometric shapes derived from traditional ironwork, would moderate climate and frame views from within the museum. The landscape design by Kathryn Gustafson of Gustafson Guthrie Nichol had been developed, emphasizing a theme of passage over water to safety. The team had revised the naturalistic linear water garden, the oculus, and a sequence of three reading groves within the north yard of the building. On the south, the main water feature adjacent to the canopy incorporated moving and still water but was now proposed to be covered with inscribed quotations resembling handwritten text.

The commission members enthusiastically supported the design but with guidance to continue refinement: the landscape should provide year-round character and remain hospitable in summer and winter; the glass base of the building below the corona should be carefully detailed; and the lacy quality of the corona must be legible at night. Artist Teresita Fernández (CFA 2011–), in her first CFA meeting, suggested that the proposed incised pattern of handwriting on the basin floor of the south entrance pool could distract from the content of the words themselves and compete with the corona itself. Michael McKinnell joined Fernández in supporting the use of actual bronze for the corona panels because of its patination over time, adding that "the essence of this whole scheme, between intimacy and monumentality...must be carried through into this exterior material in some way."[79]

Groundbreaking for the museum took place in February 2012. Although the design review process was still incomplete, the project had passed most regulatory reviews and was considered well resolved for a proposal at such a highly controversial site. The museum's expected year of completion is 2015.

Trends in Commemoration in the Monumental Core

Maya Lin's seminal Vietnam Veterans Memorial remained an influence on the typology of commemoration in the new century. Its design set the precedent of a long and horizontal form, processional and narrative in formal structure, and focused on the subjective experience of the commemorated—which, in the case of the Vietnam Veterans Memorial, were the individual names of the fallen. Over the decades, the language of commemoration continued to evolve and add complexity to memorial projects, a trend marked by the blurring of distinctions among artistic disciplines as well as between symbolic and didactic programs: no new memorial would be considered complete without a substantial component of quotations, explanatory texts, photographic images, and, ideally, a visitor center—all of which contributed to the increasingly large financial and spatial requirements for the proposed memorials. In addition, advanced technology made possible new materials and modes of representation that were, in previous generations, not typically used in commemoration: photography as the primary artistic imagery, large panels of glass to display images and text, and the almost mandatory inclusion of extensive water elements in the memorial design.[80] Finally, memorials based on narrowly focused themes, often brought forward by private, nonprofit sponsoring organizations able to financially support them, became more common in the commemorative process.

The system of bringing a memorial to being in the public setting of Washington, D.C., had always required the protracted exercise of political will; the process as defined under the Commemorative Works Act was an explicitly difficult one, with twenty-one separate steps required. Even with its augmented powers of approval provided by the act, the commission's approach remained largely constant within this changing context. As their predecessors had before them, commission members evaluated memorial proposals for their design appropriateness, examining factors such as scale, meaning, and complexity within the framework of the nation's capital. Although design quality would always be the guiding principle, the technical performance of materials was an increasingly important focus. Most significantly, the use of photography transformed the millennia-old art form of sculpture—a trend that began with the realization of Joe Rosenthal's iconic photograph of soldiers raising the flag on Iwo Jima into a bronze sculpture by Felix de Weldon in the 1950s for the U.S. Marine Corps War Memorial. It continued with the sandblasted

New Development at Military Cemeteries

As with cultural institutions, U.S. military cemeteries evolved with new programmatic changes and architectural expression in the new century. Coincident with the sixtieth anniversary of World War II, the American Battle Monuments Commission (ABMC) undertook a program in the early years of the new century to develop visitor centers at American overseas cemeteries in order to provide interpretation for the many visitors who had no direct memory of the war. The first visitor center, at Normandy, was designed by Smith Group as a neomodernist building with crisp intersecting planes of glass and stone, low in profile to avoid competing with views of

the cemetery. The CFA reviewed and enthusiastically approved the concept design in 2004, asking for resolution of the overall landscape design and access to the adjacent parking lot. In 2011, the CFA reviewed and approved several small projects to expand visitor services at ABMC cemeteries, including a neomodernist concept for a visitor center at the Sicily-Rome American Cemetery. To support the quiet addition positioned against the cemetery's perimeter walls, the CFA suggested refinement of the cemetery's entrance to control the visual intrusion of automobiles.

In the first decade of the twenty-first century, wars in Afghanistan and Iraq and the concurrent passing of many veterans of World War II, the Korean War,

and the Vietnam War placed additional demand on the land resources at Arlington National Cemetery. Based on an earlier master plan, the cemetery continued to expand its columbarium, a facility for the interment of cremated remains and a building typology providing a direct response to the growing scarcity of land at the cemetery. In 2008, the Commission of Fine Arts approved the concept design of the fifth phase of construction, which followed the original design intent for the facility; the CFA found that this consistency of approach lent dignity to the overall complex. In a separate project, the cemetery rebuilt a stone perimeter wall incorporating burial niches along its southern border, which was completed in 2008. In this period the cemetery began planning for the Millennium Tract, acquired from Fort Myer, which would also include perimeter wall and columbarium burial locations in addition to traditional interments.

Arlington National Cemetery is also the site of numerous memorials commemorating the lives of Americans lost in service to the nation. In the early 2000s, several new memorials were erected, including a memorial to the seven astronauts lost in the explosion of the space shuttle *Columbia* in February 2003. The design depicts the official insignia worn by the astronauts—an image of the spaceship—on a bronze tablet affixed to an austere, traditional granite base. The CFA reviewed the design in June 2003 suggesting that the proposed portrayal of crew members be in profile, a more typical approach to commorative portraiture. The revised design with the insignia on the front and a photograph of the crew rendered in bronze as a bas-relief on the back was approved the following month; the memorial was dedicated in 2004.

TOP: *Smith Group's 2007 design for the Normandy American Cemetery visitor center emphasized strong horizontal planes with low profiles to minimize the impact on views of the cemetery and the adjacent Omaha Beach, site of the 1944 Allied invasion.*

BOTTOM: *The proposed visitor center design of 2011 at the Sicily-Rome American Cemetery by Ottavio Di Blasi with Harry Robinson employs a neomodernist vocabulary that fits quietly within the existing complex.*

ABOVE LEFT: *The CFA found the consistency of design a dignified solution employed over numerous phases of the columbarium expansion at Arlington National Cemetery, including the fifth phase for Court 9 reviewed in 2008. The columbarium prototype was originally designed by Keyes Lethbridge & Condon Architects in the late 1960s and has been adapted over the following decades for the complex.*

ABOVE RIGHT: *The Columbia Memorial at Arlington National Cemetery as built, 2004, showing the mission insignia of the spacecraft on a traditional bronze tablet mounted on a granite slab. The 2003 concept design for the marker included a depiction of the ship's crew in relief, adapted from a photograph; the mission insignia was relocated to the front of the memorial in the approved design.*

LEFT: *The 2011 design for the Senator Edward M. Kennedy gravesite (circled in yellow) by Sasaki & Associates created a new element in a sequence of Kennedy family burial sites at Arlington National Cemetery: the circular President John F. Kennedy site by John Carl Warneke on the right; the half-circular memorial to Senator Robert F. Kennedy by I.M. Pei in the center; and the proposed soft curve for the new gravesite on the left.*

photographic images on the granite wall at the Korean War Veterans Memorial in the 1990s. By the new century, photography as a generative artistic concept was firmly established in the design of commemorative works, exemplified by such projects as the American Veterans Disabled for Life Memorial, the Martin Luther King Jr. National Memorial, and the Dwight D. Eisenhower Memorial.

PENTAGON 9/11 MEMORIAL

The design of the Pentagon 9/11 Memorial presented an expansive landscape solution commemorating the 184 victims who died at the Pentagon in the attacks of September 11, 2001. The design incorporated multiple elements including benches, water, trees, gravel footpaths, and lighting; the technical feasibility of implementing several of these features became the focus of the commission's review of the project, which had congressional, Department of Defense, and public support.

In October 2001, Congress authorized the Department of Defense to create a privately funded memorial to honor the victims of the Pentagon attack. Ten potential sites were forwarded to a family steering committee, which selected two acres on the western grounds of the Pentagon; the site was approved by the CFA in June 2002. An open and anonymous international design competition was organized with a jury comprising seven design professionals, two family members, and two former secretaries of defense, and chaired by Terry Riley, chief curator of architecture and design at the Museum of Modern Art in New York. The winning entry by New York architects Julie Beckman and Keith Kaseman, announced in March 2003, consisted of a gravel field with 184 "memorial units"—stainless steel benches each cantilevered over an illuminated reflecting pool and organized linearly along the flight path of the airplane; the field was punctuated by paperbark maple trees. Riley noted that the design appealed to the judges in part because the ordered benches recalled the rows of headstones at nearby Arlington National Cemetery.[81]

In 2003 Beckman and Kaseman first presented their design for concept review to the commission members, who raised a variety of concerns about the project. Although the CFA members had varying opinions about the relevance of the water, they agreed on the need to simplify the design, expressed significant reservations about the ongoing maintenance requirements, and questioned the functionality and appropriateness of the proposed tree specimen. David Childs summarized the concerns about water and the significant maintenance issues it posed: "You've chosen it for its light…perhaps there are other materials that could be free of maintenance and transmit light in a flickering way that might also speak of life…. I would encourage you to think about the realities of the chewing gum and the wrapper that, in fact, might desecrate…the beauty of this. At a certain point, if it's unable to be maintained, it will be changed."[82] The members also were concerned about the choice of materials, especially the epoxy polymer concrete gravel aggregate for the benches, which was sensitive to ultraviolet light and, if badly executed, could diminish the aesthetic quality of the design. The members voted to accept the concept with their concerns noted and further interim reviews encouraged, especially of the materials.

Delays in fundraising, however, prevented the team from resubmitting for three years. When they finally did, in April 2006, the commission members repeated their concerns, as the design had not changed substantively, although the bench materials had been revised to address issues of thermal expansion and the water filtration system for its ability to catch leaves and debris. The members were complimentary of the overall design, but Witold Rybczynski summarized their concern by describing it as a "Swiss watch," adding, "I admire your ingenuity, really…. But it also worries us that there is so much novelty, that there is so much that can go wrong, and that you really need to do much more homework than if you were doing something conventional."[83] The commission asked to see additional information for design development, specifically a mock-up of the bench and fountain piece.

In November, the project team returned with further developed details for a vote on the final design. Despite assurances by the design team that technical research supported the feasibility of the design elements, the commission continued to caution about the difficulty of maintaining architectural precision within a landscape setting but deferred its decision until the mock-up could be reviewed. In January 2007, the commission members visited the memorial grounds to inspect the prototype and, upon returning to the meeting, repeated their concerns, which the visit had not mitigated. The members still found the design too complex, the success of which hinged on precise construction tolerances difficult to achieve, and still questioned the feasibility of the design's long-term maintenance. Many design details remained to be refined before they could be fabricated. Members also suggested darkening the color of the pools' lining to alleviate the starkness of the white surface. Rather than take a vote on the final design, the commission chose to respond in writing, presenting its concerns and recommendations in the summary letter of the meeting to the Department of Defense.[84]

ABOVE: *Night view of the memorial as completed in 2008, featuring steel benches cantilevered over shallow illuminated pools, each forming a memorial unit within the gravel field. In its numerous reviews of the project, the CFA was concerned about many of the functional and maintenance aspects of the complex design.*

LEFT: *Plan of the winning entry for the Pentagon 9/11 Memorial by Julie Beckman and Keith Kaseman. The site was proposed as an open gravel plaza interspersed with trees and steel benches—as markers for each victim—oriented in the flight path of the downed plane.*

Aerial rendering of the 2005 concept design by Michael Verga-son Landscape Architects for the American Veterans Disabled for Life Memorial (AVDLM), showing its relationship to the Bartholdi Fountain and the Rayburn Building across Washington Avenue.

Despite the lack of a final approval by the CFA, construction proceeded, and the memorial was dedicated in September 2008.

AMERICAN VETERANS DISABLED FOR LIFE MEMORIAL

The use of photography as an expressive form as well as questions of scale and complexity were among the design issues the commission addressed in the American Veterans Disabled for Life Memorial. In September 2001, the commission approved the memorial's site on the triangle of land formed by the intersections of Washington Avenue and 2nd and C Streets, SW. The site was among the first to be selected under the planning recommendations established in the *Memorials and Museums Master Plan* and was preferred by the memorial's proponent, the Disabled Veterans' Life Memorial Foundation, for its proximity to the Capitol to remind legislators of the human cost of war. The National Park Service and the foundation returned to the commission in March 2004 with a design by landscape architect Michael Vergason, which was given concept approval with the direction to simplify and integrate the elements: a flame, grove of trees, fountain, pool, flagpole, stone and glass walls, quotations, and an art installation.

The following year, sculptor Larry Kirkland presented preliminary studies for eight-foot- tall, bronze, inverse bas-relief panels showing partial bodies to suggest loss and give "form to the sense of memory."[85] The commission was enthusiastic about the project, although Diana Balmori commented that, in his literal depiction of limbs, the designer was having "the usual problem between the abstract and representational," a "battleground" experienced by many trying to bridge the two that resulted only in ambiguity. Witold Rybczynski still found the design too complex and recommended further simplification and the establishment of a perceptual hierarchy of the elements.[86] A revised concept was presented to the commission in November 2006, incorporating a reconfigured site and related spatial adjustments to the design in response to security concerns raised by the Architect of the Capitol. The commission had few questions, mostly regarding the detailing and appearance of the pool and fountain, and approved the concept.

Three years later, at the July 2008 meeting, the team presented another revised concept with a significantly altered art component. Kirkland had changed his sculpture in response to objections raised by the foundation board and veterans who could not see themselves or their story in the impressions of body parts; his new proposal pursued an expression that combined the ideal with the real.[87] Bronze cutouts were placed in front of photographs set within five layers of glass; for example, a bronze silhouette of a charging marine framed a photograph of a young soldier with a blank expression staring into the camera. Kirkland sought to enliven the walls with qualities of light and shadow, translucence and reflectivity.

The commission reviewed and approved the revised design concept subject to the resolution of what they found to be continuing design issues. While the designer had handled the quotes in a way that the commission found presented an evocative and well-told story, the additional layers of physical and expressive forms weakened that story, leading to what John Belle called an "embarrassment of riches" that needed to be simplified. Witold Rybczynski voiced the most pointed concerns about the photographs and the nature of memorials, noting that this aspect of heightened realism was his main reservation about the design: "It seems to me that you are taking…the images so literally that there is only one way to interpret them. And it starts to feel like the medium from advertising or some commercial venue rather than a memorial." He also found the use of glass troubling as a commemorative material: "A memorial…whether it is modern or not modern, has always had a sense of being apart from the world because memorials have to be there forever…. Glass is not a traditional material for memorials precisely because it isn't there forever." He did add, however, that he was open to the design's continued exploration of the material and offered the idea of deleting the photographs, with the silhouettes alone visible through the glass. Earl Powell and architect Elizabeth Plater-Zyberk (CFA 2008–), a founding partner of the Miami-based New Urbanist design firm Duany Plater-Zyberk & Company, who had recently joined the commission, both considered the use of photography less troubling. The consensus of the commission members was for an on-site mock-up of the concept as part of any further review.[88]

During a March 2009 site inspection, the commission members viewed the mock-up of the design elements. The members commented that the glass panel with the layered images, seen at full size, produced through its reflectivity an ambiguity that would evoke a powerful response in the visitor; Diana Balmori called them "poetic" but emphasized that the simpler images were the most evocative. The members reiterated their desire for greater simplicity within the memorial, including reducing the size of the masonry wall and fountain, with further study of the memorial's views of the Capitol.[89]

The project team returned to the commission two months later with a refined concept. The wall and reflecting pool had been reduced in size and the entrances to the plaza enlarged, but some lingering concerns remained regarding

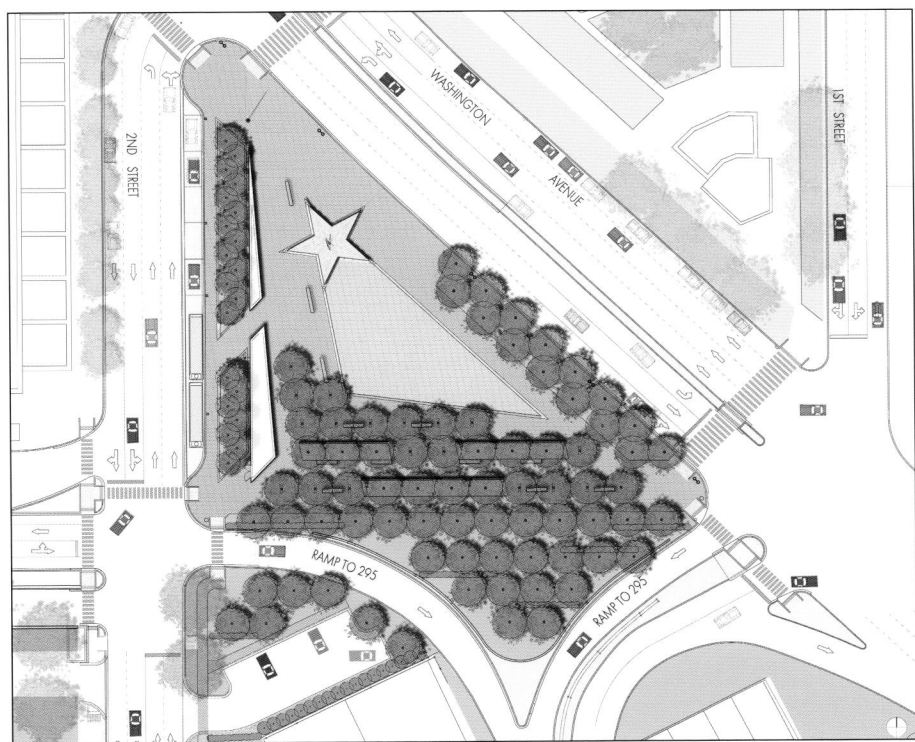

ABOVE LEFT: *Rendered site plan of the memorial illustrating Vergason's 2004 design that included a star-shaped fountain, eternal flame, and large pool within a stone plaza framed by a composition of stone walls, trees, and a series of glass walls featuring quotations and art panels.*

ABOVE RIGHT: *Preliminary study, 2005, for an inverse high-relief sculpture by artist Larry Kirkland, suggesting incomplete human forms to represent the injuries suffered by the veterans.*

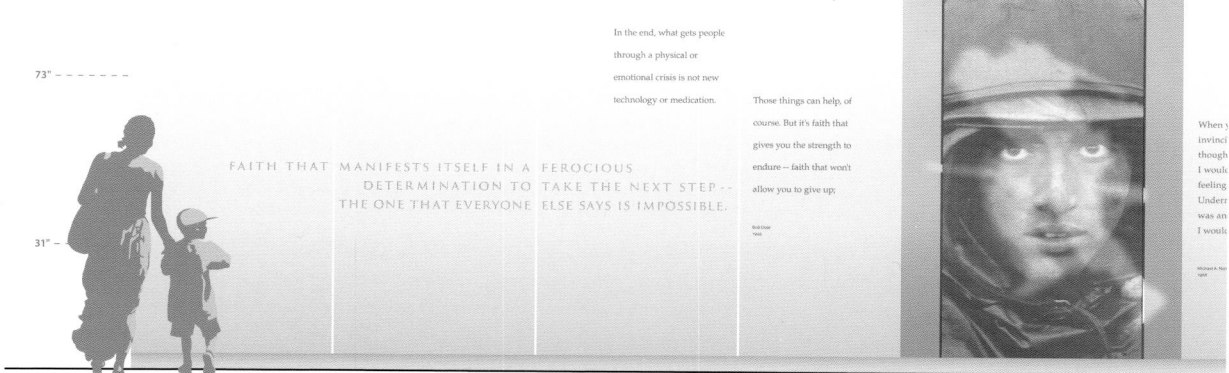

In the end, what gets people through a physical or emotional crisis is not new technology or medication. Those things can help, of course. But it's faith that gives you the strength to endure – faith that won't allow you to give up;

When y invinci though I would feeling Under was an I would

73" – – – – – –

FAITH THAT MANIFESTS ITSELF IN A FEROCIOUS DETERMINATION TO TAKE THE NEXT STEP – THE ONE THAT EVERYONE ELSE SAYS IS IMPOSSIBLE.

31" –

ABOVE: *Detail of a study model showing the extensive use of glass quotation walls punctuated by bronze negative relief panels within a grove of bald cypress trees.*

BELOW : *Rendering of a segment of the revised glass wall, approved in 2009, depicting the quotations and art panels that combined photographic images etched on glass panels superimposed with bronze silhouettes.*

the use of double images throughout the panels. The commission voted to approve the revisions with suggestions for the stone wall and paver details and with the understanding, added by Balmori, that the designers consider varying the treatment of some of the images. McKinnell supported Balmori in this suggestion, noting that varying the images would strengthen an expressive form that he found quite powerful: "I think that you have found, as artists, a way, in twenty-first century terms, to be able to introduce into the memorial the actual human content."[90] The commission reviewed and approved further refinements of design details in July 2009, and the project's final design and construction documents were reviewed and approved by delegation to the commission staff in March 2011.

MARTIN LUTHER KING JR. NATIONAL MEMORIAL

The Martin Luther King Jr. National Memorial presented several design issues during the ten-year period of its development and the commission's review, including those related to scale and iconography. However, the most challenging issues arose from the design's focus on photography as an inspiration for sculptural expression as well as the execution and appropriateness of that sculptural expression. These came to dominate the commission's concerns regarding the memorial.

In 1999, an international open design competition for the memorial was announced; the competition's information package included civil rights movement photographer Bob Fitch's 1966 photograph of King standing pensively at his desk with arms crossed and a framed portrait of Gandhi on the wall. Earlier that year, a four-acre site along the Tidal Basin had been approved by the NCPC and the CFA for the memorial, and eleven design parameters were set forth by the NCPC and agreed upon by the National Park Service and the Martin Luther King Jr. National Memorial Project Foundation. These included maintaining visual transparency between Independence Avenue and the Tidal Basin; limiting the height of any element to twenty feet; and the exclusion of any restroom, retail, or museum facility.[91]

The National Park Service and the foundation submitted the winning entry by ROMA Design Group of San Francisco, California, to the commission for an information presentation in June 2001. ROMA's landscape solution included a semicircular plaza framed by inscription walls, which also accommodated more than 500 linear feet of waterfalls, surmounted by a walkway with commemorative niches for leaders of the civil rights movement. The centerpiece of the memorial featured an expression from King's "I Have a Dream" speech delivered from the steps of the Lincoln Memorial on August 28, 1963: *With this faith, we will be able to hew out of the mountain of despair a stone of hope.* Two split stones symbolized the Mountain of Despair with a third situated ahead representing the Stone of Hope; this central stone also included a relief of King based on the Fitch photograph. When Barbaralee Diamonstein-Spielvogel asked principal designer Boris Dramov the height of the stones, he responded that, "We'd like it to be a little higher but 20 [feet] was the maximum height."[92] A second information presentation was given a

year later; at this time the commission made a variety of specific recommendations including reducing the height of the inscription walls, eliminating the elevated commemorative walk and niches, and removing the walkway bridge at the mountain gap.

Two CFA chairmanships would begin and end before October 2005, when the memorial was formally presented as a concept application; Pamela Nelson was the sole commission member who had participated in the previous discussions. Although measured drawings for the design existed by this point, the submission only included the illustrations created for the competition.[93] The design had not changed, apart from the addition of a building in the southern corner of the site. The commission members raised the same concerns mentioned in 2002 and also took issue with the vaguely defined ancillary building, variously described as a ranger kiosk, visitor center, and restrooms. Following several meetings with CFA staff and the other review agencies, the foundation simplified the design as previously directed, including the removal of the waterfalls,

Aerial view of the Martin Luther King Jr. National Memorial site on the Tidal Basin (outlined in yellow) and its relationship to other major memorials on the Mall, 1999.

RIGHT: *Model of the ROMA Design Group's concept for the memorial, which incorporated a semicircular plaza edged by inscription walls and featuring two split stones, the Mountain of Despair, and a central stone with a relief sculpture of Dr. King, the Stone of Hope.*

BELOW: *Rendered view of the memorial design in 2008 by McKissack & McKissack, illustrating a waterfall feature at the sides of the Mountain of Despair and the development of the landscape design.*

and submitted two new illustrations to the commission in March 2006. During the proceedings, Dramov spoke about his idea for the Stone of Hope: "What we have always wanted is that the Stone of Hope and Dr. King are one, that it is not a statue placed on it." He noted that the height was now "about 29 feet."[94] The project received concept approval with recommendations to study the width of the gap at the mountain and reconsider the location of the building and minimize its size.

The project returned to the commission in June 2006 with a design that reintroduced waterfalls next to the mountain. Dramov advocated for the features based on King's frequent allusions to water in his speeches and writings and as a means to reduce the impact of traffic noise from Independence Avenue. The commission members reacted negatively to the use of water, particularly regarding the use of waterfalls. Witold Rybczynski observed: "Still water is profound [a reference to the nearby Tidal Basin]. But falling water is always happy. It seems to be inappropriate to have that sentiment…. You go through those stones and it is not a happy movement. It is very tough…. For me, these afterthoughts of bubbling water really weaken the concept." He urged the designer to focus on the detailing of the metaphorical stone pieces. All agreed; Michael McKinnell summarized the point: "Everything is going to depend on the way these blocks either come off or don't." Dramov said they would bring the detailing the next time and would not pursue the water.[95]

When the foundation presented revised drawings at the October 2006 meeting, ROMA Design Group was no longer part of the project team. Ed Jackson, the foundation's executive architect, presented illustrations with a repositioned Mountain of Despair: its two pieces were no longer situated behind the inscription walls but rather in line with them, and only the last six feet of the walls incorporated waterfalls. Jackson argued that the water helped to mediate between the wall and mountain elements. The distance between the Mountain of Despair and the Stone of Hope was also diminished. The commission members agreed that reducing the distance between these elements increased the symbolic strength of the design, but recommended that the use of design elements other than water be studied to make the critical transition between the mountain and the walls.

Returning three months later in January 2007, Jackson presented a package of sketches depicting the evolution of the design at the Mountain of Despair, but he did not include a revision as earlier suggested by the commission. Both the foundation and the National Park Service reiterated the importance of water in the design, which was shown as two separate waterfalls. The commission came to agree that water could be a powerful part of the design but urged that it should be handled as a single element rather than as an aesthetic device that the members found weakened the symbolic strength of the Mountain of Despair. They voted to approve the revised concept with additional exploration of the water feature.[96]

In February 2007, the foundation presented the program of inscriptions and introduced sculptor Lei Yixin, of the People's Republic of China, who had recently been

ABOVE LEFT: *The 1966 photograph by Bob Fitch of Dr. King in his office was the inspiration for the central metaphoric image of the civil rights leader on the Stone of Hope.*

ABOVE CENTER: *Rendering of the Stone of Hope from the winning competition entry, illustrating the depth of the relief sculpture and the placement of a quotation.*

ABOVE RIGHT: *Photograph of the maquette of the Stone of Hope as realized by Chinese sculptor Lei Yixin and presented to the CFA in June 2008.*

commissioned to carve the Mountain of Despair and Stone of Hope. Lei's portfolio included colossal-scale bronze and masonry pieces, mostly for political leaders in central and east Asia, including a monumental bust of Mao Zedong. For the sculpture of Martin Luther King Jr., Lei proposed King in a frontal three-quarters-length engaged pose—arms crossed and legs apart—rather than the more pensive *contrapposto* figure based on Fitch's photograph, portraying King as emerging in a more natural stance out

of the stone. The commission members had few questions or comments on this formal concept submission of the sculpture, other than the importance of minimizing the visibility of joints in the assembly of stone pieces, and agreed with the National Park Service that full, rather than edited, quotations should be used.

That summer, the foundation retained the design services of McKissack & McKissack, who assembled for the November 2007 meeting the first comprehensive set of architectural drawings submitted to the commission. The commission members were able to review design specifics for the first time—including several that seemed to contradict the original guidelines for the site—and consequently expressed numerous concerns. They questioned why the Mountain of Despair and Stone of Hope had increased in height to thirty-two feet.[97] They recommended reducing the number of quotations, further study of lighting and paving details, and adjusting the siting of the visitor center building. They also requested material samples and documentation of joinery details; they stressed the importance of a movable, full-scale mock-up of the stone to ensure that visitors' perspectives of the colossal sculpture would not be distorted due to the constrained viewing angle created by the edge of the Tidal Basin.

In April 2008, the foundation returned with responses to the commission's previous concerns and also organized a site visit. The commission members viewed a mock-up of the Stone of Hope, which involved a hydraulic lift suspending a plywood framework wrapped in black plastic to represent the actual profile of the sculpture. At the public presentation, the project team explained that the metaphorical stones had been reduced in size. The height had been subtracted from the base of the Stone of Hope to achieve the previously presented twenty-nine-foot height; accordingly, the height of the figure itself remained unchanged while the stone's proportions became more squat.

At the conclusion of the presentation, Earl Powell inquired about the evolution of the figure of King—from Boris Dramov's competition-winning design "emerging from the stone" to Lei's interpretation that was "centralized and very static." Jackson explained that the initial rendering cut off a portion of King's shoulder, which Lei considered "inappropriate." Commission members were not comfortable with Lei's approach. To Balmori, the change was not an improvement: "[N]ow it feels as if the image of Dr. King has been…put on a stele, on a piece of stone, and is attached to it while [the competition entry figure] felt integral." Belle noted the significant difference between the two and described the new pose presented for the King statue as "confrontational."[98] McKinnell added:

I would like to comment on this because there is something I feel very strongly about here. When we were going out to the mock-up, Witold [Rybczynski] and I were talking. He said, I think correctly, 'you know, we are not experts in colossal figures. This is not something one sees very often.' I have been thinking about that ever since. Unfortunately, I have come up with examples in my mind where I have seen them recently and they have been broadcast on television and they are all being pulled down. I think that that connotation will be absolutely fatal in this instance. I think the metaphor of Dr. King being merged with

the natural force of the stone is absolutely essential to avoid the colossal monumentalization that we have been familiar with in countries that we don't need to mention. I think this is very important, the degree to which the metaphor of the stone and the man become one is absolutely imperative here. Otherwise, one risks a very unfortunate connotation.[99]

Belle's use of the word "confrontational" and McKinnell's implicit reference to a monument of former Iraqi President Saddam Hussein were noted in Secretary Luebke's summary action letter to the applicant:

In general, the Commission members found that the colossal scale and Social Realist style of the proposed statue recalls a genre of political sculpture that has recently been pulled down in other countries. They said that the proposed treatment of the sculpture—as the most iconographic and central element of the memorial to Dr. King—would be unfortunate and inappropriate as an expression of his legacy. They recommended strongly that the sculpture be reworked, both in form and modeling, to return to a more sympathetic idea of the figure growing out of the stone with increasing detail and emphasis of the upper part of the figure. The Commission cited precedents of a figure emerging from stone in the works of sculptors such as Michelangelo and Rodin.[100]

The issue of the King sculpture quickly became a point of debate in the media. James Chaffers, a professor of architecture at the University of Michigan and one of the jurors of the competition, said the project team wanted to maintain "the power and inspirational image" of Lei's design and valued its provocative nature. Chaffers told the *Washington Post*:

We see [King]…as a warrior. We see him as a warrior for peace…not as some pacifist, placid, kind of vanilla, but really a man of great conviction and strength.[101]

Two days later, *Washington Post* columnist Marc Fisher described the sculpture as "King seen in the arrogant stance of a dictator, clad in a boxy suit, with an impassive, unapproachable mien, looking more like an East Bloc Politburo member than an inspirational transformational preacher who won a war armed with nothing but truth and words."[102] Michael Nojeim, author of *Gandhi and King: The Power of Nonviolent Resistance,* wrote a letter to the editor of the *Washington Post*:

The proposed statue of the Rev. Martin Luther King Jr. fails to capture King's essence. Above all, Dr. King stood for using nonviolence to create what he called the beloved community. He was a radical reformer whose militancy was based on love, reconciliation and justice. As such, I wish to ask Ed Jackson…. Exactly where in this sculpture do you see anything remotely resembling King's principles of nonviolence, love, justice and the beloved community?[103]

However, the *Washington Post* columnist Courtland Milloy was pleased with the sculpture and walked around the Tidal Basin with a photograph of Lei's full-size clay model to ascertain public opinion about it. Milloy quoted Washingtonian Anthony McCoy in his editorial piece:

Let's be clear. If you think there is something wrong with a statue that makes Martin Luther King come off as confrontational, then there is something wrong with you. King was confrontational. If he wasn't, he'd probably still be alive.[104]

In June 2008, Jackson returned to the commission to address sculpture concerns with a submission comprising a collection of photographs of numerous statues of King and a compilation of previous commission actions. Jackson also presented slides of a modified clay maquette of the Stone of Hope with adjusted side contours. The commission members discussed the difficulty of judging sculpture from photographs and noted that a model would be more useful to better appreciate the massing. They requested a maquette of the sculpture as well as a full-size sample of the sculpture carved in the proposed granite in order for them to understand the detailing.

Two weeks before Jackson presented a comprehensive final submission to the commission in September 2008, the art critic Catesby Leigh wrote an essay on the memorial for the *Wall Street Journal*. He discussed the traditional technique of monumental sculpture and its relation to the poor artistic quality of the proposed sculpture of King:

Monumentality arises not from the size of the figure, but from a distillation and clarification of the complex topography unique to each human body—a formal technique that has all but disappeared from traditional training, which tends to focus these days on the simplistic transcription of natural appearances…. The lack of an anatomical underpinning to King's head is painfully obvious. The face is thus reduced to bulbous, schematic geometries…. The hands are rendered with greater attention to surface detail, but their modeling does not relate to that of the head. King's clothing weighs too heavily on him: The jacket looks as if it were cut from a thick sheet of rubber. The model accordingly fails to convey any sense of the structure of the body under the clothes. Nor will it be redeemed through translation into stone.[105]

At the commission meeting, the discussion again focused on the sculpture. Pamela Nelson observed that the rough finish of the mountain and the polished finish of the figure were "fighting with each other," to which Jackson responded that the foundation wanted the distinction as it opposed the idea of an "embedded" figure because then King "would give the impression that he has not freed himself…and he is not the symbol of hope."[106] Other commission members also expressed concern for the finishing treatments. John Belle noted that while the foundation had considered vertical transitions along the sculpture, it failed to appreciate the importance of horizontal variations. He recalled the metaphorical quotation and added: "It is how that man comes out of the mountain in physical, real, existential terms in the stone that we don't see at the moment. I think it is absolutely crucial to the success of this monument."[107] The commission members repeated their

desire to see a mock-up or a portion of a model. The review concluded with the commission's approval of the overall site design, planting materials, lighting detailing, and auxiliary building. Further information was requested on the inscriptions, perimeter security elements, and sculpture.

The foundation returned more than six times over the following two years to resolve outstanding issues related to perimeter security, materials, and inscriptions but did not present anything further regarding the sculpture. By the spring of 2010, the 159 granite blocks of the King statue were carved to 80 percent completion in China, in preparation for shipment to the U.S. The sculpture was completed on site and erected in the autumn of 2010; in the spring and summer of 2011, the commission reviewed lighting for the project. The memorial was opened to the public on August 28, 2011, but the formal dedication ceremonies scheduled for that day had to be postponed due to a hurricane. The official dedication took place on October 16, 2011.

A controversy also arose at the time of the dedication about a truncated quotation of Dr. King describing his role as a "drum major for justice" inscribed on the Stone of Hope. The poet Maya Angelou and others felt the alteration changed the meaning of Dr. King's words. The editing of this particular quotation had been discussed at the CFA's February 2007 meeting, and the memorial foundation had agreed to use it in its entirety. Inscriptions on the memorial were again reviewed by the CFA in September 2010, when the full "drum major" quotation was presented and approved by the CFA.[108] In early 2012, the secretary of the interior ordered the quotation to be corrected.

VIETNAM VETERANS MEMORIAL VISITOR CENTER

The Vietnam Veterans Memorial Center (VVMC)—an adjunct facility to function as a small museum for didactic elaboration of the memorial's message—generated a number of questions for the commission in its reviews: How would it affect the Mall's design integrity, would it be an appropriate adjunct to the Vietnam Memorial, and would it engender a proliferation of similar facilities? The quandary was compounded by powerful support of the project by veterans groups, former U.S. presidents and generals, and Congress, whose authorizing legislation prescribed an underground structure at a site "at or near" the Vietnam Memorial and that mandated that final approval could not be withheld.[109]

In September 2005, the Vietnam Veterans Memorial Fund (VVMF) and the National Park Service appeared before the commission as part of the site approval process.

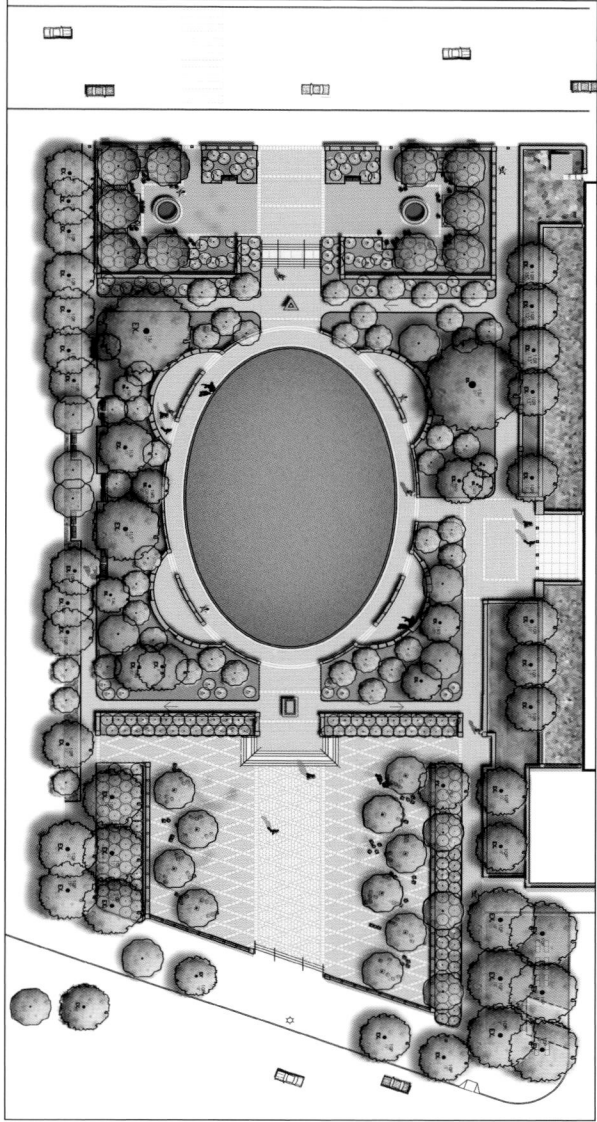

TOP LEFT: *View of the exist-*
ing John Marshall Park,
designed by landscape archi-
tect Carol Johnson in the
early 1980s, including lawn
panels, tree terraces, and
plazas, with a replica bronze
sculpture of Chief Justice John
Marshall (far left) located
near D Street.

ABOVE LEFT: *Plan view of*
the 2009 revised concept de-
sign for the park's rehabilita-
tion by Carol Johnson with an
oval central green lined with
extensive interpretive memo-
rial elements. The statue of
Marshall would be relocated
as the focus of the space closer
to Pennsylvania Avenue.

ABOVE RIGHT: *Rendered*
view of the initial 2007 concept
design showing glass benches,
glass inscription walls, and,
behind them, large arcs of di-
dactic material related to the
life and career of Marshall
on bronze panels. The CFA ap-
proved a simpler version of the
concept design in 2009 with
the amount of glass and inter-
pretative elements reduced.

CHAPTER VII | TO EVERY AGE ITS ART

Rendering of the entrance to the proposed memorial center building, 2012. The CFA had raised concerns that the sloping approach and retaining walls of the underground building might imitate the design of the Vietnam Veterans Memorial.

ing were requested, with the sense of the commission expressed by Witold Rybczynski: "We are supportive, but we are not ecstatic at this point." No formal action was taken.

A revised concept was not submitted for almost three years. At the February 2012 meeting, the CFA members reviewed the various adjustments to the design and remained critical of the project's impact on the context of adjacent memorials. The summary letter described the CFA members' consensus that the center

should be subordinate to and supportive of the visitor's experience of the Vietnam Veterans Memorial itself, not an independent destination that attracts visitors through its expressive design. They also found that the combined effect of the building's gestures in the landscape—the entrance wall, the sunken courtyard, and the arrangement of triangular skylights—together create an impact of great scale that competes visually with the actual memorial and compromises the wider commemorative setting.[115]

The CFA concluded that the skylights should be eliminated and the design of the entry elements—the length of the wall and the disposition of lights and benches—be revised to minimize the visual prominence of the center. The project remains in development; its completion will create a new precedent for large-scale visitor interpretative facilities associated with national memorials on the Mall.

JOHN MARSHALL PARK

The proposal and process to rehabilitate John Marshall Park, located in the historic right-of-way of 4th Street, NW, between D Street and Pennsylvania Avenue, illustrate a number of the design trends in the new century and the concerns that commission members had regarding the impact of these trends on civic space. The project was brought forward by the National Park Service in partnership with the John Marshall Memorial Park Foundation, a nonprofit organization dedicated to educating the public about the early nineteenth-century chief justice. The park was originally developed in the 1980s as part of the Pennsylvania Avenue Development Corporation's efforts to increase open space along Pennsylvania Avenue. Designed by Boston landscape architect Carol Johnson, the park served for three decades as the setting for a Beaux-Arts copy of a bronze statue of Marshall by William Wetmore Story, which had originally been located at the Capitol.

The rehabilitation project, submitted for review to the Commission of Fine Arts in January 2007, proposed a complete remaking of the park as an opportunity to teach the public about the life and career of one of the country's most influential jurists. The renovated park, also designed by Carol Johnson, would retain the overall organization of terraces and paths but would relocate the existing statue and introduce an expansive didactic experience featuring quotations inscribed on freestanding glass panels, an explanatory array of texts and images displayed on a suite of horizontal walls totaling some 400 feet in length, and a column commemorating the three branches of government surmounted by a bronze eagle.

The commission members voiced concerns about the extent of the didactic material, but Witold Rybczynski's remarks were the most pointed. He found that the numerous didactic elements "really don't have any place in the park.... This pedagogical impulse that everybody seems to have in public places is misplaced," he commented, adding that the glass walls in particular "don't have any artistic kind of life. They are like books that people are pushing in your face." The commission eventually voted at the meeting to approve the concept but recommended that the

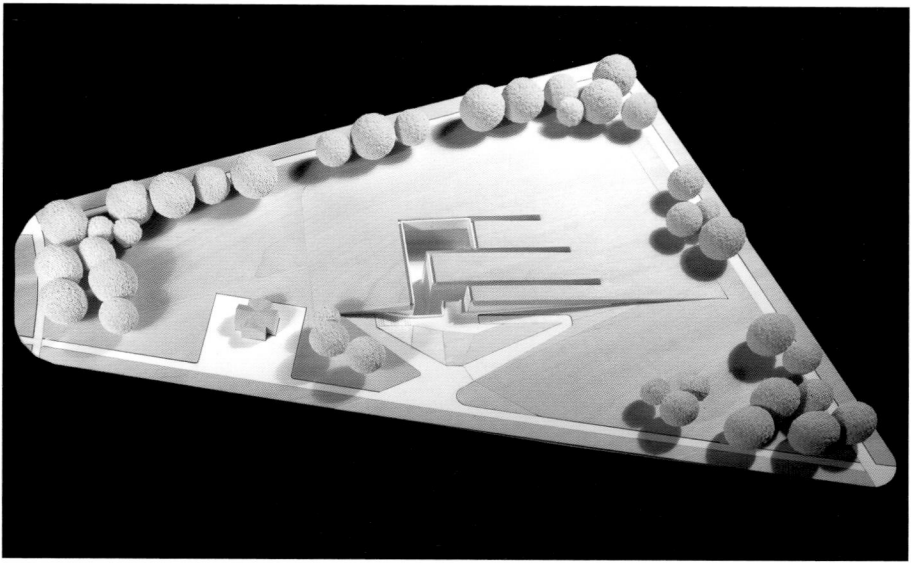

ABOVE LEFT: *Study model of the 2007 concept design showing the excavated courtyard and linear skylights of the underground visitor center, 2007.*

ABOVE RIGHT: *The 2012 revised concept design by Ennead (formerly Polshek Partnership) incorporated a curved pathway descending to the entrance; triangular skylights arrayed in the lawn toward the Lincoln Memorial replaced the linear ones from the earlier concept.*

Jan Scruggs, president of the VVMF, had tried earlier in the meeting to put to rest the issues of visitor center proliferation and site selection, noting that the VVMC would teach about values such as honor and patriotism that would speak for the other war memorials—Korean Veterans and World War II—and this was the site where that could best be achieved. However, after Belle's comments, Scruggs was more direct, citing the congressional authorization and adding:

We have been discussing sites for over a year. We can't go year after year going back to the Mall and discussing sites. This one makes sense. It makes sense to us. It makes sense to the Park Service…. Yes; it is an intervention, on this site. Yes; it is a significant site. But, you know what? We made an architectural intervention which was opposed by many on another site and that is the Viet Nam Veterans Memorial. Did the benefits outweigh the intervention? I rest my case and that is why we are here today to get the approval of the site.[111]

Commission members continued to press for clarification of the program for a building that could serve up to 2 million visitors per year. Witold Rybczynski pointed out that the project's program was creating difficulties: "I would say there is a big difference between an underground building, which is what you have been mandated to do, and a building that is covered with earth, which is not what you have been mandated to do." Ultimately, David Childs, serving at his last meeting as a commission member, crafted a motion that directed the VVMF to consider other sites, but granted conditional approval of their preferred site provided that a future building would not detract from the setting of the Lincoln Memorial or the experience of the Vietnam Veterans Memorial; this was adopted by the commission.[112]

Two years later, after design guidelines for the project

were developed and approved by the CFA and NCPC in 2006, the project team returned to the commission with a concept design for the approved site. In addition to a downward slope and raised ground plane, the Polshek design employed a sunken courtyard to accommodate ventilation and allow daylight within the visitor center. The commission reiterated concerns about the program and building size and continued to question the need for a visitor center at all. The members also expressed concern about the transition to the below-grade facility, which seemed to strongly echo the memorial itself, as noted by John Belle: "I think this is an extremely difficult design subject, and I have to commend the architects for their valiant efforts that show great sensitivity. I just am sitting here wondering whether, in successfully showing that sensitivity, they haven't, inadvertently, done something else which is to almost offer us an updated addition of the Wall, itself."[113] Other members encouraged the architect to study reducing the size of the building in order to lessen its negative effects on the site. In its discussion, however, the commission also noted the project's unusual authorizing legislation that mandated consent and reluctantly approved the concept design.[114]

When the project returned for revised concept review in April 2009, the design team had moved the building slightly north and west, but had raised the grade and shortened and simplified the ramps to mitigate visibility of the entrance from Bacon Drive. The commission still found the descent too reminiscent of the memorial and also questioned the detailing of the skylights. Of particular concern was the building's greater visibility as the design had progressed. Further studies of the design and landscape solutions to reduce the architectural impact of the build-

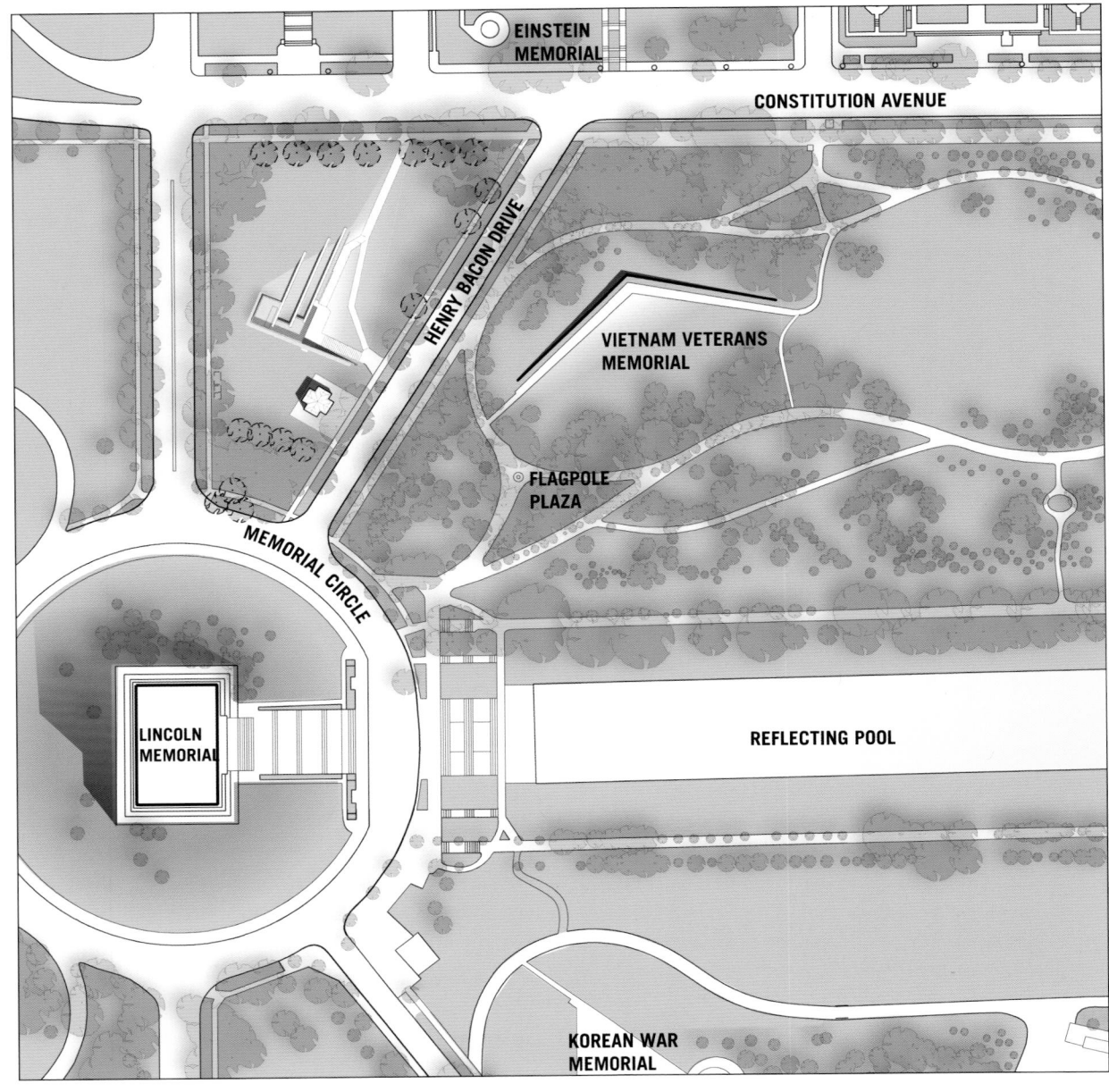

EINSTEIN MEMORIAL

CONSTITUTION AVENUE

HENRY BACON DRIVE

VIETNAM VETERANS MEMORIAL

FLAGPOLE PLAZA

MEMORIAL CIRCLE

LINCOLN MEMORIAL

REFLECTING POOL

KOREAN WAR MEMORIAL

Site plan by Polshek Partnership for the proposed subterranean Vietnam Veterans Memorial Center, across Bacon Drive from the actual memorial and in the foreground panels of the Lincoln Memorial, 2007.

Although various locations had been studied, the VVMF submitted only its preferred site to the commission: a trapezoidal parcel, part of the larger setting of the Lincoln Memorial, located between Constitution Avenue, Henry Bacon Drive, and 23rd Street. Designed by Polshek Partnership (now Ennead Architects) of New York, the 25,000-square-foot underground building would be accessed by a descending walkway, incorporate skylights, and necessitate some manipulation of the existing grades within the grass panel.

In their discussion, the commission members cautioned against establishing a precedent for education centers associated with each memorial on the Mall. They questioned the success of underground construction, noting in particular technical and lighting problems, as well as the impact on the surface plane of the Mall and the importance of preserving the landscape of flat panels as intended by the McMillan Commission and Henry Bacon. In addition, they expressed concern about the appropriateness of descending below grade, which could diminish the impact of the similar movement at the memorial itself. John Belle's comments summarized the commission's reticence regarding the site:

[Y]ou did tell us that you looked at multiple sites, and then you went into a very detailed analysis of one site. Some of us are having great difficulty in the leap of faith.... That makes it very difficult to endorse all of the things you are attempting to achieve on...the most sensitive site...which begins to create all of these problems.

He suggested it was not unreasonable for other sites to be considered.[110]

Let's be clear. If you think there is something wrong with a statue that makes Martin Luther King come off as confrontational, then there is something wrong with you. King was confrontational. If he wasn't, he'd probably still be alive.[104]

In June 2008, Jackson returned to the commission to address sculpture concerns with a submission comprising a collection of photographs of numerous statues of King and a compilation of previous commission actions. Jackson also presented slides of a modified clay maquette of the Stone of Hope with adjusted side contours. The commission members discussed the difficulty of judging sculpture from photographs and noted that a model would be more useful to better appreciate the massing. They requested a maquette of the sculpture as well as a full-size sample of the sculpture carved in the proposed granite in order for them to understand the detailing.

Two weeks before Jackson presented a comprehensive final submission to the commission in September 2008, the art critic Catesby Leigh wrote an essay on the memorial for the *Wall Street Journal*. He discussed the traditional technique of monumental sculpture and its relation to the poor artistic quality of the proposed sculpture of King:

Monumentality arises not from the size of the figure, but from a distillation and clarification of the complex topography unique to each human body—a formal technique that has all but disappeared from traditional training, which tends to focus these days on the simplistic transcription of natural appearances…. The lack of an anatomical underpinning to King's head is painfully obvious. The face is thus reduced to bulbous, schematic geometries…. The hands are rendered with greater attention to surface detail, but their modeling does not relate to that of the head. King's clothing weighs too heavily on him: The jacket looks as if it were cut from a thick sheet of rubber. The model accordingly fails to convey any sense of the structure of the body under the clothes. Nor will it be redeemed through translation into stone.[105]

At the commission meeting, the discussion again focused on the sculpture. Pamela Nelson observed that the rough finish of the mountain and the polished finish of the figure were "fighting with each other," to which Jackson responded that the foundation wanted the distinction as it opposed the idea of an "embedded" figure because then King "would give the impression that he has not freed himself…and he is not the symbol of hope."[106] Other commission members also expressed concern for the finishing treatments. John Belle noted that while the foundation had considered vertical transitions along the sculpture, it failed to appreciate the importance of horizontal variations. He recalled the metaphorical quotation and added: "It is how that man comes out of the mountain in physical, real, existential terms in the stone that we don't see at the moment. I think it is absolutely crucial to the success of this monument."[107] The commission members repeated their

desire to see a mock-up or a portion of a model. The review concluded with the commission's approval of the overall site design, planting materials, lighting detailing, and auxiliary building. Further information was requested on the inscriptions, perimeter security elements, and sculpture.

The foundation returned more than six times over the following two years to resolve outstanding issues related to perimeter security, materials, and inscriptions but did not present anything further regarding the sculpture. By the spring of 2010, the 159 granite blocks of the King statue were carved to 80 percent completion in China, in preparation for shipment to the U.S. The sculpture was completed on site and erected in the autumn of 2010; in the spring and summer of 2011, the commission reviewed lighting for the project. The memorial was opened to the public on August 28, 2011, but the formal dedication ceremonies scheduled for that day had to be postponed due to a hurricane. The official dedication took place on October 16, 2011.

A controversy also arose at the time of the dedication about a truncated quotation of Dr. King describing his role as a "drum major for justice" inscribed on the Stone of Hope. The poet Maya Angelou and others felt the alteration changed the meaning of Dr. King's words. The editing of this particular quotation had been discussed at the CFA's February 2007 meeting, and the memorial foundation had agreed to use it in its entirety. Inscriptions on the memorial were again reviewed by the CFA in September 2010, when the full "drum major" quotation was presented and approved by the CFA.[108] In early 2012, the secretary of the interior ordered the quotation to be corrected.

VIETNAM VETERANS MEMORIAL VISITOR CENTER

The Vietnam Veterans Memorial Center (VVMC)—an adjunct facility to function as a small museum for didactic elaboration of the memorial's message—generated a number of questions for the commission in its reviews: How would it affect the Mall's design integrity, would it be an appropriate adjunct to the Vietnam Memorial, and would it engender a proliferation of similar facilities? The quandary was compounded by powerful support of the project by veterans groups, former U.S. presidents and generals, and Congress, whose authorizing legislation prescribed an underground structure at a site "at or near" the Vietnam Memorial and that mandated that final approval could not be withheld.[109]

In September 2005, the Vietnam Veterans Memorial Fund (VVMF) and the National Park Service appeared before the commission as part of the site approval process.

chitectural drawings submitted to the commission. The commission members were able to review design specifics for the first time—including several that seemed to contradict the original guidelines for the site—and consequently expressed numerous concerns. They questioned why the Mountain of Despair and Stone of Hope had increased in height to thirty-two feet.[97] They recommended reducing the number of quotations, further study of lighting and paving details, and adjusting the siting of the visitor center building. They also requested material samples and documentation of joinery details; they stressed the importance of a movable, full-scale mock-up of the stone to ensure that visitors' perspectives of the colossal sculpture would not be distorted due to the constrained viewing angle created by the edge of the Tidal Basin.

In April 2008, the foundation returned with responses to the commission's previous concerns and also organized a site visit. The commission members viewed a mock-up of the Stone of Hope, which involved a hydraulic lift suspending a plywood framework wrapped in black plastic to represent the actual profile of the sculpture. At the public presentation, the project team explained that the metaphorical stones had been reduced in size. The height had been subtracted from the base of the Stone of Hope to achieve the previously presented twenty-nine-foot height; accordingly, the height of the figure itself remained unchanged while the stone's proportions became more squat.

At the conclusion of the presentation, Earl Powell inquired about the evolution of the figure of King—from Boris Dramov's competition-winning design "emerging from the stone" to Lei's interpretation that was "centralized and very static." Jackson explained that the initial rendering cut off a portion of King's shoulder, which Lei considered "inappropriate." Commission members were not comfortable with Lei's approach. To Balmori, the change was not an improvement: "[N]ow it feels as if the image of Dr. King has been…put on a stele, on a piece of stone, and is attached to it while [the competition entry figure] felt integral." Belle noted the significant difference between the two and described the new pose presented for the King statue as "confrontational."[98] McKinnell added:

I would like to comment on this because there is something I feel very strongly about here. When we were going out to the mock-up, Witold [Rybczynski] and I were talking. He said, I think correctly, 'you know, we are not experts in colossal figures. This is not something one sees very often.' I have been thinking about that ever since. Unfortunately, I have come up with examples in my mind where I have seen them recently and they have been broadcast on television and they are all being pulled down. I think that that connotation will be absolutely fatal in this instance. I think the metaphor of Dr. King being merged with

the natural force of the stone is absolutely essential to avoid the colossal monumentalization that we have been familiar with in countries that we don't need to mention. I think this is very important, the degree to which the metaphor of the stone and the man become one is absolutely imperative here. Otherwise, one risks a very unfortunate connotation.[99]

Belle's use of the word "confrontational" and McKinnell's implicit reference to a monument of former Iraqi President Saddam Hussein were noted in Secretary Luebke's summary action letter to the applicant:

In general, the Commission members found that the colossal scale and Social Realist style of the proposed statue recalls a genre of political sculpture that has recently been pulled down in other countries. They said that the proposed treatment of the sculpture—as the most iconographic and central element of the memorial to Dr. King—would be unfortunate and inappropriate as an expression of his legacy. They recommended strongly that the sculpture be reworked, both in form and modeling, to return to a more sympathetic idea of the figure growing out of the stone with increasing detail and emphasis of the upper part of the figure. The Commission cited precedents of a figure emerging from stone in the works of sculptors such as Michelangelo and Rodin.[100]

The issue of the King sculpture quickly became a point of debate in the media. James Chaffers, a professor of architecture at the University of Michigan and one of the jurors of the competition, said the project team wanted to maintain "the power and inspirational image" of Lei's design and valued its provocative nature. Chaffers told the Washington Post:

We see [King]…as a warrior. We see him as a warrior for peace…not as some pacifist, placid, kind of vanilla, but really a man of great conviction and strength.[101]

Two days later, Washington Post columnist Marc Fisher described the sculpture as "King seen in the arrogant stance of a dictator, clad in a boxy suit, with an impassive, unapproachable mien, looking more like an East Bloc Politburo member than an inspirational transformational preacher who won a war armed with nothing but truth and words."[102] Michael Nojeim, author of Gandhi and King: The Power of Nonviolent Resistance, wrote a letter to the editor of the Washington Post:

The proposed statue of the Rev. Martin Luther King Jr. fails to capture King's essence. Above all, Dr. King stood for using nonviolence to create what he called the beloved community. He was a radical reformer whose militancy was based on love, reconciliation and justice. As such, I wish to ask Ed Jackson…. Exactly where in this sculpture do you see anything remotely resembling King's principles of nonviolence, love, justice and the beloved community?[103]

However, the Washington Post columnist Courtland Milloy was pleased with the sculpture and walked around the Tidal Basin with a photograph of Lei's full-size clay model to ascertain public opinion about it. Milloy quoted Washingtonian Anthony McCoy in his editorial piece:

TOP: *View of the Martin Luther King Jr. National Memorial from the Tidal Basin as built in 2012; the granite-clad Mountain of Despair and Stone of Hope with the dark gray inscription walls are visible through the cherry trees.*

BOTTOM: *Night view of the gently curving inscription walls flanking the Mountain of Despair, which define the memorial plaza.*

commissioned to carve the Mountain of Despair and Stone of Hope. Lei's portfolio included colossal-scale bronze and masonry pieces, mostly for political leaders in central and east Asia, including a monumental bust of Mao Zedong. For the sculpture of Martin Luther King Jr., Lei proposed King in a frontal three-quarters-length engaged pose—arms crossed and legs apart—rather than the more pensive *contrapposto* figure based on Fitch's photograph, portraying King as emerging in a more natural stance out

of the stone. The commission members had few questions or comments on this formal concept submission of the sculpture, other than the importance of minimizing the visibility of joints in the assembly of stone pieces, and agreed with the National Park Service that full, rather than edited, quotations should be used.

That summer, the foundation retained the design services of McKissack & McKissack, who assembled for the November 2007 meeting the first comprehensive set of ar-

and submitted two new illustrations to the commission in March 2006. During the proceedings, Dramov spoke about his idea for the Stone of Hope: "What we have always wanted is that the Stone of Hope and Dr. King are one, that it is not a statue placed on it." He noted that the height was now "about 29 feet."[94] The project received concept approval with recommendations to study the width of the gap at the mountain and reconsider the location of the building and minimize its size.

The project returned to the commission in June 2006 with a design that reintroduced waterfalls next to the mountain. Dramov advocated for the features based on King's frequent allusions to water in his speeches and writings and as a means to reduce the impact of traffic noise from Independence Avenue. The commission members reacted negatively to the use of water, particularly regarding the use of waterfalls. Witold Rybczynski observed: "Still water is profound [a reference to the nearby Tidal Basin]. But falling water is always happy. It seems to be inappropriate to have that sentiment…. You go through those stones and it is not a happy movement. It is very tough…. For me, these afterthoughts of bubbling water really weaken the concept." He urged the designer to focus on the detailing of the metaphorical stone pieces. All agreed; Michael McKinnell summarized the point: "Everything is going to depend on the way these blocks either come off or don't." Dramov said they would bring the detailing the next time and would not pursue the water.[95]

When the foundation presented revised drawings at the October 2006 meeting, ROMA Design Group was no longer part of the project team. Ed Jackson, the foundation's executive architect, presented illustrations with a repositioned Mountain of Despair: its two pieces were no longer situated behind the inscription walls but rather in line with them, and only the last six feet of the walls incorporated waterfalls. Jackson argued that the water helped to mediate between the wall and mountain elements. The distance between the Mountain of Despair and the Stone of Hope was also diminished. The commission members agreed that reducing the distance between these elements increased the symbolic strength of the design, but recommended that the use of design elements other than water be studied to make the critical transition between the mountain and the walls.

Returning three months later in January 2007, Jackson presented a package of sketches depicting the evolution of the design at the Mountain of Despair, but he did not include a revision as earlier suggested by the commission. Both the foundation and the National Park Service reiterated the importance of water in the design, which was shown as two separate waterfalls. The commission came to agree that water could be a powerful part of the design but urged that it should be handled as a single element rather than as an aesthetic device that the members found weakened the symbolic strength of the Mountain of Despair. They voted to approve the revised concept with additional exploration of the water feature.[96]

In February 2007, the foundation presented the program of inscriptions and introduced sculptor Lei Yixin, of the People's Republic of China, who had recently been

ABOVE LEFT: *The 1966 photograph by Bob Fitch of Dr. King in his office was the inspiration for the central metaphoric image of the civil rights leader on the Stone of Hope.*

ABOVE CENTER: *Rendering of the Stone of Hope from the winning competition entry, illustrating the depth of the relief sculpture and the placement of a quotation.*

ABOVE RIGHT: *Photograph of the maquette of the Stone of Hope as realized by Chinese sculptor Lei Yixin and presented to the CFA in June 2008.*

RIGHT: *Model of the ROMA Design Group's concept for the memorial, which incorporated a semicircular plaza edged by inscription walls and featuring two split stones, the Mountain of Despair, and a central stone with a relief sculpture of Dr. King, the Stone of Hope.*

BELOW: *Rendered view of the memorial design in 2008 by McKissack & McKissack, illustrating a waterfall feature at the sides of the Mountain of Despair and the development of the landscape design.*

The National Park Service and the foundation submitted the winning entry by ROMA Design Group of San Francisco, California, to the commission for an information presentation in June 2001. ROMA's landscape solution included a semicircular plaza framed by inscription walls, which also accommodated more than 500 linear feet of waterfalls, surmounted by a walkway with commemorative niches for leaders of the civil rights movement. The centerpiece of the memorial featured an expression from King's "I Have a Dream" speech delivered from the steps of the Lincoln Memorial on August 28, 1963: *With this faith, we will be able to hew out of the mountain of despair a stone of hope.* Two split stones symbolized the Mountain of Despair with a third situated ahead representing the Stone of Hope; this central stone also included a relief of King based on the Fitch photograph. When Barbaralee Diamonstein-Spielvogel asked principal designer Boris Dramov the height of the stones, he responded that, "We'd like it to be a little higher but 20 [feet] was the maximum height."[92] A second information presentation was given a year later; at this time the commission made a variety of specific recommendations including reducing the height of the inscription walls, eliminating the elevated commemorative walk and niches, and removing the walkway bridge at the mountain gap.

Two CFA chairmanships would begin and end before October 2005, when the memorial was formally presented as a concept application; Pamela Nelson was the sole commission member who had participated in the previous discussions. Although measured drawings for the design existed by this point, the submission only included the illustrations created for the competition.[93] The design had not changed, apart from the addition of a building in the southern corner of the site. The commission members raised the same concerns mentioned in 2002 and also took issue with the vaguely defined ancillary building, variously described as a ranger kiosk, visitor center, and restrooms. Following several meetings with CFA staff and the other review agencies, the foundation simplified the design as previously directed, including the removal of the waterfalls,

Aerial view of the Martin Luther King Jr. National Memorial site on the Tidal Basin (outlined in yellow) and its relationship to other major memorials on the Mall, 1999.

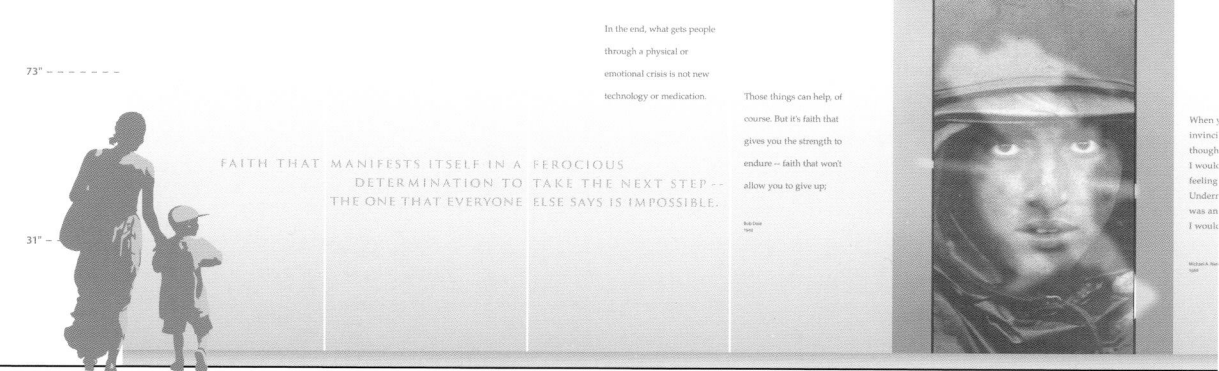

ABOVE: *Detail of a study model showing the extensive use of glass quotation walls punctuated by bronze negative relief panels within a grove of bald cypress trees.*

BELOW : *Rendering of a segment of the revised glass wall, approved in 2009, depicting the quotations and art panels that combined photographic images etched on glass panels superimposed with bronze silhouettes.*

the use of double images throughout the panels. The commission voted to approve the revisions with suggestions for the stone wall and paver details and with the understanding, added by Balmori, that the designers consider varying the treatment of some of the images. McKinnell supported Balmori in this suggestion, noting that varying the images would strengthen an expressive form that he found quite powerful: "I think that you have found, as artists, a way, in twenty-first century terms, to be able to introduce into the memorial the actual human content."[90] The commission reviewed and approved further refinements of design details in July 2009, and the project's final design and construction documents were reviewed and approved by delegation to the commission staff in March 2011.

MARTIN LUTHER KING JR. NATIONAL MEMORIAL

The Martin Luther King Jr. National Memorial presented several design issues during the ten-year period of its development and the commission's review, including those related to scale and iconography. However, the most challenging issues arose from the design's focus on photography as an inspiration for sculptural expression as well as the execution and appropriateness of that sculptural expression. These came to dominate the commission's concerns regarding the memorial.

In 1999, an international open design competition for the memorial was announced; the competition's information package included civil rights movement photographer Bob Fitch's 1966 photograph of King standing pensively at his desk with arms crossed and a framed portrait of Gandhi on the wall. Earlier that year, a four-acre site along the Tidal Basin had been approved by the NCPC and the CFA for the memorial, and eleven design parameters were set forth by the NCPC and agreed upon by the National Park Service and the Martin Luther King Jr. National Memorial Project Foundation. These included maintaining visual transparency between Independence Avenue and the Tidal Basin; limiting the height of any element to twenty feet; and the exclusion of any restroom, retail, or museum facility.[91]

within five layers of glass; for example, a bronze silhouette of a charging marine framed a photograph of a young soldier with a blank expression staring into the camera. Kirkland sought to enliven the walls with qualities of light and shadow, translucence and reflectivity.

The commission reviewed and approved the revised design concept subject to the resolution of what they found to be continuing design issues. While the designer had handled the quotes in a way that the commission found presented an evocative and well-told story, the additional layers of physical and expressive forms weakened that story, leading to what John Belle called an "embarrassment of riches" that needed to be simplified. Witold Rybczynski voiced the most pointed concerns about the photographs and the nature of memorials, noting that this aspect of heightened realism was his main reservation about the design: "It seems to me that you are taking…the images so literally that there is only one way to interpret them. And it starts to feel like the medium from advertising or some commercial venue rather than a memorial." He also found the use of glass troubling as a commemorative material: "A memorial…whether it is modern or not modern, has always had a sense of being apart from the world because memorials have to be there forever…. Glass is not a traditional material for memorials precisely because it isn't there forever." He did add, however, that he was open to the design's continued exploration of the material and offered the idea of deleting the photographs, with the silhouettes alone visible through the glass. Earl Powell and architect Elizabeth Plater-Zyberk (CFA 2008–), a founding partner of the Miami-based New Urbanist design firm Duany Plater-Zyberk & Company, who had recently joined the commission, both considered the use of photography less troubling. The consensus of the commission members was for an on-site mock-up of the concept as part of any further review.[88]

During a March 2009 site inspection, the commission members viewed the mock-up of the design elements. The members commented that the glass panel with the layered images, seen at full size, produced through its reflectivity an ambiguity that would evoke a powerful response in the visitor; Diana Balmori called them "poetic" but emphasized that the simpler images were the most evocative. The members reiterated their desire for greater simplicity within the memorial, including reducing the size of the masonry wall and fountain, with further study of the memorial's views of the Capitol.[89]

The project team returned to the commission two months later with a refined concept. The wall and reflecting pool had been reduced in size and the entrances to the plaza enlarged, but some lingering concerns remained regarding

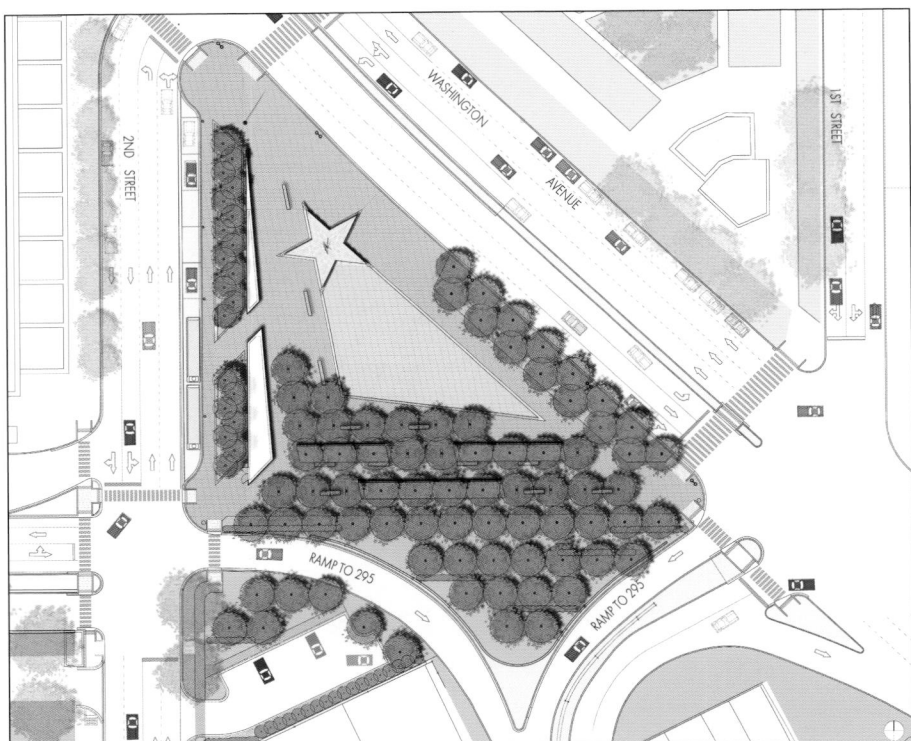

ABOVE LEFT: *Rendered site plan of the memorial illustrating Vergason's 2004 design that included a star-shaped fountain, eternal flame, and large pool within a stone plaza framed by a composition of stone walls, trees, and a series of glass walls featuring quotations and art panels.*

ABOVE RIGHT: *Preliminary study, 2005, for an inverse high-relief sculpture by artist Larry Kirkland, suggesting incomplete human forms to represent the injuries suffered by the veterans.*

Aerial rendering of the 2005 concept design by Michael Vergason Landscape Architects for the American Veterans Disabled for Life Memorial (AVDLM), showing its relationship to the Bartholdi Fountain and the Rayburn Building across Washington Avenue.

Despite the lack of a final approval by the CFA, construction proceeded, and the memorial was dedicated in September 2008.

AMERICAN VETERANS DISABLED FOR LIFE MEMORIAL

The use of photography as an expressive form as well as questions of scale and complexity were among the design issues the commission addressed in the American Veterans Disabled for Life Memorial. In September 2001, the commission approved the memorial's site on the triangle of land formed by the intersections of Washington Avenue and 2nd and C Streets, SW. The site was among the first to be selected under the planning recommendations established in the *Memorials and Museums Master Plan* and was preferred by the memorial's proponent, the Disabled Veterans' Life Memorial Foundation, for its proximity to the Capitol to remind legislators of the human cost of war. The National Park Service and the foundation returned to the commission in March 2004 with a design by landscape architect Michael Vergason, which was given concept approval with the direction to simplify and integrate the elements: a flame, grove of trees, fountain, pool, flagpole, stone and glass walls, quotations, and an art installation.

The following year, sculptor Larry Kirkland presented preliminary studies for eight-foot- tall, bronze, inverse bas-relief panels showing partial bodies to suggest loss and give "form to the sense of memory."[85] The commission was enthusiastic about the project, although Diana Balmori commented that, in his literal depiction of limbs, the designer was having "the usual problem between the abstract and representational," a "battleground" experienced by many trying to bridge the two that resulted only in ambiguity. Witold Rybczynski still found the design too complex and recommended further simplification and the establishment of a perceptual hierarchy of the elements.[86] A revised concept was presented to the commission in November 2006, incorporating a reconfigured site and related spatial adjustments to the design in response to security concerns raised by the Architect of the Capitol. The commission had few questions, mostly regarding the detailing and appearance of the pool and fountain, and approved the concept.

Three years later, at the July 2008 meeting, the team presented another revised concept with a significantly altered art component. Kirkland had changed his sculpture in response to objections raised by the foundation board and veterans who could not see themselves or their story in the impressions of body parts; his new proposal pursued an expression that combined the ideal with the real.[87] Bronze cutouts were placed in front of photographs set

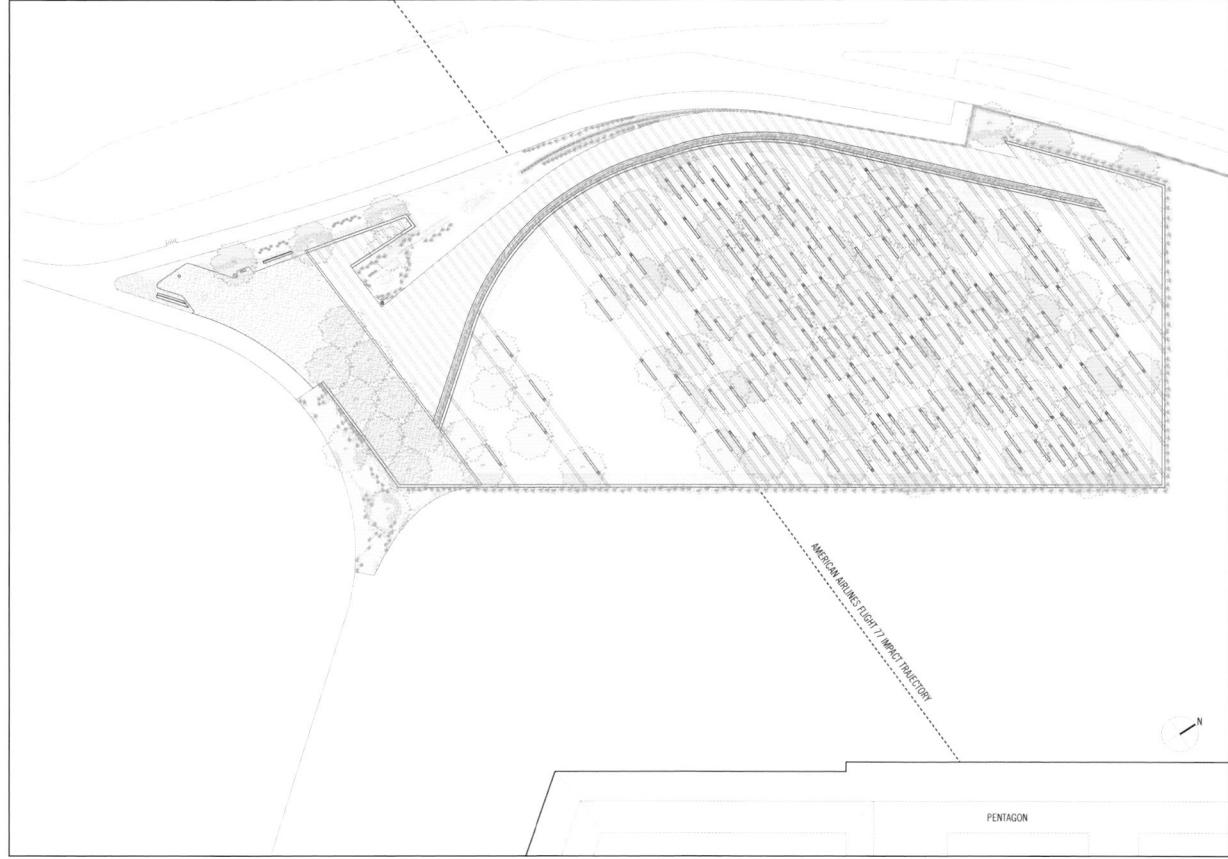

ABOVE: *Night view of the memorial as completed in 2008, featuring steel benches cantilevered over shallow illuminated pools, each forming a memorial unit within the gravel field. In its numerous reviews of the project, the CFA was concerned about many of the functional and maintenance aspects of the complex design.*

LEFT: *Plan of the winning entry for the Pentagon 9/11 Memorial by Julie Beckman and Keith Kaseman. The site was proposed as an open gravel plaza interspersed with trees and steel benches— as markers for each victim— oriented in the flight path of the downed plane.*

photographic images on the granite wall at the Korean War Veterans Memorial in the 1990s. By the new century, photography as a generative artistic concept was firmly established in the design of commemorative works, exemplified by such projects as the American Veterans Disabled for Life Memorial, the Martin Luther King Jr. National Memorial, and the Dwight D. Eisenhower Memorial.

PENTAGON 9/11 MEMORIAL

The design of the Pentagon 9/11 Memorial presented an expansive landscape solution commemorating the 184 victims who died at the Pentagon in the attacks of September 11, 2001. The design incorporated multiple elements including benches, water, trees, gravel footpaths, and lighting; the technical feasibility of implementing several of these features became the focus of the commission's review of the project, which had congressional, Department of Defense, and public support.

In October 2001, Congress authorized the Department of Defense to create a privately funded memorial to honor the victims of the Pentagon attack. Ten potential sites were forwarded to a family steering committee, which selected two acres on the western grounds of the Pentagon; the site was approved by the CFA in June 2002. An open and anonymous international design competition was organized with a jury comprising seven design professionals, two family members, and two former secretaries of defense, and chaired by Terry Riley, chief curator of architecture and design at the Museum of Modern Art in New York. The winning entry by New York architects Julie Beckman and Keith Kaseman, announced in March 2003, consisted of a gravel field with 184 "memorial units"—stainless steel benches each cantilevered over an illuminated reflecting pool and organized linearly along the flight path of the airplane; the field was punctuated by paperbark maple trees. Riley noted that the design appealed to the judges in part because the ordered benches recalled the rows of headstones at nearby Arlington National Cemetery.[81]

In 2003 Beckman and Kaseman first presented their design for concept review to the commission members, who raised a variety of concerns about the project. Although the CFA members had varying opinions about the relevance of the water, they agreed on the need to simplify the design, expressed significant reservations about the ongoing maintenance requirements, and questioned the functionality and appropriateness of the proposed tree specimen. David Childs summarized the concerns about water and the significant maintenance issues it posed: "You've chosen it for its light…perhaps there are other materials that could be free of maintenance and transmit light in a flickering way that might also speak of life…. I would encourage you to think about the realities of the chewing gum and the wrapper that, in fact, might desecrate…the beauty of this. At a certain point, if it's unable to be maintained, it will be changed."[82] The members also were concerned about the choice of materials, especially the epoxy polymer concrete gravel aggregate for the benches, which was sensitive to ultraviolet light and, if badly executed, could diminish the aesthetic quality of the design. The members voted to accept the concept with their concerns noted and further interim reviews encouraged, especially of the materials.

Delays in fundraising, however, prevented the team from resubmitting for three years. When they finally did, in April 2006, the commission members repeated their concerns, as the design had not changed substantively, although the bench materials had been revised to address issues of thermal expansion and the water filtration system for its ability to catch leaves and debris. The members were complimentary of the overall design, but Witold Rybczynski summarized their concern by describing it as a "Swiss watch," adding, "I admire your ingenuity, really…. But it also worries us that there is so much novelty, that there is so much that can go wrong, and that you really need to do much more homework than if you were doing something conventional."[83] The commission asked to see additional information for design development, specifically a mock-up of the bench and fountain piece.

In November, the project team returned with further developed details for a vote on the final design. Despite assurances by the design team that technical research supported the feasibility of the design elements, the commission continued to caution about the difficulty of maintaining architectural precision within a landscape setting but deferred its decision until the mock-up could be reviewed. In January 2007, the commission members visited the memorial grounds to inspect the prototype and, upon returning to the meeting, repeated their concerns, which the visit had not mitigated. The members still found the design too complex, the success of which hinged on precise construction tolerances difficult to achieve, and still questioned the feasibility of the design's long-term maintenance. Many design details remained to be refined before they could be fabricated. Members also suggested darkening the color of the pools' lining to alleviate the starkness of the white surface. Rather than take a vote on the final design, the commission chose to respond in writing, presenting its concerns and recommendations in the summary letter of the meeting to the Department of Defense.[84]

ABOVE LEFT: The CFA found the consistency of design a dignified solution employed over numerous phases of the columbarium expansion at Arlington National Cemetery, including the fifth phase for Court 9 reviewed in 2008. The columbarium prototype was originally designed by Keyes Lethbridge & Condon Architects in the late 1960s and has been adapted over the following decades for the complex.

ABOVE RIGHT: The Columbia Memorial at Arlington National Cemetery as built, 2004, showing the mission insignia of the spacecraft on a traditional bronze tablet mounted on a granite slab. The 2003 concept design for the marker included a depiction of the ship's crew in relief, adapted from a photograph; the mission insignia was relocated to the front of the memorial in the approved design.

LEFT: The 2011 design for the Senator Edward M. Kennedy gravesite (circled in yellow) by Sasaki & Associates created a new element in a sequence of Kennedy family burial sites at Arlington National Cemetery: the circular President John F. Kennedy site by John Carl Warneke on the right; the half-circular memorial to Senator Robert F. Kennedy by I.M. Pei in the center; and the proposed soft curve for the new gravesite on the left.

New Development at Military Cemeteries

As with cultural institutions, U.S. military cemeteries evolved with new programmatic changes and architectural expression in the new century. Coincident with the sixtieth anniversary of World War II, the American Battle Monuments Commission (ABMC) undertook a program in the early years of the new century to develop visitor centers at American overseas cemeteries in order to provide interpretation for the many visitors who had no direct memory of the war. The first visitor center, at Normandy, was designed by Smith Group as a neomodernist building with crisp intersecting planes of glass and stone, low in profile to avoid competing with views of

the cemetery. The CFA reviewed and enthusiastically approved the concept design in 2004, asking for resolution of the overall landscape design and access to the adjacent parking lot. In 2011, the CFA reviewed and approved several small projects to expand visitor services at ABMC cemeteries, including a neomodernist concept for a visitor center at the Sicily-Rome American Cemetery. To support the quiet addition positioned against the cemetery's perimeter walls, the CFA suggested refinement of the cemetery's entrance to control the visual intrusion of automobiles.

In the first decade of the twenty-first century, wars in Afghanistan and Iraq and the concurrent passing of many veterans of World War II, the Korean War,

and the Vietnam War placed additional demand on the land resources at Arlington National Cemetery. Based on an earlier master plan, the cemetery continued to expand its columbarium, a facility for the interment of cremated remains and a building typology providing a direct response to the growing scarcity of land at the cemetery. In 2008, the Commission of Fine Arts approved the concept design of the fifth phase of construction, which followed the original design intent for the facility; the CFA found that this consistency of approach lent dignity to the overall complex. In a separate project, the cemetery rebuilt a stone perimeter wall incorporating burial niches along its southern border, which was completed in 2008. In this period the cemetery began planning for the Millennium Tract, acquired from Fort Myer, which would also include perimeter wall and columbarium burial locations in addition to traditional interments.

Arlington National Cemetery is also the site of numerous memorials commemorating the lives of Americans lost in service to the nation. In the early 2000s, several new memorials were erected, including a memorial to the seven astronauts lost in the explosion of the space shuttle *Columbia* in February 2003. The design depicts the official insignia worn by the astronauts—an image of the spaceship—on a bronze tablet affixed to an austere, traditional granite base. The CFA reviewed the design in June 2003 suggesting that the proposed portrayal of crew members be in profile, a more typical approach to commorative portraiture. The revised design with the insignia on the front and a photograph of the crew rendered in bronze as a bas-relief on the back was approved the following month; the memorial was dedicated in 2004.

TOP: *Smith Group's 2007 design for the Normandy American Cemetery visitor center emphasized strong horizontal planes with low profiles to minimize the impact on views of the cemetery and the adjacent Omaha Beach, site of the 1944 Allied invasion.*

BOTTOM: *The proposed visitor center design of 2011 at the Sicily-Rome American Cemetery by Ottavio Di Blasi with Harry Robinson employs a neomodernist vocabulary that fits quietly within the existing complex.*

noting that the naturalistic pond and rain garden there appeared incongruous with the urban quality of the street. The members also praised the direction that the designers were taking with the canopy and corona design and made suggestions for additional detailing. The revised concept was approved with the commendation that "the development of the design now illustrates how this museum will become part of the community of other buildings along the National Mall."[78]

In October 2011, the design team returned with a revised concept design that addressed many of the issues raised regarding the impact of the building: its height had been adjusted to align with various roof and balustrade lines of the Federal Triangle, and the projection of the front porch was reduced. Adjaye's design of the corona, now proposed as a shell of patterned cast metal panels pierced by geometric shapes derived from traditional ironwork, would moderate climate and frame views from within the museum. The landscape design by Kathryn Gustafson of Gustafson Guthrie Nichol had been developed, emphasizing a theme of passage over water to safety. The team had revised the naturalistic linear water garden, the oculus, and a sequence of three reading groves within the north yard of the building. On the south, the main water feature adjacent to the canopy incorporated moving and still water but was now proposed to be covered with inscribed quotations resembling handwritten text.

The commission members enthusiastically supported the design but with guidance to continue refinement: the landscape should provide year-round character and remain hospitable in summer and winter; the glass base of the building below the corona should be carefully detailed; and the lacy quality of the corona must be legible at night. Artist Teresita Fernández (CFA 2011–), in her first CFA meeting, suggested that the proposed incised pattern of handwriting on the basin floor of the south entrance pool could distract from the content of the words themselves and compete with the corona itself. Michael McKinnell joined Fernández in supporting the use of actual bronze for the corona panels because of its patination over time, adding that "the essence of this whole scheme, between intimacy and monumentality…must be carried through into this exterior material in some way."[79]

Groundbreaking for the museum took place in February 2012. Although the design review process was still incomplete, the project had passed most regulatory reviews and was considered well resolved for a proposal at such a highly controversial site. The museum's expected year of completion is 2015.

Trends in Commemoration in the Monumental Core

Maya Lin's seminal Vietnam Veterans Memorial remained an influence on the typology of commemoration in the new century. Its design set the precedent of a long and horizontal form, processional and narrative in formal structure, and focused on the subjective experience of the commemorated—which, in the case of the Vietnam Veterans Memorial, were the individual names of the fallen. Over the decades, the language of commemoration continued to evolve and add complexity to memorial projects, a trend marked by the blurring of distinctions among artistic disciplines as well as between symbolic and didactic programs: no new memorial would be considered complete without a substantial component of quotations, explanatory texts, photographic images, and, ideally, a visitor center—all of which contributed to the increasingly large financial and spatial requirements for the proposed memorials. In addition, advanced technology made possible new materials and modes of representation that were, in previous generations, not typically used in commemoration: photography as the primary artistic imagery, large panels of glass to display images and text, and the almost mandatory inclusion of extensive water elements in the memorial design.[80] Finally, memorials based on narrowly focused themes, often brought forward by private, nonprofit sponsoring organizations able to financially support them, became more common in the commemorative process.

The system of bringing a memorial to being in the public setting of Washington, D.C., had always required the protracted exercise of political will; the process as defined under the Commemorative Works Act was an explicitly difficult one, with twenty-one separate steps required. Even with its augmented powers of approval provided by the act, the commission's approach remained largely constant within this changing context. As their predecessors had before them, commission members evaluated memorial proposals for their design appropriateness, examining factors such as scale, meaning, and complexity within the framework of the nation's capital. Although design quality would always be the guiding principle, the technical performance of materials was an increasingly important focus. Most significantly, the use of photography transformed the millennia-old art form of sculpture—a trend that began with the realization of Joe Rosenthal's iconic photograph of soldiers raising the flag on Iwo Jima into a bronze sculpture by Felix de Weldon in the 1950s for the U.S. Marine Corps War Memorial. It continued with the sandblasted

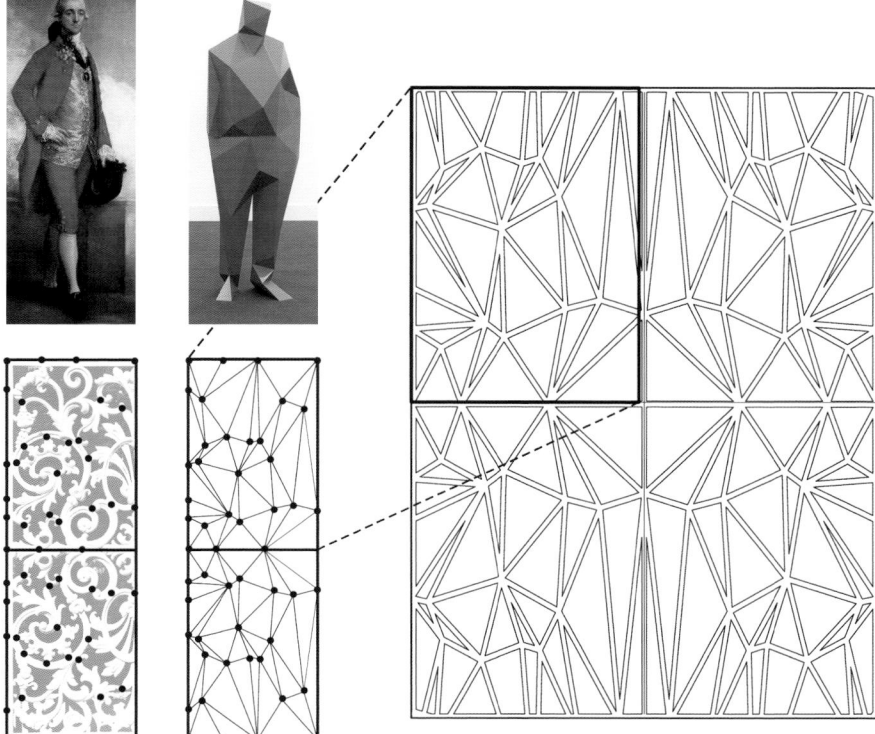

ABOVE: *Rendering of the revised concept design, October 2011, showing the south entrance porch viewed from the southwest, creating a cantilevered overhang above the reflecting pool.*

RIGHT: *Study from the October 2011 presentation by Freelon Adjaye Bond showing the development of the corona screen design derived from the geometric abstraction of traditional figures of cast-iron railings.*

LEFT: *Maquette presented at the CFA meeting of September 2012 as a study for a bronze-finished cast-aluminum corona screen unit developed from the abstract geometric design.*

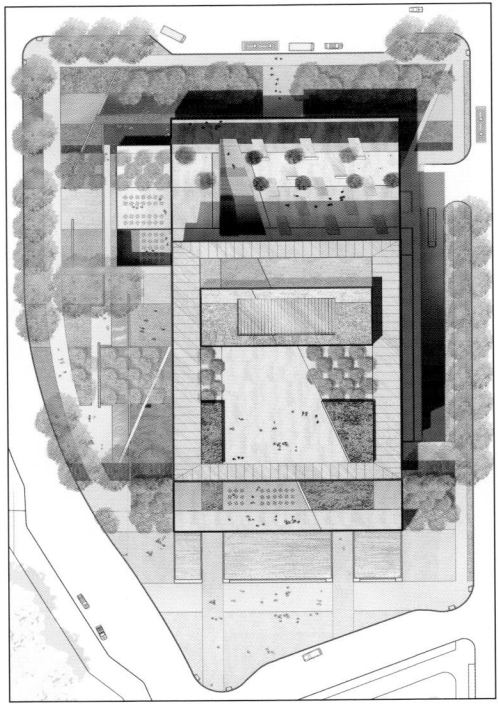

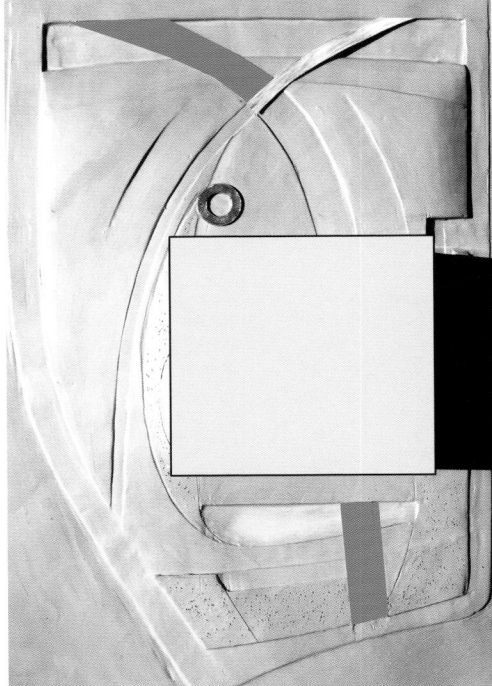

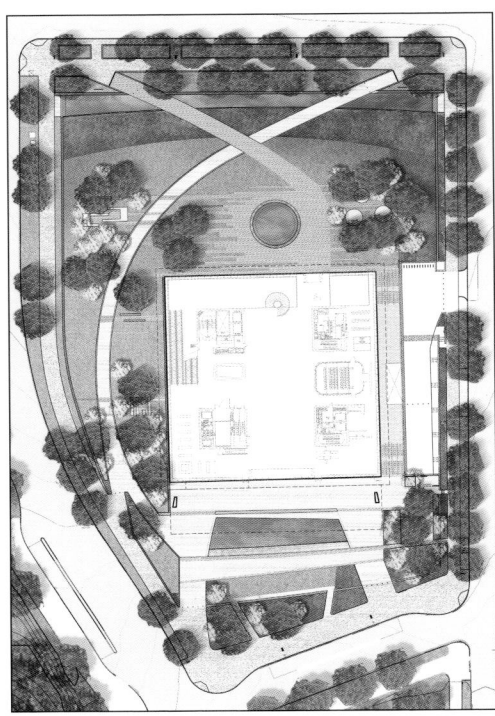

Rendering of the revised concept design for the museum as viewed from Constitution Avenue, March 2011. Freelon Adjaye Bond/Smith Group

simplified the design after restudying the transparency and material of the building's base and corona.

ABOVE LEFT: *Site plan by Gustafson Guthrie Nichol from the 2009 winning design showing a geometrically patterned landscape surrounding the building.*

ABOVE CENTER: *Concept model in plaster for the site and landscape design, 2011, by Gustafson Guthrie Nichol. The square plan of the corona is mediated within the irregular site with gently curving walks inspired by the Washington Monument Grounds; an oculus in the north building yard would provide illumination to the extensive below-grade galleries.*

ABOVE RIGHT: *Final rendered landscape site plan, October 2011, featuring a linear water garden along the Constitution Avenue frontage and a wide reflecting pool on the south side of the main entrance facing the Mall.*

ABOVE: *Rendering of the winning competition entry for the NMAAHC by Freelon Adjaye Bond. The multistory corona and extended podium are prominent in this view from Constitution Avenue.*

RIGHT: *David Adjaye and Kathryn Gustafson presented their concept designs for the NMAAHC building and landscape to the Commission of Fine Arts in April 2010. Shown discussing the model are (from left): David Adjaye, John Belle, Thomas Luebke, Kathryn Gustafson, Witold Rybczynski, Michael McKinnell, and Pamela Nelson.*

how to build on a site that had been vacant since the L'Enfant era, one within the perceived landscape of the National Mall, and in the shadow of Washington's most iconic memorial—but a site that, in the McMillan Plan, was illustrated as a location for a building.

Congress enacted legislation to establish the National Museum of African American History and Culture and set up a commission to determine a site "on or adjacent to" the Mall in December 2001.[73] The museum commission gave an informational presentation to the CFA in February 2003 to present the eleven sites studied, of which five were designated as preferred.[74] The members of the Commission of Fine Arts enthusiastically supported the concept of the museum but cautioned about protecting the open space on the Mall. Harry Robinson pointed out the conundrum of locating the museum on the monument site:

It is the perfect site in terms of presence in terms of the importance of the issue that's going to be housed in this museum . . . . But in terms of the front yard of the Washington Monument, I think it'll create a problem . . . to essentially truncate the front yard of the Washington Monument as the building is currently laid out may be a mistake.[75]

A year later, Congress authorized the Smithsonian Institution Board of Regents to select the site, and in April 2005 the Smithsonian gave an informational presentation to the Commission of Fine Arts on the site selection process. The CFA members commented that the Washington Monument site was problematic in that it had four fronts, creating difficulties of access and service. They shared thoughts on several of the other sites considered, noting that the Liberty Loan building and Banneker Overlook sites offered high visibility and recommending that the Arts and Industries Building, which occupied an exceptional location, be further analyzed for the new museum. However, the regents confirmed the highly prominent five-acre monument site as their choice in January 2006.

In an information presentation to the CFA three years later—February 2009—the Smithsonian project team discussed the established design principles that were distributed to six design teams competing for the project. The new building would serve as a "hinge point" between the line of Mall buildings and the Federal Triangle, and the design would need to address the building's relationship to the Mall's axis, the Washington Monument, and the larger context of the city as well as urban design issues of scale, views, current use patterns, and landscape. The Smithsonian noted that the commission's staff had been involved in the information development regarding the site and these design principles and had provided input for the Section 106 Historic Preservation Review.[76] The Smithsonian's project leaders commented that, in addition to a design

proposal, they wanted to understand how the architect worked, because they intended to select a designer rather than a design.[77]

The design collaborative of three architectural design firms, Freelon Adjaye Bond, won the competition in April 2009. Their proposal, submitted to the commission for informational purposes later that year, drew inspiration from the role of the porch in African American life and the Yoruban column of West African architecture, represented by a large podium with open ends supporting a "corona" of two inverted pyramidal segments. As part of the federal environmental review process, the project team had to design three alternative schemes, which were presented to the commission in April 2010. Each option incorporated a corona with different relationships to the site and with or without a podium. The commission members preferred the boldness of the simplest alternative with the corona atop a transparent base as well as a location for the building mass that centered on the adjacent buildings across 14th Street and Constitution Avenue. The CFA also commented that the building program was too large for the site, requested more information on the landscape design, and cautioned against a scheme with large water elements as being contrary to the character of the reflecting pools on the National Mall.

In September 2010, the design team presented a revised concept proposal that addressed many of the commission's issues: it incorporated the bronze-colored corona on a transparent base with a canopy, and the site design was further developed with curvilinear pathways related to the overall context of the monument grounds. The commission members encouraged the design team to further explore the relationship between the museum and the buildings on the north side of the Mall, the remnants of the monument grounds, and the urban grid. They expressed support for the picturesque approach to the landscape scheme and paths but raised concerns about the size of the water elements. The CFA members advised the architect to give careful study to the material, color, and transparency of the corona; they also suggested coordination with the National Museum of American History for service access to the site to avoid the unsightly necessity of a ramp along the building on 14th Street.

The commission members reviewed a revised concept in March 2011, following a visit to view a mock-up of elements on site. Overall, the designs for both the landscape setting and the building itself had been further refined and simplified, which the members found responded well to their earlier suggestions. However, they recommended reconsideration of the site design at Constitution Avenue,

David Adjaye's concept design was inspired in part by a carved wooden veranda post by the West African (Yoruba) artist Ọ́lọ́wẹ̀ of Isẹ̀, depicting a mounted hunter with a tiered headdress whose stepped form was expressed in the winning competition design as its most iconic element, the "corona."

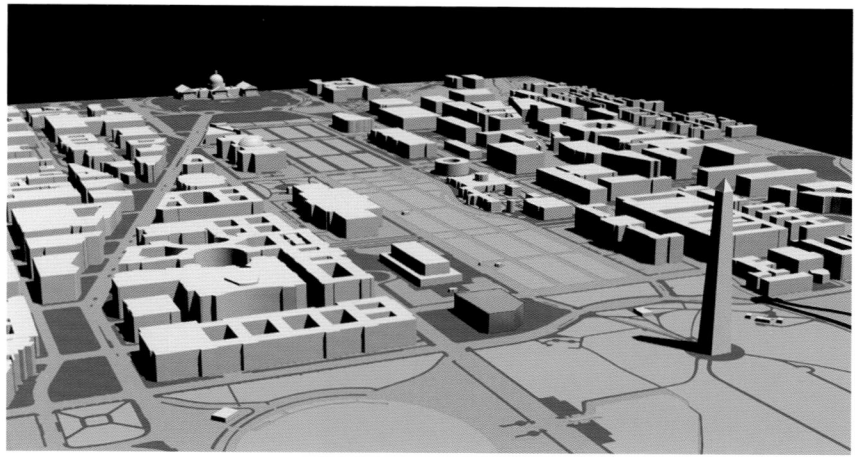

TOP LEFT: *Analysis drawing of the 15th Street and Constitution Avenue site of the Smithsonian National Museum of African American History and Culture (NMAAHC), 2005, occupying a corner of the Washington Monument Grounds.*

CLOCKWISE FROM TOP RIGHT: *Competition entries of five of the six finalists for the NMAAHC, 2009. Diller Scofidio & Renfro; Moody Nolan in association with Antoine Predock Architect (center right); Devrouax & Purnell Architects/Planners and Pei Cobb Freed & Partners (bottom right); Moshe Safdie & Associates (bottom left); Foster & Partners (center left).*

CHAPTER VII | TO EVERY AGE ITS ART

TOP LEFT: *Stereograph image from the 1890s illustrates how the stairway of the Patent Office's F Street entrance was modified when the street was lowered. This configuration remained in place until the 1930s, when the stair was demolished, and a new entrance was created at the street level.*

TOP RIGHT: *Late twentieth-century view of the Old Patent Office F Street portico and entrance. In addition to the courtyard enclosure, the building underwent a comprehensive renovation from 2000 to 2006.*

LEFT: *Photomontage of the proposed design by Hartman-Cox for a replacement stairway at the F Street entry to the building. The contested replication of the 1870s stairway remained unbuilt at the time the courtyard reopened.*

approval of the stairway, which was a requirement of the NCPC's approval, but the commission declined, referring to its previous decision, which the applicant noted put them "between a rock and a hard place."[72]

The commission finally gave its approval to the stairway at the March 2006 meeting with an expressed preference for allowing public access to the stairs and landing at least during daylight hours. Following further refinement of the courtyard scheme, the commission gave its final approval of that design a few months later. When the renovated building reopened to the public in July 2006 as the Donald W. Reynolds Center for American Art and Portraiture, plans to construct the F Street stairway had not been undertaken, and it remained unbuilt in 2012.

The new interior space—the Robert and Arlene Kogod Courtyard—features planters, white marble benches, and a water scrim under the gridded glass canopy and acts as a common orientation space for the museum.

NATIONAL MUSEUM OF AFRICAN AMERICAN HISTORY AND CULTURE

A major new project for the Smithsonian Institution, the National Museum of African American History and Culture presented the complex architectural problem of building a new museum within a highly sensitive historic landscape: the northeastern corner of the Washington Monument Grounds. The selected site involved the balancing of many delicate issues of historic preservation:

Interior view of the completed canopy and courtyard landscape featuring large marble planters and seating platforms as well as a shallow scrim of water, 2008.

By June, the canopy project had become more enmeshed in repercussions from the preservation review. That month, Earl Powell, the newly elected commission chairman, summarized the CFA's actions regarding both the enclosure and the stair in testimony before the NCPC, which was reviewing the final plans for the canopy. However, the NCPC did not give its final approval because of misgivings about the canopy's impact on the historic building expressed by the Advisory Council for Historic Preservation, a federal historic preservation advisory agency. The Smithsonian and its designers met twice more with the NCPC to show additional design revisions. Of special concern was light from the courtyard overpowering the building at night; the revisions assured that the classical build-

ing itself would be well lit.[70] By September, the NCPC had approved revisions for a final design but still required the stairway to mitigate for the enclosure; it also approved a landscape scheme for the courtyard.[71]

The CFA reviewed this revised canopy at its September meeting, giving final approval to the design although expressing concern regarding the visual impact of shadows cast on the walls of the historic courtyard by the thick ribs of the gridded roof structure. The members also reviewed the courtyard landscape design by Gustafson Guthrie Nichol, which—with its shallow scrims of water, water jets, planters and climbing vines, and blue glass balcony— they found too complex in its segmentation of the space, and asked for revisions. The Smithsonian also requested

ABOVE: *Section model of the 2005 concept design by Foster & Partners of the warped steel and glass lattice canopy to cover the historic courtyard. Supported by eight columns without bearing on the historic Patent Office structure, the enclosure was intended to create a common atrium for the Smithsonian's National Portrait Gallery and American Art Museum; a new auditorium was proposed beneath it.*

TOP LEFT: *A photograph of the south facade of the Old Patent Office on F Street, the principal commercial street of Washington, c. 1869. The original monumental stairway of Robert Mills's design is evident, though it would be demolished in the 1870s when F Street was lowered.*

TOP RIGHT: *The Old Patent Office courtyard in 1968, with its simple landscape of two fountains, lawn panels, and trees, had remained intact for more than a century.*

ABOVE LEFT: *The billowing forms of the courtyard skylight hovering above the historic building as completed in 2007. Although the initial scheme was endorsed by the CFA, the mounded profiles of the skylight structure design were lowered slightly in response to historic preservation concerns.*

ABOVE RIGHT: *Courtyard landscape plan by Gustafson Guthrie Nichol, 2004.*

materials and an emphasis on simplicity, the CFA voted in favor of the concept. In October 2011, the CFA approved a revised design with recommendations to refine the landscape design at the level of the parkway.[64]

NATIONAL PORTRAIT GALLERY AND
SMITHSONIAN AMERICAN ART MUSEUM
RENOVATION

As part of its extensive renovation and restoration of the National Portrait Gallery and the Smithsonian American Art Museum, begun in 2000, the Smithsonian Institution proposed covering the historic open courtyard with a contemporary roof designed by the London architecture firm of Foster & Partners. The gallery and museum were housed in the landmark Old Patent Office, a mid-nineteenth-century Greek Revival government office building by Robert Mills. Located on the slightly elevated block at 7th and F Streets, NW, the building was assigned to the Smithsonian Institution in the early 1960s for use as a museum, which opened to the public in 1968. Plans for the expressive, undulating roof structure were met with enthusiasm by the Commission of Fine Arts. However, questions raised through the historic preservation review process led to mitigation measures that the commission found far less acceptable.

In 2003, the Smithsonian Institution invited seven design firms to submit plans to enclose the courtyard. Foster & Partners won the competition with a warped lattice steel canopy of glass—dubbed a "magic carpet"—that seemed to float over the courtyard without touching the walls of the structure. The goal was to create a flexible, enclosed public space in the courtyard that could serve a variety of uses from catered functions to recitals or educational programs. Associated with the courtyard enclosure project, a new 346-seat auditorium was to be constructed beneath the courtyard, which required its demolition.

When the concept proposal was presented to the commission in June 2004, it generated a warm response from the members, who thought the design was a positive addition to the historic building. David Childs's remarks were representative: "The attitude of this roof, floating over the space…is entirely appropriate…you've been able to separate out this modern piece from something that is a wonderful old building." The members' questions revolved around technical aspects of the project, such as roof drainage; detailing of elements, such as further study of the supporting columns to enhance their sense of lightness; and the control of possible light pollution emanating through the canopy at night. The commission voted for concept approval and looked forward to seeing the project again as the detailing was further developed.[65]

Significantly, the Smithsonian had not completed the mandatory Section 106 review under the National Historic Preservation Act and had demolished the historic courtyard without the necessary approvals. As a result, the NCPC and the District's Historic Preservation Office, under the mandate specified in their preservation review processes, determined that mitigation measures for the enclosure of the courtyard should include reduction of the canopy height and the addition of a new element in the Smithsonian's overall renovation project—the reintroduction of a monumental stone stairway on the F Street facade that had been demolished in the 1930s.

The revised canopy design was presented to the commission for final approval in January 2005. The members found the grace and ethereal quality of the original design somewhat reduced by the lowered height, but their enthusiasm for the project remained, and again they praised it as a welcome addition to Washington. Rather, their comments focused on how the canopy would be accomplished—structural solutions and ventilation—and details such as the color of the stone flooring, treatment of the "service wall" for catering functions and storage, and the level of transparency and color of the roof's glass. The commission requested additional study of these detail items.[66]

The meeting's next agenda item was concept review of the proposed reconstruction of the building's south exterior stair, now required as mitigation for the loss of the historic courtyard. Designed by Hartman-Cox Architects, the scheme replicated a staircase added in the early 1870s when the streets around the building were lowered; the entrance to which the stairs once led, however, would remain closed. The stairway design tried to present a historically accurate duplication of the original stair, with modifications based on grade change and modern code requirements of the Americans with Disabilities Act.[67] The main access to the museum would be through three new entry doors at street level cut into one of the museum's original stone walls.

David Childs noted the dilemma that this posed for the commission: "We want to be constructive in our responsibilities, but we also want to make clear our feelings … leave it alone, is our opinion."[68] The commission found the scheme "unwarranted and inappropriate" for a number of reasons: the CFA considered the building's period of significance earlier than the 1870s; the scheme modified original building material and altered the street grid; and it did not reopen the portico entrance at the top of the reintroduced stairway, creating a confusing message about access to the building. The commission's vote was unanimous against approval of the submission.[69]

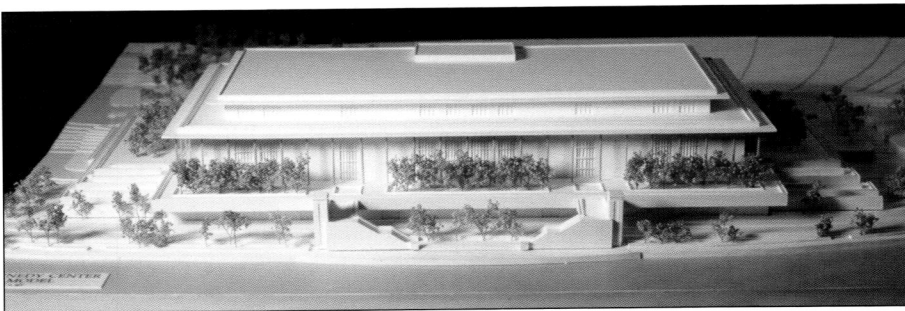

ment actively supported the reestablishment of Washington as a waterfront city. One manifestation of this vision was an access study undertaken with the Federal Highway Administration with the support of the Kennedy Center. Released in 2005, the study supported many of the goals of the Viñoly scheme, including air-rights development, a public plaza, and improved connections to the street grid. The study also continued to emphasize the need for a pedestrian link between the Kennedy Center terrace and the river. By 2007, the District's Department of Transportation, in cooperation with the National Park Service and the Kennedy Center, had engaged KGP Design Studio to revisit the idea of a pedestrian connection between the center's west terrace and the riverfront path leading to Georgetown.

KGP's concept, presented to the CFA in October 2007, reinterpreted the earlier Hartman-Cox diagram of delicate walkways leading to a pair of stairways—but in a modern expression of metal and glass. As in earlier concepts, elevator towers, now articulated in translucent glass, were integrated with the stairs; the stairs were proposed as gradually arcing trusses with glass treads and side panels. The commission was enthusiastic about the design, finding it a graceful complement to the floating quality of the terrace; with some suggestions regarding careful selection of

TOP LEFT: *Arthur Cotton Moore's concept proposed a grand masonry stairway from the Kennedy Center terrace to the Potomac shoreline that was flanked by monumental piers.*

ABOVE LEFT: *The Hartman-Cox concept of 1995 incorporated two narrower flights of stairs turned parallel to*

the river, rather than a single, steeply pitched central stairway.

TOP RIGHT: *The 2003 concept design by Rafael Viñoly for Kennedy Center expansion included decking over highway ramps and creating an enormous elliptical terrace cantilevered above the existing roadway along the river.*

ABOVE: *As part of a larger project of parking and access improvements for the Kennedy Center in 1997, Benjamin Thompson Associates and Sasaki Associates presented another scheme with two curving stairways connecting at a lower plaza.*

In an early design for the Kennedy Center for the Performing Arts, Edward Durell Stone presented an exuberantly curved building, massive in size, with a terrace extended over Rock Creek Parkway to the Potomac River. Later scaled back due to cost, the building was realized as a modernist marble-clad box that retained a western terrace cantilevered over a portion of the parkway but without a connection to the park and pathway along the river's shore. This condition—coupled with the center's isolation from the street grid by highway structures on the east and south—would cause a reexamination of the center's connections to the city and waterfront during the late twentieth and early twenty-first centuries.

A concept presented by Arthur Cotton Moore to the CFA for an informal review in July 1992 extended the center portion of the existing terrace outward as a monumental 250-foot-wide staircase descending to the narrow strip of embankment below. The stairway was bracketed by masonry elevator towers providing vertical access for those pedestrians who could not negotiate the stairs. The CFA members supported a connection between the Kennedy Center and the river, calling it "a good urban amenity," but found the steps themselves too steep and the elevation change inadequately accommodated.[61] Three years later, in October 1995, the Kennedy Center formally submitted a concept design, part of a larger scope to expand parking facilities and renovate the concert hall, by the architecture firms of Hartman-Cox and Quinn Evans. Instead of the grand monumental staircase, however, the new proposal created two narrower flights of stairs parallel to the river, leaving a maximum amount of space along the river's edge. Small elevator towers were integrated with the stairways and connected to the existing terrace with minimal walkways, allowing the terrace's floating character to remain legible. The CFA again expressed support for connecting the center to the river and found that the design respected the building's horizontality without overwhelming it but suggested shifting the base of the stairways slightly toward the river.

In 1997 and 1998, Benjamin Thompson Associates and Sasaki Associates presented concept studies to the CFA for parking expansion and improved approaches to the center that included renderings with a split stairway connection to the river. However, budget constraints prevented the Kennedy Center from including the stairway connection as part of the project.[62]

By 2003, the Kennedy Center hired Rafael Viñoly to develop a plan for the facility's expansion. Viñoly's design pushed development eastward toward the city, adding new buildings on decking over the coils of highway ramps; the Kennedy Center itself would be encircled by an ellipse-shaped terrace connected to a new trumpet-shaped plaza and water feature at the east. The new elliptical terrace on the west would cantilever over the parkway to the river with ramped connections to the embankment. The CFA approved the concept design in February 2003. Although in support of the project, the Federal Highway Administration noted that decking over the federal roadways would be a budget-driven, long-term project; in fact, Congress did not appropriate funding for the project.[63]

In the same period, the District of Columbia govern-

In 2011, the CFA approved a design by KGP Design Studio for a pair of cantilevered stairways, lightly articulated in glass and steel, to connect the floating terrace to the river's edge.

first century, the existing complex was perceived as programmatically obsolete. Concurrent with the city's plans to revitalize the Southwest waterfront, the management of the Arena Stage complex decided to renovate and expand the existing facility. The result—a sensuously sculptural glass, wood, and concrete expression of contemporary architecture—was designed by Bing Thom Architects and reconceived as the Arena Stage at the Mead Center for American Theater, a keystone in the revitalized urbanism of the waterfront.

Under the Shipstead-Luce Act, the project was first reviewed at the CFA's July 2002 meeting, following a site inspection earlier in the day to examine the context and conditions. Thom's concept proposed the two existing theater spaces, the Fichandler and the Kreeger, be joined by a new theater, all under a single curvilinear roof pointing toward the Washington Monument. The three building components, plus related service, administrative, and public spaces beneath the roof, would be wrapped in a glass curtain wall; recycled heavy timbers would support the roof. The CFA members noted the light-filled and transparent treatment of the structure, raising questions about the materials and technology of the singular design. Chairman Harry Robinson's remarks summarized the commission's response:

"[It's] a wonderful jewel box…. I think we're all in love with the project." The concept was approved.[58]

The concept, described by the architect as "three temples on the mount of the Acropolis," was further developed over the next three years, and even as the membership of the commission changed, the response of CFA members remained enthusiastic.[59] In April 2003, the CFA reviewed design refinements that included a tension structure to support the large cantilevered roof and increased roof height. Again, the members' comments focused on more specific elements such as materials and signage. Chairman David Childs described the added height and glass walls as appropriate, adding that he liked the "confusion of inside and outside." Pamela Nelson found the design theatrical, but appropriately so: "It's perfect for what it is… it's going to add so much to the area of town."[60] The members unanimously approved the refinements. The waterfall at Maine Avenue was later deleted due to maintenance concerns and replaced by a ramp with the lettering "Arena Stage" as a supergraphic visible to drivers along Maine Avenue. The final design was approved in September 2005; review of adjustments to the roof profile was delegated to staff and approved in November 2008, and the building was completed in 2010.

The new theater complex, completed in 2010, presents a dramatic swooping roofline along Maine Avenue, SW.

walls be eliminated and the amount of information reduced to avoid "an inappropriate barrage of information in a civic landscape."[116]

In June, a modestly revised version of the proposal returned to the commission, which still found it far too didactic and expansive, "a conflation of a park with a memorial, and a memorial with a park." The commission questioned whether the content of the proposed concept exceeded Congress's original 1882 authorization to "place a statue of Marshall in a public reserve," and therefore needed separate authorization under the Commemorative Works Act.[117]

A more significantly modified concept was presented two years later at the commission's November 2009 meeting; the NPS noted that it was still reviewing the question of congressional authorization. The general layout of the design was similar to the earlier approach, but the didactic material had been halved. The walls were still arranged to form "rooms," but were now granite instead of glass, and the commemorative column had been simplified and shortened. The commission members suggested ways to reduce the "general heaviness of the design" and voted to approve the revised concept.[118]

DWIGHT D. EISENHOWER MEMORIAL

At the end of the decade, the design of the Dwight D. Eisenhower Memorial presented a new discussion about photographic images in commemoration, incorporated new technology and materials, and raised questions about appropriate scale and urban placemaking. In 2006, the NCPC and CFA approved the four acres south of Independence Avenue between 4th and 6th Streets, SW, abutting the Department of Education building, for the memorial. In November 2008, the National Park Service and the Dwight D. Eisenhower Memorial Commission gave an information presentation to the CFA on a design program that tentatively called for the closing of Maryland Avenue, which diagonally bisected the parcel. The Eisenhower Memorial Commission recognized that its memorial would be the first presidential memorial in the twenty-first century and sought to sponsor a design that honored three themes in Eisenhower's life: military leadership, the presidency, and his role as public servant. The CFA recommended developing a design that emphasized a single theme, avoided adding elements to the program over time, and enhanced the urban context. The Commission of Fine Arts drew a parallel between the proposed memorial site and London's Trafalgar Square—which commemorates the 1805 Battle of Trafalgar and incorporates a memorial to Admiral Horatio Nelson—suggesting that, the com-

memorative element occur within a spatial composition that acknowledged the urban quality of the site.[119]

The Los Angeles-based architecture firm Gehry Partners with the landscape firm EDAW (now AECOM) won the multistage design competition. Frank Gehry and members of the design team made an information presentation of the three initial design concepts to the CFA in May 2010. Of the three concepts, the scheme preferred by the memorial commission and the design team included colossal columns defining a plaza; Gehry said that grain silos near Eisenhower's childhood home had been the source of inspiration. Gehry also drew inspiration from the work of artist Chuck Close to propose sixty-foot-tall metal "tapestries" supported by the columns to form a backdrop to the space, demarcating it from the Department of Education building. Composed of woven stainless steel wires, the tapestries would reinterpret, at great scale, black-and-white photographs portraying aspects of Eisenhower's life. The largest of the tapestries would measure about five hundred feet long, with their tops about eighty feet above the ground. All three schemes shared the idea of a central contemplative garden space with an undetermined grouping of abstract sculptural elements, quotations, and a small water feature.

The CFA expressed general support for the design but recommended further study of the relationships among the elements and the closed fragment of Maryland Avenue. Several members brought up the scale of the columns, cautioning that their relationship with the smaller elements within the garden had to be carefully analyzed. However, Michael McKinnell countered with strong support for the idea, which he found to be "something quite incredible because…it is like the absence of the presence of the building that could have been there." Elizabeth Plater-Zyberk agreed: "This is a site which is surrounded by what we have had named in other parts of Washington 'overly resolved' buildings. I think it actually establishes a sense of place because these columns are in the scale of those large buildings. So in a place where you might think it would be hopeless to do that, I think you succeeded." The discussion of the tapestries themselves focused on their expressive qualities rather than the images upon them or their technical feasibility. Commission members also suggested simplifying the number of elements in the design and further consideration of perimeter security, street configurations, and the impact of weather on the design elements.[120]

The project returned to the commission in January 2011 for concept design approval of the column-tapestry scheme. Adjustments had been made to the number of columns, but much of the design study had centered on the

ABOVE LEFT: *Site of the proposed Dwight D. Eisenhower National Memorial within the existing context of federal office and museum buildings in 2008; the memorial site would encompass a portion of Maryland Avenue.*

ABOVE RIGHT: *The January 1963 issue of* Architectural Forum, *a special issue on Washington, D.C., included an article by architect Paul Rudolph in which he proposed a "Madison Gateway" to Maryland Avenue, SW, using monumental columns (noted as C).*

ABOVE CENTER: *Model by Gehry Partners of one of the initial alternative design concepts for the memorial, which comprised a central plaza defined by monumental columns, 2010.*

ABOVE: *Model of the 2010 preferred design concept by Gehry Partners that located the monumental columns on the long sides of the site; most of the columns would be linked with mesh screen* "tapestries" *depicting images from Eisenhower's life as the Allied forces general and U.S. president.*

LEFT: *Frank Gehry presenting his memorial designs to the CFA in May 2010 in the reconfigured meeting room. Seated (from left): Thomas Luebke (secretary), Elizabeth Plater-Zyberk, Diana Balmori, John Belle, and Chairman Earl A. Powell III; with Vice Chairman Pamela Nelson, Michael McKinnell, and Witold Rybczynski partially hidden at right.*

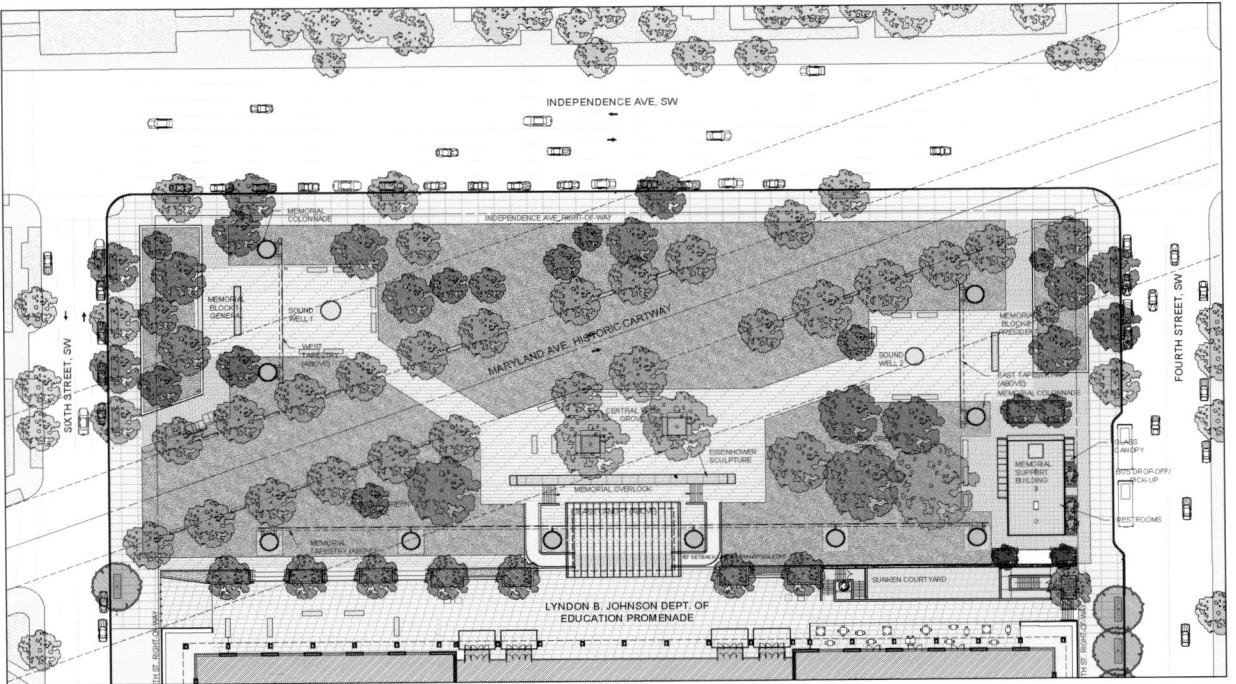

LEFT CENTER: *In September 2011, Gehry revised the design with fewer columns arranged along three sides of the site, framing the alignment of Maryland Avenue. The site plan illustrates the greensward through the site along the avenue's axis with memorial elements at the center adjacent to the Department of Education and a service building on the southeastern corner of the site.*

LEFT BOTTOM: *Model of Gehry's revised design of September 2011 illustrates the columns and tapestries—now depicting the landscape of Eisenhower's boyhood home in Abilene, Kansas—defining a central space encompassing lawn, trees, and memorial elements.*

TOP: *View of the 2011 concept design model looking toward the Capitol, with the eighty-foot-high columns framing the axis of Maryland Avenue.*

ABOVE: *Gehry Partners proposed this composite photograph of the Kansas landscape with Eisenhower's childhood home as the subject for the metal tapestries.*

RIGHT: *Mock-ups of the stainless steel tapestries with images from the Kansas landscape were presented to the CFA in September 2011 and demonstrated the mesh material's transparency during daytime and nighttime conditions.*

expressive quality and technical details of the tapestries. These also became the focus of the commission's discussion, as did the choice of photographic imagery to depict. There was agreement among the members that the scale of the proposed tapestries posed the risk of creating billboards rather than a memorial. Of the photographs suggested, they found the Kansas landscape of Eisenhower's boyhood the most evocative but urged the designers to consider less literal depictions, possibly even a commissioned work of art. They also suggested studying deleting the tapestries altogether or reducing their number, along with adjustments to the arrangement of the columns and refinement of the landscape design. However, while the commission members raised concerns about the tapestries, they found much that they liked, such as the use and scale of the columns to define the space and the central memorial, whose elements were becoming more focused. Michael McKinnell suggested that the colossal scale of the columns was an appropriate design for a memorial:

[T]here is an issue conceptually as to whether or not the definition of a place can constitute a memorial. I think that you prove with this that it can…. But, obviously, you know, you will make it work…. I am not worried about that because, if I can be facetious, the tapestry, when you and I are long since gone, will disintegrate and the columns will be left and it will be like Paestum and it will be marvelous.[121]

The commission voted to approve the preliminary concept, endorsing "the proposed combination of large-scale gestures to capture the overall site."[122]

TOP: *Rendering of memorial elements at the center of the revised memorial show the introduction of photographic images translated as relief images in stone panels; a white statue of Eisenhower as a youth was proposed on the rear wall of the memorial plaza level.*

CLOCKWISE FROM ABOVE LEFT. *Photographic source material for the various sculptural elements depicting Eisenhower proposed within the memorial: as a young man, c. 1904, was the inspiration for the solitary sculpture on the wall; as "The Elder Statesman" photographed by Yousuf Karsh, 1966; as general and supreme commander of Allied forces in Europe during the D-Day invasion, June 6, 1944.*

In September 2011, Frank Gehry returned to the CFA with a modified concept design that included significant changes addressing the commission members' previous comments. Instead of the proscenium-like configuration, the design team had altered the placement of the columns and tapestries on the edges of the site's three sides to suggest an urban room, and the side panels were slightly offset from one another to frame the diagonal alignment of Maryland Avenue. Responding to concerns made in the multiagency historic preservation regulatory review, the line of columns on the south side of the site had been reduced in length to improve the visibility of the Department of Education building's corners. While the diameter of the columns had been reduced, Gehry explained he had decided not to lower their height to avoid weakening their relationship to the relatively uniform height of nearby buildings.

The design of the tapestries had also advanced: the team had developed different technologies for creating the woven metal tapestry panels mounted twenty feet above the plaza, each roughly sixty feet tall and spanning seventy-six feet between the columns. Mock-ups of three different techniques were erected on the future memorial site and were viewed by the commission prior to the meeting. Gehry said he had initially preferred a Jacquard-type weaving method, but now found it unsatisfactory because he couldn't achieve the transparency he desired. Instead, he was trying to develop a handwoven technique of applied diagonal weft derived from Renaissance-era etching. Diana Balmori commented that the horizon line would constitute the most powerful feature, continuing across all three tapestries and unifying the design elements. She said the mock-ups had demonstrated that the handwoven stainless steel alternative gave the best transparency combined with a complex appearance when seen up close. However, she cautioned that the image of the Kansas landscape might resemble the realism of a photograph and recommended that its appearance be more interpretive as a work of art.

Balmori also emphasized the importance of creating an appropriate design for the central area to achieve an overall coherence for the memorial. The design team explained that the intent of using the tapestries was to create a garden in a temple, rather than the more usual temple in a garden; an informal allée of sycamore trees would define Maryland Avenue's diagonal alignment through the site, and other areas would have an informal, romantic character. At the center of the memorial, Gehry said, the design team had sought to present the "essence" of Eisenhower, focusing on the president's combination of modesty and powerful leadership: he proposed a "very modest memorial," a park

defined with a backdrop of Eisenhower's boyhood landscape from Abilene, Kansas. He added that ways of incorporating representations of Eisenhower as a military leader and as president—whether through bas-reliefs or other techniques—were still being considered with the aim of creating a single, unified memorial experience. The centerpiece could be a relatively small sculpture of Eisenhower as a boy. Balmori commented that she thought the design "is going in a good direction. It depends a lot on what happens in that center piece. You know, it sort of has a lot of the whole story put together. So, in a way, the comments should wait until then."[123]

The commission voted to approve the concept with its comments, specifically requesting further definition of the central elements of the memorial's design. Michael McKinnell concluded the discussion:

[T]he space achieves, in my view, an autonomy now that it didn't have before…. I think, in a curious way, this will be actually not overly monumental but actually a very gentle intrusion, intervention, into Washington with this scrim. I think it is absolutely magical. [124]

By the beginning of 2012, however, public criticism emerged regarding the Gehry design: many opinions were against the scale of the monument; others found the proposed focus on Eisenhower's youth as the thematic lens for the future leader's career to be inappropriate; still others found the aesthetic qualities of the metal-mesh tapestries evocative of imprisoning fences. In a congressional subcommittee hearing on March 20, 2012, Susan Eisenhower, the former president's granddaughter, testified, criticizing the memorial design as relying "on a romantic Horatio Alger notion, a young Eisenhower viewing his future career." Advocates of a classical design for the memorial suggested that the Eisenhower Memorial Commission's selection of the designer through a qualifications-based process managed by the GSA instead of an open competition was inappropriate for a national memorial. Witold Rybczynski addressed many of these comments in an editorial published in the *New York Times*:

Ever since the Vietnam Veterans Memorial competition was won by Maya Lin, then a college student, it is taken for granted that the best memorial designs are the result of open competitions, in which hundreds of (largely unqualified) individuals compete. But the accepted wisdom is wrong—the Vietnam Veterans Memorial is an exception. It's worth remembering that the Lincoln Memorial was the result of a competition between only two young architects—Henry Bacon and John Russell Pope—and the loser, Pope, was later invited to design the Jefferson Memorial; no one else was invited.

Presidential memorials take a long time to come to fruition—the Lincoln Memorial took more than 12 years—and the design team will continue refining its design for the Eisenhower memorial. Mr. Gehry, our finest living architect, has already shown himself willing to listen

As part of the controversy over Gehry's design, the National Civic Art Society held an Eisenhower Memorial counterproposal design competition in 2011. The winning entry by Daniel W. Cook featured a classical triumphal arch flanked by two colossal columns topped by allegorical figures.

Urban Memorials under the Commemorative Works Act

I n addition to the larger memorials in Washington's monumental core, the CFA also reviewed proposals for memorials that were submitted to it under the Commemorative Works Act during the first ten years of the new century. These memorials have typically been devoted to international subjects, often commemorating political figures or victims of repressive political regimes. Although located outside the central Mall precinct on relatively small urban parcels, the commemorative messages are amplified by sites situated at prominent intersections with good pedestrian accessibility and visual connections to related memorials or landmarks. The memorial designs have focused on a single statue or sculptural work within a plaza, which the CFA has supported for simplicity and appropriateness.

The memorial to Tomáš Masaryk (2002), the first president of an independent Czechoslovakia following the demise of the Austro-Hungarian Empire in 1918, is located on a triangle of land at the intersection of Q Street and Florida and Massachusetts Avenues, NW, diagonally across from the Gandhi Memorial. It is also near the home of President Woodrow Wilson, who had supported the creation of a free Czechoslovakia during the peace talks that ended World War I. The central element of the memorial is a sculpture of Masaryk cast in 1968 from the model of a 1937 work by Vincenc Makovský. Like the Gandhi statue, the Masaryk piece had already been completed, limiting the CFA's review to the site and its landscaping. The commission recommended a rectilinear rather than a curved site design and a base height for the statue that would make it more easily visible to pedestrians.

The Victims of Communism Memorial (2007) features *Democracy,* a bronze sculpture by Thomas Marsh, adapted from the temporary papier-mâché *Goddess of Democracy* erected by students during the 1989 Tiananmen Square uprising in Beijing, which was itself modeled after *Liberty Enlightening the World* by Frédéric Bartholdi, known more familiarly as the Statue of Liberty. The CFA unanimously approved the memorial's site at the intersection of Massachusetts and New Jersey Avenues, NW, with its visual relationship to the Capitol and the Statue of Freedom by Thomas Crawford atop the dome, and later approved the concept design with support for its appropriateness.

The Memorial to the Victims of the Ukrainian Holodomor of 1932–1933 commemorates the 10 million Ukrainians who starved to death during Josef Stalin's campaign of subjugation to Soviet rule. The CFA first approved the memorial's location at the intersection of Massachusetts Avenue and North Capitol and F Streets, one block from the Victims of Communism Memorial, in September 2008 for its high visibility and minimal impact to adjacent property owners. The concept design—a six-foot tall, bronze bas-relief titled *Field of Wheat* by Ukranian American architect and designer Larysa Kurylas and mounted on a low granite plinth set by a slate plaza—was endorsed by the CFA in October 2011 from among the several alternatives presented; the commission recommended improving the setting of the panel within the context of street trees and sight lines.

TOP LEFT: *The memorial to Tomáš Masaryk, designed by* EDAW *and completed in 2002, includes a casting of a 1937 sculpture by Vincenc Makovský of the first president of the independent state of Czechoslovakia.*

TOP RIGHT: Democracy *by sculptor Thomas Marsh, based on the papier-mâché* Goddess of Democracy *erected at the 1989 Tiananmen Square uprising in Beijing, is the central element of the Victims of Communism Memorial, completed in 2007.*

ABOVE: *The 2011 concept design by the Larysa Kurylas Studio with Hartman-Cox Architects for the Memorial to the Victims of the Ukranian Holodomor features* Field of Wheat *as the focal sculptural element commemorating the starvation of millions of Ukranians in the 1930s.*

to critical suggestions. But in this case, too many cooks will definitely spoil the broth. Compromise and consensus are important when devising legislation, but they are a poor recipe for creating a memorial.[125]

In the spring of 2012, preliminary review of the proposal by the NCPC was postponed into the summer, although the regulatory issues of historic preservation and environmental impact had progressed to resolution of the necessary agreements. While the Eisenhower Memorial Commission and Gehry were reportedly revising the design to address the concerns of the Eisenhower family, the critical issue remained to resolve the memorial's proposed artistic conception with symbolic and narrative content. Unlike the Martin Luther King Jr. National Memorial, the tightly defined metaphoric theme of which was focused on a central sculpture, Gehry's Eisenhower Memorial design presented a more particular artistic idea—the urban tapestries—which proved to require the accommodation of a more explicit story in order to achieve public support.

Coins and Medals in the New Century

For most of the twentieth century, the commemorative role of American coin design followed a traditional focus on political leaders and allegorical figures representing abstract ideals. Beginning in the 1980s, the range of subject matter expanded to include subjects such as women, historical events, and even buildings and landscapes. Likewise, the number of commemorative coins and medals authorized by Congress had increased substantially: between 1990 and 2010, seventy-eight commemorative coins were produced by the U.S. Mint; the number of Congressional Gold Medals, created to honor humanitarian and artistic achievement, soared from four or five per decade for most of its history to an average of almost twenty in the 1980s, 1990s, and 2000s.[126] In fact, Congress passed the Commemorative Coin Reform Act in 1996 to address these issues, limiting the production of commemoratives to two per year and establishing the Citizens Commemorative Coin Advisory Committee—renamed the Citizens Coinage Advisory Committee (CCAC) in 2003—to advise on thematic, technical, and design issues related to the production of coins. Just as with physical memorials, new typologies and artistic approaches emerged around the century's end, creating a new paradigm in numismatic design characterized by a mingling of traditional symbolism with didactic content and the production of images derived directly from photography and mediated by new graphic technologies.

The most visible—and arguably most successful—commemorative production of the U.S. Mint, the 50 State

Quarters Program, was authorized in the late 1990s and would continue through 2008. Producing five coins each year by order of each state's admission into the Union, the Mint presented multiple designs for review by the Commission of Fine Arts as well as the CCAC and the governor of each state. The designs presented in the earlier years of the series, notably those for Delaware, Connecticut, and Maryland, are generally simpler and more iconic in their compositions. Following the initial success of the program, many later designs became more complex, reflecting a wider level of public interest and desire for the representation of multiple constituencies; examples include the multiple elements evident in the quarters for Florida, Wisconsin, and Arkansas. In the later years of the program, coins created for Western states often depicted characteristic landscape elements—such as the Grand Canyon for Arizona and the Front Range of the Rockies for Colorado—that were difficult to represent legibly at the scale of a quarter-dollar coin. In its reviews, the CFA questioned the appropriateness of trying to tell complex stories in the small space available on a coin and, given that complexity, the quality of the coins' design.

A similar challenge began in 2009 with the America the Beautiful Quarters Program series: national parks and natural sites from all fifty states—typically monumental landscapes—would be represented on an area smaller than one square inch. Based on the popular success of the 50 State Quarters Program, the U.S. Mint was authorized to continue collectible circulating coins that would, by virtue of the language in their authorization by Congress, favor complex narratives. In fact, the traditional commemorative role of numismatics may be seen as being eclipsed by didactic purposes: for example, the Mint's Web site provided lesson plans for teachers based on the narrative content of the coins. Inevitably, the response to accommodating multiple roles has resulted in coin design favoring ever more complex compositions.

Presidential commemoration also became an important theme in the designs produced by the U.S. Mint in the first decade of the century with a series of coins portraying the presidents and the first ladies. In 2005, President Bush signed the Presidential One Dollar Coin Act of 2005, ostensibly to introduce popular coins for low value transactions, public transportation, and parking meters—as well as to educate the public about American history. The act included provisions for one-dollar presidential coins, First Spouse bullion coins and medals, and the Abraham Lincoln Bicentennial one-cent coin redesign. Beginning in January 2007, the Mint began the development of a one-dollar coin for circulation for each

America the Beautiful Quarters Program series, Chaco Culture National Historic Park (New Mexico), reverse, 2012. The image presents a complex juxtaposition of human construction, landscape, and geoglogic elements.

president beginning with George Washington. The distribution of four presidents per year would serve as an educational tool and as a means to increase demand for the coins. A portrait of the president would be represented on the obverse, and all coins would incorporate an image of the Statue of Liberty on the reverse. The noncirculating bullion coins and medals for first ladies were issued in conjunction with their husband's coin. The obverse depicted an image of the first spouse, and the reverse reflected a narrative representing an aspect of her life, sometimes based on scant biographical information.

The commission typically found the design quality of these coins lacking in simplicity, too often based on photographic images that were overly complex for the coins' size, or reliant on full or three-quarters facial views rather than the more traditional profile. The First Spouse reverses were found to be problematic in that they did not present meaningful information that might differentiate the subject from other first spouses—all within the context of the face of a coin. However, the presidential coin series, except for a small production of collector's editions, was discontinued in 2011 by Congress, which cited a lack of sales of the coins as evidence of waning public interest in the program.

Commemorative efforts in the new century also led to the redesign of a coin that many viewed as iconic—the Lincoln penny—although it had already been modified several times over the last one hundred years. The redesign

ABOVE: *Presidential One Dollar Coin, Franklin Pierce, obverse, 2010. A three-quarters view, rather than the more traditional profile, is used for the presidential portrait.*

BELOW, LEFT AND RIGHT: *First Spouse Gold Coins, Julia Tyler, obverse and reverse, 2009. In accordance with the Mint's didactic and source requirements for the coin series, a frontal view portrait of Julia Tyler on the obverse and the presidential couple dancing on the reverse replace more traditional compositions and symbolic representations typically seen in coinage.*

of the one-cent coin, the first American coinage to show a portrait of a historic figure, was initiated to commemorate the bicentennial of Lincoln's birth in 2009. The original one-cent coin featuring an Indian head was issued from 1859 to 1909; President Theodore Roosevelt had selected medallic designer Victor Brenner's profile of Lincoln for the obverse of the redesigned penny to celebrate the centennial of Lincoln's birth, and the reverse featured a bundle of wheat. In honor of the sesquicentennial of Lincoln's birth in 1959, the reverse was redesigned with an image of the Lincoln Memorial. The 2005 legislation called for the Mint to issue the one-cent coin with four reverse designs representing different periods of Lincoln's life, while the relief on the obverse would continue to reflect Brenner's profile of the president.

The commission evaluated five designs for the period from Lincoln's birth through his early years in Kentucky, ten designs for his formative years in Indiana, sixteen designs for his professional years in Illinois, and seven designs for his presidency in Washington, D.C. In general, the commission members selected a building for the reverse designs, such as the cabin of his frontier upbringing and the Capitol dome under construction to represent his presidential years. The Citizens Coinage Advisory Com-

mittee rejected the Capitol dome design, and thus the Mint returned to the commission in January 2008 with seventeen additional alternatives. The commission reiterated its support for the unfinished dome, but acknowledged that an image of the completed dome might be more legible. When the Mint submitted revised designs the following month, however, none represented a completed dome, and all but one included the figure of Lincoln, which the commission had earlier said was redundant with Lincoln's portrait on the obverse. The commission found it "regrettable" that the Mint did not return with a design that was appropriately scaled or clearer and more thoughtful in its narrative.[127] Instead, the Mint produced a shield and scroll design for the reverse derived from a Civil War–era decorative design.

The commission's frustration with the poor design extended to other commemorative coins as well; in review after review, the members continued to urge simplicity of expression and better design. Following a presentation by the U.S. Mint for the Medal of Honor Commemorative Coin Program, the United States Army Commemorative Coin Program, the one-dollar silver coin, and the half-dollar clad coin to the commission in May 2010, the members again found the lack of artistic merit so disappointing that

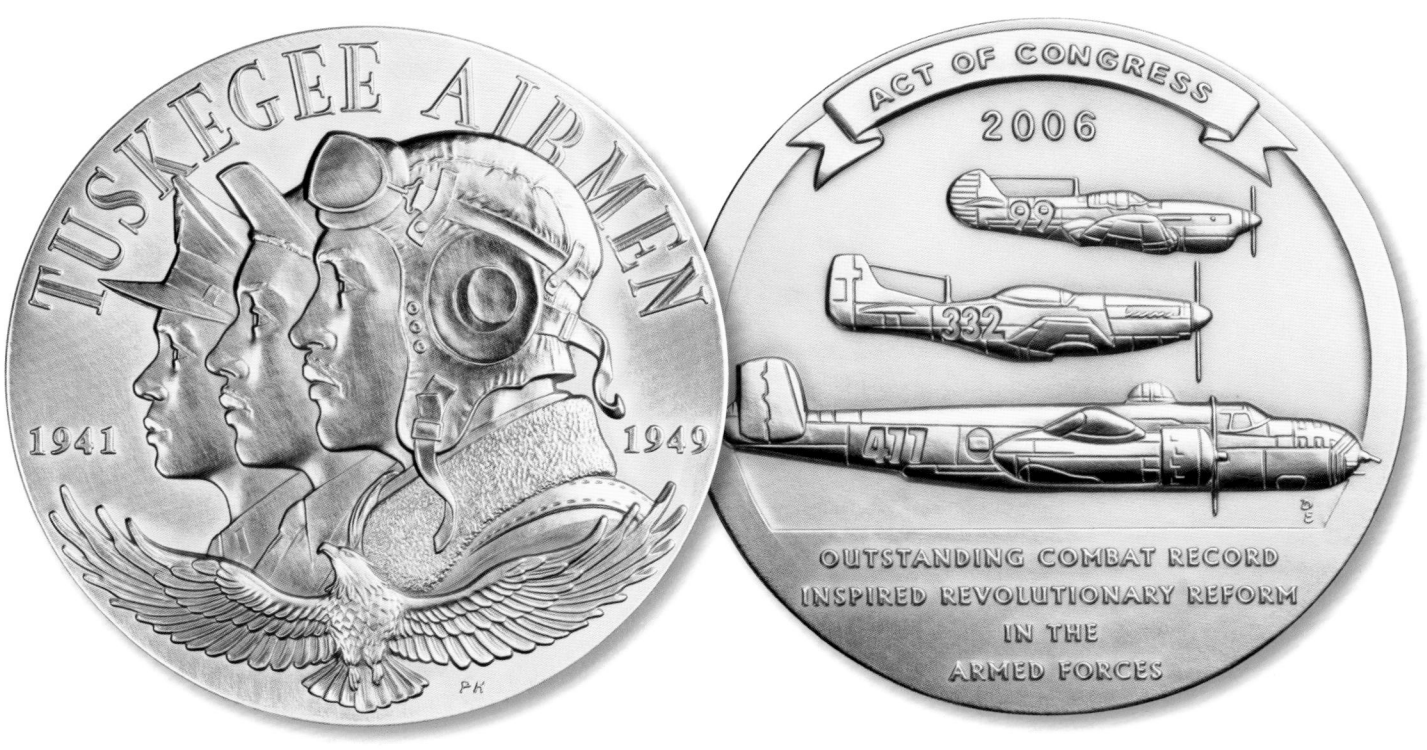

ABOVE, LEFT AND RIGHT: *Congressional Gold Medal, Tuskegee Airmen, obverse and reverse, 2006. The obverse features three figures in profile,* *a traditional approach to commemorative portraiture; the reverse was simplified to focus on the three airplanes and the inscription.*

ABOVE, LEFT AND RIGHT: *Congressional Gold Medal, Dr. Norman E. Borlaug, obverse and reverse, 2007. The CFA recommended a simple, iconic treatment of the* *humanitarian subject on the obverse and a full version of the quotation presented on the reverse.*

they did not recommend any of the designs for the half-dollar and one-dollar silver coins. In a letter to the Mint summarizing the commission's review, Secretary Luebke reported that the CFA members had emphasized that

coins and medals should distill the subject to its essence, rather than present a confusing collage of multiple elements…[and] the importance of treating the obverse and reverse as a unified design…. The U.S. Mint should approach the design process as the creation of small pieces of sculpture held in the hand.[128]

Congressional Gold Medals—the highest civilian honor award program, active since the American Revolution, which honors national achievement in patriotic, humanitarian, and artistic endeavors—had also evolved with new subjects and artistic styles. One example is the Tuskegee Airmen Congressional Gold Medal, reviewed by the CFA in September 2006. The commission supported the classic composition showing three airmen in profile view on the obverse, and they advised refining the awkward rendering of a cloud on the reverse because it detracted from the portrayal of three airplanes; the cloud was eliminated from the design. The following year, the commission considered the Mint's design for a Congressional Gold Medal commemorating Dr. Norman E. Borlaug, American agronomist and winner of the Nobel Peace Prize, whose development of improved strains of wheat is credited with

saving more than a billion lives worldwide. Borlaug is depicted on the obverse standing before a field of wheat; the commission recommended providing a defined border to contain the image from the edge of the coin. For the reverse, which portrayed a pair of hands with the globe and stalks of wheat, it advised that the hands be redrawn to appear to hold the world as well as the wheat, instead of having all fingers visible. The CFA also recommended modifying the inscription on the reverse from a fragmentary quotation made by Borlaug into a complete sentence. Of these, only the last change was made.

Security, Sustainability, and Preservation: Design Issues in Federal Office Development

By the end of the twentieth century, the designs of federal office properties reviewed by the commission reflected a new mix of concerns that would have been unimaginable by the architects of the Beaux-Arts period or even the mid-century modernists and were dominated by three overwhelming issues: security, preservation, and sustainability. Added to these components were the remarkable advances of the General Services Administration, begun in the 1990s to revive design quality for federal buildings, that yielded numerous examples of high-quality architecture

President Barack Obama signed Executive Order 13514 on October 5, 2009, which established sustainability goals for federal properties, including increased energy efficiency, decreased greenhouse emissions, and more efficient water use. Standing behind President Obama (from left): CEQ Chairman Nancy Sutley, Assistant Secretary of the Treasury Dan Tangherlini, OMB Deputy Director Jeffrey Zients, GSA Public Buildings Administrator Robert Peck, Secretary of Energy Steven Chu, and EPA Administrator Lisa Jackson.

Higher standards of design quality established by the GSA, as well as new sustainability goals and a focus on security, have influenced new federal building design nationwide; many federal buildings have been recognized for outstanding design. For several decades, the majority of the GSA's new building construction has been to accommodate security-related, law enforcement, and judicial functions.

TOP: *Wayne Lyman Morse U.S. Courthouse, Eugene, Oregon, by Morphosis, 2006.*

LEFT: *U.S. Land Port of Entry, Warroad, Minnesota, by Julie Snow Architects, 2010.*

TOP: *Model of the concept design for the Bureau of Alcohol, Tobacco, Firearms and Explosives headquarters by Moshe Safdie & Associates, 2002. The office portions of the building are protected from blast threat by a massive curved "garden wall"; windows are minimized to vertical slots on the outward-facing elevations.*

ABOVE: *As built in 2008, the curving monumental wall of the law enforcement agency complex presents a large-scale sculptural gesture at the intersection of New York Avenue and 1st Street, NE, a threshold of entry to Washington's historic L'Enfant core.*

nationally, particularly in new courthouse buildings, which generally embraced a neomodern expression.

Increasingly, these three components became integrated into the review process, requiring significantly greater involvement of the CFA staff who participated actively in interagency regulatory meetings for new projects as legally defined consulting parties under the processes stipulated by the National Environmental Protection Act (NEPA) and Section 106 of the National Historic Preservation Act. In 2010 alone, CFA staff members participated individually in 148 NEPA and Section 106 meetings for projects submitted by the federal government, a 40 percent increase from the previous year.[129] Much of the increase in meetings associated with federal buildings at the end of the decade, such as the St. Elizabeths campus redevelopment, may be explained by the simultaneous funding of "shovel-ready" projects under the American Reinvestment and Recovery Act (ARRA) of 2009.

BUREAU OF ALCOHOL, TOBACCO, FIREARMS AND EXPLOSIVES HEADQUARTERS

A prominent example of security-dominated design was the General Services Administration's proposal for a new headquarters for the Bureau of Alcohol, Tobacco, Firearms and Explosives, submitted to the commission for concept review in November 2001. The five-acre site was located at the intersection of Florida and New York Avenues, NE. Although deteriorated, the neighborhood held a high potential for redevelopment, encouraged by the New York Avenue Metro station to be constructed across from the site. The area's appearance also marred the experience of New York Avenue—a principal access route—as a gateway into the city.

The project, designed by the Boston architectural firm of Moshe Safdie & Associates, required the highest level of security, including one-hundred-foot setbacks from the property line. This requirement posed a significant urban design challenge: how to avoid the incongruous and anti-urban configuration of a building in the center of a site surrounded by open space. Safdie's approach included focusing the building toward the Metro entrance and adjacent proposed development and creating an urban edge using an eighteen-foot-high curved "garden wall" demarcating a landscaped park and retail space beyond which the building was set back. The program was distributed into a crescent-shaped building with a glazed atrium of clear security glass, allowing natural light into much of the structure. The natural grade of the site was incorporated into the security plan to reduce the need for perimeter fencing. There were few questions from the commission at the meeting, mostly for clarification regarding plant materials for the green roof, an element of the concept that was not ultimately built. The CFA members were enthusiastic about the design, found the security requirements deftly handled, and commended the GSA for a design that would help to catalyze redevelopment in the neighborhood.[130] The concept was unanimously approved; the building was completed in 2008.

ADDITIONS TO FEDERAL BUILDINGS

The government's portfolio of existing twentieth-century buildings within the monumental core posed particular challenges in improving security and adapting facilities to contemporary program needs. The William B. Bryant Annex to the E. Barrett Prettyman Federal Courthouse, designed by a joint venture of Michael Graves & Associates and Smith Group, provided additional courtrooms and other spaces for the Prettyman Courthouse, a building at Pennsylvania and Constitution Avenues designed by Louis

Justement and completed in 1952. Justement's design expressed a modernist vocabulary influenced by the earlier stripped classicism of the 1930s. The Graves design team, selected through the GSA's Design Excellence Program, first came before the commission in March 1998 in an informational presentation. The team showed three schemes for the annex, which would be located across Pennsylvania Avenue from the East Building of the National Gallery of Art and with a direct view of the U.S. Capitol. Each scheme included an atrium that connected but also clearly differentiated the annex from the older building.

Of the three schemes, the commission favored one incorporating a circular element at Pennsylvania Avenue—referred to as the rotunda—for the strong urban design relationships it established with other buildings in the monumental core: it echoed the curved element of the Federal Trade Commission as the apex of Federal Triangle, complemented the angular expression of the East Building, and

ABOVE: *View of the William B. Bryant Annex to the E. Barrett Prettyman Federal Courthouse by Michael Graves & Associates, completed in 2005, includes a low cylindrical form facing Pennsylvania Avenue and barrel-vaulted pavilions clad in a wide range of color and materials along 3rd Street, NW.*

LEFT: *A series of bas-relief panels by sculptor Mark Lineweaver were proposed for the annex's upper pavilions in 2000, intending to integrate artwork into the architecture; the designs comprised heroic human figures struggling with abstract rectangular masses to represent the citizens' relationship to the law. Noting*

the ambiguity of the message imparted by the proposal, the CFA did not approve the sculptures.

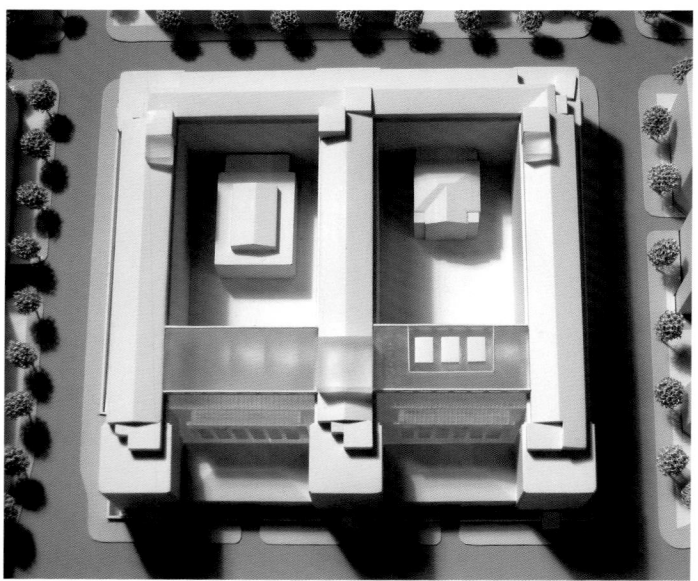

TOP: *Rendering of the 2010 revised concept design for the* GSA *headquarters illustrating the glass and steel infill structure and the addition of retail space at the street level.*

ABOVE LEFT: *Plan view of a study model of the 2005 concept design by Shalom Baranes Architects for an addition to the original 1917 building*

and GSA *headquarters, which inserted a new glassy structure between the building's masonry wings.*

ABOVE RIGHT: *The 2009 concept design for a proposed addition to the Martin annex of the Federal Reserve System headquarters by Karn, Charuhas, Chapman & Twohey encloses most of the original*

building's ground-level support pylons and extends out from the building on three sides to accommodate conference areas.

framed the existing Prettyman Courthouse.[131] The Graves design also referred to the classical influences in Justement's design, with the subtle inclusion of security elements such as blast-proof and bulletproof glass and a metal panel system into the building's bright material palette of white, red, and green.[132] This scheme evolved as the preferred option and, with refinements, was approved at the concept and later stages by the commission. The annex was completed in 2005 with significant perimeter security elements along its street frontage.

The proposed renovation and addition to the William McChesney Martin Jr. building of the Federal Reserve System presented the more difficult problem of how to modify a modernist design so highly resolved in expression it left few options for change. The original Federal Reserve System headquarters at 20th Street and Constitution Avenue, NW—the Marriner S. Eccles Federal Reserve Board building—was designed by Paul Cret in the stripped classical art deco mode and was completed in 1937. A little less than three decades later, Harbeson, Hough, Livingston & Larson was commissioned in 1962 to design the Martin annex across C Street from the Eccles building, a flat-roofed modernist white box atop pilotis punctuated by a deeply recessed grid of windows and further raised six feet above the street on a podium. Construction was delayed because of national economic conditions, and the building was finally dedicated in 1974.[133]

Upgraded security requirements and the need for additional meeting space led to proposed changes to the Martin building by 2009. The design by Karn, Charuhas, Chapman & Twohey added a new visitor screening facility on the south side of the annex, which also would serve the Eccles building, and two conference center pavilions on the east and west sides of the existing building. The additions would be largely glass, but would include stone cladding and a heavy roofline. Most of the space between the pilotis would be filled in. When they first reviewed the concept for approval in July 2009, the members acknowledged the difficulty inherent in adding to a modernist building but found the design presented particularly unsympathetic to the existing annex. They suggested ways to mitigate closing in the pilotis, expressing the pavilions as purer glass boxes, and emphasizing verticality. The more minimalist revised concept reviewed at the September meeting continued to raise concerns about the relationships between the existing and new; Elizabeth Plater-Zyberk remarked that the addition resembled "drawers" coming out from beneath the building.[134] The commission encouraged further refinement, such as inserting the additions below the podium and drawing on the expressive white masonry frame of the existing building. A third attempt at revision was presented in November 2009; certain of the commission's suggestions such as developing below the podium had been examined and proved unfeasible. The compromise scheme, which the commission approved, treated the additions as three distinct pavilions rather than extensions of the existing building, further distinguished from it by polished granite spandrels that referenced the Eccles building.[135]

The issues of preservation, security, and design quality were also prominent in the modernization and expansion of the GSA's headquarters building at 1800 F Street, NW. The existing building, a massive E-shaped, masonry, Beaux-

Arts structure spanning the block between E and F Streets, NW, and 18th and 19th Streets, NW, was constructed in 1917 for the Department of the Interior; the E Street facade on the south side of the building faced Rawlins Park, an underused amenity in the area. The proposal to insert 100,000 square feet of new office space within the courtyards was first presented to the commission in February 2005. The design by Shalom Baranes expressed the infill in a glass and steel structure articulated in a transparent, modernist vocabulary inserted between the existing masonry wings, with the glass facade echoing the rhythm of the fenestration in the historic building. An existing small secondary entry in the center of the south facade would be expanded and a lobby inserted to emphasize this entrance, with an atrium incorporated into the new infill segments if funding allowed. Although the addition differed drastically from the vocabulary of the original, the CFA found that its design respected the historic building and approved the concept as the correct approach.[136]

Rendering of the 2011 concept design of the U.S. State Department Diplomacy Center by Beyer Blinder Belle. Inserted into the forecourt of the original State Department building, the largely transparent addition engages the street and incorporates security screening as well as exhibition space and visitor services.

Five years later, in June 2010, the courtyard infill design received final approval from the commission. The presentation also included a concept design by Shalom Baranes for 20,000 square feet of restaurant space at the base of the existing building with access along E Street, and the elimination of perimeter security except at the parking garage entries, both significant departures from earlier security protocols for federal buildings. Robert Peck, commissioner of public buildings of the GSA, had directed that the headquarters modernization serve as an example for federal projects in the promotion of active streetscapes and in the reduction of perimeter security, both allowed by changes in federal security requirements.[137] The CFA welcomed the newly revised policy, which would help enliven the Rawlins Park area.

In meetings in June and October 2010, the design of the glassy retail bays and their detailing in relation to the existing masonry building dominated the commission's discussion. The CFA members' guidance to create a uniform height of the bays as well as maintaining the detailing of historic masonry openings conflicted with the approaches recommended by the District of Columbia's Historic Preservation Office and other review agencies; the CFA staff was directed to work with the architect and the other agency staffs to resolve the lingering areas of disagreement.[138] In January 2011, the commission reviewed a revised concept for the retail bays: window openings had been expanded, and the existing masonry that remained served as piers between the bays; the glass facades of the retail bays also were more transparent and supported by an interior steel frame. Generally, the design of the courtyard infill served as a more visible influence on the handling of the retail bays, as the commission had suggested. The commission members approved the revised concept, finding it elegant and well resolved, and final review was delegated to staff.[139]

TRANSFORMING THE SOUTHEAST FEDERAL CENTER

The redevelopment of the Southeast Federal Center (SEFC) along the Anacostia waterfront added a fourth consideration to the issues of security, sustainability, and preservation in federal projects within the District: economic benefit. The roughly sixty-acre industrial site east of 1st Street, SE, and south of M Street on the Anacostia River, known as the Navy Yard Annex, supported the navy's program of munitions research and development from World War I through the 1950s and was the site of the Naval Gun Factory. In the early 1960s, this site immediately west of the Navy Yard at Isaac Hull Avenue was transferred to the GSA

for reuse. During the next forty years, several master plans were developed for the site the content of which mirrored the evolution in thinking regarding urban planning and design and the role of federal development in urban revitalization within the District.

An early plan, produced in 1968, envisioned the area cleared and redeveloped as a new enclave of federal government office buildings in order to encourage general redevelopment in the area. By 1985, little had resulted from that early approach, and a new master plan was in development by Keyes, Condon & Florance (KCF) for the GSA. The CFA initially reviewed the proposed plan in April 1985; while still envisioned for federal office buildings, the KCF plan embraced the relatively new concept of adaptive reuse of existing buildings supplemented with infill development of various heights. New Jersey Avenue—an original L'Enfant Plan radial street—would be extended into the site and a two-lane road for automobiles introduced along a tree-edged waterfront. The CFA commended the plan's efforts to reconnect this neglected area to the rest of the city but cautioned that the street system and waterfront needed to be carefully coordinated with adjacent proposed development. The commission also urged greater pedestrian access to the waterfront and more public open space throughout the complex. In a prescient comment, CFA member Edward D. Stone Jr. said the plan should also include residential development.[140] These concerns—the need to increase pedestrian access and to introduce housing or hotel uses to enliven the area at night—would be repeated by the commission in its review and approval of the final draft master plan in October 1989 and in its approval of the area design guidelines in January 1995.

While federal development in the area remained stalled, concurrent private investment in other areas of the city was growing due to an improved economy and the acceptance of mixed-use and transit-oriented development principles and incentives by the city. By the early twenty-first century, the Southeast waterfront—a mile from the Capitol and served by public transit—came under increased study by District and federal planning agencies as a neighborhood that could accommodate residential, office, commercial, and recreational uses. To encourage this change, the District's representative in Congress, Eleanor Holmes Norton, sponsored the Southeast Federal Center Public-Private Development Act of 2000, which allowed the GSA to enhance the property's value by selling it to the private sector and leasing back developed buildings for federal use. The GSA worked closely with the city's Office of Planning to define a new street grid, mix of uses, and open space and to have the zoning

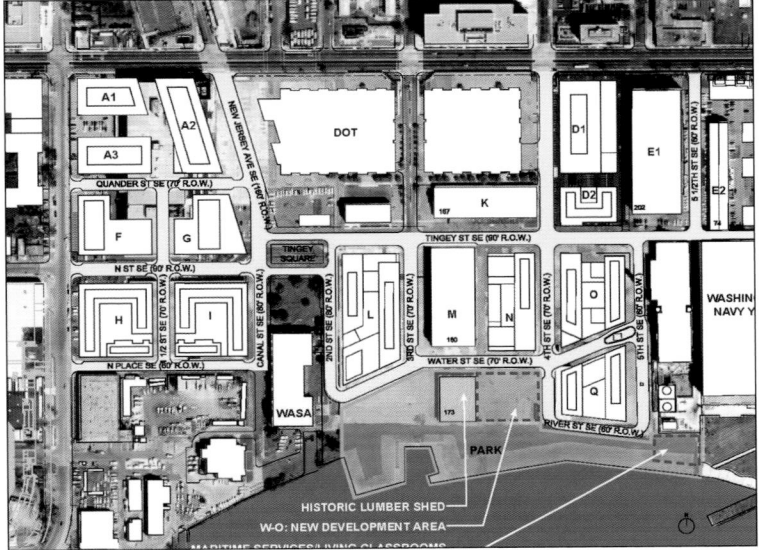

TOP: *Aerial view of the Washington Navy Yard in 1948. Much of the former industrial site's waterfront would be converted to parkland, and many of the surviving historic buildings were adaptively reused in early twenty-first-century redevelopment.*

ABOVE LEFT: *Final draft master plan of 1989 by Keyes, Condon & Florance for the Southeast Federal Center redevelopment. The plan proposed the adaptive reuse of many industrial buildings and extended New Jersey Avenue into the site, but it provided little public space along the waterfront or within the development.*

ABOVE RIGHT: *Concept site plan for the Southeast waterfront park by M. Paul Friedberg & Partners, 2009. Following the GSA's approved development plan of 2005 by Shalom Baranes Architects for Forest City Washington, a finer street grid was introduced with more of the waterfront devoted to parkland.*

TOP: *Aerial rendering of The Yards development based on the 2005 master plan, illustrating the proposed park elements by M. Friedberg & Partners along the waterfront as well as the mixed-use building redevelopment of the former industrial site.*

ABOVE: *U.S. Department of Transportation building by Michael Graves & Associates as built, 2006. The federal agency headquarters is next to the private, mixed-use redevelopment of the Southeast waterfront and was the first large-scale investment in the precinct.*

code streamlined to allow these changes to occur.

As part of the development, the GSA entered into an agreement with JBG/SEFC Venture to build a massive new headquarters for the Department of Transportation on eleven acres of the old Navy Annex, to be surrounded below M Street by a massive new private, mixed-use project planned for the area. Given the nature of the development agreement, the CFA did not have advisory authority for the new headquarters project, but the GSA and the developers made an information presentation to the commission in November 2003. As designed by Michael Graves & Associates, the 1.45 million-square-foot building for 5,500 federal employees was organized into two wings along M Street, separated by 3rd Street with a portico entrance at New Jersey Avenue. Security requirements called for a fifty-foot setback around the building, and retail uses could not be placed within the building. To compensate for the impact of security, a linear park was designed within the setback, and retail uses were to be accommodated within a separate small historic building and another small new building on site. As part of the zoning package for the project, the developer was contributing funds for a nearby park at the site of the old Washington Canal and interpretive panels for describing the history of the area. The CFA was pleased with the emphasis on public space and historic interpretation in the project. Its official remarks, however, were limited by the GSA to exterior materials, specifically the architect's choice of vividly colored concrete panels on

Views of the completed waterfront Yards Park by M. Paul Friedberg & Partners, 2010. Adaptively reused historic buildings form a backdrop to the park's sequence of fountains, esplanade and pedestrian bridge, terraced gardens, and signature light tower.

the facade. The CFA liked the samples presented but cautioned that care would be necessary in their fabrication to assure the long-term durability of the colors. The project was completed in 2006 and was the first large-scale redevelopment to begin the revitalization of the waterfront area.

Although the privatization of development removed the CFA from direct purview over design in the area, the GSA remained a party of interest and entered into a memorandum of agreement with the commission, finalized in June 2005, for conceptual review of the remaining portion of the site, a forty-two-acre, mixed-use development at the Southeast Federal Center by Forest City Washington. During the drafting of that agreement, the preliminary urban design and development plan for the project, now known as The Yards, by architect Shalom Baranes was presented to the CFA in June 2004. The commission found the plan—with its mix of housing, office, and retail space in adaptively reused buildings and new construction—appropriate for the SEFC, but urged that the waterfront park be a lively and exciting place that contained some reference to the area's industrial past. From 2007 through 2010, the CFA reviewed concepts for the buildings— supporting the designers' respect of the area's industrial character— and for the public spaces. In its January 2008 review of the waterfront park, designed by M. Paul Friedberg & Partners, the CFA endorsed the design but suggested simplification and clarification of hierarchy, larger gathering places, and additional shade. A year later, the CFA reviewed

and approved the landscape design, which acknowledged the commission's earlier suggestions, and enthusiastically approved the sixty-foot-tall light tower designed by James Carpenter. The Yards Park opened in 2010, followed by the first housing component in 2011; several retail uses were set to open in 2012. When the multiphase project is completed by the early 2020s, The Yards is expected to incorporate 2,800 residential units, 1.8 million square feet of office space, and 400,000 square feet of retail.[141]

REDEVELOPMENT OF ST. ELIZABETHS HOSPITAL

The redevelopment of the west campus of St. Elizabeths Hospital was by far the largest project of the decade and among the largest federal projects reviewed by the commission since the War Department proposed the Pentagon in 1941. The project best exemplifies the nexus of design issues generated by security, sustainability, and preservation requirements.[142] Developed and operated by the federal government as a mental hospital for more than 130 years, the entire property was deeded to the District in the 1980s for use as a mental health facility. The city's financial difficulties prompted the federal government to take back the west campus in 2004; the east campus remains under the District's control.

Together, the hospital's historic east and west campuses encompass 336 acres in southeast Washington, including a significant component of the remaining topographic ring

TOP: *Photograph of the main entrance of the Gothic Revival Center Building by Thomas Ustick Walter, the first building complex of the St. Elizabeths Hospital campus and built in the 1850s with a commanding view of the city's monumental core, c. 1910.*

ABOVE: *Significant portions of the 350-acre medical campus were built in the early twentieth century. The Administration building was designed by Shepley, Rutan & Coolidge and built in 1903 as the focus of a second quadrangle on the west campus.*

of wooded hills that surrounds the District. The property sits on a plateau that overlooks the Anacostia and Potomac Rivers and the skylines of Alexandria and Rosslyn in Virginia, Mount Alban in the District, and downtown Washington, D.C. Designated a National Historic Landmark in 1990 for the hospital's role in the development of national standards for the treatment of mental health, the historic district includes a significant collection of nineteenth- and early twentieth-century buildings, including the immense neo-Gothic Center Building by Thomas U. Walter, architect of the U.S. Capitol dome. In 2002, the National Trust for Historic Preservation listed St. Elizabeths as one of the country's "11 Most Endangered Places." The West Campus, which falls under the purview of the General Services Administration, comprises 176 acres with seventy buildings, many of them historic; a cemetery; and an overlook with dramatic views of the national capital. Strong reciprocal views down the Washington Channel from the heart of the city's monumental core gave the site tremendous potential as a future extension of the national commemorative landscape.

The Department of Homeland Security had been created in 2002 in direct response to the attacks of September 11, 2001, partly through a reorganization of many existing agencies. The site selection process conducted by the GSA to centralize the elements of the sprawling agency was cursory and quickly settled on the St. Elizabeths West Campus as the best site: it was available, within the District of Columbia, and large enough to accommodate the vast scale and high security requirements for the new cabinet-level department. After nearly two years of negotiations with consulting parties, including CFA staff as part of the federal historic preservation review process, the GSA submitted a draft master plan for the development. In June 2007, the commission visited the site and also received an information presentation on the master plan. It proposed 6.4 million square feet of office space and structured parking, including a 1.3-million-square-foot building for the U.S. Coast Guard located on the western slope of the property; access roads necessitating massive retaining walls; a series of parallel security fences separated by no-vegetation zones; restricted public access to the overlook; and impacts to the historic architecture and grounds. The Coast Guard project would be built first, although its leadership opposed relocating the agency to the St. Elizabeths site by itself without the Homeland Security departmental headquarters.

The commission members found the master plan a fundamentally flawed document. The development alternatives proposed were insufficiently differentiated, and the

Washington Monument

National Cathedral

Old Post Office

US Capitol Building

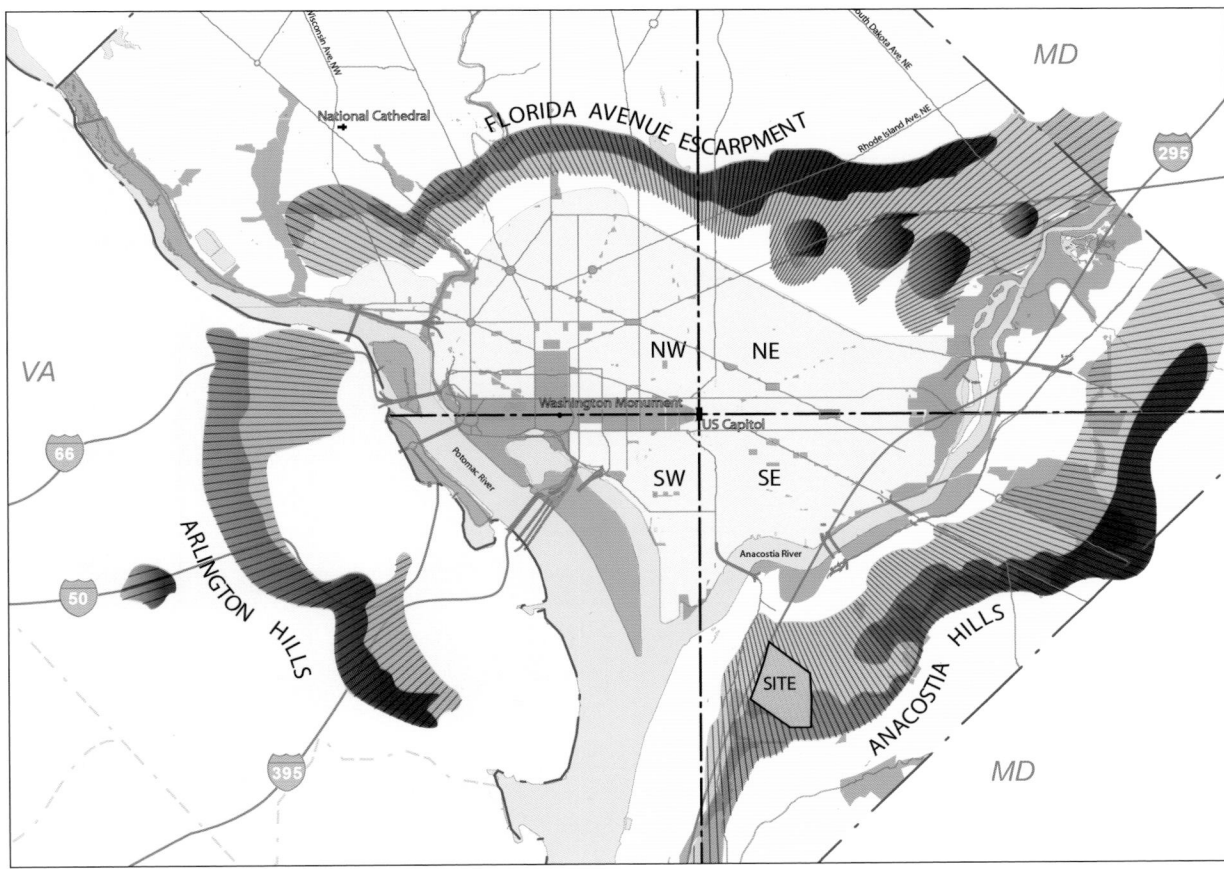

MD

National Cathedral

FLORIDA AVENUE ESCARPMENT

Rhode Island Ave NE

South Dakota Ave NE

Wisconsin Ave NW

295

VA

66

NW

NE

Washington Monument

US Capitol

Potomac River

SW

SE

ARLINGTON HILLS

50

Anacostia River

SITE

ANACOSTIA HILLS

395

MD

ABOVE: *View of monumental Washington from the overlook promontory on the St. Elizabeths West Campus, c. 2005.*

LEFT: *The design of the GSA-led consolidation of 6.3 million square feet of development for the new Department of Homeland Security headquarters began in 2005 at the St. Elizabeths West Campus (in orange), a National Historic Landmark located in the Anacostia Hills overlooking the topographic bowl of central Washington.*

limited amount of information provided in the submission materials impeded adequate analysis. Overall, the members were critical of the amount of construction proposed, its impact on the landscape and wildlife, the extensive transportation issues it created, and the weak site planning. John Belle's remarks are illustrative:

There is an important distinction here between . . . summarizing a very complex and lengthy study so that we can understand it in short time and doing so to the expense of not sharing with us very critical information. . . . It is very hard to just sign off on some of the assumptions you have made without that information. It is a . . . critically important project . . . perhaps the most important for decades. But I don't think, because of the overarching issue of national security, that it is exempt from master planning, from planning, from urban design, from good design, more or less than any other project. It is not exempt.[143]

The GSA submitted its preliminary draft master plan and a draft perimeter security master plan for formal review four months later. The commission members reiterated the concerns voiced during the information presentation, especially their frustration regarding the lack of alternative schemes. However, the remarks of some commission members focused on the preservation of the site's landscape features—essentially the visual backdrop for the capital and its environs—rather than the preservation of buildings or the site's social history. Michael McKinnell's comments were representative:

I don't think—and this is very heretical, I am sure—I don't think that the buildings on the site are of really extraordinarily fine and worthy character to be preserved. . . . I do think that it is really unfortunate in

ABOVE: *The 2008 final master plan by Smith Group for the U.S. Coast Guard headquarters (in yellow) was contentious, proposing a 1.3 million-square-foot office complex on the steeply sloping flank of the site adjacent to the lower-scale Gothic Revival buildings of the historic campus (in brown) and a Civil War-era cemetery.*

BELOW: *Site plan of the design for the Coast Guard headquarters on the West Campus by Perkins & Will with Andropogon landscape architects, 2009, illustrating the sequence of internal courts, rain gardens, and stormwater management ponds intended to integrate the building complex into the Anacostia escarpment.*

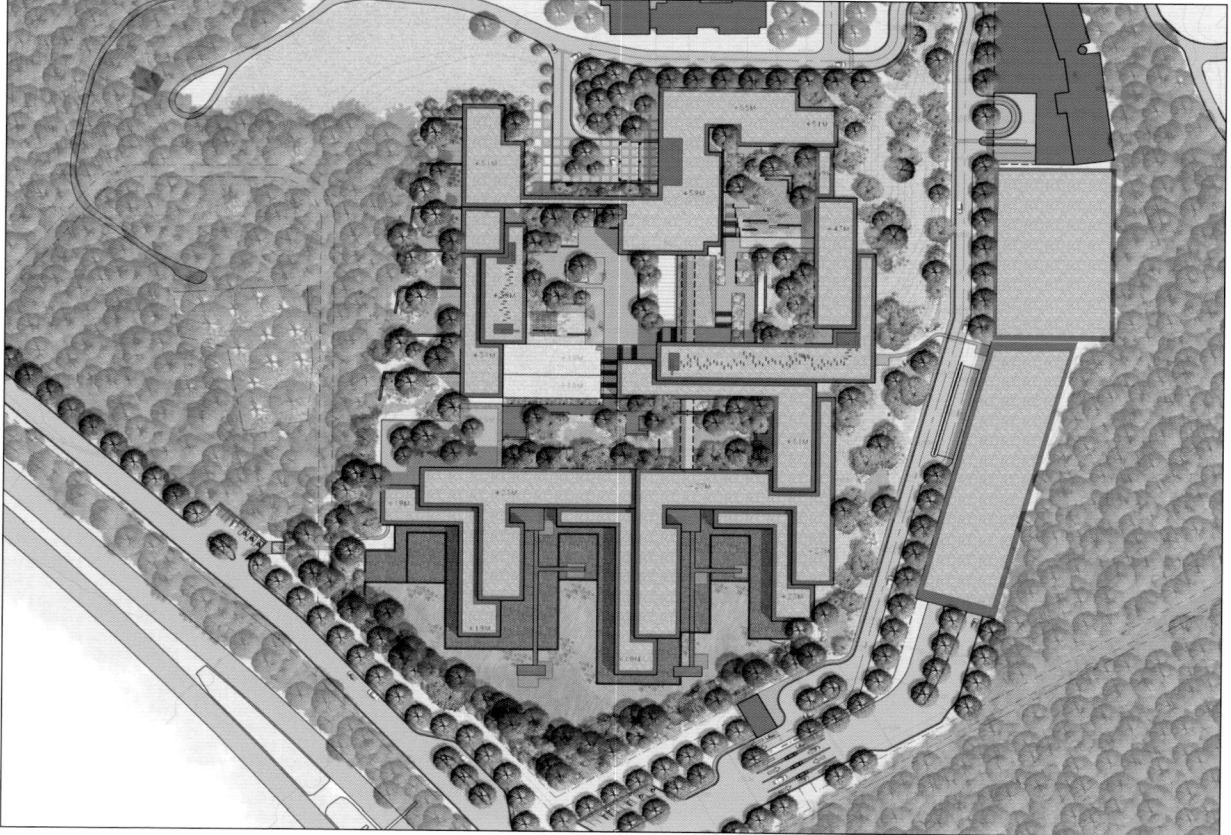

ABOVE: *Rendering of the concept design for the U.S. Coast Guard headquarters building by Perkins & Will with* HOK *and* WDG *Architecture, 2009. The complex presents itself in multiple cascading tiers treated in a composition of glassy volumes with integrated sunshades in the upper portions over lower masonry-clad forms.*

BELOW: *Rendering of the principal pavilion of the Coast Guard complex as seen from an internal courtyard, 2010, showing a lighter treatment following the* CFA's *recommendation.*

*a master plan of this scale and in terms of its topographical promi-
nence in the Washington area…that we are actually presented with
literally no alternatives except moving around the blocks a little bit.*[144]

At the meeting, a variety of parties in opposition to the
extent of the proposed development testified, including
representatives from the National Trust for Historic
Preservation, the D.C. Preservation League, the Committee of 100 on the Federal City, the D.C. Office of Planning, and the Brookings Institution. Following these coordinated and well-articulated statements, CFA chairman
Earl Powell directed the GSA to meet with these parties to
discuss ways to resolve at least some of the differences.[145]

The commission staff transmitted its official comments
regarding the GSA's Draft Environmental Impact Statement of the proposed development in mid-November
2007, noting:

*In its review of the proposal at its October 18, 2007 public meeting, the
Commission members commented that the primary resource of the St.
Elizabeths West Campus lies in its great prominence in the design and
setting of the National Capital. They also affirmed the consensus of
many professional and public organizations that have concluded that
the scale and extent of proposed development would permanently alter or destroy the character of the National Historic Landmark. They
recommended that GSA reconsider the basic assumptions for development on the site—its overall configuration, the retention of historic
buildings, and especially the size of the building program—to create
meaningful alternatives that the Commission could, in good conscience, accept as worthy of the site.*[146]

Following dozens of additional meetings with the interested parties, the GSA submitted the master plan for final review a year later with little substantive change. The
most significant modification was the relocation of 1 million square feet of development from the west campus to
the east campus—in coordination with the District government, which had identified development areas there—
while retaining 5 million square feet on the west campus.
The commission expressed its appreciation for the GSA's
efforts to revise the scheme, but continued to voice concerns about circulation and transportation issues. John
Belle again emphasized the significance of the project:

*What is there that is unique, if you will, about the master plan that
is…before us today? I think the answers are depressing because I don't
think there is a great deal that is unique. I don't think there is a great
deal of innovation in the plan…. I don't think there is a great deal of
hope there.*[147]

He concluded by advocating that the plan not be approved. However, his views proved to be in the minority
among the members, who seemed resigned to the unlike-
lihood of achieving substantial changes to the plan. Pamela
Nelson said she could not envision another entity being
interested in the property due to the weak economy but

regretted the project's impact on the landscape, noting
that the development "is going to set a different tone about
security, having it up on the horizon, that times are different. Maybe that is part of what we have to accept with different times."[148] Witold Rybczynski took the stance that
St. Elizabeths was not a typical national landmark because
it had never been open to the public and argued that some
of the impacts to the landscape could be attributed to the
requirements to save many old buildings:

*I think if you knock down half the buildings on the site, perhaps you
wouldn't need to cover the slope with the Coast Guard building. But
that would raise furor. So, in some ways, I see [GSA] trying to respond
to—and sort of not making anybody happy. But that is the way of the
world…. It would be nice if they went away somewhere else, but that
would just create a huge problem for somebody else. So I don't see that
as a solution either.*[149]

Rybczynski, noting he did not believe alternatives existed, made a motion to approve the master plan. The motion carried with John Belle voting against approval. Michael
McKinnell had recused himself since his firm was competing for work associated with the project.

Over the next several years, individual projects for the
campus were reviewed; with most of the program and its
associated elements dictated by security needs, the commission's comments generally focused on design details
and materials. Among these was the required perimeter security system for the west campus that included more than
two miles of parallel no-climb fences with periodic security stations and anti-vehicle barriers. Each side of the fence
was flanked by a ten-foot-wide cleared zone; a twenty-foot-
wide cleared swath would separate the parallel fence elements. There would be eighteen-foot-high retaining walls
and an eight-foot-wide path for security vehicles across
what had been the green Shepherd Parkway reservation of
the National Park Service—part of Washington's historic
landscape setting. The commission approved the concept
design by Perkins & Will at its February 2010 meeting, although it recommended a more comprehensively developed landscape plan that provided a more logical approach
to the location of new trees, for example, and reduced the
amount of asphalt. The final design presented the following month showed some refinements based on the CFA's
comments, and it was approved.[150]

The commission also reviewed the 1.3-million-square-
foot Coast Guard headquarters building and associated
parking structures for the west campus, located on a project site of more than thirty acres. The building was designed to cascade down the Anacostia escarpment, and its
architectural expression was influenced by sustainable features such as green screens, sunshades, and rain gardens.

The Coast Guard headquarters under construction, 2011. The project—part of the largest single building project in Washington's history since the Pentagon—required extensive excavation of the campus's west slope.

Ironically, the project received a gold rating for sustainability by the Leadership in Energy and Environmental Design (LEED) system administered by the U.S. Green Building Council, yet its construction required the removal of 1.6 million cubic feet of soil—700,000 cubic feet of which were contaminated—and, following clearing of vegetation from the hillside, portions of the upper plateau threatened to collapse into the construction site.[151] As with the perimeter security system, the commission's recommendations dealt with materials and details. However, by 2011, fiscal pressures had put a halt to development on the west campus except for the Coast Guard building, postponing indefinitely further consolidation of the Homeland Security agencies. Sadly, one of the largest federal construction projects in the history of the District of Columbia has been left

unresolved, falling short for virtually every party in achieving its goals: the Department of Homeland Security was not able to consolidate its headquarters, and the U.S. Coast Guard relocated to the site alone; the National Park Service ceded a significant strip of the forested Shepherd Parkway for the access road; the GSA continued to hold and maintain the campus without a clear future purpose for the extensive ensemble of historic buildings; the District of Columbia—which had advocated in favor of the development for its economic benefits—would only realize a fraction of the promised employment; and the federal design and planning agencies lost the long-term opportunity for the site—with its linear relationship with the Washington Channel and sweeping views of the city—as an extension of the monumental core on available federal land.

Reinvestment in the City: Public Projects by the District of Columbia

The national capital began to experience profound economic growth beginning in the late 1990s and continuing through the next decade. In part due to federal government spending in the Washington area—more than doubling from $79 billion in 2001 to $170 billion in 2010—the city emerged as the top-performing real estate market and the second-largest office market in the decade of the 2000s and beyond, which was reflected in a flourishing commercial sector and a resurgence in residential development downtown.[152] New restaurants and shops, sidewalk cafes and bars, galleries, and theaters enlivened the city. By the end of the decade, Washington, D.C., had emerged as one the nation's most vibrant urban centers, a destination for young professionals, families, and empty nesters wanting to live in a walkable city environment. The 2010 census confirmed the city's renewed vigor: the number of residents grew by more than 5 percent since 2000, to more than 600,000, the first ten-year increase in the city's population in six decades.[153]

As part of the city's upward trend, the District of Columbia government began the new century with an ambitious program of reinvestment in its institutions and facilities, made possible by a revitalized culture of professionalism within its bureaucracy under Mayors Anthony Williams (1999–2007), Adrian Fenty (2007–11), and Vincent Gray (2011–), and fueled by Washington's strength as an attractive commercial and residential real estate market. Numerous projects to correct the deferred maintenance of public facilities such as schools, parks, and libraries, as well as transportation infrastructure were undertaken citywide. The District's Department of Transportation was particularly active in implementing policies—such as bike lanes, bike sharing, a new streetcar system, and traffic control—to encourage new and alternative transportation. The Office of Planning, under the leadership of Andrew Altman and Harriet Tregoning, also worked to increase density, livability, and sustainability; in addition to its work in the commercial core, the agency focused on redevelopment plans and policies beyond the traditional downtown, including the Mount Vernon Triangle and North of Massachusetts Avenue (NOMA) neighborhoods, the Southwest D.C. Capitol Waterfront area, the Near Southeast neighborhood, and Anacostia.

The Commission of Fine Arts generally supported the city's efforts, especially its decision to introduce more

The restaurant patio at the W Hotel, formerly the Hotel Washington, at 15th Street and Pennsylvania Avenue, NW, adjacent to the Department of the Treasury, is an example of renewed urban vitality neighboring the monumental core, 2012.

ABOVE LEFT: *New bicycle transit center at Union Station by* KGP *Design Studio, completed in 2009, introduces a bold new vocabulary into the setting of a Washington, D.C., landmark.*

ABOVE RIGHT: *A 2012 concept design by* TEN *Arquitectos for redevelopment of Square 50 by EastBanc in the city's West End neighborhood uses striking contemporary expression to define the elements of the combined fire station at street level, squash courts in the middle, and residential units on the top floors.*

Washington, D.C., experienced an unusually high level of redevelopment in the decade of the 2000s, including the NOMA *district north of Union Station, where 16 million square feet of office, residential, hotel, and retail space were in development or completed by 2012. In the foreground, the* ATFE *headquarters marks the threshold of the rapidly changing area with New York Avenue on the right; the monumental core is visible in the distance.*

contemporary architectural expression in neighborhood
facilities. Siting, urban design, and detailing—particularly
in their relationship to placemaking and public gathering—were among the design elements in these projects
most commented upon in the commission's reviews.

NATIONALS PARK

Reinvestment by the District government occurred across
the city in a variety of projects. Among the most prominent was a city-supported major league baseball stadium
along South Capitol Street in the Capitol Waterfront
neighborhood roughly one block from the Anacostia
River, an area identified in the NCPC's *Extending the Legacy*
plan as appropriate for new development. The District approached this monumental project as a fast-track development proposal with an intended opening of spring 2008,
and it was reviewed only once by the commission—for
concept approval—in July 2006. The design presentation,
by competition winners HOK and Devrouax & Purnell, focused on the urban design elements of the project: how it
would address the various street frontages, access to the
nearby Metro station, and engage pedestrians. Dominant
forms of the stadium would express separate functions,
such as a curvilinear form delineating the stadium's bowl
and a triangular pavilion housing a conference center and
team offices. A monumental stairway would connect the
stadium to new parks to be developed along the Anacostia River, and retail uses would be located along the building's 1st Street facade. A mix of housing and other retail
uses was planned elsewhere on the site. The commission's
comments were brief but wide ranging, from the need to

carefully address the complex design conditions posed by
the urban site to the economic viability of the related mix
of uses. Voicing support for the project and its significant
role in creating the urban context of the area, the CFA
members voted to approve the concept.[154]

PUBLIC LIBRARIES

The D.C. Public Library system undertook a capital improvement campaign to create state-of-the-art branch libraries throughout the city. The library initiative resulted
in contemporary architectural design by nationally prominent architects in many neighborhoods that had not seen
significant development in decades. The sequencing of the
projects was based on the condition of the existing buildings; the first four—Anacostia, Tenley-Friendship, Ben-
ning, and Watha T. Daniel/Shaw—were deemed to be the
most in need of replacement. At the commission's February 2008 meeting, Davis Brody Bond Aedas presented designs for the first two, and the Freelon Group Architects
submitted designs for the latter. The commission members
applauded the proposals in general while offering some specific suggestions for the architectural refinements of each
project. They also commended the District's head librarian
for pursuing design excellence at neighborhood libraries.

For the Watha T. Daniel Library in the Shaw neighborhood, Davis Brody Bond Aedas proposed building a
transparent glass and metal volume on the foundations of
the existing brutalist-style triangular building. The commission commended the design and suggested simplification of the screen-clad glass skin for maintenance reasons. The Washington Highlands and Francis Gregory

TOP LEFT: *The Francis Gregory Library in the Southeast sector of the city, completed in 2012, was designed by Adjaye Associates and incorporates a gridded harlequin pattern of clear and mirrored glass to create a bold tension between interior transparency and the reflection of the neighboring park.*

TOP RIGHT: *The Watha T. Daniel Library in the Shaw neighborhood of Northwest designed by Davis Brody Bond Aedas and completed in 2011 uses simple, strong geometric forms and transparency to emphasize the building's relationship to the community.*

ABOVE: *The Freelon Group wrapped the masonry and glass geometric forms of the 2012 Anacostia Library with a metal roof and included a light tower as a strong vertical element to promote the building's visibility and importance within the neighborhood.*

RIGHT: *The renovation of the Mount Pleasant Library on 16th Street, NW, by Henry Myerberg with CORE Architects included a modern addition at the rear of the building designed to reinterpret the materials of the historic Renaissance Revival design with terra-cotta panels, 2012.*

neighborhood libraries were the next pair slated for replacement; proposals were submitted to the commission in May 2009. The Francis Gregory Library designed by Adjaye Associates—also part of the winning team selected in April 2009 to design the National Museum of African American History and Culture—was located at the edge of the heavily wooded Fort Davis Park. In response to this green setting, the design established a transparent pavilion sited within the park. The two-story rectangular structure featured a curtain wall of an alternating harlequin pattern of mirrored and transparent glass panels under a thin cantilevered roof. The commission members expressed enthusiasm for the proposal and the goal to raise the design standard for civic buildings in the neighborhoods, but they cautioned the project team to be prepared with alternatives if budget constraints arose.

RENOVATION OF D.C. PUBLIC SCHOOLS

The District of Columbia also undertook an ambitious program to renovate its public schools, facilitated by a specially created deputy mayoral agency, the Office of Public Education Facilities Modernization (OPEFM), under the leadership of Alan Lew, the District's manager for the recently completed Nationals Park. In a period of three years, the program proposed renovating or rebuilding several of the city's high schools; these included a new facil-

ity to replace the dilapidated Woodson and Dunbar High Schools and preservation-oriented renovations of Eastern, Cardozo, and Wilson High Schools.

The renovation of Wilson High School was a complex case that dealt with planning and deferred maintenance issues for a campus that included four Georgian Revival buildings erected in 1935. Cox Graae & Spack submitted concept plans for the renovation and expansion to the CFA in November 2009. The commission members endorsed the site planning but recommended further study of the entrance, circulation patterns, and the development of an overall proportional system to unify the historic structures with the new construction. They also encouraged the preservation of the power plant building, which was proposed for demolition. When the revised concept was presented to the commission in February 2010, changes included the rehabilitation of the power plant as a fitness center, raising the entrance plaza, and adding a projecting lobby. The CFA members characterized the proposal as well conceived and noted the successful ways in which the scale had been broken down and the spaces connected to each other. The design was approved, and the renovated school reopened in August 2011.

Across the District in the Deanwood neighborhood, OPEFM brought about the complete replacement of the Howard D. Woodson High School, known as the "Tower

The extensive renovation of the Wilson High School complex in the Tenleytown neighborhood by Cox Graae & Spack, completed in 2011, included a new modern entrance to what had been the rear of the Colonial Revival–style building.

The central exterior courtyard of the Wilson High School was enclosed with a skylight structure to create an interior student commons.

TOP LEFT: *The brutalist concrete Howard D. Woodson High School by Bryant & Bryant in the Deanwood neighborhood, known as the "Tower of Power," was built in the 1970s and demolished in 2008.*

ABOVE LEFT: *Aerial rendering of the 2010 Cox, Graae & Spack revised design for Woodson High School, which was symmetrically reorganized and made more compact with the main entry clearly defined at the street.*

TOP RIGHT: *Concept design model for the new Woodson High School by SHW Group, 2008; the building was asymmetrical in plan with multiple entries and the primary academic wing located along the adjacent Marvin Gaye Park.*

ABOVE RIGHT: *The new Woodson High School by Cox, Graae & Spack, with its distinctive columnar entrance, was completed in 2011.*

of Power." The school's site in Northeast Washington is adjacent to the linear Marvin Gaye Park, only recently developed but already popular with the community. A first attempt to replace the 1970s brutalist-style, six-story facility had been made in 2002 but was not carried out. In May 2008, another concept for a replacement building organized around a STEM (science, technology, engineering, and mathematics) curriculum by the SHW Group was submitted to the CFA for review. The SHW proposal placed the school at the east edge of the site, facing 55th Street and adjacent to the park. The plan was sprawling and asymmetrical, organized along a pair of north-south corridors with the STEM classrooms and labs occupying a large, three-story wing facing the park, with auditorium, arts, and athletic spaces located to the north. The building had multiple entries, with the student entrance in the east elevation, recessed beneath a large canopy, leading to a two-story atrium. The commission members pointed out the di-

LEFT: *The Walker-Jones Education Campus in the Mount Vernon Triangle, completed in 2009, was designed by Hord Coplan Macht Architects as a complete redevelopment of a city block with an elementary and junior high school, community center, and athletic facilities. The CFA recommended that the building use pattern and detail, such as this basket-weave brickwork, to maintain a sense of finish and civic importance.*

ABOVE: *The renovation of the 1925 Colonial Revival Janney Elementary School in the Tenleytown neighborhood, designed by Devrouax & Purnell, included an addition to the historic building with modern accommodations for science, arts, media, and assembly programs and was completed in 2011.*

chotomy between the north and south parts of building, and observed that the composition would lead to confusion about what was the building's public entrance. They also criticized the school's lack of integration with the park but approved the concept, subject to their comments.

SHW Group returned for review two more times in 2008 with revisions to the design, reconfiguring the entrance plaza, replacing the canopy, and redesigning the classroom elevations. The CFA members continued to criticize the building's complexity and unresolved relationship to its setting—whether the street frontage, the parking lot, or the park. Witold Rybczynski pointed out that the building's organization resembled a suburban shopping mall, offering multiple entrances without any hierarchy; this was in contrast to the diagram of the typical urban school, which had a street facade with one clear entrance.

Dissatisfied with the problematic design, Alan Lew replaced SHW with Cox, Graae & Spack—by this time working on the Wilson project—who submitted an entirely new proposal to the commission in September 2009. The plan was symmetrically organized around an east-west axis, with a central block containing academic spaces and a single well-defined entrance, and the community functions of pool and auditorium placed in two flanking wings, thereby allowing community access when the school was closed. The concept was sufficiently clear that the commission found that only minor changes—mostly to the front plaza, its stairways, and landscape—were necessary to arrive at a successful solution. While Rybczynski called the two-story entrance block with its canted metal columns overly monumental, Plater-Zyberk said its grand scale would elevate the students' experience of attending school. The project returned once more in March 2010, incorporating suggested changes by the CFA that refined the front landscape and entrance canopy. The project was approved, and OPEFM completed the project in August 2011.

Public Art in a Revitalized City

From a Model to a Rainbow, *Italian hand-blown glass tile mosaic by Sam Gilliam at the Takoma Metro Station, 2011.*

A s many areas within Washington experienced substantial redevelopment in the first decade of the century, public art continued to help define the identity of the city, reaching beyond the monumental core into the urban fabric of the neighborhoods. A number of District, federal, and other entities sponsored projects to bring art into the public realm, that were intended to enliven and humanize these spaces and enrich the quality of life in the city. The Commission of Fine Arts provided advice on the design and placement of these public art projects as part of its long-standing mission.

The District of Columbia Commission on the Arts and Humanities (DCCAH) sponsored many of these art projects, including *Transit* by sculptor Wendy Ross (2007). The welded steel work combines rods and spheres suspended from an exterior arcade of the Washington Convention Center, also marking an entrance to the Mount Vernon Square Metro Station. The artist reconfigured the design at the recommendation of the CFA to allow the piece to be suspended from the building, rather than mounted from the floor. In cooperation with the Washington Metropolitan Area Transit Authority's Metro Art in Transit program, the DCCAH commissioned a glass tile mosaic by artist Sam Gilliam for the Takoma Metro Station. The four hundred-square-foot piece, *From a Model to a Rainbow* (2011), is a rendition of an earlier abstract painting by Gilliam. Following a discussion regarding placement on the station wall and durability of materials, the CFA enthusiastically approved the piece, com-

One of the sculptures that constitutes Les Trois Grâces (The Three Graces), *by Niki de Saint Phalle (1999), part of a program of temporary art installed along New York Avenue in 2010.*

mending the sponsors for engaging an artist of such stature for a public art installation in a city neighborhood.

The DCCAH also sponsored public art installations at significant redevelopment sites in cooperation with the city's Office of Planning and private developers. One example is *Lift Off* by David Black (2009) for a new public plaza at the City Vista development at 5th and K Streets, NW. The CFA recommended that the sculpture be made taller and directly anchored to the ground rather than to stone bases, advising that the plaza details should be developed with the involvement of the artist. *Resonance* by Jann Rosen-Queralt (2009), a series of tile installations set in pavement and as part of a fountain, is a focal piece of public art in the redeveloping Columbia Heights neighborhood at 14th Street and Park Road, NW, and was also supported by the DCCAH with the District Department of Transportation (DDOT). Given the urban char-

acter and the space's level of use, the CFA recommended that the elements be made larger and bolder to better respond to the context.

Public art has also played a placemaking role in the redevelopment of the Southeast Federal Center on the Anacostia waterfront, a long-term project involving federal agencies, the District government, and a private developer. The project's first phase included a new waterfront park by M. Paul Friedberg & Partners (2010) with an iconic sixty-foot-tall glass light tower, *Prismatic Marker,* at the water's edge. The CFA found this vertical sculptural element by designer James Carpenter a particularly elegant component within the waterfront setting.

At its June 2008 meeting, the CFA approved the concept design for the Dr. Carter G. Woodson Memorial submitted by DDOT and the DCCAH. The piece, funded through a program of the National Trust for Historic Preservation, is

FAR LEFT: Transit, *a series of welded steel orbs by Wendy Ross at the Mount Vernon Square Metro Station entrance, 2007.*

LEFT: Prismatic Marker, *glass light tower by James Carpenter at the Yards Park, 2011.*

to be located at the intersection of Rhode Island Avenue and Q and 9th Streets, NW. The CFA commended sculptor Ray Kaskey for his use of the exedra form and suggested that the agencies work with the city's Department of Parks and Recreation to develop the landscape setting within one of Washington's characteristic triangular parks. The following year, the CFA also commended the organizers of the New York Avenue Public Art Program—the D.C. Office of Planning, the National Museum of Women in the Arts, the DCCAH, and the Downtown D.C. Business Improvement District—who created a program of temporary sculptural works by noted artists in the median of New York Avenue, NW, between 9th and 13th Streets. The CFA approved the concept proposal, emphasizing the need for careful maintenance and management of the project; the first pieces installed from 2010 to 2011 were whimsical tile-encrusted figures by sculptor Niki de Saint Phalle.

LEFT: Lift Off, *painted steel sculpture by David Black in the public plaza at City Vista in the Mount Vernon Triangle neighborhood, 2009.*

BELOW: *Maquette for the unbuilt Dr. Carter G. Woodson Memorial in the Shaw neighborhood by sculptor Ray Kaskey, approved by the CFA in 2008.*

Development and Preservation in Old Georgetown

As elsewhere in the city, development pressure on properties in Old Georgetown during the first decade of the new century continued to grow. This trend was reflected in the number of applications submitted to the commission during this time, from 330 cases reviewed in 2000 to 413 at its peak in 2008. A significant portion of these applications were for alterations to residential properties throughout Georgetown; the typical project comprised a two-story addition to expand what was, by contemporary standards, a small house into a larger multi-bedroom, multi-bathroom residence with an improved kitchen. Just as the scale of the proposed addition could be sizeable compared to the historic structure, the architectural language could also be aggrandizing, with the effect of elaborating the style beyond the property's historic character. The concomitant result of this increase in living area was a reduction of the property's existing open space, often lead-ing to the loss of mature trees; a few notable submissions even proposed extensive underground additions. The commission staff testified in several appeal cases of this type before the mayor's agent of the District of Columbia, arguing that the mature landscape proposed to be removed contributed to the character of the historic district.

Since the establishment of the Old Georgetown historic district in 1950, a historicist attitude toward new architecture had always been the prevailing approach among design practitioners, whether in the recreation of faux Colonial detailing in prior decades or in the application of high-style classical vocabularies to simple nineteenth-century houses. While some architects attempted modern design in the 1960s and 1970s, most proposals of the following decades were strictly historicist. In a few cases, however, architects worked to accommodate new construction with more tempered modernism, seeking to respect the existing historic context in scale without the literal replication or extension of historic detail. One distinguished example is a project at 2727 Q Street, NW, involving the

ABOVE: *Section rendering of a proposed addition to the rear of 3333 Q Street, NW, by Robert M. Gurney Architect, 2012. The project, combining two adjacent houses with extensive underground construction for a garage and modernist additions to the rear, illustrates the trend in historic Georgetown to create larger residences with more amenities.*

RIGHT: *Addition to the rear of 2727 Q Street, NW, by Cunningham Quill Architects, a simply detailed geometric form complimentary to the restored exterior of the 1893 Colonial Revival house, 2009.*

renovation of an 1893 Colonial Revival house—substantially altered in the twentieth century—and a new addition to the rear of the structure. The project, designed by Cunningham Quill Architects, comprised the restoration of lost elements of the historic house, such as the front porch and widow's walk. The rear addition is a simple cubic volume of brick and large glass windows that maintain the scale and rhythm of the historic wood mullions. Another notable example of residential development was a project involving the joining of two historic structures on one lot, substantial underground construction, and modern architecture. The property at 3333 Q Street, designed by Robert Gurney, combined many controversial trends, creating a larger luxury dwelling from smaller independent pieces and accommodating off-street parking with a large subterranean garage. During the process of the Old Georgetown Board (OGB) review in 2011, a third-floor addition and the extent of the rear additions were substantially reduced; the OGB supported the modern character of the architecture.

EXPANSION OF GEORGETOWN'S INSTITUTIONS

Following a series of master plans produced for its campus in the 1970s and 1980s, Georgetown University retained Robert A.M. Stern Architects to revise the campus plan in the late 1990s to accommodate further development of the campus, particularly in its southwestern quadrant. In 1998, Stern presented a plan that would reinforce the grid established by the town streets—once more prominent in the campus plan—and create a new vehicular entrance to the campus from Canal Road. Stern was also selected as the design architect for the Southwest Quadrangle building, a substantial neo-Gothic structure that included a student dormitory and dining facility on top of a parking garage and maintenance facility. The commission supported the master plan as well as Stern's traditional architecture; however, it was more critical of the adjacent Jesuit residence by Einhorn, Yaffee & Prescott asking for refinement of the Ruskinian Gothic tower that would serve as a visual terminus for Prospect Street. The Southwest Quadrangle building and the Jesuit residence were completed in 2003. Beginning in 2001, the commission reviewed plans for a new administration building and performing arts center by Hardy Holzman Pfeiffer Associates that was situated at a steeply sloping site near the center of campus. Completed in 2006, the project's use of patterned brickwork was commended by the CFA. Further development followed with the construction of a multisport facility and the new McDonough School of Business building by Goody Clancy, completed in 2009. In 2007, the 153,000-square-foot science center,

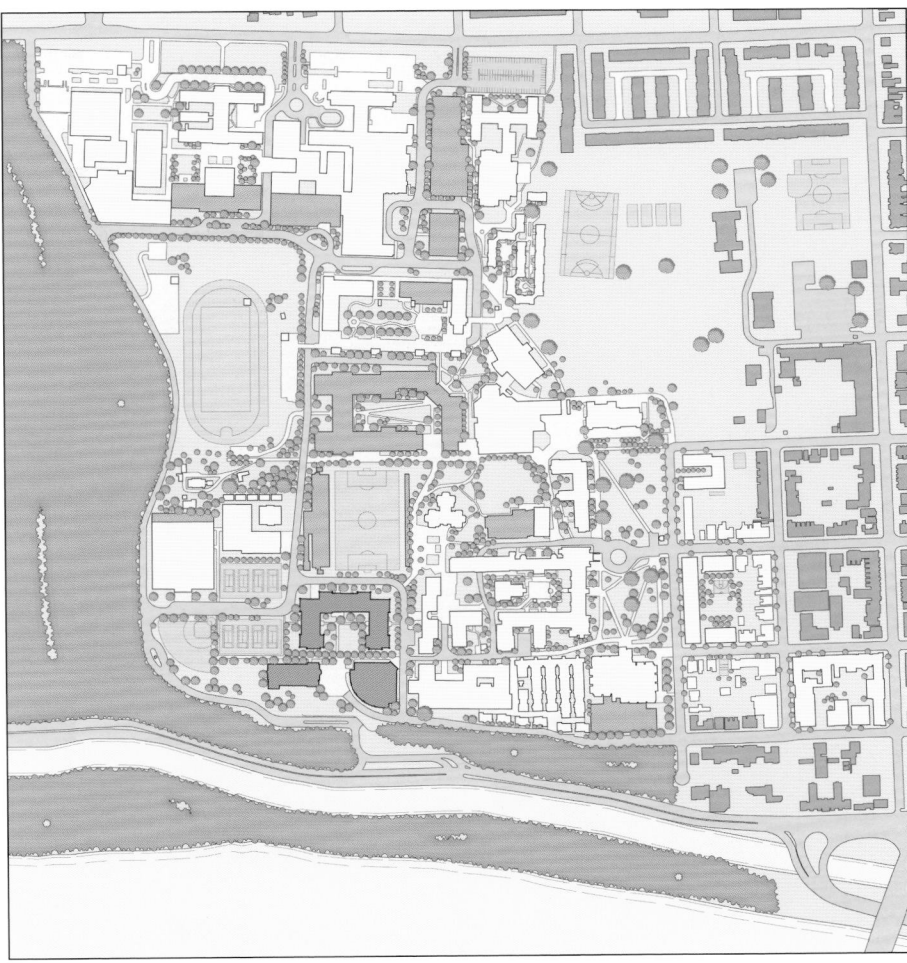

Regents Hall, by the architecture firm Payette Associates was presented to the commission, the final building planned to complete this quadrangle. The CFA supported the OGB's recommendation to emphasize the entrance, to refine the building's distinctive split-gable roof in order to better conceal the mechanical equipment, and to develop the quadrangle's terraced lawn for sustainable operation while acting as a new focus of student activity on the campus; it was completed in 2012.

Several of Georgetown's significant surviving estates had been converted to institutional ownership during the twentieth century; by the twenty-first century, plans were put forward to expand these institutional uses on the properties. Tudor Place, the Federal-era house designed by William Thornton, had become a historic house museum in the 1980s. In 2009, the museum organization operating the property began an ambitious master plan process to improve its collections, display, educational, and visitor services with a series of new accessory buildings and additions at the perimeter of the site. The OGB reviewed the case in 2011; its initial advice to reexamine program needs and minimize visual impact resulted in an

The 1999 campus plan for Georgetown University by Robert A.M. Stern Architects reinforced the historic street grid though the campus and expanded development into the school's southwest quadrant.

TOP LEFT: *Southwest Quad-rangle buildings at George-town University by Robert A.M. Stern Architects reinter-preted the traditional archi-tecture of the campus in this new dormitory (right) and cafeteria, 2003.*

TOP RIGHT: *Completed in 2003, the Jesuit residence by Einhorn, Yaffee & Prescott, part of the expansion of the southwest quadrant, quoted the neo-Gothic style of earlier campus buildings. The building sits atop an underground park-ing garage with access from a new campus entrance drive connecting to Canal Road.*

ABOVE LEFT: *The McDo-nough School of Business by Goody Clancy, completed in 2009, combines a historicist Collegiate Gothic building with an expressively modern wing facing a new elevated quadrangle.*

ABOVE RIGHT: *The construc-tion of Regents Hall, the new science center by Payette Asso-ciates, completed the develop-ment of the university's south-west quadrant in 2012.*

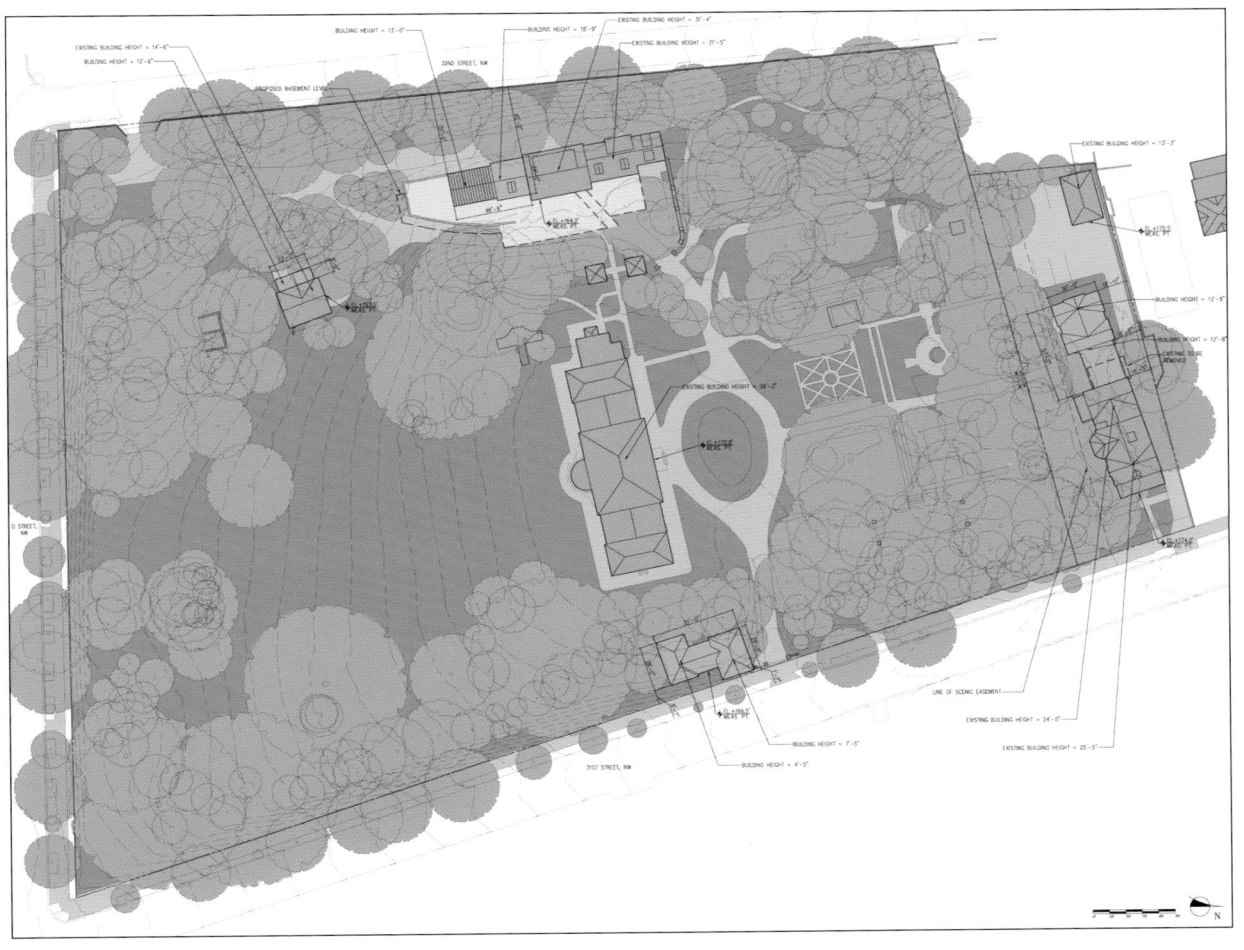

TOP: *The master plan for Tudor Place developed by Mary Oehrlein and Hartman-Cox Architects was approved in 2012; it located expanded facilities associated with the historic house museum to the edges of the property.*

BOTTOM: *A 1962 photograph of the Federal-era Tudor Place, designed by William Thornton, was taken while the property was still a private residence.*

TOP: *View of the Dumbarton Oaks house in 2000 as seen from the North Vista lawn, part of the historic gardens designed by Beatrix Farrand in the 1920s.*

CENTER: *Rendered section drawing of the 1999 design for a library addition by Richard Williams Architects showing the new structure located beneath the North Vista lawn.*

BOTTOM: *Rendering of a concept proposal for the library by Hartman-Cox Architects on a new site at the northwest corner of the property presented a terraced building in the historicist vocabulary of existing accessory buildings, 2000.*

approved master plan in 2012 to add a visitor entry building, an education center, and a curatorial and collections addition to the historic garage complex. The Dumbarton Oaks property, including the extensive notable landscape design by Beatrix Farrand, was acquired by Harvard University in 1940 as a study center for pre-Columbian and Byzantine art. Continuing its ongoing program of additions made in the late twentieth century, Dumbarton Oaks began planning a project for a new library addition in 1999. An early proposal by Richard Williams Architects for an underground addition located beneath the terraced North

Vista lawn was rejected. A different concept design by Hartman-Cox in 2000, a symmetrical pavilion featuring a hipped roof and reminiscent of the other accessory buildings on the property set upon a series of terraces, was approved by the commission. In March 2002, however, Robert Venturi was engaged to present yet another design featuring a slightly asymmetrical box with a flat roof and an articulated brick pattern on the exterior walls. Chairman J. Carter Brown criticized many aspects of the design, comparing the project negatively to the historicist Hartman-Cox design with its sloping roof, traditional windows, and arcuated terraces. By July 2002, Brown had died, and the commission reviewed the changes Venturi had made in response to Brown's critique; under new leadership, the commission voted to return to Venturi's previous concept design, which was given final approval in 2003.

NEW PATTERNS IN REDEVELOPMENT FOR COMMERCIAL PROPERTIES

Applications for review of commercial projects in Georgetown continued in the new century, often at a great pace: proposals for signs and storefront replacements were submitted at the rate of roughly fifteen in a typical month for review by the OGB. While most infill commercial development on Wisconsin Avenue and M Street followed a historicist approach, some projects attempted a more modern idiom in creating new architecture within the existing context. An early redevelopment project on the main commercial spine of M Street was 3233–3235 M Street by Kress Cox Associates, completed in 1999, which included a renovation of an existing building and an addition the proportions and horizontal lines of which drew upon the rhythm and materials of the historic district in a manner derivative of midcentury modern design—and in sympa-

thy with the commercial character of M Street's western blocks.

The most progressive new retail project of the decade was the Design Center West complex, also known as Cady's Alley, occupying much of the south side of the 3300 block of M Street. The developer, Anthony Lanier of EastBanc Inc., retained several local architects to renovate late nineteenth- and early twentieth-century commercial buildings and warehouses in order to create more than 120,000 square feet of retail space and a small number of residential units. The development reused the historic buildings, taking advantage of the change in grade between M Street and the C&O Canal to insert retail spaces and a pedestrian courtyard around the existing alley without either overtly historicist or aggressively modernist design. In contrast to many of the megablock retail projects of previous decades, the scale of redevelopment was more similar to the fabric of historic Georgetown, allowing pedestrian and vehicular access through the site. The OGB reviewed the various components of the development between 1999 and 2003 and was generally supportive of the component project designs, but, following the review of the first case, the board requested that additional architectural detail be

ABOVE: *The redevelopment of Cady's Alley by EastBanc Inc., largely completed by 2004, incorporated the designs of several architects in adjacent projects along an alley to achieve the adaptive reuse of existing industrial buildings south of M Street.*

RIGHT: *The project to renovate and add to a historic commercial building at 3233 M Street by Kress Cox Architects incorporated the rhythm and proportions of the existing structure into the addition (right), 1999.*

The controversial Apple store project involved new construction within a highly intact row of nineteenth-century commercial buildings along Wisconsin Avenue in the heart of the Georgetown historic district.

LEFT, TOP TO BOTTOM.
TOP: *Photomontage of the July 2008 concept design by Bohlin Cywinski Jackson depicted the new store as a minimalist glass volume recessed between flanking piers of masonry to reveal a single-story retail space inside.*

CENTER: *Bohlin Cywinski Jackson's revised concept design of December 2008 expressed the storefront as a billboard-like facade, incised with the Apple logo, above a recessed first-floor storefront of frameless glass.*

BOTTOM: *The revised concept design presented in February 2009 depicted a fenestrated brick facade above an unarticulated glass storefront rem-*

iniscent of the 2007 scheme; with refinements to the storefront, a version of this design was eventually approved by the OGB.

TOP RIGHT: *A concept design by local architect George Gordon in 2007 incorporated an expansive storefront at street level beneath neotraditional upper stories.*

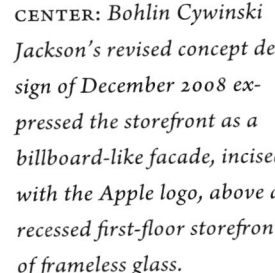

TOP: *A new residential condominium at 3303 Water Street by Frank Schlesinger and Handel Architects, completed in 2004, responded to the industrial scale and character of existing buildings along the C&O Canal.*

ABOVE: *The new Safeway store, designed by Torti Gallas & Partners, was inspired by nineteenth-century market buildings and recreated a strong urban edge to Wisconsin Avenue, 2010.*

added to create a compatible scale.

The most controversial project of the decade—inflaming a discussion on design in the historic district in the news media and Internet—was a new retail store for Apple Inc. at 1229 Wisconsin Avenue. As had been shown in other projects in the historic district, contemporary design could be compatible with historic preservation if it respected existing context. The Apple store proposal, however, revealed a conflict between the values of protecting the historic environment and supporting the widely admired design aesthetic of the highly successful brand of information technology products.

Proposed for a site then occupied by a 1980s-era postmodern commercial building on a double lot, the project was first presented to the OGB in September 2007 by local architect George Gordon for an anonymous client. The design would raze the existing building and replace it with a two-story building following a typical scheme for the commercial frontages in Georgetown: a glass storefront at the sidewalk with a brick second story with five punched windows. While the OGB supported the demolition of the existing building, it was unanimous in its rejection of the concept design, specifically objecting to the expression of the glass storefront with unarticulated full-width glass, to the incongruous scale of the proposal in relation to the adjacent historic buildings, and to the awkward juxtaposition between the modern design of the first story and the historicist second-story design featuring double-hung windows. Instead, the OGB members recommended using a modern aesthetic and emphasized that the issue of architectural scale was paramount.

In July 2008, Apple openly submitted a new design for the property by the nationally prominent firm Bohlin Cywinski Jackson (BCJ), architects of Apple's large, high-profile stores in Manhattan, London, Boston, and other cities. The architects had experience designing Apple stores in historic contexts; these involved either retrofitting historically significant buildings or new construction on streets of significantly larger scale than in Georgetown. The setting most similar to Wisconsin Avenue was Boylston Street in Boston's Back Bay neighborhood, where the store is located amid historic and modern buildings with a diverse range of widths and heights. Significantly, however, the site in Georgetown was within a highly intact historic streetscape with a consistency of scale and narrow range of buildings' ages.

The BCJ proposal for the Georgetown store was decisively minimalist, featuring a two-story, mullionless glass plane set between two stone piers; the glass wall also returned some six feet to create a glass roof at the front. The

OGB members repeated their support for a modern aesthetic but reiterated their concern of articulating architectural scale in relationship to the historic context. Five months later, BCJ submitted a revised design that included a continuous butt-glazed storefront at the sidewalk beneath a smooth white masonry plane approximately thirty-five feet long by twenty-five feet high, featuring an eight-foot-tall window in the shape of an apple, the company's widely recognized logo. The OGB rejected the proposal as too reminiscent of a commercial billboard, but repeated its appreciation of a modern aesthetic, restated its concern about compatible architectural scale, and encouraged the designers to submit alternatives in order to allow for more productive dialogue. One OGB member also questioned the social responsibility of building a one-story structure in a dense, mixed-use commercial district.[155]

In February 2009, a design similar to the schematic elevation presented in September 2007 was submitted, a reworking of the first anonymous proposal: an unarticulated glass storefront at the ground level with four openings in a brick-clad, false-front second story with mildly historicist details. While the OGB had never encouraged a historicist solution, it continued to criticize the lack of detail creating an architectural scale consistent with this prominent block in the heart of Georgetown's commercial district. After the February presentation, the national media picked up the story from the local press.[156] Online fans of Apple posted numerous opinions, criticizing the OGB erroneously for demanding historicist design or making critical remarks about historic preservation in general. Ironically, the *Washington Post* conducted a Web site survey for viewers to vote on their favorite design, generating more than 4,700 responses; the more historicist first and fourth schemes were the most popular.[157] The resolution came one month later when BCJ submitted a design that introduced a steel storefront system—a product used in other Apple stores—and revised the proportions and details of the false-front second story. The OGB recommended approval of this concept; the final design was approved in September 2009, and the store opened in June 2010.

Further north on Wisconsin Avenue, a significant redevelopment project of the decade was the Safeway store, where a suburban paradigm of parking in front of a retail building was inverted to restore a more traditional relationship of building to street frontage. The existing building, opened in 1981, was proposed to be demolished and replaced with a new 67,000-square-foot retail facility on an upper level, with smaller retail suites along Wisconsin Avenue and a two-level parking garage in the rear. Based on

TOP: *Concept model for the 2003 development proposal of a site adjacent to the Washington Harbour complex and Rock Creek involved two buildings: a new building for the Embassy of Sweden (left) and a residential building by Arthur Cotton Moore (right).*

CENTER: *Rendering of the 2003 concept design by Wingårdh Architects for House of Sweden, a neo-modernist composition contrasting with Moore's postmodern Washington Harbour complex directly behind.*

ABOVE: *The House of Sweden by Wingårdh Architects, completed 2006. The third-level volume, intended to be clad in maple veneer panels, was instead built with glass panels featuring an oversized silk-screened wood grain pattern reminiscent of Swedish faux wood painting.*

architectural precedents of nineteenth-century market buildings, the design by the local architecture and planning firm Torti Gallas & Partners presented a highly articulated facade along the street with brick piers, metal details, and a corner entrance tower. The OGB reviewed the building in 2008 and supported a contemporary design character, requesting refinement of the window articulation, reductions in the signage, and screening of the rear parking structure from the adjacent Dumbarton Oaks Park.

In the waterfront neighborhood south of the C&O Canal, large-scale redevelopment continued in the new decade to transform the industrial waterfront area into premium commercial and residential projects. Building on the success of luxury waterfront residential projects such as Washington Harbour and 3100 South Street (the Georgetown incinerator development), a massive residential condominium development was completed in 2004 at 3303 Water Street, immediately adjacent to the canal. Designed by Washington architect Frank Schlesinger with New York-based Handel Architects, 3303 Water Street offered a combination of brick planes and glazed corners articulated by steel grids that responded to the industrial scale and character of the canal location without overwhelming the finer grain of the neighborhood. While J. Carter Brown had raised concerns that the project was "too industrial" in character, the CFA later approved the project after Brown's death in 2002, embracing instead the industrial heritage of the Potomac waterfront to inform appropriate architectural character.

Another large-scale development on the Georgetown waterfront was for a site along Rock Creek, extending from K Street to the Potomac River and facing 30th Street. Numerous proposals for this parcel had been submitted to the commission since 1984 and had been envisioned as part of the Washington Harbour development designed by Arthur Cotton Moore. In April 2003, Moore submitted an entirely new concept proposal for the commercial real estate development company Lano International, headed by former CFA member Alan Novak, comprising two structures above grade linked by an underground garage. The southern structure would be occupied by the Embassy of Sweden, designed by the prominent Swedish firm Wingårdh Architects, and the northern structure, designed by Moore, would house commercial offices. The OGB was critical of Moore's proposal to locate the entrance level of the north building a half level below the street as well as other issues of architectural scale and site planning. Moore successfully appealed the review process directly to the commission—although it, too, had concerns about scale and building relationships—and a revised concept and later a

final design for various components of the north building were approved in 2004 and 2005.[158]

Wingårdh's design for the south structure—known as the House of Sweden—featured a white marble–clad podium supporting four stories of glassy construction with expansive views of the Potomac River. The design expressed subtly changing transparencies and an innovative use of materials exemplified by a decorative projecting band of glass panels encasing a veneer of maple wood. The commission recommended further study of the transparency on the top floors and building illumination but enthusiastically supported the wood panel band. However, when the commission reviewed the material mock-ups for the embassy in October 2005, the maple veneer—which had been determined to be unstable in this application—was substituted with a plastic interlayer silkscreened with an enlarged wood grain pattern between the sheets of laminated glass. The architect explained that the artifice made reference to a Swedish tradition of faux painting; the commission approved the change.

GEORGETOWN WATERFRONT PARK

On the other side of the Washington Harbour development, the Georgetown Waterfront Park comprises a ten-acre strip of land extending north along the Potomac River from the Key Bridge to 34th Street. The area, once the location of shipping and industrial activity, had been considered for decades as a redevelopment opportunity like the adjacent Washington Harbour. In 1973, CFA chairman J. Carter Brown testified before the D.C. Zoning Commission that the waterfront west of 31st Street should be treated entirely as a park, urban in character with possible amenities such as restaurants, boating facilities, and an outdoor theater. In 1975, Brown wrote to D.C. mayor Walter Washington, again urging the recreational use of the site and accepting interim parking on the parcel only to assure its future as a park. Over the next decade, Brown and CFA secretary Charles Atherton continued to advocate for the area's reservation as a public amenity, particularly since the adjacent mixed-used development was already built.[159] A design by EDAW for Phase I of the park, between 31st Street and Wisconsin Avenue, was presented to the commission in April and June of 1985; the CFA approved the design for a passive park with virtually no ancillary structures and recommended a reduction in the amount of paving.

In fact, the parcel was given over to parking, a "temporary" condition that lasted for decades due to complications in the transfer of land ownership from the District government to the National Park Service. After years of inactivity, the National Park Service returned to the CFA in

LEFT: *A c. 1982 concept for the Georgetown Waterfront Park Phase I by* EDAW *envisioned a largely passive open space with curving pathways between groupings of trees.*

BELOW: *Wallace, Roberts & Todd developed a new concept design for the waterfront park in 2003. The new plan punctuated the former industrial site as segments related to the street grid, each bisected by a diagonal path; the landscape features included a paved labyrinth, a fountain overlook at the terminus of Wisconsin Avenue, and trellises along the esplanade with metal structures reminiscent of ship masts and sails by artist Jody Pinto.*

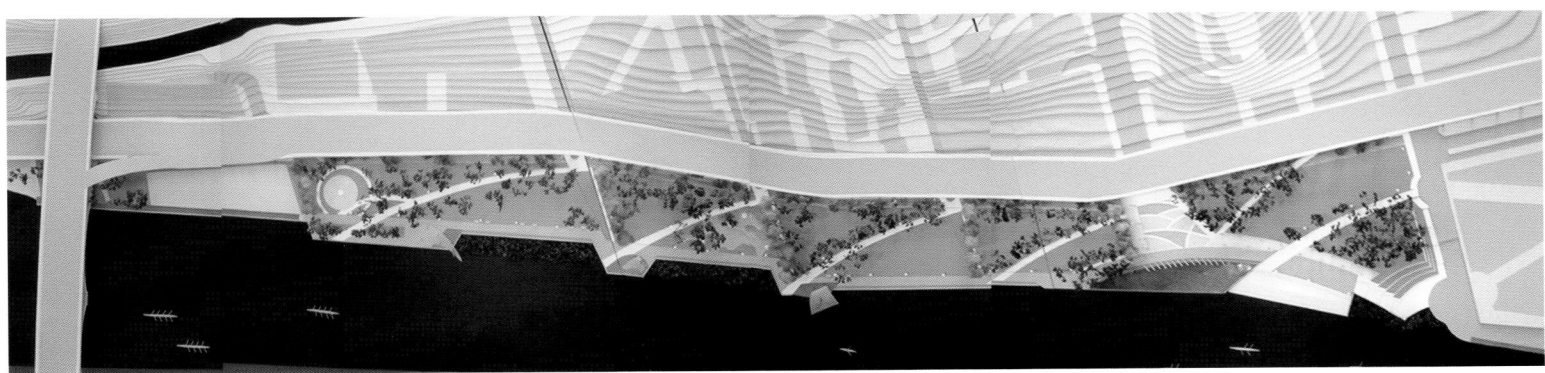

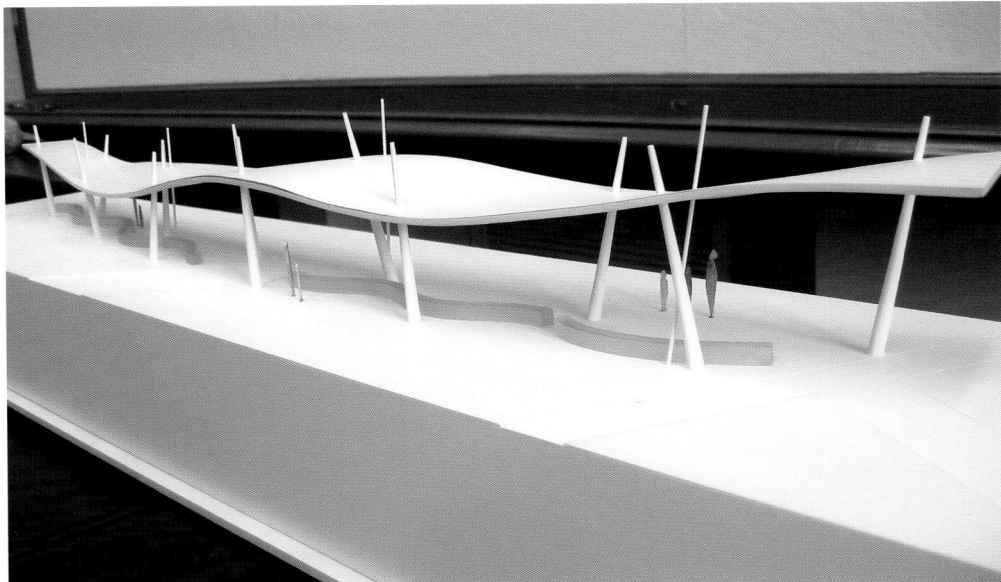

LEFT AND ABOVE: *Model of sail-like structures (left) and trellises (right) at overlooks proposed by Pinto, 2004.*

TOP: *Rendering from the revised concept by Wallace, Roberts & Todd in 2008 that simplified the design and replaced Pinto's masts and undulating structures with mesh pergolas on canted supports.*

BOTTOM: *The Georgetown Waterfront Park as completed in 2010 realized a decades-long effort to transform the industrial waterfront into public recreation space.*

2003 with a park design by landscape architect Ignacio Bunster-Ossa of Wallace, Roberts & Todd and sculptor Jody Pinto. The design featured diagonal walks that divided the park into linear sections, a promenade along the river, a fountain plaza, a stairway down the river bank from which to view regattas, and a labyrinth that was included at the request of the community. The paving of walks leading south to the river changed in a sequence symbolizing Georgetown's history, while certain plantings followed an east to west progression from formal to natural. The commission found the design too complex for the size of the park and recommended simplification of the forms and metaphors.

The most striking—and contentious—feature of the 2003 design was the three trellis structures along the river shore, designed by Pinto as seventy-five-foot-tall sloping stainless steel masts, each supporting a fiberglass sail. The style and scale of the sculptural forms—meant to evoke the sailing ships of Georgetown's maritime past—led to resistance from the community. The CFA also questioned the pavilions' scale, height, and durability, and whether their sails would cast sufficient shade; eventually, the commission recommended that they be simplified or eliminated. By September 2005, Pinto had left the project, and the pavilions had been entirely redesigned as projecting platforms with granite seats and interpretive panels; three undulating pergolas supported on canted posts lined the inland side of the promenade. While the community again expressed its dissatisfaction with the aesthetic character of the structures, the commission approved the pergolas with slight modifications. The park was finally built in 2010—completing, along with the House of Sweden, the redevelopment of Georgetown's waterfront from Rock Creek to Key Bridge, a process in which the CFA had exerted a guiding influence for nearly fifty years.

Private Development and the Shipstead-Luce Act

Through its jurisdiction under the Shipstead-Luce Act, the Commission of Fine Arts has continued to adjudicate matters of design in areas of federal interest, such as properties within the monumental core of the city, along the Potomac waterfront, and facing the parks along Rock Creek. Charged under the 1930 legislation to "prevent reasonably avoidable impairment of the public values" associated with public buildings and parks, the CFA has reviewed an increasing number of commercial, residential, and institutional projects—a number that may rise further as development in the District of Columbia continues to surge.

DEVELOPMENT ADJACENT TO FEDERAL PARKLAND

The relationship of the built environment to the Rock Creek valley has remained a core concern for the commission. A prominent case in the 1990s was a proposal for a new chancery for the Italian government on Whitehaven Street at Massachusetts Avenue, NW, a partially wooded five-acre site abutting Rock Creek and Potomac Parkway with a view of the Washington Monument. Designed by Italian architect Piero Sartogo in association with Leo A Daly, the building reflected the typology of a Tuscan villa bisected with a diagonal axis oriented to the monument. At the first review of the project in July 1993, the CFA focused on the building's relation to the site and neighborhood, near other embassies and residential properties high above the parkway. Chairman J. Carter Brown noted the mismatch between the public chancery functions and the quiet residential context and questioned the fortress-like image presented as contrary to the openness incumbent on the design of embassies; George Hartman suggested that a better site design would situate the building closer to the street with a more developed landscape garden opening to the parkland at the rear. By the final review in April 1995, the building had been reduced in size and the formal Italian garden elements omitted; although completed before the infamous U.S. embassy bombings in 1998, the project anticipated the protective and inwardly-focused requirements of embassy design in the new century.

In the first decade of the twenty-first century, significant increases in housing prices created a boom in the residential real estate market across the District, with investment ranging from home improvement to the subdivision of larger, often historic, properties and redevelopment with new homes. Depending on their location and extent, many of these projects also came under the commission's purview. In one well-publicized case in May 2006, the District of Columbia government had neglected to refer to the CFA for review a significant redevelopment project in North Portal Estates—an established neighborhood of

The Italian Embassy by Piero Sartogo with Leo A Daly as built in 2000 on its wooded site facing Massachusetts Avenue adjacent to Rock Creek Park.

generally mid-twentieth-century single-family houses adjacent to Rock Creek Park in the far northern corner of the city. The neighbors, unhappy with the insertion of two new three-story houses in their midst, advocated successfully for CFA review under the Shipstead-Luce Act. The CFA comments noted that the buildings were not in character with the established order of the houses on lots facing the public park areas that are tributary to the Rock Creek Park system. The District of Columbia eventually enforced the demolition of one of the new houses as a result.

Another important residential case reviewed under the commission's Shipstead-Luce authority was in a tributary valley of Rock Creek Park: Tregaron (originally called The Causeway), a twenty-acre estate in Cleveland Park designed by architect Charles A. Platt with landscape architect Ellen Biddle Shipman beginning in 1912. Located next to Klingle Valley Parkway, a forested stream valley, the estate had been divided in 1980 into a six-acre parcel, in-

cluding the historic residence and auxiliary structures for use as a private secondary school, and a fourteen-acre parcel with the majority of the designed landscape. In 2004, the entity that owned the larger landscaped parcel, which had become overgrown and its garden deteriorated, began pursuing a planned unit development to build sixteen new residences on the site. In February 2004, the project team of architects Miller Hull and landscape architects Oehme van Sweden submitted a master plan to the commission that located two lots at the northwest corner of the property and the others along a new road that would cross a meadow at the middle of the site.

The case revealed divergent views among commission members regarding the significance of the garden and the preservation of historic landscapes. Chairman David Childs opened the discussion by referring to the parcel as a remnant of the estate and commended the designers' concept. Diana Balmori, the landscape architect on the

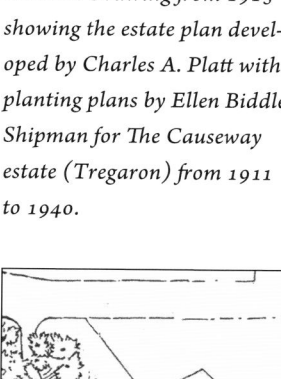

BELOW: *Drawing from 1915 showing the estate plan developed by Charles A. Platt with planting plans by Ellen Biddle Shipman for The Causeway estate (Tregaron) from 1911 to 1940.*

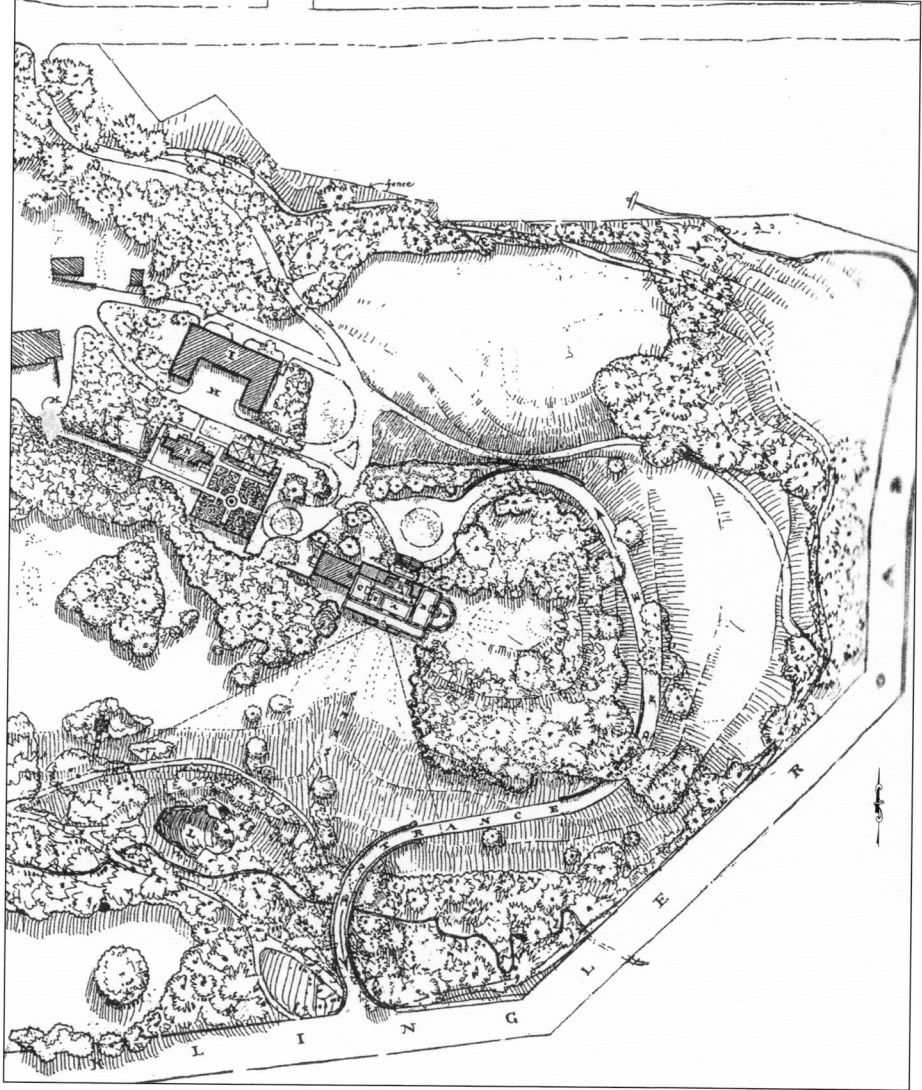

TOP RIGHT AND ABOVE: *View of the formal garden at The Causeway looking east toward the house, 1919; View* *looking west across the lawn and wooded landscape with the National Cathedral in the distance, c. 1915.*

The 2008 revised master plan by Miller Hull with Heritage Landscapes reduced the number of houses and located new development at the eastern edge of the Tregaron property close to Klingle Road; an earlier plan would have developed the meadow with sixteen houses and an access road, encompassing a significant area of the remaining garden.

commission, acknowledged that landscapes change over time but questioned the location of the proposed road and the number of houses. She further noted the importance of Shipman's design work and advocated for the restoration of her garden, adding that it would be wonderful if Washington could be the home of both a "great" Shipman garden as well as Beatrix Farrand's design at Dumbarton Oaks.[160]

After others spoke, Childs concluded by describing the project as a model development and did not call for a motion. The following week, the D.C. Historic Preservation Review Board, which must approve subdivisions of historic landmarks, recommended against all of the new

lots except for the two at the northwest corner of the property along Macomb Street.

In September, a revised master plan was submitted that reduced the number of residences from sixteen to nine. It included the two lots along Macomb Street and seven houses accessed by driveways off Klingle Road; these houses would be largely invisible from the historic residence since they were situated below the steepest slope of the property in Shipman's Wild Garden fronting Rock Creek Park. The commission members visited the site in the morning before their meeting. After the architect presented the new scheme, a representative from the National Park Service spoke in opposition to the project because of the severe stormwater management issues associated with the property. The president of the Friends of Tregaron Foundation, a neighborhood group, testified that the revised master plan had a more significant impact on Rock Creek Park and therefore conflicted with the intent of the Shipstead-Luce Act.

Childs began the discussion by expressing his disappointment that the previous plan had been disapproved by the D.C. government and then noted that fewer residences meant less money to restore the historic garden with further deterioration the result of more delay. Balmori emphasized the value of Shipman's surviving landscape. Other commission members acknowledged the scarcity of available land in Washington, the inevitability of development, and the poor condition of the landscape; but Balmori reminded them that the development plan did not address the problematic conditions throughout the entire site. Recognizing that her views were not supported by her colleagues, she remarked that "there is an enormous amount of protection of pieces of architecture and practically none of pieces of landscape architecture. This is a significant piece of landscape architecture."[161]

In 2006, thirteen of the fourteen acres owned by the Tregaron Limited Partnership were donated to the Tregaron Conservancy (formerly the Friends of Tregaron Foundation), whose mission is to restore the gardens to Shipman's design with public access. The remaining acre was subdivided into eight house lots around the edge of the site; construction of the first two of these properties began in 2012.

ARCHITECTURAL EVOLUTION IN COMMERCIAL WASHINGTON

In the downtown areas adjacent to or within the city's monumental core, economic growth continued into the early twenty-first century, bringing with it projects to redevelop many existing buildings with additions, to reclad existing structures with new skins, or to rebuild entire sites; measures of sustainable performance were often cited as informing many of the design decisions. A noteworthy example of large-scale redevelopment involving an existing historic structure was the design for a substantial addition to the headquarters of the American Pharmaceutical Association, a building on Constitution Avenue designed in an austere Beaux-Arts style by John Russell Pope in 1933. The addition by Hartman-Cox Architects, completed in 2009, provided a subdued historicist backdrop to the earlier building, which is a National Historic Landmark. In its reviews of the concept in 2002 and 2003, the CFA found the new structure to be respectful of the Pope building and suggested some additional study of the connection between the new and the old buildings to enhance their separation.

The greater trend over the last ten years in new office construction in the District has been toward an expression of neomodernist architecture characterized by the use of significant amounts of glass in facades. During one CFA review of a new office building proposal, Michael McKinnell commented on this growing trend of "glass buildings, [the] proliferation of them in Washington…at what point is the limestone masonry city going to reach a tipping point and change its received character?"[162]

A project located at 51 Louisiana Avenue, NW, by Richard Rogers & Partners, included a new ten-story office building addition on the former site of a parking garage connected to the existing Acacia Building (1935) and an earlier addition (1953) through the insertion of a seven-story triangular atrium element in a former courtyard. The expressive design employs glazed facades to heighten the transparency of the new structures. The CFA approved the initial concept in November 2004, noting its appreciation of the proposal's clarity and strong statement of contemporary aesthetics. Later revisions due to zoning requirements were also approved, and the project was completed in 2009.

A prominent example of recladding an existing property was the redevelopment of the Nassif building, the former headquarters of the U.S. Department of Transportation at 400 7th Street, SW. Named after its developer, David Nassif, the ten-story structure was designed by Edward Durell Stone in 1968 in a formalist International Style of masonry pilotis, heavy overhang, vertical glass windows, and panels of white marble—the largest private-sector office building in Washington at that time. By 2005, the building was slated for a complete renovation due to chronic issues, such as poor interior air quality and the weakening structural system of the facade panels; it was to be redeveloped as the Constitution Center with modest corner additions and an enclosed interior courtyard. In its July 2005 review of the renovation concept by Smith Group, the CFA lamented the loss of Stone's design and suggested that the new design, which it found overly complex, should retain some of the character of the original building. The commission later approved the revised design, which responded to members' comments to refine the curtain wall elements. The renovation was completed in 2009 and was positioned to accommodate a large, high-security tenant, such as the U.S. Coast Guard, although that entity was instead located on the St. Elizabeths west campus.

Two other projects illustrate the trend of site redevelopment with glass facades, often with strong sustainability performance goals. Completed in 2009, the Lafayette

TOP: *The 2009 Hartman-Cox addition to the American Pharmaceutical Association headquarters is stylistically derived from the smaller Beaux-Arts building by John Russell Pope.*

BOTTOM: *A seven-story atrium links the neomodernist office building at 51 Louisiana Avenue, NW, by Richard Rogers & Partners in 2009—a composition of striking angles and transparent glass—to the existing neoclassical architecture of the 1930s Acacia Building and its 1950s addition.*

TOP LEFT: *At the time of its completion in 1968, the Nassif building, designed in a formalist International Style by Edward Durell Stone, was the largest private-sector office building in Washington and home to the U.S. Department of Transportation for more than three decades.*

ABOVE LEFT: *Renovated by Smith Group in 2009, the marble panels of the Edward Durell Stone building were removed, and the Nassif building was redesigned as a largely transparent glass box with solid corners.*

TOP RIGHT: *Lafayette Tower at 801 17th Street, NW, by Kevin Roche John Dinkeloo & Associates, completed in 2009, recalls the graphic forms and reflective palette of late modern architecture.*

ABOVE RIGHT: *PNC Place at 800 17th Street, NW, by Gensler was completed in 2012 in a minimalist neomodern vocabulary.*

Tower at 801 17th Street, NW, by Kevin Roche John Dinkeloo & Associates, is a taut-skinned glass box with sculptural recesses relieving the facade. In September 2006, the CFA approved a revised concept design that responded to its earlier advice to reconsider the location of the facade recesses and to establish a better relationship with adjacent buildings through adjustments to the curtain wall design. Immediately across the street at 800 17th Street, NW, located within view of the White House and Washington Monument, is a new twelve-story, glass-walled office building, PNC Place, by Gensler. The CFA approved the concept design in November 2007, commending its elegance but noting that the simplicity of the glass facades would require careful detailing.

LARGE-SCALE MIXED-USE DEVELOPMENT

Due to the building up of the city's central commercial districts in the late twentieth century, significant commercial growth has been planned for the redevelopment of areas adjacent to the downtown, often as air-rights development

over existing infrastructure or the intensification of older projects. Although reviewed as a District of Columbia-sponsored project, City Center by Hines Interests, designed by Foster & Partners with Shalom Baranes, is a redevelopment of the ten-acre former convention center site near Mount Vernon Square containing 2.5 million square feet of retail, office, and residential space. The CFA's review in March 2008 was highly supportive of the mixed-use proposal to recreate city blocks lined with retail and supporting significant public spaces. Prominent examples in the Southwest sector of Washington reviewed under the Shipstead-Luce Act include the Portals project by Republic Properties, planned and designed beginning in the 1990s by Arthur Cotton Moore and others on a former rail yard immediately south of the Department of Agriculture Annex, as well as a series of proposals to improve the L'Enfant Plaza complex. The L'Enfant Plaza proposals included a 2005 unbuilt project for a new museum and office building by Cesar Pelli within the courtyard of the 1960s-era complex, substantial renovation of the complex's lower-level re-

tail mall and plaza entrance in 2011, and the development of the two vacant corners of the property as a high-rise hotel and an office building. The CFA was supportive of these proposals to intensify the existing development. In the case of the hotel building by Smith Group and ZGF's office building proposal, both reviewed from 2011 to 2012, the commission members encouraged bold, contemporary design but with minor changes in the new buildings' massing to respect the formal composition of the original I.M. Pei-designed L'Enfant Plaza hotel and the adjacent Department of Housing and Urban Development by Marcel Breuer.

Nearby, along the Washington Channel waterfront, the District of Columbia government pursued the redevelopment of a consolidated twenty-three-acre property. With a row of low-rise restaurants dating from the 1960s, the site was an underdeveloped area the earlier industrial and commercial buildings of which had been demolished under the urban renewal efforts of the 1950s; the site was added to the Shipstead-Luce jurisdiction in 1961 to control future private development on the waterfront. Reconceived as

Photomontage of the Portals project by Arthur Cotton Moore, 1996, a redevelopment centered on Maryland Avenue above a former rail yard and parking lots. By 2007, most of the megaproject parcels, designed by Moore and others, had been built.

RIGHT: *Concept design for City Center, a massive mixed-use development on the former site of the convention center by Foster & Partners with Shalom Baranes Architects, 2008.*

BELOW: *Cesar Pelli's 2005 proposal for an office building and new National Children's Museum was located in the central courtyard of L'Enfant Plaza; redevelopment also included new buildings at the northeast and southeast corners of the parcel abutting the iconic HUD headquarters building.*

RIGHT: *Rendering of the 2012 concept design for an office building on the southeast corner of the L'Enfant Plaza parcel by ZGF Architects, showing the inflected planes of the* building's *form designed to minimize proximity to the HUD building at left.*

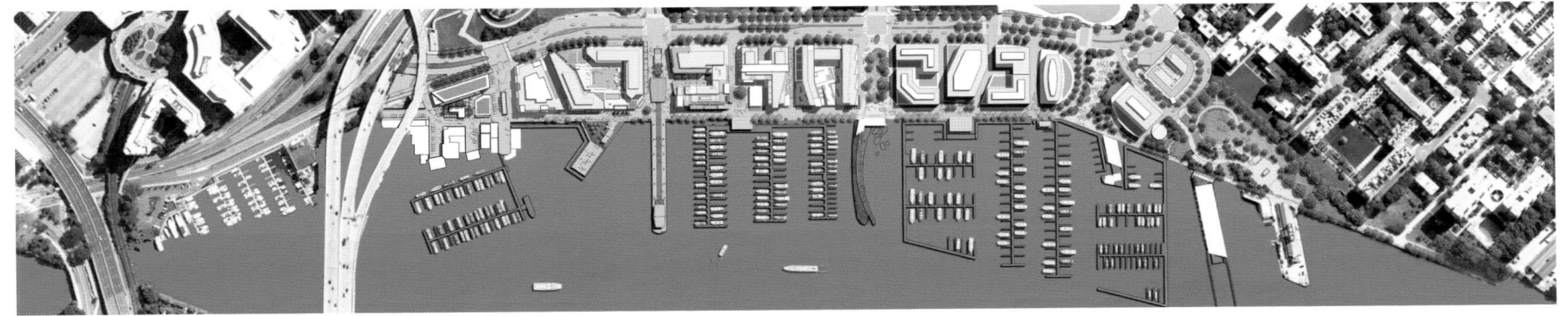

TOP: *District of Columbia–sponsored redevelopment of the Southwest waterfront resulted in a 2011 master plan by EE&K/Perkins Eastman for P.N. Hoffman, comprising multiple block-sized parcels containing 2.5 million square feet of residential, hotel, office, entertainment, and retail uses above underground parking and roughly thirteen acres of public spaces.*

ABOVE: *Rendering of The Wharf project by EE&K/ Perkins Eastman and others, 2012. After numerous reviews for the twenty-five-acre development, in July 2012, the CFA gave concept approval to all elements of the project, which addressed its advice to simplify the exuberantly commercial design character.*

LEFT: *Aerial view of the Southwest waterfront, 1992, showing the low intensity of development along the Washington Channel, which remained for five decades following the extensive demolition of the 1950s.*

The Wharf, the parcel was developed by P. N. Hoffman with a master plan by EE&K/Perkins Eastman as a series of urban blocks with a redesigned wharf frontage and new piers; reconfigured boat slips; new public squares; office, residential, and hotel buildings with underground parking; and a large performance hall—a total of 2.5 million square feet of new development. In an initial information presentation in November 2011, the CFA members expressed support for creating a new image for the city on the waterfront and stressed the importance of the physical and visual links from the National Mall to the proposed waterfront development through the 10th Street corridor. The components of the project were reviewed by the CFA in several phases in 2012, and all parts received a recommendation for concept approval by July 2012; construction of the project constitutes a significant step in realizing the goals of the *Monumental Core Framework Plan* and the Southwest Ecodistrict Initiative.

As the city continues to grow, areas near the monumental core will also continue to experience pressure for redevelopment. Currently announced are other multi-block proposals to create mixed-use air-rights developments adjacent to or within the Shipstead-Luce Act jurisdiction. One is a 2.3 million-square-foot project to recreate three urban blocks over the I-395 Center Leg between E Street and Massachusetts Avenue, NW, by SOM for Property Group Partners; another is Burnham Place by Akridge Companies and designed by Shalom Baranes for roughly 3 million square feet of development above the rail yard serving Union Station, creating a new front to the multimodal transportation hub facing H Street, N.E. Both projects demonstrate that development in Washington, D.C. is pushing outward from its historic central commercial core; underdeveloped contiguous areas are now being in-

tegrated into a larger, more organic city with the monumental core at its heart.

The Commission in its Second Century

For more than a century, the Commission of Fine Arts has built upon a tradition of bringing together nationally prominent planners, architects, and artists in creating and protecting a vision for the physical symbols of the American nation: its monuments, its coins, and its capital city—its civic art. As the commission begins its second century, new issues and challenges unforeseen by previous generations will continue to arise as the nation seeks to express its collective memory, political aspirations, and civic values in its symbols. The impact of a rapidly changing technological environment informs all aspects of these and will no doubt drive further the evolution of design—whether urban, architectural, institutional, numismatic, or commemorative—in the future.

In 2011, President Barack Obama announced three new appointments to the commission, concluding a period of relatively little change in its membership. The new members included Edwin Schlossberg, a New York-based exhibit designer and author; sculptor and visual artist Teresita Fernández, also of New York; and architect Philip Freelon of North Carolina, whose practice focused on institutional and cultural facilities and included several of Washington, D.C.'s new libraries as well as the forthcoming National Museum of African American History and Culture of the Smithsonian Institution. Architect, urban designer, and educator Elizabeth Plater-Zyberk was elected vice chairman in October 2011, joining Chairman Earl A. Powell III in leading the commission. Powell was reappointed by President Obama for a third term in 2012. The

BELOW LEFT: *The members of the U.S. Commission of Fine Arts, February 2012 (from left): Witold Rybczynski, Edwin Schlossberg, Vice Chairman Elizabeth Plater-Zyberk, Chairman Earl A. Powell III, Diana Balmori, Teresita Fernández, Philip Freelon, and Secretary Thomas Luebke.*

BELOW RIGHT: *Commission of Fine Arts staff, May 2010 (from left): Sarah Batcheler, Phyllis Roderer, Frederick Lindstrom, Susan Raposa, Mary Konsoulis, Thomas Luebke, Raksha Patel, Eve Barsoum, José Martínez Canino, and Kay Fanning.*

Rendering by ZGF of the Southwest Ecodistrict initiative, a cooperative planning effort led by the NCPC to extend sustainable development from the monumental core to the waterfront, 2012, following the direction of the Monumental Core Framework Plan *and Executive Order 13514.*

president also appointed two new members who began their service on the commission in October 2012: Alex Krieger, the Boston-based architect, urban designer, and educator; and Elizabeth K. Meyer, a theorist and professor of landscape architecture at the University of Virginia in Charlottesville.

A new decade has brought wider changes in government culture, manifesting new issues in all aspects of design reviewed by the commission. In planning, the federal government has increased its commitment to sustainable practices, following the Obama administration's Executive Order 13514 on Federal Leadership in Environmental, Energy, and Economic Performance, requiring federal agencies to increase energy efficiency, conserve water and fuel, reduce waste and emissions, support sustainable communities, and leverage federal purchasing power to promote environmentally responsible products and technologies. The Southwest Ecodistrict—a cooperative effort among the CFA and the General Services Administration, the National Capital Planning Commission, the Department of Agriculture, and the D.C. Office of Planning begun in 2009—is an initiative proceeding from the recommendations of the *Monumental Core Framework Plan* to link the symbolic landscape of the National Mall to the city's waterfront. The new plan is informed by performance-based criteria to optimize energy and water consumption, maximize efficiency of land use, and improve access and walkability through coordinated improvements of buildings and infrastructure, such as the redevelopment of the Department of Energy complex, the creation of an urban linear park above the railroad right-of-way on Maryland Avenue, and the redesign of the 10th Street corridor with a mix of uses and low-impact design landscape.

For federal facilities generally, the new decade of the 2010s appears to indicate a shift away from an overwhelming concern with security—the defining issue of the previous decade—to one of aggressive policies to reduce the federal government's footprint, both in terms of energy use as well as its physical use of real estate. The GSA's new policies will no doubt have far-reaching effects upon the future of the programming, location, and design of federal buildings through mandating transit-oriented locations, substantial reductions in space allocated for each employee, and the institution of high-energy performance requirements. Virtually all of these new directions in policy for housing the federal government may be seen as emerging from an increasingly automated workplace, where communications technologies obviate the need for the full-time physical presence of all employees or sophisticated building operations information systems can be used to control energy consumption. And as the federal government redevelops its facilities to create a more sustainable environment, there is also a concomitant impetus toward density, walkability, and livability. In Washington, this may bring about a blurring of the boundaries between the monumental, federal core and the city around it. Rather than the separate symbolic precinct envisioned by the McMillan Commission documents of the early twentieth century,

The 2011 competition conducted by the Trust for the National Mall in cooperation with the National Park Service proposed transformations of three significant landscapes within the monumental core of Washington.

ABOVE: The competition-winning entry for the redesign of Constitution Gardens by Rogers Marvel Architects and Peter Walker & Partners included skating on the lake and a long-planned restaurant pavilion for visitors, 2012.

RIGHT: The winning entry for the redesign of the Sylvan Theater on the Washington Monument Grounds by OLIN with Weiss Manfredi would rework the design, access, and setting of the amphitheater with raised earthworks and a potential connection to the Tidal Basin, 2012.

the future federal presence may be a more vibrant and integrated part of the city.

With its enormous inventory of historic properties, the federal government will face an increasing challenge of improving, maintaining, or disposing of these resources as it implements policies of planning and energy efficiency and compatibility of the physical structures with these goals. New concerns also affect decision making: for example, the great majority of the properties in the CFA's Washington, D.C., jurisdiction—now including many midcentury modern buildings—are defined as historic. As the controversy over the Georgetown Apple computer store revealed, there may be shifting attitudes about the importance of historic preservation, possibly showing a reverse in a thirty-year trend of public sympathy for the preservation of the old in favor of the expression of the new.

For the CFA, the institutionalized review process has changed from a closed council promulgating a single stylistic paradigm to an open deliberative body that considers multiple approaches, embracing a gamut of aesthetic expression ranging from classical or historicist to modern and abstract. Changing artistic sensibilities have always underlain each generation's estimation of the qualities of the built environment; the CFA of the future will continue to evolve in its assessment of design of the public realm but will, by necessity, accommodate newer aesthetics informed by technology.

At the core of the mission of the Commission of Fine Arts is a concern with the representation of national civic values as expressed in physical symbols, public institutions, and commemorative works the existence of which is mandated by a complex political governmental structure. While the subjects of national symbolism may not change fundamentally, the typologies of their representation have evolved considerably and will certainly continue to do so, particularly as our basic means of information gathering, dissemination, and public debate is radically changed by the Internet. However, as our cultural expression changes, the manifestations of its civic symbols and structures will certainly evolve with it. In one hundred years, the Commission of Fine Arts has been constant as a steward of the unique and living cultural heritage represented by the national capital in Washington. Its mission for high standards of design will continue in the future, accommodating changing aesthetic trends and political forces to express the transcendent symbols of American democracy.

The development of Washington will go on so long as the Republic endures. The problems of the future will be multiplied and will be different from those of the past.... The remedy lies not in the words but in good design, faithfully carried out.[163]

—CHARLES MOORE, 1939

The winning entry for the third site in the competition for Union Square at the western side of the U.S. Capitol was Gustafson Guthrie Nichol with Davis Brody Bond, 2012. At the location where the Mall meets the Capitol Grounds, the design would reconfigure the 1970s SOM reflecting pool as a linear extension of the Mall's lawn panels defined by terraces, groves, and gardens to accommodate events while incorporating perimeter security for the Capitol complex. Jurisdiction of Union Square was transferred from the National Park Service to the Architect of the Capitol before the competition winners were announced in 2012.

Legislative history

1910   An Act Establishing a Commission of Fine Arts (CFA), May 17, 1910, ch. 243, 36 Stat. 371 (codified at 40 U.S.C. §§ 9101–9104 (2011)).

1910   Executive Order 1259, October 25, 1910, 45 C.F.R § 2101(a)(1) (2011). CFA review of public buildings in the District of Columbia proposed by the federal or District of Columbia governments established.

1913   Executive Order 1862, November 28, 1913, 45 C.F.R. §§ 2101 (a)(1), 2101(f) (2011). CFA review of new structures and matters of art proposed by the federal government in the District of Columbia established.

1921   Executive Order 3524, July 28, 1921, 45 C.F.R. §§ 2101(a)(2), 2101(d) (2011). CFA review of the design of medals, insignia, and coins produced by the federal government and the designs of statues, fountains, and monuments in the District of Columbia established.

1923   American Battle Monuments Act of March 4, 1923, ch. 283, sec. 3, 42 Stat. 1509, 1510 (codified as amended at 36 U.S.C. § 2105(d) (2011)). CFA review and approval of the design of memorials in American cemeteries outside the United States commemorating the service of American Armed Forces established.

1930   Shipstead-Luce Act of May 16, 1930, ch. 291, sec. 1, 46 Stat. 366 (codified as amended at 40 U.S.C. § 8104 (2011)). CFA review of plans for construction or alteration of private and semipublic buildings fronting or abutting certain public areas in Washington, D.C., established.

1939   Act of July 31, 1939, ch. 400, 53 Stat. 1144 (codified as amended at 40 U.S.C. § 8104 (2011)). Shipstead-Luce Act amended to include Lafayette Park within the geographic area of the act's jurisdiction.

1946   Act of June 26, 1946, ch. 502, sec. 3, 60 Stat. 317 (codified as amended at 36 U.S.C. § 2105 (2011)). CFA approval of memorials commemorating the service of American Armed Forces extended to all battlefields and cemeteries outside the United States.

1950   Old Georgetown Act of September 22, 1950, ch. 984, 64 Stat. 903 (codified at D.C. ST. §§ 6-1201–1204 (West) (2012)). CFA review and approval of plans for construction, alteration, reconstruction, or razing of any building within a defined geographic area in Georgetown established.

1952   National Capital Planning Act of July 19, 1952, ch. 949, 66 Stat. 781 (codified as amended at 40 U.S.C. §§ 8701 et seq. (2011)). The National Capital Planning Commission created requiring CFA advice on selection of lands suitable for the development of the National Capital park, parkway, and playground system.

1955   Act of May 25, 1955, ch. 76, 69 Stat. 66 (codified as amended at 40 U.S.C. § 9104 (2011)). CFA appropriations authorized.

1956   Act of July 25, 1956, ch. 721, sec. 3(c), 70 Stat. 640, 641 (codified at 36 U.S.C. § 2105 (2011)). CFA authority regarding memorials commemorating the service of American Armed Forces under the American Battle Monuments Act amended.

1957   Act of September 2, 1957, sec 1(1), 71 Stat. 589 (codified at 10 U.S.C. § 4594 (2011)). Provision of heraldic services by the Secretary of the Army authorized, with CFA advisory design review upon request established.

1958   National Cultural Center Act of September 2, 1958, sec. 3, 72 Stat. 1698, 1699 (codified as amended at 20 U.S.C. § 76i (2011)). The National Cultural Center within the Smithsonian Institution established requiring CFA approval of building plans and specifications.

1960   Act of May 13, 1960, 74 Stat. 128 (codified as amended at 40 U.S.C. § 9104 (2011)). CFA appropriations authorized.

1964   Act of January 23, 1964, 78 Stat. 4 (codified as amended at 20 U.S.C. § 76i (2011)). The National Cultural Center renamed John F. Kennedy Center for the Performing Arts; CFA chairman named ex officio member of the board.

1964   Executive Order 11145, March 7, 1964, 3 C.F.R. 1964–1965 Comp, 184. A curator for the White House and a Committee for the Preservation of the White House, including participation by the CFA chairman, created.

1965   National Foundation of the Arts and the Humanities Act of 1965, 79 Stat. 845, 851 (codified as amended at 20 U.S.C. §§ 951–960 (2011)). The National Foundation for the Arts and Humanities with a Federal Council to advise the foundation, including participation by the CFA chairman, created.

1975   Arts and Artifacts Indemnity Act, 89 Stat. 844 (codified as amended at 20 U.S.C. §§ 971–976 (2011)). Indemnity agreements for loans of art on exhibition in the United States and elsewhere entered into by the Federal Council, including participation by the CFA chairman, authorized.

1986   National Capital Memorials and Commemorative Works Act of November 14, 1986, 100 Stat. 3650 (codified as amended at 40 U.S.C. §§ 8901–8909 (2011)). Standards for the placement of commemorative works on federal lands within the District of Columbia established; CFA approval of site and design proposals for commemorative works required.

1987   Act of December 22, 1987, Title II, sec. 201, 101 Stat. 1329–214, 1329–250 (codified as amended at 20 U.S.C. §§ 956a (2011)). Administration of program (National Capital Arts and Cultural Affairs) to support artistic and cultural programs in the National Capital transferred from National Endowment for the Humanities to CFA.

1991   45 C.F.R. §§ 1160. –1160.12 (2011). Regulations to implement the Arts and Artifacts Indemnity Act, including participation by the CFA chairman, adopted.

2003   Commemorative Works Clarification and Revision Act of 2003, Title II, secs. 201–206, 117 Stat. 1348, 1349 (codified as amended at 40 U.S.C. §§ 8901–8909 (2011)). Definitions, siting, and design review processes, and other aspects of the CWA revised and clarified.

2007   Consolidated Appropriations Act, 2007, Title IV, sec 426, 121 Stat.1844, 2151 (codified as amended at 20 U.S.C. §§ 972, 974 (2011)). Limits of coverage for indemnification agreements authorized by the Arts and Artifacts Indemnity Act amended.

2012   Honoring America's Veterans and Caring for Camp Lejeune Families Act of August 8, 2012, Title IV, sec. 604, 126 Stat. 1165, 1201. CFA advisory role in review of the design of monuments in Arlington National Cemetery formalized.

APPENDIX B

Biographies of the U.S. Commission of Fine Arts, Old Georgetown Board, Contributing Staff, and Essayists

THE U.S. COMMISSION OF FINE ARTS, 1910–2012

COMMISSION MEMBERS

In chronological order of service.

Daniel H. Burnham, 1910–12; chairman 1910–12
Francis D. Millet, 1910–12
Daniel Chester French, 1910–15; chairman 1912–15
Cass Gilbert, 1910–16
Thomas Hastings, 1910–17
Frederick Law Olmsted Jr., 1910–18
Charles Moore, 1910–40; chairman 1915–37
Peirce Anderson, 1912–16
Edwin H. Blashfield, 1912–16
Herbert Adams, 1915–20
J. Alden Weir, 1916–19
Charles A. Platt, 1916–21
William Mitchell Kendall, 1916–21
John Russell Pope, 1917–22
James L. Greenleaf, 1918–27
William Sergeant Kendall, 1920–21
James E. Fraser, 1920–25
Henry Bacon, 1921–24
Louis Ayres, 1921–25
H. Siddons Mowbray, 1921–28
Milton B. Medary Jr., 1922–27
William Adams Delano, 1924–28
Lorado Taft, 1925–29
Abram Garfield, 1925–30
Benjamin W. Morris III, 1927–31
Ferruccio Vitale, 1927–32
John W. Cross, 1928–33
Ezra Winter, 1928–33
Adolph Weinman, 1929–33
John L. Mauran, 1930–33
Egerton Swartwout, 1931–16
Gilmore D. Clarke, 1932–50; chairman 1937–50
Charles A. Coolidge, 1933–36
John Mead Howells, 1933–37
Eugene F. Savage, 1933–41
Lee Lawrie, 1933–37; 1945–50
Charles L. Borie Jr., 1936–40
Henry R. Shepley, 1936–40
Paul Manship, 1937–41
William F. Lamb, 1937–45
Edward Bruce, 1940–43
Paul P. Cret, 1940–45
John A. Holabird, 1940–45
Ralph Stackpole, 1941–45
Henry V. Poor III, 1941–45
David E. Finley, 1943–63; chairman 1950–63

William T. Aldrich, 1945–50
L. Andrew Reinhard, 1945–50
Frederick V. Murphy, 1945–50
Maurice Sterne, 1945–50
Joseph Hudnut, 1950–55
Edward F. Neild Sr., 1950–55
Pietro Belluschi, 1950–55
Elbert Peets, 1950–58
Felix W. de Weldon, 1950–63
George Biddle, 1950–51; 1953–55
Wallace K. Harrison, 1955–59
Emily Muir, 1955–59
Douglas W. Orr, 1955–63
William G. Perry, 1955–63
Michael Rapuano, 1958–62
Ralph Walker, 1959–63
Peter Hurd, 1959–63
Hideo Sasaki, 1962–71
Burnham Kelly, 1963–67
John Carl Warnecke, 1963–67
Theodore Roszak, 1963–69
William Walton, 1963–71; chairman 1963–71
Aline B. Saarinen, 1963–71
Gordon Bunshaft, 1963–72
John Walker, 1967–71
Chloethiel W. Smith, 1967–76
Kevin Roche, 1969–80
Nicolas Arroyo, 1971–76
Jane Dart, 1971–76
Edward D. Stone Jr., 1971–85
J. Carter Brown, 1971–2002; chairman 1971–2002
George A. Weymouth, 1972–77
Victorine du Pont Homsey, 1976–80
Eli S. Jacobs, 1976–80
Frederick Doveton Nichols, 1976–81
Philip W. Buchen, 1977–81
John S. Chase, 1980–85
Walter A. Netsch, 1980–85
Sondra G. Myers, 1980–85
Harold Burson, 1981–85
Alan R. Novak, 1981–85
Frederick E. Hart, 1985–89
Pascal Regan, 1985–89
Roy M. Goodman, 1985–89
Carolyn J. Deaver, 1985–90
Diane Wolf, 1985–90
Neil H. Porterfield, 1985–92
Adele Chatfield-Taylor, 1989–94
George E. Hartman, 1989–94
Joan Abrahamson, 1990–94
Robert A. Peck, 1990–94
Jeannine Smith Clark, 1992–96
Susan Porter Rose, 1993–97
Rex M. Ball, 1994–96

Carolyn S. Brody, 1994–2003
Harry G. Robinson III, 1994–2003; chairman 2002–03
Eden D. Rafshoon, 1994–2003
Barbaralee Diamonstein-Spielvogel, 1996–2005
Ann Todd Free, 1997–2001
Emily Malino, 1997–2001
Pamela Nelson, 2001–11
Donald A. Capoccia, 2001–04
David M. Childs, 2002–05; chairman 2003–05
Diana Balmori, 2003–12
Elyn Zimmerman, 2003–08
Earl A. Powell III, 2003–; chairman 2005–
Witold Rybczynski, 2004–12
John Belle, 2005–11
N. Michael McKinnell, 2005–12
Elizabeth Plater-Zyberk, 2008–
Edwin Schlossberg 2011–
Teresita Fernández, 2011–
Philip Freelon, 2012–
Alex Krieger, 2012–
Elizabeth K. Meyer, 2012–

EX OFFICIO SECRETARIES OF THE U.S. COMMISSION OF FINE ARTS, U.S. ARMY CORPS OF ENGINEERS, OFFICE OF PUBLIC BUILDINGS AND GROUNDS

Col. Spencer Cosby, 1910–13
Col. William W. Harts, 1913–17
Col. Clarence S. Ridley, 1917–21
Lt. Col. Clarence O. Sherrill, 1921–22

U.S. COMMISSION OF FINE ARTS SECRETARIES

H. P. Caemmerer, 1922–54
Linton R. Wilson, 1954–64
Charles H. Atherton, 1965–2004
Thomas E. Luebke, 2005–

A

JOAN ABRAHAMSON (1951–) CFA 1990–94

Joan Abrahamson has long been active in organizations advocating human rights, literacy, and the arts. She has a doctorate in education from Harvard University (1977) and a law degree from the University of California, Berkeley (1980). In the 1980s, Abrahamson served as associate counsel and assistant chief of staff to Vice President George H. W. Bush. In 1985, she was named a MacArthur Fellow; she has been a board member of the National Geographic Society, the California Institute for the Arts, and UNICEF. She is the president of the Jefferson Institute—a public policy institute dedicated to current policy issues, such as the future of cities—and the Jonas Salk Foundation, both located in Los Angeles, California.

HERBERT ADAMS (1858–1945) CFA 1915–20;
VICE CHAIRMAN 1918–20

Herbert Adams was a sculptor whose notable works in bronze include the doors and statues of the Library of Congress, the door of St. Bartholomew's Church in New York City, and the McMillan Fountain in Washington, D.C. Adams was a graduate of the Massachusetts Normal Art School and studied with Antonin Mercié in Paris (1885–90); he taught at the Pratt Institute from 1890 to 1898. He was affiliated with the National Academy of Design and served as president of the American Academy of Arts and Letters.

WILLIAM T. ALDRICH (1880–1966) CFA 1945–50

William Truman Aldrich, FAIA, received his degree in architecture from the Massachusetts Institute of Technology (MIT) in 1901 and a diploma from the École des Beaux-Arts in 1909. Following his studies in Paris, he worked at Carrère & Hastings in New York City until 1911 and later established his own firm in Boston. His notable works include the Rhode Island School of Design Museum and the Worchester Art Museum. Aldrich was affiliated with the National Academy of Design, the American School of Classical Studies, and the New York Society of Beaux-Arts Architects.

PEIRCE ANDERSON (1870–1924) CFA 1912–16

After completing his undergraduate degree and additional studies in engineering at Harvard University, William Peirce Anderson studied architecture at the École des Beaux-Arts, earning a diploma in 1899. Anderson joined the Chicago architectural firm of Daniel H. Burnham & Co. in 1912 and remained with the successor firms, Graham, Anderson & Co. and Graham, Anderson, Probst & White, throughout his career. Anderson was involved in the development of city plans for Manila and Baguio in the Philippines. His firm's notable architectural projects include the Equitable Building in New York and the Wrigley Building in Chicago. Anderson was a member of the Architectural League and the National Sculptors Society. His papers are located in the Ryerson and Burnham Archives at the Art Institute of Chicago.

NICOLAS ARROYO (1917–2008) CFA 1971–76

Nicolas Arroyo received his architecture degree from the University of Havana in 1941 and practiced in Cuba until 1959, during which time he also served as Cuba's minister of public works, and was the Cuban ambassador to the United States from 1957 to 1958. After the 1959 Cuban revolution, he settled in Washington, D.C., and established an architectural practice focused on residential and commercial projects; he also had business interests in South America and Arlington, Virginia. Arroyo was a member of the American Institute of Architects.

CHARLES H. ATHERTON (1932–2005) CFA SECRETARY
1965–2004; ASSISTANT SECRETARY 1960–65

Charles Henry Atherton, FAIA, served as secretary of the Commission of Fine Arts for nearly forty years. He joined the commission in 1960 as assistant secretary and was named secretary in 1965 after Linton Wilson's retirement; he retired in 2004. Atherton was educated at Princeton University, receiving both an undergraduate degree in architecture in 1954 and a master's degree in fine arts in architecture in 1957. He then served in the U.S. Naval Reserve and worked as an architect for the Central Intelligence Agency for three years before joining the commission staff in 1960. The size and professional culture of the CFA staff grew under Atherton's long tenure; the Commission took on a greater role in historic research, project analysis, presentations, and coordination with other federal agencies. Atherton also initiated the CFA publications program, which produced a series of books and publications on the architectural history of the national capital city. He was involved in numerous organizations, including the Parks and History Association, the Navy Art Foundation, the Historical Society of Washington, the Columbia Historical Society, and the National Endowment for the Arts; he served as the president of the Washington, D.C., chapter of the American Institute of Architects. Among his many honors were the Centennial Award of the D.C. chapter of the American Institute of Architects (1993), the District of Columbia Mayor's Award for Excellence in Historic Preservation (2004), and a Committee of 100 Lifetime Achievement Award. He was named a Fellow of the American Institute of Architects in 1984 and was awarded the organization's Thomas Jefferson Award for Public Architecture in 2005.

LOUIS AYRES (1874–1947) CFA 1921–25

After graduating from the School of Engineering at Rutgers University in 1896, William Louis Ayres, FAIA, worked at the noted architectural firm, McKim, Mead & White in New York City; he left in 1901 to join York & Sawyer. His work includes numerous bank buildings in New York and Washington, D.C., and the Department of Commerce building, completed in 1932, which was part of the Federal Triangle development project. Ayres served on the Federal Triangle Board of Architectural Consultants, was a trustee of the American Academy in Rome, and was elected to the National Institute of Arts and Letters. He also served as a juror for the Prix de Rome with William Mitchell Kendall and John Russell Pope in 1934.

B

HENRY BACON (1866–1924) CFA 1921–24

Henry Bacon, FAIA, a distinguished practitioner of the Beaux-Arts style of architecture, is best known for his design of the Lincoln Memorial. Bacon earned his undergraduate degree from the University of Illinois at Urbana in 1885 and later studied at the École des Beaux-Arts. He was also a recipient of the Rotch Traveling Scholarship, which funded his study in Europe from 1889 to 1891. He worked briefly at McKim, Mead & White, but by 1903 had formed his own practice in New York City. During his career he developed a varied portfolio of projects including libraries, academic buildings, banks, and mansions. In addition to the Lincoln Memorial, Bacon collaborated with sculptor Daniel Chester French on the Dupont Circle fountain and numerous other memorials around the country. Bacon also worked with other well-known sculptors of the day such as Augustus Saint-Gaudens and James E. Fraser. His professional affiliations included the National Academy of Design, and he was elected to the National Institute of Arts and Letters and the American Academy of Arts and Letters. In 1923, President Warren G. Harding presented him with the American Institute of Architects Gold Medal in a ceremony at the Lincoln Memorial.

REX M. BALL (1934–2010) CFA 1994–97

Rex Martin Ball, FAIA, joined the Oklahoma-based architecture and engineering firm HTB Inc. in 1958, eventually becoming its CEO; in 1994, he became chairman emeritus of the firm. During his tenure, the firm's work included the renovation of the National Press Building in Washington, D.C., modernization and renovation projects for the U.S. military, and numerous projects in Oklahoma. Ball served on the Tulsa Metropolitan Area Planning Commission from 1969 to 1971 and later was a member of the Oklahoma City and Tulsa Chambers of Commerce. He was the president of the Tulsa Historic Preservation Commission and the cofounder and president of the Tulsa Art Deco Society. He served

NOTE: *The abbreviation of professional honors is listed following the subject's name, including election as a Fellow of the American Institute of Architects, indicated by* FAIA; *as a Fellow of the American Society of Landscape Architects, indicated by* FASLA; *or membership in the Royal Institute of British Architects, indicated by* RIBA.

on the University of Oklahoma's Board of Visitors for the College of Architecture for two terms and was also a long-standing member of the Urban Land Institute and the American Institute of Certified Planners. Ball received his undergraduate degree in architecture from Oklahoma State University in 1956 and a master's degree in architecture from the Massachusetts Institute of Technology in 1958.

DIANA BALMORI (1932–) CFA 2003–12

Diana Balmori is a noted author and scholar, landscape and urban designer, and design principal of Balmori Associates in New York City and is recognized for her innovative and sustainable landscape designs. She studied architecture at the University of Tucuman in Argentina; received a doctorate in urban history from the University of California, Los Angeles, in 1973; and later studied landscape design at Radcliffe College. In addition to her professional practice, Balmori holds joint appointments in the School of Architecture and the School of Forestry and Environmental Studies at Yale University. She is a senior fellow in garden and landscape studies at the Dumbarton Oaks Research Library in Washington, D.C., and has been the recipient of numerous honors and awards including grants from both the National Endowment for the Arts and the National Endowment for the Humanities. From 1981 to 1990, she was a partner in the architectural firm Cesar Pelli & Associates.

JOHN BELLE (1932–) CFA 2005–11

John Belle, FAIA, is a founding partner of Beyer Blinder Belle Architects & Planners. Belle's work has focused on the restoration and revitalization of historically significant structures such as Grand Central Terminal in New York City, the Delaware Aqueduct in Pennsylvania, the Ellis Island Museum of Immigration—projects for which he was honored with the Presidential Design Award—Rockefeller Center, Old City Hall in Washington, D.C., and the Cathedral of the Blessed Sacrament in California. He was the master planner of Indiana University's eight campuses and completed numerous projects for the State University of New York (SUNY) at Stony Brook. In 2000, SUNY Stony Brook awarded Belle an honorary doctorate in fine arts for his achievements in architecture and preservation. Belle has served as president of the New York Landmarks Conservancy, is a member of the Royal Institute of British Architects, and is an honorary Fellow of the Royal Society of Architects in Wales. He received his training at the Architectural Association in London.

PIETRO BELLUSCHI (1899–1994) CFA 1950–55

Born in Ancona, Italy, Pietro Belluschi served in the Italian military during World War I. He received a doctorate in civil engineering from the University of Rome in 1922 before emigrating the next year to the United States, where he continued his studies at the Massachusetts Institute of Technology (MIT). He became the design principal of his own architectural firm, which he founded in 1943 following seventeen years of practice with Albert E. Doyle in Portland, Oregon, and it eventually was merged into the firm of Skidmore, Owings & Merrill. Belluschi's notable projects include the Juilliard School of Music, Alice Tully Hall, and the Pan Am building in New York City; the Portland Art Museum and the Equitable Building in Portland, Oregon; Bank of America in San Francisco; and libraries for Reed College and Willamette University. From 1951 to 1965, Belluschi was dean of the School of Architecture at MIT and he was a resident in architecture at the American Academy in Rome in 1954. He was elected to the National Institute of Arts and Letters and was awarded an American Institute of Architects Gold Medal in 1972 and a National Medal of Arts in 1991.

GEORGE BIDDLE (1885–1973) CFA 1950–55

After earning a law degree from Harvard University in 1911, George Biddle turned to painting, studying at the Pennsylvania Academy of Fine Arts in Philadelphia and completing a degree there in 1913. He studied at the Académie Julian in Paris; following service in World War I, he lived abroad and returned to the United States in 1932. A proponent of art for the masses and a friend of Franklin Roosevelt, Biddle is credited with convincing the president to develop a publicly supported arts program as part of the New Deal, which became the Federal Art Project. Biddle, whose painting was influenced by the social realism of Diego Rivera, completed a mural, *The Tenement,* in the U.S. Department of Justice as part of that program. Biddle was also the author of several books, and his paintings are in the permanent collection of numerous museums, including the Metropolitan Museum of Art, the Museum of Modern Art, and the Whitney Museum. In 1952 Biddle was named a resident in visual arts at the American Academy of Rome. His papers are in the Smithsonian Archives of American Art.

EDWIN H. BLASHFIELD (1848–1936) CFA 1912–16

Edwin Howland Blashfield was a painter and muralist of the late nineteenth and early twentieth centuries. He studied painting at the Pennsylvania Academy of Fine Arts after initial coursework in engineering at the Massachusetts Institute of Technology. He moved to Europe in 1867 to study with Leon Bonnat in Paris and remained abroad until 1881, traveling, painting, and exhibiting his work in salon shows. Following his early success as a genre painter, Blashfield became a widely admired muralist whose work adorned the dome of the Manufacturer's and Liberal Arts building at the World's Columbian Exposition of 1893, several state capitols, and the central dome of the Library of Congress. He was a member of numerous arts organizations including the National Academy of Design, the Society of Mural Painters, the American Academy of Arts and Letters, and the National Institute of Arts and Letters. Among his many honors, Blashfield was awarded a Gold Medal by the National Academy of Design in 1934, an honorary membership in the American Institute of Architecture, and an honorary doctorate of fine arts by New York University in 1926. His circle of friends included sculptor Daniel Chester French, painters John Singer Sargent and Maxfield Parrish, and architect Cass Gilbert.

CHARLES L. BORIE JR. (1870–1943) CFA 1936–40

Charles Louis Borie Jr., FAIA, studied civil engineering at the University of Pennsylvania in the early 1890s and worked for several years in banking. By 1905 he had formed an architectural practice in Philadelphia with Clarence Zantzinger; Milton Medary joined the partnership in 1910. The firm's projects include the Philadelphia Museum of Art with Horace Trumbauer, hospitals, educational buildings, and other public projects in the classical vocabulary. Perhaps the most notable of the firm's work was the Department of Justice building in Washington, D.C., which was part of the Federal Triangle redevelopment. Borie's affiliations included the Council of the American Academy in Rome and the Smithsonian Gallery of Art Commission; he was elected to the National Institute of Arts and Letters and the American Academy of Arts and Letters. During the Great Depression he also served as an advisor to the Philadelphia Housing Authority.

CAROLYN S. BRODY (1949–) CFA 1994–2003

Carolyn Schwenker Brody earned a graduate degree in city planning from the University of Pennsylvania in 1976 and was a city planner in Portland, Maine, for several years before earning a master's degree in business administration at Harvard University in 1983. Brody worked in real estate investment in Boston and New York and later worked as a real estate consultant to the World Bank in Washington, D.C., in the 1990s. She has served on the boards of numerous arts organizations including the Alvin Ailey American Dance Theater, the Phillips Collection, and the National Building Museum, where she served as chairman of the board from 2000 to 2006.

J. CARTER BROWN (1934–2002) CFA 1971–2002; CHAIRMAN 1971–2002

For more than thirty years, John Carter Brown led the Commission of Fine Arts, guiding the organization as it helped shape the national capital at a time of rapid change in design taste, economic outlook, and sensitivity to the past. Brown, a descendent of the illustrious and socially prominent Brown family of Rhode Island, was trained in both art history and business administration: He earned his undergraduate degree from Harvard University in 1956, received an MBA from Harvard University in 1958, and completed coursework in art history at both New York University and the École du Louvre in Paris. He was appointed director of the National Gallery of Art in Washington, D.C., in 1969, a position he held until 1992. During his tenure at the gallery, Brown introduced the concept of large and lavish exhibitions that appealed to both connoisseurs and the general public. He wrote numerous articles on art and culture and helped found Ovation, a cable television arts station. Brown was the recipient of more than a dozen honorary degrees, a National Arts Society Gold Medal (1972), a National Medal of the Arts (1991), and the National Building Museum Honor Award (1993). He was also an honorary fellow of the Royal Academy of Arts and an honorary member of the American Institute of Architects.

EDWARD BRUCE (1879–1943) CFA 1940–43
The painter Edward Bruce was trained as a lawyer, receiving his degree from Columbia University School of Law in 1904, and worked as an attorney and businessman in New York and the Philippines. In the early 1920s he moved to Italy to study art with Maurice Sterne, where he remained until 1929; he returned to the United States and continued his painting in California until 1932, when he moved to Washington, D.C., to work briefly as a lobbyist. In 1933 Bruce was named director of the Public Works of Art Project, and in 1934 he became head of the Treasury Department Section of Painting and Sculpture. Bruce received numerous honors for his paintings, including a medal for excellence from Columbia University in 1937 and an honorary doctorate in fine arts from Harvard University in 1938; he was also elected to the National Institute of Arts and Letters. Bruce's paintings are in the permanent collection of the Whitney Museum of American Art, the Phillips Collection, and the San Francisco Museum of Art, and his papers are in the Smithsonian Archives of American Art.

PHILIP W. BUCHEN (1916–2001) CFA 1977–81
An attorney, Philip William Buchen received his law degree in 1941 from the University of Michigan, where he met and befriended Gerald Ford, with whom he formed a law practice in Grand Rapids, Michigan, in the early 1940s. Buchen continued to practice law in Grand Rapids until 1974 when he came to Washington to serve on Vice President Ford's staff; later that year he became White House counsel to President Ford and served until 1977. After Ford left office, Buchen remained in Washington, practicing law with the firm of Dewey Ballantine until 1995.

GORDON BUNSHAFT (1909–90) CFA 1963–72
Gordon Bunshaft, FAIA, is recognized as a leading proponent of modern design in the mid-twentieth century. A partner in the architectural firm SOM, Bunshaft joined the firm in 1937 and remained for more than forty years; the long list of his notable buildings includes the Hirshhorn Museum in Washington, D.C.; Lever House in New York; Beinecke Library at Yale University; the Lyndon Baines Johnson Library in Texas; and the National Commercial Bank in Jeddah, Saudi Arabia. Bunshaft received both his undergraduate (1933) and master's (1935) degrees from the Massachusetts Institute of Technology, studied in Europe on a Rotch Traveling Scholarship from 1935 to 1937, and worked briefly for Edward Durrell Stone and Raymond Loewy before joining SOM. Bunshaft was elected to the National Institute of Arts and Letters and was the recipient of numerous other honors and awards, including the American Institute of Architects Twenty-five Year Award for Lever House in 1980 and the Pritzker Architecture Prize in 1988. His papers are archived at Columbia University in the Avery Architecture and Fine Arts Library.

DANIEL H. BURNHAM (1846–1912) CFA 1910–12; CHAIRMAN 1910–12
One of the most prominent architects of the late nineteenth and early twentieth centuries, Daniel Hudson Burnham, FAIA, began his career as a draftsman with the Chicago architecture firm Loring & Jenney in 1868.

He later joined Carter, Drake & Wright before opening his own firm with fellow draftsman John Wellborn Root in 1873. Burnham & Root earned prominence in Chicago with such buildings as the Rookery, the Monadnock Building, and the Rand McNally Building. In 1890, the firm was commissioned to coordinate the massive World's Columbian Exposition of 1893; following Root's death in 1891, Burnham took over as chief of construction and director of works for the fair. The exposition became a seminal influence on architecture and urban design, helping to establish the Beaux-Arts style for public buildings and city development. After 1891, Burnham operated the firm under his own name, D. H. Burnham & Co., and went on to design such renowned works as the Flatiron Building in New York and Union Station in Washington, D.C. Burnham was also an influential member of the McMillan Commission, which developed a Beaux-Arts plan for the monumental core of Washington, and he later developed a Beaux-Arts plan for the city of Chicago. Burnham became the first chairman of the U.S. Commission of Fine Arts, helping to assure the implementation of the McMillan Plan's vision. He was elected to the National Institute of Arts and Letters, was a cofounder of the American Academy in Rome, and served two terms as president of the American Institute of Architects. Burnham's papers are in the Ryerson and Burnham Archives at the Art Institute of Chicago.

HAROLD BURSON (1921–) CFA 1981–85
Harold Burson is a founding partner of the world's largest public relations agency, Burson-Marsteller. Early in his career, Burson worked as a reporter, and he completed his undergraduate degree at the University of Mississippi in 1940. From 1941 to 1943, he worked for an engineering and building company in New York City, and then served in the army in World War II as a combat engineer and correspondent. Following the war he started his own public relations firm in New York City. In 1953 he partnered with advertising executive William Marsteller to create Burson-Marsteller. Burson has long been active in professional, civic, and cultural organizations, and he has received numerous awards and honors for his public service.

C

H. P. CAEMMERER (1884–1962) CFA SECRETARY 1922–54
Hans Paul Caemmerer was the first civilian secretary of the U.S. Commission of Fine Arts. Unlike his predecessors, he was not an engineer: He had a master's degree in art and archaeology from George Washington University (1917), a law degree from Georgetown University (1924), and a doctorate from American University (1937). He was an assistant to the postmaster general for the U.S. Postal Service from 1906 until he joined the Commission of Fine Arts as a clerk and assistant in 1919, replacing his brother, Arno Cammerer, who had served as clerk to the commission since 1910 and left the position to become assistant director of the National Park Service. H.P. Caemmerer remained with the commission for more than thirty years; during this time, he wrote several books on the history of Washington, D.C., including *Washington: The National Capital* (1932) and *A Manual on the Origin and Development of Washington* (1939). He was affiliated with the Archaeological Institute of America, the Columbia Historical Society, the American Federation of the Arts, and the American Civic Association.

DONALD A. CAPOCCIA (1955–) CFA 2001–04; VICE CHAIRMAN 2003–04
Donald A. Capoccia is a partner with BFC Partners, a development company specializing in affordable and mixed-income housing in New York City, and is president of BFC Construction Company. He is also a founder and president of the New York State Association for Affordable Housing. Capoccia graduated in 1979 from the State University of New York at Buffalo with an undergraduate degree in urban affairs and later earned a master's degree in urban planning from Hunter College in 1982. He has served on the boards of numerous civic and arts organizations, including the New York State Council for the Arts. He has been a member of the United Nations Development Corporation and the

Board of Governors of the Real Estate Board of New York, and was appointed in 2011 to the Battery Park City Authority.

JOHN S. CHASE JR. (1925–2012) CFA 1980–85

John Saunders Chase Jr., FAIA, was the first African American graduate student at the University of Texas, that state's first African American registered architect, and the first African American member of the U.S. Commission of Fine Arts. In 1950 Chase completed a bachelor of science in architectural engineering from Hampton Institute and enrolled in the master of architecture program at the University of Texas at Austin shortly after the U.S. Supreme Court ordered the state university system to desegregate its graduate and professional programs. Chase completed his master's degree in 1952 and soon after opened his own practice in Houston, which he led until retiring in 2006. His work includes numerous churches, residences, schools, banks, major public buildings such as the George E. Brown Convention Center, and several buildings at Texas Southern University, where he also taught. Chase was active in civic and cultural organizations and received many honors for his achievements including the University of Texas Distinguished Alumnus Award and the American Institute of Architects Whitney M. Young Citation.

ADELE CHATFIELD-TAYLOR (1945–) CFA 1989–94

Preservationist and arts administrator Adele Chatfield-Taylor received her undergraduate degree in art history from Manhattanville College (1966) and a graduate degree in historic preservation from Columbia University (1973). She was a cofounder of the New York firm Urban Deadline Architects in 1968 and, five years later, joined the New York Landmarks Preservation Commission. She served as director of the New York Landmarks Preservation Foundation from 1980 to 1984 and was director of the Design Arts Program of the National Endowment for the Arts from 1984 to 1988. Since 1988, Chatfield-Taylor has been president of the American Academy in Rome. Her many honors and awards include a Loeb Fellowship from Harvard University in 1978, a Rome Prize from the American Academy in Rome in 1983, and the Vincent Scully Prize from the National Building Museum in 2010. She has been an adjunct member of the faculty at the Graduate School of Architecture, Planning, and Preservation at Columbia University. Her many affiliations include Preservation ACTION, the National Alliance of Preservation Commissions, and the US/International Council on Monuments and Sites.

DAVID M. CHILDS (1941–) CFA 2002–05; CHAIRMAN 2003–05

David Magie Childs, FAIA, is a consulting design partner with the architectural firm Skidmore, Owings & Merrill (SOM). He joined the Washington, D.C., office of the firm in 1971, after working with Nathaniel Owings and Daniel Patrick Moynihan on plans for the redevelopment of Pennsylvania Avenue. Childs was a design partner of the firm in Washington until 1984, when he moved to SOM's New York office. His projects in Washington include 1201 Pennsylvania Avenue, the Four Seasons Hotel, Constitution Gardens, master plans for the Mall, Metro Center, U.S. News and World Report headquarters, and National Geographic headquarters; in New York, Worldwide Plaza, 450 Lexington Avenue, Bertelsmann Tower, and One World Trade Center; and internationally, the U.S. embassy in Ottawa, Canada, and the Changi international terminal in Shanghai. He served as chairman of the National Capital Planning Commission from 1975 to 1981. Childs graduated from Yale University in 1963 and earned a master's degree from its School of Art and Architecture in 1967. He was the recipient of a Rome Prize in 2004; named a senior fellow of the Design Futures Council in 2010; and has served on the boards of the Municipal Arts Society, the Museum of Modern Art, and the American Academy in Rome.

JEANNINE SMITH CLARK (1928–) CFA 1992–96

Active in both local and national cultural organizations, Jeannine Smith Clark received her undergraduate degree in German and English and a master's degree in African studies from Howard University, and studied at the University of Wisconsin. She taught German at Sidwell Friends School and Dunbar High School, both in the District of Columbia. Her affiliations include the D.C. Urban League, the Historical Society of Washington, the National Museum of Women in the Arts, and the Phillips Collection. She is a regent emeritus of the Smithsonian Institution, a past chair of the National Portrait Gallery Commission, and a director emeritus of the White House Historical Association.

GILMORE D. CLARKE (1892–1982) CFA 1932–50; VICE CHAIRMAN 1936–37, CHAIRMAN 1937–50

Gilmore David Clarke (FASLA), was a 1913 graduate of Cornell University, where he studied both landscape architecture and civil engineering. He joined the faculty of the School of Architecture at the university in 1935 as a professor of city and regional planning; in 1938, he became dean of the school, a position he held until retiring in 1950. In his professional practice, Clarke was involved in the design of the parkway system in Westchester County, New York, and as a consultant to the New York City Park Department on projects at the Central Park Zoo and Riverside Park. With Michael Rapuano, he formed Clarke & Rapuano in White Plains, New York, in 1939; he retired from the firm in 1972. Among Clarke's best-known works are the landscape architectural designs of the 1939 and 1964 World's Fairs in New York and the Garden State Parkway in New Jersey; he was also a consultant for the United Nations headquarters project. Clarke was a member of the National Institute of Arts and Letters, a trustee of both the American Academy in Rome and the American Museum of Natural History, and served on the Architectural Advisory Board of the U.S. Capitol. He was honored by the Architectural League of New York with a Gold Medal in 1931 and by the Municipal Arts Society of New York with a citation of merit in 1949.

CHARLES A. COOLIDGE (1858–1936) CFA 1933–36

Architect Charles Allerton Coolidge, FAIA, was a founding partner of the firm Shepley, Rutan & Coolidge in 1886. After graduating from Harvard University in 1881 with additional study in architecture at the Massachusetts Institute of Technology, Coolidge worked for H. H. Richardson before forming his own office. His firm would later undergo several name changes: Coolidge & Shattuck; Coolidge, Shepley, Bulfinch & Abbott; and Coolidge & Hodgdon. Coolidge was known for his design of academic buildings and libraries at Stanford, Yale, and Brown Universities; the hospital and medical schools at Vanderbilt University and the University of Chicago; and for the law and medical schools and Fogg Art Museum at Harvard University. He also designed the Art Institute of Chicago and that city's public library, and served as the consulting architect for Constantinople College in Turkey. He was a trustee of both the American Academy in Rome and the Art Institute of Chicago. For his work on the Paris Exposition of 1899, Coolidge was named a Chevalier of the French Legion of Honor. He was awarded an honorary doctorate of arts by Harvard University in 1906.

COL. SPENCER COSBY (1867–1962) EX OFFICIO CFA SECRETARY 1910–13

Spencer Cosby graduated from the U.S. Military Academy at West Point in 1887 and served in the Corps of Engineers. As officer-in-charge of the Office of Public Buildings and Grounds for Washington, D.C., Cosby oversaw the construction of new executive offices at the White House, including the Oval Office (1909–13), and served as the first secretary of the U.S. Commission of Fine Arts. He later became the military attaché at the American Embassy in Paris.

PAUL P. CRET (1876–1945) CFA 1940–45

Trained at the École des Beaux-Arts in Lyon and Paris in the 1890s, Paul Philippe Cret, FAIA, is regarded as a practitioner of early modernism. Before he settled in the United States in 1903 to teach at the University of Pennsylvania, Cret's reputation in France was already well established, and he was the recipient of numerous architectural prizes. Once in the United States, he formed his own office in Philadelphia, where he worked until shortly before his death. Cret's portfolio includes significant public buildings throughout the country and several World War I memorials at American military cemeteries in France and Belgium. Among his most noted works in Washington, D.C., are the Pan American building with Albert Kelsey, the Federal Reserve Board building, Central Heating Plant, the Calvert Street Bridge, and the Folger Shakespeare Library. Cret was elected to the American Academy of Arts and Letters, and his many awards include a medal of honor from the Architectural League of New York in 1928 and an American Institute of Architects Gold Medal in 1938 as well as honorary degrees from Harvard and Brown Universities and the University of Pennsylvania. Cret's papers are archived at the University of Pennsylvania.

JOHN W. CROSS (1878–1951) CFA 1928–33

John Walter Cross, FAIA, received his undergraduate degree from Yale University in 1900 and studied at the School of Mines at Columbia University until 1902; he later studied architecture at the École des Beaux-Arts. Following his return from France in 1907, he formed an architectural firm in New York City, Cross & Cross, with his brother, Eliot; it was renamed Cross & Son in 1946. John Cross remained with the firm until shortly before his death. He designed numerous buildings in New York and Connecticut during his career and served as the chief architect for the Department of Labor's U.S. Housing Corporation, which developed housing for war workers during World War I. Cross was a member of the National Institute of Arts and Letters and was affiliated with the Art Commission of New York City, the Architectural League, and the Beaux-Arts Institute of Design.

D

JANE DART (1918–2009) CFA 1971–76

Jane O'Brien Dart was active in public service, the arts, and philanthropic organizations, including the Los Angeles County Museum of Science and Industry, where she served as a trustee, the California State Arts Council, and the Monterey Museum of Art. As a young woman in the late 1930s and early 1940s, she was an actor with Warner Brothers; she performed under the stage name Jane Bryan and appeared in twenty films with such stars as Paul Muni, Ronald Reagan, Jane Wyman, Humphrey Bogart, and Bette Davis.

FELIX W. DE WELDON (1907–2003) CFA 1950–63

Felix Weihs de Weldon was a prominent sculptor of the mid-twentieth century. Born in Austria and trained in Vienna, his early work was exhibited in Vienna and at the Paris Salon. He came to the United States before the outbreak of World War II and served in the U.S. Navy during the war. While still in military service, he crafted a small model of Joe Rosenthal's famous photograph of the raising of the American flag on Iwo Jima's Mt. Suribachi; the sculpture inspired a congressional commission to recreate the work as the Marine Corps Memorial. During his ensuing career, de Weldon completed numerous other works in Washington, D.C., including an inaugural bust of President Truman, the American Red Cross Memorial, the Seabees Monument, the National Guard Monument, and the equestrian statue of Simon Bolivar.

CAROLYN J. DEAVER (1939–) CFA 1985–90

Carolyn J. Deaver is active in art and philanthropic organizations. She received her undergraduate degree from the University of California, Berkeley, in 1960, and has worked as a public relations consultant in Washington, D.C. Deaver has served as a council member of the Phillips Collection and is currently an advisory board member of the Morris and Gwendolyn Cafritz Foundation, a charitable organization in Washington, D.C.

WILLIAM ADAMS DELANO (1874–1960) CFA 1924–28; VICE CHAIRMAN 1928

An architect associated with the Beaux-Arts style, William Adams Delano, FAIA, earned his undergraduate degree from Yale University in 1895 and worked at the New York architecture firm Carrère & Hastings.

He also studied at the École des Beaux-Arts, receiving a diploma in 1903. After returning from Europe, Delano formed his own architectural practice, Delano & Aldrich, and taught at Columbia University from 1903 to 1910. Delano's work was far-ranging; it included homes for Otto Kahn and the Rockefeller family, academic buildings at Yale, private schools in New York City, the Union Club in New York, the American Embassy in Paris, terminals at LaGuardia and Miami airports, Epinal American Cemetery in France, the Post Office building in the Federal Triangle redevelopment, and the controversial Truman Balcony at the White House. In addition to his design work, he served on the National Capital Planning Commission and on the board of design for the 1939 New York World's Fair and was president of the Beaux-Arts Society of Architects. Delano's many awards and honors include election to the American Academy of Arts and Letters, a Gold Medal from the National Institute of Arts and Letters in 1940, and an American Institute of Architects Gold Medal in 1953; he was also named an officer by the French Legion of Honor and was an academician of the National Academy of Design. The Delano & Aldrich collection is located at the Avery Library, Columbia University; Delano's papers from 1947 to 1954 are archived at the New York Historical Society.

BARBARALEE DIAMONSTEIN-SPIELVOGEL (1937–) CFA 1996–2005; VICE CHAIRMAN 2002–03

The first woman to serve in a leadership position on the U.S. Commission of Fine Arts, Barbaralee Diamonstein-Spielvogel is a preservationist and advocate for the arts and the author of twenty books, media programs, and numerous articles on the arts, architecture, design, and public policy. She received a doctorate from New York University in 1963 and became a staff assistant at the White House involved in the development of the White House Fellows and Presidential Scholars Programs. In 1966, Diamonstein-Spielvogel became the first director of cultural affairs for the City of New York, a position she held for five years, followed by fifteen years on the New York City Landmarks Preservation Commission (1972–87) and eight years as chairman of the New York Landmarks Preservation Foundation (1987–95). She was also a founding board member of the New York Landmarks Conservancy and chairman of the Historic Landmarks Preservation Center. She is a member of the New York State Council on the Arts and an advisor on public art and architecture to the New York Port Authority at the World Trade Center. She has taught at Hunter College, the New School-Parsons School of Design, and Duke University. Diamonstein-Spielvogel is an honorary member of the American Institute of Architects and has received honorary degrees from the Maryland Institute of Art and Baltimore College of Art. Her papers are in the Rare Book and Manuscript Library at Duke University.

F

TERESITA FERNÁNDEZ (1968–) CFA 2011–

Teresita Fernández, recipient of a 2005 MacArthur Foundation Fellowship, is a sculptor and visual artist whose works—often large in scale and inspired by landscape and natural phenomena—explore issues of perception and seeing. Her commissions include the site-specific installation *Blind Blue Landscape* at the Bennesee Art site in Naoshima, Japan; *Ring of Fire* at the Fabric Workshop and Museum in Philadelphia; and *Seattle Cloud Cover,* a permanent installation commissioned by the Seattle Art Museum for the Olympic Sculpture Park. Her works are also included in numerous private collections and in the permanent collections of the San Francisco Museum of Modern Art; MoCA, Miami; Walker Art Center, Minneapolis; and the Museum of Modern Art in New York. She has been featured in solo exhibitions at the Corcoran Gallery of Art, Washington, D.C.; the Institute for Contemporary Art, Philadelphia; the Miami Art Museum; the Museum of Modern Art in Forth Worth, Texas; and the Castello di Rivoli in Turin, Italy. Fernández was awarded a Guggenheim Fellowship in 2003 and a Louis Comfort Tiffany Biennial Award in 1999; she had a resident affiliated fellowship at the American Academy in Rome in 1999. She earned an undergraduate degree in fine art in 1990 from Florida International University, a master's degree in fine art from Virginia Commonwealth University in 1992, and has been a visiting artist at Princeton University.

DAVID E. FINLEY (1890–1977) CFA 1943–63; VICE CHAIRMAN 1945–50, CHAIRMAN 1950–63

David Edward Finley was the first director of the National Gallery of Art, a position he held from 1938 to 1956. After receiving his undergraduate degree from the University of South Carolina in 1910, Finley moved to Washington, D.C., to attend George Washington University School of Law, graduating in 1913, and practiced law before joining the army during World War I. After the war, Finley returned to Washington to work in federal service as a special assistant to Secretary of the Treasury Andrew Mellon from 1927 to 1932. This relationship led to Finley's position with the National Gallery, which Mellon founded in the late 1930s. During his tenure at the National Gallery Finley also assumed leadership positions with a number of arts and preservation organizations, including president of the American Association of Museums from 1945 to 1949, founding chairman of the National Trust for Historic Preservation from 1950 to 1962, and founding chairman of the White House Historical Association, which he led from 1961 to 1977. Among his many awards and honors, Finley received a Smithsonian Henry Medal in 1968 and a Theodore Roosevelt Distinguished Service Medal as well as honorary degrees from Yale and Georgetown Universities. Both the Library of Congress and the National Gallery of Art are repositories for Finley's papers.

JAMES E. FRASER (1876–1953) CFA 1920–25

The work of sculptor James Earle Fraser, adorning many of Washington's most iconic structures, includes *The Authority of Law and The Contemplation of Justice,* U.S. Supreme Court; south pediment and statues, National Archives; *Music and Harvest and Aspiration and Literature,* Arlington Memorial Bridge; *Alexander Hamilton* and *Albert Gallatin,* U.S. Treasury; and the Second Division Monument. His commissions also include coins and medals such as the Victory Medal, Navy Cross, and Indian head (Buffalo) nickel. Among his earliest work were sculptural pieces at the World's Columbian Exposition in 1893 and, for the San Francisco Exposition in 1915, one of his most famous pieces, *End of the Trail.* Fraser was influenced by his classical training at the Art Institute of Chicago, completed in 1890, and his studies at the École des Beaux-Arts and Académie Julien in Paris in the late nineteenth century. Early in his career, Fraser served as an assistant to Richard Bock and Augustus Saint-Gaudens; he formed his own studio in 1902. He also taught at the Art Students League in New York City beginning in 1906 and later became its director. Fraser was a member of the National Academy, the National Sculpture Society, and the Architectural League. His numerous awards and honors include election to the National Institute of Arts and Letters and a gold medal from the Architectural League in 1925. The papers of James Earle Fraser and those of his wife, sculptor Laura Gardin Fraser, can be found in the Special Collections Research Center at Syracuse University Library and at the Smithsonian Archives of American Art.

ANN TODD FREE (1947–) CFA 1997–2001

Ann Todd Free has been active in preservation organizations in Washington, D.C., serving as president of the Vice President's Residence Foundation, a nonprofit organization dedicated to assisting in the preservation and furnishing of the vice president's official home. She also served as president of the Sheraton-Kalorama Neighborhood Council, which seeks to preserve historic land uses in the neighborhood. Early in her career, Free worked for the American Bankers Association and in the congressional offices of James R. Mann (D-SC) and Butler Derrick (D-SC). She received her undergraduate degree in English literature from Salem College in North Carolina.

PHILIP G. FREELON (1952–) CFA 2012–

Philip G. Freelon, FAIA, founded The Freelon Group in 1990, an architecture firm focused on higher education, science and technology, and museum and cultural center projects. The firm has completed major museum projects in Baltimore, San Francisco, and Charlotte and, as part of the joint venture design team Freelon Adjaye Bond, is the designer of the National Museum of African American History and Culture on the National Mall. Freelon's work has received dozens of design awards, and his firm received the Outstanding Firm Award from the American Institute of Architects (AIA) North Carolina chapter in 2001. Freelon earned his undergraduate degree in environmental design from North Carolina State University and a master's degree in architecture from MIT. He has served as an adjunct professor at North Carolina State University and at MIT's School of Architecture and Planning. In 1989, Freelon was selected as a Loeb Fellow at Harvard University's Graduate School of Design. He received the National AIA Thomas Jefferson Award for Public Architecture in 2009 and a gold medal from the AIA North Carolina chapter.

DANIEL CHESTER FRENCH (1850–1931) CFA 1910–15; CHAIRMAN 1912–15

Daniel Chester French, one of the most prolific and acclaimed sculptors of the late nineteenth and early twentieth centuries, is best known for his monumental work, the statue of Abraham Lincoln in the Lincoln Memorial, completed in 1922. French's early education included training in anatomy with William Rimmer and in drawing with William Morris Hunt; he spent a year studying at the Massachusetts Institute of Technology and also several years in Florence, Italy, studying in the studio of Thomas Ball. French first earned acclaim for *Minute Man,* commissioned by the city of Concord, Massachusetts, in 1875. He soon established his own studio, first in Washington, D.C., moving later to Boston and then New York City. French's reputation grew with his *Statue of the Republic* for the World's Columbian Exposition in 1893. Other memorable works by French include the First Division Monument and the Butt-Millet Memorial Fountain in Washington, D.C.; *John Harvard,* Cambridge, Massachusetts; bronze doors for the Boston Public Library; *The Four Continents* at the U.S. Custom House, New York; and the Pulitzer Prize Medal. In addition to the Lincoln Memorial, French collaborated with architect Henry Bacon on numerous memorials around the country and on the Dupont Circle fountain in Washington, D.C. French was a trustee of the Metropolitan Museum of Art; honorary president of the National Sculpture Society; cofounder of the American Academy in Rome; and affiliated with the National Academy, the Architectural League, and the Accademia di San Luca, Rome. His many honors included election to the American Academy of Arts and Letters; Chevalier, the French Legion of Honor; a medal of honor from the Paris Exposition of 1900; and honorary degrees from Dartmouth, Yale, Harvard, and Columbia Universities.

G

ABRAM GARFIELD (1872–1958) CFA 1925–30; VICE CHAIRMAN 1929–30

Abram Garfield, the youngest son of President James A. Garfield, received a bachelor of arts from Williams College in 1893 and a bachelor of science in architecture at the Massachusetts Institute of Technology three years later. By 1898, Garfield had joined with Frank Meade to form the architectural firm Meade & Garfield in Cleveland, Ohio; the firm was noted for its residential designs. When the partnership ended in 1905, Garfield opened his own firm, which he ran until 1951. Garfield specialized in residential architecture, designing large residences in Shaker Heights and other Cleveland suburbs, but his work also included more modest homes for the Cleveland Metropolitan Housing Authority and institutional projects such as schools and a hospital. Garfield served as chairman of the Cleveland Planning Commission from 1930 to 1942 and was a founder and first president of the Cleveland School of Architecture, which became part of Case Western Reserve University in 1941.

He was named a trustee of the university that year and two years later was made an honorary lifetime member of the board; he received an honorary doctorate from the university in 1945. Garfield was also a director of the American Institute of Architects from 1919 to 1922.

CASS GILBERT (1859–1934) CFA 1910–16

Despite his achievement as a classical architect, Cass Gilbert, FAIA, had little formal training in architecture. He began his education in 1876 as an apprentice in the architectural office of Abraham Radcliffe in St. Paul, Minnesota. By 1878, he had left St. Paul for a two-year program in architecture at the Massachusetts Institute of Technology but stayed only a year, leaving to work as a surveyor and to travel in Europe. In the early 1880s he worked for several years in New York as an assistant to Stanford White, a partner in the firm of McKim, Mead & White. Gilbert returned to St. Paul and by 1885 formed a practice with James Knox Taylor; the firm completed numerous projects in the Midwest, including residences, train stations, commercial buildings, and schools. The partnership lasted until 1891 when Gilbert opened his own firm. He first gained national attention for his design of the Minnesota State Capitol in 1895. By the end of the century, Gilbert had returned to New York City to design the U.S. Custom House. His fame grew with his distinctive early skyscraper, the Woolworth Building, completed in 1913, the tallest building in the world at the time. Gilbert's many buildings include the New York Life Insurance Company, the Brooklyn Army Terminal, and the Federal Courthouse in New York City; the West Virginia State Capitol; the St. Louis Public Library; and the Federal Reserve Bank in Minneapolis. His work in Washington, D.C., contributes to the city's monumental Beaux-Arts image, including the U.S. Chamber of Commerce building, the U.S. Treasury Annex, the First Division Memorial, and the U.S. Supreme Court. Gilbert's many affiliations included service on the National Jury of Fine Arts for the World's Columbian Exposition of 1893; president of the American Institute of Architects, 1908–09; founder and president of the Architectural League of New York; and president of the National Academy of Design. He was president of the National Institute of Arts and Letters and was elected a member of the Academy of Arts and Letters; he was also an honorary member of the Royal Institute of British Architects Canada and a Chevalier of the French Legion of Honor.

ROY M. GOODMAN (1930–) CFA 1985–89

Roy M. Goodman served as a senator in the New York state legislature from 1967 to 2002, representing the twenty-sixth district of Manhattan, where he served as chairman of the Senate Committee on Housing and Urban Development for nine years. He was appointed by Mayor Michael R. Bloomberg in 2002 to serve as president of the United Nations Development Corporation, a public agency overseeing building projects at the United Nation's complex. Goodman received his undergraduate degree from Harvard University in 1951 and a master's degree in business administration in 1953. Early in his career, Goodman served as New York City's director of finance during the administration of John V. Lindsey. He has been active in philanthropic and arts organizations including the Metropolitan Opera, the New York Philharmonic Society, and the National Council on the Arts, and is president of the Goodman Family Foundation. He was also honored as a Fellow for Life by the Metropolitan Museum of Art.

JAMES L. GREENLEAF (1857–1933) CFA 1918–27; VICE CHAIRMAN 1922–27

The landscape architect James Leal Greenleaf was trained as a civil engineer, receiving a degree from Columbia University's School of Mines in 1880; he subsequently taught at the university in the School of Engineering from 1882 to 1894. At the end of the century, he established his practice in landscape architecture and became a designer of estate gardens in Westchester County, Long Island, New Jersey, and Connecticut, including the Italian gardens of the Vanderbilt mansion in Hyde Park, New York. He oversaw the design of American military cemeteries in France after World War I and advised on the landscaping

of the Lincoln Memorial in 1922; he also consulted on the landscape design for Arlington Memorial Bridge and the 1921 plan for the expansion of Arlington National Cemetery. He left his practice in 1927 to devote his time to painting and travel; his art was exhibited at the National Academy of Design in New York. Greenleaf also served as president of the American Society of Landscape Architects.

H

WALLACE K. HARRISON (1895–1981) CFA 1955–59

The architect Wallace Kirkman Harrison's work in the mid-twentieth century is characterized by large, modernist public projects and office buildings. As a young man, Harrison took classes in engineering at Worcester Polytechnic Institute and in architecture at the Boston Architectural Club; he studied at the École des Beaux-Arts in the early 1920s. He worked for McKim, Mead & White and Bertram Grosvenor Goodhue from 1916 to 1923, and later formed a series of architectural partnerships until 1941, when he joined with Max Abramowitz to form the firm of Harrison & Abramowitz. Harrison participated with the architectural teams designing the art deco Rockefeller Center complex in New York City, which was completed in 1939. Through this project, Harrison met Nelson Rockefeller, for whom he would later serve as a designer and architectural advisor, notably in the years when Rockefeller was governor of New York. Among Harrison's most noted projects are the United Nations complex, the Metropolitan Opera House at the Lincoln Center for the Performing Arts, and the Empire State Mall in Albany. He also developed the design for the Pershing Memorial in Washington, D.C. Harrison's honors and awards include a Rotch Traveling Scholarship in 1922 and an American Institute of Architects Gold Medal in 1967.

FREDERICK E. HART (1943–99) CFA 1985–89

Frederick Elliott Hart was a late twentieth-century sculptor whose work recalled the figurative tradition of the late nineteenth and early twentieth centuries. Hart studied at the University of South Carolina, American University, and the Corcoran School of Art, and was an apprentice to ornamental plasterer George Gianetti and to sculptor Felix de Weldon. In the late 1960s, he became an apprentice stone carver at the Washington National Cathedral. In 1974, he won the design competition for tympana based on the creation story for the cathedral's main facade, a work that took more than a decade to complete; he also sculpted statues of St. Paul, St. Peter, and Adam for the cathedral. Hart's most widely known work is the *Three Servicemen*, a controversial sculptural addition to the Vietnam Veterans Memorial. In his later career, Hart sculpted with acrylic resins in a process that he patented. Hart was awarded an honorary degree from the University of South Carolina and received a National Sculpture Society Henry Hering Award in 1987 and a Presidential Design Excellence Award in 1988.

GEORGE E. HARTMAN (1936–) CFA 1989–94; VICE CHAIRMAN 1993–94

George Eitel Hartman Jr., FAIA, is principal emeritus of the Washington, D.C., firm, Hartman-Cox, which he founded with Warren Cox in 1965. Hartman contributed to the revitalization of the city with a range of new construction and preservation projects. He has been recognized for his work by numerous honors and awards, including selection by the American Academy in Rome as a fellow in 1977 and as a resident in architecture in 1996, and he received the 2005 Centennial Award from the American Institute of Architects (AIA) Washington, D.C., Chapter. His firm, Hartman-Cox, was named AIA Firm of the Year in 1988 and was the recipient of the American Institute of Classical Architecture firm award in 2006. Hartman has served as president of the AIA Washington, D.C., chapter, and was a member of the Architectural Advisory Board of the Foreign Buildings Office of the U.S. Department of State, the AIA Task Force of the West Front of the U.S. Capitol, and the Joint Committee on Landmarks. He was educated at Princeton University, receiving an undergraduate degree in 1957 and a master of fine arts degree in 1960. Hartman has also taught at the Catholic University of America, the University of Maryland, and North Carolina State University.

COL. WILLIAM W. HARTS (1866–1961) EX OFFICIO CFA
SECRETARY 1913–17

William W. Harts, a colonel in the U.S. Army Corps of Engineers, graduated in 1889 from the U.S. Military Academy at West Point. He was stationed in San Francisco during the 1906 earthquake and helped with the rebuilding efforts, including developing designs for prefabricated housing. He served as part of the American Expeditionary Forces during World War I and was the recipient of the Distinguished Service Medal. Harts retired from the army in 1930 with the rank of brigadier general.

THOMAS HASTINGS (1860–1929) CFA 1910–17

In 1885, Thomas Hastings, FAIA, with John Merven Carrère, founded one of the most influential architectural firms of the late nineteenth and early twentieth centuries, Carrère & Hastings. Following Carrère's death in 1911, Hastings continued on with the firm until his own death in 1929. Hastings studied at Columbia University and then went to Paris to study at the École des Beaux–Arts, where he became acquainted with Carrère; they both worked for McKim, Mead & White in the mid-1880s before opening their own firm. Their Beaux-Arts training is apparent in the firm's work, which includes the New York Public Library; the Cannon House Office and Russell Senate Office Buildings; the interior of the Metropolitan Opera House; and the Mary Scott Townsend Mansion, now the Cosmos Club, in Washington, D.C. Following Carrère's death, Hastings continued to design numerous landmarks, including the Henry Clay Frick mansion and the Victory Arch in Madison Square in New York City; the American Embassy and Devonshire House in London; the Memorial Amphitheater at Arlington National Cemetery; and the Butt-Millet Memorial Fountain with Daniel Chester French in Washington, D.C. Hastings was active in the National Academy, the Society of Beaux-Arts Architects, the Beaux-Arts Institute of Design, Institut de France, and the Architectural League of New York; he also served as treasurer of the American Academy of Arts and Letters. Among his many honors, he was made a Chevalier of the French Legion of Honor, received a Royal Institute of British Architects Royal Gold Medal in 1922, and was awarded several honorary doctorate degrees. Papers and drawings of Carrère & Hastings (1899–1930) are housed at Avery Library, Columbia University.

JOHN A. HOLABIRD (1886–1945) CFA 1940–45

John Augur Holabird, FAIA, was trained as an engineer, graduating from the U.S. Military Academy in 1907, with further study at the Washington Barracks Engineers School in 1909. By 1913, he completed study at the École des Beaux-Arts. His father, William Holabird, had formed the architectural firm Holabird & Roche in Chicago in 1883, and the younger Holabird joined the firm in 1914. Following the deaths of William Holabird and Martin Roche in the late 1920s, John Holabird and John Wellborn Root Jr., who also joined the firm in 1914, became the name partners of Holabird & Root. The firm became known for buildings in the art deco style, particularly Chicago skyscrapers, including 333 North Michigan Avenue, the Palmolive Building, the Chicago Daily News building, the Chicago Board of Trade, and the Henry Crown Field House, as well as the North Dakota State Capitol. Holabird was a member of the Chicago Planning Commission, a trustee of the Art Institute of Chicago, and a designer of the Century of Progress Exposition in Chicago, 1933–34. The Chicago History Museum houses collections of both Holabird & Roche and Holabird & Root.

VICTORINE DU PONT HOMSEY (1900–1998) CFA 1976–80

Victorine du Pont Homsey, FAIA, received an undergraduate degree in 1923 from Wellesley College and a master's degree in architecture from Smith College in 1925. With her husband, Samuel Eldon Homsey, she founded an architectural firm in Wilmington, Delaware, in 1929 and was in practice for fifty years. She completed a number of wartime federal housing projects, including war worker housing at Greenbelt, Maryland, as well as schools, churches, homes, and gardens in Delaware and projects at Winterthur Museum and Longwood Gardens. She was active in

the Greater Wilmington Development Council, the Historic American Buildings Survey, the Historical Society of Delaware, the Society of Architectural Historians, and the National Trust for Historic Preservation. The records of Victorine & Samuel Homsey, Inc., are located at the Hagley Museum and Library.

JOHN MEAD HOWELLS (1868–1959) CFA 1933–37

The architect John Mead Howells, FAIA, earned an undergraduate degree from Harvard University in 1891 and completed further architectural studies there in 1894 before studying at the École des Beaux-Arts, where he earned a diploma in 1897. He returned to New York and formed the architectural firm Howell & Stokes with I. N. Stokes, who had also studied at the École. The partnership, which designed such works as St. Paul's Chapel at Columbia University, ended in 1913. After 1913, Howell focused his practice on office buildings in the art deco style, many of which he completed with Raymond Hood, whom he had met during his time at the École. These projects include the Tribune Tower in Chicago and the Daily News Building and Beekman Tower, both in New York City. Howells also designed the plan for the University of Brussels in Belgium in 1922 at the request of U.S. Commerce Secretary Herbert Hoover. Howells served as president of the Society of Beaux-Arts Architects and the Society of Architects Diplômes. He was also elected to the National Institute of Arts and Letters, named a Chevalier by the French Legion of Honor, and made an officer of Belgium's Order of the Crown. Howells, son of American author William Dean Howells, wrote several books on architectural history.

JOSEPH HUDNUT (1886–1968) CFA 1950–55

Architect, scholar, and educator Joseph F. Hudnut received an undergraduate degree from Harvard University in 1909 and a bachelor of architecture from the University of Michigan in 1912. He taught at Alabama Polytechnic Institute from 1912 to 1916, leaving to study at Columbia University, where he received a master of science in 1917. He opened an architectural practice in New York in 1919 but left to return to academia in 1923, teaching architecture at the University of Virginia and serving as director of the university's McIntyre School of Fine Arts. In 1926, Hudnut became a professor at Columbia University's School of Architecture and the school's dean in 1933. He became dean of the newly created Graduate School of Design at Harvard University in 1936, where he remained until retiring in 1953. Hudnut brought noted Bauhaus modernists Walter Gropius and Marcel Breuer to the Harvard faculty. He also wrote several books on architecture and art, including *Architecture and the Spirit of Man, Three Lamps of Modern Architecture,* and *Modern Sculpture,* as well as numerous articles, and continued to lecture on architecture after his retirement.

PETER HURD (1904–84) CFA 1959–63

The painter Peter Hurd was born in New Mexico, and the scenery of the Southwest would be a significant theme of his work. Hurd studied at the U.S. Military Academy at West Point from 1921 to 1923, leaving to study at Haverford College; he attended the Pennsylvania Academy of Fine Arts and studied with N.C. Wyeth from 1924 to 1926. Hurd married Wyeth's daughter, Henriette, in 1929, and the couple returned to New Mexico in the late 1930s. His paintings, primarily watercolors, chronicled the landscape of the region. In the early 1950s, he collaborated on a series of fresco murals at Texas Technological College (Texas Tech University). He was also a portrait painter, completing paintings of President Lyndon Baines Johnson and King Faisal of Saudi Arabia. Hurd's interest in folk music led him to collaborate on an album, *Spanish Folk Songs of New Mexico* in 1957. His paintings are in a number of collections, including the Metropolitan Museum, the Museum of the National Academy of Design, and the Art Institute of Chicago. He was affiliated with the National Academy, the Wilmington Society of Fine Arts, and the American Watercolor Society; he received a first prize award for watercolors from the Art Institute of Chicago in 1937. The Smithsonian Archives of American Art holds many of his papers.

ELI S. JACOBS (1937–) CFA 1976–80

Eli Solomon Jacobs, an attorney and businessman, attended Yale University, receiving his undergraduate degree in 1959 and a law degree in 1962. He worked for the investment bank White, Weld & Co. in New York City from 1964 to 1971, becoming a general partner in 1968. He continued in investment banking and other business ventures after leaving the firm. In 1965, he was named to the Mayor's Task Force on Urban Design and the Mayor's Task Force on Development of Roosevelt Island, both in New York City. He was also majority owner of the Baltimore Orioles baseball team in the early 1990s, during which time the Camden Yards baseball park was built. He has been extensively involved in defense and intelligence matters, including affiliations with the Defense Policy Board, the Academy of Political Science, the Association of Intelligence Officers, and the Council on Foreign Relations. Jacobs served as an appointed member of the General Advisory Committee of the United States Arms Control and Disarmament Agency under President Ronald Reagan.

BURNHAM KELLY (1912–99) CFA 1963–67;
VICE CHAIRMAN 1963–67

Urban planner Burnham Kelly was dean of the College of Architecture, Art, and Planning at Cornell University from 1960 to 1971. Kelly, whose maternal grandfather was Daniel Burnham, received his undergraduate degree in 1933 from Williams College, following study at the University of Paris, where he received a diploma in 1932. He completed a law degree at the Harvard University School of Law in 1936 and worked for two years at the Providence, Rhode Island, law firm Greenough, Lyman & Cross, before studying city planning at the Massachusetts Institute of Technology (MIT), where he received his master's degree in 1941. During his military service in World War II, he was a member of the Advisory Commission for the Office of Civil Defense and the Commission on Fortification; he also worked in army intelligence in Europe. After the war, Kelly taught at, where he remained until joining the Cornell faculty in 1960. Kelly wrote numerous journal articles and two books on prefabricated homes. He was active in many organizations related to planning and design, including the American Institute of Planning, the American Institute of Architects, the American Society of Planning Officials, the Housing Association of Metropolitan Boston, the New York State Council on Architecture, the National Institute of Arts and Letters, and the American Law Institute Model Land Development Code Advisory Committee. His papers are archived at Cornell University.

WILLIAM MITCHELL KENDALL (1856–1941)
CFA 1916–21

William Mitchell Kendall, FAIA, spent his architectural career with the New York firm McKim, Mead & White from 1882 until his death in 1941. Kendall's work exemplified the Beaux-Arts principles for which the firm was known, which included Madison Square Garden, the Morgan Library, the Washington Arch, and the Main Post Office, all in New York City; Arlington Memorial Bridge and the restoration of St. John's Church, both in Washington, D.C.; the American Academy in Rome; Harvard University School of Business; and the Plymouth Rock Memorial. He received his undergraduate degree from Harvard University in 1876, studied at the Massachusetts Institute of Technology from 1876 to 1878, and completed a year of travel and study in France and Italy. He was a member of the Committee for Beautification of Permanent American Military Cemeteries in France and England and designed war memorials at several of the cemeteries. Kendall was a member of the National Institute of Arts and Letters and elected to the American Academy of Arts and Letters; served as a trustee of the American Academy in Rome; was a member of the National Academy and the Society of Mayflower Descendants; and served on the 1934 Prix de Rome jury with Louis Ayres and John Russell Pope. He was honored with a merit award

from the New York Chapter of the American Institute of Architects in 1929.

WILLIAM SERGEANT KENDALL (1869–1938) CFA 1920–21

The painter William Sergeant Kendall was known for his evocative scenes of domestic life; his wife and daughters were frequent subjects in his early work. He began his training at the Brooklyn Art Guild and the Pennsylvania Academy of Fine Arts as a student of Thomas Eakins, returning to New York City in 1886 to study at the Art Students League. He moved to Europe in 1888 for further study, including a period at the École des Beaux-Arts, and continued to paint, earning recognition at the Paris Salon in 1891. A year later he returned to New York and established his studio. Kendall and his family eventually moved to Newport, Rhode Island and then to New Haven, Connecticut, where he was a professor and head of the School of Fine Arts at Yale University from 1913 to 1922. He left the university in 1922 and relocated to rural Bath County, Virginia, where he continued to paint until his death. He was the recipient of numerous prizes and awards for his work and was a member of the National Institute of Arts and Letters. His papers from 1900 to 1936 are housed at the Smithsonian Archives of American Art.

ALEX KRIEGER (1951–) CFA 2012–

Alex Krieger, FAIA, is an architect and urban designer whose career has combined teaching and practice in working to improve the quality of place in major urban areas. He is a founding principal of Chan Krieger Sieniewicz, a design firm established in 1984 that spanned the disciplines of architecture, urban design, and public space planning, and merged with NBBJ in 2010. Krieger is a professor at the Harvard Graduate School of Design, where he has taught since 1977, and served as associate chairman of the Department of Architecture and chairman of the Department of Urban Planning and Design. He has written and edited several books and essays on American cities, including *A Design Primer for Towns and Cities* (1990), *Mapping Boston* (1999), *Remaking the Urban Waterfront* (2004), and *Urban Design* (2009). He is a frequent advisor to mayors and their planning staffs, and has served on many civic boards and public commissions such as the Boston Civic Design Commission, the Providence Capital Center Commission, the Large City Planners Institute, and the Joseph Riley Institute. Krieger is a graduate of Cornell University and Harvard University; he served as an advisory panel member of the Mayor's Institute on City Design of the National Endowment for the Arts, and continues to serve as a design peer reviewer for the U.S. General Services Administration.

WILLIAM F. LAMB (1883–1952) CFA 1937–45;
VICE CHAIRMAN 1941–45

William Frederick Lamb, FAIA, joined the New York architecture firm Carrère & Hastings, in 1911, shortly after returning from Paris where he earned a diploma at the École des Beaux-Arts. Lamb became a partner in 1920; the firm would be known as Shreve & Lamb from 1924 to 1929 and thereafter as Shreve, Lamb & Harmon. Lamb's notable projects include the Empire State Building, the Standard Oil Building, 521 Fifth Avenue, the Forbes Magazine Building, and the General Motors Building in New York City; the Acacia Mutual Life Insurance Building in Washington, D.C.; and academic buildings for Connecticut College for Women, Williams College, Cornell University, and Wesleyan University. In addition to his studies at the École, Lamb received a bachelor's degree from Williams College in 1904 and did graduate work at the School of Architecture, Columbia University, from 1904 to 1906. Lamb received an honorary doctorate from his undergraduate alma mater in 1932; other honors include two gold medals from the Fifth Avenue Association (1930, 1931), a medal from the Architectural League of New York (1931), and a medal of honor from the New York Chapter of the American Institute of Architects (1932). He was a member of the American Academy of Arts and Letters, the Art Commission of the City of New York, the Beaux-Arts Institute of Design, and the Architectural League of New York.

LEE LAWRIE (1877–1963) CFA 1933–37, 1945–50
The work of sculptor Lee Lawrie is associated with some of America's most noted buildings of the first half of the twentieth century. His stylistic approach evolved with the building styles, ranging from Beaux-Arts to neo-Gothic to art deco. Many of his architectural sculptures were completed for buildings by Bertram Goodhue of Cram & Goodhue, including the chapel at West Point; the National Academy of Sciences in Washington, D.C.; the Nebraska State Capitol; the Los Angeles Public Library; St. Bartholomew's Church in New York; and Rockefeller Chapel at the University of Chicago. The sculpture *Atlas* at Rockefeller Center in New York City is one of his best-known works. He did numerous pieces in Washington, D.C., including the bronze doors of the Adams Building of the Library of Congress, the Octagon House memorial relief, the National Shrine of the Immaculate Conception south entrance portal, and the interior sculpture of George Washington at the National Cathedral. Lawrie served as a consultant to the 1932 Century of Progress Exposition in Chicago, and he was a member of the National Institute of Arts and Letters, the American Academy of Arts and Letters, the National Academy of Design, and the Architectural League of New York. Among his many awards was an American Institute of Architects Gold Medal in 1921 and 1927, a medal of honor from the Architectural League in 1931, and an honorary degree from Yale University. Lawrie began his artistic training in the studios of noted sculptors in the 1890s, including Augustus Saint-Gaudens. He received a bachelor's degree in fine arts from Yale University in 1910. He was an instructor in Yale's School of Fine Arts from 1908 to 1919 and taught in the architecture program at Harvard University from 1910 to 1912.

THOMAS E. LUEBKE (1962–) CFA SECRETARY 2005–
Thomas Eric Luebke, FAIA, was selected by the Commission of Fine Arts in 2005 to serve as secretary following the retirement of Charles Atherton. Luebke came to the position with extensive experience as an architect in both the public and private sectors. He had served as the city architect for Alexandria, Virginia, since 2002, where he was responsible for the design review of all new architecture projects in the city, including the Potomac Yard and Carlyle district redevelopment projects. Prior to his work with the City of Alexandria, Luebke had been a senior design architect with the firm Leo A Daly from 1996 to 2002, where he focused on institutional, commercial, and high-rise projects, including the forty-five-story First National Tower in Omaha, Nebraska, completed in 2002. Earlier in his career Luebke worked at Hartman-Cox Architects, Skidmore Owings & Merrill, and William Rawn Associates in Boston as well as serving as executive director of the Mayors' Institute on City Design, an urban design forum sponsored by the National Endowment for the Arts. He served as an assistant to the undersecretary of the Department of the Treasury from 1985 to 1987 and as an architectural historian for the restoration of the Pension Building and the Eisenhower Executive Office Building. He has been active in the Washington, D.C., chapter of the American Institute of Architects, serving on its board and as president of its nonprofit affiliate, the Washington Architectural Foundation. Luebke received an undergraduate degree in history from Washington University in St. Louis in 1984 and a master's degree in architecture from the Harvard University Graduate School of Design in 1991. He was a visiting scholar at the American Academy in Rome in 2010.

M

EMILY MALINO (1925–2007) CFA 1997–2001
Emily Malino (Scheuer) practiced as an interior designer in New York and Washington, D.C., specializing in medical facilities, libraries, and commercial buildings. She was a designer with the architecture firm Hellmuth, Obata & Kassabaum, a vice president of Perkins & Will, and a principal of Malino & Metcalf. She later served as a senior design consultant with Tobey & Davis in Washington, D.C. She was a syndicated columnist on design for United Features Syndicate, chaired the leg-

islative and education committees of the American Society of Interior Designers, and was also active in leadership positions with numerous arts and cultural organizations, including the Architectural League of New York, the President's Committee on the Arts and the Humanities, the Shakespeare Theatre in Washington, D.C., Gracie Mansion Conservancy, and the Aspen International Conference. She received an undergraduate degree from Vassar College and later earned a master's degree in American literature from George Washington University (2001).

PAUL MANSHIP (1885–1966) CFA 1937–41
The sculptor Paul Manship studied at the St. Paul Institute of Art and the Pennsylvania Academy of Fine Arts. While a student, he also worked as a studio assistant to Solon Borglum, Isidore Konti, and Charles Grafly. He was awarded a Rome Prize in 1909 and, in 1912, was named a fellow in sculpture at the American Academy in Rome, where his work was influenced by Assyrian, Egyptian, and early Greek precedents. In 1913, he returned to the United States, and his career was established by exhibitions at the Architectural League and Pennsylvania Academy. Among his best known public pieces are the gates for the Bronx Zoo and *Prometheus* at Rockefeller Center in New York City. Near the time of his death, Manship completed the statue of Theodore Roosevelt for the memorial to the twenty-sixth president at Roosevelt Island in Washington, D.C. He was affiliated with the National Academy, the National Sculpture Society, and the American Academy of Arts and Letters. His many honors include a Pierpont Morgan fellowship, a Widener Gold Medal from the Pennsylvania Academy of Fine Arts, and the award of Chevalier from the French Legion of Honor. His papers are in the Smithsonian Archives of American Art.

JOHN L. MAURAN (1866–1933) CFA 1930–33;
VICE CHAIRMAN, 1933
John Lawrence Mauran, FAIA, began his architectural career with the firm Shepley, Rutan & Coolidge in 1890, rising to partner of the St. Louis office. While with that firm, he helped design the Art Institute of Chicago and the Chicago Public Library. In 1900 Mauran opened his own firm, Mauran, Russell & Garden in St. Louis; it became Mauran, Russell & Crowell in 1911. His firm designed numerous buildings throughout the Midwest but was most well known for its buildings in St. Louis, among them the Federal Reserve Bank, Union Market, the St. Louis Globe-Democrat Building, and the Federal Courts Building. Mauran studied at the Massachusetts Institute of Technology (MIT) from 1885 to 1889, then traveled and studied in Europe until 1890; he later taught at MIT. He was active in many civic and professional organizations, and he served as president of the American Institute of Architects and president and secretary of the St. Louis chapter. He was also a member of the Council of Fine Arts, the predecessor to the Commission of Fine Arts.

MICHAEL MCKINNELL (1935–) CFA 2005–11
N. Michael McKinnell, FAIA, is the cofounder of the Boston firm of Kallmann McKinnell & Wood Architects, which he formed in 1962 with fellow architect Gerhard Kallmann upon winning the competition for the design of Boston City Hall. The firm received eight honor awards and the 1984 Firm of the Year Award from the American Institute of Architects. McKinnell's projects have included Boston's Hynes Convention Center, the American Academy of Arts and Sciences headquarters in Cambridge, and the Independence Visitor Center in Philadelphia as well as embassies, courthouses, libraries, and buildings at numerous universities, including Harvard, Yale, Princeton, and Emory. McKinnell graduated from the University of Manchester, England, in 1958 and received a master in architecture from Columbia University in 1960. He served on the faculty of Harvard University's Graduate School of Design for twenty-five years and as the professor of the practice of architecture at the Massachusetts Institute of Technology. McKinnell has lectured and taught at many other universities and in 1989 was the Architect in Residence at the American Academy in Rome. He was a Fulbright Scholar, received the Royal Manchester Institute Silver Medal, is an associate member of

Royal Institute of British Architects, and was recognized by the Boston Society of Architects with an Award of Honor in 1994.

MILTON B. MEDARY JR. (1874–1929) CFA 1922–27
Milton Bennett Medary Jr., FAIA, attended the University of Pennsylvania for one year before joining the Philadelphia architecture firm of Frank Miles Day in 1891. He remained there until 1894, when he opened his own firm in that city, Field & Medary; that firm would eventually become Zantzinger, Borie & Medary in 1910. Medary was a design consultant to several universities, the Roosevelt Memorial Association, and Mount Vernon. He was the designer of numerous buildings, including the Pennsylvania Athletic Club, Bryn Mawr Hospital, and, with Paul Cret, the Detroit Institute of Fine Arts. Medary served as chairman of the Department of Labor's United States Housing Corporation during World War I and was selected in 1927 by Secretary of the Treasury Paul Mellon to serve on the Board of Architectural Consultants, which was advising the department on the design of the Federal Triangle redevelopment. He served on the National Capital Park and Planning Commission in Washington, D.C., was president of both the American Institute of Architects (AIA) and its Philadelphia chapter, and was affiliated with the Foundation for Architecture and Landscape Architecture and the Pennsylvania Academy of Fine Arts. He was honored by the AIA with a gold medal in 1929, by the Philadelphia Art Club with a gold medal in 1927, and was awarded an honorary doctorate by the University of Pennsylvania in 1927.

ELIZABETH K. MEYER (1956–) CFA 2012–
Elizabeth Meyer, FASLA, is an associate professor of landscape architecture at the University of Virginia School of Architecture, where she has taught since 1993, serving as department chairman and the director of the graduate landscape architecture program. She holds degrees from the University of Virginia and Cornell University; she taught previously at Cornell and the Harvard University Graduate School of Design and worked as a landscape architect for the EDAW and Hanna/Olin design firms. Meyer is engaged nationally as a studio critic and lecturer; she has published widely on contemporary landscape design practice and theory, exploring such issues as the social and aesthetic implications of creating new parks on toxic industrial sites and the role of aesthetics in sustainable design. A recipient of a Dumbarton Oaks Fellowship, she is currently completing a book, *Groundwork: Practices of Landscape Architecture*. She was a member of the competition-winning team in 2010 for the grounds of the St. Louis Gateway Arch and recently served on the jury for the National Mall Design Competition sponsored by the Trust for the National Mall. She was named a fellow of the Council of Educators in Landscape Architecture in 2012.

FRANCIS D. MILLET (1846–1912) CFA 1910–12;
VICE CHAIRMAN 1910–12
Francis Davis Millet was a painter and muralist whose works are in the collections of major museums, including the National Gallery in London, the Metropolitan Museum, and the Detroit Museum. His work also appeared in the World's Columbian Exposition of 1893 and in the Government Pavilion of the Paris Exposition of 1900. In addition to painting, Millet designed U.S. military medals for veterans of the Civil War, the Spanish-American War, and the Philippine Insurrection. Following service in the Union Army during the Civil War, Millet received an undergraduate degree in 1869 and a master's degree in 1872, both from Harvard University. He studied painting at the Royal Academy in Antwerp from 1871 to 1873, traveled extensively, and reported on the Turkish War for the *New York Herald* from 1877 to 1878. He was secretary of the American Academy of Arts and Letters, a member of the American Academy of Arts and Letters in Rome, a member of the National Academy of Design as well as numerous other painting, muralist, and art societies in the United States and England. The multitalented Millet also wrote travel books, translated Tolstoy, and, with Daniel Burnham in 1890, wrote a book on the planning and design of the World's Fair. Millet died in the sinking of the *Titanic* and is memorialized with his friend,

Archibald Butt, in the Butt-Millet Memorial Fountain in Washington, D.C. Millet's papers are collected in the Smithsonian Archives of American Art.

CHARLES MOORE (1855–1942) CFA 1910–40;
CHAIRMAN 1915–37
Charles Moore began his career as a journalist and writer in Detroit. From 1889 to 1902, he served as secretary to U.S. Senator James McMillan and played a significant role with the McMillan Commission and its report on the development of Washington in 1901. Moore was a founding member of the Commission of Fine Arts in 1910 and would remain a member for thirty years, twenty-two of them as chairman. During this time, Moore also served as director of the Detroit Museum of Art (1914–17) and as a consultant to and later chief of the Manuscripts Division at the Library of Congress (1917–27). He was also a prolific writer, writing numerous essays, articles, and histories, many related to city planning and architecture, as well as biographies of Daniel Burnham, Charles McKim, and George Washington. He was a cofounder of the American Academy in Rome and a member of the National Conference on City Planning, the Detroit City Plan and Improvement Commission, and the American Institute of Arts and Letters as well as the New York Architectural League and the Michigan Historical Commission. He received an undergraduate degree from Harvard University in 1878 and a doctorate from George Washington University in 1900. Moore received many awards and honors during his long career, including honorary membership in the American Institute of Architects, and was named a Chevalier of the French Legion of Honor in 1924.

BENJAMIN W. MORRIS III (1870–1944) CFA 1927–31;
VICE CHAIRMAN 1931
Benjamin Wister Morris III, FAIA, studied architecture at Columbia University, with further study at the École des Beaux-Arts from 1894 to 1896. He joined the New York architecture firm of Carrère & Hastings until he founded his own firm, Morris, Butler & Rodman in 1900. The firm would undergo several name changes until 1915, when it became Morris & O'Connor. Morris designed many banks and insurance company buildings as well as an annex to the J. P. Morgan Library, a dormitory at Princeton University, the Cunard Building in New York, and the interiors of the RMS *Queen Mary*. He was a member of the American Academy of Arts and Letters and was affiliated with the Beaux-Arts Institute of Design, the Beaux-Arts Society of Architects, the Architectural League of New York, and the New York City Art Commission. He received a gold medal from the Architectural League of New York in 1918 and an honorary degree from Trinity College in 1906. Morris's architectural drawings from 1893 to 1936 are housed at Avery Library, Columbia University.

H. SIDDONS MOWBRAY (1858–1928) CFA 1921–28
Murals by the painter Henry Siddons Mowbray were often commissioned as decoration in the homes of the wealthy, including those of F. W. Vanderbilt, J. P. Morgan, C. P. Huntington, and Larz Anderson. His works also were found in the Appellate Courthouse, University Club Library, and Morgan Library in New York City as well as the U.S. Federal Court building in Cleveland, Ohio. Mowbray graduated from the U.S. Military Academy in 1875 but soon after turned to art, studying painting in the Bonnat Studio in Paris. He opened his own studio in New York City in 1878. Mowbray received the Clark Prize in 1888, served as a director of the American Academy in Rome in 1903, and was a member of the National Academy. His papers are in the Smithsonian Archives of American Art.

EMILY MUIR (1904–2003) CFA 1955–59
Emily Lansingh Muir, the first woman to serve on the Commission of Fine Arts, was a painter who drew her inspiration from the life and landscape of coastal Maine. She attended Vassar College and studied painting at the Art Students League in New York with Richard Lahey. In 1939,

she and her husband, the sculptor William Muir, moved to Stonington, Maine, where she established her studio and worked for more than sixty years. She was also an accomplished designer of houses, building more than forty on Deer Isle in Maine. Muir's paintings are in the collections of the Brooklyn Museum, the Portland Museum of Art, the University of Maine, and the Farnsworth Art Museum as well as many private collections. She served on the Advisory Committee for the Kennedy Center for the Performing Arts and was also a member of the Maine Coastal Heritage Trust, the Stonington Town Planning Board, and the Portland Society of Art. The papers of William and Emily Muir are located in the Smithsonian Archives of American Art.

FREDERICK V. MURPHY (1879–1958) CFA 1945–50

Frederick Vernon Murphy, FAIA, was the first architect based in Washington, D.C., to serve on the Commission of Fine Arts. Murphy was employed in the Office of the Supervising Architect, Department of the Treasury, from 1899 to 1911. He founded his first firm in Washington in 1911 as Murphy & Olmsted, worked on his own from 1932 to 1940, and eventually formed Murphy & Locraft, which he operated until 1954. Murphy worked mostly in Washington, D.C., on projects related to the Catholic Church; these include numerous buildings at the Catholic University of America, the Georgetown University School of Foreign Service, the Shrine of the Sacred Heart, and the National Shrine of the Immaculate Conception (with Maginnes & Walsh). He also designed the American World War II cemetery in Saint Avold, France. Walsh studied at the Art Institute of Chicago with additional coursework in architecture at George Washington University. He was accepted to the École des Beaux-Arts in 1905 and received a diploma in 1909. In 1911, he founded the School of Architecture at Catholic University, served as its dean, and taught in the school until 1949. He was a member of the Beaux-Arts Institute of Design in New York, an associate member of the National Academy of Design, and a member of the House of Representatives Office Building Design Committee. He was a Chevalier of the French Legion of Honor and the recipient of honors and awards from organizations related to the Catholic Church.

SONDRA G. MYERS (1934–) CFA 1980–85

Arts and humanities advisor Sondra Gelb Myers graduated from Connecticut College with an undergraduate degree in philosophy in 1955 and undertook graduate studies at New York University, the New School for Social Research, and Oxford University. Before her appointment to the Commission of Fine Arts in 1980, she served as chairman of the Commission on Architecture and Urban Design for the city of Scranton, Pennsylvania. She was a cultural advisor to the governor of Pennsylvania from 1987 to 1993, worked at the National Endowment for the Humanities from 1993 to 1995, and was a senior advisor to the president of Connecticut College until 2000. She joined the University of Maryland Democracy Collaborative as a senior associate in 2001, leaving in 2006 to become a senior fellow at the University of Scranton's Schemel Forum, where she serves as director. Myers has written extensively on the issues of democracy and interdependence. She has served as chair and president of the Federation of State Humanities Councils and has been affiliated with numerous other arts and humanities organizations. She was a Rapoport Democracy Fellow from 2000 to 2001 at Rutgers University and has been awarded several honorary degrees.

N

EDWARD F. NEILD SR. (1884–1955) CFA 1950–55; VICE CHAIRMAN 1951–55

Edward Fairfax Neild Sr., FAIA, graduated from the Tulane University School of Engineering in 1906. He established his own architectural practice in Shreveport, Louisiana, which became Neild-Somdal Associates in 1934; he remained with the firm until his death in 1955. Neild designed numerous residential, civic, and academic buildings in Louisiana, including the State Office Building and Louisiana State Museum in Baton Rouge. He also designed the Maricopa County Courthouse in Arizona. Neild was a friend and advisor to President Harry Truman, consulting on the renovations to the White House, and was the designer of the Truman Library. Neild also served as the director of the Shreveport Chamber of Commerce.

PAMELA NELSON (1947–) CFA 2001–11; VICE CHAIRMAN 2005–11

Pamela Nelson is an artist and educator based in Dallas, Texas. Her work has been exhibited in New York City and throughout Texas, and she has created numerous public art projects in the Dallas-Fort Worth area, including at the Dallas-Fort Worth Airport and light rail stations in the Dallas Area Rapid Transit System. She also participated in the Dallas City Center TIF Streetscape Project, for which she was honored with a City of Dallas Urban Design Award in 2000. She received a Legend Award from the Dallas Visual Art Center in 2000 and a Merit Award from the American Institute of Architects in 1994. Nelson was director of the Open Art Project at Stewpot Shelter in Dallas from 1994 to 2009 and served on the Public Art Committee for the city of Dallas from 2000 to 2005. She received a bachelor's degree in fine arts from Southern Methodist University in 1974.

WALTER A. NETSCH (1920–2008) CFA 1980–85

Walter Andrew Netsch Jr., FAIA, joined the architecture firm Skidmore, Owings & Merrill (SOM) in 1947, shortly after serving in the U.S. Army Corps of Engineers during World War II. Netsch remained in the SOM San Francisco office until 1954, when he moved to the firm's Chicago office. He became a partner in the firm and remained with SOM until 1979; he established his own practice in 1981. Netsch's work complimented the firm's modernist approach in the postwar era; among his most noted projects are the U.S. Air Force Academy Chapel; the East Wing of the Art Institute of Chicago; the Inland Steel Building; the Miami University of Ohio Art Museum; and the campus and buildings of Montgomery College in Takoma Park, Maryland, and the University of Illinois–Chicago. Netsch earned his bachelor of architecture from the Massachusetts Institute of Technology in 1943 and was a visiting professor at the University of Minnesota and the University of Illinois, Champaign–Urbana. He served as president of the Chicago Park District and was also affiliated with the Art Institute of Chicago and the Landmarks Preservation Council, Chicago. He was the recipient of several honorary degrees and the Bartlett Award from the Art Institute of Chicago.

FREDERICK DOVETON NICHOLS (1911–95) CFA 1976–81

Frederick Doveton Nichols, FAIA, was an architect, educator, and historian. He studied for two years at Colorado College and completed his undergraduate degree in fine arts from Yale University in 1935. He joined the National Park Service, becoming regional director of the Historic American Buildings Survey. He became director of architectural studies at the University of Hawaii in 1941; after service in the U.S. Army Air Force during World War II, he returned to Hawaii. In 1950 he became a professor and later chairman of the School of Architecture at the University of Virginia until his retirement in 1982. Nichols wrote several books on the architectural history of Georgia and Virginia and on Thomas Jefferson as a designer. He was a Guggenheim fellow in 1963 and received the University of Virginia Thomas Jefferson Award in 1979 as well as other fellowships and awards. Nichols was a member of the Thomas Jefferson Memorial Foundation, the American Institute of Architects Task Force on the U.S. Capitol West Front, the Virginia Historic Landmarks Commission, and the Monticello Restoration Society.

ALAN R. NOVAK (1934–) CFA 1981–85

Alan Richard Novak, an attorney and businessman, was the developer of the Ritz-Carlton, Aspen, and Mandarin Oriental Hotels in Washington, D.C. He is currently involved in energy and venture capital projects. Novak received his undergraduate degree in 1955 from Yale University as a Navy Scholar. He attended Oxford University as a Marshall Scholar and received a master's degree in 1960 and returned to Yale to earn a law degree in 1963. Novak spent a year as clerk to Supreme Court

Justice Potter Stewart before joining the law firm of Cravath, Swain & Moore until 1965, when he began a career in public service. He was a legislative aide to Senator Edward Kennedy (1965–66); executive assistant to Undersecretary Walter Rostow, U.S. Department of State; member of the White House Communications Task Force (1967–68); and advisor to the White House chief of staff (1980). He also taught at the Cardozo School of Law Yeshiva University in New York City. He was the recipient of Yale University Law School's traveling fellowship in 1962.

O

FREDERICK LAW OLMSTED JR. (1870–1957)
CFA 1910–18; VICE CHAIRMAN 1912–18

The noted landscape architect Frederick Law Olmsted Jr., FASLA, served as a young man on the McMillan Commission with Daniel Burnham and Charles Moore to create the plan that established the modern image of the nation's capital city. He was an original member of the Commission of Fine Arts. Olmsted joined the design practice started by his father, Frederick Law Olmsted Sr., in 1895, which became Olmsted Brothers in 1897 following the death of partner Charles Eliot; the younger Olmsted remained with the firm until 1950. Throughout his career, he worked on many projects, including the metropolitan park system in Boston, the Biltmore Estate, and landscape plans for the National Mall, Jefferson Memorial, Rock Creek Park, and the White House grounds. He prepared a master plan for Cornell University and was involved in the planning of Forest Hills Gardens. He was a founding member of the American Society of Landscape Architects and a member of the American Institute of Architects as well as actively involved in numerous planning and design organizations and commissions, including the Baltimore Park Commission, National Park Service Board of Advisors for Yosemite, National Conference on City Planning, American City Planning Institute, National Institute of Arts and Letters, and the American Academy in Rome. Olmsted was the recipient of many awards and honors during his long career, among them the American Academy Gold Medal (1949) and the U.S. Department of the Interior Conservation Service Award (1956).

DOUGLAS W. ORR (1892–1966) CFA 1955–63;
VICE CHAIRMAN 1955–63

Douglas William Orr, FAIA and RIBA (Hon.), opened his architectural practice in 1919 in New Haven, Connecticut, after receiving his undergraduate degree from Yale University; he would complete a master's degree in fine arts at Yale in 1927. Orr designed the Taft Memorial Tower, Harkness Memorial Hall, and Connecticut Hall at Yale University. He was also involved in the renovations of the White House and the historic Octagon House in Washington, D.C. His portfolio included many academic projects, among them buildings at Mt. Holyoke and Hollins Colleges and memorial chapels at the Coast Guard and Merchant Marine Academies. He was a member of the Commission on the Renovation of the Executive Mansion, the Advisory Commission on Presidential Office Space, and the Smithsonian Art Commission. Orr was also an academician of the American Architectural Foundation and a member of the National Academy of Design.

P

ROBERT A. PECK (1948–) CFA 1990–94

Robert A. Peck, AIA (Hon.), ASLA (Hon.), is an attorney whose career in public service and in the private sector has been focused on the built environment. He earned a bachelor's degree in economics at the University of Pennsylvania in 1969 and a law degree at Yale University in 1972. He worked at the Office of Management and Budget and the National Endowment for the Arts in its Federal Design Program before his work in Congress, first as assistant counsel to the Senate Committee on Environment and Public Works and eventually as chief of staff to Senator Daniel Patrick Moynihan. Leaving the Senate staff in 1986, he worked as a real estate investment executive and as a land-use attorney for several Washington, D.C., law firms; he also served as vice president for public affairs at the American Institute of Architects. He was appointed commissioner of the Public Buildings Service of the General Services Administration in 1995, where he served until 2001 and again from 2009 to 2012; he was instrumental in establishing the Design Excellence, First Impressions, and Urban Development/Good Neighbor design programs. From 2001 to 2005, he was president of the Greater Washington Board of Trade and a consultant at two national real estate brokerage firms. In 2012, he became regional director of workplace consulting at the architecture firm Gensler. Peck served in the U.S. Army Reserve as a Special Forces officer. In his volunteer work, Peck has been president of the D.C. Preservation League and a board member of the American Architectural Foundation and the National Building Museum. He has been a visiting lecturer at Yale University, a Loeb Fellow at the Harvard University Graduate School of Design, and a resource panelist for the Mayors' Institute on City Design. He was a 2012 recipient of the Thomas Jefferson Award for Public Architecture of the American Institute of Architects.

ELBERT PEETS (1886–1968) CFA 1950–58

Elbert Peets was a landscape architect, city planner, and author who contributed significantly to garden city development in the U.S. in the early twentieth century and to the understanding of civic art. In 1916 he opened an office with architect Werner Hegemann; the two worked together until the early 1920s, when Hegemann returned to Europe. In 1922 they published a seminal work, *The American Vitruvius: An Architect's Handbook of Civic Art*. Peets continued to practice on his own until the mid-1930s, and he continued to write, producing books on city planning and tree care. During the Great Depression, he joined the U.S. Farm Resettlement Administration (1935–38) and then became the chief of the site planning section, U.S. Housing Authority, until 1944. After World War II he worked as a consultant to such clients as the National Capital Planning Commission. He taught at Harvard and Yale Universities from 1950 to 1960. His projects include the new towns of Kohler, Washington Highlands, and Greendale in Wisconsin; Park Forest, Illinois; Bannockburn, Maryland; and Wyomissing Park and Reading, Pennsylvania. Late in his career, he developed the site plan for the Capitol Columns at the U.S. National Arboretum in Washington, D.C. Peets received an undergraduate degree from Western Reserve University in 1912 and a master's degree in landscape architecture from Harvard University in 1915. His papers are in the collection of Cornell University.

WILLIAM G. PERRY (1883–1975) CFA 1955–63

The Boston architect William Graves Perry, FAIA, formed the partnership Perry, Shaw & Hepburn in 1919 following several years in solo practice and two years with the architecture firm Shepley, Rutan & Coolidge. Perry designed Roxbury Latin School in Boston; several buildings at Harvard University, Radcliffe College, and the Massachusetts Institute of Technology (MIT); the student union at Williams College; and the American ambassador's residence in London. His firm carried out the restoration and reconstruction of Colonial Williamsburg for the foundation created by John D. Rockefeller Jr. and was involved in architectural studies for the redevelopment of Lafayette Square in the 1950s. Perry was a trustee of Colonial Williamsburg and a member of the Massachusetts Building Congress, the Historic American Buildings Survey, and the National Academy of Design. Perry earned a bachelor's degree from Harvard University in 1905 and a bachelor's degree in science from MIT in 1907; he received a Rotch Traveling Scholarship and studied at the École des Beaux-Arts, where he earned a diploma in 1913. He was an instructor at Harvard from 1915 to 1916. He received the Elise Willing Bach medal from the Colonial Dames of America in 1933. Colonial Williamsburg has a collection of Perry's papers dating from 1930 to 1940.

ELIZABETH PLATER-ZYBERK (1950–) CFA 2008–;
VICE CHAIRMAN 2011–

Elizabeth Plater-Zyberk, FAIA, is dean of the University of Miami's School of Architecture, where she has taught since 1979, and is a founding principal of Duany Plater-Zyberk & Company, Architects and Town Planners (DPZ). In her work at DPZ, Plater-Zyberk has been a principal in the creation of the Traditional Neighborhood Development ordinance, a prescription for pedestrian-oriented, mixed-use, compact urban growth, which has been incorporated into zoning codes across the country. Her recent publications include *The New Civic Art and Suburban Nation: The Rise of Sprawl and the Decline of the American Dream.* She is a founder and emeritus board member of the Congress for the New Urbanism and a board member of the Institute for Classical Architecture & Classical America. Plater-Zyberk received a bachelor of arts in architecture and urban planning from Princeton University in 1972 and a master of architecture from Yale University in 1974. Among her many awards and commendations are fourteen honorary degrees, the Thomas Jefferson Memorial Medal of Architecture from the University of Virginia, the Vincent J. Scully Prize for exemplary practice and scholarship, the Brandeis Award for Architecture, and the Seaside Prize for contributions to community planning and design from the Seaside Institute.

CHARLES A. PLATT (1861–1933) CFA 1916–21;
VICE CHAIRMAN 1920–21

Charles Adams Platt, FAIA, was an architect, painter, and etcher. He studied at the Art Students League and National Academy of Design in the late 1870s, followed by further study in Paris. His paintings were exhibited widely, including in the Paris Salon of the Societé des Artistes Français of 1885 and 1886. Platt's work is now in the collections of the Freer and Corcoran Galleries of Art. Platt returned to the United States and opened a studio in New York in the early twentieth century, where he continued to work until his death in 1933. In Washington, D.C., Platt designed the Freer Gallery of Art, an estate for James Parmelee now known as Tregaron, an addition to the Corcoran Museum, and the McMillan Fountain (with Herbert Adams). His work includes campus and buildings for Phillips Academy as well as several projects for Vincent Astor. Platt was president of the American Academy in Rome and the Augustus Saint-Gaudens Memorial, a member of the National Academy of Design, and a member of the Cornish Art Colony, whose other members included Augustus Saint-Gaudens, Herbert Adams, and Paul Manship. Platt's architectural record and papers are located at the Avery Library, Columbia University.

HENRY V. POOR III (1888–1970) CFA 1941–45

The ceramicist, painter, and muralist Henry Varnum Poor III received an undergraduate degree from Stanford University in 1910 and studied art in both London and Paris. He returned to the United States in 1911 and taught art at Stanford before moving to San Francisco to teach at the San Francisco Art Association. Following military service in World War I, he settled in Rockland County, New York, and focused on ceramics; he also designed and built his own house and designed homes for friends. In the late 1920s, Poor gained recognition as a painter and eventually turned to murals; he was commissioned to paint twelve murals in the U.S. Department of Justice and the mural *Conservation of American Wild Life* in the Department of the Interior during the 1930s. During World War II he was head of the War Art Unit of the Corps of Engineers. In 1946 he was one of the founders of the Skowhegan School of Painting and Sculpture and taught at Columbia University. Poor was a member of the American Academy of Arts and Letters and was a resident fellow in visual arts at the American Academy in Rome from 1950 to 1951. The Metropolitan Museum of Art, Whitney Museum, and Phillips Collection are among the many museums that include Poor's work in their collections. Poor's papers are in the Smithsonian Archives of American Art.

JOHN RUSSELL POPE (1874–1937) CFA 1917–22;
VICE CHAIRMAN 1921–22

John Russell Pope, FAIA and RIBA (Hon.), was one of the most celebrated classical architects of the early twentieth century for his design practice based in the Beaux-Arts tradition. His projects include the Baltimore Museum of Art, the Natural History Museum in New York City, and additions to the British Museum and the Tate Gallery in London. He is the designer of many monumental Beaux-Arts buildings in Washington, D.C., including the Scottish Rite Temple, Constitution Hall, the American Institute of Pharmacy building, the National Archives, the National Gallery of Art, and the Thomas Jefferson Memorial. After studying medicine at the College of New York City, Pope earned a doctorate in the School of Mines at Columbia University in 1894, then became the first recipient of a fellowship in architecture from the American Academy in Rome (1894–97). He also studied at the École des Beaux-Arts, returning to New York in 1900 where he opened his architectural practice. Pope later served as president of the American Academy in Rome; his many other affiliations include the National Academy of Arts and Letters, the Beaux-Arts Institute of Design, the Architectural League of New York, and the Federal Board of Consulting Architects. He was the recipient of numerous honorary degrees, awards, and medals, among them the American Institute of Architects New York Chapter Gold Medal, National Academician, and Chevalier of the French Legion of Honor.

NEIL H. PORTERFIELD (1936–) CFA 1985–92;
VICE CHAIRMAN 1986–1992

The landscape architect and educator Neil H. Porterfield, FASLA, helped establish the School of Architecture and Landscape Architecture at Penn State University in 1997 in order to encourage collaboration and a multidisciplinary approach in these fields of study. Porterfield earned an undergraduate degree in landscape architecture in 1958 from Penn State and completed a master's degree in landscape architecture from the University of Pennsylvania in 1964. His professional experience includes more than twenty years of work at the design firm Hellmuth, Obata & Kassabaum, where he was involved in the design of the National Air and Space Museum. His many other projects include an urban improvement plan for Doha, Qatar; a visual impact analysis for the Trans-Alaska pipeline; a campus plan for King Saud University in Riyadh, Saudi Arabia; and a master plan for Tortuga Island. Porterfield joined the Penn State faculty and became head of the Department of Landscape Architecture in the School of Architecture in 1985. He was dean of the College of Arts and Architecture at Penn State from 1993 to 2000, and the Neil H. Porterfield Endowment for the School of Architecture and Landscape Architecture was established in his honor in 2004. Porterfield was also honored by the Council of Educators in Landscape Architecture as an outstanding educator in 2008. After his service to the university, Porterfield continued to practice, opening his own firm, The Porterfield Group, in Boalsburg, Pennsylvania.

EARL A. POWELL III (1943–) CFA 2003–;
VICE CHAIRMAN 2004–05, CHAIRMAN 2005–

Earl A. Powell III, an expert in nineteenth- and twentieth-century European and American art, has been director of the National Gallery of Art since 1992. He was an assistant professor of art history at the University of Texas in Austin from 1974 to 1976 and, between 1976 and 1980, held curatorial posts at the National Gallery. From 1980 to 1992, Powell was director of the Los Angeles County Museum of Art. He serves as a trustee of the American Federation of the Arts, the National Trust for Historic Preservation, the White House Historical Association, and the Georgia O'Keeffe Foundation, among others. He is a member of numerous arts organizations, including the Federal Council on the Arts and the Humanities, the National Portrait Gallery Commission, and the American Philosophical Society. Powell graduated with honors from Williams College and received his master's and doctoral degrees from the Fogg Art Museum, Harvard University. He also holds honorary doctoral degrees in fine arts from Otis Parsons Art Institute and Williams College. In addition to writing many journal articles and exhibition catalogue essays, Powell is the author of a monograph on the nineteenth-century American artist Thomas Cole. He served as an officer in the U.S. Navy from 1966 to 1969 and in the Naval Reserve from 1969 to 1980. Powell's awards include Norway's King Olav Medal and the Chevalier of the French Legion of Honor.

R

EDEN D. RAFSHOON (1943–) CFA 1994–2003
Eden Donohue Rafshoon is active in cultural organizations in Washington, D.C. She is president of the board of directors of the Foundation for Art and Preservation in Embassies and has served on the boards of the Shakespeare Theater and the Washington Ballet. Rafshoon also chaired the International Sculpture Conference and Exhibition in 1980. She was a partner in the Atlanta design firms Design Ampersand from 1970 to 1974 and Donohue & Travis from 1975 to 1978. In 1978 she established her own interior design firm, Eden Donohue Interiors, in Washington, D.C., and was a production design consultant at Turner Network Television films in 1989. Rafshoon received a bachelor's degree in art from Hollins College in 1965 and a master's degree in art history from George Washington University in 1988.

MICHAEL RAPUANO (1904–75) CFA 1958–62
With Gilmore Clarke, Michael Rapuano, FASLA, formed the landscape architecture firm Clarke & Rapuano in 1939. In addition to city planning and campus planning projects, the firm became known for its work on the design of parkways. Rapuano was involved in the design of many highway projects, including portions of the Bronx River and Henry Hudson Parkways in New York. He also participated in the landscape design of the United Nations Headquarters and in the design of the World War II American Military Cemetery in Florence, Italy. Rapuano received a bachelor's degree in landscape architecture from Cornell University in 1927 and spent three years at the American Academy in Rome as a fellow in landscape architecture. His early years of employment included work with the Westchester County Park Commission and the New York City Park Commission as well as Madigan-Hyland Engineers. Rapuano was a trustee of the American Academy in Rome and a member of the National Institute of Arts and Letters; the Bucks County, Pennsylvania, Park Commission; and the Municipal Art Commission in New York.

PASCAL REGAN (1914–) CFA 1985–89
The glass sculptor Suzanne Pascal Regan, daughter of the French painter Charles Pascal, spent her childhood unable to hear and used art as a means of communication; her hearing was partially restored in her late teens. She studied art in Italy and Paris in the 1920s, and her early works were mostly paintings. She turned to glass as a sculptural medium in her late thirties, but found the material difficult to work with until the early 1960s, when she began sculpting with a process using old glass that had been tempered by a century of exposure in an abandoned foundry in Pennsylvania. Her studio was a converted garage in her home in Beverly Hills, California. Her pieces became widely exhibited and collected; Ronald Reagan, Armand Hammer, Paul Newman, and Frank Sinatra owned her sculptures. Her work is in the permanent collections of the Corcoran Gallery of Art, the Los Angeles County Museum, and the American embassies in Tokyo and London.

L. ANDREW REINHARD (1891–1964) CFA 1945–50
The architect L. Andrew Reinhard, FAIA, formed Reinhard & Hofmeister with Henry Hofmeister in 1928. After studying at the Mechanics Institute, the Beaux-Arts Institute of Design, and Columbia University, Reinhard worked for a time with architects Benjamin Morris and Raymond Hood; he also worked for the developer John R. Todd in New York City prior to forming his firm with Hofmeister. Through their acquaintance with Todd, Reinhard and Hofmeister became involved as designers for Rockefeller Center. The firm also designed the Chrysler Building East, the John F. Kennedy Airport Federal Building, the Chase Manhattan Bank buildings, and buildings at Columbia University as well as numerous office interiors. After World War II, the firm designed the Ardennes American Cemetery and Memorial in Belgium for the American Battle Monuments Commission. Reinhard was a member of the Architectural League of New York, the Municipal Art Society, and the Bronxville Zoning Board, and was the recipient of the International Exposition Paris Grande Prix (1937) and an Architectural League Gold Medal.

COL. CLARENCE S. RIDLEY (1883–1969) EX OFFICIO
CFA SECRETARY 1917–21
Clarence S. Ridley, U.S. Army Corps of Engineers, was director of the Office of Public Buildings and Grounds (OPBG) from 1917 to 1921. He was a senior military aide to President Woodrow Wilson and, as head of the OPBG, oversaw the construction of the Lincoln Memorial. Ridley left Washington in 1921 to serve in the Panama Canal Zone as an engineer; he became governor of the Canal Zone in 1936, a position he held until 1940. He retired from the military in 1947.

HARRY G. ROBINSON III (1942–) CFA 1994–2003; VICE
CHAIRMAN 1995–2002, CHAIRMAN 2002–03
Harry G. Robinson III, FAIA, is professor of urban design and dean emeritus in the School of Architecture and Design, Howard University. He also served at Howard University as vice president for academic affairs and vice president for university administration, and is the author of a university history. He heads TRG Consulting, an interdisciplinary design practice where he works currently as a consulting executive architect to the American Battle Monuments Commission. He has been president of two national architectural organizations: the National Council of Architectural Registration Boards (1992) and the National Architectural Accrediting Board (1996). Robinson has served as director of the Vietnam Veterans Memorial Fund; as a member of the Committee for the Preservation of the White House; chairman of the UNESCO International Commission for the Goree Memorial and Museum, Dakar, Senegal; secretary and trustee of the National Building Museum; and trustee of the Smithsonian Institution's Cooper-Hewitt National Design Museum. Among his many honors and awards are the American Institute of Architects 1990 Whitney M. Young Jr. Citation and the 2003 Centennial Medal by the Washington, D.C., chapter of the AIA. He is the recipient of the Bronze Star and the Purple Heart Medals, awarded during his Army service in Vietnam. Robinson received both a bachelor of architecture and a master in city planning from Howard University and a master in city planning in urban design from the Harvard University Graduate School of Design.

KEVIN ROCHE (1922–) CFA 1969–80
Eamonn Kevin Roche, FAIA, is a prominent architect recognized for his professional work during the last half of the twentieth century. A Pritzker Prize winner in 1982, he was also the recipient of the American Institute of Architects (AIA) Gold Medal in 1993, the American Academy and Institute of Arts and Letters Gold Medal for Architecture in 1990, and an American Institute of Arts and Letters Brunner Award in 1965. His firm, Kevin Roche John Dinkeloo & Associates was formed in 1966 and won an AIA Twenty-five Year Award for the design of the Ford Foundation building in New York City. Roche graduated from the National University of Ireland in 1945 and studied at the Illinois Institute of Technology with Ludwig Mies van der Rohe. He worked briefly with the United Nations Planning Office in New York before joining Eero Saarinen & Associates in 1950. He became principal design associate to Eero Saarinen in 1954 and worked on many high-profile projects in the office, completing several after the death of Saarinen in 1961, including the TWA Flight Center at John F. Kennedy Airport, the CBS Headquarters building, Dulles International Airport, the John Deere headquarters, and the St. Louis Arch. The firm of Roche & Dinkeloo designed numerous corporate headquarters, office buildings, banks, museums, and arts centers. Roche served as a trustee of the American Academy in

Rome, president of the American Academy of Arts and Letters, and a member of the National Academy of Design.

SUSAN PORTER ROSE (1941–) CFA 1993–97

Susan Porter Rose is a public administrator whose career has centered on service in a series of presidential administrations. She worked briefly as assistant dean at the George School in Newtown, Pennsylvania, before becoming assistant dean of admissions at Mount Holyoke College from 1966 to 1971. She was director of scheduling and correspondence for First Lady Patricia Nixon from 1971 to 1974 and served as chief of staff to Barbara Bush from 1981 to 1993, during the Reagan administration and during Mrs. Bush's position as First Lady. Rose received her undergraduate degree in 1963 from Earlham College in Indiana and a master's degree from Indiana State University in 1970. She was affiliated with the Barbara Bush Foundation for Family Literacy from 1993 to 2000 and was a trustee of the George H.W. Bush Presidential Library during that same period. In 1991, she received a distinguished alumni award from Indiana State University.

THEODORE ROSZAK (1907–81) CFA 1963–69

Theodore Roszak was a sculptor and painter whose work is in the collection of the Whitney Museum, Museum of Modern Art, Hirshhorn Museum, the Art Institute of Chicago, Tate Modern in London, and many others. His early work reflected the influence of the Constructivist movement; his pieces after World War II were considered to be more expressionistic. In the 1920s he studied art at the Art Institute of Chicago and the National Academy of Design and philosophy at Columbia University. He established a studio in New York City in 1932 and worked as an artist for the Works Progress Administration during the Great Depression. He had a long career as an art teacher beginning at the Art Institute of Chicago in the late 1920s, later teaching at Sarah Lawrence College from 1941 to 1956, and at Columbia University from 1970 to 1973. He was affiliated with the Skowhegan School of Painting and Sculpture, the National Institute of Arts and Letters, the American Academy in Rome, and the National Academy of Design and was the recipient of the Art Institute of Chicago Eisendrath Award (1934), the Logan Medal of Arts (1930), and a Tiffany Foundation Fellowship (1931).

WITOLD RYBCZYNSKI (1943–) CFA 2004–2012

Witold Rybczynski, FAIA, is a prominent writer and thinker on topics involving the built environment. He is the author of several books and frequently contributes to publications such as the *New York Times, Atlantic Monthly, Architectural Record, Slate,* and *Preservation.* His books include *The Perfect House: A Journey with the Renaissance Master Andrea Palladio; The Look of Architecture; City Life: Urban Expectations in a New World; Last Harvest: From Cornfield to New Town;* and *Home: A Short History of an Idea.* Rybczynski's book, *A Clearing in the Distance: Frederick Law Olmsted and America in the Nineteenth Century,* won numerous awards, including the J. Anthony Lukas Book Prize and the Christopher Award. He was a senior fellow of the Design Futures Institute in 2003; a member of the Institute of Classical Architecture & Classical America council of advisors and of the Monuments, Memorials and Museums Consultant Group; and an advisor to the Library of American Landscape History. Rybczynski received a bachelor's degree in architecture in 1966 and a master's degree in architecture in 1972, both from McGill University. He worked for a time at Moshe Safdie & Associates in the late 1960s and, from 1970 to 1982, had his own architectural practice. He was a professor at McGill University from 1975 to 1993 before joining the University of Pennsylvania faculty, where he has served as the Martin and Margy Meyerson Professor of Urbanism.

S

ALINE B. SAARINEN (1914–72) CFA 1963–71

Aline Bernstein Saarinen was a prominent journalist, art critic, author, and advocate for modern architecture. Early in her career, she was a contributor and managing editor of *Art News,* and, during the 1950s, she was an associate art editor and associate art critic for the *New York Times.*

In the 1960s, she joined NBC as an art and architecture editor and was the art critic for the Today show; later, she became a correspondent with NBC News and served as bureau chief in Paris from 1971 to 1972. In 1954 she married architect Eero Saarinen and became director of information services for his firm, remaining in that position until 1963, two years after her husband's death. Saarinen wrote numerous articles and two books on art and collectors of art as well as a book on her husband's work. She served on the Federal Aviation Administration's Design Advisory Committee, the New York State Council on the Arts, and the American Revolution Bicentennial Commission. Saarinen graduated in 1935 from Vassar College with an undergraduate degree in English and art and received a master's degree in architectural history from New York University, Institute of Fine Arts in 1939. Saarinen was a Guggenheim Fellow in 1957 and was awarded the Venice Biennale 1951 Best Foreign Criticism Award; she also received numerous honorary degrees.

HIDEO SASAKI (1919–2000) CFA 1962–71

Hideo Sasaki, FASLA, was a prominent landscape architect and educator. His work ranges from corporate projects for Upjohn, John Deere, Bell Labs, and others to major public spaces such as Copley Square in Boston, Constitution Plaza in Hartford, and Greenacre Park in New York City. He designed landscapes for numerous university projects and city parks as well as Walt Disney World in Florida. In 1957 Sasaki and Peter Walker moved their firm from San Francisco to Watertown, Massachusetts; it would later become SWA Group. Sasaki was a professor and chairman of landscape architecture at the Harvard University Graduate School of Design from 1950 to 1968. He was on the Redevelopment Land Authority's Design Advisory Panel in Washington, D.C., and served as a member of the John F. Kennedy Memorial Library Advisory Committee on Arts and Architecture, the U.S. National Arboretum Advisory Council, and others. Sasaki attended the University of California, Los Angeles, and the University of California, Berkeley, before being sent to an internment camp during World War II. He continued his education after the war, earning a bachelor of arts in landscape architecture from the University of Illinois in 1946 and a master's degree in landscape architecture from the Harvard University Graduate School of Design in 1948. He was the first recipient of the American Society of Landscape Architects Medal in 1971 and was awarded the Allied Professions Medal by the American Institute of Architects in 1973.

EUGENE F. SAVAGE (1883–1978) CFA 1933–41

The painter, muralist, and sculptor Eugene Francis Savage produced many prominent works, including murals for the New York State Court of Appeals dome, the Indiana State House, Columbia and Yale Universities, and the Post Office building in Federal Triangle. Savage also sculpted the Bailey Memorial Fountain in the Grand Army Plaza, Brooklyn, New York. Savage studied at the Art Institute of Chicago and was a fellow in visual arts at the American Academy in Rome in 1915. He later earned a bachelor's degree (1924) and master's degree in fine arts (1927) from Yale University, where he also taught during the 1920s. He was a member of the National Academy of Design, the National Institute of Arts and Letters, and an honorary member of the American Institute of Architects; he served as a trustee of the American Academy in Rome. Savage was awarded many honors during his career, including the Prix de Rome in 1912, the Clarke Prize of the National Academy of Design in 1923, and the 1921 Architectural League Medal of Honor.

EDWIN SCHLOSSBERG (1945–) CFA 2011–

Edwin A. Schlossberg is the founder and principal of ESI Design, a firm that designs interactive environments for learning, discovery, and communication. His practice specializes in integrated experiential museums, large-scale cultural facilities, and numerous children's museums and science exhibits as well as the design of collaborative public experiences, knowledge-sharing networks, and communications platforms for a variety of companies and institutions. His recent projects include the Shanghai Corporate Pavilion for the 2010 World Expo and the Ellis Island National Immigration History Museum in New York. Mr.

Schlossberg received his undergraduate degree from Columbia College, Columbia University, in 1967 and in 1971 a doctorate in science and literature from Columbia University. He teaches courses in design at Columbia University and the School of the Visual Arts in New York City. He is the author of more than ten published works, including *Interactive Excellence: Defining and Developing New Standards for the Twenty-First Century,* and is a visual artist whose works have appeared in a number of solo exhibitions and museum collections around the world. He is on several nonprofit boards and is a founding advisor of designNYC, a partnership that matches designers' services with community organizations in need of pro bono design support. Mr. Schlossberg serves as a board member of the John F. Kennedy Foundation and Library.

HENRY R. SHEPLEY (1887–1962) CFA 1936–40; VICE CHAIRMAN 1938–40

Henry Richardson Shepley, FAIA, joined his father's Boston architectural firm, Shepley, Rutan & Coolidge, in 1914; that firm had been established in 1886 as a successor to the office founded by H. H. Richardson, who was Shepley's maternal grandfather. The firm's name has evolved over many decades, becoming Shepley Bulfinch Richardson & Abbott in 1952, and is now known as Shepley Bulfinch. Many of Shepley's projects were medical or academic buildings, including New York Hospital-Cornell Medical Center and Massachusetts General Hospital as well as buildings at Wellesley, Smith, and Vassar Colleges and Northeastern and Dartmouth Universities. His portfolio also included buildings at Harvard University, among them the Fogg Art Museum. Shepley received an undergraduate degree from Harvard University in 1910 and a diploma from the École des Beaux-Arts in 1914. He was active in design and professional organizations, including the Boston Society of Architects, the Boston Architectural Center, the National Institute of Arts and Letters, the Academy of Arts and Letters, the Society of Beaux-Arts Architects, and the National Academy of Design. Shepley served as a trustee of the American Academy in Rome and on advisory commissions for the Departments of Treasury, State, and War, for the Architect of the Capitol, and for the Federal Projects Division of the Public Works Administration. He was the recipient of the New York Architectural League Medal (1933), the French Legion of Honor (1953), and the American Academy of Arts and Letters Gold Medal (1958).

LT. COL. CLARENCE O. SHERRILL (1876–1959) EX OFFICIO CFA SECRETARY 1921–22

Clarence Osborne Sherrill graduated from the U.S. Military Academy at West Point with a degree in civil engineering in 1901. He taught at several service schools between 1907 and 1910 and wrote a textbook on topography for the army. During World War I, he served in France and was awarded the Distinguished Service Medal and Croix de Guerre with Palm. In 1921 Sherrill was named director of the Office of Public Buildings and Grounds, a position he held until 1925. During this time he oversaw the completion of the Lincoln Memorial and the construction of the Grant Memorial, the Meade Memorial, and the Rock Creek and Potomac Parkway. He was chief military aide to Presidents Warren G. Harding and Calvin Coolidge, and was the last Corps of Engineers officer to serve as secretary to the U.S. Commission of Fine Arts, which became an administratively independent agency in 1922. After retiring from the army in 1926, Sherrill served two terms as city manager of Cincinnati, Ohio (1926–30 and 1937–44).

CHLOETHIEL WOODARD SMITH (1910–93) CFA 1967–76

Architect Chloethiel Woodard Smith, FAIA, was an influential mid-century modernist based in Washington, D.C. She developed a plan in 1952 for the redevelopment of Washington's Southwest quadrant with Louis Justement. She completed several projects in the redevelopment, including Capitol Park, Harbour Square, and Waterside Mall, and developed a proposal for a bridge with shops and restaurants spanning Washington Channel inspired by the Ponte Vecchio in Florence, Italy. She also designed the Waterview townhouses in the planned community of Reston, Virginia. Her office projects in the District included the Blake Building and 1100 Connecticut Avenue; overseas, she designed the U.S. Embassy in Paraguay and developed a master plan for Quito, Ecuador. Early in her career, Smith worked for the Federal Housing Authority and in the 1940s for Berla & Abel. She formed Keyes, Smith & Satterlee in 1950, and from 1963 to 1983 she practiced in her own firm, Chloethiel Woodard Smith & Associates. Smith was a founding trustee of the National Building Museum and served on numerous boards and commissions, including the Kennedy Center, President's Council on Pennsylvania Avenue, National Commission on Urban Problems, and Committee of 100 for the Federal City. Smith earned her undergraduate degree in architecture from the University of Oregon in 1932 and a master's degree in architecture from Washington University in St. Louis in 1933. She was a professor of architecture at the University de San Andres in La Paz, Bolivia, from 1942 to 1944. She was named a Guggenheim Fellow in 1944 and was awarded the Centennial Award of the D.C. chapter of the American Institute of Architects in 1987.

RALPH STACKPOLE (1885–1973) CFA 1941–45

Sculptor, muralist, and painter Ralph Stackpole was the first West Coast-based appointee to the Commission of Fine Arts. Influenced by the artistic movements of art moderne and, later, social realism, Stackpole lived in San Francisco and completed many works in the area including sculptures for the 1915 Panama-Pacific Exposition, monumental sculpture for the San Francisco Stock Exchange, and *Pacifica* for the Golden Gate Pacific Exposition in 1939. During the Great Depression, Stackpole painted murals for Coit Tower as part of the Federal Art Project of the Works Progress Administration. For nearly two decades, beginning in the mid-1920s, he was an instructor at the California School of Fine Arts. Stackpole received his early art training in San Francisco, followed by studies at the École des Beaux-Arts from 1906 to 1908; while in Paris, he met and became friends with the muralist Diego Rivera. In 1911, he completed a year of training at the Robert Henri School of Art in New York and established his studio in San Francisco where he became recognized as a leading artist. Stackpole moved to France in 1949 where he lived until his death in 1973.

MAURICE STERNE (1878–1957) CFA 1945–50

The Latvian-born painter Maurice Sterne was a modernist who rose to prominence in the early twentieth century in New York. In addition to his murals in the library of the Department of Justice in Washington, D.C., his works are in the collections of the Metropolitan Museum, the Carnegie Institute, the Art Institute of Chicago, the Corcoran Gallery of Art, and the Phillips Collection. In the late 1890s, Sterne studied under Alfred Maurer and Thomas Eakins at the National Academy of Design and then traveled widely in Europe and the Far East. Many of his works are based on his travels and his bohemian life in the early decades of the twentieth century, which included a brief marriage to the American philanthropist Mabel Dodge (Luhan). His reputation was established by a show at the Scott and Fowles Gallery in 1926 and furthered by a retrospective at the Museum of Modern Art in 1933. In the mid-1930s, Sterne lived in San Francisco and taught at the California School of Fine Arts. He returned to the East Coast in 1945 and established a studio in Mt. Kisco, New York, where he worked until his death in 1957. He was named to the American Academy of Arts and Letters in 1938.

EDWARD D. STONE JR. (1932–2009) CFA 1971–85

Edward Durell Stone Jr., FASLA, opened his landscape architecture practice, Edward D. Stone Jr. & Associates (EDSA) in Fort Lauderdale, Florida, in 1960. He had worked in the New York office of his father, the architect Edward Durell Stone, and with the landscape architect Frederic Stresau in Fort Lauderdale. A modernist, Stone completed many projects, including Lady Bird Johnson Park and the Kennedy Center, with Hideo Sasaki, in Washington, D.C.; Riverwalk in Fort Lauderdale; and PepsiCo Headquarters in Purchase, New York. He also worked on several projects for the Walt Disney Company, including Euro Disney and the western portion of Disney World. Stone received an undergraduate degree in architecture from Yale University in 1954 and a master's degree in landscape architecture from the Harvard University Graduate School of Design in 1959. He was a visiting professor at the Universities of Georgia, Miami, and Florida and at Texas A&M. Stone served as a consultant to the Committee for a More Beautiful Capital and the Governor's Conference on Environmental Quality in Florida. He was awarded the 1994 Medal of the American Society of Landscape Architects.

EGERTON SWARTWOUT (1870–1943) CFA 1931–36; VICE CHAIRMAN 1933–36

The architect Egerton Swartwout, FAIA, earned his undergraduate degree from Yale University in 1891 and soon after joined McKim, Mead & White as a draftsman. He and Evarts Tracy, also at the firm, opened their own practice, Tracy & Swartwout, in New York in 1900. The firm operated under various names until Tracy's death in 1922; Swartwout then practiced on his own until 1941. His buildings were in the neoclassical style and include the National Baptist Memorial Church in Washington, D.C., the Yale University art gallery, the Elks National Memorial in Chicago, and the U.S. Post Office and Courthouse in Denver. With sculptor Eugene Savage he designed the Bailey Memorial Fountain of the Grand Army Plaza in Brooklyn, New York. Swartwout wrote several books, including *The Classical Orders in Architecture* and *The Use of the Order in Modern Architecture*. He served as president of the New York chapter of the American Institute of Architects and was a director of the Fine Arts Federation of New York. He was a member of the American Academy of Arts and Letters, the National Academy of Design, and the Societe Nationale des Beaux-Arts, Paris. Swartwout was awarded the Gold Medal by the American Institute of Architects in 1920.

T

LORADO TAFT (1860–1936) CFA 1925–29

The sculptor Lorado Taft is known for his well-crafted civic works, often in commemorative settings. He received his initial training at the University of Illinois at Urbana and studied at the École des Beaux-Arts from 1880 to 1883. Upon his return to the United States, he established his studio in Chicago, where he worked for more than fifty years. Taft designed the Columbus Fountain at Union Station in Washington, D.C., and works for the World's Columbian Exposition in 1893, both in collaboration with Daniel Burnham, as well as the Fountain of Time for Chicago's Midway Plaisance. Taft combined his artistic pursuits with an active teaching career, serving as a lecturer and instructor at the Art Institute of Chicago from 1886 to 1929, lecturer at the University of Chicago from 1893 to 1900, and as a professor of art at the University of Illinois from 1919 onward, and he was a popular lecturer on sculpture across the country. He wrote the seminal work on nineteenth-century American sculpture, *The History of American Sculpture,* and the later work *Modern Tendencies in Sculpture.* He was a member of the National Academy, the National Institute of Arts and Letters, and the American Academy of Arts and Letters; headed the National Sculpture Society in the 1920s; and served on the Board of Art Advisors of Illinois. He was the recipient of numerous awards and prizes and honorary degrees and was an honorary member of the American Institute of Architects. Taft's papers reside in collections at the Smithsonian Archives of American Art, the University of Illinois, and the Art Institute of Chicago.

V

FERRUCCIO VITALE (1875–1933) CFA 1927–32

The landscape architect Ferruccio Vitale, FASLA, is best known for developing the planting plan for Meridian Hill Park in Washington, D.C. He completed town plans for Scarsdale and Pleasantville in New York and the designs for gardens at many private estates. He began his career as a military engineer, training at the Royal Military Academy in his native Italy, and he served as the Italian military attaché in Washington, D.C., in the late 1890s. He then turned to landscape architecture, which he studied in Italy and Paris from 1900 to 1904, and worked at his father's architectural firm in Florence during this period. In 1904 Vitale moved to New York and worked briefly at Parsons & Pentacost before estab-

lishing his own firm, Pentacost & Vitale, in 1905. He would operate a firm under his own name or with partners for the next ten years, including Vitale, Brinkerhoff & Geiffert in 1917; the firm became Vitale & Geiffert in 1924 and continued under that name until Vitale's death in 1933. He was active in many professional organizations, including serving as president of the New York chapter of the American Society of Landscape Architects and a member of the Foundation for Architecture and Landscape Architecture. He was a member of the Architectural Commission for Chicago's Century of Progress Exposition and was a trustee of the American Academy in Rome and founder of its Department of Landscape Architecture. He was awarded the 1920 Gold Medal of the Architectural League of New York and awarded the Order of the Crown of Italy; he was an honorary member of the American Institute of Architects.

W

JOHN WALKER (1906–95) CFA 1967–71

John Walker was an art curator whose work as the second director of the National Gallery of Art in Washington developed the collections and stature of the museum. He received an undergraduate degree in art history from Harvard University and studied at Villa I Tatti in Florence with Bernard Berenson. He served as a professor and assistant director of the American Academy in Rome from 1935 to 1939. Walker became chief curator of the National Gallery of Art in 1939 and was involved in identifying works of art looted by the Nazis following World War II. In 1956 he was named director of the National Gallery, succeeding David Finley, and remained in the position until his retirement in 1969. During his tenure at the National Gallery, Walker cultivated donor relationships with collectors such as the Mellon family, Joseph Widener, Armand Hammer, and Chester Dale; his significant acquisitions included Rembrandt's *Aristotle with the Bust of Homer,* Fragonard's *La Liseuse,* El Greco's *Laocoon,* and the *Ginevra de' Benci* by Leonardo da Vinci. He wrote six books, including *Bellini and Titian at Ferrara* and his autobiography, *Self-Portrait with Donors.*

RALPH WALKER (1889–1973) CFA 1959–63

Ralph Thomas Walker, FAIA and RIBA (Hon.), was a prominent New York architect called "The Architect of the Century" by the *New York Times* in 1957 upon his receiving the inaugural Centennial Gold Medal of the American Institute of Architects, where he served for two years as president. Although he was the designer of many buildings ranging from commercial art deco to modern in style, Walker is relatively unknown today. Trained initially as an apprentice, he received his undergraduate degree in architecture from the Massachusetts Institute of Technology in 1911 and worked at several firms, including Warren & Wetmore and York & Sawyer, in New York City. He was awarded a Rotch Traveling Scholarship in 1916 and served in World War I. Walker joined McKenzie, Voorhees & Gmelin in 1916, becoming a partner in 1926; he remained with the firm until his retirement. Walker's projects include the AFL-CIO building and Belgian Chancery in Washington, D.C; the Prudential Building and Bell Telephone Lab building in New Jersey; the Brooklyn Edison, Irving Trust Co., and Western Union Telegraph Buildings in New York City; and the IBM Research Center in Poughkeepsie, New York. He was involved in the planning of the 1933 Century of Progress Exposition in Chicago and in the 1939 New York World's Fair. He was associated with the Architectural League, the Beaux-Arts Institute of Design, and the Municipal Art Society of New York and was the author of several books on architecture. Walker was a Chevalier of the French Legion of Honor and a member of the American Academy of Arts and Letters. He was awarded the 1927 Gold Medal of the Architectural League of New York.

WILLIAM WALTON (1909–1994) CFA 1963–71; CHAIRMAN 1963–71

William Walton began his career as a journalist working for the Associated Press in the 1930s and was a combat correspondent during World War II. After the war he worked for Time-Life and was the Washington editor for *New Republic* magazine. In 1949 he turned to painting, opening a studio first in Washington, D.C., and later in New York City in 1975; he continued to paint in New York until the end of his life. Walton was the New York campaign coordinator for John F. Kennedy's presidential campaign in 1960 and remained a close friend of the Kennedys; he was an informal advisor on architecture to both President Kennedy and President Johnson and to Mrs. Kennedy on the selection of art for the White House and historic preservation at Lafayette Square. Walton also served on the art advisory panel for the Federal Aviation Administration. He was the author of two books, one on the history of Washington and the other on the Civil War. He was a 1931 graduate of the University of Wisconsin with a bachelor's degree in journalism.

JOHN CARL WARNECKE (1919–2010) CFA 1963–67

In Washington, D.C., John Carl Warnecke, FAIA, is best known for his work at Lafayette Square. Warnecke, who was a friend and informal architecture advisor to the Kennedys, designed the redevelopment of Lafayette Square and President Kennedy's gravesite. His other projects include the Hart Senate Office Building, Lauinger Library at Georgetown University, the Hawaii State Capitol and Civic Center, and the South Terminal at Boston's Logan Airport. Warnecke's practice was based in San Francisco; he opened his first firm in the early 1940s and John Carl Warnecke & Associates in 1958. After graduating from Stanford University with an undergraduate degree in 1941, he enrolled in the Harvard University Graduate School of Design, studying under Walter Gropius and completing his master's degree in architecture in one year. Warnecke was affiliated with the National Academy of Design and was the recipient of many awards, including a National Institute of Arts and Letters prize in 1957 and the Brunner Memorial Prize in 1958.

ADOLPH WEINMAN (1870–1952) CFA 1929–33

Adolph Alexander Weinman executed numerous architectural sculptures and was known for his association with Beaux-Arts projects—many by McKim, Mead & White. In Washington, D.C., his works include the sphinxes for the Scottish Rite Temple, figures for the Post Office building and the Straus Fountain, and the pediments for the National Archives and the Thomas Jefferson Memorial. The range of Weinman's work also includes the eagles for New York's Pennsylvania Station; a statue for the American World War I Military Cemetery in Montfaucon, France; and the design of the 1916 dime and half-dollar. A neoclassicist, Weinman trained at the Cooper Union in New York and in the studios of both Augustus Saint-Gaudens and Daniel Chester French and opened his own studio in Forest Hills, New York, in 1904. He served as president of the National Sculpture Society and was a member of the National Institute of Arts and Letters and the National Academy. Among his many honors was the Saltus Award from the American Numismatic Society in 1920. Weinman's papers are in the Smithsonian Archives of American Art.

J. ALDEN WEIR (1852–1919) CFA 1916–19

Julian Alden Weir was a landscape painter who helped found the American Impressionism movement. Weir studied at the National Academy of Design and then spent four years, from 1873 to 1877, at the École des Beaux-Arts in Paris and in the studio of Jean-Léon Gérôme; during this time, his work was shown at the Paris Salon. Returning to New York, he taught at the Art Students League and became friends with painters William Merritt Chase and Winslow Homer. In the 1880s and 1890s, Weir—influenced by the French Impressionists, Japanese art, and the observation of nature—turned to landscape painting and helped form a group of like-minded painters, "The Ten," which included Childe Hassam and John Twachtman. His farm in Branchville, Connecticut, now a National Historic Site, became a favored retreat for Weir, his family, and his circle of friends, including painters John Singer Sargent and Albert Pinkham Ryder. Weir was president of the National Acad-

emy of Design, served on the board of the Metropolitan Museum of Art, and was a member of the American Academy of Arts and Letters. He received numerous honors and awards, including honorary degrees from Princeton and Yale Universities. His papers are in the Smithsonian Archives of American Art.

GEORGE A. WEYMOUTH (1936–) CFA 1972–77

George Alexis Weymouth is a painter of portraits and landscapes and is also noted for helping found the Brandywine Conservancy, an organization dedicated to land conservation and cultural preservation in the Brandywine Valley of Pennsylvania; he serves as its board chairman. Weymouth, a member of the du Pont family, was a close friend of Andrew Wyeth and also helped found the Brandywine Museum, which is dedicated to American art; the collection includes a number of paintings by members of the Wyeth family. Weymouth served on the Visual Arts Panel of the Pennsylvania Council of the Arts and is the recipient of many awards, including the Cliveden Heritage Preservation Award and the University of Delaware Merit Award for Community Service. He received his undergraduate degree in American studies from Yale University in 1958.

LINTON R. WILSON (1903–66) CFA SECRETARY 1954–64

Linton Rayburn Wilson received both an undergraduate degree (1925) and a master's degree in fine arts (1928) from Princeton University. He was employed by the architecture firm Voorhees, Walker, Foley & Smith in New York (1928–40) where he worked on projects in Scandinavia and on the 1939 World's Fair. He designed the Swedish classroom in the National Rooms of the University of Pittsburgh's Cathedral of Learning, dedicated in 1938. He joined the navy in 1941 and remained in the service until 1954. On the recommendation of future CFA member Ralph Walker, Wilson was hired as secretary of the commission; he remained in the position until his retirement in 1964.

EZRA WINTER (1886–1949) CFA 1928–33

Ezra Augustus Winter was a prominent muralist of the first half of the twentieth century. Among his best known works are *The Canterbury Tales* in the Library of Congress and *Fountain of Youth* in the foyer of Radio City Music Hall. He also completed murals for the U.S. Supreme Court, the U.S. Chamber of Commerce, the University of Rochester and Eastman School of Music, and a six-story work for the Guardian Building in Detroit. During World War I, Winter was a camouflage designer for the U.S. Shipping Board. He later taught at the Grand Central School of Art and kept a studio in Falls Village, Connecticut. He studied art at the Chicago Academy of Fine Arts and was a fellow in visual arts at the American Academy in Rome in 1914. Winter was affiliated with the National Society of Mural Painters and the Architectural League of New York, served on the Connecticut State Commission of Sculpture, and was a member of the National Institute of Arts and Letters. His papers are in the Smithsonian Archives of American Art.

DIANE WOLF (1954–2008) CFA 1985–90

Diane Wolf was an arts patron who served on the boards of the National Archives, the Kennedy Center for the Performing Arts, and National Public Radio and was a supporter of the Library of Congress, the Smithsonian Institution, the Washington National Opera, and the National Symphony Orchestra. She also served on the Metropolitan Museum of Art Junior Committee and the Whitney Museum Friends Council and was a supporter of the Frick Museum, all in New York City. Through her work on the Commission of Fine Arts, she became an outspoken advocate for the redesign of American coinage. Wolf received her undergraduate degree from the University of Pennsylvania in 1976 and a master's degree in early childhood education from Columbia University in 1980. She earned a law degree from Georgetown University Law Center in 1995.

ELYN ZIMMERMAN (1945–) CFA 2003–08

The artist Elyn Zimmerman works in a variety of media: Her photographs, sculptures, and paintings are in a number of private, public, and corporate collections, including the Whitney Museum, the Los Angeles Museum of Art, the Museum of Modern Art, and Chase Manhattan Bank. Among her best-known, large-scale outdoor sculptures are pieces at the National Geographic Society headquarters in Washington, D.C., and the Institute for Advanced Studies in Princeton, New Jersey. She also created a stone fountain for the World Trade Center in 1995 to commemorate the 1993 bombing of the buildings; the piece was destroyed in the attack of September 11, 2001. Zimmerman has been active in leadership roles within the arts community, including serving as a commissioner of the Massachusetts Museum of Contemporary Art and a member of the board of directors of the Los Angeles Institute of Contemporary Art, Creative Time, Inc., and the International Sculpture Center. She has received many awards and honors, including National Endowment for the Arts fellowships, recognition from the Maryland chapter of the American Society of Landscape Architects, and a residency at the American Academy in Rome. Zimmerman earned a bachelor's degree in psychology from the University of California, Los Angeles, in 1968 as well as a master's degree in painting and photography in 1972.

OLD GEORGETOWN BOARD, 1950–2012

In chronological order of service.

William Dewey Foster, 1950–53
Lorenzo S. Winslow, 1950–55
Walter M. Macomber, 1950–55, 1956–58, 1960–62
Walter G. Peter Jr., 1953–58
Louis A. Simon, 1955–57
Gertrude Sawyer, 1955–56; 1962–63
Henry H. Saylor, 1957–58; 1960–65
John B. Coughlin, 1958
Gerald A. Purcell, 1960–64
William Max Haussman, 1963–69
Frank W. Cole, 1964–69
Mario Campioli, 1965–71
Thomas J. Stohlman, 1969–75
Wynant D. Vanderpool Jr., 1969–79
Warren J. Cox, 1971–75
David R. Rosenthal, 1975
Anne Vytlacil, 1975–79, 1989–96
David N. Condon, 1978–79
Thomas W. D. Wright, 1975–82
Theodore A. Sande, 1979–81
David N. Yerkes, 1979–82
Hugh C. Miller, 1981–89
John R. Andrews, 1982–91
Peter Vercelli, 1982–89
Elliott Carroll, 1989–98
Stephen A. Muse, 1991–2000, 2012–
Mary Oehrlein, 1996–2008
John E. McCartney, 1998–2007
Heather Cass, 2000–06
Stephen J. Vanze, 2006–12
David Cox, 2007–
Anne McCutcheon Lewis 2008–

JOHN R. ANDREWS (1929–95) OGB 1982–91

John Richard Andrews, AIA, earned a bachelor's degree in science in architecture from the University of Virginia before serving in the U.S. Marine Corps from 1954 to 1956. He established an architectural practice in Washington, D.C., in 1960, which he ran until his retirement in 1980; his projects included residences, office buildings, schools, and health care facilities. He consulted with Arthur Cotton Moore on the Inland Steel redevelopment project, Georgetown Harbour, on the Potomac waterfront in the 1970s.

MARIO CAMPIOLI (1910–81) OGB 1965–71

Born in Italy, Mario Ettore Campioli, FAIA, earned a bachelor's degree in architecture at New York University and joined the New York design firm Eggers & Higgins in 1940. He eventually served as the director of architecture at Colonial Williamsburg from 1949 to 1957, when he joined the Washington, D.C., architectural firm of DeWitt, Poor & Shelton, where he directed the West Front extension of the Capitol. In 1959, he became assistant Architect of the Capitol and director of architecture, a position he held until 1980, and served as architect in charge of the restoration of the original Senate and Supreme Court chambers.

ELLIOTT CARROLL (1923–2004) OGB 1989–98

Marshall Elliott Carroll, FAIA, earned bachelor's and master's degrees of architecture from Harvard University. He served as a submarine officer in the U.S. Navy during World War II and the Korean War, and continued to serve as an officer in the U.S. Naval Reserve until 1973. He practiced architecture in North Carolina before moving to Washington, D.C., in 1960 to join the executive staff of the American Institute of Architects, where he served as deputy executive vice president. He was a partner in the architectural practice of Vincent G. Kling & Partners of Philadelphia and served as executive assistant to the Architect of the Capitol from 1973 to 1988, where he was responsible for several major preservation projects, including the master plan for the Capitol from 1976 to 1981.

HEATHER CASS (1947–) OGB 2000–06

Heather Willson Cass, FAIA, earned a bachelor of arts degree from Mount Holyoke College and a master of architecture degree from Yale University; she joined the Washington, D.C. architecture firm of Keyes, Lethbridge & Condon in 1972 before establishing her own practice in 1976 with Patrick Pinnell and her solo practice after 1988. She won a Henry Luce Foundation Scholarship in 1974 in Tokyo, Japan, where she worked in the office of Fumihiko Maki. She was assistant professor of architecture at the University of Maryland and has been a visiting professor in architecture at the University of California, Berkeley, Ohio State University, and the University of Miami.

FRANK W. COLE (1901–83) OGB 1964–69

Frank William Cole, AIA, earned a bachelor's degree from Princeton University and a master's degree in architecture from the Massachusetts Institute of Technology. He established his own firm in the 1930s and worked for the War Production Board and the Reconstruction Finance Corporation during World War II. He became a partner with Horace W. Peaslee, FAIA, from 1948 to1959, when he formed Frank W. Cole Consulting Architect. His work focused on additions and renovations of historic buildings, including St. John's Episcopal Church in Georgetown and the Cosmos Club, and on small public projects. He also served on the committee that reviewed the 1952 Justement-Smith proposal for redevelopment of Southwest Washington, D.C.

DAVID H. CONDON (1916–96) OGB 1978–79

David Holt Condon, FAIA, earned a bachelor's degree in architecture from the University of California, Berkeley, before serving as an officer in the U.S. Navy during World War II. After the war, he worked in Washington as an associate of Charles Goodman Associates, where he collaborated on the design of the Hollin Hills development in Fairfax County, Virginia. In 1952 he joined the firm of Keyes, Smith, Satterlee & Lethbridge and was a partner of that firm in 1957 and its successor firm, Keyes, Condon & Florance, until 1992. Condon's work includes the Tiber Island and Carrollsburg Square developments in Southwest Washington, D.C.; renovations of the Cosmos Club and National Gallery of Art; and buildings at American University and the Catholic University of America. He was the recipient of the 1992 Centennial Award given by the Washington, D.C., chapter of the American Institute of Architects.

JOHN B. COUGHLIN (1914–96) OGB 1958

John Bernard Coughlin, AIA, earned degrees from the University of New Hampshire and the Catholic University of America prior to his work with the New York architecture firm Allen, Collens & Willis and the office of Francis C. Almirall in the late 1930s. He became a partner with Almirall in 1940, forming an architectural practice in Washington, D.C., and Cleveland; the firm's work included residential, service institutional, and office projects. He served in the U.S. Army Corps of Engineers during World War II.

DAVID COX (1942–) OGB 2007–

David Cox, FAIA, earned a bachelor's degree in architecture from the University of Illinois and a master's degree in architecture from the University of Pennsylvania, where he was a student of Louis Kahn. He served as a captain in the U.S. Army Medical Service Corps from 1968 to 1971 and worked with Arthur Cotton Moore in Washington, D.C., before founding the firm Kress Cox Associates in 1981; the firm became Cox, Graae & Spack Architects in 1999. His firm's work in Washington, D.C., includes buildings at Georgetown Visitation Preparatory and St. Anselm's Abby Schools, an addition to the Phillips Collection, the renovation and preservation of the DAR Hall, and the renovation and expansion of Wilson High School. He has been a visiting design critic at the University of Maryland and the Catholic University of America and was the recipient of the 2009 Centennial Award given by the Washington, D.C., chapter of the American Institute of Architects.

WARREN J. COX (1935–) OGB 1971–75

Warren Jacob Cox, FAIA, earned a bachelor's degree and a master's of architecture from Yale University and worked as the technology editor for *Architectural Forum* from 1961 to 1962. He worked as a designer for the Washington, D.C., architecture firm Keyes, Lethbridge & Condon from 1962 to 1965 before establishing Hartman-Cox Architects in 1965 with George Hartman. The firm's practice areas include office and institutional buildings in urban or historic settings such as the Euram Building, Market Square, the Georgetown University Law Library, and the Folger Shakespeare Library in Washington, D.C., as well as many university libraries and professional school buildings nationally. The firm has been honored with numerous design awards, was named Firm of the Year by the American Institute of Architects in 1988, and was honored with the American Institute of Classical Architecture firm award in 2006. Cox was the recipient of the 2006 Centennial Award given by the Washington, D.C., chapter of the American Institute of Architects.

WILLIAM DEWEY FOSTER (1890–1958) OGB 1950–54

William Dewey Foster, AIA, earned bachelor's and master's of science degrees at the Massachusetts Institute of Technology and was a draftsman in several New York architectural firms before his service in World War I with the U.S. Army 40th Engineers. He established his own firm, Foster & Vassar, in New York in 1922, and he served as consulting architect to the Office of the Supervising Architect from 1934 to 1942. In partnership with Gilbert Stanley Underwood, he was the consulting design architect to the Office of the Supervising Architect for the War Department building, completed in 1940, as well as the West Heating Plant in Georgetown, completed in 1948. He formed the architectural firm of Howe, Foster & Snyder in 1947. In his later career, he completed numerous residential projects in the Colonial Revival style and worked ex-

tensively in Georgetown; Foster participated in the restoration of Octagon House and was a founder of the Committee to Preserve the Capitol.

WILLIAM M. HAUSSMAN (1906–89) OGB 1963–69

William Max Haussman, AIA, earned a bachelor of architecture at the University of Pennsylvania and joined the National Capital Office of Design and Construction of the National Park Service in 1931, where he remained for thirty years, including service as chief architect. In that role, he directed the restoration of the Old Stone House and Great Falls Tavern. He became an associate with the Washington, D.C., firm of Macomber & Peter in 1963 and formed his own practice in 1965.

ANNE LEWIS (1943–) OGB 2008–

Anne McCutcheon Lewis, FAIA, earned a bachelor's degree and master's degree in architecture at Harvard University and studied with Reyner Banham at the University of London. She worked in the Washington, D.C., architecture offices of Skidmore, Owings & Merrill and Keyes, Lethbridge & Condon before establishing her own practice in 1976. She worked in partnership with Jack McCartney from 1981 to 1998 in a practice focused on residential architecture. She served as a professional architect member of the District of Columbia Historic Preservation Review Board from 2003 to 2008; she served on the boards of Friends Nonprofit Housing Inc., the Washington Humane Society, and the Jackson Art Center, and is the founder of City Wildlife, Inc.

WALTER M. MACOMBER (1895–1987) OGB 1950–55, 1956–58, 1960–62

Walter Mayo Macomber apprenticed at the Boston Architectural Club and with his father, who was an architect, cabinetmaker, and builder. He served in the French ambulance corps during World War I prior to joining the Boston architecture firm Perry, Shaw & Hepburn. In 1928 he became the resident architect at Colonial Williamsburg, supervising its restoration and reconstruction until 1934; he then became the resident architect at Mount Vernon for thirty years. He formed an architectural practice in Washington, D.C., in 1958 with Walter Peter Jr. and, after 1964, practiced in his own firm. He designed numerous restoration projects for historic properties, including Stratford Hall, President Monroe's law library, and the Fairfax County Court House; he completed the installation of the historicist diplomatic reception rooms at the Department of State in 1985 at age ninety.

JACK McCARTNEY (1938–) OGB 1998–2007

John Edward (Jack) McCartney, FAIA, earned a bachelor's degree in architecture from the Catholic University of America and served in the U.S. Army Medical Corps from 1960 to 1962. He worked in the architectural firms of Neer & Graef Architects in Alexandria, Virginia, and Keyes, Lethbridge & Condon in Washington, D.C., becoming a partner at Keyes, Condon & Florance in 1975. He established his own firm in 1977 and worked in partnership with Anne Lewis from 1981 to 1998, when he reestablished his solo practice with a focus on residential architecture. He has been a studio instructor at the Catholic University of America and the University of Maryland.

HUGH C. MILLER (1929–) OGB 1981–89

Hugh Clark Miller, FAIA, earned a master's degree in architecture from the University of Pennsylvania Graduate School of Fine Arts and served in the U.S. Army Corps of Engineers in France and Germany before joining the National Park Service as an architect in 1960. Specializing in the restoration of historic properties in the United States and the Middle East, he became a senior staff historical architect of the National Park Service in 1971 and was named the agency's chief historical architect in 1979. In 1989 he became director of the Virginia State Department of Historic Resources; he also served on the executive committee of the U.S. Committee of the International Council on Monuments and Sites.

STEPHEN A. MUSE (1950–) OGB 1991–2000, 2012–

Stephen A. Muse, FAIA, earned a bachelor's degree in architecture from the University of Maryland and a master's degree in architecture from

Cornell University. He practiced in the office of Hartman-Cox Architects in Washington, D.C., and established his firm, Muse Architects, in 1983, working in partnership with Gregory Wiedemann from 1985 to 1994. Muse has been an architecture faculty member at the University of Maryland, Cornell University, and Harvard University. He has been a member of the board of directors of the Washington, D.C., chapter of the American Institute of Architects and the Washington Architectural Foundation.

MARY OEHRLEIN (1950–) OGB 1996–2008
Mary L. Oehrlein, FAIA, earned a bachelor's degree in architecture from Iowa State University and joined the Historic American Buildings Survey as a staff architect in 1972. She worked as an architectural conservator for Universal Restoration, Inc., before becoming vice president of Building Conservation Technology, a subsidiary of The Ehrenkrantz Group in 1975. She worked as director and senior associate of The Ehrenkrantz Group's Washington, D.C., office from 1978 to 1983 and formed her own practice, Oehrlein & Associates Architects, in 1984. Her practice focused on historic preservation and technical restoration services for historic buildings and structures, including the Tomb of the Unknowns, the Washington Monument, Mount Vernon, and the Pentagon following its damage in September 2011. She joined the staff of the Architect of the Capitol in 2011 as its historic preservation officer. Oehrlein is a founder of the Washington Architectural Forum and a co-founder of the Washington, D.C., chapter of the Association for Preservation Technology. She was the president of the Washington, D.C., chapter of the American Institute of Architects and has served as a board member of the Virginia State Review Board for Historic Landmarks, the D.C. Preservation League, and the Washington Architectural Foundation.

WALTER G. PETER JR. (1908–1971) OGB 1954–58
Walter Gibson Peter Jr., FAIA, earned a bachelor's degree in architecture from George Washington University and served in the U.S. Navy during World War II. He worked as an architect for the National Park Service and formed his own practice in 1953. He worked in partnership with Walter Macomber from 1958 to 1964 and returned to solo practice until 1971. He was involved in the restoration of numerous historic buildings in Washington, D.C., including the City Tavern, Ford's Theater, the Octagon House, and Decatur House. He also served as chairman of the Georgetown Planning Council and was a committee member of the National Trust for Historic Preservation.

GERALD A. PURCELL (1901–85) OGB 1960–64
Gerald A. Purcell, AIA, was a registered architect and worked as an architect-engineer and liaison officer for the District of Columbia Department of Buildings and Grounds. He was designated by the D.C. government to serve on the Old Georgetown Board following the resolution of the legal jurisdiction of the Commission of Fine Arts in the Georgetown historic district.

DAVID R. ROSENTHAL (1927–2006) OGB 1975
David Richard Rosenthal, AIA, earned an undergraduate degree in architecture from the Catholic University of America and became a registered architect practicing in Virginia, where he also served on the City of Alexandria Planning Commission and Board of Zoning Appeals in the mid-1970s. He was a partner in the Architects Group Practice in Alexandria from 1972 to 1975, when he established his own firm, David R. Rosenthal Associates. His work includes numerous restoration projects in Alexandria and Fauquier County, Virginia, where he moved in 1984.

THEODORE A. SANDE (1933–) OGB 1979–81
Theodore Anton Sande, PhD, AIA, earned a bachelor of science dregree in architecture at the Rhode Island School of Design, a master of architecture degree at Yale University, and a doctoral degree from the University of Pennsylvania. After military service in the U.S. Navy from 1956 to 1960, he worked in the Rhode Island architectural firm Turoff Associates, where he became a partner in 1968. He established his own

consulting practice in architecture in 1970 and joined the staff of the National Trust for Historic Preservation in 1975, where he served in various positions, including director of professional services, director of planning and development, and vice president. In 1981 he became the executive director of the Western Reserve Historical Society in Cleveland, Ohio. The author of several books and articles on historic preservation and industrial archeology, he was the founder and first president of the Society for Industrial Archaeology.

GERTRUDE SAWYER (1895–1996) OGB 1955–56, 1962–63
Gertrude Elizabeth Sawyer, AIA, earned a bachelor's degree in landscape architecture at the University of Illinois and a master of architecture degree in 1919 from the Cambridge School of Architecture and Landscape Design for Women. She worked in Washington, D.C., as a designer in the office of Horace Peaslee from the 1920s to the early 1930s before establishing her own architectural practice in Georgetown, where she remained active until her retirement in 1969. Her architectural work was focused on historic restoration and residences for socially prominent clients, often in Colonial, Federal, and Renaissance Revival styles. Her most prominent work is the twenty-six-building Point Farm complex in Calvert County, Maryland, which includes a Colonial Revival main house and outbuildings, now a park and museum operated by the State of Maryland.

HENRY H. SAYLOR (1880–1967) OGB 1957–58; 1960–65
Henry Hodgman Saylor, FAIA, studied architecture at the Massachusetts Institute of Technology and worked as a draftsman in the Philadelphia architecture firms of Cope & Stewardson and Edgar V. Seeler before becoming editor of *Architectural Review* in 1904. In his long career with architectural publications, he was editor of *Country Life in America, House & Garden,* and the *Journal of the American Institute of Architects;* he also wrote numerous books on architecture for the general public. He was the author of publications for the American Institute of Architects (AIA), including the *Dictionary of Architecture* (1952) and *The AIA's First Hundred Years* (1957); he was the 1954 recipient of the AIA's Edward C. Kemper Award for distinguished service.

LOUIS A. SIMON (1867–1958) OGB 1955–57
Louis Adolphe Simon, FAIA, studied architecture at the Massachusetts Institute of Technology and joined the Office of the Supervising Architect of the Treasury in Washington, D.C., in 1896. He became chief of the office's engineering and drafting division in 1915, where he assumed responsibility for all architectural work and led the designs of hundreds of federal buildings across the U.S. Beginning in 1933, he served as supervising architect of the Public Buildings Administration, where he oversaw development of the Federal Triangle and served on the Board of Architectural Consultants; he retired from his position in 1941 but continued as an architectural consultant until 1944. He designed the Franklin D. Roosevelt Library in Hyde Park, New York, with strong influence from the president. He was named the first gold medalist of the Association of Federal Architects in 1938 and served on the American Institute of Architects committee overseeing restoration of the Octagon House.

THOMAS J. STOHLMAN (1927–2001) OGB 1969–75
Thomas Joseph Stohlman, AIA, earned a bachelor's degree in architecture from the University of Pennsylvania. He worked for the Washington, D.C., architecture firms of Chatelain, Gauger & Nolen and Walter G. Peter Jr. before establishing his own architectural practice in Washington in 1964. He was active in the Washington, D.C., chapter of the American Institute of Architects, including serving as president in 1967.

WYNANT D. VANDERPOOL JR. (1914–86) OGB 1969–79
Wynant Davis Vanderpool Jr., AIA, earned bachelor of arts and master of fine arts degrees in architecture from Princeton University and served during World War II in the U. S. Navy. He worked for Skidmore, Owings & Merrill and other firms in New York before establishing his own firm in the New York City area in 1947. He joined the firm of Wash-

ington, D.C., architect Avery Faulkner in 1964 and worked in partnership with him from 1967 to 1982, when he reestablished his solo practice. He designed many restoration projects in Washington, including St. John's Episcopal Church in Lafayette Square and the Victorian Hall of the National Portrait Gallery; he served as president of the Foundation for the Preservation of Historic Georgetown.

STEPHEN J. VANZE (1952–) OGB 2006–12
Stephen James Vanze, FAIA, earned a bachelor of arts degree from Brown University and a master of architecture degree from the University of Virginia. He worked for the Washington, D.C., architecture firms of Skidmore, Owings & Merrill and Hartman-Cox Architects before establishing his own firm, Barnes Vanze Architects, in partnership with Anthony Barnes in 1989. With offices in Washington and Middleburg, Virginia, the firm focuses on residential architecture and institutional planning projects. Vanze is active with the Washington, D.C., chapter of the American Institute of Architects, including service as president (2001), and served as president of the Washington Architectural Foundation.

PETER VERCELLI (1928–) OGB 1982–89
Peter J. Vercelli, AIA, earned a degree in architecture from the University of London and a master of architecture in urban design degree from Harvard University before working in London for Heysham & Partners from 1949 to 1954 on the restoration of historic buildings and monuments damaged during World War II. He moved to the United States and worked briefly for The Architects Collaborative in Cambridge, Massachusetts, before becoming an assistant professor at the Yale University School of Architecture in 1958. In 1969, he was the founding principal of the International Consortium of Architects (ICON) in Washington, D.C., established a solo practice in 1982 in Washington, D.C., and relocated in 1989 to Connecticut, where he continues to practice. His notable buildings in Washington include the Flour Mill redevelopment on the Georgetown waterfront and 1911 Pennsylvania Avenue, NW, for the Embassy of Mexico.

ANNE VYTLACIL (1936–2009) OGB 1975–78, 1978–79, 1989–96
Anne Bozena Vytlacil, AIA, earned a bachelor's degree and master of architecture degree from Harvard University and worked as a designer from 1963 to 1968 in architecture firms in San Francisco and New York City, including William Lescaze & Associates. She worked as an associate with Keyes, Lethbridge & Condon in Washington, D.C., from 1968 to 1977, when she formed her own practice focused on residential, commercial, and institutional renovation or rehabilitation projects in historic settings. She was an adjunct lecturer at the California Polytechnic State University–San Luis Obispo and an associate of the National Preservation Institute in 1989.

LORENZO S. WINSLOW (1892–1976) OGB 1950–55
Lorenzo Simmons Winslow, AIA, studied architecture and engineering at the Massachusetts Institute of Technology before serving in the U.S. Army Corps of Engineers during World War I. Following further architectural studies in Paris, he worked in Greensboro, North Carolina, on civic and residential architecture projects, establishing his own firm in 1927 and specializing in Tudor and Colonial Revival homes. In 1932, he joined the Office of Public Buildings and Public Parks in Washington, D.C., and was named White House architect by President Franklin Roosevelt in 1933, where he remained for twenty years, overseeing reconstruction of the West Wing, the Truman Balcony, and the White House reconstruction from 1948 1952. He formed a private architectural practice in Washington, D.C, in 1953; his projects include the remodeling of the Georgetown Presbyterian Church.

THOMAS W. D. WRIGHT (1919–2005) OGB 1975–82
Thomas William Dunstan Wright, FAIA, earned a bachelor's degree and a master's degree in architecture from Harvard University before serving in the U.S. Navy during World War II. He practiced architecture

with Leon Brown in Washington, D.C., beginning in 1951, and as a partner of the firm Brown & Wright until 1980, when he established a solo practice. His projects included single- and multifamily housing, public housing, restaurants and shopping centers, historic restorations, and chanceries for the U.S. Department of State. He was active in planning and housing organizations, serving on the District of Columbia Planning Commission and as president of the Washington chapter of the American Institute of Architects.

DAVID N. YERKES (1911–2011) OGB 1979–82
David Norton Yerkes, FAIA, earned a bachelor's degree from Harvard University and a master's degree in architecture from Yale University before serving in the U.S. Army Corps of Engineers and the Office of Strategic Services during World War II. He worked as a partner in the Washington, D.C., architecture firms of Deigert & Yerkes from 1947 to 1969; David N. Yerkes & Associates from 1970 to 1979; Yerkes, Pappas & Parker from 1979 to 1983; and Yerkes & Parker thereafter. His work includes U.S. embassies, residential, and institutional projects. He was active in the American Institute of Architects (AIA), including service as chairman of the Octagon House Committee and president of the AIA Foundation; he received the institute's 1972 Edward C. Kemper Award for Distinguished Service.

U.S. COMMISSION OF FINE ARTS CONTRIBUTING STAFF

EVE BARSOUM, CONTRIBUTING WRITER
Before joining the Commission of Fine Arts staff as an architectural historian in 2006, Eve Barsoum worked for the National Conference of State Historic Preservation Officers and the National Park Service, writing, documenting, and reviewing nominations to the National Register of Historic Places. She has worked as an independent architectural historian, providing evaluations and technical assistance for historic structures and for the District of Columbia Historic Preservation Office from 1994 to 2000, reviewing and negotiating building permit applications affecting properties in the city's historic districts. She has presented scholarly papers on the Georgetown historic district and on sculpture in the nation's capital and wrote a chapter on Georgetown in *Recreating the American Past: Essays on the Colonial Revival,* published by the University of Virginia Press. Barsoum received a bachelor's degree in city planning and a master's degree in architectural history from the University of Virginia.

SARAH BATCHELER, ILLUSTRATION EDITOR
Prior to joining the Commission of Fine Arts staff in 2008 as the Shipstead-Luce Architect, Sarah Batcheler, AIA, LEED, was an architect and associate with MGA Partners Architects (formerly Mitchell/Giurgola Architects) in Philadelphia, Pennsylvania, for more than a decade. Her work focused on the careful integration of new construction in the renovation of or addition to historic structures and included programming, design, documentation, and client and jurisdictional reviews. Her responsibilities also encompassed project management and business development as well as management of the photography program for the thirty-five-member firm. Batcheler chaired the governmental affairs committee of her local civic association, reviewing all zoning board applications within the association's boundaries, advising applicants on design, and making recommendations regarding the association's position on cases. She received her undergraduate degree from Bryn Mawr College and a master's degree in architecture from Columbia University.

KAY FANNING, CONTRIBUTING WRITER
Kay Fanning, PhD, joined the Commission of Fine Arts staff as historian in 2008 after working as a landscape historian for the Cultural Landscapes Program of the National Park Service National Capital Region, where her principal work was researching, writing, and editing cultural landscape inventories for various sections of the National Mall. In

addition, she wrote National Register of Historic Places nominations for Dumbarton Oaks Park and Theodore Roosevelt Island. She received her undergraduate degree from the College of Wooster in Ohio and her master's and doctoral degrees in architectural history from the University of Virginia. She has been an invited lecturer, published numerous book reviews in scholarly journals, and written entries for *American National Biography*.

MARY KONSOULIS, MANAGING EDITOR AND CONTRIBUTING WRITER

Mary Konsoulis, AICP, joined the Commission of Fine Arts staff in 2009 to manage the agency's centennial history project, which included her work as guest curator of the 2010 exhibition, *A Century of Design: The U.S. Commission of Fine Arts, 1910–2010*, in cooperation with the National Building Museum in Washington, D.C. She worked previously as a curator at the National Building Museum, developing exhibitions that explored the spatial, political, cultural, and technological influences on the design and development of American cities. Her professional experience includes ten years as an urban planner in the Washington, D.C., office of Skidmore, Owings & Merrill. Konsoulis is an adjunct faculty member in the University of Maryland's School of Architecture, Planning, and Preservation and has taught graduate courses in the historic preservation and real estate development programs. She has been published in *Urban Land* and *Planning* magazines and was a senior editor of *Real Estate Review*, produced by the University of Maryland and published by Thomson/West. She has a master's degree in city and regional planning from Harvard University and an undergraduate degree in American studies from Wellesley College.

THOMAS LUEBKE, EDITOR
See biographical entry on page 548.

CONTRIBUTING ESSAYISTS

WILLIAM B. BUSHONG

William B. Bushong, PHD, is the historian and webmaster of the White House Historical Association, where he develops public history materials, exhibits, and publications as well as electronic media promoting the history of the President's House. Before assuming that position in 1997, he was a historian with the National Register of Historic Places of the National Park Service and an independent author and historic preservation consultant, where his major projects included a historic resource study of Rock Creek Park and a lead research role in the National Building Museum exhibition on contemporary federal design, *From Mars to Main Street*. He has contributed to numerous publications including *North Carolina's Executive Mansion: The First 100 Years* (1991); *Uncle Sam's Architects: Builders of the Capitol* (1994); and an annotated edition of *Glenn Brown's History of the United States Capitol* (2008). Bushong received a bachelor of arts in history from North Carolina State University, a master of arts in history from Appalachian State University, and a doctorate in American civilization from George Washington University.

ARLEYN A. LEVEE

Arleyn A. Levee is an independent landscape historian and preservation consultant specializing in the work of the Olmsted firm. She is the author of numerous articles on topics of landscape history, particularly concerning the professionals of the Olmsted firm, and has written cultural and historic landscape reports for public- and private-sector clients across the country. She also lectures widely on aspects of landscape history, research, and preservation. Levee is a trustee of Historic New England and serves as a board member of The Cultural Landscape Foundation and the Stewardship Council of the Emerald Necklace Conservancy. Since 1981, she has served in various capacities with the National Association for Olmsted Parks. She received degrees from Wellesley College, Harvard University, and the Radcliffe Seminars Program in landscape design.

ZACHARY M. SCHRAG

Zachary M. Schrag, PHD, is a professor of history at George Mason University. Earning his doctorate in history from Columbia University in 2002, he taught at Baruch College and Columbia University before joining the George Mason University faculty in 2004. Schrag is the author of *The Great Society Subway: A History of the Washington Metro* and *Ethical Imperialism: Institutional Review Boards and the Social Sciences, 1965–2009*. His many articles and essays have appeared in a variety of scholarly publications, including the *Journal of Policy History*, the *Journal of Urban History*, *Technology and Culture*, *Washington History*, and the *Washington Post*. He has served as editor of *Washington History* and has received fellowships from the National Science Foundation, the Gerald Ford Foundation, and the Library of Congress.

PAMELA SCOTT

Pamela Scott is an independent architectural historian specializing in the history of Washington's planning and built environment. She has taught in affiliation with several universities and has curated exhibits on the history of Washington architecture for the Library of Congress, the National Building Museum, the Capitol Historical Society, the Historical Society of Washington, and the Department of the Interior Museum. Scott lectures frequently on many aspects of Washington's public buildings and their symbolism and has received fellowships from Winterthur Museum, the U.S. Capitol Historical Society, the White House Historical Association, and the Organization of American Historians. Her books include exhibit catalogues (*Temple of Liberty*), archival compilations (directories of District of Columbia architects and builders), guidebooks (*Buildings of the District of Columbia* with Antoinette J. Lee), and scholarly works (*Designing the Nation's Capital: The 1901 Plan for Washington, D.C.,* co-editor with Sue Kohler). She received a bachelor of arts degree from the University of Wisconsin and a master of arts degree from the University of Delaware.

CARROLL WILLIAM WESTFALL

Carroll William Westfall, PHD, was appointed as Frank Montana Professor of the University of Notre Dame in 1998 and served as chairman of the School of Architecture until 2002. His prior professional career included positions at Amherst College, the University of Illinois in Chicago, and the University of Virginia for two decades. His undergraduate degree from the University of California was followed by a master's degree from the University of Manchester and a doctorate from Columbia University. His publications include numerous articles on topics ranging from antiquity to the present day and two books, *In This Most Perfect Paradise*, a study of early Renaissance Rome (1974), and *Architectural Principles in the Age of Historicism* (1991), written with Robert Jan van Pelt. His special interest is the reciprocity between political life and the urban and architectural elements that serve the needs of citizens, especially in the contemporary American city.

RICHARD GUY WILSON

Richard Guy Wilson, PHD, holds the Commonwealth Professor's Chair in Architectural History at the University of Virginia. A frequent lecturer for universities, museums, and professional groups, he has been a television commentator for *America's Castles*, *American Experience*, and the History Channel. His many publications include *The American Renaissance* (1979), *McKim, Mead & White Architects* (1983), *The Making of Virginia Architecture* (1992), *Thomas Jefferson's Academical Village* (1993, 2008), *The University of Virginia: Campus Guide* (1999), the Society of Architectural Historians Buildings of the United States volume *Buildings of Virginia: Tidewater and Piedmont* (2002), *The Colonial Revival House* (2004), and *Harbor Hill: Portrait of a House* (2008). Wilson has led the Victorian Society in America's Summer School in Newport, Rhode Island, for twenty-nine years. He received the Outstanding Professor award from the University of Virginia in 2001 and was the Thomas Jefferson Fellow at Cambridge University, England, in 2007.

NOTES

Notes for sidebars and essays follow those of the chapter.

CHAPTER I

1   See Arthur Drexler, ed. *The Architecture of the École des Beaux-Arts* (New York: The Museum of Modern Art, 1977); Donald Egbert, *The Beaux-Arts Tradition in French Architecture* (Princeton, NJ: Princeton University Press, 1980); and James Noffsinger, *The Influence of the École des Beaux-Arts on the Architects of the United States*, (Washington, DC: Catholic University of America Press, 1955).

2   Philadelphia's Fairmont Park was begun in 1865, San Francisco established Golden Gate Park in 1870, and Boston created The Fens in 1878. Yellowstone, the first national park, located in Wyoming, Montana, and Idaho, was established in 1872.

3   These companies included the Eckington and Soldiers' Home Railway, Rock Creek Railway, Brightwood Railway, Georgetown and Tenallytown Railway, and the Washington & Glen Echo Railway.

4   The Senate Committee on Public Buildings and Grounds directed Michler to study sites of at least one hundred acres for a new home for the president—with convenient access to the city, a potential park, and a source for clean water. Michler's 1867 report recommended the upper Rock Creek valley as the preeminent place to establish a park for the nation's capital and concluded that it should be established in the valley north of Piney Branch. See 39th Cong., 2nd Sess. S. Mis. Doc. 21(1867).

5   William Bushong, *Rock Creek Park, District of Columbia: Historic Resource Study* (Washington, DC: Department of the Interior, National Park Service, August 1990), 65. Senator Brown was a member of the Union Universalist Party.

6   "Won for the People: How Rock Creek Park Was Gained for the People," *Evening Star*, October 4, 1890.

7   John Hemphill to Charles Carroll Glover, October 1, 1890. President Benjamin Harrison signed the bill on September 27, 1890. A copy of the October 1, 1890, letter is located in the Washington Board of Trade Papers, (Record Group I, Box I) Special Collections, Gelman Library, George Washington University.

8   Quoted in Elizabeth Lampl and Kimberly Williams, *Chevy Chase: A Home Suburb for the Nation's Capital* (Crownsville, MD: Maryland Historical Trust Press, 1998), 26. In 1899, Representative Newlands wrote a letter to Representative Cannon asking for an increase in the appropriation for the entrance to the zoo. He claimed he was uncomfortable doing so because of his nearby land holdings, but noted that "[Secretary of the Smithsonian] Langley was inept." In 1904, Glover donated land to the District commissioners at the southern end of the park "to facilitate the extension of Rock Creek Park and the Zoo to the northern line of Massachusetts Avenue Extended." This land eventually became the northern terminus of the Rock Creek and Potomac Parkway, established in 1913 by Congress to connect the Mall and Potomac Park to the National Zoological Park and Rock Creek Park. See Scrapbook, p. 114, Charles Carroll Glover Papers, The Historical Society of Washington, DC, and *Report of the Rock Creek and Potomac Parkway Commission: 1916,* H. Doc. 1114, (1916).

9   Ruth Boorstin, ed. *The Daniel J. Boorstin Reader* (New York: The Modern Library, 1995), 110.

10 Newlands founded the Rock Creek Railway Company in 1888 along Connecticut Avenue Extended. (In 1895, the Rock Creek Railway merged with the Washington and Georgetown Railroad Company—Glover served on its Board—to form the Capital Traction Company.) Seeing the potential for greatly increased profits in the development of suburban land, he quietly began acquiring property along Connecticut Avenue (Connecticut Avenue Extended). When his activity came to light, he was forced to incorporate and founded the Chevy Chase Land Company in 1890. In the same year, Glover began to purchase land west of Massachusetts Avenue Extended for his country estate, Westover, which by 1903 would encompass 108 acres. During this same period, American University and the National Cathedral were established along upper Massachusetts Avenue in part due to Glover's advocacy, and, coincidentally, not far from his land holdings.

11 Tony P. Wrenn, "The American Institute of Architects Convention of 1900: Its Influence on the Senate Park Commission Plan," in *Designing the Nation's Capital: The 1901 Plan for Washington, D.C.,* ed. Sue A. Kohler and Pamela Scott (Washington, DC: U.S. Commission of Fine Arts, 2006), 67.

12 Glenn Brown, *Papers Relating to the Improvement of the City of Washington, District of Columbia* (Washington, DC: Government Printing Office, 1901), 9.

13 John Reps, *Washington on View: The Nation's Capital Since 1790* (Chapel Hill: University of North Carolina Press, 1991), 240n200.

14 Thomas S. Hines, *Burnham of Chicago: Architect and Planner* (Chicago: University of Chicago Press, 2009), 73–81. Also see Erik Larson, *Devil in the White City* (New York: Crown Publishers, 2003), 77.

15 For an extensive analysis of the plan, see Sue A. Kohler and Pamela Scott, eds., *Designing the Nation's Capital: The 1901 Plan for Washington, D.C.* (Washington, DC: U.S. Commission of Fine Arts, 2006).

16 Hines, *Burnham of Chicago*, 150–51.

17 See Reps, *Washington on View*, 256 and Cynthia Field and Jeffrey Tilman, "Creating a Model for the National Mall: The Design of the National Museum of Natural History," *Journal of the Society of Architectural Historians* 63, no. 1 (March 2004): 52–73n2.

18 Constance McLaughlin Green, *Washington: A History of the Capital, 1800–1950* (Princeton, NJ: Princeton University Press, 1976), 137–38.

19 Hines, *Burnham of Chicago*, 148.

20 Charles Moore, *Daniel H. Burnham: Architect, Planner of Cities* (Boston: Houghton Mifflin Company, 1921), 2: 197.

21 Field and Tilman, "Creating a Model for the National Mall," 52–73.

22 See Dana G. Dalrymple, "Agriculture, Architects, and the Mall, 1901–1905: The Plan Is Tested" in *Designing the Nation's Capital: The 1901 Plan for Washington, D.C.,* ed. Sue A. Kohler and Pamela Scott (Washington, DC: U.S. Commission of Fine Arts, 2006), 207–243.

23 Francis G. Newlands to Glenn Brown, January 1904, Box 6, Folder 62, Francis Griffith Newlands Papers, Manuscripts and Archives, Yale University Library (hereafter cited as Newlands MSS).

24 Charles Moore to Newlands, March, 12, 1904, Box 6, Folder 64, Newlands MSS.

25 Daniel H. Burnham to Newlands, March 15, 1904, Box 6, Folder 64, Newlands MSS.

26 Charles F. McKim to Newlands, March 31, 1904, Box 6, Folder 64, Newlands MSS. Emphasis McKim.

27 Newlands to McKim, December 19, 1904, Box 7, Folder 72, Newlands MSS.

28 McKim to Newlands, March 3, 1905, Box 8, Folder 77, Newlands MSS.

29 Newlands to Burnham, October 7, 1906, Box 10, Folder 95, Newlands MSS.

30 Burnham to Newlands, October 13, 1906, Box 10, Folder 95, Newlands MSS.

31 Executive Order No. 306, March 14, 1905.

32 Daniel H. Burnham to Charles F. McKim, February 5, 1907, Box 2, Folder 50, Daniel H. Burnham Collection, Ryerson and Burnham Archives, the Art Institute of Chicago (hereafter cited as Burnham MSS).

33 McKim to Burnham, February 13, 1907, Box 2, Folder 50, Burnham MSS.

34 Burnham to McKim, February 13, 1907, Box 2, Folder 50, Burnham MSS.

35 William H. Taft to Burnham, February 14, 1907, Box 3, Folder 66, Burnham MSS.

36 "A Showy Sham, The Concoction of a Sham Commission," *Evening Star*, January 14, 1908, 4.

37 In addition to Trowbridge and Brown, the committee included George B. Post, William A. Boring, Robert S. Peabody, and C. Grant La Farge. See Brown to Newlands, January 9, 1908, Box 12, Folder 118, Newlands MSS.

38 60th Cong. 2nd Sess. S. Doc. 665 at 7–10.

39 60th Cong. 2nd Sess. S. Doc. 665 at 21.

40 S. B. P. Trowbridge to Newlands, January 11, 1909, Box 16, Folder 155, Newlands MSS.

41 Trowbridge to Newlands, January 21, 1909, Box 16, Folder 156, Newlands MSS.

42 Military aide Archibald Butt wrote about many Washington personalities to his sister-in-law, Clara Butt, beginning in 1909 until he died in 1912 in the sinking of the *Titanic*. Archibald Willingham Butt was born in Augusta, Georgia, on September 9, 1865. He attended the Summerville Academy near Augusta and then the University of the South at Sewanee, Tennessee, majoring in journalism. He worked for two southern newspapers before becoming the Washington correspondent for the *Augusta Chronicle*. During this time, he met General Matt W. Ransom, a former Confederate officer and U.S. Senator from North Carolina. In 1895, Ransom became the U.S. Minister to Mexico, and Butt entered the diplomatic world as his private secretary. With the outbreak of the Spanish-American War, Butt returned to the States and first entered the U.S. Army as a first lieutenant. After the war, he remained in the army and ultimately gained the rank of major, serving for six years in the Philippines, where he met Taft, and then in Cuba, before President Theodore Roosevelt selected him to be one of his military aides. President Taft was less interested in employing military aides; however, he asked Butt to continue to serve in this capacity. Butt wrote to his sister-in-law, in part, it seems, for future generations. See Archibald Butt, *Taft and Roosevelt: The Intimate Letters of Archie Butt* (Garden City, NY: Doubleday, Doran & Company, 1930), 2:540.

43 Butt, *Taft and Roosevelt*, 2:746–47.

44 "Francis G. Newlands," *Washington Post*, December 26, 1917, 6.

45 Christian F. Reisner, *Roosevelt's Religion* (New York: Abingdon Press, 1922), 204–05.

46 Reisner, *Roosevelt's Religion*, 209.

47 Sue A. Kohler, "The Commission of Fine Arts: Implementing the Senate Park Commission's Vision," in Kohler and Scott, *Designing the Nation's Capital*, 255.

48 Quoted in Sue A. Kohler, "The Commission of Fine Arts: Implementing the Senate Park Commission's Vision," Kohler and Scott, *Designing the Nation's Capital*, 255.

49 See Commission on Fine Arts, H.R. Rep. 407 (February 8, 1910); Commission of Fine Arts, H.R. Rep. 1292 (May 9, 1910).

50 The Committee on the Library had oversight of the congressional library, congressional art collection, and U.S. Botanic Garden.

51 Gilbert, Cook, Trowbridge, Burnham, Millet, Blashfield, French, and Olmsted had also been named to Roosevelt's Council of Fine Arts.

52 R. S. Owen to William H. Taft, May 25, 1910, and H. D. Money to Taft, May 27, 1910, Series 5, Reel 333, Case file 801, William Howard Taft Papers, Manuscript Division, Library of Congress (hereafter cited as Taft MSS).

53 Daniel H. Burnham to George P. Wetmore, May 19, 1910, Series 5, Reel 333, Case file 801, Taft MSS.

54 Burnham to Wetmore, May 19, 1910, Taft MSS. Anderson and Bennett had worked for Burnham and Bennett was his co-author for the Chicago Plan of 1909.

55 Burnham to Wetmore, May 19, 1910, Taft MSS.

56 Burnham to Francis D. Millet, May 19, 1910, Series 5, Reel 333, Case file 801, Taft MSS.

57 Newlands to William H. Taft, May 25, 1910, Box 21, Folder 208, Newlands MSS. Taft to Newlands, May 26, 1910, Series 8, Reel 502, Taft MSS.

58 See May 1910, Series 5, Reel 333, Case file 801, Taft MSS and certificate, June 15, 1910, OP 11, Burnham MSS.

59 "Waiting for Judson," *Evening Star*, March 15, 1909.

60 Burnham to Charles Norton, July 20, 1910, Series 6, Reel 372, Case file 187, Taft MSS.

61 Burnham to Norton, August 8, 1910, Series 6, Reel 372, Case file 187, Taft MSS.

ESSAY BY ARLEYN A. LEVEE

1 Most projects in the Olmsted firm files were assigned an individual job number. However, for the numerous Washington, D.C., projects, particularly for the public work, the numbering reflects a complex system that indicates the point of origin or organizational sponsorship of the work. Thus, subsumed under the File #2843 assigned to the Commission of Fine Arts projects is a complicated list of major projects and consultations covering decades of work. Moreover, some projects became independent work and are given separate job numbers; so, for example, Rock Creek Park is assigned File #2837; Rock Creek & Potomac Parkway is assigned File #2843 RC; and yet another Rock Creek folder is numbered File #2843-Folder C-4. As a result there exists today in the Olmsted records a byzantine series of overlapping administrative records concerning Washington.

2 In 1901, architect and planner Daniel H. Burnham (1846–1912) was nearly fifty-four; architect Charles Follen McKim (1847–1909) was a year younger; sculptor Augustus Saint-Gaudens (1848–1907) was nearly fifty-two. Charles Moore (1855–1942), Senator McMillan's secretary who was responsible for much of the organization concerning the McMillan Commission and who would go on to chair the Commission of Fine Arts, was closest in age to Olmsted at forty-five.

3 Laura Wood Roper, *FLO: A Biography of Frederick Law Olmsted* (Baltimore: Johns Hopkins University Press, 1973), 338. Mrs. Roper cites a conversation with Frederick Law Olmsted Jr. as a source, but correspondence as late as 1877 continues to indicate confusion over the youngest son's name. Frederick Law Olmsted Sr., writing to John Charles Olmsted in England in October 1877, discusses "sending Rick there (Henry, Frederick, 'Erick', Rick)" See Charles E. Beveridge et al., eds., *The Papers of Frederick Law Olmsted: Volume VII Parks, Politics, and Patronage, 1874–1882* (Baltimore: Johns Hopkins University Press, 2007), 335, 337. Several incidents in the mid-1870s may have influenced the senior Olmsted's concern over a legacy name, including the death of his own father, John, in 1873 and the commencement of one of the most significant design commissions of his career for the U.S. Capitol Grounds.

4   The Olmsted family at the time of Rick's birth consisted of his full sister Marion (1861–1948); his half sister Charlotte (1855–1908); and two half brothers, John Charles (1852–1920) and Owen Frederick (1857–81). His half siblings were the children of his mother, Mary Cleveland Perkins Olmsted (1830–1921), and her first husband, Dr. John Hull Olmsted (1825–57), Frederick Law's younger brother who had died of tuberculosis. Frederick Law Olmsted married his brother's widow in 1859 and adopted her children. John Charles Olmsted would become Rick's partner in the firm of Olmsted Brothers.

5   In addition to the New York parks, Olmsted Sr. and his partner, Calvert Vaux, had advised on park work in Newark, New Jersey, Buffalo, New York, New Britain, Connecticut, Philadelphia, Pennsylvania, Fall River, Massachusetts, etc; had planned several subdivisions including Riverside, Illinois, and Tarrytown, New York; and had worked on various academic and residential institutions. After the dissolution of their partnership in 1872, Olmsted's work expanded to include the U.S. Capitol Grounds and the capitol grounds for Hartford, Connecticut, and Albany, New York; park work, in Boston, Massachusetts, Detroit, Michigan, and at Niagara Falls, New York; numerous institutional projects; residential subdivisions; and estate work and railroad station grounds for the Boston and Albany Railroad.

6   Roper, FLO, 435.

7   Susan L. Klaus, "Intelligent and Comprehensive Planning of the Common Sense Kind: Frederick Law Olmsted Jr. and the Emergence of Comprehensive Planning in America, 1900–1920" (master's thesis, George Washington University, 1988), 32.

8   Payroll Ledger #1, PR-1, Administrative Records, Frederick Law Olmsted National Historic Site.

9   Pamela Scott, "Two Centuries of Architectural Practice in Washington," in Buildings of the District of Columbia, ed. Pamela Scott and Antoinette J. Lee (New York: Oxford University Press, 1993), 14–19.

10 Frederick Law Olmsted (Sr.) (hereafter "Olmsted Sr.") to J. R. Morrill, chairman of the Committee for Public Grounds, U.S. Senate, January 22, 1874, Frederick Law Olmsted Papers Manuscript Division, Library of Congress (hereafter cited as Olmsted MSS).

11 At this time, remnants of earlier design treatments and prior uses decorated the mall. Various buildings intruded into the space at the periphery. The Tiber Creek and the Botanic Garden were immediately west of the Capitol Grounds, followed by an inchoate area of erratic tree groups, crossing paths, and railroad appurtenances. Andrew Jackson Downing's picturesque park of meandering paths and arboreal excesses fronted the Smithsonian Institution, while to its west, gardenesque flower beds and miscellaneous greenhouses covered the grounds of the Department of Agriculture. The still incomplete Washington Monument was surrounded by construction with tidal marshes close by its southern side.

12 Olmsted Sr. to William Hammond Hall, March 28, 1874, Olmsted MSS.

13 The confused layering of jurisdictional controls over public structures and landscapes in the nation's capital, the intricate political maneuvering to develop the Senate Park Commission, and the creation of the Commission of Fine Arts are well addressed in various essays in Sue A. Kohler and Pamela Scott, eds., Designing the Nation's Capital: The 1901 Plan for Washington, D.C. (Washington, DC: U.S. Commission of Fine Arts, 2006).

14 Frederick Gutheim and Antoinette J. Lee, Worthy of the Nation: Washington, D.C., from L'Enfant to the National Capital Planning Commission, 2nd ed. (Baltimore: Johns Hopkins University Press, 2006), 178–181, chapter 8.

15 Frederick Law Olmsted Jr., "Landscape in Connection With Public Buildings in Washington," in Glenn Brown, comp., Papers Relating to the Improvement of the City of Washington, District of Columbia (Washington, DC: Government Printing Office, 1901), 28, 34.

16 Frederick Law Olmsted Jr., "Landscape in Connection With Public Buildings in Washington," in Brown, comp., Papers Relating to the Improvement of the City of Washington, 34.

17 Jon A. Peterson, The Birth of City Planning in the United States, 1840–1917 (Baltimore: Johns Hopkins University Press, 2003), 69–71. See also Mel Scott, American City Planning Since 1890 (Berkeley: University of California Press, 1969), 31–37. More than the importance of exemplary architecture and landscapes arranged into trend-setting groupings, the World's Columbian Exposition was notable for what has been labeled its "Renaissance ideal of artistic collaboration among architects, sculptors, painters, and fine craftsmen" who labored over this enterprise. Jon A. Peterson, "The Hidden Origins of the McMillan Plan for Washington, D.C., 1900–1902," in Historical Perspectives on Urban Design: Washington, D.C. 1890–1910, ed. Antoinette J. Lee (Washington, DC: Center for Washington Area Studies, George Washington University, 1983), 8.

18 Jon A. Peterson, "The Senate Park Commission Plan for Washington, D.C.: A New Vision for the Capital and the Nation," in Kohler and Scott, Designing the Nation's Capital, 1–19; Gutheim and Lee, Worthy of the Nation, 122–27; Charles Moore, Daniel H. Burnham: Architect, Planner of Cities, vol. 2 (Boston: Houghton Mifflin Company, 1921), 147; and Thomas S. Hines, Burnham of Chicago: Architect and Planner (Chicago: University of Chicago Press, 1979), 401n8.

19 Harvard College Class of 1894, 25th Anniversary Report, 1894–1919 (Norwood, MA: Plimpton Press, 1919), 346.

20 Charles Moore, "Makers of Washington," (unpublished manuscript) as quoted in Klaus, "Intelligent and Comprehensive Planning," 75.

21 "Appendix G: List of Lands in the District of Columbia Devoted to Public Use"; "Appendix H: List of Proposed Additional Reservations"; and "Appendix I: Proposed Additions to Existing Parks," in Charles Moore, ed., The Improvement of the Park System of the District of Columbia Report (Washington, DC: Government Printing Office, 1902), 155–71.

22 Gutheim and Lee, Worthy of the Nation, 201–05, 214–15, 254–55. See also National Park Service," The Fort Park System," part II, chapter III, in Civil War Defenses of Washington, [D.C.]: Historic Resource Study (www.nps.gov/history/online_books/civil war/hrs1,2-3.htm). In the spring of 1947, Gilmore Clarke as chairman of the Commission of Fine Arts, made a valiant last stand to forestall the D.C. commissioners from their plan to abandon "the so-called Fort Drive Project [for] the recapture lands already acquired by the Federal Government" for new uses or to be "'returned to taxation.'" The claim at the time was that this project was no longer economically feasible to provide for the city's necessary transportation needs. Clarke's plea that Fort Drive was of significance in Washington's history and as a component of the plan for Washington fell on deaf ears. Gilmore D. Clarke to John Russell Young, president, Board of Commissioners, March 11, 1947; Young to Clarke, April 4, 1947, Records of the Commission of Fine Arts, Record Group 66, Entry 17, Box 60, National Archives Building, Washington, D.C. (hereafter cited NAB).

23 From 1905 to 1909, the Consultative Board established by President Roosevelt and later enlarged into a Council of Fine Arts, attempted to protect the artistic effect of new public structures and statuary; but the legal jurisdiction of these bodies was dubious. The board members lobbied to fulfill the heroic agreement for Union Station, removing the trains from the Mall; and they negotiated with an intransigent secretary of agriculture to prevent his new building from infiltrating the Mall's sacred greensward, enlisting President Roosevelt to enforce the sanctity of its centerline. Finally, after the election of William Howard Taft, legislation was successful to establish a permanent advisory Commission of Fine Arts. See Sue A. Kohler, "The Commission of Fine Arts: Implementing the Senate Park Commission's Vision," in Kohler and Scott, Designing the Nation's Capital, 245–73. Relevant correspondence is found in Files

#2823 and #2839, Olmsted Associates Records, Manuscript Division, Library of Congress (hereafter cited OAR).

24 See File #2838, OAR, especially Charles Moore, "Some Popular Misconceptions Corrected," November 1907. In this document, Moore also makes a plea for a municipal art commission like other cities have, noting, "The city of Washington, which should be a model for other cities, seems not able to even profit by their example." See also Kay Fanning, *Cultural Landscape Inventory for National Mall & Memorial Parks: Union Square* (Washington, DC: Department of the Interior, National Park Service, 2006).

25 Frederick Law Olmsted Jr. (hereafter "Olmsted") to Daniel H. Burnham, August 2, 1907, File #2839, OAR. This letter was in response to earlier Olmsted correspondence with Burnham. In West Potomac Park, Olmsted had tried to refine the haphazard filling, road building, and tree planting of the army corps, which was in haste to open this section for public use. Considering a compromise over establishing lines and grades, Rick aroused a sharp rebuke from Burnham, who admonished him to "stand for the real thing" for the west end of the Mall, as this would "be a virtual adoption of the whole plan" to settle the Mall against all future attacks. Burnham to Olmsted, July 29, 1907, File #2839, OAR.

26 In addition, during this time Olmsted also maintained a full teaching schedule at Harvard, developing the first courses in landscape architecture; wrote several city planning reports (for Queens and Utica, New York, Holyoke, Massachusetts, and Detroit, Michigan) and periodical articles; and was an active organizer and lecturer for the American Civic Association and later the National Conference on City Planning. A sampling of his design and planning commissions for this period includes park systems in Baltimore and Hartford; a network of playground parks in Chicago's south side; continued implementation of Boston's metropolitan parks; plans for numerous educational institutions, among them the Taft School, in Watertown, Connecticut (for President Taft's brother); and residential designs for numerous private clients.

27 Olmsted to Colonel Charles S. Bromwell, January 14, 1907, File #2839, OAR. Frederick Law Olmsted, "City Plan for the City of Washington," *Journal of Proceedings of the Thirty-Sixth Annual Convention,* American Institute of Architects (1902), 55. A photograph of Langdon's plan for East Potomac Park can be found in the Commission of Fine Arts collection. Langdon presented his plans for review to the commission in 1915. Commission of Fine Arts minutes, October 2, 1915 (hereafter CFA Minutes). Copies of all minutes are held in the offices of the Commission of Fine Arts, Washington, D.C. James G. Langdon began as an employee of the Olmsted firm in 1892, coming to Washington with Frederick Law Olmsted Jr. to be his draftsman for the McMillan Commission work. Langdon remained in the Washington-Baltimore area, designing a number of public projects, many of which were collaborations with the Olmsted firm.

28 Senator McMillan died unexpectedly on August 10, 1902. Given his involvement in legislation to protect the District's water system, the area around this reservoir, which he had sponsored, was designated by President Taft as an appropriate location for a neighborhood park, also in recognition of McMillan's work for the improvement of the park system. Little remains today of the Olmsted design on the ground, and the elegant sculptural fountain designed by Herbert Adams and Charles Platt is reputed to be in storage. See File #2840, OAR and NARA, Record Group 66, Box 101. In 1934, the Commission of Fine Arts forestalled an inappropriately placed playground that impinged on the fountain. CFA minutes, January 25, 1934, letter from Charles Moore to Major Arthur.

29 The new appointees were architects Thomas Hastings and Cass Gilbert, sculptor Daniel Chester French, and artist Francis D. Millet. They were chosen from among a considerable list of suggested candidates. Sue A. Kohler, "The Commission of Fine Arts," in Kohler and Scott, *Designing the Nation's Capital*, 257–59.

30 Olmsted even traveled as far as Panama in 1914 with fellow commissioner Daniel Chester French to advise Colonel Goethals on beautification possibilities around the canal and its newly constructed communities. CFA minutes, November 15, 1912–May 9, 1913; Sue A. Kohler, "The Commission of Fine Arts," in Kohler and Scott, *Designing the Nation's Capital*, 259–62. Olmsted made several working tours of the small parks and reservations, altering plans from the Office of Public Buildings and Grounds. CFA minutes, January 23, 1914–1917. He paid special attention to the transformation of the former Boyce mansion grounds into Montrose Park, trying to blend the character of its plantings and forested slope with the new user amenities. CFA minutes, 1912–1918. Meridian Hill Park received careful scrutiny from Olmsted and fellow commissioners Cass Gilbert and Charles Platt over its spatial arrangements, constructed details, and plantings, as its unique Italianate form emerged. CFA minutes, April 4, 1913–February 24, 1922.

31 CFA minutes, May 20, 1915; July 29, 1915; October 2, 1915; December 3, 1915; September 5, 1916; and October 6, 1916.

32 Gutheim and Lee, *Worthy of the Nation*, 168–181. Park efforts during this period included encouraging donations of land or funds to fulfill the park system goals. In 1923–24, Charles Glover and Anne Archbold gave considerable acreage of the Foundry Branch valley to become part of the D.C. park system. Together with other members of NCPPC, Olmsted examined this property, preparing a report in April 1930. He praised the "sylvan mystery" and spiritual refreshment of this woodland, analyzed the character of its various component parts, and recommended management procedures to protect beauty while enabling its use as a public park. Gutheim and Lee, *Worthy of the Nation*, 178, 201–05; File #2844, Folder F-9, OAR.

33 CFA minutes, October 2, 1915; December 4, 1915; September 5, 1916; and October 6, 1916; File # 2843, Folder C-7, OAR.

34 Considerations of East Potomac Park, Rock Creek Park, and, finally, Mount Hamilton and Anacostia were reviewed by the commission with recommendations for the latter. CFA minutes, January 23, 1914; and CFA minutes, September 18, 1917, letter from Colonel William W. Harts to Representative James L. Slayden, 45–62; and File #2845, OAR.

35 Olmsted Sr., "Part of Draft Report Preliminary to Plan for National Zoological Park," addressed to Dr. Frank Baker, c. 1890, Olmsted MSS; Moore, *The Improvement of the Park System of the District of Columbia,* 87; and File #2822, OAR.

36 Moore, *The Improvement of the Park System*, 85–86, 88–89 and File #2837, OAR. For a thorough exploration of the development of the Rock Creek and Potomac Parkway, see Timothy Davis, "Rock Creek and Potomac Parkway, Washington, D.C.: The Evolution of a Contested Urban Landscape," *Studies in the History of Gardens & Designed Landscapes* 19:2 (Summer 1999): 123–237.

37 Olmsted, "Report for Senator Wetmore on the Rock Creek Matter," March 17, 1911, File #2843, Folder C-4, OAR; CFA minutes, November 28, 1916, letter from Charles Moore to Representative James L. Slayden, 390; and CFA minutes, September 18, 1917, letter from Colonel Harts to Representative James L. Slayden, 45–62.

38 Olmsted Brothers (hereafter "OB") to the Board of Control of Rock Creek Park, December 1917, File #2837, OAR; and Timothy Davis, "Beyond the Mall: The Senate Park Commission's Plans for Washington's Park System," in Kohler and Scott, *Designing the Nation's Capital*, 137–81. Following Humphrey Repton's "Redbook" practice of illustrating before-and-after views for his landscape proposals, many of these Rock Creek Park images showed extant conditions with an overlay of idealized improvements.

39 OB, December 1917 Rock Creek Park Report, File #283, OAR. In the Olmsted Brothers collaborative practice, individual work was subsumed under the Olmsted rubric. At the time of this report, 1917–18, as his tenure was ending on the Commission of Fine Arts, Olmsted was heavily engaged in the wartime planning for military and industrial workers' housing. Characteristic of his energy during

this 1910–20 decade, Olmsted had managed, around his continuing teaching schedule and his monthly meetings for the CFA, to write several influential planning reports for cities such as Pittsburgh, Pennsylvania, and Rochester, New York (both of which involved Whiting's analysis), and to maintain his active involvement in lecturing and writing for city planning organizations. As scholars have noted, however, his earlier enthusiasm for planning as a comprehensive panacea for urban ills was waning in the face of increasing reliance on "the expert" approach, rather than on a more multidisciplined collaboration. See Klaus, "Intelligent and Comprehensive Planning," and John J. Pittari Jr. "Practical Idealism: Frederick Law Olmsted Jr. and Modern American City Planning Movement," (PhD diss., University of Washington, 1997). His professional landscape practice for private clients continued to grow, now with several substantial community residential commissions: a landmark design for Forest Hills Gardens in New York and planning for resort communities such as Mountain Lake, Florida, and Palos Verdes, California. Both of these latter projects would be extensive, complex, and long-term endeavors, reaching fruition over the following decades.

40 Olmsted to Warren H. Manning, December 27, 1920, and Olmsted to Representative Robert Luce, April 28, 1921, File #2845, OAR.

41 File #2845, OAR. Having acquired the land, attempts to establish procedures for design and construction and an efficient arboretum management under the Department of Agriculture were constantly beset with delays, to the continual frustration of both Olmsted and Frederic Delano, chair of the NCPPC, who joined him on the Arboretum Advisory Council.

42 "The National Arboretum," Olmsted to Frederick T. Coville, May 8, 1927, File #2845, OAR.

43 CFA minutes, September 1931, exhibit D, letter from Commission of Fine Arts to Senator Simeon D. Fess, November 2, 1931, 24–26.

44 Pamela Scott, "'A City Designed as a Work of Art': The Emergence of the Senate Park Commission's Monumental Core," in Kohler and Scott, Designing the Nation's Capital, 107–11.

45 CFA minutes, October 4, 1932–November 29, 1932 (NCPPC minutes of November 17–19, 1932 are filed with CFA minutes, November 18–19, 1932); Olmsted to Frederic A. Delano, October 18, 1932, NCPPC minutes, appendix H. See also File # 2848, OAR and Thomas C. Jeffers, "The Washington Monument: Various Plans for Improvement of Its Surroundings," Landscape Architecture 39 (July 1949): 157–63.

46 Olmsted to Frederic A. Delano, October 18, 1932, NCPPC minutes, appendix H.; Delano to "My Colleagues on the Park and Planning Commission," October 7, 1932, NCPPC minutes; CFA minutes, January 6, 1933, letter from Henry V. Hubbard to Gilmore D. Clarke, January 3, 1933. See also File #2843, Folder MG, and File #2844, Folder 2, OAR.

47 Olmsted to A. B. Cammerer, September 27, 1933, File #2843 M.Un., OAR.

48 See File #2838, OAR.

49 Olmsted, "Memorandum as to Data for Union Square, Washington," October 11, 1933; Olmsted, "Statement in Regard to General Plan for Union Square, Washington, D.C.," April 19, 1934; and Olmsted to Cammerer, June 21, 1944, all found in File #2843 M.Un., OAR.

50 Regarding the sanctity of the 1901 plans, Olmsted noted that there are parts "which McKim and I never did thrash out as thoroughly as we did most of the other parts of the central scheme (except the Capitol cascades)." Olmsted to C. Grant La Farge, October 30, 1923, File #2847, OAR. A January 1935 memorandum about the Union Square project noted: "Introduction of cascade too grandiose and out of character with Capitol." [Olmsted], "Memorandum," January 1935, File #2843 M.Un., OAR; CFA minutes, April 24, June 1, June 19, September 17, 1934; and Olmsted to A. B. Cammerer, June 21, 1934, File #2843 M.Un., OAR.

51 Olmsted, "Statement in Regard to General Plan for Union Square, Washington, D.C.," April 19, 1934, File #2843 M.Un., OAR; and CFA

minutes, June 19, 1934 and October 10, 1934.

52 Olmsted, Report of Meeting, September 17, 1934, File #2834 M.Un., OAR; and CFA minutes, September 17, 1934, and October 19, 1934.

53 Harvard College Class of 1894, 50th Anniversary Report, 1894–1944 (Norwood, MA: Plimpton Press, 1944), 407.

54 File #2843 M.Un., OAR and Kay Fanning, Cultural Landscape Inventory for National Mall & Memorial Parks: Union Square.

55 Olmsted to Colonel U.S. Grant III, January 24, 1928, File #2843 EX, OAR.

56 CFA minutes, October 19, 1934.

57 CFA minutes January 31, 1936; Olmsted to G. Marshall Finnan, June 12, 1934, File #2843 EX, OAR; and Thomas E. Beaman Jr., "Williams, Morley Jeffers," in Pioneers of American Landscape Design, ed. Charles A. Birnbaum and Robin Karson (New York: McGraw-Hill, 2000), 455–457.

58 OB, "Report to the President of the United States on Improvements and Policy of Maintenance for the Executive Mansion Grounds," October 1935, File #2843 EX, OAR.

59 Hubbard to Moore, May 14, 1935, File #2843 EX, OAR.

60 File #2843 EX, Folders 1 and 2, OAR; Moore to the President, May 14, 1935, File #2843 EX, OAR; CFA minutes, January 29, 1937 and CFA minutes, January 29, 1937, exhibit A, letter from Clarke to Moore, March 2, 1936.

61 CFA minutes, April 25, 1935.

62 Olmsted to C. Grant La Farge, October 30, 1923, File #2847, OAR; quoted in Sue A. Kohler, The Commission of Fine Arts: A Brief History, 1910–1995 (Washington, DC: Government Printing Office, 1996), 69–71.

63 Olmsted to Cammerer, "Memorandum Report by Frederick Law Olmsted on Proposed Sites for a Memorial to Thomas Jefferson in the National Capital," July 22, 1935, File #2843 PPJ, OAR.

64 CFA minutes, March 20, 1937, including minutes of joint meeting with NCPPC and Olmsted to Harlean James, April 18, 1937, File #2843 PPJ, OAR.

65 CFA minutes, September 29, 1937.

66 CFA minutes, March 20, 1937; February 3, 1938; and March 24, 1938; exchange of correspondence between Hubbard and Fiske Kimball in October and November 1938, File #2843 PPJ, OAR.

67 Hubbard to Otto Eggers, July 25, 1938; Kimball to Hubbard, October 19, 1938; and Hubbard to Kimball, November 22, 1938, File #2843 PPJ, OAR.

68 Clarke to Newton Drury, March 4, 1941; Hubbard to Olmsted, March 31, 1941; Olmsted to Drury, April 16, 1941; Olmsted to A. E. Demaray, August 5, 1941; and Clarke to Olmsted, August 11, 1941, File #2843 PPJ, OAR.

69 Eggers to OB, July 14, 1942; Carl Rust Parker to Olmsted, July 16, 1942; and Olmsted, "Report of Visit," July 28, 1942, File #2843 PPJ.

70 Moore, Improvement of the Park System, 58.

71 Olmsted to F. A. Delano, July 2, 1936, File #2843 AI, OAR; Kay Fanning, "National Register of Historic Places Registration Form for Theodore Roosevelt Island," January 31, 1999, section 8, 46–47.

72 Hermann Hagedorn to John Russell Pope and Olmsted, May 10, 1932; Olmsted to Hagedorn, May 13, 1932, File #2843-AI, OAR.

73 Olmsted to Hagedorn, May 5, 1932; OB [HVH], "Notes on Certain Considerations Affecting the Design," December 22, 1932, File #2843-AI, OAR.

74 CFA minutes, December 15, 1933, and January 18–19, 1934 and Olmsted, "Outline of Projected Improvement Work by the C.C.C.," June 18, 1935, File #2843-AI, OAR.

75 An extensive number of plans was produced for this project, of which at least 273 are extant in the Olmsted National Historic Site, Brookline, Massachusetts, collection. Some were produced by the Olmsted office; others came either from the Office of Public Buildings and Public Parks, the NCPPC, or from another federal agency. Given its waterfront location along the Virginia shore, work on Analostan Island involved multiple jurisdictions. The preliminary general plan #2843-

AI-625 was dated in early 1936. It remained as a draft until it was revised in spring 1945 and again in October 1946, when it was issued as Plan #2843-AI-815.

76 Olmsted, "Draft of Preliminary Report Upon a Plan for the Permanent Development of Roosevelt Island," May 16, 1934, File #2843-AI, OAR.

77 OB to General Frank R. McCoy, June 13, 1947; Olmsted, "Report of Visit," June 4, 1943; and Olmsted to Hagedorn, 17 May 17, 1947, File #2843-AI, OAR.

78 Hagedorn to the secretary of the Interior, quoted in Kay Fanning, "National Register Registration Form," Section 8, 58.

79 Fanning, "National Register Registration Form," Section 8, 60–61.

80 "Olmsted, "National Parks and Forest: Inherent Values," Edward Clark Whiting and William Lyman Phillips, "Frederick Law Olmsted—1870–1957: An Appreciation of the Man and His Achievements," *Landscape Architecture* 48 (April 1958): 155; and Olmsted, "Vacation in the National Parks and Forests," *Landscape Architecture* 12 (January 1922): 107–11.

81 Harvard Class of 1894, *50th Anniversary Report,* 408–09; and "Remarks at the Dedication of Olmsted Grove 24 July, 1953," *Landscape Architecture* 44 (October 1953): 38.

CHAPTER II

1 See Richard Guy Wilson, *The American Renaissance 1876–1917* (New York: The Brooklyn Museum, 1979).

2 "Taft for Single Head but Against Suffrage," *Washington Post,* May 9, 1909, 1, 3, and 12.

3 A 1908 Sundry Civil bill provided an appropriation for the District commissioners to exhume L'Enfant from an unmarked grave at Green Hill in Prince George's County, Maryland. The task was carried out on April 22, 1909, and the body was held at Mount Olivet Cemetery until the morning of April 28, 1909, when it was taken to the Capitol where he laid in state for three hours. See James Morgan, "The Reinterment of Major Pierre Charles L'Enfant," *Records of the Columbia Historical Society* (1910) 13:119–125; "Dedicate Memorial to Major L'Enfant," *New York Times,* May 23, 1911; and Sara Butler, "The Monument as Manifesto: The Pierre Charles L'Enfant Memorial, 1909–1911," *Journal of Planning History* 6, no. 4 (November 2007): 283–310.

4 William Howard Taft, "Washington: Its Beginning, Its Growth, and Its Future," *National Geographic Magazine,* 27, no. 3 (March 1915): 221–92.

5 Daniel H. Burnham to Charles Norton, June 20, 1910, Series 5, Reel 333, Case file 801, William Howard Taft Papers, Manuscript Division, Library of Congress (hereafter cited as Taft MSS). The Office of Public Buildings and Grounds (OPBG) was created in 1867 when Congress transferred the authority over public buildings and grounds in the District of Columbia from the commissioner of Public Buildings in the Department of the Interior. The chief of engineers of the U.S. Army was designated as the head of OPBG. The office existed until 1925 when Congress transferred its authority to the Office of Public Buildings and Public Parks. The head of the OPBG served as the commission's secretary until 1922, when a separate position was created.

6 Burnham to Francis Millet, May 19, 1910, Taft MSS.

7 Daniel H. Burnham to Elizabeth Burnham, May 11, 1868, Box 25, Folder 2, Daniel H. Burnham Collection, Ryerson and Burnham Archives, Art Institute of Chicago (hereafter cited as Burnham MSS). Burnham was twenty-two years old at the time.

8 Louis Sullivan, *The Autobiography of an Idea* (New York: Dover Publications, Inc., 1956), 286.

9 Charles Moore, *Daniel H. Burnham: Architect, Planner of Cities* (Boston: Houghton Mifflin Company, 1921) 2:164. John Burnham

was Daniel's great-grandfather; he served as an officer in the Revolutionary War.

10 Quoted in Kristen Schaffer, "The Plan of Chicago as a Map of Heaven: The Influence of Burnham's Swedenborgianism," *Chicago Architectural Journal* 10 (2002): 75.

11 Schaffer, "The Plan of Chicago as a Map of Heaven," 74.

12 Speech, "On the Necessity of Dreaming," 1 ff., Box 63, Folder 23, Burnham MSS. The audience and date of the speech are not known. The Court of Honor was the principal space at the 1893 World's Columbian Exposition.

13 The statement has ambiguous origins and may have been an amalgamation of Burnham's statements assembled by his friend, San Francisco architect Willis Polk, after Burnham had died. See Thomas S. Hines, *Burnham of Chicago: Architect and Planner* (Chicago: University of Chicago Press, 2009) 401n8.

14 Executive Order No. 1259, October 25, 1910. Only the Bureau of Engraving and Printing was built.

15 This dollar amount and all subsequent amounts were calculated at www.measuringworth.com using the consumer price index.

16 Cammerer received his bachelor of law degree in 1911; he served as the director of the National Park Service from 1933 to 1940.

17 This four-story, molded-brick commercial building, erected between 1890 and 1891, was built for a printing company and razed in 1971 to make way for the new headquarters of the American Institute of Architects.

18 "Note for Convention of Art Commissions held May 13, 1913," Daniel Chester French Papers, Manuscript Division, Library of Congress (hereafter French MSS).

19 See Sue A. Kohler and Pamela Scott, eds. *Designing the Nation's Capital: The 1901 Plan for Washington, D.C.* (Washington, DC: U.S. Commission of Fine Arts, 2006), 207 ff.

20 Burnham to Millet, July 26, 1910, Box 63, Folder 5, Burnham MSS.

21 At that time, they were stored in the basement of the Library of Congress; many were damaged, and some had been lost.

22 See Archibald Butt, *Taft and Roosevelt: The Intimate Letters of Archie Butt* (Garden City, NY: Doubleday, Doran & Co., 1930) 1:228.

23 Burnham to Elihu Root, February 29, 1912, Box 63, Folder 7, Burnham MSS.

24 The commission moved twice more, to Lafayette Square in 1970 and to its present location in the National Building Museum, the former Pension Building, in 1990.

25 For a comprehensive analysis of the Lincoln Memorial, see Christopher Thomas, *The Lincoln Memorial & American Life* (Princeton, NJ: Princeton University Press, 2002).

26 The L'Enfant Plan's general notes indicated that each of the fifteen states was to be assigned a square and held responsible for embellishing it with statues, columns, obelisks, or other ornaments.

27 The library committees had oversight of the congressional library, congressional art collections, and the U.S. Botanic Garden.

28 Quoted in Thomas, *Lincoln Memorial,* 26.

29 Joseph Cannon to Burnham, March 6, 1911, Box 1, Folder 13, Burnham MSS. The Peace Monument, also known as the Naval Monument, dedicated in 1877, was located at Pennsylvania Avenue and First Street, NW.

30 Burnham to William H. Taft, June 13, 1911, Series 6, Reel 372, Case File 187, Taft MSS.

31 Millet to Burnham, June 19, 1911, Box 63, Folder 6, Burnham MSS.

32 Burnham to Millet, June 20, 1911, Box 63, Folder 6, Burnham MSS.

33 Taft to Burnham, June 28, 1911, Series 6, Reel 372, Case File 187, Taft MSS.

34 "Report of the Commission of Fine Arts to the Lincoln Memorial Commission, July 17, 1911," in *Commission of Fine Arts Annual Report, Fiscal Year 1912* (Washington, DC: Government Printing Office) 16–22.

35 Commission of Fine Arts minutes, July 31, 1911, 90.

36 Christopher A. Thomas, "The Lincoln Memorial and its Architect, Henry Bacon (1866–1924)" (PhD diss., Yale University, 1990) 99.

37 Henry Bacon to Burnham, August 14, 1911, Box 1, Folder 3, Burnham MSS.

38 Quoted in Thomas, *Lincoln Memorial*, 73.

39 "A Memorial to Lincoln Worthy Alike of the Nation and the Man," *New York Tribune*, January 7, 1912, Pt. II, 1.

40 Willliam H. Taft to Daniel H. Burnham, February 9, 1912, Series 6, Reel 372, Case file 187, Taft MSS.

41 Daniel Chester French to Burnham, February 21, 1912, Box 1, Folder 31, Burnham MSS.

42 Herbert Adams to Millet, February 28, 1912, Box 1, Folder 1, Burnham MSS.

43 Erik Larson, *Devil in the White City* (New York: Crown Publishers, 2003) 389.

44 Moore, *Daniel H. Burnham*, 2:151–53.

45 Quoted in Thomas, *Lincoln Memorial*, 119.

46 Henry Lodge to Taft, April 29, 1912, Series 6, Reel 372, Case file 187, Taft MSS.

47 Spencer Cosby to Taft, May 16, 1912, and Thomas Hastings to Taft, May 20, 1912, Series 6, Reel 372, Case file 187, Taft MSS.

48 Taft to Root, May 26, 1912 and Root to Taft, May 30, 1912, Series 6, Reel 372, Case file 187, Taft MSS.

49 George Wetmore to Taft, June 7, 1912, Series 6, Reel 372, Case file 187, Taft MSS.

50 The third partner, prominent designer Stanford White, had died in 1906.

51 Taft to Cosby, June 10, 1912, and Cosby to Taft, June 22, 1912 Series 6, Reel 372, Case file 187, Taft MSS.

52 Nicholas Henry Butler to Taft, June 25, 1912, and Richard B. Chase to Taft, June 28, 1912, Series 6, Reel 372, Case file 187, Taft MSS. Austin Lord was a principal in the firm of Lord, Hewlett & Tallant. He had served as the first director of the American School of Architecture in Rome from 1894 to 1896 (renamed the American Academy in Rome in 1896). He had been appointed the architect for the Panama Canal (1912–13) and served as the director of the School of Architecture at Columbia University (1912–15).

53 Taft Memorandum, July 3, 1912, Series 6, Reel 372, Case file 187, Taft MSS.

54 Margaret French Cresson, *Journey into Fame: The Life of Daniel Chester French* (Cambridge, MA: Harvard University Press, 1947), 227.

55 In November, the commission members selected a medal designed by John Flanagan. They may have been inclined to choose the design submitted by James Fraser, but he did not make a submission for the obverse side of the medal and therefore was disqualified. See Daniel Chester French to Spencer Cosby, November 20, 1912, Folder June–November 1912, French MSS. In 1921, President Warren Harding would sign an executive order requiring design review of all new medals, insignia, and coins.

56 The monument, featuring two allegorical figures, was approved as a final design in January 1913. It was erected on the east side of the Ellipse later that year.

57 CFA minutes, November 21, 1913, 11. The *Titanic* Memorial (1916) was erected along the Potomac River at the original terminus of New Hampshire Avenue; it was relocated to the Southwest Waterfront Park in 1968.

58 "Mrs. H. P. Whitney Wins: Her Design for the *Titanic* Memorial Chosen in Sculptors' Contest," *New York Times*, January 8, 1914. See French to William Harts, January 9, 1914, Folder January 1914, and French to Harts, February 4 and February 13, 1914, Folder February 1914, French MSS.

59 French to Cosby, December 12, 1912, Folder December 1912, and French to Cosby, January 4, January 14, and January 19, 1913, Folder January 1913, French MSS.

60 Panama Canal Report Draft, February 26, 1913, Folder April 1913, French MSS.

61 The commission's recommendations focused on a breakwater light and fog signal. They were not carried out due to cost and space. See CFA minutes, September 25, 1913, 3.

62 Executive Order No. 1862, found in Sue A. Kohler, *The Commission of Fine Arts: A Brief History* 1910–1995 (Washington, DC: Government Printing Office, 1996), 242.

63 CFA minutes, November 15, 1912, 181. The fact that the commission called for a restoration of the Federal-era building in the Colonial style reflects the then-commonly-held belief that the styles were synonymous.

64 U. S. Army Corps of Engineers, *1913 Annual Report of the Office of Public Buildings and Public Park* (Washington, DC: Government Printing Office), 3210. An appreciation of Burnap's design intent can also be ascertained from various statements in his 1915 book *Parks: Their Design, Equipment and Use* (1915, repr.; Philadelphia: J.B. Lippincott Co., 1916), 71, 98, 106, and 225.

65 See "Old-Time Mansion Falls into Decay," *Washington Star*, January 8, 1914, 3.

66 By the middle of 1915, a significant amount of landscaping had been done as well as the construction of two tennis courts and the pergola, the repair of the summerhouse, and the relocation of a Victorian-era lodge that stood previously in Lincoln Park on Capitol Hill. See U. S. Army Corps of Engineers, *1915 Annual Report of the Office of Public Buildings and Public Parks* (Washington, DC: Government Printing Office), 3714.

67 French to Fredrick Law Olmsted Jr., May 25, 1915, Folder May 1915, French MSS.

68 Olmsted Jr. to French, May 27, 1915, Folder May 1915, French MSS.

69 *Report of the Commission of Fine Arts, Fiscal Year ending June 1916* (Washington, DC: Government Printing Office, 1917), 15.

70 The following decisions were made at the July meeting: demolish the kitchen wing-turned-comfort station; relocate the summerhouse; reduce the width of the ropewalk; thin the Osage orange hedge along the walk to allow vistas across the entire park; eliminate one tennis court; and the approval of the elliptical pool at the formal entrance. See CFA minutes, July 13, 1917, 6–8.

71 *Report of the Commission of Fine Arts: Eighth Report Jan. 1, 1918–July 1, 1919* (Washington, DC: Government Printing Office, 1920), 120.

72 French to Harts, December 12, 1914, Folder December 1914, French MSS.

73 French to Harts, January 9, 1915, Folder December 1914, French MSS.

74 French to Harts, January 18, 1915, Folder January 2–21, French MSS.

75 French to Harts, January 27, 1915, Folder January 22–31, French MSS.

76 CFA minutes, December 3–4, 1915, 4.

77 Olmsted Jr. to French, January 21, 1915, Reel 18, Folder Lincoln Memorial 1, French MSS.

78 French to Harts, February 20, 1914, Folder February 1914, French MSS.

79 See French to Reverend Teunis Hamlin, Folder March 1907, French MSS. The subject arose in this letter to Hamlin, who was associated with the Presbyterian Congregation at 1316 Connecticut Avenue, NW, regarding the commission for the Dr. John Witherspoon statue. French turned the commission down the following month.

80 Just as the 1893 World's Columbian Exposition proved to be the stimulus for the injection of Beaux-Arts principles into American planning, architecture, and sculpture, the 1913 International Exhibition of Modern Art in New York—better known as the Armory Show—changed the outlook of American art. Organized by the Association of American Painters and Sculptors, the show provided a cross section of contemporary art, with a number of younger and more radical artists dominating the roster of exhibitors, including Constantin Brancusi, Pablo Picasso, Alexander Archipenko, and Wilhelm

Lehmbruck. However, academic sculpture was also well represented by James Earle Fraser, Arthur Lee, Robert Aitken, and others.

81   Henry Bacon to Franklin Hooper, May 23, 1913, Reel 18, Folder Lincoln Memorial 1, French MSS.

82   French to Harts, December 21, 1914, Reel 18, Folder Lincoln Memorial 1, French MSS.

83   French to William H. Taft, January 15, 1915, Reel 18, Folder Lincoln Memorial 1, French MSS.

84   French to Mr. President, June 1, 1915, Folder May 1915, French MSS. The folder also includes a resignation letter dated May 26, 1915.

85   French to Harts, June 5, 1915, Reel 18, Folder Lincoln Memorial 1, French MSS.

86   French to Herbert Adams, June 10, 1915, Reel 18, Folder Lincoln Memorial 1, French MSS.

ESSAY BY PAMELA SCOTT

1   Glenn Brown, *Glenn Brown's History of the United States Capitol,* annotated by William B. Bushong (Washington, DC: U.S. Capitol Preservation Commission, 2008), 29.

2   Alan Lessoff, "Washington Insider: The Early Career of Charles Moore," *Washington History 6,* no.2 (Fall/Winter 1994–1995): 64–80.

3   Charles Moore, "The Government of the City of Washington by Congress," *Daughters of the American Revolution Magazine* 58, no.4 (April 1924): 199, and Charles Moore, "Norton, Charles Eliot," undated typescript, Records of the Commission of Fine Arts, Record Group 66, Entry 5, Box 8, pp. 5, 7, National Archives Building, Washington, D.C. (hereafter cited NAB).

4   Charles Moore, "Standards of Taste," *American Magazine of Art* 21, no.7 (July 1930): 367.

5   Senate Committee on the District of Columbia, Commission to Consider Certain Improvements in the District of Columbia, S. Rep. 1919 at 1–2.

6   Commission to Consider Certain Improvements, 2–4.

7   Sally Kress Tompkins, *A Quest for Grandeur: Charles Moore and the Federal Triangle* (Washington, DC: Smithsonian Institution Press, 1993), 43–44, and Pamela Scott, "'A City Designed as a Work of Art': The Emergence of the Senate Park Commission's Monumental Core," in *Designing the Nation's Capital: The 1901 Plan for Washington, D.C.,* ed. Sue A. Kohler and Pamela Scott (Washington, DC: U.S. Commission of Fine Arts, 2006), 79.

8   Tompkins, *A Quest for Grandeur,* 83–84.

9   Tompkins, *A Quest for Grandeur,* 91–130 passim.

10 Charles Moore, "The Improvement of Washington City. First Paper," *Century Magazine* 63, no.4 (February 1902): 221–28.

11 Moore, "The Improvement of Washington City," 222, 228.

12 Moore, "The Improvement of Washington City."

13 Charles Moore, *The Life and Times of Charles Follen McKim* (Boston: Houghton Mifflin Company, 1929), 71; and Tompkins, *A Quest for Grandeur,* 9.

14 Edward F. Conklin, *The Lincoln Memorial, Washington* (Washington, DC: Government Printing Office, 1927), 30–31.

15 Moore, *McKim,* 61; Christopher A. Thomas, *The Lincoln Memorial and Its Architect, Henry Bacon* (Ph.D. diss., Yale University, 1990), 422–9; and Kathryn Fanning, *American Temples: Presidential Memorials of the American Renaissance* (PhD diss., University of Virginia, 1996), 109–47.

16 Joanna Zangrando, *Monumental Bridge Design in Washington, D.C., as a Reflection of American Culture, 1886–1932* (PhD diss., George Washington University, 1974), 304–400.

17 Zangrando, *Monumental Bridge Design,* 356.

18 Zangrando, *Monumental Bridge Design,* 356–62.

19 CFA minutes, September 7, 1922, exhibit B, letter from Charles Moore to Lieutenant Colonel Sherrill, July 7, 1922, 2.

20 CFA minutes, 4; Zangrando, *Monumental Bridge Design,* 360–62; "Arts Commission Turns Down Site for New Bridge," *Evening Star,* September 12, 1922, 1; and "Highway to Unite City with West," *Washington Post,* September 7, 1922, 2.

21 Warren G. Harding to Charles Moore, September 25, 1922, Box 10, Charles Moore Papers, Manuscript Division, Library of Congress (hereafter cited Moore MSS); Zangrando, *Monumental Bridge Design,* 262–63.

22 "Lincoln Memorial Selected as the Site for New Bridge," *Evening Star,* December 18, 1922, 2.

23 Zangrando, *Monumental Bridge Design,* 362–72.

24 Tompkins, *A Quest for Grandeur,* 26.

25 Tompkins, *A Quest for Grandeur,* 26–49.

26 [Charles Moore?], "Garden Club of America," typescript lecture, Box 13, Moore MSS; "Beautify City, Garden Club Speakers Urge," *Washington Post,* October 25, 1922, 3.

27 Charles Moore, "The Washington Monument Gardens," *Journal of the American Institute of Architects* (1932), 11–13.

28 CFA minutes, April 25, 1935, 3–5.

29 Fanning, *American Temples,* 147–162.

30 Moore to Egerton Swartwout, March 10, 1937, Record Group 66, Entry 5, General Correspondence, Box 9, NAB.

31 Moore to Gilmore Clarke, Record Group 66, Entry 5, Box 9, NAB.

32 Moore to Clarke, Record Group 66, Entry 5, Box 9, pp. 4–5, NAB; "Report of Meetings," April 12–May 14, 1935, Synopsis of Meetings, Thomas Jefferson Memorial Commission Records, Papers of Howard W. Smith, Box 265, Accession #8731, Special Collections, University of Virginia Library (hereafter cited TJMC Records); CFA minutes, May 20, 1935, 1–2; "Meeting of June 5, 1935," pp. 73, 83, 85–86, 97, TJMC; Frederick Law Olmsted Jr., "Memorandum with Reference to Proposed Sites for a Memorial to Thomas Jefferson," August 8, 1935, TJMC Records.

33 CFA minutes, May 27, 1937, exhibit F, letter from Charles Moore to John J. Boylan, April 8, 1937; CFA minutes, May 27, 1937, 17–18; CFA minutes, June 21, 1937, 14.

34 CFA minutes, September 29, 1937, 1–3.

35 F. A. Whiting Jr., "Jefferson Memorial Chronology," *Washington Post,* May 20, 1938, X9; and Steven McLeod Bedford, *John Russell Pope, Architect of Empire* (New York: Rizzoli, 1998), 222.

36 "Boylan Denies Keeping Shrine Plans in Dark," *Washington Post,* May 25, 1938, X3.

37 Moore to William Adams Delano, February 22, 1939, Record Group 66, Charles Moore Papers, Box 2, NAB.

CHAPTER III

1   In addition to his work on the commission, Moore held the position of consultant to the librarian of Congress and, from 1918 to 1927, was acting chief of the Division of Manuscripts at the library. He also was an editor, historian, and biographer, authoring numerous books and articles, many pertaining to the history of Washington, D.C. Moore wrote biographies of both Daniel Burnham and Charles McKim: *A Life of Daniel H. Burnham, Architect and Planner of Cities,* 2 vols. (Boston: Houghton Mifflin, 1921) and *The Life and Times of Charles Follen McKim* (Boston: Houghton Mifflin, 1929). His undergraduate degree was from Harvard University and he earned a doctorate from Columbian University, now known as George Washington University.

2   Many of the architects and artists presenting projects in these years were members of the conservative design fraternity; often, they were past members of the Commission of Fine Arts or had worked for McKim, Mead & White.

3   After leaving the Commission of Fine Arts, Olmsted continued his work in the design of Washington as a founding member of the National Capital Park and Planning Commission, created by the fed-

eral government in 1926 to address the increasing prominence of planning in city design and the growing acceptance of the professional discipline of planning. The NCPPC directed planning throughout the metropolitan region. Its mandate was broadened from its predecessor agency, the National Capital Park Commission established in 1924, which had overseen the growth of recreational lands only.

4   Caemmerer replaced his adoptive brother, Arno Cammerer [sic], who left the CFA to become the assistant director and then the third director of the National Park Service. Before coming to the CFA, Caemmerer had been secretary or "confidential stenographer" to the postmaster general. During his years as commission secretary, he earned a master's degree at George Washington University and a doctorate at American University, also studying law for two years at Georgetown University. For most of Caemmerer's years with the commission, the staff was tiny: He was assisted only by a stenographer-typist, sometimes a messenger. See "HPC's position description as of August 10, 1951," Caemmerer's own official two-page written description of his job, in "Hans Paul Caemmerer," CFA staff files.

5   Caemmerer's appointment became effective in July 1922. CFA minutes, May 30–31, 1922, exhibit A, letter from Charles Moore to the secretary of the Treasury, June 1, 1922.

6   "Resolution of the Commission of Fine Arts on the Death of Hans Paul Caemmerer," CFA staff files, c. June 1962.

7   "HPC's position description as of August 10, 1951," in HPC CFA staff files. The two Washington histories include *Washington: The Nation's Capital,* a large, lavishly illustrated volume published by the Government Printing Office in 1932.

8   This section is adapted from Kay Fanning, *The Mall, National Mall & Memorial Parks, Cultural Landscape Inventory* (Washington, DC: Department of the Interior, National Park Service, 2006).

9   Charles Moore, ed. *The Improvement of the Park System of the District of Columbia* (Washington, DC: Government Printing Office, 1902), 12.

10 As a junior army officer assigned to Washington with the Office of Public Buildings and Grounds, Grant filled in as secretary for the Commission of Fine Arts in Spencer Cosby's absence on several occasions between 1910 and 1912. He later was appointed executive secretary and disbursing officer of the Arlington Memorial Bridge Commission and served as director of the NCPPC from 1942 to 1949.

11 CFA minutes, July 9, 1920, 9. See also Kirk Savage, "Inventing Public Space," in *Monument Wars: Washington, D.C., the National Mall, and the Transformation of the Memorial Landscape* (Berkeley: University of California Press, 2009), 147–192. It is noteworthy that the CFA's seal, designed by Lee Lawrie in 1950, features the Washington Monument as the ultimate symbol of the national capital.

12 *Ninth Report of the Commission of Fine Arts* (Washington, DC: Government Printing Office, 1923), 16. The architect and planner for the tempos was Horace Peaslee. Information on the power plant is from Fanning, *The Mall Cultural Landscape Inventory,* 65, 69–70, and from a series of mid-1930s photos depicting the power plant in the holdings of the Museum Resource Center, National Park Service, National Capital Region, and reproduced in *The Mall Cultural Landscape Inventory.*

13 An Act to provide for the enlarging of the Capitol Grounds, Pub. L. No. 1036, H. R. 13929 (March 4, 1929).

14 Olmsted and Eliot wrote a series of reports on this subject for the NCPPC.

15 Charles Moore to U. S. Grant III, June 2, 1931, and Grant to Henry V. Hubbard, May 23, 1932, Series 66A-1097, Box 26, Folder 1460/Mall–20 Grading & Drainage, the Mall, Federal Records Center (hereafter cited Mall FRC); and John Nolen to Arno Cammerer, October 13, 1933, Series 64-A-42, Box 46, Folder 1460/Mall-5, Admin. Main. & Protection, Mall FRC.

16 NCPPC minutes, December 1932, appendix, letter from William A. Delano to U. S. Grant III, November 23, 1932.

17 CFA minutes, October 6–7, 1933; and CFA minutes, November 17–19, 1932, exhibit H, letter from Frederick Law Olmsted Jr. to Frederic A. Delano, October 18, 1932.

18 CFA minutes, May 28, 1934; and "Federal Public Works Project for Development of the Mall Is Nearing Completion," c. September 1936, Series 64-A-42, Box 46, Folder 1460/Mall, Nov. 1917–April 1955, p. 5, Mall FRC.

19 CFA minutes, July 9, 1920. See also James M. Goode, *Washington Sculpture* (Baltimore: Johns Hopkins University Press, 2008), 274–79. Congress had appropriated funding for a memorial statue to Grant as early as 1895. In McKim's scheme, the three generals would have faced west, standing in the center of a plaza composed of symmetrical arrangement of walks, fountains, and small lawn panels. The extensive paving for the square proposed by the McMillan Plan would have interrupted the continuity of the Mall landscape with the Capitol Grounds but was never built. The equestrian statue to Sherman was built in 1903 on a site south of the Treasury Building. The memorial to Sheridan was built in 1908 in the eponymous circle on Massachusetts Avenue, NW. The enormous memorial, its platform measuring 252 feet long by 71 feet wide, was the second largest equestrian monument in the world (after the monument to Victor Emmanuel in Rome, 1895–1911).

20 See Goode, *Washington Sculpture,* 442–45.

21 CFA minutes, November 20, 1920, 1, and exhibit A, letter from C. S. Ridley to Simon & Simon, December 2, 1920. See also the Grant Memorial Commission, *The Grant Memorial in Washington* (Washington, DC: Government Printing Office, 1924). Controversy followed the project through site selection. Several locations were considered; the Ellipse was the strongest contender. McMillan Commission members Frederick Law Olmsted Jr. and Charles McKim strenuously opposed any site on the 16th Street axis, in order to maintain the axis as depicted in the McMillan Plan. The old Botanic Garden was finally chosen, but disagreement about the site still mired the project: The threatened loss of several specimen and memorial trees prompted a congressional inquiry and public outcry led by the *Washington Star,* delaying construction until 1908.

22 CFA minutes, April 19, 1934.

23 CFA minutes, April 23, 1934, 12.

24 CFA minutes, June 19, 1934, 13.

25 "Plans, unsigned and undated history of Mall," Series 64-A-42, Box 46, Folder 1460/Mall-5, Adm. Main. & Prot. Supl., FRC.

26 CFA minutes, September 17, 1934.

27 Ibid.

28 Kay Fanning, *Cultural Landscape Inventory for National Mall & Memorial Parks: Union Square* (Washington, DC: Department of the Interior, National Park Service, 2006), 33–34.

29 CFA minutes, October 19, 1934, 8–9.

30 Commission/History, www.ABMC.gov, July 2, 2010.

31 See James Edwards Peters, *Arlington National Cemetery: Shrine to America's Heroes* (Kensington, MD: Woodbine House, 1986): 295–98.

32 CFA minutes, May 10, 1912, exhibit B, document from Spencer Cosby to secretary to assistant secretary of war, "13 indorsement, The Commission of Fine Arts," May 11, 1912. See also Peters, *Arlington National Cemetery,* 295–298.

33 Planning and designs for cemetery structures were handled by the Graves Registration Service, an office later folded into the Office of the Quartermaster General; both were in the Department of War, and the secretary of war himself occasionally became involved with design questions before the commission. Landscape architect George Gibbs Jr., of the Graves Registration Service, prepared the cemetery's first comprehensive plan in the early 1920s. A large complex of columbaria has been built at the eastern end of this axis, at the cemetery's boundary.

34 CFA minutes, July 20, 1922, exhibit B, July 31, 1922. Available documents do not describe the War Department submission.

35 CFA minutes, December 14, 1923, exhibit H, letter from Charles Moore to secretary of war, December 19, 1923, cover letter for "Statement Accompanying the Report Made to the Honorable the Secretary of War by the Commission of Fine Arts on the Location and Design of the Monument to the Unknown Soldier."

36 See CFA minutes, April 5, 1923, 5; and CFA minutes, February 1, 1924, quoted letter from Secretary of War John W. Weeks, January 15, 1924, 18.

37 July 3, 1926 (Public Resolution No. 44, 69th Cong.). Hastings protested to the CFA and to various officials that the commission was his and that he had never been paid for the existing tomb. The CFA supported his claim for restitution but admitted they had never been happy with his proposed sculpture. Moore argued Hastings's case with congressional committee chairmen and Secretary of War Davis, but little could be done since Congress had already approved the act for a competition. CFA minutes, September 15 and 16, 1927, and January 6, 1928.

38 CFA minutes, December 6, 1928, 9–11. Lorimer Rich had trained with McKim, Mead & White. Thomas Hudson Jones had designed a maquette for one of the allegorical figures that were originally intended to line Arlington Memorial Bridge. Jones's figure represented agriculture, and the maquette is still in the collection of the CFA. The members of the jury were Charles A. Coolidge, chair (CFA 1933–36), Daniel H. Burnham, Paul P. Cret, Assistant Secretary of War Hanford MacNider, and Mrs. William D. Rock; the architectural advisor was Victor Mindeleff. See CFA minutes, December 6, 1928, "Report of the Jury of Award for the Completion of the Tomb of the Unknown Soldier at Arlington National Cemetery, Arlington, Virginia, under the Supervision of the Secretary of War," November 11, 1928.

39 "Unknown Soldier's Tomb to Have This Appearance When Finished," article from *The World* inset into bound minutes before December 6, 1928. See description in James Goode, *Washington Sculpture*, 686–87. CFA minutes, December 6, 1928, 9.

40 CFA minutes, July 1, 1930, 13, and July 23, 1930, 5–6.

41 CFA minutes, April 26, 1932.

42 Arlington Memorial Bridge Commission, *Report* (Government Printing Office: 1924), 32, quoted by William Mitchell Kendall in CFA minutes, November 11, 1928, 2, during a discussion with the CFA about which attributes should be symbolized by the sculptural groups at the plaza behind the Lincoln Memorial.

43 The bridge was also considered in relation to the contemporary plan to restore Arlington Mansion: "Colonel Sherrill stated that in connection with the plan to restore the Mansion he desired to ask the advice of the commission regarding plans for the Arlington Memorial Bridge." CFA minutes, September 22–23, 1921, 2.

44 Lieutenant Colonel C. O. Sherrill became secretary of the CFA on March 31, 1921, and left on June 30, 1922, to serve as executive and disbursing officer of the Arlington Memorial Bridge Commission; he also remained director of the Office of Buildings and Grounds. Sherrill was later replaced as executive and disbursing officer for the AMBC by Ulysses S. Grant III. In September 1921, the AMBC asked the CFA whether the design that had won an 1899 competition for the bridge should still be accepted. Charles Moore replied that the situation had changed since completion of the Lincoln Memorial, and now the bridge would need to harmonize with the monument.

45 CFA minutes, September 7, 1922, exhibit B, report to Arlington Memorial Bridge Commission, 6.

46 CFA minutes, December 18–19, 1927, 10.

47 CFA minutes, September 15–16, 1927, 22.

48 CFA minutes, December 8–9, 1927, 13–14, and exhibit O, Charles Moore to AMBC, December 22, 1927.

49 CFA minutes, December 18–19, 1927, 7–10.

50 CFA minutes, March 15, 1928, 2, letter from McKim, Mead & White to CFA, March 10, 1928 (Kendall, White and Dennis J. VanderBent); letter from McKim, Mead & White to U. S. Grant III, AMBC, October 3, 1927, 3.

51 CFA minutes, March 15, 1928, 17–18 (Medary), 4–6 (Delano), and 6–10 (Olmsted).

52 CFA minutes, March 15, 1928, 28.

53 CFA minutes, March 15, 1928, 28. Moore formulated eight points (exhibit A), which were sent to the AMBC: "1. Reasonable reduction is to be made in the width of the steps. 2. Retaining walls on each side of the steps joining them with the parapets of the bridge and the Rock Creek Parkway connections. 3. Omit tunnel under the steps. 4. Move the steps back as far as the granite work of the bridge will permit. 5. The arch under the abutment of the bridge to be cut at right angles with the bridge, with a corresponding treatment of the arch under the Rock Creek Parkway connection. 6. Arrange for roadway at the foot of the steps, connecting the arches. This driveway to be considered as part of the architectural scheme rather than as a roadway in the true sense. 7. From this lower level of the steps, a study should be made of supplementary steps to care for the rise and fall of the water. 8. If it should be found necessary to care for the flotsam and jetsam, it should be provided for by an architectural barrier to be in harmony with the scheme of the competition."

54 CFA minutes, April 20, 1928, 8+.

55 Kendall reduced their size from roughly 48 feet by 13 by 13 to 43 feet by 12 by 12. CFA minutes, July 2, 1928, 1-2.

56 Eventually, following a design competition and many further years of study, two pairs of mounted equestrian sculptures made of gilded bronze were placed at the entrances to the bridge and the parkway in 1951, representing the *Arts of War* (Leo Friedlander) and the *Arts of Peace* (James Earle Fraser). Delays were partly caused by wartime shortages; the statues were eventually cast in Italy. See Goode, *Washington Sculpture*, 514, 516–17.

57 CFA minutes, September 22–23, 1921. The recommendation was stated in the minutes but does not seem to have been issued to any official body or in response to any request.

58 CFA minutes, March 27, 1925, exhibit B; CFA minutes, April 25, 1925; and CFA minutes, January 6, 1931. The memorial was approved apparently without objection to the provision of dormer windows in the dome, which fortunately were never built. CFA minutes, May 21, 1925.

59 CFA minutes, January 6, 1928.

60 CFA minutes, April 20, 1928, 7, and exhibit E, ref. to AMBC Report, 6

61 CFA minutes, May 24, 1928, exhibit E. The CFA retained Howard to advise them on treatment of the approaches and grounds of the memorial. Both the Howard plan and the McMillan Plan showed features in these locations north and south of the Reflecting Pool. See Christopher A. Thomas, *The Lincoln Memorial & American Life* (Princeton, NJ: Princeton University Press, 2002), 132–33.

62 CFA minutes, August 6, 1928.

63 CFA minutes, January 7, 1921. Gilbert was one of the original members of the CFA, and French—sculptor of the seated figure of Lincoln in the Lincoln Memorial—was a former chairman.

64 Moore also mentioned that the CFA had met with the War Department in late 1919, and together they had decided that there should be "one great National World War Memorial" in Washington.

65 CFA minutes, April 7, 1922, letter from C. P. Summerall to Charles Moore, April 8, 1922.

66 CFA minutes, March 27, 1925, exhibit C, letter from Charles Moore to Colonel C. O. Sherrill, officer in charge, Office of Public Buildings and Parks, April 25, 1925.

67 The American Battle Monuments Commission still exists to maintain America's overseas cemeteries and battle monuments.

68 CFA minutes, June 9, 1921.

69 CFA minutes, September 27, 1923, exhibit H, September 27, 1923.

70 CFA minutes, September 9, 1920, 4.

71 In the CFA minutes of September 3, 1920, Charles Moore reported on a meeting of the council held on August 30. See also Keith N. Morgan, *Charles A. Platt: The Artist as Architect* (New York: The Architectural History Foundation and MIT Press, 1985), 161n3; CFA minutes, November 21, 1919, exhibit A, letter from Charles Moore

to Charles Platt, October 18, 1919; and CFA minutes, October 9, 1920, 3.

72 The CFA, in response, asked the chief of the Army Cemeterial Division to engage sculptor Leo Friedlander, known for his architectural sculpture, to make plaster study models of these motifs, which the Cemeterial Division reviewed but did not adopt. See CFA minutes, July 26, 1921, exhibit D, letter from Charles Moore to Colonel George H. Penrose.

73 CFA minutes, January 13, 1922, 4–5.

74 CFA minutes, September 1928.

75 CFA minutes, June 17, 1926, 3, *Public Buildings Report*, 1917, 64.

76 CFA minutes, February 6, 1928, 16.

77 Lynn said the U.S. Supreme Court Building Commission was considering its purchase. CFA minutes, March 21, 1929, 1.

78 A letter from Moore to David Lynn suggests he wrote all former architect members of the commission. CFA minutes, March 21, 1929, exhibit C1, letter from Charles Moore to David Lynn, March 22, 1929.

79 CFA minutes, July 23, 1930.

80 Two books have explored the construction of the Federal Triangle in depth, and much of the information in this section is based on them: George Gurney, *Sculpture and the Federal Triangle* (Washington, DC: Smithsonian Institution Press, 1985) and Sally Kress Tompkins, *A Quest for Grandeur: Charles Moore and the Federal Triangle* (Washington, DC: Smithsonian Institution Press, 1993). Tompkins's study closely examines the role of the commission, particularly of Charles Moore, and analyzes the CFA's composition during its first thirty years.

81 Tompkins, *A Quest for Grandeur*, 25–26, 28, 31. The only members with design or planning experience were the architect of the Capitol and the supervising architect of the Treasury.

82 CFA, *Report of the Commission of Fine Arts, June 30, 1916–January 1, 1918* (Washington, DC: Government Printing Office, 1918), 6–25. Preparation of the report is briefly discussed in the CFA minutes of September 10, 1917; October 13, 1917; October 27, 1917; and December 21, 1917. Tompkins writes: "Despite its lack of official approval, the report would prove a solid base on which to build after the war." Tompkins, *A Quest for Grandeur*, 28.

83 Tompkins, *A Quest for Grandeur*, 38.

84 Ibid. As well as heading the CFA, Moore helped establish the NCPPC and the Zoning Commission. He cultivated relationships with Republican presidents from Harding to Hoover, becoming particularly close to the Coolidges. Moore had first become friendly with the Coolidges when the future president was governor of Massachusetts and had developed an especially close connection with Grace Coolidge. Moore received many invitations to formal functions at the Harding White House, and after Calvin Coolidge became president in August 1923, Moore was invited to even more events at the mansion, both formal and informal. See Tompkins, *A Quest for Grandeur*, 32–33. Moore resigned from his job as acting chief of the Library of Congress's Division of Manuscripts in 1922 "to devote himself full time to the commission's role in the public buildings program." Tompkins, *A Quest for Grandeur*, 13.

85 Tompkins, *A Quest for Grandeur*, 37, 39–40. The joint meeting was held on May 28, 1926.

86 Tompkins, *A Quest for Grandeur*, 42. Bennett was also a former director of the National City Planning Institute. As a principal of Bennett, Parsons & Frost, he was in these years responsible for many projects on the Capitol Grounds.

87 Gurney, *Sculpture*, 51; and CFA minutes, April 14–15, 1927; cited in Tompkins, *A Quest for Grandeur*, 43.

88 Gurney, *Sculpture*, 51; and Tompkins, *A Quest for Grandeur*, 43.

89 Tompkins, *A Quest for Grandeur*, 56; and Gurney, *Sculpture*, 52–53, 58.

90 Tompkins, *A Quest for Grandeur*, 54.

91 Gurney writes that the BAC plan "must have closely approximated the one proposed by the Commission of Fine Arts." Gurney,

Sculpture, 54. Tompkins on "freshness." CFA minutes, May 28, 1929, 10; cited in Tompkins, A Quest for Grandeur, 54.

92 Tompkins, *A Quest for Grandeur*, 53.

93 Tompkins, *A Quest for Grandeur*, 56–58.

94 Gurney writes: "The National Archives Building thus took on a new importance, and Pope made it into a symbol of America's heritage." Gurney, Sculpture, 62. Tompkins believes that Pope refused to design a building that would be simply one of a group. CFA minutes, July 1, 1931, exhibit D; approval; Tompkins, *A Quest for Grandeur*, 57.

95 CFA minutes, December 17, 1931. At first meant to house the Coast Guard, the Apex Building was later also called the Independent Offices Building because it was intended to provide office space for smaller federal agencies such as the Federal Trade Commission, the National Capital Park and Planning Commission, and the Commission of Fine Arts itself, which was never located there; the building became the home exclusively of the FTC.

96 CFA minutes, December 15, 1933, Moore reporting on recent meeting with President Franklin D. Roosevelt and Secretary of the Interior Harold Ickes. In the 1930s, the CFA sought to keep new construction in this area compatible with the buildings of the Federal Triangle: classical limestone structures that recognized the relationship of the District government within the federal government. Asserting the necessity of keeping the axis of 4½ Street open to preserve the vista from the Mall to the Old City Hall, the CFA prevented a planned municipal auditorium from being built directly on the alignment.

97 "The primary argument against the Apex Building was that it would lessen the attractiveness of Pope's neighboring Archives Building." Tompkins, *A Quest for Grandeur*, 60.

98 CFA minutes, December 15, 1933, 5. The reference to the Justice Department building as the west half of the frame is from CFA minutes of a joint meeting with the NCPPC, January 18–20, 1934, 10. CFA minutes, December 15, 1933, exhibit A1, letter from Charles Moore to Bennett, Parsons & Frost, December 19, 1933, and exhibit. A, letter from Charles Moore to Franklin Delano Roosevelt, December 19, 1933.

99 Tompkins cites Moore in the *Washington Star*, March 14, 1937. Tompkins writes: "There is no doubt that the attitude of the Commission of Fine Arts and Moore toward Bennett and the work of his firm, which prolonged the work on the plaza indefinitely, left it vulnerable to growing space pressures and resulted in its never being occupied." Also, "The characteristics that made the commission as effective as it was were the same that slowed progress on the Triangle, weakened its overall plan, and resulted in its remaining incomplete. These characteristics . . . allowed them to dictate location, general plan, style and architects of the Triangle. Its recommendations became mandates, its disapprovals were tantamount to vetoes." See Tompkins, *A Quest for Grandeur*, 61n67, 60, and 69.

100 CFA minutes, May 16, 1930, 10.

101 The CFA photo file "State Department" contains correspondence between Moore and Brunner and from Moore to Sherrill, along with blueprints of the floor plan for the building on Lafayette Square. Additional information was provided by Pamela Scott.

102 This account is taken from William D. Rhoads, "Roosevelt and Washington Architecture," *Records of the Columbia Historical Society*, vol. 52 (Charlottesville: University Press of Virginia, 1989), 106–107.

103 This project is discussed in greater detail in Lois Craig and the staff of the Federal Architecture Project, *The Federal Presence: Architecture, Politics, and Symbols in United States* (Cambridge, MA: MIT Press, 1978), 288. Also see CFA minutes, September 16, 1930; October 16, 1930; and January 6, 1931.

104 CFA minutes, November 7, 1930, exhibit M, November 19, 1930, 4, 5. The report noted improvements were already planned for Foggy Bottom, much of which was presently a slum. CFA minutes, November 7, 1930, 13, and exhibit M, November 19, 1930.

105 CFA minutes, December 15, 1933, 2. The meeting had occurred on December 7, 1933. Moore had concluded that the War and Navy Departments would not require much future expansion.

106 CFA minutes, December 17, 1931, exhibit D, letter from Charles Moore to Rear Admiral A. E. Parsons, chief, Bureau of Yards and Docks, Navy Department., December 22, 1931, 2.

107 The commission feared a proposal redevelopment of the Naval Hospital site, by the Allied Architects of Washington, would overshadow the monument. The CFA concluded there was no room for expansion and Moore said, "The two buildings are mutually antagonistic in design as well as in purpose." CFA minutes, December 17, 1931, pp. 7–8, and exhibit D, Moore to Rear Admiral A. E. Parsons, Chief, Bureau of Yards and Docks, Navy Dept., December 22, 1931. In 1939, Clarke met with Franklin Roosevelt at the White House to hear the president's proposal for the Naval Hospital: "As near as I get it the President wants to put the Navy building down there at the water front back of the hill where the old Naval Hospital stands that will be removed before long. Then the President wants to connect the War and Navy Buildings with a colonnade in front of the hill along Constitution Avenue facing the Lincoln Memorial." CFA minutes, June 9, 1939.

108 The story is told in Richard Oliver, Bertram Grosvenor Goodhue (New York: The Architectural History Foundation, 1985), 175–82. Oliver characterized these renderings as dry, lifeless, and academic.

109 CFA minutes, March 26, 1920, 7.

110 CFA minutes, February 1, 1924.

111 The commission encouraged the American Pharmaceutical Association (APA) to acquire all the lots between 22nd and 23rd Streets in order to control the building's setting. The APA purchased most of the lots, and the government bought those remaining; Congress passed legislation closing Upper Water Street. CFA minutes, March 19, 1931.

112 CFA minutes, September 16, 1930; CFA minutes, April 23, 1934, exhibit F; and CFA minutes, October 6 and 7, 1933, exhibit E2; Moore paraphrased Clarke in a letter to F. A. Birgfeld, chief clerk, Treasury Department, October 23, 1933. Landscape plans were prepared by Wheelwright & Stephenson of Philadelphia.

113 CFA minutes, August 8, 1935, 4.

114 Pamela Scott and Antoinette J. Lee, Buildings of the District of Columbia (New York: Oxford University Press, 1993), 210. The original building, a romantic fantasy following strict Beaux-Arts planning (1908–10), occupied a prime location at the corner of 17th Street and Constitution Avenue, NW. A second structure by Cret and Kelsey, a "Spanish villa," was set behind the first on the 18th Street corner of the lot.

115 CFA minutes, January 22, 1929, 11.

116 CFA minutes, December 10, 1935; and CFA minutes, February 18, 1948, exhibit B, letter from Gilmore Clarke to Julius A. King, February 3, 1948.

117 Scott and Lee, Buildings of the District of Columbia, 216.

118 CFA minutes, May 16, 1930, 10.

119 See CFA minutes, January 6, 1931, exhibit O, Moore report to Public Buildings Commission, December 29, 1930; and CFA minutes, May 28, 1931, exhibit H, CFA report, letter from Charles Moore to U. S. Grant III, June 10, 1931. On NCPPC preference for Foggy Bottom, see CFA minutes, September 24–26, 1931; and CFA minutes, January 18–19, 1934, 16+.

120 CFA minutes, October 19, 1934, secretary of war approval of building. On closing of New York Avenue, see CFA minutes, September 29, 1938. On the decision to leave Virginia Avenue open, see CFA minutes, September 29, 1938.

As late as 1940, the CFA said it "felt building should not be considered a permanent State Department building," expressing the hope that the State Department might yet occupy a "dignified building" on the west side of Lafayette Square. CFA minutes, February 24, 1940.

121 This description is based on Scott and Lee, Buildings of the District of Columbia, 212.

122 CFA minutes, August 10, 1938, reference to letter from F. A. Delano to Louis Simon, August 6, 1938; CFA minutes, October 15 1938, 14, exhibit G; and CFA minutes, January 27, 1938, 6–7.

123 Sixteenth Street marked a longitudinal meridian through the District of Columbia that passed through the White House; Meridian Hill is situated on this line. All information on Mary Henderson from Sue A. Kohler and Jeffrey R. Carson, eds., Sixteenth Street Architecture, vol. 1 (Washington, DC: U.S. Commission of Fine Arts, 1978), 323–35, 339, and from Scott and Lee, Buildings of the District of Columbia, 297–300.

124 Kohler and Carson, Sixteenth Street Architecture, I: xvii.

125 CFA minutes, June 24, 1924, exhibit F, letter from Charles Moore to Horace Peaslee, June 25, 1924; and CFA minutes, April 4, 1913.

126 Goode, Washington Sculpture, 537. A site in Potomac Park had been suggested by "the persons having the gift in charge," but this location, the CFA advised, "would be open only to an American citizen who had rendered conspicuous service to the United States." CFA minutes, August 3, 1921, 3–4.

127 Goode, Washington Sculpture, 588–89; and CFA minutes, January 7, 1921, 2. The commission was later consulted on plans to move the statue to another site in the park where the view would not be encumbered by trees or slope, but on Moore's recommendation it remained in its original location. CFA minutes, May 1, 1936, 6–7, and May 28, 1936, 12.

128 Goode, Washington Sculpture, 536; CFA minutes, November 15, 1912; September 25, 1913; and May 20, 1915.

129 According to James Goode, the Noyes Armillary Sphere disappeared from a National Park Service storage facility in the early 1980s. Goode, Washington Sculpture, 760.

130 CFA minutes, February 11, 1924, 14. A congressional act authorizing the memorial was passed on February 16, 1924, and it was brought before the CFA through the Joint Committee on the Library. The association first conceived of the memorial as honoring the sailors of the navy, merchant marine, and coast guard who had drowned at sea; they later changed this to include all Americans lost at sea.

131 CFA minutes, March 21–22, 1924.

132 CFA minutes, January 7, 1926, 3–6.

133 In A Quest for Grandeur, Sally Kress Tompkins writes: "To Moore, the L'Enfant plan was a public sacred cow used mainly to gain adherence to the 1901 plan, which had supposedly restored L'Enfant's design." In reference to Moore's paraphrasing of Elbert Peets's criticism of the Federal Triangle design (printed in the Washington Sunday Star, February 2, 1930), Tompkins says: "Peets accused the commission and others of lauding [the L'Enfant plan] in public while cutting up in private." Tompkins, A Quest for Grandeur, 57–58.

134 CFA minutes, April 26, 1932, 13. The gallery opened on April 23, 1932.

135 The Smithsonian collection was called the National Gallery of Art until the 1937 bequest by Treasury Secretary Andrew Mellon, when it was renamed the National Collection of Fine Arts. See "About the American Art Museum and the Renwick Gallery: Plans for a Permanent Home," http://americanart.si.edu/visit/about/architecture/plans/, accessed October 15, 2010. CFA minutes, December 16, 1937, 10–15. Charles Borie offered a resolution to the CFA asking for approval of this site (rather than another location on the Mall's north side between 12th and 14th Streets) and also suggesting that it should be designed by a "distinguished architect." The commission readily approved.

136 Eeva-Liisa Pelkonen and Donald Albrecht, eds., Eero Saarinen: Shaping the Future (New Haven, CT: Yale University Press, 2006), 74.

137 CFA minutes, July 20, 1939, exhibit J1, "Personal and Confidential, En Route to Naples," letter from Gilmore Clarke to Frederic A. Delano.

138 CFA minutes, September 15, 1939, exhibit C, letter from Charles Moore to Gilmore Clarke, August 28, 1939.

139 CFA minutes, October 20, 1939, exhibit J1, letter from Gilmore Clarke to Frederic A. Delano, July 22, 1939. Clarke concluded by saying: "Judging from reactions that have come to my attention as the result of publishing the final competition designs, if any attempt is made

to carry out the present Saarinen design on the Mall, the explosion that follows will make the Jefferson Memorial controversy sound like a half-penny firecracker in comparison."

140 Clarke claimed that he had been the one to recommend, directly to the secretary of the Smithsonian, that the Saarinens be considered winners of the competition rather than of a winning design, but the letter to Clarke from Frederic A. Delano suggests that this stipulation had already been included in the competition program. CFA minutes, September 15, 1939, 5.

141 CFA minutes, October 20, 1939, exhibit J, letter from Frederic A. Delano to Gilmore Clarke, October 9, 1939, 1–2. Delano reported that to his surprise Borie had agreed with it and that it was generally approved by others. He added that Edward Bruce, later a member of the CFA, had "fathered the legislation" and had promised to do what he could to get private donations.

142 CFA minutes, December 14, 1939, exhibit I, Frederic A. Delano to Charles L. Borie, chairman, Smithsonian Art Commission, November 25, 1939.

143 Steven McLeod Bedford, *John Russell Pope: Architect of Empire* (New York: Rizzoli, 1998), 192.

144 The site had long been reserved for the George Washington National Memorial, a project by Egerton Swartwout and Evarts Tracy for a massive classical building containing an auditorium and meeting rooms. The project, however, had never raised sufficient money, and after decades of planning only the foundation had been laid.

145 CFA minutes, January 1937.

146 Bedford, *John Russell Pope*, 196.

147 Bedford says they were "enraged." The architects' letter, if not Clarke's, may have been written at the suggestion of Moore himself; Bedford *John Russell Pope*, 194.

148 CFA minutes, April 8, 1937, 4–11.

149 CFA minutes, May 27, 1937, 2–3, Clarke, 4.

150 CFA minutes, May 27, 1937; and Bedford, *John Russell Pope*, 198.

151 CFA minutes, June 21, 1937, 2, letter from Andrew Mellon to Charles Moore, June 16, 1937.

152 CFA minutes, June 21, 1937, 2, letter from Mellon to Moore, June 16, 1937; CFA minutes, June 21, 1937, 3, Pope's statement.

153 CFA minutes, June 21, 1937, 9–10, and exhibit A-1, letter from Andrew Mellon to Charles Moore, June 16, 1937; and exhibit A, letter from John Russell Pope to Trustees, A. W. Mellon Educational and Charitable Trust.

154 Clarke called for "something fresh, something more indicative of Jefferson's character," in a joint meeting of the CFA and the NCP-PC. CFA minutes, March 20, 1937, 20.

WORLD WAR I MEDALS

1 CFA, *Eighth Report*, January 1, 1918–July 1, 1919, 27–28, 32.

2 CFA minutes, April 25, 1919, exhibit E, letter from General Staff of the Army to CFA, March 28, 1919.

3 CFA minutes, November 21, 1919.

4 Service medals, agency seals, and government logos can be submitted by any of the executive departments; today they are primarily developed by the U.S. Army's Institute of Heraldry, established in 1960.

5 CFA minutes May 27–29, 1927, 26.

6 The first design was by the chief engraver of the U.S. Mint, John Sinnock, and the other, the design that was adopted, was developed by two employees of the quartermaster general's office, A. E. DuBois and Elizabeth Will. CFA minutes, May 27–28, 1927, exhibit N, letter from Charles Moore to quartermaster general, May 31, 1927; and CFA minutes, November 8, 1928, exhibit F, letter from Charles Moore to secretary of war, November 12, 1928.

7 CFA minutes, December 6, 1928, include the letter from Senator Hiram Bingham to Charles Moore, November 30, 1928, and the joint letter from Assistant Secretary of War F. Trubee Davison and Assistant Secretary of the Navy Edward P. Warner, December 4, 1928,

which said: "We are peculiarly anxious that its form should be satisfactory…to the less tutored eyes of the associates of those who will win the right to wear the cross." CFA minutes, December 6, 1928, exhibit B, letter from Charles Moore to Senator Hiram Bingham, December 1, 1928.

8 CFA minutes, January 22, 1929, exhibit A, letter from Charles Moore to F. Trubee Davison and Edward P. Warner, January 24, 1929. The commission's evaluation of these small art objects has been noteworthy for the persistence of certain problems since 1921, suggesting a lack of institutional memory in the submitting agencies and certain inadequacies in the training or competence of American artists. The commission had often been displeased with submitted designs. Decade after decade, they admonished agencies to follow one recommendation in particular: Select designers who are skilled in the medallic arts and who will prepare designs that are appropriate for their small size— strong, simple, and clear. The commission had also often faulted agencies for procedural problems, such as the common practice of submitting designs when there was insufficient time to make recommended changes because of the pressure of production deadlines.

ART IN ARCHITECTURE

1 CFA minutes, July 28, 1933, exhibit F, letter from George Biddle to Eleanor Roosevelt describing his request to Franklin Delano Roosevelt; Don Adams and Arlene Goldbard, "New Deal Cultural Programs: Experiments in Cultural Democracy," accessed December 8, 2009, www.wwcd.org/policy/US/newdeal.html. Adams and Goldbard write: "Franklin Delano Roosevelt's New Deal cultural programs marked the U.S. government's first big, direct investment in cultural development."

2 Through all bureaucratic changes, Edward Bruce remained the program's highly popular director. Bruce had left law to devote himself to art, spending six years in Italy studying painting. With this background, Bruce was a natural choice among Treasury staff to head the Section of Fine Arts. Bruce's influence increased through his appointment in January 1940 to replace Charles Moore on the Commission of Fine Arts. He presented many Section projects to the commission, recusing himself from the review. See "Edward Bruce," CFA member files, and Edward Bruce and Forbes Watson, eds., *Art in Federal Buildings: An Illustrated Record of the Treasury Department's New Program in Painting and Sculpture, vol. I: Mural Designs, 1934–1936* (Washington, DC: Art in Federal Buildings Inc., 1936).

3 The Section was renamed the Section of Fine Arts, from 1938 to 1939 and in 1939 was moved from the Treasury to the Federal Works Agency, where it remained in existence until 1943, "History of the New Deal Art Projects," www.wpamurals.com/history.html, accessed December 8, 2009.

4 Information on the project is from Gurney, *Sculpture and the Federal Triangle*, (Washington, DC: Smithsonian Institution Press,1985), 374–402.

5 For this interpretation, see Gurney, *Sculpture*, 401.

SHIPSTEAD-LUCE ACT

1 Sue A. Kohler, *The Commission of Fine Arts: A Brief History, 1910–1995*, (Washington, DC: Government Printing Office, 1996), 74.

ESSAY BY CARROLL WILLIAM WESTFALL

1 William Mullen, "Burnham's Mandala, II: Mandala of the Mall," *American Arts Quarterly* 19, no. 4 (Fall 2009): 55–60.

2 "Alexander Richter's Washington Notes," *Pencil Points* 18 (May 1937): 20. This piece reported that John Russell Pope's proposal had produced a "controversy [that] has divided the city as no other single issue since the Civil War." The story is told in various sources, most extensively in Kathryn Fanning, *American Temples: Presidential*

Memorials of the American Renaissance (PhD diss., University of Virginia, 1996), 177–222; an abbreviated version is in Fanning, "On Kimball and the Jefferson Memorial," *Papers from Fiske Kimball: Creator of an American Architecture: A Symposium* (University of Virginia, Charlottesville, November 19, 1995), www2.lib.virginia.edu/finearts/exhibits/fiske/conference/Fanning.html, accessed 1/12/2010. Others are the following sources: Sue A. Kohler, *The Commission of Fine Arts: A Brief History, 1910–1995* (Washington, DC: Government Printing Office, 1996), 68–74; Hugh Howard, *Dr. Kimball and Mr. Jefferson* (New York: Bloomsbury, 2006), 230–50, who draws on Kimball archives, including those in Philadelphia that I have not consulted; Steven McLeod Bedford, *John Russell Pope: Architect of Empire* (New York: Rizzoli, 1998), 216–22, with reproductions of four proposed schemes, 8:15–18; and Richard Guy Wilson, "High Noon on the Mall," in *The Mall in Washington, 1791–1991*, ed. Richard Longstreth (Washington, DC: National Gallery of Art, 1991), 143–67.

3 CFA minutes, January 18, 1934.

4 The legislation, Public Law 49, 73rd Cong., 1st Sess. (June 26, 1934), charged the commission with "the purpose of considering and formulating plans for designing and constructing a permanent memorial in the city of Washington." It named a site "on the apex block, Constitution and Pennsylvania Avenues," but authorized the CFA to look elsewhere, which it quickly did.

5 After he died on October 5, 1938, his successor as chairman, the commission's executive director Stuart G. Gibboney, a Virginian, a lawyer in New York, and, between 1923 and 1944, the president of the foundation, would say of Boylan, "He was about the best that ever came out of Tammany Hall.... [He] was as fine a type of man as I ever met." Stenographic minutes of the Thomas Jefferson Memorial Commission, March 2, 1939, Papers of Howard W. Smith, Box 267, Accession #8731, Special Collections, University of Virginia Library (hereafter cited TJMC Records). Smith was the Thomas Jefferson Memorial Commission's secretary, and his files became the depository for its business. This cache includes forty-four stunning renderings by Otto Eggers prepared in Pope's office.

6 The other advisory commission, the National Capital Park and Planning Commission, was often represented by its chairman, Frederic A. Delano, the president's uncle. The time and place of the meetings were published, but according to Boylan few attended. House Committee on the Library, *Site for the Thomas Jefferson Memorial*, 75th Cong., 1st Sess., April 27, 1937, 67.

7 TJMC minutes, March 2 and March 24, 1936, TJMC Records. On March 24, the commission established the figure of $3 million as Pope's outside cost. Representative Francis D. Culkin, a member of the commission, recalled later that Charles Moore, then chairman of the CFA, recommended Pope. House Committee on Appropriations, Subcommittee on Deficiency Appropriations, *Second Deficiency Appropriation Bill for 1938, Thomas Jefferson Memorial Commission Hearing*, 75th Cong., 3rd Sess., May 27, 1938, 918–19.

8 A statement to the TJMC by Pope (read into the record by his assistant because Pope was in the hospital) referred to the two in this way: "The great prototypes of these forms are probably best illustrated by two buildings that he [Jefferson] seemed to be most familiar with—the Pantheon in Rome and the Villa Rotunda near Vicenza." Steno record, TJMC minutes, December 1, 1936, Box 265, TJMC Records. A briefer version of these remarks with exterior and interior renderings was published with the comment, "The plan has not yet been released for publication." See "The Proposed Jefferson Memorial," *Pencil Points* 18 (April, 1937): 233–34.

9 TJMC minutes, February 18, 1937, Box 265, TJMC Records, p. 272 for Pantheon, p. 275 for Pope as architect, and p. 275–87 for discussion and approval of the National Park Service as executor of construction; all votes were unanimous. The publication was, among others, in the *New York Times* and the *Washington Post*. The *Magazine of Art*, 30, no. 3 (March 1937): 186, published in Washington, announced the approval with no photo on the same page that it published a rendering of the National Gallery and the news that Walter Gropius had accepted a professorship at Harvard University. See Fanning, *American Temples*, 205–08, for the congressional tempest. The president requested from the Congress authorization for the TJMC to "execute plans" and $500,000 of the expected total cost of $3 million "for commencing construction." *Communication from the President*, 75th Cong., 1st Sess., April 9, 1937, H. Doc. 210.

10 See Fanning, *American Temples*, 215–17, regarding the cherry trees. The outcry about the trees came to a head in late November 1938, even after foundation work on the memorial, reduced and moved to accommodate them, had begun. See extensive press clippings, including Delbert Clark, "Tree Feud Revives Jefferson Art Row," *New York Times*, November 27, 1938, an article reporting that women chained themselves to the trees and that President Roosevelt promised to transplant the women with the trees; compiled in League for Progress in Architecture Records, MS2198, Boxes 2, Special Collections Research Center, The George Washington University (hereafter cited LPA Records). See also letters addressed to the TJMC in Boxes 266 and 268, TJMC Records.

11 TJMC minutes, February 18, 1937, 272, in Box 265, TJMC Records. The commission agreed to reject "anything that is gymnastic," as Commissioner Tumulty put it. It also agreed with Tumulty that "if you open it up to public hearings you will never close it." The sentiment for something utilitarian was certainly in the air, as can be noted in the February 19, 1937, report in the *Washington Post* that "climaxing" weeks of controversy over both the character and location of the structure, a congressional commission had decided on a memorial that was "nonutilitarian, but Jefferson basically designed it himself." LPA Records.

12 TJMC minutes, March 24, 1936, Box 265, TJMC Records.

13 CFA minutes, March 20, 1937, appendix, transcription of joint meeting with the National Capital Park and Planning Commission, 1–47. The reference to the Olmsted memorandum is at p. 32; Clarke's comments are at p. 18. Clarke's complaint is given featured billing in *The Report to the Senate and the House of Representatives concerning the Thomas Jefferson Memorial* (Washington, DC: Commission of Fine Arts, February, 1939), 1–2, exhibit B. Clarke was a Hoover appointee and landscape architect. A Cornell graduate, he joined the Cornell faculty in 1935 and was named dean in 1938. "Gilmore Clarke," CFA member files.

14 CFA minutes, March 20, 1937, 4–5.

15 CFA minutes, April 8, 1937, where the CFA suggested the adaptation. For it, see Roosevelt Memorial Association, *Plan and Design for the Roosevelt Memorial in the City of Washington, John Russell Pope Architect* (New York: The Pynson Printers, Inc., 1925); Fanning, *American Temples*, 147–62; and Bedford, *John Russell Pope*, 215.

16 CFA minutes, March 20, 1937; CFA minutes, February 3, 1938, 8, 11, exhibit F-2, and exhibit F-1, letter from Gilmore Clarke to John J. Boylan, February 5, 1938, in which Clarke states that the commission finds it "would be unfortunate to erect as a Memorial still another Pantheon in Washington enclosing a portrait statue of Jefferson."

17 Frederick Gutheim was also very busy. This informal group organized to fight the memorial kept the press supplied with commentary and organized testimony at congressional hearings. Its papers are in the League for Progress in Architecture Records, which reveal that many whom the league attempted to enlist (there were more than four dozen) declined.

18 House Committee, *Site for the Thomas Jefferson Memorial*, 67. Representative Otha Wearin's House Joint Resolution No. 322 that would require a competition for the Jefferson Memorial occupied the hearing on April 23, 1937. He had made the argument in the House in June, 1936, when the initial appropriation was being sought and reiterated it here at p. 4–6. He also argued for it in "The Competition Principle," American Architect 151 (November 1937): 22–24; and in "Wanted: Competitions for Federal Buildings," *Magazine of Art*

31 (May 1938): 266–67, 314. His proposed resolution was rendered moot after it was realized that there was already a contractual agreement with Pope, but it would resurface a year later; see below. The next several days of the hearings were devoted to questions concerning the site.

The House Committee hearings in April 1937 put on record the objections from professionals in letters addressed to Wearin. These also found other venues for publication. See House Committee, *Site for the Thomas Jefferson Memorial*, 21–27, and LPA Records. Joseph Hudnut, dean of the faculty of design at Harvard, wrote in the *Washington News* on March 3, 1937 that he joins with others in calling for a competition. In the *Washington Post*, April 3, 1937, he wrote that Pope has been dead for six months. "[T]here are at least 100 architects whose talents and professional accomplishments and competence give them an equal right to the consideration of the Commission." A National Competition Committee through William Lescaze as secretary followed this with an endorsement of Hudnut's letter and added the further endorsement of several important schools of architecture including those of Columbia and Princeton. In a letter dated December 1, 1938, Henry S. Churchill, chairman of the National Competitions Committee for Architecture and the Allied Arts, forwarded to Arno Cammerer copies of letters addressed to President Roosevelt with the same message from his committee, from the Sculptors Guild; the American Society of Painters, Sculptors and Gravers; and the College Art Association.

19 *Thomas Jefferson Memorial Site*, 75th Cong., 1st Sess., H. R. 1301 (July 23, 1937).

20 TJMC minutes, Box 268 covering April 20, April 22, and July 13 discussions of modifications with a hiatus in meetings until January 1938, TJMC Records. Present at Boylan's meeting on April 22 were Kimball, Cammerer, and John Nolan from the National Park and Planning Commission; Moore and Clarke from the CFA; John Nagle, superintendent of memorials, National Park Service; and Pope, Higgins, and I. D. Matthews from Pope's office. TJMC minutes, Box 268, April 22, 1937, TJMC Records.

21 Ibid.

22 TJMC minutes, Box 268, TJMC Records. The CFA had commended to the Memorial Commission the report Olmsted had written March 22, 1935. Olmsted's involvement brought balm to the controversy, as Pamela Scott's essay, "The Improvement of Washington City: Charles Moore and Washington's Monumental Core," elsewhere in this volume, suggests. CFA minutes, March 20, 1937, 32ff.

23 This occurred four day before Pope's death, Bedford, *John Russell Pope*, 222; and won the editorial praise of the *Washington Herald* on August 29, House Committee, *Site for the Thomas Jefferson Memorial*, 128–29.

24 Commissioners Culkins and Kimball cited the CFA's change of membership (William F. Lamb and Paul Manship joined the CFA in early 1937) and of chairmen as the whole reason the controversy came about; House Subcommittee, *Second Deficiency Appropriations Bill 1938, Thomas Jefferson Memorial Commission*, 918–19.

25 CFA minutes, September 29, 1937, 5.

26 Attending the meeting were Delano for the National Capital Park and Planning Commission; Cammerer and H. Paul Caemmerer from the CFA; and Eggers and two others (Nagel and Young) from Pope's office; TJMC minutes, Box 268, TJMC Records; and CFA minutes, February 3, 1938, exhibit F-1, letter from Gilmore Clarke to John J. Boylan.

27 CFA minutes, February 3, 1938; it includes the concurrence about the site from the NCPPC, which expressed its unanimous opinion "that the architectural base of the memorial should come to the water's edge on its northern site." It also includes a letter and memoranda dated February 5 from Clarke advocating the split colonnades scheme.

28 CFA minutes, February 17, 1938. Clarke, Borie, Shepley, Lamb, and Manship "all spoke in favor of the semicircular colonnade."

29 Ibid. See also the chronology in House Subcommittee, *Second Deficiency Appropriations Bill 1938, Thomas Jefferson Memorial Com-*

mission, 921; and Kimball's testimony on p. 930; and on p. 931, Kimball's referral to it as "looking like the entrance to a real estate development, with glorified gate posts." Boylan must have found it ironic that he had worked vigorously to squash using that site for the Theodore Roosevelt memorial in order to make it available at some future time for a memorial to Jefferson only to have its reappearance recommended with a new dedication. Fanning, *American Temples*, 158.

30 Kimball's handwritten notes reveal his anger; and a letter from Stuart Gibboney to Kimball on March 8 commented: "Hell broke loose from an unexpected quarter, namely, Mrs. Pope." Jefferson Memorial Commission Folder, 1938 (Jan.–May), papers of Marie Goebel Kimball, Box 12, Accession #5232, Special Collections, University of Virginia Library (hereafter cited "Marie Kimball Folder" and Marie Kimball MSS."

31 Delano would later report that he "talked with Mrs. Pope for 20 minutes about the segmental colonnade scheme . . . but she refused to allow it to be used." The commission has "heard that if they do so Mrs. Pope will give information to the press and say the design was stolen." See CFA minutes, March 24, 1938, 14. Kimball had Clarke have Moore, "an old friend of the Pope family," intercede. See Commission of Fine Arts, *Report to the Senate and the House*, 7. On March 16, 1938, Clarke relayed to Kimball in a letter Moore's telegram reciting his lack of success: "I hope my complete failure to win Mrs. Pope over will disappoint you no more than it does me." Marie Kimball Folder, Marie Kimball MSS.

32 CFA minutes, March 24, 1938, 11ff and addendum, March 29, 1938.

33 Neither Kimball nor Gibboney would agree to go to the meeting, so the task fell to the executive officer Arno Cammerer. TJMC minutes, March 22, 1938, TJMC Records; CFA minutes, March 24, 1938. In a letter to Gibboney, March 26, 1938, mentioning the suggestion of a planetarium opposite the National Archives building and responding by suggesting an aquarium at the Great Falls of the Potomac, Kimball opined that their "absurdity . . . show[s] they are in a last ditch of bewildered desperation," Marie Kimball Folder, Marie Kimball MSS.

34 *Communication from the President*, 75th Cong., 3rd Sess., April 1, 1938, H. Doc. 567; House Subcommittee, *Second Deficiency Appropriations Bill 1938*, Thomas Jefferson Memorial Commission, 921.

35 "The publicity recently given to the fact that the CFA had not approved the design which is being recommended by the Thomas Jefferson Memorial Commission was regarded as a good step and the action of the Chairman in this matter was commended." CFA minutes, May 7, 1938. In Congress, Representative Ortha Wearin of Iowa led the opposition with a bill, H.R. 10217, requiring that the memorial commission be disbanded and that the chairmen of the National Capital Park and Planning Commission and of the CFA and the supervising architect of the Department of the Treasury constitute a commission to conduct a competition. H. P. Caemmerer, secretary of CFA, reported that the commission "heartily" endorsed the bill. House Committee on the Library, *Thomas Jefferson Memorial*, 75th Cong., 3rd Sess. H. R. 2489, 5, (May 26, 1938). The report's language was vicious: it "would be a national eyesore," "quite unworthy," a "travesty," "merely a replica of the center of [Pope's] National Gallery of Art, and "a toadstool on the meadow."

36 Edward Alden Jewell, "Capital Architecture," April 18, 1937, LPA Records (the clipping in the LPA carries a different title).

37 Kohler, *A Brief History*, 43.

38 Henry-Russell Hitchcock, *Modern Architecture: Romanticism and Reintegration* (New York: Payson and Clarke, 1929), 103. A 1932 poll conducted among fifty architects put the Folger in tenth place (the Lincoln Memorial was first); "What are the Outstanding Buildings?," *The Federal Architect* 2, no. 4 (April 1932): 7–10. A 1948 poll of five hundred architects put the Folger in first place. Edwin Bateman Morris, "What Buildings Give You a Thrill?," *Journal of the American Institute of Architects* x, no. 6 (December 1948): 272–7.

These polls are referred to, and the building is discussed, in Richard Guy Wilson, "Modernized Classicism and Washington, D.C.," in *American Public Architecture: European Roots and Native Expressions,* ed. Craig Zabel and Susan Scott Munshower, Papers in Art History from the Pennsylvania State University, vol. 5 (University Park, PA: Pennsylvania State University, 1989), 272–303.

39 Hitchcock, *Modern Architecture,* 208.

40 For the preparation of the purgation, see Marie Frank, "The Theory of Pure Design and American Architectural Education in the Early Twentieth Century" *Journal of the Society of Architectural Historians* 67 (2008): 248–273. The purge was incomplete, although the content's identity could be transient, as seen when later in the century classicism came to be associated with totalitarianism and modernism with democratic liberalism. Consider the detailed review of the political battles in Los Angeles stemming from identifying modernist art with anti-American communism in the McCarthy era; Sarah Schrank, *Art and the City: Civic Imagination and Cultural Authority in Los Angeles* (Philadelphia: University of Pennsylvania Press, 2009), chapter 3. The identity of modernist architecture with collectivist social reform remained explicit well into the twentieth century. In the general strike conducted by the three major labor unions in a rare joint undertaking in Italy in 1970, the wall posters plastered on walls in Rome that presented their social demands used as its background Le Corbusier's Unité de Habitation set in a verdant landscape. See also Terence Riley, *"The International Style," Exhibition 15, and the Museum of Modern Art* (New York: Rizzoli, 1992).

41 Giedion's *Space, Time, and Architecture,* which is still in print is based on his lectures at Harvard in 1938 and 1939.

42 A sample from LPA clippings: Frank Lloyd Wright: "[S]hameful ... one more miscarriage of grace ... arrogant insult" to Jefferson; *Washington Herald,* April 4, 1937; and "Had [Jefferson] lived until now we would not find his face turned toward the rear to encourage the gangrene of sentimentality his mind closed to the superb achievement of the scientific art of building," *Washington News,* April 3, 1937. Other objectors in various venues included Carroll Meiggs; Marquis W. Childs; Harold Sterner; Milton Horn, representing himself, the Society of American Sculptors, and the Society of American Painters, Sculptors, and Engravers; Gutheim; Designers of Shelter in America; and the painter Max Weber. Also weighing in were Alfred H. Baar Jr., Eli Jacques Kahn, and most of the faculty at Columbia University: "[A] lamentable misfit both in time and place," *Washington Post,* April 2, 1937. Furthermore, eight modernists (Catherine Bauer, Henry S. Churchill, Carl Feiss, Talbot Hamlin, Hudnut, Lescaze, Lewis Mumford, and William Zorach) signed a letter, "The Jefferson Memorial," *The New Republic* 90 (April 7, 1937), 265–66.

43 "Twilight of the Gods," *Magazine of Art,* 30 (1937): 480–84, 522–24. Also representative: Pope's proposed memorial "is aesthetically intolerable, is inappropriate to Jefferson, and does not express our own age." Voices from outside included that of Eames MacVeagh, son of Franklin MacVeagh, President Taft's secretary of the Treasury, who said through the *Washington Star,* March 18, 1937, that the CFA was dominated by the "reactionary," Charles Moore. "We are living in a transcendental era, and we should have architecture to interpret this epoch. We now have in Washington a petrified forest of Greek and Roman columns ... [a] kind of Roman Forum ... [it should] be entirely modern in the simplicity of its lines" and have "smooth surfaces." The Folger Library is an example. Four days later, the same newspaper reported him as saying that in the past, the CFA did good work but "to stand still is to go backward." He repeated much of this in his testimony in the House hearings. See *Washington Star* in LPA Records, and House Committee, *Thomas Jefferson Memorial,* H.R. 2489.

44 This is the common understanding on the topic; Wilson's is the most prominent example. Richard Guy Wilson, *The American Renaissance, 1876–1917,* (New York: The Brooklyn Museum and Pantheon Books, 1979), 12, 70. Wilson has argued, "The American Renaissance, by

both definition and action, was intensely nationalistic.... America became the culmination of history for an age that believed in progress." But it had run its course by 1917.

45 Notes indicate that discussions about whom to hire occurred on March 22, 1938. Folder "Statements," Box 12, Marie Kimball MSS. In a letter of April 14, 1938, Kimball reported to Gibboney that Hamilton Wright, the New York publicist, "will be in this thing on our behalf with both feet." Kimball later reported to Wright that Gibboney had had a long talk at the White House with Charles Michelson, chairman of the Democratic National Committee, who was to be kept informed and who said it would be a mistake to make this a partisan issue. Kimball agreed. Letters of April 14 and May 27, 1938, Marie Kimball MSS.

46 The bill passed two-to-one. It did not hurt that Sam Rayburn, Majority Leader in the House, would write to Gibboney on May 2, 1938, "I am doing all I can to bring about the building of this memorial." Marie Kimball Folder, Marie Kimball MSS. The first funding covered only the pile foundations. Even as they were being driven, opponents sought to thwart the project by pleading for a competition for a different building to be raised on them. The CFA advocated that the domeless colonnade be built on the foundation, but Eggers in a letter to the memorial commission pointed out that it would not fit and "might well give the impression of a glorified confining cage of the columns for a statue of Thomas Jefferson." Letter dated March 11, 1939, Box 265, TJMC Records.

47 House Subcommittee, *Second Deficiency Appropriations Bill 1938, Thomas Jefferson Memorial Commission,* 915.

48 Fiske Kimball, *American Architecture* (Indianapolis and New York: Bobbs-Merrill, 1928), 69–70.

49 Ibid., 71.

50 Ibid. Earlier Kimball had written this about the architecture of the American colonies: There were "local dialects," but "the ideal of the Colonial style remained always in conformity to current English usage.... A truly American contribution to architectural style appeared only after the Revolution, and then it assumed a historical importance which has been little recognized." Kimball, *Domestic Architecture of the American Colonies and of the Early Republic* (New York: Scribner's, 1922), 141. See also Kimball, "The Restoration of Colonial Williamsburg in Virginia," *Architectural Record* 78, no. 6 (December, 1935), published as a separate book, (New York: *Architectural Record,* 1935), 359.

51 Kimball, *American Architecture,* 75.

52 Ibid., 159–163

53 Ibid., chapter XIII, "The Triumph of Classical Form," 187.

54 Ibid., 203, and chapter XIV. Henry-Russell Hitchcock, *Modern Architecture: Romanticism and Reintegration* (New York: Payson and Clarke, 1929), 116–18, 218ff, also stressed the role of founders of cycles, in which successors had diminished vigor, but his founders launched a new tradition rather than invigorating a tradition they inherited. Otherwise in disagreement, they agreed that Wright did not stand at the head of a tradition or of a cycle.

55 Kimball, *American Architecture,* 209.

56 Richard Oliver, *Bertram Grosvenor Goodhue* (Cambridge, MA, and London: MIT Press, 1983), 178 and 273n 4, presents critical comments from the CFA minutes, December 21, 1917. Wilson, "High Noon," 156–57, discusses the dispute and its context.

57 See Kohler, *A Brief History,* 74, for the Archives. The word "enthusiastically" is in Wilson, "High Noon," 158. In April, 1932, the CFA characterized the Folger "as 'somewhat modern [-istic is crossed out in the minutes] but ... designed as a building which should be considered of the classical order." Richard Guy Wilson, "Modernized Classicism and Washington, D.C.," in Zabel and Munshower, *American Public Architecture,* 272–303. Cret would be a member of the commission between 1940 and 1945. Kimball's judgment on Goodhue is in *American Architecture,* 209.

58 TJMC minutes, March 24, 1936, 234–36, TJMC Records. Kimball points out here that he had "never met Mr. Pope before I urged him on this Commission." Boylan would later put it this way: "If you are ill you get the best specialist you can." House Committee, *Site for the Thomas Jefferson Memorial*, 69. The only person Kimball might have considered was Arthur Brown Jr. who shared a birth year with Pope. Swartwout, who was four years older, would later observe in a letter of April 19, 1937, to Charles Moore, that those "who were opposed to the design . . . were 'architects and engineers that were on relief. Nobody of consequence at all, but they make a great deal of noise like all minorities.'" Quoted without indication of source in Bedford, *John Russell Pope*, 222.

59 Marquis W. Childs, "Mr. Pope's Memorial," *Magazine of Art* 30, no. 4 (April 1937): 200–02, who also gives Boylan's opinion. LPA files include other expressions of approval. Examples can be found in letters from Archibald Manning Brown, head of the Architecture League of New York; Julian Clarence Levi, former head of the League; A. A. Weinman, sculptor ("any other style of architecture would be 'ruinous to the Tidal Basin set-up'"); James Earle Frazer, member of the CFA with Pope under President Wilson; Lawrence White of McKim, Mead, & White; William H. MacMurray, an associate of Harvey Wiley Corbett; and James Gamble Rogers in a letter in the *New York Times* April 4, 1937. Pope's *Washington Post* obituary intoned, "It is the mode in some circles today to deprecate his borrowings from the ancient. No 'American' design, however, has yet qualified as an equal substitute in this city." In the *Washington Post* March 20, 1938, Waddy Wood asked, who could beat out Pope in a competition?

60 CFA minutes, September 29, 1938, exhibit G, letter from Gilmore Clarke to Franklin D. Roosevelt, October 1, 1938 (emphasis added). Backing him was a resolution from the Committee on Architecture and Industrial Art of the Museum of Modern Art that reiterated the now-familiar criticism and added that the "design was repeatedly disapproved by those authorities—the CFA and the National Park and Planning Commission—which are specifically authorized to represent in Washington the professions of architecture, landscape architecture, city planning, sculpture and painting." The resolution misspoke when it included the National Capital Park and Planning Commission, which never passed on the building and approved the site while making suggestions about its modification. The signatories were a who's who of modernism: Alfred H. Barr Jr., T. D. Mabry, J. McAndrews, Philip Goodwin, Winslow Ames, Catherine Bauer, John Coolidge, Carl Feiss, Talbot Hamlin, Henry-Russell Hitchcock, Joseph Hudnut, Edgar Kaufmann Jr., George Nelson, and Stamo Papadaki. Undated copy (its being addressed to Representative Edward T. Taylor, chairman of the appropriations committee, suggests March 1938), Box 267, TJMC Records.

61 House Committee, *Site for the Thomas Jefferson Memorial*, 68.

62 "In Defense of the Jefferson Memorial," *Magazine of Art* 30 (June 1937): 362–65. This Pope was unrelated to the architect. Reactions by Milton Horn and Frederick Gutheim appeared in appeared in the same article, pp. 400–02.

63 House Subcommittee, *Second Deficiency Appropriations Bill 1938, Thomas Jefferson Memorial Commission*, 915.

64 Ibid., 926.

65 The doctrine of imitation is so distant from current understandings, it is difficult to recover it. James Ackerman, "Imitation," in *Origins, Imitation, Conventions* (Cambridge, MA, and London: MIT Press, 2002) 125–42, presents a brief, clear-headed essay juxtaposing the older way of thinking about buildings as products of imitation against current historiographical orthodoxy that seeks influences. In seeing critics, historians, artists, and architects shifting in tandem from imitation to influence throughout the western tradition ever since the doctrine was promulgated in the Enlightenment, he follows current orthodoxy. But as the present study makes clear, that view did not gain a prominent footing in the United States until the 1930s, when

the confrontation produced the controversy that "divided the city as no other single issue since the Civil War."

66 Kimball, *American Architecture*, 172.

67 The reference to the friendship is in a later letter in the *Magazine of Art* 31 (May 1938): 315–17. In it Kimball pointed out that he was the first "to celebrate" Wright's achievement, citing his 1917 general history of architecture. In response to this letter the Commission of Fine Arts suggested skullduggery by the memorial commission: "Facts from the Fine Arts Commission," *Magazine of Art* 31 (June, 1938): 348–49 and 372–74; with separate responses from Hudnut and Wright, p. 368. In a letter to the *New York Times* on April 17, 1938, Kimball had expressed his admiration for Wright; a typewritten copy titled "Facts about the Proposed Site and Design For Jefferson Memorial" is in Box 265, TJMC Records.

68 Fiske Kimball, "John Russell Pope, 1874–1937," *American Architect* 151 (October 1937): 87. In Marie Kimball Folder, "Statements," Marie Kimball MSS. (See also the excellent summary by Howard, *Dr. Kimball*, 245–46. As he notes, this "obituary (nay, essay) . . . emerged in an outpouring, as few scratchouts marred the flow of his handwriting" and uncharacteristically with "even fewer edits" in the typescript and proofs.) Responses to Kimball came from Hudnut: "Has he considered that the alternative to a bad piece of architecture is a good piece of architecture? [It is] a bumptious replica of that insufferable monument [the Roman Pantheon]." In other words, have a competition! Wright also responded: "The sort of special pleading Fiske Kimball addresses to the timorous reactionaries of our time is painfully familiar to me." *Magazine of Art* 31 (June 1938): 368.

69 Kimball, letter, *Magazine of Art* 31 (May 1938): 315–17. In using the term "petrified forest" Kimball is borrowing from the opponents' rhetoric. It appears often in LPA material.

70 Gilmore Clarke added, "as architectural designs are simplified, we make room for rich embellishment by sculptor and by painter" that will "tend to make them wholly American in flavor," clearly a job that architecture no longer needed to do. Kohler, *A Brief History*, 45. Well after he had left the commission, he wrote that, when we see the Kennedy Center, the L'Enfant Plaza, the Air and Space Museum, and the Hirshhorn Museum, we "witness Washington being 'violated by illiterate vandals.'" Letter, *Washington Post*, April 26, 1973, quoting Wolf von Eckhardt, architecture critic of the *Washington Post*.

71 Letter, *Washington Post*, A31.

72 Fiske Kimball, *The Creation of the Rococo* (Philadelphia: Philadelphia Museum of Art, 1943), 6–7. In addition to Wölfflin's mechanistic Hegelianism, Kimball would surely have found repugnant his dependence on racial explanations, a not uncommon heuristic tool in German art historical literature before Hitler gave new meaning to racial interpretations. See for example Heinrich Wölfflin, *Die Kunst der Renaissance: Italien und das deutsche Formgefühl* (Munich: F. Bruckmann, 1931), translated by Alice Muehsam and Norma A. Shatan as *The Sense of Form in Art: A Comparative Psychological Study* (New York: Chelsea Publishing Co., 1958), and Wölfflin's largely neglected *Gedanken zur Kunstgeschichte, Gedrucktes und Ungedrucktes* (Basel: Schwabe, 1941). Giedion had earlier applied Hegelianism to the successor style of the Rococo in his *Spätbarocker und romantischer Klassizismus* (Munich: F. Bruckmann, 1922).

CHAPTER IV

1 During his years on the commission, Gilmore Clarke also served as dean of the College of Architecture at Cornell University (1935–50) and from 1939 maintained an active landscape and civil engineering practice in New York with landscape architect Michael Rapuano (CFA 1958–62). Their firm was responsible for the design of the Henry Hudson River Parkway, the restoration of Central and Bryant Parks, and the plan for Mammoth Hot Springs, and Clarke also con-

sulted on the United Nations project. He was active in the national and the New York state chapter of the American Society of Landscape Architects and in many other professional organizations, including, like so many other commission members, the American Academy in Rome.

2   Clarke had a particular interest in the design of stone-clad concrete bridges for parkway landscapes; see Domenico Annese, "Gilmore David Clarke," in *Pioneers of American Landscape Design,* ed. Charles A. Birnbaum, FASLA, and Robin Karson (New York: McGraw-Hill, 2000), 56. See also the material in Clarke's file at the CFA, particularly his obituary from the *Washington Post,* August 11, 1982. Clarke was supervisor of construction for the Bronx River Parkway (1916–23, landscape architect Herman Merkel). The success of this project led to the establishment of the Westchester County Park Commission in 1922, with Clarke placed in charge of its Department of Planning, Landscape, and Architecture Design: "By 1934 the commission had completed a system of parks and parkways unparalleled in the United States, indeed in the world," (Domenico Annese, "Gilmore David Clarke," in Birnbaum and Karson, *Pioneers,* 56).

3   During World War I, Clarke served with the American army in France, rising to the rank of captain; for many years he had the rank of major in the Army Reserve, Corps of Engineers, and he used this as his title. Typescript commendation of Clarke, "Gilmore D. Clarke," CFA member files, undated.

4   The Joint Committee included representatives from the American Planning and Civic Association, the American Institute of Architects, the Garden Club of America, the National Society of Mural Painters, the American Institute of Planning, etc. Gilmore D. Clarke, "Aesthetic Standards for the National Capital" address delivered before the members and guests of the Joint Committee on the National Capital, Washington, D.C., Friday, February 18, 1944.

5   Pamela Scott and Antoinette J. Lee, *Buildings of the District of Columbia* (New York: Oxford University Press, 1993), 235.

6   CFA minutes, September 29, 1938, exhibit F, letter from Frederic Delano to Gilmore Clarke defending the fishbone plan in comparison with the open-court type.

7   Another Klauder building was the Railroad Retirement building, south of the Social Security building.

8   CFA minutes, July 28, 1938, 8.

9   CFA minutes, August 10, 1938, "Central Composition," 11.

10   CFA minutes, July 28, 1938; CFA minutes, August 10, 1938, exhibit D1, letter from Gilmore Clarke to Louis Simon, August 12, 1938; and CFA minutes, November 8, 1940. The former Social Security building is now called the Wilbur J. Cohen Federal Building and houses the Voice of America.

11   CFA minutes, November 8, 1940, 8.

12   Manship's comments can be found in CFA minutes, January 19, 1940, exhibit P, letter from Gilmore Clarke to Edward Bruce, January 31, 1940; and CFA minutes, November 8, 1940, 7, report from Paul Manship to Gilmore Clarke, October 16, 1940.

13   Charles Moore, ed., *The Improvement of the Park System of the District of Columbia* (Washington, DC: Government Printing Office, 1902), 59.

14   CFA minutes, August 1, 1941, exhibit B, "Memorandum for the Press," 2, from recommendations submitted by the CFA to Major General Harry L. Rogers, Quartermaster General, U.S. Army, reprinted in *Ninth Report of the National Commission of Fine Arts, July 1, 1919, to June 30, 1921* (Washington, DC: Government Printing Office, 1921),115–19.

15   See the full and lively account of the battle in Steve Vogel, *The Pentagon: A History* (New York: Random House, 2007), 60–119. On Clarke as a "firebrand" during the controversy, see Vogel, p. 72. Clarke also loathed the design, calling it a "bull's eye" and "about as bad a plan as could be designed"; see Vogel, p. 73, citing NCPPC minutes, August 1, 1941.

16   Vogel, *The Pentagon,* 73.

17   CFA minutes, August 1, 1941, exhibit B, 2.

18   CFA minutes, August 1, 1941, and exhibit B, 3. Presciently, the CFA added: "We are sure that there are other and better solutions to this particular problem which, incidentally, might result in decentralizing the offices of the Army to prevent that remote possibility of wiping out the whole establishment incident to the dropping of two or three bombs."

19   Vogel, *The Pentagon,* 79–81.

20   Ibid., 77. Clarke's informant was Jay Downer, his frequent collaborator on parkway projects and now a consultant with the Public Roads Administration.

21   Ibid., 90.

22   Roosevelt's decision about cutting the number of employees resulted from a meeting with his budget director, Harold Smith, and his uncle, NCPPC chairman Frederic A. Delano; see Vogel, *The Pentagon,* 71–72, 74. On the trip, see Vogel, 100–101. The representative of NCPPC was Jay Downer.

23   CFA minutes, September 2, 1941; and CFA minutes, September 18, 1941, and October 18, 1941.

24   CFA minutes, September 2, 1941, exhibit A; and CFA minutes, September 2, 1941, exhibit B.

25   The Office of the Supervising Architect was originally part of the Treasury Department; it was transferred to the Public Buildings Administration of the Federal Works Agency in 1940 and then to the Public Buildings Service of the General Services Administration after that agency was established in 1949.

26   James M. Goode, *Washington Sculpture: A Cultural History of Outdoor Sculpture in the Nation's Capital* (Baltimore, MD: Johns Hopkins University Press, 2008), 253.

27   CFA minutes, June 19, 1947.

28   CFA minutes, June 14, 1956, 15.

29   See David Brinkley, *Washington Goes to War* (New York: Knopf, 1988), 227. Brinkley writes that the population of the District of Columbia almost doubled between 1940, when it was 663,091, and 1945; the 1950 census records the population as 802,178.

30   CFA minutes, March 17, 1941, exhibit A, letter from Gilmore Clarke to Louis A. Simon, March 19, 1941.

31   CFA minutes, November 8, 1940, 5.

32   U.S. Commission of Fine Arts, *Report on War Memorials* (Washington, DC: Government Printing Office, 1947).

33   The tract had been acquired following World War I by Avon M. Nevius, a clerk in Washington's Riggs Bank. Historic documents suggest that Lieutenant Colonel C. O. Sherrill, secretary of the CFA from 1921 to 1922 and the first executive officer of the National Capital Park Commission, was involved with Nevius in these transactions, and that they intended to keep the land out of speculative development until it could be sold to the federal government. See George Kennedy, "Mr. Nevius Had a Sharp Eye for Scenery—and It Paid Off," *Evening Star,* August 26, 1951; Raymond L. Freeman, "Land Adjacent to Nevius Tract," March 19, 1959, unpublished historical timeline, Box 29, Folder 1460/Nevius Tract, File 66A-1097, Federal Records Center (hereafter cited as FRC 1460-1; box has been transferred to National Park Service Records, Memorials Liaison Office, Lands, Resources and Planning Division, National Capital Region, National Park Service); and Land Record 91 in Land Records files, Lands, Resources and Planning Division, National Capital Region, National Park Service. Other serious development proposals for the Nevius Tract were a Veterans Administration hospital and a private apartment block.

34   This section is based in part on Kay Fanning, *Arlington Ridge Park, George Washington Memorial Parkway, Cultural Landscape Inventory* (Washington, DC: Department of the Interior, National Park Service, 2002, rev. 2003).

35   Karal Ann Marling and John Wetenhall, *Iwo Jima: Monuments, Memories, and the American Hero* (Cambridge, MA: Harvard Universi-

ty Press, 1991), 89–92; and Fanning, *Arlington Ridge Park,* Part 1, 18, and Part 2b, 2, 5.

36 CFA minutes, February 22, 1946, exhibit C1, letter from Gilmore Clarke to Representative Fritz G. Lanham, March 4, 1946.

37 Fanning, *Arlington Ridge Park,* Part 2b, 5.

38 CFA minutes, August 28, 1947; and October 29–30, 1947, and exhibit H3, letter from Gilmore Clarke to Colonel Frank Halford, USMC, Marine Corps League, October 30, 1947.

39 CFA minutes, October 29–30, 1947, and exhibit H, letter from B. H. Griffin, airport administrator, Washington National Airport, to Gilmore Clarke, September 9, 1947; and CFA minutes, November 25, 1947.

40 CFA minutes, November 25, 1947, exhibit D, letter from Gilmore Clarke to General A. A. Vandegrift, Commandant of Marine Corps, December 2, 1947.

41 CFA minutes, January 10, 1952, 10–12 (Finley on p. 11, Hudnut on p. 12).

42 Fanning, *Arlington Ridge Park,* Part 2b, 8; and CFA minutes, March 11, 1954.

43 Fanning, *Arlington Ridge Park,* Part 2b, 10, and Part 3b, 13.

44 CFA minutes, September 10, 1940. On changes to the statues' material, see also CFA minutes, May 28, 1936; and CFA minutes, November 6, 1937. See also Goode, *Washington Sculpture,* 514.

45 Fanning, *Arlington Ridge Park,* Part 2b, 7; and CFA minutes, April 8, 1954, exhibit H, 3, and May 6, 1954.

46 CFA minutes, January 28, 1954; and CFA minutes, March 11, 1954, exhibit G, "Notes on Design Criteria for the Nevius Tract Prepared by Elbert Peets," 1, 3.

47 CFA minutes, January 24, 1957; and David Finley to Conrad Wirth, April 23, 1957, FRC 1460-1.

48 Orme Lewis, assistant secretary of the interior, to A. L. Miller, chairman, Committee on Interior and Insular Affairs, House of Representatives, December 22, 1953, FRC 1460-1; and William M. Haussmann to Harry T. Thompson, September 27, 1954, Nevius Tract, and Harry T. Thompson to Horace Peaslee, January 14, 1954, Box 8, Folder 1430 (unlabeled, with letters on concessions, ceremonies, etc.), File 66A-1097, Federal Records Center, now located in National Park Service Records, Memorials Liaison Office, Lands, Resources and Planning Division, National Capital Region, National Park Service. The Freedom Shrine probably originated with a 1940s proposal by architect Eric Gugler and First Lady Eleanor Roosevelt for the "Hall of our History," intended for Warm Springs, Georgia, the location of Franklin D. Roosevelt's rehabilitation hospital for polio patients. Fanning, *Arlington Ridge Park,* Part 2b, 8.

49 Ironically, Gilmore Clarke designed the landscape after being abruptly dismissed from the Commission of Fine Arts four years earlier and after his years of leading the fight to keep the Virginia land open. CFA minutes, July 8, 1959, exhibit J, "unduly crowded"; and CFA minutes, August 19, 1959, exhibit A, David E. Finley to Senator Gordon Allott, August 19, 1959.

50 CFA minutes, August 28, 1947, 5, and exhibit F, letter from Gilmore Clarke to Howell G. Crim, August 28, 1947.

51 CFA minutes, October 29–30, 1947, exhibit B, Memorandum for the Commission, September 23, 1947.

52 CFA minutes, November 25, 1947, exhibit A, letter from Gilmore Clarke (for the CFA) to President Truman, November 26, 1947.

53 CFA minutes, January 14, 1948, exhibit C, Truman to Clarke, December 2, 1947.

54 CFA minutes, January 14, 1948, exhibit C, Clarke to Truman, December 15, 1947; and CFA minutes, January 14, 1948, exhibit C, Truman to Clarke, December 19, 1947.

55 CFA minutes, January 14, 1948, exhibit C, "Memo for the Press," January 5, 1948; "That White House Balcony," *Washington Star,* January 4, 1948; and "By-Passing the Commission," *Washington Star,* January 6, 1948.

56 "Mr. Truman's Taste," *Washington Post,* January 12, 1948; "White House Porch," *New York Times,* January 6, 1948; and "The Truman Balcony," *New York Herald Tribune,* January 6, 1948.

57 Much of the material removed from the White House found its way into the hands of the public through the White House Mementos Project, established by the Commission on the Renovation of the Executive Mansion. From January through November 1951, some 30,000 kits of authenticated material taken from the White House—offered in combinations of brick, wood, and even nails—were distributed to members of the public who had requested the souvenirs. See William G. Allman, "To Own a Piece of the White House: The Souvenir Program of the Truman Renovation," *White House History, Collection Set 1* (2004): 301–7.

58 Robert J. Lewis, "Finley Favors Downtown Subway," *Washington Star,* March 31, 1963. On Finley, see David A. Doheny, *David E. Finley: Statesman of the Arts* (Washington, DC: National Trust for Historic Preservation, 1999) and Doheny, *David E. Finley: Quiet Force for America's Arts* (Washington, DC: National Trust for Historic Preservation, 2006).

59 Robert J. Lewis, *Washington Star,* March 31, 1963.

60 However, Hudnut and Gropius were not completely in accord; for a history of their complex interactions over the Graduate School of Design at Harvard, see Jill Pearlman, "Joseph Hudnut's Other Modernism at the 'Harvard Bauhaus,'" *Journal of the Society of Architectural Historians* 56 (December 1997): 452–77; and Jill Pearlman, *Inventing American Architecture: Joseph Hudnut, Walter Gropius, and the Bauhaus Legacy at Harvard* (Charlottesville: University of Virginia Press, 2007).

61 Information from material in CFA staff file, "Linton Wilson," including Linton obituary, "Linton Wilson, Arts Board Aide," *Washington Post and Times-Herald,* August 27, 1966, B6.

62 The surveying and plat were completed on February 27, 1752; the town was bounded by Thomas Jefferson at Frederick (34th), and Prospect Streets.

63 Historically, the "heights" of Georgetown extended from West (now P) Street to Mount Alban.

64 Etta Taggart founded the Progressive Citizens Association of Georgetown in 1926 to promote the interests of Georgetown residents in response to the business-oriented Georgetown Citizens' Association established in 1899. The two organizations merged in 1963 to form the Citizens Association of Georgetown.

65 See Eve L. Barsoum, "Colonial Georgetown: The Power of Myth," in *Re-creating the American Past: Essays on the Colonial Revival,* ed. Richard Guy Wilson, Shaun Eyring, and Kenny Marotta (Charlottesville: University of Virginia Press, 2006), 180–99.

66 The house, built in 1795 by Thomas Clarke, was located at 3516 M Street. Francis Scott Key (1780–1843) and his family lived there from approximately 1805 to 1830; a one-story wing served as Key's law office until his death. Although the house was greatly altered in the late nineteenth and early twentieth centuries, Key's fame as the author of *The Star-Spangled Banner* resulted in a significant outcry at the proposed demolition to make way for a Whitehurst Freeway ramp. Accordingly, the house was dismantled in 1947 to allow for later reconstruction or the reuse of the materials; however, the storage disappeared in the following decades.

67 See "Georgetown 'Charm' Balloons Realty Prices," *The Christian Science Monitor,* May 28, 1943, 3; and Henry Pringle and Katherine Pringle, "Georgetown on the Potomac," Saturday Evening Post, March 20, 1948, 33.

68 Charleston, South Carolina, was the first historic district in the nation (1931), followed by the Vieux Carré in New Orleans in 1936, Alexandria, Virginia, in 1946, and Old Salem, North Carolina, in 1948.

69 The National Council merged with the National Trust for Historic Preservation in 1954. Finley also had been elected chairman of the board of trustees of the National Trust at its initial meeting in May

1950, following the federal legislation establishing the private, non-profit organization in October 1949.

70 CFA minutes, June 21, 1949, exhibit I-1.

71 William Wurster to Gilmore Clarke, August 5, 1949; Clarke to David Finley, August 9, 1949; Finley to Clarke, August 18, 1949, Container 5, Folder 1947–1949, David E. Finley Papers, Manuscripts Division, Library of Congress (hereafter cited as Finley MSS).

72 H. P. Caemmerer to Finley, September 14, 1949, Container 5, Folder 1947–1949, Finley MSS.

73 CFA "Georgetown Files," letter from Gilmore Clarke to Director, Bureau of the Budget, Executive Office, October 31, 1949.

74 House Committee on the District of Columbia, Subcommittee on the Judiciary, *To Regulate the Height, Exterior Design, and Construction of Private and Semipublic Buildings in the Georgetown Area of the National Capital: Hearings on H.R. 7670,* 81st Cong., 2nd Sess. (1950), 4.

75 House Committee on the District of Columbia, *To Regulate the Height,* 67. Mount Zion Methodist Church, founded in 1816, was located at 1334 29th Street. Restrictive covenants on residential property—typically based on race or religion—had been commonplace in Washington neighborhoods until declared unenforceable by the U.S. Supreme Court in 1948 in *Shelley v. Kraemer.*

76 Macomber worked at Williamsburg from 1928 to 1934 and at Mount Vernon from 1941 to 1974. Winslow was the White House architect from 1933 to 1953. Foster also lived in Georgetown.

77 Katherine Gibbs, D.C. Registration #437, October 2, 1942. She received her B.Arch. from Smith College, which at that time was associated with the Cambridge School of Domestic Architecture and Landscape Architecture.

78 George Kennedy, "Georgetown Architecture Becomes a Matter of Law Instead of Builder's Choice," *Sunday Star,* July 15, 1951.

79 CFA minutes, July 19–20, 1951, exhibit B.

80 House Committee on the District of Columbia, *To Regulate the Height,* 46.

81 CFA minutes, August 17, 1951, exhibit E, 1–4. Exhibit E is not part of the bound minutes; a copy of the exhibit is located in Folder "Old Georgetown," Container 9, Finley MSS.

82 Exhibit E, 13, Folder "Old Georgetown," Container 9, Finley MSS. See also Folder "Old Georgetown Act."

83 Exhibit E, 17, Folder "Old Georgetown," Container 9, Finley MSS. Interestingly, the elimination of ornamental detail was one of the hallmarks of modern architecture. Over the years, Hudnut's attitude toward modern architecture changed. He was among the first critics of the style, but he also brought famed modernist Walter Gropius—a central figure at Germany's Bauhaus—to Harvard in 1937, instigating the transformation of architectural education in America. See: Jill Pearlman, *Inventing American Architecture,* 6.

84 Exhibit E, 18–21, Folder "Old Georgetown," Container 9, Finley MSS. Enactment of the nation's first historic preservation ordinance in 1931 in Charleston, South Carolina, initiated the legal struggle between a community's power to preserve and regulate cultural patrimony and the property rights of an individual. The Vieux Carré district of New Orleans was designated in 1936. Two early important decisions occurred in 1941 when the Louisiana Supreme Court decided *City of New Orleans v. Impastato,* which established the principle that a preservation commission could regulate, unless precluded otherwise, all exterior alterations as opposed to only those visible from public streets; and *City of New Orleans v. Pergament,* which recognized that a preservation commission could regulate both historic and nonhistoric structures in a designated historic district. However, legal challenges to historic preservation remained an ongoing concern.

85 Exhibit E, 22, Folder "Old Georgetown," Container 9, Finley MSS.

86 Dorothy Schaffter, *The Presbyterian Congregation in George Town 1780–1970* (Washington, DC: n. p. 1971), 81.

87 The D.C. commissioners had granted the raze applications for 2732 Dumbarton Avenue, 3601–3603 O Street, 3053 M Street, and 3033 P Street. In addition, they had recently approved a sign for a gas station at Wisconsin Avenue and Q Street that the board and commission had recommended.

88 The opinion was issued by Chester H. Gray to the D.C. commissioners on March 6, 1957.

89 See "Georgetown-D.C. Dispute Erupts as 3 Architect-Advisers Resign," *Washington Post and Times-Herald,* October 17, 1958; and "City Heads Get Aid Offer on New Georgetown Law: 3 Architects Quit in Protest at D.C. Ruling," *Washington Star,* October 17, 1958. At the time, the board was composed of Water Macomber, Henry Saylor, and John Coughlin. Uncommonly, the commission allowed journalists to be present at the meeting.

90 CFA minutes, January 19, 1960, exhibit G, letter from Attorney General William P. Rogers to President Dwight D. Eisenhower, January 15, 1960. One of the cases Rogers cited to support his position was *City of New Orleans v. Pergament,* which established the concept of *tout ensemble:* "The purpose of the ordinance is not only to preserve the old buildings themselves, but to preserve the antiquity of the whole French and Spanish quarter, the tout ensemble, so to speak, by defending this relic against iconoclasm or vandalism. Preventing or prohibiting eyesores in such a locality is within the police power and within the scope of this municipal ordinance."

91 See George Beveridge, "New Bill to Preserve Old Georgetown Drawn," *Washington Star,* February 20, 1959; and Jack Eisen, "Planning Group's Aid Sought in Georgetown," *Washington Post,* October 6, 1959. The amendments to the act, concerning sections two and five, were never sponsored in Congress.

92 "Halt Hinted in Improving Georgetown," *Washington Star,* March 12, 1959.

93 Henry Saylor and William Macomber agreed to serve again. Gerald Purcell of the D.C. Department of Buildings and Grounds filled the third opening on the board. Saylor was the historian of the AIA and the former editor of the *AIA Journal.*

94 CFA minutes, March 16, 1960, exhibit G3.

95 See Frederick Gutheim and Antoinette J. Lee, *Worthy of the Nation: Washington, D.C. from L'Enfant to the National Capital Planning Commission,* 2nd ed. (Baltimore, MD: Johns Hopkins University Press, 2006), 246–49.

96 Because of the dearth of important architectural projects, and to save costs, the commission met much less frequently during the war and for many years thereafter. While there were twelve CFA meetings in 1941 (including one special meeting on the Pentagon), in 1942 there were seven and in 1943 only four, and a five-month gap elapsed between the meetings of September 1943 and February 1944. The numbers slowly climbed postwar, averaging six per year through the 1950s; nine meetings were held in 1957 and in 1959.

97 Preceding the opening was a dinner for about 150 people, at which William A. Delano spoke on the history of the NCPPC and Gilmore Clarke discussed the CFA, CFA minutes, December 18, 1941; and CFA minutes, January 8, 1942.

98 CFA minutes, December 10, 1948; and CFA minutes, February 26, 1952.

99 CFA minutes, February 6, 1928, 13; the CFA passed a resolution to preserve the river's "scenic beauties." CFA minutes, February 6, 1928, exhibit G, letter from Charles Moore to the Federal Power Commission. Moore reports on the resolution and refers to the *Senate Park Commission Report,* which had explicitly called for preservation of the river valley up to Great Falls.

100 CFA minutes, February 18, 1944, exhibit K, Gilmore Clarke, "Aesthetic Standards for the National Capital."

101 Information on the Theodore Roosevelt Memorial Association from Kay Fanning, "Theodore Roosevelt Island," *National Register Nomination,* February 16, 2001. See also James G. Deane, "Choice of

Bridge Site Runs Afoul Roosevelt Island Restrictions," *Washington Star,* February 13, 1952.

102 "Roosevelt Island Row Brews: 'There Is No Place Like It in the East,'" *Washington Daily News,* February 7, 1952. This was after the TRMA's proposal to build an enormous memorial designed by John Russell Pope on the Tidal Basin was rejected by Congress in favor of the Jefferson Memorial.

103 Roosevelt Memorial Association [*sic*], untitled pamphlet on microfilm, c. 1951, Olmsted Papers, Manuscript Division, Library of Congress.

104 George Beveridge, "Trustees Okay Bridge over Roosevelt Island," *Washington Star,* July 8, 1955;

105 Robert C. Albrook, "Roosevelt Island Trustees Reopen Bridge Site Question," *Washington Post,* July 9, 1955; and Fanning, "Theodore Roosevelt Island," *Nomination,* Section 8, 58.

106 CFA minutes, October 17, 1957, 4; CFA minutes, December 19, 1957, exhibit C, letter from David Finley to Commissioner Colonel A. C. Welling, November 22, 1957, 2; and CFA minutes, December 19, 1957, exhibit H, Finley to Welling, 1.

107 CFA minutes, December 19, 1957, exhibit H, "Statement by the Commission of Fine Arts," December 19, 1957.

108 CFA minutes, January 21, 1959; and CFA minutes, October 16, 1958, 6.

109 CFA minutes, October 14, 1959, and exhibit G, statement by David Finley, October 14, 1959.

110 The author has extrapolated this conclusion from the CFA minutes, which are not explicit about the resolution of the matter; however, the CFA began to approve aspects of the design, including approach structures, while issuing a press release stating it did not approve the location. On this subject, see CFA minutes May 17, 1960; October 18, 1960; February 14, 1961; March 14, 1961, exhibit C; March 15, 1961, exhibit C, news release, March 15, 1961; April 18 and 19, 1961; May 16, 1961; and September 19, 1961.

111 The first time an Inner Loop project was presented, it was recorded in the minutes under the heading "Inner Loop Threat to Lincoln Memorial Area." See CFA minutes, September 13, 1956, 7.

112 Bob Levey and Jane Freundel Levey, "End of the Roads," *Washington Post Magazine,* November 26, 2000, 10.

113 CFA minutes, August 19, 1959, exhibit H, David Finley to Commissioner Brigadier General A. C. Welling, August 26, 1959. Like the highways, the bridge was a project of the D.C. Department of Highways. The first proposal was by engineers Howard, Needles, Tammen & Bergendoff; engineer Paul Weidlinger and architect A. Gordon Lorimer assisted on the revised design. See also Donald Beekman Myer, *Bridges and the City of Washington* (Washington, DC: U.S. Commission of Fine Arts, 1974, reprint 1992), 35–38.

114 CFA minutes, January 25, 1967.

115 CFA minutes, April 19, 1967, exhibit I, CFA transcript, 201 (Walton) and 208 (Bunshaft). Copies of meeting transcripts held in the offices of the Commission of Fine Arts, Washington, D.C. (hereafter CFA transcript).

116 CFA minutes, September 19, 1967, and September 20, 1967, exhibit A, William Walton to Thomas F. Airis, director, D. C. Department of Highways and Traffic, September 20, 1967. See also CFA minutes, February 28, 1967, exhibit G2, letter from Walton to Airis, January 26, 1967.

117 CFA minutes, September 20, 1960, exhibit B, David Finley to Conrad Wirth, September 23, 1960.

118 CFA minutes, September 14, 1965.

119 CFA minutes, September 20, 1967, exhibit B, letter from William Walton to Thomas Airis, October 3, 1967.

120 CFA minutes, March 27, 1958, exhibit F, David Finley to A. C. Welling, March 31, 1958; CFA minutes, October 16, 1958, 4; and CFA minutes, December 16, 1959, exhibit D, letter from Finely to Welling, December 25, 1959.

121 CFA minutes, August 19, 1956, 8; and CFA minutes, December 15, 1959.

122 CFA minutes, November 17, 1959, exhibit L, press release, November 18, 1959.

123 Levey and Levey, "End of the Roads," 24.

124 Kathryn Schneider Smith, ed., *Washington at Home: An Illustrated History of Neighborhoods in the National Capital,* 2nd ed. (Baltimore, MD: Johns Hopkins University Press, 2010), 95–97.

125 CFA minutes, March 14, 1942, 10–11, and exhibits N and N-1. Also see Gutheim and Lee, *Worthy of the Nation,* 260–61. Goodwillie's report, "Rehabilitation of Southwest Washington as a War Housing Measure," proposed a significant amount of rehabilitation along with new construction to increase the residential density of Southwest and address wartime shortages of building materials.

126 See CFA minutes, March 19 and 20, 1963; and January 10 and 11, 1961, including January 11, 1961, exhibit C, letter from David Finley to Neville Miller, January 18, 1961. The CFA also approved the removal of the *Titanic* Memorial to Southwest from its original location on the river north of the Lincoln Memorial, the site of the Kennedy Center; CFA minutes, April 19, 1967, exhibit B, letter from William Walton to L. Thomas Appleby, executive director, DC Redevelopment Land Agency (RLA), April 27, 1967, and exhibit B2, letter from William Walton to T. Sutton Jett, regional director, National Capital Region, National Park Service, April 27, 1967.

127 For a more thorough discussion of these plans and the operation of the RLA, see Gutheim and Lee, *Worthy of the Nation,* 262ff.

128 CFA minutes, September 8, 1955, 3.

129 CFA minutes, May 9, 1956, exhibit C, letter from David Finley to Robert E. McLaughlin, May 11, 1956.

130 Chicago architect Harry Weese, who later designed Washington's Metro system, also advised on the Zeckendorf proposals.

131 Most of the FOBs—there were probably only eleven in all, about half located in Suitland—have since been given names: FOBS 10A and 10B have been named for the Wright Brothers and FOB 6 has been renamed the Lyndon B. Johnson Building. Some have been demolished. The only remaining FOB to be designated as such is FOB 8. E-mail from Michael McGill, General Services Administration (GSA), to Tom Luebke, secretary, Commission of Fine Arts, August 10, 2010.

132 CFA minutes, May 23, 1957, exhibit H, letter from David Finley to F. Moran McConihe, commissioner of public buildings, GSA, May 25, 1957. Two special meetings also were held to discuss FOBs in Southwest. The first took place in D.C. on August 1, 1957, and the second in New York City on August 13, 1957. See CFA minutes, August 1, 1957, unnumbered exhibit, excerpt from transcript of August 1 meeting as "The Position of the Commission of Fine Arts," 1–92. Regarding the August 13 meeting, see CFA minutes, September 12, 1957, exhibit D, memo from Douglas Orr to L. R. Wilson, August 14, 1957; exhibit E, Public Buildings Service, GSA, "Memo of Record," August 21, 1957; and exhibit F, letter from Finley to McConihe, October 3, 1957. For discussion of FOB 6 plaza, see CFA minutes, November 11, 1957, exhibit H, letter from Wilson to McConihe, January 16, 1958.

133 CFA minutes, May 23, 1957, exhibit H, letter from David Finley to F. Moran McConihe, May 24, 1957.

134 CFA minutes, September 12, 1957, 3; CFA minutes, June 27, 1957, 3; CFA minutes, October 17, 1957; and CFA minutes, May 23, 1957, exhibit H.

135 CFA minutes, May 23, 1957, exhibit H; and CFA minutes, August 1, 1957, unnumbered exhibit, excerpt from transcript of meeting, 1–92.

136 To address its concerns, the commission discussed preparing a general report to Congress presenting the commission's views on the city's planning needs, but apparently this was not done.

137 CFA minutes, September 12, 1957, exhibit D, memo from Douglas Orr to Linton Wilson, August 14, 1957, 1.

138 CFA minutes, October 16, 1958, exhibit E, David Finley to Harland Bartholomew, NCPC, November 5, 1958. In addition, Finley wrote:

"Although we do not favor in general displacing the relationships established by the approved plans for the Mall area, we do not believe the proposed direction will materially affect the overall appearance of the Mall."

139 CFA minutes, February 11, 1958, and exhibit E, letter from Linton Wilson to F. Moran McConihe, February 11, 1958; and CFA minutes, May 23, 1957, exhibit H, David Finley to F. Moran McConihe, March 24, 1957.

140 CFA minutes, October 16, 1958, 1, and exhibit A, letter from J. R. Wiggins to David Finley, September 19, 1958; and CFA minutes, April 14, 1959.

141 Editorial, "Power of Persuasion," *Washington Star,* April 8, 1963.

MEDALS AND COINS AS COMMEMORATIVE OBECTS

1 CFA minutes, June 19, 1942, 4, letter from Gilmore Clarke to Franklin D. Roosevelt, May 18, 1942, and exhibit C1, Roosevelt to Clarke, June 19, 1942.

2 CFA minutes, May 2, 1942, 3, and exhibit C1.

3 CFA minutes, November 30, 1945, 6. CFA member painter Maurice Sterne commented that "the head of Roosevelt was not one the people of the country would like to see on a Dime." See also CFA minutes, January 28, 1946, exhibit D, letter from Gilmore Clarke to Nellie Tayloe Ross, director of the Mint, January 18, 1946, and exhibit D1, letter from Clarke to Ross, February 5, 1946.

4 CFA minutes, November 19, 1958, exhibit D, memo from Linton Wilson to CFA, November 6, 1958, and exhibit D4, David Finley, memo for files; and CFA minutes, November 6, 1958, exhibit D5, letter from Linton Wilson to William H. Brett, director of the Mint.

ESSAY BY WILLIAN B. BUSHONG

1 William B. Rhoads, "Franklin D. Roosevelt and Washington Architecture," *Records of the Columbia Historical Society* 52 (1989): 104–62.

2 William Seale, *The President's House,* vol. 2 (Washington, DC: White House Historical Association, 2008), 191–204; and The *White House: The History of an American Idea* (Washington, DC: White House Historical Association, 2000), 217–77.

3 William B. Bushong, "Glenn Brown, the White House, and the Urban Renaissance of Washington, D.C.," *White House History,* Collection Set 2, nos. 7–12 (2004): 304–18.

4 Antoniette J. Lee, "The White House in the Monumental City," *White House History,* Collection Set 2, (2004): 294–303.

5 CFA minutes, December 15, 1933, 1–4 (microfilm copy), Record Group 66, U.S. Commission of Fine Arts, National Archives Building, Washington, D.C. (hereafter cited CFA NAB)

6 Nothing in Washington, D.C., planning is simple, however. Architects, planners, and politicians would argue for decades over whether to concentrate major public buildings in the monumental core or to disperse them into the suburbs. For a discussion of the planning history in this period, see Frederick Gutheim and Antoinette J. Lee, *Worthy of the Nation: Washington, D.C., from L'Enfant to the National Capital Planning Commission* (Baltimore, MD: John Hopkins Press, 2006), 202–5. Contemporary comment can be found in "The Proposed War Department Building," and "Editorial Comment: A Sorry Story," *Planning and Civic Comment,* 7, no. 3 (October 1941): 1–6.

7 Roosevelt had admired Pope's sketch of the remodeling plan when he was assistant secretary of the navy in 1917. However, the pressing need for wartime office space and restrictive economic conditions prompted Roosevelt to support the construction of a vast temporary Navy building and an adjacent Munitions building for the army on the Mall west of the Washington Monument in 1918. Rhoads, "Franklin D. Roosevelt and Washington Architecture," 107. For a

planning history of the White House environs, see Lee, "The White House in the Monumental City," 294–303; and for the plans for remodeling the State, War, and Navy Building between 1917 and 1930, see Sue A. Kohler, *The Commission of Fine Arts: A Brief History* (Washington, DC: Government Printing Office, 1992), 43–45.

8 Rhoads, "Franklin D. Roosevelt and Washington Architecture," 132. See also the chapter on the saga of this siting battle in Steve Vogel, *The Pentagon: A History* (New York: Random House, 2007), 79–103.

9 Rhoads, "Franklin D. Roosevelt and Washington Architecture," 119–21. For President Roosevelt's views on the preservation of Blair and Decatur Houses, see President Roosevelt to Hon. Sumner Welles, Department of State, December 1, 1942, President's Office File 3715, Franklin D. Roosevelt Library, Hyde Park, New York (hereafter cited Roosevelt MSS). Marie Beale bequeathed Decatur House to the National Trust in 1956 and, through the efforts of President and Mrs. John F. Kennedy, an executive office building complex planned by John Carl Warnecke & Associates and erected on the site preserved the Decatur House and many of the historic row houses on Jackson Place. See Kohler, *A Brief History,* 83–84.

10 Roosevelt's Reorganization Act of 1933 dissolved the Office of Public Buildings and Public Parks, turning stewardship of the White House and its grounds over to the National Park Service within the Department of the Interior. Winslow began his career at the White House with the Office of Public Buildings and Public Parks, then worked for its successor agency, the National Park Service, until a 1935 transfer to the Public Buildings Administration (precursor to the General Services Administration). William B. Bushong, "Lorenzo Simmons Winslow: Architect of the White House, 1933–1952," *White House History,* Collection Set 1, nos. 1–6 (2004): 273–82.

11 Ibid.

12 Seale, *The President's House,* 190; and Rhoads, "Franklin D. Roosevelt and Washington Architecture," 112–13.

13 CFA minutes, April 23, 1934, 1.

14 Eric Gugler Papers, "West Wing 1934 Memoir and Enclosures," typescript, 2, White House Collection, Office of the White House Curator, The White House, Washington, D.C. (hereafter cited Gugler Papers).

15 Ibid.

16 Seale, *The President's House,* 191–204.

17 Gugler later recalled, "I've forgotten now how a meeting with the President was arranged, perhaps through Moore, anyway, I've forgotten." "West Wing 1934 Memoirs and Enclosures," typescript, 2, Gugler Papers.

18 Ibid., 3.

19 Ibid., 7.

20 CFA minutes, May 7, 1934, 4.

21 "A Model of the President's Workshop After Alterations," *New York Times,* July 29, 1934, 1; and "White House Remodeling Increases Office Space," *Evening Star,* B-4. See also Seale, *The White House,* 220–30.

22 "Enlargement of the Offices—White House, August 2, 1934," typescript report by the Building Management, General Services Division (900), White House Collection, Office of the White House Curator, The White House, Washington, D.C.; see also "Work Progressing on the White House," *New York Times,* September 16, 1934, II 3–5.

23 CFA minutes, October 19, 1934, 15; "Roosevelt Office Ready," *New York Times,* November 24, 1934, 3–1; and "New White House Offices Finished," Evening Star, November 26, 1934, 4–7.

24 William Seale, *The White House Garden* (Washington, DC: White House Historical Association, 1996), 62–67.

25 From 1867 to 1933, the U.S. Army Corps of Engineers, under various agency names, was responsible for the care and maintenance of the White House. Colonel U. S. Grant III, head of the Office of Public Buildings and Public Parks of the National Capital from 1925

26 to 1933, sent the Olmsted report to First Lady Grace Coolidge because of her interest in the White House gardens. She passed the report to Lou Hoover, and it remained in the First Lady's office without action until it was found by Mrs. Roosevelt.

26 "Roosevelt Inspects White House Grounds," *Washington Post*, October 10, 1934, 6.

27 Seale, *The President's House*, 214–15.

28 CFA minutes, January 16, 1935, 1.

29 CFA minutes, December 19, 1933, exhibit A, letter from Charles Moore to President Franklin Roosevelt, December 19, 1933, 1; CFA minutes, January 18–19, 1934, "Memorandum from the President for Hon. Charles Moore, Chairman of the Commission of Fine Arts," January 18, 1934, incorporated on pp. 23–24, and exhibit H, letter from Charles Moore to President Roosevelt, 1–2; Rhoads, "Franklin D. Roosevelt and Washington Architecture," 122–26.

30 "Moore, Veteran Member of Fine Arts Board, Resigns as Chairman; Clarke Is His Successor," *Washington Post*, October 17, 1937, 12. In her essay in this volume, Pamela Scott speculates that Moore's resignation included a quiet deal that with the commission's acceptance of the Pantheon design, Moore would fade away.

31 Thomas W. Ennis, "Gilmore D. Clarke, 90, is Dead; Designed Major Public Works," *New York Times*, August 10, 1982, B-19.

32 The Jefferson Memorial Commission had ignored a "custom of more than 25 years" by not consulting or requesting advice from the Commission of Fine Arts before making its decision. See "The Lost Cause," *Washington Post*, March 19, 1939, B8.

33 Eleanor Roosevelt, "My Day," October 1, 1939, unidentified newspaper clipping, Gugler Papers.

34 The letter relates President Roosevelt's desire to appoint a "100% New Deal Democrat." See Graham Barnfield, "Federal Arts Policy and Political Legitimation," in *Franklin D. Roosevelt and the Shaping of American Political Culture*, ed. Nancy Beck Young, William D. Peterson, and Byron W. Danes (New York: M.E. Sharpe, Inc., 2001), 52–53.

35 Frederic A. Delano to Gen. Edwin M. Watson, aide to the president, May 3, 1939. President's Office File 187, Roosevelt MSS.

36 "Excellent Selection," *Washington Post*, January 23, 1940, 8.

37 Quoted in Lois A. Craig and the Staff of the Federal Architecture Project, *The Federal Presence: Architecture, Politics and National Design* (Cambridge, MA: The MIT Press, 1978), 335.

38 Richard Guy Wilson, "High Noon on the Mall: Traditionalism versus Modernism, 1910–1970," in *The Mall in Washington*, ed. Richard Longstreth (Hanover and London: University Press of New England, 1991), 143–63. Wilson describes the 1939 competition and its historic context, 1791–1991.

39 Graham Barnfield, "Federal Arts Policy and Political Legitimation," in Young, Peterson, and Danes, *Franklin D. Roosevelt*, 48–54.

40 CFA minutes, September 9, 1942, typescript copy of letter from Franklin D. Roosevelt to Gilmore D. Clarke, 2–3.

41 CFA minutes, November 30, 1945, 13–17.

42 CFA minutes, November 30, 1945, exhibit B-1, 2.

43 At a press conference on January 25, 1946, Truman made the remark that the whole affair was a "tempest in a teapot." Elizabeth Beard Goldsmith, "Tempest in a Teapot: Truman's Failed Attempt at an Office Addition, *White House History*, Collection Set 1, nos. 1–6 (2004): 263–72.

44 A sample of news articles on the office expansion controversy include Edward T. Folliard, "President Recalls How Memorial Led To Fetters on Bushes," *Washington Post*, January 25, 1946, 1–2; L. H. Robbins, "Will It Still Be the White House?," *New York Times*, February 10, 1946, 91; and John F. Gerrity, "White House Plan Subject of New Fight," *Washington Post*, January 28, 1946, 1.

45 CFA minutes, January 28, 1946, 2, exhibit B. Goldsmith, "Tempest in a Teapot," 272.

46 CFA Minutes, August 28, 1947, 3–5.

47 Truman provided reporters a lesson in architecture at a press conference explaining that Jefferson had a balcony addition in mind when he planned the White House porticoes. See Marshall Andrews, "Jefferson's Idea Originally, Truman Says of Balcony," *Washington Post*, April 16, 1948, 23.

48 An oddity in the history of the Commission of Fine Arts, the White House Furnishings Committee was formed in 1925 with First Lady Grace Coolidge's backing and was the first recognition of the White House's function as a museum. At Charles Moore's insistence, the panel served as a subcommittee of the Commission of Fine Arts beginning in the Hoover administration. The chairman was Mrs. Harold I. Pratt, a Republican and wealthy furniture collector. During the Roosevelt administration, the committee was reappointed and composed of members of the Commission of Fine Arts, the wives of donors, the chief usher of the White House, White House architect Lorenzo Winslow, and a representative from the president's office. For background on the composition and work of the furnishings committee, see CFA minutes, January 28, 1946, exhibit M, "Minutes of the Committee on White House Furnishings," 1–3.

49 CFA minutes, October 29–30, 1947, exhibit A and B, 1–2; and Seale, *The President's House*, 260–61.

50 Andrews, "Jefferson's Idea Originally, Truman Says of Balcony," 23.

51 President Harry S. Truman to Gilmore D. Clarke, Washington, December 2, 1947, Harry S. Truman Library, quoted in Seale, *The President's House*, 261–62.

52 Ibid.

53 CFA minutes, January 14, 1948, exhibit C, a selection of negative editorials were collected and added to the commission's minutes. Examples include "That White House Balacony," *Evening Star*, January 4, 1948; "Mr. Truman's Taste," *Washington Post*, January 12, 1948; and "The Back Porch," *New York Herald Tribune*, January 15, 1948. See also a collection of professional opinions, "The South Portico of the White House," *AIA Journal* 9 (February 1948): 64–72.

54 CFA minutes, December 10, 1948, exhibit F, letter from Gilmore D. Clarke to David Finley, November 8, 1948.

55 Seale, *The President's House*, 250.

56 CFA minutes, December 10, 1948, 3, and exhibit E, memorandum, "Restoration of the White House."

57 The appropriation to fund the Truman renovation was approved by Congress on June 23, 1949. A copy of the legislation without mention of the commission was entered in the Commission of Fine Arts minutes; see CFA minutes, June 21, 1949, 3.

58 Anthony Leviero, "Truman Shakes Up Arts Commission," *New York Times*, June 20, 1950, 25.

59 Lee Grove, "Four Named to Arts Board," *Washington Post*, June 20, 1950, 1.

60 Seale, *The President's House*, 284–95.

61 "President Believed on the Point of Packing Fine Arts Board," *Washington Post*, August 20, 1949, 1; "Fifth Fine Arts Commission Term Expires," *Washington Post*, December 2, 1949, 17; and Lee Grove, "Four Named to Arts Board," *Washington Post*, June 20, 1950, 1. Sculptor Felix de Weldon, appointed by Truman after the balcony controversy in 1950, supported Truman interpreting the transition as a need for change and recalled: "I don't think they were not reappointed because of their objection, because they just had been on the Commission for too long, and it's important to get new blood on the Commission, which I think the President realized." Oral History Interview with Felix de Weldon, Washington, D.C., January 22, 1969, by Jerry N. Hess accessed 10/15/2010, www.trumanlibrary.org/oralhist/deweldon.htm.

62 Seale, *The President's House*, 284–95.

63 David A. Doheny, *David Finley: Quiet Force for America's Arts* (Washington, DC: National Trust for Historic Preservation, 2006), 294–301.

1 Meryle Secreste, "Aline Saarinen Is Crusading to Save Washington," *Washington Post,* September 22, 1963, in "Aline Saarinen," CFA member files. Aline Saarinen once made a list of the "six worst man-made objects": the Pan Am building, Salvador Dali's *Last Supper,* the "typical suburban tacky house," the glass sculpture at Lincoln Center, a lamp with a violin base, and Mount Rushmore. See Alden Whitman, "Aline Saarinen, Art Critic, Dies at 58," *New York Times,* July 15, 1972, 26.

2 Thomas J. Leuck, "William Walton Is Dead at 84; Headed Fine Arts Panel," *New York Times,* December 20, 1994. Walton was often called the son of a newspaper publisher, although his own handwritten biographical notes say his father was editor of an Illinois newspaper, the *Jacksonville Journal;* see letter from William Walton to Charles Atherton, July 30, 1984, in "William Walton," CFA member files. In 1966, Walton published *The Evidence of Washington,* a photographic history of the District of Columbia.

3 Letter from Wolf von Eckardt to the Chairman of the Jury for Honorary AIA, September 2, 1984, in "William Walton," CFA member files.

4 Information on Bunshaft from the following sources: Nicholas Adams, *Skidmore, Owings & Merrill: SOM since 1936* (Milan: Electa, 2006); Carol Herselle Krinsky, *Gordon Bunshaft of Skidmore, Owings & Merrill* (Cambridge, MA: Architectural History Foundation and MIT Press, 1988); and "Oral History of Gordon Bunshaft," interview by Betty J. Blum, Chicago Architects Oral History Project, The Ernest R. Graham Study Center for Architectural Drawings, Department of Architecture, Art Institute of Chicago, 1990. Bunshaft was awarded the Pritzker Prize in 1988.

5 Obituary, "Bunshaft Remembered," *Architecture* 79, no. 9 (September 1990): 35.

6 Ibid., quoting an unnamed "senior SOM partner."

7 This section is adapted from the article by Kurt Helferich, "Modernism for Washington? The Kennedys and the Redesign of Lafayette Square," *Washington History* 8 (Spring/Summer 1996): 16–37. Helferich prepared his article as an intern with the CFA. On Finley, Helferich writes: "Finley's personal taste and long experience in the federal government made him the ideal shepherd for what would become the first major federal involvement in adaptive reuse."

8 Ibid., 21.

9 Ibid., 22.

10 As a principal of one of the Boston firms commissioned to design the buildings, William Perry recused himself from Commission of Fine Arts reviews. On one occasion—a special meeting on the subject with the NCPC—former member Walter Harrison sat in for Perry; see CFA minutes of special meeting, September 8, 1960, 1.

11 Helferich, "Modernism for Washington?" 24.

12 Ibid., 28–33.

13 CFA minutes, October 16, 1962, exhibit B, discussion of Lafayette Square in transcript of meeting, 47–69.

14 Laurence Stern, "President Backs $425 Million U.S. Offices Plan for D.C.," *Washington Post,* June 1, 1962, and "Avenue Visioned as Ceremonial Street," *Washington Post,* June 1, 1962. Goldberg was a prominent labor lawyer who had been general counsel for the Congress of Industrial Organizations (CIO) and the steelworkers. Moynihan, a future senator from New York, was a social scientist and politician with particular interests in labor and urban issues. On Goldberg, see Daniel L. Stebenne, "Goldberg, Arthur Joseph," *American National Biography (ANB) Online,* February 2000, www.anb.org/articles/11/11-00334.html, accessed March 22, 2010. On Moynihan, see Ann T. Keene, "Moynihan, Daniel Patrick," ANB Online, May Update 2008, www.anb.org/articles/07-07-00807.html, accessed September 12, 2009. On Owings, see Lisa A. Torrance, "Owings, Nathaniel Alexander," ANB Online, February 2000, www.anb.org/articles/17/17-01056.html, accessed March 22, 2010. American National Biography Online is a publication of the American Council of Learned Societies in association with Oxford University Press.

15 John Parsons, interview by Kay Fanning, Washington, D.C., April 26, 2006.

16 CFA minutes, September 20, 1966; CFA minutes, November 16, 1966; and CFA minutes, June 20, 1967.

17 Weese had briefly worked under Gordon Bunshaft at SOM. He practiced a direct, no-frills modernism based on careful site analysis and consideration of social and urban needs. On Weese, see the entry in Paul Heyer, *Architects on Architecture: New Directions in America* (New York: Walker and Company, 1978); and "Oral History of Harry Mohr Weese," interview by Betty J. Blum, Chicago Architects Oral History Project, 1991, rev. 2001.

18 CFA minutes, September 21, 1966.

19 CFA transcript, June 21, 1967, 51–59; and CFA transcript, September 19, 1967, 123–39.

20 CFA transcript, April 18, 1967, 100–1.

21 CFA minutes, June 21, 1967, 1–2.

22 CFA minutes, June 21, 1967, 2.

23 Weese said he was working within limitations, but there wasn't a required budget per station; CFA minutes, June 21, 1967, exhibit A, excerpt from transcript of meeting, 158–63.

24 CFA transcript, September 19, 1967, 69.

25 Ibid., 124.

26 Ibid., 134.

27 CFA minutes, October 17, 1967, 4, 6. The approval was for the Judiciary Square and G Street (Metro Center) stations specifically, with the understanding that the design would be applied to all others.

28 CFA transcript, October 17, 1967, 37. In executive session before Weese joined the meeting, Bunshaft suggested ways of detailing the mezzanine railings to strengthen their sculptural quality and stressed the need for a continuity of treatment among mezzanines and escalators. Saarinen alluded to her late husband's work: "The thing that is good about TWA, if I may say so, is it's all one family of things."

29 Stanley A. Allen, "Third Presentation," Chapter V in *For the Glory of Washington, December 1965–November 1967* (Chicago: Harry Weese Associates, 1994).

30 CFA minutes, May 17, 1961, exhibit A, letter from David Finley to John R. Searles Jr., executive director, RLA, May 31, 1961, on the River Park Cooperative Apartments; CFA minutes, September 20, 1961, exhibit E, Finley to Searles, September 27, 1961, on Tiber Island; CFA minutes, February 21, 1962, exhibit A, letter from Finley to Neville Miller, chairman, RLA, on Carrollsburg Square; and CFA minutes, October 16, 1962, exhibit D, letter from William Walton to Phil A. Doyle, executive director, RLA, October 22, 1963, on Harbour Square. The commission was somewhat more critical of Town Center Park (Wallace, McHarg, Roberts & Todd, landscape architects), calling it "far too complicated"; see CFA minutes, April 23, 1969.

31 CFA minutes, March 14, 1961; and CFA minutes, March 15, 1961, exhibit F.

32 The partners were John Walker Wright, C. Preston Andrade, William A. Amenta, and John Frederick Gane. See AIA, *The AIA Historical Directory of American Architects,* 3rd ed., 1970, communities. AIA.org/sites/hdoaa/wiki/Wiki%20Pages/1970%20American%20Architects%20Directory.aspx, accessed November 29, 2010.

33 CFA minutes, February 17, 1965, exhibit A, letter from William Walton to L. Thomas Appleby, executive director, RLA, March 10, 1965.

34 CFA minutes, April 13, 1965, 8.

35 CFA minutes, March 16, 1965; and CFA minutes April 13, 1965, exhibit L, letter from William Walton to Phil A. Doyle, executive director, RLA, April 28, 1965. At the CFA's direction, the cascade was later replaced by a low clipped hedge; see CFA minutes, April 21, 1971.

36 CFA minutes, September 21, 1966. The date of the Ponte Vecchio project appears in Robert J. Lewis, "Southwest's 'Marvelous Mile' Is in Deep Trouble," *Washington Star,* July 26, 1967.

37 CFA minutes, January 26, 1967, 3.

38 CFA minutes, April 18, 1967; and CFA minutes, April 19, 1967, exhibit A. The park was dedicated by the National Park Service in honor of Benjamin Banneker—the self-taught African American scientist who assisted L'Enfant in surveying the District of Columbia in 1792 and 1793—but it had fallen into disrepair by the early 2000s. Interestingly, the project became the focus of attention by both District and federal governments as a key feature in redevelopment for the Southwest district: A multimodal transit hub has been proposed below the level of the overlook and a memorial or significant cultural institution on the upper level, with a monumental stair connecting the site to the waterfront.

39 CFA minutes, December 19, 1961, exhibit C, letter from David Finley to Bernard L. Boutin, GSA, December 28, 1961.

40 CFA minutes, April 16, 1963, 4, and exhibit A1, excerpt from transcript of meeting, 150–67.

41 CFA minutes, April 17, 1963, 1–2, and exhibit A2, Finley to Boutin, April 25, 1963.

42 CFA minutes, September 17, 1963, 2.

43 CFA minutes, September 18, 1963, and exhibit A, letter from William Walton to Bernard L. Boutin, GSA, September 27, 1963; and CFA minutes, October 15 and 16, 1963.

44 CFA minutes, October 16, 1963, and exhibit A, excerpt from transcript of meeting, 44.

45 CFA minutes, November 20, 1963, and exhibit A, Walton to Boutin, November 21, 1963.

46 CFA minutes, January 8, 1964, 2; and CFA minutes, January 9, 1964, FOB 5 discussion at a joint meeting with NCPC, 1–2, and exhibit B, excerpt from transcript of meeting, 9–17.

47 The pilotis were set at sixty feet across the building's length and forty feet across the width.

48 See CFA minutes and transcripts for May 20, 1964; September 15, 1964; and January 12, 1965. Also see CFA transcript, November 17, 1964, 48, for "wallpaper."

48 CFA transcript, June 23, 1964, 86. Breuer told the commission that the hotel's footprint included a platform and the actual building footprint would not be quite as large.

50 CFA transcript, June 23, 1964, 80. Breuer had considered courtyard and fishbone plans, but rejected a fishbone configuration because it broke up spaces "into small courtyards, and also windows look diagonally into each other."

51 CFA transcript, June 23, 1964, 17–18, 21, 87.

52 CFA minutes, June 23, 1964, exhibit J, Walton to Boutin, July 9, 1964. The CFA also encouraged a reduction in the amount of parking.

53 CFA minutes, September 20, 1966. Before it had a tenant, the headquarters building for Health, Education, and Welfare was known as the Air Rights building and then the South Portal Office building.

54 CFA transcript, September 20, 1966, 108.

55 The meeting was chummy; in closed session beforehand, the commission decided to invite Breuer to lunch, and I. M. Pei, too, if he was available to join them.

56 CFA transcript, January 15, 1969, 104–5.

57 CFA transcript, November 14, 1967, 26.

58 CFA minutes, October 19, 1965, 12, for "Excessive heaviness"; CFA minutes, October 21, 1964; CFA minutes, November 15, 1966; and CFA minutes, November 16, 1966.

59 E-mail from Zachary Schrag to Kay Fanning, CFA, December 8, 2010; CFA transcript, November 14, 1967, 28.

60 CFA minutes and transcript, February 15, 1966. The associated architect from Mies's firm was Gene Summers.

61 CFA transcript, February 15, 1966, 24.

62 Ibid., 81.

63 Ibid., 24, 76.

64 Ibid., 80.

65 Kim Williams, Anne Brockett, and Emily Paulus, "National Register of Historic Places Registration Form for the Martin Luther King Memorial Library," November 2, 2005, Section 8, 8; and e-mail from David Maloney, D.C. historic preservation officer, to Kay Fanning, CFA, April 18, 2011.

66 CFA minutes, November 16, 1965.

67 CFA minutes, November 17, 1965, exhibit B, letter from William Walton to Lawson B. Knott, GSA administrator, November 30, 1965.

68 U.S. Government Services Administration, "U.S. Tax Court Building, Washington, D.C.," brochure produced by the Office of the Chief Architect, Center for Historic Buildings, Public Buildings Heritage Program, undated.

69 CFA minutes, December 16, 1965, exhibit B, Walton to Knott, December 27, 1965. Details of materials were easily approved the next year.

70 CFA minutes, November 16, 1966, 4, quotation and exhibit F, Walton to Knott, November 29, 1966; see also CFA minutes, September 15, 1971, on reorientation of the building.

71 CFA minutes, December 15, 1959.

72 CFA minutes, October 14, 1959, exhibit C, statement of David E. Finley in news release, October 14, 1959.

73 CFA minutes, September 18, 1962.

74 Part of the proposed site was owned by the Island Vista Corporation, the developers of the Watergate, and another section by the Watergate restaurant. At this meeting on September 18, 1962, a CFA member asked Stone if he was concerned about the potential impact of the Watergate complex. Stone said he was not, as long as the southernmost building would not be much higher than 138 feet, the proposed height of the Cultural Center, about eighteen inches lower than the Lincoln Memorial. In 1967, the Kennedy Center Board of Trustees came to the CFA with strenuous objections to the proposed height of the Watergate building, estimated at about 40 feet above the Kennedy Center, arguing that it would not be suitable now that the center had been designated a presidential memorial and asked that the Watergate structure be eliminated. The CFA recommended restricting the height of the southern Watergate building to no more than 140 feet. See CFA minutes, September 20, 1967, exhibits E and F, and meeting transcript for that date; and CFA minutes, November 14, 1967.

75 CFA minutes, June 14, 1956. The design was approved in November 1957. CFA minutes, May 22, 1958; with the assistance of the commission, former member Paul Manship coordinated the sculpture program.

76 This was described on the original L'Enfant Plan as a fountain but depicted on the 1792 Thackara and Vallance version with a "scale and architectural complexity suggest[ing] a more important function." The official description of the L'Enfant Plan was published in The Gazette of the United States, Philadelphia, January 4, 1792; it appeared on the second Thackara and Vallance map, fall 1792. L'Enfant also located on this axis the National Pantheon and the Naval Itinerary Column. A National Pantheon that was never built was meant for the site later occupied by the Patent Office building (1836). A Naval Itinerary Column, also never built, was designated for the banks of the Potomac River between 7th and 9th Streets, SW. See Pamela Scott, "'This Vast Empire': The Iconography of the Mall, 1791–1848," in The Mall in Washington, 1791–1991, ed. Richard Longstreth (Hanover and London: National Gallery of Art, 1991), 41, 55n6.

77 Also in 1969, the Dr. Samuel D. Gross Memorial statue by A. Sterling Calder (1897), which had stood in front of the Army Medical Museum, was loaned to Thomas Jefferson University in Philadelphia.

78 "A New Art Gallery for the Capitol Mall, Washington D.C.," Architectural Record, (December 1967): 112–15. The unidentified author referred to their "eccentric radii."

79 Obituary, "Bunshaft Remembered," 114.

80 CFA transcript, June 20, 1967, 84.

81 CFA transcript, June 20, 1967, 18. On FOB 10, see Pamela Scott and Antoinette J. Lee, Buildings of the District of Columbia (New York: Oxford University Press, 1993), 235–36.

82 CFA minutes, June 20, 1967, 81.

83 CFA minutes, June 20, 1967, exhibit T2, Walton to Knott, July 13, 1967.

84 CFA transcript, November 14, 1967, 13.

85 The Smithsonian Institution, "Report by the Committee on House Administration pursuant to Public Law 601," 79th Cong., 2nd Sess., H.R. 91-801 (Washington, DC: Government Printing Office, December 30, 1970), 5–8.

86 CFA minutes, April 21, 1971, 3.

87 CFA transcript, September 16, 1964, 142.

88 From 1949, the NCPPC consulted with the CFA on possible locations for the air museum. In 1957, the CFA agreed that it should not be located outside the District—suburban Maryland was being considered—but should be situated near the other Smithsonian museums for visitors' convenience; see CFA minutes, August 1, 1957, exhibit G, letter from L. R. Wilson to Representative Charles A. Buckley, September 4, 1957. The commission noted that the air museum would displace the long-anticipated contemporary art museum on the south side of the Mall across from the National Gallery of Art. Although reluctant to see this relationship abandoned, the CFA recognized that this was the last available site on the Mall. However, the CFA decided the site was too small and said it would attempt to find another. But Leonard Carmichael, secretary of the Smithsonian, was determined to build the museum there; see CFA minutes, October 17, 1957, exhibits H, letter from David E. Finley to Representative Charles A. Buckley, August 15, 1957, and H1, letter from Finley to Senator Dennis Chavez, August 15, 1957. The CFA agreed that the five blocks at the north end of 10th Street, SW, should be studied as a possible location. This area, soon to be turned over to the GSA by the Redevelopment Land Agency, had formerly been designated for museums but was now tentatively approved for office development.

89 HOK was founded in 1955 with Obata as the design partner.

90 CFA minutes, June 24, 1964, exhibit A, letter from William Walton to Bernard L. Boutin, July 9, 1964; the CFA minutes record Obata incorrectly saying that the National Gallery of Art was clad in granite rather than marble.

91 CFA transcript, September 16, 1964, 142, 147, and exhibit A. Similarly, four months later John Carl Warnecke said: "I think this is the most singularly important building this Commission has looked at"; see CFA transcript, January 12, 1965, 57.

92 CFA minutes, October 21, 1964, 1–2; CFA transcript, October 21, 1964, 109; and CFA transcript, January 12, 1965, 54–55.

93 CFA transcript, January 13, 1965, 233–34; and CFA minutes, January 12 and 13, 1965.

94 Gyo Obata, "Issues Relative to the Mall in Designing the National Air and Space Museum," in The Mall in Washington, 1791-1991, ed. Richard Longstreth (Hanover and London: National Gallery of Art, 1991), 309.

95 Valerie J. Nelson, "Jane O'Brien Dies at 90; Actress and her Husband were in Reagan's Inner Circle," Los Angeles Times, April 11, 2009. Dart possessed no design training, although she was a patron of various California cultural institutions.

96 CFA transcript, November 17, 1971, 155ff.

97 This would seem to suggest that the CFA had seen this project before November 1971, but no record of this can be found.

98 CFA minutes, January 19, 1972, 2.

99 CFA transcript, February 16, 1972, 4–13. Roche added: "The problem comes when you start to take the man's hand and try to lead him through."

100 CFA minutes, April 19, 1972, 1, 6. See also CFA minutes, April 19, 1972, exhibit J, letter from J. Carter Brown to Arthur F. Sampson, PBS commissioner, GSA, May 8, 1972, in which Brown repeats the point.

101 CFA transcript, April 19, 1972, 9–19. When Roche asked if there was any alternative to accepting this design, Bunshaft responded: "The Commission could commit suicide and get a new Commission that won't approve it."

102 CFA minutes, May 17, 1972; and CFA transcript, May 17, 1972, 7.

103 See Neil Harris, "Reinventing the National Gallery," in A Modernist Museum in Perspective: The East Building, National Gallery of Art, ed. Anthony Alofsin (Washington, DC: National Gallery of Art, 2009), 23–45.

104 Discussed in Réjean Legault, "I. M. Pei's East Building and the Postwar Cultural of Materials," in Alofsin, A Modernist Museum in Perspective, 81–105.

105 These issues are discussed in depth in Alona Nitzan-Shiftan, "Toward a Modernist Civic Monument: Pei's East Building and the City of Washington," in Alofsin, A Modernist Museum in Perspective, 135–47.

106 Assistance in determining the genesis of the Mall plans was generously provided by a number of people with the National Capital Region of the National Park Service: memorials liaison Glenn DeMarr; regional historical landscape architect Maureen Joseph; former chief of cultural resources Darwina Neal; former associate director of lands, resources, and planning John Parsons; chief historian Gary Scott; and current chief of cultural resources Perry Wheelock. Also helpful: "Status of Plans for the Mall," an internal document produced circa 1971 for the National Capital Region; and the National Capital Planning Commission, "The Mall: General Development Plan—Report of Park, Recreation, and Open Space Committee," September 1966. Copies of both documents were provided by Glenn DeMarr.

107 David Childs, telephone interview by Kay Fanning, May 2, 2011. Childs was chairman of the NCPC from 1976 to 1982.

108 The four Mall roads were Jefferson, Adams, Washington, and Madison Drives; Adams and Washington Drives were later changed to pedestrian walks. Skidmore, Owings & Merrill (SOM), "The Washington Mall Master Plan," National Park Service, 1966, 6.

109 In addition, the Mall would have been lined on either side by sloping banks planted with flowers. This configuration may have been meant to resemble L'Enfant's design for the Grand Avenue, although the report does not mention this; SOM, "Mall Master Plan," 11.

110 CFA minutes, November 15, 1966; and CFA minutes, November 16, 1966, 5.

111 Skidmore, Owings & Merrill (SOM), "The Washington Mall Circulation System," National Park Service, 1973, 3, 10.

112 SOM, "Mall Circulation System," 14, 20.

113 Ibid., 5, 14, 23–24. This new row of trees was recommended for two reasons: because of the loss of elms to Dutch elm disease and because removal of east-west drives "would change the proportional relationships between the tree panels and the greensward" (p. 23). According to SOM's analysis, the elms served two uses: They provided shade for visitors and a contrast with the open center panel, and they defined the edges of the center panel. The loss of elms was destroying the formal character of the Mall, making it more pastoral like the Washington Monument grounds: "Much of the aesthetic pleasure of the Mall landscaping is derived from this very juxtaposition of the romantic pastoral landscape with the more formal garden, and the contrast should be preserved" (p. 24). However, the Mall axis still required a strong edge.

114 Ibid., 18, 20.

115 Parsons interview, April 26, 2006.

116 Peter Penczer, interview by Kay Fanning, Bethesda, Maryland, June 13, 2006, and Nathaniel Owings, The Spaces in Between: An Architect's Journey (Boston: Houghton Mifflin, 1973), 239.

117 CFA minutes, September 20, 1966, 9.

118 CFA minutes, November 15, 1966; and CFA minutes, November 16, 1966, exhibit I, excerpt from meeting transcript, p. 180, in which Walton observed that the appropriate place for a skating rink was probably in the area of the Munitions tempo building, since it was near the closest residential area to the Mall (Foggy Bottom) and "it will be a raw material area that we can do anything we want to with it. We are not limited by some existing building."

119 CFA transcript, September 20, 1966, 117–22.

120 CFA minutes, September 20, 1966, 9; and CFA minutes, November 17, 1971, exhibit E.

121 Charles Moore, ed., *The Improvement of the Park System of the District of Columbia* (Washington, DC: Government Printing Office, 1902), 51. Later in the document, the section on the Washington Embankment and Potomac Park adds: "The form and situation of the land suggest at once the landscape of natural river bottoms—a suggestion that can be hardly improved upon as a guide in the development of the park. Of the many types of river-bottom scenery, the one which seems best adapted to the conditions is that of great, open meadows, fringed by trees along the waterside and diversified by occasional outstanding masses and single trees serving to focus the meadow area into a series of connecting compositions without completely obscuring its extent" (p. 118). However, this passage may refer primarily to Hains Point.

122 "Annual Report of the Office of Public Buildings & Grounds," in the *Annual Report of the Chief of Engineers, U.S. Army Corps of Engineers* (Washington, DC: Government Printing Office, 1918 and 1930).

123 Paul Hodge, "Trees, Shrubs Drown in Washington's Newest Park," *Washington Post,* March 3, 1977, 3; Naval Historical Center, www. history.navy.mil/photos/pl-usa/pl-dc/nav-fac/mn-mun.htm accessed December 21, 2006. (Name of organization now Naval History and Heritage Compound, www.navy.mil/local/navhist).

124 Hodge, "Trees, Shrubs Drown in Washington's Newest Park," *Washington Post,* March 3, 1977, 3; and Judith Robinson, Robinson & Associates, "East and West Potomac Park National Register Nomination," 2001, Section 7, 19. The NCPPC updated Mall plans in 1937, 1939, and 1941, showing changes to the footprint of the Reflecting Pool and completion of Constitution Avenue. The 1937 and 1941 studies illustrate landscape development of Potomac Park; both show a similar treatment for the areas south and north of the Reflecting Pool. In the 1937 study, trees are massed around the perimeters of blocks, surrounding central lawns; in the 1941 study (prepared with the assistance of Gilmore Clarke), the lines of trees are broken and irregular, extending into the central lawns and with openings along the block boundaries. See Maureen DeLay Joseph and Perry Wheelock, "Lincoln Memorial Cultural Landscape Report," U.S. Department of the Interior, National Park Service, National Capital Region, 1999, 52; NCPPC, "The Mall, Central Area, Study for Development," in *The Mall in Washington, 1791–1991,* ed. Richard Longstreth (Hanover and London: National Gallery of Art, 1991), 225, plate XCIV; and NCPPC, Gilmore Clarke, consultant, "Development of the Central Area West and East of the Capitol, Washington, D.C.," in Longstreth, *The Mall in Washington,* 225, plate XCV.

125 Joseph and Wheelock, "Lincoln Memorial Cultural Landscape Report," 56n65; and Commission of Fine Arts, *15th Report, July 1, 1944 to June 30, 1948* (Washington, DC: Government Printing Office, 1948), 91.

126 Constitution Gardens Cultural Resource files, under "Description/Research," National Park Service, National Capital Region, National Mall and Memorial Parks (NAMA), undated. Other bicentennial projects included the construction of a $1.8 million sports pavilion in Anacostia Park and a $3.5 million indoor ice-skating rink and sports complex in Fort Dupont Park. See "Bicentennial Parks," *Washington Post,* June 6, 1976, 38.

127 SOM, "Mall Circulation System," 24.

128 Other designers involved included consulting landscape architect Dan Kiley; landscape architect Henry Arnold of Arnold Associates; and architect Richard Giegengack and landscape architect George Dickie, both of SOM. See Obituary, "Richard Giegengack," *Washington Post,* January 17, 2007, B7; and Ed Desautels, "The Art of Democracy," *Penn Stater* 1–2, no. 94 (January–February 1994): 23.

129 National Park Service, Technical Information Center, Denver Service Center, Plan TIC 801/84082, Constitution Gardens base plan, undated. The idea was First Lady Patricia Nixon's. John Parsons, in-

130 terview by Kay Fanning, April 26, 2006; and David Childs, interview by Kay Fanning, September 6, 2006.

130 CFA minutes December 15, 1971, 2; and CFA minutes February 16, 1972, 3.

131 CFA minutes, February 16, 1972, exhibit A, letter from J. Carter Brown to Secretary of the Interior Rogers C. B. Morton, February 23, 1972.

132 Paul Hodge, "Constitution Gardens: A Bicentennial Gift to Us," *Washington Post,* May 28, 1976, C7; and John Parsons, interview by Kay Fanning, April 26, 2006. This was partly in hopes of creating a permanent home for the Smithsonian Folklife Festival, which had been held south of the Reflecting Pool in 1973.

133 CFA minutes, March 20, 1974, exhibit 4, letter from J. Carter Brown to Manus J. Fish, March 25, 1974.

134 Hodge, "Constitution Gardens," May 28, 1976, C1. Hodge quotes Childs: "It's a Romantic park, not a formal classical park like the Mall, and is similar to Hyde Park in London and the Bois de Boulogne in Paris." Precedents included the woodland paths of the Bois de Boulogne, and the walks in the Tuileries, where lines of trees were planted within the edges of gravel walks. The contrast of informal garden rooms with a formal feature was adapted from the gardens of Versailles, and is seen at Constitution Gardens in the contrast of the curving lake with the rectilinear Reflecting Pool just south of the park. Spreckels Lake, in Golden Gate Park in San Francisco, a small, irregularly-shaped pond used for model boat sailing, was another inspiration. J. Carter Brown later wrote: "Childs drew inspiration from the work of Andre Le Notre; I confess I had Saint James's Park in London much more in mind." See J. Carter Brown, "The Mall and the Commission of Fine Arts," in Longstreth, *The Mall in Washington,* 251–53.

135 The soil was heavily reworked and amended but has always posed problems with drainage; trees have difficulty growing. The lake has persistent problems with water quality.

136 J. Carter Brown, "The Mall and the Commission of Fine Arts," in Longstreth, *The Mall in Washington,* 251–53.

137 CFA minutes, January 26, 1967.

138 CFA minutes, February 20, 1968, exhibit E, excerpt from transcript of meeting, and exhibit F, memo of action.

139 CFA minutes, April 17, 1968, exhibit I, excerpt from transcript of meeting, 63; Bunshaft said he doubted that Giurgola could design a building the commission would like.

140 Issue discussed in the following documents: CFA minutes, June 4, 1968, exhibit I, excerpt from transcript of meeting; September 17, 1968; and September 17, 1968, exhibit G, excerpt from transcript of meeting, "abdicating our integrity," 76.

141 CFA minutes, January 21, 1970; and CFA transcript, January 21, 1970, 50, for "terrible."

142 CFA minutes, November 19, 1969; and CFA minutes, January 21, 1970.

143 CFA transcript, April 15, 1970.

144 Warnecke was a member of the commission at the time and thus recused himself from the review.

145 CFA transcript, November 15, 1966, 116.

146 See Commission of Fine Arts, O.G case file 67-76, letter from Charles Atherton to Julian Green, November 15, 1966.

147 The discussion and the following quotations from that joint session are found in CFA minutes, April 18, 1967, exhibit R, 57–60, 63–65, 70, 73.

148 NCPC, "The Georgetown Waterfront: A Summary Report and Development Proposal," October 1961, 2.

149 This documentation series includes *Georgetown Commercial Architecture—M Street* (1967), *Georgetown Commercial Architecture—Wisconsin Avenue* (1967), *Georgetown Historic Waterfront* (1968), *Georgetown Architecture—The Waterfront* (1968), *Georgetown Residential Architecture—Northeast* (1969), *Georgetown Architecture—Northwest* (1970), and *Georgetown Architecture* (1970).

150 Robinson & Associates, a private architectural history firm, compiled the first comprehensive record with a financial grant from the D.C. State Historic Preservation Office in 1993.

151 Charles Coyer was a Washington developer and W. Burton Guy was a Baltimore realtor and mortgage banker.

152 Moore's office was located in the warehouse.

153 Wolf von Eckardt, "The Great Fence Hints the Future," *Washington Post,* August 17, 1969, H-6.

154 The Potomac Valley Chapter of the AIA conferred an honor award on Canal Square in 1970, *Progressive Architecture* featured the development as the cover story of its April 1971 issue, and the national AIA gave it an honor award in 1977.

155 CFA minutes, February 25, 1970, exhibit A.

PRESIDENTIAL COMMEMORATION IN MIDCENTURY

1 CFA transcript, June 24, 1964, 199–201. See also "Artists at Odds on Kennedy Tomb," *New York Times,* October 7, 1964.

ESSAY BY ZACHARY M. SHRAG

1 *Public Buildings and Grounds—1962: Hearing Before a Subcommittee of the Committee on Public Works,* 87th Cong., 2nd Sess. 2 (1962); and Jerald terHorst, "FBI Fortress Casts a Shadow," *Chicago Tribune,* October 5, 1975.

2 CFA transcript, June 1967, 42, Records of the Commission of Fine Arts, Record Group 66, National Archives Building, Washington, D.C. (hereafter cited CFA NAB).

3 G. Martin Moeller Jr., *AIA Guide to the Architecture of Washington,* 4th ed. (Baltimore, MD: Johns Hopkins University Press, 2006), 128.

4 Benjamin Forgey, "Government Buildings: Will They 'Go Public'?," *Washington Star,* August 27, 1976.

5 Harry Kelly, "Hoover's Memory Lives in Monolith He Called Monstrous," *Chicago Tribune,* October 1, 1975.

6 Wolf von Eckardt, "New FBI Building: Perfect Stage Set for Orwell's '1984'," *Washington Post,* July 12, 1975.

7 Sarah Booth Conroy, "Facelift for FBI Building?," *Washington Post,* February 13, 1986.

8 Val Lewton, letter to the editor, "The Writing on the Wall," *Washington Post,* February 20, 1986.

9 Chelsea Delnero, "Sister Preaches for End of Death Penalty," *The Equinox,* October 18, 2007, www.prejean.org/PressClippings/Equinox.html , accessed May 13, 2010.

10 *The Need of Architectural Improvement in the Design of Federal Buildings: Hearing Before the Subcommittee on Public Works, United State Senate,* 95th Cong., 1st Sess. 57 (1977) (statement of Wolf von Echardt).

11 William Walton, *The Evidence of Washington* (New York: Harper & Row, 1966), 51.

12 Kurt Helfrich, "Modernism for Washington? The Kennedys and the Redesign of Lafayette Square," *Washington History* 8 (Spring/Summer 1996): 22.

13 William Walton, interview by Megan Floyd Desnoyers, New York, March 30, 1993, 38, John F. Kennedy Library Oral History Program, John F. Kennedy Library and Museum, Boston, Massachusetts (hereafter cited JFK OHP).

14 Daniel P. Moynihan, forward to *Pennsylvania Avenue,* by the President's Temporary Commission on Pennsylvania Avenue (Washington, DC: Government Printing Office, 1969), 2.

15 Donald Canty, "How Washington is Run: An Ungovernment Without Top or Bottom," *Architectural Forum* 118 (January 1963): 56.

16 Witold Rybczynski, "Builder in Chief," *Slate,* June 20, 2007, www.slate.com/articles/arts/architecture/2007, accessed January 9, 2012.

17 Gary O. Larson, *The Reluctant Patron: The United States Government and the Arts, 1935–1965* (Philadelphia: University of Pennsylvania Press, 1983), 164.

18 August Heckscher, interview by Wolf von Eckardt, New York, December 10, 1965, JFK OHP.

19 "Yasko Cites Excellence in New Federal Buildings," *Architectural Record* 137 (January 1965): 23.

20 Helfrich, "Modernism for Washington?," 30, 37.

21 William Grimes, "John Carl Warnecke, Architect to Kennedy, Dies at 91," *New York Times,* April 22, 2010; and John Carl Warnecke, interview by Zachary Schrag, San Francisco, January 5, 2002.

22 Franze Schulze, *Philip Johnson: Life and Work* (Chicago: University of Chicago Press, 1996), 136–44, 163; and Warnecke interview, January 5, 2002.

23 Jean White, "New Arts Advisor Is No Dilettante," *Washington Post,* June 24, 1963.

24 Charles H. Atherton, interview by Zachary Schrag, Washington, D.C., February 15, 2000.

25 Warnecke interview, January 5, 2002.

26 Atherton interview, February 15, 2000.

27 CFA transcript, October 1965, 152.

28 Zachary M. Schrag, *The Great Society Subway: A History of the Washington Metro* (Baltimore, MD: Johns Hopkins University Press, 2006), 83–93.

29 CFA transcript, December 1965, 29

30 Executive Order No. 1259, in Sue A. Kohler, *The Commission of Fine Arts: A Brief History, 1910–1976, with Additions, 1977–1984* (Washington, DC: Government Printing Office, 1985), 160.

31 *Public Buildings in the District of Columbia: Report of the Public Buildings Commission,* 65th Cong., 2nd Sess., S. Doc. 65-155 at 3 (1917).

32 Kohler, *Commission of Fine Arts,* 52–66.

33 House Committee on Public Works, *Report to the President by the Ad Hoc Committee on Federal Office Space,* 87th Cong., 2nd Sess., H.R. 87-21, at 1 (1962).

34 National Capital Planning Commission, transcript, May 1962, 18, Transcript of Proceedings and Minutes of Meeting, 1924–1999, Records of the NCPC NAB), Group 328.

35 Walton, *Evidence of Washington,* 45.

36 Nathan Glazer, *From a Cause to a Style: Modernist Architecture's Encounter with the American City* (Princeton: Princeton University Press, 2007), 149–50.

37 House Committee on Public Works, *Report to the President by the Ad Hoc Committee on Federal Office Space,* 11–12.

38 Elmer Staats, interview by Robert C. Turner, Washington, D.C., July 13, 1964, JFK OHP; Warnecke interview, January 5, 2002; Karel Yasko, interview by William McHugh, Washington, D.C., December 14, 1966, JFK OHP; and Wolf von Eckardt, "Washington's Chance for Splendor," *Harper's* (September 1963): 62.

39 CFA transcript, May 1964, 128.

40 CFA transcript, September 1964, 24; CFA transcript, November 1964, 48; and CFA transcript, June 1967, 9–11.

41 Warnecke interview, January 5, 2002.

42 *Department of the Interior and Related Agencies Appropriations for Fiscal Year 1970: Hearings on H.R. 12781 Before a Subcommittee of the Committee on Appropriations, United States Senate,* 91st Cong., 1st Sess., at 1323 (1969) (statements of William Walton and Karl Mundt).

43 William Walton to Lawson B. Knott Jr., November 30, 1965, Box 66, CFA NAB.

44 Senate Committee on Public Works, *Authorizing Use of Space Over and Under 10th Street Southwest in District of Columbia in Connection with Federal Office Building,* 87th Cong., 2nd Sess., S. Rep. No. 87-1776 at 3 (1962).

45 CFA transcript, November 20, 1963, 24, 35.

46 CFA transcript, September 1964, 6.

47 Ibid., 20.

CHAPTER VI

48 CFA transcript, September 1964, 20, 25.

49 *Department of the Interior and Related Agencies Appropriations for Fiscal Year 1970: Hearings on H.R. 12781, Part 3 Before a Subcommittee of the Committee on Appropriations, House of Representatives,* 91st Cong., 1st Sess., at 12 (1969) (statement of William Walton).

50 *Department of the Interior and Related Agencies Appropriations for Fiscal Year 1970: Hearings on H.R. 12781, Part 3 Before a Subcommittee of the Committee on Appropriations, House of Representatives,* 91st Cong., 1st Sess., at 11 (1969) (statement of William Walton).

51 CFA transcript, June 1967, 43.

52 CFA transcript, November 1964, 49.

53 CFA transcript, October 1964, 20–24.

54 Warnecke interview, January 5, 2002.

55 CFA transcript, January 1964, 14.

56 National Capital Planning Commission transcript, June 1964, NCPC NAB.

57 National Capital Planning Commission transcript, November 1965, 18–19, and January 1966, 65–67, NCPC NAB.

58 National Capital Planning Commission transcript, February 1963 and June 1963, NCPC NAB.

59 CFA transcript, October 1965, 151.

60 CFA transcript, September 1963, 99.

61 National Capital Planning Commission transcript, July 1963, NCPC NAB.

62 Carter Manny, interview by Franz Schulze, 1992, Chicago Architects Oral History Project, 241, www.artic.edu, accessed July 2, 2010.

63 Edward L. Goldman to William Walton, May 10, 1967, Box 26, CFA NAB.

64 CFA transcript, November 1965, 141.

65 Beverly Gage, *The Day Wall Street Exploded: A Story of America in Its First Age of Terror* (New York: Oxford University Press, 2009), 127–30.

66 John H. Burgee to Leonard L. Hunter, May 9, 1967, CFA project files, CFA NAB.

67 CFA transcript, June 1967, 18.

68 Ibid., 40.

69 William Walton to Lawson B. Knott Jr., April 27, 1967, Box 26, CFA NAB.

70 Walton to Knott, December 27, 1965, Box 26, CFA NAB.

71 William Walton to Karel H. Yasko, November 2, 1965, Box 26, CFA NAB.

72 Roger K. Lewis, "A Daunting but Worthy Mission for the FBI," *Washington Post,* June 13, 2009.

73 CFA transcript, October 1965, 136.

74 CFA transcript, October 1964, 146.

75 CFA transcript, December 1965, 140.

76 CFA transcript, October 1965, 141.

77 Manny interview, 1992, 245–46.

78 CFA transcript, November 1965, 144.

79 CFA transcript, October 1965, 142.

80 Ibid., 148.

81 Ibid., 135.

82 Richard Severo, "Plans Approved for FBI Building," *Washington Post,* September 15, 1967.

83 C. H. Atherton to Gaylord Nelson, October 5, 1967, Box 27, CFA NAB.

84 *Department of the Interior and Related Agencies Appropriations for Fiscal Year 1970: Hearings on H.R. 12781, Part 3 Before a Subcommittee of the Committee on Appropriations, House of Representatives,* 91st Cong., 1st Sess., at 9 (1969) (statement of William Walton).

85 Ada Louise Huxtable, "The F.B.I. Building," *New York Times,* January 24, 1972.

86 National Capital Planning Commission and U.S. Commission of Fine Arts, *Monumental Core Framework Plan* (2009), 70, www.ncpc.gov/DocumentDepot/Publications/Framework, accessed January 10, 2012.

1   William H. Jones, "1976 Bicentennial May Trigger Boom," *Washington Post Times-Herald,* January 9, 1972.

2   The National Historic Preservation Act was passed by Congress in 1966. Federal tax reform in 1977 enabled the National Park Service to create the Federal Historic Preservation Tax Incentives Program. At the local level, the District of Columbia passed a Historic Landmark and Historic District Protection Act in 1978. By the 1990s, the city was also using localized taxation tools, such as tax increment financing (TIF), as an incentive to attract development.

3   Kathryn Welch Howe, "Private Sector Involvement in Historic Preservation," in *A Richer Heritage: Historic Preservation in the Twenty-First Century,* ed. Robert E. Stipe (Chapel Hill: The University of North Carolina Press, 2003), 279–81, 286–89.

4   Michael Grunwald, "D.C.'s Fear of Heights," *Washington Post,* July 2, 2006. Also, as noted in the Staff Report for the Committee on the District of Columbia, House of Representatives, *Building Height Limitations,* 94th Cong., 2nd Sess. (April 1, 1976), 15–17, 55–57, generally this meant a maximum height of 130 feet for "business streets" and 80 feet (later amended to 90 feet in 1925) for residential uses. The law also contained an exemption on the north side of Pennsylvania Avenue roughly between the Capitol and the Department of the Treasury, allowing up to 160 feet, but the city's zoning code did not allow the maximum height in this area. The report said congressional action built upon a height regulation passed by the city's Board of Commissioners in 1894, which a news article of the time attributes to protests from neighbors of the newly built, 160-foot Cairo Hotel at 1615 Q Street, who claimed it was a fire hazard and reduced their access to light and air (p. 15). The report also references an article in the April–June 1895 issue of *Architectural Record* that raised the issue of the Cairo's impact on "the beauty of Washington." The report added that a local newspaper, the *Evening Star,* lauded the new regulation for setting both a minimum and maximum height and "bringing about a very desirable condition of uniformity" (pp. 16–17).

5   *Building Height Limitations,* 57–58.

6   John B. Willman, "It's Happening in Real Estate—Suburban Buildings Climb Modestly While D.C. Lives Under 1910 Rules," *Washington Post,* June 12, 1971, found in *Building Height Limitations,* 170–71.

7   Thomas W. Fletcher, assistant to Commissioner Walter E. Washington, Government of the District of Columbia, to Honorable John L. McMillan, October 20, 1969, found in *Building Height Limitations,* 134–36.

8   CFA transcript, November 17, 1971, 17, 23.

9   Ibid., 27.

10 Following Brown's statement at the November 17, 1971, meeting, CFA Secretary Charles Atherton shared with the members a CFA resolution passed on March 11, 1953, and sent to the D.C. Zoning Commission on the occasion of an earlier effort to increase building heights: *The Commission of Fine Arts is not concerned with the legal, financial or technical aspects of building height limitations. We are concerned only with the aesthetic factor and in Washington, that is a very important one. We believe that Washington is fortunate in being a relatively low construction city. Low construction adds to the city's order and dignity, gives us plenty of light and air, makes an appropriate setting for the monumental buildings, and helps to attract visitors. In our opinion the present legal height limitations in the central area have reached—and perhaps exceeded—the aesthetically desirable limits. We believe that Washington gains aesthetically by every decision that maintains the low construction character of the city.* (CFA transcript, November 17, 1971, 28)

11 Kirk Scharfenberg, "Twenty-five Story Buildings Proposed—Mayor to Ask Hill to Raise Height Limit," *Washington Post,* February 13, 1972, found in *Building Height Limitations,* 173.

12 Staff Report for the Committee on the District of Columbia, House of Representatives, *Impediments to the Economic, Functional, and Aesthetic Development of the District of Columbia, the Nation's Capital,* 94th Cong., 2nd Sess. (December 20, 1976), 15, 159.

13 Ibid., 15.

14 CFA minutes, July 25, 1978, exhibit C, statement of Charles Atherton to the Arlington County Planning Commission.

15 CFA transcript, August 22, 1978, 8.

16 CFA transcript, October 24, 1978, 13.

17 Ibid., 15.

18 Sandra G. Boodman, "Pentagon City Tower Is Approved: Office Structure Part of Protested Major Development," *Washington Post,* January 7, 1979.

19 Ibid.

20 Sandra G. Boodman, "Rosslyn High-Rise Suit by Interior Dept. Is Rejected," *Washington Post,* February 21, 1979.

21 Ibid.

22 Pub. L. No. 92-578, 92nd Cong., H.R. 10751 (October 27, 1972), as amended.

23 The advisory panel included the chairman of the NCPC, the architect of the Capitol, and the director of the District's Department of Housing and Community Development.

24 Ron Eichner, former assistant to the PADC executive director, telephone interview by Mary Konsoulis, October 1, 2010.

25 CFA PADC files, folder A-ORG-PADC correspondence, memorandum from Donald B. Myer, assistant secretary, to Charles H. Atherton, secretary, regarding PADC board meeting, March 15, 1977: "General Quesada [PADC executive director] raved about the assistance given PADC and the potential service in the future from the Commission of Fine Arts. He included with the agenda a copy of Carter's statement at the House Appropriations committee hearing. He attributed the survival of PADC in part to the Commission of Fine Arts' testimony."

26 CFA transcript, May 15, 1974, 35.

27 CFA minutes, May 15, 1974, exhibit 3, letter with attachment of findings from J. Carter Brown to Mayor Walter Washington, May 18, 1974.

28 CFA transcript, March 20, 1974, 28.

29 Ibid., 12–13, 29, 39, 96. The presentations were made by the memorial's architect, Wallace K. Harrison (CFA 1955–59), who had been involved with the project since the 1950s, and its sponsor, the American Battle Monuments Commission (ABMC). The meeting also was significant because Brown briefed the CFA members on the PADC board meeting of March 18, 1974, where a preliminary plan for Pennsylvania Avenue was approved. He noted that he had received "a verbal guarantee" that the CFA would review the plan and resulting projects, and the PADC "indicated . . . that they will want the Fine Arts Commission to be the sole design review body and that they will come to us as things develop" (p. 8). Brown then reviewed the plan elements, noting that National Square had been reduced; housing was being introduced; and the Willard Hotel, Evening Star building, and Old Post Office were to be retained. A sticking point for Brown and others was the plan's proposed depression of Constitution Avenue at the National Gallery; Kevin Roche and Edward D. Stone Jr., in particular, were concerned that the issue needed to be addressed sooner rather than later to avoid suggesting support through silence. Brown directed that the minutes reflect a CFA resolution against the tunnel (pp. 12–13). See also CFA minutes, June 12, 1974, exhibit 10, letter from J. Carter Brown (signed by Charles Atherton) to Colonel William Jones of the American Battle Monuments Commission, June 14, 1974, recommending that the concept should be changed to a "landscape solution."

30 CFA minutes, July 30, 1975, exhibit G, letter from J. Carter Brown to Colonel Frederick Badger, American Battle Monuments Commission, August 13, 1975.

31 CFA transcript, September 17, 1975, 32.

32 CFA transcript, March 20, 1974, 11–12. This new plaza would also provide a setting for the District Building. CFA staff was aware of an earlier proposal put forth by the District as an alternative to the PADC plan. At the CFA meeting of March 20, 1974, Donald Myer, CFA assistant secretary, noted that the District planning office suggested including an addition to the District Building and a new adjacent building: "They are talking about pulling it into alignment with the District Building and leaving this piece off so that a square is formed here as well as here so that you'd have sort of a District Square. . . . They are talking in terms of strolling troubadours and very lively aspects of the Avenue as well."

33 CFA minutes, September 17, 1975, 3–4.

34 CFA transcript, July 30, 1975, 143–44.

35 CFA transcript, September 17, 1975, 5.

36 CFA transcript, October 15, 1975, 33.

37 Ibid., 44.

38 John Woodbridge, telephone interview by Mary Konsoulis, October 13, 2010.

39 CFA transcript, November 19, 1975, 63, 67.

40 CFA minutes, November 19, 1975, exhibit C, letter from J. Carter Brown to E. R. Quesada, chairman, PADC, December 8, 1975.

41 CFA transcript, January 27, 1976, 20.

42 Ibid., 21.

43 Ibid., 47.

44 CFA transcript, April 21, 1976, 54–55.

45 Dorothy Webb, "Pennsylvania Avenue: What Development Will Really Do," *Washington Post,* July 30, 1977.

46 CFA transcript, February 17, 1982, 62–63. The PADC also initiated a ten-year streetscape improvements program in 1976 to upgrade lighting, paving, curbs, and landscaping along Pennsylvania Avenue, all of which were reviewed by the CFA.

47 PADC, "The Avenue Report," December 1977, 1–2, found in CFA PADC files, folder A-org-PADC clippings, news releases, staff notes.

48 Ronald Eichner, telephone interview by Mary Konsoulis, October 1, 2010. For additional information about this episode, see The Cultural Landscape Foundation, M. Paul Friedberg oral history interview transcript at www.tclf.org/pioneer/oral-history-project; Annette Michaelson, Richard Serra, and Clara Weyerhoff, "The Films of Richard Serra: An Interview," in *Writings/Interviews,* ed. Richard Serra (Chicago: University of Chicago Press, 1994), 94–95n10; and Grace Glueck, "Art People: A Tale of Two Pylons," *New York Times,* April 7, 1978.

49 Joann Neuhaus, telephone interview by Mary Konsoulis, September 27, 2010; and Ronald Eichner, telephone interview by Mary Konsoulis, October 1, 2010.

50 Grace Glueck, "Art People: A Tale of Two Pylons."

51 CFA transcript, March 2, 1978, 42–44.

52 Ibid., 47–50.

53 This experience was a far cry from Venturi's earlier experience before the CFA in 1968 for an office and retail project in the Southwest redevelopment area. Then, he had proposed a design that spoke in terms of the complexities of the site and the new architectural vision of postmodernism: "I think it involves an entirely different philosophy from that which much of modern architecture is judged. . . . It does not have to be a building which is a whole in itself, discrete and separated from the other buildings around it. It does not have to sit in a space; it can be a building which makes urban space around it." The CFA, then under the leadership of William Walton and counting among its members Gordon Bunshaft and Hideo Sasaki, didn't buy into his theories, with blunt-spoken Bunshaft going so far as to call it "baloney." The scheme was rejected. The project eventually was given to another architectural firm. See CFA transcript, June 4, 1968, 80–81, 90. Regarding Brown's comments about the flagpole, see CFA minutes, March 2, 1978, 6.

54 CFA minutes, May 23, 1978, 82, and exhibit D, *The Plaza for the Western Sector of Pennsylvania Avenue.*

55   CFA PADC files, folder S-R PLAN PADC Jurisdictional Units Maps–
     Western Sector 7/78, letter from Leland Allen, PADC director of de-
     sign, to Charles Atherton, July 25, 1978.

56   CFA PADC files, folder S&R LND–PADC Western Sector Design Guide-
     lines 26 July 1977, letter from Ben W. Gilbert, director, Municipal
     Planning Office, to Mr. [sic] Elwood Quesada, chairman, PADC, Sep-
     tember 19, 1978. See also CFA PADC files, folder A-org-PADC cor-
     respondence, handwritten cover letter from John Fondersmith, Mu-
     nicipal Planning Office, to Donald Myer, CFA, June 8, 1977, with at-
     tachment Design Concepts for the Western Sector of Pennsylvania Av-
     enue (Draft); and CFA transcript, July 26, 1977, 67–68.

57   Joann Neuhaus, telephone interview by Mary Konsoulis, Septem-
     ber 27, 2010. See also interview with Ronald Eichner, October 1,
     2010.

58   CFA PADC files, folder S&R-BLD-PADC Western Plaza ’78, letter from
     Cyril B. Paumier Jr., Land Design/Research, Inc., to J. Carter Brown,
     chairman, Commission of Fine Arts, February 9, 1979, with
     attached cover memo from J. Carter Brown to Charles Atherton, Feb-
     ruary 20, 1979, that reads: “Told Andy [W. Anderson Barnes, PADC
     executive director] about Olson’s lobbying on West Plaza—he said
     he was aware that the Soc. of Landscape Architects is after a land-
     scape solution—natch—and he’ll tell Sasaki & Co. who work for
     PADC to quit the back-pressure.”

59   CFA transcript, March 27, 1979, 25–38.

60   CFA minutes, September 20, 1979, 3.

61   As an example, see Wolf von Eckardt, “Bare and Square Western
     Plaza: Venturi’s Literary Traffic Island,” Washington Post, Decem-
     ber 20, 1980.

62   CFA minutes, January 20, 1994, 6, and exhibit F, letter from J. Carter
     Brown to Richard Hauser, chairman, PADC board, January 31, 1994.
     The minutes indicate that Brown supported the idea, suggesting an
     interesting “what if” scenario: “The Chairman said he thought the
     idea of using the plaza for a World War II memorial was a good one.
     It would avoid another large memorial on the Mall and in dignity
     and importance of location the site could not be surpassed. It would
     also complete Venturi’s original design, which the Commission had
     supported although it had not gained approval from the other agen-
     cies involved” (p. 6). A memo from Charles Atherton to Brown dat-
     ed November 24, 1989, suggests the two were contemplating the idea
     of a proposed World War II memorial in the plaza even earlier, and
     in relation to the PADC’s suggested changes: “If we are at all seri-
     ous about suggesting Freedom Plaza as a site for the soon-to-be-
     authorized major memorial to World War II, then I think the tim-
     ing on this fountain competition raises very serious questions.” See
     CFA PADC files, folder PADC: Freedom Plaza Fountain Redesign Com-
     petition.
        In the 1980s, Brown was expressing irritation with Venturi and
     attempts at redesign: “Given our past experience with this partic-
     ular architect, I can say that flexibility may not be as characteristic
     as other talents” (CFA transcript, February 8, 1983, 118–19, 122–23).
     Despite modifications to the design, Brown appears to remain un-
     convinced regarding the outcome. During a discussion about sig-
     nage for the National Theater across from Western Plaza, Brown re-
     ferred to it as “our problem child plaza” and thought the theater sig-
     nage would bring needed liveliness to the area (CFA transcript, July
     12, 1983, 63).

63   The Pershing Memorial took another few years to complete. The CFA
     approved Robert White as sculptor of the Pershing statue at its Oc-
     tober 1979 meeting and reviewed the modeling and casting of the
     piece during 1982 and 1983; it was installed by the end of 1983.

64   CFA transcript, March 27, 1979, 30.

65   CFA transcript, April 21, 1976, 28–31. New public open space pro-
     posed for Indiana Avenue was also reviewed at this meeting.

66   Ibid., 34.

67   CFA transcript, July 24, 1979, 10–12.

68   CFA transcript, February 17, 1982, 64. The PADC would pay for pub-
     lic improvements in the park while the Navy Memorial Foundation
     would pay for the costs associated with the memorial itself through
     privately raised funding.

69   CFA transcript, February 17, 1982, 68–70.

70   Ibid., 79–86, 88, 91–92. Sondra Myers noted her “reservations about
     the appropriateness of…the triumphal arch, as a contemporary state-
     ment and the traditional design of it with not much recognition [of]
     the time it is being built in,” and Harold Burson concurred, finding
     the design of a classical arch confusing: “Why would you build an
     arch that looks like that right now?” Countering these views, Alan
     Novak thought the arch “looks backward and yet is of our time,” al-
     though he did find that the area surrounding the arch required better
     definition. Edward D. Stone Jr. wondered if the acoustic panels would
     work as intended, but he did think the arcade appropriate for Wash-
     ington’s climate. The remaining members, architect Walter Netsch
     and architect John Chase, were not at the meeting.

71   Ibid., 88, 92, 94.

72   Ibid., 95.

73   CFA transcript, July 12, 1983, 64–65. Building height for the proposed
     new development on the north side of Market Square also was
     changed to seventy-five feet, which the PADC considered more com-
     patible with the scale of the Archives and nearby historic structures
     at Indiana Avenue.

74   Ibid., 67–74.

75   Ibid., 89.

76   Ibid., 91.

77   CFA minutes, December 11, 1985, 12.

78   Six of the seven members of the CFA were newly appointed in 1985
     by President Reagan and included two sculptors, a landscape architect,
     a business consultant, a politician, and a lawyer. For the first time
     in its history, the CFA did not have an architect among its members.

79   CFA minutes, December 11, 1986, exhibit D, letter from J. Carter
     Brown to James Brodie, PADC, January 3, 1986.

80   Kirk Scharfenberg, “Restoration Considered for Post Office Build-
     ing,” Washington Post, July 1, 1971. Georgetown Inland Corpora-
     tion, a subsidiary of Inland Steel Corporation and already active in
     the redevelopment of the Georgetown waterfront, expressed interest
     in leasing the building from the government for renovation into a
     hotel, office, and retail complex. The Federal Advisory Council on
     Historic Preservation, a group of government officials and private
     citizens, had already come out in support of preserving the build-
     ing and converting it into a new commercial-retail use. (The reno-
     vation that did take place toward the end of the 1970s did not in-
     clude a hotel.)

81   Scott G. Shultz, “America’s Watchtower: Saving the Old Post Office,”
     CRM Magazine 21, no. 2 (1998): 24.

82   CFA minutes, January 19, 1978, exhibit E, letter from J. Carter Brown
     to Joel W. (Jay) Solomon, administrator, GSA, January 26, 1978; and
     CFA minutes, January 19, 1978, 3.

83   CFA minutes, March 27, 1979, exhibit B, letter from J. Carter Brown
     to Ray Nixon, GSA, April 6, 1979.

84   CFA transcript, April 21, 1982, 14.

85   CFA minutes, April 21, 1982, 3–4.

86   CFA minutes, April 21, 1982, exhibit H, letter from J. Carter Brown
     to Bertrand G. Berube, regional administrator, GSA, May 13, 1982.

87   CFA transcript, April 16, 1987, 88–90, 96.

88   Ibid., 108, 117–18. It’s interesting to note that at this point in time,
     aside from Hart’s concerns about density consuming open space, the
     building’s square footage prompted only a few questions from mem-
     bers asking for clarification of the numbers and the change in size
     since the 1982 plan.

89   CFA transcript, April 21, 1988, 34–39.

90   CFA minutes, April 21, 1988, 4.

91   CFA transcript, April 21, 1988, 45.

92 Ibid., 69. Brown was able to do this but not before an exasperated exchange with Diane Wolf, a CFA member with a keen interest in coins and medals, who had strayed far afield in the conversation. He finally retorted, "There is so much money in this. It is not like designing a coin."

93 CFA transcript, October 19, 1989, 79.

94 Ibid., 81–82. The team also included the Washington architectural and engineering firm Ellerbe Becket and the landscape architect Peter Walker.

95 CFA minutes, November 15, 1989, 3–4.

96 CFA transcript, November 15, 1989, 43–44, 47.

97 CFA minutes, November 15, 1989, exhibit A, letter from J. Carter Brown to Richard Hauser, chairman, PADC, November 29, 1989.

98 Most of the CFA membership had changed by this time. New members were Joan Abrahamson, an attorney and painter; Adele Chatfield-Taylor, a preservationist; Robert Peck, an attorney and GSA public buildings commissioner; and George Hartman, an architect. J. Carter Brown and Neil Porterfield remained from the previous commission. One position was vacant until 1992.

99 CFA minutes, February 21, 1991, 4, and exhibit A, letter from J. Carter Brown to Richard Hauser, chairman, PADC, March 5, 1991.

100 CFA minutes, June 26, 1991, exhibit C, letter from J. Carter Brown to Richard Hauser, chairman, PADC, July 11, 1991.

101 The firm's founding partners had formerly worked for the Harry Weese & Associates office in Washington, D.C. For a discussion of the events leading to KCCT's split from Weese & Associates in 1983, see Robert Bruegman, *The Architecture of Harry Weese* (New York: W. W. Norton & Company, 2010), 72.

102 CFA minutes, October 25, 1990, 6–7, and exhibit D, letter from J. Carter Brown to Mr. Crichlow, GSA, November 5, 1990.

103 CFA minutes, December 19, 1974, exhibit G, letter from J. Carter Brown to Larry Roush, commissioner, Public Buildings Service, GSA, December 23, 1974.

104 The CFA had supported the adaptation of the Pension Building into the National Building Museum, reviewing and approving concepts for the exterior restoration and landscaping in April 1986 with further review of a revised landscape plan in November 1991. While the CFA approved the plan, it recommended simplifying the design and expressed reluctance with the idea of closing F Street to create a park connected to the National Law Enforcement Officers Memorial. The CFA did not approve a proposed glass canopy on G Street, recommending a canvas canopy instead. See CFA minutes, November 1991, 5–7, and exhibit D, letter from J. Carter Brown to James C. Handley, regional administrator, GSA, December 9, 1991.

105 CFA minutes, July 23, 1992, 10, and exhibit G, letter from J. Carter Brown to Thomas M. Sherman, assistant regional director, Public Building Service, GSA, July 29, 1992.

106 CFA minutes, September 24, 1992, 9.

107 CFA minutes, May 19, 1994, exhibit H, letter from J. Carter Brown to Jack Finberg, GSA, June 1, 1994.

108 CFA minutes, September 19, 1995, 8.

109 Ibid., exhibit C, letter from J. Carter Brown to James E. Kerr, project director, Arena Task Force, October 4, 1995.

110 CFA minutes, May 16, 1996, exhibit H, letter from Brown to Kerr, June 3, 1996.

111 CFA minutes, June 19, 1997, exhibit A, letter from J. Carter Brown to Allen Yew, managing director of development, Washington Convention Center Authority, June 30, 1997.

112 The facades of the buildings in the 2000 block of I Street were eventually incorporated into the Red Lion Row project, which placed a large, modern building behind the nineteenth-century facades and contributed to the disfavor among preservationists for "facadomies."

113 CFA transcript, May 20, 1976, 10–12.

114 Ibid., 12–13.

115 CFA transcript, July 28, 1976, 77.

116 "Needless Demolition," *Washington Post*, August 18, 1976.

117 CFA transcript, December 21, 1976, 119. CFA members architect Victorine du Pont Homsey (CFA 1976–80), architect Frederick Doveton Nichols, and painter George Weymouth were concerned that so little of the G Street houses were being retained. George Weymouth's remarks were succinct regarding the artificiality of the solution: "You have got the whole street along there, to take it all down and pretend you can put it back is a false front."

118 Oliver T. Carr Jr., "Save Metropolitan Square," *Washington Post*, October 9, 1983.

119 CFA transcript, March 2, 1978, 60.

120 Ibid., 73–74.

121 CFA transcript, September 26, 1978, 89.

122 Ibid., 86, 93–94.

123 Ibid., 94–95.

124 CFA minutes, April 24, 1979, exhibit A, letter from J. Carter Brown to Mayor Marion Barry, May 2, 1979.

125 CFA minutes, May 22, 1979, 2. Earlier, the Committee to Save Rhodes Tavern had pursued litigation against the CFA for improper compliance under Section 106 of the Historic Preservation Act in its decision to support demolition. The suit was dismissed by the U.S. District Court based on lack of federal jurisdiction, and in May 1979 the committee's request for reversal was also dismissed.

126 In "Save Metropolitan Square," published in the *Washington Post* on October 9, 1983, developer Oliver T. Carr Jr. stated that the company did not receive financial support from the city to preserve the bank and theater facades and the interior of the Old Ebbitt Grill: "With the plan completed by 1979, the company agreed to finance—without any public or private contributions—the preservation of three of the four landmarks on the site: the Metropolitan Bank facade, the Keith Albee Building facade and the interior of the Old Ebbitt Grill. The company entered into contractual understandings with the D.C. government and Don't Tear It Down to formalize this accord. The city government agreed to contribute nonfinancial support."

127 CFA minutes, October 23, 1979, 8–9.

128 Oliver T. Carr Jr., "Save Metropolitan Square," *Washington Post*, October 9, 1983.

129 CFA transcript, May 10, 1983, 72–73.

130 Ibid., 86, 111.

131 Ibid., 87–88.

132 Ibid., 87–89.

133 Ibid., 112–13.

134 CFA minutes, June 17, 1999, exhibit 7, "Dedication of Rhodes Tavern Commemorative Plaque Remarks of Charles H. Atherton, Secretary," June 1999.

135 These include the Tax Reform Act of 1976, the Revenue Act of 1978, and the Economic Recovery Tax Act of 1981. Some incentives were diminished by the Tax Reform Act of 1986. See Norman Tyler, *Historic Preservation: An Introduction to its History, Principles, and Practice* (New York: W. W. Norton & Company, 2000), 58.

136 Kirk Scharfenberg, "Arts Panel Opposes Georgetown Office," *Washington Post Times-Herald,* April 20, 1972.

137 CFA minutes, September 19, 1973, exhibit A, excerpt from transcript of meeting, 203–04.

138 Ibid., 205.

139 William Marlin, "Georgetown's Nice New Neighbor," *Architectural Record* (February 1977): 98.

140 CFA transcript, April 19, 1972, 105, 108.

141 Ibid., 108.

142 CFA transcript, May 17, 1972, 38, 40.

143 CFA transcript, November 23, 1976, 59.

144 Ibid., 62–63.

145 CFA transcript, March 10, 1981, 142.

146 Paul Goldberger, "It's not politics they're talking about in D.C.; it's an urban mall." See the *Baltimore Sun*, October 26, 1981.

147 Benjamin Forgey, "The New City in Town," *Washington Post*, October 24, 1981.

148 CFA transcript, April 21, 1976, 116.

149 CFA transcript, May 24, 1977, 85; and Wolf von Eckardt, "A Clockwork Lemon," *Washington Post*, October 6, 1979.

150 CFA transcript, October 18, 1972, 7.

151 Ibid., 20.

152 Ibid., 24.

153 CFA minutes, September 27, 1977, 8.

154 In time, representatives from the Commission of Fine Arts resigned from the task force because the proposals were becoming too architecturally prescriptive, whereas the Citizens Association of Georgetown withdrew from the committee in opposition to the excessive size of the proposed building envelope.

155 96th Cong., 2nd Sess., S. 1495 and H.R. 4947.

156 CFA transcript, December 11, 1979, 123, 125, 128.

157 CFA minutes, March 10, 1981, 118–19.

158 CFA transcript, March 10, 1981, 122.

159 Letter from Sondra Myers to J. Carter Brown, March 16, 1981, in "Sondra Gelb Myers," CFA member file.

160 Letter from Senator Mark Hatfield to J. Carter Brown, April 8, 1981, RG2C1, Records of the Office of the Director, J. Carter Brown, Box 33, Folder "Waterfront 1981," in National Gallery of Art Archives.

161 Mayor's Agent for D.C. Law 2-144, the Historic Landmark and Historic District Protection Act of 1978, order issued September 11, 1981, HPA No. 81-244.

162 CFA transcript, March 19, 1998, 142–44.

163 CFA minutes, May 20, 1976. The CFA also supported the passage of city legislation—D.C. Bill 1-228 in 1976—that required closer scrutiny of subdivision requests in historic districts.

164 Sue A. Kohler, *The Commission of Fine Arts: A Brief History 1910–1995* (Washington, DC: Government Printing Office, 1996), 195.

165 CFA transcript, November 20, 1997, 106.

166 The Old Georgetown Board reviewed all applications, but only new construction applications were presented to the commission.

167 CFA transcript, March 19, 1998, 93–94, 107–08. The architectural historian was Eve Barsoum.

168 The U.S. House of Representatives sought to eliminate the NCACA program from the 2012 fiscal year budget, but it was funded at the reduced level of $2 million.

169 *Commemorative Works Act of 1986*, 40 USC 1001, sec. 8901.

170 The site had been proposed for the Smithsonian's history and technology museum in the 1920s and, from World War I to the opening of the National Air and Space Museum in 1975, had housed the Institution's Air Museum in a Quonset structure. See CFA minutes, April 8, 1980, 8.

171 CFA minutes, April 24, 1979, 8, and exhibit G, letter from J. Carter Brown to Senator Claiborne Pell, April 27, 1979.

172 CFA minutes, April 8, 1980, 9, and exhibit D, letter from J. Carter Brown to Philip Reiss, director, Office of Facilities Planning and Engineering Services, Smithsonian Institution, April 17, 1980.

173 CFA minutes, September 16, 1981, 4.

174 Ibid., and exhibit C, letter from Brown to Reiss, September 30, 1981.

175 CFA minutes, December 15, 1981, 2–3, and exhibit B, letter from Brown to Reiss, January 12, 1982.

176 CFA minutes, July 13, 1982, exhibit C, letter from J. Carter Brown to Phillip S. Hughes, under secretary, Smithsonian Institution, August 5, 1982.

177 CFA minutes, December 14, 1982, 2, and exhibit B, letter from J. Carter Brown to S. Dillon Ripley, secretary, Smithsonian Institution, January 4, 1983.

178 CFA transcript, February 20, 1992, 107–09.

179 CFA minutes, February 20, 1992, 8.

180 Ibid., exhibit D, letter from J. Carter Brown to Robert P. Dillman, P.E., director, Office of Design and Construction, Smithsonian Institution, March 9, 1992.

181 CFA minutes, September 19, 1999, 10–11.

182 Ibid., 10–14, and exhibit F, letter from J. Carter Brown to William L. Thomas, acting director, Office of Design and Construction, Smithsonian Institution, October 4, 1995.

183 CFA minutes, October 17, 1996, exhibit A, letter from J. Carter Brown to Patrick Miller, director, Office of Physical Plan, Smithsonian Institution, October 25, 1996.

184 Benjamin Forgey, "A Step in the Wrong Direction; Smithsonian Fails to Match Vision of Fired Architect," *Washington Post*, April 24, 1999.

185 Tobey & Davis, a local firm, was associated with Polshek Partnership on the NMAI project. Several consultants of Native American lineage who had worked on the project with Cardinal remained on the team, including architect Johnpaul Jones. See CFA minutes, April 21, 1999, 2–3.

186 CFA minutes, April 21, 1991, 6–7, and exhibit C, letter from J. Carter Brown to I. Michael Heyman, secretary, Smithsonian Institution, April 27, 1999.

187 CFA minutes, June 17, 1999, 3, and exhibit C, letter from Brown to Heyman, June 22, 1999.

188 CFA minutes, September 19, 2002, exhibit B, letter from Harry G. Robinson III, Faia, chairman, to Harry Rombach, R.A., associate director, Facilities and Planning and Assessment, Smithsonian Institution, October 4, 2002.

189 CFA transcript, May 15, 1985, 30.

190 CFA minutes, May 15, 1985, 3–6.

191 CFA minutes, June 28, 1985, exhibit A, letter from J. Carter Brown to Honorable Donald P. Hodel, secretary, U.S. Department of the Interior, July 24, 1985, 1.

192 Bill Hannah consulted on the landscape design. Notter, Feingold & Alexander remained on the project as associated architects and later designed associated space for the memorial museum in an existing building near the site, known as Annex 3, which had initially been considered expendable during the design phase of the memorial museum. See CFA minutes, May 22, 1987, 2, and exhibit A, letter from Brown to Hodel, June 2, 1987; and CFA minutes, July 26, 1990, 2.

193 CFA minutes, May 22, 1987, 2.

194 CFA minutes, February 18, 1988, 3.

195 CFA minutes, March 17, 1988, 3–4.

196 Ibid., 4–5.

197 CFA minutes, April 28, 1988, 3.

198 See "In Memory of Franklin Delano Roosevelt," Historical Marker Date Base, www.HMdb.org, accessed April 13, 2011; and FDR Memorial, Trust for the National Mall, www.nationalmall.org, accessed April 13, 2011.

199 The advisory committee for the site included Pietro Belluschi; he and Joseph Hudnut served on the jury. See William A. Millen, "FDR Memorial Will Receive Early Action," *Washington Star*, January 30, 1959.

200 Public Law 86-214, September 1, 1959.

201 In 1964, Paul Tilney left the firm, and it was renamed William F. Pedersen & Associates, which remained in operation until Pedersen retired in 1989. See William Pedersen, "Modern Homes Survey," www.preservationnation.org, accessed April 12, 2011. William Pedersen's firm is unrelated to the New York architecture firm Kohn Pedersen Fox Associates, which was founded in 1976.

202 Architecture critic Wolf von Eckardt quoted the December 31, 1960, *Washington Post* editorial in his column, "*AIA Journal* Likes FDR Memorial Plan," *Washington Post*, January 23, 1961; the column by Frederick Gutheim, "FDR Tribute Like Book Ends, out of Deep Freeze," appeared in the *Washington Post* on the same day, December 31, 1960.

203 CFA files, Franklin D. Roosevelt Memorial binder 1, "Statement of the Commission of Fine Arts, Regarding the Design of the Franklin Delano Roosevelt Memorial," February 21, 1962, 1–2. Most material reviewed for the Franklin Delano Roosevelt Memorial is contained in two binders in the CFA office, which include copies of CFA

minutes, some transcripts, action letters, numerous newspaper and magazine articles, and other materials.

204 Douglas Haskell, "The Slow Progress of Architecture in Washington," *Architectural Forum* (April 1962): 75. The commission's decision led to a claim by Douglas Haskell, editor of *Architectural Forum*, that the members had not been unanimously opposed to the memorial design—and the commission not open to modern architecture: *Another argument for competitions is that they upset cliquishness by government bodies responsible for art. The group from which these pick their artists tends ever to narrow. The Commission of Fine Arts reflects this in the way it has been bestowing or withholding its approval. It knocked out the splendid winning design of the other big national competition for a Washington government building that it was called on to review: the 1939 design for a Smithsonian Gallery of Art by the late world-famous architect Eliel Saarinen. Beaux Arts designs seem always to get through, even when they are architecturally as vacuous as the New Senate Office building. The record threatens to become permanent: Beaux Arts designs in, living architecture out.*

Also see CFA minutes, April 17, 1962, exhibit F, excerpt from transcript of meeting, unpaginated. Ralph Walker was pointed in his remarks in response to Haskell's comments about the commission and the Roosevelt memorial's design: *There was no question about it…that this was a dramatic idea. The only thing is that it was too damn bad and wrong and not appropriate to that spot…. We are willing to see change if the change moves the spirit which we think is appropriate for the city…. This is something which I think is very important for the history of this Commission, that we are willing to see new things. We just don't turn things down because of the fact that we do not like them.*

205 CFA files, Franklin D. Roosevelt Memorial binder 1, "Statement of David E. Finley, Chairman, Commission of Fine Arts, at the hearing before the Committee on House Administration of the House of Representatives, on the design of the Franklin Delano Roosevelt Memorial, June 8, 1962," and "Statement of David E. Finley, chairman, Commission of Fine Arts, at the hearing before the subcommittee on Enrolled Bills and Library of the Committee on House Administration of the House of Representatives, on June 8, 1962."

206 CFA minutes, May 20, 1964, 3–4, and exhibit E, excerpt from transcript of meeting, unpaginated.

207 CFA minutes, June 23, 1964, 2; exhibit A, excerpt from transcript of meeting, 40, 42; and exhibit B, letter from James Roosevelt to William Walton, June 23, 1964. The transcript records Gordon Bunshaft calling the design wonderful. Walton saw the commission as the city's protector even if it meant being out of step with the standards of others: "Our function is not to encourage the architectural profession or the arts in general. It is to protect the city and to try to make it as beautiful as possible. This would include bringing it up to date. I am including modern concepts in it, but we can never judge this project by a standard of saying, 'Well, I would hate to not be on record for it,' or 'I'd hate to not encourage competitions to create good designs.' That cannot be our final criterion for this decision" (p. 42).

208 CFA minutes, January 25, 1967, exhibit A, excerpt from transcript of meeting, 13–14. John Carl Warnecke called the previous design "far superior" (p. 13), and Bunshaft said, "I think myself it is typical of Breuer. I think Breuer is a nice man, not as deep an architect as we all give him credit for being" (p. 14). Aline Saarinen said it plagiarized the original design, and the slabs had "lost all meaning" (p. 14). The CFA issued a press release on January 27, 1967.

209 CFA minutes, April 16, 1975.

210 A national rose garden had also been an element of the Breuer design.

211 CFA minutes, June 25, 1975. See also Lawrence Halprin, *The Franklin Delano Roosevelt Memorial* (San Francisco: Chronicle Books, 1997).

212 CFA minutes, June 25, 1975.

213 CFA minutes, June 25, 1975, exhibit B, letter from J. Carter Brown to Manus J. Fish, June 27, 1975, for the terms "evocative and unified."

214 CFA minutes, July 30, 1975, exhibit L, letter from Brown to Fish, August 14, 1975.

215 CFA minutes, May 20, 1976.

216 Ibid., exhibit F, letter from Brown to Fish, May 25, 1976.

217 CFA minutes, February 22, 1977.

218 Ibid.

219 The sculptors were George Segal, Leonard Baskin, Robert Graham, and Neil Estern.

220 CFA minutes, November 22, 1977, exhibit A, letter from Brown to Fish, December 9, 1977.

221 CFA minutes, July 25, 1978, exhibit B, letter from J. Carter Brown to Senator Claiborne Pell, July 21, 1978.

222 CFA minutes, September 20, 1979, exhibit K, letter from J. Carter Brown to Eugene J. Keogh, chairman, Franklin D. Roosevelt Memorial Commission, October 10, 1979.

223 Editorial, "The Interior Department Repents," *Washington Star*, February 26, 1979; and Paul Hodge, "Interior Says FDR Memorial Too Costly, Withdraws Support," *Washington Post*, February 22, 1979. Charles Atherton is quoted: "We've never been married to this concept…although we approved it."

224 CFA minutes, April 19, 1990, exhibit B, excerpt from transcript of meeting, 40, 58–59; Robert Peck asked Halprin to "allow some sense of space to leap through."

225 CFA minutes, April 19, 1990, 5.

226 CFA minutes, June 21, 1990.

227 The delay was caused primarily by difficulties with Leonard Baskin's rendition of Roosevelt's First Inaugural; finally the Baskin work was replaced by an image by Robert Graham. Then a furor erupted over the perceived failure to adequately represent the fact that Roosevelt had been handicapped. After an extensive public campaign, advocates for the disabled succeeded in gaining President Clinton's backing to pass legislation requiring the representation of a wheelchair in the memorial. The CFA unanimously approved the idea, and Robert Graham prepared a life-size bronze figure of Roosevelt sitting in a wheelchair that would be placed in a new entrance room designed by Halprin. The commission was dissatisfied with Graham's inclusion of a "box-like object" between the rear wheels that Graham claimed was necessary to give weight to the composition. Brown said it was difficult for a sculpture to be both abstract and real, and if Graham used a real chair as a model, he must be historically accurate. While approving the new room, the commission required Graham to restudy the wheelchair. See CFA minutes, June 18, 1998, and May 18, 2000.

228 Binders on most of the major memorials of the last twenty years are located in the CFA office. These binders include copies of CFA minutes and action letters, numerous newspaper and magazine articles, and occasionally copies of meeting transcripts and citizens' letters sent to the commission. Most material reviewed for the Vietnam Veterans Memorial is contained in the binder of that name in the CFA office.

229 CFA minutes, July 7, 1981, excerpt from transcript, 23–24. The authorizing legislation for the memorial was S.J. Res. 119, 96th Cong. The professional advisor to the competition was Washington architect Paul Spreiregen.

230 CFA minutes, October 13, 1981, 4; exhibit E, letter from James Webb to members of the U.S. Commission of Fine Arts, October 12, 1981; and exhibit E-1, statement of Thomas Carhart to the U.S. Commission of Fine Arts, October 13, 1981. Carhart, a civilian lawyer at the Pentagon, was not trained as an artist or architect but had submitted a design to the competition.

231 CFA minutes, October 13, 1981, exhibit E-3, excerpt from transcript of meeting, 40.

232 Ibid., 46.

233 CFA minutes, November 10, 1981.

234 CFA minutes, March 9, 1982, exhibit A1, letter from J. Carter Brown to Secretary James C. Watt, Department of the Interior, March 9,

1982, suggesting that the statues could perhaps be grouped with the bronze locator box that would hold the directory guiding visitors to names on the wall.

235 CFA minutes, October 13, 1982, exhibit E1, excerpt from transcript of meeting, 58–191.

236 They disapproved the design of the locator.

237 CFA minutes, February 8, 1983.

238 CFA minutes, October 16, 1984, exhibit G.

239 CFA minutes, April 19, 1983; and transcript of meeting, 22.

240 CFA minutes, July 1992, exhibit E.

241 CFA minutes, October 16, 1984; and transcript of meeting, 101.

242 CFA minutes, October 22, 1987. The sculptor was Roger Brodin.

243 Brown added that the proliferation of elements was a problem recognized in the Commemorative Works Act. Only Roy Goodman, a state senator from New York, voted in favor of this statue.

244 CFA minutes, April 19, 1990.

245 CFA minutes, September 19, 1991; and transcript of meeting, 7. Glenna Goodacre had actually won an honorable mention; she was selected after the two winners, who had submitted a landscape design and a design for a statue of a woman in military dress, had been asked to combine their concepts. They were unable to do this, and a modified version of Goodacre's design was chosen.

246 Penn State Department of Landscape Architecture, www.larch.psu.edu/faculty/george-dickie, accessed April 25, 2011.

247 CFA minutes, September 19, 1991; and transcript of meeting, 7, 28, 30–31, 337.

248 CFA minutes, April 16, 1992; and transcript of meeting, 108.

249 CFA files, "Design Competition Description and Rules for a Korean War Veterans Memorial in Washington, D.C.," November 1988, Korean War Veterans Memorial binder (hereafter cited KWVM binder). Most material reviewed for the Korean War Veterans Memorial is contained in this binder, which includes copies of CFA minutes and action letters, numerous newspaper and magazine articles, and other materials. Paul C. Harbeson was the consulting architect to the ABMC and the competition's professional advisor.

250 The team included architects Veronica Burns Lucas and her husband John Paul Lucas, Don Alvaro Leon, and landscape architect Eliza Pennypacker Oberholtzer.

251 CFA minutes, July 26, 1989, 3–4. Neil Porterfield recused himself from voting at this and subsequent meetings because he was chair of the landscape architecture department at Penn State, but he took part in discussions. Covering all the bases, the ABMC added that it would pay tribute to those who had served in all wars.

252 CFA minutes, July 26, 1989, exhibit A, letter from J. Carter Brown to Robert Stanton, regional director, National Capital Region, National Park Service, August 9, 1989.

253 Letter from Burns Lucas Leon Lucas Architects to J. Carter Brown, October 21, 1990, KWVM binder.

254 Burns Lucas Leon Lucas quoted in Benjamin Forgey, "War Memorial Changes Blasted," Washington Post, October 25, 1990. CFA Secretary Charles Atherton was also quoted in the Forgey article as admitting there had been problems with the design. See also W. Kent Cooper, "An Analysis of Change Made to the Concept Design for the Korean War Veterans Memorial in the Period April through Sept. 1990," October 4, 1990, KWVM binder.

255 Henry Arnold had been one of the designers of Constitution Gardens and the landscape architect for the Vietnam Veterans Memorial.

256 CFA minutes, December 13, 1990, 7.

257 CFA minutes, January 17, 1991, 6, 43.

258 CFA minutes, February 21, 1991, exhibit F, letter from J. Carter Brown to Colonel Badger, ABMC, March 5, 1991; and CFA minutes, June 26, 1991, exhibit A, letter from J. Carter Brown to General Paul X. Kelly, chairman, ABMC, July 12, 1991. The term "chapel" was used by Burns Lucas Leon Lucas in the preliminary review by the CFA in July 1989. See also CFA minutes, December 13, 1990, 3, for term used by Cooper.

259 CFA minutes, December 13, 1990, 39. Veronica Burns Lucas made this statement at the meeting.

260 CFA minutes, January 16, 1992.

261 CFA minutes, September 14, 1994, 4–5. For quote, see CFA transcript, September 14, 1994, 41.

262 See Linda Wheeler, "Marines Balk at Air Force Memorial," Washington Post, August 9, 1997; and Beatriz Perez, "Groups Argue Over Military Memorial Site," Prince George's Journal, August 21, 1997.

263 Freed had also won the original competition for the memorial at Arlington Ridge, but the Air Force Memorial Foundation held a new open competition for the second site.

264 CFA transcript, April 15, 2004, 166.

265 Most of the material reviewed for the World War II Memorial is contained in two binders in the CFA office prepared by CFA staff—Binder 1: 1988-May 1999 and Binder 2: Oct. 1999- (hereafter cited WWII binder 1 or WWII binder 2). Collated material includes photocopies of CFA meeting minutes and official letters, submission materials, correspondence, congressional legislation, CFA position papers, and newspaper and periodical articles.

266 CFA minutes, April 21, 1988, exhibit J, letter from J. Carter Brown to Representative Marcy Kaptur, chair, Subcommittee on Housing and Memorial Affairs, May 9, 1988. The proposal for the memorial originated with Kaptur.

267 Instead, the bill required the Smithsonian Institution and other national museums to mark the fiftieth anniversary of the war in some manner. CFA minutes, June 22, 1989.

268 "World War II Memorial Chronology," www.wwiimemorial.com/archives/factsheets/Chronology.htm, accessed April 26, 2011.

269 Memo from Regional Director Robert Stanton, National Capital Region (NCR), National Park Service, to Director Roger G. Kennedy, National Park Service, July 18, 1995, included in September 4, 2003, fax with cover memo from Nancy Young, NCR, to Charles Atherton, photocopy in WWII binder 1.

270 NCMAC meeting transcript, September 20, 1995, 51–71 (Atherton quotation p. 63), included in September 4, 2003, fax with cover memo from Nancy Young, NCR, to Charles Atherton, photocopy in WWII binder 1.

271 CFA minutes, July 27, 1995, 3–5, for discussion of project and quotations presented.

272 CFA minutes, July 27, 1995, exhibit A4, letter from J. Carter Brown to Colonel Kevin Kelley, project manager, World War II Memorial, ABMC, August 3, 1995.

273 CFA minutes, September 19, 1995.

274 Ibid., 3.

275 Ibid., 3–4.

276 Ibid., 5, in response to a suggestion from columnist Sarah McClendon, member of the World War II Memorial Advisory Board.

277 CFA minutes, September 19, 1995, exhibit A, letter from J. Carter Brown to Colonel Kevin Kelley, American Battle Monuments Commission (ABMC), October 4, 1995.

278 CFA minutes, July 25, 1996, exhibit B, letter from J. Carter Brown to General John G. Herrling, ABMC, August 5, 1996.

279 CFA minutes, January 16, 1997. The ABMC did not wish to reveal the name of the architect because President Clinton was announcing it the next day.

280 The Rainbow Pool was entirely rebuilt in the same footprint but reduced 15 percent in size, although it was described by the architect and others as "restored." CFA transcript, July 24, 1997, 63 (Fredrich St. Floran), 36 (Admiral Haydn Williams, ABMC). At the same meeting, J. Carter Brown said it would be "preserved" (transcript, p. 15).

281 CFA minutes, July 24, 1997, 3, 7.

282 CFA minutes, July 24, 1997, 22.

283 CFA minutes, July 24, 1997, exhibit A, letter from J. Carter Brown to General Frederick F. Woerner Jr., ABMC, July 30, 1997.

284 CFA minutes, May 21, 1998.

285 Ibid., exhibit A, letter from J. Carter Brown to Haydn Williams, ABMC, May 26, 1998.

286 Frederick Lindstrom, assistant secretary, U.S. Commission of Fine Arts, interview by Mary Konsoulis, Washington, D.C., May 23, 2011.

287 The idea for a flame was first mentioned by an unnamed CFA member and J. Carter Brown at the project's concept review two years earlier on July 24, 1997. The minutes of that meeting summarize Brown's statement as "the Commission would entertain that idea if it came in but didn't know if it would be considered duplicative of the one in Arlington; he noted that it was very effective in Paris." The record indicates that the commission itself neither recommended nor advised against the flame. CFA minutes, July 24, 1997, 24.

288 CFA minutes, May 20, 1999, 5, 8–9.

289 Ibid., exhibit A, letter from J. Carter Brown to Terry Carlstrom, National Park Service, May 25, 1999.

290 CFA minutes, July 20, 2000.

DOWNTOWN'S REVIVAL ON AND OFF PENNSYLNANIA AVENUE

1 CFA transcript, December 11, 1979, 146–48.

2 CFA transcript, January 13, 1981, 62, 64, 69.

3 CFA minutes, May 16, 1984, 3–4.

4 CFA minutes, December 12, 1984, 2–3.

POSTMODERNISM AND INFILL PROJECTS IN GEORGETOWN

1 CFA transcript, June 28, 1984, 84–85.

MEMORIALS UNDER THE COMMEMORATIVE WORKS ACT

1 CFA minutes, February 23, 1989, 6.

ESSAY BY RICHARD GUY WILSON

1 Angela M. LoRé, interview by Richard Guy Wilson, Washington, D.C., December 9, 2009.

2 As noted, postmodernism's definition can be difficult. The standard text is Charles Jencks, *The Language of Post-Modern Architecture* (New York: Rizzoli, 1977), with many later editions.

3 J. Carter Brown, "Remarks before the Federal City Council," April 30, 1985, National Gallery of Art Archives, Box 32 (hereafter cited NGA). See also J. Carter Brown, "The Mall and the Commission of Fine Arts," in *The Mall in Washington, 1791–1991*, ed. Richard Longstreth (Hanover and London: National Gallery of Art, distributed by University Press of New England, 1991).

4 J. Carter Brown, "Remarks before the Federal City Council," NGA.

5 Sue A. Kohler, interview by Richard Guy Wilson, Washington, D.C., December 9, 2009. For background materials, see Sue A. Kohler, *The Commission of Fine Arts, A Brief History, 1910–1995* (Washington, DC: Government Printing Office, 1996).

6 Letter from J. Carter Brown to Jim King, director of personnel, White House, May 20, 1977, Box 32, NGA; "Statement of J. Carter Brown, chairman, Commission of Fine Arts, before the Senate Subcommittee on Appropriations for the Department of the Interior and Related Agencies, May 13, 1981, Box 34, NGA; and "Impediments to the Economic, Functional and Aesthetic Development of the District of Columbia, the Nation's Capital," House Committee on the District of Columbia, 94th Cong., 2nd Sess., December 20, 1976 (Washington, DC: Government Printing Office, 1977), 157. See also Jack Fisher, "26 Years in Commission of a Memorial," *Washington Post,* September 15, 1981.

7 Several staff members frequently assisted Charles Atherton, including Donald Myer, Sue Kohler, and Jeffrey Carson.

8 Paul Schwartzman, "Struck D.C. Pedestrian Has Critical Injuries, $5 Ticket," *Washington Post,* December 3, 2005; Roger K. Lewis, "Widespread Use of Design Review Would be a Fitting Legacy," *Washington Post,* December 10, 2005; and Matt Schudel, "A Local Life: Charles H. Atherton, He Quietly Beautified Washington," *Washington Post,* December 18, 2005.

9 Donald Myer, telephone interview by Richard Guy Wilson, January 18, 2010.

10 Dietrich Neumann, ed., *Richard Neutra's Windshield House* (New Haven, CT: Yale University Press, 2001). An exhibition at the Graduate School of Design, Harvard University, and the Museum of the Rhode Island School of Design accompanied the book. See also Fred Bernstein, "When Modern Married Money," *New York Times,* February 3, 2002.

11 Quoted in Calvin Tomkins, "Profiles for the Nation," *New Yorker,* September 3, 1990, 58.

12 Sue A. Kohler, interview by Richard Guy Wilson, Washington D.C., January 15, 2010; and LoRé interview, December 9, 2009.

13 J. Carter Brown, "The Designing of the National Gallery of Art's East Building," in *The Mall in Washington, 1791–1991*, ed. Richard Longstreth (Hanover and London: National Gallery of Art, distributed by University Press of New England, 1991).

14 Neil Harris, "Reinventing the National Gallery," in *A Modernist Museum in Perspective: The East Building, National Gallery of Art*, ed. Anthony Alofsin (New Haven and London: National Gallery of Art, distributed by Yale University Press, 2009), 23–45.

15 I. M. Pei, "J. Carter Brown," *Proceedings of the American Philosophical Society,* 148, no. 3 (September 2004): 371; this is a transcript of Pei's remarks at the National Cathedral, Washington, D.C., on July 17, 2002.

16 Letter from J. Carter Brown to I. M Pei, July 5, 1973, in "J. Carter Brown 1985 and Earlier," CFA member files.

17 J. Carter Brown, "J. Carter Brown's Washington," *Providence Journal,* January 19, 1986, Box 34, NGA.

18 Ibid.

19 J. Carter Brown, "Remarks before the Federal City Council," NGA.

20 CFA minutes, September 19, 1995, 3–4.

21 "Notes on Washington Streets," November 30, 1976, Box 32, NGA.

22 Ibid; LoRé interview, December 9, 2009.

23 "Notes on Washington Streets," November 30, 1976, Box 32, NGA; editorial, "Needless Demolition," *Washington Post,* August 18, 1976; letter from Lloyd H. Elliott, president, George Washington University, to J. Carter Brown, August 19, 1976, in "J. Carter Brown 1985 and Earlier," CFA member files; and CFA minutes, July 28, 1976, exhibit D, letter from J. Carter Brown to Lorenzo W. Jacobs Jr., acting director, Department of Economic Development, District of Columbia, August 4, 1976.

24 Sandra G. Boodman, "High-Rise Va. Buildings Held an Act of Urban Vandalism," *Washington Post,* January 23, 1979, Box 33, NGA.

25 Donald Myer, telephone interview by Richard Guy Wilson, January 18, 2010.

26 J. Carter Brown quoted in Sarah Booth Conroy, "Post Office Remodeling Hitch," *Washington Post,* January 20, 1978. Also see CFA minutes, July 7, 1981, exhibit B, letter from J. Carter Brown to James B. Stewart, General Services Administration, July 22, 1981.

27 Friedrich St. Florian, telephone interview by Richard Guy Wilson, February 19, 2010. See also J. Carter Brown, "Why This Design Is a Winner," *Washington Post,* June 6, 2001. There is extensive material on the memorial; in particular see Kirk Savage, *Monument Wars: Washington D.C., the National Mall, and the Transformation of the Memorial Landscape* (Berkeley: University of California Press, 2009).

28 Testimony of Denys Peter Meyers in Demolition Permit Applications, November 30, 1982, Government of the District of Columbia, Before the Mayor's Agent for D.C. Law 2-144, Box 32, NGA.

29 CFA minutes, September 26, 1978, 6.

30 Quoted in Clyde H. Penn Jr., "Lawyer Struggling to Save Old Tavern," *Los Angeles Times,* July 29, 1981.

31 Kohler interview, December 9, 2009.

32 Judy Scott Feldman, telephone interview by Richard Guy Wilson, April 11, 2010.

33 CFA minutes, September 14, 1994, 41.

34 Rowan Scarborough, "Marines Endure a New 'Affront.'" *Washington Times,* March 7, 1998; "Marine Commandant Defends War Memorial," *Washington Times,* March 10, 1998; Mike Feinsilber, "Anger after Iwo Jima Comment," *Washington Post,* March 10, 1998; Ken Ringle, "Art Criticism Meets a Few Angry Marines," *Washington Post,* March 11, 1998; and Larry Van Dyne, "Over My Dead Body," *Washingtonian,* November 1999, 54–57, 151–60.

35 Atherton quoted in Scarborough, "Marines Endure a New 'Affront,'" *Washington Times,* March 7, 1998.

36 CFA minutes, September 14, 1994, 41.

37 CFA minutes, July 24, 1997, 2.

38 Letter from J. Carter Brown to Honorable Fred Schwengel, U.S. House of Representatives, December 24, 1969, Box 32, NGA.

39 J. Carter Brown, "The Designing of National Gallery of Art's East Building," in Longstreth, *The Mall in Washington,* 258.

CHAPTER VII

1   Quoted in Patti Gallagher and Alex Krieger, "Security with Dignity," *Urban Land* (March 2003).

2   In 1995, prior to its closure, the avenue handled an average of 29,000 vehicular trips a day. District government officials and local businesses strongly opposed the closure.

3   *The National Capital Urban Design and Security Plan* won the American Planning Association's 2005 Current Topic Award for Safe Growth.

4   CFA transcript, June 21, 2001, 129–30; and CFA transcript, November 21, 2002, 134.

5   CFA transcript, June 21, 2001, 129.

6   Ibid., 12–13.

7   Landscape gardener and horticulturalist Andrew Jackson Downing (1815–52) created a design for the Mall, Washington Monument Park, and President's Park in 1851. He was instrumental in guiding American taste away from geometrical or classically inspired gardens in favor of picturesque designs. Today, the Ellipse, located south of the White House, is the only remnant of Downing's design. Landscape architect and author Samuel Parsons Jr. (1844–1923) was commissioned by Colonel Theodore Bingham, head of the Office of Public Buildings and Grounds, to develop plans for the Mall and its connection via a parkway to Rock Creek Park. Parsons's 1900 plan incorporated a series of elliptical paths extending from the Capitol to the Washington Monument. Parsons had worked with Calvert Vaux on New York's Central Park and was one of the founders of the American Society of Landscape Architects.

8   The sunken walls were referred to as ha-has, a landscaped barrier designed not to interrupt a view, but to control animals, consisting of a ditch with a masonry revetment retaining sloped turf.

9   Security officials were concerned that an individual would enter the monument and use the viewing platform as a shooting platform, hence the need for security screening of visitors.

10 CFA transcript, February 21, 2002, 31, 33.

11 CFA minutes, February 21, 2002, exhibit A-2, letter from J. Carter Brown to Joseph M. Lawler, acting regional director, National Capital Region, National Park Service (hereafter cited NCR, NPS), March 5, 2002.

12 CFA transcript, March 21, 2002, 69.

13 Ibid., 79–81. The Committee of 100 on the Federal City was founded in 1923 to advocate responsible planning and land use to uphold the values derived from the tradition of the L'Enfant Plan and the McMillan Commission.

14 Jonathan Yardley, "On the Mall, Entrenched Thinking," *Washington Post,* May 6, 2002. Regarding the World War II Memorial, Yardley also implicated the American Battle Monuments Commission.

15 CFA minutes, May 16, 2002, 2.

16 CFA transcript, May 16, 2002, 40.

17 CFA transcript, June 21, 2001, 130; and CFA transcript May 16, 2002, 58.

18 Spencer Hsu, "Arts Panel Cools on Underground Center," *Washington Post,* May 17, 2002.

19 Benjamin Forgey, "Washington's Tunnel Vision for Tourists," *Washington Post,* May 18, 2002. In the article, Forgey also mentioned the underground visitor entrance under construction at the U.S. Capitol, a proposed 15th Street tunnel for visitors to enter the White House, and the underground Vietnam Veterans Memorial Visitor Center, to be located near this memorial.

20 For their submission, see Wilfried Wang, ed., *SOM Journal* 2 (Berlin, Germany: Hatje Cantz Publishers, 2003), 141–51.

21 CFA transcript, September 19, 2002, 59.

22 Ibid., 85–86. The Washington Monument, 555 feet tall, was designed by Robert Mills and constructed between 1848 and 1884. Ascending to the top was an especially popular attraction when the monument opened. Soon after, the steam elevator used for construction materials was converted to accommodate people; the trip took twenty minutes, and only men could ride the elevator as it was considered unsafe for women and children.

23 Ibid., 87–88.

24 Ibid., 89.

25 Ibid., 88. Given Childs's comments, it's interesting to note that the Balmori-Childs design for the Washington Monument competition in fact established a monumental approach to the base of the monument and thus raised the level of importance for the observation platform function.

26 CFA minutes, October 21, 2010, 6–10.

27 CFA minutes, February 17, 2005, 3–4.

28 CFA transcript, March 17, 2005, 57, 60.

29 Ibid., 68.

30 Letter from David Childs to John Parsons, April 26, 2005. This letter is not located in the CFA minutes; a copy can be found in the commission's Lincoln Memorial project file CFA 17/Mar/05-3.

31 The plan addressed museums located between 4th and 14th Streets as the design for the National Museum of the American Indian included security elements.

32 CFA transcript, January 15, 2004, 133.

33 Pamela Scott and Antoinette J. Lee, *Buildings of the District of Columbia* (New York: Oxford University Press, 1993), 183.

34 CFA transcript, March 18, 2004, 38.

35 CFA minutes, November 17, 2005, 6, and exhibit B, letter from Thomas E. Luebke to Craig W. Floyd, chairman, National Law Enforcement Officers Memorial Fund.

36 Frederick J. Lindstrom, assistant secretary since November 2001, served as acting secretary during the interim.

37 Memorandum from Charles Atherton to Joshua Bolton, director, Office of Management and Budget, December 3, 2003, found in the FY2005 Budget Request file, CFA office.

38 Statistic calculated from reviewing the commission's meeting agendas from FY2006 to FY2012.

39 The Commemorative Works Act specifies the requirements for development, approval, and location of new memorials and monuments in the District of Columbia and its environs in areas administered by the National Park Service and the General Services Administration. Pub. L. No. 99-652 (1986), recodified by Pub. L. No. 107-217 (2002), amended November 2003.

40 Pub. L. No. 108-126, 117 Stat. 1349 (2003). The designated boundaries of the Reserve were slightly more expansive than those recommended in the 2001 *Memorials and Museums Master Plan.*

41 Scott and Lee, *Buildings of the District of Columbia,* 207.

42 CFA transcript, October 18, 2001, 10–11.

43 Ibid., 38–39.

44 Ibid., 42–44. The Nabataen city of Petra, dating from the first century BC, is carved out of cliffs in the Jordanian desert and is reached through a long narrow gorge.

45 Benjamin Forgey, "The Corcoran Gallery's Soaring Wing," *Washington Post,* October 17, 2001.

46 CFA transcript, October 18, 2001, 44–45.

47 CFA transcript, April 22, 2003, 65.

48 CFA transcript, February 20, 2003, 156.

49 CFA transcript, November 21, 2002, 162–69.

50 Ibid., 194. John Russell Pope designed the National Gallery of Art located across the street and the National Archives one block away.

51 CFA transcript, December 19, 2002, 15–16.

52 Ibid., 47.

53 Ibid., 48–49.

54 Ibid., 76.

55 CFA transcript, February 20, 2003, 219–36.

56 Apparently the historic design guideline for the Northwest Rectangle that buildings on Constitution Avenue should be built of marble and only those behind them should be built of limestone had been forgotten.

57 Arena Stage, www.arenastage.org, accessed March 28, 2012. See section under "Plan Your Visit/Mead Center/Architect."

58 CFA transcript, July 18, 2002, 278.

59 CFA minutes, April 22, 2003, 11.

60 CFA transcript, April 22, 2003, 84–85.

61 CFA minutes, July 23, 1992, exhibit D, letter from J. Carter Brown to Robert G. Stanton, regional director, NCR, NPS, July 29, 1992.

62 CFA minutes, July 23, 1998, 4.

63 CFA minutes, March 18, 2004, 12.

64 CFA minutes, October 18, 2007, exhibit E, letter from Thomas E. Luebke to Ardeshir Nafici, acting associate director, Infrastructure Project Management Administration, District of Columbia Department of Transportation, October 26, 2007.

65 CFA transcript, June 17, 2004, 52–56.

66 CFA minutes, January 25, 2005, exhibit E, letter from Frederick J. Lindstrom, acting secretary, to Harry Rombach, associate director for facilities master planning, Smithsonian Institution, February 10, 2005.

67 CFA transcript, March 16, 2006, 34–35.

69 CFA transcript, January 25, 2005, 188.

69 CFA minutes, January 25, 2005, exhibit F, letter from Frederick J. Lindstrom, acting secretary, to Harry Rombach, associate director for facilities master planning, Smithsonian Institution, February 10, 2005. When F Street was widened in 1936, the entry was moved one level lower than the original entrance.

70 CFA transcript, September 15, 2005, 32. During the canopy's review process, the designers had informational meetings with the staffs of both the NCPC and the CFA for feedback on the design.

71 CFA minutes, September 15, 2005, 3.

72 Ibid., 6.

73 Pub. L. No. 107-106, 115 Stat. 1009 (2001).

74 The five were Capitol site at Pennsylvania Avenue and 1st Street, NW; monument site at Constitution Avenue and 14th Street, NW; Liberty Loan site at 14th and D Streets, SW; Banneker Overlook site at the southern end of 10th Street, SW; and the Arts and Industries Building on the Mall.

75 CFA transcript, February 20, 2003, 141–42.

76 CFA minutes, February 19, 2009, 9–11. The six participating teams were Philip Freelon, David Adjaye and the late Max Bond; Devrouax & Purnell with Pei Cobb Freed; Diller Scofidio with KlingStubbins; Moody Nolan with Antoine Predock; and Moshe Safdie with Sultan Campbell Britt & Associates.

77 CFA transcript, February 19, 2009, 122.

78 CFA minutes, March 17, 2011, letter from Thomas E. Luebke to Ann Trowbridge, associate director of planning, Smithsonian Institution, March 25, 2011.

79 CFA transcript, October 20, 2011, 71.

80 In Washington, an early influence of photography on commemorative language and the millennia-old art form of sculpture can be traced to the mid-twentieth century with the realization of Joe Rosenthal's iconic photograph of soldiers raising the flag on Iwo Jima into a bronze sculpture by Felix de Weldon (CFA 1950–63) in the 1950s for the U. S. Marine Corps War Memorial. The influence continued with the sandblasted photographic images on the granite wall at the Korean War Veterans Memorial in the 1990s.

81 "Pentagon Memorial Design Unveiled," *Sculpture* (April 2003).

82 CFA transcript, June 12, 2003, 125.

83 CFA transcript, April 20, 2006, 56.

84 CFA transcript, January 18, 2007, 10–44.

85 CFA transcript, July 21, 2005, 23.

86 Ibid., 35, 39.

87 CFA transcript, July 17, 2008, 114.

88 Ibid., 122–30.

89 CFA transcript, March 19, 2009, 8–15.

90 CFA transcript, May 21, 2009, 93–103.

91 CFA minutes, December 16, 1999, exhibit A attachment, letter from Reginald Griffith, National Capital Planning Commission, to John Carter, Martin Luther King Jr. National Memorial Project Foundation, October 21, 1999. The Commemorative Works Act (40 U.S.C. Chapter 89), Section 8905 (b)(6) established that the CFA and the NCPC could set mutually agreed upon guidelines for site development. The CFA has sometimes preferred to not adopt these criteria formally.

92 CFA transcript, June 21, 2001, 76.

93 See CFA case file 18/Jan/07. The "Chronology of Design" submitted for the January 2007 meeting included scaled design development drawings dated April 27, 2005.

94 CFA transcript, March 16, 2006, 25–26.

95 CFA transcript, June 15, 2006, 35–36, 42–43.

96 CFA transcript, January 18, 2007, 44–66.

97 For comparison, the standing Thomas Jefferson in the Jefferson Memorial across the Tidal Basin is nineteen feet tall. The seated Lincoln at the Lincoln Memorial and the Statue of Freedom standing atop the U.S. Capitol dome are nineteen feet six inches tall.

98 CFA transcript, April 17, 2008, 78–81.

99 Ibid., 81–82. McKinnell's implicit reference was to the toppling of the colossal statuary of Saddam Hussein when his government was overthrown in 2003 as well as that of the communist leaders Vladimir Lenin, head of the Soviet Union immediately after the 1917 revolution, and Nicolau Ceaușescu, the dictator of Romania.

100 CFA minutes, April 17, 2008, exhibit D, letter from Thomas E. Luebke to Joseph M. Lawler, regional director, NCR, NPS, April 25, 2008.

101 Michael Ruane, "Unhappy with 'Confrontational' Image, U.S. Panel Wants King Statue Reworked," *Washington Post,* May 9, 2008.

102 Marc Fisher, "At This Point, MLK Memorial Needs a Fresh Start," *Washington Post,* May 11, 2008.

103 Michael Nojeim, letter to the editor, *Washington Post,* May 13, 2008.

104 Courtland Milloy, "From Many Points of View, Statue is True to King's Image," *Washington Post,* May 14, 2008.

105 Catesby Leigh, "An Inflated, Ossified Memorial," *Wall Street Journal,* September 4, 2008.

106 CFA transcript, September 18, 2008, 32–33.

107 Ibid., 36.

108 CFA transcript, February 15, 2007, 24–25; and CFA transcript, September 16, 2010, 97–99.

109 Pub. L. No. 108-126 (2003), Sec. 6.(a)(1): "In general—The Vietnam Veterans Memorial Fund, Inc., is authorized to construct a visitor center at or near the Vietnam Veterans Memorial on Federal land

in the District of Columbia, or its environs, subject to the provisions of this section, in order to better inform and educate the public about the Vietnam Veterans Memorial and Vietnam War."

110 CFA transcript, September 15, 2005, 131, 144.

111 Ibid., 86, 134.

112 Ibid., 138, 152–53.

113 CFA transcript, October 18, 2007, 67–68.

114 Pub. L. No. 108-126, 117 Stat. 1349 (2003), Sec. 6.(b)(1): "final approval of the visitor center shall not be withheld."

115 CFA minutes, February 16, 2012, letter from Thomas E. Luebke to Steve Whitesall, regional director, NCR, NPS, February 24, 2012.

116 CFA minutes, January 18, 2007, 98–100, and exhibit C, letter from Thomas E. Luebke to Lisa A. Mendelson-Ielmini, acting regional director, NCR, NPS, January 25, 2007.

117 CFA minutes, June 21, 2007, exhibit B, letter from Thomas E. Luebke to Joseph M. Lawler, regional director, NCR, NPS, June 29, 2007.

118 CFA minutes, November 19, 2009, 11, and letter from Thomas E. Luebke to Margaret O'Dell, regional director, NCR, NPS, November 30, 2009.

119 CFA minutes, November 20, 2008, exhibit A, letter from Thomas E. Luebke to Margaret O'Dell, regional director, NCR, NPS, November 28, 2008.

120 CFA transcript, May 20, 2010, 48–51.

121 CFA transcript, January 20, 2011, 41.

122 CFA minutes, January 20, 2011, letter from Thomas E. Luebke to Margaret O'Dell, regional director, NCR, NPS, January 27, 2011.

123 CFA transcript, September 15, 2011, 37.

124 Ibid., 39–40.

125 Witold Rybczynski, "I like Ike (and his memorial)," *New York Times,* March 22, 2012.

126 Stephen W. Stathis, "Congressional Gold Medals, 1776–2008," updated July 15, 2008, Congressional Research Service, www.policy archive.org/handle/10207/bitstreams/19835_Previous_Version_ 2008-07-15, accessed June 19, 2012.

127 CFA minutes, February 21, 2008, exhibit C, letter from Thomas E. Luebke to Edmund C. Moy, director, U.S. Mint, February 29, 2008.

128 CFA minutes, May 20, 2010, letter from Thomas E. Luebke to Edmund C. Moy, director, U.S. Mint, May 28, 2010, 1.

129 CFA internal file, "Commission of Fine Arts Budget Justification for FY 2012," submitted to the Office of Management and Budget, February 2, 2011.

130 CFA transcript, November 15, 2001, 71–73.

131 CFA minutes, March 19, 1998, 6.

132 "E. Barrett Prettyman Federal Courthouse," *Glass Magazine,* www.glassmagazine.com/article/commercial/e-barrett-prettyman-federal-courthouse, accessed July 6, 2011.

133 Dedication pamphlet, William McChesney Martin Jr. building, November 19, 1974, 5, http://fraser.stlouisfed.org/docs/historical/ martin/20_05_19741119.pdf, accessed July 6, 2011.

134 CFA transcript, September 17, 2009, 45.

135 CFA minutes, November 19, 2009, William McChesney Martin Jr. building, CFA 19/Nov/09-8.

136 CFA minutes, February 17, 2005, 8; and exhibit F, letter from Frederick J. Lindstrom, acting secretary, to Michael S. McGill, special assistant for regional coordination, General Services Administration, February 25, 2005.

137 CFA minutes, June 17, 2010, CFA 17/Jun/10-3.

138 CFA minutes, October 21, 2010, CFA 21/Oct/10-8.

139 CFA minutes, January 20, 2011, CFA 20/Jan/11-2.

140 CFA minutes, April 10, 1985, 3–4.

141 Capitol Riverfront Development–The Yards, Washington, D.C., www.dcyards.com, accessed March 28, 2012.

142 Chartered by Congress in 1852, the hospital was one of the country's earliest institutions for the treatment of mental illness. The Center Building opened in 1855 and was designed by Thomas U. Walter—best known for the U.S. Capitol extensions and dome. During the Civil War, the facility was used as a military hospital. Buildings were added to the grounds throughout the rest of the century, and a major expansion began in 1903 by the architectural firm of Shepley, Rutan & Coolidge.

143 CFA transcript, June 21, 2007, 90–91.

144 CFA transcript, October 18, 2007, 165–66.

145 Ibid., 190.

146 Ibid., exhibit B-1, letter from Thomas E. Luebke to Denise Decker, General Services Administration, November 12, 2007.

147 CFA transcript, November 20, 2008, 92–93.

148 Ibid., 96.

149 Ibid., 94-95.

150 CFA minutes, March 18, 2010, CFA 18/Mar/10-3.

151 Notes by Thomas E. Luebke from Section 106 Consulting Parties meeting e-mailed to Mary Konsoulis and Eve Barsoum, June 14, 2011.

152 Stephen Fuller, "Is This a Recovery or What? The Outlook for 2012," (presentation, 2012 Economic Forecast Conference, George Mason University Center for Regional Analysis, January 13, 2012), www.cra.gmu.edu, accessed June 19, 2012.

153 DCist: Washington, D.C. News, Food, Arts & Events, http://dcist. com/2010/12/dc_breaks_600000_barrier_in_census.php, accessed July 7, 2011.

154 CFA minutes, July 27, 2006, exhibit G, letter from Thomas E. Luebke to Edward J. Rich, Robins, Kaplan, Miller & Ciresi L.L.P., August 4, 2006.

155 Each of the proposed designs had a two-story shallow atrium structure in front of a one-story structure.

156 See: Carol Buckley, "Apple Can't Clear Georgetown Review," *Georgetown Current,* December 24, 2008; and Yukari Kane, "Georgetown Not Smiling on Apple Store," *Wall Street Journal,* December 29, 2008.

157 Carol Buckley, "Apple Earns Fourth 'No' from Board," *Georgetown Current,* February 11, 2009. Also see Paul Schwartzman, "Apple Tries, Tries Again to Open in Georgetown," *Washington Post,* February 5, 2009. Several Web sites also carried comments regarding the store's design review, including D.C. Wire at http//voices.washingtonpost. com/dc/2009/02/apple_in_georgetown.html; *Washington City Paper* at www.washingtoncitypaper.com/blogs/citdesk/2008/12/29/ no-apple-store-for-dc; and Mac Observer at www.macobserver.com /tmo/article/georgetown_nixes_apple_store_design_again/, accessed March 19, 2012.

158 In December 2003, with Vice Chairman Donald Capoccia presiding and only two other members present, the revised concept design was approved with an abbreviated presentation and little discussion. At the end of the presentation, Arthur Cotton Moore asked if he could return directly to the commission rather than to the Old Georgetown Board in an effort to accelerate the review process. The commission agreed to the irregular procedure, and thus when the project returned to the commission in June 2004 for final review, it did not have the benefit of a recommendation from the OGB.

159 CFA minutes, September 17, 1975, exhibit A-2, letter from J. Carter Brown to Hon. Walter E. Washington, mayor, District of Columbia, September 26, 1975.

160 CFA transcript, February 19, 2004, 178–79. Beatrix Farrand designed the renowned gardens at Dumbarton Oaks in Georgetown.

161 CFA transcript, September 21, 2004, 277.

162 CFA transcript, October 20, 2011, 232. Michael McKinnell's remarks were made during the review of 500 L'Enfant Plaza, SW, an office building designed by ZGF.

163 CFA minutes, March 9, 1939, exhibit C, letter from Charles Moore to William Adams Delano, March 1939.

LIST OF ABBREVIATIONS AND ACRONYMS

ABMC	American Battle Monuments Commission		KCCT	Karn, Charuhas, Chapman & Twohey
AIA	American Institute of Architects		KCF	Keyes, Condon & Florance
AMBC	Arlington Memorial Bridge Commission		LEED	Leadership in Energy and Environmental Design
ANC	Arlington National Cemetery; Advisory Neighborhood Commission		NCACA	National Capital Arts and Cultural Affairs Program
ARRA	American Reinvestment and Recovery Act		NCMAC	National Capital Memorial Advisory Commission
ASLA	American Society of Landscape Architects		NCPC	National Capital Planning Commission
ATFE	(Bureau of) Alcohol, Tobacco, Firearms and Explosives		NCPPC	National Capital Park and Planning Commission
BAC	Board of Architectural Consultants		NEPA	National Environmental Protection Act
BCJ	Bohlin Cywinski Jackson		NHPA	National Historic Preservation Act
B&O	Baltimore & Ohio Railroad		NMAI	National Museum of the American Indian
B&P	Baltimore & Potomac Railroad		NOMA	North of Massachusetts Avenue
CCAC	Citizens Coinage Advisory Committee		NPS	National Park Service
CEQ	Council on Environmental Quality		OEOB	Old Executive Office Building
CFA	Commission of Fine Arts		OGB	Old Georgetown Board
C&O	Chesapeake & Ohio Canal		OMB	Office of Management and Budget
CWA	Commemorative Works Act		OPBG	Office of Public Buildings and Grounds
DCCAH	District of Columbia Commission on the Arts and Humanities		OPEFM	Office of Public Education Facilities Modernization
DDOT	District Department of Transportation		OSA	Office of the Supervising Architect
DHS	Department of Homeland Security		PADC	Pennsylvania Avenue Development Corporation
EEOB	Eisenhower Executive Office Building		PBA	Public Buildings Administration
EPA	Environmental Protection Angency		PBC	Public Buildings Commission
FBI	Federal Bureau of Investigation		PBS	Public Buildings Service
FDMC	First Division Memorial Commission		PCAG	Progressive Citizens Association of Georgetown
FOB	Federal Office Building		PWAP	Public Works of Art Program
GAO	Government Accountability Office (formerly General Accounting Office)		RLA	Redevelopment Land Agency
GSA	General Services Administration		SEFC	Southeast Federal Center
HABS	Historic American Buildings Survey		SOM	Skidmore, Owings & Merrill
HEW	(Department of) Health, Education, and Welfare		STEM	Science, Technology, Engineering, and Mathematics
HHFA	Housing and Home Financing Agency		TAC	The Architects Collaborative
HOK	Hellmuth, Obata & Kassabaum		TJMC	Thomas Jefferson Memorial Commission
HUD	(Department of) Housing and Urban Development		TRMA	Theodore Roosevelt Memorial Commission
ICTC	International Cultural and Trade Center		USIP	United States Institute of Peace
			VVMC	Vietnam Veterans Memorial Center
			VVMF	Vietnam Veterans Memorial Fund

INDEX

ILLUSTRATION CREDITS

The illustrations in this volume are from the collections of the U.S. Commission of Fine Arts unless otherwise noted; case numbers and other source information for CFA images are also noted if known.

FOREWORD

viii Luis Gomez Photos, Washington, DC.

CHAPTER I

10 TOP: Library of Congress, Prints & Photographs Division, Detroit Publishing Company Collection, LC-USZ62-75859. BOTTOM: Library of Congress, Prints & Photographs Division, LC-USZ62-94559.

12 TOP: Reprinted from *Records of the Columbia Historical Society*, Vol. 24, 1922: plate facing page 192. BOTTOM: Library of Congress, Geography and Map Division, g3850.ct000514.

13 TOP: Library of Congress, Geography and Map Division, g3851 fm.gct00191. BOTTOM: Library of Congress, Prints & Photographs Division, LC-USZ62-15878.

15 TOP: Reprinted from Charles Moore, ed., *The Improvement of the Park System of the District of Columbia* (Washington, DC: Government Printing Office, 1902).

16 TOP LEFT: Library of Congress, Prints & Photographs Division, detail from photograph by Harris & Ewing, LC-DIG-hec-05647. TOP CENTER: Library of Congress, Prints & Photographs Division, detail from photograph by Harris & Ewing, LC-DIG-hec-07811. BOTTOM LEFT: Reprinted from Fulton R. Gordon, *Connecticut Avenue Highlands at the Nation's Capital* (1903). Collection of the Library of Congress, F202.C7 G6/unk83001191.

18 LEFT: Library of Congress, Prints & Photographs Division, LC-J698-4947. RIGHT: Reprinted from *Papers Relating to the Improvement of the City of Washington*, 56th Cong., 2nd Sess., 1901, S. Doc. 94.

19 TOP: Reprinted from F. W. Fitzpatrick, "Beautifying Washington," *The Inland Architect and News Record* 35 (March 1900). Photograph courtesy of The Fine Arts Library, Harvard College Library. BOTTOM: The New York Historical Society, McKim, Mead & White Collection, Neg. #75563.

20 Library of Congress, Prints & Photographs Division, photograph by Harris & Ewing, LC-DIG-hec-15306.

21 TOP LEFT: Library of Congress, Prints & Photographs Division, LC-USZ62-36686 (detail). TOP RIGHT: U.S. Department of the Interior, National Park Service, Saint-Gaudens National Historic Site, Cornish, NH.

22 BOTTOM: The New York Historical Society, McKim, Mead & White Collection, Neg. #75565.

25 Reprinted from D. H. Burnham and E. H. Bennett, *Plan of Chicago* (Chicago: Commercial Club of Chicago, 1908).

27 Library of Congress, Prints & Photographs Division, LC-D4-191 44 A.

28 TOP: Library of Congress, Prints & Photographs Division, Detroit Publishing Company Collection, LC-D4-62804. BOTTOM LEFT: DC Public Library, Washingtoniana Division, E. B. Thompson Collection.

29 TOP LEFT: Library of Congress, Prints & Photographs Division, Theodor Horydczak Collection, LC-H824-T-1144-004. BOTTOM LEFT: DC Public Library, Washingtoniana Division, E. B. Thompson Collection.

30 TOP: Library of Congress, Prints & Photographs Division, John Parrington Earley model, LOT 11534/LC-USZ62-58725-58745. BOTTOM: Library of Congress, Prints & Photographs Division, LC-DIG-ppmsc-09954.

31 LEFT: Library of Congress, Prints & Photographs Division, LC-USZ62-92495. RIGHT: Library of Congress, Prints & Photographs Division, Theodor Horydczak Collection, LC-H814-T01-A01-007.

32 TOP: Library of Congress, Prints & Photographs Division, LC-USZ62-76768. BOTTOM: Library of Congress, Prints & Photographs Division, LC-USZ62-58986.

35 Library of Congress, Prints & Photographs Division, LC-USZ62-7757.

36 TOP, SECOND FROM LEFT: Photograph by Underwood & Underwood Studios, NY. CFA collection. TOP RIGHT: The New York Public Library Archives, The New York Public Library, Astor, Lenox and Tilden Foundations. BOTTOM LEFT: Courtesy of the National Park Service, Frederick Law Olmsted National Historic Site (detail). BOTTOM, SECOND FROM LEFT: Francis D. Millet, c. 1910/unidentified photographer (detail). Francis Davis Millet and Millet family papers, Archives of American Art, Smithsonian Institution. BOTTOM RIGHT: Library of Congress, Prints & Photographs Division, LC-USZ62-45955 (detail).

ESSAY BY ARLEYN A. LEVEE

38 Courtesy of Historic New England.

40 Architect of the Capitol.

41 Smithsonian Institution Archives, RU 79, Box 9, Folder 5, Negative #24711.

44 Courtesy of the National Park Service, Frederick Law Olmsted National Historic Site.

45 LEFT AND RIGHT: Courtesy of the National Park Service, Frederick Law Olmsted National Historic Site.

46 TOP AND BOTTOM: Reprinted from Thomas C. Jeffers, "The Washington Monument: Various Plans for Improvement of its Surroundings," *Landscape Architecture* 39 (July 1949): 160, 161.

47 National Archives and Records Administration, Washington, DC.

49 TOP: National Archives and Records Administration, Washington, DC. BOTTOM: Courtesy of the National Park Service, Frederick Law Olmsted National Historic Site.

50 LEFT AND RIGHT: Courtesy of the National Park Service, Frederick Law Olmsted National Historic Site.

52 Courtesy of the National Park Service, Frederick Law Olmsted National Historic Site.

54 TOP AND BOTTOM: Courtesy of the National Park Service, Frederick Law Olmsted National Historic Site.

55 Library of Congress, Prints & Photographs Division, LC-USZ62-53608.

CHAPTER II

56 Library of Congress, Prints & Photographs Division, Theodor Horydczak Collection, LC-H834-2852-X.

58 BOTTOM LEFT: Burnham Green, Luneta, Rizal Park, Manila, Philippines, 1914. Daniel H. Burnham, designer. Archival Image

Collection, Ryerson and Burnham Archives, the Art Institute of Chicago. Digital File #194301.081203-06 (detail). Courtesy of the Art Institute of Chicago.

63 TOP LEFT, TOP RIGHT, AND BOTTOM: Photograph by the Commercial Photo Co. CFA collection.

64 DC Public Library, Washingtoniana Division, E. B. Thompson Collection.

66 TOP LEFT: Library of Congress, Prints & Photographs Division, LC-DIG-npcc-00103. TOP RIGHT: Library of Congress, Prints & Photographs Division, LC-DIG-npcc-00104. BOTTOM: Library of Congress, Prints & Photographs Division, LC-USZ62-138698.

67 BOTTOM: Reprinted from Charles Moore, ed., *The Improvement of the Park System of the District of Columbia* (Washington, DC: Government Printing Office, 1902).

68 Library of Congress, Prints & Photographs Division, LC-DIG-npcc-01185.

70 TOP: Henry Bacon Collection, Wesleyan University Library, Special Collections & Archives. BOTTOM: National Archives and Records Administration, Cartographic and Architectural Branch, Records of the Office of the Public Buildings and Public Parks of the National Capital, Record Group 42, Lincoln Memorial, folder 2, item 5.

71 Henry Bacon Collection, Wesleyan University Library, Special Collections & Archives.

73 TOP AND BOTTOM: National Archives and Records Administration, Washington, DC.

74 TOP: Library of Congress, Prints & Photographs Division, photograph by Harris & Ewing, LC-DIG-hec-05419. BOTTOM: Library of Congress, Prints & Photographs Division, LC-USZ62-77389.

75 Library of Congress, Prints & Photographs Division, LC-USZ62-111420.

76 Library of Congress, Prints & Photographs Division, detail from photograph by Harris & Ewing, LC-DIG-hec-05052.

77 BOTTOM: Photograph by Harris & Ewing. CFA collection.

78 Photograph courtesy of the Office of Public Buildings and Public Parks of the National Capital. CFA collection.

80 TOP: Library of Congress, Prints & Photographs Division, James M. Goode Collection, LC-G7-269. BOTTOM: Reprinted from George Burnap, *Parks: Their Design, Equipment, and Use* (Philadelphia: Lippincott, 1916). Collection of the Library of Congress, SB481.B8.

81 National Park Service, National Capital Region, Prints & Drawings Collection, #891/80032.

ESSAY BY PAMELA SCOTT

84 Library of Congress, Prints & Photographs Division, LC-USZ62-90838.

85 Library of Congress, Prints & Photographs Division, LC-USZ62-94989 (detail).

86 Reprinted from Charles Moore, "The Improvement of Washington City," *Century Magazine* (February 1902).

87 Reprinted from Charles Moore, "The Improvement of Washington City," *Century Magazine* (February 1902).

91 Cornell University Faculty Biographical Files, #47-10-3394 (detail). Division of Rare and Manuscript Collections, Cornell University Library.

92 BOTTOM: Courtesy of the National Park Service, Museum Resource Center.

CHAPTER III

96 BOTTOM: Library of Congress, Prints & Photographs Division, photograph by Harris & Ewing, LC-DIG-hec-20552.

97 TOP LEFT: Library of Congress, Prints & Photographs Division, LC-DIG-npcc-06838. TOP RIGHT: Library of Congress, Prints & Photographs Division, LC-DIG-npcc-06527.

99 Photograph by U.S. Army Air Corps. CFA collection.

100 TOP LEFT: Detail from photograph by the Commercial Photo Co. CFA collection. BOTTOM RIGHT: Courtesy of the National Park Service, Museum Resource Center.

101 United States Patent and Trademark Office.

103 BOTTOM: Courtesy of the National Park Service, Denver Service Center, Technical Information Center, TIC 802/89058.

105 TOP LEFT: Photograph by the U.S. Signal Corps. CFA collection. BOTTOM RIGHT: Photograph by Peter A. Juley & Son. CFA collection.

106 TOP: Photograph by U.S. Army Air Corps. CFA collection.

107 TOP: Library of Congress, Prints & Photographs Division, LC-DIG-ppmsca-31532 (detail).

109 Photograph by Carol Clayton. CFA collection.

111 Photograph by the Commercial Photo Co. CFA collection.

112 Library of Congress, Prints & Photographs Division, Detroit Publishing Company Collection, LC-D4-32554 (detail).

117 RIGHT: Photograph by Anna Frame. CFA collection.

118 Photograph by U.S. Army, courtesy of Arlington National Cemetery, Arlington, VA.

120 BOTTOM RIGHT: Photograph by Theodor Horydczak. CFA collection.

121 TOP: Reprinted from Charles Moore, ed., *The Improvement of the Park System of the District of Columbia* (Washington, DC: Government Printing Office, 1902).

122 LEFT: Photograph by Underwood & Underwood. CFA collection.

125 CENTER: Photograph by the Commercial Photo Co. CFA collection. BOTTOM: Photograph by Theodor Horydczak. CFA collection.

126 BOTTOM: Photograph by the Commercial Photo Co. CFA collection.

128 TOP LEFT: Photograph by the Commercial Photo Co. CFA collection. TOP RIGHT: Library of Congress, Prints & Photographs Division, Theodor Horydczak Collection, LC-H824-T-3002-B-X (detail). BOTTOM RIGHT: Detail from photograph by the Commercial Photo Co. CFA collection.

129 Photograph by Fairchild Aerial Surveys, Inc. CFA collection.

132 Edward Bruce, c. 1930/unidentified photographer. Edward Bruce papers, Archives of American Art, Smithsonian Institution.

133 TOP: Library of Congress, Prints & Photographs Division, photograph by Carol M. Highsmith, LC-DIG-highsm-02881. BOTTOM RIGHT: Library of Congress, Prints & Photographs Division, photograph by Carol M. Highsmith, LC-DIG-highsm-02865.

135 Reprinted from Frederick Gutheim, *Worthy of the Nation: The History of Planning for the National Capital* (Washington, DC: Smithsonian Institution Press, 1977).

139 TOP AND BOTTOM: Photograph by the Commercial Photo Co. CFA collection.

142 BOTTOM: Photograph by the Commercial Photo Co. CFA collection.

143 TOP RIGHT: Detail from photograph by the Commercial Photo Co. CFA collection. BOTTOM: Courtesy of the National Park Service, Museum Resource Center, ROCR Collection.

144 Library of Congress, Prints & Photographs Division, LC-USZ62-47191.

145 Reprinted from *The Shipstead-Luce Act: Rules and Regulations Administered by the National Commission of Fine Arts, Washington, DC* (Washington, DC: Government Printing Office, 1938).

146 Photograph by the Commercial Photo Co. CFA collection.

147 TOP: Copyright Cranbrook Archives, Richard P. Raseman, photographer, 5476-7.

148 Library of Congress, Prints & Photographs Division, LC-DIG-ggbain-38375.

149 John Russell Pope and Otto R. Eggers, *National Gallery of Art*, 1936. Acquired from Eggers and Higgins, Architects, National Gallery of Art.

151 TOP: Reprinted from Charles Moore, ed., *The Improvement of the Park System of the District of Columbia* (Washington, DC: Government Printing Office, 1902). BOTTOM: Papers of Howard Worth Smith, Accession #8731, Albert and Shirley Small Special Collections Library, University of Virginia, Charlottesville, VA.

152 BOTTOM: Photograph courtesy of the National Park Service. CFA collection.

153 LEFT: Library of Congress, Prints & Photographs Division, Theodor Horydczak Collection, LC-H814-T-2521-002-x (detail).

ESSAY BY CARROLL WILLIAM WESTFALL

154 Photograph of commissioners, including Fiske Kimball, February 1937; Jefferson Memorial Commission; Architectural Projects; Fiske Kimball Papers; Philadelphia Museum of Art, Archives.

155 Papers of Howard Worth Smith, Accession #8731, Albert and Shirley Small Special Collections Library, University of Virginia, Charlottesville, VA.

156 TOP AND BOTTOM: Papers of Howard Worth Smith, Accession #8731, Albert and Shirley Small Special Collections Library, University of Virginia, Charlottesville, VA.

157 Papers of Howard Worth Smith, Accession #8731, Albert and Shirley Small Special Collections Library, University of Virginia, Charlottesville, VA.

158 Papers of Howard Worth Smith, Accession #8731, Albert and Shirley Small Special Collections Library, University of Virginia, Charlottesville, VA.

159 TOP, CENTER, AND BOTTOM: Papers of Howard Worth Smith, Accession #8731, Albert and Shirley Small Special Collections Library, University of Virginia, Charlottesville, VA.

160 Papers of Howard Worth Smith, Accession #8731, Albert and Shirley Small Special Collections Library, University of Virginia, Charlottesville, VA.

CHAPTER IV

164 Photograph by Abbie Rowe, courtesy of the National Park Service. CFA collection.

168 LEFT: Detail from photograph by the Commercial Photo Co. CFA collection.

170 TOP, LEFT AND RIGHT: Courtesy of the Section of Fine Arts, Public Buildings Administration. CFA collection. BOTTOM, LEFT AND RIGHT: Fine Arts Program, Public Buildings Service, U.S. General Services Administration.

171 Fine Arts Program, Public Buildings Service, U.S. General Services Administration.

172 LEFT: Reprinted from the *Evening Star*, August 8, 1941. CFA collection. RIGHT: Library of Congress, Prints & Photographs Division, LC-USZ62-39600.

173 BOTTOM: Photograph by Press Association, Inc. CFA collection.

174 Photograph by the U.S. Signal Corps. CFA collection.

177 TOP: National Archives and Records Administration, Cartographic and Architectural Branch, Records of the National Capital Planning Commission, Record Group 328: New Series; 1.30 (5.20)1251.

178 BOTTOM: Courtesy of the Public Buildings Service, U.S. General Services Administration. CFA collection.

180 Photograph by J. Alexander. CFA collection.

181 TOP LEFT: Photograph by Joe Rosenthal, collection of Odom Fanning. TOP RIGHT: Office of War Information, courtesy of Harry S. Truman Library. BOTTOM: Library of Congress, Prints & Photographs Division, Historic American Landscapes Survey, HALS VA-9-4 (detail).

182 TOP: Photograph by Herman Manasse, courtesy of the American Battle Monuments Commission, Arlington, VA. BOTTOM: Cour-

tesy of the American Battle Monuments Commission, Arlington, VA.

183 TOP AND BOTTOM: Courtesy of the American Battle Monuments Commission, Arlington, VA.

185 LEFT: Photograph by Louis H. Dreyer. CFA collection. RIGHT: Photograph by Abbie Rowe, courtesy of the National Park Service. CFA collection.

187 TOP LEFT AND CENTER RIGHT: Photograph by Anna Frame. CFA collection. BOTTOM, LEFT AND RIGHT: Photograph by Carol Clayton. CFA collection.

188 TOP LEFT: Courtesy of the National Park Service, National Capital Region, Museum Resource Center, "Freedom Shrine" 2821-1G. TOP RIGHT: Courtesy of the National Park Service, National Capital Region, Museum Resource Center, "Freedom Shrine" 2821-Y. BOTTOM RIGHT: Courtesy of the National Park Service, National Capital Region, Museum Resource Center, "Freedom Shrine" 2821-1F.

190 Detail from photograph by the Commercial Photo Co., National Archives and Records Administration, Records of the Chief Signal Officer, RG111:80747. CFA collection.

191 Photograph by Abbie Rowe, courtesy of the National Park Service, 1700-D. CFA collection.

192 Photograph by Abbie Rowe, National Park Service, collection of the Harry S. Truman Library & Museum, courtesy of the White House Historical Association.

195 BOTTOM: Library of Congress, Prints & Photographs Division, Historic American Buildings Survey, HABS DC, GEO, 3-4 (detail).

196 RIGHT: DC Public Library, Washingtoniana Division, E. B. Thompson Collection (detail).

197 TOP: Photograph by Buckingham Studio, Inc. CFA collection. BOTTOM: Detail from photograph by J. Alexander, B3399-79. CFA collection.

198 RIGHT: Library of Congress, Prints & Photographs Division, Historic American Buildings Survey, HABS DC, GEO, 112-1.

199 TOP: Map provided courtesy of the Georgetown Map Project, © 1993 Outerbridge Horsey, Florence Stone, Merle Thorpe. All rights reserved. Old Georgetown boundary line added with permission. BOTTOM LEFT: Courtesy of Mount Vernon Ladies' Association. Photograph by Robert B. Fisher. BOTTOM RIGHT: Abbie Rowe, National Park Service, courtesy of the Office of the Curator, The White House.

201 Library of Congress, Prints & Photographs Division, Farm Security Administration/Office of War Information Collection, LC-USF33-000414-M2.

202 TOP: Courtesy of The Presbyterian Congregation in George-Town. BOTTOM: Photograph by Jerry A. McCoy, Peabody Room, DC Public Library.

203 Library of Congress, Prints & Photographs Division, Historic American Buildings Survey, HABS DC, GEO, 234-11.

205 TOP: Photograph by Francis Routt, *Washington Star*. CFA collection.

206 RIGHT: Photograph by J. Alexander, B3399-91. CFA collection.

208 Mary Alice, photographer. CFA collection.

209 TOP: Photograph by Campbell Photo Service, 698-18. CFA collection. BOTTOM: Photograph by Paul Schmick, Star Collection, DC Public Library; © Washington Post.

210 Photograph by Francis Routt, Star Collection, DC Public Library; © Washington Post.

211 Photograph by Fairchild Aerial Surveys, Inc., 45502. CFA collection.

212 TOP: Library of Congress, Prints & Photographs Division, FSA/OWI Collection, LC-USF34-015931-D. BOTTOM: Photograph by Vic Casamento, Star Collection, DC Public Library; © Washington Post.

213 TOP AND CENTER: Reprinted from *Housing and Redevelopment: A Portion of the Comprehensive Plan for the National Capital and*

288 The Historical Society of Washington, D.C., Emil A. Press Slide Collection.

289 BOTTOM LEFT: Photograph by Norman McGrath. CFA collection.

ESSAY BY ZACHARY M. SHRAG

292 Cartoon by Edward Sorel, reprinted from Donald Canty, "How Washington Is Run: An Ungovernment Without Top or Bottom," *Architectural Forum* (January 1963).

293 Zachary Schrag.

297 Reprinted from *Pennsylvania Avenue: Report of the President's Council on Pennsylvania Avenue* (1964).

299 Image provided courtesy of the National Capital Planning Commission.

CHAPTER VI

300 © David Coleman.

305 Library of Congress, Prints & Photographs Division, photograph by Carol M. Highsmith, LC-DIG-highsm-04798.

307 TOP: Reprinted from Pennsylvania Avenue Development Corporation, *The Pennsylvania Avenue Plan 1974* (October 1974). CENTER: Courtesy of the Pennsylvania Avenue Development Corporation. CFA collection.

310 The Architectural Archives, University of Pennsylvania, by the gift of Robert Venturi and Denise Scott Brown.

311 Detail from photograph courtesy of Venturi, Rauch & Scott Brown. CFA collection.

312 BOTTOM: Photograph by Sue Kohler. CFA collection.

314 TOP: MPFP/M. Paul Friedberg and Partners. BOTTOM LEFT: Photograph by Ron Green, courtesy of MPFP/M. Paul Friedberg and Partners. BOTTOM RIGHT: American Battle Monuments Commission, Arlington, VA.

316 LEFT: Reprinted from *Pennsylvania Avenue: Report of the President's Temporary Commission on Pennsylvania Avenue* (1969). RIGHT: Reprinted from Pennsylvania Avenue Development Corporation, *The Pennsylvania Avenue Plan 1974* (October 1974).

318 CENTER: CFA submission file CFA 17/FEB/82-8. BOTTOM: CFA submission file CFA 12/JUL/83-6.

319 BOTTOM: Photograph by Wally Gobetz via flickr.com.

320 TOP RIGHT: Photograph by Carol M. Highsmith/PADC, CFA collection.

321 TOP AND BOTTOM: Photograph by Lawrence S. Williams, Inc., CFA collection.

323 TOP RIGHT AND CENTER RIGHT: Photograph by Carol M. Highsmith/PADC, CFA collection.

324 Photograph © Nathaniel Lieberman, CFA collection.

327 TOP: © Timothy Hursley (detail). BOTTOM LEFT: Library of Congress, Prints & Photographs Division, Historic American Buildings Survey, HABS DC, WASH, 657-8.

328 Detail from photograph © Robert Lautman, Collection of the National Building Museum. Image provided by Art in Architecture Program, Public Buildings Service, U.S. General Services Administration.

329 TOP LEFT: Library of Congress, Prints & Photographs Division, detail from photograph by Carol M. Highsmith, LC-DIG-highsm-12536. BOTTOM LEFT: Library of Congress, Prints & Photographs Division, photograph by Carol M. Highsmith, LC-DIG-highsm-13143. BOTTOM RIGHT: © Franz Jantzen, photographer.

330 BOTTOM: © Franz Jantzen, photographer.

331 LEFT: Skidmore, Owings & Merrill LLP. RIGHT: Photograph by Alan Karchmer, courtesy of Hellmuth, Obata + Kassabaum.

332 TOP: Library of Congress, Prints & Photographs Division, photograph by Carol M. Highsmith, LC-DIG-highsm-16465. BOTTOM: Photograph by Brian Gassel/tvsdesign.

334 TOP: CFA submission file SL 81-43. BOTTOM: CFA submission file SL 79-12.

335 TOP: Photograph © Peerce Phish & Photo, CFA collection. CENTER: CFA submission file SL 80-44. BOTTOM: © Franz Jantzen, photographer.

337 RIGHT: Wolfgang Hoyt/Esto, courtesy of Skidmore, Owings & Merrill LLP.

339 TOP LEFT: Library of Congress, Prints & Photographs Division, photograph by Harris & Ewing, LC-DIG-hec-10326. BOTTOM RIGHT: Detail from photograph courtesy of Oliver T. Carr Co., CFA collection.

342 TOP: *Evening Star* photograph, CFA collection.

344 BOTTOM: CFA submission file OG 79-80.

345 BOTTOM: Skidmore, Owings & Merrill LLP.

347 CFA submission file OG 79-168.

348 TOP AND CENTER: CFA submission file OG 80-6. BOTTOM: Rendering by Peter Hasselman, CFA collection.

350 Courtesy of Arthur Cotton Moore.

351 LEFT: CFA submission file OG 84-65. TOP RIGHT: Photograph by Daniel D. Reiff, CFA collection. BOTTOM RIGHT: CFA submission file OG 82-98.

352 TOP: CFA submission file OG 98-66. BOTTOM: CFA submission file OG 98-217.

353 © Maxwell MacKenzie, courtesy of Shalom Baranes.

354 TOP: Library of Congress, Prints & Photographs Division, Historic American Buildings Survey, HABS DC, GEO, 116-1.

355 TOP: CFA submission file OG 86-195. BOTTOM CENTER: Courtesy of Arthur Cotton Moore (detail). BOTTOM RIGHT: Photograph by Peter R. Penczer, B. F. Saul Company Archives.

356 TOP LEFT: The Historical Society of Washington, DC, John P. Wymer Photograph Collection. TOP RIGHT, CENTER, AND BOTTOM: CFA submission file OG 98-94.

357 TOP LEFT: The Historical Society of Washington, DC, General Photographic Collection. BOTTOM LEFT: Stavropoulos Associates Architects. TOP RIGHT AND BOTTOM RIGHT: CFA submission file OG 98-24.

361 TOP: CFA submission file CFA 8/APR/80-6.

362 BOTTOM: Library of Congress, Prints & Photographs Division, photograph by Carol M. Highsmith, LC-DIG-highsm-04863.

363 CFA submission file CFA 19/SEP/95-9.

364 TOP: CFA submission file CFA 21/APR/99-1. BOTTOM: CFA submission file CFA 16/MAY/96-1.

365 TOP: Library of Congress, Prints & Photographs Division, detail from photograph by Carol M. Highsmith, LC-DIG-highsm-12698. BOTTOM: Mike Barber.

366 TOP AND CENTER: Image courtesy of the United States Mint. BOTTOM: Photograph by Lee Anderson, *Numismatic News*.

367 All images courtesy of the United States Mint.

369 TOP LEFT: CFA submission file CFA 15/MAY/85-1. TOP RIGHT: CFA submission file CFA 22/MAY/87-1. BOTTOM LEFT: CFA submission file CFA 18/FEB/88-1 (detail). BOTTOM RIGHT: © Timothy Hursley, CFA submission file CFA 15/JUN/95-3.

370 © Timothy Hursley, CFA submission file CFA 15/JUN/95-3.

371 National Archives and Records Administration, Washington, DC, reprinted from Charles Suddarth Kelly, *Washington, D.C., Then and Now: 69 Sites Photographed in the Past and Present* (New York: Dover Publications, Inc., 1984).

375 Hugh Ferriss collection, Drawings and Archives, Avery Architectural and Fine Arts Library, Columbia University.

377 TOP LEFT: CFA submission file CFA 16/FEB/81-3. TOP RIGHT: Library of Congress, Prints & Photographs Division, photograph by Carol M. Highsmith, LC-DIG-highsm-04256. BOTTOM LEFT: Library of Congress, Prints & Photographs Division, photograph by Carol M. Highsmith, LC-DIG-highsm-12404. BOTTOM RIGHT: Library of Congress, Prints & Photographs Division, photograph by Carol M. Highsmith, LC-DIG-highsm-12409.

379 TOP LEFT: Library of Congress, Prints & Photographs Division, Vietnam Veterans Memorial Fund Slide Collection, LC-USZC4-4915. BOTTOM LEFT: CFA submission file CFA 7/JUL/81-1.

380 TOP: Photograph courtesy of National Park Service, CFA collection. BOTTOM: Photograph by Win McNamee/Getty Images.

384 TOP: CFA submission file CFA 26/JUL/89-1. CENTER: CFA submission file CFA 13/DEC/90-1. BOTTOM: CFA submission file CFA 21/MAY/92-1.

385 TOP LEFT: Library of Congress, Prints & Photographs Division, photograph by Carol M. Highsmith, LC-DIG-highsm-13978. BOTTOM: Library of Congress, Prints & Photographs Division, photograph by Carol M. Highsmith, LC-DIG-highsm-04298.

387 TOP: © Eric Schiller, CFA collection. BOTTOM: CFA submission file CFA 20/MAR/03-3.

388 LEFT: Photograph courtesy of Zenos Frudakis. RIGHT: Photograph by Wally Gobetz via flickr.com.

390 LEFT: CFA submission file CFA 20/APR/95-1. RIGHT: Photograph by Robert Lautman, courtesy of Davis Buckley Architects & Planners.

391 TOP: © Maxwell MacKenzie, courtesy of Davis Buckley Architects and Planners. BOTTOM: Photograph by James P. Beirne, courtesy of Wendy M. Ross. RIGHT: Library of Congress, Prints & Photographs Division, photograph by Carol M. Highsmith, LC-DIG-highsm-12389.

392 CFA submission file CFA 19/SEP/95-1.

395 BOTTOM: CFA submission file CFA 21/MAR/02-1.

396 David Bjorgen.

397 LEFT: Detail from photograph by NCinDC via flickr.com. RIGHT: Photograph by Mark Wilson/Getty Images.

ESSAY BY RICHARD GUY WILSON

399 Photograph by James C. Benfield, CFA collection.

400 J. Carter Brown papers, Ms. 2007-020, John Hay Library, Brown University.

401 Photograph by Phil Charles, National Gallery of Art, Washington, DC, Gallery Archives.

405 BOTTOM: © Richard Latoff/Latoff.com.

CHAPTER VII

406 Detail from photograph by Joseph Romeo, courtesy of Beyer Blinder Belle Architects & Planners LLP.

408 LEFT: Cable Risdon Photography. RIGHT: Photograph by Greg Betz, courtesy of Skidmore, Owings & Merrill LLP.

409 Architect of the Capitol.

410 LEFT: Detail from photograph by Robert A. Reeder/*The Washington Post*/Getty Images. RIGHT: Detail from photograph by Elizabeth Felicella, courtesy of Michael van Valkenburgh Associates.

411 TOP: Department of Defense photograph by Tech. Sgt. Andy Dunaway, courtesy of the U.S. Navy Office of Information, Washington, DC. BOTTOM: Photograph by Peter R. Penczer, image provided courtesy of the National Capital Planning Commission.

412 © OLIN.

414 RIGHT: Rendering by V. Yeleseyev, courtesy of Hartman-Cox Architects.

415 TOP: Hartman-Cox Architects. CENTER: Library of Congress, Prints & Photographs Division, photograph by Carol M. Highsmith, LC-DIG-highsm-04799. BOTTOM LEFT: Photograph by Paul Jutton, image provided courtesy of the National Capital Planning Commission. BOTTOM RIGHT: Model by ArchiBIM, photograph by Joseph Romeo, courtesy of Beyer Blinder Belle Architects & Planners LLP.

417 TOP: Library of Congress, Prints & Photographs Division, LC-F82-8853. BOTTOM RIGHT: CFA submission file CFA 17/NOV/05-3.

418 TOP AND BOTTOM: CFA submission file CFA 18/FEB/10-2.

419 Sasaki Associates, Inc.

420 TOP LEFT: National Park Service, National Capital Region. BOTTOM LEFT: © OLIN. TOP, CENTER, AND BOTTOM RIGHT: CFA submission file CFA 15/APR/10-2.

421 TOP: CFA submission file CFA 16/SEP/10-4. BOTTOM: WRT.

423 TOP, LEFT AND RIGHT: Beyer Blinder Belle Architects & Planners LLP. BOTTOM LEFT: Skidmore, Owings & Merrill LLP. CENTER RIGHT AND BOTTOM RIGHT: Detail from photograph by Joseph Romeo, courtesy of Beyer Blinder Belle Architects & Planners LLP.

424 TOP: Architect of the Capitol.

425 TOP: Rendering by Richard Chenoweth, courtesy of Beyer, Blinder, Belle Architects & Planners LLP. CENTER: Photograph by Joseph Romeo, courtesy of Beyer Blinder Belle Architects & Planners LLP. BOTTOM: Davis Buckley Architects and Planners.

426 Photograph by Dennis Brack, courtesy of the National Gallery of Art, Washington, DC, Gallery Archives.

427 TOP AND BOTTOM: Photograph by Carol Clayton. CFA collection.

428 TOP AND BOTTOM: Renderings by Michael McCann, images provided courtesy of the National Capital Planning Commission.

429 Image provided courtesy of the National Capital Planning Commission.

430 Image provided courtesy of the National Capital Planning Commission.

431 TOP, CENTER, AND BOTTOM: Renderings by Michael McCann, images provided courtesy of the National Capital Planning Commission.

432 LEFT: National Park Service, National Capital Region. TOP RIGHT: William V. Walsh Construction Co., Inc. BOTTOM RIGHT: ehpien via flickr.com.

433 TOP: National Park Service, National Capital Region. BOTTOM LEFT: Photograph by Greg Sorensen for the National Park Service. BOTTOM CENTER: CFA submission file CFA 16/FEB/12-2. BOTTOM RIGHT: Detail from photograph by Rob Shelley, National Gallery of Art, Washington, DC, Gallery Archives.

434 CFA submission file CFA 18/FEB/10-4.

435 Photograph by Sarah Chilcott via flickr.com.

436 TOP RIGHT: Photograph by Whit Preston, © Gehry Partners. CFA collection.

437 LEFT: Rendering by Curt Willard, courtesy of Hartman-Cox Architects. RIGHT: CFA submission file SL 12-015.

438 BOTTOM: CFA submission file SL 04-057.

439 © Ennead Architects.

440 Detail from photomontage courtesy of Safdie Architects.

441 TOP: Rendering courtesy of Safdie Architects. BOTTOM: © Timothy Hursley.

442 TOP: Library of Congress, Prints & Photographs Division, Historic American Buildings Survey, HABS DC-856-7 (detail). CENTER AND BOTTOM: Photograph by Colin Goldie, courtesy of Bing Thom Architects.

443 Photograph by Nic Lehoux, courtesy of Bing Thom Architects.

444 CFA submission file CFA 20/OCT/11-3.

445 TOP LEFT: © Arthur Cotton Moore/Associates. CFA collection. TOP RIGHT: Detail from rendering courtesy of Rafael Viñoly Architects.

447 TOP LEFT: The Historical Society of Washington, DC, General Photograph Collection. TOP RIGHT: Library of Congress, Prints & Photographs Division, Historic American Buildings Survey, HABS DC, WASH, 503-2. CENTER LEFT: Detail from photograph by Nigel Young/Foster + Partners. CENTER RIGHT: Gustafson Guthrie Nichol Ltd. BOTTOM: © Richard Davies, courtesy of Foster + Partners.

448 Gustafson Guthrie Nichol Ltd.

449 TOP LEFT: Detail from photograph by William Herman Rau, Robert N. Dennis Collection of Stereoscopic Views, Miriam and Ira D. Wallach Division of Art, Prints and Photographs, The New York Public Library, Astor, Lenox and Tilden Foundations. TOP RIGHT: Courtesy of the Smithsonian Institution Libraries, Washington, DC. BOTTOM: Hartman-Cox Architects.

450 TOP LEFT: CFA submission file CFA 20/OCT/05-2. TOP RIGHT: Diller Scofidio + Renfro. CENTER LEFT: Foster + Partners. CENTER RIGHT: Moody Nolan in association with Antoine Predock Architect. BOTTOM LEFT: Moshe Safdie & Associates. BOTTOM RIGHT: Devrouax & Purnell Architects/Planners and Pei Cobb Freed & Partners Architects.

451 Collection of the Staatliches Museum für Völkerkunde, Munich. Photograph from the archives of the National Museum, Lagos, Nigeria, reprinted from Roslyn A. Walker, *Olówè of Isè: A Yoruba Sculptor to Kings* (Washington, DC: National Museum of African Art, 1998).

452 TOP: Freelon Adjaye Bond/SmithGroup.

453 TOP, LEFT AND RIGHT: Freelon Adjaye Bond/SmithGroup. TOP CENTER: Gustafson Guthrie Nichol Ltd. BOTTOM: Freelon Adjaye Bond/SmithGroup.

454 TOP AND BOTTOM LEFT: Freelon Adjaye Bond/SmithGroup. BOTTOM RIGHT: Composite diagram by Freelon Adjaye Bond/SmithGroup, including details from *Captain William Wade* (Thomas Gainsborough, 1771), *Richard Rogers* (Xavier Veilhan, 2009), and a nineteeth-century cast-iron gate.

456 TOP: Photograph by Roland Halbe, courtesy of SmithGroupJJR. BOTTOM: CFA submission file CFA 19/MAY/11-2.

457 TOP RIGHT: Photograph by Wally Gobetz via flickr.com. BOTTOM: Sasaki Associates, Inc.

459 TOP: Bill O'Leary/The Washington Post/Getty Images. BOTTOM: KBAS LLC.

460 Rendering by Michael McCann, courtesy of Michael Vergason Landscape Architects, Ltd.

461 TOP: CFA submission file CFA 16/JUL/09-1. BOTTOM: Photograph by Craig Collins, courtesy of Larry Kirkland.

462 TOP: CFA submission file CFA 16/JUL/09-1. BOTTOM: Michael Vergason Landscape Architects, Ltd.

463 CFA submission file CFA 18/FEB/99-1.

464 TOP: Photograph by Gerald Ratto, courtesy of ROMA Design Group. BOTTOM: Rendering by Dariush Vaziri, courtesy of McKissack & McKissack.

465 LEFT: © Bob Fitch Photo. CENTER: Detail from rendering by Christopher Grubbs, courtesy of ROMA Design Group. RIGHT: CFA submission file CFA 19/JUN/08-1.

466 TOP: Photograph by Anice Hoachlander, courtesy of McKissack & McKissack. BOTTOM: SANYPICTURES/Hassan Ali.

469 © Ennead Architects

470 LEFT: © Ennead Architects. RIGHT: CFA submission file CFA 16/FEB/12–1.

471 CFA submission file CFA 16/FEB/12–1.

472 TOP LEFT AND BOTTOM LEFT: Image courtesy of Carol R. Johnson Associates. RIGHT: CFA submission file CFA 19/NOV/09-3.

474 TOP LEFT: Skidmore, Owings & Merrill LLP. TOP RIGHT: Library of Congress, Prints & Photographs Division, unprocessed in PMR-3181-8. CENTER AND BOTTOM: Gehry Partners, LLP.

475 CENTER AND BOTTOM: Gehry Partners, LLP.

476 TOP, CENTER AND BOTTOM: Gehry Partners, LLP.

477 TOP: Gehry Partners, LLP. CENTER LEFT: Dwight D. Eisenhower Presidential Library & Museum. BOTTOM LEFT: Detail from photograph by U.S. Army Signal Corps, courtesy of the Dwight D. Eisenhower Presidential Library & Museum. CENTER RIGHT: © Estate of Yousuf Karsh.

478 Daniel W. Cook.

479 TOP LEFT: Detail from photograph by Bel St. John, AECOM. TOP RIGHT: © Andrew Blasko (detail). BOTTOM: Courtesy of Hartman-Cox Architects.

480 Courtesy of the United States Mint.

481 All images courtesy of the United States Mint.

482 All images courtesy of the United States Mint.

483 All images courtesy of the United States Mint.

484 Detail from official White House photograph by Pete Souza.

485 TOP: Photography © Frank Ooms. BOTTOM: Detail from photograph by Paul Crosby, courtesy of Julie Snow Architects Inc.

486 TOP: Model photograph courtesy of Safdie Architects. BOTTOM: © Timothy Hursley.

487 TOP: © Maxwell MacKenzie, courtesy of Michael Graves & Associates.

488 TOP: Shalom Baranes Associates Architects. BOTTOM RIGHT: Karn, Charuhas, Chapman & Twohey.

489 Rendering by ArchiBIM, courtesy of Beyer Blinder Belle Architects & Planners LLP.

491 TOP: Naval History & Heritage Command Photographic Department (detail). BOTTOM LEFT: CFA submission file CFA 19/OCT/89-2. BOTTOM RIGHT: MPFP/M. Paul Friedberg and Partners.

492 TOP: MPFP/M. Paul Friedberg and Partners. BOTTOM: © Maxwell MacKenzie, courtesy of Michael Graves & Associates.

493 Photograph by Michael A. Parisi, courtesy of MPFP/M. Paul Friedberg and Partners.

494 TOP: Library of Congress, Prints & Photographs Division, LC-USZ62-104691. BOTTOM: National Archives at College Park, College Park, MD, Record Group 418 Image G-2.

495 TOP AND BOTTOM: Courtesy of SmithGroupJJR.

496 TOP: Courtesy of SmithGroupJJR. BOTTOM: Designed and rendered by Perkins + Will.

497 TOP AND BOTTOM: Designed and rendered by Perkins + Will.

499 USDA FSA Aerial Photography Field Office (detail).

500 Culinary Concepts Hospitality Group.

501 TOP LEFT: KGP Design Studio. TOP RIGHT: TEN Arquitectos image reprinted with permission of EastBanc W.D.C. (detail). BOTTOM: NoMa Business Improvement District.

502 Photograph by Ken Wyner, courtesy of Devrouax & Purnell, PLLC.

503 TOP LEFT: Photograph by Edmund Sumner, courtesy of Adjaye Associates. BOTTOM LEFT: © Mark Herboth Photography. TOP RIGHT: Photograph by Paul Rivera, Arch Photo, Inc., courtesy of Davis Brody Bond. BOTTOM RIGHT: CORE Architecture + Design.

504 Robert Creamer Photography.

505 Robert Creamer Photography.

506 TOP LEFT: Darrow Montgomery/*Washington City Paper*. TOP RIGHT: CFA submission file CFA 15/MAY/08-9. BOTTOM LEFT: © cox graae + spack architects. BOTTOM RIGHT: Robert Creamer Photography.

507 TOP: CFA submission file CFA 21/JAN/10-6. BOTTOM: Detail from photograph by Ken Wyner, courtesy of Hord Coplan Macht.

508 LEFT: Library of Congress, Prints & Photographs Division, detail from photograph by Carol M. Highsmith, LC-DIG-highsm-10443. RIGHT: Photograph by Max Freitch, courtesy of Marsha Mateyka Gallery.

509 TOP LEFT: Photograph by Wendy M. Ross. TOP RIGHT: © JCDA, Joseph Welker. CENTER: Elvert Barnes, <divxmlns:cc="http://creativecommons.org/ns#"about="http://www.ipernity.com/doc/elvetbarnes/7674617/in/keyword/836586/self"><arel="cc:attributionURL"property="cc:attributionName"href="http://www.ipernity.com/home/elvertbarnes/">ElvertBarnes</a>/<arel="license"href="http://creativecommons.org/licenses/by-sa/3.0/">CCBY-SA 3.0</a> ?. BOTTOM: Raymond Kaskey, Kaskey Studio.

510 TOP: Robert M. Gurney, FAIA. BOTTOM: © Maxwell MacKenzie, courtesy of Cunningham Quill Architects.

511 Robert A.M. Stern Architects, LLP.

512 TOP LEFT: Photograph by Peter Aaron/OTTO, courtesy of Robert A.M. Stern Architects, LLP. BOTTOM LEFT: © Anton Grassl/Esto. TOP RIGHT: Peter Aaron/OTTO. BOTTOM RIGHT: Payette.

513 TOP: Hartman-Cox Architects. BOTTOM: Library of Congress, Prints & Photographs Division, Historic American Buildings Survey, HABS DC,GEO,2-5.

514 TOP: Library of Congress, Prints & Photographs Division, Historic American Buildings Survey, HABS DC,GEO,234-25(CT) (detail). CENTER: Richard Williams Architects, PLLC. BOTTOM: Rendering

by Michael McCann, courtesy of Archives, Dumbarton Oaks Research Library and Collection, Washington, DC.

515 TOP: Venturi, Scott Brown & Associates, Inc. BOTTOM: Matt Wargo, courtesy of Venturi, Scott Brown & Associates, Inc.

516 LEFT: Photograph by Russell Hirshon, courtesy of EastBanc W.D.C. RIGHT: Photograph by Kenneth Wyner, courtesy of cox graae + spack architects.

517 TOP, CENTER, AND BOTTOM LEFT: CFA submission file OG 08-225. RIGHT: CFA submission file OG 07-201.

518 TOP: © Maxwell MacKenzie, courtesy of Handel Architects LLP. BOTTOM: © Maxwell MacKenzie, courtesy of Torti Gallas and Partners, Inc.

519 TOP: CFA submission file OG 03-133. CENTER: Rendering by Wingårdh Arkitektkontor, courtesy of National Property Board Sweden. BOTTOM: Photograph by Åke E:son Lindman, courtesy of National Property Board Sweden.

521 TOP: AECOM. CENTER: WRT. BOTTOM LEFT: Photograph by James Dee, model by Joseph Hutchinson, image provided courtesy of Jody Pinto.

522 TOP: WRT. BOTTOM: © Patrick O'Brien, courtesy of WRT.

523 © Alan Karchmer.

524 LEFT: Reprinted from Samuel Howe, *American Country Houses of To-Day* (New York: Architectural Book Publishing, 1915). Image provided courtesy of Heritage Landscapes LLC. TOP RIGHT: Library of Congress, Prints & Photographs Division, LC-J717-X110-

158. BOTTOM RIGHT: Ellen McGowan Biddle Shipman papers, #1259. Division of Rare and Manuscript Collections, Cornell University Library.

525 Heritage Landscapes LLC.

527 TOP: Photograph by Bryan Becker, courtesy of Hartman-Cox Architects. BOTTOM: Photograph by Katsuhisa Kida, courtesy of Rogers Stirk Harbour + Partners.

528 TOP LEFT: Photograph by John A. Volpe Construction, courtesy of SmithGroupJJR. BOTTOM LEFT: © Maxwell MacKenzie, courtesy of SmithGroupJJR. TOP RIGHT: Office of Kevin Roche John Dinkeloo and Associates, LLC. BOTTOM RIGHT: © Prakash Patel.

529 © Harlan Hambright, image courtesy of Republic Properties. CFA collection.

530 TOP: Rendering by Neoscape, courtesy of Shalom Baranes Architects. BOTTOM LEFT: Courtesy of Pelli Clarke Pelli Architects. BOTTOM RIGHT: CFA submission file SL 12-058.

531 TOP AND CENTER: CFA submission files SL 12-101-105, 110. BOTTOM: Library of Congress, Prints & Photographs Division, Historic American Buildings Survey, HABS DC, WASH, 612-8 (detail).

532 LEFT AND RIGHT: Photograph by Carol Clayton. CFA collection.

533 CFA submission file CFA 19/JUL/12–1.

534 TOP: PWP Landscape Architecture & Rogers Marvel Architects. BOTTOM: OLIN & Weiss/Manfredi.

535 Gustafson Guthrie Nichol & Davis Brody Bond.

CIVIC ART

A Centennial History Of The U.S. Commission Of Fine Arts

Designed by Marc Alain Meadows

Composed using QuarkXpress v8.1.6 on an iMac running OSX v10.5.8,
this book is typeset in a new multi-dimentional OpenType font named Arno Pro,
released by the Adobe Type foundry in 2007. Designed by Robert Slimbach,
this very readable font incorporates the best attributes of early humanist types of the
15th and 16th centuries. Well-crafted in the classic style of Venetian book types
(and named for the river that runs through Florence, Italy), Arno is nonetheless
quite a contemporary typeface with its clean refined characteristics,
and offers extensive expert character and glyph sets, available in five optical
size ranges, many of which are used in this book.

Printed by S&S Graphics dba Westland, Laurel, Maryland,
on Sterling Premium 100-pound dull text, made by NewPage Corporation.

Bound by Advantage Book Binding, Inc., Glen Burnie, Maryland,
in Cialux and stamped in gold.